MACMILLAN LITERATURE SERIES

SIGNATURE EDITION

DISCOVERING LITERATURE

INTRODUCING LITERATURE

ENJOYING LITERATURE

UNDERSTANDING LITERATURE

APPRECIATING LITERATURE

AMERICAN LITERATURE

ENGLISH LITERATURE
WITH WORLD MASTERPIECES

WORLD LITERATURE

FRONT COVER, detail, and BACK COVER: *Allies Day, May 1917*, 1917, oil on canvas, Childe Hassam, American (1859–1935).

National Gallery of Art, Washington, D.C. Gift of Ethelyn McKinney in memory of her brother, Glenn Ford McKinney.

GENERAL ADVISERS

READING AND INSTRUCTIONAL METHODS

Jack Cassidy
Professor of Education
Millersville University
Millersville, Pennsylvania

TEACHER'S PROFESSIONAL RESOURCES

Robert DiYanni
Professor of English
Pace University
Pleasantville, New York

SPEAKING AND LISTENING SKILLS

R. Brian Loxley
Communications Consultant
New York, New York

THINKING SKILLS

Eric Cooper
Former Director, Comprehension and Cognition Project, The College Board
New York, New York

LITERATURE AND CURRICULUM

George Kearns
Associate Professor of English
Rutgers University
New Brunswick, New Jersey

CONSULTANTS

Elizabeth Ackley, Teacher, Indian Hill High School, Cincinnati, Ohio
Wanda N. Cain, English Department Head and Teacher, Waxahachie High School, Waxahachie, Texas
Paula A. Calabrese, Principal, Espe School, North Allegheny School District, Pennsylvania
Sandra A. Cavender, English Teacher and Former Chairperson, Nathan Hale High School, West Allis, Wisconsin
Meg Durham, English Department Chairman, South Houston High School, South Houston, Texas
Robert Flores, California Assessment Program–Language Arts: Mentor Teacher, San Diego, California
Carolyn Dennis Jones, Chairperson, Martin Luther King, Jr., National Network of Schools, Englewood, New Jersey
Beverly Merrill, Language Program Specialist, Mesa Unified School District, Arizona
Jo Ann Patton, English Teacher, Berkner High School, Richardson Independent School District, Texas
Judi Purvis, Secondary Language Arts Appraiser, Carrollton–Farmers Branch Independent School District, Texas
Robert S. Ranta, Supervisor of Languages, Lacey Township High School, Lanoka Harbor, New Jersey
Pearl Thomas, NYC Board of Communication Arts—Adviser (Martin Luther King, Jr., Network of Schools)
Ruth Townsend, Teacher, Yorktown High School, Yorktown Heights, New York
Kathleen M. Keitert Wilkinson, Department Chair, Judson High School, Judson Independent School District, Texas
Marjory Carter Willis, Teacher, Midlothian High School, Midlothian, Virginia

WRITERS

Instructional Text
Elizabeth Ackley, English Teacher
Cosmo F. Ferrara, Writer and Consultant, Former Department Chair
Gale Cornelia Flynn, Poet and Writer, Former English Teacher
Philip McFarland, English Teacher
Gail Mack, Educational Writer
Brian McLaughlin, Educational Writer
Eileen Hillary Oshinsky, Educational Writer

WRITERS

Thinking Skills Handbook
Beau F. Jones-Davis, North Central Regional Educational Laboratory, Elmhurst, Illinois
Susan Sardy, Yeshiva University, New York, New York
John Sherk, University of Missouri, Kansas City, Missouri

Writing About Literature Handbook
Catherine Sagan, English Department Chair

Research Paper Casebook
Sharon Shaloo, Educational Writer, Boston, Massachusetts

Teacher's Classroom Resources
Stanlee Brimberg, Bank Street School for Children, New York, New York
Ellen Davis, Friendswood Independent School District, Texas
Judith H. McGee, Coordinator of Secondary Education, Athens Independent School District, Texas
David Nicholson, Riverdale Country School, Bronx, New York

The publisher is grateful for assistance and comments from the following people:

Jack V. Booch, Theatre Guild, New York, New York
Mrs. Rosalie Clark, Austin High School, Decatur, Alabama
Mr. Albert G. Craz, Northport–East Northport High School, Northport, New York
Gerald Dwight, Cherry Hill High School West, Cherry Hill, New Jersey
José Flores, Center for Mexican American Studies, University of Texas, Austin
Mrs. Doris E. R. Gilbert, Syracuse City Schools, Syracuse, New York
William Ince, Stuyvesant High School, New York, New York
Francisco Jiménez, Santa Clara University, Santa Clara, California
Iris Gates McAnear, Austin High School, Decatur, Alabama

MACMILLAN LITERATURE SERIES

AMERICAN LITERATURE

SIGNATURE EDITION

GLENCOE/McGRAW-HILL
A Macmillan/McGraw-Hill Company
Mission Hills, California

Send all inquiries to:
Glencoe/McGraw-Hill
15319 Chatsworth Street
P.O. Box 9509
Mission Hills, CA 91395-9509

Pupil's Edition ISBN 0-02-635091-2/11
Teacher's Annotated Edition ISBN 0-02-635092-0/11

2 3 4 5 6 7 8 9 97 96 95 94

ACKNOWLEDGMENTS

Grateful acknowledgment is given authors, publishers, and agents for permission to reprint the following copyrighted material. Every effort has been made to determine copyright owners. In the case of any omissions, the Publisher will be pleased to make suitable acknowledgments in future editions.

Margaret Walker Alexander
MARGARET WALKER ALEXANDER: "Lineage" from *For My People.* Reprinted by permission of Margaret Walker Alexander.

Robert Bly
ROBERT BLY: "Driving to Town Late to Mail a Letter" from *Silence in the Snowy Fields.* Published by Wesleyan University Press, 1962. Copyright © 1962 by Robert Bly. Reprinted by permission of Robert Bly.

Brandt & Brandt Literary Agents, Inc.
JEROME WEIDMAN: "My Father Sits in the Dark" from *My Father Sits in the Dark & Other Stories.* Copyright 1934 and renewed 1962 by Jerome Weidman. Reprinted by permission of Brandt & Brandt Literary Agents, Inc.

PEARL BUCK

1892–1973

•

Buck was born in West Virginia but grew up in China. Many of her works, such as *The Good Earth,* take place in China. The stories by this Nobel Prize recipient create better understanding among people.

Student's Edition

GUIDE STUDENTS THROUGH EXCITING LITERATURE.

rom Beowulf to James Michener, from Emily Dickinson to Dante, *Macmillan Literature Series* presents the most thought-provoking classic and contemporary selections, crossing periods, cultures, and genres. Selections were chosen and organized in response to surveys of 5,200 English teachers.

STUDENTS BECOME ACTIVE READERS THROUGH STUDY AND RESPONSE ACTIVITIES.

After each selection, a three-part questioning strategy leads students through various levels of thinking:

1 Recalling: students recall literal facts.
2 Interpreting: students apply critical thinking skills.
3 Extending: students explore selection ideas.

Challenge and Viewpoint activities encourage different types of response.

Comparing Activities encourage students to look at literature in new ways.

SPEAKING AND LISTENING HANDBOOK *Grades 7–12*

Includes lessons on how to present orally, listen effectively, and interact in collaborative learning activities.

THINKING SKILLS HANDBOOK *Grades 7–12*

Provides lessons on how to apply higher order thinking skills.

READING AND STUDY SKILLS HANDBOOK *Grades 7–10*

Lessons reinforce the skills essential to demonstrating comprehension.

BENJAMIN FRANKLIN

1706–1790

•

Franklin educated himself by reading widely. He published his first essay as a teenager. He moved penniless from Boston to Philadelphia, where he became a civic leader.

Student's Edition

BY WRITING ABOUT LITERATURE, READERS BECOME GOOD WRITERS.

riting assignments challenge students at different levels. At the end of selections, students have a choice of two different writing assignments—an analytical composition about the selection or a creative writing project.

The *Writing About Literature Handbook* encourages writing about the selections.

The Research Paper Casebook

Grades 11–12

Guides students through the specific steps needed to produce a successful research paper.

EVALUATE STUDENT PROGRESS WITH UNIT REVIEWS AND ACTIVITIES TO ENSURE COMPREHENSION.

The *Model for Active Reading* and follow-up activities help students extract meaning and enjoyment from the selections in each unit.

Literary Skills Reviews and *Themes Reviews* reinforce the unit lessons.

Student's Resources

Lessons in Active Learning

In the Student Resources handbooks at the back of the Student's Edition are guides for independent learning and evaluation.

ROBERT FROST
1874–1963

•

Frost is closely identified with New England even though he was born in San Francisco and moved to New Hampshire as a child. He received many honors, including four Pulitzer Prizes.

Teacher's Annotated Edition

IT IS MORE THAN JUST A PLANNING TOOL!
IT IS A PRACTICAL GUIDE WITH
TIME-SAVING FEATURES.

Every feature in the Teacher's Annotated Edition can be immediately used and applied in the classroom.

On-the-page annotations

1 provide on-the-spot help in directing class discussion
2 include ideas that can be shared with students of various abilities
3 save time for busy teachers rather than demand more time

INTRODUCE STUDENTS TO GREAT LITERATURE WITH EFFECTIVE PREREADING STRATEGIES.

Lead students into the literature with the help of these prereading features:

1 *At a Glance* summarizes major developments on the page; teachers can see "what happens where" without having to read the entire selection.
2 *Literary Options* lists the most obvious literary elements associated with the selection allowing teachers to focus on one or more dominant elements or techniques.
3 *Thematic Options* lets teachers select one or more themes to focus on in the teaching of the selection.

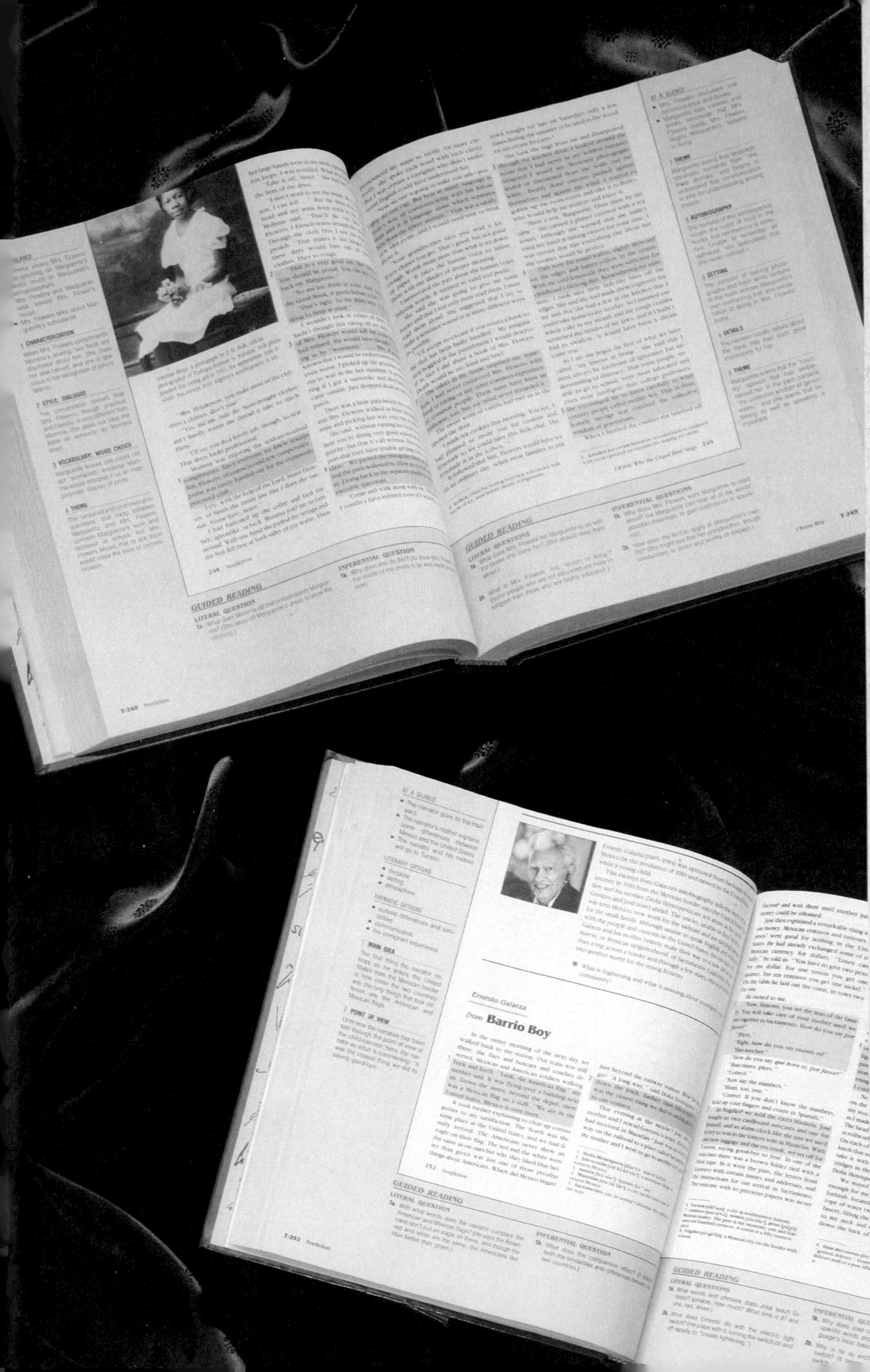

GWENDOLYN
BROOKS

1917–

•

Brooks was the first black woman to win a Pulitzer Prize. She began writing poetry that was quite traditional, but in her later work she often uses free verse and open forms.

Teacher's Annotated Edition

THE HELPFUL ANNOTATIONS ARE EASY TO FIND AND USE.

eyed-to-text annotations highlight passages in the selection for the teacher. Similar to marginal notes that any teacher keeps, these annotations

1. give insight about the passage and its relation to the selection as a whole
2. enrich class discussion
3. are brief enough to be used while teaching

These keyed-to-text annotations include literary elements, background, vocabulary, paraphrases, reading skills, and response journal.

Response Journal offers suggestions for student writing about a specific passage in a selection.
Reflecting on the Selection suggests overview questions that allow students to respond in general before beginning a detailed post-selection analysis.
Guided Reading questions address thinking skills and check students' comprehension page by page, helping prepare them for end-of-selection study questions.

CHALLENGE STUDENTS WITH ACTIVITIES AND REVIEWS THAT DEVELOP THEIR THINKING SKILLS AS THEY RESPOND TO LITERATURE.

Unit teaching notes offer activities for the *Model for Active Reading* feature in the student text.

Answers to themes review help to encourage class discussion.
Answers to end-of-selection questions appear on the Teacher's Annotated Edition page, so there's no more juggling separate answer keys.
Annotations at the beginning of each Student's Resources handbook explain the philosophy, structure, or application of the lessons.

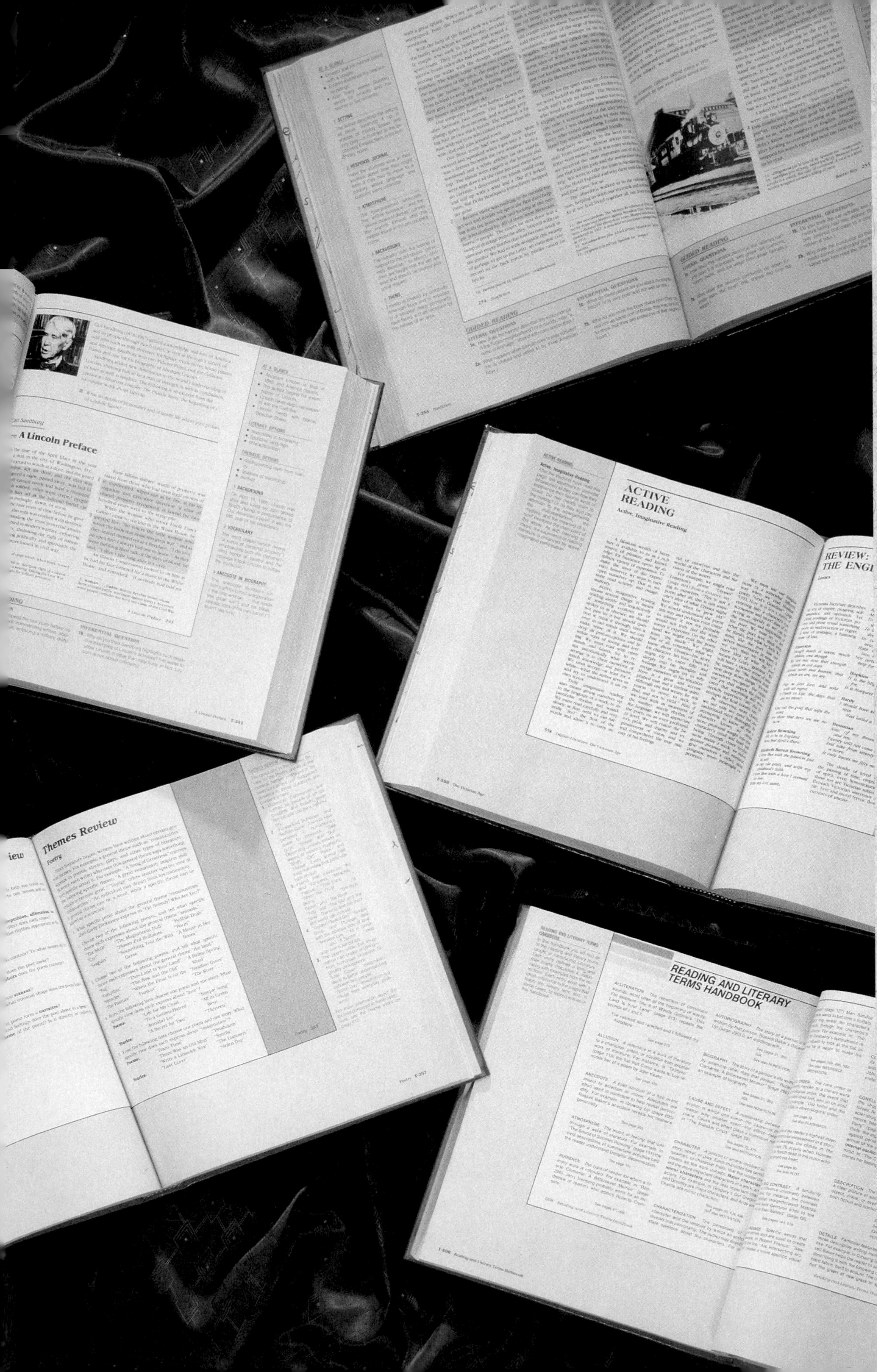

ANTON CHEKHOV

1860–1904

•

Chekhov was the grandson of a Russian serf. While at medical school he began to write, launching a brilliant literary career.

Teacher's Annotated Edition

PROVISION FOR EVALUATION AND WRITING ABOUT LITERATURE TEACH STUDENTS SKILLS TO HELP THEM IN ALL CURRICULUM AREAS.

On-the-page *Suggestions for Critiques* of the two-part composition assignments suggested in the student text save you time in assessing student writing.

It is easy to assess student achievement with a variety of reviews and checkpoints:

1 Selection End: three-level study questions feature recall, interpretation, and extension.
2 Unit End: Literary Skills Review encourages students to look at literature in a broad context.

WILLIAM
SHAKESPEARE
1564–1616

•

Shakespeare, poet and playwright, is said to be the world's favorite author. No other writer's plays have been produced so often and read so widely all over the world.

Teacher's Classroom Resources

THE LESSON PLAN BOOKLETS—PREREADING, READING, RESPONDING, AND EVALUATING—BRING IT ALL TOGETHER.

These booklets in the Teacher's Classroom Resources specify when to use each component while teaching a selection.

1 One-page lesson plans begin with clearly stated objectives.
2 Each lesson plan lists materials and activities by lesson elements: *Prereading, Reading and Response, Composition, Closure and Transfer, Reteaching, Enrichment and Extension, and Evaluation.*

The *Macmillan Literature Series* Lesson Plans make teaching manageable by providing step-by-step management of each and every component.

UNIT BOOKLETS HELP STUDENTS BECOME ACTIVE READERS AND IN-DEPTH THINKERS.

For teaching each selection, teachers will find in the Unit Booklets:

A Teaching Chart to identify features in the Student's Edition, Teacher's Annotated Edition, and Teacher's Classroom Resources (including Overhead Transparencies) for use before, during, and after reading a selection.

Teaching Notes
1 Author notes to help teachers provide additional background and context for the selection.
2 A Statement of Theme or Main Idea and Synopsis.
3 Motivation suggestions to engage students' interest before reading.
4 Words in Glossary to show teachers the selection words that appear in the Glossary in the Student's Edition.
5 Additional Projects to help students work in a novel, often nonverbal, way to further explore the selection.

A Prereading Vocabulary blackline master to introduce and provide practice with difficult words from the selection using various strategies.
A Reading Guide blackline master to keep less-able readers focused on the selection and help them note key points as they read.
A Check Test blackline master to give teachers a quick sense of students' grasp of the selection on a literal level.
A Writing Process Guide blackline master to help students complete the analytical composition assignments in the Student's Edition.
A Selection Test blackline master including vocabulary test items to help teachers evaluate the students' understanding.

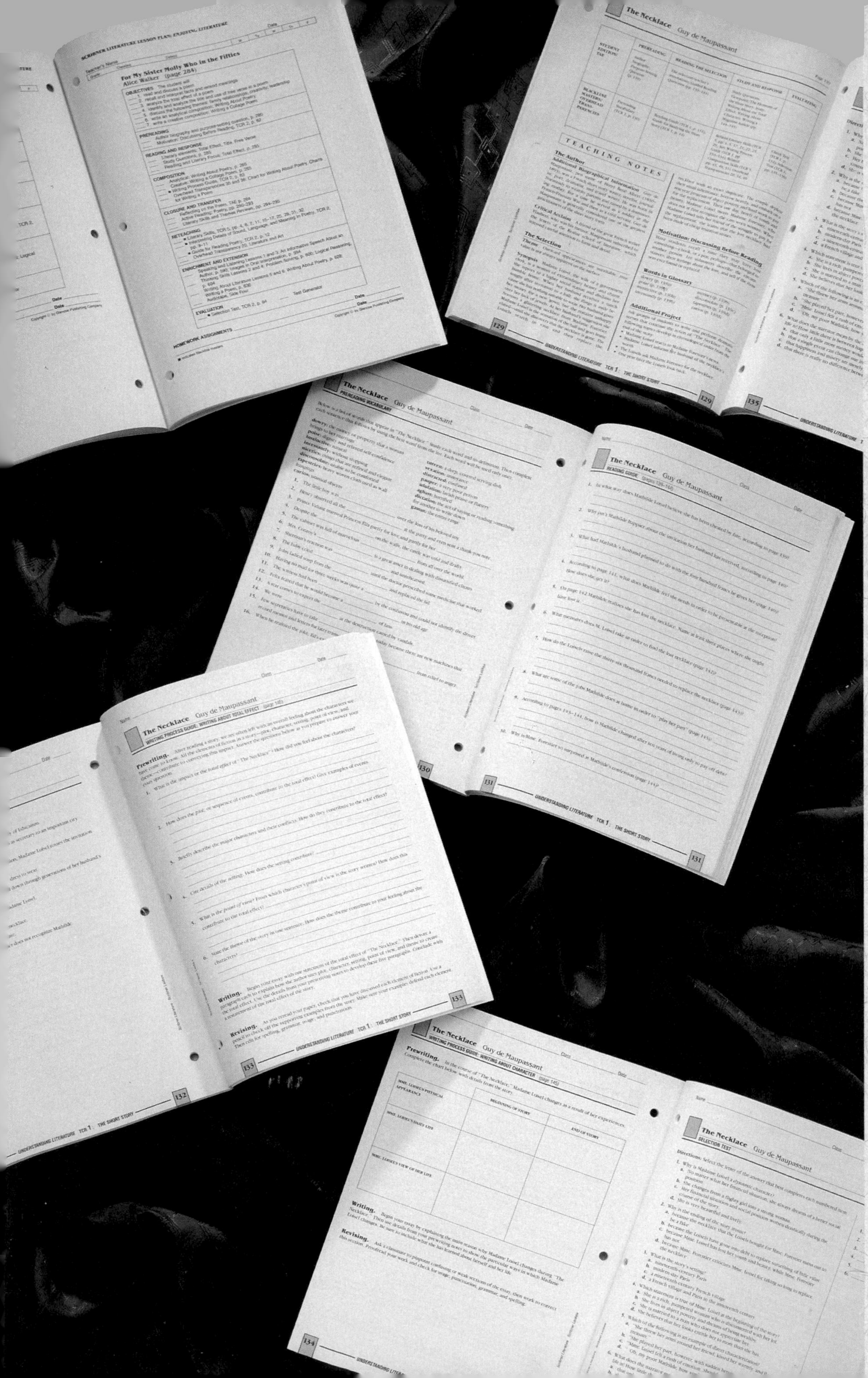

TEACHER'S CLASSROOM RESOURCES

These resources offer everything a teacher needs for planning and teaching lessons for Grades 6–12.

Teacher's Classroom Resources

THE LITERATURE IS MADE ACCESSIBLE TO ALL THE STUDENTS.

Literary Skills and *Active-Learning Guides* provide opportunities for students to become actively involved with literary terms and elements as well as reinforcement of *Student's Resources Lessons in Active Learning*.

An *Answer Key booklet* is a quick reference that provides answers and guidelines for evaluation.

Overhead Transparencies provide an alternative medium for instruction while students are actively involved with great literature.

Teacher's Professional Resources booklet contains helpful articles about the teaching of literature.

Models of Student Writing cover twelve types of writing and exemplify the writing process and the teacher's evaluation of that process.

Additional Teaching Materials complete a comprehensive literature program.

Macmillan Literature Series Test Generator provides individual test items that can be selected from the computer data bank so that tests can be customized.

Macmillan Literature Novel and Drama Guides enable students to apply independently their literary and vocabulary skills.

The Macmillan Literature Series Video Library supports classroom instruction and brings literature to life by showing how to integrate videotapes with reading.

The Macmillan Literature Series Audiotapes expand students' literary experiences with outstanding presentations and active reader comments.

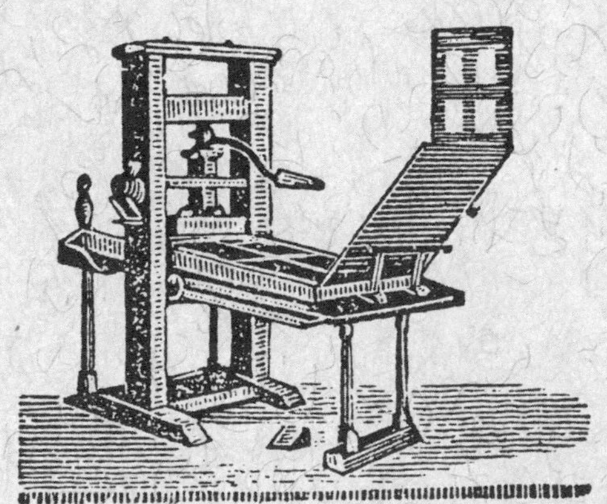

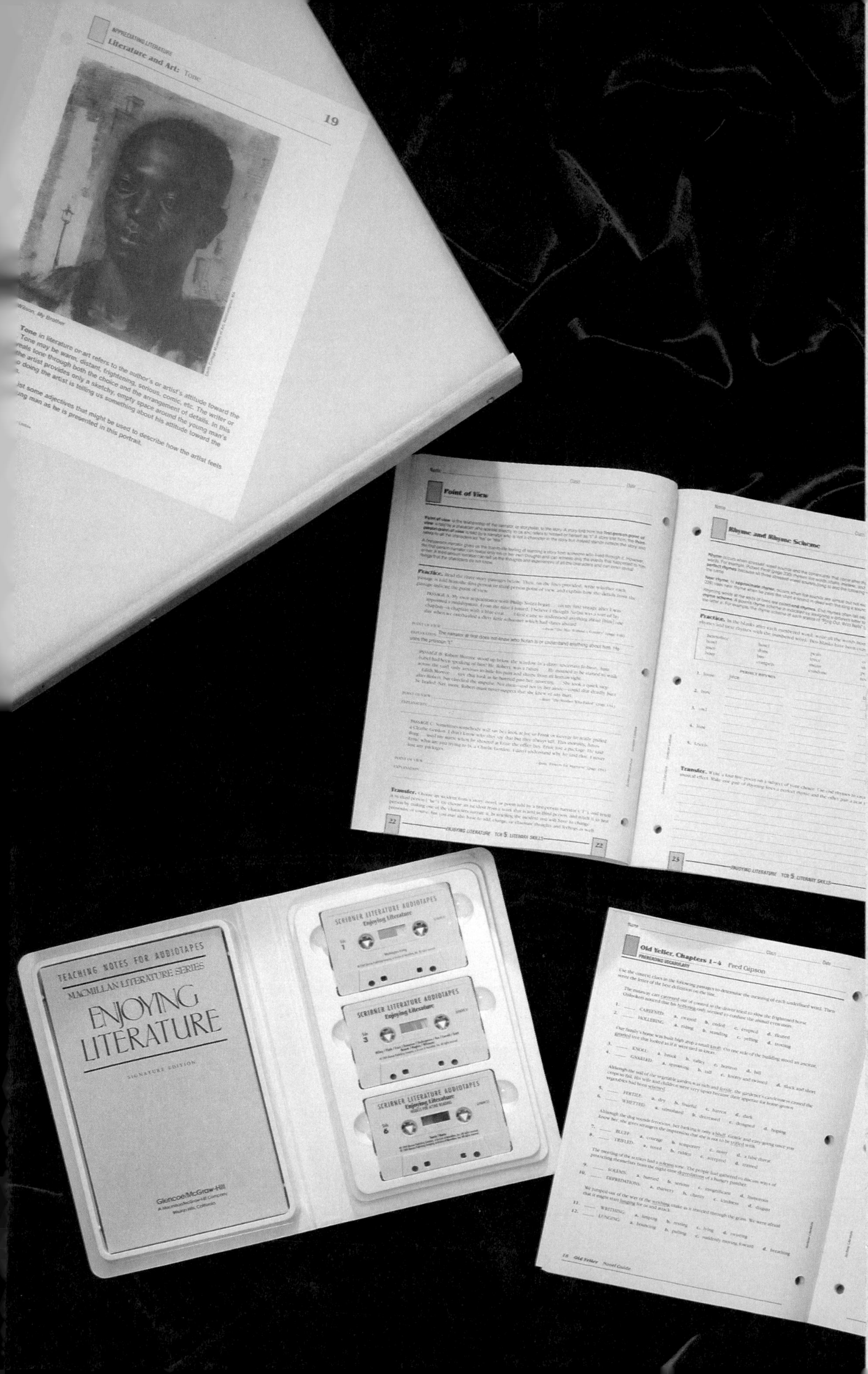

MARK TWAIN

1835–1910

Mark Twain, who was born Samuel Clemens, did not just write a story. He told it. His mastery of American speech and his ability to spin a yarn are unsurpassed.

Scope and Sequence

MACMILLAN LITERATURE SERIES

All the components fit together to make MACMILLAN LITERATURE SERIES, Signature Edition, a comprehensive language arts program.

Reading and Literary Skills	**Discovering Literature**	**Introducing Literature**	**Enjoying Literature**	**Understanding Literature**	**Appreciating Literature**	**American Literature**	**English Literature with World Masterpieces**	**World Literature**
allegory						181, 936	56, 120, 287, 290, 893	
alliteration		219, 274, 598	224, 282, 628, 630, 646	195, 720, 724, 730	200, 788, 792	131, 936	18, 26, 430, 996, 1020	
allusion		430, 598	453, 646	487, 724	200, 792	29, 936	276, 285, 286, 656, 1020	
analogy					332, 792	39, 936	1020	
antagonist					792	665, 936	1020	
assonance			227, 646	195, 720, 724	192, 788, 792	131, 937	430, 996, 1020	
atmosphere		131, 172, 598	92, 165, 646	75, 304, 724	58, 792	148–149	225, 756, 1020	
audience		47, 289, 322, 598	25, 297, 330, 486, 646	233, 261, 327	263, 353	68	236	
autobiography, biography		21, 289, 295, 303, 333, 598	11, 297, 304, 312, 646	234, 240, 245, 251, 716, 724	264, 270, 277, 346, 792	58, 244, 937	365, 498, 1021	
ballad, song				171, 724	225, 792	7, 12–14, 170–171, 236–238, 286	5, 49, 52, 55, 141, 143, 266, 313, 366, 372, 394–395, 554, 651, 804, 1021	
blank verse				356, 724	196, 491, 793	123, 937	165, 277, 285, 286, 1021	
cause and effect		72, 479, 598	47, 318, 341, 494, 646					
character		105, 171, 368, 404, 434, 447, 498, 574, 598	67, 77, 430, 462, 468, 496, 566, 622, 624, 646	53, 63, 145, 157, 326–327, 374, 428, 613, 708, 724	44, 134, 432, 512, 612, 772, 793	114, 323, 339, 710, 937	78, 225, 502, 510, 640, 701, 712, 724, 731, 904, 913, 1021	
characterization		95, 109, 170, 404, 434, 498, 532, 574, 598	67, 85, 160, 406, 430, 622, 624, 646, 647	40, 47, 613, 725	39, 793	323, 512, 600–601, 937	78, 79, 104, 698, 712, 724, 819, 1021–1022	
chronological order		72, 308, 599	47, 159, 318, 332, 647					
Classicism						101, 937	311–313, 1022	
climax		65, 172, 308, 332, 404, 599	41, 166, 430, 647	10, 273, 326, 427, 725	20, 448, 793	323, 711, 937	224, 711, 1022, 1028	
comedy			349, 350, 647	293, 725	353, 384, 793	665, 667	132–133, 242–243, 313, 569, 913, 1022	
comparison/contrast		143, 519, 599	211, 647	708	345, 346	92, 896–897	986	
concrete language		235, 599	238, 647	277, 725	320			
conflict		79, 85, 170, 308, 330, 404, 451, 508, 599	52, 165, 430, 647	26, 33, 273, 326, 427, 458, 592, 725	28, 134, 448, 491, 793	323, 365–366, 938	224, 701, 1022, 1028	
consonance				720	192, 788	131, 938	430, 996, 1022	
description		289, 312, 327, 599	297, 323, 333, 648	240, 725	794	92, 311, 938	1023	
details		100, 138, 202, 282, 312, 406, 599	73, 96, 212, 290, 291, 292, 323, 432, 434, 618, 648	69, 158, 240	58, 103, 174, 296, 320	92, 150	42, 78, 79, 104	
dialogue		45, 161, 171, 341, 355, 600	22, 189, 344, 349, 364, 642, 648	33, 273, 293, 326, 726	309, 354, 382, 794	665, 939	52, 476, 933, 1023	
drama		44, 341, 404, 592, 594, 600	22, 349, 364, 430, 432, 433, 640, 642, 648	293, 726	353, 354, 794	665, 710–711, 753, 939	144–145, 236, 242, 391, 826, 1023	
dramatic monologue					235, 794	414, 419, 939	502, 507, 1023	
elegy						261	38, 274, 366, 371, 498, 1024	
epic				433, 726	225, 576, 794	939	5, 8, 120, 277, 285, 351, 786, 820, 1024, 1027	
essay		21, 289, 317, 600	11, 297, 318, 323, 327, 331, 648	263, 273, 277, 280, 285, 726	290, 296, 309, 313, 319, 325, 339, 346, 794	664, 939	228, 332, 339, 461, 466, 1024	
exposition (in plot)				10, 273, 326, 427, 726	20, 296, 448, 794	323, 710, 848, 939	224, 711, 1024, 1028	
fable		145, 455, 600	471, 649	114, 727	90, 795	303, 939–940	732, 1024	

Scope and Sequence

MACMILLAN LITERATURE SERIES

The heart of your language arts program.

Reading and Literary Skills	Discovering Literature	Introducing Literature	Enjoying Literature	Understanding Literature	Appreciating Literature	American Literature	English Literature with World Masterpieces	World Literature
fact vs. opinion		334	342, 343, 651					
falling action				10, 273, 326, 427, 727	20, 448, 795	323, 711	224, 711, 1024, 1028	
figurative language		273, 601	245, 247, 248, 282, 628, 630, 649, 650, 651, 654	63, 196, 727	201, 289, 346, 788, 795	164, 940	140, 177, 448, 1024–1025	
figure of speech		601	649	196, 727	177, 201, 209, 211, 213, 219, 249, 795	164, 220, 940	140, 448, 1025	
foil					795	600–601, 940	903	
folk literature		413, 461, 601	469, 471, 486, 649	75	575, 644	7, 12–14, 70, 170, 236, 426	49, 52, 55, 103, 554, 641, 651, 804, 827, 1025, 1027	
foot				185, 727	795	123, 940	119, 165, 540, 940, 1025	
foreshadowing		91, 172, 369, 508, 601	57, 130, 160, 458, 566, 649	26, 639, 727	20, 795	810, 940	18, 1025	
frame				126, 727	90, 664, 795	298, 613, 940	57, 1025	
free verse			260, 649	727	198, 246, 260, 795	260–261, 265, 404, 413, 426, 940	232, 563, 656, 1025	
hero, protagonist		466, 601	449, 650	433, 467, 726	460, 568, 576, 606, 794, 798	323, 665, 711, 944	5, 146, 224, 351, 433, 436, 861, 1029, 1031	
heroic couplet						87, 170, 941	291, 352, 438, 1025	
imagery, sensory language		16, 233, 274, 498, 601	7, 238, 282, 628, 650	196, 199, 277, 399, 428, 728, 731	75, 205, 249, 320, 346, 796	32, 34, 92, 132, 164, 227, 274, 404, 413, 426, 574, 941	177, 246, 286, 652, 687, 1025–1026	
Imagism						401–402, 404, 409, 413, 427, 450, 783, 941		
inferring		100, 138, 170, 203, 283, 472, 601	73, 96, 213, 292, 406, 650	290	350	536	384	
irony		178, 602	189, 650	145, 428, 728	129, 133, 416, 612, 784, 796	391, 474, 496, 941	225, 640, 1026	
literal language				63, 196, 728	796	164, 942	177	
local color				40, 728	167, 796	311, 315, 334, 340, 395		
lyric poetry		271, 602	275, 650	208, 222, 730	177, 222, 231, 249, 796	286–287, 942	8, 38, 110, 557, 1026	
main idea		317, 324	327, 335, 634	114, 285	90, 780	323, 534, 947	698, 764, 1031	
metaphor		243, 602	247, 628, 630, 650	63, 203, 720, 728	213, 215, 217, 289, 788, 796	39, 164, 942	140, 242, 448, 893, 996, 1026	
meter				185, 728	192, 796	122–123, 215, 942	119, 165, 501, 540, 563, 1026	
Middle English							40, 56–57, 96–97, 1026	
mock-epic						286	351, 439, 1026	
Modernism						401–405, 409, 421, 429, 442, 446, 450, 459, 464, 489, 540, 545, 575, 666–667, 758, 767, 942	563–565, 651, 655, 683	
mood		131	92	729	58, 383, 774, 797	148–149, 621	165, 177, 225, 756, 1027	
myth/legend		413, 422, 602	439, 440, 650–651	439	575–580, 794	7	103, 827, 877, 1026, 1027	
narration		169, 209, 308, 324, 602	297, 318, 332, 651	729	225, 296, 797	113, 844, 942	1027	
narrative poetry		258, 264, 602	273, 651	162, 222, 730	177, 222, 225, 249, 797	286, 942	38, 553, 557, 1027	
narrator		115, 126, 532, 602	107, 120, 550, 651	85, 729	75, 612, 797	319, 333, 753, 942	553, 689, 716, 1027	
Naturalism						311, 396, 399, 942	487, 541, 545, 1027	
nonfiction		21, 289, 308, 312, 317, 322, 586, 588, 603	10, 297, 318, 323, 327, 330, 634, 636, 651	233, 729	263, 346, 786, 797	58, 244, 664	228, 332, 339, 365, 461, 498	
novel		91, 485, 603	501, 651	491, 729	611, 612, 797	114, 156, 395, 943	313, 321, 391, 514, 665, 894, 1027–1028	
Old English							3, 5, 40–41, 1028	
onomatopoeia		228, 603	234, 628, 630, 651	188, 720, 729	200, 788, 797	131, 436, 943	431, 996, 1028	

Scope and Sequence

MACMILLAN LITERATURE SERIES

The heart of your language arts program.

Reading and Literary Skills	Discovering Literature	Introducing Literature	Enjoying Literature	Understanding Literature	Appreciating Literature	American Literature	English Literature with World Masterpieces	World Literature
oral tradition		216, 341, 418, 603	349	433	579	7, 14, 943	5, 18, 49, 52, 55, 804, 820, 862, 1028	
oratory					331	65, 68–69, 96, 255, 943	225	
parallelism				195, 729	194, 331, 346, 797	84, 943	1028	
parody						566, 943	323, 338, 1028	
personification			248, 628, 630, 651	201, 720, 729	209, 788, 798	220, 943	448, 996, 1028	
persuasion		322, 336, 603	297, 330, 344, 652	263, 280, 729	326, 798	84, 943	1028	
plot		57, 65, 404, 532, 572, 603	41, 47, 52, 57, 63, 157, 430, 458, 501, 566, 581, 620, 624, 652	10, 26, 138, 145, 151, 273, 427, 592, 704, 729–730	20, 104, 134, 448, 612, 770, 798	323, 794, 943	224, 391, 514, 639–640, 698, 711, 725, 731, 750, 827, 1028	
point of view		115, 126	107, 120, 157, 550, 652	85, 94, 109, 145, 151, 509, 565, 712, 730	75, 82, 86, 134, 612, 776, 798	333, 384, 613, 943–944	689, 698, 716, 731, 1029	
predicting outcomes		91, 204, 369, 508	57, 214, 566, 620	26, 639, 727	20, 795	810, 940	1025	
purpose		47, 289, 295, 322, 604	25, 297, 305, 652	233, 273, 277, 280, 285, 718	263, 277, 290, 313, 346, 786	69, 83	990	
Realism						310–311, 367, 388, 395–396, 399, 666, 669, 944	487, 488, 545, 563, 1029	
resolution		65, 172, 604	41, 167, 620, 653	10, 273, 326, 427, 730	20, 798	323, 711	224, 711, 1028, 1029	
rhyme		16, 221, 604	7, 228, 628, 653	187, 356, 720, 725, 730	192, 239, 250, 260, 261, 798, 799	131, 170, 286, 552, 944	119, 430, 996, 1029	
rhyme scheme			228, 653	187, 730	239, 241, 799	170, 945	119, 458	
rhythm		16, 225, 274, 604	7, 231, 282, 628, 630, 653	185, 356, 720	177, 192, 196, 260, 261, 491, 788, 799	87, 122–123, 170, 215, 228, 265, 426, 436, 758, 945	57, 119, 165, 258, 327, 352, 439, 501, 540, 554, 563, 684, 996, 1029, 1030	
rising action				10, 273, 326, 427, 730	20, 799	323, 711, 945	224, 711, 1028	
romance					579, 799	156, 945	49, 353, 441, 894	
Romanticism						101, 119, 132, 437, 567, 570, 628, 666, 945	366, 372, 376, 387, 389–391, 394–395, 408, 432–433, 442, 487, 1029	
satire					663, 722, 799	483, 548, 945	242, 243, 295, 312, 331, 340, 732, 894, 903, 1030	
setting		131, 169, 186, 404, 532, 605	92, 101, 157, 164, 349, 430, 502, 581, 624, 653	69, 75, 145, 304, 428, 509, 710, 731	58, 68, 134, 383, 612, 774, 799	148–149, 323, 945	225, 514, 640, 698, 756, 1030	
short story		13, 53, 576, 605	4, 31, 624, 653	1, 145, 158, 159, 731	1, 149, 153, 166, 174, 799	323, 945–946	565, 698, 1030	
simile		240, 605	245, 628, 630, 654	63, 202, 487, 720, 727, 731	211, 289, 788, 799	39, 164, 946	140, 820, 996, 1024, 1025, 1030	
skimming and scanning		49, 604, 605	27, 653, 654	185		123, 945		
soliloquy				399, 731	512, 799	946	145, 165, 612, 1030	
sonnet					236, 239, 241, 799, 800	392, 394, 946	114, 119, 139, 251, 274, 396, 442, 1030	
speaker			279, 654	175, 177, 720, 731	178, 181, 249, 788, 800	946	116, 165, 557, 996	
stage directions and staging		45, 341, 385, 605	22, 349, 365, 642, 654	293, 304, 326–327, 430, 731	354, 383, 432, 465, 536, 800	665, 669, 710, 946	236, 1030	
stanza		16, 252, 605	7, 258, 654	161, 171, 731	177, 239, 241, 800	170–171, 552, 946	55, 127, 371, 406, 438, 439, 458, 883, 1021, 1031	
stream of consciousness						403–404, 575, 582–583, 639, 946	563, 565, 725, 731, 1028, 1031	

Scope and Sequence

MACMILLAN LITERATURE SERIES

The heart of your language arts program.

Reading and Literary Skills	Discovering Literature	Introducing Literature	Enjoying Literature	Understanding Literature	Appreciating Literature	American Literature	English Literature with World Masterpieces	World Literature
style		47	25	233, 277, 731	263, 800	3, 23, 384, 464, 496, 772–773, 946	243, 246, 277, 285, 286, 653, 683, 752, 1031	
symbol			287	436	114, 134, 173, 219, 782, 800	190–191, 650–651, 902–903, 947	376, 382, 383, 640, 650, 717, 992, 1031	
theme		145, 156, 174, 178, 186, 200, 209, 267, 269, 342, 368, 371, 404, 605	4, 7, 139, 145, 157, 276, 277, 279, 282, 287, 350, 366, 430, 502, 654	114, 118, 126, 145, 157, 188, 327, 428, 540, 714, 731	90, 98, 134, 536, 612, 780, 800	323, 384, 534, 650–651, 710–711, 904–905, 947	225, 514, 698, 764, 994, 1031	
thesis statement		317, 324, 606	327, 335, 618, 654	285, 702	339, 769, 800	894	984	
tone					82, 134, 178, 186, 263, 778, 800	474, 870, 947	246, 265, 285, 312, 640, 658, 676, 756, 1002, 1031	
topic sentence		322, 331, 606	305, 335, 655	285, 703	769			
total effect		178, 186, 200, 277, 323, 404, 532	157, 178, 211, 285, 331, 430, 581, 628	127, 220, 222, 227, 286, 427, 540, 668	134, 247, 253, 346, 459, 569, 605, 661, 734, 790	306, 908–909	224–225, 639, 998	
tragedy			350, 655	293, 331, 731	353, 462, 568, 800	665	133, 146, 224, 313, 826, 861, 1031	
Transcendentalism						154–155, 260, 947		
word choice		47, 238	25, 243, 655	181, 728, 731	178, 181, 249, 800	211	395, 502, 554, 569, 651, 663, 679, 683, 756	

Composition Skills	Discovering Literature	Introducing Literature	Enjoying Literature	Understanding Literature	Appreciating Literature	American Literature	English Literature with World Masterpieces	World Literature
ANALYTICAL (Students are asked to write about the following literary genres, techniques, elements, and terms.)								
autobiography, biography		295, 586	305, 634	240, 245, 251, 257, 716	270, 277, 281	64		
character		105, 115, 156, 174, 369, 447, 472, 574	67, 77, 107, 270, 365, 468, 622	40, 47, 53, 63, 109, 126, 145, 157, 429, 669, 706, 708	39, 44, 52, 154, 460, 570, 662, 772	211, 339, 441, 512	41, 79, 103, 726, 731	
comparison/contrast		265, 369	67	63, 669, 708	52, 570, 662, 772	29, 39, 95, 391, 496, 588, 605, 621, 632, 896–897	127, 269, 507, 650, 701, 893, 913, 937, 951, 986	
diction and sentence structure						171, 827	249	
drama		45, 405, 592	23, 431, 640		383	711	225, 640	
figures of speech				205	114, 117	220		
imagery		233, 240	238, 247, 628	216	207, 213, 251	227	143	
irony					129, 784	391	351	
nonfiction		295, 312, 586	305, 323, 328, 634	262, 273, 277, 280, 285, 289, 718	296, 309, 320, 323, 326, 332, 339, 349, 786	180, 244, 844, 853, 900–901	231, 339, 465, 705, 990	
plot		57, 72, 85, 126, 167, 279, 443, 461, 572	41, 52, 243, 273, 620	26, 138, 151, 704	28, 770	113, 583	764	
poetry		218, 269, 277, 281, 580	225, 234, 285, 289, 628	167, 173, 178, 205, 212, 215, 217, 225, 226, 720	181, 194, 198, 206, 215, 217, 227, 230, 233, 235, 239, 255, 788	134, 273, 287, 387, 413, 420, 426, 449, 463, 779, 906–907	452, 527, 537, 545, 646, 671, 679, 685, 996	
point of view				85, 94 ,151, 178, 712	75, 776	801		
purpose				245, 257, 280, 285	270	653, 660, 853	339, 990	
review of a book or drama		45, 405, 533, 592	23, 431, 582, 640					
setting		131, 182	92, 167, 482	69, 75, 80, 710	58, 68, 774	324		
symbol					114, 117, 345, 782	333, 627, 832, 840, 902–903	431, 501, 667, 688, 724, 992	
theme		145	189	114, 118, 157, 540, 714	90, 99, 108, 780	124, 475, 535, 810, 904–905	285, 756, 803, 873, 994	
tone					86, 154, 289, 778	305	656	
total effect			189, 628	145, 429, 540, 669, 722	141, 167, 259, 570, 735, 790	149, 637, 651, 908–909	225, 640, 998	

Scope and Sequence

MACMILLAN LITERATURE SERIES

The heart of your language arts program.

Composition Skills	**Discovering Literature**	**Introducing Literature**	**Enjoying Literature**	**Understanding Literature**	**Appreciating Literature**	**American Literature**	**English Literature with World Masterpieces**	**World Literature**
CREATIVE (Students are asked to create the following kinds of written materials.)								
anecdote				126	270	588		
aphorisms						64		
article				145	108, 114, 606			
description		156, 182, 216, 265, 269, 312, 447, 466, 472, 477	67, 77, 92, 273, 323, 462, 482, 493	69, 75, 94, 151, 205, 216, 277, 289	58, 68, 99, 117, 141, 192, 206, 207, 251, 320, 323, 383	45, 92, 118, 149, 191, 339, 366, 463, 475, 512, 621, 660	41, 103, 294, 406, 431, 527, 545	
dialogue		150, 423, 443	243, 468	109	20, 52, 570	711	933	
diary, journal entry		105	52, 582	33, 47, 262	133	29, 252, 651	305, 711, 756	
drama		45, 126, 369, 594	23, 189, 431, 468, 642	138, 304	75	420, 711	507, 861, 877, 913	
essay		295, 312, 322	305, 323, 328	273, 280, 285	296, 309, 326, 339, 349	171, 180, 844, 869	231, 339, 705	
fable		145, 455	139	118	90	305		
figurative language, imagery			238	63	213, 217	220, 387	143, 342, 667	
narrative, story		14, 72, 115, 174, 279, 308, 451, 461, 576	5, 107, 167, 624	53, 80, 85, 151, 157, 225, 429, 540	150, 281, 309	449, 482, 496, 613	286, 514, 724, 893	
opinion				245, 280	129	69, 353, 653		
persuasion		238, 322	365	280	44, 167, 326, 332	39, 84, 605		
poem		131, 218, 226, 233, 240, 257, 277, 281, 582	229, 265, 275, 279, 285, 630	167, 215, 217, 226, 327	181, 183, 186, 194, 198, 213, 215, 227, 230, 233, 235, 239, 244, 251, 255, 259	273, 413, 426, 459, 552, 765	127, 646, 650, 656, 662, 671, 679, 683, 825, 937	
point of view				173, 178, 669	309	113	685, 873	
setting			92, 487	304	68, 320	333, 637		
sketch				240, 251, 487	270	118, 211, 324	365, 701	
speech				114	44, 332, 460	257, 420, 827	225, 507	

Vocabulary Skills	**Discovering Literature**	**Introducing Literature**	**Enjoying Literature**	**Understanding Literature**	**Appreciating Literature**	**American Literature**	**English Literature with World Masterpieces**	**World Literature**
analogies		182, 317	73, 328	262	154, 309, 662	287, 560, 660	469, 501, 925, 937, 961	
antonyms		135, 150, 447	156, 232, 449	26, 114, 157	114, 296, 332	39, 124, 366, 601, 711	286, 358, 540, 764, 913, 955	
connotation/denotation			453	213	200	149, 211		
context clues		22, 95, 201	11, 86, 365, 458, 581	85	99, 150, 320			
dialect		238	102	126, 210	606	324	640	
dictionary		80	58, 482					
etymology		267, 385, 477	260, 318	75, 151, 487	39, 270, 339, 460	14, 92, 420, 773, 785	97, 305, 873	
glossary		138	96					
jargon, technical words, slang		369	305	181, 728	735	512		
pronunciation key		303	393					
sentence completions		65, 115, 161, 186, 265, 279, 461	47, 227	273	44, 133, 326	29, 87, 535, 651	861	
synonyms		14, 58, 107, 221, 295	5, 41, 130, 312	10, 40, 245	20, 75, 345	22, 64, 455, 832	89, 231, 331, 481, 650, 929	
thesaurus		252	179					
word choice		252	179	185, 251, 280	129, 188, 200, 227, 232, 289, 735	80, 171, 227, 257, 366, 512, 563	371, 431, 679	
word development, invention				190	167, 246, 270, 339	273	903	

Glencoe/McGraw-Hill
A Macmillan/McGraw-Hill Company
15319 Chatsworth Street
Mission Hills, California 91345

Capra Press
RAYMOND CARVER: "Everything Stuck to Him" from *Fires: Essays, Poems, Stories.* Copyright © 1983 by Raymond Carver. Reprinted by permission of Capra Press, Santa Barbara.

Carnegie-Mellon University Press
RITA DOVE: "Geometry" from *The Yellow House on the Corner.* Copyright © 1980 by Rita Dove. By permission of Carnegie-Mellon University Press.

Diana Chang
DIANA CHANG: "Most Satisfied by Snow" from *Asian-American Heritage—An Anthology of Prose and Poetry* edited by David Hsin-Fu Wand. Copyright © 1974 by David Hsin-Fu Wand. Reprinted by permission of Diana Chang.

Chatto and Windus Ltd.
WILLIAM FAULKNER: "The Bear" from *Go Down Moses.* Reprinted by permission of the Estate of William Faulkner and Chatto and Windus Ltd.
BERNARD MALAMUD: "The First Seven Years" from *The Magic Barrel.* Reprinted by permission of Bernard Malamud and Chatto and Windus Ltd.

Lucha Corpi
LUCHA CORPI: "Emily Dickinson" from *Palabras de Mediodia/Noon Words,* translated by Catherine Rodríguez-Nieto. Reprinted by permission of Lucha Corpi and Catherine Rodríguez-Nieto.

Delacorte Press/Seymour Lawrence
MARK HELPRIN: "White Gardens" from *Ellis Island and Other Stories.* Copyright © 1981 by Mark Helprin. Reprinted by permission of Delacorte Press/Seymour Lawrence.

Dodd, Mead & Company, Inc.
PAUL LAURENCE DUNBAR: "Douglass" from *The Complete Poems of Paul Laurence Dunbar,* 1968. Reprinted by permission of Dodd, Mead & Company, Inc.

Doubleday & Company, Inc.
THEODORE ROETHKE: "Big Wind." Copyright 1947 by The Saturday Review Association, Inc. "The Waking." Copyright 1953 by Theodore Roethke. Both selections from *The Selected Poems of Theodore Roethke.*
The preceding selections were reprinted by permission of Doubleday, a division of Bantam, Doubleday, Dell Publishing Group, Inc.

Ernst Cane Berner & Gitlin
SINCLAIR LEWIS: "The Hack Driver" from *Selected Short Stories of Sinclair Lewis.* Copyright 1923 by Sinclair Lewis. Reprinted by permission of Ernst Cane Berner & Gitlin.

Norma Millay Ellis
EDNA ST. VINCENT MILLAY: "Recuerdo" from *Collected Poems.* Copyright 1922, 1923, 1950, 1951 by Edna St. Vincent Millay and Norma Millay Ellis. Reprinted by permission of Norma Millay Ellis.

Faber and Faber Ltd.
W. H. AUDEN: "If I Could Tell You" and "The Unknown Citizen" from *Collected Poems.*
T. S. ELIOT: "The Love Song of J. Alfred Prufrock" from *Collected Poems 1909–1962.*
The preceding selections were reprinted by permission of Faber and Faber Ltd.

Farrar, Straus and Giroux, Inc.
ELIZABETH BISHOP: "The Fish" from *Elizabeth Bishop: The Complete Poems.* Copyright © 1940, 1969 by Elizabeth Bishop.
RANDALL JARRELL: "The Death of the Ball-Turret Gunner" from *Randall Jarrell: The Complete Poems.* Copyright 1945, 1969 by Mrs. Randall Jarrell. Copyright renewed © 1973 by Mrs. Randall Jarrell.
ROBERT LOWELL: "Hawthorne" from *For the Union Dead.* Copyright © 1956, 1960, 1961, 1962, 1963, 1964 by Robert Lowell.
BERNARD MALAMUD: "The First Seven Years" from *The Magic Barrel.* Copyright © 1950, 1958 by Bernard Malamud. Copyright renewed © 1978 by Bernard Malamud.
The preceding selections were reprinted by permission of Farrar, Straus and Giroux, Inc.

A. C. Greene

A. C. GREENE: "The Girl at Cabe Ranch" from *The Highland Park Woman*. Copyright © 1983 by A. C. Greene and reprinted by permission of the author.

GRM Associates Inc.

COUNTEE CULLEN: "Any Human to Another" from *On These I Stand* by Countee Cullen. Copyright © 1947 Harper & Brothers. Copyright renewed 1975 by Ida M. Cullen. Reprinted by permission of GRM Associates Inc., agents for the estate of Ida M. Cullen.

Grosset & Dunlap, Inc.

JAMES AGEE: "Knoxville: Summer, 1915" from *A Death in the Family*. Copyright © 1957 by The James Agee Trust. Reprinted by permission of Grosset & Dunlap, Inc.

Grove Press, Inc.

JACK KEROUAC: From pp. 121–130 in *Lonesome Traveler*. Copyright © 1960 by Jack Kerouac. Reprinted by permission of Grove Press, Inc.

Harcourt Brace Jovanovich, Inc.

T. S. ELIOT: "The Love Song of J. Alfred Prufrock" from *Collected Poems 1901–1962*. Copyright 1936 by Harcourt Brace Jovanovich, Inc.; copyright © 1963, 1964 by T. S. Eliot.

ELIZABETH ENRIGHT: "The Signature" from *The Riddle of the Fly and Other Stories*. Copyright © 1956 bt Elizabeth Enright.

KENNETH FEARING: "Cracked Record Blues" from *Afternoon of a Pawnbroker and Other Poems*. Copyright 1942 by Kenneth Fearing; renewed 1970 by Bruce Fearing.

KATHERINE ANNE PORTER: "The Jilting of Granny Weatherall" from *Flowering Judas and Other Stories*. Copyright 1930, 1958 by Katherine Anne Porter.

CARL SANDBURG: "Chicago" from *Chicago Poems*. Copyright 1916 by Holt, Rinehart and Winston, Inc.; copyright 1944 by Carl Sandburg. Excerpt from *The People, Yes*. Copyright 1936 by Harcourt Brace Jovanovich, Inc.; renewed 1964 by Carl Sandburg. "Jazz Fantasia" from *Smoke and Steel*. Copyright 1920 by Harcourt Brace Jovanovich, Inc.; copyright 1948 by Carl Sandburg.

EUDORA WELTY: "A Worn Path" from *A Curtain of Green and Other Stories*. Copyright 1941, 1969 by Eudora Welty.

RICHARD WILBUR: "Year's End" from *Ceremony and Other Poems*. First published in *The New Yorker*. Copyright 1949, 1977 by Richard Wilbur.

The preceding selections were reprinted by permission of Harcourt Brace Jovanovich, Inc.

Harper & Row Publishers, Inc.

GWENDOLYN BROOKS: "Strong Men, Riding Horses" from *The World of Gwendolyn Brooks*. Copyright © 1959 by Gwendolyn Brooks.

ANNIE DILLARD: Excerpt (pages 45–49) from *An American Childhood*. Copyright © 1987 by Annie Dillard. Reprinted by permission of Harper & Row, Publishers, Inc.

SIMON ORTIZ: "My Mother and My Sisters" from *Going for the Rain*. Copyright © 1976 by Simon J. Ortiz.

SYLVIA PLATH: "Blackberrying" from *The Collected Poems*. Copyright © 1962 by Ted Hughes. First appeared in *The New Yorker*.

WILLIAM STAFFORD: "Father and Son" from *Stories That Could Be True*. Copyright © 1972 by William Stafford.

THORNTON WILDER: The play *Our Town*. Copyright © 1938, 1957 by Thornton Wilder. Caution! *Our Town* is the sole property of the author and is fully protected by copyright. It may not be acted by professionals or amateurs without formal permission and the payment of a royalty. All rights, including professional, amateur, stock, radio and television, broadcasting, motion picture, recitation, lecturing, public reading, and the rights of translation into foreign languages are reserved. All professional inquiries should be addressed to the author's agent: Harold Freedman, Brandt & Brandt Dramatic Department, Inc., 101 Park Avenue, New York, NY 10017. All requests for amateur rights should be addressed to Samuel French, 45 West 25th Street, New York, NY 10010.

The preceding selections were reprinted by permission of Harper & Row, Publishers, Inc.

Harvard University Press

ANNE BRADSTREET: "To My Dear and Loving Husband" from *The Works of Anne Bradstreet* edited by Jeanine Hensley. Copyright 1967 by the President and Fellows of Harvard College.

WILLIAM BYRD: "A Progress to the Mines" from *The Prose Works of William Byrd of Westover*. Copyright 1966 by the President and Fellows of Harvard College.

The preceding selections were reprinted by permission of the Harvard University Press.

EMILY DICKINSON: "Apparently with no surprise," "Because I could not stop for Death—" "The Bustle in a House," "I dwell in Possibility—" "I felt a funeral, in my Brain," "I heard a fly buzz," "I never saw a Moor—" "My life closed twice before its close," " 'Nature' is what we see—" "The Soul selects her own Society—" "Success is counted sweetest," "There's a certain Slant of light,"

"This is my Letter to the World," and "This World is not Conclusion" from *The Poems of Emily Dickinson,* edited by Thomas H. Johnson, Cambridge, Mass.: The Belknap Press of Harvard University Press. Copyright 1951, © 1955, 1979 by the President and Fellows of Harvard College. Reprinted by permission of the publishers and the Trustees of Amherst College.

Henry Holt & Company

ROBERT FROST: "Acquainted with the Night," "Birches," "Desert Places," "Fire and Ice," "Mending Wall," "Nothing Gold Can Stay," "The Road Not Taken," and "Stopping by Woods on a Snowy Evening" from *The Poetry of Robert Frost* edited by Edward Connery Lathem. Copyright 1916, 1923, 1928, 1930, 1939, © 1969 by Holt, Rinehart and Winston. Copyright 1936, 1944, 1951, © 1956, 1958 by Robert Frost. Copyright © 1964, 1967 by Lesley Frost Ballantine. Reprinted by permission of Henry Holt & Company.

Houghton Mifflin Company

ARCHIBALD MACLEISH: "Ars Poetica" from *New and Collected Poems 1917–1976.* Copyright © 1976 by Archibald MacLeish.

CARSON MCCULLERS: Excerpt from *The Mortgaged Heart.* Copyright © 1963 by Carson McCullers. Copyright © 1971 by Floria V. Lasky.

AMERICO PAREDES, RAYMUND PAREDES, and HARVEY R. GRANITE: "Dichos" from *Mexican-American Authors,* pp. 27–34. Copyright © 1976, 1972 by Houghton Mifflin Company. Adapted by permission of the publisher.

ANNE SEXTON: "What's That" from *To Bedlam and Part Way Back.* Copyright © 1960 by Anne Sexton.

REED WHITTTEMORE: "The Fall of the House of Usher" from *The Mother's Breast and the Father's House.* Copyright © 1974 by Reed Whittemore.

The preceding selections were reprinted by permission of Houghton Mifflin Company.

Olwyn Hughes

SYLVIA PLATH: "Blackberrying" from *Crossing the Water.* Published by Faber & Faber Ltd., London. Copyright © 1971 by Ted Hughes. Reprinted by permission of Olwyn Hughes.

International Creative Management

WALTER VAN TILBURG CLARK: "The Portable Phonograph" from *The Watchful Gods and Other Stories.* Copyright © 1941, 1969 by Walter Van Tilburg Clark.

WILLIAM GOYEN: "The Moss Rose" from *The Collected Stories of William Goyen.* Copyright © 1975 by William Goyen.

The preceding selections were reprinted by permission of International Creative Management, Inc.

Alfred A. Knopf, Inc.

WILLIAM BRADFORD: From *Of Plymouth Plantation,* edited by Samuel Eliot Morison. Copyright 1952 by Samuel Eliot Morison.

WILLA CATHER: "Neighbor Rosicky" from *Obscure Destinies.* Copyright 1932 by Willa Cather and renewed 1960 by Executors of the Estate of Willa Cather.

LANGSTON HUGHES: "Dream Variations" from *Selected Poems of Langston Hughes.* Copyright 1926 by Alfred A. Knopf, Inc. and renewed 1954 by Langston Hughes.

JOHN CROWE RANSOM: "Janet Waking" from *Selected Poems, Third Edition, Revised and Enlarged.* Copyright 1927 by Alfred A. Knopf, Inc. and renewed 1955 by John Crowe Ransom.

WALLACE STEVENS: "Anecdote of the Jar" and "The Load of Sugar Cane" from *The Collected Poems of Wallace Stevens.* Copyright 1923 and renewed 1951 by Wallace Stevens.

JOHN UPDIKE: "The Slump" from *Museums and Women and Other Stories.* Copyright © 1968 by John Updike.

The preceding selections were reprinted by permission of Alfred A. Knopf, Inc.

Liveright Publishing Corporation

E. E. CUMMINGS: "r-p-o-p-h-e-s-s-a-g-r" from *No Thanks.* Copyright 1935 by E. E. Cummings. Copyright © 1968 by Marion Morehouse Cummings. Copyright © 1973, 1976 by Nancy T. Andrews. Copyright © 1973, 1978 by George James Firmage. Copyright © 1978 by Richard S. Kennedy. "since feeling is first" from *IS 5 Poems.* Copyright 1926 by Horace Liveright Publisher. Copyright renewed 1953 by E. E. Cummings. "your little voice" from *Tulips & Chimneys.* Copyright 1923, 1925 and renewed 1951, 1953 by E. E. Cummings. Copyright © 1973, 1976 by Nancy T. Andrews. Copyright © 1973, 1976 by George James Firmage.

ROBERT HAYDEN: "Those Winter Sundays" from *Angle of Ascent, New and Selected Poems.* Copyright © 1975, 1972, 1970, 1966 by Robert Hayden.

JEAN TOOMER: "November Cotton Flower" from *Cane.* Copyright 1923 by Boni & Liveright. Copyright renewed 1951 by Jean Toomer.

The preceding selections were reprinted by permission of Liveright Publishing Corporation.

Macmillan Publishing Company

MARIANNE MOORE: "Poetry" from *Collected Poems.* Copyright 1935 by Marianne Moore, renewed 1963 by Marianne Moore and T. S. Eliot. Reprinted by permission of Macmillan Publishing Company.

Ellen C. Masters

EDGAR LEE MASTERS: "Cassius Hueffer" and "Lucinda Matlock" from *Spoon River Anthology.* Reprinted by permission of Ellen C. Masters.

CREDITS

Illustration Credits:
Lloyd Bloom, 184; Debbi Chabrian, 590, 595, 599; Steve Chalker, 788, 791; William Cigliano, 514, 519, 525, 531; Mike Dean, 821; Lulu Delacre, 327, 331; Donna Diamond, 608, 611; Teresa Fasolino, 276, 278–279, 280, 282; Donald Gates, 643, 647; Hiroko, 625; Chet Jezierski, 16–17; Ed Martinez, 576, 587; Bob Masheris, 831; Michael McNelly, 390, 825; Robert Olson, 804; Alexis Oussenko, 396, 397; Winslow Pels, 137, 140, 147; Jerry Pinkney, 616, 619; Larry Raymond, 498, 503, 509; Thom Ricks, 4, 5, 6, 53, 54, 55, 102, 103, 157, 158, 234, 235, 312, 313, 314, 406, 407, 408, 542, 543, 544, 746, 747; Mike Rodericks, 813, 814; Roger Roth, 107, 108, 112; Bob Shore, 204, 209; Robert Steele, 415, 416, 417, 418; Terry Suhre, 557; Kurt Wallace, 242–243; John Wallner, 7; Chuck Wimmer, 301, 484; Lisa Young, 197.

Photo Credits: Akron Beacon Journal, 782. © Ann Atwood, 465. Art Color Slides, Inc. Francis G. Mayer (Metropolitan Museum of Art) 49T, 49B, 98TL, 98BR, 99T, 230CR. Courtesy of The Art Institute of Chicago: © 1981 Arizona Board of Regents, Center for Creative Photography, Edward Weston, 219. AT&T Co., 308TC. The Bettmann Archive, Inc.: xxCL, 15, 165, 310, 311, 316, 403, 404, 405, 440, 478, 538TR, 539B, 545, 589. Black Star: © Mark Ferstein, 756C; © Shelly Katz, 797C; © Andy Levin, 777; © Laurence Nelson, 778; © Flip Schulke, 797B; © Tom Tracy, 756TL. © Bernd Bohner, 784. © Michael Campbell, 565. The Collection of Mr. & Mrs. Leo Castelli, 816 Essex Institute, 153T. Sterling and Francine Clark Art Institute, all rights reserved, Acc. No. 8, detail, 372. Bruce Coleman, Inc.: © Bruce Coleman, 550; © Michael P. Gadomski, 155, 169; © M. Timothy O'Keefe, 559. © Nancy Crampton, 1987, 841, 859. Culver Pictures, Inc.: 23, 52, 56, 65, 76, 81, 104, 114, 119, 125, 159, 172, 181, 203, 230CB, 239, 258, 260, 274, 288, 315, 367, 386, 400TC, BR, 402, 429, 432, 437, 439, 444T, 483, 497, 602, 638, 668. © Walker Evans Estate, 540. © Marlene Foster-Ortiz, 780. Friends Historical Library of Swarthmore College, 393. Courtesy, Gainesville Hall Chamber of Commerce, 386–387. Thomas Gilcrease Institute of American History and Art, Tulsa, Oklahoma: photograph by Mark Haynes, 230TR, 259, 308BR. The Granger Collection: cover, xxTL, TC, CR, BC, 1C, 3, 19, 20, 24, 40, 48TR, TC, CL, BL, BC, BR, 49C, 61, 66, 70, 82, 85, 88, 98C, BL, 99C, 101, 152TL, TR, CL, BL, 153B, 217, 230CL, BL, 231T, C, 232, 233, 238, 245, 249, 253, 255, 308TL, TR, CL, CR, BL, 309C, 392, 394, 400BL, 456, 476, 513, 538C, 622. Courtesy, John Hancock Mutual Life Insurance, 796. Historical Picture Service, Chicago: 2, 27, 32, 50, 93, 153C, 216, 221, 223, 251, 291, 325, 434, 492. The Image Bank: © Art Wolfe, 843. Joslyn Liberal Arts Society, 603. Knoxville-Knox County Public Library: from the McClung Historical Collection, 631. Library of the American Library Association, 633. Life Magazine © 1944 Time Inc.: © Alfred Eisenstaedt, 791. Magnum Photos, Inc.: 421; © Dennis Stock, 447. © Bob Marshak, 722, 729, 741, 749. Maryland Historical Society, 48TL. The Metropolitan Museum of Art: Gift of Mrs. J. Insley Blair, 1950, 44, 603; The Harris Brisbane Dick Fund, 1929, 247; Gift of George A. Hearn, 1910, 309B, (10.64.5) detail, 378; Gift of George A. Hearn in Memory of Arthur Hoppock Hearne, 1911, 160; Purchase of Dikran G. Kelekian Gift, 1922 (22.27.1) detail, 382; The Alfred Stieglitz Collection, 1949, 401C, 424–425. Missouri Historical Society: photograph by Oscar Ruehn, 295. Monkmeyer Press Photo: © Frieda Leinwand, 851. Museum of Art, Rhode Island School of Design: Gift of Walter Callender, Henry D. Sharpe, Howard L. Clark, William Gammell, Isaac Bate, Acc. No. 06.002.337. Museum of The City of New York, Theatre Collection, 667. Courtesy, Museum of Fine Arts, Boston: Gift of W.G. Russell Allen, 100, 126; Gift of Samuel Bradstreet, 1B, 51. NASA Photo, 756. National Academy of Design, detail, 152C. National Gallery, London: Tate Gallery Publications, 369. National Parks Service, 168. Courtesy of The New York Historical Society, 99B. The New York Public Library: 30, 36, 224, 225, 226, 334; Photographic Service, 122; Picture Collection, 35, 89, 538CL; Prints Division, 98TR. Courtesy, New York State Museum, 73. ©

Miguel Pagliere, 796. Courtesy of the Pennsylvania Academy of The Fine Arts, 231B. Photo Researchers, Inc.: © John Bryson, 401B, 489; © Jules Bucher, 270; © David R. Frazier, 213; © Farrell Grehan, 154, 256, 462; © Dan Guravich, 443; © Ned Haines/Rapho Division, 156, 555; © Tom Hollyman, 401T, 464; © P.B. Kaplan, 428; © Paolo Koch, 539C; © Michael Phillip Manheim, 568; © Lynn McLaren, 275; © W.T. Morgan/National Audubon Division, 355, 363; © J.J. Audubon/National Audubon Division, cover, 764; © Bruce Roberts, 33; © Douglas R. Shane, 98LC; © Michael Uffer, 410; © M.E. Warren, 756. Courtesy of The Pierpont Morgan Library, back cover. © Ben Rosenthal, 713. © Anne Sager, 783. The St. Louis Art Museum: 266, 309T. Collection of San Diego Museum of Art: Mrs. Henry A. Everett Bequest, 400CL. Shostal Associates: © Martin Bordner, 222; © Ernest Manewal, 571; © Fletcher Manley, 363; © Ozzie Sweet, 214. Smithsonian Institution: Cooper-Hewitt Museum, National Museum of Design, Gift of Mrs. Margaret Carnegie Miller, 1977, 400BC; Gift of Edgar William & Bernice Chrysler Garbisch, 230BR; National Gallery of Art, 152BR, 400TR; National Museum of American Art, Gift of Mrs. Joseph Harrison Jr., xxBL; National Portrait Gallery, on loan from Serena Williams Miles Van Rennesselar, 245. © Bob & Ira Spring, 656, 656–657, 657. © Martha Swope, 455, 670L&R, 674, 694, 698, 704, 707. Sygma: © Michael Childers, 712; © Y. Coatsalion, 862; © E. Feinblatt, 818. © Gregory Thorp, 458, 472. United Press International: 442, 448, 539T, 556, 563, 654, 661, 815, 849, 854, 866. University of Nebraska, F.M. Hall Collection, Sheldon Memorial Art Gallery, 538CR. University of Texas at Austin, 847. Vassar Alumnae Magazine, 230TL. © Peter Veit/E.P.D., 775. Courtesy, Wadsworth Atheneum, Gift of William Warren in memory of Florence Paul Berger, 1976, 31. From Collection of Sam Wagstaff: © Art Sinsabaugh, 1962, 344–345. Wheelright Museum of The American Indian, Santa Fe, New Mexico: photograph by Herb Lotz, 1T, 12, 780. Collection of Whitney Museum of American Art: photo, Geoffrey Clements, 430, 444, 538BR; Juliana Force Purchase, 663; Gift of The Friends of the Whitney Museum of American Art, 759; Gift of The Friends of the Whitney Museum of American Art, Mr. & Mrs. Eugene M. Schwartz, Mrs. Samuel A. Seave, Charles Simon Purchase, 541; Gift of Mr. & Mrs. Roy R. Neuberger, 450B. Wide World Photos: 354, 388, 628, 767, 788, 828. H.W. Wilson, from the book, Living Authors, 427. © Kelly Wise, 833. © William D. Wittlift, 811. Worcester Art Museum: xxTR, 98TR. © Yale University Art Gallery, 77. Drawing by Ziegler, © 1983 The New Yorker Magazine, 758.

A LETTER TO THE STUDENT

American Literature is an anthology, a collection, of fiction, poetry, drama, and nonfiction. Three organizing ideas stand behind this anthology, and understanding them will help you to see how the book is put together.

First, all the selections are by Americans, to draw a vivid portrait of the unique and varied culture that is America. Second, the selections are strung together chronologically—that is, in order of time—to trace the changes in attitudes, ideas, and styles that have occurred in our culture over the past several centuries. Third, the selections represent some of the finest writing by the finest authors America has produced, to offer you examples of the greatest ideas and the most influential creations of the American mind.

Whether you are writing it or reading it, literature demands thinking. In fact, along with enjoyment, *thinking about literature* should be one of your principal goals as you read. To help you think in an organized way, this book provides you with short biographies of the authors and a statement to focus your thinking. After each selection, three kinds of Study Questions help you *recall* the details of a selection, *interpret* the meaning of those details, and *extend* that meaning into your own experience. A special feature called Viewpoint will introduce you to other people's thoughts about what you have read and will encourage you to think further. Another special feature called Model for Active Reading shows you how reading and thinking form a valuable partnership.

Near the back of this book you will find a special section called "Student's Resources: Lessons in Active Learning." The handbooks that make up this section are practical guides for responding to literature by speaking, thinking, researching, and writing. Each handbook lesson is designed to help you grow as an active, independent reader and thinker. The Research Paper Casebook offers you both instruction and sources for writing a full-fledged literary research paper.

The purpose of *American Literature,* then, is to introduce you to some highly enjoyable writing and to help you think logically and creatively about it. In fact, as the writers in this book so powerfully demonstrate, the more you think about literature, the richer your insights will be.

CONTENTS

The selections in American Literature *were carefully chosen. The annotations indicate the literary form or the idea that each selection illustrates.*

Native Grounds 1800–1840

New England Renaissance 1840–1855

Regionalism and Realism 1880–1910

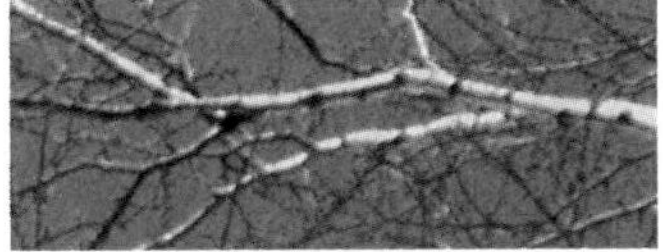

New Directions 1910–1930

Modernist short story
Short story: characterization
Short story: theme
Villanelle
Satire
Lyric of remembrance
Villanelle
Lyric portrait
Jazz lyric
Descriptive lyric
Ironic war poem
Modern poets' view of the past
Poetic parody
Lyric: meditation
Lyric: nature
Lyric: unanswered questions
Stream-of-consciousness story
Anecdote as modern story
Story of an American hero
Short story: theme and character
Frame story: point of view

STUDENT'S RESOURCES

Related blackline masters in *Teacher's Classroom Resources.*

Instruction and literature-based activities for oral/aural skills. Students may use lessons with *any* selection.

Definition, example, explanation for each skill plus procedures for application to literature. Students may use lessons with *any* selection.

Composition assignments throughout the text refer to these lessons, which reinforce prewriting, writing, and revising skills.

Complete instruction on all phases of producing a literary research paper—followed by secondary sources related to Frost's poetry.

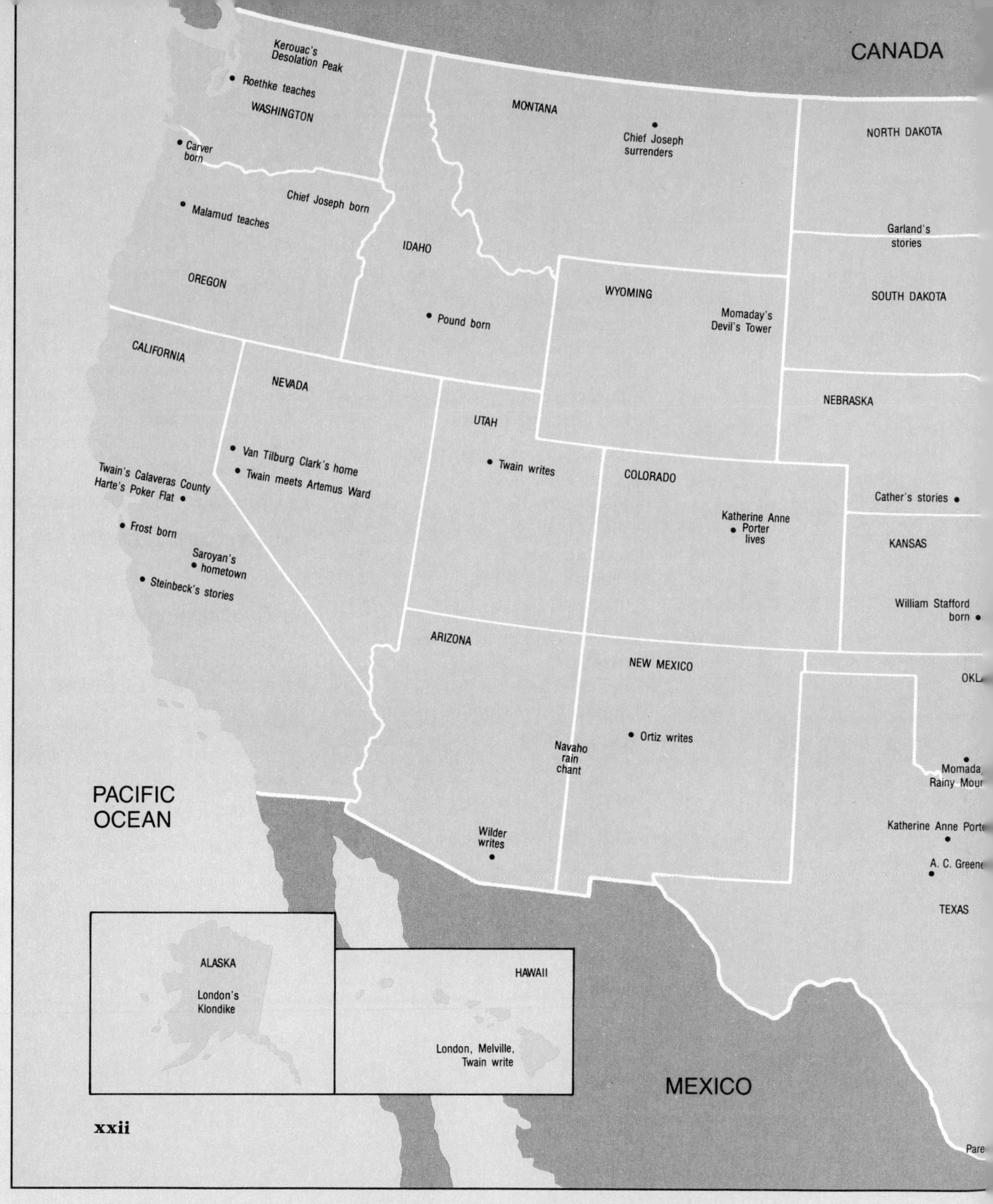
CANADA
Kerouac's Desolation Peak
Roethke teaches
WASHINGTON
Carver born
MONTANA
Chief Joseph surrenders
NORTH DAKOTA
Chief Joseph born
Malamud teaches
IDAHO
OREGON
Garland's stories
SOUTH DAKOTA
WYOMING
Momaday's Devil's Tower
Pound born
CALIFORNIA
NEVADA
NEBRASKA
UTAH
Van Tilburg Clark's home
Twain meets Artemus Ward
Twain writes
COLORADO
Twain's Calaveras County
Harte's Poker Flat
Cather's stories
Katherine Anne Porter lives
KANSAS
Frost born
Saroyan's hometown
Steinbeck's stories
William Stafford born
ARIZONA
NEW MEXICO
Ortiz writes
Navaho rain chant
PACIFIC OCEAN
Wilder writes
ALASKA
London's Klondike
HAWAII
London, Melville, Twain write
TEXAS
MEXICO

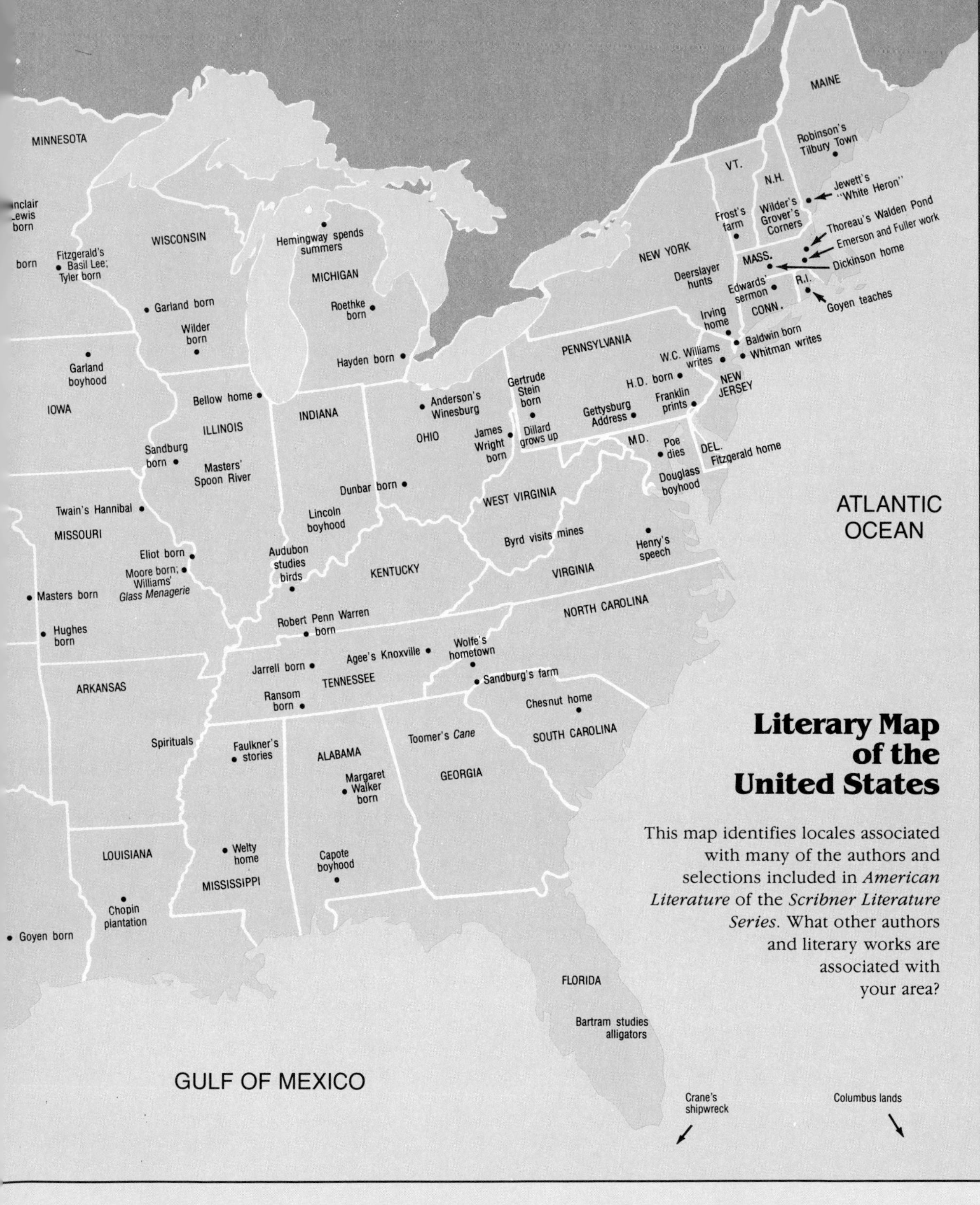

Literary Map of the United States

This map identifies locales associated with many of the authors and selections included in *American Literature* of the *Scribner Literature Series*. What other authors and literary works are associated with your area?

Key to Illustrations appears on page 47.

EARLY AMERICA

To 1750

American Beginnings

America has always been a land of beginnings. After Europeans "discovered" America in the fifteenth century, the mysterious New World became for many people a genuine hope of a new life, an escape from poverty and persecution, a chance to start again. We can say that, as a nation, America begins with that hope. When, however, does American *literature* begin?

American literature begins with American experiences. Long before the first colonists arrived, before Christopher Columbus, before the Northmen who "found" America about the year 1000, Native Americans lived here. Each tribe's literature was tightly woven into the fabric of daily life and reflected the unmistakably American experience of living with the land. Another kind of experience, one filled with fear and excitement, found its expression in the reports that Columbus and other explorers sent home in Spanish, French, and English. In addition, the journals of the people who lived and died in the New England wilderness tell unforgettable tales of hard and sometimes heartbreaking experiences of those early years.

Experience, then, is the key to early American literature. The New World provided a great variety of experiences, and these experiences demanded a wide variety of expressions by an even wider variety of early American writers. These

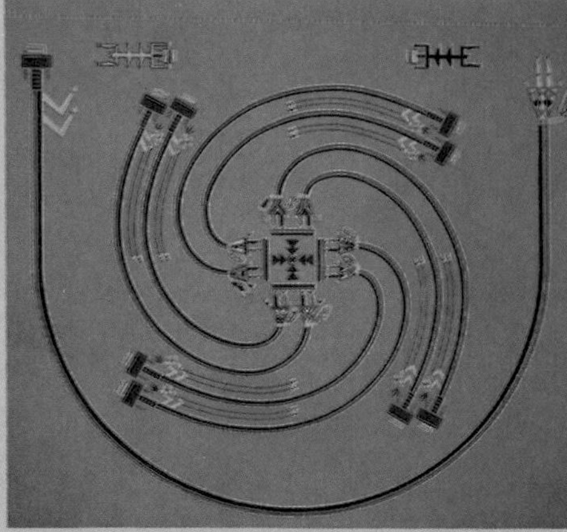

INTRODUCTION

After the students have read the introduction to the unit, ask them to think for a minute about *beginnings*—moving to a new house, for example, or meeting someone special for the first time. Elicit the understanding that at the beginning there is no knowledge of how things are going to turn out—no hindsight—only hope, wonder, uncertainty, and probably fear. Tell the students that the literature they will be reading in the unit on early America is a record of a people's beginnings.

Point out that early American writers did what writers always do: relate their experiences of life. As a concerted voice the Puritans dominate early American literature, and their influence on American letters and culture has been enormous. You might list the following contributions:

- theology—the concepts of grace and salvation
- social thinking—the vision of a utopia, or New Jerusalem
- economics—the work ethic
- politics—the democratic principles of the *Mayflower* compact and New England town meetings
- literary style—the Plain Style

Note that the southern English colonies present another way of life. Unlike Puritan New England, with its growing towns and cities, there were few communities in the South. Moreover, southern settlers were not usually radicals who sought to sever ties with Britain but members of the Church of England with stronger attachments to their mother country. Southern literature is thus decidedly different in character from that of New England: It is witty, urbane, and largely imitative of British models.

Key Ideas in This Period

- discovery
- grace and salvation
- utopias
- the American landscape
- democratic principles
- practicality

Title page of *The General History of Virginia, New England, and the Summer Isles,* John Smith, 1624.

THE
GENERALL HISTORIE
OF
Virginia, New-England, and the Summer
Isles: with the names of the Adventurers,
Planters, and Governours from their
first beginning An: 1584. to this
present 1624.
With the Procedings of those Severall Colonies
and the Accidents that befell them in all their
Journyes and Discoveries.
Also the Maps and Descriptions of all those
Countryes, their Commodities, people,
Government, Customes, and Religion
yet knowne.
Divided into sixe Bookes.
By Captaine John Smith sometymes Governour
in those Countryes & Admirall
of New England.
LONDON.
Printed by I.D. and
I.H. for Michael
Sparkes.
1624.

writers included John Smith (page 19), who spent only about two-and-one-half years on the American continent. They included Jonathan Edwards (page 40) and William Byrd (page 35), who thought of themselves as British subjects, never suspecting a revolution that would create a United States of America with a literature of its own. American Indians, explorers, Pilgrims, Puritan ministers, frontier wives, plantation owners—they are all the creators of the first American literature.

The Puritans

The ship *Mayflower* carried about one hundred passengers (their leader called them Pilgrims, or travelers) and took sixty-six days to beat its way across the Atlantic. In December of 1620, the *Mayflower* put the Pilgrims ashore at Plymouth, Massachusetts. Before the unrelenting winter was over, half of them were dead. Within the next few years, however, those who survived were joined by more settlers from England. Only some of these first colonists were *Puritans,* but it was the Puritans, led by their clergymen, who dominated the government, the religious outlook, and the literature of the communities they established.

Who were these extraordinary people? The Puritans were devout Christians who wanted to *purify* their lives and their church of what they saw as the corruptions of English society and its state religion, the Church of England. They called themselves Saints or Separatists, but they are now generally called Puritans—a name that became a sign of their separateness.

The Puritans believed in an all-powerful God who freely granted to his "Saints" the gift of *grace.* Grace was a complicated matter for the Puritans, but it can be described as the spirit that would guarantee salvation—eternal happiness with God. In their daily lives the Puritans wanted to demonstrate at every moment that they possessed grace or that they were worthy of it.

For the Puritans everything was, ideally, aimed at personal salvation and the building of a new, God-centered society. They were willing to risk their lives for such a world. It would be a place where they would practice their religion freely and raise their children free from the frivolities and temptations of the Old World. As we listen to their language, which refers to the Bible easily and frequently, their passionate desire to establish a New Jerusalem becomes clear. In their dreams they would build the City of God on earth.

Life for the average Puritan in the New World was essentially a life of work and prayer, but it was not a fanatically austere life. The Puritans worked long and hard under extremely difficult conditions so that their farms and trading enterprises would prosper. In fact, they believed prosperity was a sign of *election,* or God's special favor. Nevertheless, they did not turn away from eating and drinking, the pleasure of social gatherings, and the joys of a close family life. They simply kept reminding themselves that their souls were the constant battlegrounds of God and Satan and that every act and thought had to be judged according to whether or not it truly glorified God.

In the pursuit of virtue, the Puritans passed laws against many activities that would distract good souls from their real task. Certain "delights" were forbidden, such as bowling, Maypole dancing, gambling, attending plays, and "unprofitable" hunting (for someone who was a bad shot, it was a sin to waste time and ammunition). Virtue was learned primarily at home, where the father had complete authority. The family was the center of activity; the aged were always cared for; young people were apprenticed to learn trades the community needed.

Writing was an important part of Puritan life; it was often

an extension of religion. In fact, the first book published in America was the *Bay Psalm Book* (1640), a translation of the biblical Psalms. Many Puritans kept journals to help them carefully examine their spiritual lives. These journals and diaries, detailed and intense, were usually meant to be purely private writings. Even when they did write for a public, however, the Puritans wrote to instruct others or to testify to their experience of divine grace; they wrote spiritual autobiographies.

Puritan writing, in other words, was *practical*. The writers were not merely providing entertainment; they were deeply involved with their spiritual selves and attempts to improve them. They wrote no fiction, nor did they even approve of reading fiction, and they wrote no plays because they disapproved violently of the theater. Their writings consisted largely of journals, sermons, hymns, histories, and poems.

Just as the Puritans sought to purify their lives, so too they sought to purify their language. Everything they wrote avoided **Ornate Style,** the complicated and decorative style of their European contemporaries. They preferred to write in what they called **Plain Style,** even as they strove for plainness in their architecture, clothing, food, and household furnishings. Plain Style was meant simply to communicate ideas as clearly as possible. Writing was not a way of showing off cleverness or learning but a way of serving God and the community. The whole Puritan way of life is summed up in William Bradford's desire to tell the story of Plymouth Plantation (page 24) in "a plain style, with singular regard unto the simple truth in all things."

A page of the rhymed alphabet from the earliest extant edition of *The New England Primer*, Boston, 1727

G As runs the Glass Mans life doth pass.

H My Book and Heart Shall never part.

J Job feels the Rod Yet blesses GOD.

K Our KING the good No man of blood.

L The Lion bold The Lamb doth hold.

M The Moon gives light In time of night.

The Southern Colonies

Life in the southern colonies, begun in 1607 with Jamestown, Virginia, developed quite differently from life in New England. Unlike the Puritans, who lived fairly closely together, much of the southern population lived on farms or plantations that were distant from one another. Often like little colonies of their own, these plantations were largely self-sufficient.

The larger estates were owned and operated by wealthy and well-educated colonists who developed a more social and outgoing way of life than the Puritans. Different things became important to them: cultivation of nature and of society, sophistication, and public service.

Southern colonial literature reflects that experience. For the most part, southern gentlemen and ladies carried on correspondence with friends who often lived at great distances from them, as well as with family and friends back in England. Many of the southern colonists belonged to the Church of England, the church that the Puritans had attempted to reform, and their ties with the Old World were stronger. As a result, they did not have the reasons the Puritans had to create a literature of their own.

Still, in their letters, journals, and public reports, southern writers recorded the details of their way of life. The realities of science and politics blend, in their writings, with a New World sense of excitement and discovery. After all, the southern wilderness too had to be explored, mapped, and described.

Of course, not all the residents of the southern colonies were the prosperous owners of plantations. Most were hardworking tradespeople, artisans, small farmers, indentured servants, and slaves. Yet the sophisticated gentleman and lady dominate our sense of the early southern colonies as we meet them in literature. We can hear at once, in the voice of a man like William Byrd (page 35), a strong contrast between the more worldly and witty southerners and the intense, self-examining Puritans. This contrast, too, is an important part of the American experience.

TIME LINE

1400–1599 AMERICAN EVENTS

pre-1400 Hundreds of American Indian tribes inhabit the Americas before European explorers arrive

1492 Columbus lands in New World

1509 New World named America after Amerigo Vespucci

1540 Coronado explores Southwest

1541 De Soto explores the Mississippi

1565 Spanish found St. Augustine, Florida, oldest permanent settlement in what is now the United States

WORLD EVENTS 1400–1599

1519–1522 Magellan sails around the world

1600–1649 AMERICAN EVENTS

1607 Jamestown, Va., founded

1608 John Smith, *A True Relation of Virginia*

1609 Henry Hudson explores Hudson River

1610 Colonial population estimate: 210

1616 John Smith, *A Description of New England*

1620 Pilgrims land at Plymouth, Mass.

1624 Dutch establish New Amsterdam

WORLD EVENTS 1600–1649

1603 England: Bubonic plague kills 30,000 people

1605 England: Shakespeare completes *Macbeth*

1609 Italy: Galileo builds first telescope

1611 England: King James translation of Bible

1616 England and Spain: Deaths of Shakespeare and Cervantes

1600–1649 AMERICAN EVENTS / WORLD EVENTS 1600–1649

	American Events		World Events
		1628	England: William Harvey describes circulation of blood
1630	William Bradford begins *History of Plymouth Plantation*	1630	France: Beginning of public advertising
	John Winthrop settles Boston		
1635	First public school in America		
1636	Harvard, first college in America		
1638	First printing press in America at Cambridge, Mass.		
1640	*Bay Psalm Book,* first book published in America		
	Colonial population estimate: 27,950		
1643	Roger Williams, *A Key to the Language of America*		
	First American restaurant opens in Boston		
		1644	China: Ming Dynasty falls
			France: Blaise Pascal completes calculating device, forerunner of modern digital calculator

1650–1699

	American Events		World Events
1650	Anne Bradstreet, *The Tenth Muse Lately Sprung Up in America*		
1653	John Eliot, *Catechism in the Indian Language*		
		1663	Germany: First electric generator invented
1664	English capture New Amsterdam, rename it New York		
		1667	England: John Milton completes *Paradise Lost*
1669	La Salle explores Great Lakes		
1670	Colonial population estimate: 114,500		
1671	Edward Taylor becomes minister of Westfield, Mass.		

1673 Regular New York–Boston mail service

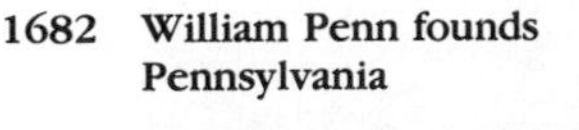

1674 Holland: Leeuwenhoek observes bacteria

1680 France: King Louis XIV at height of power

1682 William Penn founds Pennsylvania

La Salle explores Mississippi

1690 *New England Primer*

Paper money issued for first time in America

1692 Witchcraft trials in Salem, Mass.

1700–1750

1701 Detroit founded

1704 First American newspaper, *Boston News Letter*

1714 Tea introduced in colonies

1718 New Orleans founded

1729 Baltimore founded

First arithmetic textbook in America published in Boston

1731 First public library in America founded in Philadelphia

1732 William Byrd, *Progress to the Mines*

1737 William Byrd founds Richmond, Va.

1741 Jonathan Edwards, *Sinners in the Hands of an Angry God*

1749 Franklin invents lightning rod

1750 Colonial population estimate: 1,207,000

1709 Germany: Gabriel Fahrenheit invents thermometer

1719 England: Daniel Defoe, *Robinson Crusoe*

1726 England: Jonathan Swift, *Gulliver's Travels*

American Indians

When European explorers first set foot in the New World, they encountered people who had been native to the Americas for thousands of years. Because the Europeans thought they had landed in the "Indies," or the Far East, they called the natives Indians. No one name, however, would adequately describe the variety of cultures that flourished from one end of America to the other.

Generation after generation these Native Americans had told stories, sung songs, and recited groups of tales that embodied their past and told of their close relationship with the natural world. Their mythologies, songs, and ritual chants were rarely written down, though some tribes, such as the Delaware, did develop forms of writing. Most of these works of literature survived through oral tradition, each generation transmitting its literature to its young people by word of mouth. The result is a literature that is timeless, a literature created by no one author. It is a literature made by its people.

Some American Indian tribes of the New World.

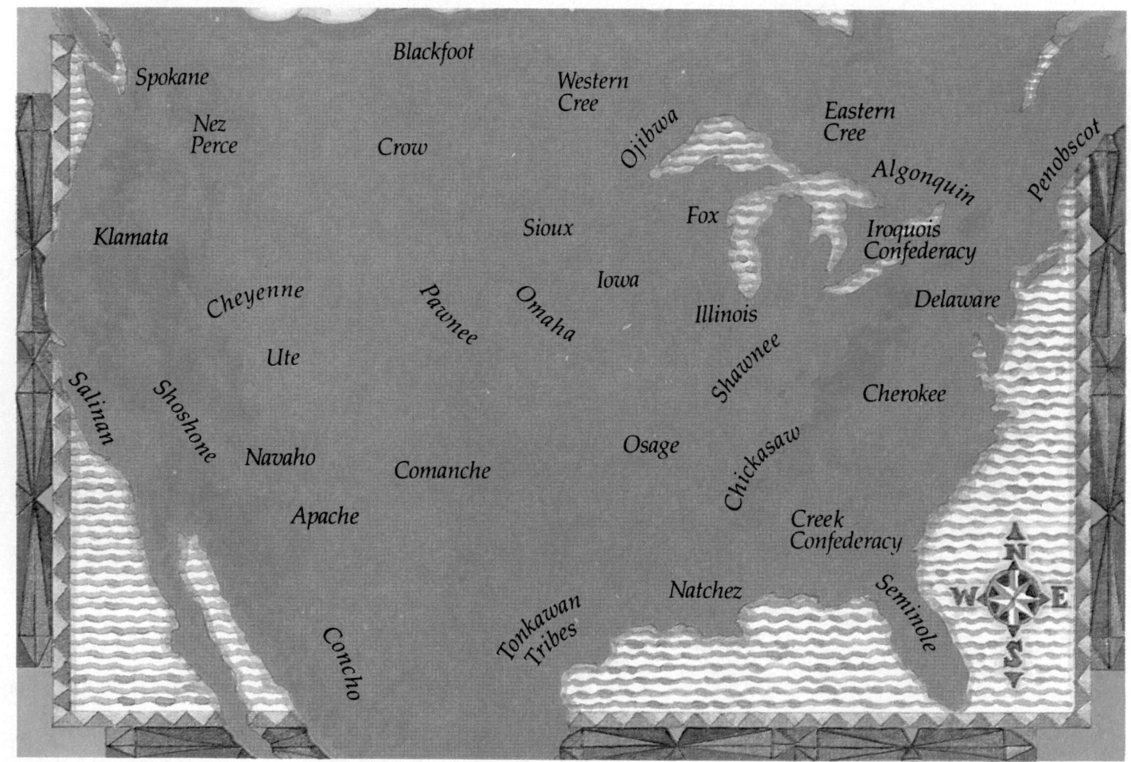

AT A GLANCE

- The great Manito exists in a timeless realm.
- The earth was fog before creation.
- The great Manito inhabits the entire universe.

LITERARY OPTIONS

- folk literature
- imagery

THEMATIC OPTIONS

- the creation of the world
- good *vs.* evil

1 AUDIENCE

Note that these pictographs were intended as a permanent record of the creation, to be described aloud to the Delaware of subsequent generations.

The *Walum Olum* is a creation myth of the Delaware, a people who lived in the areas we now call New Jersey, Delaware, and parts of New York and Pennsylvania. The *Walum Olum* ("Painted Record") is a chronicle of the beginning of the world and the origins of the Delaware people in the far Northwest.

Through this myth the Delaware kept in touch with their own past and placed themselves within a framework of history as they remembered it. The ancient words also celebrated the Manito, the supernatural force, or spirit, believed by the Delaware to be the source of both good and evil.

The form of writing developed by the Delaware was not based on a phonetic representation of sounds, as English is, but upon a kind of picture writing. In the following passage each of the original drawings, or pictographs, is accompanied by an English translation of its meaning. In some of these pictographs, we can clearly see the meaning. We can easily find the sun, men, women, fish, and birds. However, other pictographs demand a detailed knowledge of the Delaware language—or an act of imagination.

- Think about the various creation myths you have read. How does the Delaware myth differ? How is it similar?

1

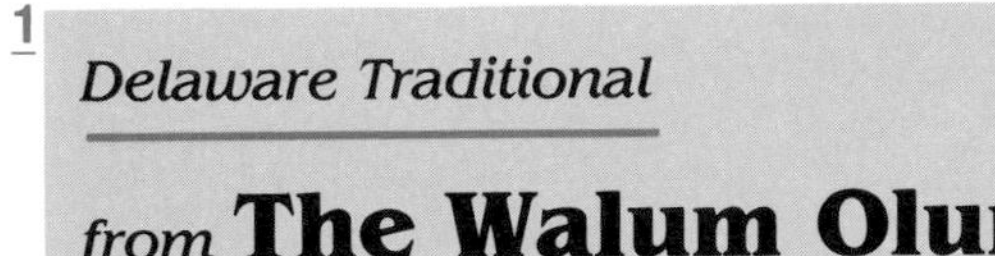

Delaware Traditional

from The Walum Olum

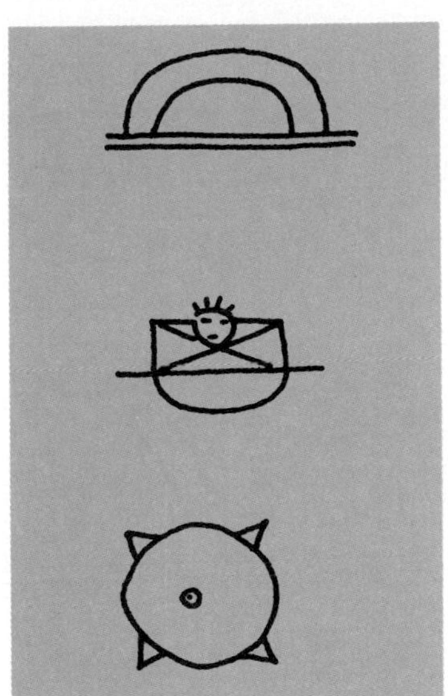

At first, in that place, at all times, above the earth,

On the earth, an extended fog, and there the great Manito was.

At first, forever, lost in space, everywhere, the great Manito was.

GUIDED READING

LITERAL QUESTION

1a. According to the translation of the first picture, where was the great Manito before the earth was created? ("in that place . . . above the earth")

INFERENTIAL QUESTION

1b. Which modern English words might a writer use for the great Manito's location before creation? (Answers will vary; examples include *Heaven; sky; the universe.*)

He made the extended land and the sky.

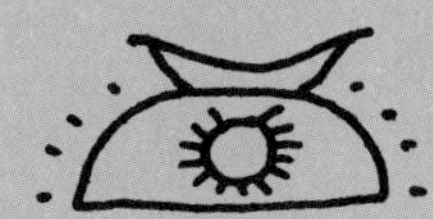

1 He made the sun, the moon, the stars.

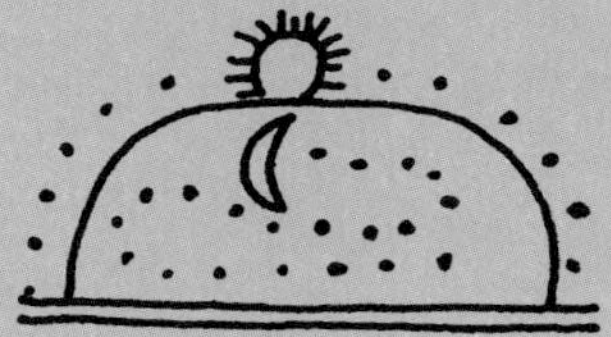

2 He made them all to move evenly.

Then the wind blew violently, and it cleared, and the water flowed off far and strong.

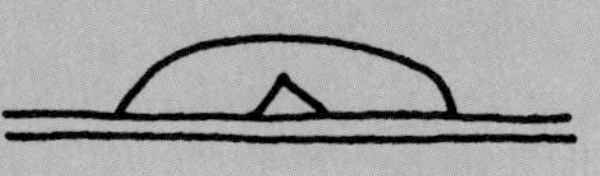

And groups of islands grew newly, and there remained.

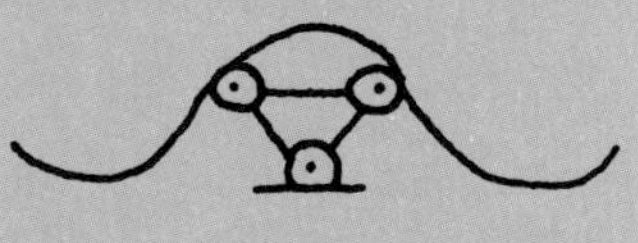

3 Anew spoke the great Manito, a manito to manitos,

To beings, mortals, souls and all,

AT A GLANCE

- The great Manito created a harmonious universe.
- Land appeared after a great storm.
- The great Manito spoke to all his creations.

1 RESPONSE JOURNAL

Ask students to compose a three-drawing symbolic picture story with a written translation, describing the creation of the earth.

2 THEME

The great Manito's benevolence is apparent in the underlying harmony with which he created the universe.

3 TRADITIONAL LITERATURE

The permanent record of the pictographs allows the great Manito to "speak" to future generations of the Delaware, just as he spoke to the first Delaware.

GUIDED READING

LITERAL QUESTION

1a. Which picture and translation illustrate the great Manito's ultimate supremacy in the universe? (the ninth, which describes him as a "manito to manitos.")

INFERENTIAL QUESTION

1b. Imagine that you are the translator of this picture. What words would you use to express the great Manito's supremacy? (Answers will vary; *Almighty; Divine Spirit; Great Spirit* are some possible choices.)

AT A GLANCE

- The great Manito created woman and a variety of natural creatures.
- An evil Manito made evil creatures.
- At first the world was a good and happy place.

1 IMAGERY

The depiction of the great Manito as a grandfather underscores his essential benevolence and kindness.

2 THEME

The earth is a good place at first because all beings live in harmony.

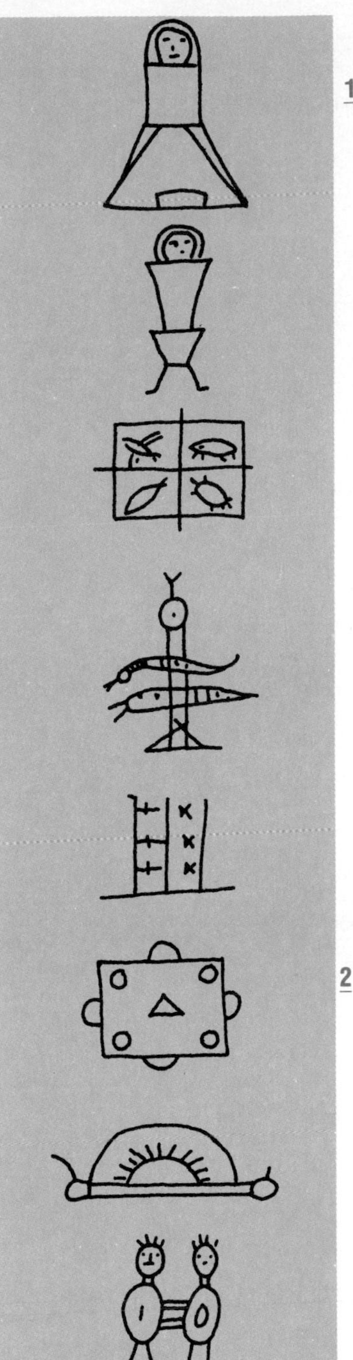

1 And ever after he was a manito to men, and their grandfather.

He gave the first mother, the mother of beings.

He gave the fish, he gave the turtles, he gave the beasts, he gave the birds.

But an evil Manito made evil beings only, monsters.

He made the flies, he made the gnats.

2 All beings were then friendly.

Truly the manitos were active and kindly

To those very first men, and to those first mothers; fetched them wives,

GUIDED READING

LITERAL QUESTION

1a. List three creatures that the evil Manito brought into the world. (*monsters; flies; gnats*)

INFERENTIAL QUESTION

1b. Why do you think these creatures are considered evil? (They upset the original harmony and balance of the universe.)

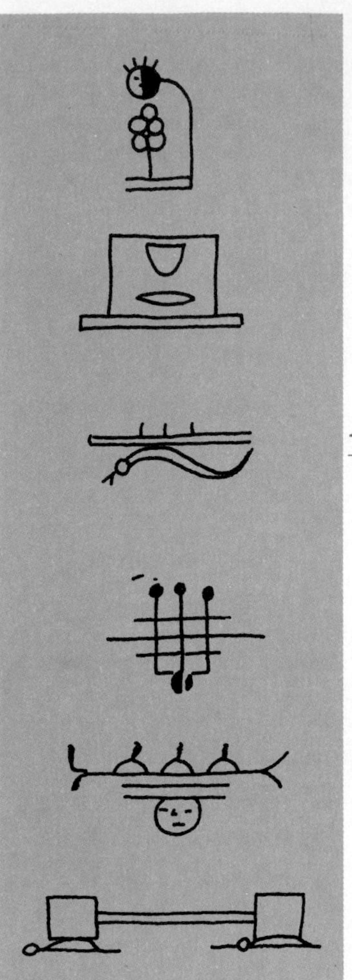

And fetched them food, when first they desired it.

All had cheerful knowledge, all had leisure, all thought in gladness.

1 But very secretly an evil being, a mighty magician, came on earth,

And with him brought badness, quarreling, unhappiness,

Brought bad weather, brought sickness, brought death.

All this took place of old on the earth, beyond the great tide water, at the first.

STUDY QUESTIONS

Recalling

1. According to the *Walum Olum,* how were good things and evil things created?
2. List three good things and three evil things that the manitos did for mortals.

Interpreting

3. What kind of relationship is depicted between the manitos, or spiritual forces, and mortals?
4. Identify two pictographs in which there is a clear relationship between the picture and the translated meaning. Then find two abstract pictographs in which the relationship between picture and meaning is not obvious. For one of the abstract pictographs, tell how it nevertheless suggests the meaning given in the translation.

AT A GLANCE

- The first humans lived in a paradise.
- An evil being came to earth, bringing evil with him.
- Evil came into the world at the very beginning.

1 THEME

The evil brought to earth by the evil Manito destroys forever the paradise that existed at first.

REFLECTING ON THE SELECTION

What purpose do you think this pictograph account served for those who saw it? (It answered questions; it gave the Delaware a sense of identity and security.)

STUDY QUESTIONS

1. good things by the great Manito; evil things by an evil Manito
2. *good things:* wives, food, leisure; *evil things:* monsters, flies, unhappiness, death
3. Manitos are kindly, create humans, care for needs, are responsible for all good; evil Manito brings evil, unhappiness.
4. *clear:* lines 5, 6, 12, 13, 18; *abstract:* possible answers may include first pictograph and line

GUIDED READING

LITERAL QUESTION

1a. Which picture and translation convey the sense of earth as a paradise? (the twentieth, showing that all beings had cheerful knowledge, leisure, and gladness)

INFERENTIAL QUESTION

1b. How do you think people would treat each other in a paradise? (with respect, kindness, understanding and compassion)

AT A GLANCE

- A thunderstorm is observed in the distance.
- Its place in the natural order of things is considered.

LITERARY OPTIONS

- oral tradition
- rhythm

THEMATIC OPTIONS

- interdependence in nature
- cyclical aspects of life

MAIN IDEA

The image of the crops "tied" to the rain illustrates how all aspects of nature work together. (l. 4).

PERSONIFICATION

Attributing the quality of *voice* to the song of a bluebird reminds the listeners that they, too, are a part of the natural order.

ORAL TRADITION

The emphatic tone of the repeated command to *listen* for the rain underscores both the oral framework of the song and the importance of rain itself (ll. 5 and 11).

RHYTHM

The rhythm created by the repetition and parallel structure of line 12 conveys a sense of cyclical order that suggests that this ritual song is itself an aspect of the natural world.

REFLECTING ON THE POEM

In view of the importance of rain, how do you think nature is characterized in this song? Explain. (as a positive force because it is the source of life)

The Navaho are a large and varied group who settled in the American Southwest, where their culture still flourishes. An agricultural people, the Navaho composed ritual songs like "Listen! Rain Approaches!" to celebrate the growth of crops and to control the coming of the vitally important rains. The repetition of words and lines (sometimes with variations) is characteristic of Native American ritual chants and songs.

- What purposes do repeated words and phrases serve in literature transmitted through the oral tradition?

Navaho Traditional

Listen! Rain Approaches!

Truly in the East
The white bean
And the great corn plant
Are tied with the white lightning.
Listen! It approaches!
The voice of the bluebird is heard.

Truly in the East
The white bean
And the great squash
Are tied with the rainbow.
Listen! It approaches!
The voice of the bluebird is heard.

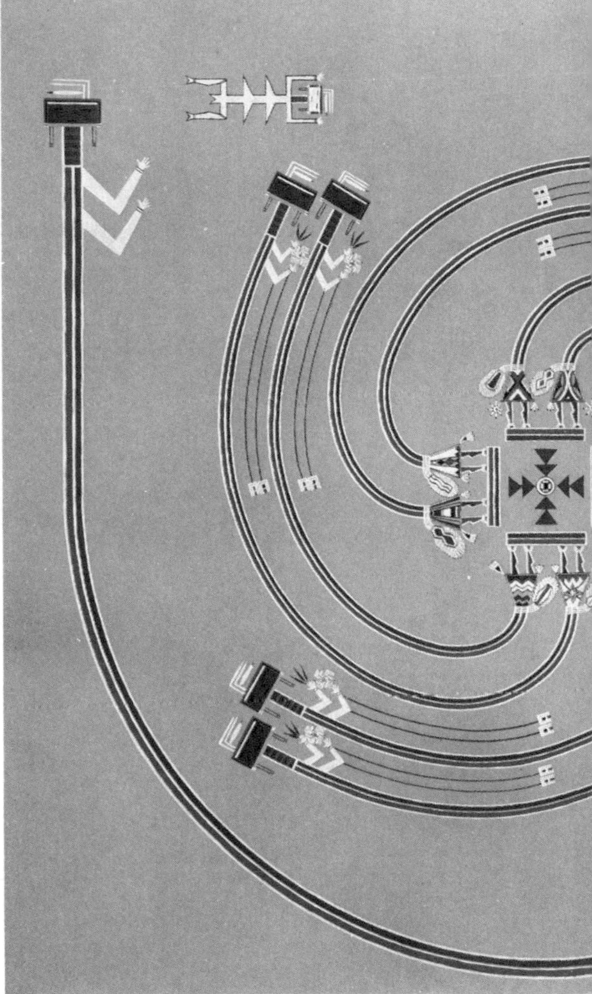

Whirling Rainbow People, 1948. This sand painting shows eight rainbow goddesses swirling clockwise around a dark, cloud-covered lake.

"Calling One's Own" is a song of the Ojibwa, also known as the Chippewa, a group of people who lived around the Great Lakes and throughout the Great Plains. It is a song that sounds much like the love songs of English-language poetry. The imagery of the song is drawn from the natural world, showing the close relationship between the Ojibwa and the landscape of waters, flowers, trees, and skies that surrounded them.

■ If you were to address a poem to some of the things you love, to what would you speak?

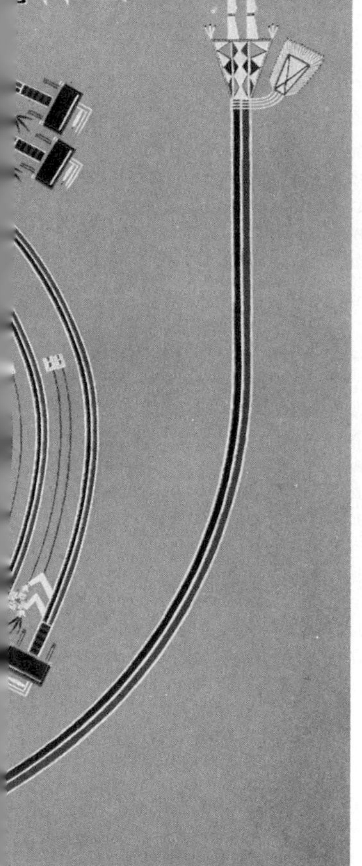
Wheelright Museum of the American Indian

Ojibwa Traditional

Calling One's Own

Awake! Flower of the forest, sky treading bird of the prairie.

Awake! Awake! Wonderful fawn-eyed One.
When you look upon me I am satisfied, as flowers that drink dew.
The breath of your mouth is the fragrance of flowers in the morning,
Your breath is their fragrance at evening in the moon of fading-leaf.

Do not the red streams of my veins run toward you
As forest streams to the sun in the moon of bright nights?
When you are beside me my heart sings; a branch it is, dancing,
Dancing before the Wind spirit in the moon of strawberries.

When you frown upon me, beloved, my heart grows dark—
A shining river the shadows of clouds darken;
Then with your smiles comes the sun and makes to look like gold
Furrows the cold wind drew in the water's face.

Myself! Behold me! Blood of my beating heart.
Earth smiles—the waters smile—even the sky of clouds smiles—but I,
I lose the way of smiling when you are not near.
Awake! Awake! My beloved.

AT A GLANCE

The singer calls for his love to awaken and describes her in terms of the natural world.

LITERARY OPTIONS

- lyric poetry
- imagery

THEMATIC OPTIONS

- romantic love
- nature

LYRIC POETRY

The imploring, repeated command to awake dramatizes the speaker's passionate intensity and the yearning quality of his love song (l. 1).

SIMILE

By comparing the effect of his lover's glance to the nourishment that flowers draw from dew, the singer suggests the benevolent power of love (l. 3).

IMAGERY

Images from the natural world (a cloud-darkened river, golden sunbeams) emphasize the intense, transforming power of love and demonstrate the connection between romantic love and nature (ll. 10–13).

REFLECTING ON THE POEM

What do the images that describe love indicate about the Ojibwa's relationship to nature? (They lived in harmony with nature and saw themselves as an integral part of the natural world.)

STUDY QUESTIONS

Listen! Rain Approaches!

1. *repeated:* lines 1, 2, 5, 6; *varied:* lines 3 and 4
2. lightning, rainbow
3. *tied:* unity of nature; *repetition:* eternality, changelessness of relationships
4. onset, departure; nature as cyclical or eternal
5. Answers will vary; may include binding people to tradition, religion, nature, others.

Calling One's Own

1. *beloved:* flower, bird; *heart:* branch in wind
2. clouds darken a shining river; sun makes water look like gold
3. nature; affects every aspect of life; Ojibwa as part of nature
4. Answers will vary, should include reasons.
5. sentiments expressed, ardor of speaker, use of imagery; imagery direct and powerful in evocation of nature

LITERARY FOCUS

"Listen . . .": 1, 2, 5, 6, most of 3, 4 repeated; "Calling": *awake, breath,* and other words; adds to imagery, echo effect; portrayal of nature as cyclical

VOCABULARY

- *totem:* Ojibwa Algonquian; a clan emblem; "his brother-sister kin"
- *powwow:* Algonquian; magician; "he dreams"
- *squash:* Algonquian for the vegetable; "vegetables eaten green"
- *Chicago:* Algonquian; "wild onion place"
- *Miami:* Muskogean; "very large"
- *hominy:* Algonquian; parched corn
- *skunk:* Algonquian for the animal
- *hammock:* Carib/Taino (West Indian); a swinging bed
- *Savannah:* Taino; a treeless plain

STUDY QUESTIONS

Listen! Rain Approaches!

Recalling

1. Which lines in the first stanza are repeated in the second stanza? Which lines are varied?
2. What two specific elements of a rainstorm does the song mention in lines 4 and 10?

Interpreting

3. What does the verb repeated in lines 4 and 10 imply about the relationship of things in nature? In what way does the other repetition in the poem contribute to this idea?
4. What stages of a storm does the variation in lines 4 and 10 represent? What broader characteristic of nature do these lines suggest?

Extending

5. What purposes, besides bringing rain, do you think someone might have for singing a ritual song?

Calling One's Own

Recalling

1. With what phrases is the beloved described in the first two lines? To what does the speaker compare his singing heart in stanza 2?
2. According to stanza 3, what happens in nature when the beloved frowns? When the beloved smiles?

Interpreting

3. What is the one general thing that the speaker and the beloved are compared to throughout the poem? What seems to be its importance in the life of the Ojibwa?
4. Which images of the beloved do you find most moving or expressive, and why?

Extending

5. Remember that this song is a translation from an Indian language. How is it like English-language love poems that you have read? In what ways, if any, is it different?

LITERARY FOCUS

Techniques of Oral Literature

Imagine yourself in a time and a place where there are no books to read. Anything you want to record, any event or story or song, must live in your memory and the memories of the people around you. You depend upon oral tradition.

Oral tradition is the name we give to the process of passing on literature by word of mouth. If a prayer or a history or a myth is important to a group, someone in the group must remember it. Otherwise, it will fade into oblivion. Its power and its pleasure will be lost.

Traditionally, it was the tribal poet whose job it was to remember the tribe's history, its line of leaders, its victories, its gods and rituals. In a sense the first poets were memory banks, able to call up the treasure of the tribe's past whenever asked to do so. To make recitation surer, the poets used certain formulas and memory tricks.

One technique was to repeat certain lines, sometimes varying one word or part of a word. Another technique was to make sure that each line had a certain number of syllables or a certain number of rhythmic beats. Sometimes a poet used standard words to represent things commonly referred to, and these stock words became so common that the listeners came to expect to hear them. In fact, the poet was eventually not allowed to leave out a certain word or deviate from the expected pattern.

Thinking About Oral Literature

- Find examples of words and parts of lines that are repeated throughout "Listen! Rain Approaches!" and "Calling One's Own." Why do you think these particular words are repeated?

VOCABULARY

Native American Words

Native American languages have contributed a large number of words to the American vocabulary. The map of North America, for example, is dotted with Indian place names. *Mississippi* means "great river" in Ojibwa, *Oklahoma* means "red people" in Choctaw, and *Ohio* means "beautiful river" in Iroquois.

We have also incorporated many American Indian common nouns into our everyday speech. The Algonquian language family contributed *chipmunk* and *toboggan.* The Aztec language, known as Nahuatl, gave us *tomato* and *avocado.*

Look up the following words in a dictionary or a book of word origins, and tell what they mean and which Indian language they come from.

totem	Chicago	skunk
powwow	Miami	hammock
squash	hominy	savannah

Christopher Columbus *1451–1506*

The dramatic story of the Italian explorer Christopher Columbus has become a familiar part of our culture. For years Columbus tried to convince his patrons that he could reach the riches of the East by sailing west, that he would not sail off the edge of the earth. Finally, with the support of Spain's Queen Isabella, he was able to pursue his dream with his three ships, the *Niña,* the *Pinta,* and the *Santa Maria.*

The discovery of the New World brought Columbus fame and an appointment as Admiral of the Ocean Sea. His later attempts to establish colonies in America were not successful, however, and his last years were filled with disappointments and a sense of failure.

Here is Columbus' own account, from his journal, of the final days of his first and most extraordinary voyage and the landing on the island of San Salvador in 1492. Columbus' nonfiction, real-life adventure might be considered the first American story—both a quest for a dream and a record of hard fact.

This version from the Spanish was made by the twentieth-century American poet William Carlos Williams.

■ Imagine keeping a diary while on a boat lost at sea. What sorts of entries might you make?

Christopher Columbus

from The Journal

A Modern Version by William Carlos Williams

The seventeenth of September, Monday, I proceeded on the west course and made over fifty leagues[1] in the day and night, counting only forty-seven. A favorable current aided us on our way. . . .

1 At dawn we observed much more weed appearing, like herbs from a river, in which one of the men discovered a live crab. This I kept that all might see it and believe on the land. The sea water was found to be less salt than it had been since leaving the Canaries.[2] This I caused many to taste. The breezes were always soft. Everyone was pleased and the best sailors went ahead to sight the first land. Many tunnyfish passed on all sides of us and the crew of the *Niña* killed one. All these signs came from the west, in which direction I trust in that high God in whose hands are all victories that very soon we shall see land. On that morning there appeared a white bird, called boatswainbird, which is not in the habit of sleeping on the sea. . . .

2 Saturday, September twenty-second, I shaped my course W.N.W. more or less, her head turning from one to the other point, and made thirty leagues. This contrary wind was very necessary to me because my people had become much excited at the thought that in

1. **leagues:** One league is about three miles. Columbus deliberately underestimates the distance for his crew.
2. **the Canaries:** the Canary Islands, off the coast of northwestern Africa.

AT A GLANCE

- Monday, September 17, 1492: Columbus misleads his crew about the distance they cover.
- Columbus and his crew make observations that indicate the nearness of land.
- Columbus affirms his faith in God.
- Saturday, September 22: Columbus changes course and finds a new wind that reassures his crew.

LITERARY OPTIONS

- description
- comparison/contrast

THEMATIC OPTIONS

- discovery
- confronting hardships
- responses to nature

1 SETTING

Columbus' detailed description of the weed and single live crab highlight the physical and emotional isolation that he and the crew feel.

2 DESCRIPTION

The detailed citation of date, change in course, and distance covered underscore the duration of Columbus' journey and the meticulousness of Columbus himself.

GUIDED READING

LITERAL QUESTION

1a. How many leagues does the ship cover on September 17, and how many does Columbus count? (The ship covers over 50 leagues, but Columbus counts only 47.)

INFERENTIAL QUESTION

1b. Why might Columbus underestimate daily progress in this way? (His men are extremely concerned about reaching land, and Columbus does not want to discourage them by revealing just how far they have traveled without sighting land.)

AT A GLANCE

- Sunset, Tuesday, September 25, 1492: Martin Alonzo thinks he sees land, and Columbus thanks God.
- Wednesday morning, September 26: The land is discovered to be a cloud formation.
- The crew despair, but the journey continues at Columbus' urging.

1 COMPARISON/CONTRAST

Columbus' description of Alonzo's joy and his own grateful thanksgiving to God contrasts sharply with the feeling of despair that pervades the crew.

2 THEME

Columbus' ardent exhortation to the crew underscores the idea that the ultimate discovery of land will put an end to the present hardship and suffering.

these seas no wind ever blew in the direction of Spain. In the morning there was no weed but in the afternoon it was very thick. . . .

Tuesday, calm and afterwards wind. . . .
1 At sunset Martin Alonzo went up on the poop of his ship and with joy called out that he had sighted land. I fell on my knees and gave thanks to the Lord, so heavy had been my burdens these latter days at the despair among the men and the murmurs going among them that I should have to turn back. And Martin Alonzo said the *Gloria in Excelsis*[3] with his people. My own crew did the same. Those of the *Niña* all went up on the mast and into the rigging and declared that it was land. It seemed distant twenty-five leagues. So it appeared until night. I ordered the course to be altered from west to S.W. in which direction the land had appeared. Four leagues that day on a west course and seventeen S.W. during the night, in all twenty-one, but I told the men that thirteen was the distance made good. The sea was very smooth so that many sailors bathed alongside. We saw many giltheads and other fish.

Wednesday, what had been said to be land was only clouds and I continued on the west course till afternoon, then altered to S.W. Day and night thirty-one leagues, counting twenty-four for the people. The sea was like a river,
2 the air pleasant and mild. The despair of the crew redoubled at this disappointment but I comforted them as best I could, begging them to endure a while longer for all that would be theirs in the end. . . .

Tuesday, west, day and night thirty-nine leagues, counted for the crew thirty. The weed, many thanks to God, coming from east to west, contrary to the usual course. Many fish seen and one killed. A white bird like a gull.

Wednesday, still the west course, and made good forty-seven leagues, counted forty. Sandpipers appeared, and much weed, some old and

3. ***Gloria in Excelsis*** [glôr′ē ə in ek sel′ sis]: *Glory in the Highest,* a Latin prayer of praise to God.

GUIDED READING

LITERAL QUESTION

1a. What does Columbus do when the crew realize that they have not sighted land after all? (He comforts them and begs them to endure.)

INFERENTIAL QUESTION

1b. What does his response suggest about his ability as a leader? (He seems to be a good leader, able to support and motivate his crew.)

some quite fresh and having fruit. No birds. So I gave it out that we had left the islands behind that were depicted on the chart. Here many called upon me to turn about and search for the land but I did not wish to keep the ships beating about, although I had certain information of islands in this region. It would not have been good sense to do this since the weather was favorable and the chief intention was to go in search of the Indies by way of the west. This was what I had promised to the King and Queen, and they had sent me for this purpose.

Thursday, west sixty-three leagues, counted
1 forty-six. . . . The crew here became even louder in their complaints but I gave as little heed as I was able though many were now openly mutinous and would have done me harm if they dared. . . .

Thursday, eleventh of October. The course was W.S.W. More sea than there had been during the whole of the voyage. Sandpipers and a green reed near the ship. And for this I gave thanks to God as it was a sure sign of
2 land. Those of the *Pinta* saw a cane and a pole, and they took up another small pole which appeared to be worked[4] with iron; also another bit of cane, a land plant and a small board. The crew of the caravel *Niña* also saw signs of land, and a small plant covered with berries.

After sunset I returned to the west course. Up to two hours past midnight we had gone ninety miles, when the *Pinta,* which was the fastest sailer and had gone ahead, found the
3 land and gave the signals. The land was first seen by Rodrigo de Triana. . . .

On Friday, the twelfth of October, we anchored before the land and made ready to go on shore. Presently we saw naked people on the beach. I went ashore in the armed boat and took the royal standard and Martin Alonzo and Vincent Yañez, his brother, who was captain of the *Niña.* And we saw the trees very

4. **worked:** carved or shaped.

AT A GLANCE

- Wednesday, October 2, 1492: The crew beg Columbus to turn back.
- Columbus refuses, determined to keep his promise to the King and Queen.
- Thursday, October 3: The crew become openly mutinous.
- Two hours past midnight, the *Pinta* sights land.
- Friday, October 12: Columbus, Alonzo, and Vincent Yañez go ashore to greet the inhabitants.

1 CHARACTERIZATION

Columbus' unemotional report of the crew's mutinous behavior illustrates the degree of his personal courage and fortitude.

2 DESCRIPTION

The accumulation of detailed information about the crew's sightings creates a visual picture that both informs the reader and builds a sense of anticipation.

3 CLIMAX AND TONE

Columbus' announcement of the sighting of land seems matter-of-fact and unemotional. By this point they have seen so many indications of land that the sighting has become inevitable.

GUIDED READING

LITERAL QUESTION

1a. Cite two reasons Columbus gives for not turning back to search for land. (The weather is good; he wants to keep his promise to the King and Queen.)

INFERENTIAL QUESTION

1b. What does this reasoning suggest about Columbus' character? (He is judicious, reasonable, loyal, and highly motivated.)

green, and much water and fruits of divers[5] kinds. Presently many of the inhabitants assembled. I gave to some red caps and glass beads to put round their necks, and many other things of little value. They came to the ships' boats afterward, where we were, swimming and bringing us parrots, cotton threads in skeins, darts—what they had, with good will. . . .

On Saturday, as dawn broke, many of these people came to the beach, all youths. Their legs are very straight, all in one line and no belly. They came to the ship in canoes, made out of the trunk of a tree, all in one piece, and wonderfully worked, propelled with a paddle like a baker's shovel, and go at a marvelous speed.

Bright green trees, the whole land so green that it is a pleasure to look on it. Gardens of the most beautiful trees I ever saw. . . . I
1 saw many trees very unlike those of our country. Branches growing in different ways and all from one trunk; one twig is one form and another is a different shape and so unlike that it is the greatest wonder in the world to see the diversity; thus one branch has leaves like those of a cane, and others like those of a mastic tree; and on a single tree there are five different kinds. The fish so unlike ours that it is wonderful. Some are the shape of dories and of the finest colors, so bright that there is not a man who would not be astounded, and would not take great delight in seeing them. There are also whales. I saw no beasts on land save parrots and lizards.

On shore I sent the people for water, some with arms, and others with casks; and as it was some little distance, I waited two hours for them.

During that time I walked among the trees which was the most beautiful thing which I had ever seen.

5. **divers** [dī′vərz]: diverse or various.

STUDY QUESTIONS

Recalling

1. According to the entry for September 22, why was the "contrary wind" necessary for Columbus?
2. What event took place on Tuesday, September 25? What happened the following day?
3. Summarize the important events described in the entry for October 11.
4. From the entry for Saturday, October 13, list several adjectives that Columbus uses to describe the land, trees, and fish that he encountered.

Interpreting

5. In what way did Columbus report the distance traveled each day to his crew? What reason would he have for reporting the distance in this manner?
6. Based on the entry for October 13, how would you characterize Columbus' general impression of the New World?

Extending

7. Why do you think so many early explorers and settlers described the New World as Columbus did? What hopes might they have had for this land?

AT A GLANCE

- Columbus and the Native Americans exchange gifts.
- Saturday, October 13, 1492: Columbus sees a bark canoe for the first time.
- Columbus compares the new land to his home and concludes that it is a paradise.

1 COMPARISON/CONTRAST

Columbus' comparison and contrast of the lush vegetation in the new land with that of his native landscape dramatizes his sense of wonder. Furthermore, in contrast to his factual account of the journey, Columbus' emotional description of the fish adds intensity to his depiction of the new land as a natural paradise.

REFLECTING ON THE SELECTION

What kinds of feelings do you think Columbus' journal might have inspired in his contemporaries at home? (admiration for him; curiosity about the new world; a desire to travel)

STUDY QUESTIONS

1. to convince the crew that a return voyage was possible
2. land sighted; land discovered to be clouds
3. Crew sees many signs of land; land sighted at 2 A.M.
4. *marvelous, bright, green*
5. underestimated it; keep crew from becoming discouraged
6. impressed with its beauty
7. Possible answers: New World as new Eden; make voyage seem successful; encourage others to settle and explore; relief

GUIDED READING

LITERAL QUESTION

1a. List three adjectives Columbus uses to describe what he finds in the new land. (*marvelous; bright green; wonderful*)

INFERENTIAL QUESTION

1b. What do these adjectives convey about Columbus' feelings about the new land? (It is like a paradise, full of wonder, abundance, and dazzling sights and experiences.)

John Smith *1580–1631*

John Smith lived a life crammed with adventure and achievement during a great age of exploration. It had not taken long for adventurers and merchants to begin to explore the New World Columbus had discovered. The Spanish to the south, the French to the north, the English along the mid-Atlantic coast, the Dutch, the Swedes, the Portuguese––all of Europe seemed to be moving west. By Smith's time, about 1600, exploration and the search for gold were still important, but the desire to establish permanent settlements was growing. Smith—strong-willed, imaginative, a born leader—was in the right place at the right time.

In 1585 Sir Walter Raleigh had commissioned an English settlement on Roanoke Island, off the coast of what is now North Carolina, but it lasted only a year. In 1587 another colony was established on Roanoke, but when the English ships returned in 1590, the colony had mysteriously disappeared. Success finally came in 1607 when the first permanent English settlement, Jamestown, Virginia, was founded. It was made up of one hundred men and four boys, and the man in charge was the twenty-seven-year-old Captain John Smith.

It was at Jamestown that Smith may or may not have had the most famous of his adventures. Scholars are still not sure to what extent he was embroidering the truth when he claimed to have been captured by Chief Powhatan and rescued from death by the chief's beautiful daughter, Pocahontas. The story seemed to grow more romantic and exciting each time Smith related it. There is no doubt, however, of the quality of Smith's leadership; the colony would not have survived without him. As it was, over half the colonists died during the first winter. After two years in Jamestown, Smith returned to England.

In 1614 a group of English merchants, who hoped to get rich from gold, whale oil, and furs, financed a six-month expedition to New England for Smith. He explored the coast from Maine to Cape Cod, made maps, traded with Indians, and went back to England, never to return to America.

Yet Smith wanted to return, as we can see from his *Description of New England,* published in 1616. Although he calls this work a description, Smith's main purpose is not to describe but to persuade. This pamphlet is essentially an advertisement, a kind of seventeenth-century "commercial."

■ If you were trying to persuade foreigners to settle in America today, what specifics would you use to entice them to leave their homeland?

AT A GLANCE

- Smith extols the advantages for England's poor working classes of working their own land.
- He enumerates the virtues and benefits of settling New England.
- He compares the abundance of nature and freedom in New England with life in England.

LITERARY OPTIONS

- persuasion
- comparison and contrast

THEMATIC OPTIONS

- New England as a paradise
- virtues and rewards of honest labor

1 VOCABULARY: CONNOTATION

In using the word *magnanimity,* Smith suggests both the abundance of the new land and the high, noble purpose that can be achieved in its settlement. His use of the word furthers his persuasive purpose.

2 READING SKILL: CONTRAST

Smith contrasts the natural abundance and freedom in New England with the difficulties of life in England to strengthen his argument about the benefits of settling New England.

The Peaceable Kingdom, Edward Hicks, c. 1839.

John Smith

from A Description of New England

Who can desire more content, that has small means or but only his merit to advance his fortune, than to tread and plant that ground he has purchased by the hazard[1] of his life? If
1 he have but the taste of virtue and magnanimity, what to such a mind can be more pleasant than planting and building a foundation for his posterity, got from the rude earth by God's blessing and his own industry, without prejudice to any? If he have any grain of faith or zeal in religion, what can he do less hurtful to any or more agreeable to God than to seek to convert those poor savages[2] to know Christ and humanity? . . . What so truly suits with honor and honesty as the discovering things unknown, erecting towns, peopling countries, informing the ignorant, reforming things unjust, teaching virtue, and gain to our native mother-country a kingdom to attend her, find employment for those that are idle because they know not what to do? [This is] so far from wronging any as to cause posterity to remember thee, and remembering thee, ever honor that remembrance with praise. . . .

2 Here nature and liberty afford us that freely which in England we want,[3] or it costs us dearly. What pleasure can be more than (being tired with any occasion ashore, in planting

1. **hazard:** risk.
2. **savages:** The earliest European settlers considered the Native Americans savages because they lacked what seemed to Europeans the advantages of "civilization."
3. **want:** lack.

GUIDED READING

LITERAL QUESTION

1a. According to Smith, what specific benefits will England enjoy if many settlers come to New England? (England will gain a new land to serve her needs and a place to send her unemployed.)

INFERENTIAL QUESTION

1b. Whom do you think Smith is addressing when he discusses England's gains from settling New England? Why? (He addresses people with money, political power, and social prestige, so that he can raise money and get political backing for more settlements.)

1 vines, fruits, or herbs, in contriving their own grounds, to the pleasure of their own minds, their fields, gardens, orchards, buildings, ships, and other works, etc.) to recreate themselves before their own doors, in their own boats upon the sea, where man, woman, and child, with a small hook and line, by angling may take divers sorts of excellent fish at their plea-
2 sures? And is it not pretty sport to pull up two pence, six pence, and twelve pence as fast as you can haul and veer[4] a line? He is a very bad fisher [who] cannot kill in one day with his hook and line, one, two, or three hundred cods, which dressed and dried, if they be sold there for ten shillings the hundred [pounds], though in England they will give more than twenty, may not both the servant, the master, and merchant be well content with this gain? If a man work but three days in seven he may get more than he can spend, unless he will be excessive. . . .

For hunting also, the woods, lakes, and rivers afford not only chase sufficient for any that delight in that kind of toil or pleasure, but such beasts to hunt that besides the delicacy of their bodies for food, their skins are so rich as may well recompense thy daily labor with a captain's pay.

For laborers, if those [in England] that sow hemp, turnips, parsnips, carrots, cabbage, and such like, give 20, 30, 40, 50 shillings yearly [rent] for an acre of ground, and meat, drink, and wages to use it and yet grow rich, [then]
3 when better or at least as good ground may be had [in New England] and cost nothing but labor, it seems strange to me any such should there grow poor.

My purpose is not to persuade children from their parents, men from their wives, nor servants from their masters, only such as with free consent may be spared. But [if] each parish or village, in city or country, that will but apparel their fatherless children of thirteen or fourteen years of age, or young married people that have small wealth to live on, here by their labor [they] may live exceeding well, provided always that first there be a sufficient power to command them, houses to receive them, means to defend them, and meet[5] provisions for them, for any place may be overlain[6] and it is most
4 necessary to have a fortress and sufficient masters (as, carpenters, masons, fishers, fowlers, gardeners, husbandmen,[7] sawyers, smiths, spinners, tailors, weavers, and such like) to take ten, twelve, or twenty, or as there is occasion, for apprentices. The masters by this may quickly grow rich; these [apprentices] may learn [by] their trades themselves to do the like, to a general and an incredible benefit for king and country, master and servant.

4. **haul and veer:** pull in and let out.

5. **meet:** sufficient.
6. **overlain:** overwhelmed by an enemy.
7. **husbandmen:** farmers.

STUDY QUESTIONS

Recalling

1. According to the first sentence, to people of what economic "means" and "fortune" is Smith addressing his words?
2. From the first paragraph name at least one attraction of life in New England that appeals to the following qualities: virtue, faith, honor.
3. Name three means of earning a living in New England that Smith discusses at length in paragraphs 2–4. Name five other trades that will be needed in New England, according to paragraph 5.
4. According to the last paragraph, whom is Smith not trying to persuade to move to New England? Who does he think should journey to America?

AT A GLANCE

- Smith enumerates the pleasures and financial rewards of settling New England, emphasizing that land is free.
- He identifies those most suited to settle New England.
- He emphasizes the importance of establishing settlements by listing the financial benefits of settling New England.

1 PERIOD IDEA

Smith's description of the personal freedom and lush natural resources in New England exemplifies the view of the New World as a paradise.

2 THEME

Smith uses the hyperbole of reeling in coins instead of fish to dramatize the abundance of the new land and underscore how easily settlers can enjoy the virtues and rewards of honest labor.

3 PERSUASION

By pointing out that land is free in New England, Smith appeals to his audience's good common sense to convince them of the advantages of settlement.

4 RESPONSE JOURNAL

Students may select one of the vocations that Smith lists and explain how that line of work might be valued in a New England settlement.

REFLECTING ON THE SELECTION

If you were living in England in 1616, would Smith's argument convince you to settle in New England? (Answers will vary: Yes, because life seems so good and so easy; no, because there is too much unknown.)

STUDY QUESTIONS

1. little or no means
2. *virtue:* make a foundation for posterity; *faith:* convert Indians; *honor:* discover unknown and build towns
3. fishing, hunting, farming; carpentry, masonry, fowling, gardening, tailoring
4. children, married men, servants; orphans, couples, laborers

5. all of England
6. wealth and ease without hard work
7. no; he wants to persuade people to go to New England
8. encourage settlement; first sentence of last paragraph; who should or should not go to New England

LITERARY FOCUS

- *settlers:* first four paragraphs; fishing, hunting, farming
- *backers:* first and last paragraphs; profit, virtue, faith, honor, patriotism

VOCABULARY

1. (a) risk
2. (c) generosity
3. (d) descendants
4. (a) fishing
5. (c) reward

5. According to the final sentence, who will benefit from the establishment of New England settlements?

Interpreting

6. What general impression does Smith give of life in New England?
7. Does Smith describe the drawbacks of settling in New England? Why or why not?
8. For what reason other than describing New England did Smith write this piece? In what paragraph and through what specific recommendations does that additional reason become most apparent?

LITERARY FOCUS

Persuasion

Persuasion attempts to sway the reader to think or act in a particular way. Although Smith says he is writing a "description," he is actually trying to persuade English men and women of the advantages of settling in the New World.

Four elements must be considered when writing or evaluating persuasion:

The writer. The persuasive writer calls upon personal experience for support. As one of the few Europeans who had been to America, Smith speaks about the New World with first-hand knowledge. His reputation as a leader and his fact-filled descriptions help convince his audience of the truth of what he says.

The audience. The persuasive writer pinpoints the people whose minds are to be changed and considers what they already believe and feel. Smith recognizes that only people without wealth and position are likely colonists, but he also addresses people who might help to finance the expedition. He stresses economic opportunities but does not neglect patriotic and religious motives.

The occasion. The persuasive writer takes advantage of current events in the mind of the reader. Smith makes the most of the curiosity of Europeans about America in the early seventeenth century. He plays upon their eagerness to know and their desire to better their own lives.

The purpose. Effective persuasion has a clear purpose: to move the reader to take a particular action. Smith's purpose is clear: He wants to persuade people "with free consent" to settle in New England.

Thinking About Persuasion

■ Which of the benefits that Smith describes seem directed at persuading people to join his expedition? Which benefits seem directed at people who might help finance a new colony?

VOCABULARY

Synonyms

Synonyms are words that have the same or nearly the same meaning. *Change* and *alter* are synonyms.

The words in capital letters are from *A Description of New England.* Choose the word that is *nearest* to the meaning of each word in capitals, *as the word is used in this selection.* Write the number of each item and the letter of your choice on a separate sheet.

1. HAZARD: (a) risk (b) choice (c) opportunity (d) desire
2. MAGNANIMITY: (a) daring (b) size (c) generosity (d) prudence
3. POSTERITY: (a) fortune (b) honor (c) ancestors (d) descendants
4. ANGLING: (a) fishing (b) carving (c) dangling (d) hunting
5. RECOMPENSE: (a) thought (b) treat (c) reward (d) correction

COMPOSITION

Developing a Thesis Statement

■ Write a brief essay about Smith's technique of piling up details. First create a thesis statement about this technique. Then demonstrate with examples how Smith adds detail after detail, not stopping with one noun or one adjective. Finally describe the effect you think Smith's technique would have had on a reader's view of the New World. *For help with this assignment, refer to Lesson 1 in the Writing About Literature Handbook at the back of this book.*

Writing a Letter

■ Assume the role of an English person in 1616. A copy of Smith's *Description* has fallen into your hands. Write a letter to a friend in which you react to Smith's appeals, discussing the positive and the negative aspects of joining Smith's proposed expedition.

COMPOSITION: GUIDELINES FOR EVALUATION

DEVELOPING A THESIS STATEMENT

Objective

To analyze a technique of persuasive writing

Guidelines for Evaluation

- suggested length: three to five paragraphs
- composition should state thesis
- should cite examples of details Smith uses to persuade readers
- should indicate overall effect of technique

WRITING A LETTER

Objective

To judge validity of persuasive writing

Guidelines for Evaluation

- suggested length: three to five paragraphs
- letter should give synopsis of selection
- should evaluate Smith's plan for settlement
- should consider negative aspects of plan
- should reach a conclusion

William Bradford *1590–1657*

While Jamestown was continuing its struggle for survival, another group of colonists, known as the Pilgrims, landed farther north. They were led by William Bradford, a Yorkshire farmer who had been converted as a teen-ager to an extreme form of Puritanism. Many Puritans hoped to remain members of the Church of England and to reform it from within. Bradford's Separatist group, however, saw no compromise and suffered heavy persecution for their beliefs. They fled to Holland and later decided to establish their own colony in Virginia.

Bradford and the Pilgrims sailed from Leyden in Holland in 1620, but because of storms they never reached Virginia. Instead, they landed their ship *Mayflower* at Plymouth on the coast of Massachusetts. In the Mayflower Compact, an agreement they signed before they left the ship, they decided to form a government and follow an elected leader. When their first governor, John Carver, died in April 1621, the people chose Bradford to take his place. He was so successful that he was reelected thirty times. In 1630 he began writing *Of Plymouth Plantation,* his history of these early Americans and their long geographical and spiritual pilgrimage.

Bradford is a gifted writer. His chronicle conveys not only facts but also feelings because he imaginatively projects himself and his readers into the experience of each moment. He makes a personal story out of the voyage, the settlement, and the grim realities of "the starving time." Through him, we share the struggle, the fears, and the victories over the elements, as well as the gradual changes that overtake the colony as people move away, as children grow up, as the original vision fades.

Year after year Bradford always keeps sight of the signs of God's judgment and providence. He sees the signs everywhere, so that, for example, the Indian interpreter Squanto becomes "an instrument sent of God for their good." For Bradford the Puritans' flight from Europe is guided by God in the same way as the Israelites' exodus from Egypt.

Bradford writes in the Puritan Plain Style, seldom using any metaphors or decorative language. Certainly he found no need to decorate a chronicle of events so charged with excitement, danger, and emotion. Bradford's plain language reflects his belief that everything in the Puritan way of life should have the power of simplicity.

■ What aspects of your community would you choose to describe to someone who knows nothing about America? Does Bradford choose very different or similar aspects of his community?

AT A GLANCE

- The Pilgrims land at Cape Cod and immediately thank God for their safe arrival.
- The Pilgrims find no welcome or shelter.

LITERARY OPTIONS

- allusion
- concrete language

THEMATIC OPTIONS

- faith overcoming adversity
- the value of friendship

1 TONE

Bradford's open invitation to the reader to share his observations of the Puritans' circumstances establishes a simple, personal, and direct tone for the history that follows.

2 ALLUSION

Despite the plain language, using a biblical allusion allows Bradford to charge his observations on the Pilgrims' plight with emotional intensity.

The Pilgrims' First Winter in Massachusetts, 1620. Nineteenth-century engraving.

William Bradford

from Of Plymouth Plantation

Arrival

After long beating at sea they fell with[1] that land which is called Cape Cod; the which being made and certainly known to be it, they were not a little joyful. . . .

Being thus arrived in a good harbor, and brought safe to land, they fell upon their knees and blessed the God of Heaven who had brought them over the vast and furious ocean, and delivered them from all the perils and miseries thereof, again to set their feet on the firm and stable earth, their proper element. . . .

1 But here I cannot but stay and make a pause, and stand half amazed at this poor people's present condition; and so I think will the reader, too, when he well considers the same. Being thus passed the vast ocean, and a sea of troubles before in their preparation (as may be remembered by that which went before), they had now no friends to welcome them nor inns to entertain or refresh their weatherbeaten bodies; no houses or much less towns to repair
2 to, to seek for succor. It is recorded in Scripture[2] as a mercy to the Apostle and his shipwrecked company, that the barbarians showed them no small kindness in refreshing them, but these savage barbarians, when they

1. **fell with:** arrived at.

2. **Scripture:** Acts of the Apostles, Chapter 28, Verse 2, tells how strangers helped Saint Paul after he was shipwrecked.

GUIDED READING

LITERAL QUESTION

1a. What kind of welcome do the Pilgrims receive when they land at Cape Cod? (It is no welcome at all. There are no friends; there is no shelter.)

INFERENTIAL QUESTION

1b. How did this situation probably affect the Pilgrims? (It probably alarmed them and forced them to rely even more on their faith and on each other.)

met with them (as after will appear) were readier to fill their sides full of arrows than otherwise. And for the season it was winter,
1 and they that know the winters of that country know them to be sharp and violent, and subject to cruel and fierce storms, dangerous to travel to known places, much more to search an unknown coast. Besides, what could they see but a hideous and desolate wilderness, full of wild beasts and wild men—and what multitudes there might be of them they knew not. Neither could they, as it were, go up to the top of Pisgah[3] to view from this wilderness a more goodly country to feed their hopes; for which way soever they turned their eyes (save upward to the heavens) they could have little solace or content in respect of any outward
2 objects. For summer being done, all things stand upon them with a weather-beaten face, and the whole country, full of woods and thickets, represented a wild and savage hue. If they looked behind them, there was the mighty ocean which they had passed and was now as a main bar and gulf to separate them from all the civil parts of the world. If it be said they had a ship to succor them, it is true; but what heard they daily from the Master[4] and company? But that with speed they should look out a place (with their shallop[5]) where they would be, at some near distance; for the season was such as he would not stir from thence till a safe harbor was discovered by them, where they would be and he might go without dan-
3 ger; and that victuals consumed apace but he must and would keep sufficient for themselves and their return. Yea, it was muttered by some[6] that if they got not a place in time, they would turn them and their goods ashore and leave them. Let it also be considered what weak hopes of supply and succor they left behind them that might bear up their minds in this sad condition and trials they were under; and they could not but be very small. It is true, indeed, the affections and love of their brethren at Leyden[7] was cordial and entire towards them, but they had little power to help them or themselves.

What could now sustain them but the Spirit of God and His grace? May not and ought not
4 the children of these fathers rightly say: "Our fathers were Englishmen which came over this great ocean, and were ready to perish in this wilderness; but they cried unto the Lord, and He heard their voice and looked on their adversity,"[8] etc. "Let them therefore praise the Lord, because He is good: and His mercies endure forever." "Yea, let them which have been redeemed of the Lord, show how He hath delivered them from the hand of the oppressor.
5 When they wandered in the desert wilderness out of the way, and found no city to dwell in, both hungry and thirsty, their soul was overwhelmed in them. Let them confess before the Lord His lovingkindness and His wonderful works before the sons of men."[9]

The Starving Time

But that which was most sad and lamentable was that in two or three months' time half of their company died, especially in January and February, being the depth of winter, and wanting houses and other comforts; being infected with the scurvy[10] and other diseases which this long voyage and their inaccommodate condition had brought upon them. So as there died some times two or three of a day in the foresaid time, that of 100 and odd persons, scarce fifty remained. And of these, in the time of most distress, there was but six or

3. **Pisgah** [piz′gə]: Moses viewed the Promised Land from Mount Pisgah (Deuteronomy 34: 1–4).
4. **Master:** Christopher Jones, the captain of the *Mayflower.*
5. **shallop** [shal′əp]: small open boat with oars or sail.
6. **some:** some of the sailors.
7. **Leyden** [līd′ən]: city in Netherlands where the Pilgrims lived before coming to America.
8. **"Our fathers . . . their adversity":** Bradford recalls Deuteronomy 26 : 5–7, the outcry of the Israelites to be delivered from Egyptian bondage.
9. **"Yea, let . . . sons of men":** Bradford paraphrases Psalm 107, comparing Puritan "captivity " and "wandering" with the captivity of the Israelites in Egypt and their wandering in the desert as they searched for the Promised Land.
10. **scurvy:** disease caused by vitamin C deficiency.

AT A GLANCE

- Bradford enumerates the hardships the Pilgrims face.
- The *Mayflower's* crew and captain, Christopher Jones, offer no help.
- The Pilgrims are sustained by their faith in God.
- Half of the Pilgrim band die within three months.

1 CONCRETE LANGUAGE

Bradford's use of spare, plain language to describe the Pilgrims' first impressions of New England reinforces the sense of their desolation.

2 IMAGERY

The simple, familiar concrete image of a weather-beaten face to describe the landscape draws a powerful, austere picture of the Pilgrims' first winter.

3 THEME

The lack of compassion and charity displayed by the *Mayflower*'s crew and captain dramatically underscores the importance of friendship during times of adversity.

4 ALLUSION

Bradford's allusion to the plight of the Israelites illustrates both the degree of the Pilgrims' hardships and the depth of their faith in God.

5 PERIOD IDEA

Bradford's comparison of the Pilgrims' "captivity" with the Israelites' wanderings underscores the Puritans' belief that faith eventually overcomes tribulations.

GUIDED READING

LITERAL QUESTIONS

1a. According to Bradford, what are the Pilgrims unable to do to "feed" their hopes when they first arrive? (go up to the top of a Mount Pisgah)

2b. What is the saddest thing that happens during the first few months after the Pilgrims' arrival? (Half of the group died.)

INFERENTIAL QUESTIONS

1a. What do Bradford's comments about the Pilgrims' hopes suggest about the way they probably felt after they arrived? (They were close to despair, disheartened, and disappointed.)

2b. What do you think sustained the Pilgrims during their time of near-despair? (their faith in God and their friendship for each other)

AT A GLANCE

- The sick Pilgrims are cared for by the few who are well, notably Myles Standish and William Brewster.
- The crew, who refuse to help, fall ill themselves.
- The Pilgrims care for the sick crewmen, who are shunned by fellow sailors.
- Some of the sick crew regret their treatment of the Pilgrims.

1 CONCRETE LANGUAGE

The straightforward account and unadorned list of chores in caring for the sick create a clear, powerful picture of the Pilgrims' plight.

2 POINT OF VIEW

Note how Bradford's Puritan belief in God's controlling influence permeates his understanding and recording of the Pilgrims' experiences.

3 STYLE: CONTRAST

Contrasting the crew's "jollity" when they were healthy with the rancor that occurs when some fall sick highlights the Pilgrims' genuine and enduring friendships with one another.

4 THEME

The boatswain's repentance underscores the inherent value of compassion and suggests the power of friendship offered in adversity.

seven sound persons who to their great commendations, be it spoken, spared no pains night nor day, but with abundance of toil and hazard
1 of their own health, fetched them wood, made them fires, dressed[11] them meat, made their beds, washed their loathsome clothes, clothed and unclothed them. In a word, did all the homely[12] and necessary offices for them which dainty and queasy stomachs cannot endure to hear named; and all this willingly and cheerfully, without any grudging in the least, showing herein their true love unto their friends and brethren; a rare example and worthy to be remembered. Two of these seven were Mr. William Brewster, their reverend Elder, and Myles Standish, their Captain and military commander, unto whom myself and many others were much beholden in our low and sick con-
2 dition. And yet the Lord so upheld these persons as in this general calamity they were not at all infected either with sickness or lameness. And what I have said of these I may say of many others who died in this general visitation,[13] and others yet living; that whilst they had health, yea, or any strength continuing, they were not wanting to any that had need of them. And I doubt not but their recompense is with the Lord.

But I may not here pass by another remarkable passage not to be forgotten. As this calamity fell among the passengers that were to be left here to plant, and were hasted ashore and made to drink water that the seamen might have the more beer, and one[14] in his sickness desiring but a small can of beer, it was answered that if he were their own father he should have none. The disease began to fall amongst them[15] also, so as almost half of their company died before they went away, and many of their officers and lustiest[16] men, as the boatswain, gunner, three quartermasters, the
3 cook and others. At which the Master was something stricken and sent to the sick ashore and told the Governor he should send for beer for them that had need of it, though he drunk water homeward bound.

But now amongst his company there was far another kind of carriage[17] in this misery than amongst the passengers. For they that before had been boon[18] companions in drinking and jollity in the time of their health and welfare began now to desert one another in this calamity, saying they would not hazard their lives for them: they should be infected by coming to help them in their cabins, and so, after they came to lie by it, would do little or nothing for them but, "if they died, let them die." But such of the passengers as were yet aboard showed them what mercy they could, which made some of their hearts relent, as the boatswain (and some others) who was a proud young man and would often curse and scoff at
4 the passengers. But when he grew weak, they had compassion on him and helped him; then he confessed he did not deserve it at their hands, he had abused them in word and deed. "Oh!" (saith he) "you, I now see, show your love like Christians indeed one to another, but we let one another lie and die like dogs." Another lay cursing his wife, saying if it had not been for her he had never come this unlucky voyage, and anon cursing his fellows, saying he had done this and that for some of them; he had spent so much and so much amongst them, and they were now weary of him and did not help him, having need. Another gave his companion all he had, if he died, to help him in his weakness; he went and got a little spice and made him a mess[19] of meat once or twice. And because he died not so soon as he expected, he went amongst his fellows and swore the rogue would cozen[20] him, he would see him choked before he made him any more meat; and yet the poor fellow died before morning.

11. **dressed:** prepared.
12. **homely:** domestic and everyday.
13. **visitation:** affliction or disaster.
14. **one:** Bradford notes that this "one" was himself.
15. **them:** the sailors.
16. **lustiest:** healthiest and strongest.
17. **carriage:** behavior.
18. **boon:** merry.
19. **mess:** a meal.
20. **cozen** [kuz′ən]: cheat.

GUIDED READING

LITERAL QUESTIONS

1a. How does Bradford think the Pilgrims who cared for their sick friends will be rewarded? (by God)

2a. What does the ship's captain tell the governor after his crew fall sick? (to send for beer, even if that means the captain must drink water on the return trip)

INFERENTIAL QUESTIONS

1b. What do Bradford's thoughts about rewards suggest about the Pilgrims' philosophy toward good deeds? (Good deeds are acts of love that are rewarded in heaven, if not on earth.)

2b. Why does the captain have a change of heart? (The fact that his own men fall sick may frighten him and move him toward less selfish behavior.)

Squanto Teaching the Pilgrims How to Plant Corn, C. W. Jefferys.

Compact with the Indians

All this while the Indians came skulking about them, and would sometimes show themselves aloof off, but when any approached near them, they would run away; and once they stole away their tools where they had been at work and were gone to dinner. But about the 16th of
1 March, a certain Indian came boldly amongst them and spoke to them in broken English, which they could well understand but marveled at it. At length they understood by discourse with him that he was not of these parts, but belonged to the eastern parts where some English ships came to fish, with whom he was acquainted and could name sundry of them by their names, amongst whom he had got his language. He be-
2 came profitable to them in acquainting them with many things concerning the state of the country in the east parts where he lived, which was afterwards profitable unto them; as also of the people here, of their names, number and strength, of their situation and distance from this place, and who was chief amongst them. His name was Samoset. He told them also of another Indian whose name was Squanto, a native of this place, who had been in England and could speak better English than himself.

Being, after some time of entertainment and gifts, dismissed, a while after he came again, and

AT A GLANCE

- The Indians, who once stole tools, are curious but aloof.
- Samoset, who speaks some English, becomes a helpful ally.
- Samoset tells the Puritans about Squanto, who speaks better English.

1 RESPONSE JOURNAL

Students may summarize what they feel Bradford's journal indicates about the Pilgrims' understanding of the Indians and their culture.

2 VOCABULARY: WORD CHOICE

Bradford's repeated use of the single word *profitable* to describe the range of Samoset's helpful behavior reflects his practical, austere view of the world.

GUIDED READING

LITERAL QUESTION

1a. How did Samoset learn to speak English? (from the crews of English fishing ships)

INFERENTIAL QUESTION

1b. Why might the Pilgrims have considered Samoset a godsend? (Not only could he give the Pilgrims helpful information, but he also could help the Indians and Pilgrims learn more about each other and become friends.)

AT A GLANCE

- Chief Massasoit signs a peace treaty with the Pilgrims.
- Brought by the chief, Squanto remains with the Pilgrims, a helpful ally until his death.

1 THEME

In helping the Pilgrims to realize their dream of building a new, God-centered society, Squanto illustrates the fundamental value of friendship.

REFLECTING ON THE SELECTION

How do you think the Pilgrims' religious beliefs helped them to face the challenge of life in the new land? (Their faith, the value they placed on love and friendship, and their strong sense of community allowed them to overcome hardships and to make friends with the Indians.)

STUDY QUESTIONS

1. prayer
2. no friends, no shelter, hostile Indians, harsh winter; "the Spirit of God"
3. put the Pilgrims ashore to save provisions for the return voyage; helped the sick sailors
4. skulked around, stole tools; made peace; *Samoset:* the land, other Indians; *Squanto:* planting corn, fishing
5. piety, courage
6. allusion to Pisgah; all of paragraph four; description of Squanto as an instrument sent by God
7. *initial impression:* savages; *later impression:* people in similar straits as pilgrims; new perspective, fewer prejudices; help from Indians, communication
8. Answers will vary. *Necessary elements:* courage, faith, good health, community; *to be abandoned:* prejudices, dietary habits, customs

five more with him, and they brought again all the tools that were stolen away before, and made way for the coming of their great Sachem,[21] called Massasoit. Who, about four or five days after, came with the chief of his friends and other attendance, with the aforesaid Squanto. With whom, after friendly entertainment and some gifts given him, they made a peace with him (which hath now continued this twenty-four years) in these terms:

1. That neither he nor any of his should injure or do hurt to any of their people.

2. That if any of his did hurt to any of theirs, he should send the offender, that they might punish him.

3. That if anything were taken away from any of theirs, he should cause it to be restored; and they should do the like to his.

4. If any did unjustly war against him, they would aid him; if any did war against them, he should aid them.

5. He should send to his neighbors confederates to certify them of this, that they might not wrong them, but might be likewise comprised in the conditions of peace.

6. That when their men came to them, they should leave their bows and arrows behind them.

After these things he returned to his place called Sowams, some forty miles from this place, 1 but Squanto continued with them and was their interpreter and was a special instrument sent of God for their good beyond their expectation. He directed them how to set their corn, where to take fish, and to procure other commodities, and was also their pilot to bring them to unknown places for their profit, and never left them till he died.

21. **Sachem** [sā'chəm]: chief.

STUDY QUESTIONS

Recalling

1. What was the Pilgrims' first action upon landing in the New World?
2. Identify four specific hardships that the Pilgrims faced in the New World, according to the third paragraph. What sustained them, according to the fourth paragraph?
3. As "calamity fell among the passengers," what did the sailors do? When calamity struck the sailors, what did the Pilgrims still on board do?
4. How did the Indians act at first, according to Bradford? What did they do after "friendly entertainment and some gifts"? What information did Samoset and Squanto provide for the Pilgrims?

Interpreting

5. State two dominant characteristics of the *Mayflower* Pilgrims as they are pictured by Bradford during their first months of hardship in America.
6. Which words and statements by Bradford create a picture of the Pilgrims as God's "chosen people"?
7. Describe Bradford's initial attitude toward the Indians and his attitude in the section "Compact with the Indians." How has Bradford changed? What seems to have caused the change?

Extending

8. Judging from Bradford's account, what qualities do you think would be necessary for a man or woman to survive for any length of time in the American wilderness? What attitudes brought from Europe had to be abandoned?

VIEWPOINT

Throughout this book "Viewpoint" will present a quotation about an author or a selection you have read. Most of these quotations come from literary critics; some come from the authors themselves. Each quotation is followed by one or two questions to help you consider the quoted opinion in light of your own reading of the selection.

Perry Miller, an expert on early American literature, writes:

> No other writer will lead us so directly to the core of Puritanism as Bradford; none with such charm, generosity, largeness of spirit, with such calm assurance and massive strength will so completely reveal the essential frame of mind, the type of character, the quality of life that underlay the theology.
>
> —*The New England Mind*

■ Find three passages in *Of Plymouth Plantation* supporting Miller's statement that Bradford reveals the essence of Puritanism. What conclusions about Puritanism can you draw from the details of Bradford's story?

LITERARY FOCUS

Allusions: The Use of the Bible

For centuries English-speaking writers and their readers knew the Bible very well. After 1611 the version they knew best was the King James translation, which has had a powerful influence on English and American literature. Poets, storytellers, and orators referred to the Bible frequently, and phrases from the King James version became part of everyone's vocabulary. The Puritans, especially, based their religion directly on a reading of the Bible, and their writers naturally made allusions to it.

An **allusion** is a short reference to a person, a place, an event, or another work of literature. When Bradford alludes to the "top of Pisgah," he knows his audience will understand that he is referring to the mountain from which Moses saw the Promised Land.

Writers use allusions to extend the meanings of their works. Sometimes they want to show that a particular experience is also a universal experience. Sometimes they want to remind us of connections we might not have thought of ourselves.

Thinking About Allusions

■ Find the two biblical allusions in Bradford's third paragraph. Why were these specific references appropriate to the experience of the Pilgrims?

VOCABULARY

Sentence Completions

Each of the following sentences contains a blank with four possible words for completing the sentence. The words are from *Of Plymouth Plantation.* Choose the word that completes each sentence correctly, using the word *as it is used in this selection.* Write the number of each item and the letter of your choice on a separate sheet.

1. The colonists could not hope for supply and _____ in the desolate wilderness.
   (a) succor (c) shallop
   (b) scurvy (d) carriage
2. The Pilgrims faced much _____ during their hard sea voyage.
   (a) abundance (c) solace
   (b) boon (d) adversity
3. One of the many _____ that befell the settlers was death from scurvy.
   (a) recompenses (c) calamities
   (b) commendations (d) commodities
4. Many sailors did not want to risk infection or to _____ their lives.
   (a) scoff (c) relent
   (b) hazard (d) cozen
5. The Pilgrims had lengthy _____ with Samoset.
   (a) commendation (c) hue
   (b) solace (d) discourse

COMPOSITION

Writing a Comparison/Contrast

■ Compare and contrast the promises that John Smith makes in his *Description of New England* (page 20) and the reality of the settlers' lives as Bradford describes it. You may want to write first about Smith's ideal vision and then about Bradford's genuine history. *For help with this assignment, refer to Lesson 2 in the Writing About Literature Handbook at the back of this book.*

Writing a Diary

■ Imagine yourself one of the Plymouth settlers, and write a diary chronicling several days of your adventures. Consider including details of your problems with weather, animals, food, clothes, the native inhabitants, and the organization of your first government.

VIEWPOINT

second and fourth paragraphs and descriptions of healthy aiding sick; had great faith in God, saw selves as God's chosen people, were courageous, compassionate, communal

LITERARY FOCUS

"a mercy to the Apostle . . ."; "the top of Pisgah . . ."; marooned in a strange land; America as the Promised Land

VOCABULARY

1. (a) succor
2. (d) adversity
3. (c) calamities
4. (b) hazard
5. (d) discourse

COMPOSITION: GUIDELINES FOR EVALUATION

WRITING A COMPARISON/CONTRAST

Objective

To compare and contrast two works of literature

Guidelines for Evaluation

- suggested length: three to five paragraphs
- should list features of New England as described by both Smith and Bradford
- should compare the two, indicating that Smith's view does not reflect the reality of life in New England

WRITING A DIARY

Objective

To write a diary from a given point of view

Guidelines for Evaluation

- suggested length: three to four entries of one or two paragraphs
- should include facts related by Bradford
- should be from a Plymouth settler's viewpoint
- should include that settler's imagined feelings about, and experiences in, the New World

Anne Bradstreet *1612–1672*

Anne Bradstreet came to the Massachusetts Bay Colony with her husband and her parents in 1630. The Bradstreets settled in the frontier village of Andover, where Anne, under difficult conditions that tried her faith, maintained a household and raised eight children. She had to defend her right to compose verses, for many Puritans, who did not disapprove of poetry itself, wondered if a woman should write it. Yet her first book, *The Tenth Muse Lately Sprung Up in America,* was published in England in 1650 and was a great success.

Bradstreet's finest poems are those closest to her personal experience as a Puritan wife and mother living on the edge of the wilderness. Like other Puritans, she found similarities between the domestic details of daily life and the spiritual details of her religious life. For Bradstreet the everyday and the everlasting were simply two sides of the same experience.

In a poem called "Upon the Burning of Our House" Bradstreet records both her earthly sorrow and the faith that sustains her:

Thou hast a house on high erect,
Framed by that mighty Architect,
With glory richly furnished,
Stands permanent though this be fled.

* * *

The world no longer let me love,
My hope and treasure lies above.

Similarly, in her tender poem "To My Dear and Loving Husband" Bradstreet places her earthly married life within the framework of eternity. Anne Bradstreet was not an innovative poet, but her directness and her sincerity are moving.

■ What qualities do you think most people want in a husband or wife? Does Bradstreet share your opinion?

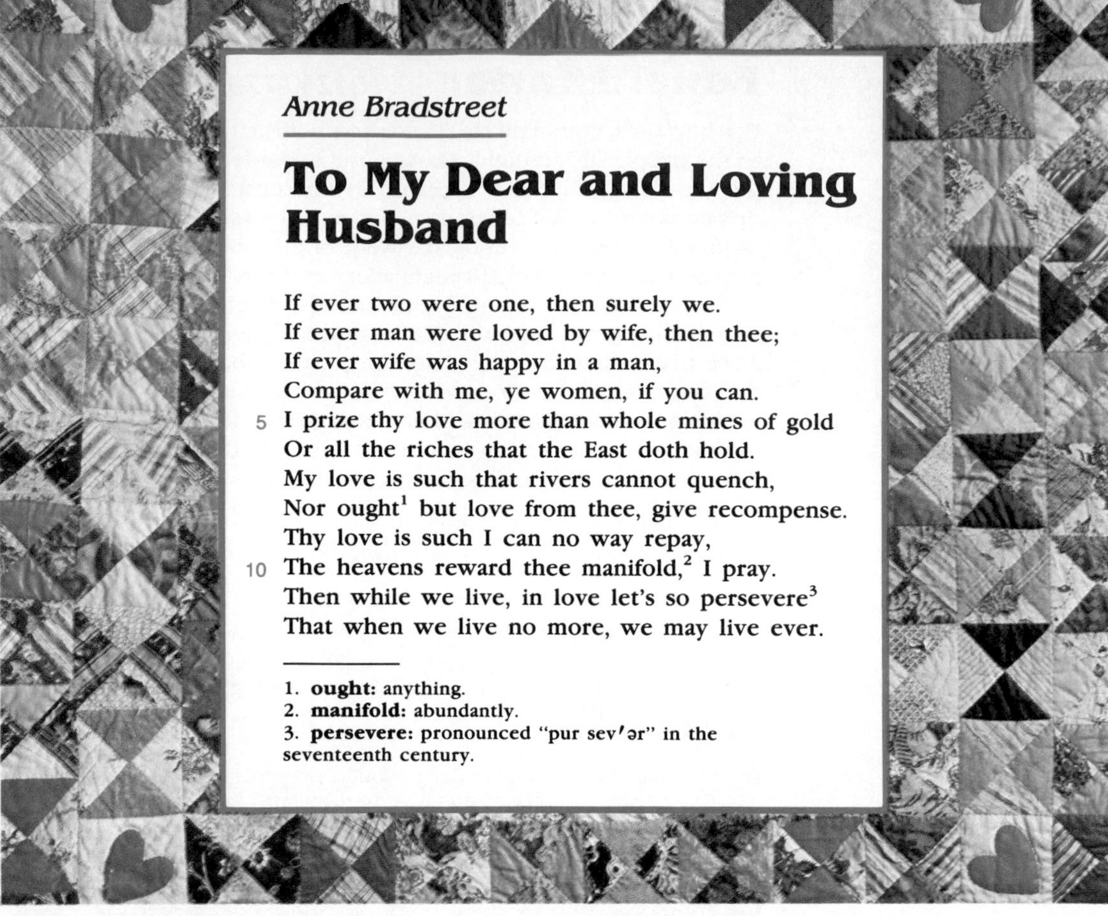

Anne Bradstreet

To My Dear and Loving Husband

If ever two were one, then surely we.
If ever man were loved by wife, then thee;
If ever wife was happy in a man,
Compare with me, ye women, if you can.
I prize thy love more than whole mines of gold
Or all the riches that the East doth hold.
My love is such that rivers cannot quench,
Nor ought[1] but love from thee, give recompense.
Thy love is such I can no way repay,
The heavens reward thee manifold,[2] I pray.
Then while we live, in love let's so persevere[3]
That when we live no more, we may live ever.

1. **ought:** anything.
2. **manifold:** abundantly.
3. **persevere:** pronounced "pur sev′ər" in the seventeenth century.

STUDY QUESTIONS

Recalling

1. What does the poet prize "more than whole mines of gold"? What is it that "rivers cannot quench"?
2. Which words tell us what will happen when she and her husband die if they persevere in love while they live?

Interpreting

3. What does Bradstreet actually mean by the seeming paradox in the last line about living "no more" yet living "ever"?
4. Besides declaring her human love for her husband during her earthly marriage, what other typical Puritan concern does this poem celebrate in lines 9–10?

VIEWPOINT

The contemporary American poet Adrienne Rich writes of Bradstreet:

> It is worth observing that Anne Bradstreet happened to be one of the first American women, inhabiting a time and place in which heroism was a necessity of life, and men and women were fighting for survival both as individuals and as a community.
>
> —Introduction to *The Works of Anne Bradstreet*

■ What personal qualities and beliefs does Bradstreet reveal in "To My Dear and Loving Husband" that made such heroism possible for her?

AT A GLANCE

The poet contemplates her love for her husband.

LITERARY OPTIONS

- rhyme scheme
- comparison and contrast

THEMATIC OPTIONS

- marital love
- everlasting life

SPEAKER

By addressing her husband directly in the poem, Bradstreet establishes a simple, highly personal tone that adds warmth and forcefulness to her declaration of love (l. 1).

RHYME SCHEME

In using the couplet form (*aa, bb,* and so on) throughout the poem, Bradstreet reinforces and highlights the strong unity that exists between herself and her husband as members of a couple (e.g., ll. 1–2).

COMPARISON AND CONTRAST

By elevating the value she places on her husband's love above the value she places on gold, Bradstreet projects both the depth of her love and its emphatically spiritual nature (ll. 5–6).

MAIN IDEA

Bradstreet suggests that in loving each other fully on earth, and thus truly reflecting divine love, she and her husband will attain everlasting love in heaven (ll. 11–12).

REFLECTING ON THE POEM

What does Bradstreet suggest are the joys of a happy marriage? (unity with another, reciprocal ardor, earthly joy, and heavenly reward)

STUDY QUESTIONS

1. her husband's love; her love for her husband
2. "we may live ever"
3. eternal life in heaven
4. grace, which she prays her husband will receive

VIEWPOINT

faith in God; love and devotion for her husband

Edward Taylor *1642–1729*

For fifty-eight years Edward Taylor was both minister and physician to the people of Westfield, Massachusetts, bordering what he called the "howling wilderness." Because Taylor considered his poems a private record of his religious experience, he asked his heirs never to publish them. As a result, the work of this major New England poet was unknown for 210 years after his death.

Perhaps another reason Taylor did not wish to publish his work was that his poetry was not written in the Plain Style of the Puritans. At first reading we can see that Taylor uses elaborate imagery. In one poem, *God's Determinations,* the poet meditates on the wonders of the created world and compares God to a builder, an ironmonger, a weaver, and a bowler rolling forth the great bowling ball of the sun. He focuses on images of God as an artisan, a maker:

His hand hath made this noble work which stands
His Glorious Handiwork not made by hands.

"Huswifery" [hoos′wif rē] is also a complicated poem, a prayer in which the poet compares God's granting of grace to the work of a housewife who spins, weaves, and dyes a piece of cloth. By *huswifery,* Taylor meant not only "housekeeping," but also "managing well."

■ What did the Puritans believe about a person's relationship to God? How does this poem reflect that belief?

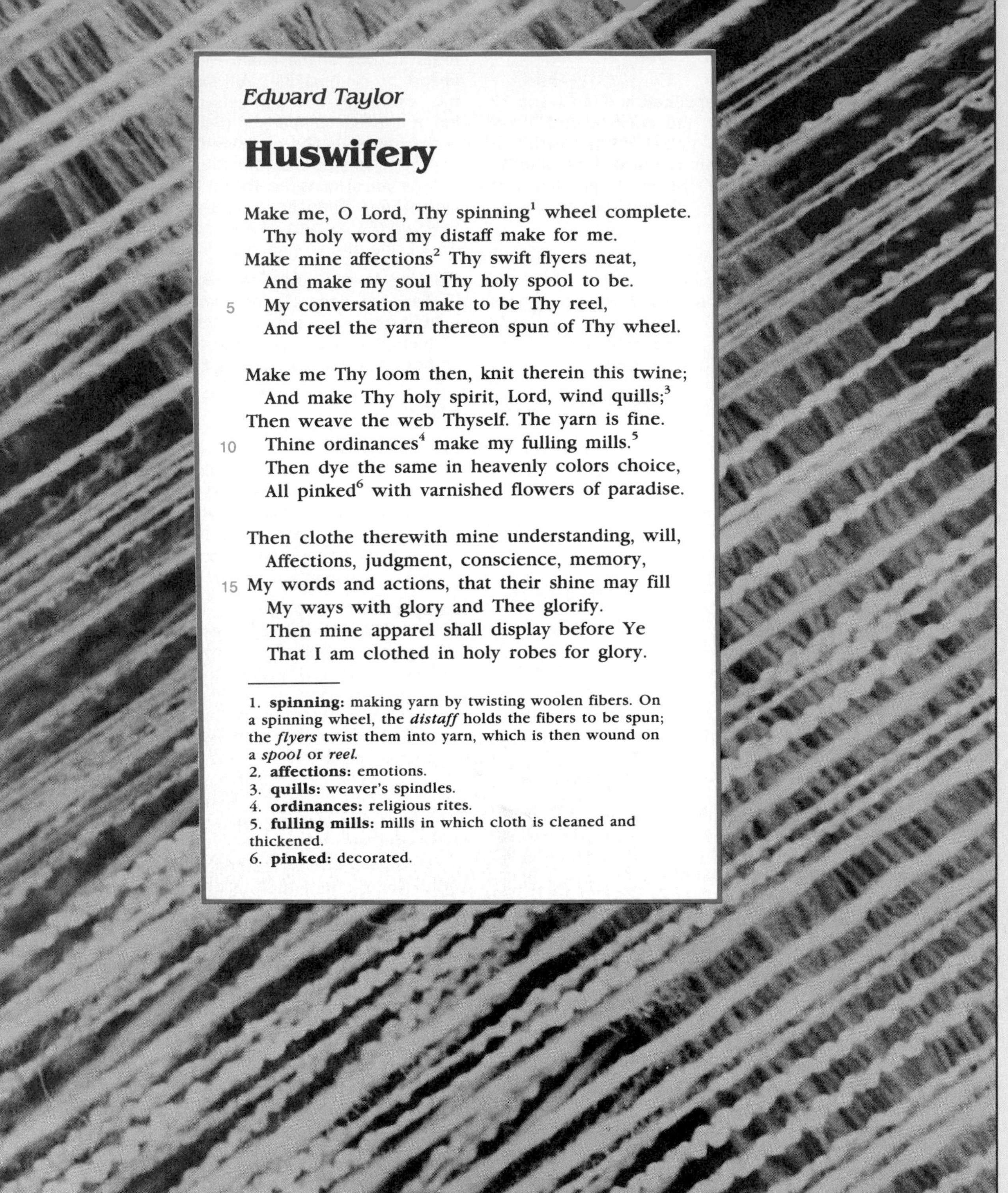

Edward Taylor

Huswifery

Make me, O Lord, Thy spinning[1] wheel complete.
Thy holy word my distaff make for me.
Make mine affections[2] Thy swift flyers neat,
And make my soul Thy holy spool to be.
My conversation make to be Thy reel,
And reel the yarn thereon spun of Thy wheel.

Make me Thy loom then, knit therein this twine;
And make Thy holy spirit, Lord, wind quills;[3]
Then weave the web Thyself. The yarn is fine.
Thine ordinances[4] make my fulling mills.[5]
Then dye the same in heavenly colors choice,
All pinked[6] with varnished flowers of paradise.

Then clothe therewith mine understanding, will,
Affections, judgment, conscience, memory,
My words and actions, that their shine may fill
My ways with glory and Thee glorify.
Then mine apparel shall display before Ye
That I am clothed in holy robes for glory.

1. **spinning:** making yarn by twisting woolen fibers. On a spinning wheel, the *distaff* holds the fibers to be spun; the *flyers* twist them into yarn, which is then wound on a *spool* or *reel.*
2. **affections:** emotions.
3. **quills:** weaver's spindles.
4. **ordinances:** religious rites.
5. **fulling mills:** mills in which cloth is cleaned and thickened.
6. **pinked:** decorated.

AT A GLANCE

- The poet prays to be drawn closer to God.
- He wants every aspect of his being to be wholly taken over and transformed.

LITERARY OPTIONS

- controlling image
- main idea

THEMATIC OPTIONS

- religious fervor
- physical and spiritual beauty

SPEAKER

The speaker's direct address to God establishes the closeness he feels to God and projects the emotional intensity of his plea (l. 1).

CONTROLLING IMAGE

Using the spinning wheel in an extended metaphor allows Taylor to connect a vision of God as Creator with concern for salvation. The conceit dramatizes how thoroughly he believes that God infuses every aspect of life on earth (ll. 1–6).

MAIN IDEA

The speaker asks God to "clothe" him with the gift of grace, thus making him an instrument of divine will, so that he can glorify God on earth and gain salvation in heaven (ll. 13–18).

REFLECTING ON THE POEM

How does the idea of a spinner operating a spinning wheel convey a relationship between God and human beings? (It shows a fundamental belief that the spirit of God permeates life on earth.)

STUDY QUESTIONS

1. spinning wheel, loom
2. "make"; *subject:* "Lord"; *object:* "me"; lines 2, 3, 4, 5, 7, 8, 10
3. show God that he is "clothed in holy robes for glory"
4. making cloth: spinning, weaving, dyeing; spinning wheel, loom, cloth; spinner, weaver, dyer
5. God as active and central dispenser of life and grace
6. receive and display God's grace, be with God, do God's work
7. gift from God; Taylor asks to be the agent of God's will and thus be endowed with grace

VIEWPOINT

Everyday occurrence of making cloth is contrasted with heavenly "clothmaker."

LITERARY FOCUS

emotions: flyers; *soul:* spool; clothmaking shows everyday tasks as charged with God's presence

COMPARING WRITERS

Answers will vary. Columbus: real world; Smith: idealized world; Puritans: material world as creation of God, heaven as ideal; American Indians: no tension between real and ideal, nature sacred; *Walum Olum:* tension in introduction of evil into originally ideal world

STUDY QUESTIONS

Recalling

1. What devices are mentioned in lines 1 and 7?
2. With what verb does the poem begin? What are the subject and object of this verb? In what lines of the poem is the verb repeated?
3. According to lines 17–18, what does the poet want his "apparel" to "display" and to whom?

Interpreting

4. What process and what stages in that process are described in the poem? What role does the poet play in this process? What role does God play?
5. What does the verb repeated throughout the poem suggest about how the poet views God's role in his life?
6. In the third stanza, particularly in line 16, what does Taylor suggest is his ultimate goal?
7. Does Taylor believe one can achieve grace through one's own efforts, or must grace come as a gift from God? Supply evidence from the poem for your answer.

VIEWPOINT

One writer who has studied the Puritans says that Edward Taylor

> brings religious vision and the actualities of earth together in his verses, striking poetic sparks from the contrast. Again and again he makes articulate the drama inherent in man's quest for a beauty which is beyond earth. . . .
>
> —*Literary History of the United States*

■ The writer, Kenneth Murdock, points to a dramatic contrast in Taylor's poetry. How does "Huswifery" contrast a heavenly vision with the everyday things of earth?

LITERARY FOCUS

Controlling Imagery

When we speak of an **image** in literature, we usually mean that the words create a "picture" in our minds. Images can be visual, of course, but they can also describe other sensory experiences, such as tasting, smelling, feeling, or hearing. Sometimes poets use a variety of images in a single poem. Sometimes they use only one, allowing it to *control*, or dominate, the poem.

In "Huswifery" Taylor controls the many separate images of the poem with the single larger image of clothmaking. An extended image like this, especially one that sets up a rather surprising or unusual comparison (God as a clothmaker), is sometimes called a **conceit.**

Taylor sets up the controlling image in the first line as he asks to be God's instrument, a spinning wheel. Then he compares the Bible ("Thy holy word") to part of the spinning wheel—the distaff, the strong stick that holds the raw wool.

Thinking About Controlling Imagery

■ To what does Taylor compare his emotions and his soul? How does the controlling image help show that, for Taylor, the earthly and the heavenly are one and the same?

COMPOSITION

Analyzing a Title

■ Write a brief essay in which you discuss the title of Taylor's poem. First tell what the title means. Then explain how the title helps to explain the poem itself. Finally tell whether you think the title is appropriate, and give reasons to support your opinion.

Using a Controlling Image

■ Write a poem that uses a conceit, or controlling image. Follow the format of Taylor's "Huswifery" or of Bradstreet's "To My Dear and Loving Husband" (page 31), keeping the same basic sentence structure but changing the key words. You may want to begin, for example, by completing this line: "Make me, _____, your _____ complete."

COMPARING WRITERS

In William Bradford, Anne Bradstreet, and Edward Taylor we find a quest for heavenly joy meeting face to face the real world of flesh and blood. Even the selections by Christopher Columbus and John Smith reveal a contrast between Eden-like dreams and the unavoidable realities of earth. This contrast between the real and the ideal is one of the most American of themes, one that will appear in every unit of this book.

■ Find passages from at least two writers in this unit that demonstrate an awareness of both the real world and an ideal one. Describe each writer's attitude toward that contrast.

COMPOSITION: GUIDELINES FOR EVALUATION

ANALYZING A TITLE

Objective

To relate the title of a poem to its meaning

Guidelines for Evaluation

- suggested length: three to four paragraphs
- should define "huswifery"
- should relate definition to specific images
- should show how title highlights meaning
- support opinion with specific references

USING A CONTROLLING IMAGE

Objective

To write a poem with a controlling image

Guidelines for Evaluation

- suggested length: eight to twelve lines
- should follow the format of Bradstreet's or Taylor's poem
- should establish a controlling image and carry it through with relevant details

William Byrd *1674–1744*

The New England Puritans wrote so much and so vividly that they tend to dominate early American literature. We should remind ourselves that not all early American settlers were Puritans. In the southern colonies, especially, other English settlers had founded prosperous plantations and communities with a style of life quite unlike that of New England.

William Byrd was one of the most brilliant of the southern landowning aristocracy. These southern gentry modeled themselves on the English upper classes, taking pride in stately homes furnished with fine china, paintings, and books. Though hard-working and religious, they were not afraid of some of the worldly pleasures that the Puritans shunned.

Byrd was born in Jamestown, which John Smith had helped establish sixty-seven years earlier. When Byrd was only seven years old, his rich father sent him to England for his education. Byrd lived in London more than half of his life, enjoying the city's society and its theaters. He was fifty-two before he returned to Virginia. There he read his Greek and Latin classics every day; owned the second largest library in America, numbering 3,600 books; entertained and visited his neighbors; and managed his huge 180,000-acre estate, upon which he founded the city of Richmond.

Byrd's writings include diaries, travel books, and poems. One of his best-known works, *The History of the Dividing Line,* recounts his experiences on a surveying trip that defined the Virginia–North Carolina border. *A Progress to the Mines* (1732), another well-known work, is Byrd's account of a trip to the iron-mining territory of western Virginia, where he visited the estate of former governor Spotswood. The Spotswoods' elegant "enchanted castle," with its pet deer leaping around and smashing the china, provides a striking contrast to New England earnestness and plain living.

■ From what you have seen on television and in film, what do you think life on a Southern plantation was like? Would Byrd concur?

AT A GLANCE

- September 27, 1732: Byrd describes the town of Germanna.
- Byrd arrives at the Spotswood home and is warmly greeted by Mrs. Spotswood.
- A pet deer breaks a mirror in the sitting room.
- Colonel Spotswood and Miss Theky, Mrs. Spotswood's sister, arrive home.

LITERARY OPTIONS

- analogy
- simile
- description

THEMATIC OPTIONS

- companionship and friendship
- the development of industry

1 DESCRIPTION

Byrd's use of concrete details and descriptive adjectives creates a clear, immediately accessible picture of the landscape as it looked more than two and a half centuries ago.

2 STYLE: IRONY

Byrd's sophisticated appreciation of language, clear in his ironic use of the word *pious*, reflects the art of conversation in the society about which he writes.

3 CHARACTERIZATION

Byrd's account of Mrs. Spotswood's reaction to the broken mirror shows her as good-natured and easygoing, despite her wealth and position.

William Byrd

from A Progress to the Mines

1 *September 27, 1732* I rode eight miles together over a stony road and had on either side continual poisoned fields, with nothing but saplings growing on them. Then I came into the main county road that leads from Fredericksburg to Germanna, which last place I reached in ten miles more.

This famous town consists of Colonel Spotswood's enchanted castle on one side of the street and a baker's dozen[1] of ruinous tenements on the other, where so many German families had dwelt some years ago, but are now removed ten miles higher, in the fork of Rappahannock,[2] to land of their own. There had also been a chapel about a bowshot from the colonel's house, at the end of an avenue of
2 cherry trees, but some pious people had lately burned it down, with intent to get another built nearer to their own homes.

Here I arrived about three o'clock and found only Mrs. Spotswood at home, who received her old acquaintance with many a gracious smile. I was carried into a room elegantly set off with pier glasses,[3] the largest of which came soon after to an odd misfortune. Amongst other favorite animals that cheered this lady's solitude, a brace[4] of tame deer ran familiarly about the house, and one of them came to stare at me as a stranger; but, unluckily spying his own figure in the glass, he made a spring over the tea table that stood under it and shattered the glass to pieces and, falling back upon the tea table, made a terrible fracas among the china. This exploit was so sudden, and accompanied with such noise, that it surprised me and perfectly frightened Mrs. Spots-
3 wood. But 'twas worth all the damage to show the moderation and good humor with which she bore this disaster.

In the evening the noble colonel came home from his mines, who saluted me very civilly, and Mrs. Spotswood's sister, Miss Theky, who had been to meet him *en cavalier,*[5] was so kind too as to bid me welcome. We talked

1. **baker's dozen:** thirteen.
2. **Rappahannock:** river flowing through northeastern Virginia.
3. **pier glasses:** tall mirrors.
4. **brace:** pair.
5. ***en cavalier*** [än ka va lyā′]: French for "on horseback."

GUIDED READING

LITERAL QUESTIONS

1a. Which buildings make up the town of Germanna? (the Spotswood house and 13 tenement houses)

2a. Who breaks the mirror in the Spotswood house? (a pet deer)

INFERENTIAL QUESTIONS

1b. What do you think life was probably like in a town of that size? (People probably had to devise their own amusements to offset the quiet, loneliness, and isolation.)

2b. What does this event suggest about the Spotswoods' life style? (The family have enough money and social standing to enjoy an easy, self-indulgent life style.)

over a legend of old stories, supped about nine, and then prattled with the ladies till 'twas time for a traveler to retire. In the meantime, I observed my old friend to be very uxorious[6] and exceedingly fond of his children. This was so opposite to the maxims he used to preach up before he was married that I could not forbear rubbing up the memory of them. But he gave a very good-natured turn to his change
1 of sentiments by alleging that whoever brings a poor gentlewoman into so solitary a place, from all her friends and acquaintance, would be ungrateful not to use her and all that belongs to her with all possible tenderness.

September 28 We all kept snug in our several apartments till nine, except Miss Theky, who was the housewife of the family. At that hour we met over a pot of coffee, which was not quite strong enough to give us the palsy.

After breakfast the colonel and I left the ladies to their domestic affairs and took a turn in the garden, which has nothing beautiful but three terrace walks that fall in slopes one below another. I let him understand that besides the pleasure of paying him a visit I came to be
2 instructed by so great a master in the mystery of making iron, wherein he had led the way and was the Tubal-cain[7] of Virginia. He corrected me a little there by assuring me he was not only the first in this country but the first in North America who had erected a regular furnace. That they ran altogether upon bloomeries[8] in New England and Pennsylvania till his example had made them attempt greater works. But in this last colony, they have so few ships to carry their iron to Great Britain that they must be content to make it only for their own use, and must be obliged to manufacture it when they have done. That he hoped he had done the country very great service by setting so good an example. . . .

Then I inquired after his own mines, and hoped, as he was the first that engaged in this great undertaking, that he had brought them to
3 the most perfection. He told me he had iron in several parts of his great tract of land, consisting of forty-five thousand acres. But that the mine he was at work upon was thirteen miles below Germanna. That his ore (which was very rich) he raised a mile from his furnace and was obliged to cart the iron, when it was made, fifteen miles to Massaponax, a plantation he had upon Rappahannock River; but that the road was exceeding good, gently declining all the way, and had no more than one hill to go up in the whole journey. . . .

But at the same time he gave me to understand that his furnace had done no great feats lately, because he had been taken up in building an air furnace at Massaponax, which he had now brought to perfection and should be thereby able to furnish the whole country with all sorts of cast iron as cheap and as good as ever came from England. I told him he must do one thing more to have a full vent for those
4 commodities: he must keep a *chaloupe*[9] running into all the rivers to carry his wares home to people's own doors. And if he would do that I would set a good example and take off a whole ton of them.

Our conversation on this subject continued till dinner, which was both elegant and plen-
5 tiful. The afternoon was devoted to the ladies, who showed me one of their most beautiful walks. They conducted me through a shady lane to the landing and by the way made me drink some very fine water that issued from a marble fountain and ran incessantly.

September 29 Having employed about two hours in retirement, I sallied out at the first summons to breakfast, where our conversation with the ladies, like whip sillabub,[10] was

---

6. **uxorious** [uk sôr′ē əs]: fond of his wife.
7. **Tubal-cain:** master ironworker and toolmaker described in the Bible, Genesis 4 : 22.
8. **bloomeries:** formerly, furnaces where iron was made directly from iron ore.
9. ***chaloupe*** [shə lo͞op′]: French for "shallop," a small boat.
10. **whip sillabub:** light, frothy dessert made of sweetened milk or cream.

AT A GLANCE

- Byrd notes Spotswood's love for his family. Spotswood comments on the loneliness of life in Germanna.
- September 28: Spotswood and Byrd walk in the garden and discuss the manufacture of iron.
- Byrd, the Spotswoods, and Miss Theky spend the afternoon walking and talking.

1 THEME

Spotswood's awareness of his wife's loneliness suggests how vitally important companionship and friendship were to the early, isolated settlers of the new land.

2 ANALOGY

Byrd's analogy between Spotswood and the biblical Tubal-cain reflects Byrd's deep respect for Spotswood's business achievements.

3 THEME

Byrd's detailed description of Spotswood's iron mines illustrates the increasingly important role that industry played in the development of the new land.

4 VOCABULARY: WORD CHOICE

Byrd's repeated use of French words reflects his European education and suggests that he is writing for an audience of his peers.

5 PERIOD IDEA

Byrd's description of the Spotswoods' gardens with their lovely walks and marble fountains echoes, to an extent, earlier portraits of America as a natural paradise. Now this paradise is being tamed.

GUIDED READING

LITERAL QUESTIONS

1a. What two reasons does Byrd give Spotswood for his visit? (He wants the pleasure of the visit; he wants to learn how to make iron.)

2a. After their business discussion, how do Byrd and Spotswood spend the afternoon? (walking and talking with the ladies)

INFERENTIAL QUESTIONS

1b. Why do you think Byrd is interested in learning how to make iron? (The growing country needs iron to develop economically, and Byrd hopes to profit by filling that need.)

2b. What do the occupants' various activities suggest about the quality of life in the Spotswood house? (Life is pleasant and balanced. There is ample time and opportunity for both work and fun.)

AT A GLANCE

- September 29: Miss Theky celebrates her birthday and wins a reprieve for her misbehaving dog.
- Byrd and Spotswood continue discussing business.
- The group enjoys dinner, more talks, and walks.
- September 30: the group goes riding, finds ginseng plants, and returns for dinner.

1 STYLE: PARALLELISM

The graceful parallel that Byrd employs to wish Miss Theky a long life illustrates both the importance of the art of conversation and Byrd's own pleasure in playing with language.

2 ANALOGY

Byrd's humor in this anecdote arises from his making analogies between Miss Theky's misbehaving dog and a criminal guilty of a terrible crime.

3 DESCRIPTION

Byrd's use of specific physical detail gives his writing the map-like clarity of a travel guide.

4 SIMILE

The use of vivid similes to describe the group's good appetites (*hungry as hawks; eat like a philosopher*) conveys not only what these early Americans do, but also how they feel.

REFLECTING ON THE SELECTION

What image of America does Byrd suggest in his description of the Spotswood home? (America seems like a land of great natural beauty and natural resources.)

STUDY QUESTIONS

1. *enchanted castle;* pier glasses, tame deer, china
2. iron making, selling iron wares
3. eating, conversing, walking, horseback riding

very pretty but had nothing in it. This it seems was Miss Theky's birthday, upon which
1 I made her my compliments and wished she might live twice as long a married woman as she had lived a maid. I did not presume to pry into the secret of her age, nor was she forward to disclose it, for this humble reason, lest I should think her wisdom fell short of her years. She contrived to make this day of her birth a day of mourning, for, having nothing better at present to set her affections upon, she had a dog that was a great favorite. It hap-
2 pened that very morning the poor cur had done something very uncleanly upon the colonel's bed, for which he was condemned to die. However, upon her entreaty, she got him a reprieve, but was so concerned that so much severity should be intended on her birthday that she was not to be comforted; and lest such another accident might oust the poor cur of his clergy, she protested she would board out her dog at a neighbor's house, where she hoped he would be more kindly treated.

Then the colonel and I took another turn in the garden to discourse farther on the subject of iron.

We had a Michaelmas[11] goose for dinner, of Miss Theky's own raising, who was now good-natured enough to forget the jeopardy of her dog. In the afternoon we walked in a meadow by the riverside, which winds in the form of a horseshoe about Germanna, making it a peninsula containing about four hundred acres.
3 Rappahannock forks about fourteen miles below this place, the northern branch being the larger and consequently must be the river that bounds My Lord Fairfax's grant of the Northern Neck.

September 30 The sun rose clear this morning, and so did I, and finished all my little affairs by breakfast. It was then resolved to wait on the ladies on horseback, since the bright sun, the fine air, and the wholesome exercise all invited us to it. We forded the river a little above the ferry and rode six miles up the neck to a fine level piece of rich land, where we found about twenty plants of ginseng, with the scarlet berries growing on the top of the middle stalk. The root of this is of wonderful virtue in many cases, particularly to raise the spirits and promote perspiration, which makes it a specific in colds and coughs. The colonel complimented me with all we found in return for my telling him the virtues of it. We were all pleased to find so much of this king of plants so near the colonel's habitation and growing, too, upon his own land, but were, however, surprised to find it upon level ground, after we had been told it grew only upon the north side of stony mountains. I carried home this treasure with as much joy as if every root had been a graft of the tree of life, and washed and dried it carefully.

4 This airing made us as hungry as so many hawks, so that, between appetite and a very good dinner, 'twas difficult to eat like a philosopher.

11. **Michaelmas:** September 29, the feast of Saint Michael.

STUDY QUESTIONS

Recalling

1. With what two words is Colonel Spotswood's home described in paragraph 2? List three details from the description of the house in paragraph 3.
2. What two related topics do Byrd and Colonel Spotswood discuss on September 28?
3. Name at least four activities described in paragraphs 4, 9, and 13 that the men and women share.

Interpreting

4. Based on Byrd's description, make three generalizations that characterize life on the Spotswood plantation.
5. What aspect of southern life does the discussion between Byrd and Colonel Spotswood illustrate?

Extending

6. How does life on Spotswood's plantation contrast with life in New England as described in the writings of the Puritans?

LITERARY FOCUS

Analogy, Simile, and Metaphor

Few things are more basic to an appreciation of literature than a sense of analogy. An **analogy** compares two things or groups of things that are similar in some ways but not in all ways. A writer uses an analogy to make an experience more vivid for the reader or to explain something unfamiliar by comparing it to something familiar.

The two most common ways in which writers make analogies are simile and metaphor. A **simile** states a comparison by using a word or phrase that clearly indicates the comparison. Most similes use *like* or *as* to indicate the comparison.

When Byrd tells us that his breakfast conversation was "*like* whip sillabub," he uses a simile. He presents an image—something we can perceive with our senses—to reinforce his abstract statement that the conversation was "very pretty but had nothing in it." The image of something light and frothy makes his abstract statement vivid and concrete.

A **metaphor** makes a comparison by identifying one thing with another. If Byrd had said that his conversation *was* whip sillabub, he would have been using a metaphor. Metaphors do not use signal words, such as *like* or *as,* to identify the comparisons they make. They are direct identifications and one of the most powerful of imaginative devices.

Using a simile or a metaphor is an imaginative act. It is a creative attempt to make an experience more intense or more universal or simply clearer. It is the kind of imaginative act that can take a journal or a history and help turn it into literature.

Thinking About Simile and Metaphor

■ What two similes occur in the last sentence of the selection? What abstract word does the first simile make concrete? What does the second simile mean? Rewrite the sentence making the first simile into a metaphor.

VOCABULARY

Antonyms

Antonyms are words that have opposite or nearly opposite meanings, such as *temporary* and *permanent.* The words in capitals are from *A Progress to the Mines.* Choose the word that is an antonym of each word in capitals, *as it is used in this selection.* Write the number of each item and the letter of your choice on a separate sheet.

1. INCESSANTLY: (a) never (b) always (c) now (d) later
2. REPRIEVE: (a) pardon (b) revise (c) remake (d) condemn
3. OUST: (a) eject (b) hurt (c) keep (d) joust
4. JEOPARDY: (a) gloom (b) danger (c) safety (d) authority
5. RESOLVED: (a) doubted (b) solved (c) decided (d) finished

COMPOSITION

Writing a Comparison/Contrast

■ Compare and contrast the Plain Style of the Puritans with the more casual and decorative writing style of Byrd. First describe the Plain Style, and cite specific examples of it. Then describe Byrd's style, and cite specific examples of it. Conclude by describing how the two styles compare or contrast. *For help with this assignment, refer to Lesson 2 in the Writing About Literature Handbook at the back of this book.*

Writing a Persuasive Advertisement

■ Write an advertisement persuading eighteenth-century Europeans to come to the southern colonies. Be sure to specify the attractions of the land and the life, as John Smith does in his *Description of New England* (page 20). Use comparison and contrast to draw for your audience a picture of how they would be able to change their lives.

4. Possibilities include wealth and elegance, appreciation of nature, enthusiasm for discovery and economic development
5. business
6.
- *Spotswood:* results in leisure, luxury, amusement, conversation
- *Puritans:* abhor luxury and pleasure for its own sake; hard work, industry
- *surroundings:* plantation *vs.* New England winter

LITERARY FOCUS

"as hungry as so many hawks"; "to eat like a philosopher"; *hungry;* to eat with moderation; example: This airing made hungry hawks of us.

VOCABULARY

1. (a) never
2. (d) condemn
3. (c) keep
4. (c) safety
5. (a) doubted

COMPOSITION: GUIDELINES FOR EVALUATION

WRITING A COMPARISON/CONTRAST

Objective

To compare and contrast two literary styles

Guidelines for Evaluation

- suggested length: three to five paragraphs
- should define the Plain Style and present examples from Bradstreet or Bradford
- should define Byrd's style, present examples
- should explain how the two styles differ
- should identify any similarities

WRITING A PERSUASIVE ADVERTISEMENT

Objective

To write a persuasive advertisement

Guidelines for Evaluation

- suggested length: three to five paragraphs
- should include details of Southern life
- should be modeled on Smith's *Description*
- should persuade the reader that the Southern colonies would be a good place to live

Jonathan Edwards *1703–1758*

Jonathan Edwards and William Byrd are the first two writers in this book who were actually born in America. In fact, Edwards is the first major American writer who was educated and lived his entire life in the New World.

Edwards was an extraordinary child who, at the age of eleven or twelve, wrote scientific essays on insects, colors, and rainbows. When he was thirteen, he entered Yale, where he experienced a religious conversion. In 1729 he succeeded his grandfather as minister in Northampton, Massachusetts. Edwards became a leading figure in the movement known as the Great Awakening, a fervent revival of religious feeling that swept America from New England to the South from about 1734 to 1749. His sermon *Sinners in the Hands of an Angry God* remains the most famous literary monument to the Great Awakening.

In 1750 some of the Northampton Puritans began to disagree with their famous minister and removed Edwards from his post. He moved, in a kind of exile, to the frontier village of Stockbridge. There he preached to the Indians and wrote many of the works that made him the most influential American writer before Franklin.

Edwards is best known, even notorious, for his sermon *Sinners in the Hands of an Angry God,* which he preached to a congregation at Enfield, Connecticut, in 1741. The Enfield sermon shows Edwards as the hell-fire preacher, but it is unfair to this learned and complex religious thinker to allow *Sinners* totally to represent him. After all, sermons such as this had been traditional for hundreds of years. Edwards' other writings appeal to his readers' reason as well as to their emotions. The lovely and equally devout essay-meditation "The Beauty of the World" shows him in a softer light. It helps to give us a more balanced view of this intense and devoted man.

■ Since the best of prose often uses poetic devices, see if you can recognize poetic elements in Edwards' prose pieces.

Model for Active Reading

In this selection, and in one selection in each unit, you will find notes in the right-hand margin that highlight parts of the selection. These notes point out important ideas of the literary period and draw your attention to literary elements and techniques covered in the Literary Focuses. Page numbers in the notes will refer you to more extensive discussions of these important ideas and elements.

Jonathan Edwards

from Sinners in the Hands of an Angry God

So that thus it is that natural men are held in the hand of God over the pit of Hell; they have deserved the fiery pit, and are already sentenced to it; and God is dreadfully provoked. His anger is as great towards them as to those that are actually suffering the executions of the fierceness of his wrath in Hell, and they have done nothing in the least to appease or abate that anger.

Neither is God in the least bound by any promise to hold 'em up one moment. The Devil is waiting for them; Hell is gaping for them; the flames gather and flash about them, and would fain[1] lay hold on them and swallow them up. The fire pent up in their own hearts is struggling to break out, and they have no interest in any mediator; there are no means within reach that can be any security to them. In short, they have no refuge, nothing to take hold of. All that preserves them every moment is the mere arbitrary will and uncovenanted unobliged forbearance of an incensed God.[2]

The use of this awful subject may be of awakening unconverted persons in this congregation. This that you have heard is the case of every one of you that are out of Christ.[3] That world of mercy, that lake of burning brimstone, is extended abroad under you. There is a dreadful pit of the glowing flames of the wrath of God; there is Hell's wide gaping mouth open; and you have nothing to stand upon, nor anything to take hold of. There is nothing between you and Hell but the air; it is only the power and mere pleasure of God that holds you up.

You probably are not sensible of this; you find you are kept out of Hell, but don't see the hand of God in it, but look at other things, as the good state of your bodily constitution, your care of your own life, and the means you use for your own preservation. But indeed these things are nothing; if God should withdraw his hand, they would avail no more to keep you from falling than the thin air to hold up a person that is suspended in it.

Your wickedness makes you as it were heavy as lead and to tend downwards with great weight and pressure towards Hell. And if God should let you go, you would immediately sink and

The occasion (p. 22): In this persuasive speech, Edwards chooses the most appropriate occasion to deliver his message: a Sunday church service.

Puritan idea: The Puritans kept reminding themselves that the soul was a constant battleground between the forces of good and evil (p. 2).

The audience (p. 22): Edwards speaks directly to the congregation he wants to persuade and emphasizes that his words apply to members of the congregation.

1. **fain:** gladly.
2. **uncovenanted . . . God:** self-control of an angry God who, Edwards says, has not promised, and is under no obligation, to grant salvation to any individual. The idea of the Covenant, a binding pact between God and his people, was much debated among the Puritans.
3. **out of Christ:** out of God's grace.

AT A GLANCE

- Edwards describes humanity's pitiful state in the hands of an angry God over the fiery pit of Hell.
- People wrongly think that forces other than God's will—such as their own bodily well-being—keep them from Hell.

LITERARY OPTIONS

- oratory
- figurative language
- theme

THEMATIC OPTIONS

- salvation
- divine wrath
- human frailty

GUIDED READING

LITERAL QUESTION

1a. In the first paragraph, what words identify the attitude of God toward "natural men"? (*provoked, anger, arbitrary will, incensed*)

INFERENTIAL QUESTION

1b. What does such language suggest about Edwards' view of God? (These words suggest that Edwards' God is frightening and capricious, implacable and unforgiving, impossible for humans to understand.)

AT A GLANCE

- Edwards depicts God as an archer aiming an arrow at each human.
- Christians—even religious ones—must undergo a "great change" in order to find salvation.
- Edwards says that God's purity makes Him view sinners as loathsome serpents.

swiftly descend and plunge into the bottomless gulf, and your healthy constitution, and your own care and prudence and best contrivance,[4] and all your righteousness would have no more influence to uphold you and keep you out of Hell than a spider's web would have to stop a falling rock. . . .

The bow of God's wrath is bent, and the arrow made ready on the string, and justice bends the arrow at your heart, and strains the bow, and it is nothing but the mere pleasure of God, and that of an angry God, without any promise or obligation at all, that keeps the arrow one moment from being made drunk with your blood.

Thus are all you that never passed under a great change of heart, by the mighty power of the spirit of God upon your souls; all that were never born again, and made new creatures, and raised from being dead in sin to a state of new, and before altogether unexperienced, light and life (however you may have reformed your life in many things, and may have had religious affections, and may keep up a form of religion in your families and closets[5] and in the house of God, and may be strict in it), you are thus in the hands of an angry God. 'Tis nothing but his mere pleasure that keeps you from being this moment swallowed up in everlasting destruction.

The God that holds you over the pit of Hell, much as one holds a spider or some loathsome insect over the fire, abhors you, and is dreadfully provoked. His wrath towards you burns like fire; he looks upon you as worthy of nothing else but to be cast into the fire; he is of purer eyes than to bear to have you in his sight; you are ten thousand times so abominable in his eyes as the most hateful venomous serpent is in ours. . . .

O sinner! Consider the fearful danger you are in: 'Tis a great furnace of wrath, a wide and bottomless pit, full of the fire of wrath, that you are held over in the hand of that God, whose wrath is provoked and incensed as much against you as against many of the damned in Hell. You hang by a slender thread, with the flames of divine wrath flashing about it, and ready every moment to singe it and burn it asunder; and you have no interest in any mediator, and nothing to lay hold of to save yourself, nothing to keep off the flames of wrath, nothing of your own, nothing that you ever have done, nothing that you can do, to induce God to spare you one moment. . . .

There is reason to think that there are many in this congregation now hearing this discourse that will actually be the subjects of this very misery to all eternity. We know not who they are, or in what seats they sit, or what thoughts they now have: It may be they are now at ease, and hear all these things without much dis-

Puritan idea: Puritans exhibited "care," "prudence," and "righteousness" in their daily lives to show that they possessed grace and would be granted salvation (p. 2).

Controlling image (p. 34): The dominant image in this paragraph is of the wrathful God as an archer.

Simile and metaphor (p. 39): Comparisons to a spider, fire, and the "hateful venomous serpent" are similes because they are directly stated with *as* or *like*. Comparisons of Hell to a "furnace" and a "bottomless pit" are metaphors. Both devices add vividness.

Repetition and rhythm (p. 14): These devices of oral recitation make the sermon more forceful.

---

4. **contrivance:** effort.
5. **closets:** small rooms, especially for meditation.

GUIDED READING

LITERAL QUESTION

1. What must each person undergo in order to please God? (a "great change")

INFERENTIAL QUESTION

1. What do you think Edwards means by this "great change"? (He probably means a sudden and intense realization of human frailty and dependence on God's mercy, an awakening of fervent religious feeling.)

turbance, and are now flattering themselves that they are not the persons, promising themselves that they shall escape. If we knew that there was one person, and but one, in the whole congregation that was to be the subject of this misery, what an awful thing would it be to think of! If we knew who it was, what an awful sight would it be to see such a person! How might all the rest of the congregation lift up a lamentable and bitter cry over him! But alas! instead of one, how many is it likely will remember this discourse in Hell?

And it would be a wonder if some that are now present should not be in Hell in a very short time, before this year is out. And it would be no wonder if some person that now sits here in some seat of this meetinghouse in health, and quiet and secure, should be there before tomorrow morning. Those of you that finally continue in a natural condition, that shall keep out of Hell longest, will be there in a little time! Your damnation does not slumber; it will come swiftly, and in all probability very suddenly upon many of you. You have reason to wonder that you are not already in Hell. 'Tis doubtless the case of some that heretofore you have seen and known, that never deserved Hell more than you, and that heretofore appeared as likely to have been now alive as you: Their case is past all hope. They are crying in extreme misery and perfect despair. But here you are in the land of the living, and in the house of God, and have an opportunity to obtain salvation. What would not those poor damned, helpless souls give for one day's such opportunity as you now enjoy!

And now you have an extraordinary opportunity, a day wherein Christ has flung the door of mercy wide open, and stands in the door calling and crying with a loud voice to poor sinners; a day, wherein many are flocking to him, and pressing into the kingdom of God. Many are daily coming from the east, west, north and south; many that were very lately in the same miserable condition that you are in, are in now a happy state, with their hearts filled with love to Him that has loved them and washed them from their sins in His own blood, and rejoicing in hope of the Glory of God. How awful is it to be left behind at such a day! To see so many others feasting, while you are pining and perishing! To see so many rejoicing and singing for joy of heart, while you have cause to mourn for sorrow of heart and howl for vexation of spirit! How can you rest one moment in such a condition? . . .

Therefore let everyone that is out of Christ now awake and fly from the wrath to come. The wrath of Almighty God is now undoubtedly hanging over a great part of this congregation: Let everyone fly out of Sodom! *Haste and escape for your lives, look not behind you, escape to the mountain, lest you be consumed.*[6]

Puritan idea: Puritans watched closely over one another, judging every act according to whether or not it truly glorified God (p. 2).

Plain Style (p. 3): Puritans tried to communicate ideas as clearly as possible, as Edwards does in the last part of this paragraph.

Allusion (p. 29): The reference to the biblical story of Sodom emphasizes the wrath of God.

6. ***Haste . . . consumed:*** In Genesis 19 : 17 the angels warn Lot, the only virtuous inhabitant of the sinful city of Sodom, to flee the city before they destroy it.

AT A GLANCE

- Edwards tells the congregation that some of them may die and face God's judgment soon.
- He reminds his listeners of their opportunity for salvation in Christ's mercy.
- He calls for those who are "out of Christ" to awake.

REFLECTING ON THE SELECTION

What effect do you think Edwards' words had upon his listeners in 1741? (They were probably terrified by his visions of hellfire and grateful for the door of mercy he describes near the end of the sermon.)

GUIDED READING

LITERAL QUESTION

1a. What does Edwards say Christ has done for poor sinners? (flung open the doors of mercy and forgiven them their sins)

INFERENTIAL QUESTION

1b. Why do you think Edwards creates such a terrifying image of God and then follows it with such a forgiving image of Jesus Christ? (He probably wants to terrify his listeners so that they are especially receptive to and grateful for Christ's mercy.)

AT A GLANCE

- The greatest beauty of the corporeal world is its resemblance to spiritual beauty.
- This beauty is peculiar to the natural world and surpasses art.
- The harmony of the planets and natural world reflects spiritual harmony.
- The beauty of the world makes suffering bearable.

LITERARY OPTIONS

- style
- theme

THEMATIC OPTIONS

- natural beauty
- physical and spiritual worlds

1 STYLE: FIGURATIVE LANGUAGE

The Platonic image of the natural world as a *shadow* of the spiritual world vividly conveys Edwards' view that natural beauty reflects spiritual beauty.

2 THEME

The harmonious circuit of the planets around the sun provides a striking and majestic image to convey the idea that the universe reflects a greater, spiritual beauty.

3 PERIOD IDEA

Edwards' explanation of how the beauty of the universe comforts even the most miserable person suggests that in its reflection of heavenly beauty the world is a kind of natural paradise.

REFLECTING ON THE SELECTION

What aspect of the natural world do you think gives Edwards the most pleasure? Why? (Edwards seems to feel the most pleasure contemplating the harmony of the universe, because he sees it as a reflection of the spirit of God.)

The Metropolitan Museum of A

Needlework from a chair, New England, c. 1725.

Jonathan Edwards

The Beauty of the World

The beauty of the world consists wholly of sweet mutual consents,[1] either within itself or with the Supreme Being. As to the corporeal[2] world, though there are many other sorts of consents, yet the sweetest and most charming beauty of it is its resemblance of spiritual
1 beauties. The reason is that spiritual beauties are infinitely the greatest, and bodies being but the shadows of beings, they must be so much the more charming as they shadow forth spiritual beauties. This beauty is peculiar to[3] natural things, surpassing the art of man.

Thus there is the resemblance of a decent trust, dependence, and acknowledgment in the
2 planets continually moving around the sun, receiving his influences by which they are made happy, bright, and beautiful: a decent attendance in the secondary planets, an image of majesty, power, glory, and beneficence in the sun in the midst of all, and so in terrestrial[4] things, as I have shown in another place.

It is very probable that that wonderful suitableness of green for the grass and plants, the blues of the sky, the white of the clouds, the colors of flowers, consists in a complicated proportion that these colors make one with another, either in their magnitude of the rays, the number of vibrations that are caused in the atmosphere, or some other way. So there is a great suitableness between the objects of dif-
3 ferent sense, as between sounds, colors, and smells; as between colors of the woods and flowers and the smells and the singing of birds, which it is probable consist in a certain proportion of the vibrations that are made in the different organs. So there are innumerable other agreeablenesses of motions, figures, etc. The gentle motions of waves, of the lily, [are] agreeable to other things that represent calmness, gentleness, and benevolence. The fields and woods seem to rejoice, and how joyful do the birds seem to be in it. How much a resemblance is there of every grace in the field covered with plants and flowers when the sun shines serenely and undisturbedly upon them; how a resemblance, I say, of every grace and beautiful disposition of mind, of an inferior towards a superior cause, preserver, benevolent benefactor, and a fountain of happiness.

How great a resemblance of a holy and virtuous soul is a calm, serene day. What an infinite number of such like beauties is there in that one thing, the light, and how complicated a harmony and proportion is it probable belongs to it.

. . . Hence the reason why almost all men, and those that seem to be very miserable, love life—because they cannot bear to lose sight of such a beautiful and lovely world. The idea, that every moment whilst we live has a beauty that we take not distinct notice of, brings a pleasure that, when we come to the trial, we had rather live in much pain and misery than lose.

1. **consents:** agreements and harmonies.
2. **corporeal:** material, physical.
3. **peculiar to:** characteristic of.
4. **terrestrial:** earthly.

GUIDED READING

LITERAL QUESTION

1a. To what does Edwards compare a calm, serene day? (a holy and virtuous soul)

INFERENTIAL QUESTION

1b. What does this comparison suggest about how Edwards sees the natural world? (He sees it as a kind of paradise, reflecting the beauty and harmony of heaven.)

STUDY QUESTIONS

Sinners in the Hands of an Angry God

Recalling

1. According to the first paragraph, over what does God hold "natural men"? What is the only thing that "preserves" them?
2. Name three things that will *not* keep them from Hell, according to the third and fourth paragraphs.
3. What opportunity do people facing Hell have, according to Edwards?

Interpreting

4. What concrete images in the first paragraph make Hell vivid? Describe the general tone of this paragraph.
5. At what point in the sermon is there a marked change in tone and topic? Describe that change. Why is the new tone appropriate to the new topic?
6. In your opinion, how effective is Edwards' sermon as an example of persuasion? Give at least two specific reasons (other than those discussed in the marginal annotations) to support your opinion.

Extending

7. What are the advantages and the disadvantages of making such an emotional appeal rather than a cool and reasoned argument? What are some occasions when an emotional appeal is best? When is reason more effective?

The Beauty of the World

Recalling

1. Of what does the beauty of the world consist, according to the first sentence?
2. According to the first paragraph, what is the "sweetest and most charming beauty" of the corporeal (material) world? To what is this beauty "peculiar"?
3. Give at least five examples of "suitableness" in nature, according to paragraph 3.
4. According to the final paragraph, why do almost all people love life?

Interpreting

5. Explain the comparison that Edwards draws in paragraph 4. What more general harmony does the comparison suggest?
6. In your own words, explain fully why the natural world is beautiful to Edwards.

Extending

7. Do you agree with Edwards' explanation of why people love life? Are there other reasons that Edwards does not mention?

VIEWPOINT

Perry Miller, a specialist on Puritans, says:

> The truth is, Edwards was infinitely more than a theologian. He was one of America's five or six major artists, who happened to work with ideas instead of with poems or novels. He was much more a psychologist and a poet than a logician.
>
> —*Jonathan Edwards*

■ Find several passages in *Sinners* or in "The Beauty of the World" that show Edwards relying more on psychology or on poetic images than on logic or reason to make his point.

COMPOSITION

Citing Evidence

■ In a short essay defend or attack this proposition: "It is difficult to believe that the same man who delivered *Sinners in the Hands of an Angry God* also wrote 'The Beauty of the World.' " If you defend the statement, cite specific passages defining the conflict between the two selections. If you attack it, cite specific passages showing how the ideas and the emotions in the two selections can be harmonized. *For help with this assignment, refer to Lesson 3 in the Writing About Literature Handbook at the back of this book.*

Writing a Description

■ Write a description of a miserable place, as Edwards does in *Sinners,* using concrete details of sight, sound, smell, and touch. Use several similes and metaphors. If you prefer, write about an inviting place instead, describing it so vividly that your reader will not want to miss it.

STUDY QUESTIONS

"Sinners . . ."

1. the pit of Hell; God's will
2. healthy constitution, care for life, righteousness
3. salvation through Christ
4. hand of God, pit of Hell; angry
5. ■ next-to-last paragraph
   ■ damnation to redemption, anger to hope
   ■ tone and topic introduce hope
6. logical structure, powerful imagery, citation of authority
7. Answers will vary: *emotional:* moves people, may unleash an uncontrollable force; *reasoned:* convinces logically, less powerful.

"The Beauty of the World"

1. sweet mutual consents
2. resemblance to the spiritual
3. green grass, blue sky, white clouds, bird songs, motions of waves, woods smells
4. unwilling to lose sight of the beauty of the world
5. virtuous soul = calm serene day; harmony between corporeal and spiritual beauty
6. Its order and harmony reflect great beauty of spiritual world.
7. Answers will vary.

VIEWPOINT

Possible answers: Edwards frightens audience, then shows a way out; he recognizes that even miserable people cling to life.

COMPOSITION: GUIDELINES FOR EVALUATION

CITING EVIDENCE

Objective

To cite evidence relating to a literary opinion

Guidelines for Evaluation

- suggested length: five to eight paragraphs
- should state point of view
- should cite specific supporting passages
- should show understanding of author's beliefs
- should base arguments on literary style as well as on author's beliefs

WRITING A DESCRIPTION

Objective

To write a vivid description

Guidelines for Evaluation

- suggested length: two to four paragraphs
- should use vivid, sensory images
- should use similes and metaphors
- should appeal to the readers' senses
- should convey horror or wonder

ACTIVE READING

The Historical Imagination

You might ask the students if they like books or films about times other than their own. Have them discuss the periods that appeal to them and explain why: What attracts them to the "Wild" West, for instance, or the future worlds of science fiction? Establish that other time periods seem romantic and intriguing. Help students see that when they read about another era, they are using their imaginations to picture the unfamiliar settings, events, and customs being described.

ACTIVE READING

The Historical Imagination

Reading literature offers us an *experience,* but to have the experience, to make the words come alive, we must read actively. We must use our imaginations, participating with the writer in producing or reproducing the experience of the literature. That experience, which is never exactly the same for all readers, or for the same reader on all occasions, is only a potential until we ourselves release it.

One kind of imagination we must bring to literature is *historical.* After all, why should we limit ourselves to the experiences of twentieth-century Americans? In many ways, we share the same basic values and emotions that people had in Homer's Greece, Shakespeare's London, and Bradford's Plymouth. Yet at other times and in other places, people also had different ideas and feelings. As we learn to read literature with an active historical imagination, we release ourselves into those other times and places, illuminating our own time and our own place.

We certainly do not have to *agree* with the world views of other people, or with the opinions of any particular writer, in order to share imaginatively the experience of literature. We do not have to agree with the beliefs of Jonathan Edwards to feel the shiver of terror that ran down the spines of those who listened to him that Sunday. We do not have to be a Puritan poet like Anne Bradstreet to know what it means to love someone. Yet the poet's expression of what it means to her helps us to see what it can mean to us. In just such a way, by using our historical imagination, we can make the past speak to us through literature.

Literature is not always an escape from our own time, nor should it be. It offers us the pleasure of learning about ourselves by learning about others. How are we different, say, from the Puritans of seventeenth-century New England? What do they still have to offer us in the way of wisdom? How can they, as people, expand our sense of the complexity and variety of human nature?

Reading the Puritan writers is not easy. They challenge us to penetrate their time and place, their minds and hearts. The task is difficult not simply because our language has changed or because the Puritans did not share our modern ideas. The task is difficult because the past *is* the past. With the aid of the historical imagination, however, we can make the past live again.

THE AMERICAN VOICE

A Natural Paradise

The writers who appear in this unit have at least one thing in common: They all lived and wrote at a time when the New World was truly new. A place of possibility, America seemed to provide a second birth to anyone who desired to build a community, establish a church, gain fame and honor, or make a new life.

The initial awe and excitement of the early Americans, however, always seemed to focus on the land itself—an enormous garden, an untouched natural paradise. Words like the following, all examples of the American voices we have heard in this unit, are a part of that myth of the American Eden:

Columbus
During that time I walked among the trees which was the most beautiful thing which I had ever seen.

Smith
Here nature and liberty afford us that freely which in England we want. . . .

Edwards
Hence the reason why almost all men, and those that seem to be very miserable, love life—because they cannot bear to lose sight of such a beautiful and lovely world.

Columbus was writing of the Caribbean, Smith of New England, and Edwards of the whole world, yet they were all inspired by the American abundance before their eyes. They saw in America a dream come true, a vision made real. As this book continues, we will hear other American writers voicing these same ideas and emotions. The abundant land is one American theme to keep in mind throughout our entire literary history.

Key to Illustrations on Page 1 and Facing Page.

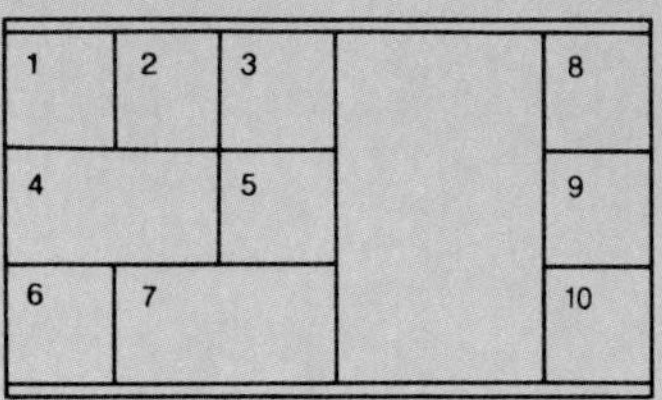

1. Captain John Smith. Nineteenth-century engraving.
2. Columbus setting sail for the New World, engraving by Theodor de Bry, 1594.
3. Portrait of Mrs. Elizabeth Freake and Baby Mary, unknown artist, c. 1670.
4. Landing at Jamestown, Virginia, 1607.
5. Colonial hornbook, a small board with the alphabet, numbers, etc., used by early American schoolchildren.
6. A chief of the Ojibwa, painting by George Catlin, 1832.
7. Pilgrims signing the Mayflower Compact, 1620. Nineteenth-century engraving.
8. *Whirling Rainbow People,* 1948 sand painting (an ancient art form still practiced by American Indians).
9. Jonathan Edwards. Nineteenth-century engraving.
10. Embroidered chair seat cover, attributed to Anne Bradstreet, seventeenth century.

THE AMERICAN VOICE

A Natural Paradise
After the students have read this section, you might have them consider the two related themes suggested by the term "natural paradise": the idea that America was a *paradise,* an Eden, a utopia; and the suggestion that life in early America was rooted in *nature,* in the land. Discuss the importance of nature to all early Americans, from the native Indian tribes and early pioneers (who lived so close to the land), to the explorers (who were awed by nature's abundance), to Jonathan Edwards (who found spiritual joy in nature's wonders).

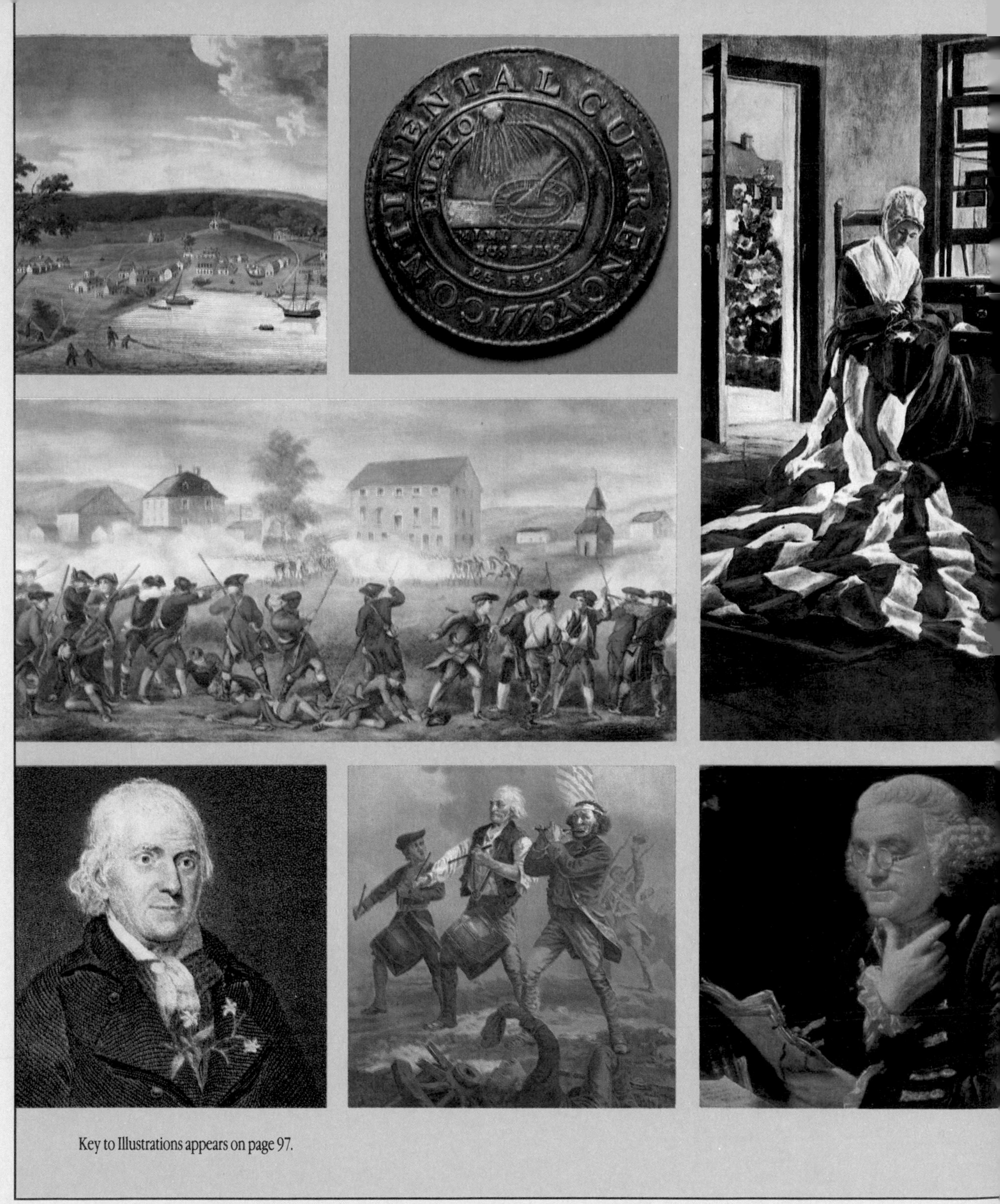

Key to Illustrations appears on page 97.

REASON AND REVOLUTION

1750–1800

A New Nation

On April 19, 1775, a group of American Minutemen faced British redcoats across the little bridge outside the village of Concord, Massachusetts. Suddenly someone—no one knows who—fired a musket shot, "the shot heard round the world," and the American Revolution began. That shot was the climax of years of frustration, anger, and preparation among the colonists.

During the half-century before the Revolution, the thirteen colonies had begun to prosper and to seem less and less like perilous settlements on the edge of a wilderness. They had begun to communicate more with one another and to grow aware of their mutual problems and feelings. They shared their anger over the oppressive political and economic policies of the British government. No one at that time, however, was thinking of revolution—not yet.

Then came a series of infuriating laws and taxes. The Stamp Act in 1765 required that the colonists buy special stamps for newspapers, licenses, pamphlets, and many other documents. The Quartering Act in 1765 forced colonists to feed and house British soldiers in their own homes. The Townshend Acts in 1767 taxed tea, glass, lead, and paper. When some of the colonial assemblies refused to abide by the new laws, the

INTRODUCTION

After the students have read the introduction to the unit, you might conduct a more detailed discussion of the factors that led to the American Revolution. The discussion might make the following points:

- The idea of representative government was in keeping with long-standing English traditions of limiting royal power.
- The writings of the British philosopher John Locke profoundly influenced America's founding fathers and eighteenth-century thought in general. Locke justified limiting royal authority and proposed that all human beings have natural rights and are entitled to political and economic freedoms regardless of birth.
- Many early immigrants to the American colonies left Europe hoping for religious, political, and economic freedoms.
- The ideas of separation of church and state owe much to the writings of Voltaire, the leading philosopher of the French Enlightenment.
- With the beginnings of the Industrial Revolution in Britain, England's factory owners sought raw materials and markets for their goods, both of which they felt the American colonies should provide. The colonists, in turn, objected to laws that discouraged factories in America.
- After the French and Indian War (1756–1763) the mother country expected the colonies to pay for their own protection and instituted taxes for this purpose. The colonists objected, for they felt that England's constant quarreling with France was not their fight.

Key Ideas in This Period
- representative government
- natural rights
- freedom
- separation of church and state
- American identity
- a national literature

British government declared those assemblies "dissolved." Violence was not far away: The Boston Massacre erupted in 1770 when British troops fired on a taunting mob. In 1773 the British Parliament insisted again on its right and power to tax Americans. The tax on tea became a symbol, and the famous Boston Tea Party became a symbol too—a symbol of American resistance—as colonists dressed as Indians dumped a shipment of British tea into Boston Harbor.

Americans protested and petitioned King George III for "no taxation without representation." They wanted only what was reasonable, they said. They wanted to share in their own government. Britain replied with the Intolerable Acts of 1774, designed to punish Massachusetts for the Boston Tea Party. Many more rights that had been granted to the colonists in their charters were revoked. Then, when Paul Revere spotted the redcoats on their way to seize American arms at Concord, Americans responded with force.

Yet it was not until January 1776 that a widely heard public voice demanded complete separation from England. The voice was that of Thomas Paine, whose pamphlet *Common Sense,* with its heated language, increased the growing demand for separation. It pointed the way toward the Declaration of Independence in July. If ever writing affected public affairs, *Common Sense* did.

Title page from the revolutionary pamphlet *Common Sense,* Thomas Paine, 1776.

COMMON SENSE;

ADDRESSED TO THE

INHABITANTS

OF

AMERICA,

On the following interesting

SUBJECTS.

I. Of the Origin and Design of Government in general, with concise Remarks on the English Constitution.

II. Of Monarchy and Hereditary Succession.

III. Thoughts on the present State of American Affairs.

IV. Of the present Ability of America, with some miscellaneous Reflections.

Man knows no Master save creating HEAVEN,
Or those whom choice and common good ordain.
THOMSON.

PHILADELPHIA:
Printed, and Sold, by R. BELL, in Third-Street.
MDCCLXXVI.

We will not be surprised to find that most American literature in the eighteenth century was political. Through newspapers, magazines, pamphlets, broadsides, and letters, colonial leaders discussed their ideas of human nature and of government. They began forging a new sense of national identity. Battles had to be fought before the thirteen colonies achieved independence. Nevertheless, for years before the first shot was fired, *language* was the source of growing American power. For those Americans it was language that connected reason and revolution. By the time the Revolutionary War was over in 1783, Americans were well on their way to establishing a literary heritage as extraordinary as their political one.

The Age of Reason

Thomas Jefferson once said that a rational society is one that "informs the mind, sweetens the temper, cheers our spirits, and promotes health." Jefferson's attitude—a firm belief in progress, common sense, and the pursuit of happiness—is typical of the period we now call the Age of Reason.

Some historians say we oversimplify the complex eighteenth century in suggesting it was a time when everyone was "reasonable." Of course everyone was not reasonable. The century was marked by fiery emotion as much as by cool logic. But it was a time when people believed in the *possibilities* of reason. It is that hope, that optimism, that gives the age its character.

Americans at this time were influenced by the European movement called the Enlightenment. Followers of Enlightenment ideas believed that people could discover truth by the light of reason alone. They shed the light of reason on the darkness of ignorance, superstition, social injustice, and political tyranny—all in a quest to build the perfect society. Through science and rational government, they thought, order could be established in the world. Above all, followers of Enlightenment ideas stressed the importance of resisting arbitrary limitations on their own free thoughts.

Enlightened Americans, like Europeans, came to trust in human potential. They began to rely on the power of their own minds to shape their own destinies, and the power of their own *language* to express what that destiny should be. They thought, wrote, and spoke with a greater self-confidence than a young nation had ever done before. Jefferson once commented that one evening spent at Ben Franklin's house in Philadelphia in the company of musicians, lawyers, and politicians was worth a whole week in Paris.

Writing and Revolution

During the 1770s no one in America could claim to be a professional novelist, poet, or playwright. Yet a great number of Americans expressed themselves on the subjects of liberty, government, law, reason, and individual and national freedom. Throughout the land, weekly "Poet's Corners" in American newspapers never lacked locally written poems, songs, and satires. Americans filled pamphlets with anonymous poems on the issues of the day. They produced a great number of political **broadsides**—sheets of paper covered with anonymous poems, songs, and essays—that could be tacked up around the city, left on doorsteps, or even read to groups on street corners. This writing was not sophisticated, but it was the writing of people whose lives were touched by the events of a turbulent time.

The policies of Great Britain helped make writers—even poets—out of many colonials. Furor over the Stamp Act of 1765 brought out poems everywhere: in political pamphlets, in newspapers, nailed to trees, slipped under doors. When British soldiers killed several Boston citizens in 1770, a flurry of broadsides protested the senseless deaths. The awkward, naive verses—written by people who were not professional writers—suggest that the pain and shock of the events were intense enough to stir even in nonliterary people the need to express their feelings.

Detail from *Boy with a Squirrel,* John Singleton Copley, 1766.

Gradually, negative protests turned into more positive expressions. Besides petitioning against "taxation without representation," more and more Americans started calling for more self-government. Paine's pamphlet *Common Sense* sold an extraordinary 100,000 copies in three months. The Declaration of Independence—the culmination of the writing of this period—carries the voice not of an individual but of a whole people. It is more than writing of the period; it defined the meaning of the Revolution.

Toward a National Literature

Americans of the eighteenth century produced a great variety of unusual forms of literature: ballads, skits, broadsides, newspaper poems, editorials, essays, private and public letters, satires, pamphlets—written by people of every social class and almost every degree of skill. The energy of the age did not express itself in the usual forms with great original poetry, fiction, drama, music, or art. Nevertheless, there were some writers, composers, and painters of note.

Joel Barlow, an urbane and sophisticated man, produced a mock-epic poem called *The Hasty Pudding.* Phillis Wheatley, a former slave, produced highly praised religious and patriotic verses; in 1773 she published what was probably the first book by a black American. Philip Freneau wrote bitter satires and fiery political poems, earning the title "Poet of the American Revolution." The composer William Billings and the painter John Singleton Copley demonstrated that music and art could also flourish in America, even though these artists imitated the formal, balanced, restrained classical style of European artists.

It would be some time before America would learn to be itself artistically, but it did make a beginning. The new nation had the desire to be new in every way possible. Political indepen-

Noah Webster, nationalist and scholar, who standardized American spelling and wrote the *American Dictionary.*

dence brought with it a desire for literary and artistic independence. In 1783 Noah Webster, a literary nationalist, declared: "America must be as independent in literature as she is in politics, as famous for the arts as for arms."

What would make an *American* book? Many writers thought that the new nation possessed at least two unique subjects, two things no European had experienced: the natural wilderness and the Revolution. They believed that the majestic, awe-inspiring landscape provided a setting and even an antagonist that would be the basis of a great literature. They also believed that the Revolution provided stories of great human experiences and the beginning of an American mythology. They began to see the possibility of typical American characters in literature: The first American comedy, Royall Tyler's *The Contrast* (1787), gave the public a homespun American who outsmarts the more "sophisticated" characters. The Yankee hero was born.

If Columbus "discovered" America, then patriots such as Franklin, Paine, and Jefferson, in the words of one historian, "invented" it. That invention of an American self and society, an American *identity,* was the greatest single imaginative creation of this period. The writing in this unit can give us some idea of the complexity and the excitement of trying to answer the question that was once posed by Jean de Crèvecoeur: "What then is the American, this new man?"

TIME LINE

1750–1800 AMERICAN EVENTS

1733–1758 Benjamin Franklin, *Poor Richard's Almanack*

1750 First playhouse in America opens in New York City

1751 First sugar cane in America grown in Louisiana

1752 Franklin performs electricity experiment with kite and key

1754 Columbia University founded in New York City

1757 First streetlights in America used in Philadelphia

1761 *The Complete Housewife,* early American cookbook

1765 British Parliament imposes Stamp Act on colonies

Chocolate is first produced in America: Dorchester, Mass.

1766 John Singleton Copley's painting *Boy with Squirrel* a great success in London

1767 Daniel Boone first explores west of Appalachians

1770 Boston Massacre

William Billings, first important American composer, publishes *The New England Psalm-Singer*

WORLD EVENTS 1750–1800

1750 Germany: Death of composer Johann Sebastian Bach

1751 France: Denis Diderot, *Encyclopédie*

1755 England: Samuel Johnson completes *Dictionary of the English Language*

1759 France: Voltaire, *Candide*

1761 Austria: Wolfgang Amadeus Mozart begins writing minuets at age five

1762 France: Jean Jacques Rousseau, *The Social Contract*

1764 England: Practice of numbering houses begun in London

1765 Scotland: James Watt invents steam engine

1769 France: Nicolas-Joseph Cugnot builds first automobile with steam-powered engine

1770 Germany: Birth of composer Ludwig van Beethoven

1772 Charles Wilson Peale completes life-size portrait of George Washington

1773 Boston Tea Party

Phillis Wheatley's *Poems on Various Subjects, Religious and Moral* published in London

1774 First Continental Congress meets in Philadelphia

First museum in America established in Philadelphia

1775 Patrick Henry delivers Speech in Virginia Convention

Revolutionary War begins

1776 Thomas Paine, *American Crisis*

Thomas Jefferson writes Declaration of Independence

1777 France: Chemist Antoine Lavoisier coins term *oxygen*

1778 Captain Cook discovers Hawaii

1780 American Academy of Arts and Sciences established in Boston

1781 England: William Herschel discovers planet Uranus

1782 Jean de Crèvecoeur, *Letters from an American Farmer*

1783 Revolution ends

Noah Webster publishes *American Spelling Book*, standardizing spelling of American English

First American edition of *Mother Goose Rhymes*

1784 Franklin invents bifocal lenses

1786 First commercially made ice cream sold in New York City

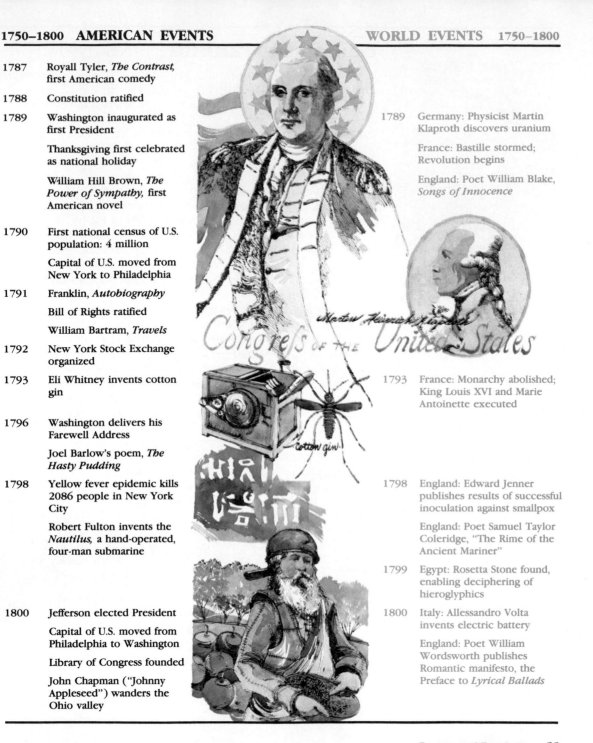

	American Events		World Events
1787	Royall Tyler, *The Contrast,* first American comedy		
1788	Constitution ratified		
1789	Washington inaugurated as first President	1789	Germany: Physicist Martin Klaproth discovers uranium
	Thanksgiving first celebrated as national holiday		France: Bastille stormed; Revolution begins
	William Hill Brown, *The Power of Sympathy,* first American novel		England: Poet William Blake, *Songs of Innocence*
1790	First national census of U.S. population: 4 million		
	Capital of U.S. moved from New York to Philadelphia		
1791	Franklin, *Autobiography*		
	Bill of Rights ratified		
	William Bartram, *Travels*		
1792	New York Stock Exchange organized		
1793	Eli Whitney invents cotton gin	1793	France: Monarchy abolished; King Louis XVI and Marie Antoinette executed
1796	Washington delivers his Farewell Address		
	Joel Barlow's poem, *The Hasty Pudding*		
1798	Yellow fever epidemic kills 2086 people in New York City	1798	England: Edward Jenner publishes results of successful inoculation against smallpox
	Robert Fulton invents the *Nautilus,* a hand-operated, four-man submarine		England: Poet Samuel Taylor Coleridge, "The Rime of the Ancient Mariner"
		1799	Egypt: Rosetta Stone found, enabling deciphering of hieroglyphics
1800	Jefferson elected President	1800	Italy: Allessandro Volta invents electric battery
	Capital of U.S. moved from Philadelphia to Washington		England: Poet William Wordsworth publishes Romantic manifesto, the Preface to *Lyrical Ballads*
	Library of Congress founded		
	John Chapman ("Johnny Appleseed") wanders the Ohio valley		

Benjamin Franklin *1706–1790*

Benjamin Franklin was born in Boston, the son of a poor craftsman who could not afford to keep him long in school. He educated himself by reading widely. As a teenager he learned the printing trade and published his first essay in his brother's newspaper. Proud, ambitious, and independent, Franklin left Boston at the age of seventeen and arrived penniless in Philadelphia. He soon established himself as a printer and a civic leader, became rich, and retired from business at the age of forty-two.

Such an outline of Franklin's life, however, does not do justice to his extraordinary range of accomplishments. After retiring from business, Franklin intended to devote the rest of his life to his deepest interest—science—the only thing, it was said, about which he was not ironic. He did make substantial contributions to the scientific knowledge of his time. In fact, his work on lightning rods, earthquakes, bifocal lenses, and electricity made him world famous, and the Franklin stove is still used in some homes. Nevertheless, it was public affairs that dominated the last half of his life.

Franklin spent many years in England and France, where he was a popular figure among intellectuals and aristocrats. Before the Revolution he represented the colonies in London, trying to persuade the British government to modify its oppressive tax policies in America. In 1776, at age seventy, he joined Thomas Jefferson, John Adams, and others on the committee that drafted the Declaration of Independence. Later he served as the American representative in Paris and helped negotiate the peace treaty with England. In his final years he was a delegate to the Constitutional Convention and worked for the ratification of the Constitution.

At the time of his death, no other American was better known or more respected. In both the Old World and the New World, Franklin was seen as a representative American: the clever, prudent, self-made man, the thrifty Yankee who works hard, who knows how to take advantage of an opportunity, and who "gets ahead."

Franklin's life was full; he lived with intensity and imagination. Even his death, according to his plan, would reflect his feeling for life. This is his **epitaph**, or tombstone inscription, for himself:

> The Body of B. Franklin, printer; Like the cover of an old Book, Its contents torn out, and stripped of its Lettering and Gilding, Lies here, Food for Worms. But the work shall not be wholly Lost: For it will, as he believed, appear once more. In a new and more perfect Edition. Corrected and amended by the Author. He was born Jan. 6, 1706. Died 17—.

■ How do the following selections show us Franklin's "wit and wisdom"?

Franklin published *Poor Richard's Almanack* every year for twenty-five years (1733–1758), pretending the attitudes and observations were those of one "Richard Saunders." An **almanac** is an annual collection of statistics, weather forecasts, current events, and other useful or entertaining information. Franklin enlivened his almanac with Poor Richard's **proverbs** and **aphorisms**, short sayings memorable for their wit and wisdom, which he later collected into a book titled *The Way to Wealth*.

Benjamin Franklin

from Poor Richard's Almanack

God helps them that help themselves.

Fish and Visitors stink after three days.

1 Beware of little Expenses: a small Leak will sink a great Ship.

No gains without pains.

Love your Neighbor; yet don't pull down your Hedge.

There are no ugly loves, nor handsome prisons.

At the working man's house hunger looks in, but dares not enter.

2 To err is human, to repent divine; to persist, devilish.

3 Keep thy shop, and thy shop will keep thee.

You may be too cunning for One, but not for All.

The Cat in Gloves catches no Mice.

Dost thou love Life? Then do not squander Time; for that's the Stuff Life is made of.

He that falls in love with himself, will have no rivals.

4 For want of a Nail the Shoe is lost;
for want of a Shoe the Horse is lost;
for want of a Horse the Rider is lost.

What you would seem to be, be really.

STUDY QUESTIONS

Interpreting

1. According to the second aphorism, why do fish and visitors have a common characteristic? According to the third aphorism, why can little expenses be compared to a leak in a ship?
2. Why are there "no ugly loves, nor handsome prisons"?
3. Which of the aphorisms stress the importance of hard work? Of thrift? Of honesty?
4. What recommendations and observations about human behavior do the other aphorisms make?

Extending

5. Which of these sayings do you find applicable today? Which do you think are amusing? Why?

AT A GLANCE

- The author offers advice in the form of proverbs and aphorisms.
- He discusses such matters as self-reliance, hard work, and honesty.

LITERARY OPTIONS

- theme
- style

THEMATIC OPTIONS

- self-improvement
- independence

1 STYLE: FIGURATIVE LANGUAGE

In using the image of a leaking ship, Franklin vividly dramatizes his admonition on the danger of accumulating debt.

2 RESPONSE JOURNAL

Students may restate this aphorism (or any aphorism in the selection) in modern language.

3 STYLE: PARALLELISM

The repeated use of the words *thy shop* in both clauses of this sentence reinforces Franklin's ideas about independence and self-reliance.

4 THEME

Franklin affirms the importance of being thrifty by building a progression of images in a parallel structure *(for want of)*.

REFLECTING ON THE SELECTION

How do you think Franklin probably felt about individuality? (He would probably approve strongly of individuals' freedom to express themselves honestly.)

STUDY QUESTIONS

1. three days for a fish to go bad, a visitor to outstay his welcome; small expenses can become a "sinking debt"
2. to one in love, beloved is beautiful; to one in prison, the prison is ugly
3. *Hard work:* 1, 4, 7, 9, 11; *Thrift:* 3, 12; *Honesty:* 10, 15
4. Visitors shouldn't overstay welcome (2); friendliness should not overcome privacy (5); emotions affect perspective (6); learn from mistakes (8); egotists are unpopular (13); for success, attend to details (14).
5. Answers will vary. Students should find most of the aphorisms timeless and universal.

AT A GLANCE

- Franklin works as an apprentice on his brother's newspaper—Boston, 1720–1721.
- Franklin publishes articles in the paper anonymously but then reveals his secret.
- His brother is jailed for publishing a politically offensive article, and Franklin is questioned by the authorities.

LITERARY OPTIONS

- autobiography
- tone

THEMATIC OPTIONS

- striving for self-improvement
- political and personal liberty

1 TONE

Franklin's plain diction establishes a warm conversational tone that helps the reader to feel a personal contact with the author.

2 AUTOBIOGRAPHY

Franklin creates a vivid account of his youth with narration of external events (listening to the writers' conversations) and commentary revealing his own emotions and thoughts.

3 THEME

Franklin's account of his brother's jailing reminds the reader that the Revolution will be fought to guarantee political freedom.

When he was sixty-five, Franklin, already internationally famous, began writing his autobiography. An **autobiography** is the story of a person's life told by the person who lived it; Franklin told his story in the form of a letter to his son. Franklin never completed his autobiography, never reaching his account of the Declaration of Independence. Yet Franklin was able to make clear that he enjoyed creating in himself "the American, this new man."

Benjamin Franklin

from The Autobiography

My Brother had in 1720 or 21, begun to print a Newspaper. It was the second that appeared in America, and was called the *New En-*
1 *gland Courant.* The only one before it was the *Boston News Letter.* I remember his being dissuaded by some of his Friends from the Undertaking, as not likely to succeed, one Newspaper being in their Judgment enough for America. At this time (1771) there are not less than five and twenty. He went on, however, with the Undertaking, and after having worked in composing the Types and printing off the Sheets, I was employed to carry the Papers through the Streets to the Customers. He had some ingenious Men among his Friends who amused themselves by writing little Pieces for this Paper, which gained it Credit, and made it more in Demand; and these Gentlemen often visited
2 us. Hearing their Conversations, and their Accounts of the Approbation[1] their Papers were received with, I was excited to try my Hand among them. But being still a Boy, and suspecting that my Brother would object to printing any Thing of mine in his Paper if he knew it to be mine, I contrived to disguise my Hand, and writing an anonymous Paper, I put it in at Night under the Door of the Printing House. It was found in the Morning and communicated to his Writing Friends when they called in as usual. They read it, commented on it in my Hearing, and I had the exquisite Pleasure of finding it met with their Approbation, and that in their different Guesses at the Author none were named but Men of some Character among us for Learning and Ingenuity.

I suppose now that I was rather lucky in my Judges: And that perhaps they were not really so very good ones as I then esteemed them. Encouraged, however, by this, I wrote and conveyed in the same Way to the Press several more Papers,[2] which were equally approved, and I kept my Secret till my small Fund of Sense for such Performances was pretty well exhausted, and then I discovered[3] it; when I began to be considered a little more by my Brother's Acquaintance, and in a manner that did not quite please him, as he thought, probably with reason, that it tended to make me too vain. . . .

3 One of the Pieces in our Newspaper, on some political Point which I have now forgotten, gave Offense to the Assembly. He was taken up, censured and imprisoned for a Month by the Speaker's Warrant, I suppose because he would not discover his Author. I too was taken up and examined before the Council; but though I did not give them any satisfaction, they contented themselves with admonishing

---

1. **Approbation:** approval.
2. **Papers:** articles.
3. **discovered:** revealed.

GUIDED READING

LITERAL QUESTION

1a. Who do his brother's friends think is the author of the articles that Franklin submits anonymously? (men with reputation for learning and ingenuity)

INFERENTIAL QUESTION

1b. What do the other newspaper writers' judgments indicate about the kind of writer Franklin was as a boy? (They suggest that he was a skillful writer.)

me, and dismissed me; considering me perhaps as an Apprentice who was bound to keep his Master's Secrets. During my Brother's Confinement, which I resented a good deal, notwith-
1 standing our private Differences, I had the Management of the Paper, and I made bold to give our Rulers some Rubs in it, which my Brother took very kindly, while others began to consider me in an unfavorable Light, as a young Genius that had a Turn for Libeling and Satyr.[4] My Brother's Discharge was accompanied with an Order of the House (a very odd one) *that James Franklin should no longer print the Paper called the New England Courant.* There was a Consultation held in our Printing House among his Friends what he should do in this Case. Some proposed to evade the Order by changing the Name of the Paper; but my Brother seeing Inconveniences in that, it was finally concluded on as a better Way, to let it be printed for the future under the Name of *Benjamin Franklin.* And to avoid the Censure of the Assembly that might fall on him, as still printing it by his Apprentice, the
2 Contrivance was that my old Indenture[5] should be returned to me with a full Discharge on the Back of it, to be shown on Occasion; but to secure to him the Benefit of my Service, I was to sign new Indentures for the Remainder of the Term, which were to be kept private. A very flimsy Scheme it was, but, however, it was immediately executed, and the Paper went on accordingly under my Name for several Months. At length a fresh Difference arising between my Brother and me, I took upon me to assert my Freedom, presuming that he would not venture to produce the new Indentures. It was not fair in me to take this Advantage, and this I therefore reckon one of the first Errata[6] of my Life: But the Unfairness of it weighed little with me, when under the Impressions of Resentment for the Blows his Passion too often urged him to bestow upon me. Though he was otherwise not an ill-natured Man: Perhaps I was too saucy[7] and provoking.

When he found I would leave him, he took care to prevent my getting Employment in any other Printing House of the Town, by going round and speaking to every Master, who accordingly refused to give me Work. I then thought of going to New York as the nearest
3 Place where there was a Printer; and I was the rather inclined to leave Boston when I reflected that I had already made myself a little obnoxious to the governing Party; and from the arbitrary Proceedings of the Assembly in my Brother's Case it was likely I might if I stayed soon bring myself into Scrapes. . . .

Selling some of his books to raise money, Franklin journeys first to New York, and then to Philadelphia. After sailing through a storm, walking about fifty miles, and finally rowing a small boat, he arrives on a Sunday morning in October 1723.

4 I was in my Working Dress, my best Clothes being to come round by Sea. I was dirty from my Journey; my Pockets were stuffed out with Shirts and Stockings; I knew no Soul, nor where to look for Lodging. I was fatigued with Traveling, Rowing and Want of Rest. I was very hungry, and my whole Stock of Cash consisted of a Dutch Dollar[8] and about a Shilling[9] in Copper. The latter I gave the People of the Boat for my Passage, who at first refused it on Account of my Rowing; but I insisted on their taking it, a Man being sometimes more generous when he has but a little Money than when he has plenty, perhaps through Fear of being thought to have but little.

Then I walked up the Street, gazing about, till near the Market House I met a Boy with Bread. I had made many a Meal on Bread, and inquiring where he got it, I went immediately to the Baker's he directed me to in Second

4. **Satyr** [sat′ īr]: satire.
5. **Indenture:** contract that binds one person to work for another, sometimes as an apprentice.
6. **Errata** [ə rā′ tə]: errors.
7. **saucy:** disrespectful.
8. **Dutch Dollar:** unit of currency in circulation before the U.S. dollar was established.
9. **Shilling:** British coin equal to one-twentieth of a pound.

AT A GLANCE

- Franklin manages the paper in his brother's absence.
- Franklin frees himself from indenture to his brother.
- After a series of harsh disagreements with his brother, Franklin leaves Boston.
- He arrives in Philadelphia with almost no money.

1 VOCABULARY: WORD CHOICE

Franklin creates a highly readable, conversational tone by using ordinary speech *(Rubs)* to describe serious situations.

2 THEME

The detailed account of the scheme that Ben and his brother work out to assure the paper's future suggests a link between personal and political freedom. It also underscores Franklin's preoccupation with the issue of liberty.

3 TONE

When Franklin calls himself "obnoxious," he adopts a humorous, ironic, self-critical tone that makes his similarly ironic criticisms of others and society seem good-natured and well taken.

4 AUTOBIOGRAPHY

Franklin's remarks about the details of his dress help him convey, with humor, just how desperate his situation was when he arrived in Philadelphia.

GUIDED READING

LITERAL QUESTIONS

1a. What is the private agreement between Franklin and his brother? (The paper is to be published under Ben's name; his brother publicly cancels Ben's indenture but privately renews it.)

2a. What does Ben say he has made many a meal on? (bread)

INFERENTIAL QUESTIONS

1b. What does Ben's reaction to the private agreement suggest about his character? (He has noticed that people who strive usually succeed. He regrets having taken advantage of his brother but acts on his own need for personal freedom.)

2b. What can you infer about Franklin's life style from his comments about his first meal in Philadelphia? (He is poor but has abundant good humor; he faces life's difficulties without bitterness.)

AT A GLANCE

- Hungry, Franklin walks through Philadelphia carrying three huge rolls; his future wife notices him for the first time.
- He dozes off in the meeting-house.
- Years later, a successful printer, he decides to achieve moral perfection.
- He lists thirteen virtues to develop.

1 TONE

Franklin draws a vivid, though unflattering, picture of his younger self, complete with comically incongruous details.

2 CHARACTERIZATION

By giving his bread to others, the penniless Franklin shows that he was generous and had an apparent trust in divine Providence.

3 THEME

Franklin's determination to arrive at moral perfection reflects his passion for self-improvement and his conviction that through reason and hard work a person can achieve any goal.

4 ENLIGHTENMENT IDEA

Franklin's lists of virtues and precepts reflect the emphasis on order that was characteristic of the Age of Reason.

Street; and asked for Biscuit, intending such as we had in Boston, but they it seems were not made in Philadelphia; then I asked for a threepenny Loaf, and was told they had none such; so not considering or knowing the Difference of Money and the greater Cheapness nor the Names of his Bread, I bade him give me threepenny worth of any sort. He gave me accordingly three great Puffy Rolls. I was surprised at the Quantity, but took it, and having no room
1 in my Pockets, walked off, with a Roll under each Arm, and eating the other. Thus I went up Market Street as far as Fourth Street, passing by the Door of Mr. Read, my future Wife's Father, when she standing at the Door saw me, and thought I made, as I certainly did, a most awkward ridiculous Appearance. Then I turned and went down Chestnut Street and part of Walnut Street, eating my Roll all the Way, and coming round, found my self again at Market Street Wharf, near the Boat I came in, to which
2 I went for a Draft[10] of the River Water, and being filled with one of my Rolls, gave the other two to a Woman and her Child that came down the River in the Boat with us and were waiting to go farther. Thus refreshed, I walked again up the Street, which by this time had many clean dressed People in it who were all walking the same Way; I joined them, and thereby was led into the great Meetinghouse of the Quakers[11] near the Market. I sat down among them, and after looking round a while and hearing nothing said,[12] being very drowsy through Labor and want of Rest the preceding Night, I fell fast asleep, and continued so till the Meeting broke up, when one was kind enough to rouse me. This was therefore the first House I was in or slept in, in Philadelphia. . . .

During the next several years Franklin becomes a successful printer and businessman.

10. **Draft:** drink.
11. **Quakers:** the Society of Friends, a Christian religious group founded in the seventeenth century.
12. **hearing . . . said:** Quaker religious meetings include long periods of silence.

In the following section of his Autobiography, *he tells how he put his practical instincts to work to achieve spiritual "success" as well.*

3 It was about this time that I conceived the bold and arduous Project of arriving at moral Perfection. I wished to live without committing any Fault at any time; I would conquer all that either Natural Inclination, Custom, or Company might lead me into. As I knew, or thought I knew, what was right and wrong, I did not see why I might not *always* do the one and avoid the other. But I soon found I had undertaken a Task of more Difficulty than I had imagined. While my Attention was taken up in guarding against one Fault, I was often surprised by another. Habit took the Advantage of Inattention. Inclination was sometimes too strong for Reason. I concluded at length that the mere speculative Conviction that it was our Interest to be completely virtuous was not sufficient to prevent our Slipping, and that the contrary Habits must be broken and good ones acquired and established, before we can have any Dependence on a steady uniform Rectitude of Conduct. For this purpose I therefore contrived the following Method.

In the various Enumerations of the moral Virtues I had met with in my Reading, I found the Catalogue more or less numerous, as different Writers included more or fewer Ideas under the same Name. Temperance, for Example, was by some confined to Eating and Drinking, while by others it was extended to mean the moderating every other Pleasure, Appetite, Inclination or Passion, bodily or mental, even to our Avarice and Ambition. I proposed to myself, for the sake of Clearness, to use rather more Names with fewer Ideas annexed to each, than a few Names with more Ideas;
4 and I included under Thirteen Names of Virtues all that at that time occurred to me as necessary or desirable, and annexed to each a short Precept,[13] which fully expressed the Extent I gave to its Meaning.

13. **Precept:** rule.

Benjamin Franklin's Experiment, June 1752, print by Currier and Ives, 1876.

GUIDED READING

LITERAL QUESTIONS

1a. What does Franklin do with his two extra rolls? (He sees a woman and child and gives the rolls to them.)

2a. How many virtues does Franklin decide are necessary or desirable? (thirteen)

INFERENTIAL QUESTIONS

1b. What does this action imply about the kind of person he is? (He is responsible and kind.)

2b. What does his list of virtues suggest about the way Franklin deals with problems? (He believes that logic and organization can solve any problem.)

AT A GLANCE

- Franklin lists the thirteen most necessary virtues.
- He designs a chart on which to track his progress to moral perfection.
- He decides to focus on one virtue a week.

1 STYLE: PLAIN LANGUAGE

Franklin's use of direct, literal language emphasizes the seriousness of his desire for self-improvement.

2 RESPONSE JOURNAL

Ask students to write about one of the old-fashioned–seeming virtues, such as silence, or frugality. Have them tell what type of experience they imagine led Franklin to consider it important.

3 DESCRIPTION

Franklin's description of the book he makes to track his progress resembles an instructional or how-to guide in its simple, direct language and close attention to procedure.

4 THEME

Franklin's attempt to achieve moral perfection reflects his belief that everyone can become the best person possible.

These Names of Virtues with their Precepts were

1. TEMPERANCE

Eat not to Dullness.
Drink not to Elevation.

1 2. SILENCE

Speak not but what may benefit others or yourself. Avoid trifling Conversation.

3. ORDER

Let all your Things have their Places. Let each Part of your Business have its Time.

4. RESOLUTION

Resolve to perform what you ought. Perform without fail what you resolve.

2 5. FRUGALITY

Make no Expense but to do good to others or yourself: i.e., Waste nothing.

6. INDUSTRY

Lose no Time. Be always employed in something useful. Cut off all unnecessary Actions.

7. SINCERITY

Use no hurtful Deceit.
Think innocently and justly; and, if you speak, speak accordingly.

8. JUSTICE

Wrong none by doing Injuries or omitting the Benefits that are your Duty.

9. MODERATION

Avoid Extremes. Forbear resenting Injuries so much as you think they deserve.

10. CLEANLINESS

Tolerate no Uncleanness in Body, Clothes or Habitation.

11. TRANQUILITY

Be not disturbed at Trifles or at Accidents common or unavoidable.

12. CHASTITY

Rarely use venery but for health or offspring, never to dullness, weakness, or the injury of your own or another's peace or reputation.

13. HUMILITY

Imitate Jesus and Socrates.[14]

3 I made a little Book in which I allotted a Page for each of the Virtues. I ruled each Page with red Ink, so as to have seven Columns, one for each Day of the Week, marking each Column with a Letter for the Day. I crossed these Columns with thirteen red Lines, marking the Beginning of each Line with the first Letter of one of the Virtues, on which Line and in its proper Column I might mark by a little black Spot every Fault I found upon Examination to have been committed respecting that Virtue upon that Day.

TEMPERANCE							
	S	M	T	W	T	F	S
T							
S	• •	•		•		•	
O	•	•	•		•	•	•
R			•			•	
F		•			•		
I			•				
S							
J							
M							
Cl.							
T							
Ch.							
H							

I determined to give a Week's strict Attention to each of the Virtues successively. Thus in the first Week my great Guard was to avoid every the least Offense against Temperance, leaving the other Virtues to their ordinary Chance, only marking every Evening the Faults
4 of the Day. Thus if in the first Week I could keep my first Line marked *T* clear of Spots, I supposed the Habit of that Virtue so much strengthened and its opposite weakened, that I might venture extending my Attention to include the next, and for the following Week keep both Lines clear of Spots. Proceeding thus to the last, I could go through a Course complete in Thirteen Weeks, and four Courses in a

14. **Socrates** [sok′rə tēz]: Greek philosopher and teacher (470?–399 B.C.).

GUIDED READING

LITERAL QUESTION

1a. How does Franklin keep track of his progress toward moral perfection? (with a diagram, or grid, with one line of squares for each virtue)

INFERENTIAL QUESTION

1b. Would Franklin be a good judge of his own character? (Yes; he seems to see his own shortcomings clearly and to want to change them.)

1 Year. And like him who having a Garden to weed does not attempt to eradicate all the bad Herbs at once, which would exceed his Reach and his Strength, but works on one of the Beds at a time, and having accomplished the first proceeds to a Second; so I should have (I hoped) the encouraging Pleasure of seeing on my Pages the Progress I made in Virtue, by clearing successively my Lines of their Spots, till in the End, by a Number of Courses, I should be happy in viewing a clean Book after a thirteen Weeks' daily Examination.

2 The Precept of *Order* requiring that *every Part of my Business should have its allotted Time,* one Page in my little Book contained the following Scheme of Employment for the Twenty-four Hours of a natural Day:

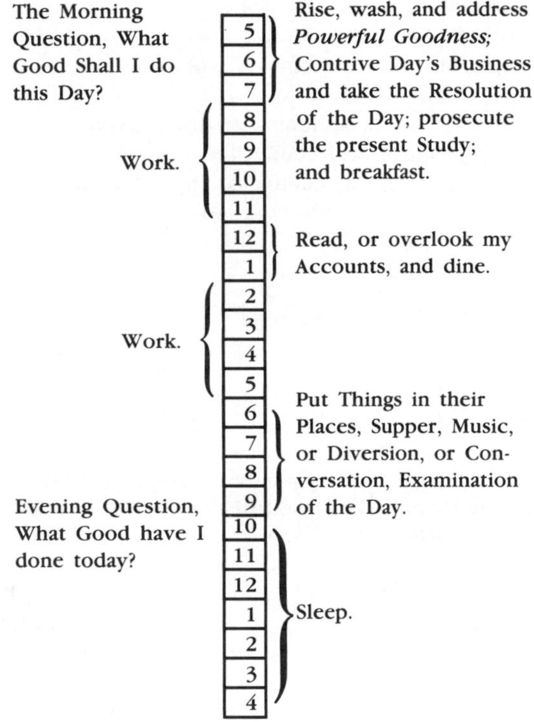

The Morning Question, What Good Shall I do this Day?
5 6 7
Rise, wash, and address *Powerful Goodness;* Contrive Day's Business and take the Resolution of the Day; prosecute the present Study; and breakfast.
Work.
8 9 10 11
12 1
Read, or overlook my Accounts, and dine.
Work.
2 3 4 5
6 7 8 9
Put Things in their Places, Supper, Music, or Diversion, or Conversation, Examination of the Day.
Evening Question, What Good have I done today?
10 11 12 1 2 3 4
Sleep.

I entered upon the Execution of this Plan for Self-Examination, and continued it with occasional Intermissions for some time. I was surprised to find myself so much fuller of Faults than I had imagined, but I had the Satisfaction of seeing them diminish. To avoid the Trouble of renewing now and then my little Book, which, by scraping out the Marks on the Paper of old Faults to make room for new Ones in a
3 new Course, became full of Holes, I transferred my Tables and Precepts to the Ivory Leaves of a Memorandum Book on which the Lines were drawn with red Ink that made a durable Stain, and on those Lines I marked my Faults with a black Lead Pencil, which Marks I could easily wipe out with a wet Sponge. After a while I went through one Course only in a Year, and afterwards only one in several Years, till at length I omitted them entirely, being employed in Voyages and Business abroad with a Multiplicity of Affairs that interfered; but I always carried my little Book with me.

My Scheme of *Order* gave me the most Trouble, and I found that though it might be practicable where a Man's Business was such as to leave him the Disposition of his Time, that of a Journeyman Printer,[15] for instance, it was not possible to be exactly observed by a Master, who must mix with the World and often receive People of Business at their own Hours. *Order* too, with regard to Places for Things, Papers, etc., I found extremely difficult to acquire. I had not been early accustomed to *Method,* and having an exceeding good Memory, I was not so sensible of the Inconvenience attending Want of Method. This Article therefore cost me much painful Attention, and my Faults in it vexed me. . . .

In Truth I found myself incorrigible with respect to *Order;* and now I am grown old, and my Memory bad, I feel very sensibly the want
4 of it. But on the whole, though I never arrived at the Perfection I had been so ambitious of obtaining, but fell far short of it, yet I was by the Endeavor a better and a happier Man than I otherwise should have been if I had not attempted it.

15. **Journeyman Printer:** worker who has completed an apprenticeship and works for a master printer.

AT A GLANCE

- Comparing himself to a gardener, Franklin works on one virtue at a time.
- He finds that he has more faults than he had thought.
- In later life Franklin affirms that his life was better for having sought perfection.

1 STYLE: SIMILE

The garden simile adds clarity to Franklin's description. Franklin also reminds us that a human life is much more complex and multidimensional than a garden.

2 AUTOBIOGRAPHY

In describing his Scheme of Employment with unadorned, diagrammatic detail, Franklin demonstrates his lifelong faith in order and simplicity.

3 TONE

By focusing on the mechanics of tracking his progress, while withholding self-judgment, Franklin achieves an unconsciously humorous tone that begs indulgence.

4 THEME

The theme of self-improvement is underscored as Franklin summarizes his attempts to achieve moral perfection.

REFLECTING ON THE SELECTION

How do you think Franklin's maturity affected his view of his early experiences? (Time and perspective may have allowed him to regard himself both critically *and* indulgently. He also was able to assess the results of his efforts over time.)

GUIDED READING

LITERAL QUESTIONS

1a. Which virtue does Franklin use to organize his day? (order)

2a. What reason does he give for not having followed his method as his career progressed? (His time was not as much under his control.)

INFERENTIAL QUESTIONS

1b. Which character trait do you think led him to focus on this virtue? (his belief in the power of reason to shape his life)

2b. What does this reasoning suggest about the limitations of his method? (Rigid or fixed plans of behavior may not be suitable to the varying needs and experiences of a complex life.)

STUDY QUESTIONS

1. slips them under the door
2. printed article critical of government; has Ben legally, but falsely, named publisher
3. James cannot reveal that Ben is only an apprentice, so Ben has him discharge his indenture. His brother keeps him from getting another job there; he has enemies in city government.
4. dirty, fatigued, hungry; he eats one, gives the others away
5. plans to achieve moral perfection by breaking bad habits; focusing on one virtue each week
6. the number of his faults; that he can diminish them; order
7. *cleverness:* success of articles; *self-reliance:* relocating in Philadelphia; *generosity:* giving away rolls; *optimism and belief in virtue:* plan for moral perfection; *industry:* adherence to plan
8. exaggeration regarding small number of newspapers in America; newspapers; reasons for leaving Boston; description of Quaker meetinghouse as first lodgings
9. reconsider one's own life; put events into perspective; recognize one's flaws, virtues; detect patterns and turning points

VIEWPOINT

Franklin was interested in grave questions but didn't treat them seriously; for example, he makes light of his assumption of tough political stands while James was jailed.

VOCABULARY

1. (b) cleverness
2. (b) scold
3. (d) disapproval
4. (a) uprightness
5. (c) un-reformable

STUDY QUESTIONS

Recalling

1. How does Ben Franklin submit his articles to the *Courant?*
2. Why does the government try to close down the *Courant?* What does Ben's brother do to evade the government order?
3. According to the third paragraph, how does Ben take advantage of his brother? For what reasons does Ben leave Boston?
4. What three adjectives in the fifth paragraph describe how Ben looked and felt when he arrived in Philadelphia? What becomes of the puffy rolls he bought?
5. According to the seventh paragraph, why does Franklin create his "Method" for "moral perfection"? Summarize the method.
6. What surprises Franklin when he begins to follow his plan for self-examination (page 63)? What satisfaction does he have? What gives him the most trouble?

Interpreting

7. State three or more dominant characteristics of Ben Franklin as a young man. Cite an incident to illustrate each characteristic.
8. Find three examples of humor or worldly wisdom that help illustrate why Franklin was regarded as one of the wittiest Americans of the eighteenth century.

Extending

9. How can writing an autobiography contribute to self-knowledge? By way of example, explain what Ben Franklin the autobiographer comes to see about Ben Franklin the young man.

VIEWPOINT

In one of his novels, Herman Melville, the nineteenth-century American writer, described Franklin in this way:

> Having carefully weighed the world, Franklin could act any part in it. By nature turned to knowledge, his mind was often grave, but never serious.
>
> —*Israel Potter*

■ Discuss Melville's distinction between *grave* and *serious.* Find one example in the selection where Franklin deals with a grave issue in a light manner.

VOCABULARY

Synonyms

A **synonym** is a word that has the same or nearly the same meaning as another word. *Journey* and *voyage* are synonyms. The words in capital letters are from the *Autobiography.* Choose the word that is *nearest* the meaning of each word in capitals, *as it is used in the selection.* Write the number of each item and the letter of your choice on a separate sheet.

1. INGENUITY: (a) approbation (b) cleverness (c) innocence (d) disturbance
2. ADMONISH: (a) finish (b) scold (c) require (d) admire
3. CENSURE: (a) freedom (b) vote (c) count (d) disapproval
4. RECTITUDE: (a) uprightness (b) custom (c) cowardice (d) indigestion
5. INCORRIGIBLE: (a) confused (b) courageous (c) unable to be reformed (d) easy

COMPOSITION

Writing About Autobiography

■ Choose one paragraph from the *Autobiography,* and write a short composition in which you show how Franklin tells his story using both objective facts and subjective feelings. First identify the facts that Franklin provides. Then describe the feelings he suggests. Conclude by explaining the total impression Franklin creates.

Writing Aphorisms

■ Write contemporary adaptations of two of the sayings of Poor Richard. First write a paraphrase, or short summary in your own words, of each of the two Poor Richard sayings. Then create a modern aphorism that conveys the same meaning.

COMPOSITION: GUIDELINES FOR EVALUATION

WRITING ABOUT AUTOBIOGRAPHY

Objective

To analyze Franklin's autobiography

Guidelines for Evaluation

- suggested length: three to four paragraphs
- should describe an incident from Franklin's autobiography
- should identify both facts and feelings, showing how they work together
- should state Franklin's tone and attitudes

WRITING APHORISMS

Objective

To interpret and update aphorisms

Guidelines for Evaluation

- suggested length: four sentences
- should state the implicit idea behind two of Franklin's aphorisms
- should restate the aphorisms in modern terms
- should retain the wit and wisdom of the original aphorisms

Patrick Henry *1736–1799*

"If this be treason, make the most of it!" Outcries like this one opposing the Stamp Act have assured Patrick Henry a place of honor among orators of the American Revolution. Born in Virginia, Henry worked as a storekeeper but ran hopelessly into debt because of his poor business sense. When he began to practice law, however, his talent as an orator won him wide recognition. Eventually, he held various positions in the public service: member of the Virginia House of Burgesses and of the Continental Congress, commander of Virginia's military forces, and governor of the new Commonwealth of Virginia from 1776 to 1779. Henry was also the major voice in the drafting of the Bill of Rights.

After his years of public service, Henry was badly in debt again, and so he returned to his law practice in 1788. Though a major figure in the Revolution, he turned down George Washington's invitations to become secretary of state and Chief Justice of the Supreme Court. A fellow Virginian said that in private Henry was "modest, mild, and in religious matters, a saint." Yet when he spoke in public, he became the "Son of Thunder."

We hear that thunder in the following speech, which he delivered in 1775 to the Virginia Convention. The delegates had assembled to discuss the British military buildup in America. Gathered in St. John's Church in Richmond on that mild March day were Virginia's greatest men, including Washington and Jefferson. The first speakers urged moderation and compromise with the British. But Henry spoke strongly, dramatically, defiantly. We have come to see his speech as a masterpiece of clear, skillful oratory, a forceful blend of argument and emotion. As we know now, Henry's speech, which begins on the following page, won the day. The Declaration of Independence was only a few months away.

■ Why is Patrick Henry's statement "Give me liberty or give me death" important to most Americans?

AT A GLANCE

- Henry sees the issues before the Virginia Convention as a matter of slavery and freedom.
- Henry affirms that the freedom to speak freely is as important to this debate as is its immediate subject.

LITERARY OPTIONS

- oratory
- allusion

THEMATIC OPTIONS

- the nature of freedom
- political action
- changing the status quo

1 ORATORY: PURPOSE AND AUDIENCE

Henry immediately reinforces the importance of not compromising with the British.

2 THEME

Henry reduces the arguments under debate to a single issue: fighting for freedom or accepting slavery.

Patrick Henry delivering a speech. Nineteenth-century engraving.

Patrick Henry

Speech in the Virginia Convention

Mr. President: No man thinks more highly than I do of the patriotism, as well as abilities, of the very worthy gentlemen who have just addressed the house. But different men often see the same subject in different lights; and,
1 therefore, I hope it will not be thought disrespectful to those gentlemen, if, entertaining, as I do, opinions of a character very opposite to theirs, I shall speak forth my sentiments freely and without reserve. This is no time for ceremony. The question before the house is one of
2 awful moment[1] to this country. For my own part, I consider it as nothing less than a question of freedom or slavery. And in proportion to the magnitude of the subject ought to be the freedom of the debate. It is only in this way that we can hope to arrive at truth, and fulfill the great responsibility which we hold to God and our country. Should I keep back my opinions at such a time, through fear of giving

1. **awful moment:** dreadful importance.

GUIDED READING

LITERAL QUESTION

1a. To whom does Henry feel responsible in debating the issue before the Convention? (to God and to country)

INFERENTIAL QUESTION

1b. How do you think this mention of responsibility affected the delivery of Henry's speech? (It was dramatic, it gave him the power of sincerity, and it made him persuasive.)

offense, I should consider myself as guilty of treason toward my country, and of an act of disloyalty toward the Majesty of Heaven, which I revere above all earthly kings.

1 Mr. President, it is natural to man to indulge in the illusions of hope. We are apt to shut our eyes against a painful truth, and listen to the song of that siren till she transforms us into beasts.[2] Is this the part of wise men, engaged in a great and arduous struggle for liberty? Are we disposed to be of the number of those who having eyes see not, and having ears hear not,[3] the things which so nearly concern their temporal[4] salvation? For my part, whatever anguish of spirit it may cost, I am willing to know the whole truth; to know the worst and to provide for it.

I have but one lamp by which my feet are guided, and that is the lamp of experience. I know of no way of judging of the future but by the past. And judging by the past, I wish to know what there has been in the conduct of the British ministry for the last ten years to justify those hopes with which gentlemen have been pleased to solace themselves and the house? Is it that insidious smile with which our petition has been lately received? Trust it not, sir; it will prove a snare to your feet. Suffer not yourselves to be betrayed with a kiss.[5] Ask yourselves how this gracious reception of our petition comports with those warlike preparations which cover our waters and darken our
2 land. Are fleets and armies necessary to a work of love and reconciliation? Have we shown ourselves so unwilling to be reconciled that force must be called in to win back our love? Let us not deceive ourselves, sir. These are the implements of war and subjugation—the last arguments to which kings resort.

I ask gentlemen, sir, what means this martial array, if its purpose be not to force us to submission? Can gentlemen assign any other possible motive for it? Has Great Britain any enemy in this quarter of the world, to call for all this accumulation of navies and armies? No, sir, she has none. They are meant for us: they
3 can be meant for no other. They are sent over to bind and rivet upon us those chains which the British ministry have been so long forging.

And what have we to oppose to them? Shall we try argument? Sir, we have been trying that for the last ten years. Have we anything new to offer upon the subject? Nothing. We have held the subject up in every light of which it is capable; but it has been all in vain. Shall we resort to entreaty and humble supplication? What terms shall we find which have not been already exhausted? Let us not, I beseech you, sir, deceive ourselves longer.

Sir, we have done everything that could be done to avert the storm which is now coming
4 on. We have petitioned; we have remonstrated; we have supplicated; we have prostrated ourselves before the throne, and have implored its interposition[6] to arrest the tyrannical hands of the ministry and Parliament. Our petitions have been slighted; our remonstrances have produced additional violence and insult; our supplications have been disregarded; and we have been spurned with contempt from the foot of the throne! In vain, after these things, may we indulge the fond[7] hope of peace and reconciliation. There is no longer any room for hope. If we wish to be free, if we mean to preserve inviolate those inestimable privileges for which we have been so long contending, if we mean not basely to abandon the noble struggle in which we have been so long engaged, and which we have pledged ourselves never to abandon until the glorious object of our contest shall be obtained—we must fight! I repeat it, sir, we must fight! An appeal to arms and to the God of Hosts is all that is left us!

2. **listen . . . beasts:** In Homer's *Odyssey* the enchantress Circe charms men with her song and then turns them into swine.
3. **having eyes . . . hear not:** In Ezekiel 12 : 2 the prophet addresses those "who have eyes to see, but see not, who have ears to hear, but hear not."
4. **temporal:** earthly.
5. **betrayed . . . kiss:** In Luke 22 : 47–48 Judas betrays Jesus with a kiss.

6. **interposition:** intervention.
7. **fond:** foolish.

AT A GLANCE

- Henry cites evidence that the British will use force against the Americans.
- He affirms the necessity of fighting for freedom since petition and argument have failed.

1 ALLUSION

The classical and biblical allusions that Henry cites place America's predicament into universal perspective.

2 ORATORY: RHETORICAL QUESTIONS

Henry's repeated rhetorical questions force his audience to weigh the intangible hopes for reconciliation against the real and present danger posed by the British military forces.

3 STYLE: METAPHOR

The image of bondage Henry conveys with such words as "bind," "rivet," "chains," and "forging" add grim intensity to his warning about British intentions.

4 ORATORY: REPETITION AND PARALLELISM

Repetition of *we* would inspire a sense of unity in the audience. Parallel constructions are a powerful device in which the symmetry and rhythm of the sentence add to the persuasiveness of the words.

GUIDED READING

LITERAL QUESTIONS

1a. What is Henry willing to know, regardless of the anguish it may cause? (the truth)

2a. What three attempts to cope with the British does Henry cite as already having failed? (argument, entreaty, and supplication)

INFERENTIAL QUESTIONS

1b. What do you think Henry means when he says he is ready to "provide" for the truth? (He is prepared to face it squarely and act on it accordingly.)

2b. Why do you think Henry focuses on these three failed attempts to deal with the British? (This reminder might help him persuade his audience that their only remaining recourse is to fight.)

They tell us, sir, that we are weak—unable to cope with so formidable an adversary. But when shall we be stronger? Will it be the next week, or the next year? Will it be when we are totally disarmed, and when a British guard shall be stationed in every house? Shall we gather strength by irresolution and inaction? Shall we acquire the means of effectual resistance by lying supinely on our backs and hugging the delusive phantom of hope until our enemies shall have bound us hand and foot? Sir, we are not weak, if we make a proper use of those means which the God of nature hath placed in our power. Three millions of people, armed in the holy cause of liberty, and in such a country as that which we possess, are invincible by any force which our enemy can send against us.
1 Besides, sir, we shall not fight our battles alone. There is a just God who presides over the destinies of nations and who will raise up friends to fight our battles for us. The battle, sir, is not to the strong alone;[8] it is to the vigilant, the active, the brave. Besides, sir, we have no election.[9] If we were base enough to desire it, it is now too late to retire from the contest. There is no retreat but in submission and slavery! Our chains are forged! Their clanging may be heard on the plains of Boston! The war is inevitable—and let it come! I repeat it, sir, let it come!

It is in vain, sir, to extenuate the matter. Gentlemen may cry, "Peace, peace"—but there is no peace. The war is actually begun! The next gale that sweeps from the north[10] will bring to our ears the clash of resounding arms!
2 Our brethren are already in the field! Why stand we here idle? What is it that gentlemen wish? What would they have? Is life so dear, or peace so sweet, as to be purchased at the price of chains and slavery? Forbid it, Almighty God! I know not what course others may take; but as for me, give me liberty or give me death!

8. **battle . . . strong alone:** "The race is not to the swift, nor the battle to the strong" (Ecclesiastes 9 : 11).

9. **election:** choice.

10. **next gale . . . north:** In Massachusetts some colonists had already begun to show open resistance against the British.

STUDY QUESTIONS

Recalling

1. Why is Henry stating his opinion at this time?
2. According to the third and fourth paragraphs, what does Henry believe is Britain's purpose in America?
3. According to the sixth paragraph, what have the colonists already done "to avert the storm"? What does Henry say they must do now?
4. According to the seventh paragraph, why is the American army "invincible"?
5. As Henry concludes, what does he say has already begun?

Interpreting

6. What does Henry accomplish through his series of questions in paragraph 7?
7. Which evidence that Henry cites in support of his argument is factual, or provable? Which evidence is opinion?
8. When Henry says, "I know not what course others may take," how is he trying to make his listeners feel? Identify at least two more instances where he appeals to his audience's emotions.

Extending

9. In what ways do you think Henry's speech illustrates the beliefs of the Age of Reason?

LITERARY FOCUS

Oratory

Oratory, the art of public speaking, played a crucial part in the American past. In an age long before radio and television, commanding the at-

AT A GLANCE

- Henry discounts allegations of American weakness.
- He proclaims that with God's help the colonists' cause is invincible.
- Henry equates retreat with slavery, a fate he calls worse than death.

1 STYLE: ALLUSION

Henry alludes to Ecclesiastes to discount fear of his countrymen's military weakness and to legitimize his call to arms.

2 ORATORY: CONCLUSION

In the memorable conclusion to his speech, Henry asks a final series of rhetorical questions, building up to a thundering answer: "Forbid it, Almighty God!"

REFLECTING ON THE SPEECH

What do you think is most powerful about Henry's speech? (Some students may point to the citation of the facts impelling Americans into revolution; others, to Henry's oratorical devices—rhythm, parallelism, figurative language.)

STUDY QUESTIONS

1. responding to those who spoke for reconciliation with Britain
2. to subdue colonists through force
3. petitioned, remonstrated, supplicated, prostrated selves before the throne; fight
4. "three million people armed in the holy cause of liberty, with God on their side"
5. the war
6. dismisses arguments against fighting
7.
   - Fact: petitions submitted; British unreceptive; increase in British forces; resistance in North
   - Opinion: no hope for reconciliation; Britain wants war; everything possible tried; Americans are strong, have God on their side
8. guilty; presenting choice between freedom or slavery; describing British reception of petitions; biblical allusions
9. logic, goal of liberty, idea that people can change history and improve their lot

tention of an audience with a powerful address was the surest way to win an election, debate public issues, sell products, and, as the sermon of Jonathan Edwards in the preceding unit illustrates, spread a religious message.

Oratory flourished in ancient Greek and Roman times, when speakers were judged by the power of their words and the way those words were presented to the public. Reasoned arguments and emotional appeals were both important. Classical orators developed intricate systems of rules and devices for speaking properly. Three of these oratorical devices, found in Henry's speech and still used today, are rhetorical questions, repetition, and improvisation.

A **rhetorical question** is a question that the speaker really does not intend as a question, or one that he means to answer himself. Henry asks, "Is this the part of wise men, engaged in a great and arduous struggle for liberty?" He expects his audience to be so sure of the answer that no one will need to think twice about the response. A rhetorical question can give a speaker a tone of confidence or a biting satiric edge. It can also act as a bridge between a speaker and an audience, implying that they understand each other perfectly.

Repetition can be as effective in oratory as it is in poetry. Henry says, "We have petitioned; we have remonstrated; we have supplicated; we have prostrated ourselves before the throne." His repetitions add force to what he says; they add the weight of accumulated evidence.

Improvisation is the skill of speaking without reading word for word from a written text. No original manuscript of Henry's speech exists, although he certainly would have prepared his speech in his mind. He probably had a scheme or outline and may even have memorized some of the best of his sentences. Yet he could not have known in advance what previous speakers were going to say, and his speech does sound like a direct reply. William Wirt, who wrote a biography of Henry, reconstructed the text of the speech from outside sources and accounts given by other delegates at the convention. The speech we now read as a finished piece of oratory was probably created in large part as it was being delivered, by a master of improvisation.

Thinking About Oratory

■ Find another rhetorical question and another example of repetition in Henry's speech.

COMPOSITION

Writing About Oratory

■ What is Henry's purpose in his speech? Cite with examples the particular techniques that Henry uses to accomplish that purpose. You may consider his use of facts, statistics, examples, and opinions. *For help with this assignment, refer to Lesson 4 in the Writing About Literature Handbook at the back of this book.*

Writing a Guest Editorial

■ Many local television and radio stations invite their audiences to express their opinions on the air. Write an editorial on a subject that is important to you or your community. Limit yourself to a speech that you can deliver in two minutes. State your case clearly, using facts, statistics, and examples wherever appropriate. Be sure your audience knows where you stand on the issue and what action you think should be taken.

LITERARY FOCUS

- *Rhetorical questions:* "Are we disposed . . .", paragraph 2; second, third, sixth, and seventh sentences in paragraph 3; first three sentences in paragraph 4; first, second, fourth, sixth, and seventh sentences in paragraph 5; second through eighth sentences in paragraph 7; fifth through eighth sentences in final paragraph
- *Repetitions:* "If we wish" and "if we mean" in paragraph 6; "we must fight" in paragraph 6; "let it come" in paragraph 7

COMPOSITION: GUIDELINES FOR EVALUATION

WRITING ABOUT ORATORY

Objective

To analyze the techniques of oratory

Guidelines for Evaluation

- suggested length: four to seven paragraphs
- should identify Henry's purpose
- should discuss use of rhetorical questions, repetition, allusion, fact, statistic, example

WRITING A GUEST EDITORIAL

Objective

To prepare an editorial for oral presentation

Guidelines for Evaluation

- suggested length: one- to two-minute presentation
- should be on an important issue
- should show awareness of audience
- should identify purpose, state case clearly
- should use facts, statistics, examples

AT A GLANCE

- The speaker sings about America's desire for liberty.
- Americans will stay loyal to King George only if he grants them liberty; if not they will rebel.
- The speaker toasts the health of brave Americans and George Washington.

LITERARY OPTIONS

- repetition
- rhyme

THEMATIC OPTIONS

- the coexistence of liberty and loyalty
- American bravery

SPEAKER

The speaker's spirited exhortation to listen to his song reflects the vigor and boldness that characterize the fighting men who seek to win America's liberty (ll. 1–2).

RHYME

The strong end rhyme *(unfold/controlled)* and internal rhyme *(bold/controlled)* add emphasis and focus to the speaker's central thesis that brave Americans refuse to accept England's restrictions on their freedom (ll. 3–4).

REPETITION

The use of parallel clauses and frequent repetition of *liberty* reinforce the idea that through either compromise or rebellion, Americans will win their freedom (ll. 5–12, 16).

REFLECTING ON THE POEM

Which idea or ideas reflected in the broadside would have made a persuasive political statement at the time? Explain your answer. (The idea of liberty through compromise would have appealed to the respect for reason; the scorn of being controlled would have appealed to the concern for freedom.)

Anonymous Broadside

"The Bold Americans" was circulated as an anonymous broadside, a large printed sheet of paper, in late 1775 or early 1776. While other songs of the time, such as "Yankee Doodle," sang out wholeheartedly for complete independence, "The Bold Americans" offered a compromise. It reminds us that those who called for complete separation from Britain were actually few in number and that a large percentage of Americans wanted *both* a measure of liberty and continued affiliation with England.

■ What conditions for liberty does this poem present to King George?

Anonymous

The Bold Americans

Come all you bold young Bostonians, come listen unto me:
I will sing you a song concerning liberty.
Concerning liberty, my boys, the truth I will unfold,
Of the bold Americans, who scorn to be controlled.

We'll honor George,[1] our sovereign, on any reasonable terms,
But if he don't grant us liberty, we'll all lay down our arms.
But if he will grant us liberty, so plainly shall you see,
We are the boys that fear no noise! Success to liberty!

We'll honor George, our sovereign, while he sits on the throne.
If he grants us liberty, no other king we'll own.
If he will grant us liberty, so plainly shall you see,
We are the boys that fear no noise! Success to liberty!

Come all you sparkling landladies, come fill the other bowl,
We'll drink a health to those brave boys who scorn to be controlled,
Another to George Washington, who fought so manfully.
So now we end our ditty, boys: Success to liberty!

1. **George:** George III (1738–1820), who was king of Great Britain, 1760–1820.

The Boston Tea Party, 1773. Nineteenth-century engraving.

STUDY QUESTIONS

Recalling

1. What do the bold Americans "scorn"?
2. For what reason will the bold Americans lay down their arms and refuse to defend the British government?
3. Whom do the bold Americans toast in the last stanza?

Interpreting

4. Describe the mixed attitude toward rebellion displayed in this song.
5. Which details make the bold Americans seem reasonable and open-minded?

Extending

6. How can songs reflect the attitudes and beliefs of a particular time and place?

STUDY QUESTIONS

1. being controlled
2. if King George does not grant them liberty
3. themselves, George Washington
4. Americans want liberty but hope it will be granted on "any reasonable terms."
5. They will honor King George on "any reasonable terms"; if George grants liberty they are willing to let bygones be bygones and be his loyal subjects; while they hope to remain George's subjects, they nevertheless respect and honor George Washington.
6. Answers will vary. Students should note that people write from experience, so songs reflect the attitudes of the time and place in which the songwriter lived.

Dekanawida

Centuries before the American colonists banded together to set up an independent government, a large group of Native Americans had established a unified government of their own called the Five Nations, also known as the Iroquois Confederacy. The Five Nations—Mohawk, Seneca, Onondaga, Oneida, and Cayuga—admitted the Tuscarora in 1724 and became the Six Nations (still commonly called the Iroquois Confederacy).

The Iroquois Confederacy, covering much of the area that is now New York State, brought together tribes with similar customs and languages. These tribes had often warred against one another and had weakened themselves against outside enemies. A great chief, Dekanawida, united the tribes and created the code of laws upon which the federation rested. What we now call the Iroquois Constitution was the remarkable civil and social system Dekanawida named the Great Binding Law.

Dekanawida traveled from tribe to tribe, organizing the confederacy, establishing the Great Peace, and persuading tribes to subscribe to the Great Law. The Great Law was a comprehensive and efficient system to protect the Five Nations from outside enemies and from themselves. It covered membership in the league, council procedures, rules for debate and decision making, and the rights and responsibilities of leaders, as well as laws relating to marriage, emigration, treason, and festivals.

In this selection Dekanawida invests the chief of the Onondaga with the responsibility of keeping the Council Fire. He then goes on to enumerate some of the aspects of the system that made the Iroquois a dominant power. The Iroquois Constitution takes its place with the other political statements in this unit: Benjamin Franklin used the Iroquois Confederacy as an example when trying to persuade American colonists to unite. It is even said that Thomas Jefferson studied the Iroquois code in his efforts to interpret the Constitution of the United States.

■ What democratic beliefs do we share with the early Indians?

New York State Museum

An Iroquois wampum belt made of polished beads, commemorating the unification of the Five Nations.

Dekanawida

from The Iroquois Constitution

The Tree of the Great Peace

I am Dekanawida and with the Five Nations' Confederate Lords I plant the Tree of the Great Peace. I plant it in your territory, Adodarho, and the Onondaga Nation, in the territory of you who are Firekeepers.

I name the tree the Tree of the Great Long Leaves. Under the shade of this Tree of the Great Peace we spread the soft white feathery down of the globe thistle as seats for you, Adodarho, and your cousin Lords.

We place you upon those seats, spread soft with the feathery down of the globe thistle, there beneath the shade of the spreading branches of the Tree of Peace. There shall you sit and watch the Council Fire of the Confederacy of the Five Nations, and all the affairs of the Five Nations shall be transacted at this place.

1 Roots have spread out from the Tree of the Great Peace, one to the north, one to the east, one to the south and one to the west. The name of these roots is the Great White Roots and their nature is Peace and Strength.

If any man or any nation outside the Five Nations shall obey the laws of the Great Peace and make known their disposition to the Lords

AT A GLANCE

- Dekanawida plants the Tree of Great Peace in the land of Adodarho, of the Onondaga Indian nation.
- Adodarho and his "cousin Lords" are to take charge of the Council Fire, and the Five Nations of the Iroquois shall be united.

LITERARY OPTIONS

- theme
- style

THEMATIC OPTIONS

- peace through unity
- mutual respect

1 STYLE: METAPHOR

The metaphor of the spreading tree roots reinforces the idea that peace and strength are nurtured by unity

GUIDED READING

LITERAL QUESTION

1a. What does Dekanawida name the tree that he plants? (Tree of the Great Long Leaves)

INFERENTIAL QUESTION

1b. What do you think the name signifies? (It suggests that the tree will spread shade over the land and offer shelter and comfort.)

AT A GLANCE

- Procedures for joining the confederacy are outlined. The confederacy includes the Mohawk, Seneca, Oneida, Cayuga, and Onondaga Nations.
- Specific laws for conducting business before the Council are stipulated.
- The original clans that comprise the Five Nations are named.

1 VOCABULARY: WORD CHOICE

The language that describes membership in the confederacy ("roots," "trace," "shelter") symbolizes the cohesion of the Five Nations.

2 THEME

In stipulating a formal ceremony of thanksgiving at the opening of every Council, the Constitution reinforces the need for harmony between people and the world they live in.

3 ENLIGHTENMENT IDEA

The by-laws of the Constitution—in their logical organization, attention to detail, and reasonable consideration of issues—suggest beliefs similar to those that characterized the Age of Reason.

4 STYLE: METAPHOR

The image of a beam to describe new laws conveys a sense of the confederacy's adaptability and openness to growth.

1 of the Confederacy, they may trace the Roots to the Tree and if their minds are clean and they are obedient and promise to obey the wishes of the Confederate Council, they shall be welcomed to take shelter beneath the Tree of the Long Leaves.

We place at the top of the Tree of the Long Leaves an Eagle who is able to see afar. If he sees in the distance any evil approaching or any danger threatening, he will at once warn the people of the Confederacy.

The Care of the Fire

The Smoke of the Confederate Council Fire shall ever ascend and pierce the sky so that other nations who may be allies may see the Council Fire of the Great Peace.

You, Adodarho, and your thirteen cousin Lords shall faithfully keep the space about the Council Fire clean and you shall allow neither dust nor dirt to accumulate. I lay a Long Wing before you as a broom. As a weapon against a crawling creature I lay a staff with you so that you may thrust it away from the Council Fire.

The Laws of the Council

2 Whenever the Confederate Lords shall assemble for the purpose of holding a council, the Onondaga Lords shall open it by expressing their gratitude to their cousin Lords and greeting them, and they shall make an address and offer thanks to the earth where men dwell, to the streams of water, the pools, the springs and the lakes, to the maize and the fruits, to the medicinal herbs and trees, to the forest trees for their usefulness, to the animals that serve as food and give their pelts for clothing, to the great winds and the lesser winds, to the Thunderers, to the Sun, the mighty warrior, to the moon, to the messengers of the Creator who reveal his wishes and to the Great Creator who dwells in the heavens above, who gives all the things useful to men, and who is the source and the ruler of health and life.

All the business of the Five Nations' Confederate Council shall be conducted by the two combined bodies of Confederate Lords. First the question shall be passed upon by the Mohawk and Seneca Lords; then it shall be discussed and passed by the Oneida and Cayuga Lords. Their decisions shall then be referred to the Onondaga Lords (Firekeepers) for final judgment.

3 When the Council of the Five Nation Lords shall convene, they shall appoint a speaker for the day. He shall be a Lord of either the Mohawk, Onondaga, or Seneca Nation.

No individual or foreign nation interested in a case, question or proposition shall have any voice in the Confederate Council except to answer a question put to him or them by the speaker for the Lords.

If the conditions which shall arise at any future time call for an addition to or change of this law, the case shall be carefully considered,
4 and if a new beam seems necessary or beneficial, the proposed change shall be voted upon and, if adopted, it shall be called, "Added to the Rafters."

The Clans

Among the Five Nations and their posterity there shall be the following original clans: Great Name Bearer, Ancient Name Bearer, Great Bear, Ancient Bear, Turtle, Painted Turtle, Standing Rock, Large Plover, Little Plover, Deer, Pigeon Hawk, Eel, Ball, Opposite-Side-of-the-Hand, and Wild Potatoes. These clans, distributed through their respective Nations, shall be the sole owners and holders of the soil of the country, and in them is it vested as a birthright.

People of the Five Nations [who are] members of a certain clan shall recognize every other member of that clan, irrespective of the Nation, as relatives.

The lineal descent of the people of the Five Nations shall run in the female line. Women

GUIDED READING

LITERAL QUESTIONS

1a. Why is an eagle placed at the top of the Tree of Long Leaves? (to warn of approaching evil and danger)

2a. How are the people of the Five Nations, regardless of their affiliation, to regard members of other clans? (as relatives)

INFERENTIAL QUESTIONS

1b. In what way does the eagle add to the benefits provided by the Tree of Long Leaves? (It adds the assurance of protection and a sense of mobility and greatness.)

2b. How do you think this idea of kinship affected the people of the Five Nations? (It gave them a sense of unity, of harmony, and of strength in numbers.)

shall be considered the progenitors of the Nation. They shall own the land and the soil. Men and women shall follow the status of the mother.

The Leaders

The Lords of the Confederacy of the Five Nations shall be mentors of the people for all time. The thickness of their skin shall be seven spans—which is to say that they shall be proof against anger, offensive actions, and criticism. Their hearts shall be full of peace and good will and their minds filled with a yearning for the welfare of the people of the Confederacy. With endless patience they shall carry out their duty, and their firmness shall be tempered with
1 a tenderness for their people. Neither anger nor fury shall find lodgment in their minds, and all their words and actions shall be marked by calm deliberation.

The Festivals

The rites and festivals of each Nation shall remain undisturbed and shall continue as before because they were given by the people of old times as useful and necessary for the good of men.

The recognized festivals of Thanksgiving shall be the Midwinter Thanksgiving, the Maple or Sugar Making Thanksgiving, the Raspberry Thanksgiving, the Strawberry Thanksgiving, the Corn Planting Thanksgiving, the Corn Hoeing Thanksgiving, the Little Festival of Green Corn, the Great Festival of Ripe Corn, and the complete Thanksgiving for the Harvest.

The Symbols

2 A large bunch of shell strings, in the making of which the Five Nations' Confederate Lords have equally contributed, shall symbolize the completeness of the union and certify the pledge of the Nations represented by the Confederate Lords of the Mohawk, the Oneida, the Onondaga, the Cayuga, and the Seneca, that all are united and formed into one body or union called the Union of the Great Law, which they have established.

Five arrows shall be bound together very strong, and each arrow shall represent one nation. As the five arrows are strongly bound, this shall symbolize the complete union of the nations. Thus are the Five Nations united completely and enfolded together, united into one head, one body, and one mind. Therefore they shall labor, legislate, and council together for the interest of future generations.

STUDY QUESTIONS

Recalling

1. What tree does Dekanawida plant in the first section? What does he say the eagle at the top will do?
2. According to the second section, what is the purpose of the Council Fire? What qualities, according to "The Leaders," should all Lords of the Five Nations possess?
3. According to "The Festivals," why should the rites and festivals of each nation remain undisturbed?
4. What two symbols of the complete union of the Five Nations Confederacy are described in the final section?

Interpreting

5. Why is a tree an appropriate symbol for peace achieved through a unification such as the Iroquois Confederacy?
6. What is Dekanawida suggesting about laws when he describes them as beams and rafters?
7. Find the part of the Iroquois Constitution that suggests each of these modern ideas: national holidays, legislative houses, parliamentary procedure, constitutional amendments.

Extending

8. Tell how the flag of the United States, like the five arrows, represents a nation "united completely and enfolded together."

AT A GLANCE

- The Constitution enumerates the characteristics of good leadership, legitimizes the Nation's rites, and stipulates festival days.
- A large bunch of shell strings and five arrows bound together symbolizes the unity of the Five Nations.

1 ENLIGHTENMENT IDEA

The qualities of good leadership enumerated here relate to Franklin's thirteen virtues, especially the importance of moderation and logical reasoning.

2 THEME

The themes of unity and mutual respect are underscored by the stipulation of an equal contribution of shell strings from each Nation.

REFLECTING ON THE SELECTION

Why do you think the Iroquois Constitution survived so long? (It articulates basic, widely held beliefs about justice, peace, and brotherhood.)

STUDY QUESTIONS

1. the Tree of the Great Peace; warn people of evil or danger
2. - Smoke shall ascend so other nations see the Council Fire.
   - peace, good-will, patience
3. They are "useful and necessary."
4. shell strings, five arrows
5. Trees are tall, majestic, deep-rooted, long-lived, and protective.
6. With a firm foundation laws can be added as one adds a new beam or rafter in enlarging a house.
7. - *National holidays:* "Festivals"
   - *Legislative houses:* "Laws," paragraph 2
   - *Parliamentary procedure:* "Laws," paragraphs 1–4
   - *Amendments:* "Laws," paragraph 5
8. As the five arrows symbolized the Five Nations, so the 13 stripes represent the 13 original colonies and the 50 stars represent the 50 states.

Thomas Jefferson *1743–1826*

Thomas Jefferson wanted John Adams to draft the Declaration of Independence. "I will not," said Adams. "What can be your reasons?" Jefferson asked. Adams replied, "You can write ten times better than I can." "Well," said Jefferson, "if you are decided, I will do as well as I can."

The author of the most famous statement of American principles was born and raised in Virginia, where he studied law, became both an excellent horseman and a competent violinist, and began his public life as a member of the Virginia House of Burgesses. Jefferson was devoted to the growth of both the American land and the American mind. This man of many talents cultivated ten thousand acres of land and built a library of ten thousand volumes, the books that were ultimately the beginning of the Library of Congress. He was a philosopher, scientist, farmer, architect, and inventor (he invented a plow that revolutionized farming); he was governor of Virginia, ambassador to France, and third President of the United States.

Despite his sophistication as a scholar and a gentleman, Jefferson put all the force of his personality behind the drive to build a society based upon equality. He refused to allow his birthday to become a national holiday or to allow coins to be stamped with his image. Democracy was a genuine way of life for him, and his vision of America was a nation in which every family would live freely, independently, and close to the land. His only published book, *Notes on the State of Virginia* (1785), is one of the most important books of its time, a record of Jefferson's beliefs, especially that "those who labor in the earth are the chosen people of God."

In the Declaration of Independence, Jefferson addresses not only his fellow Americans but the rest of the world as well. He wants "to place before mankind the common sense of the subject, in terms so plain and firm as to command their assent."

■ What does Jefferson see the "common sense of the subject" to be?

Thomas Jefferson

Declaration of Independence

1 When in the Course of human events it becomes necessary for one people to dissolve the political bands which have connected them with another, and to assume among the powers of the earth the separate and equal station to which the Laws of Nature and of Nature's God entitle them, a decent respect to the opinions of mankind requires that they should declare the causes which impel them to the separation.

We hold these truths to be self-evident: that
2 all men are created equal; that they are endowed by their Creator with certain unalienable[1] Rights; that among these are Life, Liberty and the pursuit of Happiness; That to secure these rights, Governments are instituted among Men, deriving their just powers from the consent of the governed; That whenever any Form of Government becomes destructive of these ends, it is the Right of the People to alter or to abolish it, and to institute new Government, laying its foundation on such principles, and organizing its powers in such form, as to them shall seem most likely to effect their Safety and Happiness. Prudence, indeed, will dictate that Governments long established should not be changed for light and transient causes; and accordingly all experience hath shown that mankind are more disposed to suffer while evils are sufferable than to right themselves by abolishing the forms to which
3 they are accustomed. But when a long train of abuses and usurpations,[2] pursuing invariably the same Objects, evinces a design to reduce them under absolute Despotism,[3] it is their right, it is their duty, to throw off such Government, and to provide new Guards for their future security. Such has been the patient sufferance of these Colonies; and such is now the necessity which constrains[4] them to alter their former Systems of Government. The history of the present King of Great Britain is a history of
4 repeated injuries and usurpations, all having in direct object the establishment of an absolute Tyranny over these States. To prove this, let Facts be submitted to a candid[5] world.

He has refused his Assent to Laws the most wholesome and necessary for the public good.

He has forbidden his Governors to pass Laws of immediate and pressing importance, unless suspended in their operation till his Assent should be obtained; and when so suspended, he has utterly neglected to attend to them.

He has refused to pass other Laws for the accommodation of large districts of people, unless those people would relinquish the right of Representation in the Legislature, a right inestimable to them and formidable to tyrants only.

He has called together legislative bodies at places unusual, uncomfortable, and distant from the depository of their public records, for the sole purpose of fatiguing them into compliance with his measures.

He has dissolved Representative Houses repeatedly, for opposing with manly firmness his invasions on the rights of the people.

He has refused for a long time after such dissolutions to cause others to be elected, whereby the Legislative powers, incapable of Annihilation, have returned to the People at large for their exercise, the State remaining in the mean time exposed to all the dangers of invasions from without and convulsions within.

He has endeavored to prevent the population of these States; for that purpose obstructing the Laws for Naturalization of Foreigners,

1. **unalienable:** that cannot be taken away.
2. **usurpations:** unlawful seizures of power.
3. **Despotism:** tyranny.
4. **constrains:** forces.
5. **candid:** impartial.

AT A GLANCE

- A declaration of independence requires explanation.
- Governments exist to guarantee unalienable rights to citizens.
- The British have abused their own laws in their treatment of the colonies.

LITERARY OPTIONS

- persuasion
- style

THEMATIC OPTIONS

- government by consent
- individual rights

1 ENLIGHTENMENT IDEA

The reasoned tone articulates the belief that humans can shape their own destiny.

2 STYLE: PARALLELISM

Parallel sentence structure adds conviction to the list of "self-evident" truths of which Jefferson seeks to persuade his readers.

3 TONE

Jefferson creates a calm, reasoned tone and infuses the Declaration with majesty by using straightforward adjectives *(absolute)* and highly evocative nouns *(abuses, usurpation)* and verbs *(reduce, throw off)*.

4 AUDIENCE

By identifying his audience as members of "the candid world," Jefferson seeks to legitimize America's sovereignty and enlist the approval of other nations.

GUIDED READING

LITERAL QUESTIONS

1a. Which human rights are unalienable? (life, liberty, and the pursuit of happiness)

2a. What is the aim of Britain in these injuries and usurpations? (absolute tyranny over the colonies)

INFERENTIAL QUESTIONS

1b. How would you explain the meaning of the phrase *the pursuit of happiness?* (Answers may include personal freedom to make one's own decisions and the right to choose one's own form of government.)

2b. Why do you think the colonists saw British rule as tyranny? (Students may say that it cut the colonists off from a legal process or that it did not allow them to live by their beliefs.)

AT A GLANCE

- Jefferson lists the king's abuses of the law.
- He describes the crown's use of force to subdue the colonists.
- He enumerates America's attempts to reach conciliation with England.

1 PERSUASION

Repeated use of *He* adds to Jefferson's argument, as it reinforces the idea of the king as a belligerent and aggressive force trampling on the inherent rights of the colonists.

2 PERSUASION

Jefferson persuasively underscores the reasons behind the revolt by repeating *For* in a series of indictments.

3 STYLE: WORD CHOICE

Jefferson adds emotional intensity as he shifts from more objective, legalistic language to such strong verbs as *plundered* and *ravaged* to attack the Crown.

4 THEME

Jefferson eloquently articulates his belief in people's natural right to freedom and to a voice in government as he recounts the colonists' attempts to petition the king for redress.

refusing to pass others to encourage their migration hither, and raising the conditions of new Appropriations of Lands.

He has obstructed the Administration of Justice, by refusing his Assent to Laws for establishing Judiciary powers.

He has made Judges dependent on his Will alone for the tenure of their offices, and the amount and payment of their salaries.

He has erected a multitude of New Offices, and sent hither swarms of Officers to harass our people and eat out their substance.

1 He has kept among us, in times of peace, Standing Armies, without the Consent of our legislatures.

He has affected to render the Military independent of, and superior to, the Civil power.

He has combined with others to subject us to a jurisdiction foreign to our constitutions and unacknowledged by our laws; giving his Assent to their Acts of pretended Legislation:

For quartering large bodies of armed troops among us;

For protecting them, by a mock Trial, from punishment for any Murders which they should commit on the Inhabitants of these States;

For cutting off our Trade with all parts of the world;

2 For imposing Taxes on us without our Consent;

For depriving us, in many cases, of the benefits of Trial by Jury;

For transporting us beyond Seas to be tried for pretended offenses;

For abolishing the free System of English Laws in a neighboring Province,[6] establishing therein an Arbitrary government, and enlarging its Boundaries, so as to render it at once an example and fit instrument for introducing the same absolute rule into these Colonies;

For taking away our Charters, abolishing our most valuable Laws, and altering, fundamentally, the Forms of our Governments;

For suspending our own Legislatures, and declaring themselves invested with Power to legislate for us in all cases whatsoever.

He has abdicated Government here, by declaring us out of his Protection and waging War against us.

3 He has plundered our seas, ravaged our Coasts, burned our towns, and destroyed the lives of our people.

He is at this time transporting large Armies of foreign Mercenaries to complete the works of death, desolation and tyranny, already begun with circumstances of Cruelty and perfidy[7] scarcely paralleled in the most barbarous ages, and totally unworthy the Head of a civilized nation.

He has constrained our fellow Citizens taken Captive on the high Seas to bear Arms against their Country, to become the executioners of their friends and Brethren, or to fall themselves by their Hands.

He has excited domestic insurrections amongst us, and has endeavored to bring on the inhabitants of our frontiers the merciless Indian Savages whose known rule of warfare is an undistinguished destruction of all ages, sexes, and conditions.

4 In every stage of these Oppressions We have Petitioned for Redress[8] in the most humble terms. Our repeated Petitions have been answered only by repeated injury. A Prince whose character is thus marked by every act which may define a Tyrant is unfit to be the ruler of a free people.

Nor have We been wanting in attentions to our British brethren. We have warned them from time to time of attempts by their legislature[9] to extend an unwarrantable jurisdiction over us. We have reminded them of the circumstances of our emigration and settlement here. We have appealed to their native justice and magnanimity, and we have conjured[10]

6. **abolishing . . . neighboring Province:** In 1774 the British, having captured Quebec, forced strict laws on colonists there.

7. **perfidy** [pur′fi dē]: betrayal of trust.

8. **Redress** [ri dres′]: just compensation for a wrong done.

9. **their legislature:** British Parliament.

10. **conjured:** solemnly appealed to.

GUIDED READING

LITERAL QUESTIONS

1a. In what position has the king placed military power in the colonies? (It is independent of and superior to civil power.)

2a. What does the Declaration warn the British people about? (Parliament's attempts to attain jurisdiction over the colonies)

INFERENTIAL QUESTIONS

1b. What do you think are the dangers of this type of action? (It leads to a military government; it could mean the increasing use of force; it could shut the people entirely out of the process of government.)

2b. In his arguments against British rule, why does Jefferson include pleas made earlier to the British people? (He wants the world to know that the American colonies have tried every reasonable course of action before declaring independence.)

Yale University Art Gallery

The Declaration of Independence, John Trumbull, 1786.

them by the ties of our common kindred to disavow these usurpations, which would inevitably interrupt our connections and correspondence. They too have been deaf to the voice of justice and of consanguinity.[11] We must therefore acquiesce in the necessity which denounces[12] our Separation and hold them, as we hold the rest of mankind, Enemies in War, in Peace Friends.

1 We, therefore, the Representatives of the United States of America in General Congress Assembled, appealing to the Supreme Judge of the world for the rectitude of our intentions, do in the Name and by the Authority of the good People of these Colonies, solemnly publish and declare that these United Colonies are and of right ought to be Free and Independent States; that they are Absolved from all Allegiance to the British Crown, and that all political connection between them and the State of Great Britain is and ought to be totally dis-
2 solved, and that as Free and Independent States, they have full Power to levy War, conclude Peace, contract Alliances, establish Commerce, and to do all other Acts and Things which Independent States may of right do.

And for the support of this Declaration, with a firm reliance on the protection of Divine Providence, we mutually pledge to each other our Lives, our Fortunes, and our sacred Honor.

11. **consanguinity** [kon′sang gwin′ə tē]: blood relationship.
12. **denounces:** here, announces.

AT A GLANCE

- The colonies declare their independence.
- Jefferson lists America's rights as a sovereign nation.
- The colonies' pledge of allegiance to each other concludes the Declaration.

1 PERSUASION

In affirming that God will judge the rectitude of the colonists' actions, Jefferson invokes the power of righteousness to add further weight to his proposal.

2 THEME

The enumeration of American rights, as befitting a sovereign nation, echoes the earlier citation of "unalienable rights."

REFLECTING ON THE DOCUMENT

What elements do you think contribute most to the persuasive power of the Declaration of Independence? (Answers may refer to its calm, reasoned tone; the evidence presented; the impressive style of the writing.)

STUDY QUESTIONS

1. justifying the separation when political ties are dissolved
2. All men are created equal and endowed with the rights of life, liberty, pursuit of happiness. Government's purpose is to secure these rights; a government should be replaced when it fails to do so.
3. establish tyranny; enumerates the king's tyrannical acts
4. petitioned for redress; the voice of justice
5. the independence of the colonies
6. proves by example King George's failure to secure colonists' rights and his behavior as a tyrant
7. Faith in reason is implied in the assumption that the world will understand Americans' actions if explained. People will endure evils when possible, will only revolt with good reason. Colonists' attempts at redress show them as reasonable, in contrast to King George.
8. Answers will vary. The leaders of the rebellion would have been executed, their lands confiscated, families forced to flee. Such had been the fate of Irish and Scottish rebels in the 1600s and 1700s.

VIEWPOINT

Each specific grievance helps define public happiness. For example, "He has made judges dependent on his will alone" implies that an independent judiciary is necessary.

VOCABULARY

forbidden, dissolved, obstructed, to harass, to subject, abdicated, plundered, destroyed, constrained

STUDY QUESTIONS

Recalling

1. According to the first paragraph, what does "a decent respect to the opinions of mankind" require?
2. According to the second paragraph, what truths are self-evident? What is the purpose of government, and when should a government be replaced?
3. Moving from a theory of government to the situation in 1776, what does Jefferson claim King George's "direct object" has been in the colonies? How does Jefferson set out to prove his claim?
4. What does Jefferson say the Americans have done "in every stage of these Oppressions"? To what does he say "our British brethren" have been deaf?
5. What does the final paragraph "publish and declare"?

Interpreting

6. Why does including Jefferson's bill of particulars make the Declaration more effective?
7. How is the faith in reason characteristic of the eighteenth century reflected in the opening paragraph? In Jefferson's remarks about Prudence in the second paragraph? In the description of the colonists' peaceful attempts to redress their grievances?

Extending

8. In the final sentence of the Declaration, the signers pledge their "Fortunes," or fate. What do you think their fate would have been if Britain had been the victor in the Revolution?

VIEWPOINT

The historian Garry Wills explains the following about the Declaration of Independence:

> When Jefferson spoke of pursuing happiness, he had nothing vague or private in mind. He meant a public happiness which is measurable, which is, indeed, the test and justification of any government.
>
> —*Inventing America: Jefferson's Declaration of Independence*

■ List three statements from the Declaration that suggest what Jefferson's idea of "public happiness" was.

VOCABULARY

Loaded Words

A **loaded word** has a particularly strong set of associations for the reader. Such a word arouses strong feelings and appeals to the emotions. A writer often deliberately uses loaded words to move people to action by appealing to their feelings, to their fears and prejudices, or to their hopes and illusions.

Jefferson uses very strong, loaded nouns when describing the behavior of King George. For example, he writes about *usurpations, despotism,* and *tyranny.* Jefferson also selects verbs with very negative associations. He says, for example, that King George "has refused" and "has endeavored to prevent."

■ Find five more verbs that describe the king's actions in such a way as to rouse Jefferson's audience to anger.

COMPOSITION

Citing Evidence

■ Write a brief composition in which you give three reasons why you think the Declaration of Independence is a successful political statement. Is it its clarity, its reasonableness, its passion, its rhetoric? State your opinion, and then cite specific examples to support it. *For help with this assignment, refer to Lesson 3 in the Writing About Literature Handbook at the back of this book.*

Writing a Letter to the Editor

■ Assume that you are writing a letter to the editor of your local newspaper. Using the Declaration of Independence as a basis, address the people of your community. First list three things that the Declaration means to you, and then tell what it can continue to mean for your community. Be sure to indicate in your letter the specific Age of Reason ideas and principles that are still valid and can be carried over into the twentieth century.

COMPOSITION: GUIDELINES FOR EVALUATION

CITING EVIDENCE

Objective

To support critical opinions with evidence

Guidelines for Evaluation

- suggested length: three to four paragraphs
- should give three reasons the Declaration succeeds as a political statement
- should state political purpose of each reason
- should cite specific examples from the Declaration to support each general reason

WRITING A LETTER TO THE EDITOR

Objective

To write a letter expressing an opinion

Guidelines for Evaluation

- suggested length: two to four paragraphs
- should address people of community
- should list three opinions about Declaration
- should explain Declaration's current relevance
- should show understanding of Age of Reason
- should use appropriate style for community

Thomas Paine *1737–1809*

America's most effective revolutionary propagandist failed at many jobs before he became a journalist. While he was growing up in England, he tried life as a corset maker, a grocer, a sailor, a teacher, and a tax collector. By the time he left England for America, he was thirty-seven years old and well acquainted with poverty, disappointment, and sorrow: His first wife had died after less than one year of marriage.

Paine came to America because he had met Benjamin Franklin in London. Franklin gave Paine the encouragement he desperately needed, as well as a letter of introduction praising him as an "ingenious, worthy young man." Franklin's insight certainly paid off. Within two years Tom Paine became a successful journalist, publishing anonymously the pamphlet *Common Sense* in January of 1776, the first American cry for complete independence. *Common Sense* sold almost a half million copies. Nothing that had been written in America was so widely read or so influential.

The rest of Paine's life was marked by career failures, private disappointments, and public controversies. Nevertheless, he persisted in writing against tyranny and monarchy. *The Rights of Man* (1791–1792), for example, is the work of a man who combined clear thinking with an intense feeling for human possibilities.

The American Crisis, Number 1 is the first of sixteen pamphlets Paine wrote beginning in December 1776. At that time, five months after the Declaration of Independence, Washington's forces were retreating, their morale low. The American commander had these stirring words, which begin on the following page, read to his men just before they crossed the Delaware to fight at Trenton.

■ How do we define courage and cowardice today?

AT A GLANCE

- Americans face a crisis, but real patriots will stand fast.
- British rule means slavery.
- God will aid Americans in their struggle.

LITERARY OPTIONS

- persuasion
- theme

THEMATIC OPTIONS

- freedom as a worthy cause
- personal courage
- confronting obstacles

1 AUDIENCE

Paine uses strong, blunt adjectives and verbs ("summer," "sunshine," "try," "shrink") that will appeal to working-class Americans.

2 PERSUASION

Paine's abrupt transition to the first person and his open revelation of personal opinion add sincerity and intensity to his claim of God's support.

Thomas Paine

from The American Crisis

1 These are the times that try men's souls. The summer soldier and the sunshine patriot will, in this crisis, shrink from the service of their country; but he that stands it *now,* deserves the love and thanks of man and woman. Tyranny, like hell, is not easily conquered; yet we have this consolation with us, that the harder the conflict, the more glorious the triumph. What we obtain too cheap, we esteem too lightly: it is dearness only that gives every thing its value. Heaven knows how to put a proper price upon its goods; and it would be strange indeed if so celestial an article as *freedom* should not be highly rated. Britain, with an army to enforce her tyranny, has declared that she has a right not only to *tax* but "to *bind* us in *all cases whatsoever*"; and if being *bound in that manner* is not slavery, then is there not such a thing as slavery upon earth. Even the expression is impious; for so unlimited a power can belong only to God. . . .

2 I have as little superstition in me as any man living, but my secret opinion has ever been, and still is, that God Almighty will not give up a people to military destruction, or leave them unsupportedly to perish, who have so earnestly and so repeatedly sought to avoid the calamities of war, by every decent method which wisdom could invent. Neither have I so much of the infidel[1] in me as to suppose that

1. **infidel:** unbeliever.

First Blow for Liberty, A. H. Ritchie. Nineteenth-century engraving.

GUIDED READING

LITERAL QUESTION

1a. What does Paine refer to as "impious"? (the British declaration to bind the Americans in "all cases whatsoever")

INFERENTIAL QUESTION

1b. What implications are raised by such a comment? (Britain is guilty of blasphemous pride. British attempts to dominate are irreligious; God is on the colonists' side.)

He has relinquished the government of the
world, and given us up to the care of devils;
1 and as I do not, I cannot see on what grounds
the king of Britain can look up to heaven for
help against us: a common murderer, a highwayman, or a housebreaker, has as good a pretense as he. . . .

I once felt all that kind of anger which a man ought to feel against the mean[2] principles that are held by the Tories:[3] a noted one, who kept a tavern at Amboy, was standing at his door, with as pretty a child in his hand, about eight or nine years old, as I ever saw, and after speaking his mind as freely as he thought was prudent, finished with this unfatherly expression, "Well! give me peace in my day." Not a man lives on the continent but fully believes that a separation must some time or other finally take place, and a generous parent should have said, "If there must be trouble, let it be in my day, that my child may have peace"; and this single reflection, well applied, is sufficient to awaken every man to duty. Not a place upon earth might be so happy as America. Her situation is remote from all the wrangling world, and she has nothing to do but to trade
with them. A man can distinguish himself be-
2 tween temper and principle, and I am as confident, as I am that God governs the world,
that America will never be happy till she gets
clear of foreign dominion. Wars, without ceasing, will break out till that period arrives, and
the continent must in the end be conqueror;
for though the flame of liberty may sometimes
cease to shine, the coal can never expire. . . .

2. **mean:** small-minded.
3. **Tories:** colonists loyal to Great Britain.

STUDY QUESTIONS

Recalling

1. According to the first paragraph, whom is Paine criticizing? Whom is he praising?
2. According to the first paragraph, what is the purpose of Britain's army? What has Britain declared?
3. What "secret opinion" does Paine state in his second paragraph?
4. What does the third paragraph state about the possibility of happiness in America? What does it say must be accomplished before America can be happy?

Interpreting

5. What is the price of freedom, according to Paine? For what is Paine, therefore, criticizing the "summer soldiers," the "sunshine patriots," and the tavernkeeper in Amboy?
6. To what emotions does Paine appeal when he describes the king of Britain? Where in this selection does Paine rely on reason rather than emotion?

Extending

7. The "crisis" Paine speaks of was nothing less than the potential defeat of the American armies. Do you think Paine's words have a more general application as well?

VIEWPOINT

Tom Paine himself once said that his purpose as a writer was to use plain language

> to make those who can scarcely read understand . . . [and] to fit the powers of thinking and the turn of language to the subject, so as to bring out a clear conclusion that shall hit the point in question and nothing else.

■ Cite at least one sentence from *Crisis* in which you think Paine achieves this purpose.

AT A GLANCE

- God will not aid the British.
- The colonists must fight now so that their children will be free.
- America's happiness lies in her sovereignty.

1 THEME

Comparing the king to a common criminal dramatically reinforces the presentation of the struggle for freedom as a holy cause.

2 PERSUASION

Paine balances his confidence in America's ultimate happiness with his conviction that God rules the world.

REFLECTING ON THE SELECTION

Do you think that Paine appeals more to the "head" of his audience, or to its "heart"? (He appeals more to the heart, because his arguments are chiefly emotional.)

STUDY QUESTIONS

1. summer soldier and sunshine patriot; those who fight
2. enforce tyranny; a right to bind the colonies "in all cases"
3. God will not desert Americans.
4. happiest place on Earth; "get clear" of foreign rule
5. war; selfishly leave it to others to fight
6.
   - indignation, anger
   - Paine's comments about America's remoteness from Europe support his claim that America can be the world's happiest place.
7. Possible answers include Paine's ideas about patriotism, the value of freedom, the need to fight oppression.

VIEWPOINT

any sentence in first paragraph

LITERARY FOCUS

- the anecdote about the tavernkeeper
- "not a man . . . not a place"
- vivid language ("flame of liberty"); exaggeration ("wars, without ceasing"); metaphor of the flickering flame and undying coal of liberty

COMPARING WRITERS

Answers will vary. Students should consider the techniques of persuasion discussed on pages 22 and 84. They should see that Paine appeals to emotions, Henry to reason and emotions, Jefferson chiefly to reason; that Paine and Henry are more emotional in tone than Jefferson. Paine and Henry seek to win support among Americans for the Revolution; Jefferson addresses the world and posterity.

LITERARY FOCUS

Methods of Persuasion

Paine's *Crisis* is a superb example of persuasive writing (see page 22). To persuade colonial men and women to stand firm, take courage, and continue fighting, he uses a number of methods:

Concrete examples. Good persuasion supports general statements with facts, quotations, and other examples to convince the audience that the general statements are true. In paragraph 1 Paine declares that Britain's army "enforces tyranny"; to support this statement, he quotes directly from the British themselves.

Vivid language. Vivid language and images appeal to the audience's emotions and make persuasive writing powerful. Consider how much weaker Paine's opening statement would be if he merely said, "These are bad times."

Exaggeration. Persuasive writers often exaggerate in order to rouse the emotions of their audiences. Paine says, for example, that Americans have sought to avoid war "by every decent method which wisdom could invent." By overstating, he makes his point.

Repetition. By repeating words and ideas, the persuasive writer emphasizes their importance and lodges them even more firmly in the minds of the audience. When Paine wants to say that King George has committed crimes against the Americans, he combines exaggeration and repetition: He compares the king to "a common murderer, a highwayman, or a housebreaker."

Parallelism. **Parallelism** is the repeating of phrases or sentences so that the repeated parts are alike in structure or in meaning. By using balanced sentences with parallel structures, a persuasive writer creates a rhythm that reinforces the message. Paine says, "The harder the conflict, the more glorious the triumph." Parallel structures add a feeling of completeness and sureness of thought to what the writer has to say.

Thinking About Methods of Persuasion

- What concrete example in the third paragraph illustrates Paine's feelings about the Tories? Where in the third paragraph does Paine repeat words and sentence structures? What makes his final sentence so forceful?

COMPOSITION

Writing About Persuasion

- Write a short essay in which you first state the purpose of either Henry's speech (page 66) or the Declaration of Independence (page 77). Then cite with examples the particular techniques that Henry or Jefferson uses to accomplish his purpose. *For help with this assignment, refer to Lesson 4 in the Writing About Literature Handbook at the back of this book.*

Writing Persuasion

- Compose a short speech, a newspaper editorial, or a radio or television commercial intended to persuade someone to take action on a matter of urgent public interest. You may want to analyze a few examples from today's media before writing your own. Include concrete examples, vivid language, exaggeration, repetition, and parallel structure to make your argument more persuasive.

COMPARING WRITERS

- If you had been indecisive about America's role in the years before the Revolution, which would have influenced you more to join the Revolution—Henry's speech, Jefferson's Declaration, or Paine's pamphlet? Compare at least two of these selections, citing specific examples of the arguments each uses and the emotional responses each calls up. Tell how the attitude and style of each author affects his argument, making it more or less persuasive.

COMPOSITION: GUIDELINES FOR EVALUATION

WRITING ABOUT PERSUASION

Objective

To analyze a piece of persuasive writing

Guidelines for Evaluation

- suggested length: five to seven paragraphs
- should state purpose of document
- should cite examples of vivid language, exaggeration, repetition, parallelism
- should explain how these techniques make the work persuasive

WRITING PERSUASION

Objective

To write a persuasive public statement

Guidelines for Evaluation:

- suggested length: three to five paragraphs
- should take a stand on an issue
- should recommend the audience take action
- should use examples, vivid language, exaggeration, repetition, parallel structure

Phillis Wheatley *1754?–1784*

Phillis Wheatley's life remains a testament to the triumph of talent over difficult circumstances. When she was about eight years old, she was taken from her home in Africa, brought on a slave ship to Boston, and sold to a wealthy family, the Wheatleys, who gave her their name and their religion. They also recognized her extraordinary talents. Within two years she had learned English and was reading the Bible. Soon she was reading the great English poets, such as Milton and Pope, as well as Latin writers, such as Virgil and Terence.

Wheatley was only sixteen when she published her first poem. It made her famous, and at nineteen she went to London, where she became a celebrity and where her *Poems on Various Subjects, Religious and Moral* was published in 1773. Back in Boston she continued to write, but her last years were sad ones, marked by obscurity and poverty.

"To His Excellency, General Washington" is typical of Wheatley's verse: modeled on the conventions of the English poetry of the time, formal, elegant, making frequent use of classical allusions. Thomas Paine was the first to publish the poem in his *Philadelphia Magazine* in 1775. Washington himself liked the poem so much that he wrote to Wheatley and invited her to visit him. She did meet Washington in Cambridge, Massachusetts, in 1776, but unfortunately no record exists of what these two Americans from such different backgrounds said to each other.

■ What do you imagine Wheatley and Washington most wanted to tell each other?

AT A GLANCE

- The speaker addresses herself to the angels.
- She speaks of America's glorious struggle for freedom.

LITERARY OPTIONS

- heroic couplet
- personification

THEMATIC OPTIONS

- the nobility of America
- the heroism of Washington
- the rightness of a holy cause

SPEAKER

Using a lofty and classical style for the invocation, the speaker places America's struggle in a heroic framework (ll. 1–2).

PERSONIFICATION

Attributing the feelings of a grief-stricken mother to the earth allows Wheatley to maintain classical conventions while adding emotional intensity to the depiction of America's plight (l. 5).

Phillis Wheatley

To His Excellency, General Washington

Celestial choir! enthron'd in realms of light,
Columbia's[1] scenes of glorious toils I write.
While freedom's cause her anxious breast alarms,
She flashes dreadful in refulgent[2] arms.
See mother earth her offspring's fate bemoan,
And nations gaze at scenes before unknown!

---

1. **Columbia:** goddess personifying America.
2. **refulgent** [ri ful′jənt]: brightly shining.

AT A GLANCE

- The speaker asks for poetic inspiration.
- She names George Washington as one subject of her praise.
- She acknowledges divine support of America's cause in general and Washington's strategies in particular.

SYMBOL

Wheatley uses the symbols of the olive, which represents peace, and the laurel, which stands for victory and distinction, to suggest both the fundamental nobility of America's character and the inevitability of her success (l. 10).

ALLUSION

By invoking the image of Eolus' fury, Wheatley infuses America's newly formed military forces with a powerful, divine aspect (ll. 15–16).

RHYTHM AND PARALLELISM

Wheatley uses the natural caesura in line 27 to create a parallel structure *(thy valor, thy virtues)* that balances with the stressed *thy* in line 28 to highlight Washington's virtues.

MAIN IDEA

In referring to Washington's victory over the French, Wheatley implies divine and invincible support for America's struggle (ll. 30–33).

REFLECTING ON THE POEM

What does personifying America as "Columbia" contribute to the picture of the struggle? (It makes the struggle more heroic and also more meaningful in emotional human terms.)

See the bright beams of heaven's revolving light
Involved in sorrows and the veil of night!

The goddess comes, she moves divinely fair,
Olive and laurel binds her golden hair:
Wherever shines this native of the skies,
Unnumber'd charms and recent graces rise.

Muse![3] bow propitious while my pen relates
How pour her armies through a thousand gates,
As when Eolus[4] heaven's fair face deforms,
Enwrapp'd in tempest and a night of storms;
Astonish'd ocean feels the wild uproar,
The refluent[5] surges beat the sounding shore;
Or thick as leaves in Autumn's golden reign,
Such, and so many, moves the warrior's train.
In bright array they seek the work of war,
Where high unfurl'd the ensign[6] waves in air.
Shall I to Washington their praise recite?
Enough thou know'st them in the fields of fight.
Thee, first in peace and honors—we demand
The grace and glory of thy martial band.
Fam'd for thy valor, for thy virtues more,
Hear every tongue thy guardian aid implore!

One century scarce perform'd its destined round,
When Gallic[7] powers Columbia's fury found;
And so may you, whoever dares disgrace
The land of freedom's heaven-defended race!
Fix'd are the eyes of nations on the scales,
For in their hopes Columbia's arm prevails.
Anon Britannia[8] droops the pensive head,
While round increase the rising hills of dead.
Ah! cruel blindness to Columbia's state!
Lament thy thirst of boundless power too late.

Proceed, great chief, with virtue on thy side,
Thy ev'ry action let the goddess guide.
A crown, a mansion, and a throne that shine,
With gold unfading, WASHINGTON! be thine.

3. **Muse:** Wheatley asks the aid of the goddess who presides over the creation of poetry.
4. **Eolus** [ē′ə ləs]: in Greek mythology, god of the winds.
5. **refluent** [ref′lo͞o ənt]: flowing back.
6. **ensign:** flag.
7. **Gallic:** French. Washington fought the French during the French and Indian War (1754–1763).
8. **Britannia:** goddess personifying Great Britain.

STUDY QUESTIONS

Recalling

1. What phrases does Wheatley use in lines 3–4 to describe the goddess Columbia? In lines 10–13?
2. What does Wheatley call George Washington in line 25? What does he have on his side, according to line 39?
3. According to lines 29–32, what defends America? What will happen to anyone who disgraces America?

Interpreting

4. Identify at least three positive qualities of America in Wheatley's portrait.
5. How are Washington's virtues tied to Wheatley's portrait of America? What, ultimately, makes him noble?
6. In what ways can this poem be seen as a warning? What is Wheatley suggesting about the American forces when she uses the images of the storm (lines 15–18) and the leaves (lines 19–20)?

Extending

7. Explain how Wheatley is continuing an American tradition, begun by Puritan writers, when she calls Americans a "heaven-defended race."

LITERARY FOCUS

The Heroic Couplet

Phillis Wheatley wrote most of her verse in the form that dominated English poetry in the eighteenth century, the heroic couplet. A **heroic couplet** is a pair of rhymed lines in iambic pentameter. Each line, therefore, has ten syllables and five beats, or accents:

> Anón Británnia dróops the pénsive héad
> While róund incréase the rísing hílls of dréad

To keep the regular pattern of ten syllables and five beats, however, some words give up a syllable (for example, *Britannia,* pronounced as *Bri tan'yə*).

Literary taste changes from age to age. For over two centuries poets and readers enjoyed heroic couplets and accepted them as a standard of English verse. Skillful poets have been able to make this pattern sound natural and have used it to create great poetry. The English poets Geoffrey Chaucer and Alexander Pope were masters of the heroic couplet. To the ears of some modern readers, however, the couplet may sound too regular when used for more than a few lines at a time. Nevertheless, even though this form is now mainly used for a humorous or a deliberately archaic effect, we can still hear in poems like Wheatley's the noble accents and attitudes of a time past.

Thinking About the Heroic Couplet

■ Anne Bradstreet's "To My Dear and Loving Husband" (page 31) uses the heroic couplet. Choose two of Bradstreet's couplets and point out the accented syllables and the end rhymes.

VOCABULARY

Sentence Completions

Each of the following sentences contains a blank with four possible words for completing the sentence. The words are from "To His Excellency, General Washington." Choose the word that completes each sentence correctly, using the word *as it is used in this selection.* Write the number of each item and the letter of your choice on a separate sheet.

1. Since the boss is in a generous mood, it seems a _____ time to ask him for a raise.
   (a) celestial (c) pensive
   (b) propitious (d) martial
2. The troops are in battle _____.
   (a) array (c) reign
   (b) ensign (d) laurel
3. The expression on the girl's face was _____ as she thought through her dilemma.
   (a) destined (c) unfurled
   (b) pensive (d) celestial
4. I call upon the _____ of poetry to inspire my song.
   (a) Britannia (c) Eolus
   (b) Columbia (d) Muse
5. His _____ spirit was expressed in the belligerent thrust of his jaw.
   (a) pensive (c) celestial
   (b) martial (d) propitious

STUDY QUESTIONS

1. "her anxious breast alarms/ She flashes dreadful in refulgent arms"; "Olive and laurel binds her golden hair"; "shines"; "Unnumbered charms and recent graces"
2. "first in peace and honors"; virtue
3. Heaven; will face "Columbia's fury"
4. fights for freedom; is a land of grace, glory, valor; has virtue on its side; is protected by Heaven
5. Washington and America have similar virtues, and he takes his virtues from his place in history; he is America's defender.
6. Anyone threatening America will be defeated. American forces are as strong, innumerable, and invincible as the forces of nature.
7. Answers will vary. Puritans also saw selves as under God's special protection.

LITERARY FOCUS

Answers will vary. Examples:

- If éver twó were óne, then súrely wé.
  If éver mán were lóved by wífe, then thée, . . .
  (End rhymes: *we/thee*)
- Thy lóve is súch I cán no wáy repáy;
  The héavens rewárd thee mánifóld, I práy.
  (End rhymes: *repay/pray*)

VOCABULARY

1. (b) propitious
2. (a) array
3. (b) pensive
4. (d) Muse
5. (b) martial

William Bartram *1739–1823*

William Bartram virtually grew up in the botanical garden built by his father in Philadelphia. John Bartram, the first American botanist, took William with him on explorations and scientific expeditions in search of America's plants and flowers. William's interest in observing and describing nature remained strong all his life.

In 1773 Bartram set out alone on a two-year journey through the Carolinas, Georgia, Florida, and Mississippi. He collected specimens of plants and animals, made careful drawings, observed life on the frontier, and took a special interest in the American Indians he met. As a mark of honor, the Seminole Indians of Florida named him the Flower Hunter.

Bartram's record of the journey was published in 1791 with a typical, meticulous, Age of Reason title: *Travels Through North and South Carolina, Georgia, East and West Florida, the Cherokee Country, the Extensive Territories of the Muscogulges, or Creek Confederacy, and the Country of the Chactaws.* The book was especially popular in Europe and was praised by the English poets Wordsworth and Coleridge. Like Crèvecoeur's essays (see page 93), published at about the same time, Bartram's book presented an image of America as a place truly appropriate for the "pursuit of happiness."

Bartram was a scientist, an Enlightenment man in America, but he was also something of a poet himself. His writing combines observation and adventure, objectivity and excitement. Bartram communicates his sense of the sheer *wonder* of what he saw—things few Americans had ever seen.

■ How would you describe an alligator to someone who has never seen one?

William Bartram's drawing of the alligators of east Florida.

William Bartram

from Travels

The Alligators of East Florida

1 The noise of the crocodiles[1] kept me awake the greater part of the night, but when I arose in the morning, contrary to my expectations, there was perfect peace; very few of them to be seen, and those were asleep on the shore. Yet I was not able to suppress my fears and apprehensions of being attacked by them in future; and indeed yesterday's combat with them, notwithstanding I came off in a manner victorious, or at least made a safe retreat, had left sufficient impression on my mind to damp my courage; and it seemed too much for one of my strength, being alone in a very small boat, to encounter such collected danger.

To pursue my voyage up the river, and be obliged every evening to pass such dangerous
2 defiles,[2] appeared to me as perilous as running the gauntlet[3] betwixt two rows of Indians armed with knives and firebrands. I however resolved to continue my voyage one day longer, if I possibly could with safety, and then return down the river, should I find the like difficulties to oppose. Accordingly I got everything on board, charged my gun, and set sail, cautiously, along shore. As I passed by Battle Lagoon, I began to tremble and keep a good lookout; when suddenly a huge alligator rushed out of the reeds, and with a tremendous roar came up and darted as swift as an arrow under my boat, emerging upright on my lee quarter,

1. **crocodiles:** Bartram uses *crocodile* and *alligator* interchangeably.

2. **defiles** [dē fīlz′]: narrow passages.

3. **running the gauntlet:** punishment in which an offender was beaten while running between two rows of people.

AT A GLANCE

- Bartram wakes, afraid of being attacked by crocodiles.
- Later he loads his boat.
- A large alligator charges it.

LITERARY OPTIONS

- description
- narration

THEMATIC OPTIONS

- natural wonders of the New World
- scientific investigation

1 NARRATION

Within a primarily descriptive piece Bartram establishes an inviting narrative framework when he uses chronological order and focuses on both what he sees and how he feels.

2 AUDIENCE

Bartram helps the reader to appreciate the depth of his fear by alluding to an assault by Indians, an experience that figured prominently in the imagination of most people at the time.

GUIDED READING

LITERAL QUESTION

1a. For how long does Bartram decide to continue his trip? (one more day)

INFERENTIAL QUESTION

1b. What do you think helps Bartram to overcome his fear and continue the trip? (a combination of curiosity, wonder, and dedication to science)

AT A GLANCE

- Bartram beats off an alligator with a club.
- He observes a large brood of young crocodiles.
- He describes how females care for their young.

1 DESCRIPTION

Bartram uses the senses of sight ("open jaws," "rapidity of lightning"), sound ("belching water and smoke"), and touch ("fell upon me like rain") to create a vivid account of the crocodile assault.

2 THEME

Bartram's image of the alligator as a roaring, menacing monster conveys the fearsome yet wondrous aspects of nature in the New World.

3 THEME

Bartram's determination to examine the crocodile nests demonstrates the prevalent belief in scientific investigation.

4 DESCRIPTION

Bartram helps the reader to visualize crocodile nests clearly by providing blueprintlike details of the method of their construction.

5 NARRATION

Combining scientific observation with personal opinion and speculation, Bartram creates a narrative tone that adds interest and color to his travelogue.

1 with open jaws, and belching water and smoke that fell upon me like rain in a hurricane. I laid soundly about his head with my club, and beat him off; and after plunging and darting about my boat, he went off on a straight line through the water, seemingly with the rapidity of lightning, and entered the cape of the lagoon. I now employed my time to the very best advantage in paddling close along shore, but could not forbear looking now and then behind me, and presently perceived one of them coming
2 up again. The water of the river hereabouts was shoal[4] and very clear; the monster came up with the usual roar and menaces, and passed close by the side of my boat, when I could distinctly see a young brood of alligators, to the number of one hundred or more, following after her in a long train. They kept close together in a column, without straggling off to the one side or the other; the young appeared to be of an equal size, about fifteen inches in length, almost black, with pale yellow transverse-waved clouds or blotches, much like rattlesnakes in color. I now lost sight of my enemy again.

Still keeping close along shore, on turning a point or projection of the riverbank, at once I beheld a great number of hillocks or small pyramids, resembling haycocks,[5] ranged like an encampment along the banks. They stood fifteen or twenty yards distant from the water, on a high marsh, about four feet perpendicular above the water. I knew them to be the nests of the crocodile, having had a description of them before, and now expected a furious and general attack, as I saw several large crocodiles swimming abreast of these buildings. These
3 nests being so great a curiosity to me, I was determined at all events immediately to land and examine them. Accordingly, I ran my bark[6] on shore at one of their landing places, which was a sort of nick, or little dock, from which ascended a sloping path or road up to the edge of the meadow, where their nests were; most of them were deserted, and the great thick whitish eggshells lay broken and scattered upon the ground round about them.

The nests, or hillocks, are of the form of an obtuse[7] cone, four feet high and four or five feet in diameter at their bases; they are con-
4 structed with mud, grass, and herbage. At first they lay a floor of this kind of tempered mortar on the ground, upon which they deposit a layer of eggs, and upon this a stratum of mortar, seven or eight inches in thickness, and then another layer of eggs; and in this manner, one stratum upon another, nearly to the top. I believe they commonly lay from one to two hundred eggs in a nest. These are hatched, I suppose, by the heat of the sun; and perhaps the vegetable substances mixed with the earth, being acted upon by the sun may cause a small degree of fermentation, and so increase the heat in those hillocks. The ground for several acres about these nests showed evident marks of a continual resort[8] of alligators; the grass was everywhere beaten down, hardly a blade or straw was left standing; whereas, all about, at a distance, it was five or six feet high, and as thick as it could grow together.

5 The female, as I imagine, carefully watches her own nest of eggs until they are all hatched; or perhaps while she is attending her own brood, she takes under her care and protection as many as she can get at one time, either from her own particular nest or others; but certain it is that the young are not left to shift for themselves; for I have had frequent opportunities of seeing the female alligator leading about the shores her train of young ones, just as a hen does her brood of chickens; and she is equally assiduous and courageous in defending the young, which are under her care, and providing for their subsistence; and when she is basking upon the warm banks, with her brood around her, you may hear the young ones con-

4. **shoal** [shōl]: shallow.
5. **haycocks:** small, cone-shaped haystacks.
6. **bark:** small boat.
7. **obtuse** [əb to͞os′]: blunt on top.
8. **resort:** movement.

GUIDED READING

LITERAL QUESTIONS

1a. To what does Bartram compare the skin color of the young alligator? (the skin of the rattlesnake)

2a. What characteristics does the female alligator demonstrate in the care of her young? (courage, concern, responsibility)

INFERENTIAL QUESTIONS

1b. Based on his description, what emotions do you think Bartram felt as he watched the brood of alligators? (fear, wonder, curiosity, fascination)

2b. How does Bartram's characterization of the female alligators alter his earlier description of the species? (It makes them seem less alien and less frightening.)

tinually whining and barking like young puppies. I believe but few of a brood live to the years of full growth and magnitude, as the old feed on the young as long as they can make prey of them.

The alligator when full grown is a very large and terrible creature, and of prodigious strength, activity, and swiftness in the water. I have seen them twenty feet in length, and some are supposed to be twenty-two or
1 twenty-three feet. Their body is as large as that of a horse; their shape exactly resembles that of a lizard, except their tail, which is flat or cuneiform,[9] being compressed on each side and gradually diminishing from the abdomen to the extremity, which, with the whole body, is covered with horny plates or squamae,[10] impenetrable when on the body of the live animal, even to a rifle ball, except about their head and just behind their forelegs or arms, where it is said they are only vulnerable. The head of a full-grown one is about three feet, and the mouth opens nearly the same length; their eyes are small in proportion, and seem sunk deep in the head, by means of the prominency of the brows; the nostrils are large, inflated, and prominent on the top, so that the head in the water resembles, at a distance, a great chunk of
2 wood floating about. Only the upper jaw moves, which they raise almost perpendicular, so as to form a right angle with the lower one. In the forepart of the upper jaw, on each side, just under the nostrils, are two very large, thick, strong teeth, or tusks, not very sharp, but rather the shape of a cone: These are as white as the finest polished ivory, and are not covered by any skin or lips, and always in sight, which gives the creature a frightful appearance. In the lower jaw are holes opposite
3 to these teeth, to receive them: When they clap their jaws together it causes a surprising noise, like that which is made by forcing a heavy plank with violence upon the ground, and may be heard at a great distance.

But what is yet more surprising to a stranger is the incredible loud and terrifying roar which they are capable of making, especially in the spring season, their breeding time. It most resembles very heavy distant thunder, not only shaking the air and waters, but causing the earth to tremble; and when hundreds and thousands are roaring at the same time, you can scarcely be persuaded but that the whole globe is violently and dangerously agitated.

9. **cuneiform** [kū nē′ə fôrm]: wedge-shaped.
10. **squamae** [skwā′mē]: scales.

STUDY QUESTIONS

Recalling

1. What "fears and apprehensions" does Bartram mention in the first paragraph? What happened as he passed Battle Lagoon?
2. According to the third paragraph, what did Bartram expect when he saw the alligator nests? What did he do?
3. What description of the nests does Bartram provide in the fourth paragraph? Of a female alligator in the fifth paragraph?
4. What basic facts about the alligator does Bartram provide in the sixth paragraph?
5. According to the last paragraph, what is the most "surprising" thing about alligators?

Interpreting

6. Find two sentences where Bartram writes objectively, scientifically reporting the facts of his experience. Find two sentences where he writes subjectively, attempting to convey his feelings about his experience.
7. What does Bartram reveal about the kind of person he was with the statement, "I was determined at all events to immediately land and examine them [the nests]"? Consider the context of the first two paragraphs.

AT A GLANCE

- Bartram describes in detail the body and head of the alligator.
- He describes the animal's roar.

1 ENLIGHTENMENT IDEA

In his attention to detail, logical development, and organization of facts, Bartram echoes the era's concern for precision of thought.

2 RESPONSE JOURNAL

Students may wish to compare Bartram's description of the alligator with a description in a modern science book.

3 DESCRIPTION

Bartram adds intensity by focusing on the sense of sound and using the familiar comparison of the sound that a board makes when it hits the ground.

REFLECTING ON THE SELECTION

What emotion(s) does Bartram feel toward the alligators?

STUDY QUESTIONS

1. an alligator attack; he was attacked
2. to be attacked; landed boat
3. - *nests:* cone-shaped; 4 feet high, constructed of mud, grass, "herbage"; layered
   - *alligator:* leads young like a mother hen; defends them; basks on banks with brood
4. twenty feet long (as long as a horse); lizard-shaped, with pointed tail; covered with plates; head is three feet long; small eyes, large nostrils, etc.
5. their roar
6. *Objective:* description of nests, full-grown alligator; *Subjective:* description of fear of attack, terrifying roar
7. determined, adventurous, brave; curiosity stronger than fear

8. Answers will vary. Students should note the insight Bartram gives us into the interests and adventurousness of early Americans, as well as the work's entertainment value.

LITERARY FOCUS

- *Sensory language:* "belching water and smoke," "great thick whitish eggshells," "heavy distant thunder"
- *Organized detail:* "kept close together in a column . . . "
- *Comparisons:* "like rattlesnakes in color," "as a hen does her brood," "resembles a lizard"

VOCABULARY

1. stratum: from Latin *strātum,* "covering," itself from *sternere,* "to spread out, strew"
2. magnitude: from Latin *magnitūdō,* "greatness"
3. prodigious: from Latin *prōdigiōsus,* "strange, marvelous," itself from Latin *prōdigium,* "portent, omen"
4. cuneiform: from Latin *cuneus,* "wedge"
5. vulnerable: from Latin *vulnerābilis,* "wounding," itself from *vulnus,* "wound"

Extending

8. Bartram's work no longer has scientific value because modern scientists have made more thorough studies of alligators. In your opinion, what value does his writing have today?

LITERARY FOCUS

Description

Description is writing that creates an impression of a person, a place, or a thing. Bartram uses description in this passage from his *Travels.* He uses some narrative here too, especially when he tells of rising in the morning and continuing his journey up the river, but the emphasis is on clear and vivid description. He makes it possible for us to imagine what he saw. To do so, he uses the following techniques:

Specific sensory language. Bartram gives many concrete and specific sensory details. For example, notice his precise visual description of the nests: "the form of an obtuse cone, four feet high and four or five feet in diameter at their bases; they are constructed with mud, grass and herbage." He does *not* say, "They looked like medium-sized mounds of dirt," which would give us a much less valuable picture.

Bartram's language appeals to other senses besides sight. We can almost hear the alligators as "hundreds and thousands are roaring at the same time."

Selected and organized details. In the sixth paragraph Bartram does not attempt to tell everything about the alligator at once. He separates the parts of the animal and describes them in detail in a spatial order we can follow clearly: overall size and shape, tail, hide, head. In this way he avoids a vague or jumbled impression.

Comparisons. Few of Bartram's readers had seen alligators, but all had seen horses. To emphasize the bulk of the alligators' torsos, Bartram says "their body is as large as that of a horse." He uses the familiar to help describe the unfamiliar.

Thinking About Description

- In this selection from Bartram, find another example of sensory language, of organized details, and of comparison with another animal.

VOCABULARY

Words from Latin

People who write scientific reports in English often use words derived from Latin. For example, both *penicillin* and *coronary* are medical terms that come from Latin. In his report about alligators, Bartram uses the Latin word *squamae* to refer to the scalelike parts of the animals.

In addition to supplying us with scientific terms, Latin has greatly influenced the everyday vocabulary of English speakers and writers. Look up the following words from Bartram's report, and give each word's original form and Latin meaning.

1. stratum
2. magnitude
3. prodigious
4. cuneiform
5. vulnerable

COMPOSITION

Analyzing Descriptive Writing

- Choose one of Bartram's comparisons or one of his descriptive images, and tell why you think it is appropriate or inappropriate. First make sure you tell your audience what Bartram is describing. Then explain whether the description helps you picture the item clearly. Tell why or why not.

Writing a Description

- Using the three methods Bartram uses—specific sensory language, selected and organized details, and comparisons (see preceding Literary Focus)—write a description of an animal. Assume that your reader has *never seen* the animal you choose to write about. You may want to follow Bartram's example and combine your description with a narrative of your own encounter with the animal.

COMPOSITION: GUIDELINES FOR EVALUATION

ANALYZING DESCRIPTIVE WRITING

Objective

To analyze description

Guidelines for Evaluation

- suggested length: two to four paragraphs
- should identify what is described
- should restate the comparison or images used
- should state an opinion on appropriateness of comparison or image
- should give reasons supporting opinion

WRITING A DESCRIPTION

Objective

To write a description

Guidelines for Evaluation

- suggested length: two to four paragraphs
- should describe an animal
- should use sensory language, selected and organized details, and comparisons
- should give information about size, shape, appearance and behavior of the animal

Jean de Crèvecoeur *1735–1813*

Michel-Guillaume-Jean de Crèvecoeur spent the first nineteen years of his life in France. After living in England and Canada, and traveling throughout the American colonies as a surveyor, he settled on a farm near Chester, New York, in 1769. There he began writing his *Letters from an American Farmer,* published in London in 1782.

Like most literary letters, Crèvecoeur's were addressed to a particular person—a "Mr. F. B."—but were actually intended for a large audience. In fact, Crèvecoeur's letters reached a much larger audience than he had anticipated. Europeans were eager for information about the New World, and Crèvecoeur's *Letters,* translated into several languages, made him famous. His idealized vision of a "new man" living in a land of boundless opportunities, free from the restraints and class structure of Europe, was extremely influential in shaping the Old World's image of America.

Most Americans, of course, were well aware that the human race had not escaped all its problems merely by crossing the Atlantic. George Washington, for one, thought Crèvecoeur's picture "too flattering." Yet Crèvecoeur's excitement at the *possibilities* for freedom, equality, and prosperity was genuine—and that enthusiasm is communicated in his writing, which begins on the following page.

Michel-Guillaume-Jean de Crèvecoeur [mē shel′ gē yōm′zhän də krev ko͞or′]

Model for Active Reading

In this selection, and in one selection in each unit, you will find notes in the right-hand margin that highlight parts of the selection. These notes point out important ideas of the period—in this case, the Enlightenment—and draw your attention to literary elements and techniques covered in the Literary Focuses. Page numbers in the notes will refer you to more extensive discussions of these important ideas and elements.

■ What possibilities for freedom, equality, and prosperity do you see in America today? Are today's possibilities different from those of Crèvecoeur's day?

AT A GLANCE

- The letter writer meditates on the burgeoning New World, praising its "new race of men"—Americans with varied ancestry who are free of Europe's prejudices and restrictions.
- Crèvecoeur believes that the absence of negative, Old World pressures will result in an ideal society.

LITERARY OPTIONS

- comparison and contrast
- details
- persuasion

THEMATIC OPTIONS

- American destiny
- progress and hope
- diversity

Jean de Crèvecoeur

from Letters from an American Farmer

"What then is the American?"

I wish I could be acquainted with the feelings and thoughts which must agitate the heart and present themselves to the mind of an enlightened Englishman, when he first lands on this continent. . . . Here he beholds fair cities, substantial villages, extensive fields, an immense country filled with decent houses, good roads, orchards, meadows, and bridges, where a hundred years ago all was wild, woody, and uncultivated! What a train of pleasing ideas this fair spectacle must suggest; it is a prospect which must inspire a good citizen with the most heartfelt pleasure.

Enlightenment idea: Crèvecoeur refers to enlightened people and notes that belief in progress and hope were typical of the time (p. 50).

The difficulty consists in the manner of viewing so extensive a scene. He is arrived on a new continent; a modern society offers itself to his contemplation, different from what he had hitherto seen. It is not composed, as in Europe, of great lords who possess everything, and of a herd of people who have nothing. Here are no aristocratical families, no courts, no kings, no bishops, no ecclesiastical dominion, no invisible power giving to a few a very visible one, no great manufacturers employing thousands, no great refinements of luxury. The rich and the poor are not so far removed from each other as they are in Europe. . . .

Selected and organized details (p. 92) **and Repetition** (p. 69): In this *description* Crèvecoeur provides a catalogue of Old World injustices and uses repetition to stress their absence in America.

What then is the American, this new man? He is either a European or the descendant of a European, hence that strange mixture of blood, which you will find in no other country. I could point out to you a family whose grandfather was an Englishman, whose wife was Dutch, whose son married a French woman, and whose present four sons have now four wives of different nations. *He* is an American who, leaving behind him all his ancient prejudices and manners, receives new ones from the new mode of life he has embraced, the new government he obeys, and the new rank he holds. He becomes an American by being received in the broad lap of our great *Alma Mater.*[1] Here individuals of all nations are melted into a new race of men whose labors and posterity will one day cause great changes in the world.

Rhetorical question (p. 69): Crèvecoeur answers his question himself.

Americans are the western pilgrims who are carrying along with them that great mass of arts, sciences, vigor, and industry which began long since in the east; they will finish the great circle. The Americans were once scattered all over Europe; here they are incorporated into one of the finest systems of population which has

1. ***Alma Mater*** [äl′mə mät′ər]: Latin for "foster mother," referring here to America.

GUIDED READING

LITERAL QUESTIONS

1a. What does the enlightened Englishman encounter in America? (a modern society so "different from what he had hitherto seen")

2a. What is the American, according to Crèvecoeur? (He is either a European or the descendant of a European.)

INFERENTIAL QUESTIONS

1b. How is the new society different from the Englishman's world? (There is less distance between rich and poor, no social ranking, no civil or religious dominion, no sign of the Industrial Revolution.)

2b. What do you think he means when he claims that "they will finish the great circle?" (They will use the skills and knowledge of the Old World to create and maintain a better system than the one they left.)

ever appeared, and which will hereafter become distinct by the power of the different climates they inhabit.

The American ought therefore to love this country much better than that wherein either he or his forefathers were born. Here the rewards of his industry follow with equal steps the progress of his labor; his labor is founded on the basis of nature, *self-interest;* can it want a stronger allurement? Wives and children, who before in vain demanded of him a morsel of bread, now, fat and frolicsome, gladly help their father to clear those fields whence exuberant crops are to arise to feed and to clothe them all, without any part being claimed either by a despotic prince, a rich abbot,[2] or a mighty lord. Here religion demands but little of him—a small voluntary salary to the minister and gratitude to God; can he refuse these? The American is a new man, who acts upon new principles; he must therefore entertain new ideas and form new opinions. From involuntary idleness, servile dependence, penury,[3] and useless labor, he has passed to toils of a very different nature, rewarded by ample subsistence.[4]—This is an American.

Enlightenment idea: Crèvecoeur stresses that Americans use their own powers to shape their destinies (p. 50).

Specific sensory language (p. 92): Crèvecoeur adds specific details and sensory images to his *description.*

2. **abbot:** man who heads an abbey of monks.
3. **penury** [pen′yər ē]: extreme poverty.
4. **subsistence:** livelihood.

STUDY QUESTIONS

Recalling

1. According to the first two paragraphs, what does an Englishman behold when he arrives in America? What does he *not* behold?
2. According to the third paragraph, what does the American leave behind? What does the American embrace, obey, and hold?
3. According to the last paragraph, what was the result of labor in the Old World? For what do people work in America?
4. Why must Americans "entertain new ideas and form new opinions"?

Interpreting

5. What is the effect of the long lists of details describing Europe and America in paragraphs 1 and 2?
6. What, in your own words, is Crèvecoeur's definition of an American?
7. In addition to the rhetorical question that opens the third paragraph, what other rhetorical questions does Crèvecoeur ask? Where does he exaggerate?

Extending

8. In what way is Crèvecoeur's description of America reminiscent of the writing of the earliest visitors from Europe, such as Columbus (page 15), John Smith (page 19), and William Bradford (page 23)?

COMPOSITION

Writing a Comparison/Contrast

■ Write a short essay summarizing the characteristics of an American as described by Crèvecoeur. For each characteristic that you mention, compare Crèvecoeur's "new man" to today's American. Be sure to show both what they have in common and what makes them different.

Writing a Literary Letter

■ Compose your own literary letter, addressing it to a public figure or to a fictitious character, but actually aiming it at a wider audience. First comment on a current event. Then describe your version of an ideal America and tell how you feel the event and the ideal compare.

AT A GLANCE

The American acts on his own principles, entertains new ideas, and works in his own self-interest.

REFLECTING ON THE SELECTION

What might account for Crèvecoeur's great optimism about America? (The fact that it is such an abundant land and that it offers Europeans a fresh start)

STUDY QUESTIONS

1. fair cities, substantial villages, large fields; kings, aristocrats, royal courts
2. ancient prejudices and manners; new life, government, rank
3. those in power claim part of all labor; themselves
4. They are a new people.
5. America is contrasted favorably with Europe.
6. independent, hard working, patriotic, democratic
7. last paragraph: "Can it want a stronger allurement?", "Can he refuse these?"; description in first paragraph, contrast of European and American children
8. enthusiasm for abundant land, stress and exaggeration of opportunity for settlement, Americans as a special people

COMPOSITION: GUIDELINES FOR EVALUATION

WRITING A COMPARISON/CONTRAST

Objective

To compare and contrast opinions

Guidelines for Evaluation

- suggested length: five to eight paragraphs
- should include characteristics of Crèvecoeur's "new man"
- should examine modern Americans in this light
- should use examples to support opinions
- should make analogies clarifying points

WRITING A LITERARY LETTER

Objective

To write a literary letter

Guidelines for Evaluation

- suggested length: two to four paragraphs
- should be addressed to a specific individual but be aimed at a larger audience
- should describe a significant current event
- should describe an "ideal American"
- should compare the event and the ideal

ACTIVE READING

The Sound of Prose

After the students have read the page, emphasize that the sound of prose is a significant factor even if the prose was not written for oral presentation. Have students consider the selection from Paine's *American Crisis*. Ask in what tone they would read the selection (urgent, angry, exhorting). Ask which words they would stress in Paine's first sentence (These, times, try, men's, souls) and what sort of tone they might use in stressing *summer* and *sunshine* in the second sentence (sarcastic). You might have volunteers prepare the selection by Paine, Crèvecoeur's essay, or portions of Franklin's autobiography for oral presentation. Also assign Henry's speech if no one has yet presented it.

THE AMERICAN VOICE

Liberty

After students have read the page, have them write their own definitions of liberty and share them with the class. They might then compare their ideas with the views expressed in the quotations on page 97: How have ideas about liberty changed or expanded in the last two centuries? In what ways have they remained the same?

ACTIVE READING

The Sound of Prose

Since so much of the literature in this unit is oratory, or public statement, we should remind ourselves that prose makes a *sound*. In other words, most literature begins with a speaking voice. Some people say they read mostly with their eyes, that they do not hear anything as they read. It may not matter that we do not hear a voice behind a newspaper article, an advertisement, or a legal document. Yet with any writing we call literature, the language itself is a large part of the pleasure of reading, and we will miss much of that pleasure, miss the experience, if we do not find a voice for what we read.

Reading aloud is one way not to miss that pleasure. However, most of the time we read silently. (At least we do in the modern world. A few centuries ago, silent reading was considered an amazing feat!) So we need, as always, to be imaginative and to read *aloud silently* or *silently aloud*. This technique means hearing in our mind's ear the rise and fall of a human voice, pausing, emphasizing, shifting tone. Literature is, after all, human communication. It is someone speaking to us.

There is no tape recording of how Patrick Henry delivered his speech at the Virginia Convention. Yet when we read we must give that speech a voice. Where did Henry pause? Which words did he emphasize? Where did he drop his voice, or raise it, for greater effect? We can imagine his emphases in one possible "script":

What *is* it that gentlemen wish? [Voice rising, slightly louder:] What would they *have?* Is life so *dear* [slight pause], or peace so *sweet* [slight pause], as to be purchased [with rising indignation] at the price of *chains* and *slavery?* For*bid* it, Almighty *God!* [Then more quietly, rising to the conclusion] I know not what course *others* may take; but as for *me* [pause], give me *liberty* [long pause] or give me *death!*

There is no single "correct" way of reading a sentence. In addition, prose writers have very few devices available to help readers hear their voices. They can use *italics,* exclamation points (!), or CAPITALS for emphasis. The can use commas, parentheses, or dashes for pauses. However, these devices are limited and quickly become tiresome if overused. It is up to each reader's active participation in the experience of literature if he or she is going to hear the amused voice of Franklin remembering his youth or the warm voice of Crèvecoeur filled with love of country.

THE AMERICAN VOICE

Liberty

Most of the American voices in this unit, from the famous to the anonymous, carry the message of the Declaration of Independence. They are Age of Reason voices that are strongly emotional, talking about matters of life and death, yet still logical, coherent, and organized. In particular, they share a vision of the liberty and the freedom that would allow Americans to think and feel as independent individuals long after the Revolution:

Franklin
I took upon me to assert my Freedom. . . .

Henry
If we wish to be free, if we mean to preserve inviolate those inestimable privileges . . . we must fight!

Anonymous
I will sing you a song concerning liberty.
Concerning liberty, my boys, the truth I will unfold,
Of the bold Americans, who scorn to be controlled.

Jefferson
We hold these truths to be self-evident, that all men are created equal, that they are endowed by their Creator with certain unalienable Rights, that among these are Life, Liberty and the pursuit of Happiness.

Paine
For though the flame of liberty may sometimes cease to shine, the coal can never expire.

Crèvecoeur
The American ought therefore to love this country much better than that wherein either he or his forefathers were born. Here the rewards of his industry follow with equal steps the progress of his labor; his labor is founded on the basis of nature, self-interest; *can it want a stronger allurement?*

Freedom in American literary expression had helped to create the American political system. Writing about liberty helped to make liberty possible. The literature in this unit helped to found the nation on the basis of private and public independence.

As the new United States continued to grow, American literature also continued to grow. Literature helped the nation to achieve an identity by defining its characteristics, its problems, and its goals. Liberty is one of those characteristics. It is part of the answer to Crèvecoeur's question, "What then is the American, this new man?" The American is someone free to create a new literature, to found a new tradition, to speak in a new voice.

Key to Illustrations on Pages 48–49.

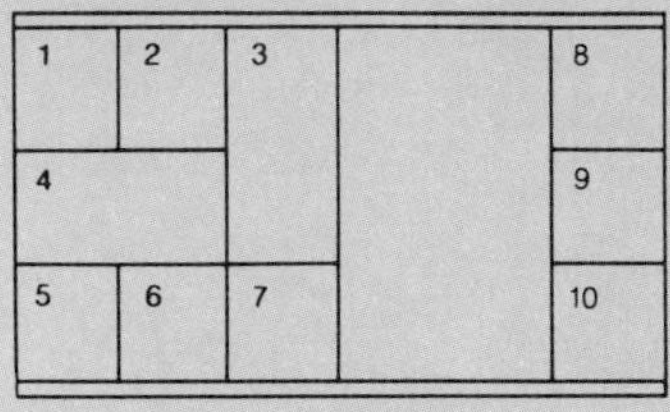

1. Baltimore, Maryland, c. 1752.
2. American Continental dollar, 1776.
3. Betsy Ross sewing the first American flag, illustration by Elizabeth Moore Hallowell.
4. *The Battle of Lexington, April 19, 1775.* Early twentieth-century engraving.
5. William Bartram. Nineteenth-century engraving.
6. *The Spirit of '76,* lithograph from a painting by Archibald M. Willard.
7. *Benjamin Franklin,* David Martin, 1766.
8. *The Midnight Ride of Paul Revere,* Grant Wood, 1931.
9. Phillis Wheatley, engraved frontispiece to her *Poems on Various Subjects, Religious and Moral,* 1773.
10. *Daniel Boone Escorting Settlers Through the Cumberland Gap,* George Caleb Bingham, 1852.

Key to Illustrations appears on page 151.

NATIVE GROUNDS

1800–1840

Growth and Prosperity

In 1789 George Washington, not only an American hero, but an international hero of freedom, was inaugurated as first President of the United States. The American Revolution had been a success. Would the new nation be equally successful? Many questions remained to be answered. Could a modern republic—a nation without a king or a hereditary aristocracy—withstand the tensions of a large and varied population? Would there be economic prosperity? Would there be real democracy? Would the new Constitution stand the test of time? In short, would the American experiment work?

Many of the nation's first problems were physical ones. In an age of few good roads and no rapid and reliable means of transportation or communication, it was difficult for the thirteen states to conceive of themselves and act as a single nation. Regional rivalries and even separate cultures had to be reconciled. As Lincoln asked years later, could a nation "conceived in liberty and dedicated to the proposition that all men are created equal . . . long endure"?

In fact the nation did prosper, did expand, and did overcome the dangers it faced. Jefferson's Louisiana Purchase in 1803 vastly enlarged the territory. The War of 1812 offered a challenge to the proud new nation, and the victory reasserted American independence. By 1821

INTRODUCTION

After the students have read the introduction to the unit, you might ask them what *nationalism* means (national pride). Stress that as a new nation, Americans needed to take pride in things American, not European. Then discuss why Americans of the time would have felt it important to have their own literature.

Ask the students what the most common meaning of *romantic* is (related to love). Then ask what *Romantic* with a capital *R* has to do with love. They should see that for the Romantic, feelings or emotions were of primary importance. Emphasize that Romanticism was a reaction to Classicism and the Age of Reason in these key ways:

Classical	*Romantic*
reason	emotion
moderation	excess
science	nature
society	self
pragmatism	idealism
cool wit	intense feeling

Point out that the Romantics were also reacting against the new industrial age.

Key Ideas in This Period

- nationalism
- Romanticism
- the industrial age
- nature
- idealism

Illustration (detail) from a French edition of Edgar Allan Poe's "The Raven," Edouard Manet. 1875.

ten new states had joined the original thirteen. Settlers moved west; roads and waterways improved. Steamships created a new network of trade and communication. New factories and mills began to move the nation away from a largely agricultural economy toward a more urban and industrialized society.

"Our Own Books"

As Americans continued to build the nation, they came increasingly to feel less like transported Europeans. The native grounds of the Old World—the European environment, its traditions and customs, its languages and literatures—gave way to the native grounds of the New World. A new culture and a new literature had to be created. With an increasing nationalism, a sense of national pride, Americans began to call for a literature that would be less dependent upon European models, one that would express their Americanism. The playwright Royall Tyler saw what was needed: "that we write our own books . . . and that they exhibit our own manners."

During the first decades of the American republic, a great deal of *writing* was done, but very little of it possessed that mysterious vitality that made it *literature.* For example, not many people today have heard of Mrs. Susannah Rowson. Yet her novel *Charlotte Temple,* published in the United States in 1794, sold fifty thousand copies by 1810 and appeared in two hundred editions before it settled into near oblivion. Better known is Charles Brockden Brown, perhaps the most original of early American novelists. Brown's *Wieland* (1798) was quite successful. He often used American locales in his tales, and he established some subjects that were to become common in American writing: settlers, Indians, forests, madness, sin, and guilt. With greater artistry, Poe, Hawthorne, Melville, and Faulkner would develop the material Brown used in the eighteenth century.

In 1820 it was still possible for a British critic, Sydney Smith, to ask, "Who reads an American book?" Smith, like many other Europeans, wondered why any intelligent person would want to bother reading books from such an unformed, uncultured, unsophisticated place as America. Yet in the same year that Smith asked his mocking question, Washington Irving's *Sketch Book* was published in England. American literature of lasting value was beginning to be created. In 1817 William Cullen Bryant gained fame for his poem "Thanatopsis." James Fenimore Cooper brought out the first of the Leatherstocking novels, *The Pioneers,* in 1823. Edgar Allan Poe published his first volume of poetry in 1827.

Who were the people who produced this first American literature, and what made their work unmistakably American? In the first place they were *writers,* not soldiers of fortune like John Smith (page 19), business leaders like Ben Franklin (page 56), or government leaders like Thomas Jefferson (page 76). Though they sometimes had to do other things to make a living, they thought of themselves as writers, and they were thought of as writers by their growing public.

Second, they began writing about American people in American places dealing with American problems. This accomplishment may seem like something to take for granted, but it is important to remember that no one had ever done it before. Their characters and settings were not *always* American, and their forms were usually British, but they did take the first steps. They wrote about the American wilderness, the Revolution, pioneers, American town and city life. They praised American heroes and American artists and told American tales. Their subjects were freedom, expansion, the individual—definitely not European subjects.

The Romantic Writers

We cannot think about Irving, Cooper, Bryant, and Poe—the writers represented in this unit—as if they were all writing about the same things in the same way. We should recognize, however, that all four writers shared some of the characteristics of Romanticism, a literary movement that began in Europe in the late eighteenth century and dominated literature on both sides of the Atlantic in the first half of the nineteenth century.

Romanticism was a reaction to **Classicism,** the Age of Reason movement in the arts that attempted to duplicate the order and balance in the art of Greece and Rome. While Classicism stressed reason over emotion and social concerns over personal ones, Romantic writers stressed personal experience and were often highly emotional. Among the earliest Romantic writers were the British poet William Wordsworth and the German poet Johann Wolfgang von Goethe.

The qualities of Romanticism vary from place to place, and few Romantic writers exhibit all of them. But there are six characteristics that can give us a general definition of **Romanticism:** (1) a profound love of nature; (2) a focus on the self and the individual; (3) a fascination with the supernatural, the mysterious, and the gothic; (4) a yearning for the picturesque and the exotic; (5) a deep-rooted idealism; and (6) a passionate nationalism, or love of country.

Natty Bumppo and the Indian chieftain Chingachgook, from an 1872 edition of *The Last of the Mohicans* by Cooper.

One quality of Romantic writers, then, is a deep feeling for nature. Close observation of the natural world usually gives a Romantic writer an insight into all life, especially human life. We can find this kind of detailed observation of nature in Irving, Cooper, and Bryant—particularly in Bryant's poems and in Cooper's breadth of feeling for the unspoiled wilderness.

Romantic writers also reveal with emotion their own personal visions and delve deeply into the individual personalities of their characters. Poe is the best representative of this strain of Romanticism, for he often displays the tortured minds and hearts of inward-looking characters. It is Poe also who demonstrates a fascination with the **gothic**—the dark, irrational side of the imagination.

One generalization about Romantic writing fits all four of the authors in this unit. Romantic writers were often interested in the picturesque and the exotic, in times and places other than their own, especially the past. Sometimes this interest in the past offers an escape from an oppressive or unromantic present. Irving's "Devil and Tom Walker" is set in and around a Boston that had vanished a century before the tale was written, and the story is wrapped in legend, rumor, suggestion, and fantasy. Cooper's hero, the frontiersman Natty Bumppo, lived in an America that was already a legendary past for Cooper's readers. Bryant's "Thanatopsis" moves deep into the past of the human race. Poe's story, "The Fall of the House of Usher," is not set in any country at all or in any time that we can easily recognize.

Irving, Cooper, and Bryant often wrote with a fervent idealism, a belief in a heroic mode of behavior that would make life worthwhile. Nationalism, too, was a part of the imaginative lives of these writers—men who were completely aware of the importance of establishing an *American* literary art.

These four writers of the first half of the nineteenth century began an American Romantic tradition that would be developed by Emerson, Hawthorne, Melville, Whitman, and Faulkner, writers you will meet later in this book. We continue to read the four writers in this unit, however, not only because of their historical importance but because they still offer exciting and meaningful imaginative experiences.

TIME LINE

1800–1840 AMERICAN EVENTS

1803 U.S. negotiates Louisiana Purchase from France

Lewis and Clark explore west of Mississippi River

1807 Robert Fulton launches steamboat *Clermont* on Hudson River

1812 War of 1812 against Great Britain begins

First lead pencils manufactured (Concord, Mass.)

1814 Francis Scott Key writes "The Star-Spangled Banner"

First school in U.S. for higher education of women (Middlebury, Conn.)

1817 William Cullen Bryant, "Thanatopsis"

1820 Washington Irving, *The Sketch Book*

First canning factory in U.S. (Boston, Mass.)

WORLD EVENTS 1800–1840

1800 England: Poet William Wordsworth publishes Romantic manifesto, the Preface to *Lyrical Ballads*

1804 France: Napoleon crowns himself Emperor

1805 England: William Wordsworth completes *The Prelude*

1808 Austria: German composer Ludwig van Beethoven, *Symphony No. 5*

1812 Germany: Jacob and Wilhelm Grimm, *Fairy Tales*

1813 England: Jane Austen, *Pride and Prejudice*

1815 Belgium: Napoleon defeated at Battle of Waterloo

1818 England: Mary Shelley, *Frankenstein*

1820 England: Sir Walter Scott, *Ivanhoe*

England: John Keats, "Ode on a Grecian Urn"

1800–1840 AMERICAN EVENTS

1823 James Fenimore Cooper, first of the Leatherstocking Tales

President Monroe issues Monroe Doctrine

1825 Erie Canal opens

1826 First overland route to California blazed

1827 James Audubon, *Birds of America*

1828 Noah Webster, *American Dictionary of the English Language*

1830 U.S. population: 12.6 million

1831 First regularly scheduled steam locomotive service

Joseph Henry builds first electric motor

Edgar Allan Poe, *Poems*

1832 First clipper ship, *Ann McKim,* launched at Baltimore

1834 Americans begin to eat tomatoes, previously considered poisonous

Cyrus McCormick patents reaper

1836 Texas declares independence from Mexico

Ralph Waldo Emerson, *Nature*

1837 Nathaniel Hawthorne, *Twice-Told Tales*

1839 First baseball diamond laid out (Cooperstown, N.Y.)

1840 Edgar Allan Poe, *Tales of the Grotesque and Arabesque*

Richard Dana, *Two Years Before the Mast*

Samuel Morse patents telegraph

WORLD EVENTS 1800–1840

1823 England: Lord Byron, *Don Juan*

1825 Russia: Bolshoi Ballet established

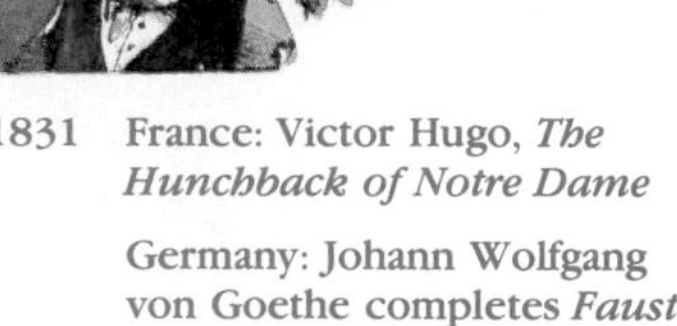

1831 France: Victor Hugo, *The Hunchback of Notre Dame*

Germany: Johann Wolfgang von Goethe completes *Faust*

1832 Russia: Alexander Pushkin, *Eugene Onegin*

1833 Slavery abolished in British Empire

1835 Denmark: Hans Christian Andersen, *Fairy Tales*

1837 England: Charles Dickens, *Oliver Twist*

Washington Irving *1783–1859*

Washington Irving, born during the Revolution and named after George Washington, was the first American storyteller to be internationally recognized as a man of letters. A member of a wealthy New York family, Irving reluctantly studied law and even managed to pass his bar examination. However, he preferred reading, roaming the countryside, and listening to the old tales told by the villagers in New York's Hudson Valley.

Like Ben Franklin in the preceding unit, Irving had begun to publish witty and satiric letters in a newspaper edited by his brother. By the time he was twenty-four, he was publishing a satiric magazine appropriately named after a spicy appetizer, *Salmagundi. Salmagundi* carried essays and sketches making fun of everything from Thomas Jefferson's politics to the latest fashions. Irving was fond of using pen names, and he signed his articles with such names as William Wizard and Anthony Evergreen.

In 1809 Irving created another pseudonym, Diedrich Knickerbocker, and published Knickerbocker's *History of New York from the Beginning of the World to the End of the Dutch Dynasty.* Knickerbocker was supposed to be an eccentric old historian who often confused fact with folklore, giving Irving an opportunity to mix old tales and satiric opinions with a bit of history. The *History* entertained its readers with hilarious sketches of the customs, manners, families, and "history" of old New York. It was enormously popular and established Irving as a celebrity.

In 1815 Irving went to Europe and spent the next seventeen years in Britain, France, Germany, Italy, and Spain, exploring local traditions, customs, and folklore. "My native country was full of youthful promise: Europe was rich in the accumulated treasures of age," he wrote in his 1820 *Sketch Book.* An elegant English gentleman named Geoffrey Crayon was supposedly the author of some of the stories in the Sketch Book, but the two most famous stories—"Rip Van Winkle" and "The Legend of Sleepy Hollow"—are told by old Knickerbocker. Both tales have become American classics even though Irving borrowed their plots from two traditional German tales before placing them in the Hudson Valley setting. In fact, it is this ability to blend European sophistication and American flavor that is the most distinctive characteristic of Irving's writing.

Irving finally settled down at Sunnyside, his estate on the bank of the Hudson. There he continued writing travel books, histories, biographies of Columbus and Washington, more tales and sketches.

■ What impression of America and Americans would Irving give to someone who had never been here?

The English novelist Thackeray summed up Irving's accomplishments when he called him "the first Ambassador from the New World of Letters to the Old."

"The Devil and Tom Walker" is one of the stories in Irving's *Tales of a Traveler* (1824). It is Irving's version of the old German legend of Faust, the man who sold his soul to the devil. Irving set the tale in New England in the 1720s—a time when Puritanism was fading and commercialism was growing. He placed it, appropriately, in the section of the book called "The Money Diggers."

Washington Irving

The Devil and Tom Walker

A few miles from Boston in Massachusetts, there is a deep inlet, winding several miles into the interior of the country from Charles Bay, and terminating in a thickly wooded swamp or morass. On one side of this inlet is a beautiful dark grove; on the opposite side the land rises abruptly from the water's edge into a high ridge, on which grow a few scattered oaks of
1 great age and immense size. Under one of these gigantic trees, according to old stories, there was a great amount of treasure buried by Kidd the pirate.[1] The inlet allowed a facility to bring the money in a boat secretly and at night to the very foot of the hill; the elevation of the place permitted a good lookout to be kept that no one was at hand; while the remarkable trees formed good landmarks by which the place might easily be found again. The old stories add, moreover, that the Devil presided at the hiding of the money, and took it under his guardianship; but this, it is well known, he always does with buried treasure, particularly when it has been ill-gotten. Be that as it may, Kidd never returned to recover his wealth, being shortly after seized at Boston, sent out to England, and there hanged for a pirate.

About the year 1727, just at the time that
2 earthquakes were prevalent in New England and shook many tall sinners down upon their knees, there lived near this place a meager, miserly fellow, of the name of Tom Walker. He had a wife as miserly as himself: they were so miserly that they even conspired to cheat each other. Whatever the woman could lay hands on she hid away; a hen could not cackle but she was on the alert to secure the new-laid egg. Her husband was continually prying about to detect her secret hoards, and many and fierce were the conflicts that took place about what ought to have been common property. They lived in a forlorn-looking house that stood alone and had an air of starvation. A few straggling savin trees, emblems of sterility, grew
3 near it; no smoke ever curled from its chimney; no traveler stopped at its door. A miserable horse, whose ribs were as articulate as the bars of a gridiron, stalked about a field, where a thin carpet of moss, scarcely covering the ragged beds of puddingstone,[2] tantalized and balked his hunger; and sometimes he would lean his head over the fence, look piteously at the passerby, and seem to petition deliverance from this land of famine.

1. **Kidd the pirate:** Captain William Kidd (1645–1701).

2. **puddingstone:** kind of rock in which pebbles are embedded like plums in a pudding.

AT A GLANCE

- The narrator describes the site where the pirate Captain Kidd purportedly buried his treasure.
- The story takes place in New England, c. 1727: Tom Walker and his wife, both misers, now live near Captain Kidd's treasure ground.

LITERARY OPTIONS

- narration
- point of view
- style

THEMATIC OPTIONS

- the effects of greed
- hypocrisy
- marital relationships

1 POINT OF VIEW

The narrator establishes a credible, omniscient point of view in his ostensibly well-informed, detailed description of where and how Kidd had buried his treasure.

2 SETTING

Setting the story in Puritan New England evokes the Puritans' concern with damnation, through the humorous reference to "many tall sinners."

3 IMAGERY

Irving vividly conveys the Walkers' miserliness in his description of their dilapidated house and skeletal horse.

GUIDED READING

LITERAL QUESTIONS

1a. According to the old stories, who presided over the hiding of Kidd's money? (the Devil)

2a. What does Tom continually try to find out about his wife? (the location of her secret hoards)

INFERENTIAL QUESTIONS

1b. In what way do the references to "old stories" and the Devil affect the narrator's account? (The references make the story sound like a folk tale or fairy tale.)

2b. What does the way in which Tom and his wife treat each other suggest about their greed? (Their greed has crowded out every emotion, including marital love.)

AT A GLANCE

- Tom and his wife fight constantly.
- Taking a shortcut through a forest swamp, Tom discovers a split skull.
- A big, dark-skinned man mysteriously appears.

1 VOCABULARY: CONNOTATION

Inmates suggests the bitterness of their lives together. *Termagant* (a harsh, scolding person) suggests that, of the two, the wife is more to blame for the situation.

2 PLOT: FORESHADOWING

The anger, meanness, and contention between Tom and his wife suggest that their lives are likely to take increasingly dark, unpleasant turns.

3 ROMANTIC IDEA

The mysterious swamp and stock occult elements (hemlock, toadlike creatures) jibe with the folk-tale framework of the story and reflect Romantic fascination with the gothic.

4 CHARACTERIZATION

Tom's unnatural lack of fear and his ease in the mysterious swamp reflect his wholly pragmatic nature.

5 NARRATION

The skull adds more gothic elements to the story and heightens the buildup to the sudden appearance of the "great black man."

1 The house and its inmates had altogether a bad name. Tom's wife was a tall termagant, fierce of temper, loud of tongue, and strong of arm. Her voice was often heard in wordy warfare with her husband; and his face sometimes showed signs that their conflicts were not confined to words. No one ventured, however, to interfere between them. The lonely wayfarer
2 shrunk within himself at the horrid clamor and clapperclawing;[3] eyed the den of discord askance; and hurried on his way, rejoicing, if a bachelor, in his celibacy.

One day that Tom Walker had been to a distant part of the neighborhood, he took what he considered a shortcut homeward, through the swamp. Like most shortcuts, it was an ill-chosen route. The swamp was thickly grown with great gloomy pines and hemlocks, some of them ninety feet high, which made it dark at noonday, and a retreat for all the owls of the neighborhood. It was full of pits and quagmires, partly covered with weeds and mosses, where the green surface often betrayed the traveler into a gulf of black, smothering mud;
3 there were also dark and stagnant pools, the abodes of the tadpole, the bullfrog, and the water snake, where the trunks of pines and hemlocks lay half drowned, half rotting, looking like alligators sleeping in the mire.

Tom had long been picking his way cautiously through this treacherous forest; stepping from tuft to tuft of rushes and roots, which afforded precarious footholds among deep sloughs; or pacing carefully, like a cat, along the prostrate trunks of trees; startled now and then by the sudden screaming of the bittern, or the quacking of a wild duck rising on the wing from some solitary pool. At length he arrived at a firm piece of ground, which ran out like a peninsula into the deep bosom of the swamp. It had been one of the strongholds of the Indians during their wars with the first colonists. Here they had thrown up a kind of fort, which they had looked upon as almost impregnable, and had used as a place of refuge for their squaws and children. Nothing remained of the old Indian fort but a few embankments, gradually sinking to the level of the surrounding earth, and already overgrown in part by oaks and other forest trees, the foliage of which formed a contrast to the dark pines and hemlocks of the swamp.

It was late in the dusk of evening when Tom Walker reached the old fort, and he
4 paused there awhile to rest himself. Anyone but he would have felt unwilling to linger in this lonely, melancholy place, for the common people had a bad opinion of it from the stories handed down from the time of the Indian wars, when it was asserted that the savages held incantations here and made sacrifices to the evil spirit.

Tom Walker, however, was not a man to be troubled with any fears of the kind. He reposed himself for some time on the trunk of a fallen hemlock, listening to the boding cry of the tree toad, and delving with his walking staff into a mound of black mold at his feet. As he turned up the soil unconsciously, his staff
5 struck against something hard. He raked it out of the vegetable mold, and lo! a cloven[4] skull, with an Indian tomahawk buried deep in it, lay before him. The rust on the weapon showed the time that had elapsed since this deathblow had been given. It was a dreary memento of the fierce struggle that had taken place in this last foothold of the Indian warriors.

"Humph!" said Tom Walker, as he gave it a kick to shake the dirt from it.

"Let that skull alone!" said a gruff voice. Tom lifted up his eyes and beheld a great black man seated directly opposite him, on the stump of a tree. He was exceedingly surprised, having neither heard nor seen anyone approach; and he was still more perplexed on observing, as well as the gathering gloom would permit, that the stranger was neither Negro nor Indian. It is true he was dressed in a rude half-Indian garb, and had a red belt or sash swathed round his body; but his face was

3. **clapperclawing:** scratching, clawing.

4. **cloven** [klō′vən]: split.

GUIDED READING

LITERAL QUESTIONS

1a. To which animal is Tom compared as he walks through the forest? (a cat)

2a. Why is Tom so surprised when the great black man speaks to him? (Tom has not seen or heard anyone approach.)

INFERENTIAL QUESTIONS

1b. How does this physical description add to the reader's perception of Tom's character? (It increases the sense that there is something not fully human about him.)

2b. What can you infer about the dark-skinned man from the mysterious way in which he makes his appearance? (There may be something supernatural about him.)

neither black nor copper color, but swarthy
1 and dingy, and begrimed with soot, as if he had been accustomed to toil among fires and forges. He had a shock of coarse black hair that stood out from his head in all directions, and bore an ax on his shoulder.

He scowled for a moment at Tom with a pair of great red eyes.

2 "What are you doing on my grounds?" said the black man, with a hoarse growling voice.

"Your grounds!" said Tom, with a sneer. "No more your grounds than mine; they belong to Deacon Peabody."

"Deacon Peabody be d——d," said the stranger, "as I flatter myself he will be, if he does not look more to his own sins and less to those of his neighbors. Look yonder, and see how Deacon Peabody is faring."

Tom looked in the direction that the
3 stranger pointed and beheld one of the great trees, fair and flourishing without, but rotten at the core, and saw that it had been nearly hewn through, so that the first high wind was likely to blow it down. On the bark of the tree was scored the name of Deacon Peabody, an eminent man, who had waxed wealthy by driving shrewd bargains with the Indians. He now looked around, and found most of the tall trees marked with the name of some great man of the colony, and all more or less scored by the
4 ax. The one on which he had been seated, and which had evidently just been hewn down, bore the name of Crowninshield; and he recollected a mighty rich man of that name, who made a vulgar display of wealth, which it was whispered he had acquired by buccaneering.

"He's just ready for burning!" said the black man, with a growl of triumph. "You see I am likely to have a good stock of firewood for winter."

"But what right have you," said Tom, "to cut down Deacon Peabody's timber?"

"The right of a prior claim," said the other. "This woodland belonged to me long before one of your whitefaced race put foot upon the soil."

"And pray, who are you, if I may be so bold?" said Tom.

5 "Oh, I go by various names. I am the wild huntsman in some countries; the black miner in others. In this neighborhood I am known by the name of the black woodsman. I am he to whom the red men consecrated this spot, and in honor of whom they now and then roasted a white man, by way of sweet-smelling sacrifice. Since the red men have been exterminated by you white savages, I amuse myself by presiding at the persecutions of Quakers and Anabaptists;[5] I am the great patron and prompter of slave dealers, and the grandmaster of the Salem witches."

"The upshot of all which is that, if I mistake not," said Tom, sturdily, "you are he commonly called Old Scratch."

"The same, at your service!" replied the black man, with a half-civil nod.

Such was the opening of this interview, according to the old story; though it has almost

5. **Quakers and Anabaptists:** two religious groups that were often persecuted for their beliefs.

AT A GLANCE

- The dark-skinned man accuses Tom of occupying his land.
- The man points out tall trees that bear the names of great men in the colony.
- Tom realizes that the mysterious stranger is the Devil.

1 IMAGERY

The image of the swarthy, sooty man toiling before a fire suggests the Devil stoking the fires of hell.

2 NARRATION

Introducing dialogue to the narration colors the rising action, as the characters reveal themselves with their own distinct voices.

3 SYMBOL

Irving makes a strong point about hypocrisy and corruption by describing the "Deacon Peabody" tree, rotting and weakened by the Devil's ax.

4 THEME

Irving uses the ill-gotten gains of Crowninshield, and his status in the colony, to attack unscrupulous businessmen of his own time and the culture that accorded them authority and honor.

5 STYLE: FIGURATIVE LANGUAGE

The concrete, evocative images of the wild huntsman, black miner, and black woodsman suggest the many manifestations of evil in the world and its timeless universality.

GUIDED READING

LITERAL QUESTIONS

1a. What does the Devil plan to burn in winter? (trees that bear the names of the colony's great men)

2a. How does the Devil amuse himself in Puritan New England? (by presiding at the persecution of Quakers and Anabaptists)

INFERENTIAL QUESTIONS

1b. What does this source of fuel suggest about the great men in the colony and their success? (that they will pay in hell for their ill-gotten earthly success)

2b. What can you infer about Irving's religious views from this characterization of the Devil? (He believes in religious tolerance.)

AT A GLANCE

- The Devil offers pirate gold in exchange for Tom's service and his soul.
- Crowninshield suddenly dies.
- Tom's wife urges him to accept the Devil's offer.

1 NARRATION

By citing oral history as his source *(It is said),* the narrator lends validity to his tale.

2 RESPONSE JOURNAL

Have students list what they think are the conditions that Tom had to meet to acquire the hidden treasure.

3 STYLE: DESCRIPTION

Detailed description and the narrator's claim to be reporting what Tom said create credibility for the supernatural events.

4 THEME

This passage reinforces the theme of hypocrisy by ironically contrasting the description of Crowninshield as a rich buccaneer and the newspaper's account of him as a great man in Israel.

5 PLOT: RISING ACTION

The quarrel between Tom and his wife adds a note of drama: Tom's contrariness may outweigh his greed.

too familiar an air to be credited. One would think that to meet with such a singular personage, in this wild, lonely place, would have shaken any man's nerves; but Tom was a hard-minded fellow, not easily daunted, and he had lived so long with a termagant wife that he did not even fear the Devil.

1 It is said that after this commencement they had a long and earnest conversation together as Tom returned homeward. The black man told him of great sums of money buried by Kidd the pirate under the oak trees on the high ridge, not far from the morass. All these were under his command, and protected by his power, so that none could find them but such as propitiated[6] his favor. These he offered to place within Tom Walker's reach, having conceived an especial kindness for him; but they were to be had only on certain conditions.
2 What these conditions were may be easily surmised, though Tom never disclosed them publicly. They must have been very hard, for he required time to think of them, and he was not a man to stick at trifles when money was in view. When they had reached the edge of the swamp, the stranger paused. "What proof have I that all you have been telling me is true?"
3 said Tom. "There's my signature," said the black man, pressing his finger on Tom's forehead. So saying, he turned off among the thickets of the swamp and seemed, as Tom said, to go down, down, down into the earth, until nothing but his head and shoulders could be seen, and so on, until he totally disappeared.

When Tom reached home, he found the black print of a finger burned, as it were, into his forehead, which nothing could obliterate.

4 The first news his wife had to tell him was the sudden death of Absalom Crowninshield, the rich buccaneer. It was announced in the papers with the usual flourish that "a great man had fallen in Israel."[7]

Tom recollected the tree which his black friend had just hewn down, and which was ready for burning. "Let the freebooter roast," said Tom. "Who cares!" He now felt convinced that all he had heard and seen was no illusion.

He was not prone to let his wife into his confidence; but as this was an uneasy secret, he willingly shared it with her. All her avarice was awakened at the mention of hidden gold, and she urged her husband to comply with the black man's terms and secure what would
5 make them wealthy for life. However Tom might have felt disposed to sell himself to the Devil, he was determined not to do so to oblige his wife; so he flatly refused, out of the mere spirit of contradiction. Many and bitter were the quarrels they had on the subject; but the more she talked, the more resolute was Tom not to be damned to please her.

At length she determined to drive the bargain on her own account, and if she succeeded, to keep all the gain to herself. Being of the

6. **propitiated** [prə pish′ē āt id]: earned, gained.
7. **Israel:** II Samuel 3 : 38. The Puritans traditionally called New England "Israel," their Promised Land.

GUIDED READING

LITERAL QUESTIONS

1a. What explanation does the narrator suggest for Tom's not being afraid of the Devil? (He has lived a long time with a bad-tempered wife.)

2a. What proof does the Devil give Tom that he is telling the truth? (He burns his signature into Tom's forehead.)

INFERENTIAL QUESTIONS

1b. What does this explanation imply in regard to marriage? (Living with a quarrelsome spouse can be like hell on earth.)

2b. What might the Devil's actions indicate about the power of evil? (That power is formidable; it scars human beings.)

same fearless temper as her husband, she set off for the old Indian fort towards the close of a summer's day. She was many hours absent. When she came back, she was reserved and sullen in her replies. She spoke something of a black man, whom she had met about twilight hewing at the root of a tall tree. He was sulky, however, and would not come to terms: she was to go again with a propitiatory offering, but what it was she forbore to say.

The next evening she set off again for the swamp, with her apron heavily laden. Tom waited and waited for her, but in vain; midnight came, but she did not make her appearance: morning, noon, night returned, but still
1 she did not come. Tom now grew uneasy for her safety, especially as he found she had carried off in her apron the silver teapot and spoons, and every portable article of value. Another night elapsed, another morning came; but no wife. In a word, she was never heard of more.

2 What was her real fate nobody knows, in consequence of so many pretending to know. It is one of those facts which have become confounded by a variety of historians. Some asserted that she lost her way among the tangled mazes of the swamp and sank into some pit or slough; others, more uncharitable, hinted that she had eloped with the household booty and made off to some other province; while others surmised that the tempter had decoyed her into a dismal quagmire, on the top of which her hat was found lying. In confirmation of this, it was said a great black man, with an ax on his shoulder, was seen late that very evening coming out of the swamp, carrying a bundle tied in a check apron, with an air of surly triumph.

The most current and probable story, however, observes that Tom Walker grew so anxious about the fate of his wife and his property that he set out at length to seek them both at the Indian fort. During a long summer's afternoon he searched about the gloomy place, but no wife was to be seen. He called her name repeatedly, but she was nowhere to be heard. The bittern alone responded to his voice as he flew screaming by; or the bullfrog croaked dolefully from a neighboring pool. At length, it
3 is said, just in the brown hour of twilight, when the owls began to hoot, and the bats to flit about, his attention was attracted by the clamor of carrion crows hovering about a cypress tree. He looked up and beheld a bundle tied in a check apron and hanging in the branches of the tree, with a great vulture perched hard by, as if keeping watch upon it. He leaped with joy; for he recognized his wife's apron, and supposed it to contain the household valuables.

"Let us get hold of the property," said he consolingly to himself, "and we will endeavor to do without the woman."

As he scrambled up the tree, the vulture spread its wide wings and sailed off, screaming, into the deep shadows of the forest. Tom seized the checked apron, but, woeful sight! found nothing but a heart and liver tied up in it!

Such, according to this most authentic old story, was all that was to be found of Tom's wife. She had probably attempted to deal with the black man as she had been accustomed to deal with her husband; but though a female scold is generally considered a match for the Devil, yet in this instance she appears to have had the worst of it. She must have died game, however; for it is said Tom noticed many prints of cloven feet deeply stamped about the tree, and found handfuls of hair that looked as if they had been plucked from the coarse black shock of the woodman. Tom knew his wife's prowess by experience. He shrugged his shoulders, as he looked at the signs of a fierce clapperclawing. "Egad," said he to himself, "Old Scratch must have had a tough time of it!"

4 Tom consoled himself for the loss of his property with the loss of his wife, for he was a man of fortitude. He even felt something like gratitude towards the black woodman, who, he considered, had done him a kindness. He sought, therefore, to cultivate a further acquaintance with him, but for some time without success; the old blacklegs played shy, for whatever people may think, he is not always to

AT A GLANCE

- Tom's wife goes to meet the Devil and disappears mysteriously.
- Tom finds a heart and liver tied up in his wife's apron.
- He looks for the Devil, with no success.

1 TONE

The narrator achieves an ironic tone when he reverses conventional expectations: Tom is concerned not because his wife has disappeared but because she has taken the family silver with her.

2 NARRATION

In recounting various historians' claims and admitting that no one really knew what had happened to Tom's wife, the narrator gives the story authenticity.

3 ATMOSPHERE

The bats and the "carrion crows" gathering at "the brown hour of twilight" create a supernatural atmosphere that foreshadows Tom's discovery of his wife's remains.

4 THEME

A primary effect of Tom and his wife's greed is the reversal of traditional marital values.

GUIDED READING

LITERAL QUESTIONS

1a. What does Tom's wife bring the Devil as a propitiary offering? (every portable item of value from her home)

2a. What does Tom find at the base of the tree after discovering his wife's apron? (prints of cloven feet and tufts of coarse black hair)

INFERENTIAL QUESTIONS

1b. What does her offering suggest about her character? (Her sense of values is entirely materialistic.)

2b. In what way does Tom's discovery add to the atmosphere of the story? (It intensifies the sense of the supernatural and reinforces the folk-tale framework.)

AT A GLANCE

- Tom bargains with the Devil but refuses to deal in slaves.
- He agrees to use Kidd's gold to become a usurer.

1 THEME

The Devil reveals that greed is his own driving motivation when he insists that Tom use the gold to further the Devil's work.

2 DIALOGUE

The intense dialogue between Tom and the Devil heightens the rising action and adds color and depth to Tom's and the Devil's characters.

3 PLOT: CLIMAX

The handshake between Tom and the Devil consummates the bargain and points toward the resolution of the conflict between the two.

4 SETTING

Details that firmly set the story in eighteenth-century New England add a realistic dimension to the tale.

be had for calling for: he knows how to play his cards when pretty sure of his game.

At length, it is said, when delay had whetted Tom's eagerness to the quick and prepared him to agree to anything rather than not gain the promised treasure, he met the black man one evening in his usual woodman's dress, with his ax on his shoulder, sauntering along the swamp and humming a tune. He affected to receive Tom's advances with great indifference, made brief replies, and went on humming his tune.

By degrees, however, Tom brought him to business, and they began to haggle about the terms on which the former was to have the pirate's treasure. There was one condition which need not be mentioned, being generally understood in all cases where the Devil grants favors; but there were others about which, though of less importance, he was inflexibly
1 obstinate. He insisted that the money found through his means should be employed in his service. He proposed, therefore, that Tom should employ it in the black traffic; that is to say, that he should fit out a slave ship. This, however, Tom resolutely refused: he was bad enough in all conscience, but the Devil himself could not tempt him to turn slave trader.

Finding Tom so squeamish on this point, he did not insist upon it, but proposed, instead, that he should turn usurer,[8] the Devil being extremely anxious for the increase of usurers, looking upon them as his peculiar[9] people.

To this no objections were made, for it was just to Tom's taste.

2 "You shall open a broker's shop in Boston next month," said the black man.

"I'll do it tomorrow, if you wish," said Tom Walker.

"You shall lend money at two per cent a month."

"Egad, I'll charge four!" replied Tom Walker.

"You shall extort bonds, foreclose mortgages, drive the merchants to bankruptcy—"

"I'll drive them to the d——l," cried Tom Walker.

"You are the usurer for my money!" said blacklegs with delight. "When will you want the rhino?"[10]

"This very night."

"Done!" said the Devil.

3 "Done!" said Tom Walker. So they shook hands and struck a bargain.

A few days' time saw Tom Walker seated behind his desk in a countinghouse in Boston.

His reputation for a ready-moneyed man who would lend money out for a good consid-
4 eration soon spread abroad. Everybody remembers the time of Governor Belcher,[11] when money was particularly scarce. It was a time of paper credit. The country had been deluged with government bills; the famous Land Bank[12] had been established; there had been a rage for speculating; the people had run mad with schemes for new settlements, for building cities in the wilderness; land jobbers[13] went about with maps of grants and townships and El Dorados,[14] lying nobody knew where, but which everybody was ready to purchase. In a word, the great speculating fever which breaks out every now and then in the country had raged to an alarming degree, and everybody was dreaming of making sudden fortunes from nothing. As usual the fever had subsided; the dream had gone off, and the imaginary fortunes with it; the patients were left in doleful plight, and the whole country resounded with the consequent cry of "hard times."

At this propitious time of public distress did Tom Walker set up as usurer in Boston.

8. **usurer** [ū′zhər ər]: one who lends money at an unfair interest rate.
9. **peculiar:** special.

10. **rhino** [rī′nō]: slang for "money."
11. **Governor Belcher:** Jonathan Belcher, governor of Massachusetts and New Hampshire from 1730 to 1741.
12. **Land Bank:** bank that loaned money to people based on mortgages controlled by the bank.
13. **land jobbers:** people who bought and sold undeveloped land as a speculation.
14. **El Dorados** [el′də rä′dōs]: places of fabulous wealth. Explorers had searched for the legendary place the Spanish called El Dorado, "the golden one."

GUIDED READING

LITERAL QUESTIONS

1a. Which of the Devil's requests does Tom refuse? (that he become a slave trader)

2a. What makes the timing of Tom's moneylending business so appropriate? (the great speculating fever then rampant in Boston)

INFERENTIAL QUESTIONS

1b. What does this refusal imply about Irving's personal views? (It suggests that slavery was so evil that even the most immoral man would not stoop to it.)

2b. What does the narrator's description of the business climate suggest about the prevailing social values? (that the country had become obsessed with making money through investments)

His door was soon thronged by customers. The needy and adventurous, the gambling speculator, the dreaming land jobber, the thriftless tradesman, the merchant with cracked credit, in short, everyone driven to raise money by desperate means and desperate sacrifices hurried to Tom Walker.

Thus Tom was the universal friend of the needy, and acted like a "friend in need"; that is to say, he always exacted good pay and good
1 security. In proportion to the distress of the applicant was the hardness of his terms. He accumulated bonds and mortgages, gradually squeezed his customers closer and closer, and sent them at length, dry as a sponge, from his door.

In this way he made money hand over hand, became a rich and mighty man, and exalted his cocked hat upon 'Change.[15] He built himself, as usual, a vast house, out of ostentation; but left the greater part of it unfinished and unfurnished, out of parsimony. He even set up a carriage in the fullness of his vainglory, though he nearly starved the horses
2 which drew it; and as the ungreased wheels groaned and screeched on the axletrees, you would have thought you heard the souls of the poor debtors he was squeezing.

As Tom waxed old, however, he grew thoughtful. Having secured the good things of this world, he began to feel anxious about those of the next. He thought with regret on the bargain he had made with his black friend, and set his wits to work to cheat him out of the conditions. He became, therefore, all of a
3 sudden, a violent churchgoer. He prayed loudly and strenuously, as if heaven were to be taken by force of lungs. Indeed, one might always tell when he had sinned most during the week by the clamor of his Sunday devotion. The quiet Christians who had been modestly and steadfastly traveling Zionward[16] were struck with self-reproach at seeing themselves so suddenly outstripped in their career by this new-made convert. Tom was as rigid in religious as in money matters; he was a stern supervisor and censurer of his neighbors, and seemed to think every sin entered up to their account became a credit on his own side of the page. He even
4 talked of the expediency of reviving the persecution of Quakers and Anabaptists. In a word, Tom's zeal became as notorious as his riches.

Still, in spite of all this strenuous attention to forms, Tom had a lurking dread that the Devil, after all, would have his due. That he might not be taken unawares, therefore, it is said he always carried a small Bible in his coat pocket. He had also a great folio Bible on his countinghouse desk, and would frequently be found reading it when people called on business; on such occasions he would lay his green spectacles in the book, to mark the place, while he turned round to drive some usurious bargain.

Some say that Tom grew a little crack-brained in his old days, and that, fancying his end approaching, he had his horse new shod, saddled and bridled, and buried with his feet uppermost; because he supposed that at the last day the world would be turned upside down, in which case he should find his horse standing ready for mounting, and he was determined at the worst to give his old friend a
5 run for it. This, however, is probably a mere old wives' fable. If he really did take such a precaution, it was totally superfluous; at least so says the authentic old legend, which closes his story in the following manner.

One hot summer afternoon in the dog days, just as a terrible black thunder-gust was coming up, Tom sat in his countinghouse, in his white linen cap and India silk morning gown. He was on the point of foreclosing a mortgage, by which he would complete the ruin of an unlucky land speculator for whom he had professed the greatest friendship. The poor land jobber begged him to grant a few months' indulgence. Tom had grown testy and irritated, and refused another day.

"My family will be ruined, and brought

15. **'Change:** the Exchange, where merchants and bankers met to do business.
16. **Zionward:** toward Heaven.

AT A GLANCE

- Tom becomes successful and wealthy but remains a miser.
- Regretting his bargain with the Devil, he becomes a churchgoer.

1 STYLE: FIGURATIVE LANGUAGE

Tom's hardness and his clients' distress are graphically conveyed in the image of Tom squeezing his victims "dry as a sponge."

2 ONOMATOPOEIA

The emphasis on sound *(groaned, screeched)* adds an anguished dimension to the allusion to the debtors.

3 THEME

Irving's humorous, exaggerated portrait of Tom at prayer illustrates that real piety is reflected better in one's daily life than in a public performance.

4 CHARACTERIZATION

Tom's talk of persecuting Quakers and Anabaptists shows, ironically, that he is still doing the Devil's work.

5 NARRATION

By reporting and then discounting other versions of Tom's demise, the narrator adds both suspense and credibility to this final version.

GUIDED READING

LITERAL QUESTIONS

1a. How does Tom treat the horses that pull his carriage? (He nearly starves them to death.)

2a. What does Tom keep on his countinghouse desk? (a big Bible)

INFERENTIAL QUESTIONS

1b. What is revealed about Tom's character from the way that he treated his horse at the beginning of the story and the way that he treats his horses now? (He hasn't changed.)

2b. What point do you think Irving makes by emphasizing this detail? (that piety cannot be judged according to outward forms of observance)

AT A GLANCE

- The Devil catches Tom without his Bible.
- Tom is last seen being carried off on a black horse to the Indian fort.
- Tom's house burns to the ground; his treasures are worthless.

1 DIALOGUE

Dialogue adds drama to the impending conclusion and helps to make the events more believable.

2 PLOT: RESOLUTION

The description of Tom's abduction in the midst of a violent storm heightens the tension and drama as the story ends.

3 NARRATION

The narrator adds credibility to his version of Tom's abduction by citing an authority to substantiate his earlier description.

4 THEME

The images of cinders, chips, shavings, and skeletons reinforce the valuelessness of earthly possessions and highlight the inherent vanity of greed.

REFLECTING ON THE STORY

What similarities between their own time and late Puritan New England do you think Irving's contemporaries were likely to see? (Students may note the importance of the work ethic or concern with the conflict between spiritual and temporal values.)

upon the parish," said the land jobber. "Charity begins at home," replied Tom; "I must take
1 care of myself in these hard times."

"You have made so much money out of me," said the speculator.

Tom lost his patience and his piety. "The Devil take me," said he, "if I have made a farthing!"

Just then there were three loud knocks at the street door. He stepped out to see who was there. A black man was holding a black horse, which neighed and stamped with impatience.

"Tom, you're come for," said the black fellow gruffly. Tom shrank back, but too late. He had left his little Bible at the bottom of his coat pocket, and his big Bible on the desk buried under the mortgage he was about to foreclose: never was sinner taken more unawares.
2 The black man whisked him like a child into the saddle, gave the horse the lash, and away he galloped, with Tom on his back, in the midst of the thunderstorm. The clerks stuck their pens behind their ears and stared after him from the windows. Away went Tom Walker, dashing down the streets, his white cap bobbing up and down, his morning gown fluttering in the wind, and his steed striking fire out of the pavement at every bound. When the clerks turned to look for the black man, he had disappeared.

Tom Walker never returned to foreclose
3 the mortgage. A countryman who lived on the border of the swamp reported that in the height of the thunder-gust he had heard a great clattering of hoofs and a howling along the road, and, running to the window, caught sight of a figure such as I have described, on a horse that galloped like mad across the fields, over the hills, and down into the black hemlock swamp towards the old Indian fort; and that shortly after a thunderbolt falling in that direction seemed to set the whole forest in a blaze.

The good people of Boston shook their heads and shrugged their shoulders, but had been so much accustomed to witches and goblins and tricks of the Devil, in all kinds of shapes, from the first settlement of the colony, that they were not so much horror-struck as might have been expected. Trustees were appointed to take charge of Tom's effects. There was nothing, however, to administer upon. On searching his coffers, all his bonds and mort-
4 gages were found reduced to cinders. In place of gold and silver, his iron chest was filled with chips and shavings; two skeletons lay in his stable instead of his half-starved horses, and the very next day his great house took fire and was burned to the ground.

Such was the end of Tom Walker and his ill-gotten wealth. Let all griping money brokers lay this story to heart. The truth of it is not to be doubted. The very hole under the oak trees, whence he dug Kidd's money, is to be seen to this day; and the neighboring swamp and old Indian fort are often haunted in stormy nights by a figure on horseback, in morning gown and white cap, which is doubtless the troubled spirit of the usurer. In fact, the story has resolved itself into a proverb, and is the origin of that popular saying, so prevalent throughout New England, of "The Devil and Tom Walker."

GUIDED READING

LITERAL QUESTIONS

1a. In what way is Tom taken unawares by the Devil's reappearance? (He has forgotten his Bible.)

2a. Why are the people in Boston not as horror-struck as might be expected? (They were used to believing in witches, goblins, and the tricks of the Devil.)

INFERENTIAL QUESTIONS

1b. What do you think is the significance of Tom's forgetfulness? (It reinforces the idea that true piety is something that must be felt within; it cannot be "carried around.")

2b. What point do you think that Irving might be making with this observation? (He seems to be satirizing the age as one in which too many people claimed to have had supernatural experiences.)

STUDY QUESTIONS

Recalling

1. What adjectives in the second paragraph describe Tom and his wife?
2. Why does Tom refuse the Devil's offer at first? As a result, what does Tom's wife do? What does Tom find when he looks for her?
3. In addition to the "one condition which need not be mentioned," what does Tom agree to do in return for the treasure?
4. According to page 111, what sort of man does Tom become after his pact with the Devil? Why does he build a big house? Why does he leave it unfinished?
5. As Tom grows old, about what does he grow anxious?
6. What does Tom say to the poor land jobber? What are Tom's last words? What becomes of his possessions?

Interpreting

7. What character trait of the Walkers is reinforced by the descriptions of their house and horse in the second paragraph? Does this trait later change? Explain.
8. What is the "one condition which need not be mentioned" (page 110)?
9. Why are Tom's last words ironic?
10. Identify in the story two elements of Romanticism described in the introduction to this unit. Which details make the story an American tale, despite its age-old theme?

Extending

11. What would you say are some of the positive human traits not possessed by Tom and his wife that Irving wants us to think about?

VIEWPOINT

Literary critic Lewis Leary points out that although Irving spent many years in other countries, he saw his own country clearly.

> With quick eye, ready tongue, and alert recognition of absurdities, he sits quietly at both ends of the American literary spectrum—an expatriate seeking reverently in Europe for sources of culture, but . . . most effective in realizing American characters enmeshed in American ideals.
>
> *—Washington Irving*

■ What qualities of Tom and his wife seem to you to be common to people of all places? What qualities seem to be particularly American? What do you think makes these two characters become victims of their "ideals"?

LITERARY FOCUS

Narration

Narration is writing that tells a story, moving from event to event, usually in chronological order. A narrative may be factual, like William Bradford's *Of Plymouth Plantation* (which appears on page 24), or fictional, like "The Devil and Tom Walker."

Sometimes a fictional narrative will have elements that make it seem factual. In "The Devil and Tom Walker" Irving uses the narrator of the story, Diedrich Knickerbocker, to help make his fictional narrative seem like fact.

Knickerbocker is supposed to be a historian, and so his reputation lends the story believability. He uses expressions like "this most authentic old story" to make us believe that this outlandish tale actually happened. He cites his sources of information and even tells us that there are a few details of which he is not quite sure (implying that everything else is absolutely correct). These devices give the narrative the ring of truth.

Thinking About Narration

■ Find two other examples in the story of "evidence" presented by the narrator to make us believe that his fictional narrative is a true story.

COMPOSITION

Summarizing a Narrative

■ Tell the story of Tom Walker and his wife in one paragraph. Include all the major events in the story and omit unimportant details. Make your sentences move smoothly from event to event, creating one connected narrative.

Retelling from a Different Point of View

■ Retell the story of Tom Walker using Mrs. Walker as the narrator. Cover only the events up to the point of her disappearance. Remember to consider her personality, the events she witnesses, her relationship to Tom, and her final meeting with Old Scratch.

STUDY QUESTIONS

1. meager, miserly
2. ■ His wife wants him to accept it.
   ■ She goes to make her own deal.
   ■ her apron, with a heart and a liver
3. become a usurer, ruin people
4. rich, mighty; ostentation; parsimony
5. his fate after death
6. ■ "Charity begins at home. I must take care of myself in these hard times."
   ■ "The Devil take me if I have made a farthing!"
   ■ become worthless, house burns
7. ■ miserliness
   ■ No—his wife is still miserly when she disappears; wealth does not change Tom.
8. Tom's soul belongs to the Devil.
9. Tom uses a figure of speech to claim falsely that he has made no money, but the Devil takes it literally.
10. fascination with supernatural, idealism; setting, references to historical figures, events
11. Possible answers: charity, generosity, sincerity

VIEWPOINT

common: greed, miserliness, contentiousness; *American:* materialism; *victims* of American drive for success, Puritan work ethic—of ideals gone astray

LITERARY FOCUS

detailed description of swamp, references to historical figures

COMPOSITION: GUIDELINES FOR EVALUATION

SUMMARIZING A NARRATIVE

Objective

To write a summary

Guidelines for Evaluation

- suggested length: one paragraph
- should include all important events in the story
- should organize the events chronologically
- should tell story smoothly, using transitions

RETELLING FROM A DIFFERENT POINT OF VIEW

Objective

To retell a story from a different point of view

Guidelines for Evaluation

- suggested length: three to six paragraphs
- should establish character of Mrs. Walker
- should relate the quarrel over Devil's offer, Mrs. Walker's first trip to the swamp, and her final meeting with Old Scratch

James Fenimore Cooper *1789–1851*

Although James Fenimore Cooper is best remembered for his novels of the American frontier, he himself never experienced the danger and struggle of pioneer life. The son of a wealthy judge, Cooper grew up in Cooperstown, a settlement established by his father in New York State. By 1789, however, the frontier had moved farther west, and there were few pioneers left. "I was never among the Indians," Cooper admitted. "All that I know of them is from reading, and from hearing my father speak of them." From his home Cooper watched wagon trains heading west; he left the rest up to his imagination.

After several years as a sailor and then as an officer, Cooper married and settled down to the life of a gentleman farmer with money inherited from his father. Tradition says that one day he tossed aside the British novel he was reading and exclaimed to his wife, "I could write a better book myself." She challenged him to do so, and Cooper produced a sentimental novel, *Precaution*. Determined to improve, he wrote a tale of the Revolution, *The Spy,* which became a great success in America and Europe.

In 1823 Cooper published *The Pioneers,* the first of the Leatherstocking Tales, five novels centering around the career of the frontiersman Natty Bumppo. Natty has many names—Leatherstocking, Deerslayer, Pathfinder—but his character never changes. He is strong, brave, resourceful, independent, and absolutely honorable, with a profound understanding of nature. The five novels—*The Deerslayer, The Last of the Mohicans, The Pathfinder, The Prairie,* and *The Pioneers*—make up an American epic, chronicling the westward march of civilization and the destruction of the wilderness.

Cooper went on to write over thirty novels, including eleven exciting adventures of the sea. His plots were often improbable and his language unrealistic, but he charged his works with an energy that made them immensely popular. He created the American historical novel, using authentic American subjects. He infused those subjects with a spirit of chivalry and romanticism like that of the British novelist Sir Walter Scott—complete with heroes and villains, picturesque settings, extraordinary adventures, and a profound love of country.

In Natty Bumppo, Cooper did what few writers ever succeed in doing: He created a character so original and so influential that it became a myth. Natty is the title character in *The Deerslayer*. At the time of the story, he is an untried youth, but one who already possesses qualities that would become typical of the American hero.

■ What impression of America and Americans would Cooper give to a newcomer to this country?

James Fenimore Cooper

from The Deerslayer

The incidents of this tale occurred between the years 1740 and 1745, when the settled portions of the colony of New York were confined to the four Atlantic counties, a narrow
1 belt of country on each side of the Hudson, extending from its mouth to the falls near its head, and to a few advanced "neighborhoods" on the Mohawk and the Schoharie. Broad belts of the virgin wilderness not only reached the shores of the first river, but they even crossed it, stretching away into New England, and affording forest covers to the noiseless moccasin of the native warrior as he trod the secret and bloody warpath. A bird's-eye view of the whole region east of the Mississippi must then have offered one vast expanse of woods, relieved by a comparatively narrow fringe of cultivation along the sea, dotted by the glittering surfaces of lakes, and intersected by the waving lines of rivers. In such a vast picture of solemn solitude, the district of country we design to paint sinks into insignificance, though we feel encouraged to proceed by the conviction that, with slight and immaterial distinctions, he who succeeds in giving an accurate idea of any portion of this wild region must necessarily convey a tolerably correct notion of the whole.

2 Whatever may be the changes produced by man, the eternal round of the seasons is unbroken. Summer and winter, seedtime and harvest, return in their stated order with a sublime precision, affording to man one of the noblest of all the occasions he enjoys of proving the high powers of his far-reaching mind, in compassing[1] the laws that control their exact uniformity, and in calculating their never-ending revolutions. Centuries of summer suns had warmed the tops of the same noble oaks and pines, sending their heats even to the tenacious roots, when voices were heard calling to each other in the depths of a forest, of which the leafy surface lay bathed in the brilliant light of a cloudless day in June, while the trunks of the trees rose in gloomy grandeur in the shades beneath. The calls were in different tones, evidently proceeding from two men who had lost their way and were searching in different directions for their path. At length a shout proclaimed success, and presently a man of gigantic mold broke out of the tangled labyrinth of a small swamp, emerging into an opening that appeared to have been formed partly by the ravages of the wind, and partly by
3 those of fire. This little area, which afforded a good view of the sky, although it was pretty well filled with dead trees, lay on the side of one of the high hills, or low mountains, into which nearly the whole surface of the adjacent country was broken.

"Here is room to breathe in!" exclaimed the liberated forester as soon as he found himself under a clear sky, shaking his huge frame
4 like a mastiff[2] that has just escaped from a snowbank: "Hurrah! Deerslayer; here is daylight at last, and yonder is the lake."

These words were scarcely uttered when the second forester dashed aside the bushes of the swamp and appeared in the area. After making a hurried adjustment of his arms and disordered dress, he joined his companion, who had already begun his dispositions for a halt.

"Do you know this spot?" demanded the one called Deerslayer, "or do you shout at the sight of the sun?"

"Both, lad, both; I know the spot, and am not sorry to see so useful a friend as the sun. Now we have got the p'ints of the compass in our minds once more, and 'twill be our own

1. **compassing:** understanding.

2. **mastiff:** large, powerful dog.

AT A GLANCE

- The narrator describes an unsettled portion of the New York colony in the 1740s.
- The voices of two lost men are heard in the forest.
- One of the men calls to his friend, Deerslayer, to join him in a clearing.

LITERARY OPTIONS

- dialect
- description

THEMATIC OPTIONS

- the noble frontiersman
- unity with nature

1 SETTING

The wilderness appealed to Cooper's readers and represented an inherent harmony and spiritual purity that contrasted with materialistic civilization.

2 THEME

The eternal, harmonious cycle of the seasons reflects the benevolent and sublime power of nature, which often goes unrecognized by the individual.

3 DESCRIPTION

Cooper paints a majestic canvas of the natural world by dispensing with specific physical details and focusing on the sky, the forest, and the surrounding mountains.

4 DIALECT

The characters' way of speaking reinforces the historical and regional setting of the story, and adds color and dramatic interest to the dialogue.

GUIDED READING

LITERAL QUESTIONS

1a. Why does the narrator feel encouraged to go on with his story in spite of the size of his subject? (He thinks that an accurate description of any part of the region can portray the whole.)

2a. To what animal does the narrator compare Hurry Harry? (a mastiff)

INFERENTIAL QUESTIONS

1b. What does this view suggest about the nature of frontier America? (Before the encroachments of civilization, there was an underlying harmony and union.)

2b. What can you infer about Hurry Harry from this physical description? (He is strong, active, energetic, and at home in the natural world.)

AT A GLANCE

- Hurry Harry and Deerslayer eat lunch.
- Hurry Harry has a noble physical bearing, while Deerslayer has a guileless manner.
- Both men wear deerskin and carry knives and guns.

1 DIALECT

Harry's colorful natural speech, with its focus on physical detail (stomach as a timepiece) and its use of dialect *(p'ints, wallet)*, reflects the self-sufficient character of the early American frontiersman.

2 CHARACTERIZATION

In explaining the origins of Harry's nickname, the narrator both places him in an historical context and anticipates the description that follows.

3 ROMANTIC IDEA

Cooper's description of Harry provides a portrait of the free-spirited, self-confident kind of hero admired during the Romantic age.

4 DESCRIPTION

The detailed description of the men's dress adds depth and a more specific historical context to Cooper's earlier description of their physical traits and personalities.

faults if we let anything turn them topsy-turvy ag'in as has just happened. My name is not Hurry Harry, if this be not the very spot where the land hunters 'camped the last summer and passed a week. See, yonder are the dead bushes of their bower, and here is the spring.
1 Much as I like the sun, boy, I've no occasion for it to tell me it is noon; this stomach of mine is as good a timepiece as is to be found in the colony, and it already p'ints to half-past twelve. So open the wallet,[3] and let us wind up for another six hours' run."

At this suggestion, both set themselves about making the preparations necessary for their usual frugal but hearty meal. We will profit by this pause in the discourse to give the reader some idea of the appearance of the men, each of whom is destined to enact no insignificant part in our legend. It would not have been easy to find a more noble specimen of vigorous manhood than was offered in the person of him who called himself Hurry Harry.
2 His real name was Henry March; but the frontiermen having caught the practice of giving *sobriquets*[4] from the Indians, the appellation of Hurry was far oftener applied to him than his proper designation, and not infrequently he was termed Hurry Skurry, a nickname he had obtained from a dashing, reckless, offhand manner, and a physical restlessness that kept him so constantly on the move as to cause him to be known along the whole line of scattered habitations that lay between the province and the Canadas. The stature of Hurry Harry exceeded six feet four, and, being unusually well-proportioned, his strength fully realized the
3 idea created by his gigantic frame. The face did no discredit to the rest of the man, for it was both good-humored and handsome. His air was free, and, though his manner necessarily partook of the rudeness of a border life, the grandeur that pervaded so noble a physique prevented it from becoming altogether vulgar.

Deerslayer, as Hurry called his companion, was a very different person in appearance, as well as in character. In stature he stood about six feet in his moccasins, but his frame was comparatively light and slender, showing muscles, however, that promised unusual agility, if not unusual strength. His face would have had little to recommend it except youth, were it not for an expression that seldom failed to win upon those who had leisure to examine it and to yield to the feeling of confidence it created. This expression was simply that of guileless truth, sustained by an earnestness of purpose and a sincerity of feeling that rendered it remarkable. At times this air of integrity seemed to be so simple as to awaken the suspicion of a want of the usual means to discriminate between artifice and truth; but few came in serious contact with the man without losing this distrust in respect for his opinions and motives.

Both these frontiermen were still young, Hurry having reached the age of six- or eight-and-twenty, while Deerslayer was several years
4 his junior. Their attire needs no particular description, though it may be well to add that it was composed in no small degree of dressed deerskins, and had the usual signs of belonging to those who pass their time between the skirts of civilized society and the boundless forests. There was, notwithstanding, some attention to smartness and the picturesque in the arrangements of Deerslayer's dress more particularly in the part connected with his arms and accouterments. His rifle was in perfect condition, the handle of his hunting knife was neatly carved, his powder horn was ornamented with suitable devices lightly cut into the material, and his shot pouch was decorated with wampum. On the other hand, Hurry Harry, either from constitutional recklessness or from a secret consciousness how little his appearance required artificial aids, wore everything in a careless, slovenly manner, as if he felt a noble scorn for the trifling accessories of dress and ornaments. Perhaps the peculiar effect of his

3. **wallet:** knapsack.
4. ***sobriquets*** [sō′ brə kā′]: French for "nicknames."

GUIDED READING

LITERAL QUESTIONS

1a. Why was Henry March called Hurry Harry? (Frontiersmen had adopted the Indian custom of using a nickname.)

2a. How are Hurry Harry and Deerslayer dressed? (in deerskin; carrying rifles, hunting knives, powder horns, and shot pouches)

INFERENTIAL QUESTIONS

1b. What are the positive connotations of this name? (that he is swift and dashing) What are the negative connotations? (that he may be reckless, perhaps undependable)

2b. What does the way in which Harry and Deerslayer dress suggest about the way in which they live? (Their clothing suggests that they live by their wits and strengths, and that they are self-reliant and at home in the outdoors.)

fine form and great stature was increased, rather than lessened, by this unstudied and disdainful air of indifference.

1 "Come, Deerslayer, fall to, and prove that you have a Delaware[5] stomach, as you say you have had a Delaware edication," cried Hurry, setting the example by opening his mouth to receive a slice of cold venison steak that would have made an entire meal for a European peasant; "fall to, lad, and prove your manhood on this poor devil of a doe with your teeth, as you've already done with your rifle."

2 "Nay, nay, Hurry, there's little manhood in killing a doe, and that too out of season; though there might be some in bringing down a painter[6] or a catamount,"[7] returned the other, disposing himself to comply. "The Delawares have given me my name not so much on account of a bold heart, as on account of a quick eye and an active foot. There may not be any cowardice in overcoming a deer, but sartain it is, there's no great valor."

"The Delawares themselves are no heroes," muttered Hurry through his teeth, the mouth being too full to permit it to be fairly opened, "or they would never have allowed them loping vagabonds, the Mingos,[8] to make them women."

3 "That matter is not rightly understood—has never been rightly explained," said Deerslayer earnestly, for he was as zealous a friend as his companion was dangerous as an enemy; "the Mengwe[9] fill the woods with their lies, and misconstruct words and treaties. I have now lived ten years with the Delawares, and know them to be as manful as any other nation when the proper time to strike comes."

---

5. **Delaware:** Indian of the Delaware River Valley.
6. **painter:** in Deerslayer's dialect, a panther or cougar.
7. **catamount** [kat′ə mount]: wild cat, such as a puma.
8. **Mingos:** Delaware name for the Iroquois, meaning "the treacherous."
9. **Mengwe:** variant of *Mingo.*

"Harkee, Master Deerslayer, since we are on the subject, we may as well open our minds to each other in a man-to-man way; answer me one question. You have had so much luck among the game as to have gotten a title, it would seem, but did you ever hit anything human or intelligible: did you ever pull trigger on an inimy that was capable of pulling one upon you?"

This question produced a singular collision between mortification and correct feeling in the bosom of the youth that was easily to be traced in the workings of his ingenuous countenance. The struggle was short, however, uprightness of heart soon getting the better of false pride and frontier boastfulness.

"To own the truth, I never did," answered Deerslayer, "seeing that a fitting occasion never offered. The Delawares have been
4 peaceable since my sojourn with 'em, and I hold it to be onlawful to take the life of man, except in open and generous warfare."

"What! did you never find a fellow thieving among your traps and skins, and do the law on him, with your own hands, by way of saving the magistrates trouble in the settlements, and the rogue himself the cost of the suit?"

"I am no trapper, Hurry," returned the young man proudly: "I live by the rifle, a we'pon at which I will not turn my back on any man of my years atween the Hudson and the St. Lawrence. I never offer a skin that has not a hole in its head besides them which natur' made to see with or to breathe through."

". . . I shall not frequent your society long, friend Natty, unless you look higher than four-footed beasts to practice your rifle on."

"Our journey is nearly ended, you say, Master March, and we can part tonight, if you see occasion. I have a fri'nd waiting for me who will think it no disgrace to consort with a fellow creatur' that has never yet slain his kind."

AT A GLANCE

- While the two men eat cold venison, Deerslayer points out that there is no valor in killing deer.
- Deerslayer states that warfare is the only time he would kill a man. Harry challenges his conviction and they quarrel.

1 DIALECT

Note that Harry's speech is colored by expressions that he coins from his frontier experiences ("a Delaware edication").

2 CHARACTERIZATION

Deerslayer's refusal to use the dead deer as proof of his manhood shows an inherent decency.

3 CONFLICT

The conflict between Harry's contempt for the Delaware Indians and Deerslayer's defense of them reflects their more serious differences of opinion.

4 THEME

Deerslayer's moral code, which acknowledges the sanctity of human life, reflects his respect for nature and his harmony with the natural world.

REFLECTING ON THE STORY

How does Hurry Harry provide insight into Deerslayer's character? (by voicing ideas and values that conflict with Deerslayer's; by forcing Deerslayer to defend his views)

GUIDED READING

LITERAL QUESTIONS

1a. Why have the Delaware named Natty the "Deerslayer"? (because of his quick eye and active foot)

2a. What struggle does Deerslayer undergo when Harry asks him if he has ever killed a man? (the struggle between telling the truth or giving in to false pride and frontier boasting)

INFERENTIAL QUESTIONS

1b. In view of his character, what is ironic about Deerslayer's name? (He does not think that killing deer takes courage.)

2b. What can you infer about Deerslayer's character from the way in which he resolves the struggle? (He is honest, honorable, and self-confident enough to act on what he believes is right.)

STUDY QUESTIONS

1. a view of "one vast expanse of woods"; the first three sentences of the paragraph
2. Hurry Harry, Deerslayer; eat
3. a "noble specimen of vigorous manhood"; shorter, thinner, younger; "earnestness of purpose and sincerity of feeling"
4. The Delaware; "a quick eye and an active foot"
5. killing deer, the character of the Delaware, killing people
6. Deerslayer; no valor: for food only, not to prove manliness
7. modesty, thoughtfulness, honor; contentious, aggressive, boastful, prejudiced
8. idealized: noble, pristine; focus on individual, idealism, yearning for picturesque past, love of country
9. Answers will vary. Students should mention that the setting, themes, and characters are exotic, escapist, and idealistic.

LITERARY FOCUS

'twill: it will; *agin:* again; *sartain:* certain; *inimy:* enemy; *harkee:* listen; *onlawful:* unlawful

STUDY QUESTIONS

Recalling

1. What "bird's-eye view" of the region east of the Mississippi does the first paragraph provide? In the second paragraph locate a description that tells of the timeless, unspoiled environment in which the narrative takes place.
2. In paragraphs 3 – 6 who are the two characters we find in the woods and what do they set about doing?
3. According to the seventh paragraph, what kind of "specimen" is Harry? According to the eighth paragraph, how is Deerslayer different from Harry? What makes Deerslayer's expression "remarkable"?
4. Who educated Deerslayer? How did he acquire his nickname?
5. On what three subjects do Harry and Deerslayer disagree in the last nine paragraphs?

Interpreting

6. Who killed the doe that Deerslayer and Harry eat? What is that marksman's attitude toward slaying a doe?
7. Identify at least three character traits that make Deerslayer admirable or heroic. In comparison, what sort of person is Harry?
8. Judging from the first two paragraphs, what is the author's attitude toward nature? Identify the other elements of Romanticism the narrative contains (see the Introduction to this unit).

Extending

9. Most of Cooper's readers lived in towns and cities. Why would a romance of the wilderness such as *The Deerslayer* appeal to them?

LITERARY FOCUS

The American Language: Dialect

A few years after Cooper began his Leatherstocking Tales, Noah Webster published the first specifically American dictionary, *The American Dictionary of the English Language* (1828). Americans were becoming aware that their language was beginning to differ from the English written and spoken in England.

Today British and American English differ somewhat in both pronunciation and vocabulary. For example, when the British speak of the "bonnet" of a car, they mean what we call the "hood." Similarly, differences in vocabulary and pronunciation grew up within different regions of the United States.

These various ways of speaking and writing particular to a specific region of the country are called **dialects.** Some people, for example, say *skillet,* while others say *frying pan.* Some pronounce *root* to rhyme with *toot;* some pronounce it to rhyme with *foot.*

American writers have always taken pleasure in recording American dialects. In *The Deerslayer* Cooper writes *atween* for *between,* and *p'ints* for *points.* In later units of this book, Mark Twain, Bret Harte, and Willa Cather use dialects very effectively in their short stories. The use of written dialects helps us to imagine speaking voices more accurately and to understand characters more fully. It brings characters to life, even though we may occasionally need a footnote to tell us that a *painter* is a *panther.*

Thinking About Dialect

■ Find three other words in *The Deerslayer* that are examples of Deerslayer's and Harry's dialect. Tell what the words mean, and indicate which words you would use in their places if you were speaking.

COMPOSITION

Writing About a Quotation

■ In *The Deerslayer* Natty says, "I hold it to be onlawful to take the life of man, except in open and generous warfare." Write a composition discussing what this quotation tells about the hero. First tell why it is significant that Deerslayer cares about what is unlawful and what is not. Then discuss the meaning of the unusual phrase "generous warfare." Conclude with a general statement of how this sentence reflects Natty's whole character. *For help with this assignment, refer to Lesson 5 in the Writing About Literature Handbook at the back of this book.*

Writing a Description of a Hero

■ Write a description of a contemporary American hero. Take your hero from literature or from real life. You may want to organize your description by asking these questions: What does the hero look like? What is the hero's personality? What qualities make him or her a hero?

COMPOSITION: GUIDELINES FOR EVALUATION

WRITING ABOUT A QUOTATION

Objective

To analyze a character by examining a quotation

Guidelines for Evaluation

- suggested length: three to five paragraphs
- should relate quotation to setting
- should show understanding of "open . . . warfare"
- should identify underlying character traits leading Natty to make and believe statement
- should draw conclusion about Natty's character

WRITING A DESCRIPTION OF A HERO

Objective

To write a description of a heroic person

Guidelines for Evaluation

- suggested length: three to four paragraphs
- should say what hero looks like
- should describe his or her personality
- should identify individual's heroic traits
- should give the reader a sense of what the hero is like

William Cullen Bryant *1794–1878*

William Cullen Bryant, the "father of American poetry," grew up in a small village in western Massachusetts. He began writing when he was very young, composing devout religious poems and even publishing one when he was thirteen. Bryant's father encouraged him to continue writing poetry but recommended that he become a lawyer in order to make a living.

After a short time as a lawyer, however, Bryant began a career as one of the nation's most distinguished journalists. He became the editor-in-chief of the influential *New York Evening Post* and used his position to put forth his strong political and social views. He supported the early labor movement, free speech, a free press, and the abolition of slavery. He was instrumental in Lincoln's election to the presidency; in fact, it was Bryant who introduced Lincoln to the voters of New York. For the last thirty years of his life, Bryant was New York City's most prominent citizen, yet he continued to write poetry. His noble and romantic verses, often based on the American landscape, established him as the first American poet to have an enduring reputation. At his death, New York City's flags flew at half-mast.

Bryant probably wrote "Thanatopsis" when he was about nineteen. Several years later his father sent it to the *North American Review,* an important Boston literary magazine. When it was published—anonymously, according to the custom of the magazine—readers could not believe that it had been written by a young man, or even by an American. Even the editors of the magazine thought that Bryant's father had actually written it. As successful as the poem was, Bryant later revised it. He added the beginning section (lines 1–17) and the ending (lines 66–81).

The title of the poem is a Greek word meaning "view of death." The poem is, however, much more than that. "Thanatopsis," which begins on the following page, is a Romantic poet's vision of what it means to be a human being—to be both a mortal individual and a part of enduring nature.

■ In what ways do you think we can respond to nature? Are there ways in which nature can respond to us?

AT A GLANCE

- Nature has various messages to meet your moods.
- When thoughts of death blight your spirit, you should listen to nature's teachings.
- When you die, you become a part of elements and do not die alone.

LITERARY OPTIONS

- meter
- personification

THEMATIC OPTIONS

- the nature of death
- the power of nature

BACKGROUND

During Bryant's youth young people died of diseases easily cured or prevented today; it would have been natural for him to become absorbed in thoughts of death. A literary influence on the young writer was Wordsworth, the great English Romantic poet of nature.

PERSONIFICATION

The poem attributes to nature the character of a benevolent woman: a teacher and nurse. It refers to her voice, her smile, her "healing sympathy." Personification is also used for particular natural phenomena such as the sun (ll. 1–8, 17–19).

MAIN IDEA

When facing death, you should take comfort in nature. Looking at the natural world, you can see the earth as everyone's final resting place (ll. 14–17, 31–34).

William Cullen Bryant

Thanatopsis

To him who in the love of Nature holds
Communion with her visible forms, she speaks
A various language; for his gayer hours
She has a voice of gladness, and a smile
And eloquence of beauty, and she glides
Into his darker musings, with a mild
And healing sympathy, that steals away
Their sharpness, ere[1] he is aware. When thoughts
Of the last bitter hour come like a blight
Over thy spirit, and sad images
Of the stern agony, and shroud, and pall,
And breathless darkness, and the narrow house,[2]
Make thee to shudder, and grow sick at heart—
Go forth, under the open sky, and list
To Nature's teachings, while from all around—
Earth and her waters, and the depths of air—
Comes a still voice.

Yet a few days, and thee
The all-beholding sun shall see no more
In all his course; nor yet in the cold ground,
Where thy pale form was laid, with many tears,
Nor in the embrace of ocean, shall exist
Thy image. Earth, that nourished thee, shall claim
Thy growth, to be resolved to earth again,
And, lost each human trace, surrendering up
Thine individual being, shalt thou go
To mix forever with the elements,
To be a brother to the insensible rock
And to the sluggish clod, which the rude swain[3]
Turns with his share[4] and treads upon. The oak
Shall send his roots abroad, and pierce thy mold.

Yet not to thine eternal resting place
Shalt thou retire alone, nor couldst thou wish
Couch[5] more magnificent. Thou shalt lie down
With patriarchs of the infant world—with kings,

1. **ere** [ār]: before.
2. **narrow house:** coffin.
3. **swain:** country youth.
4. **share:** plowshare.
5. **Couch:** bed.

Kindred Spirits, 1849, Asher B. Durand. Bryant and the painter Thomas Cole share their Romantic awe of nature.

The powerful of the earth—the wise, the good,
Fair forms, and hoary seers of ages past,
All in one mighty sepulcher. The hills
Rock-ribbed and ancient as the sun—the vales
Stretching in pensive quietness between;
The venerable woods—rivers that move
In majesty, and the complaining brooks
That make the meadows green; and, poured round all,
Old Ocean's gray and melancholy waste—
Are but the solemn decorations all
Of the great tomb of man. The golden sun,
The planets, all the infinite host of heaven,
Are shining on the sad abodes of death,
Through the still lapse of ages. All that tread
The globe are but a handful to the tribes
That slumber in its bosom. Take the wings
Of morning,[6] pierce the Barcan wilderness,[7]
Or lose thyself in the continuous woods
Where rolls the Oregon[8] and hears no sound,
Save his own dashings—yet the dead are there:
And millions in those solitudes, since first
The flight of years began, have laid them down
In their last sleep—the dead reign there alone.
So shalt thou rest, and what if thou withdraw
In silence from the living, and no friend
Take note of thy departure? All that breathe
Will share thy destiny. The gay will laugh
When thou art gone, the solemn brood of care
Plod on, and each one as before will chase
His favorite phantom; yet all these shall leave
Their mirth and their employments, and shall come
And make their bed with thee. As the long train
Of ages glides away, the sons of men,
The youth in life's fresh spring, and he who goes
In the full strength of years, matron and maid,
The speechless babe, and the gray-headed man—

---

6. **Take . . . morning:** from Psalm 139 : 9, in which the psalmist sings of flying away to distant places.
7. **Barcan** [bär′kən] **wilderness:** the deserts of Barca in North Africa.
8. **Oregon:** American Indian name for the Columbia River.

AT A GLANCE

- When you die, you will be in good company and rest with great figures of the past.
- Those who have died far outnumber the living.
- All people who live after you will eventually share your destiny and die too.

METAPHOR

Developing the poem's basic image, Bryant presents the whole earth as one vast common burial vault, "one mighty sepulcher" for humankind (ll. 35–37, 45).

PERSONIFICATION

The word *complaining* invests the brooks with a human trait (ll. 41–42).

MAIN IDEA

Although you will eventually lose your life, you are destined to acquire in death the companionship of all other mortals (ll. 58–61, 64–66).

Shall one by one be gathered to thy side,
By those, who in their turn shall follow them.

So live, that when thy summons comes to join
The innumerable caravan, which moves
To that mysterious realm where each shall take
His chamber in the silent halls of death,
Thou go not, like the quarry-slave at night,
Scourged to his dungeon, but, sustained and soothed
By an unfaltering trust, approach thy grave,
Like one who wraps the drapery of his couch
About him, and lies down to pleasant dreams.

STUDY QUESTIONS

Recalling

1. According to lines 1–8, to whom does nature speak? To what two different human moods does nature respond?
2. What do lines 14–17 recommend to those who "grow sick at heart" when they think of death?
3. According to lines 22–30, what will happen to all people? What two points should people remember, according to lines 31–33?
4. What do lines 61–66 tell the readers will happen after their own deaths?
5. What simile does Bryant use in lines 80–81 to suggest the way the reader should "approach thy grave"?

Interpreting

6. What lesson about death does the poet expect us to learn from closely observing nature? What is the overall relationship between human beings and nature, according to the poet?
7. What comforting observation about human experience does the poet make repeatedly throughout the poem (lines 31–32, 48–50, 60–61, 64–66, 70–72, and 75–76)?
8. With what emotion does Bryant suggest people face death?
9. In what way does the subject matter of the poem reflect the Romantic interest in the self, or the individual?

Extending

10. Poets often use the image of the *seasons of human life.* Tell in your own words what this expression means. How does the image of human seasons reflect the central idea of Bryant's poem?

VIEWPOINT

In his biography of Bryant, critic Charles H. Brown writes:

> To him, as he said in his lectures on poetry, "the great spring of poetry is emotion." . . . Nevertheless, Bryant's practice in composition was not to warble as a bird does, for he held that poetry not only appeals to "the passions and the imagination" but also to the understanding. —*William Cullen Bryant*

■ Find at least two passages in "Thanatopsis" that show how Bryant blends emotions and ideas. First find a controlled and thoughtful presentation of a feeling; then find an emotional presentation of an idea.

LITERARY FOCUS

Meter

All writing has rhythm. Rhythm simply means the arrangement of stressed and unstressed syllables in a work. Only poetry, however, has meter. **Meter** is a regular rhythm—that is, stressed and unstressed syllables in an arrangement that

AT A GLANCE

When you face death, do not go with bitterness; rather, be sustained by the knowledge that it is part of nature's plan.

METER

Iambic pentameter lines, approximating the cadences of ordinary speech, are especially effective in the final reassuring injunction (ll. 73–81).

REFLECTING ON THE POEM

Where in the poem does the speaker envision the natural world in its broadest and brightest aspects? (Students are likely to choose lines 45–48: "The golden sun . . . still lapse of ages.")

STUDY QUESTIONS

1. the person "who in the love of nature holds/Communion with her visible forms"; "gayer hours," "darker musings"
2. "Go forth, under the open sky, and list/To Nature's teachings"
3. die; when they die they join great figures of the past in a magnificent resting place
4. Those left behind will continue to live their lives but will eventually die too.
5. "Like one who wraps the drapery of his couch/About him, and lies down to pleasant dreams"
6. a natural part of life; humans a part of nature
7. We are not alone in death.
8. with the quiet trust felt when drifting off to sleep
9. deals with individual's feelings toward death, a personal experience
10. Answers will vary. Such images usually equate youth with spring, prime of life with summer, old age with autumn, and death with winter; however, the seasons are cyclical.

VIEWPOINT

Lines 1–8; third stanza

has a pattern. Meter is an important element of most poetry written before the twentieth century, and studying a poem's meter can help us appreciate the craft and tone of the poet.

The basic unit of meter is the **foot.** Usually a foot consists of one stressed syllable and one or two unstressed syllables. The most common foot in English-language poetry is the **iambic foot,** an unstressed syllable followed by a stressed syllable. There are five iambic feet in this line from Shakespeare's *Julius Caesar:*

> Yond Cassius has a lean and hungry look.

The stressed syllables are marked (′); the unstressed syllables are marked (˘).

A **trochaic foot** is an iambic foot in reverse: a stressed syllable followed by an unstressed syllable. This line from Poe's "Raven" illustrates eight trochaic feet:

> Once upon a midnight dreary, while I pondered, weak and weary.

An **anapestic foot** consists of two unstressed syllables followed by one stressed syllable. It is often used to capture swift movement, as in this line from "The Destruction of Sennacherib" by the British Romantic poet Lord Byron:

> The Assyrian came down like a wolf on the fold.

A **dactylic foot** is an anapestic foot in reverse: a stressed syllable followed by two unstressed syllables. Dactylic feet have a jingly, nursery-rhyme quality, illustrated in this line from a poem by E. E. Cummings:

> anyone lived in a pretty how town

Notice that Cummings ends the line without completing the final foot. Poets may also vary the feet within a line. Sometimes they use a **spondaic foot,** consisting of two stressed syllables alone, for emphasis. Spondaic feet often occur at the end of a line of poetry, as in this line from "Thanatopsis":

> In all his course; nor yet in the cold ground.

When we describe the meter of a poem, we must consider not only the kinds of feet it contains but also the number of feet in each line. We use the prefixes mono- (one), di- (two), tri- (three), tetra- (four), penta- (five), and hex- (six) to identify the number of feet in a line. The meter of "Thanatopsis," for example, is iambic pentameter: It has five iambic feet in each line.

Unrhymed iambic pentameter is sometimes called **blank verse,** one of the most common meters in British and American poetry. Blank verse attempts to sound like English as it is spoken, and so every line need not be perfectly regular. A poet using iambic pentameter will deliberately vary the stresses to avoid monotony and to use the sound of the verse to support the meaning. The line quoted above from "Thanatopsis" shows Bryant using two heavy stresses—a spondee—at the end of the line to reinforce the idea of death and finality that is in the meaning of the words themselves.

Emerson's "Concord Hymn" is written in a simpler meter, iambic tetrameter:

> On this green bank, by this soft stream,
> We set today a votive stone.

This meter seems perfect for the subject and the occasion of the poem: Emerson chose a meter that would lend itself to hymnlike singing.

Just as poets may vary types of feet, they may vary the number of feet in their lines, as Emily Dickinson does in this stanza:

> The Soul selects her own Society—
> Then—shuts the Door—
> To her divine Majority—
> Present no more—

When we mark a poem with stressed and unstressed marks to determine its meter, we are **scanning** the poem. **Scansion** is a useful tool for analyzing the rhythmic patterns of poems written in standard meters.

Thinking About Meter

1. Choose four lines from Bryant's "Thanatopsis," and scan them. Account for every syllable.
2. Choose another poem that you have read in this book. Scan four lines from the poem, and give the name of the meter the poet uses.

LITERARY FOCUS

1. Example:
To him who in the love of nature holds
Communion with her visible forms, she speaks
A various language; for his gayer hours
She has a voice of gladness, and a smile

2. Example of Phillis Wheatley's iambic pentameter:
Celestial choir! enthron'd in realms of light,
Columbia's scenes of glorious toils I write.
While Freedom's cause her anxious breast alarms,
She flashes dreadful in refulgent arms.

VOCABULARY

1. (c) health
2. (b) hills
3. (c) brightness
4. (a) aware
5. (d) youthful

VOCABULARY

Antonyms

Antonyms are words that have opposite or nearly opposite meanings. The following words in capitals are from "Thanatopsis." Choose the word that is an antonym of each word in capitals, *as the word is used in this selection.* Write the number of each item and the letter of your choice on a separate sheet.

1. BLIGHT: (a) disease (b) light (c) health (d) darkness
2. VALES: (a) dreams (b) hills (c) valleys (d) laughter
3. PALL: (a) boredom (b) paleness (c) brightness (d) shroud
4. INSENSIBLE: (a) aware (b) stupid (c) mighty (d) unconscious
5. HOARY: (a) elderly (b) white (c) frosted (d) youthful

COMPOSITION

Writing About Theme

■ Write a composition about the theme of "Thanatopsis." Begin by stating the theme. Then discuss lines 1–17 and 66–81, which Bryant added during a revision. Tell what those lines add to the poem's theme. Show how Bryant illuminates his theme through setting, through the specific events that he discusses, and through the kinds of people he refers to. *For help with this assignment, refer to Lesson 6 in the Writing About Literature Handbook at the back of this book.*

Writing About Nature

■ Like Bryant, many artists have heard the "voice" of nature. Write a paragraph describing one natural phenomenon—for example, the seasons, a storm, plants, or animals—and tell what you think the "voice" of nature seems to be saying about life itself.

COMPOSITION: GUIDELINES FOR EVALUATION

WRITING ABOUT THEME

Objective

To analyze the theme of a poem

Guidelines for Evaluation

- suggested length: three to four paragraphs
- should state the theme of the poem
- should show how lines 1–17 and 66–81 underscore the theme
- should show how settings, events, and kinds of people in the poem underscore the theme

WRITING ABOUT NATURE

Objective

To describe a natural phenomenon

Guidelines for Evaluation

- suggested length: one paragraph
- should describe a natural phenomenon
- should express an opinion about what the phenomenon "says" about life in general
- should relate the physical world to the world of ideas and feelings

Edgar Allan Poe *1809–1849*

The short, unhappy life of Edgar Allan Poe was marked by poverty, restlessness, and feverish creative activity. Nevertheless, this struggling, sometimes overwhelmingly lonely man became, after his death, one of the most widely read and influential American writers.

Edgar Poe was born in Boston, the son of traveling actors. His mother died when he was still an infant, and a wealthy Virginia couple, the Allans, became his foster parents. He received a good education and seemed to be headed for the life of a gentleman when he entered the University of Virginia. However, heavy gambling debts and a wild life forced him to drop out.

Refusing to join his foster father's business, Poe fled to Boston and, under an assumed name, joined the United States Army. At the age of eighteen, he published his first book of poetry and, in 1829, a second book. His foster father helped him win an appointment to the U.S. Military Academy at West Point, but once again a rigid life seemed incompatible with the writing Poe wanted to do. He deliberately broke rules and behaved in a way that made it necessary for West Point to expel him. His third book of poems, published soon after his expulsion, was dedicated to "the U.S. Corps of Cadets."

Poe knew that he was not going to inherit the Allans' fortune and that he would have to make his own way in the world. He moved from city to city, from job to job, usually as an editor or journalist, continuing to write poems, short stories, and reviews. His steadiest income came as the editor of a newly founded magazine, the *Southern Literary Messenger*.

In 1838 Poe published his only novel, *The Narrative of Arthur Gordon Pym,* a mysterious sea adventure. His *Tales of the Grotesque and Arabesque* came out in 1840, as he continued to contribute stories and poems to an assortment of journals. Nevertheless, Poe was unable to escape his spirit-breaking poverty. Even "The Raven," his most popular work, brought him little money. When his beloved wife, Virginia, died in 1847, Poe found his deep sorrow difficult to bear. He died in 1849, as completely "alone" as any American artist has ever been.

A few writers have found Poe's writing unpolished and juvenile: Emerson called him "the jingle man," and Mark Twain said he would read Poe only if someone paid him to do so. Yet some writers and critics, especially Europeans, have admired Poe more than any other American writer. The Irish poet W. B. Yeats considered Poe "certainly the greatest of American poets."

■ Do you find anything extraordinary in Poe's poems? Or do you find him just a "jingle man"?

Poe said that when he set out to write a poem with a melancholy effect, the word *nevermore* was the first word that came into his mind, both for its sound and for its meaning. The subject of the poem, he decided, had to be the death of a beautiful woman, "unquestionably, the most poetical topic in the world." His first thought was to have *nevermore* repeated by a parrot, but he saw greater possibilities in a raven, "the bird of ill omen," an emblem of "Mournful and Never-ending Remembrance."

Edgar Allan Poe

The Raven

Once upon a midnight dreary, while I pondered, weak and weary,
Over many a quaint and curious volume of forgotten lore—
While I nodded, nearly napping, suddenly there came a tapping,
As of someone gently rapping, rapping at my chamber door—
"'Tis some visitor," I muttered, "tapping at my chamber door—
Only this and nothing more."

Ah, distinctly I remember it was in the bleak December;
And each separate dying ember wrought its ghost upon the floor.
Eagerly I wished the morrow—vainly I had sought to borrow
From my books surcease of sorrow—sorrow for the lost Lenore—
For the rare and radiant maiden whom the angels name Lenore—
Nameless *here* for evermore.

And the silken, sad, uncertain rustling of each purple curtain
Thrilled me—filled me with fantastic terrors never felt before;
So that now, to still the beating of my heart, I stood repeating
"'Tis some visitor entreating entrance at my chamber door—
Some late visitor entreating entrance at my chamber door—
This it is and nothing more."

Presently my soul grew stronger; hesitating then no longer,
"Sir," said I, "or Madam, truly your forgiveness I implore;
But the fact is I was napping, and so gently you came rapping,
And so faintly you came tapping, tapping at my chamber door,
That I scarce was sure I heard you"—here I opened wide the door—
Darkness there and nothing more.

This lithograph was made by painter Edouard Manet (1832–1883) for a French translation of "The Raven."

AT A GLANCE

- The speaker is reading in an attempt to forget his lost love Lenore when he hears knocking at the door.
- He opens the door but sees only darkness.

LITERARY OPTIONS

- single effect
- assonance
- onomatopoeia

THEMATIC OPTIONS

- loss and recovery
- memory and time

ONOMATOPOEIA

The very sounds in certain lines of the opening stanzas convey what the speaker hears; "rapping" and "tapping" break the stillness of the night (ll. 3–5).

NARRATIVE POEM

Despite its lyric elements, this is a narrative poem. The setting is December at midnight in the speaker's chamber (ll. 1, 4, 6). The exposition includes an explanation of the speaker's sorrow over his lost love (l. 10), and the knocking on the door (ll. 3–4).

MOOD

With words that convey images of darkness, cold, and death, Poe establishes the gloomy, eerie mood that will prevail throughout the poem: *bleak December, dying ember, ghost* (ll. 7–8).

AT A GLANCE

- Hopefully, the speaker asks, "Lenore?" but no one responds.
- When the tapping begins again, he thinks it is the wind and opens the shutter; a raven flies in.
- Perched on a bust of Pallas Athena, the bird says only one word: nevermore.

CAESURA

A caesura is a pause within a line of poetry, especially necessary with lines having as many as eight feet. In the first three stanzas on this page, the break in each opening line is indicated by a comma—an appropriate aid to a poem that seems designed to be read aloud (ll. 25, 31, 37).

TROCHAIC METER

A trochee, which is a metrical foot consisting of a stressed syllable followed by an unstressed one, is the reverse of the iambic foot more commonly found in poetry. The trochaic meter of "The Raven" gives the lines a stronger, more emphatic rhythm than iambic lines would have (line 28).

ROMANTIC IDEA

The self-absorbed, tormented speaker reflects the Romantic focus on the self (l. 31).

CONTRAST

Poe juxtaposes images of darkness and light: the black "grim and ancient Raven" and the "placid" bust of Athena, goddess of wisdom and enlightenment, which may have been sculptured in white marble (ll. 38–42, 55).

Deep into that darkness peering, long I stood there wondering, fearing,
Doubting, dreaming dreams no mortal ever dared to dream before;
But the silence was unbroken, and the stillness gave no token,
And the only word there spoken was the whispered word, "Lenore?"
This I whispered, and an echo murmured back the word, "Lenore!"
Merely this and nothing more.

Back into the chamber turning, all my soul within me burning,
Soon again I heard a tapping somewhat louder than before.
"Surely," said I, "surely that is something at my window lattice;
Let me see, then, what thereat is, and this mystery explore—
Let my heart be still a moment and this mystery explore—
'Tis the wind and nothing more!"

Open here I flung the shutter, when, with many a flirt and flutter,
In there stepped a stately Raven of the saintly days of yore.
Not the least obeisance made he; not a minute stopped or stayed he;
But, with mien of lord or lady, perched above my chamber door—
Perched upon a bust of Pallas[1] just above my chamber door—
Perched, and sat, and nothing more.

Then this ebony bird beguiling my sad fancy into smiling,
By the grave and stern decorum of the countenance it wore,
"Though thy crest be shorn and shaven, thou," I said, "art sure no craven,
Ghastly grim and ancient Raven wandering from the Nightly shore—
Tell me what thy lordly name is on the Night's Plutonian[2] shore!"
Quoth the Raven "Nevermore."

Much I marveled this ungainly fowl to hear discourse so plainly,
Though its answer little meaning—little relevancy bore;
For we cannot help agreeing that no living human being
Ever yet was blessed with seeing bird above his chamber door—
Bird or beast upon the sculptured bust above his chamber door,
With such name as "Nevermore."

But the Raven, sitting lonely on the placid bust, spoke only
That one word, as if his soul in that one word he did outpour.
Nothing farther then he uttered—not a feather then he fluttered—
Till I scarcely more than muttered "Other friends have flown before—
On the morrow *he* will leave me, as my Hopes have flown before."
Then the bird said "Nevermore."

---

1. **Pallas** [pal′əs]: in Greek mythology Pallas Athena, the goddess of wisdom.
2. **Plutonian** [plo͞o tō′nē ən]: dark; referring to Pluto, Greek god of the underworld.

Startled at the stillness broken by reply so aptly spoken,
"Doubtless," said I, "what it utters is its only stock and store
Caught from some unhappy master whom unmerciful Disaster
Followed fast and followed faster till his songs one burden bore—
Till the dirges of his Hope that melancholy burden bore
Of 'Never—nevermore.' "

But the Raven still beguiling my sad fancy into smiling,
Straight I wheeled a cushioned seat in front of bird and bust and door;
Then, upon the velvet sinking, I betook myself to linking
Fancy unto fancy, thinking what this ominous bird of yore—
What this grim, ungainly, ghastly, gaunt, and ominous bird of yore
Meant in croaking "Nevermore."

This I sat engaged in guessing, but no syllable expressing
To the fowl whose fiery eyes now burned into my bosom's core;
This and more I sat divining, with my head at ease reclining
On the cushion's velvet lining that the lamplight gloated o'er,
But whose velvet violet lining with the lamplight gloating o'er,
She shall press, ah, nevermore!

Then, methought, the air grew denser, perfumed from an unseen censer
Swung by seraphim[3] whose footfalls tinkled on the tufted floor.
"Wretch," I cried, "thy God hath lent thee—by these angels he hath sent thee
Respite—respite and nepenthe[4] from thy memories of Lenore;
Quaff, oh quaff this kind nepenthe and forget this lost Lenore!"
Quoth the Raven "Nevermore."

"Prophet!" said I, "thing of evil!—prophet still, if bird or devil!—
Whether Tempter sent, or whether tempest tossed thee here ashore,
Desolate yet all undaunted, on this desert land enchanted—
On this home by Horror haunted—tell me truly, I implore—
Is there—*is* there balm in Gilead?[5]—tell me—tell me, I implore!"
Quoth the Raven "Nevermore."

"Prophet!" said I, "thing of evil!—prophet still, if bird or devil!
By that Heaven that bends above us—by that God we both adore—
Tell this soul with sorrow laden if, within the distant Aidenn,[6]
It shall clasp a sainted maiden whom the angels name Lenore—
Clasp a rare and radiant maiden whom the angels name Lenore."
Quoth the Raven "Nevermore."

3. **seraphim** [ser′ə fim′]: angels.
4. **nepenthe** [ni pen′thē]: in classical mythology a drink that banishes sorrow.
5. **balm in Gilead** [gil′ē əd]: Poe's version of "Is there no balm in Gilead?" (Jeremiah 8 : 22), referring to a healing ointment made in Gilead in ancient Palestine; therefore, a relief from suffering.
6. **Aidenn** [ā′dən]: Arabic for "Eden" or heaven.

AT A GLANCE

The bird replies "Nevermore" to all of the speaker's frenzied questions: Will he forget Lenore? Will he have relief from suffering? Will he rejoin Lenore in heaven?

STANZAIC FORM

Like the meter, the stanzaic form Poe employs here is unusual: five rather lengthy (eight-foot) lines, followed by a very short sixth line. The rhyme scheme likewise is unusual and memorable, effective in holding a listener's attention: *abcbbb* (ll. 61–66).

ROMANTIC IDEA

Phrases such as "ominous bird of yore" reflect the Romantic interest in the exotic past.

SINGLE EFFECT

The words describing the raven *(grim, ungainly, ghastly, gaunt, ominous)* add to the hypnotic and eerie gloom of the poem (l. 71).

ASSONANCE

With the device of employing similar vowel sounds in a line of poetry, Poe uses soft, light long-*a* sounds in the speaker's question about Lenore: "a s*aint*ed m*ai*den whom the *a*ngels n*a*me Lenore——/. . . a *rare* and r*a*diant m*ai*den whom the *a*ngels n*a*me Lenore" (ll. 94–95).

AT A GLANCE

- Denouncing the raven as a lying fiend, the speaker orders the bird back into the night.
- The bird does not leave but assumes a supernatural aspect, remaining forever above the speaker's door.

ALLITERATION

In the despairing, closing lines of the poem, the liquid *l* sounds have a clear, ringing sound, like the tolling of a bell, in the speaker's final cry: "And my sou*l* from out that shadow that *l*ies f*l*oating on the f*l*oor/Sha*ll* be *l*ifted—nevermore!" (ll. 107–108)

REFLECTING ON THE POEM

What main kinds of repetition do you find in "The Raven," and which is most effective? (Students may at first name the short phrases containing *nevermore* and conveying a sense of inevitable tragedy. They may also point to occurrences of the words *Lenore* and *chamber door* and their significance within the story, or refer to effective repetition of particular consonant or vowel sounds.)

STUDY QUESTIONS

1. reading; relief from sorrow; knocking is a visitor
2. only darkness; "Lenore"
3. wind at window; raven flies in
4. "nevermore"; bird's name; the only word learned from a master
5. what the bird really means when it says "nevermore"
6. "Is there balm in Gilead?"; if he will ever hold Lenore again; "Nevermore"; "Nevermore"
7. still perched on the bust in the speaker's chamber; the speaker's soul
8. No; he only says them to still the beating of his heart.
9. Lenore; speaker; air grows denser with perfume, God has sent angels to bring him relief
10. never forget Lenore, not join her in heaven; they have no meaning

"Be that word our sign of parting, bird or fiend!" I shrieked, upstarting—
"Get thee back into the tempest and the Night's Plutonian shore!
Leave no black plume as a token of that lie thy soul hath spoken!
Leave my loneliness unbroken!—quit the bust above my door!
Take thy beak from out my heart, and take thy form from off my door!"
Quoth the Raven "Nevermore."

And the Raven, never flitting, still is sitting, *still* is sitting
On the pallid bust of Pallas just above my chamber door;
And his eyes have all the seeming of a demon's that is dreaming,
And the lamplight o'er him streaming throws his shadow on the floor;
And my soul from out that shadow that lies floating on the floor
Shall be lifted—nevermore!

STUDY QUESTIONS

Recalling

1. In stanzas 1–3 what is the speaker doing when he first hears the tapping? What does he seek "to borrow"? What does he say "to still the beating" of his heart?
2. In stanzas 4–5 what does the speaker see when he opens the door? What does he whisper?
3. What does the speaker hope is making the tapping noise in stanza 6? What happens when he opens the shutter?
4. What is the only word the raven speaks? In stanza 9 to what does the speaker think the word relates? How does he explain the word when the raven first repeats it (lines 62–66)?
5. About what does the speaker begin to think when he wheels his chair in front of the raven (lines 69–72)?
6. What question does the speaker ask in lines 88–90? In lines 93–95? What does the raven reply? What does it say when ordered to leave?
7. Where is the raven now? What will never be lifted from the raven's shadow?

Interpreting

8. Does the speaker believe the words he says in lines 16–18 and line 36? How do you know?
9. Who is "she" in line 78? Who is the "wretch" in line 81? Trace the speaker's thoughts in lines 78–83.
10. What does the speaker interpret "nevermore" in line 84 and in line 96 to mean? What do you know about the raven's answers that the speaker does not realize?
11. What does the raven come to represent for the speaker? What does "Plutonian shore" (line 98) suggest about the speaker's final evaluation of the raven? Of himself?
12. Evaluate the speaker's emotional state at the beginning of the poem, in the next-to-the-last stanza, and in the last stanza. What does the future probably hold for the speaker?
13. Describe the mood of the poem. Which expressions in stanzas 1–2 help establish the mood?

Extending

14. Poe felt the death of a beautiful woman was "the most poetical topic in the world." What do you think makes a topic "poetical"? Name at least three topics you find poetical, and tell why they are suitable for poetry.

LITERARY FOCUS

Poe and the Single Effect

In a review of *Twice-Told Tales* by his contemporary, Nathaniel Hawthorne, Poe asserted that a work of literature must arrange all of its elements so that they combine to achieve a single effect. In

11. dark terror, despair; associated with the forces of darkness; damned
12. melancholy, brooding; hysterical, angry; resigned, in complete despair; despair
13. eerie, gloomy, melancholy; "midnight dreary," "bleak December," "dying ember," etc.
14. Answers will vary, but students should find topics of modern poetry broader than those of Romantic poetry.

fact, Poe believed that a poet or a short story writer must begin with an idea of a single effect and then create the characters and incidents to produce that effect. He said, "In the whole composition there should be no word written, of which the tendency, direct or indirect, is not to the one preestablished design." He added, "If [an author's] very initial sentence tend not to the outbringing of this [single] effect, then he has failed in his first step."

Poe believed, in other words, that one clear, powerfully felt emotion should carry the reader through the work. Of course, literature may display many different emotions, but Poe believed they must all ultimately combine into one overwhelming feeling for the reader.

Thinking About Single Effect

1. What is the single effect of "The Raven"?
2. Discuss the first sentence of "The Raven," pointing out how each element of it contributes to the single effect.

Sound Devices

Poe's use of sound devices in poetry is as important as his subject matter. The particular music of his verses creates mood, reveals character, and conveys ideas, in addition to providing that pleasure in sound that only poetry can provide.

Most sound devices are kinds of **repetition. Alliteration,** for example, is the repetition of consonant sounds at the beginnings of words and of sounds within words. Poe uses alliteration to create an almost hypnotic effect in phrases like "weak and weary" and "silken, sad, uncertain rustling." (**Consonance** is the repetition in nearby words of similar consonant sounds preceded by different accented vowels.)

Assonance is the repetition of vowel sounds, and Poe uses assonance mainly to create mood. The most conspicuous example in "The Raven" is the open *o* sound, with its deep mournful effect: "s*o*rrow—s*o*rrow for the lost Len*o*re."

Poe uses the assonance of the *o* sound as the basis for the poem's most common rhyme. **Rhyme** is a kind of repetition, and it also can be used to create mood. Notice, for example, how many times the poet rhymes that long moaning sound: "neverm*ore*," "d*oor*," "Len*ore*," "impl*ore*," "y*ore*," "b*ore*," and so on. Rhyme can reinforce meaning; the poet emphasizes the absence of his beloved when he rhymes *Lenore* with *nevermore*.

Internal rhyme is rhyme that occurs within a single line:

> Ah, distinctly I *remember* it was in the bleak
> *December.*

Poe uses internal rhyme as another kind of repeated sound, like alliteration or assonance, for hypnotic effect, for mood, and simply for the pleasure of the repetition itself.

Poe also employs **onomatopoeia,** the use of words with sounds that suggest their meanings. For example, the words *tapping* and *rapping,* in addition to meaning "knocking," actually suggest the sound of someone or something knocking at the door. Poe repeats the words in the first stanza, just as a knock at the door is repeated.

Thinking About Sound Devices

■ Find at least two more examples in "The Raven" of alliteration, assonance, internal rhyme, and onomatopoeia. Tell how Poe's use of each of these sound devices contributes to the meaning or the mood of the poem.

LITERARY FOCUS

Single Effect

1. hypnotic, eerie gloom
2. The phrases "midnight dreary" and "weak and weary" and the word "pondered" contribute to the eerie gloom. The internal rhyme and alliteration of *w* sounds add to the hypnotic effect.

Sound Devices

- Examples of alliteration: nodded, nearly napping (line 3); Doubting, dreaming dreams (line 26); whispered word (line 28); a flirt and flutter (line 37); grim, ungainly, gaunt (line 71)
- Examples of assonance: the long *e* in "weak and weary" (line 1); the short initial *e* in "entreating entrance" (line 17); the long *e* in "wheeled a cushioned seat" (line 68)
- Examples of internal rhyme: dreary and weary (line 1); napping, tapping, and rapping (lines 3–4); morrow, borrow, and sorrow (lines 9–10); uncertain and curtain (line 13)
- Examples of onomatopoeia: muttered (line 5); rustling (line 13); whispered (line 28); murmured (line 29)
- All of these devices contribute to the hypnotic effect that pulls the reader into the gloomy, desperate, eerie world of the speaker.

AT A GLANCE

- The speaker addresses and acclaims an idealized woman.
- He compares her beauty to that of graceful ships of the Byzantine era.
- He praises her hair and features and compares her to a water nymph.
- Statue-like, she is a shining spiritual symbol.

LITERARY OPTIONS

- alliteration/assonance
- simile

THEMATIC OPTIONS

- friendship and love
- visions and ideals

SIMILE

The speaker begins his tribute to Helen by comparing the effect of her beauty to the gentle, reassuring motion of a ship that carries a tired traveler toward home (ll. 1–5).

ALLITERATION/ASSONANCE

In the closing lines of the first stanza, the repetition of the initial consonant sound of *w* suggests ocean waves, whereas the mournful feelings of someone far from home are conveyed by long *o* sounds: "The *w*eary, *w*ay-w*o*rn *w*anderer b*o*re/To his *o*wn native sh*o*re" (ll. 4–5).

REFLECTING ON THE POEM

In what sense does the poem suggest the *maternal* aspects of the woman who was Poe's subject? (in the emphasis on the idea of *home*—the weary traveler's return, the comforting light in the window)

SELECTION FOR PRACTICE IN ACTIVE READING
(TCR 7, p. 61)

"To Helen" shows how a Romantic poet can use classical images for his own purposes. Inspired by the beauty of the mother of one of his friends, Poe uses Helen of Troy—"the face that launched a thousand ships"—to represent that beauty. Helen may also be an allusion to the Greek goddess of light, but whatever the specific reference Poe intended, she is clearly the poet's timeless ideal of pure beauty.

Edgar Allan Poe

To Helen

Helen, thy beauty is to me
  Like those Nicéan[1] barks of yore,
That gently, o'er a perfumed sea,
  The weary, way-worn wanderer bore
  To his own native shore.

On desperate seas long wont[2] to roam,
  Thy hyacinth[3] hair, thy classic face,
Thy Naiad[4] airs have brought me home
  To the glory that was Greece,
And the grandeur that was Rome.

Lo! in yon brilliant window niche
  How statue-like I see thee stand,
  The agate lamp within thy hand!
Ah, Psyche,[5] from the regions which
  Are Holy Land!

1. **Nicéan** [nī sē'ən] **barks:** Poe may be referring to boats from the shipbuilding city of Nicea in Asia Minor. It is likely, however, that he created the phrase for its melodious sound.
2. **wont** [wônt]: accustomed.
3. **hyacinth** [hī'ə sinth']: wavy and perfumed.
4. **Naiad** [nī'ad]: in classical mythology, a water nymph.
5. **Psyche** [sī'kē]: goddess of the soul.

Model for Active Reading

In this selection, and in one selection in each unit, you will find notes in the right-hand margin that highlight parts of the selection. These notes point out important ideas of the period—in this case, the Romantic movement—and draw your attention to literary elements and techniques covered in the Literary Focuses. Page numbers in the notes will refer you to more extensive discussions of these important ideas and elements.

Edgar Allan Poe

Alone

From childhood's hour I have not been
As others were—I have not seen
As others saw—I could not bring
My passions from a common spring—
From the same source I have not taken
My sorrow—I could not awaken
My heart to joy at the same tone—
And all I lov'd—*I* lov'd alone—
Then—in my childhood—in the dawn
Of a most stormy life—was drawn
From ev'ry depth of good and ill
The mystery which binds me still—
From the torrent, or the fountain—
From the red cliff of the mountain—
From the sun that 'round me roll'd
In its autumn tint of gold—
From the lightning in the sky
As it pass'd me flying by—
From the thunder, and the storm—
And the cloud that took the form
(When the rest of Heaven was blue)
Of a demon in my view—

Romantic idea: The poem focuses on the self, common in Romantic poetry (p. 101).

Alliteration, Assonance, and Rhyme (p. 131): The *l* sounds in line 8 and the *o* sounds of lines 7–8 add to the "music" of the poem. By rhyming "alone" with "tone," Poe stresses the title.

Romantic idea: The Romantic writer is often fascinated by mystery (p. 101).

Meter (p. 122): The first eight lines of the poem are iambic tetrameter. From line 11 to the end, the poem becomes trochaic, reversing its rhythm.

AT A GLANCE

- Isolation is truly terrifying and evil, the speaker says.
- He has known its horrors since a particular moment in childhood.

LITERARY OPTIONS

- imagery
- sound devices
- meter

THEMATIC OPTIONS

- isolation
- terror and evil
- mystery

REFLECTING ON THE POEM

How is the speaker's isolation different from mere solitude? (He seems to be cut off from all others because he sees and feels differently from them.)

STUDY QUESTIONS

"To Helen"

1. Nicéan barks of yore; wanderer
2. hyacinth hair, classic face, Naiad face; speaker; glory of Greece, grandeur of Rome
3. standing in a window with a lamp; Psyche; Holy Land
4. aimless and tired, homesick
5. ▪ comforts of home, feeling of belonging, glory of classical civilization, spiritual contentment
   ▪ guiding beacon to immortality, beauty, knowledge, spiritual comfort
   ▪ cured his ailing soul
6. idealizes human beauty as spiritual; concern for the individual, classical allusions

"Alone"

1. has not been like others, has not seen like others, feelings arise from a different source; since childhood
2. the mystery that still binds him
3. a demon
4. ▪ The speaker knew from childhood that he was different from others and has suffered greatly.
   ▪ lonely, odd, brooding, emotional
5. no; sees the dark side of everything, is damned or cursed; work of evil forces
6. Possible answers: experience, humility, compassion; comfort to readers

STUDY QUESTIONS

To Helen

Recalling

1. To what does the poet compare Helen's beauty in the first stanza? Who is brought "to his own native shore"?
2. What images describe Helen in the second stanza? Who is brought home in this stanza? To what is he brought home?
3. What is Helen doing in the third stanza? With whom is she associated in line 14? From where does she come?

Interpreting

4. State in your own words the condition the speaker was in before encountering Helen.
5. Considering the places to which Helen brings the speaker and the place from which she comes, name the three kinds of joys or comforts she seems to provide. What might the agate lamp represent? What has Helen done for the speaker to explain why he calls her Psyche?
6. In what way is this poem idealistic? Which of the other characteristics of Romanticism (listed in the Introduction to this unit) does this poem display?

Alone

Recalling

1. In what three ways is the speaker set apart, according to lines 1–4? From when do these differences exist?
2. What does the speaker say arose "in the dawn" of a "most stormy life"?
3. What, according to line 22, has the speaker seen in all places?

Interpreting

4. Summarize the main idea of the first eight lines in one sentence. What characteristics of the speaker are implied in these lines?
5. Do we ever learn exactly what "mystery" binds the speaker? What do lines 20–22 suggest about the speaker? About the mystery?

Extending

6. What are the insights and the positive results that may come from a poet's suffering?

COMPOSITION

Writing About Poetry

■ Write a composition in which you show how the specific techniques used in "To Helen" contribute to the meaning of the poem. First state the poem's meaning. Next identify the poem's images and allusions, and tell why they are appropriate to the meaning. Then discuss the rhythm and the rhyme, describing the overall feeling they suggest. Conclude with a general statement about the poet's effectiveness in using these devices. *For help with this assignment, refer to Lesson 7 in the Writing About Literature Handbook at the back of this book.*

Writing with Classical Allusions

■ Write a brief description of a person or a place using at least one of the following classical names to help describe your subject. You may want to look up the names in a dictionary or encyclopedia to add details to your description.

Zeus	Hercules
Olympus	Odysseus
Athena	Elysium
Penelope	Achilles
Hermes	

COMPOSITION: GUIDELINES FOR EVALUATION

WRITING ABOUT POETRY

Objective

To analyze a poem

Guidelines for Evaluation

- suggested length: four to six paragraphs
- should state poem's theme
- should cite and explain images and allusions
- should identify rhyme scheme and meter
- should tell how rhyme scheme and meter support the theme, noting effect of variation

WRITING WITH CLASSICAL ALLUSIONS

Objective

To use a classical allusion in a description

Guidelines for Evaluation

- suggested length: one paragraph
- should describe a person or place
- should include a classical allusion from list
- should show knowledge of classical reference
- should show how classical reference corresponds to an aspect of person or place described

"The Fall of the House of Usher" is one of Poe's most famous tales. Like many gothic stories, it is set in an old mansion that suggests the terrible events that will take place there. Setting, characterization, plot, theme, and style all contribute to the single effect of terror. The story, however, is much more than a tale of terror: It is a portrait of an isolated and suffering human being.

Edgar Allan Poe

The Fall of the House of Usher

Son coeur est un luth suspendu;
Sitôt qu'on le touche il résonne.[1]

De Béranger

1 During the whole of a dull, dark, and soundless day in the autumn of the year, when the clouds hung oppressively low in the heavens, I had been passing alone, on horseback, through a singularly dreary tract of country, and at length found myself, as the shades of the evening drew on, within view of the melancholy House of Usher. I know not how it was—but, with the first glimpse of the building, a sense of insufferable gloom pervaded my spirit. I say insufferable, for the feeling was unrelieved by any of that half-pleasurable, because poetic, sentiment with which the mind usually receives even the sternest natural im-
2 ages of the desolate or terrible. I looked upon the scene before me—upon the mere house and the simple landscape features of the domain—upon the bleak walls—upon the vacant eyelike windows—upon a few rank sedges[2]—and upon a few white trunks of decayed trees—with an utter depression of soul which I can compare to no earthly sensation more properly than to the afterdream of the reveler upon opium—the bitter lapse into everyday life—the hideous dropping off of the veil. There was an iciness, a sinking, a sickening of the heart—an unredeemed dreariness of thought which no goading of the imagination could torture into aught[3] of the sublime. What was it—I paused to think—what was it that so unnerved me in the contemplation of the House of Usher? It was a mystery all insoluble; nor could I grapple with the shadowy fancies
3 that crowded upon me as I pondered. I was forced to fall back upon the unsatisfactory conclusion that while, beyond doubt, there *are* combinations of very simple natural objects which have the power of thus affecting us, still the analysis of this power lies among considerations beyond our depth. It was possible, I reflected, that a mere different arrangement of the particulars of the scene, of the details of the picture, would be sufficient to modify, or perhaps to annihilate, its capacity for sorrowful impression; and, acting upon this idea, I reined my horse to the precipitous brink of a black

1. ***Son . . . resonné:*** "His heart is a suspended lute; as soon as one touches it, it resounds." From "Le Refus" by French poet Pierre-Jean Béranger (1780–1857).
2. **sedges:** grasslike plants that grow in swampy ground.
3. **aught:** anything.

AT A GLANCE

- After a solitary day's ride on his horse, the narrator first glimpses the House of Usher.
- Seeing it, he is overcome by a sense of insufferable gloom.
- He decides that combinations of simple natural objects have the power of thus affecting people.

LITERARY OPTIONS

- setting: atmosphere and mood
- plot
- style: imagery

THEMATIC OPTIONS

- incomprehensible mysteries
- inescapable fate
- terror of the unknown

1 SETTING: ATMOSPHERE AND MOOD

The first sentence—with its ominous-sounding initial three adjectives—instantly creates an atmosphere at once oppressive and depressive.

2 STYLE: IMAGERY

The images the narrator uses to describe the house and its surroundings make them mysterious as well as desolate and arouse in the reader a sense of impending doom.

3 THEME

The narrator accepts the idea that the world contains things that are beyond the analysis of reason.

GUIDED READING

LITERAL QUESTION

1a. What does the narrator feel on first glimpsing the House of Usher? ("a sense of insufferable gloom")

INFERENTIAL QUESTION

1b. How does the narrator's reaction reveal his Romantic sensibility? (It reveals his self-absorption, vulnerability to extreme feelings, and nervous sensitivity to his surroundings—all characteristic of the Romantic sensibility.)

AT A GLANCE

- The narrator is there at the written request of his childhood friend Roderick Usher.
- In his letter Usher spoke of both physical and emotional distress.
- The narrator admits that he really knows little about his friend and relates information about the Ushers.

1 SETTING: ATMOSPHERE AND MOOD

By repeating certain features of the setting, the narrator fixes them in the reader's mind, perhaps trying to re-create the same sense of depression that he feels himself.

2 PLOT: EXPOSITION

The narrator has responded to an urgent emotional appeal which is both dramatic and vague.

3 POINT OF VIEW

The first-person narration allows the reader to enter the narrator's mind and this adds a sense of immediacy to the story.

4 SETTING: ATMOSPHERE AND MOOD

The narrator aligns the setting not with the airs of heaven but with earthly decay and death.

and lurid tarn[4] that lay in unruffled luster by the dwelling, and gazed down—but with a shudder even more thrilling than before—upon
1 the remodeled and inverted images of the gray sedge, and the ghastly tree stems, and the vacant and eyelike windows.

Nevertheless, in this mansion of gloom I now proposed to myself a sojourn of some weeks. Its proprietor, Roderick Usher, had been one of my boon companions in boyhood; but many years had elapsed since our last meeting. A letter, however, had lately reached me in a distant part of the country—a letter from him—which, in its wildly importunate nature, had admitted of no other than a personal reply. The MS.[5] gave evidence of nervous ag-
2 itation. The writer spoke of acute bodily illness—of a mental disorder which oppressed him—and of an earnest desire to see me, as his best and indeed his only personal friend, with a view of attempting, by the cheerfulness of my society, some alleviation of his malady. It was the manner in which all this, and much more, was said—it was the apparent *heart* that went with his request—which allowed me no room for hesitation; and I accordingly obeyed forthwith what I still considered a very singular summons.

Although as boys we had been even intimate associates, yet I really knew little of my friend. His reserve had been always excessive and habitual. I was aware, however, that his very ancient family had been noted, time out of mind, for a peculiar sensibility of temperament, displaying itself, through long ages, in many works of exalted art, and manifested, of late, in repeated deeds of munificent[6] yet unobtrusive charity, as well as in a passionate devotion to the intricacies, perhaps even more than to the orthodox and easily recognizable beauties, of musical science. I had learned, too, the very remarkable fact that the stem of the Usher race, all time-honored as it was, had put forth at no period any enduring branch; in other words, that the entire family lay in the direct line of descent, and had always, with very trifling and very temporary variation, so lain. It was this deficiency, I considered, while running over in thought the perfect keeping of the character of the premises with the accredited character of the people, and while speculating upon the possible influence which the one, in the long lapse of centuries, might have exercised upon the other—it was this deficiency, perhaps, of collateral[7] issue, and the consequent undeviating transmission from sire to son of the patrimony[8] with the name, which had at length so identified the two as to merge the original title of the estate in the quaint and equivocal appellation of the "House of Usher"—an appellation which seemed to include, in the minds of the peasantry who used it, both the family and the family mansion.

I have said that the sole effect of my somewhat childish experiment—that of looking down within the tarn—had been to deepen the first singular impression. There can be no doubt that the consciousness of the rapid increase of my superstition—for why should I not so term it?—served mainly to accelerate the increase itself. Such, I have long known, is the paradoxical law of all sentiments having
3 terror as a basis. And it might have been for this reason only that, when I again uplifted my eyes to the house itself, from its image in the pool, there grew in my mind a strange fancy—a fancy so ridiculous, indeed, that I but mention it to show the vivid force of the sensations which oppressed me. I had so worked upon my imagination as really to believe that about the whole mansion and domain there hung an atmosphere peculiar to themselves and
4 their immediate vicinity—an atmosphere which had no affinity with the air of heaven, but which had reeked up from the decayed trees, and the gray wall, and the silent tarn—a pes-

4. **tarn:** small lake.
5. **MS.:** manuscript.
6. **munificent:** generous.
7. **collateral** [kə lat′ər əl]: descended from common ancestors, but in a different line.
8. **patrimony** [pat′rə mō′nē]: inheritance.

GUIDED READING

LITERAL QUESTIONS

1a. What is the reason for the narrator's visit? (He has come at the urgent request of his boyhood friend.)

2a. What does the narrator know about his friend? (He knows very little.)

INFERENTIAL QUESTIONS

1b. What does the narrator mean when he refers to the "apparent heart that went with the request"? (He means that Roderick Usher wrote with great feeling and sincerity.)

2b. What might this tell you about Usher? (He has secrets he wants to hide from even his closest friends.)

tilent and mystic vapor, dull, sluggish, faintly discernible, and leaden-hued.

Shaking off from my spirit what *must* have been a dream, I scanned more narrowly the real aspect of the building. Its principal feature seemed to be that of an excessive antiquity. The discoloration of ages had been great. Minute fungi overspread the whole exterior, hanging in a fine tangled webwork from the eaves. Yet all this was apart from any extraordinary dilapidation. No portion of the
1 masonry had fallen; and there appeared to be a wild inconsistency between its still perfect adaptation of parts, and the crumbling condition of the individual stones. In this there was much that reminded me of the specious totality[9] of old woodwork which has rotted for long years in some neglected vault, with no disturbance from the breath of the external air. Beyond this indication of extensive decay, however, the fabric gave little token of instability. Perhaps the eye of a scrutinizing observer might have discovered a barely perceptible fissure, which, extending from the roof of the building in front, made its way down the wall in a zigzag direction, until it became lost in the sullen waters of the tarn.

Noticing these things, I rode over a short causeway to the house. A servant-in-waiting
2 took my horse, and I entered the Gothic[10] archway of the hall. A valet, of stealthy step, thence conducted me, in silence, through many dark and intricate passages in my progress to
3 the studio of his master. Much that I encountered on the way contributed, I know not how, to heighten the vague sentiments of which I have already spoken. While the objects around me—while the carvings of the ceilings, the somber tapestries of the walls, the ebon blackness of the floors, and the phantasmagoric[11] armorial trophies which rattled as I strode, were but matters to which, or to such as which, I

9. **specious totality:** giving the illusion of being in one piece.
10. **Gothic:** tall and pointed.
11. **phantasmagoric** [fan taz′mə gôr′ik]: fantastic; dreamlike.

AT A GLANCE

- The narrator recognizes that the chief feature of the house is its excessive antiquity.
- Entering the house the narrator is conducted by a valet to Usher's studio.

1 SETTING: ATMOSPHERE AND MOOD

The narrator's reference to the "wild inconsistency" of the house adds to the mysterious atmosphere by suggesting a place where contradictory things or events exist without explanation.

2 ROMANTIC IDEA

For the Romantics a horror story would be incomplete without a Gothic setting.

3 POINT OF VIEW

The reader sees the objects in the house through the narrator's eyes and is thus invited to feel about them the same way the narrator does.

GUIDED READING

LITERAL QUESTIONS

1a. What is the chief feature of the house? (excessive antiquity)

2a. What objects does the narrator see inside the house? (ceiling carvings, wall tapestries, the floors, and armorial trophies)

INFERENTIAL QUESTIONS

1b. What Romantic preoccupations does this description of the house reflect? (a fascination with the exotic, the mysterious, and the Gothic)

2b. What is their effect on the atmosphere? (They make it seem gloomy and mysterious.)

AT A GLANCE

- To the narrator the studio seems deeply gloomy.
- He is startled and awed by the physical change in Usher.
- Usher appears excessively agitated.

1 SETTING: ATMOSPHERE AND MOOD

The description of Usher's studio reinforces the atmosphere of gloom and unreality and foreshadows the description of Usher himself.

2 DESCRIPTION

The words used to describe Usher *(ghastly pallor, miraculous luster, gossamer texture)* have an otherworldly quality about them.

3 COMPARISON

The narrator uses the word *inconsistency* to describe his impression of Usher. This is the same word used earlier in the story to describe the house, suggesting that the atmosphere of the house reflects Usher's mental and spiritual condition.

had been accustomed from my infancy—while I hesitated not to acknowledge how familiar was all this—I still wondered to find how unfamiliar were the fancies which ordinary images were stirring up. On one of the staircases, I met the physician of the family. His countenance, I thought, wore a mingled expression of low cunning and perplexity. He accosted me with trepidation and passed on. The valet now threw open a door and ushered me into the presence of his master.

The room in which I found myself was very large and lofty. The windows were long, narrow, and pointed, and at so vast a distance from the black oaken floor as to be altogether inaccessible from within. Feeble gleams of encrimsoned light made their way through the trellised panes and served to render sufficiently distinct the more prominent objects around; the eye, however, struggled in vain to reach the remoter angles of the chamber, or the recesses of the vaulted and fretted[12] ceiling.
1 Dark draperies hung upon the walls. The general furniture was profuse, comfortless, antique, and tattered. Many books and musical instruments lay scattered about, but failed to give any vitality to the scene. I felt that I breathed an atmosphere of sorrow. An air of stern, deep, and irredeemable gloom hung over and pervaded all.

Upon my entrance, Usher arose from a sofa on which he had been lying at full length and greeted me with a vivacious warmth which had much in it, I at first thought, of an overdone cordiality—of the constrained effort of the *ennuyé*[13] man of the world. A glance, however, at his countenance convinced me of his perfect sincerity. We sat down; and for some moments, while he spoke not, I gazed upon him with a feeling half of pity, half of awe. Surely, man had never before so terribly altered, in so brief a period, as had Roderick Usher! It was with difficulty that I could bring myself to admit the identity of the wan being before me with the companion of my early boyhood. Yet the character of his face had been at all times remarkable. A cadaverousness of complexion; an eye large, liquid, and luminous beyond comparison; lips somewhat thin and very pallid, but of a surpassingly beautiful curve; a nose of a delicate Hebrew model, but with a breadth of nostril unusual in similar formations; a finely molded chin, speaking, in its want of prominence, of a want of moral energy; hair of a more than weblike softness and tenuity; these features, with an inordinate expansion above the regions of the temple, made up altogether a countenance not easily to be forgotten. And now, in the mere exaggeration of the prevailing character of these features, and of the expression they were wont to convey, lay so much of change that I doubted to
2 whom I spoke. The now ghastly pallor of the skin, and the now miraculous luster of the eye, above all things startled and even awed me. The silken hair, too, had been suffered to grow all unheeded, and as, in its wild gossamer texture, it floated rather than fell about the face, I could not, even with effort, connect its Arabesque[14] expression with any idea of simple humanity.

3 In the manner of my friend I was at once struck with an incoherence—an inconsistency; and I soon found this to arise from a series of feeble and futile struggles to overcome a habitual trepidancy—an excessive nervous agitation. For something of this nature I had indeed been prepared, no less by his letter, than by reminiscences of certain boyish traits, and by conclusions deduced from his peculiar physical conformation and temperament. His action was alternately vivacious and sullen. His voice varied rapidly from a tremulous indecision (when the animal spirits seemed utterly in abeyance) to that species of energetic concision—that abrupt, weighty, unhurried, and hollow-sounding enunciation—that leaden, self-balanced and perfectly modulated guttural ut-

12. **fretted:** ornamented.
13. ***ennuyé*** [än nwē ā′]: French for "bored."
14. **Arabesque** [ar′ə besk′]: fantastic and complex, like the designs on Arab architecture.

GUIDED READING

LITERAL QUESTIONS

1a. What did the narrator's eye struggle in vain to reach? (the remoter angles of the chamber)

2a. What is the narrator unable to do even with effort? (to connect the expression on Usher's face with any idea of simple humanity)

INFERENTIAL QUESTIONS

1b. What does this suggest about the narrator? (It suggests his inability to see or penetrate the mystery surrounding the house and its master.)

2b. What does the narrator's inability suggest about Usher? (It suggests something inhuman about him.)

terance, which may be observed in the lost drunkard, or the irreclaimable eater of opium, during the periods of his most intense excitement.

It was thus that he spoke of the object of my visit, of his earnest desire to see me, and of the solace he expected me to afford him. He entered, at some length, into what he conceived to be the nature of his malady. It was, he said, a constitutional and a family evil, and one for which he despaired to find a remedy—a mere nervous affection,[15] he immediately added, which would undoubtedly soon pass. It displayed itself in a host of unnatural sensations. Some of these, as he detailed them, interested and bewildered me; although, perhaps, the terms and the general manner of the nar-
1 ration had their weight. He suffered much from a morbid acuteness of the senses; the most insipid food was alone endurable; he could wear only garments of certain texture; the odors of all flowers were oppressive; his eyes were tortured by even a faint light; and there were but peculiar sounds, and these from stringed instruments, which did not inspire him with horror.

2 To an anomalous[16] species of terror I found him a bounden slave. "I shall perish," said he, "I *must* perish in this deplorable folly. Thus, thus, and not otherwise, shall I be lost. I dread the events of the future, not in themselves, but in their results. I shudder at the thought of any, even the most trivial, incident which may operate upon this intolerable agitation of soul. I have, indeed, no abhorrence of danger, except in its absolute effect—in terror. In this unnerved—in this pitiable condition—I feel that the period will sooner or later arrive when I must abandon life and reason together, in some struggle with the grim phantasm, FEAR."

I learned, moreover, at intervals, and through broken and equivocal hints, another singular feature of his mental condition. He was enchained by certain superstitious impressions in regard to the dwelling which he tenanted, and whence, for many years, he had never ventured forth—in regard to an influence whose supposititious[17] force was conveyed in terms too shadowy here to be restated—an influence which some peculiarities
3 in the mere form and substance of his family mansion had, by dint of long sufferance, he said, obtained over his spirit—an effect which the physique of the gray walls and turrets, and of the dim tarn into which they all looked down had, at length, brought about upon the morale of his existence.

He admitted, however, although with hesitation, that much of the peculiar gloom which thus afflicted him could be traced to a more natural and far more palpable origin—to the severe and long-continued illness—indeed to the evidently approaching dissolution—of a tenderly beloved sister—his sole companion for long years—his last and only relative on earth. "Her decease," he said, with a bitterness which I can never forget, "would leave him (him the hopeless and the frail) the last of the ancient
4 race of the Ushers." While he spoke, the lady Madeline (for so was she called) passed slowly through a remote portion of the apartment, and, without having noticed my presence, disappeared. I regarded her with an utter astonishment not unmingled with dread—and yet I found it impossible to account for such feelings. A sensation of stupor oppressed me as my eyes followed her retreating steps. When a door at length closed upon her, my glance sought instinctively and eagerly the countenance of the brother—but he had buried his face in his hands, and I could only perceive that a far more than ordinary wanness had overspread the emaciated fingers through which trickled many passionate tears.

The disease of the lady Madeline had long baffled the skill of her physicians. A settled apathy, a gradual wasting away of the person, and frequent although transient affections of a par-

---

15. **affection:** affliction.
16. **anomalous** [ə nom′ə ləs]: abnormal.
17. **supposititious** [sə poz′ə tish′əs]: supposed.

AT A GLANCE

- Usher's symptoms include an acuteness of the senses.
- He also experiences an overpowering terror and has a number of superstitions regarding his house.
- He attributes much of his gloom to the illness of his sister Madeline, who makes a brief appearance in the room.

1 ROMANTIC IDEA

To the Romantics the idea of someone suffering from something as excessive (and vague) as a "morbid acuteness of the senses" was immensely appealing.

2 CONFLICT

The major conflict in the story is the struggle between Usher and the mysterious terrors that threaten him.

3 SETTING

The relationship between character and setting is fluid, with each affecting the other; thus the gloomy setting causes or increases Usher's own depression but is also an extension of his emotional state.

4 PLOT: RISING ACTION

As Usher reveals his sister's approaching death, Madeline glides before the narrator's eyes and then disappears like a ghost.

GUIDED READING

LITERAL QUESTIONS

1a. By what was Usher enchained? (certain superstitious impressions in regard to his house)

2a. How did Madeline pass through the apartment? (slowly, without noticing the narrator, then disappearing)

INFERENTIAL QUESTIONS

1b. What might be the significance of this? (The atmosphere of the house is an extension of Usher's own depressive emotional state.)

2b. What does this suggest about her? (Her ghostlike appearance suggests her impending death.)

AT A GLANCE

- That night Madeline's illness worsens and forces her to stay in bed.
- During the next few days the narrator spends time with Usher painting, reading, and playing music in hopes of alleviating Usher's melancholy.
- The narrator recalls the feverish unreality of their time together.

1 PLOT: RISING ACTION

Madeline's worsening illness is vital to the development of the plot.

2 PLOT: RISING ACTION

The narrator's futile attempt to cheer his friend testifies to the power of darkness and gloom personified in Usher.

3 ROMANTIC IDEA

The idea of feverish unreality as contrasted with the world of reason excited the Romantic imagination.

tially cataleptical[18] character were the unusual
1 diagnosis. Hitherto she had steadily borne up against the pressure of her malady, and had not betaken herself finally to bed; but on the closing in of the evening of my arrival at the house, she succumbed (as her brother told me at night with inexpressible agitation) to the prostrating power of the destroyer, and I learned that the glimpse I had obtained of her person would thus probably be the last I should obtain—that the lady, at least while living, would be seen by me no more.

For several days ensuing, her name was unmentioned by either Usher or myself, and during this period I was busied in earnest endeavors to alleviate the melancholy of my friend. We painted and read together; or I listened, as if in a dream, to the wild improvisations of his speaking guitar. And thus, as a closer and still closer intimacy admitted me more unreservedly into the recesses of his spirit, the
2 more bitterly did I perceive the futility of all attempt at cheering a mind from which darkness, as if an inherent positive quality, poured forth upon all objects of the moral and physical universe in one unceasing radiation of gloom.

I shall ever bear about me a memory of the many solemn hours I thus spent alone with the master of the House of Usher. Yet I should fail in any attempt to convey an idea of the exact character of the studies, or of the occupations, in which he involved me, or led me the way.
3 An excited and highly distempered ideality[19] threw a sulfureous[20] luster over all. His long improvised dirges will ring forever in my ears. Among other things, I hold painfully in mind a certain singular perversion and amplification of the wild air of the last waltz of von Weber.[21] From the paintings over which his elaborate fancy brooded, and which grew, touch by touch, into vaguenesses at which I shuddered

18. **cataleptical** [kat'əl ep'tik əl]: state marked by loss of consciousness and deathlike muscular rigidity.
19. **distempered ideality:** feverish unreality.
20. **sulfureous:** greenish-yellow.
21. **von Weber:** Karl Maria von Weber (1786–1826), German Romantic composer.

GUIDED READING

LITERAL QUESTION

1a. What throws its luster over everything? (an excited and highly distempered ideality)

INFERENTIAL QUESTION

1b. Why might the narrator perceive this? (Students might suggest that the strangeness of the house and the situation is affecting the narrator's perceptions.)

the more thrillingly, because I shuddered knowing not why—from these paintings (vivid as their images now are before me) I would in vain endeavor to educe more than a small portion which should lie within the compass of merely written words. By the utter simplicity, by the nakedness of his designs, he arrested and overawed attention. If ever mortal painted an idea, that mortal was Roderick Usher. For me at least—in the circumstances then surrounding me—there arose out of the pure abstractions which the hypochondriac contrived to throw upon his canvas, an intensity of intolerable awe, no shadow of which felt I ever yet in the contemplation of the certainly glowing yet too concrete reveries of Fuseli.[22]

One of the phantasmagoric conceptions of my friend, partaking not so rigidly of the spirit of abstraction, may be shadowed forth, al-
1 though feebly, in words. A small picture presented the interior of an immensely long and rectangular vault or tunnel, with low walls, smooth, white, and without interruption or device. Certain accessory points of the design served well to convey the idea that this excavation lay at an exceeding depth below the surface of the earth. No outlet was observed in any portion of its vast extent, and no torch or other artificial source of light was discernible; yet a flood of intense rays rolled throughout and bathed the whole in a ghastly and inappropriate splendor.

I have just spoken of that morbid condition of the auditory nerve which rendered all music intolerable to the sufferer with the exception of certain effects of stringed instruments. It was, perhaps, the narrow limits to which he thus confined himself upon the guitar which
2 gave birth, in great measure, to the fantastic character of his performances. But the fervid facility of his impromptus could not be so accounted for. They must have been, and were, in the notes as well as in the words of his wild fantasias (for he not unfrequently accompanied himself with rhymed verbal improvisations), the result of that intense mental collectedness and concentration to which I have previously alluded as observable only in particular moments of the highest artificial excitement. The words of one of these rhapsodies I have easily remembered. I was, perhaps, the more forcibly impressed with it as he gave it because, in the under or mystic current of its meaning, I fancied that I perceived, and for the first time, a full consciousness on the part of Usher of the tottering of his lofty reason upon her throne. The verses, which were entitled "The Haunted Palace," ran very nearly, if not accurately, thus:

I

In the greenest of our valleys,
By good angels tenanted,
3 Once a fair and stately palace—
Radiant palace—reared its head.
In the monarch Thought's dominion—
It stood there!
Never seraph spread a pinion
Over fabric half so fair.

II

Banners yellow, glorious, golden,
On its roof did float and flow;
(This—all this—was in the olden
Time long ago)
And every gentle air that dallied,
In that sweet day,
Along the ramparts plumed and pallid,
A wingèd odor went away.

III

Wanderers in that happy valley
Through two luminous windows saw
Spirits moving musically
To a lute's well-tunèd law,
Round about a throne, where sitting
(Porphyrogene!)[23]
In state his glory well befitting,
The ruler of the realm was seen.

---

22. **Fuseli:** John Henry Fuseli (1742–1825), Swiss-born English Romantic painter.

23. **Porphyrogene** [pôr fə roʹje nē]: born to the purple—that is, to royalty.

AT A GLANCE

- The narrator describes the strange pictures painted by Usher, in particular a painting of a vault.
- The narrator also describes the fantastic character of Usher's guitar improvisations.
- The narrator remembers the verses of one of them entitled "The Haunted Palace."

1 FORESHADOWING

Usher's painting of the vault foreshadows Madeline's actual burial.

2 ALLITERATION

Poe's prose style is similar to the style he uses in his poetry. Here he uses repetition of the *f* sound in words like *fantastic, fervid,* and *facility.*

3 SYMBOL

The "Haunted Palace" may symbolize the House of Usher before its decline as well as Roderick's mental state before he started to go mad.

GUIDED READING

LITERAL QUESTIONS

1a. What is the subject of Usher's small picture? (a vault or a tunnel)

2a. What words are used to describe the haunted palace in the first stanza? (fair, stately, radiant)

INFERENTIAL QUESTIONS

1b. What might this be a picture of? (the family vault)

2b. What is the significance of this description? (The palace is a sharp contrast to Usher's house.)

AT A GLANCE

- According to the song the forces of evil overcome the palace.
- Usher says that inanimate objects have the capacity to feel and cites his house as an example.
- The two men read obscure books of magic and mysticism.

1 SYMBOL

If the palace is the House of Usher, then its monarch is Usher himself, and his high estate may refer both to his social position and to his mental state.

2 VOCABULARY: WORD CHOICE

The use of the word *entombed* foreshadows Madeline's entombment as well as the death of the House of Usher itself.

3 SETTING: ATMOSPHERE AND MOOD

Usher's belief that the objects of his house intentionally act to create their own atmosphere is paralleled by Poe's attempts to make the setting as "alive" as possible.

4 VOCABULARY: LATIN ROOTS

Titles on pages 142–143 contain Latin roots. (See *Directorium Inquisitorum* [dē rāk tōr′ē o͞om ēn′ quē zē tōr′o͞om], *Directory of the Inquisition,* and *Vigiliae Mortuorum secundum Chorum Ecclesiae Maguntinae* [vē jē′lē ā mōr′to͞o ōr′o͞om sā ko͞on′do͞om kōr′o͞om ā klā′zē ā mä go͞on′tē nā], *Vigils of the Dead According to the Choir of the Church of Mayence.*) Ask students to suggest English words containing these roots: *-quis-:* "question" (inquisitive); *-vig-* "watch," "awake" (vigilant); *-mort-:* "death" (mortal).

5 ROMANTIC IDEA

The books the two men read reflect the Romantic fascination with the exotic past.

IV

And all with pearl and ruby glowing
  Was the fair palace door,
Through which came flowing, flowing, flowing,
  And sparkling evermore,
A troop of Echoes whose sweet duty
  Was but to sing,
In voices of surpassing beauty,
  The wit and wisdom of their king.

V

1 But evil things, in robes of sorrow,
  Assailed the monarch's high estate;
(Ah, let us mourn, for never morrow
  Shall dawn upon him, desolate!)
And, round about his home, the glory
  That blushed and bloomed
Is but a dim-remembered story
2   Of the old time entombed.

VI

And travelers now within that valley,
  Through the red-litten[24] windows, see
Vast forms that move fantastically
  To a discordant melody;
While, like a rapid ghastly river,
  Through the pale door,
A hideous throng rush out forever,
  And laugh—but smile no more.

I well remember that suggestions arising from this ballad led us into a train of thought wherein there became manifest an opinion of Usher's which I mention not so much on account of its novelty (for other men have thought thus) as on account of the pertinacity with which he maintained it. This opinion, in its general form, was that of the sentience[25] of all vegetable things. But, in his disordered fancy the idea had assumed a more daring character and trespassed, under certain conditions, upon the kingdom of inorganization.[26] I lack words to express the full extent or the earnest abandon of his persuasion. The belief, however, was connected (as I have previously hinted) with the gray stones of the home of his forefathers. The conditions of the sentience had been here, he imagined, fulfilled in the method of collocation of these stones—in the order of their arrangement, as well as in that of the many fungi which overspread them and of the decayed trees which stood around—above all, in the long undisturbed endurance of this arrangement and in its reduplication in the
3 still waters of the tarn. Its evidence—the evidence of the sentience—was to be seen, he said (and I here started as he spoke), in the gradual yet certain condensation of an atmosphere of their own about the waters and the walls. The result was discoverable, he added, in that silent yet importunate and terrible influence which for centuries had molded the destinies of his family, and which made *him* what I now saw him—what he was. Such opinions need no comment, and I will make none.

Our books—the books which, for years, had formed no small portion of the mental existence of the invalid—were, as might be supposed, in strict keeping with this character of phantasm. We pored together over such works
4 as the *Ververt et Chartreuse*[27] of Gresset; the *Belphegor* of Machiavelli; the *Heaven and Hell* of Swedenborg; the *Subterranean Voyage of Nicholas Klimm* by Holberg; the *Chiromancy* of Robert Flud, of Jean D'Indaginé, and of De la Chambre; the *Journey into the Blue Distance* of Tieck; and the *City of the Sun* of Campanella. One favorite volume was a small octavo edition of the *Directorium Inquisitorum* by the Dominican Eymeric de Gironne; and
5 there were passages in Pomponius Mela, about the old African Satyrs and Aegipans, over which Usher would sit dreaming for hours. His chief

24. **litten:** lighted.
25. **sentience** [sen′shəns]: capacity for feeling.
26. **inorganization:** inanimate objects.

27. ***Ververt et Chartreuse,*** etc.: Actual titles of obscure books of magic and mysticism. The last one in the paragraph is a book of "vigils for the dead."

GUIDED READING

LITERAL QUESTIONS

1a. What forces assail "The Haunted Palace"? (evil things in robes of sorrow)

2a. What does the narrator say about Usher's opinions relating to the sentience of inanimate objects? ("Such opinions need no comment, and I will make none.")

INFERENTIAL QUESTIONS

1b. What might these forces represent? (the evil that Usher feels in his house or his own madness)

2b. What does the narrator's comment indicate about how he views Usher? (He thinks Usher is mad.)

delight, however, was found in the perusal of an exceedingly rare and curious book in quarto Gothic—the manual of a forgotten church—the *Vigiliae Mortuorum secundum Chorum Ecclesiae Maguntinae.*

I could not help thinking of the wild ritual of this work, and of its probable influence upon the hypochondriac, when one evening, having informed me abruptly that the lady Madeline was no more, he stated his intention of preserving her corpse for a fortnight (previously to its final interment) in one of the numerous vaults within the main walls of the building. The worldly reason, however, assigned for this singular proceeding was one which I did not feel at liberty to dispute. The brother had been led to his resolution (so he told me) by consideration of the unusual character of the malady of the deceased, of certain obtrusive and eager inquiries on the part of her medical men, and of the remote and exposed situation of the burial ground of the family. I will not deny that when I called to mind the sinister countenance of the person whom I met upon the staircase on the day of my arrival at the house, I had no desire to oppose what I regarded as at best but a harmless, and by no means an unnatural, precaution.

At the request of Usher, I personally aided him in the arrangements for the temporary entombment. The body having been encoffined,
1 we two alone bore it to its rest. The vault in which we placed it (and which had been so long unopened that our torches, half smothered in its oppressive atmosphere, gave us little opportunity for investigation) was small, damp, and entirely without means of admission for light, lying, at great depth, immediately beneath that portion of the building in which was my own sleeping apartment. It had been used, apparently in remote feudal times, for the worst purposes of a donjon keep and in later days as a place of deposit for powder or some other highly combustible substance, as a portion of its floor and the whole interior of a long archway through which we reached it were carefully sheathed with copper. The door, of massive iron, had been also similarly protected. Its immense weight caused an unusually sharp grating sound as it moved upon its hinges.

Having deposited our mournful burden upon trestles within this region of horror, we partially turned aside the yet unscrewed lid of the coffin and looked upon the face of the ten-
2 ant. A striking similitude between the brother and sister now first arrested my attention; and Usher, divining, perhaps, my thoughts, murmured out some few words from which I learned that the deceased and himself had been twins, and that sympathies of a scarcely intelligible nature had always existed between them. Our glances, however, rested not long upon the dead—for we could not regard her unawed. The disease which had thus entombed the lady in the maturity of youth had left, as usual in all maladies of a strictly cataleptical character, the mockery of a faint blush upon the bosom and the face, and that suspiciously lingering smile upon the lip which is so terrible in death. We replaced and screwed down the lid, and, having secured the door of iron, made our way, with toil into the scarcely less gloomy apartments of the upper portion of the house.

And now, some days of bitter grief having elapsed, an observable change came over the features of the mental disorder of my friend. His ordinary manner had vanished. His ordinary occupations were neglected or forgotten. He roamed from chamber to chamber with
3 hurried, unequal, and objectless step. The pallor of his countenance had assumed, if possible, a more ghastly hue—but the luminousness of his eye had utterly gone out. The once occasional huskiness of his tone was heard no more; and a tremulous quaver, as if of extreme terror, habitually characterized his utterance. There were times, indeed, when I thought his unceasingly agitated mind was laboring with some oppressive secret, to divulge which he struggled for the necessary courage. At times,

AT A GLANCE

- Madeline dies and Usher tells the narrator that he intends to temporarily entomb her in a vault within the house.
- While assisting Usher with the entombment, the narrator discovers that Madeline was Usher's twin.

1 SETTING: ATMOSPHERE AND MOOD

Although all the areas of the house are oppressive, the vault is the most so, literally and figuratively, creating an atmosphere of "entombment."

2 PLOT: RISING ACTION

The fact that Madeline is Usher's twin adds a new dimension to the plot by suggesting an even stronger bond between them.

3 CHARACTERIZATION

After Madeline's entombment Usher's appearance becomes increasingly deathlike.

GUIDED READING

LITERAL QUESTIONS

1a. What is the narrator's reaction to Usher's decision to preserve Madeline's corpse for a fortnight? (He thinks it a harmless and natural precaution.)

2a. What does the narrator learn on looking at Madeline's face? (that she and Usher are twins)

INFERENTIAL QUESTIONS

1b. What does his reaction show about the narrator? (He does not really understand Usher.)

2b. Why is this significant? (Twins are closer than ordinary siblings and are able to communicate their thoughts and feelings without words.)

AT A GLANCE

- Late one stormy night the narrator, unable to sleep, hears his friend's step.
- A frantic Usher abruptly asks the narrator if he has "seen it."
- Usher opens the window, and they view the eerie manifestations of the storm.

1 THEME

The narrator is unable to escape the terrors that are overwhelming his friend.

2 FORESHADOWING

The rising tempest, which now invades the room, foreshadows the events that will destroy the house and its master.

3 CHARACTERIZATION

Usher is sinking further into madness.

4 STYLE: IMAGERY

The imagery of the storm enhances the supernatural tone and reflects Usher's belief that the house is somehow alive and has the capacity for feeling.

again, I was obliged to resolve all into the mere inexplicable vagaries of madness, for I beheld him gazing upon vacancy for long hours, in an attitude of the profoundest attention, as if listening to some imaginary sound. It was no wonder that his condition terrified—
1 that it infected me. I felt creeping upon me by slow yet certain degrees, the wild influences of his own fantastic yet impressive superstitions.

It was, especially, upon retiring to bed late in the night of the seventh or eighth day after the placing of the lady Madeline within the donjon, that I experienced the full power of such feelings. Sleep came not near my couch—while the hours waned and waned away. I struggled to reason off the nervousness which had dominion over me. I endeavored to believe that much, if not all, of what I felt was due to the bewildering influence of the gloomy
2 furniture of the room—of the dark and tattered draperies, which, tortured into motion by the breath of a rising tempest, swayed fitfully to and fro upon the walls, and rustled uneasily about the decorations of the bed. But my efforts were fruitless. An irrepressible tremor gradually pervaded my frame; and at length there sat upon my very heart an incubus[28] of utterly causeless alarm. Shaking this off with a gasp and a struggle, I uplifted myself upon the pillows, and, peering earnestly within the intense darkness of the chamber, harkened—I know not why, except that an instinctive spirit prompted me—to certain low and indefinite sounds which came, through the pauses of the storm, at long intervals, I knew not whence. Overpowered by an intense sentiment of horror, unaccountable yet unendurable, I threw on my clothes with haste (for I felt that I should sleep no more during the night), and endeavored to arouse myself from the pitiable condition into which I had fallen by pacing rapidly to and fro through the apartment.

I had taken but few turns in this manner when a light step on an adjoining staircase arrested my attention. I presently recognized it as that of Usher. In an instant afterward he rapped, with a gentle touch, at my door, and entered, bearing a lamp. His countenance was, as usual, cadaverously wan—but, moreover,
3 there was a species of mad hilarity in his eyes—an evidently restrained hysteria in his whole demeanor. His air appalled me—but anything was preferable to the solitude which I had so long endured, and I even welcomed his presence as a relief.

"And you have not seen it?" he said abruptly, after having stared about him for some moments in silence—"you have not then seen it?—but, stay! you shall." Thus speaking, and having carefully shaded his lamp, he hurried to one of the casements and threw it freely open to the storm.

The impetuous fury of the entering gust nearly lifted us from our feet. It was, indeed, a tempestuous yet sternly beautiful night, and one wildly singular in its terror and its beauty. A whirlwind had apparently collected its force in our vicinity, for there were frequent and violent alterations in the direction of the wind; and the exceeding density of the clouds (which hung so low as to press upon the turrets of the house) did not prevent our perceiving the lifelike velocity with which they flew careering from all points against each other, without passing away into the distance. I say that even their exceeding density did not prevent our perceiving this—yet we had no glimpse of the moon or stars—nor was there
4 any flashing forth of the lightning. But the under surfaces of the huge masses of agitated vapor, as well as all terrestrial objects immediately around us, were glowing in the unnatural light of a faintly luminous and distinctly visible gaseous exhalation which hung about and enshrouded the mansion.

"You must not—you shall not behold this!" said I, shudderingly, to Usher, as I led him, with a gentle violence, from the window to a seat. "These appearances, which bewilder you, are merely electrical phenomena not uncommon—or it may be that they have their ghastly origin in the rank miasma of the tarn. Let us

28. **incubus** [ing′kyə bəs]: nightmare.

GUIDED READING

LITERAL QUESTION

1a. What does the storm do to the narrator's apartment? (It sways the draperies and rustles the decorations on the bed.)

INFERENTIAL QUESTION

1b. What might the storm represent? (an agitated state of mind)

close this casement; the air is chilling and dangerous to your frame. Here is one of your favorite romances. I will read, and you shall listen; and so we will pass away this terrible night together."

1 The antique volume which I had taken up was the "Mad Trist"[29] of Sir Launcelot Canning; but I had called it a favorite of Usher's more in sad jest than in earnest; for in truth there is little in its uncouth and unimaginative prolixity which could have had interest for the lofty and spiritual ideality of my friend. It was, however, the only book immediately at hand; and I indulged a vague hope that the excitement which now agitated the hypochondriac might find relief (for the history of mental disorder is full of similar anomalies) even in the extremeness of the folly which I should read. Could I have judged, indeed, by the wild overstrained air of vivacity with which he harkened, or apparently harkened, to the words of the tale, I might well have congratulated myself upon the success of my design.

I had arrived at that well-known portion of the story where Ethelred, the hero of the Trist, having sought in vain for peaceable admission into the dwelling of the hermit, proceeds to make good an entrance by force. Here, it will be remembered, the words of the narrative run thus:

"And Ethelred, who was by nature of a doughty[30] heart, and who was now mighty withal, on account of the powerfulness of the wine which he had drunken, waited no longer to hold parley with the hermit, who, in sooth, was of an obstinate and maliceful turn, but, feeling the rain upon his shoulders, and fearing the rising of the tempest, uplifted his mace outright, and, with blows, made quickly room in the plankings of the door for his gauntleted hand; and now pulling therewith sturdily, he so cracked, and ripped, and tore all asunder, that the noise of the dry and hollow-sounding wood alarumed and reverberated throughout the forest."

At the termination of this sentence I started and, for a moment, paused; for it appeared to me (although I at once concluded that my excited fancy had deceived me)—it appeared to me that, from some very remote portion of the
2 mansion, there came, indistinctly to my ears, what might have been, in its exact similarity of character, the echo (but a stifled and dull one certainly) of the very cracking and ripping sound which Sir Launcelot had so particularly described. It was, beyond doubt, the coincidence alone which had arrested my attention;
3 for, amid the rattling of the sashes of the casements and the ordinary commingled noises of the still increasing storm, the sound in itself had nothing, surely, which should have interested or disturbed me. I continued the story:

"But the good champion Ethelred, now entering within the door, was sore enraged and amazed to perceive no signal of the maliceful hermit; but, in the stead thereof, a dragon of a scaly and prodigious demeanor, and of a fiery tongue, which sat in guard before a palace of gold, with a floor of silver; and upon the wall there hung a shield of shining brass with this legend enwritten—

Who entereth herein, a conqueror hath bin;
Who slayeth the dragon, the shield he shall win.

4 And Ethelred uplifted his mace, and struck upon the head of the dragon, which fell before him, and gave up his pesty breath with a shriek so horrid and harsh, and withal so piercing, that Ethelred had fain to close his ears with his hands against the dreadful noise of it, the like whereof was never before heard."

Here again I paused abruptly, and now with a feeling of wild amazement—for there could be no doubt whatever that, in this instance, I did actually hear (although from what direction it proceeded I found it impossible to say) a low and apparently distant, but harsh, protracted, and most unusual screaming or grating

29. **"Mad Trist":** The book and its author are fictional. A *trist* is a meeting.
30. **doughty** [dou′tē]: brave.

AT A GLANCE

- To calm Usher the narrator reads the "Mad Trist" to him.
- Each noise described in the story seems to be echoed by a similar noise in the house—first a cracking and ripping sound and then a scream.

1 ROMANTIC IDEA

The invented medieval romance reflects the Romantic fascination with the antique.

2 PLOT: RISING ACTION

The suspense builds as the narrator hears the noises described in the "Mad Trist" echoed by similar noises in the house.

3 STYLE: REPETITION

Here Poe uses a repetition of *s* and *sh* sounds to help reflect the narrator's growing agitation.

4 SYMBOL

Ethelred may symbolize Madeline and the hermit (or dragon) may represent Usher.

GUIDED READING

LITERAL QUESTIONS

1a. To what does the narrator attribute the first sound he hears? (to the sounds of the storm)

2a. What is the second sound the narrator hears? (a scream)

INFERENTIAL QUESTIONS

1b. Why might the narrator try to fool himself about the true nature of the sound? (He does not want to give way to terror; admitting that he heard something might mean that he is also going mad.)

2b. Who might be making this sound? (Madeline's ghost)

AT A GLANCE

- The narrator continues reading the story and once again a sound from the story is echoed by a sound in the house.
- Usher discloses that his sister is making the noises because they buried her alive.
- Madeline appears at the door with blood on her white robes.

1 CHARACTERIZATION

The narrator is a level-headed individual who is trying to be sensitive to his friends' needs.

2 STYLE: IMAGERY

The auditory sensory image precisely and realistically portrays the sound the narrator hears.

3 PLOT: CLIMAX

Roderick's revelation shows the deep bonds between himself and his twin.

sound—the exact counterpart of what my fancy had already conjured up for the dragon's unnatural shriek as described by the romancer.

1 Oppressed, as I certainly was, upon the occurrence of this second and most extraordinary coincidence, by a thousand conflicting sensations, in which wonder and extreme terror were predominant, I still retained sufficient presence of mind to avoid exciting, by any observation, the sensitive nervousness of my companion. I was by no means certain that he had noticed the sounds in question; although, assuredly, a strange alteration had, during the last few minutes, taken place in his demeanor. From a position fronting my own, he had gradually brought round his chair, so as to sit with his face to the door of the chamber; and thus I could but partially perceive his features, although I saw that his lips trembled as if he were murmuring inaudibly. His head had dropped upon his breast—yet I knew that he was not asleep from the wide and rigid opening of the eye as I caught a glance of it in profile. The motion of his body, too, was at variance with this idea—for he rocked from side to side with a gentle yet constant and uniform sway. Having rapidly taken notice of all this, I resumed the narrative of Sir Launcelot, which thus proceeded:

"And now the champion, having escaped from the terrible fury of the dragon, bethinking himself of the brazen shield and of the breaking up of the enchantment which was upon it, removed the carcass from out of the way before him, and approached valorously over the silver pavement of the castle to where the shield was upon the wall, which in sooth tarried not for his full coming, but fell down at his feet upon the silver floor with a mighty great and terrible ringing sound."

No sooner had these syllables passed my lips, than—as if a shield of brass had indeed, at the moment, fallen heavily upon the floor of
2 silver—I became aware of a distinct, hollow, metallic, and clangorous, yet apparently muffled, reverberation. Completely unnerved, I leaped to my feet; but the measured rocking movement of Usher was undisturbed. I rushed to the chair in which he sat. His eyes were bent fixedly before him, and throughout his whole countenance there reigned a stony rigidity. But, as I placed my hand upon his shoulder, there came a strong shudder over his whole person; a sickly smile quivered about his lips; and I saw that he spoke in a low, hurried, and gibbering murmur, as if unconscious of my presence. Bending closely over him, I at length drank in the hideous import of his words.

"Not hear it?—yes, I hear it, and *have* heard it. Long—long—long—many minutes, many hours, many days have I heard it—yet I dared not—oh, pity me, miserable wretch that I
3 am!—I dared not—I *dared* not speak! *We have put her living in the tomb!* Said I not that my senses were acute? I *now* tell you that I heard her first feeble movements in the hollow coffin. I heard them—many, many days ago—yet I dared not—*I dared not speak!* And now—tonight—Ethelred—ha!ha!—the breaking of the hermit's door, and the death cry of the dragon, and the clangor of the shield!—say, rather, the rending of her coffin, and the grating of the iron hinges of her prison, and her struggles within the coppered archway of the vault! Oh whither shall I fly? Will she not be here anon? Is she not hurrying to upbraid me for my haste? Have I not heard her footstep on the stair? Do I not distinguish that heavy and horrible beating of her heart? Madman!"—here he sprang furiously to his feet, and shrieked out his syllables as if in the effort he were giving up his soul—*"Madman! I tell you that she now stands without the door!"*

As if in the superhuman energy of his utterance there had been found the potency of a spell—the huge antique panels to which the speaker pointed threw slowly back, upon the instant, their ponderous and ebony jaws. It was the work of the rushing gust—but then without those doors there *did* stand the lofty and enshrouded figure of the lady Madeline of Usher. There was blood upon her white robes, and the evidence of some bitter struggle upon every portion of her emaciated frame. For a

GUIDED READING

LITERAL QUESTIONS

1a. What does Roderick reveal? (that they have buried Madeline alive)

2a. Who or what is at the door? ("the enshrouded figure of the lady Madeline")

INFERENTIAL QUESTIONS

1b. What does this revelation show about his feelings for his sister? (It shows his deep attachment to her and perhaps his guilt over her death.)

2b. Why has she come? (to claim her brother's life)

moment she remained trembling and reeling to and fro upon the threshold—then, with a low moaning cry, fell heavily inward upon the person of her brother, and in her violent and now final death agonies, bore him to the floor a
1 corpse, and a victim to the terrors he had anticipated.

From that chamber, and from that mansion,
2 I fled aghast. The storm was still abroad in all its wrath as I found myself crossing the old causeway. Suddenly there shot along the path a wild light, and I turned to see whence a gleam so unusual could have issued; for the vast house and its shadows were alone behind me. The radiance was that of the full, setting, and blood-red moon, which now shone vividly through that once barely discernible fissure, of which I have before spoken as extending from the roof of the building, in a zigzag direction, to the base. While I gazed, this fissure rapidly widened—there came a fierce breath of the whirlwind—the entire orb of the satellite burst at once upon my sight—my brain reeled as I
3 saw the mighty walls rushing asunder—there was a long tumultuous shouting sound like the voice of a thousand waters—and the deep and dank tarn at my feet closed sullenly and silently over the fragments of the *"House of Usher."*

AT A GLANCE

- Madeline falls on Roderick; they both die.
- In the midst of the storm, the narrator flees the house.
- The house collapses, and its fragments sink into the tarn.

1 PLOT: CLIMAX

Madeline (or her ghost) claims her brother; perhaps his guilt and sense of loss are simply unbearable for someone so susceptible to terror or anxiety.

2 PLOT: FALLING ACTION

The narrator's flight represents the story's falling action; there is nothing he can do but escape from this scene of misery and death.

3 PLOT: RESOLUTION

Just as Usher's fate is attached to his sister's, so is the fate of the house attached to theirs. They are the only offspring; thus literally and figuratively the house of Usher dies with them.

REFLECTING ON THE STORY

What Romantic preoccupations permeate the story? (the fascination with the antique, the mysterious, the exotic, the supernatural, and the Gothic, as well as the focus on the self)

GUIDED READING

LITERAL QUESTION

1a. To what was Usher a victim? ("to the terrors he had anticipated")

INFERENTIAL QUESTION

1b. In what way might this be true? (Students might say that Usher's years of seclusion, his brooding personality, and his obsession with his own terror lead to the events that destroy him.)

STUDY QUESTIONS

1. *melancholy;* both the family and the house

2. "a constitutional and a family evil"; "an anomalous species of terror" he believes will kill him; his sister's illness and imminent death

3.
- paint, read, listen to Roderick play guitar
- He is losing his mind.

4. resemblance between brother and sister; that they were twins

5. gives up usual occupations, becomes agitated and pale, his eyes and voice change; terrifies him

6. Sounds in story are heard in house. She was alive when entombed.

7.
- Madeline, her robes covered with blood
- Madeline collapses on him, and he dies.

8. breaks apart, sinks into tarn

9. his love for her, a mystical bond; twins closer than ordinary siblings

10.
- Possible answers: He really believed her dead; he was trying to bury his fears; she returned from death as a ghost.
- unnatural storm, sounds in story duplicated in house, collapse of house

11. nervous, sensitive, artistic; no; knew little of him in childhood, descriptions full of contradictions, impossible to understand a contradictory person

12. Possible answers: years of isolation; brooding, reserved personality; obsession with his own fear

13.
- family and house both finally destroyed
- Ushers have no other relatives, so the fall of the house is complete.

14. Answers will vary. Students might note that the single effect builds tension and helps readers suspend disbelief; effective fiction helps reader suspend disbelief through a compelling fictional reality.

STUDY QUESTIONS

Recalling

1. What adjective does the narrator first use to describe the house of Usher? According to the third paragraph, what do the peasants mean when they say "House of Usher"?
2. Upon meeting the narrator, what does Roderick say about the nature of his "malady"? To what terror is he a "slave"? What does he admit is the natural cause of his gloomy condition?
3. What three things does the narrator do in an attempt to alleviate Roderick's melancholy (page 140)? What does the narrator understand for the first time when he hears Roderick perform "The Haunted Palace"?
4. What does the narrator notice while turning aside the lid of Madeline's coffin? What does Roderick explain?
5. What "observable change" comes over Roderick after the entombment of Madeline? What does his condition do to the narrator?
6. What interruptions occur when the narrator reads passages from "Mad Trist" to Roderick? What does Roderick reveal about Madeline's entombment?
7. What does the narrator see when the doors open "their ponderous and ebony jaws"? What happens to Roderick?
8. What happens to the house in the last paragraph?

Interpreting

9. What does Roderick's condition when the narrator arrives reveal about his relationship with his sister? Why is it significant that they are twins?
10. Why might Roderick have put Madeline in the tomb while she was alive? What other mysteries or supernatural elements does the story contain?
11. Name at least three character traits the narrator reveals about Roderick, either directly or indirectly. Does the narrator really understand his friend? How do you know?
12. Try to explain Roderick's deterioration. What in his own behavior might be the cause of his destruction?
13. What is the dual meaning of the story's title? Why is it significant that the Usher family has no "collateral issue" (paragraph 3)?

Extending

14. The English Romantic writer, Samuel Taylor Coleridge, said that we experience a "willing suspension of disbelief" when we read literature. In other words, we ignore our doubts about the possibility of events happening and willingly accept what the author tells us. Did you suspend your disbelief as you read "The Fall of the House of Usher"? Do you think the suspension of disbelief is necessary for the full enjoyment of a work of fiction? Why or why not?

VIEWPOINT

An expert on Poe, Arthur Hobson Quinn, writes of this story:

> One of the most common errors in Poe criticism lies in the assumption of the absence of heart in his characters. But the narrator has come a long distance simply because the appeal of Roderick Usher has clutched at his friendship through that quality—"It was the apparent *heart* that went with his request."
>
> —*Edgar Allan Poe*

- Do you agree that the narrator and Roderick are believable characters with genuine, heartfelt emotions? Or do you find the characters artificial and mechanical? Support your opinion with details from the story itself.

LITERARY FOCUS

Setting: Atmosphere and Mood

In "The Fall of the House of Usher" the **setting**—the time and place in which the events occur—is as important as the characters themselves. It would be impossible, for example, to imagine the Ushers living anywhere else than in their ancient house near the black tarn. If they did, they would not be the same people we find in this story. As characters, they not only contribute to the setting, but they are created in part *by* the setting.

In what country is the story set? It is certainly not America, for in Poe's time the United States was not old enough to have produced this ancient family and crumbling mansion. Where is the House of Usher? Nowhere, except within the

VIEWPOINT

Answers will vary. *Negative:* Terror eclipses characters, narrator's visit is just a plot device. *Positive:* Characters are genuine, as evidenced in details of suffering, narrator's concern, details of time spent together, narrator's attempt to distract Usher from his terror.

pages of the story itself. Yet the setting seems "real," with highly specific details about the rooms and the furnishings. The setting is a combination of reality and unreality that contributes to the unearthly effect of the story.

Notice, too, how Poe uses the setting to control the atmosphere, or mood—the general feeling—of the story by surrounding almost every object with adjectives piled upon adjectives: *dull, dark, dreary, bleak, decayed, pestilent, leaden-hued.* Each adjective has a separate meaning, of course, but more important is the way they merge, building an atmosphere of gloom and unreality. That atmosphere conveys not only the physical appearance of the house, but the Ushers' mental and spiritual condition as well.

Thinking About Setting

■ Choose a passage in the story—the description of Usher's studio, for example—and point out the adjectives that create the atmosphere and mood.

VOCABULARY

Recognizing Shades of Meaning

Though several adjectives can combine to create a single effect, it is equally important to be aware of the shades of meanings of individual adjectives. *Dull* and *bleak,* for example, do not mean exactly the same thing. *Dull* suggests a quality of light; *bleak* suggests a wider picture of emptiness and hopelessness.

■ Use your dictionary to define the following words from "The Fall of the House of Usher," paying special attention to the differences in meaning among the words in each group.

Group 1: decayed, morbid, pestilent
Group 2: pallid, ghastly, insipid
Group 3: dreary, somber, grim

COMPOSITION

Writing About the Total Effect

■ Describe the total effect of "The Fall of the House of Usher." How does Poe use the following literary elements to achieve this effect: (1) the setting, (2) the characters, (3) the plot, and (4) the theme of the story? *For help with this assignment, refer to Lesson 8 in the Writing About Literature Handbook at the back of this book.*

Describing a Setting

■ Write a paragraph describing a house or another place that has its own special atmosphere. Like Poe, use strings of adjectives to help convey the atmosphere. Assume that you are creating the setting for a mystery, a science fiction story, a humorous story, or a serious contemporary story.

COMPARING WRITERS

Washington Irving, James Fenimore Cooper, William Cullen Bryant, and Edgar Allan Poe are America's early Romantic writers. They share many of the characteristics of Romanticism (see the Introduction to this unit), yet they also differ greatly from one another.

1. Compare and contrast the profound love of nature in Bryant and Cooper. What does each author think should be the relationship between people and the natural world?
2. Compare and contrast the focus on the self and the individual in Irving, Cooper, Bryant, and Poe. What does each author reveal about the effects of this intense self-concern?
3. Compare and contrast the fascination with the supernatural in Irving and Poe. What effect does each author try to achieve?

LITERARY FOCUS

Answers will vary. Usher's studio: *large, lofty, narrow, vast,* etc.

VOCABULARY

1. decayed: decomposed; morbid: relating to disease; pestilent: causing death
2. pallid: pale; ghastly: dreadful, deathly pale; insipid: lacking zest
3. dreary: dull, dismal, sad; somber: dark, gloomy, depressing; grim: stern, forbidding

COMPARING WRITERS

1. *Both* idealize nature. *Cooper* views nature in physical as well as spiritual terms; nature is pristine, but also a threat; respects nature as awe-inspiring and potentially destructive. *Bryant* views nature in spiritual terms only—nature is teacher, offering consolation, final resting place; reveres nature.
2. ▪ *Irving* is concerned with fate of individual in moderation, critical of excessive self-concern. People should not take themselves too seriously.
   ▪ *Cooper:* Individual is on quest amid forces of nature and "civilization"; individual must be strong, pure, true to ideals.
   ▪ *Bryant:* individual facing death; self as part of nature
   ▪ *Poe:* individual in torment; self-absorbed individuals isolated in grotesque world; intense self-concern destructive
3. *Irving* uses wry tone that entertains and makes point gently; uses supernatural for folk-tale effect; evil can be overcome. *Poe* uses supernatural to horrify and spurs destructiveness of self-absorbed characters—no escape from doom.

COMPOSITION: GUIDELINES FOR EVALUATION

WRITING ABOUT THE TOTAL EFFECT

Objective

To state and analyze the total effect of a story

Guidelines for Evaluation

- suggested length: four to six paragraphs
- should state total effect of story
- should describe setting, characters, and plot
- should state theme
- should show how setting, characters, plot, and theme together produce the total effect

DESCRIBING A SETTING

Objective

To describe a setting with a distinct atmosphere

Guidelines for Evaluation

- suggested length: one to three paragraphs
- should describe a setting with an appropriate atmosphere
- should use adjectives to convey the atmosphere
- should use language appropriate to atmosphere
- should achieve a single effect

ACTIVE READING

Significant Detail

After the students have read this page, you might discuss the fact that details are not chosen indiscriminately: Authors include specific details for specific reasons. Ask why Poe included so many unpleasant details in describing the house of Usher (to achieve the single effect of terror) or the "silken, sad, uncertain rustling" of purple curtains in "The Raven" (to create a musical effect). Elicit that many of Irving's and Cooper's details are historical, lending a sense of history or legend to their works.

ACTIVE READING

Significant Detail

Our greatest delight as readers lies in the details of what we are reading. In fact, the pleasure of reading literature comes from responding to the actual words as they appear before our eyes. If we fully respond to the details of "The Devil and Tom Walker," "Thanatopsis," "The Raven," or "The Fall of the House of Usher," we will sense some of the pleasure that Irving, Bryant, and Poe had as they created their texts. If we read too quickly, without attention, looking only for some abstract "meaning," reading is likely to become a chore rather than a pleasure. We must attend to the details. In fact, it is only from the details that the specific meaning arises.

Each good story or poem is different from all others, even if it shares its themes, its forms, its language with thousands of other works. That difference, that unique sound and texture, is what we try to capture as we read. We might try to sum up "Thanatopsis," for example, in this way: "We will all die, but we should be comforted by the thought that we will all be gathered into nature with every man and woman who lived before us." Here we have the main idea of the poem but none of its pleasure. If we are to enjoy "Thanatopsis," or any poem, it will be because we give ourselves up to the specific movements of its verse, to the sound carrying us from line to line, to the details and images that make us feel the thought. Our pleasure is not always in "happy" thoughts, but in the perfection, the rightness of the language:

To be a brother to the insensible rock
And to the sluggish clod, which the rude swain
Turns with his share and treads upon. The oak
Shall send his roots abroad, and pierce thy mold.

From this feeling of negation, we move *with* and *in* the language of the poem toward a more positive and comforting feeling:

So live, that when thy summons comes to join
The innumerable caravan . . .
Thou go not, like the quarry-slave at night,
Scourged to his dungeon, but, sustained and soothed
By an unfaltering trust. . . .

To take just one detail, ask yourself why *innumerable* is so right here. For one thing, *innumerable caravan* suggests a long and stately procession moving toward a definite goal, rather than a disorderly or panic-driven mob. For another, *innumerable* is the only word in the poem with as many as five syllables, and the sense that many syllables suddenly come together in one word supports the sense that many (in fact, *innumerable*) people are moving together in this caravan. In itself, *innumerable* is not a particularly interesting word at all. Yet placed within its context in this poem, it becomes a source of delight.

Consider the gridiron ribs of Tom Walker's horse. From that detail we see that Tom is so greedy that he feeds his poor horse only enough to keep it alive. Think about the doors to Roderick's room in Poe's story. They open like "ponderous and ebony jaws." That detail—jaws—continues the suggestion made at the beginning of the story—with "vacant eyelike windows"—that the house itself is almost human. Such details are sources of *meaning* and part of the *pleasure* of a text.

THE AMERICAN VOICE

Other Times, Other Places

One of the paradoxes of Romantic literature is that it can be passionately nationalistic and still long for foreign places and ancient ages. Romantic authors, like those in this unit, insist on the value of their own land, their own customs and language, their own time in history. Yet these same authors often dream of old tales and exotic settings, as the following quotations reveal:

Irving
Under one of these gigantic trees, according to old stories, there was a great amount of treasure buried by Kidd the pirate. The inlet allowed a facility to bring the money in a boat secretly and at night to the very foot of the hill; the elevation of the place permitted a good lookout to be kept that no one was at hand; while the remarkable trees formed good landmarks by which the place might easily be found again.

Cooper
The incidents of this tale occurred between the years 1740 and 1745, when the settled portions of the colony of New York were confined to the four Atlantic counties. . . . A bird's-eye view of the whole region east of the Mississippi must then have offered one vast expanse of woods, relieved by a comparatively narrow fringe of cultivation along the sea, dotted by the glittering surfaces of lakes, and intersected by the waving lines of rivers. In such a vast picture of solemn solitude, the district of country we design to paint sinks into insignificance. . . .

Bryant
. . . Thou shalt lie down
With patriarchs of the infant world—with kings,
The powerful of the earth—the wise, the good,
Fair forms, and hoary seers of ages past. . . .

Poe
Thy Naiad airs have brought me home
To the glory that was Greece,
And the grandeur that was Rome.

These writers established a national identity for American literature in the first part of the nineteenth century. They helped define the character of the New World, but they never gave up the marvels of the past.

Key to Illustrations on Pages 98–99.

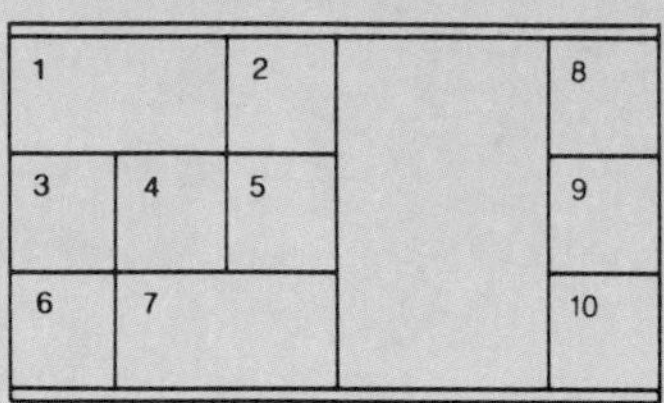

1. *Fur Traders Descending the Missouri,* George Caleb Bingham, 1851.
2. Women operating looms in a New England mill, early nineteenth century.
3. Monticello, the Virginia home of Thomas Jefferson, designed by Jefferson himself.
4. Edgar Allan Poe, daguerreotype (early photograph) by Mathew Brady.
5. *Baltimore Oriole,* colored engraving from *Birds of America* (1827–1838), John James Audubon.
6. James Fenimore Cooper, engraving, 1831.
7. *The Old House of Representatives,* Samuel F. B. Morse, 1822.
8. *Pat Lyon at the Forge,* John Neagle, 1826.
9. William Cullen Bryant. Nineteenth-century engraving.
10. The steamboat *Clermont,* built by Robert Fulton, 1807.

Other Times, Other Places
After the students have read this page, discuss how in the modern world the idea of progress and the idea of the golden age can exist simultaneously. Point out that in times of rapid change, people frequently feel insecure; it is perfectly natural to look forward with hope and back with fondness. The first half of the nineteenth century was a time of many changes in the United States, and all of the writers in this unit looked at what was happening with varying degrees of skepticism.

Key to Illustrations appears on page 229.

NEW ENGLAND RENAISSANCE

1840–1855

During the colonial and revolutionary periods American culture struggled for survival. During the early nineteenth century it struggled for individuality. By mid-century it was struggling for greatness.

A remarkable outburst of creativity marked this time, especially the years 1840 to 1855. Two famous books about this time—*American Renaissance* and *The Flowering of New England*—suggest in their titles the extraordinary quality of this period. A *renaissance* is a rebirth, a vital period in a culture, a ripeness that calls forth a concentration of great writers and artists. Such flowering periods took place in ancient Athens, in fifteenth- and sixteenth-century Italy, and in Elizabethan England. The United States, by mid-nineteenth century, began to flower. It had achieved self-confidence, prosperity, and a settled and mature culture. American expansiveness and the assertion of individualism seemed to demand a great literature to celebrate and explain—and to criticize as well—the mysterious uniqueness of American life.

As the nation consolidated and grew, its problems grew too: Slavery, materialism, child labor, and political corruption had become crucial dilemmas in America, and the Mexican-American War (1846–1848) provoked heated debates about American expansion. Yet as most Americans looked about them, they saw new states joining the union, a great movement into the central plains of the

INTRODUCTION

After the students have read the introduction to the unit, you might discuss Transcendentalism, clarifying its system of beliefs as follows:

- The human being can transcend to a higher spiritual plane.
- One "transcends" through intuition, not reason.
- One "transcends" by learning from and living in harmony with nature.
- One "transcends" as an individual.
- Every human being is capable of "transcending."
- After "transcending," one will want to do the right and moral thing and will work to better society.

In addition to the key words about Transcendentalism italicized on page 155, stress that Transcendentalists had great spiritual faith and optimism.

You might also have students consider the ideas of the New England Renaissance writers in light of those of previous literary and historical movements: In what ways was Transcendentalism an outgrowth of Romanticism? (It displayed a profound love of nature, a deep-rooted idealism, and a focus on the individual.) What ideas of their Puritan forebears do the Transcendentalists display in modified form? (They have a utopian vision, exhibit great faith and moral enthusiasm, and are concerned with reforming society.)

Key Ideas in This Period

- Transcendentalism
- Spiritualism
- nature
- individualism
- optimism
- utopian society
- American expansion

continent, and a conspicuous growth of industry, invention, technology, and trade that produced a general prosperity, pride, and confidence in the nation's future.

Democracy, a concept that in the eighteenth century few people thought would actually work, was indeed working. The election of Andrew Jackson in 1828, the first real "man of the people" to become President, dramatized the democratic spirit and the new, easy, not always graceful ways of Americans, freed from European constraints of class and tradition.

The Literary Response

Americans had always produced a vital literary response to their experience: the Native Americans, the Puritans, the planters, the revolutionaries, the early Romantics. Yet many American writers—even Irving and Cooper—seemed to be still a bit provincial, still under the influence of English and other European writers. The first steps taken by Irving, Cooper, Bryant, and Poe had to be lengthened, and now came the giant strides. A convenient historical marker is Emerson's stirring lecture *The American Scholar* (1837), often called America's intellectual declaration of independence. Emerson exclaimed, "We will walk on our own feet; we will work with our own hands; we will speak our own minds." The nation listened and took the words to heart.

The Custom House in Salem, Massachusetts, where Nathaniel Hawthorne once worked.

Increasingly, American writers, many of them directly inspired by Emerson, began to free themselves from European models. During a relatively few years, concentrating around Boston and the village of Concord, a number of writers appeared whom we now think of as "classic." Some of them, such as Emerson and Hawthorne, were well known in their time; others, like Thoreau, were uncelebrated until years after their deaths. Their influence, especially Emerson's, reached Walt Whitman in New York and Emily Dickinson in western Massachusetts. We say these writers are great because their work has for many readers a vitality and originality that endures, that transcends time and place. They produced work that has a scope and a depth that still reach us, still inspire us, still make us ask the great questions and face the most mysterious of realities. At times this literature celebrates the American, even the human, spirit. At times it criticizes the easy optimism that also marked the first half of the nineteenth century.

The Transcendentalists

Transcendentalism is a formidable term describing the movement in American culture that energized much of the literature of this period. To *transcend* something is to rise above it, to pass beyond its limits.

Transcendentalism is based on the belief that the most fundamental truths about life and death can be reached only by going beyond the world of the senses. The Transcendentalists believed—democratically—that each and every man and woman, living as a true individual, free from restraining dogma and dull habits of thought, could rise above the material world. They believed that each human mind could know something of the ultimate spiritual reality but could not know it through logic or the data of the senses. Rather, that knowledge came through a deep, free *intuition,* which they recognized as the "highest power of the Soul."

Transcendentalist is a fairly loose term referring to a large group of men and women who were very different from one another both as individuals and as writers. They did not have a strict doctrine or code to which they all subscribed. Transcendentalism is more of a tendency, an attitude, than it is a philosophy in any well-defined way. Nevertheless, we are able to define some aspects of it.

Nature played an important role in the Transcendentalist view. Nature was divine, alive with spirit; the human mind could *read* nature, find truths in it. To live in harmony with nature, to allow one's deepest intuitive being to communicate with nature, was a source of goodness and inspiration. We hear Emerson, in his rhapsodic essay *Nature,* an emotional outpouring, trying to capture in words the experience of that communication with nature:

"Standing on the bare ground—my head bathed by the blithe air and uplifted into infinite space—all mean egotism vanishes. I become a transparent eyeball; I am nothing; I see all; the currents of the Universal Being circulate through me; I am part or particle of God."

The Transcendentalists believed that this deep intuition of a spiritual reality is available to us only if we allow ourselves to be individuals, and Transcendentalist writing places a strong emphasis on *individualism.* Transcendentalism is also very *democratic,* asserting that the powers of the individual mind and soul are equally available to all people. These powers are not dependent upon wealth or background or education. We all have a potential equality as spiritual beings, and the divinity within each of us can be realized by the laborer and the farmer as well as by the learned minister and the scholar. For Emerson, every person can be a kind of poet, releasing individual imaginative power.

The rhodora, a flower that symbolized for Emerson the transcendental beauty and power of nature.

Such thoughts and feelings led the Transcendentalists to intense *moral enthusiasm* and concerns. Society, with its emphasis on material success, is often seen as a source of corruption. The Transcendentalist wants to do the right thing, the moral thing. That desire brought many Transcendentalists into efforts to *reform society,* to create a utopia—a perfect social and political system. They worked toward their ideal through utopian communities such as Brook Farm, through the antislavery movement, and through a sometimes vigorous feminism. The tone of Transcendentalist writing is often intensely optimistic and aspiring. It frequently suggests that the individual, in harmony with the divine universe, can transform the world.

The Darker Visions

The optimism of the Transcendentalists was not shared by all the great writers of the time. There were those—Hawthorne and Melville are the outstanding examples—who saw the universe as a more confusing and difficult place. Nature, they thought, is ambiguous, not easy to read, interpret, and harmonize. Evil and suffering had to be accounted for and were not to be brushed airily aside. Human nature was obstinate. Life was, as it always had been and always would be, mysterious.

Emerson could not read Hawthorne with pleasure, for he found Hawthorne's tales too gloomy. Hawthorne admired Emerson but thought him "a mystic, stretching his hand out of cloud-land, in vain search for something real." Melville had no use at all for Transcendentalism and the optimism of Emerson. To him it was all "nonsense," a much too easy dismissal of life's "disagreeable facts." For Melville life was a matter of compromises, not ideals—a spectacle of disappointment and illusion.

It is our privilege, as readers, not to need to take sides. Each of us will have preferences, perhaps recognizing part of the truth in one writer, part in another, perhaps seeing different parts at different times of our lives. Two elements, however, are common to all these writers: the power of their writing and the sincerity of their search.

Nathaniel Hawthorne's study and writing table in The Old Manse, Salem, Massachusetts.

The American Romance

An important development in American writing began to take shape with the writing of Hawthorne and Melville. This was the idea of the *romance*.

"Native Grounds" (pages 98–151) contains works of the early American Romantic writers—Irving, Cooper, Bryant, and Poe. These writers certainly exemplify many of the characteristics of the large movement called Romanticism. But it is with Hawthorne that an American writer began to make a critical distinction between a *novel* and a *romance*. This important distinction is useful in helping us to define just what it is that makes an American narrative different from a European narrative.

Hawthorne described what he meant by romance in the Preface to *The House of the Seven Gables* (1851):

"When a writer calls his work a Romance, it need hardly be observed that he wishes to claim a certain latitude, both as to its fashion and material, which he would not have felt himself entitled to assume, had he professed to be writing a Novel. The latter form of composition is presumed to aim at a very minute fidelity, not merely to the possible, but to the probable and ordinary course of man's experience. The former—while, as a work of art, it must rigidly subject itself to laws, and while it sins unpardonably so far as it may swerve aside from the truth of the human heart—has fairly a right to present that truth under circumstances, to a great extent, of the writer's own choosing or creation."

Hawthorne's statement makes clear that he thought a romance need not be totally faithful to reality. A romance can make greater use of the marvelous, the improbable, the eccentric, even the completely unbelievable. A romance need not tie itself to an accurate portrait of real people in the real social and physical world—as a novel does—as long as it is true to the human heart. Hawthorne's story "The Minister's Black Veil" is built on a highly improbable situation, but it remains faithful to larger human emotions. Melville's *Moby-Dick* contains characters and events that we never would expect to find in the real world, yet this great novel never fails to strike a reader as a voyage into authentic human experience.

As Hawthorne wrote, it would be a great mistake for a reader to try to bring "his fancy-pictures almost into positive contact with the realities of the moment." For Hawthorne—and for many of the American novelists to follow him—an American "novel" should only be judged as a romance.

The Fireside Poets

The Fireside Poets—Henry Wadsworth Longfellow, Oliver Wendell Holmes, James Russell Lowell, and John Greenleaf Whittier—also began writing during the time of Emerson, Hawthorne, and Melville. Their visions, however, were neither strictly Transcendental nor difficult and bleak. They did not form an organized group, but history has linked them for what they had in common.

The Fireside Poets were often concerned with ordinary American people, history, and values. Their poems were inspiring and easy to read; they made the reading of poetry immensely popular. The name *Fireside Poets* suggests their honored place in American homes during the 1800s. Together these poets forged a kind of national mythology—creating American scenes, telling American tales, putting into poetry a romanticized image of the American way of life. Though now they bow to the greatness of Emerson, Thoreau, Hawthorne, and Melville, they did spread an awareness of poetry throughout the country and contribute to the American Renaissance.

TIME LINE

1840–1855 AMERICAN EVENTS

1840 *The Dial,* Transcendentalist magazine, begins publication

Brook Farm, utopian community, established

1841 Ralph Waldo Emerson, *Self-Reliance* and *Essays*

1842 New York Philharmonic Symphony Orchestra established

U.S. and Seminole Indians sign peace treaty

1843 John Greenleaf Whittier, *Lays of My Home and Other Poems*

1845 First written examinations given in Boston public schools

1846 Oliver Wendell Holmes, *Poems*

Herman Melville, *Typee*

Smithsonian Institution established in Washington

Mexican-American War begins

1847 First adhesive postage stamp used in America

WORLD EVENTS 1840–1855

1841 Antarctica: Englishman James Ross explores the continent

1843 England: Charles Dickens, *A Christmas Carol*

1844 France: Alexander Dumas *père, The Three Musketeers*

1845 Ireland: Failure of potato crop causes famine

1846 Germany: Astronomers discover planet Neptune

Belgium: Adolphe Sax patents saxophone

1847 England: Charlotte Brontë, *Jane Eyre*

England: Emily Brontë, *Wuthering Heights*

1840–1855 American Events

1848 James Russell Lowell, *The Biglow Papers* and *A Fable for Critics*

California Gold Rush begins

Mexican-American War ends: U.S. adds much territory to its borders

1849 Elizabeth Blackwell becomes first woman in U.S. to receive a medical degree

Francis Parkman, *The Oregon Trail*

1850 Nathaniel Hawthorne, *The Scarlet Letter*

Congress enacts Compromise of 1850

U.S. population 23.1 million

1851 Herman Melville, *Moby-Dick*

Nathaniel Hawthorne, *The House of the Seven Gables*

The *New York Times* first published

Isaac Singer patents first continuous-stitch sewing machine

1852 Harriet Beecher Stowe, *Uncle Tom's Cabin*

1853 U.S. purchases southern New Mexico and Arizona from Mexico

1854 Henry David Thoreau, *Walden*

1855 Henry Wadsworth Longfellow, *The Song of Hiawatha*

World Events 1840–1855

1848 Belgium: Karl Marx and Friedrich Engels, *The Communist Manifesto*

1849 France: Realism movement in art begins

1850 England: Charles Dickens, *David Copperfield*

1851 Italy: Giuseppe Verdi composes the opera *Rigoletto*

1852 Europe: Crimean War begins

France: Henry Gifford makes successful flight in steam-powered airship

1854 England: Alfred, Lord Tennyson, "The Charge of the Light Brigade"

1855 Africa: David Livingstone discovers Victoria Falls

Herman Melville

Harriet Beecher Stowe

THE ESSAY: Emerson and Thoreau

Ralph Waldo Emerson *1803–1882*

Outwardly Ralph Waldo Emerson's life was quiet and well ordered, but inwardly it overflowed with new ideas. Emerson was born in Boston, the son of a Unitarian minister who died when Waldo, as he preferred to be called, was eight years old. He attended Harvard, studied theology, and became a Unitarian minister himself in 1829. In that year he was also married, but his beloved wife, Ellen, died only sixteen months later.

In 1832, for reasons of conscience, Emerson felt obliged to resign his ministry. After a trip to Europe, where he met the English writers Wordsworth, Coleridge, and Carlyle, he settled in the village of Concord, Massachusetts. He remarried and began his lifelong career as lecturer and writer. At Concord he became a member of the Transcendental Club and was surrounded by a remarkable group of men and women, including Henry David Thoreau, Bronson Alcott, and Margaret Fuller.

It was at Concord that Emerson composed his first book, *Nature* (1836). His address called *The American Scholar* (1837) has been an inspiration to generations of young Americans, but Emerson did not achieve national fame until his *Essays* appeared in 1841. Then came *Essays: Second Series* (1844), *Representative Men* (1849), and *The Conduct of Life* (1860).

When he was a young man, Emerson began writing what he called his "Savings Bank," the remarkable journals and notebooks that were not published in full until almost a century after his death. He would "deposit" in these journals his daily thoughts and observations as well as notes on his wide reading. From them he would "withdraw" the language and ideas for lectures. As he became increasingly famous as an American "prophet," he traveled widely throughout the country, delivering the lectures in a rich and beautiful voice. The lectures, polished and improved with many deliveries, often became the basis for the essays that were important influences upon so many American writers, including Thoreau, Whitman, Dickinson, and Frost. Yet Emerson's great influence extended beyond the literary community to the American people at large. His optimism, his belief in the vast possibilities of mind and spirit, and his doctrine of self-reliance well suited a democratic, progressive nation.

No single essay of Emerson's can give an adequate sense of his range of thought and mood. If at times he appears to contradict himself, it is because he wished himself and all of us to grow and to become aware of the mystery and richness of experience. "I wish to say what I think and feel today," he declared, "with the proviso that tomorrow perhaps I shall contradict it all. Freedom boundless I wish." Emerson continually redefined his own vision and fought to inspire others to have the noblest conceptions of themselves and of the "God in us."

It is easy to find oversimplified, watered-down versions of Emersonian aspiration, optimism, and individualism. Simplifications of his thought often lead toward the very opposite of what he meant. When Emerson spoke, for example, of the potential powers of the self-reliant individual—"A man is stronger than a city"—he did not mean that we should become irresponsibly obsessed with our selves. He did not mean that individualism is a license to do as we wish. Emerson would have us trust in "divine providence," live in harmony with nature and with what he called the Oversoul, the universal spirit that is the source of all unity and growth.

Nature and "Self-Reliance" are two of Emerson's best-known and most influential essays. *Nature* is a lyrical expression of the harmony Emerson felt between himself and nature. "Self-Reliance" is also at the core of Emerson's ideas—what one of his biographers calls "a twenty-one gun salute to self-reliance."

■ What does Emerson mean by "see truly" and "live truly"?

The Metropolitan Museum of Art

Spring Blossoms, George Inness, 1889.

from Nature

To go into solitude, a man needs to retire
1 as much from his chamber as from society. I am not solitary whilst I read and write, though nobody is with me. But if a man would be alone, let him look at the stars. The rays that come from those heavenly worlds will separate between him and what he touches. One might think the atmosphere was made transparent with this design, to give man, in the heavenly bodies, the perpetual presence of the sublime. Seen in the streets of cities, how great they are! If the stars should appear one night in a thousand years, how would men believe and adore, and preserve for many generations the remembrance of the city of God which had been shown! But every night come out these envoys of beauty, and light the universe with their admonishing smile.

The stars awaken a certain reverence because, though always present, they are inaccessible; but all natural objects make a kindred impression when the mind is open to their influence. Nature never wears a mean[1] appearance. Neither does the wisest man extort her secret and lose his curiosity by finding out all her perfection. Nature never became a toy to a wise spirit. The flowers, the animals, the mountains reflected the wisdom of his best hour, as much as they had delighted the simplicity of his childhood. . . .

To speak truly, few adult persons can see nature. Most persons do not see the sun. At least they have a very superficial seeing. The sun illuminates only the eye of the man, but shines into the eye and the heart of the child. The lover of nature is he whose inward and outward senses are still truly adjusted to each other, who has retained the spirit of infancy even into the era of manhood. His intercourse with heaven and earth becomes part of his daily food. In the presence of nature a wild delight runs through the man, in spite of real sor-
2 rows. Nature says: He is my creature, and maugre[2] all his impertinent griefs, he shall be glad with me. Not the sun or the summer alone, but every hour and season yields its tribute of delight; for every hour and change corresponds to and authorizes a different state of the mind, from breathless noon to grimmest midnight. Nature is a setting that fits equally well a comic or a mourning piece. In good health, the air is a cordial[3] of incredible virtue. Crossing a bare common,[4] in snow puddles, at twilight, under a clouded sky, without having in my thoughts any occurrence of special good fortune, I have enjoyed a perfect exhilaration. I am glad to the brink of fear. In the woods, too, a man casts off his years, as the snake his slough, and at what period soever of life is always a child. In the woods is perpetual youth. Within these plantations of God, a decorum[5] and sanctity reign; a perennial festival is dressed, and the guest sees not how he should tire of them in a thousand years. In the woods, we return to reason and faith. There I feel that nothing can befall me in life—no disgrace, no calamity (leaving me my eyes), which
3 nature cannot repair. Standing on the bare ground—my head bathed by the blithe air and uplifted into infinite space—all mean egotism vanishes. I become a transparent eyeball; I am nothing; I see all; the currents of the Universal Being circulate through me; I am part or particle of God. The name of the nearest friend sounds then foreign and accidental: to be brothers, to be acquaintances, master or servant, is then a trifle and a disturbance. I am the lover of uncontained and immortal beauty.

1. **mean:** shabby; miserly; ignoble.
2. **maugre** [mô′gər]: in spite of.
3. **cordial:** stimulating medicine or drink.
4. **common:** area of open public land.
5. **decorum:** rightness; harmony.

AT A GLANCE

- The stars exemplify the glories of nature.
- All manifestations of nature reflect its glory.
- To see nature truly, one must experience it fully, as a child does.
- Nature can elevate humanity to a higher experience.

LITERARY OPTIONS

- main idea
- style
- purpose

THEMATIC OPTIONS

- spiritual understanding
- the power of nature
- visions and ideals

1 PERIOD IDEA

Experiencing the natural world with unobstructed vision was a key feature of Transcendentalist philosophy.

2 STYLE: PERSONIFICATION

Nature is portrayed as a magnanimous being in comparison with whom people and their concerns are small and "impertinent." The image suggests nature as a symbol for a higher power.

3 STYLE: METAPHOR

Emerson's famous metaphor of himself as "a transparent eyeball" describes the power of nature to raise one's consciousness to a higher plane.

GUIDED READING

LITERAL QUESTIONS

1a. Who does Emerson say is the true lover of nature? (the person who retains the spirit of infancy into adulthood)

2a. How does Emerson describe what happens when his egotism vanishes in the presence of nature? ("I become a transparent eyeball; I am nothing; I see all.")

INFERENTIAL QUESTIONS

1b. Why is it necessary to experience nature as a child does? (Unencumbered by petty ambitions and cares, children are more able to delight unegotistically in nature.)

2b. With the disappearance of his egotism, what feeling does Emerson then experience? (a feeling of oneness with God and with the universe)

AT A GLANCE

- There is harmony among all living things.
- The delight people feel in the presence of nature comes from within the human spirit.

1 VOCABULARY: MULTIPLE MEANINGS

Occult is used here in its sense of "hidden" or "not easy to discover," rather than with the meaning of "supernatural" or "eerie."

2 MAIN IDEA

Emerson presents the theory that nature and the human soul cooperate to produce what we perceive as natural beauty.

REFLECTING ON THE SELECTION

What does nature seem to mean to Emerson? (Students may suggest that nature symbolizes God or the inner life of human beings.)

STUDY QUESTIONS

1. People would adore and remember "the city of God."
2. because they are inaccessible; when the mind is open to their influence
3. has attuned inward and outward senses and retained a child's spirit
4. Human beings have a mystical relationship with nature.
5. He has become a receptor to stimuli, does not allow his ego to color what he sees. He feels a part of God, with something of God in him.
6. man, or nature and man in harmony
7. Scientists seek empirical evidence, see nature as that which can be proven; mystical feelings can not influence their thinking.

In the wilderness, I find something more dear and connate[6] than in streets or villages. In the tranquil landscape, and especially in the distant line of the horizon, man beholds somewhat as beautiful as his own nature.

The greatest delight which the fields and
1 woods minister is the suggestion of an occult relation between man and the vegetable. I am not alone and unacknowledged. They nod to me, and I to them. The waving of the boughs in the storm is new to me and old. It takes me by surprise, and yet is not unknown. Its effect is like that of a higher thought or a better emotion coming over me, when I deemed I was thinking justly or doing right.

2 Yet it is certain that the power to produce this delight does not reside in nature, but in man, or in a harmony of both. It is necessary to use these pleasures with great temperance. For nature is not always tricked[7] in holiday attire; but the same scene which yesterday breathed perfume and glittered as for the frolic of the nymphs is overspread with melancholy today. Nature always wears the colors of the spirit. To a man laboring under calamity, the heat of his own fire hath sadness in it. Then there is a kind of contempt of the landscape felt by him who has just lost by death a dear friend. The sky is less grand as it shuts down over less worth in the population. . . .

6. **connate** [kon′āt]: closely related.

7. **tricked:** dressed.

STUDY QUESTIONS

Recalling

1. According to paragraph 1, what does Emerson say would happen if the stars appeared one night in a thousand years?
2. According to paragraph 2, why does Emerson believe the stars awaken a reverence in people? When do natural objects make a similar impression of reverence?
3. According to paragraph 3, how does Emerson describe the lover of nature?
4. Summarize the first sentence of paragraph 4. Be sure to use your own words in the summary.

Interpreting

5. Near the end of paragraph 3, what does Emerson mean when he describes himself as "a transparent eyeball" when in the woods? How does this state of mind affect his relationship with God?
6. Where does Emerson believe the power for a true relationship between man and God comes from, according to paragraph 5?

Extending

7. What do you think is the difference between the kind of meaning Emerson finds in nature and the meaning a botanist, a geographer, or an astrophysicist finds in nature?

Ralph Waldo Emerson

from Self-Reliance

1 Trust thyself: every heart vibrates to that iron string. Accept the place the divine providence has found for you, the society of your contemporaries, the connection of events. Great men have always done so, and confided themselves childlike to the genius[1] of their age, betraying their perception that the absolutely trustworthy was seated at their heart, working through their hands, predominating in all their
2 being. And we are now men, and must accept in the highest mind the same transcendent destiny; and not minors and invalids in a protected corner, not cowards fleeing before a revolution, but guides, redeemers, and benefactors, obeying the Almighty effort and advancing on Chaos and the Dark. . . .

3 A foolish consistency is the hobgoblin of little minds, adored by little statesmen and philosophers and divines. With consistency a great soul has simply nothing to do. He may as well concern himself with his shadow on the wall. Speak what you think now in hard words, and tomorrow speak what tomorrow thinks in hard words again, though it contradict everything you said today. "Ah, so you shall be sure to be misunderstood." Is it so bad then to be misunderstood? Pythagoras was misunderstood, and Socrates, and Jesus, and Luther, and Copernicus, and Galileo, and Newton,[2] and every pure and wise spirit that ever took flesh. To be great is to be misunderstood. . . .

Man is timid and apologetic; he is no longer upright; he dares not say, "I think," "I am," but quotes some saint or sage. He is ashamed before the blade of grass or the blowing rose. These roses under my window make no reference to former roses or to better ones; they are for what they are; they exist with God today. There is no time to them. There is simply the rose; it is perfect in every moment of
4 its existence. Before a leaf bud has burst, its whole life acts; in the full-blown flower there is no more; in the leafless root there is no less. Its nature is satisfied and it satisfies nature in all moments alike. But man postpones or remembers; he does not live in the present, but with reverted[3] eye laments the past, or, heedless of the riches that surround him, stands on tiptoe to foresee the future. He cannot be happy and strong until he too lives with nature in the present, above time.

This should be plain enough. Yet see what strong intellects dare not yet hear God himself unless he speak the phraseology of I know not what David, or Jeremiah, or Paul.[4] We shall not always set so great a price on a few texts, on a few lives. We are like children who repeat by rote the sentences of grandames and tutors and, as they grow older, of the men of talents and character they chance to see—painfully recollecting the exact words they spoke. Afterwards, when they come into the point of view which those had who uttered these sayings, they understand them and are willing to let the words go, for at any time they can use words as good when occasion comes. If we live truly, we shall see truly. It is as easy for the strong man to be strong as it is for the weak to be weak. When we have new perception, we shall gladly disburden the memory of its hoarded treasures as old rubbish. When a man lives with God, his voice shall be as sweet as the murmur of the brook and the rustle of the corn. . . .

1. **genius:** spirit.
2. **Pythagoras . . . Newton:** Individuals who made an extraordinary contribution to scientific, philosophical, or religious thinking.
3. **reverted:** backward-looking.
4. **David . . . Paul:** biblical writers.

AT A GLANCE

- One must trust oneself.
- The ideal is to exist in the present, as nature does.

LITERARY OPTIONS

- main idea
- style

THEMATIC OPTIONS

- being true to oneself
- visions and ideals

1 MAIN IDEA

Emerson believes that people have an intuitive understanding of their place in the universe and must act according to that understanding.

2 PURPOSE

Emerson sets out to persuade his readers to believe in individualism and to practice it by asserting their innate strength.

3 STYLE: METAPHOR

In this famous metaphor Emerson belittles the need for perfect continuity between present and past. Yesterday's judgments may not be appropriate to today's reality.

4 STYLE: CONTRAST

The essay contrasts the natural life of the rose with the self-conscious life of people, reaffirming the Transcendentalist view of nature as a guide to higher understanding.

REFLECTING ON THE SELECTION

How would Emerson describe a truly self-reliant person? (Possible answers: someone who follows his or her own conscience; someone who has strong personal values.)

SELECTION FOR PRACTICE IN ACTIVE READING
(TCR 7, p. 62)

GUIDED READING

LITERAL QUESTIONS

1a. What does Emerson say is the "hobgoblin" of little minds? (a foolish consistency)

2a. According to Emerson, what is the penalty for being great? (being misunderstood)

INFERENTIAL QUESTIONS

1b. What do you think Emerson meant by his statement about "little" minds? (Narrow-minded people are likely to make consistency with the past so important that they fail to perceive the truth of this moment.)

2b. How do the names Emerson mentions support his statement about greatness? (Each of these people was misunderstood in his own time; today, however, all are acknowledged to be great.)

STUDY QUESTIONS

1. "trust thyself"
2. foolish consistency; all were misunderstood
3. timid, apologetic, quotes others rather than voicing opin ion; must live "with nature in the present, above time"
4. We shall see truly.
5. self-confidence in ourselves and our convictions; speaking out without fear
6. live in the present; meet God directly
7. Answers will vary. Students should recognize Emerson's optimism, his faith in humanity's capacity for wisdom, greatness, possibility of living with God.
8. Answers will vary. Students should recognize that self-reliance characterized the Age of Exploration, Age of Reason, early settlers and pioneers, as well as the enterprising spirit that made the country prosper. Selections by Columbus, Smith, Franklin, Bartram, Crèvecoeur, and Cooper all exemplify self-reliance.

LITERARY FOCUS

- *that iron string:* emphasizes the strength of purpose involved in self-trust
- *hobgoblin:* suggests the obsession with consistency that can haunt little minds
- *shadow on the wall:* visualizes the insignificance of consistency to a great soul

STUDY QUESTIONS

Recalling

1. According to paragraph 1, to what "iron string" does every heart vibrate?
2. According to paragraph 2, what is "the hobgoblin of little minds"? What does the paragraph say about Pythagoras, Socrates, and Jesus?
3. At the beginning of paragraph 3, how is man described? According to the end of the paragraph, under what conditions will man be "happy and strong"?
4. According to the last paragraph, what will happen if we live truly?

Interpreting

5. Explain two lessons that great figures of the past teach us about the concept of self-reliance.
6. Explain two lessons that nature teaches about self-reliance.
7. In your opinion does Emerson express optimism or pessimism about human nature and human potential? What seems to be the basis of his belief? Support your answer to this question with specific references to the essay.

Extending

8. Explain to what extent the concept of self-reliance can be considered a fundamental American idea. Support your answer with references to works that you have read in this book as well as to other aspects of American life and history.

LITERARY FOCUS

Figurative Language

Literal language is language that means exactly what it says, word for word—for example, "I stand on tiptoe to reach the shelf." **Figurative language** is language that is not meant to be taken literally. For example, Emerson describes someone who "stands on tiptoe to foresee the future." Phrases using figurative language, such as similes and metaphors, are often called **figures of speech.**

The origin of *figure* is the Latin word for "form" or "shape," and figurative language gives to an idea a familiar form or shape. When Emerson says, for instance, that he becomes a "transparent eyeball," he uses figurative language. He presents a concrete image—something we can perceive with our senses—to help us understand the abstract idea of wonder.

Figurative language can also make commonplace ideas fresh and vivid. When Emerson says, "I am glad to the *brink* of fear," or when he tells us, "a man casts off his years, *as the snake his slough,*" he provides vivid pictures of emotions that otherwise might not seem unusual. By using figurative language throughout the third paragraph of *Nature,* Emerson underscores the extraordinary exhilaration he experiences in nature.

Thinking About Figurative Language

■ Find at least three examples of figurative language in "Self-Reliance." Tell why each image is appropriate to the idea it makes concrete.

Margaret Fuller *1810–1850*

American editor, essayist, poet, and social reformer Margaret Fuller rejected the conventional role assigned to women of her time. Well educated and highly intellectual, she became associated with Emerson and several other New England Transcendentalists in an informal discussion group that they called the Transcendental Club. In 1840 the club founded a magazine, *The Dial,* to give wider dissemination to Transcendentalist ideas. Fuller served as the magazine's editor in chief until 1842. Two years later, she began writing critical pieces for the New York *Tribune.* In 1846 she went to Europe. In 1850 Fuller, her husband, and their infant son drowned in a shipwreck off Fire Island, New York.

■ If you were introducing a new magazine to the public, what would you want to say about it?

Margaret Fuller and Ralph Waldo Emerson

The Announcement of *The Dial*

1 We invite the attention of our countrymen to
a new design. Probably not quite unexpected or
unannounced will our Journal appear, though
small pains have been taken to secure its welcome. Those who have immediately acted in editing the present Number cannot accuse themselves of any unbecoming forwardness in their
undertaking, but rather of a backwardness, when
they remember how often in many private circles the work was projected, how eagerly desired, and only postponed because no individual
volunteered to combine and concentrate the
2 freewill offerings of many cooperators. With
some reluctance the present conductors of this
work have yielded themselves to the wishes of
their friends, finding something sacred and not
to be withstood in the importunity which urged
the production of a Journal in a new spirit.

As they have not proposed themselves to the
work, neither can they lay any the least claim to
an option or determination of the spirit in which
it is conceived, or to what is peculiar in the design. In that respect, they have obeyed, though
with great joy, the strong current of thought and
feeling which, for a few years past, has led many
sincere persons in New England to make new
3 demands on literature, and to reprobate that
rigor of our conventions of religion and education which is turning us to stone, which re-
nounces hope, which looks only backward,
which asks only such a future as the past, which
suspects improvement and holds nothing so
much in horror as new views and the dreams of
youth.

With these terrors the conductors of the
present Journal have nothing to do—not even so
much as a word of reproach to waste. They know
4 that there is a portion of the youth and of the
adult population of this country who have not
shared them; who have in secret or in public
paid their vows to truth and freedom; who love
reality too well to care for names; and who live
by a Faith too earnest and profound to suffer
them to doubt the eternity of its object, or to
shake themselves free from its authority. Under
the fictions and customs which occupied others,

AT A GLANCE

- The editors introduce *The Dial.*
- They reject rigid conventions that hold new ideas suspect.
- They recognize the rise of the Transcendental spirit.

LITERARY OPTIONS

- purpose
- figurative language
- audience

THEMATIC OPTIONS

- the power of original thought
- visions and ideals
- self-reliance

1 AUDIENCE

The editors address their essay to their "countrymen," particularly to those imbued with the Transcendental spirit.

2 BACKGROUND

The Transcendental Club—Emerson, Fuller, Thoreau, Bronson Alcott, Theodore Parker, and Orestes Brownson—met informally to discuss ideas.

3 TRANSCENDENTAL IDEA

The rejection of rigid conservatism and the belief in the individual's ability to look at ideas in a fresh way were two of the strongest Transcendental ideals.

4 AUDIENCE

The editors appeal to the magazine's potential readership as people who believe in truth, freedom, and justice.

GUIDED READING

LITERAL QUESTION

1a. Who is the intended readership of *The Dial?* (people who have "paid their vows to truth and freedom")

INFERENTIAL QUESTION

1b. What do you think Fuller and Emerson mean when they say "that rigor of our conventions . . . is turning us to stone"? (They suggest that people grow complacent about values and beliefs and so become incapable of change.)

AT A GLANCE

- The Transcendental spirit manifests itself differently in each individual.
- The editors cannot fully predict what course their journey will take, but they feel that it will give expression to the Transcendental spirit.

1 MAIN IDEA

The current of self-reliance and optimism running through the country suggests that the time is right for a journal of Transcendental thought.

2 FIGURATIVE LANGUAGE

In comparing the Transcendental movement to Fate, to an oak tree, and to a river, the editors express their belief that Transcendentalism is satisfying on both a mystical and a natural level.

3 FIGURATIVE LANGUAGE

The personification of criticism as having a serene, not wrinkled, brow exemplifies the formal style of the essay—as well as the confidence of the editors.

4 PURPOSE

The "new design" of the journal is its focus on making readers aware of what is transcendent within themselves.

these have explored the Necessary, the Plain, the True, the Human—and so gained a vantage ground which commands the history of the past and the present.

No one can converse much with different classes of society in New England without remarking the progress of a revolution. Those who share in it have no external organization, no badge, no creed, no name. They do not vote, or print, or even meet together. They do not know each other's faces or names. They are united only in a common love of truth and love of its work. They are of all conditions and constitutions. Of these acolytes,[1] if some are happily born and well bred, many are no doubt ill dressed, ill placed, ill made—with as many scars of hereditary vice as other men. Without pomp, without trumpet, in lonely and obscure places, in solitude, in servitude, in compunctions and privations, trudging beside the team in the dusty road, or drudging a hireling in other men's cornfields, schoolmasters who teach a few children rudiments for a pittance, ministers of small parishes of the obscurer sects, lone women in dependent condition, matrons and young maidens, rich and poor, beautiful and hard-favored, without con-
1 cert or proclamation of any kind, they have silently given in their several adherence to a new hope, and in all companies do signify a greater trust in the nature and resources of man than the laws or the popular opinions will well allow.

This spirit of the time is felt by every individual with some difference—to each one casting its light upon the objects nearest to his temper and habits of thought—to one, coming in the shape of special reforms in the state; to another, in modifications of the various callings of men, and the customs of business; to a third, opening a new scope for literature and art; to a fourth, in philosophical insight; to a fifth, in the vast solitudes of prayer. It is in every form a protest against usage, and a search for principles. In all its movements, it is peaceable, and in the very lowest marked with a triumphant success. Of course, it rouses the opposition of all which it judges and condemns, but it is too confident in its tone to comprehend an objection, and so builds no outworks for possible defense against
2 contingent enemies. It has the step of Fate, and goes on existing like an oak or a river, because it must.

In literature, this influence appears not yet in new books so much as in the higher tone of criticism. The antidote to all narrowness is the comparison of the record with nature, which at once shames the record and stimulates to new attempts. Whilst we look at this, we wonder how any book has been thought worthy to be preserved. There is somewhat in all life untranslatable into language. He who keeps his eye on that will write better than others, and think less of his writing, and of all writing. Every thought has a certain imprisoning as well as uplifting quality and, in proportion to its energy on the will, refuses to become an object of intellectual contemplation. Thus what is great usually slips through our fingers, and it seems wonderful how a lifelike word ever comes to be written.

If our Journal share the impulses of the time, it cannot now prescribe its own course. It cannot foretell in orderly propositions what it shall attempt. All criticism should be poetic; unpredictable; superseding, as every new thought does, all
3 foregone thoughts, and making a new light on the whole world. Its brow is not wrinkled with circumspection, but serene, cheerful, adoring. It has all things to say, and no less than all the world for its final audience.

Our plan embraces much more than criticism; were it not so, our criticism would be naught. Everything noble is directed on life, and this is. We do not wish to say pretty or curious things, or to reiterate a few propositions in var-
4 ied forms, but, if we can, to give expression to that spirit which lifts men to a higher platform, restores to them the religious sentiment, brings them worthy aims and pure pleasures, purges the inward eye, makes life less desultory, and, though raising men to the level of nature, takes away its melancholy from the landscape, and reconciles the practical with the speculative powers.

---

1. **acolytes:** attendants; followers; helpers.

GUIDED READING

LITERAL QUESTION

1a. What do the editors say that people will notice on conversing with different classes of New England society? (a revolution)

INFERENTIAL QUESTION

1b. How does this revolution or "spirit of the time" manifest itself? (Each person reacts to the feeling according to his or her own talents and interests.)

But perhaps we are telling our little story too gravely. There are always great arguments at hand for a true action, even for the writing of a few pages. There is nothing but seems near it and prompts it—the sphere in the ecliptic, the sap in the apple tree—every fact, every appearance seem to persuade to it.

Our means correspond with the ends we have indicated. As we wish not to multiply books, but to report life, our resources are therefore not so much the pens of practiced writers, as the discourse of the living, and the portfolios which friendship has opened to us. From the beautiful recesses of private thought, from the experience and hope of spirits which are withdrawing from all old forms and seeking in all that is new somewhat to meet their inappeasable longings, from the secret confession of genius afraid to trust itself to aught but sympathy, from the conversations of fervid and mystical pietists,[2] from tear-stained diaries of sorrow and passion, from the manuscripts of young poets, and from the records of youthful taste commenting on old works of art, we hope to draw thoughts and feelings which, being alive, can impart life.

And so with diligent hands and good intent we set down our Dial on the earth. We wish it may resemble that instrument in its celebrated happiness, that of measuring no hours but those of sunshine. Let it be one cheerful rational voice amidst the din of mourners and polemics. Or to abide by our chosen image, let it be such a Dial, not as the dead face of a clock, hardly even such as the Gnomon[3] in a garden, but rather such a
1 Dial as is the Garden itself, in whose leaves and flowers and fruits the suddenly awakened sleeper is instantly apprised not what part of dead time, but what state of life and growth is now arrived and arriving.

2. **pietists** [pī'ə tists]: pious people.

3. **Gnomon** [nō'mon]: pin on sundial that casts a shadow indicating time of day.

STUDY QUESTIONS

Recalling

1. In what different ways do Fuller and Emerson refer to *The Dial* in the first paragraph?
2. According to paragraphs 1 and 2, did the idea for *The Dial* originate with the authors of the announcement? Find evidence in the two paragraphs to support your opinion.
3. What are the "terrors" the authors refer to at the beginning of paragraph 3? Who, besides the authors, have nothing to do with these terrors?
4. What are the characteristics of the "revolution" mentioned in paragraph 4? Who are the participants in this revolution? What unites them?
5. According to the second-to-last paragraph, who will write for *The Dial*? In general, what will they write about?

Interpreting

6. In your own words, explain what you think the authors mean by "This spirit of the time" at the beginning of paragraph 5.
7. Would you say that the ideas expressed in this essay are democratic? Support your opinion with references to the essay.
8. Summarize the authors' explanation of the choice of *The Dial* as a name for the new magazine.

Extending

9. Suppose a rock musician or group were to write an essay about contemporary popular music. How would the ideas in such an essay compare with the ideas expressed in Fuller and Emerson's essay on *The Dial*?

AT A GLANCE

- *The Dial* will include criticism; it also will report life, using private writings inspired by deep feeling.
- The publishers hope that the publication will provoke lively thought.

1 STYLE: SIMILE

To suggest the life with which they hope to infuse their publication, the editors compare *The Dial* to a garden across which the sun moves, continually changing the vista.

REFLECTING ON THE SELECTION

In what ways were the editors of *The Dial* taking an unusual and risky step? (by not having a set editorial policy and by promising to use private writings by new and inexperienced writers)

STUDY QUESTIONS

1. "a new design"; "our Journal"; "the present Number"; "the work"
2. no; *paragraph 1:* ". . . how often in many private circles . . ."; "have yielded themselves to the wishes of their friends . . ."; *paragraph 2:* first sentence and ". . . they have obeyed . . ."
3. the rigorous conventions of religion and education referred to at the end of paragraph 2; a portion of the youth and adult population
4. *characteristics*—no organization, badge, name, creed, meetings; participants don't know each other; *participants*—people "of all conditions and constitution"; *unity*—love of truth, adherence to a new hope and trust in humanity
5. mostly unknown writers, many of them young; reports of life
6. *Possible answers:* revolutionary; a call for a change from old ways; individualistic; optimistic
7. yes; people from all walks of life can participate in "revolution"; untried authors will be published
8. named for sun dial which works only when sun is shining
9. *Possible answers:* call for change in ways of thinking, emphasis on individual

AT A GLANCE

- Minutemen once stood at this place and fired the shot that began the Revolution.
- Now, a memorial is dedicated to their bravery.

LITERARY OPTIONS

- imagery
- stanza form

THEMATIC OPTIONS

- remembrance of American heroes
- memory and time

ALLITERATION

The repetition of *s* sounds suggests movement of the river and the slow passage of time (ll. 5–8).

IMAGERY

The visual images of a "soft stream" and "green bank" create a picture of tranquility that contrasts with the battle scene of the first stanza (l. 9).

STANZA FORM

The poem is divided into quatrains, or four-line stanzas, each following the rhyme scheme *abab*. Each stanza signals a new idea: the battle itself, the passage of time, the present ceremony, and the invocation to Time and Nature.

REFLECTING ON THE POEM

How does the poem reflect Emerson's philosophy of optimism and self-reliance? (Students may suggest that Emerson honors the Minutemen because they acted according to their beliefs.)

On July 4, 1837, a monument was unveiled in Concord, at the spot where the American Minutemen had first done battle with British troops in 1775. At the request of the Monument Committee, Emerson wrote the words to this hymn, which was sung at the memorial ceremony.

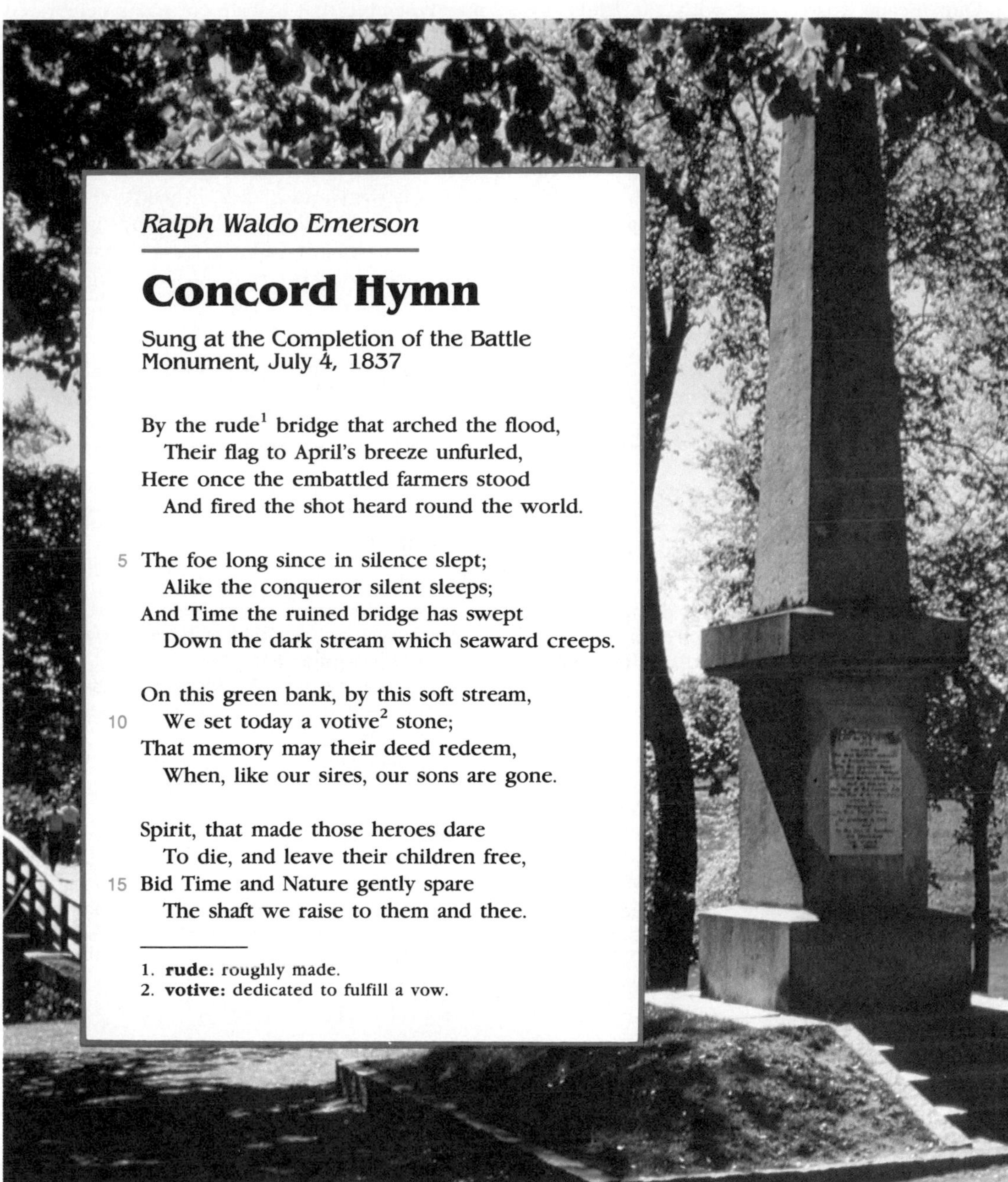

Ralph Waldo Emerson

Concord Hymn

Sung at the Completion of the Battle Monument, July 4, 1837

By the rude[1] bridge that arched the flood,
  Their flag to April's breeze unfurled,
Here once the embattled farmers stood
  And fired the shot heard round the world.

The foe long since in silence slept;
  Alike the conqueror silent sleeps;
And Time the ruined bridge has swept
  Down the dark stream which seaward creeps.

On this green bank, by this soft stream,
  We set today a votive[2] stone;
That memory may their deed redeem,
  When, like our sires, our sons are gone.

Spirit, that made those heroes dare
  To die, and leave their children free,
Bid Time and Nature gently spare
  The shaft we raise to them and thee.

1. **rude:** roughly made.
2. **votive:** dedicated to fulfill a vow.

Written while the idea for the essay *Nature* (page 161) was developing in Emerson's mind, this poem expresses the same intimacy between human nature and the surrounding world. Here the poet stops to address the rhodora, a shrub that often flowers in spring before its leaves appear.

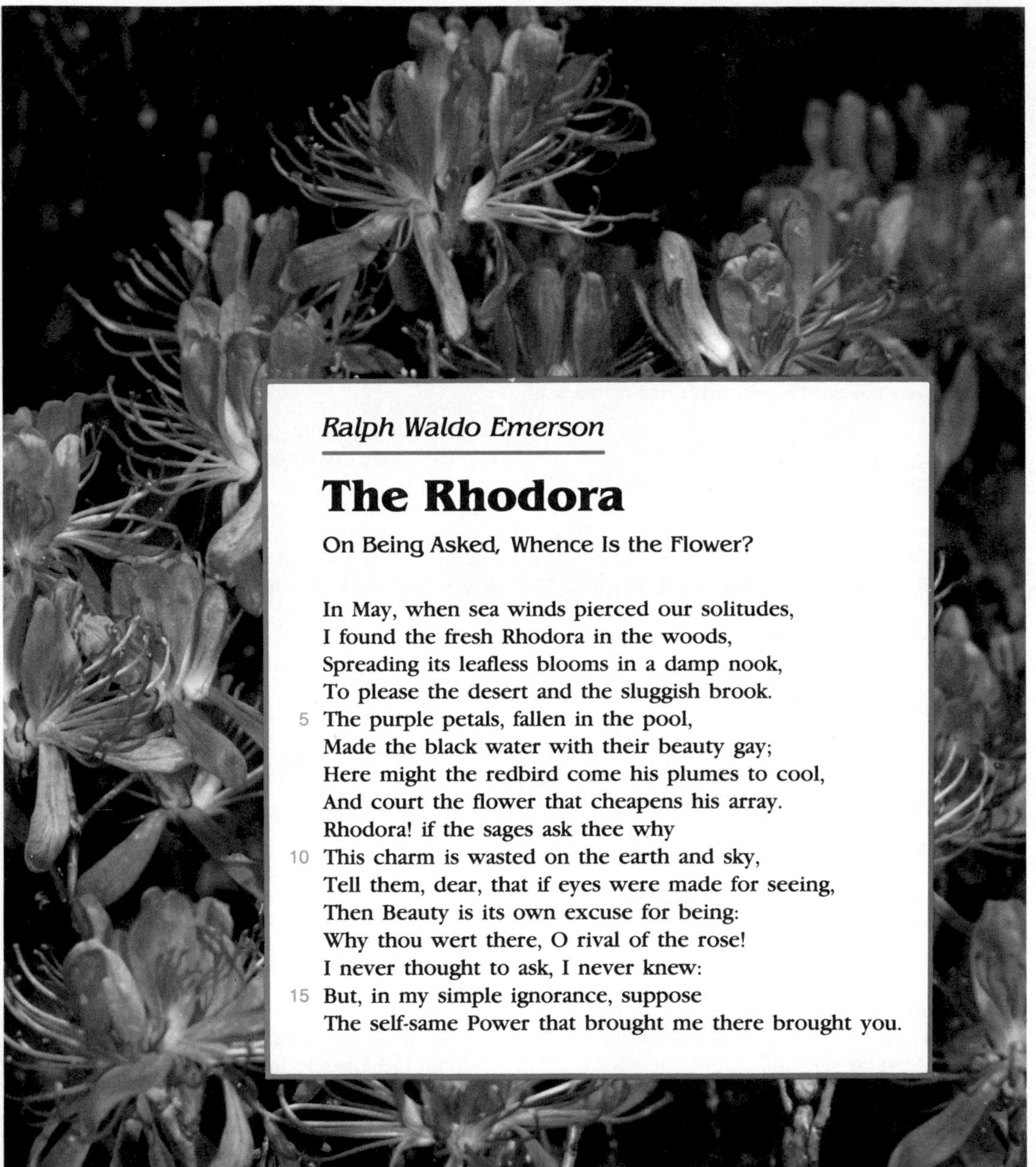

Ralph Waldo Emerson

The Rhodora

On Being Asked, Whence Is the Flower?

In May, when sea winds pierced our solitudes,
I found the fresh Rhodora in the woods,
Spreading its leafless blooms in a damp nook,
To please the desert and the sluggish brook.
The purple petals, fallen in the pool,
Made the black water with their beauty gay;
Here might the redbird come his plumes to cool,
And court the flower that cheapens his array.
Rhodora! if the sages ask thee why
This charm is wasted on the earth and sky,
Tell them, dear, that if eyes were made for seeing,
Then Beauty is its own excuse for being:
Why thou wert there, O rival of the rose!
I never thought to ask, I never knew:
But, in my simple ignorance, suppose
The self-same Power that brought me there brought you.

AT A GLANCE

- The speaker finds a rhodora in a damp part of the woods.
- He muses on why such beauty occurs in such a remote place.
- He concludes that this occasion exemplifies the harmony of life.

LITERARY OPTIONS

- imagery
- figures of speech

THEMATIC OPTIONS

- the responsive imagination
- the power of nature

BACKGROUND

The rhodora is a wild relative of the rhododendron. It blooms in the Northeast during the early spring. The poem reflects Emerson's joy at seeing this uncommon flower (l. 2).

IMAGERY

Emerson contrasts purple petals with black water for a strong visual image that illustrates the transforming power of beauty (ll. 5–6).

APOSTROPHE

Addressing the flower directly and ascribing to it the human power of response suggest the harmony between humanity and nature that is fundamental to Transcendental thought (l. 9).

REFLECTING ON THE POEM

Do you agree with Emerson's answer to the question of why such beauty is "wasted" on such a remote place? Why or why not? (Students may suggest that part of the flower's beauty lies in its rarity.)

STUDY QUESTIONS

Concord Hymn

1. "the shot heard round the world"; swept downstream "by Time"
2. memory
3. that the battle monument be spared by "Time and Nature"
4. first shot of Revolution, which inspired people everywhere
5. bravery, self-sacrifice, freedom

The Rhodora

1. "Whence is the flower?"
2. "Why is this charm wasted on the earth and sky?"; "If eyes were made for seeing, then Beauty is its own excuse for being."
3. never asked for explanation; assumed that the Rhodora was created by the same God that created him
4. nature
5. *Sages:* question flower's reason for existing; *poet:* accepts flower, revels in its beauty; suggests that a childlike, accepting attitude is needed to understand nature
6. intuitive, spiritual wisdom
7. humans and the rhodora both are God's creations, part of same scheme; harmony among all living things
8. Answers will vary. Emerson idealizes natural beauty.

VIEWPOINT

Answers will vary. Idealism may seem practical because it provides a basis for action, satisfaction of spirit; keeps "practical" activities from becoming empty and meaningless. Emerson's form of idealism may strike some as impractical: misguided, dated.

STUDY QUESTIONS

Concord Hymn

Recalling

1. According to stanzas 1 and 2, what was fired at Concord Bridge, and what has since happened to the bridge?
2. According to stanza 3, what will redeem the deaths of the heroes?
3. What is the poet's request in the last stanza?

Interpreting

4. In what sense was the shot fired at Concord Bridge "heard round the world"?
5. What ideals is the poet celebrating in lines 13–14?

The Rhodora

Recalling

1. What question prompts the poet to write?
2. What question does Emerson say the sages might ask? What answer does he say should be given to the sages?
3. According to the last four lines, what had always been the poet's own response to the rhodora?

Interpreting

4. In a larger sense, what does the rhodora represent?
5. How does the poet contrast himself with the sages? What does this contrast suggest about the kind of attitude needed to understand nature?
6. What do you think the poet really means by his "simple ignorance"?
7. Explain the meaning of line 16. What harmony does the line imply?

Extending

8. Do you agree that "Beauty is its own excuse for being"? Tell why or why not.

VIEWPOINT

Van Wyck Brooks, a well-known literary critic, summarizes the effect of Emerson's ideas:

> He addressed himself . . . especially to students and beginners in life. . . . [He] stirred them to take life strivingly in full belief that what man had done man could do, that the world was all opportunities. . . . All art was yet to be created, all literature yet to be written. All nature was new and undescribed.
>
> —*The Flowering of New England*

■ Do you think Emerson's ideas are practical as well as noble? Are they impossible ideals, or could they work in today's world?

LITERARY FOCUS

Stanza Forms

A **stanza** is a grouping together of lines of poetry into a fixed number of lines. Commonly used stanzas include:

the couplet	(2 lines)
the tercet	(3 lines)
the quatrain	(4 lines)
the cinquain	(5 lines)
the sestet	(6 lines)
the octave	(8 lines)

Groups of lines not in fixed numbers, such as those in Bryant's "Thanatopsis" (page 120), are called **verse paragraphs.**

Stanzas organize a poem into thoughts or sections, much as paragraphs help to organize prose. In using stanzas, a poet usually establishes a meter (see page 122) and a **rhyme scheme,** or pattern of end rhymes. The rhyme scheme of a poem is indicated by assigning a different letter of the alphabet to each new rhyming sound. For example, the rhyme scheme of the first stanza of "Concord Hymn" is *abab.*

Throughout the history of poetry, some special combinations of meters and rhyme schemes have proved popular with poets and readers, including:

the **heroic couplet**—two rhymed lines of iambic pentameter

the **triplet**—three rhymed lines of iambic pentameter

the **heroic stanza**—four lines of iambic pentameter with alternate lines rhyming *(abab)*

the **ballad stanza**—four lines in which tetrameter and trimeter lines alternate and only the second and fourth lines rhyme *(abcb).*

Emerson's "Concord Hymn" was originally written to be set to music, and like most songs, it employs a strict stanza pattern. Emerson uses a stanza appropriate to his subject: the **hymnal stanza**—four lines of iambic tetrameter rhyming either *abcb* or *abab.* The hymnal stanza is one of the most common poetic stanzas, largely because of its regularity; in fact, it is sometimes called **common measure.**

Emerson is skillful, however, in avoiding too much regularity. Notice, for example, how he varies the meter in line 8 and uses some rhymes that are not exact, such as *flood* and *stood.* These variations help to avoid monotony.

Thinking About Stanza Forms

1. What stanza form does Edgar Allan Poe use in the poem "To Helen" (page 132)?
2. Although Emerson's "Rhodora" is written as one stanza, indicate how you would divide the poem into separate stanzas, and tell why you would divide it in that way.

VOCABULARY

Abstract Words

Emerson was both a poet and a philosopher, expressing his ideas and feelings in a language both abstract and concrete. He often uses examples and images taken from the real world and from nature to support his concepts. His writing, though it deals with difficult ideas, thus has an immediacy that philosophical writing often does not have.

■ Each of the following abstract words appears in Emerson's *Nature.* Look up each word in a dictionary, and then define it in your own words. Give a concrete example to make the definition more complete.

1. sublime
2. exhilaration
3. decorum
4. egotism
5. harmony
6. infinite

COMPOSITION

Writing About a Sentence

■ Emerson's individual sentences often capture his thought and convey it with intensity and clarity. Choose one of Emerson's sentences, and write a short essay showing how that one sentence carries a large measure of his meaning. First define the important words in the sentence. Then summarize the main idea of Emerson's essay, and tell how the sentence expresses that idea. *For help with this assignment, refer to Lesson 5 in the Writing About Literature Handbook at the back of this book.*

Writing a Persuasive Essay

■ The Transcendentalists were sure that society could and should be improved. Write a persuasive essay on an improvement you would make in society. First clearly propose your improvement, and tell why it is important. Then detail the specific practical measures you would take to put it into effect. Conclude with an appeal to your audience to support your proposal.

LITERARY FOCUS

1. the cinquain
2. may be divided into two octaves or four quatrains; dictated by rhyme scheme, units of thought

VOCABULARY

1. exalted, inspiring
2. elation
3. conformity to social conventions
4. exaggerated self-importance
5. agreement, accord
6. having no boundaries or limits

COMPOSITION: GUIDELINES FOR EVALUATION

WRITING ABOUT A SENTENCE

Objective

To show how one sentence captures the main idea

Guidelines for Evaluation

- suggested length: one to two paragraphs
- composition should choose a sentence that captures the main idea of the essay
- should identify and define important words
- should state the main idea of the essay
- should relate the sentence to the main idea

WRITING A PERSUASIVE ESSAY

Objective

To write an essay suggesting social improvement

Guidelines for Evaluation

- suggested length: four to six paragraphs
- composition should identify the improvement
- should explain importance of improvement
- should detail practical measures to be taken
- should conclude with an emotional appeal that will rouse the audience to action

Henry David Thoreau *1817–1862*

Thoreau lived a deliberately unconventional life. "His virtues," his friend Emerson said, "sometimes ran into extremes." Thoreau marched to his own tune, or as he put it, to the beat of "a different drummer." He knew that "most men think differently from myself," but he never regretted that he did not think like his neighbors.

Of all the writers associated with Concord, Massachusetts, Thoreau was the only one born there. He attended Harvard but refused all the careers his education prepared him for, such as minister, lawyer, or merchant. To many people he appeared "irresponsible" all his life. He hated joining any organization or movement or cooperating with institutions. After graduation he came back to Concord, where he supported himself by odd jobs that left him the freedom he desired.

He tried teaching school but did not like it. His father owned a small pencil factory, and for a while Thoreau worked there; but then, so he said, one day he found that he had made "the perfect pencil." After that he wondered why he should do the same thing over and over.

For two years Thoreau lived in Emerson's house, paying for his room and board by taking care of the house while Emerson was away on lecture tours. Sometimes he worked as a land surveyor, but he did not want to own land himself: It would have tied him down.

Thoreau's actions were the actions of an individual: To whatever extent he wanted to reform society, he would do so by changing the individual lives of men and women. One year he refused to pay a small tax, making a symbolic gesture against the policies of the federal government, especially the Mexican-American War and slavery. He spent a night in jail before his aunt paid the tax for him and had him released. From that experience he wrote the great essay *Civil Disobedience,* which years later affected the course of history through its strong influence on Gandhi in India and Martin Luther King, Jr., in the United States.

Thoreau died young, and most people thought him an interesting failure. Emerson said that he lacked ambition. He published only two books during his lifetime (together with a few poems and essays), *A Week on the Concord and Merrimack Rivers* (1849) and *Walden* (1854). He had to pay for the publication of both books himself, and neither sold many copies during his lifetime. His reputation was a local one. The townsfolk who knew him as a talented but difficult friend would have been astonished to know that in the twentieth century Thoreau would be more widely read than the great Emerson himself.

Thoreau's most memorable gesture was his move to Walden Pond. He lived for two years and two months in a cabin he built with his own hands on a piece of land owned by Emerson. (The cabin, he figured, cost him exactly 28 dollars and 12 1/2 cents.) That experience gave him the material for one of the greatest of American classics, *Walden*. Much of *Walden* is Thoreau's observation of nature, Emersonian in spirit but more sharply drawn than Emerson's observations. "It was a pleasure and a privilege to walk with him," wrote Emerson of the man he always thought of as a somewhat thorny disciple. *Walden,* in fact, is not so much about living in the woods as it is about living itself.

■ What does Thoreau say we must do to live as individuals in the midst of society? Can we do that today?

Walden Pond, Concord, Massachusetts.

AT A GLANCE

- Thoreau wrote most of *Walden* in his two years at Walden Pond.
- He claims most men lead lives of quiet desperation that they often label "resignation."

LITERARY OPTIONS

- persuasion
- aphorism
- figurative language

THEMATIC OPTIONS

- simplicity and self-reliance
- individuality and conformity
- visions and ideals

Model for Active Reading

In this selection, and in one selection in each unit, you will find notes in the right-hand margin that highlight parts of the selection. These notes point out important ideas of the period—in this case, the Transcendentalist movement—and draw your attention to literary elements and techniques covered in the Literary Focuses. Page numbers in the notes will refer you to more extensive discussions of these important ideas and elements.

Henry David Thoreau

from Walden

from Economy

When I wrote the following pages, or rather the bulk of them, I lived alone, in the woods, a mile from any neighbor, in a house which I had built myself, on the shore of Walden Pond, in Concord, Massachusetts, and earned my living by the labor of my hands only. I lived there two years and two months. At present I am a sojourner[1] in civilized life again.

I should not obtrude my affairs so much on the notice of my readers if very particular inquiries had not been made by my townsmen concerning my mode of life, which some would call impertinent,[2] though they do not appear to me at all impertinent, but, considering the circumstances, very natural and pertinent. Some have asked what I got to eat; if I did not feel lonesome; if I was not afraid; and the like. Others have been curious to learn what portion of my income I devoted to charitable purposes; and some, who have large families, how many poor children I maintained. I will therefore ask those of my readers who feel no particular interest in me to pardon me if I undertake to answer some of these questions in this book. In most books, the *I,* or first person, is omitted; in this it will be retained; that, in respect to egotism, is the main difference. We commonly do not remember that it is, after all, always the first person that is speaking. I should not talk so much about myself if there were anybody else whom I knew as well. . . .

Persuasion (p. 22): Thoreau calls upon his personal experience to give greater support to his observations.

The mass of men lead lives of quiet desperation. What is called resignation is confirmed desperation. From the desperate city you go into the desperate country, and have to console yourself with the bravery of minks and muskrats. A stereotyped but unconscious

1. **sojourner:** visitor.
2. **impertinent:** irrelevant; inappropriate.

GUIDED READING

LITERAL QUESTION

1a. How does Thoreau define resignation? (confirmed desperation)

INFERENTIAL QUESTION

1b. What do you think he means by this definition? (Having no hope of living joyfully, they have surrendered to despair.)

despair is concealed even under what are called the games and amusements of mankind. There is no play in them, for this comes after work. But it is a characteristic of wisdom not to do desperate things.

When we consider what, to use the words of the catechism,[3] is the chief end of man,[4] and what are the true necessaries and means of life, it appears as if men had deliberately chosen the common mode of living because they preferred it to any other. Yet they honestly think there is no choice left. But alert and healthy natures remember that the sun rose clear. It is never too late to give up our prejudices. No way of thinking or doing, however ancient, can be trusted without proof. What everybody echoes or in silence passes by as true today may turn out to be falsehood tomorrow, mere smoke of opinion, which some had trusted for a cloud that would sprinkle fertilizing rain on their fields. What old people say you cannot do, you try and find that you can. Old deeds for old people, and new deeds for new. . . .

Transcendentalist idea: Freedom from dull habit can lead to the discovery of spiritual truths (p. 154).

One young man of my acquaintance, who has inherited some acres, told me that he thought he should live as I did, *if he had the means.* I would not have anyone adopt *my* mode of living on any account; for, beside that before he has fairly learned it I may have found out another for myself, I desire that there may be as many different persons in the world as possible; but I would have each one be very careful to find out and pursue *his own* way, and not his father's or his mother's or his neighbor's instead. The youth may build or plant or sail, only let him not be hindered from doing that which he tells me he would like to do. It is by a mathematical point only that we are wise, as the sailor or the fugitive slave keeps the polestar[5] in his eye; but that is sufficient guidance for all our life. We may not arrive at our port within a calculable period, but we would preserve the true course.

from Where I Lived, and What I Lived For

As I have said, I do not propose to write an ode to dejection, but to brag as lustily as chanticleer[6] in the morning, standing on his roost, if only to wake my neighbors up.

When first I took up my abode in the woods, that is, began to spend my nights as well as days there, which, by accident, was on Independence Day, or the Fourth of July, 1845, my house was not finished for winter, but was merely a defense against the rain, without plastering or chimney, the walls being of rough weatherstained

---

3. **catechism** [kat′ə kiz′əm]: handbook that teaches the principles of a religion through questions and answers.
4. **chief . . . man:** "What is the chief end of man?" is a question from the Shorter Catechism in the New England Primer.
5. **polestar:** Polaris, the North Star, used for navigation.
6. **chanticleer** [chan′tə klēr′]: literally, "the loud singer": a rooster.

AT A GLANCE

- Thoreau argues that people should consider alternatives before they choose their course of life.
- He says that change is possible; each must find his or her own way.
- Thoreau moved into an unfinished house on July 4, 1845.

GUIDED READING

LITERAL QUESTION

1a. When does Thoreau move into his house? (July 4, 1845)

INFERENTIAL QUESTION

1b. Why is this date significant? (Thoreau begins his experiment in independent living on Independence Day.)

AT A GLANCE

- From his rough-hewn cabin Thoreau counsels people to absorb nature's inspirational beauty, as he does.
- He exhorts his readers to understand essential truths, approach life with simplicity, and transcend the antlike wretchedness of the "unexamined life."

boards, with wide chinks, which made it cool at night. The upright white hewn studs and freshly planed door and window casings gave it a clean and airy look, especially in the morning, when its timbers were saturated with dew, so that I fancied that by noon some sweet gum would exude from them. To my imagination it retained throughout the day more or less of this auroral[7] character, reminding me of a certain house on a mountain which I had visited the year before. This was an airy and unplastered cabin, fit to entertain a traveling god, and where a goddess might trail her garments. The winds which passed over my dwelling were such as sweep over the ridges of mountains, bearing the broken strains, or celestial parts only, of terrestrial music. The morning wind forever blows, the poem of creation is uninterrupted, but few are the ears that hear it. Olympus[8] is but the outside of the earth everywhere. . . .

Description (p. 92): Thoreau uses language that appeals to the senses to make his description concrete and vivid.

I went to the woods because I wished to live deliberately, to front[9] only the essential facts of life, and see if I could not learn what it had to teach, and not, when I came to die, discover that I had not lived. I did not wish to live what was not life, living is so dear; nor did I wish to practice resignation, unless it was quite necessary. I wanted to live deep and suck out all the marrow of life, to live so sturdily and Spartan-like[10] as to put to rout all that was not life, to cut a broad swath and shave close, to drive life into a corner, and reduce it to its lowest terms, and, if it proved to be mean, why then to get the whole and genuine meanness of it, and publish its meanness to the world; or if it were sublime, to know it by experience, and be able to give a true account of it in my next excursion. For most men, it appears to me, are in a strange uncertainty about it, whether it is of the devil or of God, and have *somewhat hastily* concluded that it is the chief end of man here to "glorify God and enjoy him forever."[11]

Transcendentalist idea: Living in harmony with nature is a source of inspiration (p. 155).

Still we live meanly, like ants; though the fable tells us that we were long ago changed into men;[12] like pygmies we fight with cranes;[13] it is error upon error, and clout upon clout, and our best virtue has for its occasion a superfluous and evitable[14] wretchedness. Our life is frittered away by detail. An honest man has hardly need to count more than his ten fingers, or in extreme

Simile (p. 39): Thoreau compares human life to the life of ants to underscore what he means by "meanly."

7. **auroral** [ə rôr′əl]: resembling the dawn.
8. **Olympus:** in Greek mythology, the mountain home of the gods.
9. **front:** face.
10. **Spartan-like:** simple, hardy, and disciplined, like the life of the Spartans of ancient Greece.
11. **"glorify . . . forever":** answer to the question "What is the chief end of man?" in the New England Primer.
12. **fable . . . men:** in a Greek fable Zeus transforms ants into men.
13. **pygmies . . . cranes:** in the *Iliad* the Trojans are compared to cranes battling pygmies.
14. **evitable:** avoidable.

GUIDED READING

LITERAL QUESTIONS

1a. How does Thoreau define Olympus? ("the outside of the earth anywhere")

2a. What is a Spartanlike existence? (one that is simple, hardy, and disciplined)

INFERENTIAL QUESTIONS

1b. What does he mean? (that nature is heavenly to him)

2b. Why was such an austere life desirable to Thoreau? (because he feels that luxuries, details, and complexities would have prevented him from seeing life as it really is)

cases he may add his ten toes, and lump the rest. Simplicity, simplicity, simplicity! I say, let your affairs be as two or three, and not a hundred or a thousand; instead of a million count half a dozen, and keep your accounts on your thumbnail. In the midst of this chopping sea of civilized life, such are the clouds and storms and quicksands and thousand-and-one items to be allowed for, that a man has to live, if he would not founder and go to the bottom and not make his port at all, by dead reckoning,[15] and he must be a great calculator indeed who succeeds. Simplify, simplify. Instead of three meals a day, if it be necessary eat but one; instead of a hundred dishes, five; and reduce other things in proportion. . . .

For my part, I could easily do without the post office. I think that there are very few important communications made through it. To speak critically, I never received more than one or two letters in my life—I wrote this some years ago—that were worth the postage. The penny post is, commonly, an institution through which you seriously offer a man that penny for his thoughts which is so often safely offered in jest. And I am sure that I never read any memorable news in a newspaper. If we read of one man robbed, or murdered, or killed by accident, or one house burned, or one vessel wrecked, or one steamboat blown up, or one cow run over on the Western Railroad, or one mad dog killed, or one lot of grasshoppers in the winter—we never need read of another. One is enough. If you are acquainted with the principle, what do you care for a myriad instances and applications? To a philosopher all *news,* as it is called, is gossip, and they who edit and read it are old women over their tea. Yet not a few are greedy after this gossip. . . .

Time is but the stream I go a-fishing in. I drink at it; but while I drink, I see the sandy bottom and detect how shallow it is. Its thin current slides away, but eternity remains. I would drink deeper; fish in the sky, whose bottom is pebbly with stars. I cannot count one. I know not the first letter of the alphabet. I have always been regretting that I was not as wise as the day I was born. The intellect is a cleaver; it discerns and rifts its way into the secret of things. I do not wish to be any more busy with my hands than is necessary. My head is hands and feet. I feel all my best faculties concentrated in it. My instinct tells me that my head is an organ for burrowing, as some creatures use their snout and forepaws, and with it I would mine and burrow my way through these hills. I think that the richest vein is somewhere hereabouts; so by the divining rod[16] and thin rising vapors I judge; and here I will begin to mine.

15. **dead reckoning:** navigating without sighting the stars.
16. **divining rod:** forked stick that supposedly reveals the presence of underground minerals or water.

Transcendentalist idea: Only by simplifying our material lives and rising above the material world can we discover spiritual reality (p. 154).

Methods of persuasion (p. 84): Thoreau uses exaggeration and repetition to persuade the reader that his opinion of the post office and newspapers is justified.

Figurative language (p. 164): Thoreau compares time to a stream, using a figure of speech to make his abstract idea concrete.

AT A GLANCE

- Thoreau argues that letters are worthless, news is gossip; time is a distraction from eternity.
- He will simplify, discern the secrets of things, and recover his lost wisdom.

GUIDED READING

LITERAL QUESTION

1a. How does Thoreau define time? (as the stream he fishes in)

INFERENTIAL QUESTION

1b. What does this analogy imply? (that the flow of experience is insignificant; what is important is the occasional insight that lies hidden beneath the surface of human life)

AT A GLANCE

- Thoreau leaves the woods and his beaten path, having learned that dreams can be realized.
- Thoreau recommends that, rather than pursue success, we should go our own ways at our own pace and love our lives, however humble.

from Conclusion

I left the woods for as good a reason as I went there. Perhaps it seemed to me that I had several more lives to live, and could not spare any more time for that one. It is remarkable how easily and insensibly we fall into a particular route, and make a beaten track for ourselves. I had not lived there a week before my feet wore a path from my door to the pondside; and though it is five or six years since I trod it, it is still quite distinct. It is true, I fear that others may have fallen into it, and so helped to keep it open. The surface of the earth is soft and impressible by the feet of men; and so with the paths which the mind travels. How worn and dusty, then, must be the highways of the world, how deep the ruts of tradition and conformity! I did not wish to take a cabin passage, but rather to go before the mast and on the deck of the world, for there I could best see the moonlight amid the mountains. I do not wish to go below now.

I learned this, at least, by my experiment: that if one advances confidently in the direction of his dreams, and endeavors to live the life which he has imagined, he will meet with a success unexpected in common hours. He will put some things behind, will pass an invisible boundary; new, universal, and more liberal laws will begin to establish themselves around and within him; or the old laws be expanded, and interpreted in his favor in a more liberal sense, and he will live with the license of a higher order of beings. In proportion as he simplifies his life, the laws of the universe will appear less complex, and solitude will not be solitude, nor poverty poverty, nor weakness weakness. If you have built castles in the air, your work need not be lost; that is where they should be. Now put the foundations under them. . . .

Transcendentalist idea: Spiritual reality is available only to people living as true individuals (p. 155).

Why should we be in such desperate haste to succeed, and in such desperate enterprises? If a man does not keep pace with his companions, perhaps it is because he hears a different drummer. Let him step to the music which he hears, however measured or far away. It is not important that he should mature as soon as an apple tree or an oak. Shall he turn his spring into summer? If the condition of things which we were made for is not yet, what were any reality which we can substitute? We will not be shipwrecked on a vain reality. Shall we with pains erect a heaven of blue glass over ourselves, though when it is done we shall be sure to gaze still at the true ethereal heaven far above, as if the former were not? . . .

However mean your life is, meet it and live it; do not shun it and call it hard names. It is not so bad as you are. It looks poorest when you are richest. The faultfinder will find faults even in paradise. Love your life, poor as it is. You may perhaps have some pleasant, thrilling, glorious hours, even in a poorhouse. The setting sun is reflected from the windows of the almshouse as brightly as

GUIDED READING

LITERAL QUESTION

1a. What does Thoreau accomplish in less than a week? (He wears a path from the cabin to the pond.)

INFERENTIAL QUESTION

1b. What can be inferred from this experience? (how easily fresh experience becomes habit)

from the rich man's abode; the snow melts before its door as early in the spring. I do not see but a quiet mind may live as contentedly there, and have as cheering thoughts, as in a palace. The town's poor seem to me often to live the most independent lives of any. Maybe they are simply great enough to receive without misgiving. Most think that they are above being supported by the town; but it oftener happens that they are not above supporting themselves by dishonest means, which should be more disreputable. Cultivate poverty like a garden herb, like sage. Do not trouble yourself much to get new things, whether clothes or friends. Turn the old; return to them. Things do not change; we change. Sell your clothes and keep your thoughts. God will see that you do not want society. If I were confined to a corner of a garret all my days, like a spider, the world would be just as large to me while I had my thoughts about me. . . .

Aphorism (p. 57): Throughout *Walden,* Thoreau offers short, memorable recommendations to the reader.

The life in us is like the water in the river. It may rise this year higher than man has ever known it, and flood the parched uplands; even this may be the eventful year, which will drown out all our muskrats. It was not always dry land where we dwell. I see far inland the banks which the stream anciently washed, before science began to record its freshets. Everyone has heard the story, which has gone the rounds of New England, of a strong and beautiful bug which came out of the dry leaf of an old table of apple tree wood which had stood in a farmer's kitchen for sixty years, first in Connecticut, and afterward in Massachusetts—from an egg deposited in the living tree many years earlier still, as appeared by counting the annual layers beyond it— which was heard gnawing out for several weeks, hatched perchance by the heat of an urn. Who does not feel his faith in a resurrection and immortality strengthened by hearing of this? Who knows what beautiful and winged life, whose egg has been buried for ages under many concentric layers of woodenness in the dead dry life of society, deposited at first in the alburnum[17] of the green and living tree, which has been gradually converted into the semblance of its well-seasoned tomb—heard perchance gnawing out now for years by the astonished family of man, as they sat round the festive board—may unexpectedly come forth from amidst society's most trivial and handseled furniture, to enjoy its perfect summer life at last!

Transcendentalist idea: Society can be and should be improved (p. 155).

I do not say that John or Jonathan[18] will realize all this; but such is the character of that morrow which mere lapse of time can never make to dawn. The light which puts out our eyes is darkness to us. Only that day dawns to which we are awake. There is more day to dawn. The sun is but a morning star.

---

17. **alburnum** [al bur′nəm]: youngest part of the wood in a tree, through which the sap moves.
18. **John or Jonathan:** the average person. Thoreau is using the popular names for the average Englishman (John Bull) and the average American (Brother Jonathan).

AT A GLANCE

- Thoreau praises poverty's independence and recommends old clothes, old friends, and one's thoughts as the best companions.
- Like the egg that after sixty dormant years hatches into a beautiful creature, our spirits may bloom unexpectedly.

REFLECTING ON THE SELECTION

What feelings do you think Thoreau was trying to arouse in his readers? (a desire for change, for simplicity; perhaps disgust with their own narrow lives; hope for the future; exhilaration)

GUIDED READING

LITERAL QUESTIONS

1a. What should people cultivate? (poverty)

2a. What does Thoreau call the sun ("but a morning star")

INFERENTIAL QUESTIONS

1b. What are its rewards? (contentment, cheering thoughts, simplicity, and independence)

2b. What might he mean? (We must begin by seeing life in new, simplified terms—this is dawn. But then we must put our new insight into practice and live out the rest of the day as truly enlightened, truly human beings.)

STUDY QUESTIONS

1. lives of quiet desperation
2. He should live his own life.
3. live deliberately; face only essential facts of life; learn from life; avoid resignation; reduce life to lowest terms
4. detail; simplicity
5. He had more lives to live.
6. Trying to realize dreams yields unexpected success.
7. "Meet it and live it."
8. ■ Beautiful insect hatches from egg in sixty-year-old table.
   ■ faith in resurrection and immortality
9. joyless, empty; accepted without complaint
10. being a nonconformist
11. wonder and hope
12. to live life fully, strip away encumbrances, be true to oneself
13. Possible answers: technology, bureaucracy, mass media

VIEWPOINT

Answers will vary. Some students may criticize Thoreau for retreating from society or for his lack of ambition; others may see that he offered a vision for a better society, inspired others.

COMPARING WRITERS

- Emerson: spiritual values, communicating ideas; observed nature, drawn to it metaphysically; philosophical tone
- Thoreau: a "doer"; a nonconformist; interested only in his own development; lived in nature, drawn to it by what it could teach him; direct, often conversational tone

STUDY QUESTIONS

Recalling

1. In paragraph 3 of "Economy," what does Thoreau say most people lead?
2. According to paragraph 5 of "Economy," what are Thoreau's reasons for not wanting the young man to adopt his way of life?
3. From paragraph 3 of "Where I Lived," list at least five reasons that Thoreau gives for going to live in the woods.
4. According to paragraph 4 of "Where I Lived," by what is life "frittered away"? What does the exclamation in this paragraph call for?
5. In paragraph 1 of "Conclusion," why does Thoreau say he left the woods?
6. According to paragraph 2 of "Conclusion," what does Thoreau say he learned by his "experiment"?
7. In paragraph 4 of "Conclusion," what does Thoreau tell the reader to do, "however mean your life is"?
8. Summarize the story that has "gone the rounds of New England," which Thoreau relates in paragraph 5 of "Conclusion." According to Thoreau, what does hearing this story strengthen?

Interpreting

9. Describe in your own words what you think Thoreau means by "lives of quiet desperation."
10. Explain in your own words what Thoreau means, in paragraph 3 of "Conclusion," by hearing a "different drummer."
11. What emotions might Thoreau want to arouse in his reader with the story of the "beautiful bug"?
12. Summarize the central message Thoreau conveys in *Walden.*

Extending

13. What are some of the things that surround us in America today about which Thoreau might cry, "Simplify, simplify"?

VIEWPOINT

One of the finest essays on Thoreau is the personal one by Emerson. Defining Thoreau's greatness, Emerson also has one regret:

> Had his genius been only contemplative, he had been fitted to his life, but with his energy and practical ability he seemed born for great enterprise and for command; and I so much regret the loss of his rare powers of action, that I cannot help counting it a fault in him that he had no ambition. Wanting this, instead of engineering for all America, he was the captain of a huckleberry-party.
>
> —"Thoreau"

■ Do you agree that a person with such practical ability as Thoreau ought to take on "great enterprise"? Was the Walden "huckleberry-party" a sufficiently "great enterprise"? In what way is *Walden* itself an example of "engineering for all America"?

COMPOSITION

Writing About Nonfiction

■ Write a composition discussing the purpose of *Walden.* Cite techniques Thoreau uses to accomplish the purpose. Discuss sensory details, facts, statistics, examples, and opinions. *For help with this assignment, refer to Lesson 4 in the Writing About Literature Handbook at the back of this book.*

Writing a Personal Essay

■ Write a short personal essay keeping your style informal and directly addressing the reader. Use a sentence from *Walden* as a starting point ("Things do not change; we change," for example), or start with your own original thought. Then apply that idea to several different situations, and comment upon them. End by drawing one clear conclusion.

COMPARING WRITERS

■ Emerson and Thoreau were personal friends, shared many of the same ideas, and wrote about many of the same subjects. Yet their approaches to their experiences were quite different. Try to define the differences between these two writers. What relationship did each have to nature? What did each believe to be the most important things in life? How would you describe the tone of each?

COMPOSITION: GUIDELINES FOR EVALUATION

WRITING ABOUT NONFICTION

Objective

To analyze author's purpose in a nonfiction work

Guidelines for Evaluation

- suggested length: four to six paragraphs
- should state the author's purpose
- should recognize that Thoreau's purpose is to show readers a certain way of living life
- should cite details, facts, statistics, examples, opinions helping achieve purpose

WRITING A PERSONAL ESSAY

Objective

To write a personal essay

Guidelines for Evaluation

- suggested length: three to five paragraphs
- should open with a generalization
- should apply generalization to situations
- should comment on the situations
- should draw a conclusion on generalization
- should be informal, addressing reader directly

Nathaniel Hawthorne *1804–1864*

The same New England that gave birth to the hopeful visions of the Transcendentalists also brought forth the troubled vision of Nathaniel Hawthorne. Hawthorne, son of a sea captain, was born in Salem, Massachusetts, and raised by his mother. One of Hawthorne's ancestors had been among the judges who condemned the "witches" of Salem in 1692, and Hawthorne felt that the traits of his Puritan ancestors had "intertwined themselves" with his own character. After graduating from Bowdoin College in Maine, he was drawn back to Salem.

Yet Hawthorne was no Puritan. He looked back with distaste upon "the whole dismal severity of the Puritanic code of law." For twelve years he lived in his mother's house in Salem, a semirecluse, studying the American past, teaching himself to write. In 1837 *Twice-Told Tales,* his first collection of stories, appeared, and Hawthorne left his lonely chamber.

He worked at the Boston Custom House and then lived for a while among the Transcendental reformers and visionaries at the utopian community, Brook Farm. Later he turned the Brook Farm experience into a brilliant satiric book, *The Blithedale Romance.* In 1842 he married Sophia Peabody and moved to the Old Manse at Concord, where Emerson had lived. In 1846 he published *Mosses from an Old Manse,* another collection of stories. Unable to support himself and his wife, Hawthorne returned once again to Salem, where he received a political appointment as Surveyor of the Port.

Removed from office by a change of administrations, he began *The Scarlet Letter,* a subtle study of guilt and retribution in Puritan Boston. Published in 1850, *The Scarlet Letter* became a sensation. Hawthorne followed it with *The House of the Seven Gables.* When his college friend Franklin Pierce became President, Hawthorne was appointed American consul at Liverpool, England. After many years in Europe, he returned to America but, with the exception of *The Marble Faun* in 1860, he was unable to complete any major work during his later years.

Hawthorne listened to conversations at Emerson's house and went boating with Thoreau, but his spirit was very different from theirs. As Emerson and Thoreau assert human freedom, Hawthorne reminds us of human limitations. He called his tales "allegories of the heart." An **allegory** is a story with a symbolic meaning used to teach a moral principle. Hawthorne's allegories are stories of how pride and isolation frustrate our capacity for love and sympathy.

■ What does Hawthorne believe about individual guilt and forgiveness?

AT A GLANCE

- On Sunday morning the citizens of Milford gather for church.
- Pastor Hooper appears wearing a black veil over most of his face.
- The congregation reacts with curiosity and bewilderment, as well as alarm.

LITERARY OPTIONS

- symbol
- plot
- style

THEMATIC OPTIONS

- the failure of human understanding
- secrets of the soul
- visions and ideals

1 SETTING

Setting this story in Puritan New England alerts the reader to the possibilities of a tale that deals with strict standards of right and wrong and a strong awareness of personal guilt.

2 POINT OF VIEW

The third-person narrator is a detached observer. That Mr. Hooper is seen from the outside enhances the mystery of his actions.

3 SYMBOL

The parable has meanings on two levels: It is a narrative in which characters, actions, and objects have meanings beyond their literal ones. Here, the veil can be seen both as a simple crape veil and as a symbol of mourning or even of shame.

4 PLOT: CONFLICT

The clergyman's veil immediately creates tension between him and his congregation.

5 PLOT: RISING ACTION

The parishioners sense some meaning in the veil but cannot agree on its interpretation.

Nathaniel Hawthorne

The Minister's Black Veil

A Parable

1 The sexton stood in the porch of Milford meetinghouse, pulling lustily at the bellrope. The old people of the village came stooping along the street. Children, with bright faces, tripped merrily beside their parents, or mimicked a graver gait, in the conscious dignity of their Sunday clothes. Spruce bachelors looked sidelong at the pretty maidens and fancied that the sabbath sunshine made them prettier than on weekdays. When the throng had mostly streamed into the porch, the sexton began to toll the bell, keeping his eye on the Reverend Mr. Hooper's door. The first glimpse of the clergyman's figure was the signal for the bell to cease its summons.

"But what has good Parson Hooper got upon his face?" cried the sexton in astonishment.

All within hearing immediately turned about and beheld the semblance of Mr. Hooper, pacing slowly his meditative way towards the meetinghouse. With one accord they started, expressing more wonder than if some strange minister were coming to dust the cushions of Mr. Hooper's pulpit.

"Are you sure it is our parson?" inquired Goodman[1] Gray of the sexton.

"Of a certainty it is good Mr. Hooper," replied the sexton. "He was to have exchanged pulpits with Parson Shute of Westbury; but Parson Shute sent to excuse himself yesterday, being to preach a funeral sermon."

2 The cause of so much amazement may appear sufficiently slight. Mr. Hooper, a gentlemanly person of about thirty, though still a bachelor, was dressed with due clerical neatness, as if a careful wife had starched his band and brushed the weekly dust from his Sunday's garb. There was but one thing remarkable in his appearance. Swathed about his forehead, and hanging down over his face, so low as to
3 be shaken by his breath, Mr. Hooper had on a black veil. On a nearer view, it seemed to consist of two folds of crape,[2] which entirely concealed his features, except the mouth and chin, but probably did not intercept his sight, farther than to give a darkened aspect to all living and inanimate things. With this gloomy shade before him, good Mr. Hooper walked onward, at
4 a slow and quiet pace, stooping somewhat and looking on the ground, as is customary with abstracted[3] men, yet nodding kindly to those of his parishioners who still waited on the meetinghouse steps. But so wonderstruck were they, that his greeting hardly met with a return.

5 "I can't really feel as if good Mr. Hooper's face was behind that piece of crape," said the sexton.

"I don't like it," muttered an old woman, as she hobbled into the meetinghouse. "He has changed himself into something awful, only by hiding his face."

"Our parson has gone mad!" cried Goodman Gray, following him across the threshhold.

A rumor of some unaccountable phenomenon had preceded Mr. Hooper into the meetinghouse, and set all the congregation astir. Few could refrain from twisting their heads towards the door; many stood upright and turned directly about; while several little boys clambered upon the seats and came down again with a terrible racket. There was a general bustle, a rustling of the women's gowns and shuffling of the men's feet, greatly at variance with that hushed repose which should attend the

1. **Goodman:** a title similar to *Mister.*

2. **crape** [krāp]: black, crinkled cloth often worn as a sign of mourning.

3. **abstracted:** withdrawn and preoccupied.

GUIDED READING

LITERAL QUESTION

1a. What is the reaction of the old woman to Mr. Hooper's veil? ("He has changed himself into something awful. . . .")

INFERENTIAL QUESTION

1b. Why do you think people are so disturbed by the veil? (Some students may feel that the fact that much of the minister's face is hidden is what disturbs people, making them suspect that the face itself has been changed. Other students may feel that the black veil itself adds a frightening note to Hooper's appearance.)

entrance of the minister. But Mr. Hooper appeared not to notice the perturbation of his people. He entered with an almost noiseless step, bent his head mildly to the pews on each side, and bowed as he passed his oldest parishioner, a white-haired great-grandsire, who occupied an armchair in the center of the aisle. It was strange to observe how slowly this venerable man became conscious of something singular in the appearance of his pastor. He seemed not fully to partake of the prevailing wonder till Mr. Hooper had ascended the stairs and showed himself in the pulpit, face to face with his congregation, except for the black
1 veil. That mysterious emblem was never once withdrawn. It shook with his measured breath as he gave out the psalm; it threw its obscurity between him and the holy page as he read the Scriptures; and while he prayed, the veil lay heavily on his uplifted countenance. Did he seek to hide it from the dread Being whom he was addressing?

Such was the effect of this simple piece of crape, that more than one woman of delicate nerves was forced to leave the meetinghouse. Yet perhaps the pale-faced congregation was almost as fearful a sight to the minister as his black veil to them.

2 Mr. Hooper had the reputation of a good preacher, but not an energetic one: he strove to win his people heavenward by mild persuasive influences, rather than to drive them thither by the thunders of the Word. The sermon which he now delivered was marked by the same characteristics of style and manner, as the general series of his pulpit oratory. But there was something, either in the sentiment of the discourse itself or in the imagination of the auditors, which made it greatly the most powerful effort that they had ever heard from their pastor's lips. It was tinged, rather more darkly than usual, with the gentle gloom of Mr. Hoop-
3 er's temperament. The subject had reference to secret sin, and those sad mysteries which we hide from our nearest and dearest, and would fain conceal from our own consciousness, even forgetting that the Omniscient[4] can detect them. A subtle power was breathed into his words. Each member of the congregation, the most innocent girl, and the man of hardened breast, felt as if the preacher had crept upon them, behind his awful veil, and discovered their hoarded iniquity of deed or thought. Many spread their clasped hands on their bos-
4 oms. There was nothing terrible in what Mr. Hooper said—at least, no violence; and yet, with every tremor of his melancholy voice, the hearers quaked. An unsought pathos came hand in hand with awe. So sensible were the audience of some unwonted attribute in their minister that they longed for a breath of wind to blow aside the veil, almost believing that a stranger's visage would be discovered, though the form, gesture, and voice were those of Mr. Hooper.

At the close of the services, the people hurried out with indecorous confusion, eager to communicate their pent-up amazement, and conscious of lighter spirits the moment they lost sight of the black veil. Some gathered in little circles, huddled closely together, with their mouths all whispering in the center; some went homeward alone, wrapped in silent meditation; some talked loudly, and profaned the Sabbath day with ostentatious laughter. A few shook their sagacious heads, intimating that they could penetrate the mystery; while one or two affirmed that there was no mystery at all, but only that Mr. Hooper's eyes were so weakened by the midnight lamp as to require a shade. After a brief interval, forth came good Mr. Hooper also, in the rear of his flock. Turning his veiled face from one group to another, he paid due reverence to the hoary heads, saluted the middle-aged with kind dignity, as their friend and spiritual guide, greeted the young with mingled authority and love, and laid his hands on the little children's heads to bless them. Such was always his custom on the Sabbath day. Strange and bewildered looks repaid him for his courtesy. None, as on former occasions, aspired to the honor of walking by

4. **Omniscient** [om nish′ənt]: God; the all-knowing.

AT A GLANCE

- Mr. Hooper behaves in an ordinary way and delivers an unusually powerful sermon.
- The amazed congregation hurries out afterwards.

1 VOCABULARY: CONNOTATION

The words *mysterious*, *obscurity*, and *heavily* convey the congregation's confusion and lack of understanding.

2 CHARACTERIZATION

Mr. Hooper is consistently presented as good and mild, in contrast to the effect he is producing on his congregation.

3 THEME

In his sermon Mr. Hooper refers to the "secret sins" that people try to hide from each other and from God. The rest of this story will tell how Mr. Hooper continues to "preach" this message through his own lifestyle.

4 STYLE: AMBIGUITY

The narrator tempers the assertion that there was "nothing terrible" in Hooper's delivery; here is a disclaimer that raises doubt.

GUIDED READING

LITERAL QUESTION

1a. What two things may have made the sermon more powerful than usual? (its content and the imagination of the listeners)

INFERENTIAL QUESTION

1b. Which do you consider more important? Why? (Probably the sermon was colored by the imagination of the congregation, since the narrator says Hooper used his customary style. However, the narrator, by saying that there was "at least, no violence" in the sermon hints that the sermon itself may have contained something else that was unsettling.)

AT A GLANCE

- Mr. Hooper returns to the parsonage, with a sad smile.
- Parishioners comment upon the effects of the veil.

1 CHARACTERIZATION

The minister's "sad smile" suggests that the reaction of his congregation is painful but not unexpected.

2 PLOT: CONFLICT

The people's observations reiterate the central problem in the story: the power of the veil (and what it represents) to create feelings of fear and confusion.

their pastor's side. Old Squire Saunders, doubtless by an accidental lapse of memory, neglected to invite Mr. Hooper to his table, where the good clergyman had been wont to bless the food almost every Sunday since his settlement. He returned, therefore, to the parsonage and, at the moment of closing the door, was observed to look back upon the people, all of whom had their eyes fixed upon the minister. 1 A sad smile gleamed faintly from beneath the black veil and flickered about his mouth, glimmering as he disappeared.

"How strange," said a lady, "that a simple black veil such as any woman might wear on her bonnet should become such a terrible thing on Mr. Hooper's face!"

2 "Something must surely be amiss with Mr. Hooper's intellects," observed her husband, the physician of the village. "But the strangest part of the affair is the effect of this vagary, even on a sober-minded man like myself. The black veil, though it covers only our pastor's face, throws its influence over his whole person, and makes him ghostlike from head to foot. Do you not feel it so?"

"Truly do I," replied the lady; "and I would not be alone with him for the world. I wonder he is not afraid to be alone with himself!"

"Men sometimes are so," said her husband.

The afternoon service was attended with similar circumstances. At its conclusion, the bell tolled for the funeral of a young lady. The relatives and friends were assembled in the house, and the more distant acquaintances stood about the door, speaking of the good qualities of the deceased, when their talk was interrupted by the appearance of Mr. Hooper, still covered with his black veil. It was now an appropriate emblem. The clergyman stepped into the room where the corpse was laid, and bent over the coffin to take a last farewell of his deceased parishioner. As he stooped, the veil hung straight down from his forehead, so that, if her eyelids had not been closed for ever, the dead maiden might have seen his face. Could Mr. Hooper be fearful of her

GUIDED READING

LITERAL QUESTION

1a. What expression crosses the minister's face as he closes the door? (a sad smile)

INFERENTIAL QUESTION

1b. What do you think the minister's expression means? (He is saddened by the reaction of the people but is not angry. Perhaps in some way he has achieved the effect he intended.)

glance, that he so hastily caught back the black veil? A person who watched the interview between the dead and living scrupled not to affirm that, at the instant when the clergyman's
1 features were disclosed, the corpse had slightly shuddered, rustling the shroud and muslin cap, though the countenance retained the composure of death. A superstitious old woman was the only witness of this prodigy. From the coffin, Mr. Hooper passed into the chambers of the mourners, and thence to the head of the staircase to make the funeral prayer. It was a tender and heart-dissolving prayer, full of sorrow, yet so imbued with celestial hopes that the music of a heavenly harp, swept by the fingers of the dead, seemed faintly to be heard among the saddest accents of the minister. The people trembled, though they but darkly un-
2 derstood him, when he prayed that they, and himself, and all of mortal race, might be ready, as he trusted this young maiden had been, for the dreadful hour that should snatch the veil from their faces. The bearers went heavily forth, and the mourners followed, saddening all the street, with the dead before them, and Mr. Hooper in his black veil behind.

"Why do you look back?" said one in the procession to his partner.

"I had a fancy," replied she, "that the minister and the maiden's spirit were walking hand in hand."

"And so had I, at the same moment," said the other.

That night, the handsomest couple in Milford village were to be joined in wedlock. Though reckoned a melancholy man, Mr. Hooper had a placid cheerfulness for such occasions, which often excited a sympathetic smile where livelier merriment would have been thrown away. There was no quality of his disposition which made him more beloved than this. The company at the wedding awaited his arrival with impatience, trusting that the strange awe which had gathered over him throughout the day would now be dispelled. But such was not the result. When Mr. Hooper came, the first thing that their eyes rested on
3 was the same horrible black veil, which had added deeper gloom to the funeral, and could portend nothing but evil to the wedding. Such was its immediate effect on the guests that a cloud seemed to have rolled duskily from beneath the black crape, and dimmed the light of the candles. The bridal pair stood up before the minister. But the bride's cold fingers quivered in the tremulous hand of the bridegroom, and her deathlike paleness caused a whisper that the maiden who had been buried a few hours before was come from her grave to be married. If ever another wedding were so dismal, it was that famous one where they tolled the wedding knell.[5] After performing the ceremony, Mr. Hooper raised a glass of wine to his lips, wishing happiness to the new-married couple, in a strain of mild pleasantry that ought to have brightened the features of the guests, like a cheerful gleam from the hearth. At that instant, catching a glimpse of his figure in the looking glass, the black veil involved his own spirit in the horror with which it overwhelmed
4 all others. His frame shuddered—his lips grew white—he spilt the untasted wine upon the carpet—and rushed forth into the darkness. For the Earth, too, had on her Black Veil.

The next day, the whole village of Milford talked of little else than Parson Hooper's black veil. That, and the mystery concealed behind it, supplied a topic of discussion between acquaintances meeting in the street and good women gossiping at their open windows. It was the first item of news that the tavernkeeper told to his guests. The children babbled of it on their way to school. One imitative little imp covered his face with an old black handkerchief, thereby so affrighting his playmates that the panic seized himself, and he well nigh lost his wits by his own waggery.

It was remarkable that, of all the busybodies and impertinent people in the parish, not one ventured to put the plain question to Mr.

5. **If . . . knell:** Hawthorne is referring to his own short story, "The Wedding Knell." A *knell* usually describes the sound of a bell at a funeral.

AT A GLANCE

- The minister officiates at the funeral of a young woman and performs a wedding ceremony, wearing the veil at both occasions.
- Seeing himself in the mirror, he rushes from the wedding festivities.

1 TONE

The narrator captures the mood of whispered gossip that surrounds the minister; however, he maintains an objective tone by asserting that its source was superstitious.

2 SYMBOL

Here, the veil is the mystery that separates human beings from God—a traditional Christian symbol. At the moment of death, the veil is dissolved. The parishioners are aware of this symbolism, but they fail to relate it to the minister's actions.

3 STYLE: IMAGE PATTERN

The images of evil and darkness that some parishioners associate with the veil here create a brooding mood that conflicts with the happy occasion of the wedding.

4 PLOT: RISING ACTION

Mr. Hooper's reaction to his own reflection fuels speculation that he has something to hide.

GUIDED READING

LITERAL QUESTION

1a. What two strange impressions do people at the funeral relate regarding Mr. Hooper? (An old woman says the corpse shuddered when Hooper leaned over it, and two mourners imagine they see the corpse's spirit walking with Hooper.)

INFERENTIAL QUESTION

1b. What do these impressions suggest about the effect of the veil? (that the veil transcends the boundary between life and death)

AT A GLANCE

- A deputation of parishioners visit the minister, but they cannot bring themselves to discuss the veil.
- His fiancée confronts him.
- He tells her that the veil is a symbol he has vowed to wear forever.

1 SYMBOL

The failure of the delegation to confront the problem of the veil and find out its meaning can be interpreted as the failure of understanding in society at large.

2 CHARACTERIZATION

Elizabeth's calm directness contrasts with the confusion of the other parishioners.

3 STYLE: IMAGE PATTERN

Previously, the minister's smile was tinged with sadness as he acknowledged the consternation of his people. Here, it is tinged with expectation as he hopes for Elizabeth's understanding.

4 PLOT: RISING ACTION

Mr. Hooper's response outlines his action and his vow but leaves the meaning of the veil unexplained.

Hooper, wherefore he did this thing. Hitherto, whenever there appeared the slightest call for such interference, he had never lacked advisers, nor shown himself averse to be guided by their judgment. If he erred at all, it was by so painful a degree of self-distrust that even the mildest censure would lead him to consider an indifferent action as a crime. Yet, though so well acquainted with this amiable weakness, no individual among his parishioners chose to make the black veil a subject of friendly remonstrance. There was a feeling of dread, neither plainly confessed nor carefully concealed, which caused each to shift the responsibility upon another, till at length it was found expedient to send a deputation of the church, in order to deal with Mr. Hooper about the mystery before it should grow into a scandal. Never did an embassy so ill discharge its duties. The minister received them with friendly courtesy, but became silent after they were seated, leaving to his visitors the whole burden of introducing their important business. The topic, it might be supposed, was obvious enough. There was the black veil, swathed round Mr. Hooper's forehead, and concealing every feature above his placid mouth, on which, at times, they could perceive the glimmering of a melancholy smile. But that piece of crape, to their imagination, seemed to hang down before his heart, the symbol of a fearful secret between him and
1 them. Were the veil but cast aside, they might speak freely of it, but not till then. Thus they sat a considerable time, speechless, confused, and shrinking uneasily from Mr. Hooper's eye, which they felt to be fixed upon them with an invisible glance. Finally, the deputies returned abashed to their constituents, pronouncing the matter too weighty to be handled, except by a council of the churches if, indeed, it might not require a general synod.[6]

But there was one person in the village unappalled by the awe with which the black veil had impressed all beside herself. When the deputies returned without an explanation, or even venturing to demand one, she, with the calm energy of her character, determined to chase away the strange cloud that appeared to be settling round Mr. Hooper, every moment more darkly than before. As his plighted wife,[7] it should be her privilege to know what the black veil concealed. At the minister's first
2 visit, therefore, she entered upon the subject with a direct simplicity, which made the task easier both for him and her. After he had seated himself, she fixed her eyes steadfastly upon the veil, but could discern nothing of the dreadful gloom that had so overawed the multitude: it was but a double fold of crape, hanging down from his forehead to his mouth, and slightly stirring with his breath.

"No," said she aloud, and smiling, "there is nothing terrible in this piece of crape, except that it hides a face which I am always glad to look upon. Come, good sir, let the sun shine from behind the cloud. First lay aside your black veil: then tell me why you put it on."

3 Mr. Hooper's smile glimmered faintly.

"There is an hour to come," said he, "when all of us shall cast aside our veils. Take it not amiss, beloved friend, if I wear this piece of crape till then."

"Your words are a mystery too," returned the young lady. "Take away the veil from them, at least."

"Elizabeth, I will," said he, "so far as my
4 vow may suffer me. Know, then, this veil is a type and a symbol, and I am bound to wear it ever, both in light and darkness, in solitude and before the gaze of multitudes, and as with strangers, so with my familiar friends. No mortal eye will see it withdrawn. This dismal shade must separate me from the world: even you, Elizabeth, can never come behind it!"

"What grievous affliction hath befallen you," she earnestly inquired, "that you should thus darken your eyes forever?"

"If it be a sign of mourning," replied Mr. Hooper, "I, perhaps, like most other mortals,

6. **synod** [sin′əd]: meeting of the governing body of all the churches.

7. **plighted wife:** betrothed; fiancée.

GUIDED READING

LITERAL QUESTIONS

1a. How does the deputation from the congregation behave in the minister's presence? (They sit speechless and confused.)

2a. How does Elizabeth approach the subject of the veil? (with direct simplicity)

INFERENTIAL QUESTIONS

1b. Why, do you think, are they unable to discharge their duties? (The veil has made them too uncomfortable; they fear the explanation.)

2b. Why is Elizabeth able to do what others cannot? (She loves the minister.)

have sorrows dark enough to be typified by a black veil."

1 "But what if the world will not believe that it is the type of an innocent sorrow?" urged Elizabeth. "Beloved and respected as you are, there may be whispers that you hide your face under the consciousness of secret sin. For the sake of your holy office, do away this scandal!"

The color rose into her cheeks as she intimated the nature of the rumors that were already abroad in the village. But Mr. Hooper's mildness did not forsake him. He even smiled again—that same sad smile, which always appeared like a faint glimmering of light, proceeding from the obscurity beneath the veil.

2 "If I hide my face for sorrow, there is cause enough," he merely replied; "and if I cover it for secret sin, what mortal might not do the same?"

And with this gentle but unconquerable obstinacy did he resist all her entreaties. At length Elizabeth sat silent. For a few moments she appeared lost in thought, considering, probably, what new methods might be tried to withdraw her lover from so dark a fantasy, which, if it had no other meaning, was perhaps a symptom of mental disease. Though of a firmer character than his own, the tears rolled down her cheeks. But in an instant, as it were, a new feeling took the place of sorrow: her eyes were fixed insensibly on the black veil when, like a sudden twilight in the air, its terrors fell around her. She arose, and stood trembling before him.

"And do you feel it then at last?" said he mournfully.

She made no reply, but covered her eyes with her hand, and turned to leave the room. He rushed forward and caught her arm.

3 "Have patience with me, Elizabeth!" cried he passionately. "Do not desert me, though this veil must be between us here on earth. Be mine, and hereafter there shall be no veil over my face, no darkness between our souls! It is but a mortal veil—it is not for eternity! Oh, you know not how lonely I am and how frightened to be alone behind my black veil. Do not leave me in this miserable obscurity forever!"

"Lift the veil but once, and look me in the face," said she.

"Never! It cannot be!" replied Mr. Hooper.

"Then, farewell!" said Elizabeth.

4 She withdrew her arm from his grasp and slowly departed, pausing at the door to give one long, shuddering gaze that seemed almost to penetrate the mystery of the black veil. But even amid his grief, Mr. Hooper smiled to think that only a material emblem had separated him from happiness, though the horrors which it shadowed forth must be drawn darkly between the fondest of lovers.

From that time no attempts were made to remove Mr. Hooper's black veil or, by a direct appeal, to discover the secret which it was supposed to hide. By persons who claimed a superiority to popular prejudice, it was reckoned merely an eccentric whim, such as often mingles with the sober actions of men otherwise rational and tinges them all with its own semblance of insanity. But with the multitude, good Mr. Hooper was irreparably a bugbear.[8] He could not walk the street with any peace of mind, so conscious was he that the gentle and timid would turn aside to avoid him, and that others would make it a point of hardihood to throw themselves in his way. The impertinence of the latter class compelled him to give up his customary walk at sunset to the burial ground; for when he leaned pensively over the gate, there would always be faces behind the gravestones, peeping at his black veil. A fable went the rounds that the stare of the dead people drove him thence. It grieved him, to the very depth of his kind heart, to observe how the children fled from his approach, breaking up their merriest sports while his melancholy figure was yet afar off. Their instinctive dread caused him to feel, more strongly than aught else, that a preternatural[9]

---

8. **bugbear:** something dreaded.
9. **preternatural:** supernatural.

AT A GLANCE

- Elizabeth beseeches the minister to lift the veil, but he refuses.
- She leaves him, ending their engagement.
- The minister's solitary life continues.

1 PERIOD IDEA

Through Elizabeth's question Hawthorne challenges the Transcendentalists' glorification of the individual's conscience. Can following one's conscience be advised, he asks, if it leads to divisions among people who should work together in common cause?

2 THEME

The minister's answer suggests that the veils people take to hide their inmost selves are different, but all have the effect of preventing people from truly knowing each other.

3 THEME

Hooper argues for the redemptive power of love, which breaks down the barriers between people.

4 PLOT: CLIMAX

Elizabeth's departure marks the loss of the minister's best chance for resolving the conflict raised by the veil. It also may be read as the failure of even love to lift some veils that separate people.

GUIDED READING

LITERAL QUESTIONS

1a. Which word does the minister use to describe the veil? *(mortal)*

2a. What is the minister's response to Elizabeth's plea that he lift the veil? ("Never! It cannot be!")

INFERENTIAL QUESTIONS

1b. What does he mean? (It is earthly, not heavenly. It cannot separate their souls.)

2b. What does this response tell you about his character? (He is determined to fulfill his vow, no matter what the personal cost.)

AT A GLANCE

- Hooper's solitary life continues.
- He becomes a particularly effective clergyman.
- He grows old and approaches death.

1 STYLE: METAPHOR

The continuing effect of the veil is likened to a cloud that darkens the sun.

2 VOCABULARY: CONNOTATION

The words *shudderings, terrors, shadow, darkly, saddened, lawless,* and *dreadful* connote dark and painful feelings and convey the unhappiness of the minister's life.

3 THEME

Over time the veil seems to have fulfilled its purpose: Through its influence people have begun to catch a vision of their secret selves and their personal guilt. The vision glorifies Mr. Hooper even as the visionaries shudder at his presence.

4 SYMBOL

The veil, representing the dark secrets of the soul, seems more frightening to the dying than does death itself.

5 IRONY

The narrator objectively sums up the ironic contrasts in the minister's life.

horror was interwoven with the threads of the black crape. In truth, his own antipathy to the veil was known to be so great that he never willingly passed before a mirror nor stooped to drink at a still fountain, lest, in its peaceful bosom, he should be affrighted by himself. This was what gave plausibility to the whispers that Mr. Hooper's conscience tortured him for some great crime, too horrible to be entirely concealed or otherwise than so obscurely inti-
1 mated. Thus, from beneath the black veil, there rolled a cloud into the sunshine, an ambiguity of sin or sorrow, which enveloped the poor minister, so that love or sympathy could never reach him. It was said that ghost and fiend consorted with him there. With self-
2 shudderings and outward terrors, he walked continually in its shadow, groping darkly within his own soul, or gazing through a medium that saddened the whole world. Even the lawless wind, it was believed, respected his dreadful secret and never blew aside the veil. But still good Mr. Hooper sadly smiled at the pale visages of the worldly throng as he passed by.

Among all its bad influences, the black veil had the one desirable effect of making its wearer a very efficient clergyman. By the aid of his mysterious emblem—for there was no other apparent cause—he became a man of awful power over souls that were in agony for
3 sin. His converts always regarded him with a dread peculiar to themselves, affirming, though but figuratively, that, before he brought them to celestial light, they had been with him behind the black veil. Its gloom, indeed, enabled him to sympathize with all dark affections.[10] Dying sinners cried aloud for Mr. Hooper, and would not yield their breath till he appeared; though ever, as he stooped to whisper conso-
4 lation, they shuddered at the veiled face so near their own. Such were the terrors of the black veil, even when death had bared his visage! Strangers came long distances to attend service at his church, with the mere idle purpose of gazing at his figure, because it was forbidden them to behold his face. But many were made to quake ere they departed! Once, during Governor Belcher's[11] administration, Mr. Hooper was appointed to preach the election sermon.[12] Covered with his black veil, he stood before the chief magistrate, the council, and the representatives, and wrought so deep an impression that the legislative measures of that year were characterized by all the gloom and piety of our earliest ancestral sway.

5 In this manner Mr. Hooper spent a long life, irreproachable in outward act, yet shrouded in dismal suspicions; kind and loving, though unloved and dimly feared; a man apart from men, shunned in their health and joy, but ever summoned to their aid in mortal anguish. As years wore on, shedding their snows above his sable veil, he acquired a name throughout the New England churches, and they called him Father Hooper. Nearly all his parishioners, who were of mature age when he was settled, had been borne away by many a funeral: he had one congregation in the church, and a more crowded one in the churchyard; and having wrought so late into the evening, and done his work so well, it was now good Father Hooper's turn to rest.

Several persons were visible by the shaded candlelight in the death-chamber of the old clergyman. Natural connections[13] he had none. But there was the decorously grave, though unmoved physician, seeking only to mitigate the last pangs of the patient whom he could not save. There were the deacons, and other eminently pious members of his church. There also was the Reverend Mr. Clark of Westbury, a young and zealous divine, who had ridden in haste to pray by the bedside of the expiring minister. There was the nurse, no hired handmaiden of death, but one whose calm affection had endured thus long in secrecy, in solitude,

10. **affections:** emotions.

11. **Governor Belcher:** Jonathan Belcher, governor of Massachusetts and New Hampshire from 1730 to 1744.

12. **election sermon:** Mr. Hooper was given the honor of preaching at the governor's inaugural ceremony.

13. **natural connections:** relatives.

GUIDED READING

LITERAL QUESTIONS

1a. What is the one good effect of the veil? (It has made Mr. Hooper an effective minister.)

2a. How do his converts feel about him? (They dread him but feel that they had "been with him behind the black veil.")

INFERENTIAL QUESTIONS

1b. Why has the veil changed him? (He has become more sympathetic to the suffering brought about by guilt and sin.)

2b. What might they mean? (Their secret sins had hidden them behind figurative veils; their lifelong pretenses were like veils.)

1 amid the chill of age, and would not perish, even at the dying hour. Who but Elizabeth! And there lay the hoary head of good Father Hooper upon the death-pillow, with the black veil still swathed about his brow and reaching down over his face, so that each more difficult gasp of his faint breath caused it to stir. All through life that piece of crape had hung between him and the world: It had separated him from cheerful brotherhood and woman's love, and kept him in that saddest of all prisons, his own heart; and still it lay upon his face, as if to deepen the gloom of his darksome chamber and shade him from the sunshine of eternity.

For some time previous, his mind had been confused, wavering doubtfully between the past and the present, and hovering forward, as it were, at intervals, into the indistinctness of the world to come. There had been feverish turns, which tossed him from side to side and wore away what little strength he had. But in his most convulsive struggles, and in the wildest vagaries of his intellect, when no other thought retained its sober influence, he still showed an awful solicitude lest the black veil should slip aside. Even if his bewildered soul could have forgotten, there was a faithful woman at his pillow, who, with averted eyes, would have covered that aged face, which she had last beheld in the comeliness of manhood. At length the death-striken old man lay quietly in the torpor of mental and bodily exhaustion, with an imperceptible pulse, and breath that grew fainter and fainter, except when a long, deep, and irregular inspiration seemed to prelude the flight of his spirit.

The minister of Westbury approached the bedside.

2 "Venerable Father Hooper," said he, "the moment of your release is at hand. Are you ready for the lifting of the veil that shuts in time from eternity?"

Father Hooper at first replied merely by a feeble motion of his head; then, apprehensive, perhaps, that his meaning might be doubtful, he exerted himself to speak.

"Yea," said he, in faint accents, "my soul hath a patient weariness until that veil be lifted."

"And is it fitting," resumed the Reverend Mr. Clark, "that a man so given to prayer, of such a blameless example, holy in deed and thought so far as mortal judgment may pronounce; is it fitting that a father in the church should leave a shadow on his memory that may seem to blacken a life so pure? I pray you, my venerable brother, let not this thing be! Suffer us to be gladdened by your triumphant aspect as you go to your reward. Before the veil of eternity be lifted, let me cast aside this black veil from your face!"

And thus speaking, the Reverend Mr. Clark bent forward to reveal the mystery of so many years. But, exerting a sudden energy that made all the beholders stand aghast, Father Hooper snatched both his hands from beneath the bedclothes and pressed them strongly on the black veil, resolute to struggle if the minister of Westbury would contend with a dying man.

"Never!" cried the veiled clergyman. "On earth, never!"

3 "Dark old man!" exclaimed the affrighted minister, "with what horrible crime upon your soul are you now passing to the judgment?"

Father Hooper's breath heaved; it rattled in his throat; but, with a mighty effort, grasping forward with his hands, he caught hold of life, and held it back till he should speak. He even raised himself in bed; and there he sat, shivering with the arms of death around him, while the black veil hung down, awful, at that last moment, in the gathered terrors of a lifetime.

4 And yet the faint, sad smile, so often there, now seemed to glimmer from its obscurity and linger on Father Hooper's lips.

"Why do you tremble at me alone?" cried he, turning his veiled face round the circle of pale spectators. "Tremble also at each other! Have men avoided me, and women shown no pity, and children screamed and fled, only for my black veil? What, but the mystery which it

AT A GLANCE

- Mr. Hooper lies dying.
- The minister from Westbury attempts to remove the veil.
- Mr. Hooper rises up and refuses.

1 CHARACTERIZATION

Perhaps the most touching detail in this story is the realization that Elizabeth has waited these many decades for Mr. Hooper to break his vow, remove the veil, and return to her. The narrator explains that she has veiled this hope as a private secret.

2 STYLE: METAPHOR

The moment of death is characterized as a lifting of the veil, or division, between life and eternity.

3 IRONY

In the last moments of his life, Mr. Hooper is failed also by the church in the person of Mr. Clark, who, like the others, concludes that the veil must represent an evil secret.

4 STYLE: IMAGE PATTERN

Mr. Hooper's final smile reflects his sadness that many people have failed to learn the lesson that he has tried to teach.

GUIDED READING

LITERAL QUESTIONS

1a. What does the narrator say is "that saddest of all prisons"? (the human heart)

2a. How does Father Hooper react when Mr. Clark tries to remove his veil? (He snatches both his hands from beneath the bedclothes and holds on to the veil.)

INFERENTIAL QUESTIONS

1b. In what way might this description be true? (It is sad because the prisons people maintain for themselves are both inescapable and unnecessary.)

2b. Why does he react this way? (He is determined to fulfill his vow; most people will not give up their veils.)

obscurely typifies, has made this piece of crape so awful? When the friend shows his inmost heart to his friend; the lover to his best-beloved; when man does not vainly shrink from the eye of his Creator, loathsomely treasuring up the secret of his sin; then deem me a monster, for the symbol beneath which I have lived, and die! I look around me, and lo! on every visage a black veil!"

While his auditors shrank from one another in mutual affright, Father Hooper fell back upon his pillow, a veiled corpse, with a faint smile lingering on the lips. Still veiled, they laid him in his coffin, and a veiled corpse they bore him to the grave. The grass of many years has sprung up and withered on that grave, the burial stone is moss-grown, and good Mr. Hooper's face is dust; but awful is still the thought, that it moldered beneath the black veil!

STUDY QUESTIONS

Recalling

1. What is the subject of Mr. Hooper's sermon on the first day he wears the black veil?
2. What does Reverend Hooper tell Elizabeth the veil is? What two possible explanations for wearing the veil do they discuss?
3. What reasons does Hooper give Elizabeth not to desert him? For what reason does he smile after Elizabeth breaks their engagement and leaves?
4. What does the author say is "the one desirable effect" the black veil has?
5. On his deathbed, what does Reverend Hooper say men, women, and children have done? What does he say he sees on every face?

Interpreting

6. What human emotions are shown to fail between Elizabeth and Reverend Hooper as a result of the veil?
7. What is the chief effect that the veil has on Reverend Hooper? Support your answer with evidence from the story.
8. What might Reverend Hooper mean when he says that everyone wears a black veil?
9. List at least four possible reasons Reverend Hooper might have for wearing the veil. Why is it appropriate that we never learn the precise reason?
10. Hawthorne purposely leaves the meaning of the veil ambiguous and up to the reader. What do you think the veil means? Why?

VIEWPOINT

Critic Marius Bewley, in a study of classic American writers, writes about "The Minister's Black Veil":

> The fullness of life . . . can only come about through self-surrender, through a refusal to withhold oneself, or any part of one's personality, in a human relationship.
>
> In the last analysis, this was what Hawthorne believed was the essence of human reality. The most compelling truth of all that Mr. Hooper tried to teach by means of his dismal veil is the necessity of self-surrender.
>
> —*The Eccentric Design*

■ Do you agree that self-surrender is central to the story? Support your opinion by discussing Mr. Hooper's intended marriage and the marriage of "the handsomest couple in Milford village" in the light of this statement.

LITERARY FOCUS

Symbol

A **symbol** is something that conveys two kinds of meaning: It is simply itself, *and* it stands for something other than itself. The American eagle, for example, is an actual bird; it also represents the power and individualism of America. A symbol, in other words, is both literal and figurative. People, places, things, and even events can be used symbolically.

AT A GLANCE

- The minister explains that everyone wears a veil.
- He dies and is buried, still wearing the veil.

REFLECTING ON THE STORY

What are some possible meanings for the black veil? Why, do you think, is no precise meaning given? (The veil seems to stand for all of the many ways in which people hide from each other, from themselves, and from God.)

STUDY QUESTIONS

1. secret sin
2. "a type and a symbol"; sign of mourning, sign of secret sin
3. They will be together without the veil in heaven; he is lonely and frightened. He smiles to think that only a material emblem separated him from happiness.
4. makes Hooper a very efficient clergyman
5. avoided him, shown no pity, screamed, fled; a black veil
6. love, trust, understanding
7. The veil makes him an outcast. *Evidence:* initial behavior of parishioners; Elizabeth's breaking their engagement; his deathbed description of people's behavior toward him
8. Everyone hides the soul's secrets.
9. ■ to symbolize secret sin; as penance; to symbolize mourning; to teach a lesson
   ■ The lack of an explanation emphasizes the idea that humans cannot understand dark secrets of the soul.
10. Answers will vary. Students may note the reference to sin in the first sermon; some may suggest that the setting relates the veil to sin or guilt.

VIEWPOINT

Answers will vary. Students may note that the contrast between the wedding that takes place and the wedding that does not suggests that Hooper surrendered future happiness. Some may feel he was trying to teach a lesson about self-sacrifice. Others may feel that surrendering his life to his ideals was selfish.

Hawthorne centers "The Minister's Black Veil" on the veil and what it means to the characters. If the meaning of a symbol is obscure, that obscurity may also be part of the meaning.

A symbol is a way of telling a story and a way of conveying meaning. The best symbols are those that are believable in the lives of the characters and also convincing as they convey a meaning beyond the literal level of the story.

Thinking About Symbols

■ Discuss the veil in "The Minister's Black Veil" by considering the following questions: What do the characters think and say about it? What do they never say about it? What does the author say about it? What does the author not say about it? Is the obscurity of the symbol itself part of its meaning?

Ambiguity

Ambiguity is a way of expressing something so that its meaning is uncertain. An ambiguous statement is one that can be understood in two or more ways.

Usually, in our everyday lives, we strive for clear and unambiguous statements: "I want that sweater." Occasionally, it is useful or at least prudent to be ambiguous: "Oh, what an unusual sweater!" Writers, however, are often deliberately ambiguous—not because they want to confuse us but because they want to open up our minds to the possibilities of multiple meanings.

"The Minister's Black Veil" is an excellent example of a story in which ambiguity has been deliberately used. Hawthorne delicately hangs between one interpretation and another. To get the most from the story, we should relish the many possibilities, not resist them in favor of one limited response, one "definite" meaning.

Thinking About Ambiguity

■ Because of the veil in "The Minister's Black Veil," many of Mr. Hooper's actions seem ambiguous. Discuss the ambiguity of his final speech and of the "faint, sad smile" lingering on his lips. Tell what the story gains because of its multiple meanings.

COMPOSITION

Developing a Thesis Statement

■ Good critical writing does more than retell a story or paraphrase a poem: A thesis statement often defines a question and then attempts to answer it. For example, "Why does Mr. Hooper do what he does?" Write an interpretive essay answering this question or asking a question of your own about "The Minister's Black Veil." Develop your answer with material from the story. Conclude with a paragraph about how the question and the answer help in understanding the story. *For help with this assignment, refer to Lesson 1 in the Writing About Literature Handbook at the back of this book.*

Describing a Symbol

■ Choose a person, place, thing, or event to serve as a symbol. Then write a short composition (or a story, if you wish) describing how that symbol can mean different things to different people at different times. For example, a cane: To a boy it may symbolize his father's authority; to the father it may symbolize old age; to the mother it may symbolize elegance. Remember that the best symbols are not only universal but also a natural part of the lives of people.

LITERARY FOCUS

Symbols

- Townspeople find the veil frightening, depressing; wonder if it represents secret sin. Elizabeth wonders if Hooper has gone mad. She also discusses the veil as a symbol of mourning. Hooper calls the veil a "type and symbol" and says it will be removed only in heaven.
- The characters never say what the veil means.
- Hawthorne calls the veil a "symbol" and "emblem"; uses negative words to characterize it.

Ambiguity

All people hide something; never clarifies what or from whom; smile unexplained; eerie resonance; multiple possibilities make story richer, more profound.

COMPOSITION: GUIDELINES FOR EVALUATION

DEVELOPING A THESIS STATEMENT

Objective

To analyze a story through a thesis statement

Guidelines for Evaluation

- suggested length: four to seven paragraphs
- should define a general question
- should answer the question
- should cite evidence from the story
- should present the evidence logically
- should show how question aids understanding

DESCRIBING A SYMBOL

Objective

To write about multiple meanings of a symbol

Guidelines for Evaluation

- suggested length: two to five paragraphs
- should identify a symbol
- should present different interpretations of symbol from different peoples' points of view
- should choose a symbol that also functions as a natural part of the lives of the people

AT A GLANCE

- Aylmer, a scientist, marries the beautiful Georgiana.
- Troubled by her only flaw, a birthmark on her cheek shaped like a tiny hand, he suggests having it removed.
- Georgiana, who considers the birthmark a charm, is hurt by his suggestion.

LITERARY OPTIONS

- irony
- characterization

THEMATIC OPTIONS

- science vs. nature
- reality vs. idealism

1 SETTING

The story is set in an indeterminate place in a period of scientific discovery that makes total control over nature seem possible.

2 CHARACTERIZATION

Aylmer is presented as someone for whom science is a passion, who can love another human being only within the parameters of science.

3 SYMBOL

The birthmark is the imperfection that confirms Georgiana's humanity. To Aylmer, obsessed with perfection, it symbolizes the baseness of earthly life.

Nathaniel Hawthorne

The Birthmark

In the latter part of the last century there lived a man of science, an eminent proficient in every branch of natural philosophy,[1] who not long before our story opens had made experience of a spiritual affinity more attractive than any chemical one. He had left his laboratory to the care of an assistant, cleared his fine countenance from the furnace smoke, washed the stain of acids from his fingers, and persuaded a beauti-
1 ful woman to become his wife. In those days when the comparatively recent discovery of electricity and other kindred mysteries of Nature seemed to open paths into the region of miracle, it was not unusual for the love of science to rival the love of woman in its depth and absorbing energy. The higher intellect, the imagination, the spirit, and even the heart might all find their congenial aliment[2] in pursuits which, as some of their ardent votaries[3] believed, would ascend from one step of powerful intelligence to another, until the philosopher should lay his hand on the secret of creative force and perhaps make new worlds for himself. We know not whether Aylmer possessed this degree of faith in man's
2 ultimate control over Nature. He had devoted himself, however, too unreservedly to scientific studies ever to be weaned from them by any second passion. His love for his young wife might prove the stronger of the two; but it could only be by intertwining itself with his love of science, and uniting the strength of the latter to his own.

Such a union accordingly took place, and was attended with truly remarkable consequences and a deeply impressive moral. One day, very soon after their marriage, Aylmer sat gazing at his wife with a trouble in his countenance that grew stronger until he spoke.

"Georgiana," said he, "has it never occurred to you that the mark upon your cheek might be removed?"

"No, indeed," said she, smiling; but perceiving the seriousness of his manner, she blushed deeply. "To tell you the truth it has been so often called a charm that I was simple enough to imagine it might be so."

3 "Ah, upon another face perhaps it might," replied her husband; "but never on yours. No, dearest Georgiana, you came so nearly perfect from the hand of Nature that this slightest possible defect, which we hesitate whether to term a defect or a beauty, shocks me, as being the visible mark of earthly imperfection."

"Shocks you, my husband!" cried Georgiana, deeply hurt; at first reddening with momentary anger, but then bursting into tears. "Then why did you take me from my mother's side? You cannot love what shocks you!"

To explain this conversation it must be mentioned that in the center of Georgiana's left cheek there was a singular mark, deeply interwoven, as it were, with the texture and substance of her face. In the usual state of her complexion—a healthy though delicate bloom—the mark wore a tint of deeper crimson, which imperfectly defined its shape amid the surrounding rosiness. When she blushed it gradually became more indistinct, and finally vanished amid the triumphant rush of blood that bathed the whole cheek with its brilliant glow. But if any shifting emotion caused her to turn pale there was the mark again, a crimson stain upon the snow, in what Aylmer sometimes deemed an almost fearful distinctness. Its shape bore not a little similarity to the human hand, though of the smallest pygmy size. Georgiana's lovers were wont to say that some fairy at her birth hour had laid her tiny hand upon the infant's cheek, and left this impress there in token of the magic endowments that were to give her such sway over all hearts. Many

1. **natural philosophy:** early name for natural science.
2. **aliment:** anything that nourishes.
3. **votaries:** devoted supporters.

GUIDED READING

LITERAL QUESTIONS

1a. What is on Georgiana's left cheek? (a birthmark)

2a. What question does Aylmer ask Georgiana? ("Has it never occurred to you that the mark upon your cheek might be removed?")

INFERENTIAL QUESTIONS

1b. Is it disfiguring? How can you tell? (Apparently not; Georgiana had considered it a charm.)

2b. Why does he react in this way? (As a scientist he feels humankind can and should control nature. He views the mark as a defect of nature that science can correct.)

a desperate swain would have risked life for the privilege of pressing his lips to the mysterious hand. It must not be concealed, however, that the impression wrought by this fairy sign manual varied exceedingly, according to the difference of temperament in the beholders. Some fastidious persons—but they were exclusively of her own sex—affirmed that the bloody hand, as they chose to call it, quite destroyed the effect of Georgiana's beauty, and rendered her countenance even hideous. But it would be as reasonable to say that one of those small blue stains which sometimes occur in the purest statuary marble would convert the Eve of Powers[4] to a monster. Masculine observers, if the birthmark did not heighten their admiration, contented
1 themselves with wishing it away, that the world might possess one living specimen of ideal loveliness without the semblance of a flaw. After his marriage—for he thought little or nothing of the matter before—Aylmer discovered that this was the case with himself.

Had she been less beautiful—if Envy's self could have found aught else to sneer at—he might have felt his affection heightened by the prettiness of this mimic hand, now vaguely portrayed, now lost, now stealing forth again and glimmering to and fro with every pulse of emotion that throbbed within her heart; but seeing
2 her otherwise so perfect, he found this one defect grow more and more intolerable with every moment of their united lives. It was the fatal flaw of humanity which Nature, in one shape or another, stamps ineffaceably on all her productions, either to imply that they are temporary and finite, or that their perfection must be wrought by toil and pain. The crimson hand ex-
3 pressed the ineludible gripe in which mortality clutches the highest and purest of earthly mold, degrading them into kindred with the lowest, and even with the very brutes, like whom their visible frames return to dust. In this manner, selecting it as the symbol of his wife's liability to sin, sorrow, decay, and death, Aylmer's somber imagination was not long in rendering the birthmark a frightful object, causing him more trouble and horror than ever Georgiana's beauty, whether of soul or sense, had given him delight.

4 At all the seasons which should have been their happiest, he invariably and without intending it, nay, in spite of a purpose to the contrary, reverted to this one disastrous topic. Trifling as it at first appeared, it so connected itself with innumerable trains of thought and modes of feeling that it became the central point of all. With the morning twilight Aylmer opened his eyes upon his wife's face and recognized the symbol of imperfection; and when they sat together at the evening hearth his eyes wandered stealthily to her cheek, and beheld, flickering with the blaze of the wood fire, the spectral hand that wrote mortality where he would fain have worshiped. Georgiana soon learned to shudder at his gaze. It needed but a glance with the peculiar expression that his face often wore to change the roses of her cheek into a deathlike paleness, amid which the crimson hand was brought strongly out, like a bas-relief[5] of ruby on the whitest marble.

Late one night when the lights were growing dim, so as hardly to betray the stain on the poor wife's cheek, she herself, for the first time, voluntarily took up the subject.

"Do you remember, my dear Aylmer," said she, with a feeble attempt at a smile, "have you any recollection of a dream last night about this odious hand?"

"None! none whatever!" replied Aylmer, starting; but then he added, in a dry, cold tone, affected for the sake of concealing the real depth of his emotion, "I might well dream of it; for before I fell asleep it had taken a pretty firm hold of my fancy."

"And you did dream of it?" continued Georgiana, hastily; for she dreaded lest a gush of tears should interrupt what she had to say. "A terrible dream! I wonder that you can forget it. Is it possible to forget this one expression?—'It is in her

4. **Eve of Powers:** at the time the story is set, a renowned statue of Eve by Hiram Powers.

5. **bas-relief** [bä′ri lēf′]: sculpture in which figures are carved in a flat surface so that they project only slightly from the background.

AT A GLANCE

- Aylmer, obsessed with the birthmark, sees it as a symbol of earthly mortality and imperfection.
- His strange expression when he looks at it causes his wife to shudder.
- One night Georgiana asks him whether he dreamed of the birthmark.

1 CHARACTERIZATION

Aylmer's growing preoccupation with the birthmark and his wish to possess one specimen of ideal loveliness signify that he fails to realize Georgiana's exceptional loveliness and humanity.

2 POINT OF VIEW

The omniscient third-person narrator enters the mind of Aylmer, capturing the urgency of his preoccupation and presenting Aylmer's interpretation of the workings of nature.

3 BACKGROUND

The notion of death as the legacy of original sin was emphasized by the Puritans, whose influence figures strongly in Hawthorne's writing.

4 IRONY

Ironically, a man who always wants to be in control cannot control his own obsession.

GUIDED READING

LITERAL QUESTIONS

1a. Under what circumstances might the birthmark have heightened Aylmer's affection for Georgiana? (had she been less beautiful)

2a. What tone does Aylmer assume when he speaks to Georgiana? (cold and dry)

INFERENTIAL QUESTIONS

1b. Why would this have been the case? (If she had been less nearly perfect, removal of one birthmark would not have achieved perfection. Then Aylmer would not have been obsessed to have it removed and could have even found pleasure in it.)

2b. Why does he use such a tone? (He wants to spare her from knowing how deeply he feels about the birthmark.)

AT A GLANCE

- Aylmer recalls a dream of cutting into Georgiana's heart to remove the birthmark.
- Georgiana pleads with him to remove the birthmark despite any danger; he assures her that it can be done.
- He tells her of his plan to have them seclude themselves in living quarters that include the laboratory he used during his youth.

1 FORESHADOWING

The dream foreshadows Aylmer's actions and reveals the depth of his obsession.

2 CHARACTERIZATION

Georgiana's words show that she understands what is at stake for her. She is more clearheaded than her husband and has a better grasp of reality.

3 VOCABULARY: CONNOTATION

The words *hateful, horror, disgust, burden, dreadful,* and *wretched* connote extreme feelings of unpleasantness. These words have added impact when the reader realizes that they come from Georgiana's lips, not Aylmer's.

4 CHARACTERIZATION

Aylmer's excessive intellectual pride leads him to believe that he can correct nature.

heart now; we must have it out!' Reflect, my husband; for by all means I would have you recall that dream."

The mind is in a sad state when Sleep, the all-involving, cannot confine her specters within the dim region of her sway, but suffers them to break forth, affrighting this actual life with secrets that perchance belong to a deeper one. Ayl-
1 mer now remembered his dream. He had fancied himself with his servant Aminadab, attempting an operation for the removal of the birthmark; but the deeper went the knife, the deeper sank the hand, until at length its tiny grasp appeared to have caught hold of Georgiana's heart; whence, however, her husband was inexorably resolved to cut or wrench it away.

When the dream had shaped itself perfectly in his memory, Aylmer sat in his wife's presence with a guilty feeling. Truth often finds its way to the mind close muffled in robes of sleep, and then speaks with uncompromising directness of matters in regard to which we practice an unconscious self-deception during our waking moments. Until now he had not been aware of the tyrannizing influence acquired by one idea over his mind, and of the lengths which he might find in his heart to go for the sake of giving himself peace.

"Aylmer," resumed Georgiana, solemnly, "I know not what may be the cost to both of us to
2 rid me of this fatal birthmark. Perhaps its removal may cause cureless deformity; or it may be the stain goes as deep as life itself. Again: do we know that there is a possibility, on any terms, of unclasping the firm gripe of this little hand which was laid upon me before I came into the world?"

"Dearest Georgiana, I have spent much thought upon the subject," hastily interrupted Aylmer. "I am convinced of the perfect practicability of its removal."

"If there be the remotest possibility of it," continued Georgiana, "let the attempt be made
3 at whatever risk. Danger is nothing to me; for life, while this hateful mark makes me the object of your horror and disgust—life is a burden which I would fling down with joy. Either remove this dreadful hand, or take my wretched life! You have deep science. All the world bears witness of it. You have achieved great wonders. Cannot you remove this little, little mark, which I cover with the tips of two small fingers? Is this beyond your power, for the sake of your own peace, and to save your poor wife from madness?"

"Noblest, dearest, tenderest wife," cried Aylmer, rapturously, "doubt not my power. I have already given this matter the deepest thought—thought which might almost have enlightened me to create a being less perfect than yourself. Georgiana, you have led me deeper than ever
4 into the heart of science. I feel myself fully competent to render this dear cheek as faultless as its fellow; and then, most beloved, what will be my triumph when I shall have corrected what Nature left imperfect in her fairest work! Even Pygmalion,[6] when his sculptured woman assumed life, felt not greater ecstasy than mine will be."

"It is resolved, then," said Georgiana, faintly smiling. "And, Aylmer, spare me not, though you should find the birthmark take refuge in my heart at last."

Her husband tenderly kissed her cheek—her right cheek—not that which bore the impress of the crimson hand.

The next day Aylmer apprised his wife of a plan that he had formed whereby he might have opportunity for the intense thought and constant watchfulness which the proposed operation would require; while Georgiana, likewise, would enjoy the perfect repose essential to its success. They were to seclude themselves in the extensive apartments occupied by Aylmer as a laboratory, and where, during his toilsome youth, he had made discoveries in the elemental powers of Nature that had roused the admiration of all the learned societies in Europe. Seated calmly in this laboratory, the pale philosopher had investigated the secrets of the highest cloud region and of the profoundest mines; he had satisfied himself of

6. **Pygmalion:** in Greek legend, a king of Cyprus and sculptor, who fell in love with his statue of a maiden, later brought to life by Aphrodite at his prayer.

GUIDED READING

LITERAL QUESTIONS

1a. What circumstances does Georgiana say would justify an attempt to remove the birthmark? (even the remotest possibility of success, at whatever risk)

2a. How does Aylmer greet Georgiana's decision? (rapturously)

INFERENTIAL QUESTIONS

1b. What has brought her to this decision? (She sees removal of the mark as the only way to save her marriage.)

2b. What does this reaction reveal about his character? (He is absolutely convinced of his own powers; he is not afraid to hurt Georgiana to achieve his ends.)

the causes that kindled and kept alive the fires of the volcano; and had explained the mystery of fountains, and how it is that they gush forth, some so bright and pure, and others with such rich medicinal virtues, from the dark bosom of the earth. Here, too, at an earlier period, he had studied the wonders of the human frame, and attempted to fathom the very process by which Nature assimilates all her precious influences from earth and air, and from the spiritual world, to create and foster man, her masterpiece. The latter pursuit, however, Aylmer had long laid aside in unwilling recognition of the truth—against which all seekers sooner or later stumble—that our great creative Mother, while she amuses us with apparently working in the broadest sunshine, is yet severely careful to keep her own secrets, and, in spite of her pretended
1 openness, shows us nothing but results. She permits us, indeed, to mar, but seldom to mend, and, like a jealous patentee,[7] on no account to make. Now, however, Aylmer resumed these half-forgotten investigations; not, of course, with such hopes or wishes as first suggested them; but because they involved much physiological truth and lay in the path of his proposed scheme for the treatment of Georgiana.

As he led her over the threshold of the laboratory, Georgiana was cold and tremulous. Aylmer looked cheerfully into her face, with intent to reassure her, but was so startled with the intense glow of the birthmark upon the whiteness of her cheek that he could not restrain a strong convulsive shudder. His wife fainted.

"Aminadab! Aminadab!" shouted Aylmer, stamping violently on the floor.

Forthwith there issued from an inner apartment a man of low stature, but bulky frame, with shaggy hair hanging about his visage, which was grimed with the vapors of the furnace. This personage had been Aylmer's underworker during his whole scientific career, and was admirably fitted for that office by his great mechanical readiness, and the skill with which, while incapable of comprehending a single principle, he executed all the details of his master's experiments. With his vast strength, his shaggy hair, his smoky aspect, and the indescribable earthiness that incrusted him, he seemed to represent man's physical nature; while Aylmer's slender figure, and pale, intellectual face, were no less apt a type of the spiritual element.

"Throw open the door of the boudoir,[8] Aminadab," said Aylmer, "and burn a pastil.[9]"

2 "Yes, master," answered Aminadab, looking intently at the lifeless form of Georgiana; and then he muttered to himself, "If she were my wife, I'd never part with that birthmark."

When Georgiana recovered consciousness she found herself breathing an atmosphere of penetrating fragrance, the gentle potency of which had recalled her from her deathlike faintness. The scene around her looked like enchantment. Aylmer had converted those smoky, dingy, somber rooms, where he had spent his brightest years in recondite pursuits, into a series of beautiful apartments not unfit to be the secluded abode of a lovely woman. The walls were hung with gorgeous curtains, which imparted the combination of grandeur and grace that no other species of adornment can achieve; and as they fell from the ceiling to the floor, their rich and ponderous folds, concealing all angles and straight lines, appeared to shut in the scene from infinite space. For aught Georgiana knew, it
3 might be a pavilion among the clouds. And Aylmer, excluding the sunshine, which would have interfered with his chemical processes, had supplied its place with perfumed lamps, emitting flames of various hue, but all uniting in a soft impurpled radiance. He now knelt by his wife's side, watching her earnestly, but without alarm; for he was confident in his science, and felt that he could draw a magic circle round her within which no evil might intrude.

"Where am I? Ah, I remember," said Georgiana, faintly; and she placed her hand over her

7. **patentee:** person who has been granted a patent.

8. **boudoir** [bo͞od′wär]: woman's bedroom, dressing room, or private sitting room.

9. **pastil** [pas′til]: pellet of aromatic paste, burned for fumigating or deodorizing.

AT A GLANCE

- Aylmer takes Georgiana to their new living quarters as planned.
- She faints when he recoils from looking at her face, and he summons his assistant, Aminadab, to help.
- Georgiana awakens in a marvelously appointed boudoir.

1 THEME

Only nature can create life. The power of science is limited to making changes within the scope permitted by nature.

2 CHARACTERIZATION

Aminadab, described as representing man's physical nature, is closer to nature than is his master. Lacking Aylmer's preoccupation with perfection, he recognizes the birthmark as an enhancement of Georgiana's beauty.

3 SYMBOL

Sunlight, symbol of the natural world, is excluded by Aylmer, who has turned entirely to science.

GUIDED READING

LITERAL QUESTION

1a. According to the narrator, in what manner did Aylmer lay aside his pursuit of the ways in which nature creates human life? ("in unwilling recognition of the truth")

INFERENTIAL QUESTION

1b. What aspect of Aylmer's character led him to feel this way? (He was full of intellectual pride; he did not want to recognize the superiority of nature over science.)

AT A GLANCE

- Aylmer entertains Georgiana with scientific wonders.
- She touches a strange plant and it shrivels.
- Aylmer makes a photo of his wife; the birthmark overwhelms it.
- He tells her about alchemy, stating his belief that he can make the elixir of life.

1 CHARACTERIZATION

Aylmer now views the birthmark as a symbol of his anticipated triumph over nature. His love for his wife can only exist if it is intertwined with his love of science.

2 IRONY

By making the images too perfect, Aylmer has made them less lifelike.

3 AMBIGUITY

The death of the flower at Georgiana's touch hints that there is some flaw in her, as Aylmer believes, although the flaw may as easily lie in his science.

4 RESPONSE JOURNAL

Have students respond to the question of why physical immortality might give those possessed of it reason to curse it.

cheek to hide the terrible mark from her husband's eyes.

1 "Fear not, dearest!" exclaimed he. "Do not shrink from me! Believe me, Georgiana, I even rejoice in this single imperfection, since it will be such a rapture to remove it."

"Oh, spare me!" sadly replied his wife. "Pray do not look at it again. I never can forget that convulsive shudder."

In order to soothe Georgiana, and, as it were, to release her mind from the burden of actual things, Aylmer now put in practice some of the light and playful secrets which science had taught him among its profounder lore. Airy figures, absolutely bodiless ideas, and forms of unsubstantial beauty came and danced before her, imprinting their momentary footsteps on beams of light. Though she had some indistinct idea of the method of these optical phenomena, still the illusion was almost perfect enough to warrant the belief that her husband possessed sway over the spiritual world. Then again, when she felt a wish to look forth from her seclusion, immediately, as if her thoughts were answered, the procession of external existence flitted across a
2 screen. The scenery and the figures of actual life were perfectly represented, but with that bewitching, yet indescribable difference which always makes a picture, an image, or a shadow so much more attractive than the original. When wearied of this, Aylmer bade her cast her eyes upon a vessel containing a quantity of earth. She did so, with little interest at first; but was soon startled to perceive the germ of a plant shooting upward from the soil. Then came the slender stalk; the leaves gradually unfolded themselves; and amid them was a perfect and lovely flower.

"It is magical!" cried Georgiana. "I dare not touch it."

"Nay, pluck it," answered Aylmer—"pluck it, and inhale its brief perfume while you may. The flower will wither in a few moments and leave nothing save its brown seed vessels; but thence may be perpetuated a race as ephemeral as itself."

But Georgiana had no sooner touched the flower than the whole plant suffered a blight, its
3 leaves turning coal-black as if by the agency of fire.

"There was too powerful a stimulus," said Aylmer, thoughtfully.

To make up for this abortive experiment, he proposed to take her portrait by a scientific process of his own invention. It was to be effected by rays of light striking upon a polished plate of metal. Georgiana assented; but, on looking at the result, was affrighted to find the features of the portrait blurred and indefinable; while the minute figure of a hand appeared where the cheek should have been. Aylmer snatched the metallic plate and threw it into a jar of corrosive acid.

Soon, however, he forgot these mortifying failures. In the intervals of study and chemical experiment he came to her flushed and exhausted, but seemed invigorated by her presence, and spoke in glowing language of the resources of his art. He gave a history of the long dynasty of the alchemists,[10] who spent so many ages in quest of the universal solvent by which the golden principle might be elicited from all things vile and base. Aylmer appeared to believe that, by the plainest scientific logic, it was altogether within the limits of possibility to discover this long-sought medium; "but," he added, "a philosopher who should go deep enough to acquire the power would attain too lofty a wisdom to stoop to the exercise of it." Not less singular were his opinions in regard to the elixir vitæ.[11] He more than intimated that it was at his option to concoct a liquid that should prolong life for
4 years, perhaps interminably; but that it would produce a discord in Nature which all the world, and chiefly the quaffer of the immortal nostrum, would find cause to curse.

"Aylmer, are you in earnest?" asked Georgiana, looking at him with amazement and fear. "It is terrible to possess such power, or even to dream of possessing it."

---

10. **alchemists:** practitioners of an early form of chemistry, whose aims were to change metals into gold and to discover a substance for perpetual youth.
11. **elixir vitæ** [i lik'sər vī'tē]: "elixir of life."

GUIDED READING

LITERAL QUESTIONS

1a. What happens when Aylmer makes Georgiana's picture? (The birthmark appears where the cheek should have been.)

2a. How does Aylmer cope with the mortifying failure of his experiments? (He forgets them.)

INFERENTIAL QUESTIONS

1b. What possibilities does this detail suggest? (The birthmark has some extraordinary importance; Aylmer's science is imperfect.)

2b. What does this information suggest about Aylmer? (He neither gains humility nor learns from his failures.)

“Oh, do not tremble, my love,” said her hus-
1 band. “I would not wrong either you or myself by working such inharmonious effects upon our lives; but I would have you consider how trifling, in comparison, is the skill requisite to remove this little hand.”

At the mention of the birthmark, Georgiana, as usual, shrank as if a redhot iron had touched her cheek.

Again Aylmer applied himself to his labors.
2 She could hear his voice in the distant furnace room giving directions to Aminadab, whose harsh, uncouth, misshapen tones were audible in response, more like the grunt or growl of a brute than human speech. After hours of absence, Aylmer reappeared and proposed that she should now examine his cabinet of chemical products and natural treasures of the earth. Among the former he showed her a small vial, in which, he remarked, was contained a gentle yet most powerful fragrance, capable of impregnating all the breezes that blow across a kingdom. They were of inestimable value, the contents of that little vial; and, as he said so, he threw some of the perfume into the air and filled the room with piercing and invigorating delight.

“And what is this?” asked Georgiana, pointing to a small crystal globe containing a gold-colored liquid. “It is so beautiful to the eye that I could imagine it the elixir of life.”

“In one sense it is,” replied Aylmer; “or, rather, the elixir of immortality. It is the most precious poison that ever was concocted in this world. By its aid I could apportion the lifetime of any mortal at whom you might point your finger. The strength of the dose would determine whether he were to linger out years, or drop dead in the midst of a breath. No king on his guarded throne could keep his life if I, in my private station, should deem that the welfare of millions justified me in depriving him of it.”

“Why do you keep such a terrific[12] drug?” inquired Georgiana in horror.

12. **terrific:** terrifying.

AT A GLANCE

- Aylmer reassures Georgiana that he would not actually use the elixir of life.
- He shows her two examples of his chemical products—a marvelous perfume and a powerful poison.

1 CONTRAST

Aminadab's rough earthiness contrasts sharply with Aylmer's overrefined intellectualism.

2 ROMANTIC IDEA

The suggestion of strange, almost magical powers and the heady appeal to the senses display the influence of Romanticism.

GUIDED READING

LITERAL QUESTION

1a. What does Aylmer concoct? (a “precious poison”)

INFERENTIAL QUESTION

1b. Upon what does its safe use depend? (It depends upon Aylmer's using it wisely, likening him to nature in that he is in control of life and death.)

AT A GLANCE

- Aylmer shows his wife a cosmetic that removes freckles, but tells her that she requires a more potent treatment.
- She senses that he has begun this treatment without her knowledge.
- She discovers and reads his scientific journal, which discloses that he has never been satisfied with the outcomes of his experiments.

1 VOCABULARY: DICTION

The words *drift, conjecture,* and *fancied* convey the vagueness of Georgiana's perception.

2 CONTRAST

By juxtaposing opposites (successes/failures; diamonds/pebbles), the author emphasizes the discrepancy between Aylmer's aspirations and his achievements.

3 THEME

The limitations imposed by nature on human beings cannot be overcome by science.

"Do not mistrust me, dearest," said her husband, smiling; "its virtuous potency is yet greater than its harmful one. But see! here is a powerful cosmetic. With a few drops of this in a vase of water, freckles may be washed away as easily as the hands are cleansed. A stronger infusion would take the blood out of the cheek, and leave the rosiest beauty a pale ghost."

"Is it with this lotion that you intend to bathe my cheek?" asked Georgiana, anxiously.

"Oh, no," hastily replied her husband; "this is merely superficial. Your case demands a remedy that shall go deeper."

In his interviews with Georgiana, Aylmer generally made minute inquiries as to her sensations and whether the confinement of the rooms and the temperature of the atmosphere agreed with
1 her. These questions had such a particular drift that Georgiana began to conjecture that she was already subjected to certain physical influences, either breathed in with the fragrant air or taken with her food. She fancied likewise, but it might be altogether fancy, that there was a stirring up of her system—a strange, indefinite sensation creeping through her veins, and tingling, half painfully, half pleasurably, at her heart. Still, whenever she dared to look into the mirror, there she beheld herself pale as a white rose and with the crimson birthmark stamped upon her cheek. Not even Aylmer now hated it so much as she.

To dispel the tedium of the hours which her husband found it necessary to devote to the processes of combination and analysis, Georgiana turned over the volumes of his scientific library. In many dark old tomes she met with chapters full of romance and poetry. They were the works of the philosophers of the middle ages, such as Albertus Magnus, Cornelius Agrippa, Paracelsus, and the famous friar who created the prophetic Brazen Head. All these antique naturalists stood in advance of their centuries, yet were imbued with some of their credulity, and therefore were believed, and perhaps imagined themselves to have acquired from the investigation of Nature a power above Nature, and from physics a sway over the spiritual world. Hardly less curious and imaginative were the early volumes of the Transactions of the Royal Society, in which the members, knowing little of the limits of natural possibility, were continually recording wonders or proposing methods whereby wonders might be wrought.

But to Georgiana the most engrossing volume was a large folio[13] from her husband's own hand, in which he had recorded every experiment of his scientific career, its original aim, the methods adopted for its development, and its final success or failure, with the circumstances to which either event was attributable. The book, in truth, was both the history and emblem of his ardent, ambitious, imaginative, yet practical and laborious life. He handled physical details as if there were nothing beyond them; yet spiritualized them all, and redeemed himself from materialism by his strong and eager aspiration towards the infinite. In his grasp the veriest clod of earth assumed a soul. Georgiana, as she read, reverenced Aylmer and loved him more profoundly than ever, but with a less entire dependence on his judgment than heretofore. Much as he had accomplished, she could not but observe that his
2 most splendid successes were almost invariably failures, if compared with the ideal at which he aimed. His brightest diamonds were the merest pebbles, and felt to be so by himself, in comparison with the inestimable gems which lay hidden beyond his reach. The volume, rich with achievements that had won renown for its au-
3 thor, was yet as melancholy a record as ever mortal hand had penned. It was the sad confession and continual exemplification of the shortcomings of the composite man, the spirit burdened with clay and working in matter, and of the despair that assails the higher nature at finding itself so miserably thwarted by the earthly part. Perhaps every man of genius in whatever sphere might recognize the image of his own experience in Aylmer's journal.

So deeply did these reflections affect Georgiana that she laid her face upon the open vol-

---

13. **folio:** large-sized book.

GUIDED READING

LITERAL QUESTIONS

1a. What kind of remedy does Aylmer say that Georgiana's problem demands? ("a remedy that shall go deeper")

2a. After reading Aylmer's journal, on what did Georgiana have a "less entire dependence"? (on his judgment)

INFERENTIAL QUESTIONS

1b. What does this statement suggest about the type of remedy he will use on his wife? (It will be a drastic one.)

2b. Why does she feel this way? (She probably questions the judgment of a man who continues to try to control nature even though he has never had any real success.)

ume and burst into tears. In this situation she was found by her husband.

"It is dangerous to read in a sorcerer's books," said he, with a smile, though his countenance was uneasy and displeased. "Georgiana, there are pages in that volume which I can scarcely glance over and keep my senses. Take heed lest it prove as detrimental to you."

"It has made me worship you more than ever," said she.

"Ah, wait for this one success," rejoined he, "then worship me if you will. I shall deem myself hardly unworthy of it. But come, I have sought you for the luxury of your voice. Sing to me, dearest."

1 So she poured out the liquid music of her voice to quench the thirst of his spirit. He then took his leave with a boyish exuberance of gaiety, assuring her that her seclusion would endure but a little longer, and that the result was already certain. Scarcely had he departed when Georgiana felt irresistibly impelled to follow him. She had forgotten to inform Aylmer of a symptom which for two or three hours past had begun to excite her attention. It was a sensation in the fatal birthmark, not painful, but which induced a restlessness throughout her system. Hastening after her husband, she intruded for the first time into the laboratory.

The first thing that struck her eye was the furnace, that hot and feverish worker, with the intense glow of its fire, which by the quantities of soot clustered above it seemed to have been burning for ages. There was a distilling apparatus
2 in full operation. Around the room were retorts, tubes, cylinders, crucibles, and other apparatus of chemical research. An electrical machine stood ready for immediate use. The atmosphere felt oppressively close, and was tainted with gaseous odors which had been tormented forth by the processes of science. The severe and homely simplicity of the apartment, with its naked walls and brick pavement, looked strange, accustomed as Georgiana had become to the fantastic elegance of her boudoir. But what chiefly, indeed almost solely, drew her attention, was the aspect of Aylmer himself.

3 He was pale as death, anxious and absorbed, and hung over the furnace as if it depended upon his utmost watchfulness whether the liquid which it was distilling should be the draught of immortal happiness or misery. How different from the sanguine and joyous mien[14] that he had assumed for Georgiana's encouragement!

"Carefully now, Aminadab; carefully, thou human machine; carefully, thou man of clay!" muttered Aylmer, more to himself than his assistant. "Now, if there be a thought too much or too little, it is all over."

"Ho! ho!" mumbled Aminadab. "Look, master! look!"

Aylmer raised his eyes hastily, and at first reddened, then grew paler than ever, on beholding Georgiana. He rushed towards her and seized her arm with a gripe that left the print of his fingers upon it.

"Why do you come hither? Have you no trust in your husband?" cried he, impetuously. "Would you throw the blight of that fatal birthmark over my labors? It is not well done. Go, prying woman, go!"

"Nay, Aylmer," said Georgiana with the firmness of which she possessed no stinted endowment, "it is not you that have a right to complain. You mistrust your wife; you have concealed the anxiety with which you watch the development of this experiment. Think not so unworthily of me, my husband. Tell me all the risk we run, and fear not that I shall shrink; for my share in it is far less than your own."

"No, no, Georgiana!" said Aylmer, impatiently; "it must not be."

4 "I submit," replied she calmly. "And, Aylmer, I shall quaff whatever draft you bring me; but it will be on the same principle that would induce me to take a dose of poison if offered by your hand."

"My noble wife," said Aylmer, deeply moved, "I knew not the height and depth of your nature until now. Nothing shall be concealed. Know, then, that this crimson hand, superficial as it seems, has clutched its grasp into your being

14. **mien** [mēn]: appearance.

AT A GLANCE

- Aylmer warns his wife of the danger of reading his journal and encourages her to sing for him.
- After he leaves she follows him to the laboratory to mention a sensation in the birthmark.
- Seeing how anxious he is about the experiment, she asks him to disclose the risks involved and assures him she will not back out.

1 IMAGERY

The rich, sensory image of Georgiana's liquid voice suggests her sensuous beauty and generous nature.

2 MOOD

The harsh instruments and malodorous, bubbling chemicals create a mood of unease and tension.

3 CONTRAST

The pale, anxious man at work in the laboratory is a sharp contrast to the exuberant, carefree man who left his wife a few moments before.

4 CHARACTERIZATION

Georgiana understands that she is less important to Aylmer than is the experiment. Her words suggest that she sees more clearly than Aylmer what may happen, but she is ready for the consequences.

GUIDED READING

LITERAL QUESTION

1a. According to Georgiana, who has the greater stake in the experiment? (He does.)

INFERENTIAL QUESTION

1b. In what way is this true? (Life no longer means as much to Georgiana as science still means to Aylmer.)

AT A GLANCE

- Aylmer tells his wife that the birthmark goes deeper than he had known.
- She answers that the mark must be removed at any cost.
- He brings her a potion; she drinks it and falls asleep.

1 AMBIGUITY

What is at stake for each is different: For Aylmer, it is the success of his experiment; for Georgiana, it is her life.

2 IRONY

Georgiana's thoughts are ironic. By admiring Aylmer's "honorable love," which consists of an intolerance of imperfection, she implies that he is incapable of human love, since all humans are imperfect.

3 SYMBOL

To Georgiana mortality has come to be as burdensome as the birthmark that symbolizes it.

4 PLOT: CLIMAX

Aylmer's quest for perfection has driven out all other considerations. As Georgiana drinks the potion, he feels nothing but admiration.

with a strength of which I had no previous conception. I have already administered agents powerful enough to do aught except to change your entire physical system. Only one thing remains to be tried. If that fail us we are ruined."

"Why did you hesitate to tell me this?" asked she.

"Because, Georgiana," said Aylmer, in a low voice, "there is danger."

"Danger? There is but one danger—that this horrible stigma shall be left upon my cheek!" cried Georgiana. "Remove it, remove it, whatever be the cost, or we shall both go mad!"

"Heaven knows your words are too true," said Aylmer, sadly. "And now, dearest, return to your boudoir. In a little while all will be tested."

1 He conducted her back and took leave of her with a solemn tenderness which spoke far more than his words how much was now at stake. After his departure Georgiana became rapt in musings. She considered the character of Aylmer, and did it completer justice than at any previous moment. Her heart exulted, while it trembled, at his honorable love—so pure and lofty that it would accept nothing less than perfection nor miserably make itself contented with an earthlier na-
2 ture than he had dreamed of. She felt how much more precious was such a sentiment than that meaner kind which would have borne with the imperfection for her sake, and have been guilty of treason to holy love by degrading its perfect idea to the level of the actual; and with her whole spirit she prayed that, for a single moment, she might satisfy his highest and deepest conception. Longer than one moment she well knew it could not be; for his spirit was ever on the march, ever ascending, and each instant required something that was beyond the scope of the instant before.

The sound of her husband's footsteps aroused her. He bore a crystal goblet containing a liquor colorless as water, but bright enough to be the draft of immortality. Aylmer was pale; but it seemed rather the consequence of a highly wrought state of mind and tension of spirit than of fear or doubt.

"The concoction of the draft has been perfect," said he, in answer to Georgiana's look. "Unless all my science have deceived me, it cannot fail."

3 "Save on your account, my dearest Aylmer," observed his wife, "I might wish to put off this birthmark of mortality by relinquishing mortality itself in preference to any other mode. Life is but a sad possession to those who have attained precisely the degree of moral advancement at which I stand. Were I weaker and blinder it might be happiness. Were I stronger, it might be endured hopefully. But, being what I find myself, methinks I am of all mortals the most fit to die."

"You are fit for heaven without tasting death!" replied her husband. "But why do we speak of dying? The draft cannot fail. Behold its effect upon this plant."

On the window seat there stood a geranium diseased with yellow blotches, which had overspread all its leaves. Aylmer poured a small quantity of the liquid upon the soil in which it grew. In a little time, when the roots of the plant had taken up the moisture, the unsightly blotches began to be extinguished in a living verdure.[15]

"There needed no proof," said Georgiana, quietly. "Give me the goblet. I joyfully stake all upon your word."

4 "Drink, then, thou lofty creature!" exclaimed Aylmer, with fervid admiration. "There is no taint of imperfection on thy spirit. Thy sensible frame, too, shall soon be all perfect."

She quaffed the liquid and returned the goblet to his hand.

"It is grateful," said she with a placid smile. "Methinks it is like water from a heavenly fountain; for it contains I know not what of unobtrusive fragrance and deliciousness. It allays a feverish thirst that had parched me for many days. Now, dearest, let me sleep. My earthly senses are closing over my spirit like the leaves around the heart of a rose at sunset."

She spoke the last words with a gentle reluctance, as if it required almost more energy than she could command to pronounce the faint and lingering syllables. Scarcely had they loitered

15. **verdure** [vur'jər]: greenness.

GUIDED READING

LITERAL QUESTIONS

1a. What "one danger" does Georgiana see in the experiment? (that the birthmark will remain)

2a. What does Aylmer say that the potion cannot do? (fail)

INFERENTIAL QUESTIONS

1b. What irony is there in Aylmer's agreeing with her? (He places less value on her life than on his success.)

2b. Why is he so confident? (He has complete faith in science; his intellectual arrogance makes him believe that he can work miracles.)

through her lips ere[16] she was lost in slumber.
1 Aylmer sat by her side, watching her aspect with the emotions proper to a man the whole value of whose existence was involved in the process now to be tested. Mingled with this mood, however, was the philosophic investigation characteristic of the man of science. Not the minutest symptom escaped him. A heightened flush of the cheek, a slight irregularity of breath, a quiver of the eyelid, a hardly perceptible tremor through the frame—such were the details which, as the moments passed, he wrote down in his folio volume. Intense thought had set its stamp upon every previous page of that volume, but the thoughts of years were all concentrated upon the last.

While thus employed, he failed not to gaze often at the fatal hand, and not without a shudder. Yet once, by a strange and unaccountable impulse, he pressed it with his lips. His spirit recoiled, however, in the very act; and Georgiana, out of the midst of her deep sleep, moved uneasily and murmured as if in remonstrance. Again Aylmer resumed his watch. Nor was it without avail. The crimson hand, which at first had been strongly visible upon the marble paleness of Georgiana's cheek, now grew more faintly outlined. She remained not less pale than ever; but the birthmark, with every breath that came and went, lost somewhat of its former distinctness. Its presence had been awful; its departure was more awful still. Watch the stain of the rainbow fading out of the sky, and you will know how that mysterious symbol passed away.

"By Heaven! it is well-nigh gone!" said Aylmer to himself, in almost irrepressible ecstasy. "I can scarcely trace it now. Success! success! And now it is like the faintest rose color. The lightest flush of blood across her cheek would overcome it. But she is so pale!"

2 He drew aside the window curtain and suffered the light of natural day to fall into the room and rest upon her cheek. At the same time he heard a gross, hoarse chuckle, which he had long known as his servant Aminadab's expression of delight.

"Ah, clod! ah, earthly mass!" cried Aylmer, laughing in a sort of frenzy, "you have served me well! Matter and spirit—earth and heaven—have both done their part in this! Laugh, thing of the senses! You have earned the right to laugh."

These exclamations broke Georgiana's sleep. She slowly unclosed her eyes and gazed into the mirror which her husband had arranged for that purpose. A faint smile flitted over her lips when she recognized how barely perceptible was now that crimson hand which had once blazed forth with such disastrous brilliancy as to scare away all their happiness. But then her eyes sought Aylmer's face with a trouble and anxiety that he could by no means account for.

"My poor Aylmer!" murmured she.

"Poor? Nay, richest, happiest, most favored!" exclaimed he. "My peerless bride, it is successful! You are perfect!"

3 "My poor Aylmer," she repeated, with a more than human tenderness, "you have aimed loftily; you have done nobly. Do not repent that with so high and pure a feeling, you have rejected the best the earth could offer. Aylmer, dearest Aylmer, I am dying!"

Alas! it was too true! The fatal hand had grappled with the mystery of life, and was the bond by which an angelic spirit kept itself in union with a mortal frame. As the last crimson tint of the birthmark—that sole token of human imperfection—faded from her cheek, the parting breath of the now perfect woman passed into the atmosphere, and her soul, lingering a moment near her husband, took its heavenward flight. Then a hoarse, chuckling laugh was heard again! Thus ever does the gross fatality of earth exult in its invariable triumph over the immortal essence which, in this dim sphere of half development, demands the completeness of a higher state. Yet, had Aylmer reached a profounder wisdom, he need not thus have flung away the happiness which would have woven his mortal life of the selfsame texture with the celestial. The momentary circumstance was too strong for him; he failed to look beyond the shadowy scope of time, and, living once for all in eternity, to find the perfect future in the present.

16. **ere** [âr]: before.

AT A GLANCE

- As the birthmark begins to fade, Aylmer exults at his success.
- Georgiana awakens and tells Aylmer that she is dying.
- Perfect at last, she dies.

1 IRONY

The test of the value of Aylmer's existence lies not with saving his wife but with proving his experiment.

2 SYMBOL

The light of natural day and Aminadab's laugh (repeated a few paragraphs later) both symbolize the real, natural world.

3 THEME

Georgiana's dying words reflect the theme that life on earth depends upon acceptance of imperfections inherent in nature.

REFLECTING ON THE STORY

Why must Georgiana die as she becomes perfect? (Students may suggest that perfection is not part of human nature and that by making her perfect, Alymer has made Georgiana unfit for life on this earth.)

GUIDED READING

LITERAL QUESTIONS

1a. What characteristic behavior does Aylmer show as Georgiana sleeps? (He examines every symptom at every moment, for the sake of his "philosophic investigation.")

2a. What had Aylmer failed to reach? (profounder wisdom)

INFERENTIAL QUESTIONS

1b. What does this suggest about him? (He is unable to enter fully into the world of feeling.)

2b. If he had reached it, what would it have done for him? (He would have been able to appreciate the essence of life; he would have been able to appreciate the joys of the present moment.)

STUDY QUESTIONS

1. Aylmer can't tolerate hand-shaped birthmark on Georgiana's left cheek; that Aylmer use his scientific knowledge to remove the birthmark; explains that he will implement previously formulated plan to remove the mark
2. *Aminabad*—human physical nature; *Aylmer*—human spiritual element
3. Birthmark fades from Georgiana's cheek, but she dies.
4. *Aylmer*—perfectionism, possibly selfishness; *Georgiana*—trusting, loyal, anxious to please
5. Possible foreshadowing clues: ". . . it may be the stain goes as deep as life itself"; Georgiana's realization of Aylmer's past failures
6. Georgiana's birthmark brings about her death.
7. probably in a negative way; can be inferred from his attitude toward Aylmer's attempts to perfect Georgiana

VIEWPOINT

- Sample statements of moral: Do not expect perfection in the people and things of this world. Even science cannot bring perfection to an imperfect world.
- Story references: "It was the sad confession and continual exemplification . . ."; "Then a hoarse, chuckling laugh was heard again! Thus ever. . . ."
- Opinions of moral will vary.

COMPARING STORIES

Elizabeth's love is conditional; she can't love Hooper while he wears black veil. Georgiana's love is unconditional; she trusts Aylmer with her life. Hooper loves Elizabeth as she is, wants her to accept him as he is with the black veil. Aylmer's love for Georgiana is conditional; he can't accept her with imperfection.

STUDY QUESTIONS

Recalling

1. What conflict do Aylmer and Georgiana face after their marriage? What does Georgiana suggest to resolve the conflict? How does Aylmer react to her suggestion?
2. According to the narrator, what two different aspects of humanity do Aylmer and Aminadab represent?
3. What is the result of Aylmer's attempt to remove Georgiana's birthmark?

Interpreting

4. What character trait do Aylmer's words and actions reveal most strongly? How would you characterize Georgiana?
5. Did you suspect that Georgiana would die before you read the end of the story? At what point did you first suspect it?
6. The title "The Birthmark" could be interpreted as ironic. What irony could it suggest?

Extending

7. How do you think Hawthorne would react to modern scientific attempts to manipulate human, animal, and plant genes? Cite evidence from the story to support your opinion.

VIEWPOINT

In a renowned study of the New England Renaissance, critic F. O. Matthiessen presents his own and Herman Melville's reactions to "The Birthmark":

> Hawthorne's clear-sighted rendering of what was due to both matter and spirit emerges in "The Birthmark," at the end of which Melville wrote, "The moral here is wonderfully fine."
>
> —*American Renaissance*

- What moral did Melville find in Hawthorne's story? State the moral in your own words. Cite parts of the story that suggested the moral to you. Explain why you do or do not agree that the moral is "wonderfully fine."

COMPARING STORIES

- In both "The Minister's Black Veil" and "The Birthmark," Hawthorne presents the love between a man and a woman. Compare and contrast these treatments of human love. Does Elizabeth love Mr. Hooper in the same way Georgiana loves Aylmer? Explain how the love of the two women is similar and/or different. Describe Mr. Hooper's love for Elizabeth, and explain how it resembles or differs from Aylmer's love for Georgiana.

Herman Melville *1819–1891*

"NO! in thunder." This, according to Melville, is what the true writer, the great writer, says. With his own great "NO!" Melville set himself against the optimism of Emerson and the Transcendentalists, challenged conformity, and rejected the idea of progress and prosperity that dominated the American mind in the 1800s.

Born in New York City, Melville was the son of a prosperous merchant who died when Herman was eleven. The boy was forced to leave school when he was twelve; later, unable to find a profession, he became a sailor. His sailing years gave him the background of ships and mutinies and exotic islands that served him well in his early successes, *Typee* (1846) and *Omoo* (1847).

He quickly became a literary celebrity in both England and America, but he refused to continue producing the sort of adventure books the public wanted. At the age of thirty, Melville began a new kind of book, *Moby-Dick,* a whaling story of great complexity and power, meant to rival the work of Shakespeare. Yet it took almost a century before the novel was recognized by more than a handful of readers. The tale of the obsessed hero-villain Captain Ahab and his doomed search for the white whale, Moby Dick, is now regarded as one of the most vital stories available to the American imagination.

However, with the incomprehension that met *Moby-Dick* and the commercial failure of his next two works, *Pierre* and *The Confidence Man,* Melville saw that he could not support his family by writing. Bitter, at times acting in ways that made people think him insane, he was forced to spend twenty years at a routine job in the Custom House in New York City. Even other American writers hardly remembered him, and once when a British admirer tried to find him in New York, no one knew if he was alive or dead. He published some poems, which were ignored by the public, and at his death he left the manuscript of his short novel *Billy Budd.* Generations later, readers began to discover Melville.

Moby-Dick, often considered the greatest American novel, is a masterpiece with many layers. It is a sea adventure, an exciting chase after a destructive and mysterious creature. It is an encyclopedia of the concrete details of nineteenth-century whaling life. It is a psychological portrait of a bitter, crusty, brilliant man aching for vengeance and searching for truth. It is a myth about the place of humankind in the universe.

The portrait of Ahab given here is a sketch of the main character, Captain Ahab, in action. Ishmael, the young sailor who narrates the book, has signed aboard the *Pequod* without ever having met its captain.

■ In this excerpt how does Ahab turn a commercial voyage for whale oil into a personal voyage of vengeance?

AT A GLANCE

- The whaling ship leaves Nantucket in winter and heads south.
- The weather grows warmer.
- Captain Ahab makes his first appearance on deck.

LITERARY OPTIONS

- diction
- characterization
- plot

THEMATIC OPTIONS

- the dangers of single-mindedness
- self-reliance

1 CHARACTERIZATION

Even before he is seen, Ahab exerts a powerful influence on the crew. The speaker's description suggests that Ahab's influence is almost godlike.

2 SETTING

The winter sea and gloomy sky help to set the mood for the story. The ship tightly contains the action.

3 POINT OF VIEW

The first-person narrator is a young and impressionable sailor, watching everything going on around him with a fresh eye. His sense of foreboding helps to set the tone of the story.

Herman Melville

from Moby-Dick

Ahab

For several days after leaving Nantucket, nothing above hatches[1] was seen of Captain Ahab. The mates regularly relieved each other at the watches, and for aught that could be seen to the contrary, they seemed to be the only commanders of the ship; only they sometimes issued from the cabin with orders so sudden and peremptory that, after all, it was plain they but commanded vicariously. Yes,
1 their supreme lord and dictator was there, though hitherto unseen by any eyes not permitted to penetrate into the now sacred retreat of the cabin. . . .

Now, it being Christmas when the ship shot from out her harbor, for a space we had biting polar weather, though all the time running away from it to the southward; and by every degree and minute of latitude which we sailed, gradually leaving that merciless winter and all
2 its intolerable weather behind us. It was one of those less lowering, but still gray and gloomy enough mornings of the transition, when with a fair wind the ship was rushing through the water with a vindictive sort of leaping and melancholy rapidity, that as I mounted to the deck at the call of the fore-
3 noon watch, so soon as I leveled my glance towards the taffrail, foreboding shivers ran over me. Reality outran apprehension; Captain Ahab stood upon his quarter-deck.[2]

There seemed no sign of common bodily illness about him, nor of the recovery from

1. **above hatches:** on deck.

2. **quarter-deck:** rear upper deck, reserved for officers.

GUIDED READING

LITERAL QUESTION

1a. What kinds of orders did the mates sometimes give? (sudden and peremptory)

INFERENTIAL QUESTION

1b. What can you assume about the source of the orders? (They were issued first by the unseen captain, who must have been rather fierce.)

any. He looked like a man cut away from the stake, when the fire has overrunningly wasted all the limbs without consuming them or taking away one particle from their compacted
1 aged robustness. His whole high, broad form seemed made of solid bronze and shaped in an unalterable mold, like Cellini's cast Perseus.[3] Threading its way out from among his gray hairs and continuing right down one side of his tawny scorched face and neck, till it disappeared in his clothing, you saw a slender rodlike mark, lividly whitish. It resembled that perpendicular seam sometimes made in the straight, lofty trunk of a great tree when the upper lightning tearingly darts down it, and, without wrenching a single twig, peels and grooves out the bark from top to bottom ere running off into the soil, leaving the tree still
2 greenly alive, but branded. Whether that mark was born with him, or whether it was the scar left by some desperate wound, no one could certainly say. By some tacit consent, throughout the voyage little or no allusion was made to it, especially by the mates. But once Tashtego's senior, an old Gayhead Indian[4] among the crew, superstitiously asserted that not till he was full forty years old did Ahab become that way branded, and then it came upon him, not in the fury of any mortal fray, but in an elemental strife at sea. Yet this wild hint seemed inferentially negatived by what a gray Manxman[5] insinuated, an old sepulchral man who, having never before sailed out of Nantucket, had never ere this laid eye upon wild Ahab. Nevertheless, the old sea traditions, the immemorial credulities, popularly invested this old Manxman with preternatural powers of discernment. So that no white sailor seriously contradicted him when he said that if ever Captain Ahab should be tranquilly laid out—

3. **Cellini's** [chə lē′nēz] **cast Perseus** [pur′sē əs]: bronze-cast statue of Perseus, a hero of Greek mythology, by Italian sculptor Benvenuto Cellini.
4. **Gayhead Indian:** Indian from Gayhead, a town in Martha's Vineyard, Massachusetts.
5. **Manxman:** native of the Isle of Man, one of the British Isles.

which might hardly come to pass, so he muttered—then whoever should do that last office for the dead would find a birthmark on him from crown to sole.

3 So powerfully did the whole grim aspect of Ahab affect me, and the livid brand which streaked it, that for the first few moments I hardly noted that not a little of this overbearing grimness was owing to the barbaric white leg upon which he partly stood. It had previously come to me that this ivory leg had at sea been fashioned from the polished bone of the
4 sperm whale's jaw. "Aye, he was dismasted off Japan," said the old Gayhead Indian once; "but like his dismasted craft, he shipped another mast without coming home for it. He has a quiver of 'em."

I was struck with the singular posture he maintained. Upon each side of the *Pequod's* quarter-deck, and pretty close to the mizzen shrouds,[6] there was an auger hole bored about half an inch or so into the plank. His bone leg steadied in that hole, one arm elevated, and holding by a shroud, Captain Ahab stood erect, looking straight out beyond the ship's ever-pitching prow. There was an infinity of firmest fortitude, a determinate, unsurrenderable willfulness, in the fixed and fearless forward dedication of that glance. Not a word he spoke; nor did his officers say aught to him, though by all their minutest gestures and expressions, they plainly showed the uneasy, if not painful, consciousness of being under a troubled master-eye. And not only that, but moody stricken Ahab stood before them with a crucifixion in his face, in all the nameless regal overbearing dignity of some mighty woe.

Ere long, from his first visit in the air, he withdrew into his cabin. But after that morning, he was every day visible to the crew, either standing in his pivot hole, or seated upon an ivory stool he had, or heavily walking the deck. As the sky grew less gloomy, indeed, began to grow a little genial, he became still less and less a recluse, as if, when the ship had

6. **shrouds:** sails.

AT A GLANCE

- Ahab bears a mysterious mark, or scar, down his face and neck.
- He wears an artificial leg of ivory.
- With the tip of his peg leg steadied in a hole bored in the deck, he gazes silently out to sea; then he returns to his cabin.

1 DICTION

The comparison of Ahab to a bronze statue emphasizes his hard, unyielding nature.

2 SYMBOL

The scar that he bears makes Ahab both literally and figuratively a "marked man," different from other men. He is set apart, either by having survived an elemental struggle or by fate.

3 POINT OF VIEW

The awe that Ahab elicits in the narrator underscores the captain's commanding presence.

4 CHARACTERIZATION

Ahab's actions after losing his leg—fashioning a leg from whalebone and continuing to sail—suggest his fierce independence and self-reliance.

GUIDED READING

LITERAL QUESTIONS

1a. Of what does the narrator say Ahab seems to be made? (solid bronze)

2a. What does the mark on Ahab's face and neck resemble? (a seam left on a tree by lightning)

INFERENTIAL QUESTIONS

1b. What does this comparison suggest about Ahab? (that he is strong, hard, and uncompromising)

2b. What is significant about the mark? (Its origins are mysterious, and the sailors refuse to discuss the mark, giving rise to superstitious speculation.)

AT A GLANCE

- Ahab becomes a regular, brooding presence on the deck.
- His pacings reach a high pitch.
- He has Starbuck call the crew together; then he addresses them.

1 STYLE: METAPHOR

The brooding expression on Ahab's face is likened to layers of clouds on a mountain peak; by extension, Ahab is compared to a mountain.

2 POINT OF VIEW

The narrator's observations reiterate that Ahab is different from ordinary men.

3 DICTION

The one thought that drives Ahab to pace the deck is given the quality of pacing within his brain. The description suggests a caged animal and thus may identify the kind of thought that drives Ahab.

4 CHARACTERIZATION

Ahab's pacing shows the degree to which his obsession has taken hold of him and propels him.

5 PLOT: RISING ACTION

The steady rhythm of the ship's routine is broken by Ahab's extraordinary order to call the crew together for no apparent reason.

sailed from home, nothing but the dead wintry bleakness of the sea had then kept him so secluded. And, by and by, it came to pass that he was almost continually in the air; but, as yet, for all that he said, or perceptibly did, on the at last sunny deck, he seemed as unnecessary there as another mast. But the *Pequod* was only making a passage now, not regularly cruising; nearly all whaling preparatives needing supervision the mates were fully competent to, so that there was little or nothing out of himself to employ or excite Ahab now, and thus
1 chase away, for that one interval, the clouds that layer upon layer were piled upon his brow, as ever all clouds choose the loftiest peaks to pile themselves upon.

Nevertheless, ere long, the warm, warbling persuasiveness of the pleasant holiday weather we came to seemed gradually to charm him from his mood. For, as when the red-cheeked dancing girls, April and May, trip home to the wintry, misanthropic woods, even the barest, ruggedest, most thunder-cloven old oak will at least send forth some few green sprouts to welcome such glad-hearted visitants; so Ahab did, in the end, a little respond to the playful
2 allurings of that girlish air. More than once did he put forth the faint blossom of a look which, in any other man, would have soon flowered out in a smile.

One morning shortly after breakfast, Ahab, as was his wont, ascended the cabin gangway to the deck. There most sea captains usually walk at that hour, as country gentlemen, after the same meal, take a few turns in the garden.

Soon his steady ivory stride was heard, as to and fro he paced his old rounds, upon planks so familiar to his tread that they were all over dented, like geological stones, with the peculiar mark of his walk. Did you fixedly gaze,
3 too, upon that ribbed and dented brow, there also, you would see still stranger footprints—the footprints of his one unsleeping, ever-pacing thought.

But on the occasion in question, those dents looked deeper, even as his nervous step that morning left a deeper mark. And so full of his thought was Ahab, that at every uniform turn that he made, now at the mainmast and
4 now at the binnacle, you could almost see that thought turn in him as he turned, and pace in him as he paced; so completely possessing him, indeed, that it all but seemed the inward mold of every outer movement.

"D'ye mark him, Flask?" whispered Stubb; "the chick that's in him pecks the shell. 'Twill soon be out."

The hours wore on—Ahab now shut up within his cabin; anon, pacing the deck, with the same intense bigotry of purpose[7] in his aspect.

5 It drew near the close of day. Suddenly he came to a halt by the bulwarks and, inserting his bone leg into the auger hole there, and with one hand grasping a shroud, he ordered Starbuck to send everybody aft.[8]

"Sir!" said the mate, astonished at an order seldom or never given on shipboard except in some extraordinary case.

"Send everybody aft," repeated Ahab. "Mastheads, there! come down!"

When the entire ship's company were assembled, and with curious and not wholly unapprehensive faces were eyeing him, for he looked not unlike the weather horizon when a storm is coming up, Ahab, after rapidly glancing over the bulwarks and then darting his eyes among the crew, started from his standpoint; and as though not a soul were nigh him resumed his heavy turns upon the deck. With bent head and half-slouched hat he continued to pace, unmindful of the wondering whispering among the men; till Stubb cautiously whispered to Flask that Ahab must have summoned them there for the purpose of witnessing a pedestrian feat. But this did not last long. Vehemently pausing, he cried:

"What do ye do when ye see a whale, men?"

7. **bigotry of purpose:** total singlemindedness.
8. **aft:** rear section of a ship.

GUIDED READING

LITERAL QUESTIONS

1a. What does Stubb say to Flask about the Captain's behavior? (". . . The chick that's in him pecks the shell. 'Twill soon be out.")

2a. What order does Ahab give Starbuck? (to send everybody aft)

INFERENTIAL QUESTIONS

1b. What observation about human nature is Stubb making? (Ahab's agitation can be contained only so long; he soon will give the reason for it away.)

2b. Why do you think Ahab wants to assemble the crew? (He probably wants to make an important announcement—one that may reveal the obsession that has been driving him to pace.)

"Sing out for him!" was the impulsive rejoinder from a score of clubbed voices.

"Good!" cried Ahab, with a wild approval in his tones, observing the hearty animation into which his unexpected question had so magnetically thrown them.

"And what do ye next, men?"

"Lower away, and after him!"

"And what tune is it ye pull to, men?"

"A dead whale or a stove[9] boat!"

1 More and more strangely and fiercely glad and approving grew the countenance of the old man at every shout; while the mariners began to gaze curiously at each other, as if marveling how it was that they themselves became so excited at such seemingly purposeless questions.

But they were all eagerness again as Ahab, now half revolving in his pivot hole, with one hand reaching high up a shroud and tightly, almost convulsively, grasping it, addressed them thus:

"All ye mastheaders have before now heard me give orders about a white whale. Look ye! d'ye see this Spanish ounce of gold?"—holding up a broad bright coin to the sun—"It is a sixteen dollar piece, men—a doubloon. D'ye see it? Mr. Starbuck, hand me yon topmaul."

While the mate was getting the hammer, Ahab, without speaking, was slowly rubbing the gold piece against the skirts of his jacket, as if
2 to heighten its luster, and without using any words was meanwhile lowly humming to himself, producing a sound so strangely muffled and inarticulate that it seemed the mechanical humming of the wheels of his vitality in him.

Receiving the topmaul from Starbuck, he advanced towards the mainmast with the hammer uplifted in one hand, exhibiting the gold with the other, and with a high raised voice exclaiming: "Whosoever of ye raises me a white-headed whale with a wrinkled brow and a crooked jaw; whosoever of ye raises me that white-headed whale, with three holes punc-
3 tured in his starboard fluke[10]—look ye, whosoever of ye raises me that same white whale, he shall have this gold ounce, my boys!"

"Huzza! huzza!" cried the seamen, as with swinging tarpaulins they hailed the act of nailing the gold to the mast.

"It's a white whale, I say," resumed Ahab, as he threw down the topmaul; "a white whale. Skin your eyes for him, men; look sharp for white water; if ye see but a bubble, sing out."

4 All this while Tashtego, Daggoo, and Queequeg had looked on with even more intense interest and surprise than the rest, and at the mention of the wrinkled brow and crooked jaw they had started as if each was separately touched by some specific recollection.

"Captain Ahab," said Tashtego, "that white whale must be the same that some call Moby Dick."

"Moby Dick?" shouted Ahab. "Do ye know the white whale then, Tash?"

"Does he fantail[11] a little curious, sir, before he goes down?" said the Gayheader deliberately.

"And has he a curious spout, too," said Daggoo, "very bushy, even for a parmacetty,[12] and mighty quick, Captain Ahab?"

"And he have one, two, tree—oh! good many iron in him hide, too, Captain," cried Queequeg disjointedly, "all twiske-tee be-twisk, like him—him—" faltering hard for a word, and screwing his hand round and round as though uncorking a bottle—"like him—him—"

"Corkscrew!" cried Ahab. "Aye, Queequeg, the harpoons lie all twisted and wrenched in him; aye, Daggoo, his spout is a big one, like a whole shock of wheat, and white as a pile of our Nantucket wool after the great annual sheepshearing; aye, Tashtego, and he fantails like a split jib[13] in a squall. Death and devils!

9. **stove:** smashed.

10. **starboard fluke:** right half of a whale's tail.
11. **fantail:** spread out the tail like a fan.
12. **parmacetty:** dialect for *spermaceti,* a waxlike substance taken from oil in the head of a sperm whale; used to make cosmetics, candles, and other items.
13. **jib:** triangular sail ahead of the mainmast.

AT A GLANCE

- Ahab drills the crew about the procedure for capturing a whale.
- Ahab offers a gold doubloon to the first sailor who signals the sighting of a white whale.
- Tashtego, Daggoo, and Queequeg identify the whale as Moby Dick.

1 CHARACTERIZATION

Ahab's performance demonstrates his exceptional leadership qualities. The men follow him without knowing exactly why.

2 STYLE: FIGURATIVE LANGUAGE

Ahab is portrayed as a man possessed beyond reason, to the point of being propelled by a mechanical force.

3 PLOT: NARRATIVE HOOK

By offering the gold piece and making the hunt for the white whale a contest, Ahab has wiped all questions from the minds of most of the crew.

4 PLOT: RISING ACTION

The reaction of the three crew members is a signal that the whale is known to be a formidable creature. It will therefore be a suitable adversary for Ahab.

GUIDED READING

LITERAL QUESTIONS

1a. How do the mariners feel as Captain Ahab questions them? (excited)

2a. Which sailors seem even more interested than the rest? (Tashtego, Daggoo, and Queequeg)

INFERENTIAL QUESTIONS

1b. What causes this feeling? (They are swept along by the captain's passion and approval.)

2b. Why are they particularly interested? (Each of them apparently has had prior experience with the white whale.)

AT A GLANCE

- Starbuck reveals that Moby Dick caused the loss of Ahab's leg.
- Amidst the crew's excitement Starbuck questions the wisdom of hunting such a whale merely for revenge.
- Ahab asserts that he will never be free until he has succeeded in his quest.

1 PLOT: RISING ACTION

Ahab lays forth his plan for the voyage: He will follow the whale through the worst passages in the ocean and to Hell itself.

2 DICTION

Ahab's passionate address to his crew has him at the brink of losing control. His "God bless ye" suggests that he sees his mission as a holy one.

3 CONFLICT

Against Ahab's obsessive passion, Starbuck offers cool reason. He opposes a voyage for the purpose of vengeance.

4 THEME

This speech, culminating in the line "If man will strike, strike through the mask," may be the most famous single passage in *Moby-Dick*. Ahab's passionate plea expresses one of the novel's central themes: the assertion of human will in the face of cosmic malevolence.

5 SYMBOL

Ahab sees the whale both as a whale and as the embodiment of mindless evil. He hates the physical evil it did to him and is sworn to destroy the creature.

men, it is Moby Dick ye have seen—Moby Dick—Moby Dick!"

"Captain Ahab," said Starbuck, who, with Stubb and Flask, had thus far been eyeing his superior with increasing surprise, but at last seemed struck with a thought which somewhat explained all the wonder. "Captain Ahab, I have heard of Moby Dick—but it was not Moby Dick that took off thy leg?"

"Who told thee that?" cried Ahab; then pausing, "Aye, Starbuck; aye, my hearties all round; it was Moby Dick that dismasted me; Moby Dick that brought me to this dead stump I stand on now. Aye, aye," he shouted with a terrific, loud, animal sob, like that of a heart-stricken moose; "Aye, aye! it was that accursed white whale that razeed[14] me; made a poor pegging lubber[15] of me for ever and a day!" Then tossing both arms, with measureless im-
1 precations he shouted out: "Aye, aye! and I'll chase him round Good Hope, and round the Horn,[16] and round the Norway Maelstrom, and round perdition's flames before I give him up. And this is what ye have shipped for, men! to chase that white whale on both sides of land, and over all sides of earth, till he spouts black blood and rolls fin out. What say ye, men, will ye splice hands on it, now? I think ye do look brave."

"Aye, aye!" shouted the harpooners and seamen, running closer to the excited old man: "A sharp eye for the White Whale; a sharp lance for Moby Dick!"

2 "God bless ye," he seemed to half sob and half shout. "God bless ye, men. Steward! go draw the great measure of grog. But what's this long face about, Mr. Starbuck; wilt thou not chase the white whale? art not game for Moby Dick?"

"I am game for his crooked jaw, and for the jaws of Death too, Captain Ahab, if it fairly comes in the way of the business we follow;
3 but I came here to hunt whales, not my commander's vengeance. How many barrels will thy vengeance yield thee even if thou gettest it, Captain Ahab? it will not fetch thee much in our Nantucket market."

"Nantucket market! Hoot! But come closer, Starbuck; thou requirest a little lower layer. If money's to be the measurer, man, and the accountants have computed their great counting-house the globe, by girdling it with guineas, one to every three parts of an inch; then let me tell thee that my vengeance will fetch a great premium *here!*"

"He smites his chest," whispered Stubb. "What's that for? methinks it rings most vast, but hollow."

"Vengeance on a dumb brute!" cried Starbuck, "that simply smote thee from blindest instinct! Madness! To be enraged with a dumb thing, Captain Ahab, seems blasphemous."

"Hark ye yet again—the little lower layer.
4 All visible objects, man, are but as pasteboard masks. But in each event—in the living act, the undoubted deed—there some unknown but still reasoning thing puts forth the moldings of its features from behind the unreasoning mask. If man will strike, strike through the mask! How can the prisoner reach outside except by thrusting through the wall? To me, the white whale is that wall, shoved near to me. Sometimes I think there's naught beyond. But 'tis enough. He tasks me; he heaps me; I see in him outrageous strength, with an inscrutable
5 malice sinewing it. That inscrutable thing is chiefly what I hate; and be the white whale agent, or be the white whale principal, I will wreak that hate upon him. Talk not to me of blasphemy, man; I'd strike the sun if it insulted me. For could the sun do that, then could I do the other; since there is ever a sort of fair play herein, jealousy presiding over all creations. But not my master, man, is even that fair play. Who's over me? Truth hath no confines. Take off thine eye! More intolerable than fiends'

14. **razeed** [rā zēd′]: removed the upper deck of a ship; here, referring to Ahab's leg.
15. **lubber:** slow, clumsy person.
16. **Good Hope . . . Horn:** the Cape of Good Hope at the southern tip of Africa and Cape Horn at the southern tip of South America.

GUIDED READING

LITERAL QUESTIONS

1a. How do Starbuck, Stubb, and Flask react to Ahab's speech? (with increasing surprise)

2a. What word does Starbuck use to describe Ahab's desire for vengeance? *(blasphemous)*

INFERENTIAL QUESTIONS

1b. What is the reason for this reaction? (They are all experienced and sensible men who expect to hunt whales only for profit.)

2b. Why does he feel this way? (To Starbuck the whale is just a whale; to consider it capable of malice and want revenge on it is, to him, against the natural order of things.)

glarings is a doltish stare! So, so; thou reddenest and palest; my heat has melted thee to anger-glow. But look ye, Starbuck, what is said in heat, that thing unsays itself. There are men from whom warm words are small indignity. I meant not to incense thee. Let it go. Look! see yonder Turkish cheeks of spotted tawn—living, breathing pictures painted by the sun. The Pagan leopards—the unrecking and unworshipping things that live and seek and give no rea-
1 sons for the torrid life they feel! The crew, man, the crew! Are they not one and all with Ahab in this matter of the whale? See Stubb! he laughs! See yonder Chilean! he snorts to think of it. Stand up amid the general hurricane, thy one tossed sapling cannot, Starbuck! And what is it? Reckon it. 'Tis but to help strike a fin; no wondrous feat for Starbuck. What is it more? From this one poor hunt, then, the best lance out of all Nantucket, surely he will not hang back when every foremast hand has clutched a whetstone? Ah! constrainings seize thee; I see! the billow lifts thee! Speak, but speak!—Aye,
2 aye! thy silence, then, *that* voices thee. *(Aside)* Something shot from my dilated nostrils, he has inhaled it in his lungs. Starbuck now is mine, cannot oppose me now without rebellion."

"God keep me!—keep us all!" murmured Starbuck, lowly. But in his joy at the enchanted, tacit acquiescence of the mate, Ahab did not hear his foreboding invocation; nor yet the low laugh from the hold; nor yet the presaging vibrations of the winds in the cordage; nor yet the hollow flap of the sails against the masts, as for a moment their hearts sank in. For again Starbuck's downcast eyes lighted up with the stubbornness of life; the subterranean laugh died away; the winds blew on; the sails filled out; the ship heaved and rolled as before. Ah, ye admonitions and warnings! why stay ye not when ye come? But rather are ye predictions than warnings, ye shadows! Yet not so much predictions from without, as verifications of the foregoing things within. For with little external to constrain us, the innermost necessities in our being, these still drive us on.

STUDY QUESTIONS

Recalling

1. What does Ishmael, the narrator, call Captain Ahab in paragraph 1? How does he describe Ahab's "form" in paragraph 3?
2. What incentive does Ahab offer his crew for sighting the white whale?
3. According to Ahab, what did Moby Dick do to him? What does Ahab claim is the purpose of their voyage?
4. What is Starbuck's first objection to the hunt for Moby Dick? What does he then say seems "blasphemous"?
5. What two qualities does Ahab say he sees in the whale? What does he say about blasphemy?
6. In the last paragraph, what "foreboding invocation" does Ahab not hear? What does Ishmael ask of "admonitions and warnings"?

Interpreting

7. Identify three dominant traits of Ahab's.
8. What do we learn about Ahab's character from his statement, "I'd strike the sun if it insulted me"?
9. What deeper meaning is suggested by Ahab's desire to "strike through the mask" of things?
10. What distinction does Ahab make when he speaks of the whale as "agent" or "principal"? What does he mean by each of these terms?
11. Explain in your own words the observation about human nature that Ishmael makes in the last paragraph.

Extending

12. Why do you think the ocean and its creatures have so often provided writers with material for serious thoughts about time, evil, life, and death?

AT A GLANCE

- Ahab appeals to Starbuck's pride and practicality.
- Starbuck silently acquiesces to the captain's purpose.
- The voyage continues.

1 PLOT: CLIMAX

Ahab wins Starbuck's reluctant cooperation by pointing out that since the crew is with him Starbuck cannot effectively oppose him.

2 ASIDE

In Ahab's murmured aside, ". . . Starbuck now is mine . . ." Melville borrows a technique from drama to provide a rare *direct* glimpse into Ahab's mind.

REFLECTING ON THE SELECTION

How does Ahab's character shape the novel? (Students may suggest that Ahab's personality dominates the crew; he is so charismatic that he can get them to accept his questionable plan.)

STUDY QUESTIONS

1. "supreme lord and dictator"; high, broad, "shaped in an unalterable mold"
2. a gold doubloon
3. removed his leg; kill Moby Dick
4. one whale won't produce much money; anger towards an animal
5. strength, malice; "Talk to me not of blasphemy . . . I'd strike the sun if it insulted me."
6. "God keep me—keep us all!"; why they do not stay
7. vengeful, charismatic, proud
8. unlimited pride and fury
9. He is unwilling to accept limitations; sees himself as a truth-seeker.
10. distinguishes between the whale acting for another power and being the power itself; *agent:* representative; *principal:* prime mover
11. Without external constraints, humans are ruled by inner drives.
12. Possibilities: mystery, danger, timelessness, contrast with transience of human life

VIEWPOINT

The literary critic Richard Chase sees *Moby-Dick* in the light of Emerson's idea of self-reliance:

> It is a book about the alienation from life that results from an excessive . . . self-dependence. . . . As Newton Arvin [another critic] demonstrates, there is some reason to think of Ahab as guilty of *hubris*, in the Greek sense, or of excessive pride, in the Christian sense; but there is more reason to think of him as guilty of or victimized by a distorted "self-reliance."
>
> —*The American Novel and Its Tradition*

■ Discuss Ahab's "distorted 'self-reliance.'" What elements of self-reliance does Ahab take to an extreme? What elements of self-reliance play no part in Ahab's character?

LITERARY FOCUS

Diction

One element of *Moby-Dick* that contributes to its success as a work of art is its extraordinary diction. **Diction** is word choice: It is the use of exactly the right word to fit the character, the meaning, and the tone the writer is trying to achieve.

To define Ahab's remarkable character, Melville gives the captain the vocabulary of a sailor *and* the vocabulary of a Shakespearean hero. Ahab says:

> Aye, Starbuck; aye, my hearties all round; it was Moby Dick that dismasted me. . . . What say ye, men, will ye splice hands on it, now?

Yet Ahab also says:

> All visible objects, man, are but as pasteboard masks. But in each event—in the living act, the undoubted deed—there some unknown but still reasoning thing puts forth the moldings of its features from behind the unreasoning mask.

Ahab's diction reflects his whaler's occupation *(aye, hearties, splice)* and his philosopher's mental struggles *(visible objects, unreasoning mask).*

Thinking About Diction

■ Find two other examples in the selection from *Moby-Dick* in which diction tells something about a character.

VOCABULARY

Denotation and Connotation

Words have both **denotations,** their dictionary definitions, and **connotations,** the associations that they take on in context.

The following phrases are from *Moby-Dick.* Indicate which meaning is suggested, or *connoted,* by each italicized word as it is used in the selection.

1. an old *sepulchral* man:
   (a) entombed (c) gray
   (b) deadly (d) grim
2. the *barbaric* white leg:
   (a) pagan (c) elemental
   (b) crude (d) ornate
3. moody *stricken* Ahab:
   (a) wounded (c) crippled
   (b) slapped (d) tormented
4. like *geological* stones:
   (a) scientific (c) elemental
   (b) old (d) hard
5. vast, but *hollow:*
   (a) loud (c) heartless
   (b) empty (d) large

COMPOSITION

Writing About Character

■ Write a short composition about Ahab or another literary character. Organize your composition by first telling what we learn about the character *directly* from the author. Then tell what we learn *indirectly* from what the character and other characters say and do. Conclude with a general statement about the character.

Writing a Character Sketch

■ Write a brief character sketch of another character in this book or one of your own creation. Allow the character to be revealed both *directly,* by what you tell the reader, and *indirectly,* by the character's own words and actions.

VIEWPOINT

- Ahab takes the following to an extreme: trusts, believes in self; not afraid to speak his mind; refuses to listen to reason; takes on nature; risks others' safety.
- Ahab is not "self-reliant" in the following ways: is not ready to learn from others; is obsessively consistent; does not live in present; sees nature as an enemy.

LITERARY FOCUS

- Speeches of Stubb, Tashtego, Dagoo mark them as sailors.
- Starbuck's argument with Ahab indicates practicality, religious faith.

VOCABULARY

1. (d) grim
2. (b) crude
3. (d) tormented
4. (b) old
5. (b) empty

COMPOSITION: GUIDELINES FOR EVALUATION

WRITING ABOUT CHARACTER

Objective

To analyze a literary character

Guidelines for Evaluation

- suggested length: three to five paragraphs
- should describe those character traits stated directly and those revealed indirectly
- should conclude with a general statement about the character's personality

WRITING A CHARACTER SKETCH

Objective

To describe a character

Guidelines for Evaluation

- suggested length: three to five paragraphs
- should describe a character
- should state some character traits directly
- should reveal other traits indirectly

Henry Wadsworth Longfellow

1807–1882

Longfellow was the best-known of the Fireside Poets and the most successful American poet of his age. *Hiawatha* (1855), for instance, sold about one million copies in his lifetime—a rare achievement for a book of verse. Longfellow was so revered that his seventy-fifth birthday was celebrated in schoolrooms across the land. When he died, a memorial bust was placed in the Poet's Corner of Westminster Abbey in England. He is still the only American so honored.

Born in Maine, Longfellow attended Bowdoin College, where one of his classmates was Nathaniel Hawthorne. He loved languages and became so skilled in them that for most of his life, first at Bowdoin, later at Harvard, he taught a great variety of languages and literatures, even writing his own language textbooks. As a result of his attachment to languages and his broad knowledge of European literature, and through his work as a teacher, anthologist, and poet, Longfellow did much to bring European culture to America.

Longfellow wrote poems on a wide range of subjects, contemporary and historical, and he used many different verse forms and meters with great technical skill. His most famous works, however, are those that bring to life stories from the American past: *Evangeline* (1847), *The Courtship of Miles Standish* (1858), and "Paul Revere's Ride" (1861). Late in life, grieving over his wife's death, Longfellow also translated *The Divine Comedy,* the fourteenth-century epic by the Italian poet Dante. Throughout his life Longfellow wrote noble and elevated verse built around romanticized characters and heroic sentiments. His versatility and enthusiasm won him a large audience, but, more important, he helped to popularize poetry itself in America.

Both "A Psalm of Life" and "The Tide Rises, the Tide Falls" offer large views of life. However, the tone, or poet's attitude, is different in the two poems. In the first the young Longfellow urges us to live vigorously in spite of hardships. In the second the same poet, now older, gazes back on life with a sense of melancholy.

■ How do the following poems about life differ in tone and content? Why might they differ?

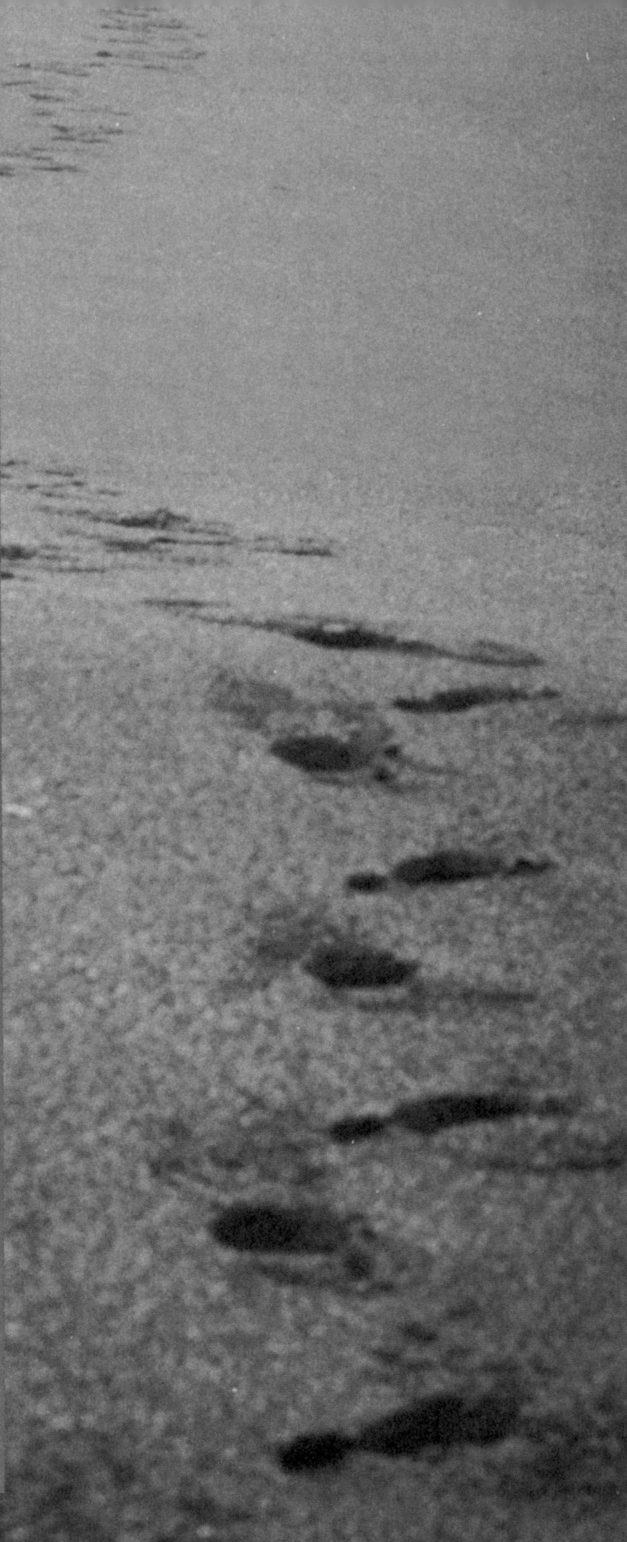

Henry Wadsworth Longfellow

A Psalm of Life

What the Heart of the Young Man Said to the Psalmist

Tell me not, in mournful numbers,[1]
Life is but an empty dream!—
For the soul is dead that slumbers,
And things are not what they seem.

Life is real! Life is earnest!
And the grave is not its goal;
Dust thou art, to dust returnest,
Was not spoken of the soul.

Not enjoyment, and not sorrow,
Is our destined end or way;
But to act, that each tomorrow
Find us farther than today.

Art is long, and Time is fleeting,
And our hearts, though stout and brave,
Still, like muffled drums, are beating
Funeral marches to the grave.

In the world's broad field of battle,
In the bivouac[2] of Life,
Be not like dumb, driven cattle!
Be a hero in the strife!

Trust no Future, howe'er pleasant!
Let the dead Past bury its dead!
Act—act in the living Present!
Heart within, and God o'erhead!

Lives of great men all remind us
We can make our lives sublime,
And, departing, leave behind us
Footprints on the sands of time;

Footprints that perhaps another,
Sailing o'er life's solemn main,[3]
A forlorn and shipwrecked brother,
Seeing, shall take heart again.

1. **numbers:** verses.
2. **bivouac:** temporary camp.
3. **main:** ocean.

AT A GLANCE

Everyone should so live each day as to advance spirituality.

LITERARY OPTIONS

- period idea
- imagery and figurative language

THEMATIC OPTIONS

- the purpose of life
- visions and ideals

SPEAKER

A young man, full of idealism, responds in his heart to the fatalistic view of life as merely a passage to death (l. 1).

PERIOD IDEA

The belief that the purpose of life is to live truly, so as to achieve spiritual growth, is a reflection of Transcendentalist idealism and self-reliance (ll. 11–12).

SIMILE

The comparison of the heartbeat to the drumbeat in a funeral march emphasizes the inevitability of death (ll. 15–16).

IMAGERY

The image of footprints in sand suggests that anyone may, by showing spiritual courage, make enough of an impression to gain some measure of immortality (l. 28).

REFLECTING ON THE POEM

In what way is this poem a "psalm [or song] of life"? (The poem is fervently optimistic and joyful, and its rhythms suggest a song.)

AT A GLANCE

A traveler leaves in the sand footprints that the tide washes away.

LITERARY OPTIONS

- repetition
- personification

THEMATIC OPTIONS

- the transient nature of human events
- the power of Nature

REPETITION

The refrain *The tide rises, the tide falls* mimics the steady, timeless rhythms of Nature.

PERSONIFICATION

The soft white hands of the waves suggest the gentle but purposeful ways in which nature eventually erases the marks left by humans (ll. 8–9). This image and idea directly contrast with the line from "A Psalm of Life" about leaving "footprints on the sands of time."

REFLECTING ON THE POEM

How do the views expressed in this poem differ from those of "A Psalm of Life"? (Students may suggest that this poem expresses less optimism about the impression that an individual can make.)

STUDY QUESTIONS

A Psalm of Life

1. not to be told life is an empty dream; life is real and earnest
2. to go further each day
3. in the living present
4. "We can make our lives sublime."
5. Live in the present, achieve whatever you can.
6. involves risks, difficulties to overcome

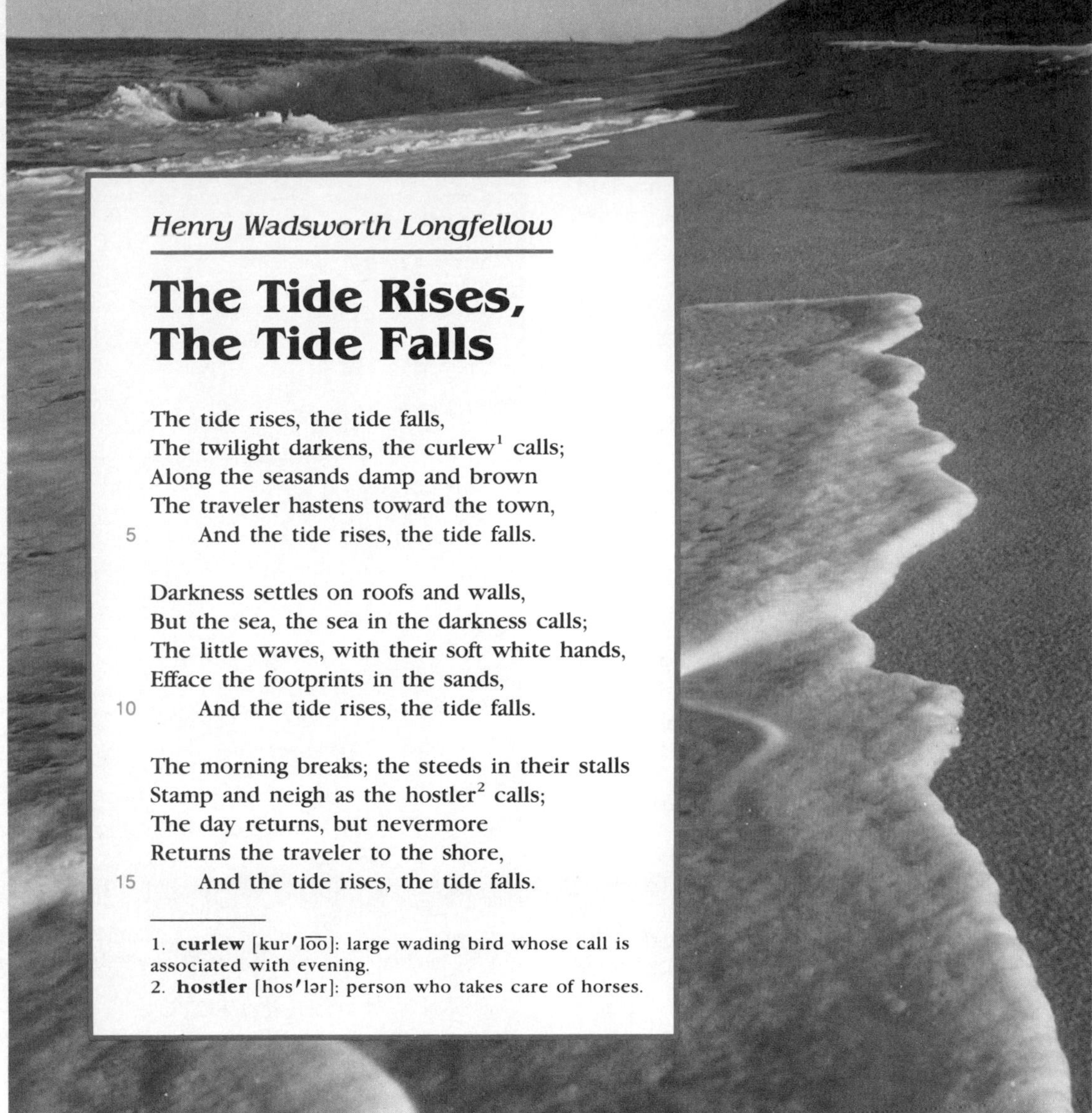

Henry Wadsworth Longfellow

The Tide Rises, The Tide Falls

The tide rises, the tide falls,
The twilight darkens, the curlew[1] calls;
Along the seasands damp and brown
The traveler hastens toward the town,
And the tide rises, the tide falls.

Darkness settles on roofs and walls,
But the sea, the sea in the darkness calls;
The little waves, with their soft white hands,
Efface the footprints in the sands,
And the tide rises, the tide falls.

The morning breaks; the steeds in their stalls
Stamp and neigh as the hostler[2] calls;
The day returns, but nevermore
Returns the traveler to the shore,
And the tide rises, the tide falls.

1. **curlew** [kur′lo͞o]: large wading bird whose call is associated with evening.
2. **hostler** [hos′lər]: person who takes care of horses.

STUDY QUESTIONS

A Psalm of Life

Recalling

1. What demand does the speaker make in lines 1–2? What opinion does he proclaim in line 5?
2. According to stanza 3, what is "our destined end or way"?
3. According to stanza 6, when should we act?
4. What do we learn from the lives of the great, according to stanza 7?

Interpreting

5. In your own words summarize the speaker's advice for living.
6. Why is the image in stanza 5 of a "field of battle" appropriate to the speaker's view of life?

7. Based on the last two stanzas, explain how the speaker feels we can help future generations. To what, specifically, might the image in line 28 refer?

Extending

8. In what respects is Emerson's ideal of self-reliance echoed by the speaker?

The Tide Rises, the Tide Falls

Recalling

1. According to stanza 1, what is the setting (time and place) of the poem?
2. According to stanza 2, what evidence does the traveler leave behind? What happens to this evidence?
3. What line is repeated throughout the poem?
4. What returns in the third stanza? What never returns?

Interpreting

5. Does the action of the tide suggest permanence or impermanence? Explain.
6. What does the poet suggest about nature and about human life in lines 13–14?
7. How does repetition underscore the meaning of the poem?

Extending

8. Longfellow wrote "A Psalm of Life" when he was young and "The Tide Rises, the Tide Falls" when he was old. How do you think the first poem represents the visions and ideals of a young person? What elements in the second poem indicate the view of a mature and experienced person looking back and assessing life?

LITERARY FOCUS

Repetition in Poetry

The most basic device of poetry—the one that gives poetry most of its musical quality—is repetition. It includes not only the repetition of sounds (see page 131) and rhythms but the repetition of words and lines.

Often individual words are repeated in a poem for emphasis. For example, in "The Tide Rises, the Tide Falls" Longfellow repeats the words *tide* and *sea* a number of times, suggesting the importance of these words to the meaning of the poem.

Entire lines may also be repeated in a poem. A repeated line or group of lines is called a **refrain.** Like a musical refrain—the chorus of a song, for example—a poetic refrain occurs at regular intervals. "The tide rises, the tide falls" is both the title and the refrain of Longfellow's poem.

Thinking About Repetition

■ Find and discuss at least two examples of word repetition in "A Psalm of Life." Tell what the repetition contributes to the meaning of the poem.

Rhythm

Rhythm is the arrangement of stressed and unstressed syllables in a poem. When the rhythm forms a regular pattern, it is called **meter** (see page 122).

The rhythm of "The Tide Rises, the Tide Falls" is irregular. For example, the first two lines of the poem swing forward and backward like a pendulum:

> The tide rises, the tide falls,
>
> The twilight darkens, the curlew calls.

This rhythm suits the meaning, suggesting the rise and fall of the tide itself.

The "rising-falling" rhythm is created in part by punctuation, usually a comma, that interrupts certain lines, such as line 1. The resulting pause, a **caesura,** accentuates the "rising" and the "falling" of the line.

Lines 3–4 of the poem have a more regular rhythm, and no comma interrupts their flow:

> Along the seasands damp and brown
>
> The traveler hastens toward the town.

The contrast between the rhythms of the first two lines and the rhythm of the next two lines echoes the contrast between the tide and the traveler that the poet wishes to make.

Sometimes the sense and the grammatical structure of a line flow into the next line, as line 3 flows into line 4. This is a **run-on** line. If a line does not flow on to another line, it is called an **end-stopped line.**

Thinking About Rhythm

■ How does the regular rhythm, or meter, of "A Psalm of Life" echo the meaning of the poem?

A Psalm of Life (*continued*)

7. inspire them through our deeds; art, religion, literature
8. spiritual self-reliance, independence, learning self-reliance from the past, optimism about human capability

The Tide Rises, the Tide Falls

1. twilight on beach near town
2. footprints; washed away
3. "The tide rises, the tide falls."
4. day; the traveler
5. It suggests both the permanence of nature (repetition) and the impermanence of individual life (washing away of footprints).
6. Nature is eternal; human life is fleeting.
7. reinforces idea of ceaseless cycle, in contrast with transient human life
8. Possible answers: The young Longfellow has hope; everything is possible; he will leave mark on world. The old Longfellow is resigned; sees the individual life as too small to leave a lasting mark.

LITERARY FOCUS

Repetition

Life, soul, dust, act, time, footprints; underscore meaning; repeating *life* (l. 5) stresses that life is real by making it sound more positive.

Rhythm

underscores idea that life has a plan or pattern, is not meaningless

Oliver Wendell Holmes *1809–1894*

Like the other Fireside Poets, Oliver Wendell Holmes was a man of extraordinary vitality and versatility. Remembered now as a man of letters, he was also a doctor, a teacher, dean of Harvard Medical School, a lecturer, a reformer, and one of America's greatest conversationalists.

Holmes, a descendant of the Puritan poet Anne Bradstreet (page 30), was born in Cambridge, Massachusetts. He was the class poet at Harvard. He studied law there but grew devoted to medicine, which he traveled to Paris to learn. In 1836, the year he received his M.D., he also published his first collection of poems. Holmes became a professor of medicine at Harvard, where he was immensely popular with his students and deeply respected by his peers as well. Among his many scientific publications was a work that helped lower the fearfully high mortality rate among newborn children.

Many people would be content with such a full and distinguished life. However, Holmes made a second career of literature. He wrote novels and published poetry in periodicals. He helped organize the Saturday Club, a group of writers and scientists who met regularly for conversation. With James Russell Lowell and John Greenleaf Whittier, he helped found the *Atlantic Monthly,* an important literary magazine that printed humorous essays by Holmes and serialized one of his most popular works, *The Autocrat of the Breakfast-Table,* a marvelous collection of wise and witty conversations.

Holmes's lyric poem "Old Ironsides" was inspired by plans to demolish the frigate *Constitution*, which had won important naval battles in the War of 1812. Its sides were not made of iron, but it had so gallantly withstood the assaults of British warships that it had won the nickname Old Ironsides. The poem, published in a Boston newspaper, aroused such protest that Old Ironsides was saved.

"The Chambered Nautilus" reveals Holmes the poet-scientist. The chambered nautilus is a sea mollusk that builds its own pearly shell, chamber by chamber, as it grows. *Nautilus* means "sailor," an appropriate term for this creature: It was once thought to send out a membrane that acted as a sail, enabling it to float across the water in the wind.

■ What particular images do you think stirred the American public to save "Old Ironsides?"

Old Ironsides

Ay, tear her tattered ensign[1] down!
Long has it waved on high,
And many an eye has danced to see
That banner in the sky;
Beneath it rung the battle shout,
And burst the cannon's roar—
The meteor of the ocean air
Shall sweep the clouds no more.

Her deck, once red with heroes' blood,
Where knelt the vanquished foe,
When winds were hurrying o'er the flood,
And waves were white below,
No more shall feel the victor's tread,
Or know the conquered knee—
The harpies[2] of the shore shall pluck
The eagle of the sea!

Oh, better that her shattered hulk
Should sink beneath the wave;
Her thunders shook the mighty deep,
And there should be her grave;
Nail to the mast her holy flag,
Set every threadbare sail,
And give her to the god of storms,
The lightning and the gale!

1. **ensign:** flag.

2. **harpies:** in Greek mythology, hideous winged creatures that carry off the souls of the dead.

U.S.S. Constitution vs. H.M.S. Guerriere, 19 July 1812, Thomas Birch.

AT A GLANCE

- The battleship known as *Old Ironsides,* which has a proud history, is to be dismantled.
- It would be more fitting to allow her a burial at sea.

LITERARY OPTIONS

- metaphor
- personification

THEMATIC OPTIONS

- patriotism
- memory and time

BACKGROUND

The U.S.S. *Constitution* won more battles and sustained less damage than any other American ship in the War of 1812. Condemned as unseaworthy in 1830, she was saved from demolition by the outcry this poem raised.

METAPHOR

The speaker compares the ship to an eagle—a symbol of pride, strength, and America itself (l. 16).

PERSONIFICATION

The conventional use of the pronoun *she* to designate a ship contributes to the impression that the *Constitution* is a human heroine who is being badly treated in her old age. It is this sense that adds poignant power to the poem's closing lines, which suggest a Viking hero being buried at sea (ll. 24–25).

REFLECTING ON THE POEM

What do you think makes this poem particularly effective? (Students may feel that it appeals to basic human emotions of pride, patriotism, and fairness.)

AT A GLANCE

- The speaker looks at an abandoned nautilus shell.
- He considers how the nautilus grew; adding ever-larger compartments.
- He draws an analogy: one should continue to grow spiritually throughout one's life.

LITERARY OPTIONS

- personification
- apostrophe

THEMATIC OPTIONS

- spiritual growth
- the power of Nature

METAPHOR

The comparison of the nautilus to a ship of pearl that sails enchanted seas suggests the fragile beauty of the shell (ll. 1–7).

PERSONIFICATION

The nautilus is portrayed as a patient builder who moves into his new home and seals off the old one (ll. 18–21).

APOSTROPHE

The speaker personifies the nautilus as a child of the sea and addresses it directly (ll. 22–24).

REFLECTING ON THE POEM

In what ways does the poem suggest Transcendentalist ideas? (Students may recognize Transcendentalist thought in the encouragement toward self-reliance and the optimistic belief in spiritual growth.)

Oliver Wendell Holmes

The Chambered Nautilus

This is the ship of pearl, which, poets feign,
  Sails the unshadowed main—
  The venturous bark that flings
On the sweet summer wind its purpled wings
In gulfs enchanted, where the Siren[1] sings,
  And coral reefs lie bare,
Where the cold sea-maids rise to sun their streaming hair.

Its webs of living gauze no more unfurl;
  Wrecked is the ship of pearl!
  And every chambered cell,
Where its dim dreaming life was wont to dwell,
As the frail tenant shaped his growing shell,
  Before thee lies revealed—
Its irised[2] ceiling rent,[3] its sunless crypt unsealed!

Year after year beheld the silent toil
  That spread his lustrous coil;
  Still, as the spiral grew,
He left the past year's dwelling for the new,
Stole with soft step its shining archway through,
  Built up its idle door,
Stretched in his last-found home, and knew the old no more.

Thanks for the heavenly message brought by thee,
  Child of the wandering sea,
  Cast from her lap, forlorn!
From thy dead lips a clearer note is born
Than ever Triton[4] blew from wreathèd horn!
  While on mine ear it rings,
Through the deep caves of thought I hear a voice that sings:

Build thee more stately mansions, O my soul,
  As the swift seasons roll!
  Leave thy low-vaulted past!
Let each new temple, nobler than the last,
Shut thee from heaven with a dome more vast,
  Till thou at length art free,
Leaving thine outgrown shell by life's unresting sea!

---

1. **Siren:** in Greek mythology, a sea goddess whose songs lured sailors to their deaths.
2. **irised:** rainbow-colored.
3. **rent:** torn apart.
4. **Triton** [trī′tən]: in Greek mythology, a sea god with the body of a man and the tail of a fish, usually pictured carrying a conch-shell trumpet.

Shell, photograph by Edward Weston.

STUDY QUESTIONS

Old Ironsides

1. meteor; eagle; heroes' blood
2. to sink in a storm
3. heroism, patriotism, self-reliance
4. is a monument to heroic past; served well, deserves heroic end; demolition insult to noble qualities it symbolizes
5. Humans should die in the battle of life, not in despair and apathy.

The Chambered Nautilus

1. *ship of pearl, venturous bark*
2. chambered cells of the shell
3. old dwelling for new; coiled its way from old cell to new until reaching final home
4. "more stately mansions"
5. beauty, courage, adventurous spirit, self-reliance
6. It has died.
7. Humans must grow and widen horizons until death.
8. Answers will vary, but most students will agree that clear description prepares the reader for the image of the human soul in more stately "mansions" until it is free of its "shell."

LITERARY FOCUS

1. nautilus as "he"; "dreaming life"; sea as "her"
2. ▪ lines 10–14 of "The Rhodora"
   ▪ Yes; it thinks and sleeps.

STUDY QUESTIONS

Old Ironsides

Recalling

1. What image does the poet use to describe Old Ironsides in line 7? In line 16? With what was the deck of the ship once red, according to line 9?
2. According to stanza 3, what does the poet consider a better end for the old battleship?

Interpreting

3. What qualities does the ship seem to symbolize for the poet?
4. Why does the poet oppose the demolition of Old Ironsides?
5. What advice about human life is suggested by the poet's preferred end to the battleship?

The Chambered Nautilus

Recalling

1. Find two phrases in stanza 1 that describe the chambered nautilus.
2. What "lies revealed" in stanza 2?
3. According to stanza 3, what did the nautilus leave year after year? Summarize the process it followed.
4. According to stanzas 4 and 5, what does the voice from the "deep caves of thought" tell the poet's soul to build?

Interpreting

5. What qualities are attributed to the chambered nautilus through the images of stanza 1?
6. What has happened to the nautilus in stanza 2?
7. According to stanza 5, what lessons about human life does the poet learn by observing the nautilus?
8. Do the details in stanza 3 prepare the reader for the comparison made in the last stanza? Explain.

LITERARY FOCUS

Personification and Apostrophe

Personification is a figure of speech in which human qualities are given to objects, animals, and ideas. Holmes personifies Old Ironsides when he says that it "No more shall feel the victor's tread." Of course, he does not mean this literally; a ship cannot really feel anything. However, through personification, Holmes convinces us for a moment that this old battleship has courage, pride, and, probably, emotions as well. We believe with him that Old Ironsides has undergone the struggles of war and deserves the respect we would give a hero.

Personification can be a powerful and moving device, because it appeals to our *human* nature. Naturally, we sympathize more readily with something that is human—and therefore like us—than with something nonhuman. Personification enables the poet to bring us one step closer to the subject. Often this device makes reading the poem a more dramatic and compelling experience.

A literary device related to personification is **apostrophe,** in which a poet directly addresses an inanimate object, an idea, or an absent person. Holmes's address to the chambered nautilus is an example of apostrophe. For centuries the most common apostrophe was the poet's address to the Muse of Poetry.

Thinking About Personification and Apostrophe

1. Find an example of personification in "The Chambered Nautilus."
2. Find an example of apostrophe in one of Emerson's poems. Does Emerson also personify the thing he addresses? Explain.

COMPOSITION

Writing About Personification

▪ Write a short essay discussing Holmes's use of personification in "The Chambered Nautilus." First identify the human qualities given to the nautilus. Then tell why they are appropriate to the poet's subject. Conclude with your comments on the emotions aroused in the reader by this use of personification.

Writing a Personification

▪ Select an object—something you own or see around you—and compose a short essay or poem in which you personify that object. You might, for example, tell what the object "sees," "hears," "feels," what it "thinks" or "regrets" or "desires."

COMPOSITION: GUIDELINES FOR EVALUATION

WRITING ABOUT PERSONIFICATION

Objective

To analyze the use of personification in a poem

Guidelines for Evaluation

- suggested length: three to five paragraphs
- should name the specific human qualities given to the nautilus
- should tell how qualities relate to theme
- should note how the use of personification affects the reader's emotions

WRITING A PERSONIFICATION

Objective

To write an essay or poem using personification

Guidelines for Evaluation

- suggested length: two to four paragraphs, six to twelve lines
- should use human traits to describe an object
- should attribute senses, emotions to object
- should choose human traits in some way appropriate to the object

James Russell Lowell *1819–1891*

James Russell Lowell was perhaps the most gifted of the Fireside Poets. He was a critic, journalist, reformer, teacher, editor, lecturer, and diplomat, as well as a poet and a wit. With Longfellow and Holmes, Lowell was one of the "Brahmins"—the name of the highest caste of Indian society, which Holmes applied to the Boston aristocracy.

Like the other Fireside Poets, Lowell lived long and accomplished much. He grew up in Cambridge, Massachusetts. A student of law at Harvard, he discovered that he greatly preferred literature. Two collections of poetry, a volume of literary essays, and some journalistic work supporting the antislavery movement established him as a noted writer by the age of twenty-seven.

Three of Lowell's best-known poetic works appeared in 1848. *The Vision of Sir Launfal* is a romantic epic about knighthood, influenced by the King Arthur legends. *A Fable for Critics* contains sharp satiric portraits of the writers of the day, including Lowell himself. *The Biglow Papers* is a collection of poems and letters, featuring a down-to-earth character named Hosea Biglow, whose clever observations are delivered in a humorous rural New England dialect.

In 1855 Lowell succeeded Longfellow as professor of modern languages at Harvard, where he taught until 1872. With Holmes and others he helped found the *Atlantic Monthly,* serving as its first editor, and co-edited the *North American Review.* Under his guidance both of these publications gained literary and intellectual prominence. Later, as the U.S. ambassador to Spain, and then to Great Britain, Lowell became a popular spokesperson for democracy.

"Auspex", which appears on the following page, reveals Lowell's lyric gift. In it he draws an extended comparison between nature's songbirds and his own poems. An "auspex," in Ancient Rome, was someone who watched for omens in the flights of birds.

■ How are songbirds and the poem alike?

AT A GLANCE

The poet compares his heart to a desolate nest from which songbirds have flown.

LITERARY OPTIONS

- speaker
- symbol

THEMATIC OPTIONS

- the transience of poetic inspiration
- visions and ideals

SPEAKER

The voice is that of a poet lamenting the loss of poetic inspiration. He represents himself as an auspex, a Roman seer who read omens in the flight of birds (l. 1).

SYMBOL

The empty nest symbolizes the loss of poetic inspiration, when the poet's heart seems filled not with song, but with dryness and cold: "dead leaves and snow" (ll. 3–6).

REFLECTING ON THE POEM

In what way is the poet an auspex, or reader of omens in the flight of birds? (Students may suggest that he foresees a time when the birds will leave and not return, that is, when he will lose his poetic inspiration.)

STUDY QUESTIONS

1. a nest with songbirds in it
2. dead leaves and snow
3. swallows; no longer feels impatience of birds' wings
4. "sweet delusion"; wild confusion of leaves covers the poet and his song
5. poems; poet, reading omen in flight of "birds"; departure of poetic inspiration
6. losing them less painful; no; poet finds songbirds wonderful, stresses how terrible their loss would be to him
7. - Momentary hovering of leaves implies they will not cover poet and song; because poems exist for the moment, poet has delusion that poetic inspiration will last forever.
   - Unpleasant forces or events in life, the poet's death, and the transience of human accomplishments—all suggested by the brown leaves—will smother poetic inspiration.

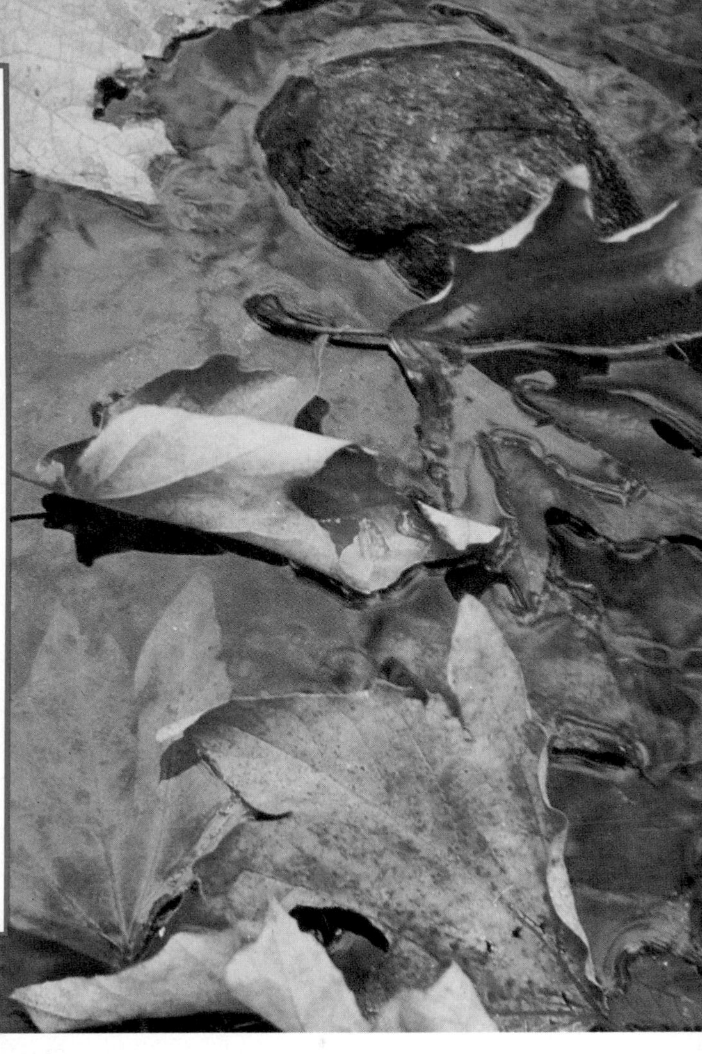

James Russell Lowell

Auspex

My heart, I cannot still it,
Nest that had songbirds in it;
And when the last shall go,
The dreary days, to fill it,
Instead of lark or linnet,[1]
Shall whirl dead leaves and snow.

Had they been swallows only,
Without the passion stronger
That skyward longs and sings—
Woe's me, I shall be lonely
When I can feel no longer
The impatience of their wings!

A moment, sweet delusion,
Like birds the brown leaves hover;
But it will not be long
Before their wild confusion
Fall wavering down to cover
The poet and his song.

1. **linnet:** small songbird.

STUDY QUESTIONS

Recalling

1. To what does the poet compare his heart in lines 1–2?
2. According to stanza 1, what will whirl in the poet's heart when the last bird has gone?
3. According to stanza 2, what birds do not fill the poet's heart? What will make the poet "lonely"?
4. What does the poet call the moment in which the birds hover? What does he say "will not be long" in happening?

Interpreting

5. What do the songbirds represent? What does the auspex represent? What is suggested by the image of the songbirds leaving the nest in the first stanza?
6. Why does the poet say that he wishes his "birds" had been ordinary swallows instead of songbirds? Does he really mean what he says? Explain.
7. Explain the "sweet delusion" in line 13. What does the poet say will occur to dispel his delusion?

John Greenleaf Whittier *1807–1892*

Like the other Fireside Poets—Longfellow, Holmes, and Lowell—John Greenleaf Whittier won fame and reverence during a long career. He was not only honored by his peers but also beloved by the nation at large. His poems were recited by students, and his books were found on the shelves of countless American homes. In 1877 the *Atlantic Monthly* celebrated Whittier's seventieth birthday with a dinner attended by virtually every noteworthy living American author. His eightieth birthday was the occasion for a national celebration.

Unlike the other Fireside Poets, however, Whittier rose from markedly humble beginnings. He grew up on a Massachusetts farm, situated on land an ancestor had cleared in 1648. Although he later idealized his boyhood in his most famous poem, *Snow-Bound,* his life on the farm was often difficult. Hard work took its toll on his health, and he later suffered from periodic physical breakdowns. His upbringing was modest in another way: His family were Quakers, whose basic principles were piety, plainness, simplicity, and love of social justice. These ideals were ever after the hallmarks of Whittier's life and his poetry.

Whittier vigorously opposed slavery. Encouraged by his lifelong friend, the abolitionist William Lloyd Garrison, he threw himself into the antislavery movement with uncommon devotion—principally as a newspaper writer and editor. In 1835 he and another abolitionist were attacked during a lecture tour in New Hampshire. Miraculously, they made their way through a barrage of gunfire and escaped unhurt.

As a poet Whittier matured late in life. Having remained a simple man with down-to-earth tastes, he wrote increasingly about what he loved best: rural America, with its local traditions, customs, and close-knit family life. *Snow-Bound* (1866), in which the poet recalls his boyhood on the farm, takes place before the time of telephones, snowplows, and snowmobiles. When a blizzard struck, the farm was instantly isolated. Outdoors was a world transformed by the miracle of snow; inside were warmth and family life, with its deep affections and simple pleasures. *Snow-Bound* is a poem of memory, a vision of youth, suggesting that the poet was remembering a kind of life that, even then, was passing away. Parts of *Snow-Bound* appear on the following pages.

■ What details help you to "see" the family as snowbound?

The engravings on pages 224–226 are from an 1874 edition of *Snow-Bound.*

AT A GLANCE

- The sky foretells the coming storm.
- The snow continues all night and through the next day.
- The watchers look out on an unfamiliar world.

LITERARY OPTIONS

- imagery
- metaphor
- personification

THEMATIC OPTIONS

- the intimacy of rural isolation
- family portraits
- memory and time

VOCABULARY: WORD CHOICE

The words *cheerless, gray, darkly, sadder,* and *waning* all suggest the foreboding that accompanies awareness of an approaching storm (ll. 2–4).

IMAGERY

Swarm and *whirl-dance* suggest that the storm is like something alive, full of swirling vigor (ll. 17–18).

SPEAKER

SPEAKER

The use of the pronouns *we* and *our* shows the speaker's feeling of unity with the others who are sharing the experience (ll. 32–33).

John Greenleaf Whittier

from Snow-Bound

The Storm

The sun that brief December day
Rose cheerless over hills of gray,
And, darkly circled, gave at noon
A sadder light than waning moon.
Slow tracing down the thickening sky
Its mute and ominous prophecy,
A portent seeming less than threat,
It sank from sight before it set.
A chill no coat, however stout,
Of homespun stuff could quite shut out,
A hard, dull bitterness of cold,
  That checked, mid-vein, the circling race
  Of lifeblood in the sharpened face,
The coming of the snowstorm told.

• • •

Unwarmed by any sunset light
The gray day darkened into night,
A night made hoary[1] with the swarm
And whirl-dance of the blinding storm,
As zigzag wavering to and fro
Crossed and recrossed the wingèd snow:
And ere the early bedtime came
The white drift piled the window frame,
And through the glass the clothesline posts
Looked in like tall and sheeted ghosts.

The First Morning

So all night long the storm roared on:
The morning broke without a sun;
In tiny spherule[2] traced with lines
Of Nature's geometric signs,
In starry flake, and pellicle,[3]
All day the hoary meteor fell;
And, when the second morning shone,
We looked upon a world unknown,
On nothing we could call our own.
Around the glistening wonder bent
The blue walls of the firmament,
No cloud above, no earth below—
A universe of sky and snow!
The old familiar sights of ours
Took marvelous shapes; strange domes and towers

---

1. **hoary** [hôr′ē]: white.
2. **spherule** [sfer′o͞ol]: small sphere.
3. **pellicle:** thin film.

GUIDED READING

LITERAL QUESTION

1a. According to "The First Morning," on what does the family look out after the snow has fallen? ("On nothing we could call our own")

INFERENTIAL QUESTION

1b. What does the speaker mean when he says that "We looked . . . /On nothing we could call our own"? (The world is so transformed by the snow that even the family's own land and home are no longer recognizable.)

Rose up where sty or corncrib stood,
Or garden wall, or belt of wood;
A smooth white mound the brushpile showed,
A fenceless drift what once was road;
The bridle post an old man sat
With loose-flung coat and high cocked hat;
The well curb had a Chinese roof;
And even the long sweep,[4] high aloof,
In its slant splendor, seemed to tell
Of Pisa's leaning miracle.[5]
A prompt, decisive man, no breath
Our father wasted: "Boys, a path!"
Well pleased (for when did farmer boy
Count such a summons less than joy?)
Our buskins[6] on our feet we drew;
  With mittened hands, and caps drawn low,
  To guard our necks and ears from snow,
We cut the solid whiteness through.
And, where the drift was deepest, made
A tunnel walled and overlaid
With dazzling crystal: we had read
Of rare Aladdin's[7] wondrous cave,
And to our own his name we gave,
With many a wish the luck were ours
To test his lamp's supernal[8] powers.

The Hearth at Night

The moon above the eastern wood
Shone at its full; the hill range stood
Transfigured in the silver flood,
Its blown snows flashing cold and keen,
Dead white, save where some sharp ravine
Took shadow, or the somber green
Of hemlocks turned to pitchy black
Against the whiteness at their back.
For such a world and such a night
Most fitting that unwarming light,
Which only seemed where'er it fell
To make the coldness visible.
Shut in from all the world without,
We sat the clean-winged hearth[9] about.
Content to let the north wind roar

4. **sweep:** pole with a bucket at one end, used to raise water from a well.
5. **Pisa's** [pē′zəz] **leaning miracle:** the famous Leaning Tower of Pisa, Italy.
6. **buskins:** high, laced, leather boots.

7. **Aladdin:** boy in the *Arabian Nights* who found treasures in a cave with the aid of a magic lamp.
8. **supernal:** supernatural.
9. **clean-winged hearth:** The hearth was cleaned with a broom made from a turkey's wing.

AT A GLANCE

- The viewers see fanciful sights in the drifted snow.
- They tunnel a path through huge drifts.
- At night, they sit around the hearth.

IMAGERY

The images that the children see in the snow reveal lively imaginations and dramatize the foreignness of a snow-covered landscape (ll. 44–49).

RESPONSE JOURNAL

Ask students to comment on the effect of Whittier's allusion to Aladdin's magical cave in describing the tunnel that the boys made (ll. 60–64).

IMAGERY

The image of "dazzling crystal" walls and ceiling captures the clear, icy coldness of the snowy world (l. 60).

IMAGE PATTERN

The stark contrast of white snow with black-appearing evergreen trees in the moonlight emphasizes the harsh cold (ll. 69–72).

GUIDED READING

LITERAL QUESTION

1a. What images of foreign lands does the family fancy that they see? (a Chinese pagoda, the Leaning Tower of Pisa)

INFERENTIAL QUESTION

1b. What does the fact that they see such images suggest about this rural American family? (Although they may be isolated physically from the world, they have read a great deal and have vivid imaginations.)

AT A GLANCE

- The speaker recalls the warm security of the firelit family hearth.
- All the family but the poet's brother have since died.
- The speaker has faith that he will meet them again.

PERSONIFICATION

The representation of the chimney as a great laughing throat conveys the speaker's sense of great happiness (ll. 85–86).

IMAGERY

Simmering cider and sputtering apples evoke both the sounds and smells of the fireside (ll. 93–94).

MAIN IDEA

The poet expresses optimism and faith by asserting that loved ones are not lost while those who loved them live and remember them (ll. 119–120).

REFLECTING ON THE POEM

How do Whittier's images of cold and warmth reinforce the meaning of the poem? (Students may suggest that the warmth of the hearth symbolizes the warmth of the family gathered around it, whereas the cold represents an outside, possibly uncaring world.)

In baffled rage at pane and door,
While the red logs before us beat
The frost line back with tropic heat;
And ever, when a louder blast
Shook beam and rafter as it passed,
The merrier up its roaring draft
The great throat of the chimney laughed.
The house dog on his paws outspread
Laid to the fire his drowsy head,
The cat's dark silhouette on the wall
A couchant[10] tiger's seemed to fall;
And, for the winter fireside meet,
Between the andirons' straddling feet,
The mug of cider simmered slow,
The apples sputtered in a row,
And, close at hand, the basket stood
With nuts from brown October's wood.
What matter how the night behaved?
What matter how the north wind raved?
Blow high, blow low, not all its snow
Could quench our hearthfire's ruddy glow.
O Time and Change!—with hair as gray
As was my sire's that winter day,
How strange it seems, with so much gone
Of life and love, to still live on!
Ah, brother![11] only I and thou
Are left of all that circle now—
The dear home faces whereupon
That fitful firelight paled and shone.

• • •

Yet Love will dream, and Faith will trust,
(Since He who knows our need is just)
That somehow, somewhere, meet we must.
Alas for him who never sees
The stars shine through his cypress trees!
Who, hopeless, lays his dead away,
Nor looks to see the breaking day
Across the mournful marbles[12] play!
Who hath not learned, in hours of faith,
The truth to flesh and sense unknown,
That Life is ever lord of Death,
  And Love can never lose its own!

10. **couchant** [kou′chənt]: lying down.

11. **brother:** the poet's brother, Matthew Whittier (1812–1883).
12. **marbles:** marble tombstones.

GUIDED READING

LITERAL QUESTION

1a. What does the speaker describe immediately before the line *O Time and Change*? (the happiness and warmth of the snowbound family around its own hearth)

INFERENTIAL QUESTION

1b. How does the speaker's tone change at this point? (The speaker shifts from reveling in the warm memories of his childhood to a quiet, bittersweet reflection on age and loss and a touching hope for reunion of the family after death.)

STUDY QUESTIONS

Recalling

1. In the section "The Storm," what details of the sunrise and the sunset foretell the storm?
2. How does the poet describe his father in the section "The First Morning"? What does the father tell the boys to do?
3. According to lines 98–100, what can the north wind not quench?
4. What does the poet address in line 101? What does he say seems strange?
5. According to the last three lines, what truth does the poet say he has learned?

Interpreting

6. What can you tell about the father's relationship to the children from lines 50–53?
7. In the section "The Hearth at Night," what emotions does Whittier suggest his family felt as they sat around the hearth?
8. State in your own words the poet's ideas about life, death, and change expressed in the final lines of the poem.

Extending

9. Whittier's memory of his boyhood is primarily a happy one. Do you think Whittier is justified in omitting the dangerous and more difficult aspects of a great winter blizzard?

LITERARY FOCUS

Imagery

Imagery is a collection of mental pictures. Although visual imagery is the most common, it is important to remember that an image can appeal to any of our physical senses. For example, Whittier uses many images of what the storm looks like. But when he writes that "all night long the storm roared on," he also suggests what the storm sounds like—perhaps a menacing beast.

A poet can suggest to our imagination a particular sight, sound, smell, taste, or feeling. Much of the pleasure of reading poetry comes from our enjoyment of images, which may be astonishing and lovely in themselves. Moreover, effective images stimulate us to consider familiar things in new ways.

Thinking About Imagery

■ Find three other images in this selection from *Snow-Bound.* At least one of these images should appeal to a sense other than sight. Describe each image in your own words, and tell what purpose it serves in the poem.

VOCABULARY

Vivid Adjectives

The beauty of Whittier's images stems in part from his careful choice of adjectives. Define each of these adjectives, *as it is used in the poem.* Then write an original sentence for each, in which you use the adjective to create an image.

1. waning (line 4)
2. ominous (line 6)
3. hoary (line 17)
4. supernal (line 64)
5. ruddy (line 100)

COMPOSITION

Writing About Imagery

■ *Snow-Bound* encompasses in its imagery many changes of scene and a variety of moods. In an essay tell how Whittier evokes contrasting emotions by using contrasting images. First tell which images describe light, which images describe darkness, and what emotional response the poet has to each image. Then do the same thing for the images of cold and warmth. Conclude with a comment about your own response to the images.

Writing a Remembrance

■ In either prose or verse, compose your own recollection of an experience or a time that was important in your life. Fill your description with sharp images that suggest what the experience or time meant to you then. End your composition, as Whittier does, with a comment about it from your point of view today.

COMPARING WRITERS

■ In the selections in this unit, Longfellow, Holmes, Lowell, and Whittier reveal their profound concern with the passage of time. Based on the poems you have read, tell what at least two of these poets have to say about time. What attitudes and emotions do these poets share?

STUDY QUESTIONS

1. cheerless sunrise; early sunset
2. prompt, decisive; shovel a path
3. hearthfire's ruddy glow
4. "Time and Change"; to live on when so much of life is gone
5. "Life is ever lord of Death, / And Love can never lose its own!"
6. Children respect and obey him.
7. love, happiness, security
8. recognizes difficulty of accepting change, particularly death; has faith we meet dead loved ones when we die; that dead live on in our memories
9. Answers will vary. Students should see that Whittier is not aiming at realism.

LITERARY FOCUS

"darkly circled" sun: gray sky with one spot of brightness, foretells coming storm; *"unwarming light":* moon on landscape, feeling of coldness; *"louder blast" of wind:* sound of wind and shaking of house, contrast with warm, peaceful scene around the hearth

VOCABULARY

1. gradual decrease (lunar cycle)
2. foreboding of evil; threatening
3. white, as from age
4. supernatural; heavenly
5. reddish; rosy

Sentences will vary.

COMPARING WRITERS

Longfellow: stresses present, optimism about future; resignation; *Holmes:* keep past alive; stresses present, optimism; *Whittier:* past preserved by love, memory; *Lowell:* resignation, great sadness

COMPOSITION: GUIDELINES FOR EVALUATION

WRITING ABOUT IMAGERY

Objective

To analyze contrasting images

Guidelines for Evaluation

- suggested length: five to eight paragraphs
- should describe poet's response to images of light and dark, cold and warmth
- should describe their own emotional responses to these images
- should recognize contrast in images

WRITING A REMEMBRANCE

Objective

To write about a remembered experience

Guidelines for Evaluation

- suggested length: four to six paragraphs, ten to thirty lines
- should describe an experience
- should use sharp images to convey emotions
- should conclude with a comment explaining present feelings about experience

ACTIVE READING

The Sound of Poetry

Extend the last paragraph on this page by asking students to prepare for oral presentation a poem or a portion of a poem in the student textbook. Tell students to consider the meanings of the individual words, the places to pause, and the overall tone of the poem—thoughtful, ironic, mysterious, joyous, and so on. Remind them to avoid a sing-song monotony.

ACTIVE READING

The Sound of Poetry

Poems began with the human voice singing or chanting. Now that we *see* most poems in print rather than *hear* them recited, we can easily forget that one of the pleasures of poetry is the sound it makes.

Perhaps we should say: the sound we make *for* it, or *of* it. A printed poem, like a musical score, is only an indication of what can happen in "performance," even if we are reading silently. Yet the sound of poetry is not pure like the sound of a piano: It is part of the words. When we read a poem, we do not want the sense to overwhelm the verse; we do not want the verse to overwhelm the sense.

Look at the rhythm of Whittier's *Snow-Bound,* for example. Possible heavy or long pauses are marked with //, and light or short pauses with /. Try these lines, taking no pause at all or just the hint of a pause at the ends of lines, unless a pause is indicated:

The moon / above the eastern wood /
Shone at its full; // the hill range stood
Transfigured in the silver flood, /
Its blown snows flashing / cold and keen, /
Dead white, // save where some sharp ravine
Took shadow, / or the somber green
Of hemlocks turned to pitchy black /
Against the whiteness at their back. //

You may disagree with this phrasing; the point, however, is that we can avoid a monotonous sing-song:

The MOON aBOVE the EASTern WOOD
Shone AT its FULL; the HILL range STOOD

—and so forth. There are subtler and more pleasant rhythms than that. At the same time we do not want to turn the poem into prose. Whittier did not write: "The moon above the eastern wood shone at its full; the hill range stood transfigured in the silver flood. . . ."

All poems do not sound alike, although the poems of a single poet do sometimes take on the "voice" of that poet. Find a "music" appropriate to some poems. Lowell's "Auspex" would be a good candidate. Allow the English language to have its natural way, but allow the verse to have its way as well.

THE AMERICAN VOICE

Self-Reliance

Self-reliance in all its forms seems always to have been a part of American culture. During the New England Renaissance, however, it was given special attention and special expression.

Emerson
Trust thyself: every heart vibrates to that iron string. Accept the place the divine providence has found for you. . . . Speak what you think now in hard words, and tomorrow speak what tomorrow thinks in hard words again, though it contradict everything you said today. . . . To be great is to be misunderstood.

Thoreau
In most books, the I, *or first person, is omitted; in this it will be retained; that, in respect to egotism, is the main difference. We commonly do not remember that it is, after all, always the first person that is speaking. I should not talk so much about myself if there were anybody else whom I knew as well. . . . If a man does not keep pace with his companions, perhaps it is because he hears a different drummer. Let him step to the music which he hears, however measured or far away.*

Hawthorne
"Oh, you know not how lonely I am and how frightened to be alone behind my black veil."

Melville
"He tasks me; he heaps me; I see in him outrageous strength, with an inscrutable malice sinewing it. That inscrutable thing is chiefly what I hate; and be the white whale agent, or be the white whale principal, I will wreak that hate upon him. Talk not to me of blasphemy, man; I'd strike the sun if it insulted me."

Longfellow
Be not like dumb, driven cattle! Be a hero in the strife!

As a true American idea self-reliance has withstood the extremes of optimism and pessimism. It has lifted some people to glorious visions and, when distorted, isolated some people to the point of destruction. It has been the basis for a great variety of philosophical ideas, and it has inspired many political thinkers. Every period of American literature, every unit in this book, reveals in some way that self-reliance is an idea continually defining and redefining the American imagination.

Key to Illustrations on Pages 152–153.

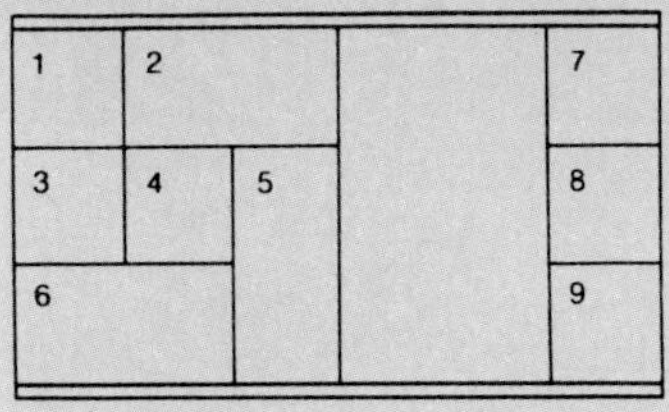

1. Ralph Waldo Emerson, photographer unknown, c. 1855.
2. *Gold Mining in California,* print by Currier and Ives, 1871.
3. Inventor Isaac Singer demonstrating his sewing machine, engraving, c. 1853.
4. The power of newspapers, painting, artist unknown, c. 1846.
5. Nineteenth-century weather vane in the form of Columbia, personification of America.
6. *The Whale Fishery,* print by Currier and Ives, c. 1845.
7. *Nathaniel Hawthorne,* Charles Osgood, 1840.
8. Illustration from the title page of Henry David Thoreau's *Walden,* original 1854 edition.
9. Henry David Thoreau, daguerreotype (early photograph) by Benjamin D. Maxham, 1856.

Self-Reliance

After the students have read this page, you might have them consider the theme of self-reliance as it is displayed in other periods of American history and literature. Elicit that self-reliance is evident in the lives and writings of the early explorers, such as Columbus and John Smith, and that it was an important idea of the Age of Reason, apparent in the writings of Franklin, Jefferson, Bartram, and Crèvecoeur, among others. Point out that the typical hero of the American frontier—whether fictional, like Cooper's Deerslayer, or real, like Daniel Boone—was a highly self-reliant individual and that the self-made businessman or businesswoman is another, more recent manifestation.

Key to Illustrations appears on page 307.

CONFLICT AND CELEBRATION

1855–1880

Near the middle of the nineteenth century, the American showman P. T. Barnum returned from a tour of Europe. The young poet Walt Whitman, then working as a reporter for the Brooklyn *Eagle,* interviewed Barnum and asked him if seeing Europe made him less impressed with America. "No! Not a bit of it!" cried Barnum. "Why, sir, you can't imagine the difference. There everything is frozen—kings and *things*—formal, but absolutely frozen: here it is *life.*"

Like so many other Americans, Barnum was aware that America was indeed flourishing and full of life. The transplantings from Europe of people, customs, and ideas had been successful. The roots had taken hold; what had been foreign had become native. Full of confidence, Americans were envisioning a nation that would reach from sea to sea. The explorations of Lewis and Clark had spurred the idea of that destiny, and thousands of men and women moved westward to homestead, enduring hardship and danger because they saw the limitless possibilities of making new lives on the American land.

At the same time that the westward expansion was beginning, the United States and the Constitution met their sternest test. That test, the Civil War, divided America against itself for the first time. It tore apart the carefully woven fabric of the *united* states.

INTRODUCTION

The Civil War was America's first "modern" war. It featured, among other things, massive popular mobilization, artillery bombardment of civilians, and the use of repeating rifles. The population in the North had been bolstered by immigrants who came to America in the wake of the Irish potato famine and German political upheaval, and by 1863 the Union had nearly one million men under arms. The South had only half that number and lacked the factories to provide sufficient armaments. Among the North's greatest difficulties were the violent protests against the new draft laws that allowed men with money to buy substitutes to replace them in the Union army. On both sides soldiers were as much threatened by disease as by guns and cannon.

For both the North and the South the death of Lincoln was a disaster of the greatest magnitude. Lincoln's reconstruction plan was aimed at healing the wounds of the war; his successor, Andrew Johnson, lacked the prestige or wisdom to enact such a plan.

Enlarged by the Mexican-American War and drawing settlers with the California Gold Rush, the West throughout this period continued to feed the American dream. It did so, however, at the expense of Native American tribes, many of whom fought for their land in what have come to be called the Indian Wars of the 1860s and 1870s.

Key Ideas in This Period

- civil war
- freedom vs. slavery
- the frontier
- leadership
- the American dream
- landscape and ownership

Cartoon of Mark Twain riding his "Celebrated Jumping Frog," Frederick Waddy, 1872.

A Nation Divided

By the middle of the century, the North had secured prosperity through manufacturing and commerce. Factories flourished; industry sought protective tariffs and a strong federal government. Cities boomed with plenty of work and plenty of workers. In the South, on the other hand, the economy had remained agricultural, depending on cotton exports, the slave system, and low tariffs. For Southerners the agrarian way of life and the rights of the individual states were cherished as the foundations of Jeffersonian democracy. As the century wore on, the Northern and the Southern ways of life seemed more and more irreconcilable. Just as Americans have always had to face the question of the place of the individual person within the whole society, so Americans before the Civil War had to face the question of the rights of individual states within a democratic union.

Every year the debates grew fiercer. Abolitionists became more and more vocal. William Lloyd Garrison attacked slavery every week in his newspaper, *The Liberator.* Harriet Beecher Stowe moved the emotions of many people with *Uncle Tom's Cabin* (1852). As each new western state entered the Union, a decision had to be made: would the state be slave or free? Compromise after compromise was reached until the tension became too great. When Abraham Lincoln was elected President in 1860, the Southern states took action. In December of 1860, South Carolina seceded from the Union; within a month six more states followed, and four others joined the new Confederacy soon after. With the firing at Fort Sumter on April 12, 1861, the Civil War began.

It is difficult to express what a civil war means to a nation: "Cousin against cousin" is a tired phrase, but it tells the truth. The young Mark Twain of Hannibal, Missouri, joined a Confederate militia; his brother accepted a Union appointment and moved to the Nevada Territory. In Maryland thousands enlisted in the Confederacy, and thousands more with the Union Army. Throughout the nation families were divided and friends became enemies.

The Civil War was fought on a scale that America had never before seen. On land and sea, in the Mississippi Valley and in the Virginia Wilderness, across Pennsylvania, Tennessee, and Georgia, in massive battles and unrecorded skirmishes—people fought and died. Bull Run, Shiloh, Chancellorsville, Gettysburg, Vicksburg, Atlanta—early Southern victories eventually gave way to Northern ones. On April 9, 1865, after a long and bitter war that some people had thought would take only a few weeks, Robert E. Lee, General of the Confederate Armies, surrendered to the Union Commander, General Ulysses S. Grant, at Appomattox Court House.

For the new nation, the Civil War, or War Between the States, was a tragedy of the greatest magnitude. The war decimated a generation and left the nation its most painful legacy.

Expansion and Celebration

The South, caught in a struggle for new power after the war, had to endure the long and painful Reconstruction Period. Elsewhere, however, the end of the war was cause for celebration. The nation had been preserved and could get on with its business. In the North cities opened their gates again.

This postwar period was named the Gilded Age by Mark Twain. It was an age that seemed to have lost some of its ideals in the chaos and hatred of war, and it filled that void with an intense materialism. The two decades after the war were a time of rapid technological progress: They witnessed the

Walt Whitman Urging the Bird of Freedom to Soar, caricature by Max Beerbohm, 1904.

completion of the transcontinental railroad and the invention of the typewriter, the ticker tape, the telephone, the light bulb, and the "horseless carriage." They were even more a time of profit, economic development, and financial wheeling-and-dealing—the age of the Robber Barons. The nation had found strength through the war, but it had lost some innocence.

The great new source of joy and inspiration, however, was the West. The West was "wild," exciting, new: It was still a frontier, with all the possibilities of an unspoiled place. Few people thought of the plight of the Indians; all that mattered was the great frontier where dreams were fulfilled and fortunes made. The newspaper editor Horace Greeley was credited with the words that symbolized the spirit of the time: "Go west, young man!"

The toil of the slaves, the bloodshed of battle, the celebration of a reunited America, the boom in technology, the populating of the American frontier, and the displacement of the Indian cultures were dramatic experiences. Out of such experiences came memorable contributions to our literature.

Three Americans

During these turbulent years three writers emerged who used the American language in new ways and who would prove to be among America's literary giants—Walt Whitman, Emily Dickinson, and Mark Twain.

Whitman. "I sound my barbaric yawp over the roofs of the world." So Walt Whitman cried out in *Song of Myself.* There was indeed something elemental, unmannered and unmannerly, in the new language American writers found themselves using. The American experience could only be described with new expressions: Whitman invented them. A new literature demanded using new rhythms and new forms: Whitman generated them. Whitman absorbed America. He became the country in his poetry, and his songs became America's new self-portrait.

Dickinson. The American language shaped the sound of Emily Dickinson's poetry as well, but it is the quieter, drier, crisper tone of New England speech we hear in her poems. Most of our early poets wrote in a language close to the "literary" style of England, but the poems of Dickinson—like those of Whitman—take on the characteristic turns and twists of American speech. Her poems deal with the profound matters that New England writers had always explored, but her voice takes on an irony and reveals a sensibility that still seems modern today.

Mark Twain. We can never think of Mark Twain as anything but a product of the American frontier. A child of the Mississippi River, the great dividing line between East and West, he sought his fortune in California. He was able to tell the world about mining camps and backwater towns, daring riverboat pilots, braggarts and adventurers, country children and their dreams—and he told of these things in the language of the people who experienced them. Steeped in his time and place, a master of dialect and rural humor, Mark Twain wrote in a language that opened a new mine of American literature.

Wherever Americans were going after the war, they were not returning to the past. The old forms and many of the old ideals had died in the war. New ones were not easily found. Perhaps Mark Twain's Huckleberry Finn best sums up the direction many Americans felt they had to take:

"But I reckon I got to light out for the Territory ahead of the rest, because Aunt Sally she's going to adopt me and sivilize me and I can't stand it. I been there before."

TIME LINE

1855–1880 AMERICAN EVENTS		WORLD EVENTS 1855–1880	
1855	Walt Whitman, *Leaves of Grass* Frederick Douglass, *My Bondage and My Freedom*	1855	Russia: Ivan Turgenev, *A Month in the Country*
1857	Dred Scott case rules Missouri Compromise unconstitutional E. G. Otis installs first safety elevator	1857	France: Gustave Flaubert, *Madame Bovary* England: Thomas Hughes, *Tom Brown's Schooldays*
1858	Oliver Wendell Holmes, *Autocrat of the Breakfast Table* First transatlantic telegraph cable laid		
1859	First oil well in U.S. drilled (Titusville, Pa.)		
1860	Abraham Lincoln elected President Pony Express established	1860	England: Florence Nightingale founds world's first nursing school
1861	Civil War begins Federal income tax instituted	1861	England: Charles Dickens, *Great Expectations*
1862	Civil War battles of Shiloh, Antietam, and Fredericksburg	1862	Russia: Ivan Turgenev, *Fathers and Sons*
1863	Lincoln issues Emancipation Proclamation Lincoln delivers Gettysburg Address		
		1864	Russia: Leo Tolstoy begins *War and Peace* France: Louis Pasteur develops pasteurization method
1865	Civil War ends Lincoln assassinated	1865	England: Lewis Carroll, *Alice in Wonderland* Austria: Franz Schubert (died 1828), first performance of *Unfinished Symphony*
1866	Cholera epidemic strikes many American cities	1866	Russia: Feodor Dostoevsky, *Crime and Punishment*
1867	U.S. buys Alaska from Russia for two cents per acre Mark Twain, "The Celebrated Jumping Frog of Calaveras County"	1867	France: Pierre Michaux begins to manufacture bicycles Sweden: Alfred Nobel patents dynamite

1855–1880 AMERICAN EVENTS

1868 First professional baseball team, Cincinnati Red Stockings, founded

Louisa May Alcott, *Little Women*

1869 National Women Suffrage Association organized

First transcontinental railroad line completed

1870 John D. Rockefeller founds Standard Oil Company

1871 P. T. Barnum opens "The Greatest Show on Earth" in New York

1872 James Whistler paints *The Artist's Mother*

1874 First U.S. zoo established (Philadelphia, Pa.)

1875 Thomas Eakins paints realistic masterpiece, *The Gross Clinic*

1876 Alexander Graham Bell invents telephone

Mark Twain, *The Adventures of Tom Sawyer*

American Centennial Exposition held in Philadelphia

1877 Thomas Edison invents phonograph

1878 Henry James, *Daisy Miller*

1879 Thomas Edison invents electric light bulb

Frank W. Woolworth opens his first store

1880 U.S. population estimate: 50 million

WORLD EVENTS 1855–1880

1868 Japan: Shogunate abolished; power returns to emperor

1869 England: Jules Verne, *Twenty Thousand Leagues Under the Sea*

Suez Canal opens, connecting Mediterranean Sea and Red Sea

1870 Franco-Prussian War begins

1871 England: George Eliot, *Middlemarch*

1872 First international soccer game played, Scotland versus England

1874 France: Impressionist painting first exhibited

1876 Russia: Peter Tchaikovsky composes *Swan Lake*

1878 England: Thomas Hardy, *The Return of the Native*

1879 England: Gilbert and Sullivan, *Pirates of Penzance*

Russia: Feodor Dostoevsky, *The Brothers Karamazov*

1880 France: Auguste Rodin exhibits *The Thinker*

Spirituals

Spirituals reflect the two deepest concerns of the black slaves who gave them birth: earthly bondage and religious faith. In fact, many of these songs have their origins in religious hymns, transformed by memories of African music. Spirituals were also taken up and sung by white Americans in camp meetings and other religious gatherings in the nineteenth century. They were collected in such books as *The Southern Harmony* (1835) and *The Sacred Harp* (1844), yet no printed version can fully convey to us now the power and the emotion of the original sound of "the sorrow songs," as they were called.

Many spirituals had double meanings and were used to transmit secret messages, especially about escape. "Go Down, Moses," for example, is based on the biblical account of the bondage of the Jews in Egypt. However, it probably also refers to Harriet Tubman, a former slave who was known as "Moses." Tubman repeatedly risked her life to help slaves escape.

"Follow the Drinking Gourd" told escaped slaves that the Big Dipper in the sky pointed to the North Star—the direction of freedom. The spiritual is based on an old gospel hymn, "Follow the Risen Lord," and was sung by those using the Underground Railroad, the network of escape that carried many slaves to freedom. The "old man" of the song may refer to a man called Peg Leg Joe, one of the "conductors," or guides, on the Underground Railroad. "Old Man," however, has also long been a nickname for the Mississippi River.

■ What songs of today give people hope for the future? How do spirituals do the same thing?

Go Down, Moses

When Israel was in Egypt land,
  Let my people go!
Oppressed so hard they could not stand,
  Let my people go!

Chorus
Go down, Moses,
  Way down in Egypt land
Tell ole Pharaoh,
  Let my people go!

Thus say the Lord, bold Moses said,
  Let my people go!
If not I'll smite your first-born dead,
  Let my people go!

Chorus
Go down, Moses,
  Way down in Egypt land
Tell ole Pharaoh,
  Let my people go!

No more shall they in bondage toil,
  Let my people go!
Let them come out with Egypt's spoil,
  Let my people go!

Chorus
Go down, Moses,
  Way down in Egypt land
Tell ole Pharaoh,
  Let my people go!

STUDY QUESTIONS

Recalling

1. In stanza 1 how are the people of Israel in Egypt described?
2. In the Chorus what specifically is Moses asked to do?
3. With what words does Moses threaten Pharaoh in stanza 2?

Interpreting

4. Who does *my* refer to in the repeated line "Let my people go"? Who tells Moses to "Go down . . . in Egypt land"?
5. What does this spiritual show about the condition and faith of the slaves who sang it? What emotions would have inspired a spiritual such as this?

Extending

6. Why do you think slaves in America sang about the captivity of the Jews in Egypt? Might there have been practical reasons for doing so?

AT A GLANCE

- The speaker sings of the Hebrews' slavery in Egypt.
- God sent Moses to tell Pharaoh to free the Israelites.

LITERARY OPTIONS

- refrain
- allusion

THEMATIC OPTIONS

- freedom vs. slavery
- visions and ideals

ALLUSION

The spiritual is a lengthy allusion to the story of Moses (Exodus 1:22–12:36). The narrative is told by the ageless voice of the black storyteller; the refrain repeats the words of the Lord (l. 4).

REFRAIN

In the oral tradition repeated lines made the song easier to learn, remember, and sing in chorus (ll. 5–8).

MAIN IDEA

The implied comparison of the bondage of American slaves with that of the Hebrews in Egypt is a powerful expression of the desire for freedom (ll. 17–19).

REFLECTING ON THE POEM

What is the effect of the repetition in the poem? (Students may recognize that the line *Let my people go!* grows stronger with each repetition.)

STUDY QUESTIONS

1. oppressed
2. go to Egypt, tell Pharaoh to let the people of Israel go
3. Lord will smite first-born dead.
4. the Lord; the Lord
5.
- Answers will vary. Students should recognize hard life and deep faith of slaves.
- hatred of slavery, longing for freedom, strong faith

6.
- Answers will vary. By analogy the slaves were singing about themselves.
- Yes; to sing about themselves would have been dangerous.

AT A GLANCE

- The song directs escaping slaves to "follow the drinking gourd" to freedom.
- The "old man" waits to take the fugitives to safety.

LITERARY OPTIONS

- allusion
- symbol

THEMATIC OPTIONS

- freedom and slavery
- visions and ideals

SYMBOL

- The Big Dipper, or "drinking gourd," is a symbol of freedom and hope because it points to the North Star (l. 2).
- The "old man" (l. 3), found frequently in spirituals, may represent the Mississippi River or may symbolize death—for many slaves, the only source of freedom.

ALLUSION

"Another river" may mean the Jordan, boundary of the Promised Land and symbol of a better life to come (l. 15).

REFLECTING ON THE POEM

What might this song have meant to those who sang it? (Students may suggest that it would have kept up their courage by giving them hope.)

STUDY QUESTIONS

1. "when the sun comes back and the first quail calls"
2. river bank; dead trees
3. junction of rivers; carry slave to freedom
4. crossing Jordan to Promised Land or going to heaven
5. hope and faith
6. Answers will vary. Students will probably be able to cite such a song.

VIEWPOINT

Answers will vary. Students might mention the nobility of the human spirit, a cry for justice, or a mournful sorrow.

Follow the Drinking Gourd

When the sun comes back and the first quail calls,
  Follow the drinking gourd,
For the old man is a-waiting for to carry you to freedom
  If you follow the drinking gourd.

Follow the drinking gourd,
  Follow the drinking gourd,
For the old man is a-waiting for to carry you to freedom
  If you follow the drinking gourd.

The river bank will make a very good road,
  The dead trees show you the way,
Left foot, peg foot traveling on
  Follow the drinking gourd.

The river ends between two hills
  Follow the drinking gourd.
There's another river on the other side,
  Follow the drinking gourd.

Where the little river meets the great big river,
  Follow the drinking gourd.
The old man is a-waiting for to carry you to freedom,
  If you follow the drinking gourd.

STUDY QUESTIONS

Recalling

1. According to stanza 1, when is the right time to begin to "follow the drinking gourd"?
2. According to stanza 3, which road should the slave take first? What landmarks show the way?
3. According to the last stanza, where is the old man waiting? For what or for whom is the old man waiting?

Interpreting

4. What larger spiritual meaning might a slave have added to the literal meaning of crossing a river to "the other side"?
5. What emotions do you think this song could have inspired in the slaves who sang it as they escaped?

Extending

6. Do people still write and sing songs to give each other courage and hope in desperate situations? Name one such song, and tell its message in your own words.

VIEWPOINT

In his autobiography the modern black poet James Weldon Johnson observes about the spirituals that

> so many of these songs contain more than mere melody; there is sounded in them that elusive undertone, the note in music which is not heard with the ears.

- Describe in your own words "that elusive undertone" of the spirituals. How would you define the music "not heard with the ears"?

Frederick Douglass *c. 1817–1895*

Frederick Douglass was born into slavery. He learned to read in the Auld household in Baltimore, at first with the support of his master's wife and later against her orders. What he read made him long for freedom.

In 1838 Douglass succeeded in his second attempt at escape. A few years later he attended a meeting of the Massachusetts Anti-Slavery Society and gave an extemporaneous speech that was so inspiring that he was engaged to be one of the society's agents. Douglass was a brilliant orator. His speeches and his 1845 autobiography, *Narrative of the Life of Frederick Douglass,* were powerful fuel for the Abolitionist cause. However, he was still a fugitive slave, and by naming names and places in his autobiography he placed himself in great danger. He went abroad, where in 1847 some English friends purchased his freedom.

Returning to America, Douglass published an antislavery magazine that urged political solutions until the war came. He also wrote an updated version of his autobiography entitled *My Bondage and My Freedom* (1855). After the war he remained committed to his people and his country, holding important positions such as that of Minister to Haiti. A final version of his autobiography, *Life and Times of Frederick Douglass,* was published in 1882.

As a writer Douglass makes his points with characteristic simplicity and dignity through the simple recitation of the facts of his life. In *My Bondage and My Freedom* Douglass tells his story plainly, letting his experience speak for itself.

■ What essential effect of slavery does Douglass point out?

AT A GLANCE

- The mistress of the house has been teaching the author, then a slave boy, to read.
- Persuaded by her husband, she stops the lessons.
- The inward struggle shows in her unhappiness.

LITERARY OPTIONS

- autobiography
- main idea
- purpose

THEMATIC OPTIONS

- slavery as unnatural
- growth and change
- conflict and resolution

1 AUTOBIOGRAPHY

The emphasis on introspection and self-interpretation of the author's life is characteristic of autobiography.

2 PERIOD IDEA: ABOLITION

The belief that natural rights are inherent for all human beings is an outgrowth of the Age of Reason.

3 STYLE: IRONY

The author's insistence that Mrs. Auld is "deficient" is ironic; she is naturally warm, kind, and humane, lacking at this point only the ability to view him as less than human.

4 PURPOSE

The author uses his own human qualities to show that slaves, like others, experienced the full range of human emotions.

Frederick Douglass

from My Bondage and My Freedom

1 I lived in the family of Master Hugh, at Baltimore, seven years, during which time—as the almanac makers say of the weather—my condition was variable. The most interesting feature of my history here was my learning to read and write, under somewhat marked disadvantages. In attaining this knowledge, I was compelled to resort to indirections by no means congenial to my nature and which were really humiliating to me. My mistress—who had begun to teach me—was suddenly checked in her benevolent design by the strong advice of her husband. In faithful compliance with this advice, the good lady had not only ceased to instruct me herself, but had set her face as a flint against my learning to read by any means. It is due, however, to my mistress to say that she did not adopt this course in all its stringency at the first. She either thought it unnecessary or she lacked the depravity indispensable to shutting me up in mental darkness. It was at least necessary for her to have some training and some hardening in the exercise of the slaveholder's prerogative to make her equal to forgetting my human nature and character, and to treating me as a thing destitute of a moral or an intellectual nature. Mrs. Auld—my mistress—was a most kind and tenderhearted woman; and, in the humanity of her heart and the simplicity of her mind, she set out, when I first went to live with her, to treat me as she supposed one human being ought to treat another.

It is easy to see that, in entering upon the duties of a slaveholder, some little experience
2 is needed. Nature has done almost nothing to prepare men and women to be either slaves or slaveholders. Nothing but rigid training, long persisted in, can perfect the character of the one or the other. One cannot easily forget to love freedom; and it is as hard to cease to respect that natural love in our fellow creatures.
3 On entering upon the career of a slaveholding mistress, Mrs. Auld was singularly deficient; nature, which fits nobody for such an office, had done less for her than any lady I had known. It was no easy matter to induce her to think and to feel that the curly-headed boy who stood by her side and even leaned on her lap, who was loved by little Tommy and who loved little Tommy in turn, sustained to her
4 only the relation of a chattel. I was *more* than that, and she felt me to be more than that. I could talk and sing; I could laugh and weep; I could reason and remember; I could love and hate. I was human, and she, dear lady, knew and felt me to be so. How could she then treat me as a brute, without a mighty struggle with all the noble powers of her own soul. That struggle came, and the will and power of the husband was victorious. Her noble soul was overthrown; but he that overthrew it did not himself escape the consequences. He, not less than the other parties, was injured in his domestic peace by the fall.

When I went into their family, it was the abode of happiness and contentment. The mistress of the house was a model of affection and tenderness. Her fervent piety and watchful uprightness made it impossible to see her without thinking and feeling—"that woman is a Christian." There was no sorrow nor suffering for which she had not a tear, and there was no innocent joy for which she had not a smile. She had bread for the hungry, clothes for the naked, and comfort for every mourner that came within her reach. Slavery soon proved its ability to divest her of these excellent qualities and her home of its early happiness. Conscience cannot stand much violence. Once thoroughly broken down, *who* is he that can repair the damage? It may be broken toward the slave on Sunday, and toward the master on Monday. It cannot endure such shocks. It must

GUIDED READING

LITERAL QUESTIONS

1a. What does the author say was the most interesting feature of his stay in the Auld household? (learning to read and write)

2a. According to the author, what was needed to perfect people's belief in their status as slaves or slaveholders? (rigid training, long persisted in)

INFERENTIAL QUESTIONS

1b. What was most "interesting" about it? (He was forced to acquire this basic knowledge in roundabout ways, and his education caused great unhappiness in the household.)

2b. Why would such action be necessary? (The whole notion of slavery runs counter to most people's innate understanding of what is right and natural.)

stand entire, or it does not stand at all. If my condition waxed bad, that of the family waxed not better. The first step, in the wrong direction, was the violence done to nature and to conscience in arresting the benevolence that would have enlightened my young mind. In ceasing to instruct me, she must begin to justify herself *to* herself; and, once consenting to take sides in such a debate, she was riveted to her position. One needs very little knowledge of moral philosophy to see *where* my mistress now landed. She finally became even more violent in her opposition to my learning to read than was her husband himself. She was not satisfied with simply doing as *well* as her husband had commanded her, but seemed resolved to
1 better his instruction. Nothing appeared to make my poor mistress—after her turning toward the downward path—more angry than seeing me, seated in some nook or corner, quietly reading a book or a newspaper. I have had her rush at me with the utmost fury, and snatch from my hand such newspaper or book, with something of the wrath and consternation which a traitor might be supposed to feel on being discovered in a plot by some dangerous spy.

2 Mrs. Auld was an apt woman, and the advice of her husband, and her own experience, soon demonstrated to her entire satisfaction that education and slavery are incompatible with each other. When this conviction was thoroughly established, I was most narrowly watched in all my movements. If I remained in a separate room from the family for any considerable length of time, I was sure to be suspected of having a book, and was at once called upon to give an account of myself. All this, however, was entirely *too late.* The first, and never to be retraced, step had been taken.
3 In teaching me the alphabet, in the days of her simplicity and kindness, my mistress had given me the "inch," and now, no ordinary precaution could prevent me from taking the "ell."[1]

Seized with a determination to learn to read at any cost, I hit upon many expedients to accomplish the desired end. The plea which I mainly adopted, and the one by which I was most successful, was that of using my young white playmates, whom I met in the street, as teachers. I used to carry, almost constantly, a copy of Webster's spelling book in my pocket; and, when sent on errands, or when play time was allowed me, I would step, with my young friends, aside, and take a lesson in spelling. I generally paid my *tuition fee* to the boys with bread, which I also carried in my pocket. For a single biscuit, any of my hungry little comrades would give me a lesson more valuable to me than bread. Not every one, however, demanded this consideration, for there were those who took pleasure in teaching me whenever I had a chance to be taught by them. I am strongly tempted to give the names of two or three of those little boys as a slight testimonial of the gratitude and affection I bear them, but prudence forbids; not that it would injure me, but it might possibly embarrass them; for it is almost an unpardonable offense to do any thing, directly or indirectly, to promote a slave's freedom in a slave state. It is enough to say of my warm-hearted little playfellows that they lived on Philpot street very near Durgin & Bailey's shipyard.

Although slavery was a delicate subject, and very cautiously talked about among grownup people in Maryland, I frequently talked about it—and that very freely—with the white boys. I would sometimes say to them, while seated on a curb stone or a cellar door, "I wish I could be free, as you will be when you get to
4 be men." "You will be free, you know, as soon as you are twenty-one and can go where you like, but I am a slave for life. Have I not as good a right to be free as you have?" Words like these, I observed, always troubled them; and I had no small satisfaction in wringing from the boys, occasionally, that fresh and bitter condemnation of slavery that springs from nature, unseared and unperverted. Of all consciences, let me have those to deal with which

1. **"ell"**: former English measure of length, used mainly for cloth, equal to forty-five inches.

AT A GLANCE

- Mrs. Auld becomes violently opposed to Douglass' reading.
- The boy determines to read at all costs.
- He barters food for lessons from white boys.

1 THEME

Mrs. Auld's irrational anger is disproportionate to the "offense" of reading. The author's reasonable understanding of her behavior contrasts with Mrs. Auld's unreasonable actions in defense of slavery.

2 THEME

Ironically, Mrs. Auld grasps the principle but fears to draw from it the conclusion that knowledge is the greater good. Recognizing the incompatibility of slavery and knowledge, she feels threatened by the boy's knowledge.

3 AUTOBIOGRAPHY

The author notes the learning of the alphabet as a turning point in his life.

4 PURPOSE

In addressing this question to the boys, Douglass is also addressing his larger audience.

GUIDED READING

LITERAL QUESTIONS

1a. What was "more valuable than bread" to Douglass? (a spelling lesson)

2a. Why does Douglass not give the names of those who helped him read? (It might embarrass them as residents of a slave state.)

INFERENTIAL QUESTIONS

1b. Why would this have been so valuable to him? (He was determined to learn at any cost; he liked reading and sensed that it could change his condition.)

2b. What might have happened if he had done so? (They could have been blamed for helping him; they probably would have become targets of anger or ridicule among their neighbors.)

AT A GLANCE

- The boys treat young Douglass much as an equal.
- He is burdened by the expectation that he will always be a slave.
- He buys a copy of the *Columbian Orator,* which contains speeches on liberty, and longs intensely for freedom.

1 AUDIENCE

Douglass engages his audience directly, as if in a dialogue, thereby reaching out for support.

2 AUTOBIOGRAPHY

The author's feelings and the effects of bondage on his spirit give the autobiography depth and create sympathy in the audience.

3 THEME

Douglass discusses how newly gained knowledge brings enlightenment that can be painful. In his dramatic comparison of a life in slavery to confinement in a pit with a monster, Douglass portrays his increasing anxiety as he grew older.

have not been bewildered by the cares of life.
I do not remember ever to have met with a
boy, while I was in slavery, who defended the
slave system; but I have often had boys to console me with the hope that something would
yet occur by which I might be made free. Over
and over again, they have told me that "they
believed *I* had as good a right to be free as
they had," and that "they did not believe God
1 ever made anyone to be a slave." The reader
will easily see that such little conversations
with my playfellows had no tendency to
weaken my love of liberty nor to render me
contented with my condition as a slave.

When I was about thirteen years old and
had succeeded in learning to read, every increase of knowledge, especially respecting the
free states, added something to the almost intolerable burden of the thought—"I am a slave
2 for life." To my bondage I saw no end. It was
a terrible reality, and I shall never be able to
tell how sadly that thought chafed my young
spirit. Fortunately, or unfortunately, about this
time in my life, I had made enough money to
buy what was then a very popular schoolbook,
the *Columbian Orator.* I bought this addition
to my library of Mr. Knight on Thames street,
Fell's Point, Baltimore, and paid him fifty cents
for it. I was first led to buy this book by hearing some little boys say that they were going
to learn some little pieces out of it for the Ex-
hibition. This volume was indeed a rich treasure, and every opportunity afforded me, for a
time, was spent in diligently perusing it. . . .
3 The dialogue and the speeches were all redolent of the principles of liberty, and poured
floods of light on the nature and character of
slavery. . . . I was no longer the light-hearted,
gleesome boy, full of mirth and play, as
when I landed first at Baltimore. Knowledge
had come. . . .

This knowledge opened my eyes to the horrible pit and revealed the teeth of the frightful dragon that was ready to pounce upon me, but it opened no way for my escape. I have often wished myself a beast or a bird—anything, rather than a slave. I was wretched and gloomy

beyond my ability to describe. I was too thoughtful to be happy. It was this everlasting thinking which distressed and tormented me; and yet there was no getting rid of the subject of my thoughts. All nature was redolent of it. Once awakened by the silver trump[2] of knowledge, my spirit was roused to eternal wakefulness. Liberty! the inestimable birthright of every man had for me converted every object into an asserter of this great right. It was heard

---

2. **trump:** trumpet.

GUIDED READING

LITERAL QUESTION

1a. What did the white boys whom Douglass knew believe about slavery? (They did not believe that God meant anyone to be a slave.)

INFERENTIAL QUESTION

1b. How does this detail support Douglass' thesis that slavery is against nature? (The boys, being younger, are speaking from natural instincts; they have not been taught to accept slavery.)

in every sound and beheld in every object. It was ever present to torment me with a sense of my wretched condition. The more beautiful and charming were the smiles of nature, the more horrible and desolate was my condition.
1 I saw nothing without seeing it, and I heard nothing without hearing it. I do not exaggerate when I say that it looked from every star, smiled in every calm, breathed in every wind, and moved in every storm.

I have no doubt that my state of mind had something to do with the change in the treatment adopted by my once kind mistress to-
2 ward me. I can easily believe that my leaden, downcast, and discontented look was very offensive to her. Poor lady! She did not know my trouble, and I dared not tell her. Could I have freely made her acquainted with the real state of my mind and given her the reasons therefor, it might have been well for both of us. Her abuse of me fell upon me like the blows of the false prophet upon his ass; she did not know that an *angel* stood in the way;[3] and—such is the relation of master and slave—I could not
3 tell her. Nature had made us *friends;* slavery made us *enemies.* My interests were in a direction opposite to hers, and we both had our private thoughts and plans. She aimed to keep me ignorant; and I resolved to know, although knowledge only increased my discontent. My feelings were not the result of any marked cruelty in the treatment I received; they sprung from the consideration of my being a slave at all. It was *slavery*—not its mere *incidents*—that I hated. I had been cheated. I saw through the attempt to keep me in ignorance; I saw that slaveholders would have gladly made me believe that they were merely acting under the authority of God in making a slave of me and in making slaves of others, and I treated them as robbers and deceivers. The feeding and clothing me well could not atone for taking my liberty from me. The smiles of my mistress could not remove the deep sorrow that dwelt in my young bosom. Indeed these, in time,
4 came only to deepen my sorrow. She had changed; and the reader will see that I had changed too. We were both victims to the same overshadowing evil—*she* as mistress, *I* as slave. I will not censure her harshly; she cannot censure me, for she knows I speak but the truth, and have acted in my opposition to slavery, just as she herself would have acted in a reverse of circumstances.

---

3. **blows . . . way:** The reference is to the biblical tale (Numbers 22 : 21–35) in which an ass, despite being beaten by her master, Balaam, cannot obey and move on because an angel blocks her way.

AT A GLANCE

- Douglass contrasts his bondage with the freedom that he sees in nature.
- His discontent chafes at Mrs. Auld.
- He sees both himself and his owners as victims of slavery.

1 STYLE: PERSONIFICATION

The personification of Liberty shows the degree to which it had become a vital presence to the writer.

2 TONE

Douglass' calm, restrained attitude and the sympathy that he shows for Mrs. Auld suggest that he is reasonable; they also may help to win over his audience.

3 THEME

Douglass returns to the basic conflict between knowledge and ignorance and their relationship to slavery.

4 THEME

Because it perverts human nature, slavery is detrimental not only to the slave but also to the slave owner.

REFLECTING ON THE SELECTION

How does Douglass persuade his readers that slavery is unnatural and demeaning? (Students may suggest that he demonstrates its effects not only on himself, but also on others, while showing himself to be a completely reasonable and logical person.)

GUIDED READING

LITERAL QUESTIONS

1a. What behavior does Douglass say he does not doubt was offensive to Mrs. Auld? (his leaden, downcast look)

2a. At the conclusion of this passage, which word does Douglass use to label both himself and Mrs. Auld? *(victims)*

INFERENTIAL QUESTIONS

1b. Why was this behavior so offensive to her? (On one level, Mrs. Auld felt justified in her treatment of Douglass; on another, she probably realized the reason for Douglass' unhappiness and felt guilty.)

2b. Why does he use this term? (He was a victim because he was a slave. Mrs. Auld was a victim because she was being forced to live in a way that robbed her of her humanity.)

STUDY QUESTIONS

1. his learning to read and write
2. kind, tender, pious; no
3. her husband; more opposed than her husband was
4. lessons from white playmates; bread and biscuits
5. *Columbian Orator;* liberty
6. learned meaning of slavery; awakened desire for liberty
7. Slavery hurt them both: Robbed him of freedom, her of compassion.
8. shows understanding; sympathetic, for he hated slavery, not individuals

LITERARY FOCUS

second paragraph, last paragraph on page 241, last two paragraphs; in relating incidents of Auld household and his dealings with playmates

STUDY QUESTIONS

Recalling

1. At the beginning of the selection, what does Douglass call "the most interesting feature" of his history in the Auld household?
2. What was Mrs. Auld like when Douglass first met her? Was she "trained" in being a slaveholder?
3. Who told Mrs. Auld to stop teaching Douglass to read? Eventually, what was her attitude toward Douglass' reading?
4. After Mrs. Auld stopped instructing him, what was Douglass' chief means for continuing his education? What "tuition fee" did he usually pay?
5. What book, in particular, does Douglass call a "rich treasure"? Of what principles does he say it was redolent?

Interpreting

6. Why was learning to read so important to Douglass?
7. What does Douglass mean when he says in the last paragraph that he and Mrs. Auld were "victims of the same overshadowing evil"?
8. What is Douglass' overall attitude toward his experiences? Does he seem bitter or sympathetic toward the Aulds and others?

LITERARY FOCUS

Autobiography

A **biography** is an account of a person's life that is factual, or at least claims to be so. It is not, however, a mere chronicle of days or events; rather, it is an overview, an attempt to place the subject in time and to explain the meaning or importance of his or her life.

An **autobiography** is also an account of a person's life, but here the subject is the author as well. The autobiographer believes that his or her life is interesting enough, important enough, or exemplary enough to merit consideration. The best autobiographies give a cogent view of the author's world and his or her place in it.

Frederick Douglass' three versions of his autobiography were written for a cause: to show the world that a black man, a slave, was a human being in the complete sense of "human"—at a time when there were those who said otherwise. Beyond what Douglass says directly about slavery, the quality of his writing, the sensitivity he displays, and the simple facts of his life are eloquent in themselves. In writing more than an antislavery tract, Douglass became not only a leader but a symbol who helped change American history.

Thinking About Autobiography

■ Where in Douglass' account does the author directly state his opinion of slavery? Where does he let the facts of his life speak for themselves?

COMPOSITION

Writing About Nonfiction

■ Write a brief essay in which you discuss Douglass' purpose in writing his autobiography. First state his purpose in your own words. Then cite examples of the techniques he uses to accomplish his purpose—for example, sensory details, facts, examples, and opinions. *For help with this assignment, refer to Lesson 4 in the Writing About Literature Handbook at the back of this book.*

Writing a Review

■ Place yourself in the days before the Civil War, and compose a short review of Douglass' *My Bondage and My Freedom* that might have appeared in a newspaper or a magazine of the time. Your review should contain quotations and examples from the extract as well as your comments on the author's style. Conclude by telling why you recommend the book or why you do not.

COMPOSITION: GUIDELINES FOR EVALUATION

WRITING ABOUT NONFICTION

Objective

To analyze author's purpose and methods

Guidelines for Evaluation

- suggested length: four to six paragraphs
- should identify author's purpose
- should cite details, facts, examples, opinions, and other techniques used to achieve this purpose

WRITING A REVIEW

Objective

To write a book review

Guidelines for Evaluation

- suggested length: five to eight paragraphs
- should be written from the point of view of a critic of Douglass' day
- should comment on the author's style
- should support opinions with quotes, examples
- should say if recommended and why or why not

National Portrait Gallery, Smithsonian

Mary Chesnut *1822–1886*

Mary Boykin Chesnut grew up with the daughters of Southern planters amid all the elegance that attended such surroundings. Her father was a proslavery politician who served as both governor of and senator from South Carolina; her mother came from an old established Carolina family.

At seventeen Mary married her childhood sweetheart, James Chesnut, Jr., a wealthy Carolina lawyer. James was elected senator from South Carolina in 1858, and though he was a moderate who did not favor secession, he stood with the Southern delegation as war approached. Later he served under General Beauregard and advised Confederate President Jefferson Davis. Thus Mary Chesnut had the advantage of personal contact with many of the leading Southern figures during the Civil War.

Mary Chesnut feared the war, and she hated to see it come. Yet when it came she was loyal to her friends and family. She visited hospitals, rejoiced in Confederate victories, and wept at Confederate defeats. Nevertheless, even in victory, her joy was tinged by grief and bitterness at the agonies and evils of warfare.

The pages of Chesnut's journal sparkle with humor and tears, for Mary Chesnut was a keen observer and a moving one. Her journal is one of the most valuable documents to come down to us.

■ What does Mary Chesnut's personal diary tell us about the Civil War that an account in a history book could not?

A Cotton Plantation on the Mississippi, 1884, Currier and Ives lithograph.

AT A GLANCE

- Chesnut watches preparations for the attack on Fort Sumter.
- She expresses annoyance with the Union occupation of the fort.

LITERARY OPTIONS

- journal
- tone
- purpose

THEMATIC OPTIONS

- the cost of war
- conflict and resolution

1 **BACKGROUND**

The Confederates felt that the continuing Union occupation of Fort Sumter was illegal. They threatened to seize it. Willing to surrender, Anderson awaited orders from his superiors.

2 **JOURNAL**

The catalog of relatively undeveloped impressions and events is typical of journal-writing style.

3 **PURPOSE**

The writer is keeping a record of an eventful period in her life and in American history, both for her own gratification and to get perspective on the events around her.

4 **TONE**

The writer's tone of annoyance reveals both a facet of her personality and her firm belief in the Confederate cause.

Mary Chesnut

from A Wartime Journal

March 1861

"Now this is positive," they say. "Fort Sumter[1] is to be relieved, and we are to have no war." Poor Sumter—not half as much as we would be!

After all, far too good to be true.

If there be no war, how triumphant Mr. Chesnut will be. He is the only man who has persisted from the first that his would be a *peaceful* revolution. Heaven grant it may prove so.

April 7, 1861

Things are happening so fast.

My husband has been made an aide-de-camp[2] of General Beauregard.

Three hours ago we were quietly packing to go home. The convention has adjourned.

1 Now he tells me the attack upon Fort Sumter may begin tonight. Depends upon Anderson and the fleet outside. The *Herald* says that this show of war outside of the bar is intended for Texas.

John Manning came in with his sword and red sash. Pleased as a boy to be on Beauregard's staff while the row goes on. He has gone with Wigfall to Captain Hartstene with instructions.

Mr. Chesnut is finishing a report he had to make to the convention.

2 Mrs. Hayne called. She had, she said, "but one feeling, pity for those who are not here."

Jack Preston, Willie Alston—"the take-life-easys," as they are called—with John Green, "the big brave," have gone down to the island—volunteered as privates.

Seven hundred men were sent over. Ammunition wagons rumbling along the streets all night. Anderson burning blue lights—signs and signals for the fleet outside, I suppose.

3 Today at dinner there was no allusion to things as they stand in Charleston Harbor. There was an undercurrent of intense excitement. There could not have been a more brilliant circle. In addition to our usual quartet (Judge Withers, Langdon Cheves, and Trescot), our two governors dined with us, Means and Manning.

These men all talked so delightfully. For once in my life I listened.

That over, business began. In earnest, Governor Means rummaged a sword and red sash from somewhere and brought it for Colonel Chesnut, who has gone to demand the surrender of Fort Sumter.

And now, patience—we must wait.

4 Why did that green goose Anderson go into Fort Sumter? Then everything began to go wrong.

Now they have intercepted a letter from him, urging them to let him surrender. He paints the horrors likely to ensue if they will not.

He ought to have thought of all that before he put his head in the hole.

April 12, 1861

Anderson will not capitulate.

Yesterday was the merriest, maddest dinner we have had yet. Men were more audaciously wise and witty. We had an unspoken foreboding it was to be our last pleasant meeting. Mr. Miles dined with us today. Mrs. Henry King rushed in: "The news, I come for the latest

1. **Fort Sumter:** fort in Charleston Harbor, southeastern South Carolina, occupied in early 1861 by Union troops under the command of Major Robert Anderson.
2. **aide-de-camp** [ād′də kamp′]: an officer who serves as an assistant to a superior officer.

GUIDED READING

LITERAL QUESTIONS

1a. On April 7 what does Mary Chesnut call the developing situation around her? (a "show of war"; a "row")

2a. What unspoken feeling does she say prevailed at the dinner party on April 12? (foreboding)

INFERENTIAL QUESTIONS

1b. What does this description convey? (the dramatic excitement of the situation)

2b. Why did the people at the table have this feeling? (The country was on the brink of war.)

news—all of the men of the King family are on the island"—of which fact she seemed proud.

1 While she was here, our peace negotiator—or envoy—came in. That is, Mr. Chesnut returned—his interview with Colonel Anderson had been deeply interesting—but was not inclined to be communicative, wanted his dinner. Felt for Anderson. Had telegraphed to President Davis[3] for instructions.

What answer to give Anderson, etc., etc. He has gone back to Fort Sumter with additional instructions.

When they were about to leave the wharf, A. H. Boykin sprang into the boat in great excitement; thought himself ill-used. A likelihood of fighting—and he to be left behind!

I do not pretend to go to sleep. How can I? If Anderson does not accept terms—at four—the orders are—he shall be fired upon.

2 I count four—St. Michael chimes. I begin to hope. At half-past four, the heavy booming of a cannon.

I sprang out of bed. And on my knees—prostrate—I prayed as I never prayed before.

There was a sound of stir all over the house—pattering of feet in the corridor—all seemed hurrying one way. I put on my double gown and a shawl and went too. It was to the housetop.

The shells were bursting. In the dark I heard a man say, "waste of ammunition."

I knew my husband was rowing about in a boat somewhere in that dark bay. And that the shells were roofing it over—bursting toward the fort. If Anderson was obstinate—he was to
3 order the forts on our side to open fire. Certainly fire had begun. The regular roar of the cannon—there it was. And who could tell what each volley accomplished of death and destruction.

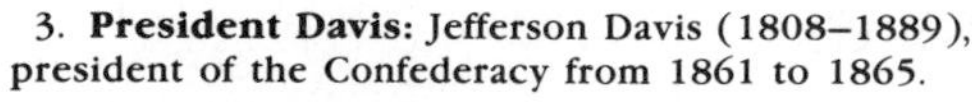

The women were wild, there on the housetop. Prayers from the women and imprecations from the men, and then a shell would light up the scene. Tonight, they say, the forces are to attempt to land.

The Metropolitan Museum of Art

Southern women making uniforms for Confederate soldiers.

The *Harriet Lane* had her wheelhouse[4] smashed and put back to sea.

We watched up there—everybody wondered. Fort Sumter did not fire a shot.

4 Today Miles and Manning, colonels now—aides to Beauregard—dined with us. The latter hoped I would keep the peace. I give him only good words, for he was to be under fire all day and night, in the bay carrying orders, etc.

Last night—or this morning truly—up on the housetop I was so weak and weary I sat down on something that looked like a black stool. "Get up, you foolish woman—your dress is on fire," cried a man. And he put me out. It was a chimney, and the sparks caught my clothes. Susan Preston and Mr. Venable then

3. **President Davis:** Jefferson Davis (1808–1889), president of the Confederacy from 1861 to 1865.

4. **wheelhouse:** enclosed area on the deck of a ship that shelters the steering equipment and the pilot.

AT A GLANCE

- Mary Chesnut's husband continues with negotiations for the surrender of Fort Sumter.
- At 4:30 A.M. she hears cannons firing on the fort.
- She watches from the roof of her home.

1 POINT OF VIEW

The writer sees the events of the war as an involved observer, not as an actual participant.

2 STYLE

The telegraphic style captures the immediacy of the scene and the author's intense emotion.

3 THEME

The roar of the cannon means the failure of the two sides to come to an agreement and immediately suggests the destructive nature of war.

4 CHARACTERIZATION

Mary Chesnut's explanation of her encouragement reveals her to be a selfless, compassionate woman.

GUIDED READING

LITERAL QUESTIONS

1a. What is James Chesnut's attitude toward the Union commander, Colonel Anderson? (sympathetic; "felt for" him)

2a. How does the writer describe the women watching the battle from the roof? (as "wild")

INFERENTIAL QUESTIONS

1b. What does this detail reveal about the effort at reconciliation? (It was sincere; Chesnut had wanted to work things out.)

2b. Why are they behaving in this way? (They were all fearful for their loved ones.)

AT A GLANCE

- The diarist learns that no one was hurt in the attack on Fort Sumter.
- Lincoln issues a call for Union funds and military recruits.
- Her husband meets with Jefferson Davis and Robert E. Lee, then goes off to war.

1 BACKGROUND

His ammunition and supplies exhausted, Anderson surrendered Fort Sumter to the Confederates. Their firing on the American flag, however, so enraged the North that an all-out war began.

2 JOURNAL

Mary Chesnut candidly portrays continual upheaval in feelings caused by living with the uncertainty of war.

3 POINT OF VIEW

The writer portrays gracious, intelligent people united for a cause dear to them. She continues to hope that they will be spared the horrors of war.

4 CHARACTERIZATION

The writer's curiosity and her impatience with the men's war council reveal her personality.

came up. But my fire had been extinguished before it broke out into a regular blaze.

Do you know, after all that noise and our tears and prayers, nobody has been hurt. Sound and fury, signifying nothing.[5] A delusion and a snare. . . .

April 13, 1861

Nobody hurt, after all. How gay we were last night.

Reaction after the dread of all the slaughter we thought those dreadful cannons were making such a noise in doing.

1 Not even a battery[6] the worse for wear.

Fort Sumter has been on fire. He has not yet silenced any of our guns. So the aides—still with swords and red sashes by way of uniform—tell us.

But the sound of those guns makes regular meals impossible. None of us go to table. But tea trays pervade the corridors, going everywhere.

Some of the anxious hearts lie on their beds and moan in solitary misery. Mrs. Wigfall and I solace ourselves with tea in my room.

These women have all a satisfying faith. . . .

But our men could not tarry with us in these cool shades and comfortable quarters—water unlimited, excellent table, etc., etc. They have gone back to Manassas,[7] and the faithful Brewster with them, to bring us the latest news. They left us in excellent spirits, which we shared until they were out of sight. We went with them to Warrenton and there heard that General Johnston was in full retreat and that a column was advancing upon Beauregard.

2 So we came back, all forlorn. If our husbands are taken prisoners, what will they do with them? . . .

Lincoln wants four hundred millions of money—and men in proportion.

Can he get them?

He will find us a heavy handful.

July 9, 1861

Our battle summer. May it be our first and our last. So-called.

3 After all, we have not had any of the horrors of war. Could there have been a gayer or pleasanter life than we led in Charleston? And Montgomery, how exciting it all was there. So many clever men and women congregated from every part of the South.

Flies and mosquitoes and a want of neatness and a want of good things to eat did drive us away.

In Richmond the girls say it is perfectly delightful. We find it so, too, but the bickering and quarreling has begun there.

July 14, 1861

Mr. C remained closeted with them—the president and General Lee[8] etc., etc.—all the afternoon. The news does not seem pleasant. At least, he is not inclined to tell me any of it. Satisfied himself with telling me how sensible and soldierly this handsome General Lee is. General Lee's military sagacity was his theme. Of course, the president dominated the party—as well by his weight of brain as by his position.

4 I did not care a fig for a description of the war council. I wanted to know what is in the wind now.

July 16, 1861

. . . I did not know there was such a "bitter cry" left in me. But I wept my heart away today when my husband went off. . . .

5. **Sound . . . nothing:** from *Macbeth*, Act V, Scene v, lines 26–28; part of Macbeth's description of life's tragedy.
6. **battery:** artillery unit.
7. **Manassas** [mə nas′əs]: a town in northeastern Virginia.
8. **General Lee:** Robert Edward Lee (1807–1870), commander in chief of the Confederate Army.

GUIDED READING

LITERAL QUESTIONS

1a. What does Mary Chesnut decide that Lincoln will find the Confederates to be? (a "heavy handful")

2a. What does she remark has begun in Richmond? ("bickering and quarreling")

INFERENTIAL QUESTIONS

1b. What does she mean? (She believes that Lincoln will find them to be more than he has bargained for, not easy to manage or defeat.)

2b. What does this remark show about the situation in Richmond? (The people are feeling the stresses of the war.)

July 22, 1861

Mrs. Davis came in so softly that I did not know she was here until she leaned over me, kissed me, and said:

1 "A great battle has been fought—Jeff Davis led the center, Joe Johnston the right wing, Beauregard the left wing of the army. Your husband is all right. Wade Hampton is wounded. Colonel Johnson of the Legion killed—so are Colonel Bee and Colonel Bartow. Kirby Smith is wounded or killed."

I had no heart to speak. She went on in that desperate calm way to which people betake themselves when under greatest excitement. "Bartow was rallying his men, leading them into the hottest of the fight—died gallantly, at the head of his regiment.

"The president telegraphs me only that 'it is a great victory.' General Cooper has all the other telegrams." Still I said nothing. I was stunned. Then I was so grateful. Those nearest and dearest to me were safe still.

Then she began in the same concentrated voice to read from a paper she held in her hand.

"Dead and dying cover the field. Sherman's[9] battery taken, Lynchburg regiment cut to pieces. Three hundred of the Legion[10] wounded."

They got me up. Times were too wild with excitement to stay in bed. We went into Mrs. Preston's room.

She made me lie down on her bed. Men, women, and children streamed in. Every living soul had a story to tell. "Complete victory" you heard everywhere.

We had been such anxious wretches! The revulsion of feeling was almost too much to bear.

9. **Sherman's:** referring to William Tecumseh Sherman (1820–1891), a colonel during the first battle of Manassas; later, a Union general.
10. **Legion:** Hampton Legion, formed and equipped by the wealthy Wade Hampton of South Carolina.

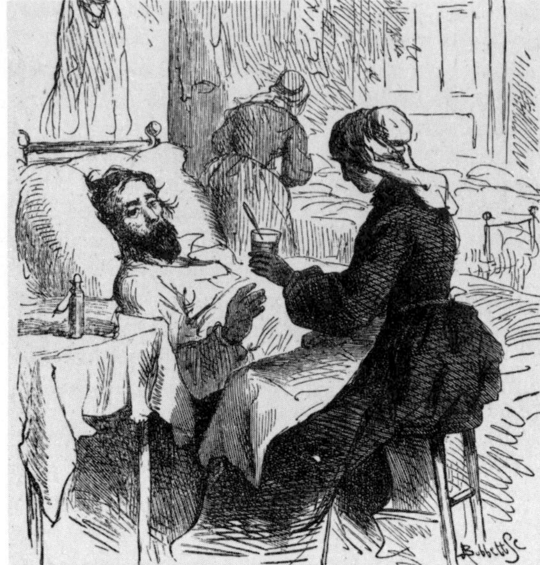
Scene in a Confederate army hospital.

August 23, 1861

But oh, such a day! since I wrote this morning.

Have been with Mrs. Randolph to all the hospitals.

2 I can never again shut out of view the sights I saw of human misery. I sit thinking, shut my eyes, and see it all. Thinking—yes, and there is enough to think about now, God knows. Gillands was the worst. Long rows of ill men on cots. Ill of typhoid fever, of every human ailment—dinner tables, eating, drinking, wounds being dressed—all horrors, to be taken in at one glance. . . .

Then we went to the St. Charles. Horrors upon horrors again—want of organization. Long rows of them dead, dying. Awful smells, awful sights.

3 A boy from home had sent for me. He was lying in a cot, ill of fever. Next him a man died in convulsions while we stood there.

I was making arrangements with a nurse, hiring him to take care of this lad. I do not remember any more, for I fainted. . . .

AT A GLANCE

- Mrs. Davis comes to Mary Chesnut with news of a major Confederate victory.
- James Chesnut has survived the battle.
- Mary Chesnut visits hospitals full of sick, wounded, and dying men.

1 BACKGROUND

The Battle of Bull Run, July 21, 1861, was won by the Confederates and greatly encouraged the South.

2 THEME

The hospital scenes make the costs of war an all-too-vivid reality, as the writer visits the wounded.

3 TONE

The objective tone with which the diarist describes the scene accentuates its horror.

GUIDED READING

LITERAL QUESTIONS

1a. What is Mary Chesnut's first reaction to news of the victory? (She is stunned and then grateful.)

2a. Where does she go with Mrs. Randolph? (to all the local hospitals)

INFERENTIAL QUESTIONS

1b. Why does she react in this way? (She has been very anxious, apparently expecting the worst.)

2b. Why does she react so strongly to what she sees there? (Thus far, her journal entries have spoken of the war as a distant crisis. This is the first time that the horrors of war have been made real to her in such a graphic way.)

AT A GLANCE

- Chesnut notes that some women are being searched, suspected of smuggling arms and information for the North.
- The war is progressing badly for the Confederates.
- She quotes General Winfield Scott on the Southern personality.

1 STYLE: PUN

Mrs. Chesnut makes a play on the word *arms,* meaning "weapons." Her ironic wit captures the grimness of the situation, in which everyone is suspect.

2 THEME

Her determination never to be forced back into the Union shows the depth of the writer's belief that the Confederate cause is just.

3 AUDIENCE

The journal is primarily an outlet for the writer's feelings and observations, but she recognizes its eventual importance as a historical document for a wider audience.

4 STYLE: ALLUSION

The use of allusions shows Mary Chesnut's intelligence and level of education. The allusions here suggest endurance in the face of great suffering and the hope that the suffering is transient.

5 JOURNAL

The author's introspection leads her to consider how little freedom anyone really has. She feels that most people are victims of their circumstances and expresses empathy for them.

August 29, 1861

Women who come before the public are in a bad box now. False hair is taken off and searched for papers. Pistols are sought for [under] "cotillons renversés."[11] Bustles are "suspect." All manner of things, they say, come over the border under the huge hoops
1 now worn. So they are ruthlessly torn off. Not legs but arms are looked for under hoops. And sad to say, found. Then women are used as detectives and searchers to see that no men come over in petticoats.

So the poor creatures coming this way are humiliated to the deepest degree.

February 11, 1862

Confederate affairs in a blue way. Roanoke taken, Fort Henry on the Tennessee River open to them, and we fear the Mississippi River, too. We have evacuated Romney—wherever that is. New armies, new fleets, swarming and threatening everywhere.

2 We ought to have as good a conceit of ourselves as they have of us—and to be willing to do as much to save ourselves from a nauseous union with them as they are willing to do by way of revengeful coercion in forcing us back.

You'll never win us back, no never—etc., etc.

England's eye is scornful and scoffing as she turns it toward us—and on our miseries. I have nervous chills every day. Bad news is killing me. . . .

March 10, 1862

3 Congaree House. Second year. Confederate independence. I write daily for my own distractions. These memoirs *pour servir*[12] may some future day afford dates, facts, and prove useful to more important people than I am. I do not wish to do any harm or to hurt anyone. If any scandalous stories creep in, they are easily burned. It is hard, in such a hurry as things are in, to separate wheat from chaff.

Now I have made my protest and written down my wishes. I can scribble on with a free will and free conscience. . . .

4 Medea—when asked: "Country, wealth, husband, children—all gone. What remains?" "Medea remains." . . .[13]

"There is a time in most men's lives when they resemble Job, sitting among the ashes[14] and drinking in the full bitterness of complicated misfortune." . . .

May 13, 1862

Read Beverley Tucker's *Partisan.*[15]

Just such a rosewater revolution he imagines as we fancied we were to have—and now the reality is hideous and an agony.

5 The color of slaves—that is all—the misery of poverty, alike everywhere, only a person can be beaten with many stripes by his own family—his father or mother—or schoolmaster or superior officer by land or sea, or master, if he is an apprentice, *or* her husband, if she is a woman—everybody who chooses, if she be a child.

Wherever there is a cry of pain, I am on the side of the one who cries.

June 11, 1862

General Scott on Southern soldiers. He says we have élan, courage, woodcraft, consummate horsemanship, endurance of pain equal to the Indians, but that we will not submit to discipline. We will not take care of things or husband our resources. Where we are, there is waste and destruction. If it could all be done

---

11. **"cotillons renversés"** [cō tē yon′rän ver sā′]: petticoats.
12. ***pour servir*** [po͞or′ser vēr′]: French for "in order to serve."
13. **"Medea remains":** from Act 2 of *Medea* by Seneca, a Roman dramatist. Medea was a suffering, tragic figure.
14. **sitting . . . ashes:** the reference is to Job 2 : 8. Job suffered greatly but retained his faith in God.
15. ***Partisan:** The Partisan Leader: A Tale of the Future,* an 1836 tale about a war to found a southern Confederacy.

GUIDED READING

LITERAL QUESTION

1a. On May 13 how does Chesnut describe the reality of revolution? ("hideous" and "agony")

INFERENTIAL QUESTION

1b. What causes her to adopt this view? (She has seen the horrors of the hospitals; the South seems to be losing the war; the Southern way of life is breaking down.)

1 by one wild desperate dash, we would do it. But he does not think we can stand the long blank months between the acts—waiting! We can bear pain without a murmur, but we will not submit to be bored. . . .

I know how it feels to die—I have felt it again and again.

For instance. Someone calls out, "Albert Sidney Johnston is killed." My heart stands still. I feel no more. I am for so many seconds, so many minutes—I know not how long—I am utterly without sensation of any kind—dead. And then there is that great throb, that keen agony of physical pain—the works are wound up again, the ticking of the clock begins anew, and I take up the burden of life once more. Someday it will stop too long, or my feeble heart will be too worn out to make that awakening jar, and all will be over. I know not—think when the end comes that there will be any difference except the miracle
2 of the new wind up, throb. And now good news is just as bad—"Hurrah—Stonewall[16] has saved us!" Pleasure that is almost pain—

June 29, 1862

Victory! Victory heads every telegram now, one reads on the bulletin board.

It is the anniversary of the battle of Fort Moultrie.[17]

They went off so quickly. I wonder if it is not a trap laid for us, to lead us away from Richmond—to some place where they can manage to do us more harm.

3 And now comes the list of killed and wounded.

Victory does not seem to soothe the sore hearts. Mrs. Haskell has five sons before the enemy's illimitable cannon. Mrs. Preston two.

A call from that dark-eyed one—Mrs. C. She has adopted a languid and helpless man-

16. **Stonewall:** Thomas Jonathan (Stonewall) Jackson (1824–1863), Confederate general.
17. **battle . . . Moultrie:** a battle of the Revolutionary War.

Soldiers in the streets of Richmond.

ner. She has taken her belle-mère example to heart, but the latter has been found out. She may talk in as silly a manner as she pleases, she will never deceive anybody into thinking her a fool anymore.

This fair one rejoices that her sons were too young to be soldiers. "Of course, one fretted and worried about one's husband—but then, everyone knew husbands had a way of taking care of themselves. But, oh—the heartbreak and misery if one's son was there."

Then she gave us details of the fight. "McClellan is routed. And we have 12,000 prisoners."

"Prisoners! And what are we to do with them? We can't feed our own people."

July 26, 1864

When I remember all the truehearted, the lighthearted, the gay and gallant boys who have come laughing, singing, dancing in my way in the three years past, I have looked into their

AT A GLANCE

- Mary Chesnut feels that she dies with each death of which she hears.
- Victories are bought at a great price.
- She hears about Union prisoners and wonders how they can be fed.

1 PURPOSE

The diarist's reflections on the Southern character show her attempt to gain perspective on the situation.

2 TONE

The writer sees a bitter irony in the fact that victory only prolongs suffering. She suggests that it would be better not to be saved.

3 THEME

The grim, matter-of-fact telling of the deaths and woundings of friends' sons reveals how quickly the glorious causes of wars degenerate into a series of personal tragedies.

GUIDED READING

LITERAL QUESTIONS

1a. What does Mary Chesnut declare that she has felt again and again? ("how it feels to die")

2a. What can victory no longer do? ("soothe the sore hearts")

INFERENTIAL QUESTIONS

1b. Although she has not served in battle, why might Chesnut feel this way? (She has seen many men die in the hospital and has also shared the grief of bereaved families.)

2b. Why is this true? (Each victory has been bought at the price of great suffering.)

AT A GLANCE

She remembers the young, dead soldiers and wonders what can be worth such sacrifice.

1 THEME

Mary Chesnut's experience with war has led her to question whether any cause, no matter how righteous, can justify the price.

REFLECTING ON THE SELECTION

How do Chesnut's feelings about war change as it progresses? (She begins with the attitude that war is necessary, although not desirable. By the end she feels that probably nothing justifies war.)

STUDY QUESTIONS

1. firing on Fort Sumter; "a delusion and a snare"
2. wept; "had no heart to speak"
3. hospitals; wounded and dying; fainted
4. to distract herself, for future generations
5. "hideous and an agony"
6. worries for their safety
7. is fearful of war and feels nothing is worth its price, yet is loyal supporter of Confederacy; no
8. woman's point of view; shows inconsistency of human reactions; personal
9. Answers will vary, but most will say yes.

LITERARY FOCUS

Answers will vary: advantages—fresh, candid; limitations—little perspective.

brave young eyes and helped them as I could every way and then seen them no more forever. They lie stark and cold, dead upon the battlefield or moldering away in hospitals or prisons—which is worse. I think, if I consider the long array of those bright youths and loyal men who have gone to their deaths almost before my very eyes, my heart might break, too.

1 Is anything worth it? This fearful sacrifice—this awful penalty we pay for war?

STUDY QUESTIONS

Recalling

1. What historic event occurred on the night of April 12? What is Chesnut's assessment of the event?
2. According to the entry for July 16, what did Mary Chesnut do when her husband went off to the war? How did she react on July 22 when Mrs. Davis told her of the battle?
3. Where did Chesnut go on August 23? What did she see there? What happened to her?
4. On March 10 for what reason does Chesnut say she kept her journal?
5. What does Chesnut say about the reality of war on May 13, 1862?

Interpreting

6. What concerns does Chesnut express about her husband and friends?
7. Briefly describe Chesnut's attitude toward the war and toward the Confederacy. Are her feelings consistent?
8. Identify at least three characteristics of Mary Chesnut's journal that make it different from histories or memoirs by important politicians or generals of the time.

Extending

9. Do you think Chesnut is honest about her feelings? Why or why not?

LITERARY FOCUS

The Journal

A **journal,** like a **diary,** is a day-to-day account that a person writes of his or her life. Millions of people keep diaries; most of them are never seen by anyone other than the writer. Some journals are written self-consciously, with an eye to readers. Some preserve ordinary thoughts in ordinary language and so have little worth to anyone other than the writer. Some preserve extraordinary thoughts in language that is alive and permanent.

The special quality of a journal is that it plunges us into the midst of life. If it sounds too self-conscious, too "literary," it loses the flavor of an immediate, spontaneous response to daily events as they are happening. However, if it merely lists dull details, it will be of little interest to anyone except perhaps a historian.

Mary Chesnut's journal is successful both as a diary and as literature. She is a moving and gifted writer whose experiences we are able to share over a hundred years after they were recorded.

Thinking About the Journal

■ What do you think are the advantages of writing down ideas and impressions in a journal day by day, as the events take place? What are the limitations of this method?

COMPOSITION

Writing About a Diary

■ Write a brief essay describing the variations in Chesnut's attitude toward war as her journal progresses. Begin by describing her initial attitude. Then tell how she changes, citing examples and details from the journal. Consider especially the entries for April 12 and 13 and those following July 22, 1861.

Writing a Journal Entry

■ Imagine that you have witnessed a public event that involved many people. Write a journal entry describing the event. Begin by giving a "bird's-eye view" of the whole event, including some objective facts. Then make the event personal, as Mary Chesnut does, by focusing on your own experience of the event.

COMPOSITION: GUIDELINES FOR EVALUATION

WRITING ABOUT A DIARY

Objective

To describe changing attitudes in a journal

Guidelines for Evaluation

- suggested length: four to six paragraphs
- should describe the variations in Chesnut's attitude
- should state how her attitude changes
- should cite examples and details from the journal

WRITING A JOURNAL ENTRY

Objective

To write a journal entry describing an event

Guidelines for Evaluation

- suggested length: three to five paragraphs
- should be written from the point of view of an eyewitness
- should describe a large public event
- should give an overview of the event
- should include personal details and comments

Robert E. Lee *1807–1870*

Robert Edward Lee was born at Stratford Hall, Virginia, into one of the oldest and most esteemed families in the nation. Thomas Lee had been a royal governor of Virginia; Richard Henry Lee was the delegate to the Continental Congress who in 1776 proposed that the colonies "are, and of right ought to be" independent. Robert's father, Light-Horse Harry Lee, was a hero of the Revolution and a governor of Virginia.

Following in his father's footsteps, Lee chose a career in the military, graduating with high honors from the United States Military Academy at West Point. During the Mexican-American War he rose to the rank of colonel and was praised as "the greatest military genius in America." In 1852 he became superintendent of West Point.

The War Between the States presented Lee with a heart-breaking dilemma. Although he supported neither slavery nor secession, he knew he could not fight against family and neighbors in his beloved Virginia. Offered the command of the Federal Army, he refused and resigned his commission. He joined the Confederate forces and took command of the Army of Northern Virginia. After brilliant victories at Manassas, Fredericksburg, and Chancellorsville, he was made general-in-chief of the Confederate armies.

On April 9, 1865, with the collapse of Confederate forces, Lee surrendered to Ulysses S. Grant at Appomattox. He told his army: "Men, we have fought through the war together. I have done my best for you; my heart is too full to say more." After the war Lee attempted to repair the damage that had been done and urged fellow Southerners to put their bitterness behind them. Adored by his troops and respected by his enemies, Lee remains a symbol of not only Southern but American dignity.

Lee was an able writer. His letters are of interest for the light they throw on historic events and for the revelations they give us into the mind and heart of a great statesman. In the following letter, written to his sister, Lee explains his reason for resigning from the Federal Army.

■ What reasons does Lee give for deserting the Union? Can you see why he made that decision?

AT A GLANCE

- Lee writes to his sister living in Maryland, a Union state.
- He will remain loyal to the Confederacy, for he cannot bring himself to fight against home and family.

LITERARY OPTIONS

- tone
- purpose

THEMATIC OPTIONS

- the nature of loyalty
- conflict and resolution

1 TONE

Lee states simply and straightforwardly the reasons for his decision.

2 THEME

The war has created an enormous conflict of loyalties: Lee must follow his conscience as to which loyalty has the greater claim.

3 PURPOSE

Lee's purpose is to explain his actions to his sister and to seek her understanding, if not her agreement. Here he shows that he understands her point of view, too.

REFLECTING ON THE SELECTION

What can you learn about Lee from the tone of his letter? (Students may suggest that Lee is forthright, devoted to his family, highly principled, and modest about his talents.)

STUDY QUESTIONS

1. whether he would fight against Virginia
2. devotion, loyalty, duty; raise his hand against his relatives and home; to resign his commission
3. to show difficulty of decision
4. torn between strong and conflicting loyalties
5. honest, noble, humble, compassionate

Robert E. Lee

Letter to His Sister

To Mrs. Anne Marshall
Baltimore, Maryland

Arlington, Virginia
April 20, 1861

My Dear Sister:

I am grieved at my inability to see you. I have been waiting for
a more convenient season, which has brought to many before me
1 deep and lasting regret. Now we are in a state of war which will
yield to nothing. The whole South is in a state of revolution, into
which Virginia, after a long struggle, has been drawn; and though I
recognize no necessity for this state of things, and would have forborne
and pleaded to the end for redress of grievances, real or supposed,
yet in my own person I had to meet the question whether
I should take part against my native State.

2 With all my devotion to the Union, and the feeling of loyalty and duty of an American citizen, I have not been able to make up my mind to raise my hand against my relatives, my children, my home. I have, therefore, resigned my commission in the Army, and, save in defense of my native State (with the sincere hope that my poor services may never be needed), I hope I may never be called upon to draw my sword.

3 I know you will blame me, but you must think as kindly as you can, and believe that I have endeavored to do what I thought right. To show you the feeling and struggle it has cost me I send you a copy of my letter of resignation. I have no time for more. May God guard and protect you and yours and shower upon you everlasting blessings, is the prayer of

Your devoted brother,
R. E. Lee

STUDY QUESTIONS

Recalling

1. According to the first paragraph, what question did Lee have to meet?
2. According to the second paragraph, what did Lee feel toward the Union and as an American citizen? What could he nevertheless *not* do? What decision did he therefore make?
3. Why does Lee say he enclosed the copy of his letter of resignation?

Interpreting

4. Briefly describe in your own words Lee's state of mind in making the decision to resign his commission from the Federal Army.
5. What kind of person does this letter reveal Lee to have been?

Abraham Lincoln *1809–1865*

"We cannot escape history," Abraham Lincoln once said. Lincoln himself was caught in history and proved to be one of history's greatest and most tragic personalities.

Born in a log cabin in Kentucky, Lincoln spent his boyhood in Indiana where he struggled to get an education, taking every opportunity to read the books that were available to him. In 1830 his family, plagued by poverty, moved to Illinois where Lincoln became interested in politics. Two years later he ran for the Illinois state legislature—and lost. He continued to pursue a political career however, and moved steadily into public view. In 1858 he debated Stephen Douglas, his opponent in the Illinois Senate race, and became nationally known as a brilliant, compelling speaker.

Elected the nation's sixteenth President in 1860, Lincoln saw as his chief duty the preservation of the Union. In speech after speech, he inspired Americans at a time of dark despair. His dream was that the nation be reunited "with malice toward none; and charity for all." But five days after Lee's surrender at Appomattox, Lincoln was shot in a Washington theater, and his plans for a harmonious reunion died with him.

Lincoln's speeches were written to express his convictions and convince others to share them. His language is masterful: plain, powerful, dignified, as in the Gettysburg Address. On November 19, 1863, Lincoln attended the dedication of a national cemetery at Gettysburg, the site of a great but costly Union victory. The main speaker was Edward Everett, one of the most admired orators in the country. Everett gave a lengthy address, and Lincoln's aim was to make a few pertinent remarks following Everett's performance. Afterward, however, Everett wrote to Lincoln: "I should be glad if I could flatter myself that I came as near to the central idea of the occasion in two hours, as you did in two minutes." In the ten sentences that appear on the following page, Lincoln gave the world a masterpiece of oratory and one of the greatest speeches ever written by an American.

■ What ideas and images in these ten famous sentences have made them so universally memorable?

AT A GLANCE

- Eighty-seven years before, the country was founded on principles of liberty and equality.
- The battlefield being dedicated has already been consecrated by those who died there.
- The living must dedicate themselves to the rebirth of the nation.

LITERARY OPTIONS

- parallelism
- tone

THEMATIC OPTIONS

- responsibilities of democracy
- loss and recovery
- visions and ideals

1 PARALLELISM AND TONE

The parallel structure and the choice of connotative words *(dedicate, consecrate, hallow)* lend a solemn, stately tone to the speech. The words are sequenced to build in emotion.

2 THEME

Lincoln's main objective is to save the Union. Here he advances the idea that the sacrifice of the soldiers places on the living a responsibility to finish the dead heroes' work.

3 PARALLELISM AND TONE

The address ends with parallel phrases that give it a hymnlike, prayerful tone.

REFLECTING ON THE SELECTION

How does Lincoln use images of birth, life, and death to give his speech coherence? (Students may note that he begins with the birth of the nation and progresses to life, death, and a prayer that from death will come rebirth.)

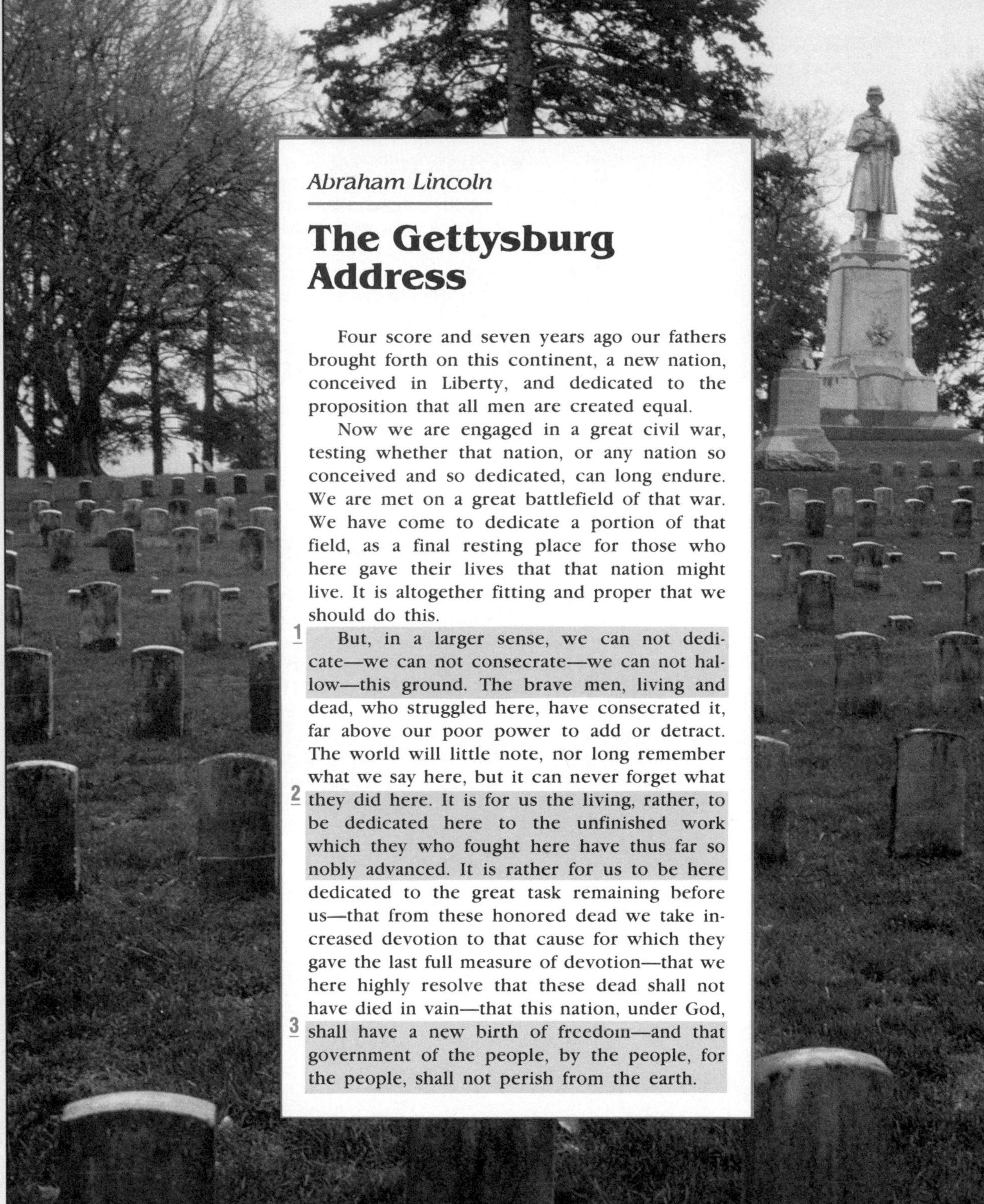

Abraham Lincoln

The Gettysburg Address

Four score and seven years ago our fathers brought forth on this continent, a new nation, conceived in Liberty, and dedicated to the proposition that all men are created equal.

Now we are engaged in a great civil war, testing whether that nation, or any nation so conceived and so dedicated, can long endure. We are met on a great battlefield of that war. We have come to dedicate a portion of that field, as a final resting place for those who here gave their lives that that nation might live. It is altogether fitting and proper that we should do this.

1 But, in a larger sense, we can not dedicate—we can not consecrate—we can not hallow—this ground. The brave men, living and dead, who struggled here, have consecrated it, far above our poor power to add or detract. The world will little note, nor long remember what we say here, but it can never forget what
2 they did here. It is for us the living, rather, to be dedicated here to the unfinished work which they who fought here have thus far so nobly advanced. It is rather for us to be here dedicated to the great task remaining before us—that from these honored dead we take increased devotion to that cause for which they gave the last full measure of devotion—that we here highly resolve that these dead shall not have died in vain—that this nation, under God,
3 shall have a new birth of freedom—and that government of the people, by the people, for the people, shall not perish from the earth.

GUIDED READING

LITERAL QUESTION

1a. What attitude does Lincoln call upon the living to have? (dedication to the task for which soldiers died)

INFERENTIAL QUESTION

1b. What task needs to be accomplished? (saving the Union and making the nation whole again)

STUDY QUESTIONS

Recalling

1. What happened "four score and seven years ago"?
2. What is happening "now," according to paragraph 2?
3. According to paragraph 3, what is the "great task remaining before us"?

Interpreting

4. State in your own words the kind of nation that Lincoln says is having its endurance tested by the Civil War.
5. In your own words, state the main point of Lincoln's speech. For what does he argue?
6. To what chief emotion or feeling does Lincoln's speech appeal?

Extending

7. Do you think the Gettysburg Address is more powerful as a written document or an oral presentation? Explain your answer.

VOCABULARY

Diction and Style

Diction, or word choice, has a significant effect on a writer's style. The words a writer chooses to use must be appropriate to the audience, the occasion, the subject, the speaker, and the tone. How different, how unmemorable, would have been Lincoln's address if he had chosen words appropriate to a casual style: "Eighty-seven years ago some folks set up a government so that everybody could be free and equal." Instead he used a formal vocabulary, noble, dignified, worthy of its subject.

■ Choose five words from the Gettysburg Address, and tell why Lincoln's use of each is appropriate. Define each word precisely, and give at least one synonym that would not be as fitting as the word Lincoln chose to use.

COMPOSITION

Analyzing Coherence

■ In a brief essay analyze Lincoln's methods for creating coherence in the Gettysburg Address. Begin by describing how Lincoln uses transition words such as *but* and *rather.* Then tell how he uses pronouns that refer to things said earlier, words that indicate a sequence in time, and repetitions of words. Show how these devices tie the sentences together and help structure the address.

Writing an Oral Tribute

■ Choose one of the people you have encountered thus far in this unit, and write a speech in which you pay tribute to him or her. The speech may be a funeral oration or a tribute to be made at a present-day ceremony. Like Lincoln, keep your speech to ten sentences. Remember that it is a *speech,* to be read aloud.

STUDY QUESTIONS

1. America became a nation.
2. Civil War being fought, testing if a nation founded on principles of liberty and equality can endure
3. insure that democracy does not perish
4. a democratic nation
5. Audience must insure preservation of democracy that soldiers have died for, continue fight to preserve Union.
6. patriotism
7. Answers will vary, but students should note the tight structure and power.

VOCABULARY

Examples:

- score (twenty years): Saying "eighty-seven years ago" instead of "four score and seven years ago" would have sounded less noble and been less memorable.
- conceived (to form or develop mentally): A synonym such as *formed* would not have the connotations of thoughtfully giving birth to a new nation.
- dedicated (devoted to a special or sacred purpose): A synonym such as *based on* would not have the connotations of devotion.
- proposition (something offered for consideration or discussion): A synonym such as *suggestion* would have been weaker than this term.
- endure (to continue to be; to suffer without yielding): A synonym such as *last* would not have the connotations of growing stronger through suffering.

COMPOSITION: GUIDELINES FOR EVALUATION

ANALYZING COHERENCE

Objective

To analyze the coherence of a speech

Guidelines for Evaluation

- suggested length: three to five paragraphs
- should cite use of transitions
- should cite pronouns tying sentences together
- should cite words indicating time sequence
- should cite instances of word repetition
- should explain how devices structure address

WRITING AN ORAL TRIBUTE

Objective

To write a tribute to be delivered orally

Guidelines for Evaluation

- suggested length: ten sentences
- should pay tribute to a person encountered in this unit
- should be appropriate for a funeral oration or a present-day ceremony honoring the person
- should use techniques of oratory

Chief Joseph *c. 1840–1904*

Chief Joseph succeeded his father as leader of the Nez Perce tribe in 1873. At that time, under a treaty of 1863, the tribal lands in the Wallowa Valley of Oregon had been ceded to the United States Government. Chief Joseph considered the treaty illegal and refused to recognize it. When the government attempted to remove the Nez Perce by force, Chief Joseph decided to fight.

Though his warriors won several battles, they were heavily outnumbered by the U.S. Army. Chief Joseph's strategy was to attempt to march across the Canadian border to join forces with the Sioux. The march was a brilliantly conducted retreat across Idaho and Montana, punctuated by battles between the Indians and federal troops. However, after traveling over a thousand miles, the band of men, women, and children were on the brink of collapse. Forty miles from the Canadian border, Chief Joseph was forced to surrender. He was taken to Leavenworth prison and, after his release, to the Indian Territory in what is now Oklahoma. He spent the last years of his life on the Colville Indian Reservation in the state of Washington.

Chief Joseph never ceased to strive for the betterment of conditions for Native Americans. In 1879 he wrote "An Indian's View of Indian Affairs" for the *North American Review;* in 1903 he made an impressive visit to Washington, D.C., on behalf of his people.

The following extract is from Chief Joseph's speech of surrender, made in October of 1877. Its natural nobility of spirit and simple language make a powerful statement about the horrors of warfare.

■ What reasons do people usually give for refusing to go to war? How do Chief Joseph's reasons differ? How are they similar?

I Will Fight No More Forever

1 Tell General Howard I know his heart. What he told me before, I have in my heart. I am tired of fighting. Our chiefs are killed. Looking Glass is dead. Toohoolhoolzote is dead. The old men are all dead. It is the young men who say yes and no. He who led on the young men is dead. It is cold and we have no blankets. The little children are freezing to death. My people, some of them, have run away to the hills and have no blankets, no food; no one knows where they are—perhaps freezing to death. I want to have time to look for my children and see how many I can find.
2 Maybe I shall find them among the dead. Hear me, my chiefs. I am tired; my heart is sick and sad. From where the sun now stands I will fight no more forever.

Thomas Gilcrease Institute

Detail from *Chief Joseph's Surrender,* Olaf C. Seltzer.

STUDY QUESTIONS

Recalling

1. Name five of the conditions that cause Chief Joseph to surrender.
2. What promise does Chief Joseph make in the last sentence?

Interpreting

3. Near the end of the speech, to whom does Chief Joseph refer when he says "my children"? What does this reference suggest about Chief Joseph's role?
4. What purpose other than surrender do you think is served by Chief Joseph's speech? How would you characterize the tone of the speech?

Extending

5. Because war is one of the most terrible of human experiences, it is one of the most difficult to write about. What qualities do you think a writer should possess to be able to communicate to readers the reality of war?

COMPARING WRITERS

■ All the people whose works appear in this section were caught in the web of history. How, in his or her own way, did each person rise above the suffering? What evidence in the writings of Douglass, Lee, Lincoln, and Chief Joseph explains why they have come to be regarded as symbols of noble ideals?

AT A GLANCE

- Chief Joseph says that he is too tired and heartsick to continue fighting.
- Many of his people are dead; many others are freezing and scattered.

LITERARY OPTIONS

- tone
- purpose

THEMATIC OPTIONS

- the costs of war
- conflict and resolution

1 TONE

In surrender Chief Joseph is dignified but mournful. His litany of the price his people have paid emphasizes his great sadness.

2 PURPOSE

Although the immediate purpose of the speech is to surrender to federal troops, Chief Joseph uses the occasion to decry the pain and destructiveness of all war.

REFLECTING ON THE SELECTION

What do the reasons that Chief Joseph gives for surrendering reveal about his character? (Students may suggest courage, responsibility, and honor.)

STUDY QUESTIONS

1. chiefs dead, cold, no blankets, no food, desire to help those who have run off to the hills
2. "I will fight no more forever."
3. his people; spiritual father of his people, responsible for their welfare
4. statement against war; resigned, mournful
5. Answers should include: ability to observe, describe, and comprehend; not be overwhelmed; honesty, compassion.

COMPARING WRITERS

- rising above suffering—*slave spirituals:* faith; *Douglass:* education, understanding, enlightenment; *Chesnut:* honesty, compassion; *Lee:* morality; *Lincoln:* preserve Union, not revenge; *Chief Joseph:* leadership, concern for people's welfare
- symbols—*Douglass:* intelligence, compassion for slaves and slave owners; *Lee:* humility, integrity; *Lincoln:* dedication; *Chief Joseph:* concern for people

THREE MAJOR WRITERS

Walt Whitman *1819–1892*

In 1855 Ralph Waldo Emerson, the most famous literary figure of his day, received a book from an unknown poet. The book was called *Leaves of Grass,* and the poet's name was Walt Whitman. A picture of the author appeared on the title page: bearded, in work pants, shirt open, wide-brimmed hat cocked at a jaunty angle. He seemed at once inviting and distanced, friendly and yet somehow alone. He seemed, indeed, as he described himself, "one of the roughs." Emerson thought the book was "the most extraordinary piece of wit and wisdom that America has yet contributed." Here was the new American voice he had been calling for. However, when he wrote to Whitman in a private letter, "I greet you at the beginning of a great career," he was startled by the young man's response. Whitman, without Emerson's permission, quoted Emerson's praise-filled remark on the cover of the next edition of *Leaves of Grass.*

Such audacity was a mark of the spirit of the man whom many now consider America's greatest poet. A great reader, he was nurtured by the Transcendentalists, yet he was no country-dwelling New Englander contemplating the quiet joys of nature. He had spent his early manhood in New York City, soaking up its sights and sounds. Later he traveled down the Mississippi, absorbing the variety of America. He listened to the talk of street gangs and working people, of farmers and soldiers, and saw in them the essence of America. He loved his country and its democracy, which allowed all forms of human spirit to flourish. His poetry extends the Transcendentalists' joy in nature to a love for humanity in all its manifestations. Whitman's verse became a sweeping catalogue of America, pouring forth like the operatic arias of which he was so fond.

Whitman was born on Long Island, New York, into a devout Quaker family. He grew up in Brooklyn, where he left school at eleven to become, in turn, an office boy, a doctor's helper, a printer's assistant, a journalist, a typesetter, and a printer. At twenty-seven he became editor of the *Brooklyn Eagle,* but he left the job when the paper took a proslavery stand. Later he taught in country schools. When in 1855 he came out with the first edition of *Leaves of Grass* (containing twelve poems), he had to set the type himself and pay for the book's publication.

Acceptance by the American public came slowly. Most readers—and there were few enough of them—were shocked by the unconventional subject matter, the unusual forms, and the break with standard rhyme and meter that Whitman's "free verse" constituted. John Greenleaf Whittier threw his copy of the book into his fireplace.

Whitman remained undaunted. He kept arranging, rearranging, and adding to *Leaves of Grass* throughout his lifetime, envisioning all of his work as one vast poem. He added the poems from his volume *Drum-Taps* (1865), which grew out of his experiences as a volunteer nurse in the Civil War. He added poems that have since been recognized as among the greatest of American expressions: the elegy to Abraham Lincoln, "When Lilacs Last in the Dooryard Bloom'd"; "Crossing Brooklyn Ferry"; and "Out of the Cradle Endlessly Rocking." Even in old age Whitman kept working, attempting to put "a Person, a human being (myself, in the latter half of the Nineteenth Century, in America) freely, fully and truly on record." In the final, "deathbed" edition of *Leaves of Grass* (1891) there were 383 titled poems, and the person they put on record was one of the most remarkable America has ever produced.

One of the poems that most fully captures the essence of Whitman is "Song of Myself." It is his celebration of individuality and of his oneness with the world.

■ If you were to write poetry that "celebrates life itself," what images would you choose to show that "celebration"?

Walt Whitman

from Song of Myself

1

I celebrate myself, and sing myself,
And what I assume you shall assume,
For every atom belonging to me as good belongs to you.

I loaf and invite my soul,
I lean and loaf at my ease observing a spear of summer grass.

My tongue, every atom of my blood, formed from this soil, this air,
Born here of parents born here from parents the same, and their
parents the same,

AT A GLANCE

- Section 1: The poet celebrates himself and all other individuals.
- He speaks as an American, born of American parents.

LITERARY OPTIONS

- diction
- imagery
- main idea

THEMATIC OPTIONS

- individualism
- self-reliance
- the power of nature

MAIN IDEA

Whitman is celebrating the infinite variety within the individual (section 1, ll. 1–3).

GUIDED READING

LITERAL QUESTION

1a. What does Whitman say that the reader should assume? (what he, the poet, assumes)

INFERENTIAL QUESTION

1b. Why should the reader do so? (In celebrating his individuality Whitman is speaking for every individual. What is true for him is true for everyone.)

AT A GLANCE

- The poet is thirty-seven years old, living freely and naturally.
- Section 4: He is observing life while living it.
- Section 6: He calls the grass a sign of hope and renewal.

SPEAKER

Whitman's voice in the poem is informal, inviting, and inclusive (section 1, ll. 12–13).

METAPHOR

The grass is the "handkerchief" of God—that is, an example of God's design and a reminder of a higher power (section 6, ll. 4–6).

SYMBOL

Grass, which dies each fall and grows again each spring, is a symbol of rebirth and renewal (section 6, l. 10).

I, now thirty-seven years old in perfect health begin,
Hoping to cease not till death.

Creeds and schools in abeyance,
Retiring back a while sufficed at what they are, but never forgotten,
I harbor for good or bad, I permit to speak at every hazard,
Nature without check with original energy.

4

. . .
Apart from the pulling and hauling stands what I am,
Stands amused, complacent, compassionating, idle, unitary,
Looks down, is erect, or bends an arm on an impalpable certain rest,
Looking with side-curved head curious what will come next,
Both in and out of the game and watching and wondering at it. . . .

6

A child said *What is the grass?* fetching it to me with full hands;
How could I answer the child? I do not know what it is any more than he.

I guess it must be the flag of my disposition, out of hopeful green
    stuff woven.

Or I guess it is the handkerchief of the Lord,
A scented gift and remembrancer[1] designedly dropped,
Bearing the owner's name someway in the corners, that we may see
    and remark, and say *Whose?*

. . .
    What do you think has become of the young and old men?
And what do you think has become of the women and children?

They are alive and well somewhere,
The smallest sprout shows there is really no death,
And if ever there was it led forward life, and does not wait at the
    end to arrest it,
And ceased the moment life appeared.

All goes onward and outward, nothing collapses,
And to die is different from what any one supposed, and luckier.

---

1. **remembrancer:** reminder.

GUIDED READING

LITERAL QUESTION

1a. In section 1 what does the poet refer to as "in abeyance"? ("Creeds and schools")

INFERENTIAL QUESTION

1b. What does this statement reveal about the perspective from which he writes? (He is writing from a natural perspective, a self-reliance like that endorsed by Emerson.)

17

These are really the thoughts of all men in all ages and lands, they are not original with me,
If they are not yours as much as mine they are nothing, or next to nothing,
If they are not the riddle and the untying of the riddle they are nothing,
If they are not just as close as they are distant they are nothing.

This is the grass that grows wherever the land is and the water is,
This the common air that bathes the globe.

42

. . .
This is the city and I am one of the citizens,
Whatever interests the rest interests me, politics, wars, markets, newspapers, schools,
The mayor and councils, banks, tariffs, steamships, factories, stocks, stores, real estate and personal estate.

The little plentiful manikins[2] skipping around in collars and tailed coats,
I am aware who they are, (they are positively not worms or fleas,)
I acknowledge the duplicates of myself, the weakest and shallowest is deathless with me,
What I do and say the same waits for them,
Every thought that flounders in me the same flounders in them.

I know perfectly well my own egotism,
Know my omnivorous[3] lines and must not write any less,
And would fetch you whoever you are flush with myself.

Not words of routine this song of mine,
But abruptly to question, to leap beyond yet nearer bring; . . .

51

The past and present wilt—I have filled them, emptied them,
And proceed to fill my next fold of the future.

Listener up there! what have you to confide to me?
Look in my face while I snuff the sidle of evening,[4]
(Talk honestly, no one else hears you, and I stay only a minute longer.)

---

2. **manikins:** little men.
3. **omnivorous** [om niv′ər əs]: taking in everything; here, covering all subjects.
4. **snuff . . . evening:** put out the light of day, which is moving sideways across the sky.

AT A GLANCE

- Section 17: The poet's thoughts are the thoughts of all people everywhere.
- Section 42: He shares the interests of other citizens.
- He recognizes his own egotism and seeks to draw his reader into it.

MAIN IDEA

The human experience, with all its riddles and mysteries, is universal, shared by all people in all times (section 17, ll. 2–4).

STYLE

The catalog of details helps to capture the vitality and variety of city life. Such lists are typical of Whitman's exuberant style (section 42, ll. 2–3).

MAIN IDEA

The poet's egotism is not self-centered; rather, it is outreaching and inclusive (section 42, ll. 9–11).

SPEAKER

In speaking directly to every reader, Whitman achieves an informality and openness (section 51, ll. 3–5).

GUIDED READING

LITERAL QUESTION

1a. In section 17 what does Whitman say about the thoughts in the poem? (They are not original; they are the thoughts of all men.)

INFERENTIAL QUESTION

1b. What comment is he thereby making about himself and others? (His experience is the experience of all people.)

AT A GLANCE

- Section 51: The poet acknowledges contradictions within himself.
- Section 52: He then compares himself to a hawk, untamed and squawking.
- He gives himself to the earth as an inheritance.

MAIN IDEA

The poet accepts contradictions. His declaration recalls Emerson's comment, in "Self-Reliance": "A foolish consistency is the hobgoblin of little minds" (section 51, ll. 6–8).

VOCABULARY: WORD CHOICE

The words *gab* and *loitering* mark Whitman's lively, informal style (section 52, l. 1).

ONOMATOPOEIA

The word *yawp* mimics the raucous cry of the hawk. Whitman suggests that he means his poetry to be jarring (section 52, ll. 1–3).

REFLECTING ON THE POEM

Who is the "I" of the poem? (Students may suggest that the "I" in the poem both is Whitman's highly personal expression of himself and includes all people in its celebration of individuality.)

Do I contradict myself?
Very well then I contradict myself,
(I am large, I contain multitudes.)

I concentrate toward them that are nigh,[5] I wait on the door-slab.
Who has done his day's work? who will soonest be through with his supper?
Who wishes to walk with me?

Will you speak before I am gone? will you prove already too late?

52

The spotted hawk swoops by and accuses me, he complains of my gab and my loitering.

I too am not a bit tamed, I too am untranslatable,
I sound my barbaric yawp over the roofs of the world.

The last scud[6] of day holds back for me,
It flings my likeness after the rest and true as any on the shadow'd wilds,
It coaxes me to the vapor and the dusk.

I depart as air, I shake my white locks at the runaway sun,
I effuse[7] my flesh in eddies, and drift it in lacy jags.

I bequeath myself to the dirt to grow from the grass I love,
If you want me again look for me under your boot soles.

You will hardly know who I am or what I mean,
But I shall be good health to you nevertheless,
And filter and fiber your blood.

Failing to fetch me at first keep encouraged,
Missing me one place search another,
I stop somewhere waiting for you.

5. **nigh:** near.
6. **scud:** low, dark, wind-driven clouds.
7. **effuse:** pour forth.

GUIDED READING

LITERAL QUESTIONS

1a. In section 52 which descriptive words does the poet use about himself? *(not a bit tamed; untranslatable)*

2a. What advice does the poet offer to someone who cannot find him at first? (continue to search somewhere else)

INFERENTIAL QUESTIONS

1b. What aspects of his personality is Whitman expressing through these words? (unconventionality, exuberance, and freedom of feeling and expression)

2b. What does this advice suggest about Whitman's view of life and death? (Life does not end with death. Past and future will one day be united.)

STUDY QUESTIONS

Recalling

1. According to line 1 of section 1, who is the poet celebrating? Whom do lines 2–3 also include in the celebration?
2. What facts about himself does Whitman reveal in lines 6–9 of section 1? With what adjectives does Whitman describe himself in section 4?
3. Who fetches the grass in section 6? What does Whitman guess the grass might be? What does the "smallest sprout" show?
4. According to section 17, are Whitman's thoughts original? Whose thoughts are they?
5. What does Whitman say he knows "perfectly well" in section 42? What does he say his song is *not?* According to this section, what *is* the purpose of his song?
6. In section 51 what explanation does the poet give for contradicting himself?
7. To what animal does Whitman compare himself in section 52? What does he sound "over the roofs of the world"? Where does he tell us to look for him if we want him again?

Interpreting

8. Describe the relationship Whitman sets up with the reader in the first section.
9. Name as many characteristics of Whitman's "self" as you can. Which characteristics seem the most prominent?
10. Consider the image of the grass in sections 6 and 52. What does the grass have to do with life and death?
11. By associating himself with the grass, what does the poet suggest about himself? Summarize Whitman's attitude toward nature.

Extending

12. Why might Whitman have called his volume of poetry *Leaves of Grass?*

LITERARY FOCUS

Free Verse

Free verse is poetry that has an irregular rhythm and line length and that attempts to avoid any predetermined verse structure; instead, it uses the cadences of natural speech. While it alternates stressed and unstressed syllables as stricter verse forms do, free verse does so in a looser way.

Whitman's poetry is an example of free verse at its most impressive. Listen, for instance, to a line from "Song of Myself":

> A child said *What is the grass?* fetching it to me with full hands;

Here, question and answer create a rising and falling effect, ending in a stop.

Whitman continues:

> How could I answer the child? I do not know what it is any more than he.

The same question-and-answer pattern is repeated, the same rising and falling effect. This is not prose but poetry. It is arranged rhythmically, tightened and loosened by the poet. It has a plan, although the plan seems to "grow" organically—like its subjects, nature and human beings.

Although free verse had been used before Whitman—notably in Italian opera and in the King James translation of the Bible—it was Whitman who pioneered the form and made it acceptable in American poetry. It has since been used by Ezra Pound, T. S. Eliot, William Carlos Williams, Wallace Stevens, and other major American poets of the twentieth century.

Thinking About Free Verse

■ Why is free verse particularly suited to Whitman's ideas? How do you think it relates to Whitman's democratic principles?

STUDY QUESTIONS

1. himself; the reader
2. ■ He is American, from an American family, thirty-seven years old, in good health.
   ■ *amused, complacent, idle, unitary*
3. child; green flag of his disposition, handkerchief of the Lord; that there is no death
4. no; "all men in all ages and lands"
5. his egotism; "words of routine"; "to question, to leap beyond yet nearer bring"
6. He is large and contains multitudes.
7. spotted hawk; "barbaric yawp"; under our boot soles
8. close, informal, intimate
9. ■ enthusiastic, curious, lusty, informal
   ■ Answers will vary.
10. final resting place for life, affirmation of renewal of life
11. "Self" is elemental, filled with wonder, constantly renewed; loves nature as source of spiritual knowledge and comfort, but sees cities and daily activities of humanity as part of nature.
12. The book contains "leaves" (pages) he associates with grass on literal and symbolic levels; grass represents joys and mysteries of life and death.

LITERARY FOCUS

- Whitman's verse sprawls exuberantly on the page, breaking standard forms, and thereby capturing his exuberance, informality, and individuality. Its organic nature reflects his organic view of life.
- Just as he believed in democracy founded on freedom and individualism and not on rigid hierarchies, so too his verse abandons rigid structures for "freedom." Its informality helps him establish his close, informal relationship with every reader.

AT A GLANCE

- The poet hears the songs of Americans.
- The carpenter, the mason, the boatman, the shoemaker, the homemaker, and others sing their songs.
- Each song is different and individual but also powerful and beautiful.

LITERARY OPTIONS

- repetition
- imagery

THEMATIC OPTIONS

- individuality
- democratic spirit
- art and imagination

IMAGERY

The image of a singing America suggests the harmony of many people, alike in enthusiasm (l. 1).

REPETITION

The parallel sentences that list the singers, along with the repetition of *singing,* give the poem form and rhythm (ll. 3–6).

MAIN IDEA

The poet emphasizes the uniqueness of each individual while also celebrating the harmonious unity that individualism creates (l. 9).

REFLECTING ON THE POEM

What does Whitman's focus on certain occupations say about his vision of America? (Students may notice that he has chosen to celebrate the work of ordinary people; his vision of America is democratic.)

Walt Whitman

I Hear America Singing

I hear America singing, the varied carols I hear,
Those of mechanics, each one singing his as it should be blithe and strong,
The carpenter singing his as he measures his plank or beam,
The mason singing his as he makes ready for work, or leaves off work,
The boatman singing what belongs to him in his boat, the deckhand singing on the steamboat deck,
The shoemaker singing as he sits on his bench, the hatter singing as he stands,
The woodcutter's song, the plowboy's on his way in the morning, or at noon intermission or at sundown,
The delicious singing of the mother, or of the young wife at work, or of the girl sewing or washing,
Each singing what belongs to him or her and to none else,
The day what belongs to the day—at night the party of young fellows, robust, friendly,
Singing with open mouths their strong melodious songs.

St. Louis Art Museum

Cradling Wheat,
Thomas Hart Benton, 1939.

When the Union army was defeated at the first battle of Bull Run in 1861, many Americans suddenly realized that the war was going to be longer and more terrible than they had thought. Whitman responded with this poem.

Beat! Beat! Drums!

Beat! beat! drums!—blow! bugles! blow!
Through the windows—through doors—burst like a ruthless force,
Into the solemn church, and scatter the congregation,
Into the school where the scholar is studying;
Leave not the bridegroom quiet—no happiness must he have now with his bride,
Nor the peaceful farmer any peace, plowing his field or gathering his grain,
So fierce you whirr and pound you drums—so shrill you bugles blow.

Beat! beat! drums!—blow! bugles! blow!
Over the traffic of cities—over the rumble of wheels in the streets;
Are beds prepared for sleepers at night in the houses? no sleepers must sleep in those beds,
No bargainers' bargains by day—no brokers or speculators[1]—would they continue?
Would the talkers be talking? would the singer attempt to sing?
Would the lawyer rise in the court to state his case before the judge?
Then rattle quicker, heavier drums—you bugles wilder blow.

Beat! beat! drums!—blow! bugles! blow!
Make no parley—stop for no expostulation,
Mind not the timid—mind not the weeper or prayer,
Mind not the old man beseeching the young man,
Let not the child's voice be heard, nor the mother's entreaties,
Make even the trestles to shake the dead where they lie awaiting the hearses,
So strong you thump O terrible drums—so loud you bugles blow.

---

1. **speculators:** people who take large risks in business transactions hoping to make large, quick profits.

AT A GLANCE

In time of war, beating drums and sounding bugles disrupt all normal courses of life.

LITERARY OPTIONS

- repetition
- style: parallelism
- onomatopoeia

THEMATIC OPTIONS

- disruptions caused by war
- conflict and resolution

PARALLELISM

The parallel structures give form to the poem, which has no regular rhyme or meter. Parallel phrasing occurs in each stanza; for example, note the parallel prepositional phrases in lines 3–4.

ONOMATOPOEIA

The words *whirr, pound,* and *shrill* imitate the sounds of machinery and suggest that war is an unfeeling, inhuman force (l. 7).

REPETITION

Each stanza begins with the same line, which becomes a refrain. Furthermore, the last line of each stanza echoes elements from the first, thus suggesting the insistent sound of drums and bugles.

REFLECTING ON THE POEM

What attitude toward war is Whitman expressing in this poem? (Students may suggest that by showing war's disruption of peaceful, innocent lives Whitman presents war as an inexorable and possibly evil force.)

LITERARY OPTIONS

- imagery
- main idea
- repetition

THEMATIC OPTIONS

- personal understanding of nature
- Lincoln's greatness
- the search for meaning

"ASTRONOMER": IMAGERY

The dry catalog of scientific proofs in the professor's lecture contrasts sharply with the "moist" air of nature (ll. 2–3, 7).

"DUST": MAIN IDEA

Lincoln's greatness grows from his actions, not his identity. Hence, the poem's subject is not identified by name.

"SPIDER": REPETITION

The poet repeats words exactly (as in *filament,* l. 4) and through synonyms (see ll. 5, 7, 8, 9–10) to signify that the search for meaning is a continuing task.

REFLECTING ON THE POEMS

How does Whitman use comparison and contrast in each of the three poems? (Whitman contrasts the dry lecture with the restorative power of nature; contrasts Lincoln's almost negligible remains—*dust*—with his heroic achievement; compares his own soul to the persistent, patient spider.)

SELECTION FOR PRACTICE IN ACTIVE READING "When I Heard the Learn'd Astronomer" (TCR 7, p. 64)

Walt Whitman

When I Heard the Learn'd Astronomer

When I heard the learn'd astronomer,
When the proofs, the figures, were ranged in columns before me,
When I was shown the charts and diagrams, to add, divide, and
measure them,
When I sitting heard the astronomer where he lectured with much
applause in the lecture room,
How soon unaccountable I became tired and sick,
Till rising and gliding out I wandered off by myself,
In the mystical moist night air, and from time to time,
Looked up in perfect silence at the stars.

This Dust Was Once the Man

This dust was once the man,
Gentle, plain, just and resolute, under whose cautious hand,
Against the foulest crime in history known in any land or age,
Was saved the Union of these States.

A Noiseless Patient Spider

A noiseless patient spider,
I marked where on a little promontory[1] it stood isolated,
Marked how to explore the vacant vast surrounding,
It launched forth filament,[2] filament, filament, out of itself,
Ever unreeling them, ever tirelessly speeding them.

And you O my soul where you stand,
Surrounded, detached, in measureless oceans of space,
Ceaselessly musing, venturing, throwing, seeking the spheres to
connect them,
Till the bridge you will need be formed, till the ductile[3] anchor hold,
Till the gossamer thread you fling catch somewhere, O my soul.

1. **promontory:** high portion of land extending out into a body of water.
2. **filament:** slender fiber or thread.
3. **ductile** [dukt'əl]: pliant; easily bent.

STUDY QUESTIONS

I Hear America Singing

Recalling

1. According to line 1, what does Whitman hear?
2. Name eight of the people that Whitman hears, according to lines 2–8.
3. According to line 9, what does each person sing?

Interpreting

4. What one word could describe in general what each person sings about?
5. What aspects of American life are being celebrated in this poem? Is the description of America "singing" literal, figurative, or both? Explain.

Beat! Beat! Drums!

Recalling

1. What people do the drums and bugles disturb in each of stanzas 1, 2, and 3?
2. What verbs and adjectives are used to describe the sounds of the drums and bugles?

Interpreting

3. Based on the description of the drums and bugles and the effect they have, what do they seem to represent? What does the simile in line 2 imply?
4. Are the people in stanzas 1 and 2 doing anything out of the ordinary? Why is this significant?
5. Why might the people in stanza 3 be praying, beseeching, and so on? What do the drums and bugles do to their prayers and pleas?
6. Explain how rhythm and repetition reinforce the meaning of the poem. In particular, consider the effect of lines 1, 8, and 15.

Extending

7. What images other than drums and bugles might Whitman have used to make his point?

When I Heard the Learn'd Astronomer

Recalling

1. What aids does the astronomer use to supplement his lecture?
2. What does the poet become as he listens?
3. Where does the poet go when he wanders off? What does he do?

Interpreting

4. What is the effect of the parallel structure and repetition in lines 1–4?
5. How does the poet contrast himself with the astronomer? What wisdom does he find that the astronomer and his audience do not have?

Extending

6. What does this poem have in common with Romantic or Transcendentalist poetry that you have read? In what ways is it different?

This Dust Was Once the Man

Recalling

1. What four adjectives describe the man?
2. What did the man save?

Interpreting

3. To what major event does "the foulest crime in history" refer?
4. Who is the man referred to in the poem?

A Noiseless Patient Spider

Recalling

1. According to stanza 1, where and how is the spider standing? What is it doing?
2. According to stanza 2, where and how is the poet's "soul" standing? What is it doing? What three things is it waiting for?

Interpreting

3. What two things are being compared in this poem? What specific similarities between the two does the poet draw?
4. Why does the soul need to form a "bridge"? To what will the bridge connect it?

STUDY QUESTIONS

I Hear America Singing

1. America singing varied carols
2. mechanics, carpenter, mason, boatman, deckhand, shoemaker, hatter, woodcutter, plowboy
3. "what belongs to him or her and to none else"
4. individuality
5. energy, democracy, freedom; both: literal hearing, figurative hearing of chorus of American democracy

Beat! Beat! Drums!

1. *1:* churchgoers, scholar, bridegroom, etc.; *2:* sleepers, bargainers, brokers, etc.; *3:* weeper, prayer, old man, child, etc.
2. *beat, blow, burst,* etc.; *ruthless, fierce, shrill, quicker,* etc.
3. war; war's cruelty
4. ▪ no
   ▪ War will disrupt everyday life, claim innocent victims.
5. for loved ones not to go, to return; drown them out
6. echo the ruthless, unrelenting force of drums, bugle; capture abrupt interruptions war causes in life
7. Answers will vary, but students should choose images representing war.

When I Heard the Learn'd Astronomer

1. proofs and figures in columns, charts, diagrams
2. tired, sick
3. into the "mystical moist night air"; looks at stars
4. reinforces sense of boredom
5. describes boredom at lecture, then shows how he examines subject; experiences stars, not merely studies them
6. love of nature, which must be experienced with childlike wonder and as source of spiritual guidance; informal, chatty, free verse, no direct statement on nature, allows reader to draw conclusions

This Dust Was Once the Man

1. *gentle, plain, just, resolute*
2. "the Union of these States"
3. the Civil War
4. Abraham Lincoln

A Noiseless Patient Spider

1. isolated on promontory; launching forth filament
2. detached in oceans of space; musing, venturing, throwing; bridge, anchor, gossamer thread
3. spider, poet's soul; detachment, isolated, need something
4. to achieve love, communication, comfort; other humans, nature, God

LITERARY OPTIONS

- rhythm
- symbol
- tone

THEMATIC OPTIONS

- honoring the dead
- the power of poetry
- love

"WOODS": RHYTHM

The brisk rhythm of the first stanza, broken with parenthetical comments, suggests the haste of the march. It contrasts with the reflective tone and slower pace of the second stanza.

"WOODS": SYMBOL

The fallen soldier, his loyalties unknown, represents all the war dead. In a larger sense he represents the triumph of love over death.

"LIFT ME": TONE

The poet establishes intimacy between himself and his reader by suggesting physical closeness and by whispering.

"LIFT ME": MAIN IDEA

The poem marks the closing of a book but can also be read as the closing of the poet's life. In either case the poem captures the deep and unending bond between poet and reader.

REFLECTING ON THE POEMS

In what way does each poem suggest that human beings triumph over death? ("Woods": The epitaph bestows a kind of immortality on the dead soldier. "Now Lift Me Close": The poet's book is almost flesh and blood—an immortal piece of himself.)

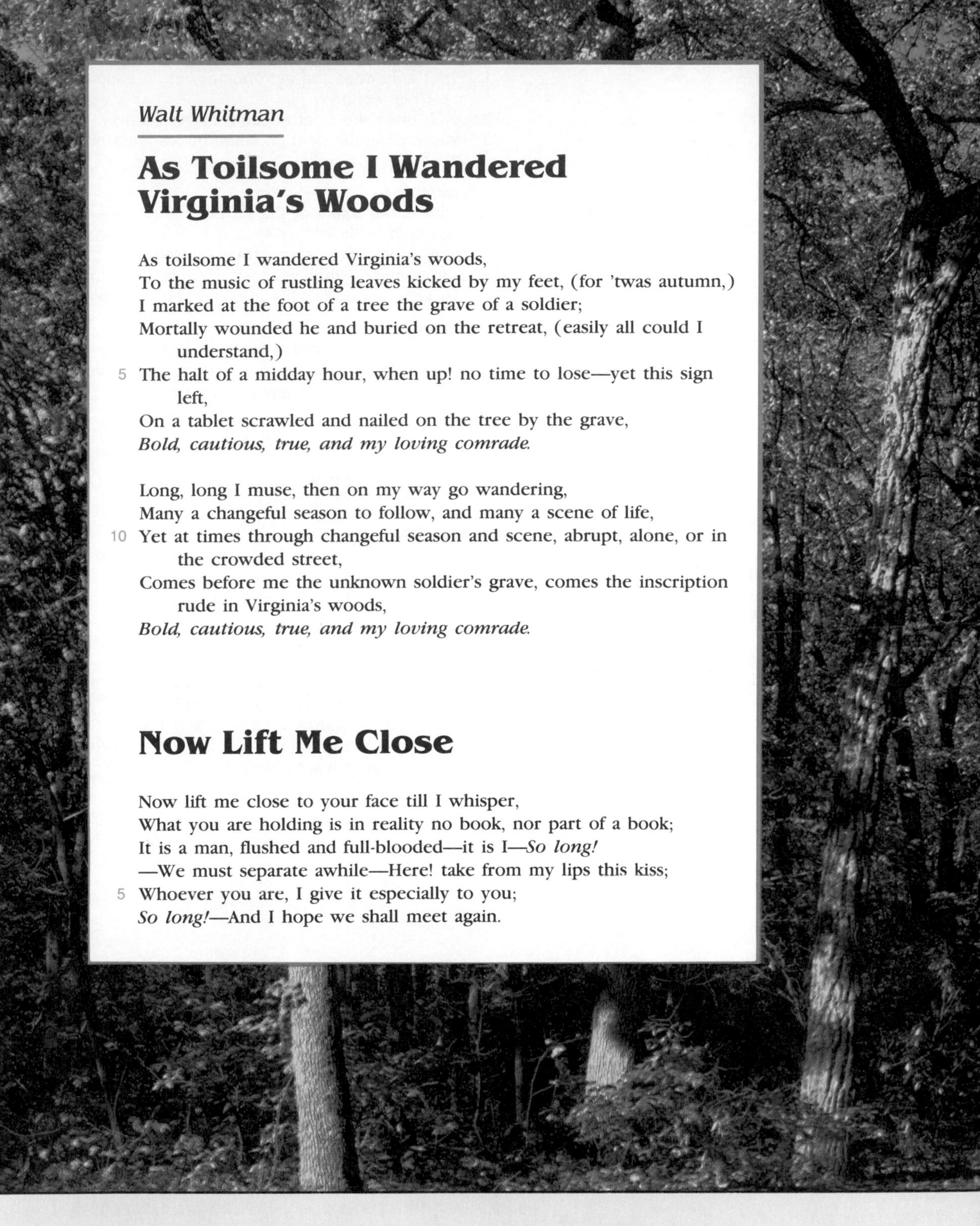

Walt Whitman

As Toilsome I Wandered Virginia's Woods

As toilsome I wandered Virginia's woods,
To the music of rustling leaves kicked by my feet, (for 'twas autumn,)
I marked at the foot of a tree the grave of a soldier;
Mortally wounded he and buried on the retreat, (easily all could I understand,)
The halt of a midday hour, when up! no time to lose—yet this sign left,
On a tablet scrawled and nailed on the tree by the grave,
Bold, cautious, true, and my loving comrade.

Long, long I muse, then on my way go wandering,
Many a changeful season to follow, and many a scene of life,
Yet at times through changeful season and scene, abrupt, alone, or in the crowded street,
Comes before me the unknown soldier's grave, comes the inscription rude in Virginia's woods,
Bold, cautious, true, and my loving comrade.

Now Lift Me Close

Now lift me close to your face till I whisper,
What you are holding is in reality no book, nor part of a book;
It is a man, flushed and full-blooded—it is I—*So long!*
—We must separate awhile—Here! take from my lips this kiss;
Whoever you are, I give it especially to you;
So long!—And I hope we shall meet again.

STUDY QUESTIONS

As Toilsome I Wandered Virginia's Woods

Recalling

1. In stanza 1 what does the poet encounter as he wanders through Virginia's woods?
2. What is written on the tablet?
3. According to stanza 2, what does the poet do before he wanders away? When does he think of the inscription again?

Interpreting

4. Why is it significant that the encounter takes place in autumn?
5. What is ironic about the word *cautious* on the tablet? With what word does *cautious* contrast? Does this paradox make sense? Explain your answer.
6. Whose "comrade" was the dead man originally? Whose comrade does the dead man become? Why?

Extending

7. Have you ever had a similar experience of years later remembering an event "abrupt, alone, or in the crowded street"?

Now Lift Me Close

Recalling

1. According to lines 2–3, what "in reality" is the "book" the poet says "you" are holding?
2. With what words does Whitman say good-by? What does he hope?

Interpreting

3. Who is the "you" addressed in the poem? What kind of relationship does the poet establish with "you"?
4. What is the poet's attitude toward "you"?

Extending

5. This poem looks toward Whitman's old age, when he would face death. Does knowing this deepen or change your reaction to the poem?

STUDY QUESTIONS

As Toilsome I Wandered Virginia's Woods

1. the grave of a soldier
2. "Bold, cautious, true, and my loving comrade"
3. muses; when alone, in a crowded street
4. season for death, change
5.
   - soldier killed in spite of caution; *bold*
   - One can be bold in actions yet cautious about chances taken, and one can be bold for oneself yet cautious for lives of others.
6.
   - soldier who buried him; poet's
   - poet empathizes with soldier and cannot forget encounter, sees soldier as symbol of bravery, transience of life, horror of war
7. Answers will vary. Students might say sensory cues prompt memories, especially of important or traumatic experiences.

Now Lift Me Close

1. the poet
2. "So long!"; meet reader again
3. reader; close, informal—intimacy of reading poems
4. loving, informal, playful
5. Answers will vary, but students should recognize the dual meanings of such phrases as "So long!" and "I hope we shall meet again": Whitman refers both to the reader's closing the book and to the close of his life.

AT A GLANCE

- The businessman bequeaths money and other valuables in a formal will.
- On the other hand, Whitman tells us that he has nothing to bequeath except for souvenirs of democracy—his poems.

LITERARY OPTIONS

- comparison and contrast
- diction
- tone

THEMATIC OPTIONS

- material wealth vs. the artistic legacy
- visions and ideals
- democratic ideal

REFLECTING ON THE POEM

In what way is Whitman's "legacy" more valuable than that of the businessman? (It is immortal; it also can be enjoyed by many.)

Model for Active Reading

In this selection, and in one selection in each unit, you will find notes in the right-hand margin that highlight parts of the selection. These notes point out important ideas of the period—in this case, the democratic idea—and draw your attention to literary elements and techniques covered in the Literary Focuses. Page numbers in the notes will refer you to more extensive discussions of these important ideas and elements.

Walt Whitman

Souvenirs of Democracy

The business man, the acquirer vast,
After assiduous years, surveying results, preparing for departure,
Devises houses and lands to his children—bequeaths stocks,
goods—funds for a school or hospital,
Leaves money to certain companions to buy tokens, souvenirs
of gems and gold;
Parceling out with care—And then, to prevent all cavil,[1]
His name to his testament[2] formally signs.

But I, my life surveying,
With nothing to show, to devise, from its idle years,
Nor houses, nor lands—nor tokens of gems or gold for my
friends,
Only these Souvenirs of Democracy—In them—in all my
songs—behind me leaving,
To You, whoever you are, (bathing, leavening[3] this leaf
especially with my breath—pressing on it a moment with
my own hands;
—Here! feel how the pulse beats in my wrists!—how my heart's
blood is swelling, contracting!)
I will You, in all, Myself, with promise to never desert you,
To which I sign my name,

Walt Whitman

Democratic idea: Whitman suggests the widespread prosperity and material success of the Gilded Age (page 232).

Autobiography (p. 244): Whitman offers his poems as a verse autobiography, the story of his life.

Apostrophe (p. 220): Whitman addresses the reader directly.

Free verse (p. 265): Whitman approximates natural speech while maintaining poetic rhythms.

Democratic idea: Whitman asserts his selfhood and independence even while he remains a part of a great nation (page 233).

1. **cavil:** trivial objections.
2. **testament:** last will and testament.
3. **leavening** [lev′ə ning]: raising.

STUDY QUESTIONS

Recalling

1. According to the first stanza, what does the "business man" leave? To whom does he leave it?
2. According to lines 10–13, what does Whitman bequeath? To whom does he bequeath it?
3. What is the poet's final promise?

Interpreting

4. What does stanza 2 suggest about the businessman of stanza 1?
5. What are the "Souvenirs of Democracy" to which Whitman refers? Why is that term appropriate?
6. Based on the evidence in stanza 2, does Whitman really believe that he has "nothing to show" for his life? Explain how he actually seems to feel about his life and work.
7. What is the effect of Whitman's unusual gesture of actually signing the poem?

Extending

8. What would you say is Whitman's greatest legacy? Which of his ideas is most appealing to you, and why?

VIEWPOINT

In the Preface to the first edition of his poems, Walt Whitman boldly says:

> The Americans of all nations at any time upon the earth have probably the fullest poetical nature. The United States themselves are essentially the greatest poem.
>
> —*Leaves of Grass*

■ What quality of American culture is Whitman trying to describe? In what sense is his statement true? In what sense can a nation be a "poem"?

VOCABULARY

Americanisms

An **Americanism** is a word or phrase that has originated in America. Americans have always been practical about language, and when a word has been needed to name a new experience or object or idea, we have invented it. Indian names, new scientific terms, brand names, slang, modified words from other languages, and colloquialisms are common sources of Americanisms.

Many dictionaries recognize this vital element of our speech and point out Americanisms: For example, *woodchuck, trick or treat, Sun Belt, clobber, megaphone, powderkeg, radar,* and *overcoat* are all Americanisms. Whitman uses the Americanism *loaf* in "Song of Myself."

■ Use your dictionary to find at least five Americanisms. Tell what each means, and identify its origin.

COMPOSITION

Writing About Poetry

■ In a brief essay examine Whitman's use of free verse, rhythm, repetition, and punctuation in one of the poems you have read. Begin by showing the ways in which certain lines capture the quality of everyday speech. Then explain how Whitman's style relates to the meaning of the poem. *For help with this assignment, refer to Lesson 7 in the Writing About Literature Handbook at the back of this book.*

Using Free Verse

■ Try writing a short poem in free verse. Remember that although rhythm and line length will be irregular, you should not lose sight of rhythm altogether. If you have difficulty in deciding on a topic for your poem, you might write an updated version of "I Hear America Singing."

STUDY QUESTIONS

1. houses, lands, stocks, etc.; his children, friends, charities
2. souvenirs of democracy, his songs; the reader
3. never to desert the reader
4. excessive, unimportant wealth
5. ■ poems
   ■ Poems express love of democracy and fellow humans, belief in universal brotherhood.
6. no; proud of work: "pulse" in it, democratic vision
7. mocks businessman's will, gives personal touch
8. Answers will vary. Possible answers: optimism; democratic spirit; original form, content; American voice

VIEWPOINT

Answers will vary, but students should see that he describes the energy, diversity, and individuality of people committed to democracy.

VOCABULARY

Answers will vary. Examples: backpack, cattle rustler, decal, flunk out, josh, passel, red cent, sidekick, tailgate, want ad

COMPOSITION: GUIDELINES FOR EVALUATION

WRITING ABOUT POETRY

Objective

To analyze a poem

Guidelines for Evaluation

- suggested length: four to seven paragraphs
- should examine use of free verse, rhythm, repetition, punctuation in one poem
- should show how certain lines capture the quality of everyday speech
- should explain relation of style to meaning

USING FREE VERSE

Objective

To write a poem using free verse

Guidelines for Evaluation

- suggested length: five to fifteen lines
- should be original poem or updated version of "I Hear America Singing"
- should use free verse that does not abandon a sense of rhythm

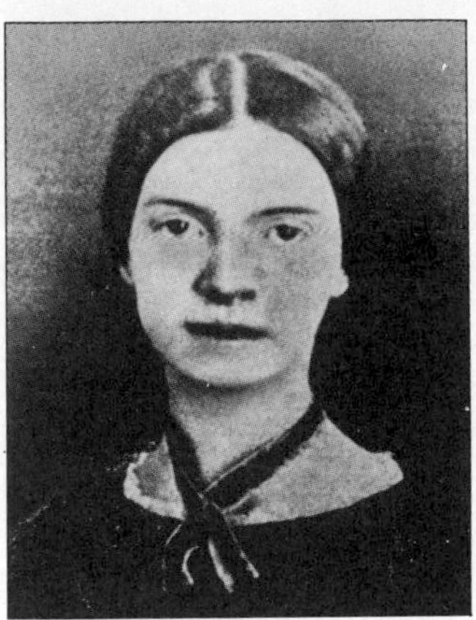

Emily Dickinson *1830–1886*

Only seven of Emily Dickinson's poems were published during her lifetime, and even those were published anonymously. Yet after her death people found in her home many small packages of her poems. Some of the poems had been carefully revised and neatly tied with ribbons; others had been scrawled on scraps of paper. In all, 1,775 poems were preserved. One of the great poets of the English language had lived and died unknown to the public.

Dickinson was born in her father's house in Amherst, Massachusetts. She attended the Mount Holyoke Female Seminary in nearby South Hadley and visited Boston, Washington, and Philadelphia when she was young. The last time she left home was in 1864, to travel to Boston for an eye examination. As she grew older, she communicated with fewer and fewer people. She dressed all in white, and her neighbors knew there was something extraordinary about this radiant yet isolated woman. At the age of fifty-six Dickinson died in the house in which she had been born.

Dickinson's poems, however, survived her. On April 15, 1862, Thomas Wentworth Higginson, a kindly but undistinguished literary critic, had received a letter from Dickinson. Higginson did not know her. Dickinson enclosed four of her poems, wondering whether they were good poems, whether they "breathed." Higginson saw that the poems had quality, but he thought they were "not for publication." They were too informal, too abrupt; even their punctuation was peculiar. Later editors of Dickinson's work were equally unperceptive. Deeming her style "not correct," they rewrote what Dickinson had written in order to make it "proper." It was not until 1955 that *The Complete Poems* were printed exactly as Dickinson had written them.

Like Whitman's, Dickinson's was a totally dedicated art, though a private one. Through her poetry she wrote what she called her "letter to the World," even though she chose to live most of her life isolated from the world. Her personality, her self—the Soul she so often writes about—was so strong and independent that she was able to write poems of genuine originality. She was influenced by the Bible, classical myths, Shakespeare, the English Romantic poet John Keats, and Ralph Waldo Emerson, but no influence overshadowed her own spirit.

Dickinson presents her poems in a wry voice, with sharp, unusual images, and a highly expressive method of punctuation. Her subjects are the great subjects—life, death, nature, God—and her special talent is to express her lofty thoughts using concrete images from everyday experience.

■ How could a recluse really see and understand the mysteries of life?

Emily Dickinson

This is my letter to the World

This is my letter to the World
That never wrote to Me—
The simple News that Nature told—
With tender Majesty

Her Message is committed
To Hands I cannot see—
For love of Her—Sweet—countrymen—
Judge tenderly—of Me

STUDY QUESTIONS

Recalling

1. According to stanza 1, to whom is the poet's letter addressed? What "News" does it contain?
2. In stanza 2, what does the poet ask her "countrymen" to do?

Interpreting

3. To what is Dickinson referring when she uses the phrase "my letter to the World"?
4. How is nature related to the poet's "letter"?
5. What does the fact that the world never wrote back suggest about Dickinson's life?
6. To what does "Her" refer in lines 5 and 7?
7. What attitude about herself and her poetry does Dickinson reveal in stanza 2? Explain your answer.

Emily Dickinson's home, Amherst, Massachusetts.

LITERARY OPTIONS

- metaphor
- tone

THEMATIC OPTIONS

- nature as poetic inspiration
- art and imagination

METAPHOR

The metaphor of the poem as a letter suggests an intimate, personal communication between the poet and her (unknown) audience.

TONE

The hesitant tone contrasts with the self-confidence of Whitman and the Transcendentalists and may reflect the poet's personal diffidence (ll. 7–8).

REFLECTING ON THE POEM

How is the poem like a letter? (Students may observe that its tone is personal and that the poet addresses the reader directly, one to one, as a letter writer would.)

STUDY QUESTIONS

1. the world; news that "Nature told— With tender Majesty"
2. Judge her tenderly.
3. her poems
4. It inspires her poems.
5. reclusive, work largely unknown
6. nature
7. shy, hesitant, humble; credits nature, not own talent, and does not assume reader's automatic acceptance

LITERARY OPTIONS

- imagery
- metaphor

THEMATIC OPTIONS

- poetry vs. prose
- the power of the imagination

METAPHOR

The house of Possibility is Poetry, the opposite of Prose. The metaphor suggests the mystery and delight of a multiroomed house with different aspects and entrances (ll. 2–4).

IMAGERY

The image of the thick, dark, impenetrable cedars underscores the private nature of the poet's world (ll. 5–6).

ROMANTIC IDEA

The boundlessness of imaginative possibilities—especially the abundance of "Windows" and "Doors" and the "Roof" of the "Sky"—places Dickinson within the Romantic tradition.

REFLECTING ON THE POEM

What does the poet's attitude toward poetry seem to be? (Her feeling of possibility seems intensely positive. The poet seems awed and enchanted by her gift.)

STUDY QUESTIONS

1. "Prose"
2. windows, doors, chambers, roofs
3. "spreading wide [her] narrow Hands / To gather Paradise"
4. poetry; that Dickinson lives in the house of poetry, that she is a poet; limitless abundance of thought and feeling
5. Poetry offers more ways of looking at world than prose; doors, more ways of shutting out the world. Students should recognize element of paradox: Dickinson's way of life is contradictory to a writer even though many poets display similar behavior.
6.
- writing poetry
- It is wonderful, ecstatic, heavenly—"narrow" poet experiences delights of poetic inspiration.

7. Answers will vary. Students might see poetry as good medium for expression.

Emily Dickinson

I dwell in Possibility—

I dwell in Possibility—
A fairer House than Prose—
More numerous of Windows—
Superior—for Doors—

Of Chambers as the Cedars—
Impregnable of Eye—
And for an Everlasting Roof
The Gambrels[1] of the Sky—

Of Visitors—the fairest—
For Occupation—This—
The spreading wide my narrow Hands
To gather Paradise—

1. **Gambrels:** angled roofs.

STUDY QUESTIONS

Recalling

1. What "House" is "Possibility" fairer than?
2. Name the four parts of the "Houses" the poet compares.
3. What is the poet's "Occupation" in the "House" of "Possibility"?

Interpreting

4. Considering the contrast in line 2, identify the thing that Dickinson is equating with "Possibility." What does line 1 therefore mean? What does the use of the word *possibility* imply?
5. What is implied by the more numerous windows? By the superior number of doors? Does this seem to be a contradiction? Explain.
6. What is the "Occupation" in the last stanza? What do lines 11–12 imply about this occupation?

Extending

7. Why do you think people write poetry?

Emily Dickinson

"Nature" is what we see—

"Nature" is what we see—
The Hill—the Afternoon—
Squirrel—Eclipse—the Bumble bee—
Nay—Nature is Heaven—
Nature is what we hear—
The Bobolink[1]—the Sea—
Thunder—the Cricket—
Nay—Nature is Harmony—
Nature is what we know—
Yet have no art to say—
So impotent Our Wisdom is
To her Simplicity.

1. **Bobolink:** variety of songbird.

I never saw a Moor—

I never saw a Moor[1]—
I never saw the Sea—
Yet know I how the Heather looks
And what a Billow[2] be.

I never spoke with God
Nor visited in Heaven—
Yet certain am I of the spot
As if the Checks[3] were given—

1. **Moor:** open, rolling land often swampy and covered with heather.
2. **Billow:** a large wave.
3. **Checks:** probably the seat checks, indicating destination, that are issued to train passengers when their tickets are collected.

STUDY QUESTIONS

"Nature" is what we see—

Recalling

1. What does the poet say nature is in line 1? In line 4?
2. What does the poet say nature is in line 5? In line 8?
3. What do lines 9–10 say nature is?
4. Compared with what is our wisdom impotent, according to lines 11–12?

Interpreting

5. Explain the relationship between the definitions of nature in lines 1 and 4 and between the definitions in lines 5 and 8. What word in line 4 and 8 makes the relationship clear?
6. In your own words explain what the last four lines suggest about nature.

I never saw a Moor—

Recalling

1. According to stanza 1, what two things has the poet never seen? What does she nevertheless know about them?
2. According to stanza 2, where has the poet never visited? Of what is she nevertheless certain?

Interpreting

3. What specific type of belief is suggested by the poet in stanza 2?
4. In what way does the poet's argument in stanza 1 affect her argument in stanza 2? Explain.
5. Where does parallel structure occur within the poem? How does this organized structure affect the poet's argument?

Extending

6. Dickinson's early editors rewrote line 4 as "And what a wave must be" and line 8 as "As if the chart were given." Do you think these changes improved the poem? Do you think editors should rewrite a poet's original compositions? Explain your answers.

LITERARY OPTIONS

- slant rhyme
- lyric poetry

THEMATIC OPTIONS

- the wonders of nature
- faith

"NATURE": LYRIC POETRY

The poet directly expresses feelings about nature and about the tension between sensory and emotional "reality."

"I NEVER SAW": TONE

Repetition and short, sturdy statements convey confidence as they structure the analogy between different ways of imagining truth.

"I NEVER SAW": SLANT RHYME

The words *never, Heaven,* and *given* all contain the *v* sound and varying short vowel sounds. Slant rhyme focuses attention on certain words by arresting the ear (ll. 5, 6, 8).

REFLECTING ON THE POEMS

How does the poet's choice of images contribute to the concreteness of her poetry? (Students may suggest that Dickinson's word choices are very precise.)

STUDY QUESTIONS

"Nature" is what we see—

1. what we see; "Heaven"
2. what we hear; "Harmony"
3. what we know but cannot say
4. nature's "Simplicity"
5. contradictory: cannot see heaven or hear harmony; the word *Nay*
6. Nature displays childlike simplicity that we can understand intuitively but cannot explain in words.

I never saw a Moor—

1. moor, sea; how heather looks, "what a Billow be"
2. heaven; the spot
3. religious faith
4. supports it; accepts existence of unseen places, accepts heaven on spiritual evidence
5. lines 2 and 4 with 1 and 3, second with first stanza; makes it more effective through its logic and simplicity
6. Answers will vary, but students should see that the original wording is more personal, imaginative, and subtle.

LITERARY OPTIONS

- personification
- tone

THEMATIC OPTIONS

- death and natural order
- the sadness of parting

"APPARENTLY": WORD CHOICE

Accidental, suggesting that nature is impersonal, indicates the speaker's ambivalent feelings about death (l. 4).

"APPARENTLY": PERSONIFICATION

The phrase *blonde assassin* captures the frost's paleness, silence, and stealth.

"APPARENTLY": MAIN IDEA

The characterization of the sun as "unmoved" and of God as "Approving" suggests that death is part of the natural order, a system alien to human emotions and needs (ll. 6–8).

"MY LIFE": TONE

The words *hopeless* and *befell* give the stanza a bleak, despairing tone (ll. 5–6).

"MY LIFE": MAIN IDEA

Death is our only window on eternity ("heaven"); it is also our saddest experience ("hell").

REFLECTING ON THE POEMS

What is the poet's attitude toward death in these two poems? (Students may say that the poet envisions death as an impersonal, inevitable event, part of an uncaring force that is alien to human feelings and needs.)

Emily Dickinson

Apparently with no surprise

Apparently with no surprise
To any happy Flower
The Frost beheads it at its play—
In accidental power—
The blonde Assassin passes on—
The Sun proceeds unmoved
To measure off another Day
For an Approving God.

My life closed twice before its close—

My life closed twice before its close—
It yet remains to see
If Immortality unveil
A third event to me

So huge, so hopeless to conceive
As these that twice befell.
Parting is all we know of heaven,
And all we need of hell.

STUDY QUESTIONS

Apparently with no surprise

Recalling

1. According to lines 3–4, what happens to the flower?
2. According to lines 6–8, how does the sun react, and how does God feel about the incident?

Interpreting

3. What might the "accidental" aspect of the frost's power suggest about nature? What might the flower's apparent lack of surprise suggest about nature?
4. Beyond the death of one flower, what is this poem about? Explain the significance of God's reaction to these events.
5. According to what the poem implies, who *is* surprised by the flower's death? Why?

Extending

6. One of Dickinson's greatest talents was her ability to find universal meanings in everyday events. Why do you think all great literature must be able to do this?

My life closed twice before its close—

Recalling

1. According to stanza 1, what has happened twice to the poet? What does she say remains to be seen?
2. How does the poet define parting in stanza 2?

Interpreting

3. What happened to cause the poet's life to "close twice before its close"? In what line is this made clear?
4. What is the "third event"? In comparing it to the first two events, what does the poet reveal about her feelings regarding the first two?
5. In what sense might parting be "all we know of heaven"? How might it be "all we need of hell"?

Extending

6. Many biographers of Dickinson have suggested that this poem was prompted by the departures of two men in whom the poet had a romantic interest. Does knowing this add to your appreciation of the poem? Do you think Dickinson might be referring to another kind of departure? Explain your answers.

STUDY QUESTIONS

Apparently with no surprise

1. "The Frost beheads it."
2. unmoved; approves
3. indifference; that death is natural
4. death of all living things, reactions to death; death part of the world God created
5. poet; cannot accept cutting down flower in happy play: death of human in midst of life
6. Answers will vary. Possible answer: Universal truths are best presented through familiar concrete applications.

My life closed twice . . .

1. Her life has closed twice; if immortality will unveil a third closing
2. "all we know of heaven, and all we need of hell"
3. a loved one departed; line 7
4. death; traumatic, painful
5. like dying, leaving world for heaven; like pain of hell
6. Answers will vary. Students might say she could be talking about the death of a loved one, or the spiritual death of an emotion or a belief.

AT A GLANCE

- A certain kind of winter light seems to cause depression and despair.
- The light arrives with a feeling of suspense and leaves with a feeling of death.

LITERARY OPTIONS

- imagery
- simile

THEMATIC OPTIONS

- the desolation of winter
- visions and ideals

SIMILE

The comparison of light to cathedral music suggests solemn organ music, which often takes sorrow and death as its theme (ll. 3–4).

IMAGERY

The depression is a sort of invisible injury with no apparent cause. Its effect, however, is to "scar" the psyche (ll. 5–8).

WORD CHOICE

Imperial affliction suggests the enormity of the poet's feeling (l. 11).

REFLECTING ON THE POEM

What does the poet mean by "internal difference, / Where the Meanings, are"? (Students may note that Dickinson is writing mainly about the emotional effect of the light, which alters the poet's state of mind.)

STUDY QUESTIONS

1. oppresses; winter afternoons
2. "Heavenly Hurt"
3. "Seal Despair," "imperial affliction"
4. "the Landscape listens," "shadows—hold their breath"; "Distance / On the look of Death"
5. Nothing grows in winter; death, emotional desolation
6. oppressive, painful, desperate, arresting
7. sudden momentary awareness of death or of great unhappiness, or a moment of spiritual doubt; suggest that the slant of light is related to death and its departure brings relief
8. Answers will vary. Students might cite holidays, changes in weather, or personal emotional experiences.

Emily Dickinson

There's a certain Slant of light

There's a certain Slant of light,
Winter Afternoons—
That oppresses, like the Heft
Of Cathedral Tunes—

Heavenly Hurt, it gives us—
We can find no scar,
But internal difference,
Where the Meanings, are—

None may teach it—Any—
'Tis the Seal Despair—
An imperial affliction
Sent us of the Air—

When it comes, the Landscape listens—
Shadows—hold their breath—
When it goes, 'tis like the Distance
On the look of Death—

STUDY QUESTIONS

Recalling

1. According to stanza 1, what does the certain slant of light do? When does it come?
2. What does the slant of light give us, according to stanza 2?
3. What two things is the slant of light called in stanza 3?
4. According to stanza 4, what happens when the slant of light comes? What is it like when it goes?

Interpreting

5. Why is it significant that the light occurs on *winter* afternoons? What might winter suggest?
6. Describe the mood or feeling that the slant of light brings.
7. What does the light seem to represent to the poet? Explain how lines 15–16 reinforce this meaning.

Extending

8. Why do you think certain seasons evoke certain moods and emotions?

Emily Dickinson

The Soul selects her own Society—

The Soul selects her own Society—
Then—shuts the Door—
To her divine Majority—
Present no more—

Unmoved—she notes the Chariots—pausing—
At her low Gate—
Unmoved—an Emperor be kneeling
Upon her Mat—

I've known her—from an ample nation—
Choose One—
Then—close the Valves of her attention—
Like Stone—

Success is counted sweetest

Success is counted sweetest
By those who ne'er succeed.
To comprehend a nectar
Requires sorest need.

Not one of all the purple Host
Who took the Flag today
Can tell the definition
So clear of Victory

As he defeated—dying—
On whose forbidden ear
The distant strains of triumph
Burst agonized and clear!

STUDY QUESTIONS

The Soul selects her own Society—

Recalling

1. According to stanza 1, what does the "Soul" select? What does she do then?
2. What two things leave the soul unmoved, according to stanza 2?
3. According to stanza 3, what does the soul choose? What does she do then?

Interpreting

4. What does the phrase "I've known her" in line 9 suggest about the identity of the soul?
5. What do the images in lines 2 and 9–10 suggest about this soul? What other lines in the poem reinforce this meaning?
6. What can we infer about this soul from her attitude toward the images of royalty in stanza 2?

Success is counted sweetest

Recalling

1. According to stanza 1, to whom is success "sweetest"? What is required to "comprehend a nectar"?
2. What does "the purple Host" achieve? What is it unable to do, according to stanza 2?

Interpreting

3. Restate the observation made in lines 1–2 in your own words. How are lines 3–4 related to this observation?
4. How is the observation about soldiers and armies in stanzas 2 and 3 related to lines 1–2?

Extending

5. Do you agree with the observation about success and human nature expressed in this poem? Why or why not?

LITERARY OPTIONS

- main idea
- metaphor

THEMATIC OPTIONS

- privacy of the soul
- perception of success

"THE SOUL": METAPHOR

The image of the closed door suggests firmness and determination (l. 2).

"THE SOUL": REPETITION

Repeating *unmoved* emphasizes the speaker's resolve and underscores the unwillingness of the soul to alter her convictions (ll. 5–8).

"SUCCESS": MAIN IDEA

Full appreciation can best be won through deprivation (ll. 1–4).

REFLECTING ON THE POEMS

What purpose does the speaker's objective stance serve in these two poems? (Students may suggest that in the first, it separates the speaker from the choice of shutting out the world; in the second, it focuses attention on the defeated, dying soldier.)

STUDY QUESTIONS

The Soul selects her own Society—

1. her own society; shuts door
2. chariots pausing at her gate; emperor kneeling upon her mat
3. "One"; closes valves of attention
4. objective description of own soul
5. privacy; lines 1, 3, 11–12
6. unimpressed by worldly status; maintains privacy despite most tempting, powerful intrusions

Success is counted sweetest

1. unsuccessful; "sorest need"
2. victory; define victory as clearly as the defeated can
3. success most valued by unsuccessful; reinforces observation
4. concrete example
5. Answers will vary. Students may feel that Dickinson's observations are based on actual experience.

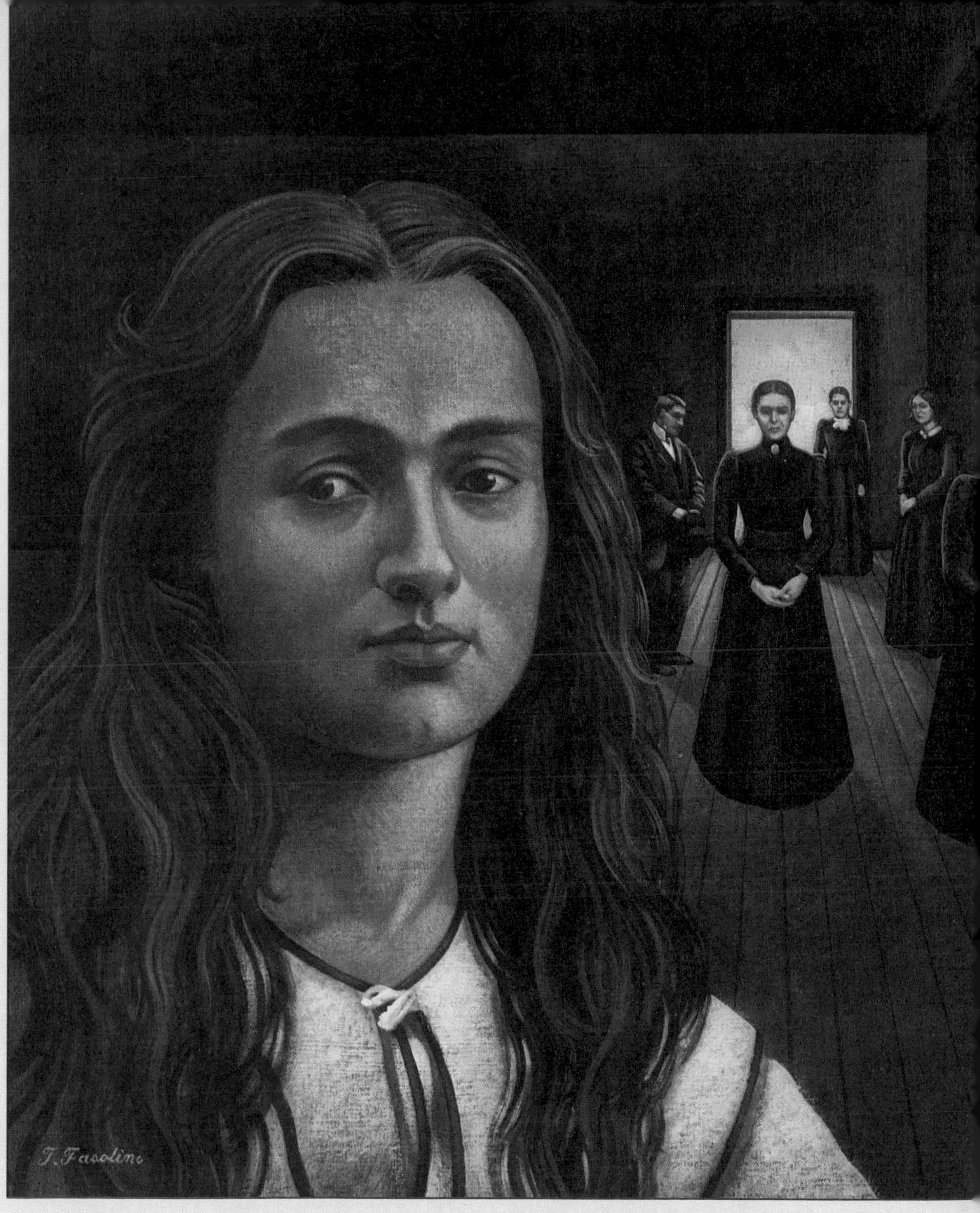
T. Fasolino

Emily Dickinson

I felt a Funeral, in my Brain

I felt a Funeral, in my Brain,
And Mourners to and fro
Kept treading—treading—till it seemed
That Sense was breaking through—

And when they all were seated,
A Service, like a Drum—
Kept beating—beating—till I thought
My Mind was going numb—

And then I heard them lift a Box
And creak across my Soul
With those same Boots of Lead, again,
Then Space—began to toll,

As all the Heavens were a Bell,
And Being, but an Ear,
And I, and Silence, some strange Race
Wrecked, solitary, here—

And then a Plank in Reason, broke,
And I dropped down, and down—
And hit a World, at every plunge,
And Finished knowing—then—

The Bustle in a House

The Bustle in a House
The Morning after Death
Is solemnest of industries
Enacted upon Earth—

The Sweeping up the Heart
And putting Love away
We shall not want to use again
Until Eternity.

STUDY QUESTIONS

I felt a Funeral, in my Brain

Recalling

1. Where does the "Funeral" take place? Who keeps treading to and fro?
2. What keeps beating? What do the mourners lift?
3. According to stanza 3, what begins to toll after the mourners leave?
4. What breaks, according to stanza 5? What happens then?

Interpreting

5. What is the "Service" in line 6? What is the "Box" in line 9?
6. Whose funeral is the speaker envisioning? What might the last two stanzas be describing?
7. Compare the images beginning in line 12 with the images of the funeral presented in lines 1–11. Which group of images is clearer? Why?

The Bustle in a House

Recalling

1. According to stanza 1, when and where does the bustle described in the poem occur?
2. According to stanza 2, what is swept up? What is put away? Until when won't we want to use the love?

Interpreting

3. What analogy does the poet make in this poem? In what line does the analogy become clear?
4. What do the images in lines 5 and 6 suggest about human reactions and needs after a death?
5. Can the first stanza be interpreted on a literal level? Explain your answer.

LITERARY OPTIONS

- imagery
- main idea
- metaphor

THEMATIC OPTIONS

- the mystery of death
- loss and recovery

"I FELT": IMAGERY

The funeral imagery—mourners, procession, tolling bell, and service—evokes emotions such as sadness, fear, and grief in the reader.

"I FELT": METAPHOR

Reason is compared to a solid platform: The breaking of a plank sends the speaker plunging into chaos (ll. 17–18).

"THE BUSTLE": MAIN IDEA

After a death we must sort out our feelings, set aside our grief, and go on with our lives. The controlling image of housecleaning reflects this main idea (ll. 5–8).

REFLECTING ON THE POEMS

What feelings do these poems about death communicate? (Students may suggest such feelings as grief, strain, loss, anguish, sadness, a sense of inevitability, and resignation.)

STUDY QUESTIONS

I felt a Funeral, in my Brain

1. speaker's brain; mourners
2. a "Service"; a "Box"
3. "Space"
4. "Plank in Reason"; speaker drops, hits a "World" at every plunge, finishes knowing
5. funeral; coffin
6. her own; journey to afterlife or return to present at vision's end
7. - first group
   - Answers will vary. If lines 12–20 represent journey to afterlife, they are beyond range of human experience. If represent end of vision, vision seemed more vivid than real world.

The Bustle in a House

1. in a house, morning after "Death"
2. heart; love; "until Eternity"
3. between cleaning a house and the ordering of emotions after death of a loved one; line 5
4. overwhelmed by grief; need to sort out emotions, keep them in check
5. yes; solemn bustle of receiving mourners, making funeral arrangements; housecleaning after death: preparation for mourners, ritual, catharsis

AT A GLANCE

- Death stops for the speaker.
- Centuries pass but seem more brief than the day the speaker died.

LITERARY OPTIONS

- slant rhyme
- personification

THEMATIC OPTIONS

- the unexpectedness of death
- time vs. eternity

PERSONIFICATION

Death comes as a courtly coachman, whose invitation cannot be refused (ll. 1–2).

SLANT RHYME

In the forced rhyming of *chill* with *tulle,* the rhymed vowels differ, but the *l* sound is the same, focusing attention on the chill of death (ll. 13–16).

REFLECTING ON THE POEM

What does the structure of the poem suggest about time and eternity? (Relegating eternity to one stanza without detail makes the "centuries" after death seem uneventful compared to the intense experience of death.)

Emily Dickinson

Because I could not stop for Death—

Because I could not stop for Death—
He kindly stopped for me—
The Carriage held but just Ourselves—
And Immortality.

We slowly drove—He knew no haste
And I had put away
My labor and my leisure too,
For His Civility—

We passed the School, where Children strove
At Recess—in the Ring—
We passed the Fields of Gazing Grain—
We passed the Setting Sun—

Or rather—He passed Us—
The Dews drew quivering and chill—
For only Gossamer, my Gown—
My Tippet[1]—only Tulle[2]—

We paused before a House that seemed
A Swelling of the Ground—
The Roof was scarcely visible—
The Cornice[3]—in the Ground—

Since then—'tis Centuries—and yet
Feels shorter than the Day
I first surmised the Horses' Heads
Were toward Eternity—

---

1. **Tippet:** scarf for the neck and shoulders, hanging down in front.
2. **Tulle** [to͞ol]: fine netting used for scarves and veils.
3. **Cornice** [kôr′ nis]: the projecting decorative molding along the top of a building.

I heard a Fly buzz—when I died—

I heard a Fly buzz—when I died—
The Stillness in the Room
Was like the Stillness in the Air—
Between the Heaves of Storm—

The Eyes around—had wrung them dry—
And Breaths were gathering firm
For that last Onset—when the King
Be witnessed—in the Room—

I willed my Keepsakes—Signed away
What portion of me be
Assignable—and then it was
There interposed a Fly—

With Blue—uncertain stumbling Buzz—
Between the light—and me—
And then the Windows failed—and then
I could not see to see—

This World is not Conclusion

This World is not Conclusion.
A Species stands beyond—
Invisible, as Music—
But positive, as Sound—
It beckons, and it baffles—
Philosophy—don't know—
And through a Riddle, at the last—
Sagacity, must go—
To guess it, puzzles scholars—
To gain it, Men have borne
Contempt of Generations
And Crucifixion, shown—
Faith slips—and laughs, and rallies—
Blushes, if any see—
Plucks at a twig of Evidence—
And asks a Vane, the way—
Much Gesture, from the Pulpit—
Strong Hallelujahs roll—
Narcotics cannot still the Tooth
That nibbles at the soul—

STUDY QUESTIONS

Because I could not stop for Death—

Recalling

1. According to stanza 1, why did Death stop for the speaker? What did Death's carriage hold?
2. What three things did the speaker and Death pass in stanza 3? Where did they pause in stanza 5?
3. According to stanza 6, how much time has passed since the day of Death's visit? What does that time feel shorter than?

Interpreting

4. Is the speaker in this poem alive or dead? What day is she describing?
5. What do lines 1–2 suggest about human behavior?
6. What might the three things the speaker passed in stanza 3 represent?
7. What is the "House" in the ground in stanza 5? Is this the speaker's final destination? Explain.
8. Why does the day described seem so long to the speaker?

I heard a Fly buzz—when I died—

Recalling

1. What does the speaker hear in stanza 1? When does she hear it?
2. According to stanza 2, what are the "Eyes" and "Breaths" doing?
3. According to stanzas 3–4, what interposes between the light and the speaker? What happens then?

I heard a Fly buzz—when I died—

1. fly buzz; when she dies
2. wringing selves dry; gathering firm for "last Onset"
3. fly; speaker cannot "see to see"

LITERARY OPTIONS

- imagery
- personification

THEMATIC OPTIONS

- the experience of death
- the mystery of the afterlife

"I HEARD A FLY": PERSONIFICATION

Death is personified as a king, suggesting not only death's wonder and majesty but also its ultimate authority (ll. 7–8).

"I HEARD A FLY": SYMBOL

The light is actual and symbolizes life; the failing light signifies both approaching death and the loss of the senses (ll. 13–16).

"THIS WORLD": IMAGERY

The tooth that gnaws the soul is ambiguous. An image of doubt, it is also a nagging will to believe in spite of doubt (ll. 19–20).

REFLECTING ON THE POEMS

What is the role of doubt in these poems? (Students may suggest that because of her doubt, the poet provides two different views of death. In the first poem, there is nothing after the light fails; the second expresses a belief in an afterlife.)

STUDY QUESTIONS

Because I could not stop . . .

1. She could not stop for Death; Death, speaker, Immortality
2. school, fields, setting sun; before a "House that seemed a Swelling of the Ground"
3. centuries; day of death
4. dead; the day she died
5. reluctance to meet death
6. *school:* childhood; *fields:* maturity; *setting sun:* old age
7. grave or crypt; no; final destination is eternity
8. sees whole life on earth, understands eternity; time later becomes meaningless

4. dying; mourners around deathbed
5. parts of bodies only; speaker's
6. solemn scene contrasted with speaker's noticing fly; randomness of death

This World is not Conclusion

1. *invisible, positive;* beckons and baffles
2. through a "riddle" at the last
3. "much Gesture"
4. "Tooth that nibbles at the soul"
5. meaning of life, death
6. philosophy, religion; cannot satisfy everyone
7. Possible answers: imagery, wording, tone, self-examination, questions rather than answers, ambiguity

VIEWPOINT

Answers will vary. There is much supporting evidence for Johnson.

LITERARY FOCUS

Slant Rhyme

- *"I heard a Fly . . .":* jarring effect until perfect rhyme *me/see;* reflects contrast between solemnity of scene and triviality of fly; underscores jarring intrusion of fly; exact rhyme *me/see* underscores harmony of death
- "Apparently . . . ": *unmoved/God;* jarring nature of flower's death contrasted with harmony of its play

Interpreting

4. What is happening to the speaker? Who are the other people in the room?
5. What is unusual about the description of the people in lines 5–6? From whose point of view are they being described?
6. Why is the fly's appearance somewhat ironic? What basic message about death is suggested to the poet by the appearance of the fly?

This World is not Conclusion

Recalling

1. What two adjectives in lines 1–4 describe the "Species" that stands beyond this world? What does this species do in line 5?
2. According to lines 7–8, where must "Sagacity" go?
3. What comes "from the Pulpit" in line 17?
4. According to the last two lines, what can narcotics not still?

Interpreting

5. What baffling question is this poem about?
6. Identify two ways through which human beings have tried to answer the question, according to the poet. What do the last two lines suggest about these answers?

Extending

7. What elements of Dickinson's poetry seem most modern to you? Does she seem old-fashioned, or does she seem like one of our contemporaries? Explain your answer.

VIEWPOINT

The scholar who edited the definitive texts of Dickinson's poems, Thomas H. Johnson, tells us:

> Emily Dickinson loved words ardently. Her feeling about them amounted to veneration and her selection of them was ritualistic.

■ What evidence do you find to support Johnson's contention? What unusual or well-chosen words add power to the poems you have read? How does Dickinson's use of everyday words help make her abstract ideas more concrete?

LITERARY FOCUS

Slant Rhyme

In **perfect,** or **exact, rhyme,** the consonants change but the vowel sounds stay the same: *be/see, talking/walking, history/mystery.* In **slant rhyme**—also called **off rhyme, near rhyme, approximate rhyme,** and **imperfect rhyme**—the vowel sounds are similar but not identical: *be/sigh, talking/working, history/mastery.*

Emily Dickinson is noted for her use of slant rhyme to achieve special effects. Consider, for example, her poem "This is my letter to the World." The first stanza builds tension because the reader expects a perfect rhyme that never comes. In the concluding line of the poem, however, it does come: "see" and "Me" rhyme exactly.

On the other hand, in "The Soul selects her own Society— " Dickinson wants to end on a jarring note. She uses the slant rhyme "One"/"Stone." The overall effect of all the slant rhymes in this poem is to create a discordant quality that mirrors the abrupt, unsociable actions of the Soul.

The jarring effect of a slant rhyme can also underscore a word's importance. In "The Bustle in a House" the importance of "Eternity" is stressed by the imperfect rhyme it completes: "away"/"Eternity."

Thinking About Slant Rhyme

■ What slant rhymes occur in "I heard a Fly buzz—when I died—" and "Apparently with no surprise"? What effects do they have? How are the slant rhymes related to the meaning of each poem?

Types of Poetry

Poetry is often classified as narrative, dramatic, or lyric. These categories are more clear-cut in some poems than in others. The category in which we place a poem will often depend on what we consider the main purpose of the poem to be.

The main purpose of a **narrative poem** is to tell a story. Narrative poetry includes the **epic,** a long poem that recounts the adventures of heroic figures in polished, elevated language. Narrative poetry also includes the **mock-epic**, a poem about a comical or foolhardy hero that parodies epic grandeur. The **ballad** is a shorter narrative poem.

The main purpose of a **dramatic poem** is to reveal character through dialogue and monologue. A dramatic poem may contain narrative elements, but it usually presents characters in a particular situation rather than in a series of events. The focus of the dramatic poem is on character, not events.

The main purpose of a **lyric poem** is to communicate the emotions of the poet. Lyric poems are generally short and attempt to achieve a single, unified effect. By far, most poetry falls into this category. Lyric poems, too, may contain narrative or dramatic elements, but the focus of the lyric is on the personal feelings of the poet.

Thinking About Types of Poetry

1. In which category—narrative, dramatic, or lyric—would you place Dickinson's poems? Why?
2. Note any examples in Dickinson of a blend of the elements of more than one type of poetry.

VOCABULARY

Analogies

Analogies are comparisons that point out relationships between items. Analogy items on vocabulary tests are usually written as two pairs of words. The words in the first pair are related to each other in the same way as those in the second pair: for example, WORD : SENTENCE : : PAGE : BOOK.

The words in capitals in the following analogies appear in Emily Dickinson's poems. Complete the analogies by choosing the pair of words that is related in the same way as the pair in capital letters.

1. ONSET : CONCLUSION : :
   (a) end : beginning (c) grief : sorrow
   (b) numbness : cold (d) plodding : dancing
2. TREADING : BEATING : :
   (a) sticks : stones (c) feet : heart
   (b) ears : eyes (d) desert : mountain
3. HEATHER : BILLOW : :
   (a) fixed : moving (c) land : ocean
   (b) rising : falling (d) grow : decline
4. HEFT : HANDS : :
   (a) jumping : legs (c) brightness : eyes
   (b) learning : reading (d) thirst : water
5. MUSIC : SOUND : :
   (a) cake : bread (c) wind : air
   (b) poetry : language (d) dancing : jumping

COMPOSITION

Analyzing Slant Rhyme

■ Choose one of Dickinson's poems, and write an analysis of the effect of the poet's use of exact and slant rhyme. Begin by telling what the rhymes are. Then explain how the rhymes work (sometimes along with capitalization and punctuation) to emphasize certain words and meanings. Conclude with a comment about the overall relationship between the rhymes and the poem's meaning.

Writing About an Abstract Idea

■ Like all great writers, Dickinson often uses concrete words to make abstract ideas clearer. In a poem or a short composition describe or explain an abstract idea or emotion. Use concrete words to create the clearest possible impression for your reader. Some abstractions you might write about are poetry, nature, joy, or success.

COMPARING WRITERS

■ Both Walt Whitman and Emily Dickinson were poets of great originality and intense emotion. Yet in temperament and life style they were almost exactly opposite. What do Whitman's and Dickinson's poems suggest about the sources of poetic inspiration? Where do they suggest the truly imaginative life can be found? What do you think made the poetry of these writers so fresh and original?

Types of Poetry

1. *lyric:* communicate feelings

2. *narrative elements:* "Apparently with no surprise," "I felt a Funeral, in my Brain," "Because I could not stop for Death—," "I heard a Fly buzz—when I died—"; *dramatic elements:* "Success is counted sweetest"

VOCABULARY

1. (a) end : beginning
2. (c) feet : heart
3. (c) land : ocean
4. (a) jumping : legs
5. (b) poetry : language

COMPARING WRITERS

Answers will vary. Students should recognize that the source of poetic inspiration knows no particular boundaries.

COMPOSITION: GUIDELINES FOR EVALUATION

ANALYZING SLANT RHYME

Objective

To analyze slant and exact rhyme in a poem

Guidelines for Evaluation

- suggested length: five to eight paragraphs
- should identify the slant rhymes and exact rhymes in the poem
- should explain how rhymes emphasize words/meanings; note capitalization/punctuation
- should explain how rhymes reflect meaning

WRITING ABOUT AN ABSTRACT IDEA

Objective

To explain abstract ideas with concrete images

Guidelines for Evaluation

- suggested length: four to twelve lines, two paragraphs
- should state an abstract idea or emotion
- should use concrete images to describe or explain the abstraction

Mark Twain *1835–1910*

Mark Twain, who was born Samuel Langhorne Clemens, spent his early life in Missouri, chiefly in the river town of Hannibal. Here he became a journeyman printer and later a riverboat pilot. So much did he love the life on the Mississippi River that he later chose a pen name that would link him with the river forever: "Mark twain!" was a river call meaning "two fathoms" and indicating that the water was deep enough for safe passage.

When the Civil War closed the Mississippi River, Sam Clemens headed for Nevada, where he dreamed of striking it rich. He did not. Instead he supported himself by newspaper reporting, specializing in humorous feature stories. Soon the pseudonym "Mark Twain" was well-known in California and Nevada and with the publication of "The Celebrated Jumping Frog of Calaveras County" (1865) in the East as well. In 1867, as a correspondent for the *Alta California,* Clemens set out for Europe and the Middle East. This journey provided the material for *Innocents Abroad* (1869), a sharp-tongued look at raw American travelers that quickly became a best seller. Another huge success, *Roughing It* (1872), recounted Clemens' experiences in the "Wild West."

By now the rough-edged westerner had married a wealthy eastern lady, and the family settled in Hartford, Connecticut, where Clemens met Charles Dudley Warner and William Dean Howells, the most influential literary critic of the day. With Warner Twain collaborated on *The Gilded Age* (1874), a satire that gave its name to the era of corrupt materialism that followed the Civil War. In Howells' *Atlantic Monthly* Twain recounted his experiences as a riverboat pilot in a series, "Old Times on the Mississippi," later called *Life on the Mississippi* (1883). *The Adventures of Tom Sawyer* (1876) established Twain as a master of fiction, and its sequel, *The Adventures of Huckleberry Finn* (1883), as one of the greatest novelists America has ever produced.

Mark Twain did not write a story; he told it. His mastery of American speech—the native vernacular—and his ability "to spin a yarn" are unrivaled; and whether his yarn spinning is aimed at pure entertainment or at social satire, his humor is irresistible. His realism and detail influenced many later writers of American fiction: Ernest Hemingway once said that "all modern American literature comes from one book by Mark Twain called *Huckleberry Finn.*"

Plagued by financial misfortunes and the deaths of loved ones, Twain's later years saw him frequently embittered, his work given to dark satire and philosophic brooding. *A Connecticut Yankee in King Arthur's Court* (1889) is a biting satire set in the Middle Ages; *Pudd'nhead Wilson* (1894) is an attack on racial discrimination. *The Man That Corrupted Hadleyburg* (1900) is probably the best of his powerful pessimistic tales.

Though Mark Twain first achieved fame as a western humorist, his greatest works—*The Adventures of Huckleberry Finn, The Adventures of Tom Sawyer,* and *Life on the Mississippi*—are set on the long river that divided the nation. Sam Clemens' boyhood dreams and memories are the sources of *Life on the Mississippi,* which begins with a vivid description of the arrival of a riverboat.

■ What makes Twain's serious narratives and his outlandish tales seem equally real? Why do we believe what he says?

Mark Twain

from Life on the Mississippi

A Boy's Ambition

1 When I was a boy, there was but one permanent ambition among my comrades in our village on the west bank of the Mississippi River. That was, to be a steamboatman. We had transient ambitions of other sorts, but they were only transient. When a circus came and went, it left us all burning to become clowns; the first Negro minstrel show that came to our section left us all suffering to try that kind of life; now and then we had a hope that if we lived and were good, God would permit us to be pirates. These ambitions faded out, each in its turn; but the ambition to be a steamboatman always remained.

Once a day a cheap, gaudy packet[1] arrived upward from St. Louis, and another downward from Keokuk.[2] Before these events had transpired, the day was glorious with expectancy; after they had transpired, the day was a dead and empty thing. Not only the boys, but the
2 whole village, felt this. After all these years I can picture that old time to myself now, just as it was then: the white town drowsing in the sunshine of a summer's morning; the streets empty, or pretty nearly so; one or two clerks sitting in front of the Water Street stores, with
3 their splint-bottomed chairs tilted back against the wall, chins on breasts, hats slouched over their faces, asleep—with shingle-shavings enough around to show what broke them down; a sow and a litter of pigs loafing along the sidewalk, doing a good business in watermelon rinds and seeds; two or three lonely little freight piles scattered about the levee;[3] a pile of skids[4] on the slope of the stone-paved wharf, and the fragrant town drunkard asleep in the shadow of them; two or three wood flats[5] at the head of the wharf, but nobody to listen to the peaceful lapping of the wavelets against them; the great Mississippi, the majestic, the magnificent Mississippi, rolling its mile-wide tide along, shining in the sun; the dense forest away on the other side; the "point" above the town, and the "point" below, bounding the river-glimpse and turning it into a sort of sea, and withal a very still and brilliant and lonely one. Presently a film of dark smoke appears above one of those remote "points"; instantly a Negro drayman,[6] famous for his quick

1. **packet:** boat that carries mail, passengers, and freight at fixed times over a fixed route.
2. **Keokuk** [kē′ə kuk′]: Mississippi River town at the southeastern tip of Iowa.
3. **levee** [lev′ ē]: landing place along the river.
4. **skids:** low, movable wooden platforms.
5. **wood flats:** small flat-bottomed boats.
6. **drayman:** driver of a dray, a low, sturdy cart with removable sides.

AT A GLANCE

- As a boy Twain wanted to be a steamboat captain.
- The arrival of a boat was the high point of the day in his sleepy Mississippi River village.

LITERARY OPTIONS

- colloquial language
- autobiography

THEMATIC OPTIONS

- the perspective of experience
- growth and change
- memory and time

1 AUTOBIOGRAPHY

The author immediately establishes that he is writing about his own boyhood and looking back on it from an adult perspective.

2 TONE

Twain is re-creating his boyhood, which he remembers with fondness and amusement. The autobiography reflects a personal, affectionate tone.

3 SETTING

The richly detailed description creates a precise and realistic picture of the sleepy town.

GUIDED READING

LITERAL QUESTION

1a. What major event transpires once a day? (the arrival of two steamboats, one heading upriver, and the other, down)

INFERENTIAL QUESTION

1b. Why is the event so important? (Very little else of interest happens in the town.)

AT A GLANCE

- The townspeople assemble; the boat arrives and leaves; the village returns to its sleepy state.
- Years later, when Twain becomes an apprentice steamboat pilot, he discovers how difficult piloting is.

1 CONTRAST

In direct contrast to the previous view of the town, this scene illustrates the dramatic effect of the arrival of the steamboat.

2 DESCRIPTION

The detailed description helps the reader imagine the steamboat as the townspeople see it.

3 THEME

In retrospect, Twain appreciates how unfounded his adolescent self-confidence was.

eye and prodigious voice, lifts up the cry, "S-t-e-a-m-boat a-comin'!" and the scene
1 changes! The town drunkard stirs, the clerks wake up, a furious clatter of drays follows, every house and store pours out a human contribution, and all in a twinkling the dead town is alive and moving. Drays, carts, men, boys, all go hurrying from many quarters to a common center, the wharf. Assembled there, the people fasten their eyes upon the coming boat as upon a wonder they are seeing for the first time.

2 And the boat *is* rather a handsome sight, too. She is long and sharp and trim and pretty; she has two tall, fancy-topped chimneys, with a gilded device of some kind swung between them; a fanciful pilothouse, all glass and "gingerbread," perched on top of the texas deck[7] behind them; the paddleboxes are gorgeous with a picture or with gilded rays above the boat's name; the boiler deck, the hurricane deck, and the texas deck are fenced and ornamented with clean white railings; there is a flag gallantly flying from the jackstaff; the furnace doors are open and the fires glaring bravely; the upper decks are black with passengers; the captain stands by the big bell, calm, imposing, the envy of all; great volumes of the blackest smoke are rolling and tumbling out of the chimneys—a husbanded grandeur created with a bit of pitch pine just before arriving at a town; the crew are grouped on the forecastle;[8] the broad stage[9] is run far out over the port bow, and an envied deckhand stands picturesquely on the end of it with a coil of rope in his hand; the pent steam is screaming through the gaugecocks; the captain lifts his hand, a bell rings, the wheels stop; then they turn back, churning the water to foam, and the steamer is at rest. Then such a scramble as there is to get aboard, and to get ashore, and to take in freight and to discharge freight, all at one and the same time; and such a yelling and cursing as the mates facilitate it all with! Ten minutes later the steamer is under way again, with no flag on the jackstaff and no black smoke issuing from the chimneys. After ten more minutes the town is dead again, and the town drunkard asleep by the skids once more.

A Cub Pilot's Experience: Learning the River

Years later, while on a trip down the Mississippi, Twain felt his boyhood ambition surface again, and he signed on as apprentice to the pilot of the Paul Jones, *Mr. Bixby.*

The *Paul Jones* was now bound for St. Louis. I planned a siege against my pilot, and at the end of three hard days he surrendered. He agreed to teach me the Mississippi River from New Orleans to St. Louis for five hundred dollars, payable out of the first wages I should receive after graduating. I entered upon the small enterprise of "learning" twelve or thirteen hundred miles of the great Mississippi River with the easy confidence of my time of
3 life. If I had really known what I was about to require of my faculties, I should not have had the courage to begin. I supposed that all a pilot had to do was to keep his boat in the river, and I did not consider that that could be much of a trick, since it was so wide.

The boat backed out from New Orleans at four in the afternoon, and it was "our watch" until eight. Mr. Bixby, my chief, "straightened her up," plowed her along past the sterns of the other boats that lay at the levee, and then said, "Here, take her; shave those steamships as close as you'd peel an apple." I took the wheel, and my heart went down into my boots; for it seemed to me that we were about to scrape the side off every ship in the line, we were so close. I held my breath and began to claw the boat away from the danger; and I had my own opinion of the pilot who had known no better than to get us into such peril, but I was too wise to express it. In half a minute I had a

7. **texas deck:** On a Mississippi River steamboat the deck adjoining the officers' cabins was called texas because the cabins there were the largest on the ship.
8. **forecastle** [fōk′səl]: upper deck.
9. **stage:** plank for loading and unloading cargo and passengers.

Steamboats on the Mississippi.

GUIDED READING

LITERAL QUESTION

1a. What does Twain say would have happened if he had known what learning the river required? (He would not have had the courage to begin.)

INFERENTIAL QUESTION

1b. What does this tell you about young Twain? (He does not look into things carefully before proceeding.)

AT A GLANCE

- Mr. Bixby reprimands young Twain for cowardice.
- Twain takes no interest in the information Mr. Bixby imparts to him.
- Twain makes the unpleasant discovery that as a pilot he must work nights.

1 STYLE: IMAGERY

The image of the huge boat hugging the shore "with affection" is both amusing and telling: Bixby is very close to the shore both literally and emotionally.

2 PURPOSE

By leaving the encounter with Bixby to the reader's imagination, Twain achieves a comic effect.

3 THEME

Experience is already beginning to change Twain's romantic adolescent view of the steamboat pilot.

wide margin of safety intervening between the *Paul Jones* and the ships; and within ten seconds more I was set aside in disgrace, and Mr. Bixby was going into danger again and flaying me alive with abuse of my cowardice. I was stung, but I was obliged to admire the easy confidence with which my chief loafed from side to side of his wheel, and trimmed the ships so closely that disaster seemed ceaselessly imminent. When he had cooled a little he told me that the easy water was close ashore and the current outside, and therefore we must hug the bank, upstream, to get the benefit of the former, and stay well out, downstream, to take advantage of the latter. In my own mind I resolved to be a downstream pilot and leave the upstreaming to people dead to prudence.

Now and then Mr. Bixby called my attention to certain things. Said he, "This is Six-Mile Point." I assented. It was pleasant enough information, but I could not see the bearing of it. I was not conscious that it was a matter of any interest to me. Another time he said, "This is Nine-Mile Point." Later he said, "This is Twelve-Mile Point." They were all about level with the water's edge; they all looked about alike to me; they were monotonously unpicturesque. I hoped Mr. Bixby would change the
1 subject. But no; he would crowd up around a point, hugging the shore with affection, and then say: "The slack water ends here, abreast this bunch of China-trees; now we cross over." So he crossed over. He gave me the wheel once or twice, but I had no luck. I either came near chipping off the edge of a sugar plantation, or else I yawed[10] too far from shore, and so I dropped back into disgrace again and got abused.

The watch was ended at last, and we took supper and went to bed. At midnight the glare of a lantern shone in my eyes, and the night watchman said:

"Come! turn out!"

10. **yawed:** unintentionally swerved outside the planned route.

And then he left. I could not understand this extraordinary procedure; so I presently gave up trying to, and dozed off to sleep. Pretty soon the watchman was back again, and this time he was gruff. I was annoyed. I said:

"What do you want to come bothering around here in the middle of the night for? Now as like as not I'll not get to sleep again tonight."

The watchman said:

"Well, if this ain't good, I'm blessed."

The "off-watch" was just turning in, and I heard some brutal laughter from them, and such remarks as, "Hello, watchman! ain't the new cub turned out yet? He's delicate, likely. Give him some sugar in a rag and send for the chambermaid to sing rock-a-by-baby to him."

2 About this time Mr. Bixby appeared on the scene. Something like a minute later I was climbing the pilot-house steps with some of my clothes on and the rest in my arms. Mr. Bixby was close behind, commenting. Here was something fresh—this thing of getting up in the middle of the night to go to work. It was a detail in piloting that had never occurred to
3 me at all. I knew that boats ran all night, but somehow I had never happened to reflect that somebody had to get up out of a warm bed to run them. I began to fear that piloting was not quite so romantic as I had imagined it was; there was something very real and worklike about this new phase of it.

It was a rather dingy night, although a fair number of stars were out. The big mate was at the wheel, and he had the old tub pointed at a star and was holding her straight up the middle of the river. The shores on either hand were not much more than a mile apart, but they seemed wonderfully far away and ever so vague and indistinct. The mate said:

"We've got to land at Jones's plantation, sir."

The vengeful spirit in me exulted. I said to myself, I wish you joy of your job, Mr. Bixby; you'll have a good time finding Mr. Jones's plantation such a night as this; and I hope you never *will* find it as long as you live.

GUIDED READING

LITERAL QUESTIONS

1a. What does Mr. Bixby do "now and then" as they travel? (calls the cub pilot's attention to certain points along the way)

2a. What kind of spirit is aroused in Twain when the mate tells Mr. Bixby that the boat has to land at Jones's plantation? (a vengeful spirit)

INFERENTIAL QUESTIONS

1b. What does Mr. Bixby expect Twain to do with this information? (memorize it so that he can learn the river)

2b. What do his feelings toward Mr. Bixby tell you about Twain? (He blames Bixby for his own incompetence and inexperience.)

Mr. Bixby said to the mate:

"Upper end of the plantation, or the lower?"

"Upper."

1 "I can't do it. The stumps there are out of water at this stage. It's no great distance to the lower, and you'll have to get along with that."

"All right, sir. If Jones don't like it he'll have to lump it, I reckon."

And then the mate left. My exultation began to cool and my wonder to come up. Here was a man who not only proposed to find this plantation on such a night, but to find either end of it you preferred. I dreadfully wanted to ask a question, but I was carrying about as many short answers as my cargo room would admit of, so I held my peace. All I desired to ask Mr. Bixby was the simple question whether he was ass enough to really imagine he was going to find that plantation on a night when all plan-
2 tations were exactly alike and all the same color. But I held in. I used to have fine inspirations of prudence in those days.

Mr. Bixby made for the shore and soon was scraping it, just the same as if it had been daylight. And not only that, but singing

"Father in heaven the day is declining," etc.

It seemed to me that I had put my life in the keeping of a peculiarly reckless outcast. Presently he turned on me and said:

"What's the name of the first point above New Orleans?"

3 I was gratified to be able to answer promptly, and I did. I said I didn't know.

"Don't *know?*"

This manner jolted me. I was down at the foot again, in a moment. But I had to say just what I had said before.

"Well, you're a smart one," said Mr. Bixby. "What's the name of the *next* point?"

Once more I didn't know.

"Well this beats anything. Tell me the name of *any* point or place I told you."

I studied a while and decided that I couldn't.

"Look-a-here! What do you start out from, above Twelve-Mile Point, to cross over?"

"I—I—don't know."

"You—you—don't know?" mimicking my drawling manner of speech. "What *do* you know?"

"I—I—nothing, for certain."

"By the great Caesar's ghost I believe you! You're the stupidest dunderhead I ever saw or ever heard of, so help me Moses! The idea of *you* being a pilot—*you!* Why, you don't know enough to pilot a cow down a lane."

4 Oh, but his wrath was up! He was a nervous man, and he shuffled from one side of his wheel to the other as if the floor was hot. He would boil a while to himself, and then overflow and scald me again.

"Look-a-here! What do you suppose I told you the names of those points for?"

I tremblingly considered a moment, and then the devil of temptation provoked me to say:

"Well—to—to—be entertaining, I thought."

This was a red rag to the bull. He raged and stormed so (he was crossing the river at the time) that I judge it made him blind, because he ran over the steering oar of a trading scow.[11] Of course the traders sent up a volley of red-hot profanity. Never was a man so grateful as Mr. Bixby was: because he was brim full, and here were subjects who would *talk back.* He threw open a window, thrust his head out, and such an irruption followed as I never had heard before. The fainter and farther away the scowmen's curses drifted, the higher Mr. Bixby lifted his voice and the weightier his adjectives grew. When he closed the window he was empty. You could have drawn a seine[12] through his system and not caught curses enough to disturb your mother with. Presently he said to me in the gentlest way:

"My boy, you must get a little memorandum book, and every time I tell you a thing,

11. **trading scow:** a large, flat-bottomed boat with square ends used for carrying coal and other cargo.
12. **seine** [sān]: large fishing net.

AT A GLANCE

- Bixby begins to quiz Twain on the names of the points he provided earlier.
- Bixby becomes enraged when Twain does not remember the names of any of the points.
- When he calms down, Bixby tells Twain to write everything down.

1 COLLOQUIAL LANGUAGE

The plain, slangy speech of Mr. Bixby and the mate lend authenticity to the tale and help to show their personalities.

2 TONE

The author's comment on his prudence is one of good-humored mockery and reflects the amusing, personal tone of the selection.

3 IRONY

It is ironic that Twain would be gratified to answer promptly when he does not know the answer.

4 STYLE: METAPHOR

Mr. Bixby in his state of wrath is compared to a bubbling pot that periodically boils over.

GUIDED READING

LITERAL QUESTIONS

1a. What "simple question" does Twain want to ask Mr. Bixby? (whether Bixby really expects to find the plantation on such a night)

2a. What provokes Twain to say that he thought that Mr. Bixby was being entertaining? (the "devil of temptation")

INFERENTIAL QUESTIONS

1b. Why was it better for him not to ask the question? (It would have been insulting to the pilot.)

2b. Why did Twain characterize his answer in this way? (He knew that it would provoke Mr. Bixby.)

AT A GLANCE

- Twain's notebook contains more information than his mind can hold.
- He and Bixby go to a grander boat for the trip downstream.
- Twain realizes that he now must learn the river in reverse.

1 AUTOBIOGRAPHY

At this point in the autobiography, Twain offers an objective assessment of his progress from the perspective of maturity.

2 READING SKILLS: COMPARISONS

The detailed description creates a sharp contrast between the *Paul Jones* and the New Orleans boat.

3 AUDIENCE

Speaking directly to his audience, Twain creates intimacy and brings his readers into the story.

4 STYLE: IMAGERY

The image of the boy tangled up in a knot suggests his utter bafflement and frustration with all the things he has to learn.

put it down right away. There's only one way to be a pilot, and that is to get this entire river by heart. You have to know it just like A B C."

That was a dismal revelation to me; for my memory was never loaded with anything but blank cartridges. . . .

1 By the time we had gone seven or eight hundred miles up the river, I had learned to be a tolerably plucky upstream steersman, in daylight, and before we reached St. Louis I had made a trifle of progress in night work, but only a trifle. I had a notebook that fairly bristled with the names of towns, "points," bars, islands, bends, reaches, etc.; but the information was to be found only in the notebook—none of it was in my head. It made my heart ache to think I had only got half of the river set down; for as our watch was four hours off and four hours on, day and night, there was a long four-hour gap in my book for every time I had slept since the voyage began.

My chief was presently hired to go on a big New Orleans boat, and I packed my satchel and went with him. She was a grand affair. When I stood in her pilothouse I was so far above the water that I seemed perched on a mountain; and her decks stretched so far away, fore and aft, below me, that I wondered how I could ever have considered the little *Paul Jones* a large craft. There were other differ-
2 ences, too. The *Paul Jones*'s pilothouse was a cheap, dingy, battered rattletrap, cramped for room: but here was a sumptuous glass temple; room enough to have a dance in; showy red and gold window curtains; an imposing sofa; leather cushions and a back to the high bench where visiting pilots sit, to spin yarns and "look at the river"; bright, fanciful "cuspadors"[13] instead of a broad wooden box filled with sawdust; nice new oilcloth on the floor; a hospitable big stove for winter; a wheel as high as my head, costly with inlaid work; a wire tiller rope; bright brass knobs for the bells; and a tidy, white-aproned, black "texas tender,"[14] to bring up tarts and ices and coffee during midwatch, day and night. Now this was "something like"; and so I began to take heart once more to believe that piloting was a romantic sort of occupation after all. The moment we were under way I began to prowl about the great steamer and fill myself with joy. She was as clean and as dainty as a drawing room; when I looked down her long, gilded saloon, it was like gazing through a splendid tunnel; she had an oil picture, by some gifted sign painter, on every stateroom door; she glittered with no end of prism-fringed chandeliers; the clerk's office was elegant, the bar was marvelous, and the barkeeper had been barbered and upholstered at incredible cost. The boiler deck (i.e., the second story of the boat, so to speak) was as spacious as a church, it seemed to me; so with the forecastle; and there was no pitiful handful of deckhands, firemen, and roustabouts[15] down there, but a whole battalion of men. The fires were fiercely glaring from a long row of furnaces, and over them were eight huge boilers! This was unutterable pomp. The mighty engines—but enough of this. I had never felt so fine before. And when I found that the regiment of natty servants respectfully "sir'd" me, my satisfaction was complete.

3 When I returned to the pilothouse St. Louis was gone and I was lost. Here was a piece of river which was all down in my book, but I could make neither head nor tail of it: you understand, it was turned around. I had seen it, when coming upstream, but I had never faced about to see how it looked when it was behind me. My heart broke again, for it was plain that I had got to learn this troublesome river *both ways.*

A Dangerous Crossing

4 My late voyage's notebooking was but a confusion of meaningless names. It had tangled me all up in a knot every time I had looked at it in the daytime. I now hoped for respite in sleep; but no, it reveled all through my head

13. **"cuspadors"** [kus′pə dôrz′]: spittoons.
14. **"texas tender":** a servant of the officers on texas deck.
15. **roustabouts:** laborers on a ship.

GUIDED READING

LITERAL QUESTION

1a. What conclusion does Twain come to when he finds that his book will be of little use to him going downstream? (He concludes that he must learn the river both ways.)

INFERENTIAL QUESTION

1b. What failings of Twain's make this a heartbreaking discovery? (He is poor at memorizing and does not like hard work.)

Levee at St. Louis, photo by Oscar Kuehn, 1904.

till sunrise again, a frantic and tireless nightmare.

Next morning I felt pretty rusty and low-spirited. We went booming along, taking a good many chances, for we were anxious to "get out of the river" (as getting out to Cairo[16] was called) before night should overtake us.
1 But Mr. Bixby's partner, the other pilot, presently grounded the boat, and we lost so much time getting her off that it was plain the darkness would overtake us a good long way above the mouth. This was a great misfortune, especially to certain of our visiting pilots, whose boats would have to wait for their return, no matter how long that might be. It sobered the
2 pilothouse talk a good deal. Coming upstream, pilots did not mind low water or any kind of darkness; nothing stopped them but fog. But downstream work was different; a boat was too nearly helpless, with a stiff current pushing behind her; so it was not customary to run downstream at night in low water.

There seemed to be one small hope, however: if we could get through the intricate and dangerous Hat Island crossing before night, we could venture the rest, for we would have plainer sailing and better water. But it would be insanity to attempt Hat Island at night. So there was a deal of looking at watches all the rest of the day, and a constant ciphering upon the speed we were making; Hat Island was the eternal subject; sometimes hope was high and sometimes we were delayed in a bad crossing,

16. **Cairo:** Mississippi River town at the southern tip of Illinois.

AT A GLANCE

- On the way downstream, a grounding makes them late.
- Darkness, the current, and low water make the passage dangerous.
- To make the difficult Hat Island crossing before dark is their best hope.

1 READING SKILLS: CAUSE AND EFFECT

The cause is the grounding of the boat. The effects of this cause are the loss of time and approaching darkness.

2 TONE

Twain provides the background information necessary for his audience to appreciate the story. His tone is straightforward and businesslike.

GUIDED READING

LITERAL QUESTION

1a. How does Twain feel the morning after his nightmare? ("pretty rusty and low-spirited")

INFERENTIAL QUESTION

1b. Why does he feel that way? (He probably realizes that he still has a long way to go before becoming a pilot.)

AT A GLANCE

- Mr. Bixby takes the wheel.
- The sun goes down, but Bixby continues to head for Hat Island.
- Bixby steers between the reefs and drifts toward the head of the island.

1 AUTOBIOGRAPHY

Twain's memory of feeling unable to get a deep breath conveys the tension on the boat as he experienced it.

2 STYLE: IMAGERY

The image of bell notes floating on air gives them a palpable quality and suggests the heaviness of the atmosphere around the boat.

3 VOCABULARY: JARGON

The use of riverboat jargon adds realism and tension.

4 COLLOQUIAL LANGUAGE

The colloquial, expressive words of the boatmen tell Twain's story for him. They provide realism, a sense of being there.

and down it went again. For hours all hands lay under the burden of this suppressed excitement; it was even communicated to me, and I got to feeling so solicitous about Hat Island, and under such an awful pressure of responsi-
1 bility, that I wished I might have five minutes on shore to draw a good, full, relieving breath, and start over again. We were standing no regular watches. Each of our pilots ran such portions of the river as he had run when coming upstream, because of his greater familiarity with it; but both remained in the pilothouse constantly.

An hour before sunset, Mr. Bixby took the wheel and Mr. W——— stepped aside. For the next thirty minutes every man held his watch in his hand and was restless, silent, and uneasy. At last somebody said, with a doomful sigh:

"Well, yonder's Hat Island—and we can't make it."

All the watches closed with a snap, everybody sighed and muttered something about its being "too bad, too bad—ah, if we could *only* have got here half an hour sooner!" and the place was thick with the atmosphere of disappointment. Some started to go out, but loitered, hearing no bell tap to land. The sun dipped behind the horizon, the boat went on. Inquiring looks passed from one guest to another; and one who had his hand on the doorknob, and had turned it, waited, then presently took away his hand and let the knob turn back again. We bore steadily down the bend. More looks were exchanged, and nods of surprised admiration—but no words. Insensibly the men drew together behind Mr. Bixby as the sky darkened and one or two dim stars came out. The dead silence and sense of waiting became
2 oppressive. Mr. Bixby pulled the cord, and two deep, mellow notes from the big bell floated off on the night. Then a pause, and one more note was struck. The watchman's voice followed, from the hurricane deck:

"Labboard[17] lead, there! Stabboard[18] lead!"

17. **labboard:** larboard, the left side of the ship.
18. **stabboard:** starboard, the right side of the ship.

The cries of the leadsmen[19] began to rise out of the distance, and were gruffly repeated by the wordpassers on the hurricane deck.

3 "M-a-r-k[20] three! M-a-r-k three! Quarter-less-three! Half twain! Quarter twain! M-a-r-k twain! Quarter-less"—

Mr. Bixby pulled two bellropes, and was answered by faint jinglings far below in the engineroom, and our speed slackened. The steam began to whistle through the gaugecocks. The cries of the leadsmen went on—and it is a weird sound, always, in the night. Every pilot in the lot was watching, now, with fixed eyes, and talking under his breath. Nobody was calm and easy but Mr. Bixby. He would put his wheel down and stand on a spoke, and as the steamer swung into her (to me) utterly invisible marks—for we seemed to be in the midst of a wide and gloomy sea—he would meet and fasten her there. Talk was going on, now, in low voices:

4 "There; she's over the first reef all right!"

After a pause, another subdued voice:

"Her stern's coming down just *exactly* right, by *George!* Now she's in the marks;[21] over she goes!"

Somebody else muttered:

"Oh, it was done beautiful—*beautiful!*"

Now the engines were stopped altogether, and we drifted with the current. Not that I could see the boat drift, for I could not, the stars being all gone by this time. This drifting was the dismalest work; it held one's heart still. Presently I discovered a blacker gloom than that which surrounded us. It was the head of the island. We were closing right down upon it. We entered its deeper shadow, and so imminent seemed the peril that I was likely to suffocate; and I had the strongest impulse to do *something,* anything, to save the vessel. But still Mr. Bixby stood by his wheel, silent, intent

19. **leadsmen** [ledz′mən]: men who use a lead line, a weighted line for measuring water depth.
20. **Mark:** one of the markers on a lead line to indicate depth in fathoms (a fathom equals six feet). "Mark twain" indicates two fathoms.
21. **marks:** safe water.

GUIDED READING

LITERAL QUESTIONS

1a. Who is the only "calm and easy" person during the crossing? (Mr. Bixby)

2a. What does Twain call "the dismalest work"? (drifting)

INFERENTIAL QUESTIONS

1b. Why is he able to remain calm? (He is a competent pilot, sure of his abilities.)

2b. What makes it dismal? (They are adrift and unable to see; he feels helpless and in danger.)

as a cat, and all the pilots stood shoulder to shoulder at his back.

"She'll not make it!" somebody whispered.

The water grew shoaler[22] and shoaler by the leadsmen's cries, till it was down to—

1 "Eight-and-a-half! E-i-g-h-t feet! E-i-g-h-t feet! Seven-and"—

Mr. Bixby said warningly through his speaking tube to the engineer:

"Stand by, now!"

"Aye-aye, sir."

"Seven-and-a-half! Seven feet! *Six*-and"—

We touched bottom! Instantly Mr. Bixby set a lot of bells ringing, shouted through the tube, "*Now* let her have it—every ounce you've got!" then to his partner, "Put her hard down! snatch her! snatch her!" The boat rasped and ground her way through the sand, hung upon the apex of disaster a single tremendous instant, and then over she went! And such a shout as went up at Mr. Bixby's back never loosened the roof of a pilothouse before!

2 There was no more trouble after that. Mr. Bixby was a hero that night; and it was some little time, too, before his exploit ceased to be talked about by river men.

Fully to realize the marvelous precision required in laying the great steamer in her marks in that murky waste of water, one should know that not only must she pick her intricate way through snags and blind reefs, and then shave the head of the island so closely as to brush the overhanging foliage with her stern, but at one place she must pass almost within arm's reach of a sunken and invisible wreck that would snatch the hull timbers from under her if she should strike it, and destroy a quarter of a million dollars' worth of steamboat and cargo in five minutes, and maybe a hundred and fifty human lives into the bargain.

The last remark I heard that night was a compliment to Mr. Bixby, uttered in soliloquy and with unction by one of our guests. He said:

"By the Shadow of Death, but he's a lightning pilot!"

22. **shoaler:** shallower.

STUDY QUESTIONS

Recalling

1. According to the opening paragraphs, what was the one permanent ambition of the writer and all his childhood friends? What daily events did all Hannibal look forward to?
2. What adjectives does Twain use to describe the Mississippi River in the second paragraph?
3. According to the section "A Cub Pilot's Experience," upon what enterprise did Twain enter with the "easy confidence" of youth? Who agreed to train him?
4. What is the method that Mr. Bixby recommended for learning to be a pilot?
5. Identify five differences between the *Paul Jones* and the New Orleans boat on which Twain traveled back from St. Louis. What "heart-breaking" realization did he have as he headed downstream?

Interpreting

6. Describe Twain's attitude as a boy toward the Mississippi River and toward the profession of riverboat pilot.
7. What is Twain's general attitude toward himself as a youth as evidenced by the tone of this selection? Cite details to support your answer.
8. Who is the "hero" of this selection? What details lead you to this conclusion?
9. What clues does this selection give you toward understanding why Samuel Clemens chose the pen name "Mark Twain"?

Extending

10. What aspects of Twain's excitement about learning a new skill seem authentic?

AT A GLANCE

- When the boat touches bottom, Bixby calls for power and completes the crossing.
- Bixby is hailed as hero by both crew and passengers.

1 DIALOGUE

The clipped calls of the boatmen add to the suspense of the situation.

2 RESPONSE JOURNAL

Ask students to argue in favor of or against Bixby's decision to make the crossing; have them speculate about why he did it.

REFLECTING ON THE SELECTION

How does Twain's tone in this selection contribute to its humor? (Students may suggest that in mocking and laughing at himself, Twain gives the reader permission to do so, too.)

STUDY QUESTIONS

1. become steamboatmen; arrival of two steamboats
2. *great, majestic, magnificent*
3. learning to be a pilot; Mr. Bixby
4. learn entire river by heart
5. bigger, cleaner, more elegant, better pilot house, greater engines; learn river both ways
6. romanticized; glamorous
7. amused by naivety and foolishness; "easy confidence" remark, surprise at being awakened at night
8. Mr. Bixby; skill, Twain's admiration
9. explains leadsman's cry, shows excitement; Twain's admiration for river, riverboat pilots
10. Answers will vary. Students should note realistic details.

AT A GLANCE

- The narrator meets Simon Wheeler, a talkative old Westerner.
- He asks Wheeler about Leonidas W. Smiley.
- Wheeler, thereby reminded of a *Jim* Smiley, begins a tall tale.

LITERARY OPTIONS

- style: dialect
- point of view
- setting

THEMATIC OPTIONS

- the Wild West
- art and imagination

1 POINT OF VIEW

The unnamed narrator begins to tell his story using a first-person point of view. The narrator's choice of language—*personage, conjectured, exasperating, tedious*—suggests that he is a pompous individual.

2 SETTING

Angel's Camp is dilapidated and decayed, the kind of place where outcasts collected near the exhausted mines of the Old West.

3 POINT OF VIEW

The first narrator gives way to Wheeler—an early old westerner—whose story turns out to be a tall tale.

"The Celebrated Jumping Frog of Calaveras County" is Mark Twain's most famous western tale. It is actually a story within a frame story: The first narrator introduces us to a second narrator, Simon Wheeler, who then tells the tale. Our pleasure is in the company of Wheeler himself, a man who loves to talk and who could, as we see at the end, go on spinning his tall tales forever.

Mark Twain

The Celebrated Jumping Frog of Calaveras County

In compliance with the request of a friend of mine, who wrote me from the East, I called on good-natured, garrulous old Simon Wheeler, and inquired after my friend's friend, Leonidas W. Smiley, as requested to do, and I hereunto append the result. I have a lurking suspicion
1 that *Leonidas W.* Smiley is a myth; that my friend never knew such a personage; and that he only conjectured that if I asked old Wheeler about him, it would remind him of his infamous *Jim* Smiley, and he would go to work and bore me to death with some exasperating reminiscence of him as long and as tedious as it should be useless to me. If that was the design, it succeeded.

2 I found Simon Wheeler dozing comfortably by the barroom stove of the dilapidated tavern in the decayed mining camp of Angel's, and I noticed that he was fat and baldheaded, and had an expression of winning gentleness and simplicity upon his tranquil countenance. He roused up, and gave me good day. I told him that a friend of mine had commissioned me to make some inquiries about a cherished companion of his boyhood named *Leonidas W.* Smiley—*Rev. Leonidas W.* Smiley, a young minister of the gospel, who he had heard was at one time a resident of Angel's Camp. I added that if Mr. Wheeler could tell me anything about this Rev. Leonidas W. Smiley, I would feel under many obligations to him.

Simon Wheeler backed me into a corner and blockaded me there with his chair, and then sat down and reeled off the monotonous narrative which follows this paragraph. He never smiled, he never frowned, he never changed his voice from the gentle-flowing key to which he tuned his initial sentence, he never betrayed the slightest suspicion of enthusiasm; but all through the interminable narrative there ran a vein of impressive earnestness and sincerity, which showed me plainly that, so far from his imagining that there was anything ridiculous or funny about his story, he regarded it as a really important matter, and admired its two heroes as men of transcendent genius in *finesse.* I let him go on in his own way, and never interrupted him once.

3 "Rev. Leonidas W. H'm, Reverend Le—well, there was a feller here once by the name of *Jim* Smiley, in the winter of '49—or maybe it was the spring of '50—I don't recollect exactly, somehow, though what makes me think it was one or the other is because I remember

GUIDED READING

LITERAL QUESTION

1a. What adjective does the narrator use to describe the narrative that follows? *(monotonous)*

INFERENTIAL QUESTION

1b. Do you think Twain agrees with his narrator? Why or why not? (No; if he had believed the story to be monotonous, he would not be relating it.)

the big flume[1] warn't finished when he first come to the camp; but anyway, he was the curiousest man about always betting on anything that turned up you ever see, if he could get anybody to bet on the other side; and if he
1 couldn't he'd change sides. Any way that suited the other man would suit *him*—any way just so's he got a bet, *he* was satisfied. But still he was lucky, uncommon lucky; he most always come out winner. He was always ready and laying for a chance; there couldn't be no solit'ry thing mentioned but that feller'd offer to bet on it, and take ary side you please, as I was just telling you. If there was a horse race, you'd find him flush or you'd find him busted at the end of it; if there was a dog fight, he'd
2 bet on it; if there was a cat fight, he'd bet on it; if there was a chicken fight, he'd bet on it; why, if there was two birds setting on a fence, he would bet you which one would fly first; or if there was a camp meeting,[2] he would be there reg'lar to bet on Parson Walker, which he judged to be the best exhorter about here, and so he was too, and a good man. If he even see a straddle bug[3] start to go anywheres, he would bet you how long it would take him to get to—to wherever he was going to, and if you took him up, he would foller that straddle bug to Mexico but what he would find out where he was bound for and how long he was on the road. Lots of the boys here has seen that Smiley, and can tell you about him. Why, it never made no difference to *him*—he'd bet on *any* thing—the dangdest feller. Parson Walker's wife laid very sick once, for a good while, and it seemed as if they warn't going to save her; but one morning he come in, and Smiley up and asked him how she was, and he said she was considerable better—thank the Lord for his inf'nite mercy—and coming on so smart that with the blessing of Prov'dence she'd get well yet; and Smiley, before he thought, says, 'Well, I'll resk two-and-a-half she don't anyway.'

"Thish-yer Smiley had a mare—the boys called her the fifteen-minute nag, but that was only in fun, you know, because of course she was faster than that—and he used to win money on that horse, for all she was so slow and always had the asthma, or the distemper, or the consumption, or something of that kind. They used to give her two or three hundred yards' start, and then pass her underway; but always at the fag end[4] of the race she'd get excited and desperate like, and come cavorting and straddling up, and scattering her legs around limber, sometimes in the air, and sometimes out to one side among the fences, and kicking up m-o-r-e dust and raising m-o-r-e racket with her coughing and sneezing and blowing her nose—and *always* fetch up at the stand just about a neck ahead, as near as you could cipher it down.

"And he had a little small bull pup, that to look at him you'd think he warn't worth a cent but to set around and look ornery and lay for a chance to steal something. But as soon as money was up on him he was a different dog;
3 his underjaw'd begin to stick out like the fo'castle[5] of a steamboat, and his teeth would uncover and shine like the furnaces. And a dog might tackle him and bullyrag him, and bite him, and throw him over his shoulder two or three times, and Andrew Jackson[6]—which was the name of the pup—Andrew Jackson would never let on but what *he* was satisfied, and hadn't expected nothing else—and the bets being doubled and doubled on the other side all the time, till the money was all up; and then all of a sudden he would grab that other dog jest by the j'int of his hind leg and freeze to it—not chaw, you understand, but only just grip and hang on till they throwed up the sponge, if it was a year. Smiley always come out winner on that pup, till he harnessed a dog

1. **flume** [floom]: artificial inclined channel for conducting water to provide power and transport objects.
2. **camp meeting:** religious meeting and service held in the mining camp.
3. **straddle bug:** long-legged beetle.
4. **fag end:** last part.
5. **fo'castle:** forecastle; upper deck.
6. **Andrew Jackson:** after the general and seventh President of the United States.

AT A GLANCE

- Jim Smiley would bet on anything.
- He won money betting on his rundown horse.
- He had a bull pup that looked unimpressive but beat any dog it fought.

1 STYLE: DIALECT

The contractions, regionalisms, and nonstandard usage in Wheeler's speech mark him as uneducated; the language gives the story its folksy local color.

2 CHARACTERIZATION

Wheeler's litany reveals his own garrulousness as much as it does Smiley's behavior. In the long sentence, Wheeler seems barely to pause for breath.

3 STYLE: FIGURES OF SPEECH

Wheeler comically compares the dog's underjaw to the forecastle of a steamboat and says that his teeth would shine like the furnaces.

GUIDED READING

LITERAL QUESTION

1a. What does Jim Smiley say to Parson Walker after the Parson tells him that Mrs. Walker will "get well yet"? ("I'll resk two-and-a-half she don't anyway.")

INFERENTIAL QUESTION

1b. In what way does this emphasize Smiley's obsession with gambling? (Because betting is uppermost in his mind, he makes a very inappropriate comment.)

AT A GLANCE

- Pitted against a dog with no hind legs to seize, Smiley's pup loses.
- Smiley starts training a frog to jump.
- He brags to a stranger that the frog, Dan'l, can outjump any other in the county.

1 THEME

Wheeler's depiction of the dog dying of a broken heart is typical of the exaggeration used in the tall tales of the American West.

2 STYLE: DIALECT

Wheeler's colloquial speech adds color to his tale by helping the reader to picture him.

3 HUMOR

Wheeler endows the frog with human modesty, along with extraordinary talent.

once that didn't have no hind legs, because they'd been sawed off in a circular saw, and when the thing had gone along far enough, and the money was all up, and he come to make a snatch for his pet holt,[7] he see in a minute how he'd been imposed on, and how the other dog had him in the door, so to speak, and he 'peared surprised, and then he looked sorter discouraged-like, and didn't try no more to win
1 the fight, and so he got shucked out bad. He give Smiley a look, as much as to say his heart was broke, and it was *his* fault, for putting up a dog that hadn't no hind legs for him to take holt of, which was his main dependence in a fight, and then he limped off a piece and laid down and died. It was a good pup, was that Andrew Jackson, and would have made a name for hisself if he'd lived, for the stuff was in him and he had genius—I know it, because he hadn't no opportunities to speak of, and it don't stand to reason that a dog could make such a fight as he could under them circumstances if he hadn't no talent. It always makes me feel sorry when I think of that last fight of his'n, and the way it turned out.

2 "Well, thish-yer Smiley had rat terriers[8] and chicken cocks[9] and tomcats and all them kind of things, till you couldn't rest, and you couldn't fetch nothing for him to bet on but he'd match you. He ketched a frog one day, and took him home, and said he cal'lated to educate him; and so he never done nothing for three months but set in his back yard and learn that frog to jump. And you bet you he *did* learn him, too. He'd give him a little punch behind, and the next minute you'd see that frog whirling in the air like a doughnut—see him turn one summerset, or maybe a couple, if he got a good start, and come down flatfooted and all right, like a cat. He got him up so in the matter of ketching flies, and kep' him in practice so constant, that he'd nail a fly every time as fur as he could see him. Smiley said all a frog wanted was education, and he could do 'most anything—and I believe him. Why, I've seen him set Dan'l Webster[10] down here on this floor—Dan'l Webster was the name of the frog—and sing out, 'Flies, Dan'l, flies!' and quicker'n you could wink he'd spring straight up and snake a fly off'n the counter there, and flop down on the floor ag'in as solid as a gob of mud, and fall to scratching the side of his
3 head with his hind foot as indifferent as if he hadn't no idea he'd been doin' any more'n any frog might do. You never see a frog so modest and straightfor'ard as he was, for all he was so gifted. And when it come to fair and square jumping on a dead level, he could get over more ground at one straddle than any animal of his breed you ever see. Jumping on a dead level was his strong suit, you understand; and when it come to that, Smiley would ante up money on him as long as he had a red.[11] Smiley was monstrous proud of his frog, and well he might be, for fellers that had traveled and been everywheres all said he laid over any frog that ever *they* see.

"Well, Smiley kep' the beast in a little lattice box, and he used to fetch him downtown sometimes and lay for a bet. One day a feller—a stranger in the camp, he was—come acrost him with his box, and says:

" 'What might it be that you've got in the box?'

"And Smiley says, sorter indifferent-like, 'It might be a parrot, or it might be a canary, maybe, but it ain't—it's only just a frog.'

"And the feller took it, and looked at it careful, and turned it round this way and that, and says, 'H'm—so 'tis. Well, what's *he* good for?'

" 'Well,' Smiley says, easy and careless, 'he's good enough for *one* thing, I should judge—he can outjump any frog in Calaveras County.'

"The feller took the box again, and took another long, particular look, and give it back to Smiley, and says, very deliberate, 'Well,' he

7. **holt:** hold.
8. **rat terriers:** dogs skilled in catching rats.
9. **chicken cocks:** here, roosters trained for fights on which bets were made.
10. **Dan'l Webster:** after Daniel Webster, the American statesman and orator.
11. **a red:** a red cent; any money.

GUIDED READING

LITERAL QUESTION

1a. What does Wheeler say finally caused the death of Smiley's dog? (Its heart was broken; it was Smiley's fault for putting Andrew Jackson up against a dog with no hind legs.)

INFERENTIAL QUESTION

1b. What makes this situation humorous? (It is an exaggeration: it is very unlikely that a dog with no hind legs could win a fight or that Andrew Jackson would have died of a broken heart after losing.)

says, 'I don't see no p'ints about that frog that's any better'n any other frog.'

" 'Maybe you don't,' Smiley says. 'Maybe you understand frogs and maybe you don't understand 'em; maybe you've had experience, and maybe you ain't only a amature, as it were. Anyways, I've got *my* opinion, and I'll resk forty dollars that he can outjump any frog in Calaveras County.'

"And the feller studied a minute, and then says, kinder sad-like, 'Well, I'm only a stranger here, and I ain't got no frog; but if I had a frog, I'd bet you.'

1 "And then Smiley says, 'That's all right—that's all right—if you'll hold my box a minute, I'll go and get you a frog.' And so the feller took the box, and put up his forty dollars along with Smiley's, and set down to wait.

2 "So he set there a good while thinking and thinking to himself, and then he got the frog out and prized his mouth open and took a teaspoon and filled him full of quailshot[12]—filled him pretty near up to his chin—and set him on the floor. Smiley he went to the swamp and slopped around in the mud for a long time, and finally he ketched a frog, and fetched him in, and give him to this feller, and says:

" 'Now, if you're ready, set him alongside of Dan'l, with his fore paws just even with Dan'l's, and I'll give the word.' Then he says, 'One—two—three—*git!*' and him and the feller touched up the frogs from behind, and the new frog hopped off lively, but Dan'l give a heave, and hysted up his shoulders—so—like a

12. **quailshot:** small lead pellets used for shooting quail.

AT A GLANCE

- Smiley wants to bet the stranger forty dollars on Dan'l.
- Because the stranger has no frog, Smiley goes off to find him one.
- In Smiley's absence, the stranger feeds quailshot to Dan'l.
- The contest begins with the stranger's frog hopping off.

1 CHARACTER

Smiley's mind is so intent on his bet that he does not realize the danger in leaving his frog with the stranger.

2 INFERENCES

From the amount of time that the stranger sat thinking, the reader can infer that he did not have the quailshot in mind when he first made the bet.

GUIDED READING

LITERAL QUESTION

1a. What does the stranger do to Dan'l Webster? (fills him with quailshot, out of Smiley's sight)

INFERENTIAL QUESTION

1b. What effect will the stranger's actions have? (It will make the frog too heavy to jump at all.)

AT A GLANCE

- Dan'l cannot jump.
- The stranger takes Smiley's money and leaves.
- Too late, Smiley discovers the quailshot.
- Wheeler would go on talking, but the narrator takes his leave.

1 POINT OF VIEW

The point of view returns to the first narrator, closing the frame of the story.

REFLECTING ON THE STORY

What does the personality of the unnamed narrator add to the story? (Students may say that Twain provides humor through contrast: The pompous narrator is forced to listen to the earthy Wheeler.)

STUDY QUESTIONS

1. *good-natured* and *garrulous; exasperating*
2. Leonidas W. Smiley; Jim Smiley
3. would bet on anything
4. winning fights despite size; lost to dog with no hind legs, died of a broken heart
5. outjump other frogs; filled frog with quailshot; puzzled, then very angry
6. no; Twain would not devote such space to Wheeler's tale if he thought so
7. no, highly improbable; does not matter; aim is humor through exaggeration
8. gambler; colorful, tricky; activities exaggerated
9. Simon Wheeler; captures flavor of Old West; Jim Smiley's story cut off in middle
10. Answers will vary. Students should find tall tales inventive and entertaining.

Frenchman, but it warn't no use—he couldn't budge; he was planted as solid as a church, and he couldn't no more stir than if he was anchored out. Smiley was a good deal surprised, and he was disgusted too, but he didn't have no idea what the matter was, of course.

"The feller took the money and started away; and when he was going out at the door, he sorter jerked his thumb over his shoulder—so—at Dan'l, and says again, very deliberate, 'Well,' he says, 'I don't see no p'ints about that frog that's any better'n any other frog.'

"Smiley he stood scratching his head and looking down at Dan'l a long time, and at last he says, 'I do wonder what in the nation that frog throw'd off for—I wonder if there ain't something the matter with him—he 'pears to look mighty baggy, somehow.' And he ketched Dan'l by the nap of the neck, and hefted him, and says, 'Why blame my cats if he don't weigh five pound!' and turned him upside down and he belched out a double handful of shot. And then he see how it was, and he was the maddest man—he set the frog down and took out after that feller, but he never ketched him. And—"

1 Here Simon Wheeler heard his name called from the front yard, and got up to see what was wanted. And turning to me as he moved away, he said: "Just set where you are, stranger, and rest easy—I ain't going to be gone a second."

But, by your leave, I did not think that a continuation of the history of the enterprising vagabond *Jim* Smiley would be likely to afford me much information concerning the Rev. *Leonidas W.* Smiley, and so I started away.

At the door I met the sociable Wheeler returning, and he buttonholed me and recommenced:

"Well, thish-yer Smiley had a yaller one-eyed cow that didn't have no tail, only just a short stump like a bannanner, and—"

However, lacking both time and inclination, I did not wait to hear about the afflicted cow, but took my leave.

STUDY QUESTIONS

Recalling

1. With what adjectives does the narrator describe Wheeler and Wheeler's reminiscences in the first paragraph?
2. About whom does the narrator ask Wheeler? About whom does Wheeler speak?
3. According to Wheeler's opening paragraph, about what was Jim Smiley "the curiousest man"?
4. How did Smiley's bullpup surprise people? What eventually became of the dog?
5. What did Smiley train his frog to do? Summarize what the stranger did to the frog and Smiley's reaction.

Interpreting

6. The narrator tells us that Wheeler bored him to death. Do you think Twain expects the reader to have the same reaction? How can you tell?
7. Does Wheeler's account of what happened to Smiley's dog make sense? Does it matter? Why or why not?
8. What kind of person is Jim Smiley, as Wheeler presents him?
9. Who is really the main character in this story, and why?

Extending

10. Why do you think people love to tell tall tales—and to listen to them?

A **fable** is a tale in which animals behave as if they were human beings; it usually ends with a moral. Here Mark Twain adopts the traditional fable format and in the simple language of fables gives us his view of art and our ways of experiencing it.

Mark Twain

A Fable

1 Once upon a time an artist who had painted a small and very beautiful picture placed it so that he could see it in the mirror. He said, "This doubles the distance and softens it, and it is twice as lovely as it was before."

The animals out in the woods heard of this through the housecat, who was greatly admired by them because he was so learned, and so refined and civilized, and so polite and high-bred, and could tell them so much which they didn't know before, and were not certain about afterward. They were much excited about this new piece of gossip, and they asked questions, so as to get at a full understanding of it. They asked what a picture was, and the cat explained.

"It is a flat thing," he said; "wonderfully flat, marvelously flat, enchantingly flat and elegant. And, oh, so beautiful!"

That excited them almost to a frenzy, and they said they would give the world to see it. Then the bear asked:

"What is it that makes it so beautiful?"

"It is the looks of it," said the cat.

This filled them with admiration and uncertainty, and they were more excited than ever. Then the cow asked:

"What is a mirror?"

2 "It is a hole in the wall," said the cat. "You look in it, and there you see the picture, and it is so dainty and charming and ethereal and inspiring in its unimaginable beauty that your head turns round and round, and you almost swoon with ecstasy."

The ass had not said anything as yet; he now began to throw doubts. He said there had never been anything as beautiful as this before, and probably wasn't now. He said that when it took a whole basketful of sesquipedalian[1] adjectives to whoop up a thing of beauty, it was time for suspicion.

It was easy to see that these doubts were having an effect upon the animals, so the cat went off offended. The subject was dropped for
3 a couple of days, but in the meantime curiosity was taking a fresh start, and there was a revival of interest perceptible. Then the animals assailed the ass for spoiling what could possibly have been a pleasure to them, on a mere suspicion that the picture was not beautiful, without any evidence that such was the case. The ass was not troubled; he was calm, and said there was one way to find out who was in the right, himself or the cat: he would go and look in that hole, and come back and tell what he found there. The animals felt relieved and grateful, and asked him to go at once—which he did.

But he did not know where he ought to stand; and so, through error, he stood between the picture and the mirror. The result was that the picture had no chance, and didn't show up. He returned home and said:

"The cat lied. There was nothing in that

1. **sesquipedalian** [ses′ kwi pi dā′lē ən]: having many syllables.

AT A GLANCE

- An artist paints a picture and hangs it so it can be seen in a mirror.
- His cat tells other animals how marvelous the picture is.
- The ass doubts the cat and goes to see for himself.
- He stands between the mirror and the picture.

LITERARY OPTIONS

- theme
- satire

THEMATIC OPTIONS

- art and imagination
- self-absorption vs. openness

1 SETTING

The opening words signal a tale in a traditional form, set in a timeless fantasy land.

2 CHARACTERIZATION

The cat is given to hyperbole and neither defines nor describes the mirror. His explanation belies his reputation for being learned.

3 TONE

The author good-naturedly mocks the very human behavior of the animals.

GUIDED READING

LITERAL QUESTIONS

1a. What is the animals' attitude toward the cat? (He is greatly admired.)

2a. Which animal throws doubts on the cat's explanation? (the ass)

INFERENTIAL QUESTIONS

1b. Is their opinion justified? Why or why not? (Probably not; he seems not to be as learned as they think and is rather shallow.)

2b. Why is this animal an appropriate choice for such an action? (Rough and brash, compared to the over-refined housecat, the ass is a practical and hardworking animal.)

AT A GLANCE

- The ass sees his own reflection and reports seeing only an ass.
- The other animals go in turn; each sees only itself.
- The cat remarks that you find in a text what you bring to it; if you stand too close, you see only yourself.

1 SATIRE

Twain pokes fun at both pomposity (as displayed by the cat) and gullibility (as displayed by the other animals).

2 THEME

The cat recognizes that to appreciate art one must stand far enough back to let imagination work.

REFLECTING ON THE FABLE

What kinds of people might the cat and the ass represent in the fable? (Students may suggest that the cat is a snob who does not necessarily know what he is talking about; the ass is an ordinary person, skeptical of exaggerated-sounding reports.)

STUDY QUESTIONS

1. *small, beautiful;* doubles distance, softens picture
2. housecat; learned, refined
3. donkey; he has never seen anything so beautiful; suspicious of too many "sesquipedalian" adjectives
4. himself
5. "You can find in a text whatever you bring, if you will stand between it and the mirror of your imagination."
6. snob; gullible
7. - If it takes many fancy words to tell how great something is, it probably is not great.
   - Answers will vary. Students might say that greatness speaks for itself.
8. imagination; interject selves, do not use imaginations
9. Answers will vary. Possible purpose is to strike the imagination.

hole but an ass. There wasn't a sign of a flat thing visible. It was a handsome ass, and friendly, but just an ass, and nothing more."

The elephant asked:

"Did you see it good and clear? Were you close to it?"

"I saw it good and clear, O Hathi, King of Beasts. I was so close that I touched noses with it."

1 "This is very strange," said the elephant; "the cat was always truthful before—as far as we could make out. Let another witness try. Go, Baloo, look in the hole, and come and report."

So the bear went. When he came back, he said:

"Both the cat and the ass have lied; there was nothing in the hole but a bear."

Great was the surprise and puzzlement of the animals. Each was now anxious to make the test himself and get at the straight truth. The elephant sent them one at a time.

First, the cow. She found nothing in the hole but a cow.

The tiger found nothing in it but a tiger.

The lion found nothing in it but a lion.

The leopard found nothing in it but a leopard.

The camel found a camel, and nothing more.

Then Hathi was wroth,[2] and said he would have the truth, if he had to go and fetch it himself. When he returned, he abused his whole subjectry for liars, and was in an unappeasable fury with the moral and mental blindness of the cat. He said that anybody but a nearsighted fool could see that there was nothing in the hole but an elephant.

MORAL, BY THE CAT

2 You can find in a text whatever you bring, if you will stand between it and the mirror of your imagination. You may not see your ears, but they will be there.

2. **wroth** [rôth]: very angry.

STUDY QUESTIONS

Recalling

1. What adjectives in the first paragraph describe the artist's picture? What does the artist say is the effect of viewing his picture in a mirror?
2. Who tells the animals in the woods about the picture? According to the second paragraph, why is this newsbearer admired by the other animals?
3. Who does not believe that such a beautiful picture exists? What reason does he give for his suspicions?
4. What does each animal see when he looks in the mirror?
5. According to the cat, what is the moral?

Interpreting

6. What criticism of the housecat may be inferred from the second paragraph? Of the forest animals?
7. Explain the donkey's statement in your own words. Do you agree with him? Why or why not?
8. What does the cat's moral suggest about the chief necessity for appreciating art? Why, then, can the forest animals not appreciate the beautiful picture?

Extending

9. How would you describe the purpose of a work of art, for example a painting, a story, a poem, or a song?

VIEWPOINT

Justin Kaplan, one of Twain's biographers, tells us that Twain's "preferred form" is

> the oral, humorous story, which . . . relies for its effectiveness on the manner of the telling instead of the outcome. . . . It is de-

livered gravely and unsuspectingly, with no overt cues for laughter, and it may wander around as much as it pleases.

—Introduction to *The Great Short Works of Mark Twain*

■ According to Kaplan's definition, which selection by Twain most clearly illustrates an "oral, humorous story," and why? Does the same "grave delivery" apply to the humor in the other selections? If so, where?

LITERARY FOCUS

Colloquial Language

Colloquial language is the everyday language we use in our conversation. It is sometimes ungrammatical, and it may contain slang words and phrases. It varies from place to place and among ethnic groups.

Rendering colloquial speech in print is an art, an art that Mark Twain mastered. Not only was he able to capture dialect realistically, but he had a knack for knowing when to use colloquial language and when to avoid it. The first narrator in "The Celebrated Jumping Frog of Calaveras County" has an educated, slightly pompous way of speaking: "I hereunto append," "personage," "conjectured." His language is not colloquial; it is quite formal English. Simon Wheeler, on the other hand, speaks in colloquial language; he uses a western dialect: "fellers," "curiousest," "This-yer." Wheeler's language is especially delightful to us because we see that Twain and his narrator enjoy it so much themselves.

Twain is also careful not to overdo the colloquial language. Wheeler's speech has the *suggestion* of western dialect; it is not an accurate recording. If it were, it would bore and confuse the reader, who would find it largely unintelligible. Twain's aim is to capture the colloquial American voice, not to make a study of it. He succeeds so well in "The Jumping Frog" that Wheeler's speech not only makes the tale, it *is* the tale.

Thinking About Colloquial Language

■ Find instances of colloquial language in *Life on the Mississippi.* How does Twain's use of colloquial conversation make his memories seem more realistic and exciting?

COMPOSITION

Analyzing Contrasting Tones

■ Write a brief essay contrasting the romantic or nostalgic parts of *Life on the Mississippi* with the more realistic ones. Begin by defining the two different tones of the selection. Then give examples of each. Conclude with a comment on how Twain uses language to achieve these different tones.

Writing a Fable

■ Write a fable of your own in which you use animal characters to make a point about human nature. Try to get something of Twain's graceful humor and simplicity of language into your writing. Like Twain, you might begin your fable with "Once upon a time. . . ."

COMPARING WRITERS

■ Whitman, Dickinson, and Twain all helped develop American literature as a singular expression of American life. How do the styles and subjects of these three writers differ from those of the American authors who preceded them? What do you think makes Whitman, Dickinson, and Twain so distinctly American?

VIEWPOINT

- "Celebrated Jumping Frog . . . "; composed of tall tale spoken to narrator
- Others also employ grave delivery.
- *Life on the Mississippi:* adult Twain understates foibles of young Sam for humorous effects
- "A Fable": description of housecat delivered seriously but implies mockery

LITERARY FOCUS

Most dialogues and some phrases applied to steamboats and piloting are colloquial. The language approximates real language of steamboatmen and adds to suspense in Hat Island crossing.

COMPARING WRITERS

Answers will vary. Students should recognize informality and originality that preceding authors lacked. Informality is displayed in elliptical and colloquial language and in personal attitude toward readers.

COMPOSITION: GUIDELINES FOR EVALUATION

ANALYZING CONTRASTING TONES

Objective

To analyze contrasting tones in a work

Guidelines for Evaluation

- suggested length: four to six paragraphs
- should identify contrasting tones as nostalgic or romantic and realistic
- should provide examples of each tone
- should state how Twain uses language to achieve these different tones

WRITING A FABLE

Objective

To write a fable

Guidelines for Evaluation

- suggested length: five to ten paragraphs
- should use animals to make point about human nature
- should have animals behave as human beings
- should use graceful humor and simple language
- should conclude with a moral

ACTIVE READING

Meaning

After the students have read this page, ask them to think of a poem, a story, or a song of which they are particularly fond, one to which they have listened or that they have read more than once. Did its meaning stay the same each time, or did each experience with the work prompt new ideas and meanings? Discuss how sometimes the meaning of a work can change for readers as they grow older and more experienced.

ACTIVE READING

Meaning

As we read, most of us ask some version of the question, "What does it mean?" But in order to get the most out of what we read, we ought to first stop and ask ourselves the odd question, "What do we *mean* by 'mean'?" It will help to make a few distinctions.

To begin with, we should recognize the fact that no statement *about* a poem or a story, no summary of it, can take the place of the work itself. For convenience we sometimes make such statements and summaries. To do so is fine as long as we know that they are not the same as the poem or story *as it is written.*

Surely, we want to interpret a work so that as many of its multiple meanings as possible are brought to light. These meanings will include much more than whatever "message" we may find—and we must not turn ourselves exclusively into "message seekers." The meanings of a work will also include the way the specific language works, the tone of a work, its shape, its movements. In short, the complete meaning of a work of literature is its *total effect.*

As we read we must ask not only *what does this say,* but also *how does this work,* and *what happens in it?* For the way the poem or story happens is part of its meaning. We may say, for example, that Whitman's "As Toilsome I Wander'd Virginia's Woods" can be paraphrased, or restated, as follows: "The poet remembers coming across the grave of an unknown soldier in the woods and an inscription nailed to a nearby tree. Long after that incident he still sees the grave and the inscription. The memory comes back to him suddenly." Compare this version of the poem with the poem itself. You will sense at once how much of the *meaning* is missing.

In the paraphrase, for one thing, the repeated refrain is missing—the important line that makes its effect by its very repetition. All the poem's rhythms disappear in a paraphrase, and you can hear at once how the phrasing of the words creates the poem's effect. In the refrain, for example, there are three short words—"Bold," "cautious," "true"—followed by a long phrase—"and my loving comrade"—which suggests the sudden rush of emotion that sprang into the poet's heart. If you are moved by the way that phrase is positioned twice within the poem, then you will see how hard it is to isolate meaning from the total effect of the work. The meaning is what happens in the poem *as it happens.*

THE AMERICAN VOICE

The Shadow of War

The writers in this unit lived through a turbulent time in American history. The Civil War brought many Americans face to face with suffering and death. It also shocked many people into an intense awareness of the value of human life itself. Whether they faced war's violence publicly as soldiers or privately as poets, the writers in this unit confronted the harsh facts of war with honesty and courage. They found strength and refuge in a larger vision of the compassionate individual.

Chesnut
I think, if I consider the long array of those bright youths and loyal men who have gone to their deaths almost before my very eyes, my heart might break, too.

Lee
I hope I may never be called upon to draw my sword.

Lincoln
It is rather for us to be here dedicated to the great task remaining before us—that from these honored dead we take increased devotion to that cause for which they gave the last full measure of devotion—that we here highly resolve that these dead shall not have died in vain.

Chief Joseph
Hear me, my chiefs. I am tired; my heart is sick and sad. From where the sun now stands I will fight no more forever.

Whitman
Beat! beat! drums!—blow! bugles! blow!
Through the windows—through doors—burst like a ruthless force,
Into the solemn church, and scatter the solemn congregation
Into the school where the scholar is studying.

Dickinson
Not one of all the purple Host
Who took the Flag today
Can tell the definition
So clear of Victory

As he defeated—dying—
On whose forbidden ear
The distant strains of triumph
Burst agonized and clear!

Americans endured the war with a combination of realism and idealism. The American voice spoke of victory and of defeat, of compassion deeply felt, and of hard lessons learned. The period to come would reflect in its realistic literature both that surviving compassion and the effects of those hard lessons.

Key to Illustrations on Pages 230–231.

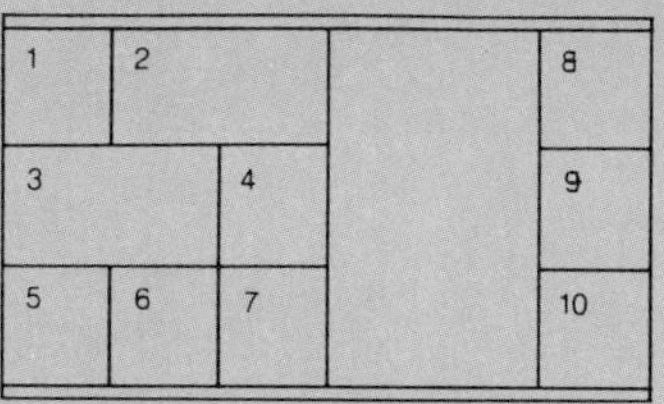

1. Photograph of Emily Dickinson, 1847.
2. *Coming and Going of the Pony Express,* Frederick Remington, 1906.
3. *Bombardment of Island Number Ten in the Mississippi River,* print by Currier and Ives, 1862.
4. *Portrait of the Artist's Mother,* James Abbott McNeill Whistler, 1871.
5. *Frederick Douglass,* Elisha Hammond, 1844.
6. An early typewriter, from a 1908 advertisement.
7. *Manhantango Valley Farm,* artist unknown, c. 1860.
8. Drawing of Mark Twain, from an early twentieth-century box label.
9. *Across the Continent—Westward the Course of Empire Takes Its Way,* print by Currier and Ives, 1868.
10. *Walt Whitman,* Thomas Eakins, 1887.

The Shadow of War
In conjunction with this page, discuss the conflicting image of war as a destroyer of innocence and a test of character. Elicit that the writers in this unit lost something of their innocence in facing war, but that at the same time they displayed compassion and courage.

Key to Illustrations appears on page 399.

REGIONALISM AND REALISM

1880–1910

In the decades around the turn of the century, America continued its energetic expansion and its growth in population, wealth, and military power. The Civil War had challenged the nation's self-confidence and had put an end to the optimism of the mid-nineteenth century. After the war a new, more varied, bewildering America emerged. In the Puritan age, in the revolutionary age, in the age of the western frontier, America seemed to have a single, clear direction. Now it seemed to be moving in many different directions at once.

The war had devastated the nation. Throughout the South people suffered from the continued effects of economic collapse. In the North industry flourished, having been spurred by the production demands of the war. The movement west continued as established American families and new immigrants searching for a better life spread out and populated new territories. The isolated frontier was becoming only a memory as railroads continued to crisscross the continent.

The great cities, too, expanded rapidly: The population of Philadelphia tripled between 1870 and 1910; that of New York quadrupled. Chicago's population multiplied an astounding twenty times as the new capital of the Midwest became, in the poet Carl Sandburg's words, "the Nation's Freight Handler."

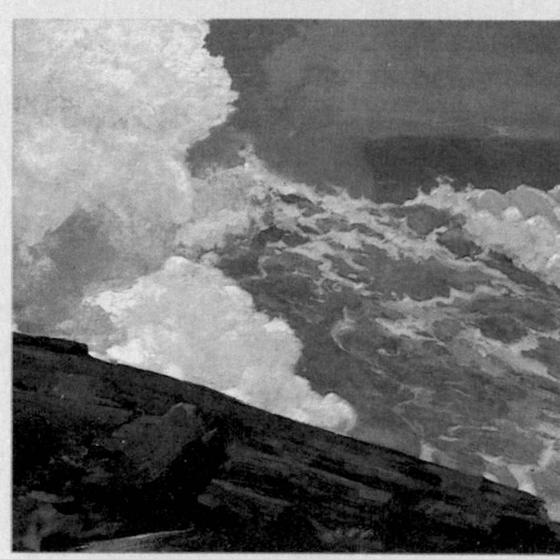

INTRODUCTION

After having students read the introduction, you might focus discussion in the following ways:

- Ask students how the events of this era might have caused people to lose the optimism and confidence that marked the earlier years of the nineteenth century. (Students might mention the continued effects of economic collapse in the South, urban poverty, natural disasters affecting farmers in the Midwest, political corruption, and corrupt business practices.)
- Ask students to distinguish Realism from another kind of writing, such as romance, fantasy, or science fiction.
- Modern life has done much to eliminate the distinctions between regions; nevertheless, ask students to name some things that are distinctive of your particular region of the country.

Key Ideas in This Period

- regionalism
- local landscapes
- aftermath of war
- realism
- social reform
- Naturalism

Affluence—its origins as well as its effects on Americans—was frequently a subject of the writing of this time.

Thomas Jefferson's dream of an agrarian America, with small towns and family farms, was vanishing. The United States was becoming a wealthy industrial nation.

By the 1890s there were over four thousand American millionaires, and some whose wealth greatly exceeded a mere million dollars—men like Andrew Carnegie, who made his fortune in iron and steel; J. P. Morgan, the great financier; and John D. Rockefeller, founder of the Standard Oil Company. The Gilded Age, as Mark Twain called it in a satirical novel, was a time of fabulous display of wealth, larger and larger corporations and industrial monopolies, and a widening gap between haves and have-nots among the American people.

Indeed, as wealth grew more conspicuous, poverty became more visible. In the Midwest a series of natural disasters forced farmers to move from state to state in order to eke from the soil the barest means of existence. In the West wheat growers battled the railroads, whose owners were condemned in works such as Frank Norris' *The Octopus* (1901). Drawing the most criticism were the burgeoning urban centers: Journalist Lincoln Steffens called poverty and slums "the shame of the cities," attacking too the urban phenomenon of political corruption and "bossism." Other "muckraking" journalists, such as Upton Sinclair and Ida Tarbell, criticized corrupt business practices and urged governmental reforms.

The literature of the decades just before and after 1900 responded to the new conditions of American life by turning from Romanticism and Transcendental optimism toward a franker portrayal of society and of human nature. The major literary movements of this period were Realism, Regionalism, and an offshoot of Realism called Naturalism.

Realism

The elements of Realism are so familiar to us today that we may have difficulty in seeing Realism as a specific movement in literature. What, then, did Realism mean to the writers for whom it was something new?

In part, Realism was a reaction against Romanticism. Realism turned from an emphasis on the strange toward a faithful rendering of the ordinary, a slice of life as it is really lived. The Realist writers avoided the improbabilities of such Romantic tales as Washington Irving's "Devil and Tom Walker" (page 105) and Edgar Allan Poe's "Fall of the House of Usher" (page 135). As the American novelist Frank Norris said: "Realism is the kind of fiction that confines itself to the type of normal life." Or as William Dean Howells, one of the earliest exponents of Realism, put it: "Let fiction cease to lie about life; let it portray men and women as they are."

Realism frequently provided an outlet for a writer's democratic sympathies. Middle- and lower-class people were often its subjects, and the Realist writers took their characters' lives as seriously as they took the lives of the rich and powerful. For example, Stephen Crane's novel *The Red Badge of Courage* focused on an ordinary soldier; earlier war stories dealt not with common soldiers but with kings, nobles, and generals.

Yet if things are *too* normal, *too* ordinary, there may be no imaginative lure to the writing. It is more accurate to say that Realist literature finds the drama and the tension beneath the ordinary surface of life. A Realist writer is more objective than subjective, more descriptive than symbolic. A Realist writer gets to the heart of human experience without ever swerving too far from verisimilitude, or lifelikeness. Realists looked for Truth in everyday truths.

Many Realist writers found the greatest sources for litera-

Poverty—its causes and its effects—was also a fundamental subject for American Realist writers.

ture in the daily life that immediately surrounded them. Some were called Regional writers: They set their literature in the region they knew best, the area where they lived.

Regionalism

In an age when transportation and communication were not what they are today, Regional literature was especially popular, for it satisfied Americans' demand to know how people lived in other parts of the country. Mark Twain and Bret Harte illustrated for the whole nation the rough excitement of the "Wild West." Kate Chopin's stories portrayed the colorful mixture of languages and cultures in Louisiana. Sarah Orne Jewett wrote quiet, well-observed sketches of rural New England life.

However, in reading Regional literature, Americans found more than a travel guide. The aim of most Regional fiction was to capture the special atmosphere, the "local color," of the area and people it portrayed. As the midwestern writer Hamlin Garland, in an essay called "Local Color in Art," explains:

". . . I am using local color to mean something more than a forced study of the picturesque scenery of a state. Local color in a novel means that it has such quality and background that it could not have been written in any other place, or by anyone [other] than a native."

Like Realist fiction, Regional literature generally deals with the lives of ordinary people. Accurate descriptions of the characters' activities and realistic use of dialect are important in capturing the local color of the region. Equally important are accurate descriptions of nature, of the physical appearance of the environment being portrayed. Good Regionalist writing used all the elements of the local scene to extend insights and observations to the universal.

Naturalism

Environment also plays an important role in Naturalism, an outgrowth of Realism that responded to theories in science, psychology, human behavior, and social thought current in the late nineteenth century.

In Naturalist fiction people are often caught within forces of nature or society that are beyond their understanding or control. For instance, the hero of Jack London's "To Build a Fire" is crushed by the overwhelming force of the Arctic cold. Tim Haskins, a farmer in Hamlin Garland's "Under the Lion's Paw," suffers beneath an economic force that he is not equipped to fight. In Stephen Crane's story "The Open Boat," the four shipwrecked men experience the relentlessness of the sea; they face "the unconcern of the universe." In Theodore Dreiser's novels the characters' actions are determined by uncontrollable social and physical factors.

Naturalist writing uses a facts-only approach, a style made of detailed observation of the "truth" of human experiences. Romantic illusions, sentiments, and idealistic solutions to problems are all absent from Naturalistic writing. Poets as well as novelists participated in this movement: Edwin Arlington Robinson, for example, showed his characters in the harsh light of day, unromanticized, often unhappy and unfulfilled.

Although Naturalist literature described the world with sometimes brutal realism, it sometimes also aimed at bettering the world through social reform. For example, Frank Norris and Hamlin Garland, in portraying the plight of the western and midwestern farmer, hoped to bring a desperate situation to the eyes of the American public and so to improve it. This combination of grim reality and desire for improvement is typical of America as it moved into the twentieth century.

TIME LINE

1880–1910 AMERICAN EVENTS

1880 Andrew Carnegie begins establishing libraries

Sidney Lanier, *Science of English Verse*

1881 Henry James, *Portrait of a Lady* and *Washington Square*

Booker T. Washington founds Tuskegee Institute (Alabama)

Clara Barton founds American Red Cross

1883 Sidney Lanier, "Song of the Chattahoochee"

Thomas Edison discovers that electric current can be sent through space

"Buffalo Bill" Cody opens his first Wild West show

1884 Mark Twain, *The Adventures of Huckleberry Finn*

1885 William Dean Howells, *The Rise of Silas Lapham*

1886 Sarah Orne Jewett, "A White Heron"

Statue of Liberty dedicated

1889 Reporter Nellie Bly begins record trip around the world (72 days, 6 hours, 11 minutes)

1890 William James, *Principles of Psychology*

Ladybugs imported from Australia to save California citrus crop

1891 Hamlin Garland, *Main-Travelled Roads*

James A. Naismith invents game of basketball

WORLD EVENTS 1880–1910

1880 Russia: Peter Ilyich Tchaikovsky, "1812 Overture"

1881 Cuba: Doctor Carlos Finlay discovers that mosquitoes transmit yellow fever

1883 England: Robert Louis Stevenson, *Treasure Island*

Paris–Istanbul: Orient Express train makes first run

1886 France: Georges Seurat exhibits pointillist painting, *La Grande Jatte*

1887 Italy: Giuseppe Verdi, *Otello*

England: Arthur Conan Doyle, *A Study in Scarlet,* first Sherlock Holmes novel

1889 Japan: Physician Shibasabura Kitasato isolates the bacillus that causes tetanus

1890 Norway: Henrik Ibsen, *Hedda Gabler*

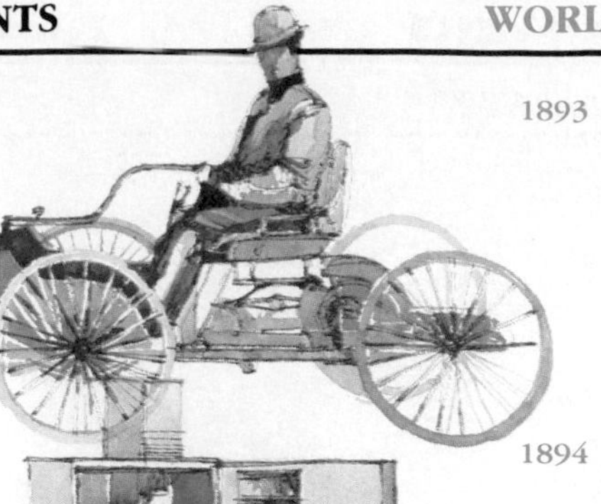

AMERICAN EVENTS

1893 World's Columbian Exposition opens in Chicago

Katherine Lee Bates writes "America the Beautiful"

Colorado first state to grant women right to vote

Henry Ford builds his first automobile

1894 Kate Chopin, *Bayou Folk*

1895 Stephen Crane, *The Red Badge of Courage*

1896 Sarah Orne Jewett, *The Country of the Pointed Firs*

Paul Laurence Dunbar, *Lyrics of a Lowly Life*

1897 Edwin Arlington Robinson, "Richard Cory"

Klondike Gold Rush begins

1898 Henry James, *The Turn of the Screw*

Spanish-American War

1899 Frank Norris, *McTeague*

Scott Joplin, "Maple Leaf Rag"

1900 L. Frank Baum, *The Wonderful Wizard of Oz*

Theodore Dreiser, *Sister Carrie*

1901 Frank Norris, *The Octopus*

1902 Muckraking movement begins

WORLD EVENTS

1893 Ireland: W. B. Yeats, *The Celtic Twilight*

1894 Germany: Rudolf Diesel invents diesel engine

England: Rudyard Kipling, *The Jungle Book*

1895 France: Lumière brothers project moving pictures on screen for first time

Italy: Guglielmo Marconi invents wireless telegraph

England: Oscar Wilde, *The Importance of Being Earnest*

1897 England: H. G. Wells, *The Invisible Man*

England: Irish-born playwright George Bernard Shaw, *Candida*

Ireland: Bram Stoker, *Dracula*

1898 France: Polish-born physicist Marie Curie discovers radium

1900 Austria: Sigmund Freud, *The Interpretation of Dreams*

China: Boxer Rebellion against foreign influence

1901 Russia: Anton Chekhov, *The Three Sisters*

American Events

1903 Orville and Wilbur Wright make first successful flight in motorized airplane

First World Series played

Henry James, *The Ambassadors*

Jack London, *The Call of the Wild*

1906 Charles Ives composes "The Unanswered Question"

First musical radio program broadcast in U.S.

1907 Mother's Day first celebrated

Commercial plastic produced

1908 Jack London, "To Build a Fire"

1909 First animated cartoon, *Gertie the Dinosaur,* produced

Explorers Robert Peary and Matthew Henson are first to reach North Pole

Frank Lloyd Wright designs Robie House in Chicago

1910 Edwin Arlington Robinson, "Miniver Cheevy"

Halley's Comet does not destroy the earth as many people had expected

U.S. population: 92 million

World Events

1903 Beginning of Russo-Japanese War

1905 Germany: Physicist Albert Einstein proposes special theory of relativity and equation $E=mc^2$

1906 John Galsworthy begins *The Forsyte Saga*

1907 France: Pablo Picasso paints *Les Demoiselles d'Avignon,* beginning of Cubism

1908 France: Marcel Proust begins *Remembrance of Things Past*

1910 China: Slavery abolished

Russia: Composer Igor Stravinsky completes ballet *The Firebird*

Bret Harte *1836–1902*

Bret Harte was born an Easterner, yet in a handful of stories, he captured much of the humor and romance that make up our myth of the American West. Although his finest stories were written during the 1860s, Harte stands as the first writer of the local color movement that continued until approximately the turn of the century.

Harte was born in Albany, New York, but he ventured west in 1854, when he was only eighteen. In California he tried prospecting, rode "shotgun" on a stagecoach, and then found work in journalism, first as a typesetter, then as an editor, and finally as a writer.

In the 1850s California was a booming, turbulent, and colorful frontier. The discovery of gold in 1848 had drawn prospectors and adventurers from all over the United States and the rest of the world. Mining towns had sprung up; small towns had turned into cities; fortunes had been made and lost; and people from all walks of life had been thrown together in rough, sometimes violent circumstances. History was being made, and a whole new way of life was being forged. The colorful incidents of western life and vivid anecdotes of "old-timers" fired the imagination of Bret Harte, who began to turn this material into fiction.

While serving as editor of the *Overland Monthly,* a literary magazine, Harte wrote a story that made him famous across the land, "The Luck of Roaring Camp" (1868). Soon after came "The Outcasts of Poker Flat." These stories were spectacularly successful both here and in England, among readers eager for descriptions of California and the Wild West. As a result, the prestigious Boston literary magazine the *Atlantic Monthly* offered Harte a special contract for any twelve selections he would like to contribute. The return east was a disappointment, however: Harte's later stories did not match the early ones in quality and were less successful with readers. Harte spent most of his remaining years abroad, in Germany, Scotland, and England, continuing to write and working as a diplomat.

Yet in those early stories, particularly in "The Outcasts of Poker Flat," Harte painted a romantic portrait of the West that has endured. Characters like John Oakhurst, the gambler with nerves of steel, have become fixtures in America's collective imagination.

■ What do you think of when you picture the Old West? As you read, are your ideas reinforced?

AT A GLANCE

- The story begins in Poker Flat, a frontier town near the Sierra Nevadas, in November, 1850.
- John Oakhurst, a gambler, senses an ominous change in the town.
- A vigilance committee determines to administer its own form of justice to persons deemed "improper."

LITERARY OPTIONS

- characterization
- style
- theme

THEMATIC OPTIONS

- the nature of heroism
- fate and chance
- sacrifice and redemption

1 FORESHADOWING

This threatening talk against Oakhurst at the opening of the story prepares the reader to encounter a different kind of threat later on.

2 STYLE

The narrator outlines the threat to Oakhurst by using the western style of understated, offhanded speech to describe the demise of two other "undesirables."

Main street in a western town, c. 1870.

Bret Harte

The Outcasts of Poker Flat

As Mr. John Oakhurst, gambler, stepped into the main street of Poker Flat on the morn-
1 ing of the twenty-third of November, 1850, he was conscious of a change in its moral atmosphere from the preceding night. Two or three men, conversing earnestly together, ceased as he approached, and exchanged significant glances. There was a Sabbath lull in the air, which, in a settlement unused to Sabbath influences, looked ominous.

Mr. Oakhurst's calm, handsome face betrayed small concern of these indications. Whether he was conscious of any predisposing cause, was another question. "I reckon they're after somebody," he reflected; "likely it's me." He returned to his pocket the handkerchief with which he had been whipping away the red dust of Poker Flat from his neat boots, and quietly discharged his mind of any further conjecture.

In point of fact, Poker Flat was "after somebody." It had lately suffered the loss of several thousand dollars, two valuable horses, and a prominent citizen. It was experiencing a spasm of virtuous reaction, quite as lawless and ungovernable as any of the acts that had pro-
2 voked it. A secret committee[1] had determined to rid the town of all improper persons. This was done permanently in regard of two men who were then hanging from the boughs of a sycamore in the gulch, and temporarily in the banishment of certain other objectionable char-

1. **secret committee:** vigilance committee, a group of citizens that bands together to punish criminals when usual law enforcement agencies are lacking.

GUIDED READING

LITERAL QUESTION

1a. What is Oakhurst doing as he reflects on the change of mood in Poker Flat? (cleaning his boots with his handkerchief)

INFERENTIAL QUESTION

1b. What does this action say about Oakhurst's attitude toward the change in Poker Flat? (He is coolly unconcerned—almost disdainful.)

acters. I regret to say that some of these were ladies. It is but due to the sex, however, to state that their impropriety was professional, and it was only in such easily established standards of evil that Poker Flat ventured to sit in judgment.

Mr. Oakhurst was right in supposing that he was included in this category. A few of the committee had urged hanging him as a possible example, and a sure method of reimbursing themselves from his pockets of the sums he
1 had won from them. "It's agin[2] justice," said Jim Wheeler, "to let this yer young man from Roaring Camp—an entire stranger—carry away our money." But a crude sentiment of equity residing in the breasts of those who had been fortunate enough to win from Mr. Oakhurst, overruled this narrower local prejudice.

2 Mr. Oakhurst received his sentence with philosophic calmness, none the less coolly that he was aware of the hesitation of his judges. He was too much of a gambler not to accept Fate. With him life was at best an uncertain game, and he recognized the usual percentage in favor of the dealer.

A body of armed men accompanied the deported wickedness of Poker Flat to the outskirts of the settlement. Besides Mr. Oakhurst, who was known to be a coolly desperate man, and for whose intimidation the armed escort was intended, the expatriated party consisted of a young woman familiarly known as "The Duchess"; another, who had gained the infelicitous title of "Mother Shipton";[3] and "Uncle Billy," a suspected sluice-robber[4] and confirmed drunkard. The cavalcade provoked no comments from the spectators, nor was any
3 word uttered by the escort. Only when the gulch which marked the uttermost limit of Poker Flat was reached, the leader spoke briefly and to the point. The exiles were forbidden to return at the peril of their lives.

2. **agin** [ə gin′]: dialect variation of *against*.
3. **"Mother Shipton":** English woman accused of witchcraft (1488–1560).
4. **sluice** [slo͞os]**-robber:** one who steals from sluices. A sluice is a long sloping trough used for washing gold ore.

As the escort disappeared, their pent-up feelings found vent in a few hysterical tears from the Duchess, some bad language from Mother Shipton, and a Parthian[5] volley of ex-
4 pletives from Uncle Billy. The philosophic Oakhurst alone remained silent. He listened calmly to Mother Shipton's desire to cut somebody's heart out, to the repeated statements of the Duchess that she would die in the road, and to the alarming oaths that seemed to be bumped out of Uncle Billy as he rode forward. With the easy good humor characteristic of his class, he insisted upon exchanging his own riding horse, "Five Spot," for the sorry mule which the Duchess rode. But even this act did not draw the party into any closer sympathy. The young woman readjusted her somewhat draggled plumes with a feeble, faded coquetry; Mother Shipton eyed the possessor of "Five Spot" with malevolence, and Uncle Billy included the whole party in one sweeping anathema.

5 The road to Sandy Bar—a camp that not having as yet experienced the regenerating influences of Poker Flat, consequently seemed to offer some invitation to the emigrants—lay over a steep mountain range. It was distant a day's severe journey. In that advanced season, the party soon passed out of the moist, temperate regions of the foothills, into the dry, cold, bracing air of the Sierras.[6] The trail was narrow and difficult. At noon the Duchess, rolling out of her saddle upon the ground, declared her intention of going no further, and the party halted.

The spot was singularly wild and impressive. A wooded amphitheater, surrounded on three sides by precipitous cliffs of naked granite, sloped gently toward the crest of another precipice that overlooked the valley. It was undoubtedly the most suitable spot for a camp, had camping been advisable. But Mr. Oakhurst knew that scarcely half the journey to Sandy

5. **Parthian** [pär′thē ən]: referring to an ancient people of southwest Asia, whose cavalry was noted for shooting at an enemy while retreating or pretending to retreat.
6. **Sierras** [sē er′əz]: Sierra Nevada mountain range in eastern California.

AT A GLANCE

- The vigilantes decide to exile, rather than kill, Oakhurst and three others, known as the Duchess, Uncle Billy and Mother Shipton.
- The group heads toward Sandy Bar, about a day's ride from Poker Flat.
- Unused to rough conditions, the exhausted Duchess soon makes the group stop near a canyon.

1 REGIONALISM

Dialect brings to life the supposedly righteous citizens who oppose Oakhurst.

2 THEME

Oakhurst sees fate (the "dealer" in the "game" of life) in terms of his gambling experience.

3 PLOT: NARRATIVE HOOK

The undesirables are thrown together and thrown out of town. At this point the main action of the story begins.

4 POINT OF VIEW

During this part of the story, the narrator enters only the mind of Oakhurst. The reactions of the exiles to their fate are shown through what Oakhurst sees and hears.

5 STYLE: IMAGERY

The geographical setting is described in careful, accurate detail. The details appeal primarily to the sense of touch and hint at the form that the trouble to come will take.

GUIDED READING

LITERAL QUESTIONS

1a. How are the citizens who discuss Oakhurst divided? (Those who lost money to him want him hanged; those who won money from him support him.)

2a. How does each of the outcasts react to his or her fate? (Oakhurst is silent; the Duchess weeps; Mother Shipton threatens; Uncle Billy curses.)

INFERENTIAL QUESTIONS

1b. What does the discussion suggest about the narrator's opinion of frontier justice? (It reinforces the earlier statement that the justice itself is lawless.)

2b. What general conclusion can you draw about the exiles, based on their reactions? (Except for Oakhurst, they all seem to be weak, villainous grumblers.)

AT A GLANCE

- Oakhurst watches the other outcasts drink themselves to sleep.
- He encounters a guileless young man, Tom Simson, and Piney Woods, a girl with whom Tom has run away.
- Against Oakhurst's advice, the Innocent decides to camp and to share his supplies with the group.

1 CHARACTERIZATION

Except for Oakhurst, the outcasts do not have the common sense to postpone their pleasure and do not appear to have the fortitude to be survivors.

2 CHARACTERIZATION

Watching the other outcasts makes Oakhurst consider the limitations of the life he has chosen for himself. Such thoughts are not characteristic of Oakhurst; rather, they come to him "for the first time."

3 FLASHBACK

An earlier generosity extended by Oakhurst to the Innocent both explains Tom's admiration for Oakhurst and shows Oakhurst's basic decency.

4 BACKGROUND

The temperance movement, strong in nineteenth-century America, established inns and hotels to appeal to "decent" citizens. Piney's employment at such a place emphasizes the contrast between the outcasts and the new arrivals.

Bar was accomplished, and the party were not equipped or provisioned for delay. This fact
1 he pointed out to his companions curtly, with a philosophic commentary on the folly of "throwing up their hand before the game was played out." But they were furnished with liquor, which in this emergency stood them in place of food, fuel, rest and prescience. In spite of his remonstrances, it was not long before they were more or less under its influence. Uncle Billy passed rapidly from a bellicose state into one of stupor, the Duchess became maudlin, and Mother Shipton snored. Mr. Oakhurst alone remained erect, leaning against a rock, calmly surveying them.

Mr. Oakhurst did not drink. It interfered with a profession which required coolness, impassiveness and presence of mind, and, in his
2 own language, he "couldn't afford it." As he gazed at his recumbent fellow exiles, the loneliness begotten of his pariah trade,[7] his habits of life, his very vices, for the first time seriously oppressed him. He bestirred himself in dusting his black clothes, washing his hands and face, and other acts characteristic of his studiously neat habits, and for a moment forgot his annoyance. The thought of deserting his weaker and more pitiable companions never perhaps occurred to him. Yet he could not help feeling the want of that excitement, which singularly enough was most conducive to that calm equanimity for which he was notorious. He looked at the gloomy walls that rose a thousand feet sheer above the circling pines around him; at the sky, ominously clouded; at the valley below, already deepening into shadow. And doing so, suddenly he heard his own name called.

A horseman slowly ascended the trail. In the fresh, open face of the newcomer, Mr. Oakhurst recognized Tom Simson, otherwise known as "The Innocent" of Sandy Bar. He had met him some months before over a "little game," and had, with perfect equanimity, won the entire fortune—amounting to some forty dollars—of that guileless youth. After the game
3 was finished, Mr. Oakhurst drew the youthful speculator behind the door and thus addressed him: "Tommy, you're a good little man, but you can't gamble worth a cent. Don't try it over again." He then handed him his money back, pushed him gently from the room, and so made a devoted slave of Tom Simson.

There was a remembrance of this in his boyish and enthusiastic greeting of Mr. Oakhurst. He had started, he said, to go to Poker Flat to seek his fortune. "Alone?" No, not ex-
4 actly alone; in fact—a giggle—he had run away with Piney Woods. Didn't Mr. Oakhurst remember Piney? She that used to wait on the table at the Temperance House? They had been engaged a long time, but old Jake Woods had objected, and so they had run away, and were going to Poker Flat to be married, and here they were. And they were tired out, and how lucky it was they had found a place to camp and company. All this the Innocent delivered rapidly, while Piney—a stout, comely damsel of fifteen—emerged from behind the pine tree, where she had been blushing unseen, and rode to the side of her lover.

Mr. Oakhurst seldom troubled himself with sentiment. Still less with propriety. But he had a vague idea that the situation was not felicitous. He retained, however, his presence of mind sufficiently to kick Uncle Billy, who was about to say something, and Uncle Billy was sober enough to recognize in Mr. Oakhurst's kick a superior power that would not bear trifling. He then endeavored to dissuade Tom Simson from delaying further, but in vain. He even pointed out the fact that there was no provision nor means of making a camp. But, unluckily, the Innocent met this objection by assuring the party that he was provided with an extra mule loaded with provisions, and by the discovery of a rude attempt at a log house near the trail. "Piney can stay with Mrs. Oakhurst," said the Innocent, pointing to the Duchess, "and I can shift for myself."

Nothing but Mr. Oakhurst's admonishing

7. **pariah** [pə rī′ə]**trade:** despicable occupation. A pariah is one who is despised; an outcast.

GUIDED READING

LITERAL QUESTIONS

1a. What fact does Oakhurst mention to encourage the group to continue to Sandy Bar instead of making camp? (They have no supplies.)

2a. How does the Innocent respond to Oakhurst's objection that he and Piney not stay? (He says that he has an extra mule with supplies.)

INFERENTIAL QUESTIONS

1b. Why do the other outcasts not listen to Oakhurst? (They are weaker than he and quickly succumb to the temptation to drink away their troubles.)

2b. Why is Tom said to respond "unluckily"? (Oakhurst probably suspects that the others may take unfair advantage of Tom and Piney's generosity.)

foot saved Uncle Billy from bursting into a roar of laughter. As it was, he felt compelled to retire up the cañon[8] until he could recover his gravity. There he confided the joke to the tall pine trees, with many slaps of his leg, contortions of his face, and the usual profanity. But
1 when he returned to the party, he found them seated by a fire—for the air had grown strangely chill and the sky overcast—in apparently amicable conversation. Piney was actually talking in an impulsive, girlish fashion to the Duchess, who was listening with an interest and animation she had not shown for many days. The Innocent was holding forth, apparently with equal effect, to Mr. Oakhurst and Mother Shipton, who was actually relaxing into amiability. "Is this yer a d——d picnic?" said
2 Uncle Billy, with inward scorn, as he surveyed the sylvan[9] group, the glancing firelight and the tethered animals in the foreground. Suddenly an idea mingled with the alcoholic fumes that disturbed his brain. It was apparently of a jocular nature, for he felt impelled to slap his leg again and cram his fist into his mouth.

As the shadows crept slowly up the mountain, a slight breeze rocked the tops of the pine trees, and moaned through their long and gloomy aisles. The ruined cabin, patched and covered with pine boughs, was set apart for the ladies. As the lovers parted, they unaffectedly exchanged a parting kiss, so honest and sincere that it might have been heard above the swaying pines. The frail Duchess and the malevolent Mother Shipton were probably too stunned to remark upon this last evidence of simplicity, and so turned without a word to the hut. The fire was replenished, the men lay down before the door, and in a few minutes were asleep.

Mr. Oakhurst was a light sleeper. Toward morning he awoke benumbed and cold. As he stirred the dying fire, the wind, which was now blowing strongly, brought to his cheek that which caused the blood to leave it—snow!

He started to his feet with the intention of awakening the sleepers, for there was no time to lose. But turning to where Uncle Billy had been lying he found him gone. A suspicion leaped to his brain and a curse to his lips. He ran to the spot where the mules had been tethered; they were no longer there. The tracks were already rapidly disappearing in the snow.

3 The momentary excitement brought Mr. Oakhurst back to the fire with his usual calm. He did not waken the sleepers. The Innocent slumbered peacefully, with a smile on his good-humored, freckled face; the virgin Piney slept beside her frailer sisters as sweetly as though attended by celestial guardians, and Mr. Oakhurst, drawing his blanket over his shoulders, stroked his mustachios and waited for the dawn. It came slowly in a whirling mist of snowflakes that dazzled and confused the eye. What could be seen of the landscape appeared magically changed. He looked over the valley, and summed up the present and future in two words—"Snowed in!"

A careful inventory of the provisions, which, fortunately for the party, had been stored within the hut, and so escaped the felonious fingers of Uncle Billy, disclosed the fact that with care and prudence they might last ten days longer. "That is," said Mr. Oakhurst, *sotto voce*[10] to The Innocent, "if you're willing to board us. If you aint—and perhaps you'd better not—you can wait till Uncle Billy gets back with provisions." For some occult reason, Mr. Oakhurst could not bring himself to disclose Uncle Billy's rascality, and so offered the hypothesis that he had wandered from the camp and had accidentally stampeded the animals. He dropped a warning to the Duchess and Mother Shipton, who of course knew the facts of their associate's defection. "They'll find out the truth about us *all,* when they find out anything," he added, significantly, "and there's no good frightening them now."

Tom Simson not only put all his worldly

8. **cañon** [kan′yən]: variant of *canyon.*
9. **sylvan** [sil′vən]: characteristic of the woods.

10. ***sotto voce*** [sot′ō vō′chē]: Italian for "under the voice"; in an undertone.

AT A GLANCE

- Except for Uncle Billy, the outcasts seem to welcome Tom and Piney.
- The outcasts and the new arrivals go to sleep.
- The next morning, Oakhurst is awakened by snow. He discovers that Uncle Billy—and the mules—are gone.
- The five who remain are snowed in, with ten days' provisions.

1 PLOT: RISING ACTION

A storm may be brewing. The threat is suggested again at the beginning of the next paragraph. Although the characters are unaffected by the threat at this point, it prepares the way for their rising tension later.

2 PLOT: SUSPENSE

Uncle Billy's amusement at the possibilities bodes ill for his companions and increases the reader's tension.

3 CHARACTERIZATION

Despite the desperateness of the situation, Oakhurst remains calm as he awaits the dawn. He neither wakes the others in panic nor chases recklessly after Uncle Billy.

GUIDED READING

LITERAL QUESTIONS

1a. What does Uncle Billy do during the night? (He steals the mules.)

2a. What warning does Oakhurst give the Duchess and Mother Shipton? (not to tell Tom and Piney the truth about Uncle Billy's defection—or their own unsavory past)

INFERENTIAL QUESTIONS

1b. What new detail about Uncle Billy's character does this action indicate? (He is a coward, for he sneaks off at night and leaves his companions to fend for themselves.)

2b. Why does Oakhurst want to keep information from Tom and Piney? (Their innocence may appeal to him, especially when he thinks of his own lost innocence. Protecting these two may make him feel that he is somehow redeeming himself.)

AT A GLANCE

- The group decides to fix up the hut and make the best of being snowed in.
- In the evening, the group sings songs, including a hymn.
- Oakhurst takes watch duty and talks to Tom about luck.

1 CHARACTERIZATION

The Duchess and Mother Shipton's embarrassment suggests that Piney's innocence and good will have made them ashamed of the lives they have led.

2 THEME

The enthusiasm with which the outcasts sing the hymn indicates that they are being changed—even redeemed—by their ordeal. Harte describes the natural surroundings to augment the spiritual feeling at that moment.

3 THEME

Oakhurst continues to view fate in gambling terms, but his view has changed. Here he tells Tom that a bad fate awaits those who depend entirely on luck, whereas a good fate awaits those who "live in the service of the Lord."

4 IRONY

The "kindly warmth" of the morning sun stands in bitter contrast to the group's increasing state of deprivation.

store at the disposal of Mr. Oakhurst, but seemed to enjoy the prospect of their enforced seclusion. "We'll have a good camp for a week, and then the snow'll melt, and we'll all go back together." The cheerful gaiety of the young man and Mr. Oakhurst's calm infected the others. The Innocent, with the aid of pine boughs, extemporized a thatch for the roofless cabin, and the Duchess directed Piney in the rearrangement of the interior with a taste and tact that opened the blue eyes of that provincial
1 maiden to their fullest extent. "I reckon now you're used to fine things at Poker Flat," said Piney. The Duchess turned away sharply to conceal something that reddened her cheeks through its professional tint, and Mother Shipton requested Piney not to "chatter." But when Mr. Oakhurst returned from a weary search for the trail, he heard the sound of happy laughter echoed from the rocks. He stopped in some alarm, and his thoughts first naturally reverted to the whiskey—which he had prudently *cachéd.*[11] "And yet it don't somehow sound like whiskey," said the gambler. It was not until he caught sight of the blazing fire through the still blinding storm, and the group around it, that he settled to the conviction that it was "square fun."

Whether Mr. Oakhurst had *cachéd* his cards with the whiskey as something debarred the free access of the community, I cannot say. It was certain that, in Mother Shipton's words, he "didn't say cards once" during that evening. Haply the time was beguiled by an accordion, produced somewhat ostentatiously by Tom Simson, from his pack. Notwithstanding some difficulties attending the manipulation of this instrument, Piney Woods managed to pluck several reluctant melodies from its keys, to an accompaniment by the Innocent on a pair of bone castanets. But the crowning festivity of the evening was reached in a rude camp meeting hymn, which the lovers, joining hands, sang with great earnestness and vociferation. I fear that a certain defiant tone and Covenanter's swing[12] to its chorus, rather than any devotional quality, caused it to speedily infect the others, who at last joined in the refrain:

2 I'm proud to live in the service of the Lord,
And I'm bound to die in His army.[13]

The pines rocked, the storm eddied and whirled above the miserable group, and the flames of their altar leaped heavenward, as if in token of the vow.

At midnight the storm abated, the rolling clouds parted, and the stars glittered keenly above the sleeping camp. Mr. Oakhurst, whose professional habits had enabled him to live on the smallest possible amount of sleep, in dividing the watch with Tom Simson, somehow managed to take upon himself the greater part of that duty. He excused himself to the Innocent, by saying that he had "often been a week without sleep." "Doing what?" asked Tom. "Poker!" replied Oakhurst, sententiously;
3 "when a man gets a streak of luck, he don't get tired. The luck gives in first. Luck," continued the gambler, reflectively, "is a mighty queer thing. All you know about it for certain is that it's bound to change. And it's finding out when it's going to change that makes you. We've had a streak of bad luck since we left Poker Flat—you come along and slap you get into it, too. If you can hold your cards right along you're all right. For," added the gambler, with cheerful irrelevance,

I'm proud to live in the service of the Lord,
And I'm bound to die in His army.

The third day came, and the sun, looking through the white-curtained valley, saw the outcasts divide their slowly decreasing store of
4 provisions for the morning meal. It was one of the peculiarities of that mountain climate that its rays diffused a kindly warmth over the wintry landscape, as if in regretful commiseration

11. ***cachéd*** [ka shād′]: modified French for "hidden."

12. **Covenanter's** [kuv′ə nan′tərz] **swing:** implying a lively rhythm. Covenanters were Scottish Presbyterians who demanded separation from the Church of England.

13. **"I'm . . . army":** The lines are from "Service of the Lord," an early American spiritual.

GUIDED READING

LITERAL QUESTION

1a. Who takes the longer part of the watch duty? (Oakhurst)

INFERENTIAL QUESTION

1b. Why does Oakhurst want the watch to be divided this way? (He seems to be continuing in his desire to look out for the Innocent.)

of the past. But it revealed drift on drift of snow, piled high around the hut; a hopeless, uncharted, trackless sea of white lying below the rocky shores to which the castaways still clung. Through the marvelously clear air, the smoke of the pastoral village of Poker Flat rose miles away. Mother Shipton saw it, and from a remote pinnacle of her rocky fastness, hurled in that direction a final malediction. It was her last vituperative attempt, and perhaps for that reason was invested with a certain degree of sublimity. It did her good, she privately informed the Duchess. "Just you go out there
1 and cuss, and see." She then set herself to the task of amusing "the child," as she and the Duchess were pleased to call Piney. Piney was no chicken, but it was a soothing and ingenious theory of the pair to thus account for the fact that she didn't swear and wasn't improper.

2 When night crept up again through the gorges, the reedy notes of the accordion rose and fell in fitful spasms and long-drawn gasps by the flickering campfire. But music failed to fill entirely the aching void left by insufficient food, and a new diversion was proposed by Piney —storytelling. Neither Mr. Oakhurst nor his female companions caring to relate their personal experiences, this plan would have failed, too, but for the Innocent. Some months before he had chanced upon a stray copy of Mr. Pope's[14] ingenious translation of the *Iliad.*[15] He now proposed to narrate the principal incidents of that poem—having thoroughly mastered the argument and fairly forgotten the words—in the current vernacular of Sandy Bar.
3 And so for the rest of that night the Homeric demigods again walked the earth. Trojan bully and wily Greek wrestled in the winds, and the great pines in the cañon seemed to bow to the wrath of the son of Peleus.[16] Mr. Oakhurst listened with quiet satisfaction. Most especially was he interested in the fate of "Ash-heels,"[17] as the Innocent persisted in denominating the "swift-footed Achilles."

So with small food and much of Homer and the accordion, a week passed over the heads of the outcasts. The sun again forsook them, and again from leaden skies the snowflakes were sifted over the land. Day by day closer around them drew the snowy circle, until at last they looked from their prison over drifted walls of dazzling white, that towered twenty feet above their heads. It became more and more difficult to replenish their fires, even from the fallen trees beside them, now half-hidden in the drifts. And yet no one complained. The lovers turned from the dreary prospect and looked into each other's eyes, and were happy. Mr. Oakhurst settled himself coolly to the losing game before him. The Duchess, more cheerful than she had been, assumed the care of Piney. Only Mother Shipton—once the strongest of the party—seemed to sicken and fade. At midnight on the tenth day she called Oakhurst to her side. "I'm going," she said, in a voice of querulous weakness, "but don't say anything about it. Don't waken the kids. Take the bundle from under my head and open it." Mr. Oak-
4 hurst did so. It contained Mother Shipton's rations for the last week, untouched. "Give 'em to the child," she said, pointing to the sleeping Piney. "You've starved yourself," said the gambler. "That's what they call it," said the woman querulously, as she lay down again, and turning her face to the wall, passed quietly away.

The accordion and the bones were put aside that day, and Homer was forgotten. When the body of Mother Shipton had been commit-
5 ted to the snow, Mr. Oakhurst took the Innocent aside, and showed him a pair of snowshoes, which he had fashioned from the old pack saddle. "There's one chance in a hundred to save her yet," he said, pointing to Piney; "but it's there," he added, pointing toward

14. **Mr. Pope's:** referring to Alexander Pope (1688–1744), an English poet.
15. ***Iliad*** [il'ē əd]: Greek epic poem by Homer, describing the war between the Trojans, natives of ancient Troy, and the Greeks.
16. **son of Peleus** [pēl'yo͞os]: Achilles [ə kil'ēz], Greek warrior hero in the Trojan War.

17. **"Ash-heels":** mispronunciation of *Achilles,* emphasizing his one vulnerable spot, his heel.

AT A GLANCE

- Mother Shipton and the Duchess begin to mother Piney.
- Tom entertains the others by retelling the *Iliad.*
- Mother Shipton weakens quickly and dies because she has been saving her own rations for Piney.
- Oakhurst gives Tom the snowshoes he has made and tells him to go for help.

1 CHARACTERIZATION

The "mothering" of Piney shows that both the Duchess and Mother Shipton have broken through the selfishness that characterized them when they left Poker Flat.

2 STYLE: PERSONIFICATION

The "fitful spasms" and "long-drawn gasps" of the accordion suggest the bodily suffering of the starving party.

3 ALLUSION

The references to Homer's battles and heroes suggest that the outcasts themselves are engaged in a heroic struggle of their own.

4 THEME

Mother Shipton's unexpected sacrifice makes her death touchingly meaningful; the manner of her death atones for the life she has led.

5 THEME

Oakhurst's offer of the snowshoes means that he has now sacrificed any attempt to save himself.

GUIDED READING

LITERAL QUESTIONS

1a. What has Mother Shipton done with her rations? (She has hidden them away for Piney instead of eating them herself.)

2a. What has Oakhurst made from the abandoned pack saddle? (a pair of snowshoes)

INFERENTIAL QUESTIONS

1b. Why has she done this? (She has developed a real affection for Piney. Evidently she feels that Piney's life is more worth saving than her own.)

2b. What does the fact that Oakhurst had worked in secret show about his change in character? (He probably had intended to use the snowshoes himself. Now, however, he seems to realize that there may be value in sacrificing oneself so that someone better might survive.)

AT A GLANCE

- Oakhurst and Tom leave the camp.
- Piney and the Duchess huddle together as the storm rages.
- Rescuers find Piney and the Duchess dead, still embracing.
- The body of Oakhurst, who has shot himself, is found beneath the tree that bears his epitaph.

1 CHARACTERIZATION

The same Duchess who had wept openly along the trail as she was being put out of town now hides her tears from Piney as she faces death.

2 STYLE: FIGURATIVE LANGUAGE

Death comes to Piney and the Duchess with the gentleness of the feathery snow that is settling around them.

3 THEME

Through her compassion, bravery, and sacrifice, the Duchess, too, has been redeemed and transformed—in death, she seems as pure as Piney herself.

4 PLOT: RESOLUTION

The rescuers discover that Oakhurst has handled his suicide as he had handled events in his past—coolly and calmly.

REFLECTING ON THE STORY

In what sense was Oakhurst both the strongest and the weakest of the outcasts? (The key may be his compassion, which gave him the strength to forfeit his only chance to survive but which made him find the prospect of his own slow death and that of the women too much to bear.)

Poker Flat. "If you can reach there in two days she's safe." "And you?" asked Tom Simson. "I'll stay here," was the curt reply.

The lovers parted with a long embrace. "You are not going, too," said the Duchess, as she saw Mr. Oakhurst apparently waiting to accompany him. "As far as the cañon," he replied. He turned suddenly, and kissed the Duchess, leaving her pallid face aflame, and her trembling limbs rigid with amazement.

Night came, but not Mr. Oakhurst. It brought the storm again and the whirling
1 snow. Then the Duchess, feeding the fire, found that some one had quietly piled beside the hut enough fuel to last a few days longer. The tears rose to her eyes, but she hid them from Piney.

The women slept but little. In the morning, looking into each other's faces, they read their fate. Neither spoke; but Piney, accepting the position of the stronger, drew near and placed her arm around the Duchess's waist. They kept this attitude for the rest of the day. That night the storm reached its greatest fury, and rending asunder the protecting pines, invaded the very hut.

Toward morning they found themselves unable to feed the fire, which gradually died away. As the embers slowly blackened, the Duchess crept closer to Piney, and broke the silence of many hours: "Piney, can you pray?" "No, dear," said Piney, simply. The Duchess, without knowing exactly why, felt relieved, and putting her head upon Piney's shoulder, spoke no more. And so reclining, the younger and purer pillowing the head of her soiled sister upon her virgin breast, they fell asleep.

2 The wind lulled as if it feared to waken them. Feathery drifts of snow, shaken from the long pine boughs, flew like white-winged birds, and settled about them as they slept. The moon through the rifted clouds looked down upon what had been the camp. But all human stain, all trace of earthly travail, was hidden beneath the spotless mantle mercifully flung from above.

3 They slept all that day and the next, nor did they waken when voices and footsteps broke the silence of the camp. And when pitying fingers brushed the snow from their wan faces, you could scarcely have told from the equal peace that dwelt upon them, which was she that had sinned. Even the Law of Poker Flat recognized this, and turned away, leaving them still locked in each other's arms.

But at the head of the gulch, on one of the largest pine trees, they found the deuce of clubs[18] pinned to the bark with a bowie knife. It bore the following, written in pencil, in a firm hand:

†
BENEATH THIS TREE
LIES THE BODY
OF
JOHN OAKHURST,
WHO STRUCK A STREAK OF BAD LUCK
ON THE 23D OF NOVEMBER, 1850,
AND
HANDED IN HIS CHECKS
ON THE 7TH DECEMBER, 1850
†

4 And pulseless and cold, with a Derringer[19] by his side and a bullet in his heart, though still calm as in life, beneath the snow, lay he who was at once the strongest and yet the weakest of the outcasts of Poker Flat.

18. **deuce of clubs:** two of clubs, considered to have the lowest value in a deck of cards.
19. **Derringer** [der′in jər]: small short-barreled pistol, named after Henry Deringer (1806–1868), an American gunsmith.

GUIDED READING

LITERAL QUESTIONS

1a. What event makes the Duchess want to cry? (her discovery of the fuel that someone has piled outside the hut)

2a. On what does Oakhurst write his epitaph? (a playing card—the deuce of clubs)

INFERENTIAL QUESTIONS

1b. For whom does the Duchess cry? (Because it is this discovery that brings tears, one can assume that she cries for Oakhurst. She realizes that he probably will not return to the camp.)

2b. Why is his choice of "stationery" significant? (He knows that this card is the least valuable. It is a fitting choice for a gambler whose sacrifice demonstrates that he has counted his own life as less important than those of his companions.)

STUDY QUESTIONS

Recalling

1. As the story opens, what has the secret committee of Poker Flat decided to do? Who is directly affected by the committee's decision?
2. What is John Oakhurst's "profession"? How does he receive his "sentence," according to the fifth paragraph?
3. Why are Tom Simson and Piney Woods going to Poker Flat? What natural event puts them and the outcasts in danger?
4. What does Mother Shipton do to help Piney? Why does Tom leave the group?
5. When the rescue party arrives, what do they find?

Interpreting

6. Briefly describe John Oakhurst and his attitude toward life. Explain how his final actions relate to his philosophy of life.
7. What are Tom and Piney like? What effect do they have on Mother Shipton and on Oakhurst?
8. What forces do all the characters have to face? How do all of them except Uncle Billy behave in this crisis?

Extending

9. Which elements of this story are common elements of western fiction that you have encountered in films, TV shows, or other works about the West?

LITERARY FOCUS

The Short Story

A **short story** is a brief prose fiction, usually one that can be read in a single sitting. It generally contains the six major elements of fiction—characterization, setting, theme, plot, point of view, and style.

Characterization refers to the way an author develops the personalities of the characters. In a short story there is usually only one character whose personality is fully developed; there are rarely more than two or three. The main character is often called the **protagonist.**

The **setting** is the time and place in which the events occur. Most short stories have only one setting that is described in great detail and rarely more than two or three settings.

The **theme** is the main idea that the writer communicates to the reader. In a short story there is usually one theme.

The **plot** is the series of events that takes us from a beginning to an end. Each event in the plot is related to the **conflict,** the struggle that the main character undergoes. Traditionally, the short story opens with **exposition,** background information vital to our understanding of what will follow. The events in the story follow a **rising action** until they reach a **climax**—the point of highest dramatic tension or excitement. After the climax a **falling action** leads to a **resolution**—a conclusion in which the conflict is resolved and the "knot" of the plot is untied. The resolution of the story is sometimes called the **denouement** (dā'nōō män'), a French word meaning "untying."

Thinking About the Short Story

■ Trace the structure of "The Outcasts of Poker Flat." First identify the exposition, the events that make up the rising action, and the climax. Then identify the events that make up the falling action and the resolution. What is the chief conflict in the story?

Flat and Round Characters

The English novelist E. M. Forster described fictional characters as either flat or round. A **flat character** is built around a single trait, quality, or idea. This type of character is immediately recognizable and never changes or surprises us. Flat characters include **stereotypes,** or **stock characters,** such as the noble hero, the innocent young lover, the fiendish villain, and the faithful friend. Stories of hard-boiled detectives and dashing secret agents involve flat characters; they may of course be wonderfully entertaining stories, but they are still predictable.

A round character, on the other hand, satisfies our sense of the actual richness and complexity of human nature. **Round characters** are developed by the author; they change and grow. They often exhibit contradictory traits, and, like real human beings, frequently surprise us. The greatest characters in literature are those that are most "round."

"The Outcasts of Poker Flat" is an example of an effective story with several flat characters. For example, Uncle Billy is dishonest, devious, and selfish throughout. Some of the characters are "rounder" than Uncle Billy, but all the characters are clearly defined types.

STUDY QUESTIONS

1. rid town of improper persons; hanged men, Oakhurst, Duchess, Mother Shipton, Uncle Billy
2. gambler; calmly
3. to get married; snowstorm
4. saves her food; to get help
5. Piney and Duchess dead, Oakhurst buried in snow at foot of tree he marked with a card
6. gambler, believes in Fate: sees life as a game with odds against him; thinking luck has deserted him, concedes defeat and kills himself
7. innocent; become protective, willing to die for them
8. isolation from society, storm; show cheer and concern for companions
9. vigilante justice, stock characters, rugged terrain

LITERARY FOCUS

The Short Story

exposition: vigilante justice, introduction of outcasts; *rising action:* journey, meeting with Tom and Piney, desertion of Uncle Billy, snowed in; *climax:* Mother Shipton's death; *falling action:* Tom's leaving, Oakhurst's disappearance, deaths, arrival of rescuers; *resolution:* finding of Oakhurst's body, epitaph; *chief conflict:* characters vs. storm

Thinking About Flat and Round Characters

1. In what way are Tom and Piney flat characters?
2. Mother Shipton and the Duchess may be considered "rounder" because they begin with one set of traits and end with another. Describe the change in these two characters.
3. What seems contradictory in Oakhurst? Comment on the last sentence of the story.
4. Select one flat character and one round character from other stories you have read. Describe the characters, and tell why they are flat or round.

VOCABULARY

Regionalisms

A **regionalism** is a word or phrase peculiar to a particular region of the country. Every region invents its own words and phrases, and sometimes these new expressions are so unusual that they can be understood only by the people who live in the region.

A writer will use regionalisms to make his characters' speech more vivid, more believable, and more closely tied to the time and place of the story. When Oakhurst, for example, reflects, "I reckon they're after somebody," we know from his expression that he is a man of the West.

Thinking About Regionalisms

1. Find another regionalism in "The Outcasts of Poker Flat."
2. Make a list of expressions that are part of the speech of your own region. Which ones do you think would not be easily understood by someone living somewhere else? Which ones do you think would be universally understood? Why?

COMPOSITION

Applying a Statement About Literature

■ The Regionalist Hamlin Garland said that local color in a story "means that it has such quality and background that it could not have been written in any other place" (see page 311). Write an essay applying this statement to "The Outcasts of Poker Flat." First cite the details of setting, or background, in the story. Then explain how this background is particularly fitting for these characters and, therefore, for the story. *For help with this assignment, refer to Lesson 9 in the Writing About Literature Handbook at the back of this book.*

Writing a Character Sketch

■ Write a short character sketch of a real or a fictional person. Begin by describing one or two traits of the person. Then illustrate the traits by showing the character in action, participating in an event or performing a specific action. Make the character as "round" as possible; that is, give the character enough qualities and complexity to make him or her genuinely human. Remember that round characters, like people, often experience many emotions.

Flat and Round Characters

1. personalities do not change
2. *Shipton:* at first foul-mouthed, malevolent; then self-sacrificing; *Duchess:* at first coquettish complainer; then as pure as Piney, faces death without complaint
3. recognizes danger, but does little to avert it; leader of group, but gives in to Fate; acts to save Tom, but has no faith in rescue; "philosophical calmness" is both strength and tragic flaw
4. Answers will vary. Students might pick Tom Walker as a flat character who is miserly, quarrelsome, and mean. Ahab is a round character, proud, angry, avenging, and endlessly complex.

VOCABULARY

1. Almost every instance of dialogue contains regionalisms. Examples include:
   - Oakhurst: "That is if you're willing to board us. If you ain't . . ."
   - The Duchess: "Just you go out there and cuss, and see."
2. Answers will vary. You might point out that *hoagy, hero, grinder,* and *submarine* are regionalisms for the same kind of sandwich.

COMPOSITION: GUIDELINES FOR EVALUATION

APPLYING A STATEMENT ABOUT LITERATURE

Objective

To show how local color applies to Harte

Guidelines for Evaluation

- suggested length: three to five paragraphs
- should include Garland's quotation
- should cite details of setting
- should discuss how expulsion and isolation enable characters to interact as they do

WRITING A CHARACTER SKETCH

Objective

To develop a round character

Guidelines for Evaluation

- suggested length: 350–400 words
- should clearly describe two or more traits of the character
- should illustrate traits through actions
- should include dialogue illustrating traits

Sarah Orne Jewett *1849–1909*

Sarah Orne Jewett wrote compassionately and gracefully about the part of the world she knew best—her native New England. Jewett was born in the village of South Berwick, on the Maine coast. As a young girl she accompanied her father, a local doctor, on his visits to remote farms and small fishing towns. Her imagination was stirred by the life styles and personalities she encountered and by her father's anecdotes. Soon she set out to collect local legends, examine the family histories of nearby fishermen and farmers, and study their manners and speech.

At the age of fourteen, she started writing sketches with the material she had gathered. By the time she was twenty, her stories were polished enough for the pages of the *Atlantic Monthly,* America's most distinguished literary journal. *Deephaven* (1877), a collection of her tales and sketches, was the first of more than twenty works, including her masterpiece, *The Country of the Pointed Firs* (1896).

In her stories and novels Sarah Orne Jewett sought to preserve a way of life that was passing and a natural landscape that was changing.

■ Have you ever felt protective toward an animal? How far would you go to protect it? What does Sylvia risk in this story?

Sarah Orne Jewett

A White Heron

1 The woods were already filled with shadows one June evening, just before eight o'clock, though a bright sunset still glimmered faintly among the trunks of the trees. A little girl was driving home her cow, a plodding, dilatory, provoking creature in her behavior, but a valued companion for all that. They were going away from the western light, and striking deep into the dark woods, but their feet were familiar with the path, and it was no matter whether their eyes could see it or not.

There was hardly a night the summer through when the old cow could be found waiting at the pasture bars; on the contrary, it was her greatest pleasure to hide herself away among the high huckleberry bushes, and
though she wore a loud bell she had made the
discovery that if one stood perfectly still it
2 would not ring. So Sylvia had to hunt for her
until she found her, and call "Co'! Co'!" with
never an answering "Moo," until her childish
patience was quite spent. If the creature had
not given good milk and plenty of it, the case
would have seemed very different to her own-
3 ers. Besides, Sylvia had all the time there was,
and very little use to make of it. Sometimes in pleasant weather it was a consolation to look upon the cow's pranks as an intelligent attempt to play hide and seek, and as the child had no playmates she lent herself to this amusement with a good deal of zest. Though this chase had been so long that the wary animal herself

AT A GLANCE

Sylvia, a young girl, drives her cow home through the woods one evening in June.

LITERARY OPTIONS

- point of view
- internal conflict
- setting

THEMATIC OPTIONS

- our relationship to nature
- friendship
- maturity and independence

1 SETTING

With specific details concerning the sunset that "still glimmered," Jewett creates a picture of nature that suggests serenity and affection.

2 VOCABULARY: ROOT WORD

The name *Sylvia* comes from the Latin word for woods, *silva*—fitting for a girl who is most at home in the forest.

3 CHARACTERIZATION

Sylvia copes with her loneliness and need for companionship by making a game of hunting for the cow.

GUIDED READING

LITERAL QUESTION

1a. What human attributes has the narrator given to the cow? (It feels pleasure at hiding and has realized it can keep its bell from ringing by not moving.)

INFERENTIAL QUESTION

1b. What do these attributes suggest about the relationship between humans and animals? (They bridge the gap between humans and animals, suggesting that they share many of the same feelings.)

AT A GLANCE

- Sylvia's lateness does not concern her grandmother, Mrs. Tilley.
- Sylvia recalls her early years in a factory town.
- The cow stops for a drink and Sylvia revels in the forest world.
- A hunter whistles to get her attention and frightens her.

1 CHARACTERIZATION

Sylvia's affection for the cow is shown by the playful name given to her—Mistress Moolly.

2 STYLE: SENSORY DETAIL

By invoking several sensations *(cool, softly, stirring),* Jewett helps the reader to share Sylvia's experience and thus to better understand her attachment to the environment.

3 THEME

Rather than feeling isolated or frightened in the darkening forest, Sylvia feels a part of the natural scene.

4 CHARACTERIZATION

Sylvia's reaction to the whistle confirms her grandmother's remark that Sylvia is "afraid of folks."

had given an unusual signal of her where-
1 abouts, Sylvia had only laughed when she came upon Mistress Moolly at the swampside, and urged her affectionately homeward with a twig of birch leaves. The old cow was not inclined to wander farther, she even turned in the right direction for once as they left the pasture, and stepped along the road at a good pace. She was quite ready to be milked now, and seldom stopped to browse. Sylvia wondered what her grandmother would say because they were so late. It was a great while since she had left home at half past five o'clock, but everybody knew the difficulty of making this errand a short one. Mrs. Tilley had chased the horned torment too many summer evenings herself to blame anyone else for lingering, and was only thankful as she waited that she had Sylvia, nowadays, to give such valuable assistance. The good woman suspected that Sylvia loitered occasionally on her own account; there never was such a child for straying about out-of-doors since the world was made! Everybody said that it was a good change for a little maid who had tried to grow for eight years in a crowded manufacturing town, but, as for Sylvia herself, it seemed as if she never had been alive at all before she came to live at the farm. She thought often with wistful compassion of a wretched dry geranium that belonged to a town neighbor.

" 'Afraid of folks,' " old Mrs. Tilley said to herself, with a smile, after she had made the unlikely choice of Sylvia from her daughter's houseful of children, and was returning to the farm. " 'Afraid of folks,' they said! I guess she won't be troubled no great with 'em up to the old place!" When they reached the door of the lonely house and stopped to unlock it, and the cat came to purr loudly, and rub against them, a deserted pussy, indeed, but fat with young robins, Sylvia whispered that this was a beautiful place to live in, and she never should wish to go home.

The companions followed the shady wood-road, the cow taking slow steps, and the child very fast ones. The cow stopped long at the brook to drink, as if the pasture were not half a swamp, and Sylvia stood still and waited, let-
2 ting her bare feet cool themselves in the shoal water, while the great twilight moths struck softly against her. She waded on through the brook as the cow moved away, and listened to the thrushes with a heart that beat fast with pleasure. There was a stirring in the great boughs overhead. They were full of little birds and beasts that seemed to be wide awake, and going about their world, or else saying goodnight to each other in sleepy twitters. Sylvia herself felt sleepy as she walked along. However, it was not much farther to the house, and
3 the air was soft and sweet. She was not often in the woods so late as this, and it made her feel as if she were a part of the gray shadows and the moving leaves. She was just thinking how long it seemed since she first came to the farm a year ago, and wondering if everything went on in the noisy town just the same as when she was there; the thought of the great red-faced boy who used to chase and frighten her made her hurry along the path to escape from the shadow of the trees.

Suddenly this little woods girl is horror stricken to hear a clear whistle not very far away. Not a bird's whistle, which would have a sort of friendliness, but a boy's whistle, determined, and somewhat aggressive. Sylvia left the cow to whatever sad fate might await her, and stepped discreetly aside into the bushes, but
4 she was just too late. The enemy had discovered her, and called out in a very cheerful and persuasive tone, "Halloa, little girl, how far is it to the road?" and trembling Sylvia answered almost inaudibly, "A good ways."

She did not dare to look boldly at the tall young man, who carried a gun over his shoulder, but she came out of her bush and again followed the cow, while he walked alongside.

"I have been hunting for some birds," the stranger said kindly, "and I have lost my way, and need a friend very much. Don't be afraid," he added gallantly. "Speak up and tell me what your name is, and whether you think I can

GUIDED READING

LITERAL QUESTIONS

1a. When Sylvia recalls a geranium that belonged to a town neighbor, what words does she use to describe it? *(wretched, dry)*

2a. When Sylvia recalls the red-faced boy, what does she do? (She starts walking faster.)

INFERENTIAL QUESTIONS

1b. Why do you think she uses these words? (She probably thinks that by comparison with the bursting life in the country, the flowers in town are pitiful.)

2b. Why does she do this? (The memory of town life arouses her fear of "folks," intrudes on the scene around her, and makes the forest appear threatening.)

spend the night at your house, and go out gunning early in the morning."

Sylvia was more alarmed than before. Would not her grandmother consider her much to blame? But who could have foreseen
1 such an accident as this? It did not appear to be her fault, and she hung her head as if the stem of it were broken, but managed to answer "Sylvy," with much effort when her companion again asked her name.

Mrs. Tilley was standing in the doorway when the trio came into view. The cow gave a loud moo by way of explanation.

"Yes, you'd better speak up for yourself, you old trial! Where'd she tuck herself away
2 this time, Sylvy?" Sylvia kept an awed silence; she knew by instinct that her grandmother did not comprehend the gravity of the situation. She must be mistaking the stranger for one of the farmer lads of the region.

The young man stood his gun beside the door, and dropped a heavy game bag beside it; then he bade Mrs. Tilley good evening, and repeated his wayfarer's story, and asked if he could have a night's lodging.

3 "Put me anywhere you like," he said. "I must be off early in the morning, before day; but I am very hungry, indeed. You can give me some milk at any rate, that's plain."

"Dear sakes, yes," responded the hostess,

AT A GLANCE

- Sylvia leads the traveler to her grandmother's house.
- Mrs. Tilley agrees to the traveler's request for food and lodging.

1 STYLE: FIGURATIVE LANGUAGE

Jewett reinforces Sylvia's connection with the world of nature by describing her as a flower with a broken stem.

2 INTERNAL CONFLICT

Although Sylvia feels that the stranger's presence is a threat, she is unable to express her concern to her grandmother.

3 BACKGROUND

In nineteenth-century rural America, it was not uncommon for travelers to ask for—and be given—bed and dinner, even from total strangers.

GUIDED READING

LITERAL QUESTION

1a. How does Sylvia react to the young man's request to spend the night at her house? (She becomes even more frightened.)

INFERENTIAL QUESTION

1b. Why does she react this way? (Her fear of people and the solitariness of life in the woods seem to make any stranger appear dangerous.)

AT A GLANCE

- Grandmother welcomes the stranger.
- Grandmother, the young man, and Sylvia eat supper and then sit in the doorway and talk.
- The young man explains that he is interested in birds and is looking for a rare white heron.

1 CHARACTERIZATION

Grandmother's immediate acceptance of the young man shows she does not see him (as Sylvia did) as a grave threat.

2 POINT OF VIEW

The narrator enters the young man's mind, showing the attitude of a town person toward rural life.

3 VOCABULARY: DIALECT

Grandmother's rural speech sets her apart from the young man with his educated, "town" speech.

4 THEME

So close is Sylvia to the world of nature that she would eat less in order to be able to feed the birds.

5 THEME

Instinctively the young man seems to realize and accept Sylvia's friendship with the natural world.

whose long slumbering hospitality seemed to be easily awakened. "You might fare better if you went out on the main road a mile or so,
1 but you're welcome to what we've got. I'll milk right off, and you make yourself at home. You can sleep on husks or feathers," she proffered graciously. "I raised them all myself. There's good pasturing for geese just below here towards the ma'sh. Now step round and set a plate for the gentleman, Sylvy!" And Sylvia promptly stepped. She was glad to have something to do, and she was hungry herself.

2 It was a surprise to find so clean and comfortable a little dwelling in this New England wilderness. The young man had known the horrors of its most primitive housekeeping, and the dreary squalor of that level of society which does not rebel at the companionship of hens. This was the best thrift of an old-fashioned farmstead, though on such a small scale that it seemed like a hermitage.[1] He listened eagerly to the old woman's quaint talk, he watched Sylvia's pale face and shining gray eyes with ever growing enthusiasm, and insisted that this was the best supper he had eaten for a month; then, afterward, the new-made friends sat down in the doorway together while the moon came up.

Soon it would be berry time, and Sylvia was a great help at picking. The cow was a good milker, though a plaguy[2] thing to keep track of, the hostess gossiped frankly, adding presently that she had buried four children, so that Sylvia's mother, and a son (who might be dead) in California were all the children she had left. "Dan, my boy, was a great hand to go gun-
3 ning," she explained sadly. "I never wanted for pa'tridges or gray squer'ls while he was to home. He's been a great wand'rer, I expect, and he's no hand to write letters. There, I don't blame him, I'd ha' seen the world myself if it had been so I could.

"Sylvia takes after him," the grandmother continued affectionately, after a minute's pause. "There ain't a foot o' ground she don't know her way over, and the wild creaturs counts her one o' themselves. Squer'ls she'll tame to come an' feed right out o' her hands,
4 and all sorts o' birds. Last winter she got the jaybirds to bangeing[3] here, and I believe she'd 'a' scanted herself of her own meals to have plenty to throw out amongst 'em, if I hadn't kep' watch. Anything but crows, I tell her, I'm willin' to help support—though Dan he went an' tamed one o' them that did seem to have reason same as folks. It was round here a good spell after he went away. Dan an' his father they didn't hitch[4]—but he never held up his head ag'in after Dan had dared him an' gone off."

The guest did not notice this hint of family sorrows in his eager interest in something else.

"So Sylvy knows all about birds, does she?" he exclaimed, as he looked round at the little girl who sat, very demure but increasingly sleepy, in the moonlight. "I am making a collection of birds myself. I have been at it ever since I was a boy." (Mrs. Tilley smiled.) "There are two or three very rare ones I have been hunting for these five years. I mean to get them on my own ground if they can be found."

"Do you cage 'em up?" asked Mrs. Tilley doubtfully, in response to this enthusiastic announcement.

"Oh, no, they're stuffed and preserved, dozens and dozens of them," said the ornithologist,[5] "and I have shot or snared every one myself. I caught a glimpse of a white heron three miles from here on Saturday, and I have followed it in this direction. They have never
5 been found in this district at all. The little white heron, it is," and he turned again to look at Sylvia with the hope of discovering that the rare bird was one of her acquaintances.

But Sylvia was watching a hoptoad in the narrow footpath.

"You would know the heron if you saw it," the stranger continued eagerly. "A queer tall

1. **hermitage:** home of a hermit, someone who lives alone in an isolated place, often for religious reasons.
2. **plaguy** [plā′gē]: annoying.
3. **bangeing** [ban′jing]: lounging about.
4. **hitch:** get along well with each other.
5. **ornithologist** [ôr′nə thol′ə jist]: expert on birds.

GUIDED READING

LITERAL QUESTIONS

1a. According to Grandmother, whom does Sylvia take after? (Sylvia's uncle Dan)

2a. What is the young man looking for, and what does he plan to do with it? (a white heron; he will kill it and add it to his extensive collection)

INFERENTIAL QUESTIONS

1b. In what way does Sylvia take after this person? (Like Dan, she knows and cares for the land and the creatures who live on it.)

2b. What do you think about the hunter's plan? (Answers will vary. Some students may find his goal worthy and interesting; others may find it brutal.)

white bird with soft feathers and long thin legs. And it would have a nest perhaps in the top of a high tree, made of sticks, something like a hawk's nest."

Sylvia's heart gave a wild beat; she knew that strange white bird, and had once stolen softly near where it stood in some bright green swamp grass, away over at the other side of the woods. There was an open place where the sunshine always seemed strangely yellow and hot, where tall, nodding rushes grew, and her grandmother had warned her that she might sink in the soft black mud underneath and never be heard of more. Not far beyond were the salt marshes and beyond those was the sea, the sea which Sylvia wondered and dreamed about, but never had looked upon, though its great voice could often be heard above the noise of the woods on stormy nights.

"I can't think of anything I should like so much as to find that heron's nest," the hand-
1 some stranger was saying. "I would give ten dollars to anybody who could show it to me," he added desperately, "and I mean to spend my whole vacation hunting for it if need be. Perhaps it was only migrating, or had been chased out of its own region by some bird of prey."

Mrs. Tilley gave amazed attention to all this, but Sylvia still watched the toad, not divining, as she might have done at some calmer time, that the creature wished to get to its hole under the doorstep, and was much hindered by the unusual spectators at that hour of the evening. No amount of thought, that night, could decide how many wished-for treasures the ten dollars, so lightly spoken of, would buy.

The next day the young sportsman hovered about the woods, and Sylvia kept him company, having lost her first fear of the friendly lad, who proved to be most kind and sympa-
2 thetic. He told her many things about the birds and what they knew and where they lived and what they did with themselves. And he gave her a jackknife, which she thought as great a treasure as if she were a desert islander. All day long he did not once make her troubled or afraid except when he brought down some un-
3 suspecting singing creature from its bough. Sylvia would have liked him vastly better without his gun; she could not understand why he killed the very birds he seemed to like so much. But as the day waned, Sylvia still watched the young man with loving admiration. She had never seen anybody so charming and delightful; the woman's heart, asleep in the child, was vaguely thrilled by a dream of love. Some premonition of that great power stirred and swayed these young foresters who traversed the solemn woodlands with soft-footed silent care. They stopped to listen to a bird's song; they pressed forward again eagerly, parting the branches, speaking to each other rarely and in whispers; the young man going first and Sylvia following, fascinated, a few steps behind, with her gray eyes dark with excitement.

She grieved because the longed-for white heron was elusive, but she did not lead the guest, she only followed, and there was no such thing as speaking first. The sound of her own unquestioned voice would have terrified her—it was hard enough to answer yes or no when there was need of that. At last evening began to fall, and they drove the cow home together, and Sylvia smiled with pleasure when they came to the place where she heard the whistle and was afraid only the night before.

Half a mile from home, at the farther edge of the woods, where the land was highest, a great pine tree stood, the last of its generation. Whether it was left for a boundary mark, or for what reason, no one could say; the woodchoppers who had felled its mates were dead and gone long ago, and a whole forest of sturdy trees, pines and oaks and maples, had grown again. But the stately head of this old pine towered above them all and made a landmark for sea and shore miles and miles away. Sylvia
4 knew it well. She had always believed that whoever climbed to the top of it could see the ocean; and the little girl had often laid her hand on the great rough trunk and looked up wistfully at those dark boughs that the wind always stirred, no matter how hot and still the air might be below. Now she thought of the

AT A GLANCE

- Sylvia, too, has seen the white heron in the area.
- The young man offers ten dollars to anyone who can show him the bird's nest.
- The next day, Sylvia and the young man search the woods.
- They see a great pine tree that stands above the rest.

1 THEME

To the desperate young man, nature is a collection of items to be bought, possessed, and studied at leisure.

2 CHARACTERIZATION

The young man's charm and knowledge of birds and the present of the knife erase Sylvia's fears and make her begin to like him.

3 INTERNAL CONFLICT

Sylvia's feeling for the young man is tempered by her distaste for his desire to kill the birds she loves.

4 SYMBOL

The pine tree is the doorway to new worlds; climbing it extends the horizon figuratively as well as literally.

GUIDED READING

LITERAL QUESTIONS

1a. What one thing about the young man does Sylvia not like? (She does not understand why he killed the very birds he seemed to like so much.)

2a. What stands alone at the edge of the forest? (an old and very tall pine tree)

INFERENTIAL QUESTIONS

1b. Why does she find this behavior contradictory? (Sylvia's love of nature does not include possessing or killing anything of nature, and she cannot understand that feeling in the young man.)

2b. Why do you think Sylvia looks up through the tree wistfully? (The tree represents an as-yet-untried connection to the faraway places Sylvia longs to see.)

AT A GLANCE

- Sylvia decides to climb the great pine in order to find the heron's nest.
- Sylvia slips out before dawn, makes her way to the tree, and climbs to the top.

1 POINT OF VIEW

The narrator goes beyond simply observing events and provides a personal opinion: It would be unfortunate for Sylvia to let her attraction to the young man ruin her special relationship with the natural world.

2 PLOT: RISING ACTION

The climb is difficult, making the reader wonder if Sylvia can reach the top before dawn.

3 THEME

So at one with nature is Sylvia that the tree itself seems to help her to climb by making itself steady beneath her.

4 PLOT: RISING ACTION

Sylvia sees the sea for the first time. Her sense of triumph may include an even greater appreciation of the marvels of nature, as symbolized by the dazzling sea and the slow-moving hawks.

tree with a new excitement, for why, if one climbed it at break of day, could not one see all the world, and easily discover whence the white heron flew, and mark the place, and find the hidden nest?

What a spirit of adventure, what wild ambition! What fancied triumph and delight and glory for the later morning when she could make known the secret! It was almost too real and too great for the childish heart to bear.

All night the door of the little house stood open, and the whippoorwills came and sang upon the very step. The young sportsman and his old hostess were sound asleep, but Sylvia's great design kept her broad awake and watching. She forgot to think of sleep. The short summer night seemed as long as the winter darkness, and at last when the whippoorwills ceased, and she was afraid the morning would after all come too soon, she stole out of the house and followed the pasture path through the woods, hastening toward the open ground beyond, listening with a sense of comfort and companionship to the drowsy twitter of a half-awakened bird, whose perch she had jarred in
1 passing. Alas, if the great wave of human interest which flooded for the first time this dull little life should sweep away the satisfactions of an existence heart to heart with nature and the dumb[6] life of the forest!

There was the huge tree asleep yet in the paling moonlight, and small and hopeful Sylvia began with utmost bravery to mount to the top of it, with tingling, eager blood coursing the channels of her whole frame, with her bare feet and fingers, that pinched and held like bird's claws to the monstrous ladder reaching up, up, almost to the sky itself. First she must mount the white oak tree that grew alongside, where she was almost lost among the dark branches and the green leaves heavy and wet with dew; a bird fluttered off its nest, and a red squirrel ran to and fro and scolded pettishly at the harmless housebreaker. Sylvia felt her way easily. She had often climbed there, and knew that higher still one of the oak's upper branches chafed against the pine trunk, just where its lower boughs were set close together. There, when she made the dangerous pass from one tree to the other, the great enterprise would really begin.

She crept out along the swaying oak limb at last, and took the daring step across into the
2 old pine tree. The way was harder than she thought; she must reach far and hold fast, the sharp dry twigs caught and held her and scratched her like angry talons, the pitch made her thin little fingers clumsy and stiff as she went round and round the tree's great stem, higher and higher upward. The sparrows and robins in the woods below were beginning to wake and twitter to the dawn, yet it seemed much lighter there aloft in the pine tree, and the child knew that she must hurry if her project were to be of any use.

The tree seemed to lengthen itself out as she went up, and to reach farther and farther upward. It was like a great mainmast to the voyaging earth; it must truly have been amazed that morning through all its ponderous frame as it felt this determined spark of human spirit creeping and climbing from higher branch to
3 branch. Who knows how steadily the least twigs held themselves to advantage this light, weak creature on her way! The old pine must have loved his new dependent. More than all the hawks, and bats, and moths, and even the sweet-voiced thrushes, was the brave, beating heart of the solitary gray-eyed child. And the tree stood still and held away the winds that June morning while the dawn grew bright in the east.

Sylvia's face was like a pale star, if one had seen it from the ground, when the last thorny
4 bough was past, and she stood trembling and tired but wholly triumphant, high in the treetop. Yes, there was the sea with the dawning sun making a golden dazzle over it, and toward that glorious east flew two hawks with slow-moving pinions.[7] How low they looked in the

6. **dumb:** silent.

7. **pinions** [pin′yənz]: wings.

GUIDED READING

LITERAL QUESTIONS

1a. What is Sylvia's plan for finding the heron's nest? (to climb the great pine tree at dawn and watch for the heron leaving its nest)

2a. How does Sylvia reach the lower boughs of the pine tree? (by climbing an oak next to the pine)

INFERENTIAL QUESTIONS

1b. Why does she keep her plan a secret? (She has probably decided to surprise the young man—and perhaps to cement their friendship—by leading him to the heron's nest.)

2b. Why does the "great enterprise . . . really begin" when she reaches the pine boughs? (When she starts to climb the pine, she enters the unknown; she has often climbed the oak.)

air from that height when before one had only seen them far up, and dark against the blue sky. Their gray feathers were as soft as moths; they seemed only a little way from the tree,
1 and Sylvia felt as if she too could go flying away among the clouds. Westward, the woodlands and farms reached miles and miles into the distance; here and there were church steeples, and white villages; truly it was a vast and awesome world.

The birds sang louder and louder. At last the sun came up bewilderingly bright. Sylvia could see the white sails of ships out at sea, and the clouds that were purple and rose-colored and yellow at first began to fade away. Where was the white heron's nest in the sea of green branches, and was this wonderful sight and pageant of the world the only reward for
2 having climbed to such a giddy height? Now look down again, Sylvia, where the green marsh is set among the shining birches and dark hemlocks; there where you saw the white heron once you will see him again; look, look! a white spot of him like a single floating feather comes up from the dead hemlock and grows larger, and rises, and comes close at last, and goes by the landmark pine with steady sweep of wing and outstretched slender neck
3 and crested head. And wait! wait! do not move a foot or finger, little girl, do not send an arrow of light and consciousness from your two eager eyes, for the heron has perched on a pine bough not far beyond yours, and cries back to his mate on the nest, and plumes his feathers for the new day!

The child gives a long sigh a minute later when a company of shouting catbirds comes also to the tree, and vexed by their fluttering and lawlessness the solemn heron goes away. She knows his secret now, the wild, light, slender bird that floats and wavers, and goes back like an arrow presently to his home in the

AT A GLANCE

- Sylvia looks out from the top of the pine and spots the heron.
- The heron flies near her and calls to its mate.
- A noisy group of catbirds appears, and the heron flies off.

1 RESPONSE JOURNAL

Students may wish to recall a moment at which they realized that they were a part of "a vast and awesome world."

2 POINT OF VIEW

The narrator speaks to Sylvia, as if to help her find the heron. This unusual shift from the narrator's usual tone helps prepare for the story's climax. Note also that the narrator's switch to the present tense increases the excitement of this passage.

3 CLIMAX

The story's climax occurs when the heron perches in the pine tree near Sylvia.

GUIDED READING

LITERAL QUESTION

1a. When does Sylvia finally see the white heron? (when she looks down from the pine tree)

INFERENTIAL QUESTION

1b. Why is it fitting that Sylvia of all people is permitted to see this rare bird? (because of her special closeness to and love of nature—her ability to become one with it)

AT A GLANCE

- Sylvia returns, considering how to tell the young man about the heron.
- Sylvia finally refuses to say anything about what she has seen, even though she is urged to speak by both her grandmother and the young man.
- The young man leaves, and Sylvia is left lonely once again.

1 INTERNAL CONFLICT

The rebukes of the grandmother and the appeals of the young man show externally the conflict Sylvia feels inside.

2 THEME

The love of nature—a love that does not seek to possess—outweighs "mere" human interests.

3 THEME

Because she has sacrificed a friendship, says the narrator, the world of nature should reward Sylvia with its special wisdom.

REFLECTING ON THE STORY

What is the heron's "secret" that Sylvia cannot tell? (It seems to be something more than the location of its nest. Perhaps it has to do with the spirit that makes a person feel at one with nature rather than at odds with it.)

STUDY QUESTIONS

1. "afraid of folks"; "little woods-girl"
2. hides; almost inaudible
3. ornithology; ten dollars
4. from top of tall pine tree; no
5. whether birds are better friends than the hunter might have been
6. shy loner, loves wandering in woods; shy, unusual

green world beneath. Then Sylvia, well satisfied, makes her perilous way down again, not daring to look far below the branch she stands on, ready to cry sometimes because her fingers ache and her lamed feet slip. Wondering over and over again what the stranger would say to her, and what he would think when she told him how to find his way straight to the heron's nest.

"Sylvy, Sylvy!" called the busy old grandmother again and again, but nobody answered, and the small husk bed was empty, and Sylvia had disappeared.

The guest waked from a dream, and remembering his day's pleasure hurried to dress himself that it might sooner begin. He was sure from the way the shy little girl looked once or twice yesterday that she had at least seen the white heron, and now she must really be persuaded to tell. Here she comes now, paler than ever, and her worn old frock is torn and tattered, and smeared with pine pitch. The grandmother and the sportsman stand in the door together and question her, and the splendid moment has come to speak of the dead hemlock tree by the green marsh.

1 But Sylvia does not speak after all, though the old grandmother fretfully rebukes her, and the young man's kind appealing eyes are looking straight in her own. He can make them rich with money; he has promised it, and they are poor now. He is so well worth making happy, and he waits to hear the story she can tell.

No, she must keep silence! What is it that suddenly forbids her and makes her dumb? Has she been nine years growing, and now, when the great world for the first time puts out a hand to her, must she thrust it aside for a
2 bird's sake? The murmur of the pine's green branches is in her ears, she remembers how the white heron came flying through the golden air and how they watched the sea and the morning together, and Sylvia cannot speak; she cannot tell the heron's secret and give its life away.

Dear loyalty, that suffered a sharp pang as the guest went away disappointed later in the day, that could have served and followed him and loved him as a dog loves! Many a night Sylvia heard the echo of his whistle haunting the pasture path as she came home with the loitering cow. She forgot even her sorrow at the sharp report of his gun and the piteous sight of thrushes and sparrows dropping silent to the ground, their songs hushed and their pretty feathers stained and wet with blood. Were the birds better friends than their hunter might
3 have been—who can tell? Whatever treasures were lost to her, woodlands and summertime, remember! Bring your gifts and graces and tell your secrets to this lonely country child.

STUDY QUESTIONS

Recalling

1. How did Sylvia's family describe Sylvia to her grandmother, according to the third paragraph? What does the author call Sylvia in the fifth paragraph?
2. How does Sylvia react when she first hears the young man's whistle? In what kind of voice does she answer his question in the fifth paragraph?
3. What is the young man's hobby? What does he offer to give Sylvia if she helps him find the white heron?
4. How does Sylvia finally sight the white heron? Does she tell the young man of her discovery?
5. What question does the author ask in the last paragraph?

Interpreting

6. Identify Sylvia's chief character trait, as de-

veloped in the opening paragraphs of the story. In what ways is Sylvia like the white heron?

7. Consider the meaning of the name *Sylvia* or the word *sylvan*. How does Sylvia feel about nature? How do her feelings compare to the young man's?
8. What new senses are awakened in Sylvia as a result of her friendship? What ideas come into conflict in this story?
9. In making her choice at the end of the story, what new experience is Sylvia ending? In more general terms, between what is she choosing?

Extending

10. Do you think Sylvia had an obligation to help her new friend by telling him what he wanted to know, or to help her grandmother by taking the money?

VIEWPOINT

In a discussion of Sarah Orne Jewett's work, the twentieth-century author Willa Cather writes:

> Miss Jewett wrote of the people who grew out of the soil and the life of the country near her heart, not about exceptional individuals at war with their environment.
>
> —Preface to *The Country of the Pointed Firs*

■ How would you describe the relationship between Sylvia and her environment? What are the advantages and limitations of such a relationship? Do you think Sylvia is nevertheless an "exceptional individual"? Why or why not?

LITERARY FOCUS

Point of View

The writer of fiction must decide from which point of view to tell a story. A story has a **first-person point of view** if one of the characters tells the tale in his or her own words, using the first-person pronoun *I*. A story has a **third-person point of view** if the narrator stands back from the events and uses the third-person pronouns *he* and *she* to refer to the characters. A narrator who tells us the thoughts of many characters and who also tells us things that no character could know uses the **omniscient** ("all-knowing") **third-person point of view.**

In "A White Heron" Jewett could have employed a first-person point of view by having Sylvia tell us in her own voice what happened to her and what she was thinking. This point of view might have made Sylvia's dilemma more immediate and realistic, but we could then know only what Sylvia herself knew and felt; we could not learn, for example, that the young man thinks Sylvia is "pale," "tattered," and "dirty" and that he suspects she knows the home of the heron.

By using the omniscient third-person point of view, the narrator of "A White Heron" can tell us the thoughts of all the characters and can jump out of the characters' heads to describe them objectively. The narrator can even *intrude* on the story with personal opinion, as on page 330 ("Alas, if . . . ").

Thinking about Point of View

1. Find another instance where the narrator reveals the young man's thoughts. What do his thoughts reveal about his character?
2. Find another instance where the narrator intrudes on the story. What does the intrusion suggest about the narrator's attitude toward Sylvia and her secret?

COMPOSITION

Writing About a Symbol

■ In an essay discuss what you think the white heron symbolizes. First discuss what the color white suggests about the bird, and tell why it is important that the bird is unusual and rarely seen. Go on to tell what qualities of Sylvia herself the heron represents. Then discuss the significance of the white heron in the work as a whole, explaining how it relates to the theme of the work. *For help with this assignment, refer to Lesson 5 in the Writing About Literature Handbook at the back of this book.*

Creating a Setting

■ In a paragraph or two describe a place about which you have strong feelings, as Jewett obviously has for the Maine wilderness. First describe the general area you want your reader to see. Then fill out your description with details of sights and sounds and any other physical impressions that can make the setting vivid. Conclude by telling how you feel about the setting.

7.
- *Sylvia* from Latin *sylva*, meaning "forest"
- close bond
- man: willing to destroy to possess; Sylvia: part of nature, guards its secrets

8. love for a man; conflict between guarding life of solitude and developing friendship with stranger

9. friendship and love; choosing nature, heron, and solitude over the outside world

10. Students might argue that her friendship and responsibility to her grandmother obligated Sylvia to reveal the location of the heron to get money. Others might cite an obligation to uphold principles.

VIEWPOINT

- close
- enriches her life and animates her spirit but cuts her off from human relationships and society
- Answers will vary as to whether Sylvia is exceptional.

LITERARY FOCUS

1. thinks house is "clean and comfortable" and listens "eagerly" to grandmother's "quaint talk"; orderly, inquiring mind

2.
- The narrator directly addresses Sylvia when she climbs the tall pine. This implies shared wonder and excitement.
- The intrusion in the final paragraph suggests approval of Sylvia's choice.

COMPOSITION: GUIDELINES FOR EVALUATION

WRITING ABOUT A SYMBOL

Objective

To explain symbolic meaning of white heron

Guidelines for Evaluation

- suggested length: four to six paragraphs
- should state that white suggests purity
- should discuss significance of heron's rarity and reclusiveness
- should compare Sylvia and heron
- should show how heron elucidates theme

CREATING A SETTING

Objective

To describe a setting

Guidelines for Evaluation

- suggested length: one to two paragraphs
- should relate general description of area
- should use vivid adjectives and sensory details to create unified tone and impression
- should convey student's feelings about place

Kate Chopin *1851–1904*

Delicate, objective, and *poignant* are words often used to describe the local color stories of Kate Chopin. Born in St. Louis, Missouri, Kate O'Flaherty Chopin married at nineteen and went to live in New Orleans, Louisiana. During the more than ten years she spent there, she became fascinated by the variety of Louisiana life, the rich mixture of cultures, and the many languages and dialects. After her husband's death in 1882, she returned to St. Louis with her six children and began to write.

Just as Bret Harte gave the world a vision of the American West and Sarah Orne Jewett wrote delicate sketches of rural New England, Kate Chopin was chiefly interested in Louisiana. The characters who inhabit Chopin's world are generally Louisiana Creoles, descendants of the original French and Spanish colonists, and Cajuns, descendants of Louisiana's French Canadian settlers. While Chopin is interested in capturing the flavor of Louisiana life as she knew it—as she does in her collection of stories, *Bayou Folk* (1894)—she moves beyond local color to explore the characters of her time and place.

Chopin cared deeply about the roles of women in society and she often writes about a woman's responsibilities to her family, her community, and herself. It is this theme that dominates her most famous novel, *The Awakening* (1899). "A Pair of Silk Stockings" offers a sensitive portrait of another woman who also cares deeply about her responsibilities.

■ How long have women been concerned about their own roles and responsibilities? How have those concerns changed in the last hundred years?

Kate Chopin

A Pair of Silk Stockings

Little Mrs. Sommers one day found herself the unexpected possessor of fifteen dollars. It seemed to her a very large amount of money, and the way in which it stuffed and bulged her worn old *porte-monnaie*[1] gave her a feeling of importance such as she had not enjoyed for years.

The question of investment was one that occupied her greatly. For a day or two she
1 walked about apparently in a dreamy state, but really absorbed in speculation and calculation. She did not wish to act hastily, to do anything she might afterward regret. But it was during the still hours of the night when she lay awake revolving plans in her mind that she seemed to see her way clearly toward a proper and judicious use of the money.

A dollar or two should be added to the
2 price usually paid for Janie's shoes, which would insure their lasting an appreciable time longer than they usually did. She would buy so and so many yards of percale for new shirt-waists for the boys and Janie and Mag. She had intended to make the old ones do by skillful patching. Mag should have another gown. She had seen some beautiful patterns, veritable bargains in the shop windows. And still there would be left enough for new stockings—two pairs apiece—and what darning that would save for a while! She would get caps for the boys and sailor hats for the girls. The vision of her little brood looking fresh and dainty and new for once in their lives excited her and made her restless and wakeful with anticipation.

The neighbors sometimes talked of certain "better days" that little Mrs. Sommers had known before she had ever thought of being Mrs. Sommers. She herself indulged in no such
3 morbid retrospection. She had no time—no second of time to devote to the past. The needs of the present absorbed her every faculty. A vision of the future like some dim, gaunt monster sometimes appalled her, but luckily tomorrow never comes.

Mrs. Sommers was one who knew the value of bargains; who could stand for hours making her way inch by inch toward the desired object that was selling below cost. She could elbow her way if need be; she had learned to clutch a piece of goods and hold it and stick to it with persistence and determination till her turn came to be served, no matter when it came.

But that day she was a little faint and tired.
4 She had swallowed a light luncheon—no! when she came to think of it, between getting the children fed and the place righted, and preparing herself for the shopping bout, she had actually forgotten to eat any luncheon at all!

She sat herself upon a revolving stool before a counter that was comparatively deserted, trying to gather strength and courage to charge through an eager multitude that was besieging breastworks[2] of shirting[3] and figured lawn.[4] An all-gone limp feeling had come over her and she rested her hand aimlessly upon the counter. She wore no gloves. By degrees she grew aware that her hand had encountered something very soothing, very pleasant to touch. She looked down to see that her hand lay upon a pile of silk stockings. A placard nearby announced that they had been reduced in price from two dollars and fifty cents to one dollar and ninety-eight cents; and a young girl who stood behind the counter asked her if she wished to examine their line of silk hosiery.

1. ***porte-monnaie*** [pôrt mō nä′]: French for "change purse."

2. **breastworks:** low, hastily built defense walls; here, merchandise displays.
3. **shirting:** material for making shirts.
4. **figured lawn:** fine, sheer, patterned cloth.

AT A GLANCE

- Mrs. Sommers plans how she will spend fifteen dollars.
- The narrator describes the needs of her family and her skill at getting bargains.
- Waiting at a store counter, she happens to touch a pair of silk stockings.

LITERARY OPTIONS

- character motivation
- symbol
- Naturalism

THEMATIC OPTIONS

- duty vs. self-fulfillment
- making choices

1 CHARACTER MOTIVATION

That deciding how to spend this money most appropriately could keep Mrs. Sommers awake at night indicates how strongly she is motivated by a sense of duty.

2 PLOT: EXPOSITION

The information about the family's needs makes clear the economic standing of Mrs. Sommers and explains her frugality.

3 CHARACTER MOTIVATION

Her refusal to bemoan the past and to be daunted by the specter of the future shows how driven she is by the demands of the present.

4 POINT OF VIEW

The narrator (limited third-person) gives us access to the thoughts of only Mrs. Sommers, thus isolating her within the wall of concerns that press on her mind.

GUIDED READING

LITERAL QUESTIONS

1a. How does the sudden possession of fifteen dollars affect Mrs. Sommers? (It keeps her awake nights planning how the money should be spent.)

2a. Which two words does the author use to describe Mrs. Sommers' feeling just before she touches the silk stockings? *(all-gone, limp)*

INFERENTIAL QUESTIONS

1b. Why does the money affect her this way? (There are many things for which she needs to spend the money, and she has a strong sense of duty.)

2b. Why do you think touching the silk stockings soothes her? (Perhaps the luxury and elegance of the stockings remind her of a time when she was not poor or encumbered by responsibilities.)

AT A GLANCE

- Without really knowing why, Mrs. Sommers buys a pair of silk stockings and puts them on.
- She buys expensive shoes, fitted gloves, and two high-priced magazines.

1 SYMBOL

The sensual description of the stockings and the way in which Mrs. Sommers looks at and handles them show that the stockings have a deep significance for her; perhaps they evoke remembrances of the "better life" of her past.

2 PLOT: RISING ACTION

Once she has bought the stockings, Mrs. Sommers abandons her well-thought-out plan and turns away from the bargain counter.

3 NATURALISM

Mrs. Sommers is moved by forces that she neither controls nor understands, apparently oblivious to the psychological factors affecting her behavior.

4 CONFLICT

The reaction of the clerk, finding that the stockings do not match the shoes, parallels Mrs. Sommers' inner conflict between what she wants and what life has dictated that she can have.

5 STYLE: SENTENCE STRUCTURE

Through its structure (the expletive *there* and the use of passive verbs), the sentence distances Mrs. Sommers from any decision to continue the shopping spree; she is merely carried along.

She smiled, just as if she had been asked to inspect a tiara[5] of diamonds with the ultimate
1 view of purchasing it: But she went on feeling the soft, sheeny luxurious things—with both hands now, holding them up to see them glisten, and to feel them glide serpent-like through her fingers.

Two hectic blotches came suddenly into her pale cheeks. She looked up at the girl.

"Do you think there are any eights-and-a-half among these?"

There were any number of eights-and-a-half. In fact, there were more of that size than any other. Here was a light blue pair; there were some lavender, some all black and various shades of tan and gray. Mrs. Sommers selected a black pair and looked at them very long and closely. She pretended to be examining their texture, which the clerk assured her was excellent.

"A dollar and ninety-eight cents," she mused aloud. "Well, I'll take this pair." She handed the girl a five-dollar bill and waited for her change and for her parcel. What a very small parcel it was! It seemed lost in the depths of her shabby old shopping bag.

2 Mrs. Sommers after that did not move in the direction of the bargain counter. She took the elevator, which carried her to an upper floor into the region of the ladies' waiting rooms. Here, in a retired corner, she exchanged her cotton stockings for the new silk ones which she had just bought. She was not going through any acute mental process or reasoning with herself, nor was she striving to explain to her satisfaction the motive of her ac-
3 tion. She was not thinking at all. She seemed for the time to be taking a rest from that laborious and fatiguing function and to have abandoned herself to some mechanical impulse that directed her actions and freed her of responsibility.

How good was the touch of the raw silk to her flesh! She felt like lying back in the cushioned chair and reveling for a while in the luxury of it. She did for a little while. Then she replaced her shoes, rolled the cotton stockings together and thrust them into her bag. After doing this she crossed straight over to the shoe department and took her seat to be fitted.

4 She was fastidious. The clerk could not make her out; he could not reconcile her shoes with her stockings, and she was not too easily pleased. She held back her skirts and turned her feet one way and her head another way as she glanced down at the polished, pointed-tipped boots. Her foot and ankle looked very pretty. She could not realize that they belonged to her and were a part of herself. She wanted an excellent and stylish fit, she told the young fellow who served her, and she did not mind the difference of a dollar or two more in the price so long as she got what she desired.

It was a long time since Mrs. Sommers had been fitted with gloves. On rare occasions when she had bought a pair they were always bargains, so cheap that it would have been preposterous and unreasonable to have expected them to be fitted to the hand.

Now she rested her elbow on the cushion of the glove counter, and a pretty, pleasant young creature, delicate and deft of touch, drew a long-wristed kid[6] over Mrs. Sommers' hand. She smoothed it down over the wrist and buttoned it neatly, and both lost themselves for a second or two in admiring contemplation of
5 the little symmetrical gloved hand. But there were other places where money might be spent.

There were books and magazines piled up in the window of a stall a few paces down the street. Mrs. Sommers bought two high-priced magazines such as she had been accustomed to read in the days when she had been accustomed to other pleasant things. She carried them without wrapping. As well as she could she lifted her skirts at the crossings. Her stockings and boots and well fitting gloves had

5. **tiara** [tē ar′ə]: woman's crownlike headdress.

6. **kid:** soft glove made of goatskin.

GUIDED READING

LITERAL QUESTION

1a. What kinds of magazines does she buy? (high-priced—the kind she used to read often)

INFERENTIAL QUESTION

1b. What do the magazines suggest about her motivation for spending the money on luxuries? (She may be trying to recapture the carefree happiness of her younger days; she may be trying to deny those circumstances that have caused her to go without "pleasant things.")

Detail, *The Black Hat,* Frank Benson, 1904.

AT A GLANCE

- Mrs. Sommers dines in an elegant restaurant and attends a play.
- Riding a cable car home, she wishes that the ride would never end.

1 CHARACTERIZATION

The change wrought by spending the money on herself shows not only Mrs. Sommers' desire for fine things but also the alienation she feels in not having them.

2 INTERNAL CONFLICT

Mrs. Sommers alternates between feeling like an imposter, as here, and feeling like the woman of leisure she once was.

3 SYMBOL

The silk stockings have come to stand for all the things Mrs. Sommers once had and has now been denied.

4 RESPONSE JOURNAL

Students may speculate as to whether Mrs. Sommers, having tasted "the good life," will successfully readjust to her life at home.

REFLECTING ON THE STORY

Would Mrs. Sommers ever have gone on such a spree if she had not touched the silk stockings? (Some students may argue that the stockings seduced her; others, that her desires would eventually have expressed themselves anyway.)

1 worked marvels in her bearing—had given her a feeling of assurance, a sense of belonging to the well-dressed multitude.

She was very hungry. Another time she would have stilled the cravings for food until reaching her own home, where she would have brewed herself a cup of tea and taken a snack of anything that was available. But the impulse that was guiding her would not suffer her to entertain any such thought.

There was a restaurant at the corner. She had never entered its doors; from the outside she had sometimes caught glimpses of spotless damask[7] and shining crystal, and soft-stepping waiters serving people of fashion.

2 When she entered her appearance created no surprise, no consternation, as she had half feared it might. She seated herself at a small table alone, and an attentive waiter at once approached to take her order. She did not want a profusion; she craved a nice and tasty bite—a half dozen blue-points,[8] a plump chop with cress, a something sweet—a crème-frappée,[9] for instance; a glass of Rhine wine, and after all a small cup of black coffee.

While waiting to be served she removed her gloves very leisurely and laid them beside her. Then she picked up a magazine and glanced through it, cutting the pages with a blunt edge of her knife.[10] It was all very agreeable. The damask was even more spotless than it had seemed through the window, and the crystal more sparkling. There were quiet ladies and gentlemen, who did not notice her, lunching at the small tables like her own. A soft, pleasing strain of music could be heard, and a gentle breeze was blowing through the win-
3 dow. She tasted a bite, and she read a word or two, and she sipped the amber wine and wiggled her toes in the silk stockings. The price of it made no difference. She counted the money out to the waiter and left an extra coin on his tray, whereupon he bowed before her as before a princess of royal blood.

There was still money in her purse, and her next temptation presented itself in the shape of a matinee poster.

It was a little later when she entered the theater, the play had begun and the house seemed to her to be packed. But there were vacant seats here and there, and into one of them she was ushered, between brilliantly dressed women who had gone there to kill time and eat candy and display their gaudy attire. There were many others who were there solely for the play and acting. It is safe to say there was no one present who bore quite the attitude which Mrs. Sommers did to her surroundings. She gathered in the whole—stage and players and people in one wide impression, and absorbed it and enjoyed it. She laughed at the comedy and wept—she and the gaudy woman next to her wept over the tragedy. And they talked a little together over it. And the gaudy woman wiped her eyes and sniffled on a tiny square of filmy, perfumed lace and passed little Mrs. Sommers her box of candy.

The play was over, the music ceased, the crowd filed out. It was like a dream ended. People scattered in all directions. Mrs. Sommers went to the corner and waited for the cable car.

A man with keen eyes, who sat opposite to her, seemed to like the study of her small, pale face. It puzzled him to decipher what he saw
4 there. In truth, he saw nothing—unless he were wizard enough to detect a poignant wish, a powerful longing that the cable car would never stop anywhere, but go on and on with her forever.

7. **damask** [dam′əsk]: durable, lustrous, reversible fabric, often used for table linen.
8. **blue-points:** oysters.
9. **crème-frappée** [krem fra pā′]: French for "whipped cream."
10. **cutting . . . knife:** The pages of certain elegant magazines had to be slit open at the outer edges by the reader.

GUIDED READING

LITERAL QUESTIONS

1a. What is Mrs. Sommers' fear as she enters the restaurant? (She fears being out of place or the object of stares.)

2a. At the end, what is Mrs. Sommers' wish? (She wishes that the cable car would never stop.)

INFERENTIAL QUESTIONS

1b. Why does she have this fear? (In part, she may be thinking that her clothes—despite the shoes, stockings, and gloves—are not fine enough; she probably also feels guilty and out of place and expects others to take note.)

2b. Why does she feel this way? (When the cable car stops, she has to return to her life of selflessness, penny-pinching, bargain counters, and unattractive clothes.)

STUDY QUESTIONS

Recalling

1. How does Mrs. Sommers feel about unexpectedly possessing fifteen dollars, according to the opening paragraph? According to the third paragraph, how does she plan to spend the money?
2. What do the neighbors say about Mrs. Sommers, according to the fourth paragraph? Why does Mrs. Sommers not indulge in such "morbid retrospection"?
3. On the day on which this story takes place, how does Mrs. Sommers feel (paragraph 6)? How is she resting her hand on the counter when "an all-gone limp feeling" comes over her (paragraph 7)?
4. How does Mrs. Sommers spend the fifteen dollars? As Mrs. Sommers takes the cable car home, what is her "poignant wish"?

Interpreting

5. Describe Mrs. Sommers' life as a wife and mother. Does her life seem to have been different before she married? If so, how was it different?
6. Does Mrs. Sommers buy the silk stockings deliberately—that is, calmly and with forethought? Explain.
7. Why is this day special for Mrs. Sommers? Why does she long for the cable car to "go on and on with her forever"? Why is this wish called "poignant"?

Extending

8. Do you consider Mrs. Sommers justified in thinking of her own needs and desires? Why or why not?

LITERARY FOCUS

Character Motivation

In order for fictional characters to appear true to life and to be interesting, they must act in ways that we can understand. That is, the writer must supply adequate **motivation**, stating or implying the reasons for their behavior. A character may surprise us, may act in an unexpected or inconsistent way, but we must be convinced that the action is plausible.

At the beginning of "A Pair of Silk Stockings," we are told that Mrs. Sommers is careful about the "proper and judicious use of money." Her entire past life leads us to expect her to act in a certain way—specifically, to spend her extra fifteen dollars on buying things for her children. We are surprised to discover that she spends the money on herself instead.

Kate Chopin never states *directly* why Mrs. Sommers changes her mind. Rather, the motivation is *implied.* For instance, we learn that Mrs. Sommers is tired and has eaten no lunch. "An all-gone limp feeling" overwhelms her just as she rests her hand upon a pile of silk stockings. At this point, her original plans for the money seem to vanish; her weariness and the smooth, pleasant sensation of the silk against her skin suddenly make her think of herself and her own wishes.

Since we have probably had similar experiences, we can imagine why Mrs. Sommers acts as she does. Although Kate Chopin does not name the reasons, she makes us feel that Mrs. Sommers is adequately motivated.

Thinking About Character Motivation

■ Choose another character from a story you have read in this book. What are the character's motives for action? Are they believable? Do any of the motives conflict with others?

COMPOSITION

Writing About Character

■ Write an essay about the character of Mrs. Sommers. Begin by discussing whether she is a flat character or a round one (see page 309). Then tell what we learn about the character by what she says, does, thinks, and feels. Describe her motivations and what they tell about the kind of woman she is. Conclude with your own opinion of the character.

Describing a Character's Movements

■ Much of this story depends on detailed descriptions of Mrs. Sommers' actions. Imagine a character in a situation. Then describe in detail the character's physical movements as he or she performs a single, specific action, such as painting a picture, watering a plant, or eating a meal.

STUDY QUESTIONS

1. important; clothes for children
2. had known better days; no time to devote to past
3. faint, tired; aimlessly
4. stockings, shoes, gloves, magazines, lunch, theater ticket; that the cable car would go on forever
5. life is hard, works in house and makes do with little, no mention of husband, friends; yes, better; was accustomed to finer things
6. No; her action is compulsive, arising out of deep, unexpressed need.
7. She has indulged herself; she does not want to return to drudgery or face the fact she wasted money; she realizes that her feelings on life will evermore be in conflict, while we feel compassion for her.
8. Some might say she needed to maintain her sense of self-worth; others will find her actions weak and selfish.

LITERARY FOCUS

Answers will vary. Possible answers: Reverend Hooper, "The Minister's Black Veil"; Oakhurst, "Outcasts of Poker Flat"; Sylvia, "White Heron"

COMPOSITION: GUIDELINES FOR EVALUATION

WRITING ABOUT CHARACTER

Objective

To analyze the character of Mrs. Sommers

Guidelines for Evaluation

- suggested length: four to six paragraphs
- should establish Mrs. Sommers as a round character; complex, contradictory
- should cite what we learn about her
- should cite conflict as basis of motivation
- should state writer's opinion of character

DESCRIBING A CHARACTER'S MOVEMENTS

Objective

To describe a character's movements

Guidelines for Evaluation

- suggested length: one to two paragraphs
- should focus on action rather than character's appearance or personality
- should use precise verbs and adverbs to describe a single, specific action
- should develop a single mood

Hamlin Garland *1860–1940*

Hamlin Garland grew up among poor farmers in the Midwest. He watched his family and friends move from farm to farm, from state to state, trying to make a living despite harsh economic conditions and a series of natural disasters. Garland himself fled the Midwest when he was in his twenties and settled in Boston to complete his education. On a visit home he was struck again by the poverty of rural America, and this world became the backdrop for most of his writing.

Working for East Coast journals, he produced from his memories of youth a series of stories depicting the everyday lives of simple midwestern farmers. The stories were gathered together in 1891 and published under the title *Main-Travelled Roads.* Other, similar collections followed soon after.

Garland was firmly convinced that fiction should be realistic and drawn from personal experience. In *Crumbling Idols* (1894), a collection of essays, he argues that truth in literature is best achieved by writers who flavor their stories with the "local color" of the region they know best. Many of Garland's later works are biographical. They include his autobiography, *A Son of the Middle Border* (1917), and the story of his wife's family, *A Daughter of the Middle Border* (1921), which won Garland the Pulitzer Prize.

Hand in hand with his concern for truth in literature was Garland's belief that literature could be a means of achieving economic and social reform. "Under the Lion's Paw," his most famous story, is written with a sense of outrage at the plight of the midwestern farmer. The tale is a far cry from the Romantic writings of Washington Irving and James Fenimore Cooper. With almost brutal realism, Garland brings to life the desperate situation of the struggling farmers and casts the harsh light of reality on the relationship between Americans and the land.

Model for Active Reading

In this selection, and in one selection in each unit, you will find notes in the right-hand margin that highlight parts of the selection. These notes point out important ideas of the period—in this case, Realist, Regionalist, and Naturalist ideas—and draw your attention to literary elements and techniques covered in the Literary Focuses. Page numbers in the notes will refer you to more extensive discussions of these important ideas and elements.

■ Has "life on the farm" really been the idyllic existence so often portrayed in movies and on television?

Hamlin Garland

Under the Lion's Paw

I

It was the last of autumn and first day of winter coming together. All day long the plowmen on their prairie farms had moved to and fro in their wide level fields through the falling snow, which melted as it fell, wetting them to the skin—all day, notwithstanding the frequent squalls of snow, the dripping, desolate clouds, and the muck of the furrows, black and tenacious as tar.

Under their dripping harness the horses swung to and fro silently, with that marvelous uncomplaining patience which marks the horse. All day the wild geese, honking wildly, as they sprawled sidewise down the wind, seemed to be fleeing from an enemy behind, and with neck outthrust and wings extended, sailed down the wind, soon lost to sight.

Yet the plowman behind his plow, though the snow lay on his ragged greatcoat, and the cold clinging mud rose on his heavy boots, fettering him like gyves,[1] whistled in the very beard of the gale. As day passed, the snow, ceasing to melt, lay along the plowed land, and lodged in the depth of the stubble, till on each slow round the last furrow stood out black and shining as jet[2] between the plowed land and the gray stubble.

When night began to fall, and the geese, flying low, began to alight invisibly in the near cornfield, Stephen Council was still at work "finishing a land."[3] He rode on his sulky plow[4] when going with the wind, but walked when facing it. Sitting bent and cold but cheery under his slouch hat, he talked encouragingly to his four-in-hand.[5]

"Come round there, boys!—Round agin! We got t' finish this land. Come in there, Dan! *Stiddy,* Kate,—stiddy! None o' y'r tantrums, Kittie. It's purty tuff, but got a be did. *Tchk! tchk!* Step along, Pete! Don't let Katie git y'r single-tree[6] on the wheel. *Once* more!"

They seemed to know what he meant, and that this was the last round, for they worked with greater vigor than before.

"Once more, boys, an' then, sez I, oats an' a nice warm stall, an' sleep f'r all."

By the time the last furrow was turned on the land it was too dark to see the house, and the snow was changing to rain again.

Mood (p. 148): Strings of adjectives help establish an atmosphere for the setting of the story.

Regionalist idea: Accurate descriptions of the characters' activities are important in capturing the "local color" of the region (p. 311).

Dialect (p. 311): Characters' conversation is written in the dialect of the region to support the "local color."

---

1. **gyves** [jīvz]: shackles, chains.
2. **jet:** velvet black, coallike mineral.
3. **"finishing a land":** completing work on a section of a farm.
4. **sulky plow:** plow having wheels and a driver's seat.
5. **four-in-hand:** team of four horses driven by one person.

AT A GLANCE

Plowing all day in mud, snow, and rain, farmer Stephen Council coaxes his horses good-naturedly.

LITERARY OPTIONS

- conflict
- mood
- characterization

THEMATIC OPTIONS

- human beings vs. nature
- the individual vs. society
- gains and losses

GUIDED READING

LITERAL QUESTIONS

1a. Under what conditions does Council work? (snow, rain, muck, and cold)

2a. Who are Council's companions? (geese and horses)

INFERENTIAL QUESTIONS

1b. What conflict do these details suggest? (human beings vs. nature)

2b. What does the fact that Council works alone suggest about his economic condition? (He is too poor to hire help.)

AT A GLANCE

- A stranger appears, asking lodging for his family.
- Council agrees, and Mrs. Council welcomes them in the kitchen with food and fire.

The tired and hungry man could see the light from the kitchen shining through the leafless hedge, and he lifted a great shout, "Supper f'r a half a dozen!"

It was nearly eight o'clock by the time he had finished his chores and started for supper. He was picking his way carefully through the mud, when the tall form of a man loomed up before him with a premonitory cough.

"Waddy ye want?" was the rather startled question of the farmer.

"Well, ye see," began the stranger, in a deprecating tone, "we'd like t' git in f'r the night. We've tried every house f'r the last two miles, but they hadn't any room f'r us. My wife's jest about sick, 'n' the children are cold and hungry—"

"Oh, y' want 'o stay all night, eh?"

"Yes, sir; it 'ud be a great accom—"

"Waal, I don't make it a practice t' turn anybuddy way hungry, not on sech nights as this. Drive right in. We ain't got much, but sech as it is—"

But the stranger had disappeared. And soon his steaming, weary team, with drooping heads and swinging single-trees, moved past the well to the block beside the path. Council stood at the side of the schooner[7] and helped the children out—two little half-sleeping children—and then a small woman with a babe in her arms.

"There ye go!" he shouted jovially, to the children. "*Now* we're all right! Run right along to the house there, an' tell Mam' Council you wants sumpthin' t' eat. Right this way, Mis'—keep right off t' the right there. I'll go an' git a lantern. Come," he said to the dazed and silent group at his side.

"Mother," he shouted, as he neared the fragrant and warmly lighted kitchen, "here are some wayfarers an' folks who need sumpthin' t' eat an' a place t' snooze." He ended by pushing them all in.

Mrs. Council, a large, jolly, rather coarse-looking woman, took the children in her arms. "Come right in, you little rabbits. 'Most asleep, hey? Now here's a drink o' milk f'r each o' ye. I'll have s'm tea in a minute. Take off y'r things and set up t' the fire."

While she set the children to drinking milk, Council got out his lantern and went out to the barn to help the stranger about his team, where his loud, hearty voice could be heard as it came and went between the haymow and the stalls.

The woman came to light as a small, timid, and discouraged-looking woman, but still pretty, in a thin and sorrowful way.

"Land sakes! An' you've traveled all the way from Clear Lake

---

6. **single-tree:** pivoted swinging bar to which the traces of a harness are fastened and by which a vehicle is pulled.
7. **schooner:** prairie schooner, a broad-wheeled covered wagon.

GUIDED READING

LITERAL QUESTIONS

1a. What does the stranger want of Council? (shelter for the night)

2a. As he and the stranger near the kitchen, what does Council do? (tells his wife some wayfarers need food and beds)

INFERENTIAL QUESTIONS

1b. What does the strangers' plight suggest about the times? (Adversity seems widespread.)

2b. What does Mrs. Council's response reveal about her character? (She is warm, sympathetic, and generous.)

t'-day in this mud! Waal! waal! No wonder you're all tired out. Don't wait f'r the men, Mis'—" She hesitated, waiting for the name.

"Haskins."

"Mis' Haskins, set right up to the table an' take a good swig o' tea whilst I make y' s'm toast. It's green tea, an' it's good. I tell Council as I git older I don't seem to enjoy Young Hyson n'r Gunpowder.[8] I want the reel green tea, jest as it comes off'n the vines. Seems t'have more heart in it, some way. Don't s'pose it has. Council says it's all in m' eye." Going on in this easy way, she soon had the children filled with bread and milk and the woman thoroughly at home, eating some toast and sweetmelon pickles, and sipping the tea.

"See the little rats!" she laughed at the children. "They're full as they can stick now, and they want to go to bed. Now, don't git up, Mis' Haskins; set right where you are an' let me look after 'em. I know all about young ones, though I'm all alone now. Jane went an' married last fall. But, as I tell Council, it's lucky we keep our health. Set right there, Mis' Haskins; I won't have you stir a finger."

It was an unmeasured pleasure to sit there in the warm, homely kitchen, the jovial chatter of the housewife driving out and holding at bay the growl of the impotent, cheated wind.

Realist idea: Realistic fiction turned from the Romantic emphasis on the strange toward a faithful rendering of the ordinary (p. 310).

The little woman's eyes filled with tears which fell down upon the sleeping baby in her arms. The world was not so desolate and cold and hopeless, after all.

"Now I hope Council won't stop out there and talk politics all night. He's the greatest man to talk politics an' read the *Tribune*—How old is it?"

She broke off and peered down at the face of the babe.

"Two months 'n' five days," said the mother, with a mother's exactness.

"Ye don't say! I want 'o know! The dear little pudzy-wudzy!" she went on, stirring it up in the neighborhood of the ribs with her fat forefinger. "Pooty tough on 'oo to go galivant'n' 'cross lots this way—"

"Yes, that's so; a man can't lift a mountain," said Council, entering the door. "Mother, this is Mr. Haskins, from Kansas. He's been eat up 'n' drove out by grasshoppers."

"Glad t' see yeh!—Pa, empty that washbasin 'n' give him a chance t' wash."

Haskins was a tall man, with a thin, gloomy face. His hair was a reddish brown, like his coat, and seemed equally faded by the wind and sun, and his sallow face, though hard and set, was pathetic somehow. You would have felt that he had suffered much by the line of his mouth showing under his thin, yellow mustache.

8. **Young Hyson . . . Gunpowder:** types of Chinese green tea.

AT A GLANCE

- The Councils care for the hungry Haskins family, who in turn are greatly touched by their generosity.
- Haskins tells Council he has come from Kansas, where grasshoppers devastated his crops.

GUIDED READING

LITERAL QUESTION

1a. What happened to the Haskins family in Kansas? (They were "eat up 'n' drove out by grasshoppers.")

INFERENTIAL QUESTION

1b. What does this information reveal about the farmer's lot at that time? (Farming was highly risky, subject to natural disasters.)

AT A GLANCE

Haskins tells of his four-year losing battle with grasshoppers.

"Hain't Ike got home yet, Sairy?"

"Hain't seen 'im."

"W-a-a-l, set right up, Mr. Haskins; wade right into what we've got; 'tain't much, but we manage to live on it—she gits fat on it," laughed Council, pointing his thumb at his wife.

After supper, while the women put the children to bed, Haskins and Council talked on, seated near the huge cooking stove, the steam rising from their wet clothing. In the Western fashion Council told as much of his own life as he drew from his guest. He asked but few questions, but by and by the story of Haskins' struggles and defeat came out. The story was a terrible one, but he told it quietly, seated with his elbows on his knees, gazing most of the time at the hearth.

"I didn't like the looks of the country, anyhow," Haskins said, partly rising and glancing at his wife. "I was ust t' northern Ingyannie,[9] where we have lots o' timber 'n' lots o' rain, 'n' I didn't like the looks o' that dry prairie. What galled me the worst was goin' s' far away acrosst so much fine land layin' all through here vacant."

"And the 'hoppers eat ye four years, hand runnin', did they?"

"Eat! They wiped us out. They chawed everything that was green. They jest set around waitin' f'r us to die t' eat us, too. My God! I ust t' dream of 'em sittin' 'round on the bedpost, six feet long, workin' their jaws. They eet the fork handles. They got worse 'n' worse till they jest rolled on one another, piled up like snow in winter. Well, it ain't no use. If I was t' talk all winter I couldn't tell nawthin'. But all the while I couldn't help thinkin' of all that land back here that nobuddy was usin' that I ought 'o had 'stead o' bein' out there in that cussed country."

Naturalist idea: People are shown struggling with forces of nature that are beyond their control (p. 311).

"Waal, why didn't ye stop an' settle here?" asked Ike, who had come in and was eating his supper.

"Fer the simple reason that you fellers wantid ten 'r fifteen dollars an acre fer the bare land, and I hadn't no money fer that kind o' thing."

"Yes, I do my own work," Mrs. Council was heard to say in the pause that followed. "I'm a-gettin' purty heavy t' be on m' laigs all day, but we can't afford t' hire, so I keep rackin' around somehow, like a foundered horse. S' lame—I tell Council he can't tell how lame I am, f'r I'm jest as lame in one laig as t' other." And the good soul laughed at the joke on herself as she took a handful of flour and dusted the biscuit board to keep the dough from sticking.

"Well, I hain't *never* been very strong," said Mrs. Haskins. "Our folks was Canadians an' small-boned, and then since my last child I hain't got up again fairly. I don't like t' complain. Tim has about all he can bear now—but they was days this week when I jes wanted to lay right down an' die."

9. **Ingyannie** [in' gē an'ē]: dialect form of *Indiana.*

GUIDED READING

LITERAL QUESTION

1a. What does Haskins most regret about his hardships? (He might have avoided them by buying better land.)

INFERENTIAL QUESTION

1b. What does Haskins' glance at his wife suggest? (Perhaps he bought the Kansas land to please her.)

AT A GLANCE

Council suggests that Haskins rent a rundown farm from Jim Butler, a hard-working grocer turned land speculator.

"Waal, now, I'll tell ye," said Council, from his side of the stove, silencing everybody with his good-natured roar, "I'd go down and *see* Butler, *anyway,* if I was you. I guess he'd let you have his place purty cheap; the farm's all run down. He's ben anxious t' let t' somebuddy next year. It 'ud be a good chance fer you. Anyhow, you go to bed and sleep like a babe. I've got some plowin' t' do, anyhow, an' we'll see if somethin' can't be done about your case. Ike, you go out an' see if the horses is all right, an' I'll show the folks t' bed."

When the tired husband and wife were lying under the generous quilts of the spare bed, Haskins listened a moment to the wind in the eaves, and then said, with a slow and solemn tone, "There are people in this world who are good enough t' be angels, an' only haff t' die to *be* angels."

II

Flat character (p. 323): Butler is "one of those men"—that is, he is a stereotype.

Jim Butler was one of those men called in the West "land poor."[10] Early in the history of Rock River he had come into the town and started in the grocery business in a small way, occupying a small building in a mean[11] part of the town. At this period of his life he earned all he got, and was up early and late sorting beans, working over butter, and carting his goods to and from the station. But a change came over him at the end of the second year, when he sold a lot of land for four times what he paid for it. From that time forward he believed in land speculation[12] as the surest way of

10. **"land poor":** owning land but having little money.
11. **mean:** poor.
12. **land speculation:** buying and selling land for a profit.

GUIDED READING

LITERAL QUESTION

1a. How does Haskins characterize the Councils to his wife? (They are "good enough to be angels.")

INFERENTIAL QUESTION

1b. Why would he think this? (Poor themselves, the Councils are still generous and helpful to those who are in worse straits.)

AT A GLANCE

- Butler has acquired many farms by means of forced sales or mortgages.
- He usually retains former owners as tenants.
- Council encourages Haskins to bargain shrewdly with Butler for the purchase of Higley's failed farm.

getting rich. Every cent he could save or spare from his trade he put into land at forced sale,[13] or mortgages on land, which were "just as good as the wheat," he was accustomed to say.

Farm after farm fell into his hands, until he was recognized as one of the leading landowners of the county. His mortgages were scattered all over Cedar County, and as they slowly but surely fell in he sought usually to retain the former owner as tenant.

He was not ready to foreclose; indeed, he had the name of being one of the "easiest" men in the town. He let the debtor off again and again, extending the time whenever possible.

"I don't want y'r land," he said. "All I'm after is the int'rest on my money—that's all. Now, if y' want 'o stay on the farm, why, I'll give y' a good chance. I can't have the land layin' vacant." And in many cases the owner remained as tenant.

In the meantime he had sold his store; he couldn't spend time in it; he was mainly occupied now with sitting around town on rainy days smoking and "gassin' with the boys," or in riding to and from his farms. In fishing time he fished a good deal. Doc Grimes, Ben Ashley, and Cal Cheatham were his cronies on these fishing excursions or hunting trips in the time of chickens or partridges. In winter they went to northern Wisconsin to shoot deer.

In spite of all these signs of easy life Butler persisted in saying he "hadn't enough money to pay taxes on his land," and was careful to convey the impression that he was poor in spite of his twenty farms. At one time he was said to be worth fifty thousand dollars, but land had been a little slow of sale of late, so that he was not worth so much.

A fine farm, known as the Higley place, had fallen into his hands in the usual way the previous year, and he had not been able to find a tenant for it. Poor Higley, after working himself nearly to death on it in the attempt to lift the mortgage, had gone off to Dakota, leaving the farm and his curse to Butler. This was the farm which Council advised Haskins to apply for; and the next day Council hitched up his team and drove down town to see Butler.

"You jest let *me* do the talkin'," he said. "We'll find him wearin' out his pants on some salt barrel somew'ers; and if he thought you *wanted* a place he'd sock it to you hot and heavy. You jest keep quiet; I'll fix 'im."

Round character (p. 323): Stephen Council is a "rounder" character than Butler, with more facets to his personality.

Butler was seated in Ben Ashley's store telling fish yarns when Council sauntered in casually.

"Hello, But; lyin' agin, hey!"

"Hello, Steve! how goes it?"

"Oh, so-so. Too dang much rain these days. I thought it was goin' t' freeze up f'r good last night. Tight squeak if I get m' plowin' done. How's farmin' with *you* these days?"

---

13. **forced sale:** buying cheaply from someone who is forced to sell.

GUIDED READING

LITERAL QUESTIONS

1a. Why is Butler known as "easy"? (He is slow to foreclose, tries to keep the original owners as tenants.)

2a. How does Council advise Haskins to act with Butler? (keep quiet and let Council do the talking)

INFERENTIAL QUESTIONS

1b. Why is Butler slow to foreclose? (As he waits, the land increases in value.)

2b. What facets of Council's character does this advice reveal? (He is shrewd and benevolent, helpful and resourceful.)

"Bad. Plowin' ain't half done."

"It 'ud be a religious idee f'r you t' go out an' take a hand y'rself."

"I don't haff to," said Butler, with a wink.

"Got anybody on the Higley place?"

"No. Know anybody?"

"Waal, no; not eggsackly. I've got a relation back t' Michigan who's ben hot an' cold on the idee o' comin' West f'r some time. *Might* come if he could get a good layout. What do you talk on the farm?"

"Well, I d'know. I'll rent it on shares or I'll rent it money rent."

"Waal, how much money, say?"

"Well, say ten per cent, on the price—two-fifty."

"Waal, that ain't bad. Wait on 'im till 'e thrashes?"[14]

Haskins listened eagerly to his important question, but Council was coolly eating a dried apple which he had speared out of a barrel with his knife. Butler studied him carefully.

"Well, knocks me out of twenty-five dollars interest."

"My relation'll need all he's got t' git his crops in," said Council, in the safe, indifferent way.

"Well, all right; *say* wait," concluded Butler.

"All right; this is the man. Haskins, this is Mr. Butler—no relation to Ben—the hardest-working man in Cedar County."

On the way home Haskins said: "I ain't much better off. I'd like that farm; it's a good farm, but it's all run down, an' so 'm I. I could make a good farm of it if I had half a show. But I can't stock it n'r seed it."

"Waal, now, don't you worry," roared Council in his ear. "We'll pull y' through somehow till next harvest. He's agreed t' hire it plowed, an' you can earn a hundred dollars plowin' an' y' c'n git the seed o' me, an' pay me back when y' can."

Haskins was silent with emotion, but at last he said, "I ain't got nothin' t' live on."

"Now, don't you worry 'bout that. You jest make your headquarters at ol' Steve Council's. Mother'll take a pile o' comfort in havin' y'r wife an' children 'round. Y' see, Jane's married off lately, an' Ike's away a good 'eal, so we'll be darn glad t' have y' stop with us this winter. Nex' spring we'll see if y' can't git a start agin." And he chirruped to the team, which sprang forward with the rumbling, clattering wagon.

"Say, looky here, Council, you can't do this. I never saw—" shouted Haskins in his neighbor's ear.

Council moved about uneasily in his seat and stopped his stammering gratitude by saying: "Hold on now: don't make such a fuss over a little thing. When I see a man down, an' things all on top

14. **Wait . . . thrashes:** await rent payment until the harvest is in.

Point of view (p. 333): Garland uses the omniscient point of view, and so the narrator has the freedom to tell how any of the characters are reacting.

AT A GLANCE

- Council maneuvers Butler into renting Haskins the farm and awaiting payment until harvest.
- Council offers Haskins seed and a winter home.

GUIDED READING

LITERAL QUESTIONS

1a. Initially, whom does Council propose as a tenant? (an undecided Michigan relative)

2a. Why is Haskins doubtful about the bargain? (The farm is run-down, and he has no money.)

INFERENTIAL QUESTIONS

1b. Why does he begin in this way? (to strike a better bargain by not seeming eager)

2b. What does Council's response reveal about his character? (generosity and tact about offering his charity)

AT A GLANCE

- Haskins, overcome with gratitude toward the Councils for their neighborly spirit, promises to repay them in time.
- Council says accepting repayment is against his religion.
- By June the house is mended, the lawn is seeded, and the garden is planted.

of'm, I jest like t' kick 'em off an' help 'm up. That's the kind of religion I got, an' it's about the *only* kind."

They rode the rest of the way home in silence. And when the red light of the lamp shone out into the darkness of the cold and windy night, and he thought of this refuge for his children and wife, Haskins could have put his arm around the neck of his burly companion and squeezed him like a lover. But he contented himself with saying, "Steve Council, you'll git y'r pay f'r this some day."

"Don't want any pay. My religion ain't run on such business principles."

The wind was growing colder, and the ground was covered with a white frost, as they turned into the gate of the Council farm, and the children came rushing out, shouting, "Papa's come!" They hardly looked like the same children who had sat at the table the night before. Their torpidity, under the influence of sunshine and Mother Council, had given way to a sort of spasmodic cheerfulness, as insects in winter revive when laid on the hearth.

III

Haskins worked like a fiend, and his wife, like the heroic woman that she was, bore also uncomplainingly the most terrible burdens. They rose early and toiled without intermission till the darkness fell on the plain, then tumbled into bed, every bone and muscle aching with fatigue, to rise with the sun next morning to the same round of the same ferocity of labor.

The eldest boy drove a team all through the spring, plowing and seeding, milked the cows, and did chores innumerable, in most ways taking the place of a man.

An infinitely pathetic but common figure, this boy on the American farm, where there is no law against child labor. To see him in his coarse clothing, his huge boots, and his ragged cap, as he staggered with a pail of water from the well, or trudged in the cold and cheerless dawn out into the frosty field behind his team, gave the city-bred visitor a sharp pang of sympathetic pain. Yet Haskins loved his boy, and would have saved him from this if he could, but he could not.

Point of view (p. 333): The omniscient narrator can intrude on the story with a general comment, as Garland does here

By June the first year the result of such Herculean[15] toil began to show on the farm. The yard was cleaned up and sown to grass, the garden plowed and planted, and the house mended.

Council had given them four of his cows.

"Take 'em an' run 'em on shares. I don't want 'o milk s' many. Ike's away s' much now, Sat'd'ys an' Sund'ys, I can't stand the bother anyhow."

15. **Herculean** [hur′kyə lē′ən]: requiring great strength; referring to the Greek hero Hercules.

GUIDED READING

LITERAL QUESTIONS

1a. Why doesn't Council want pay for his kindness? (His religion isn't run on business principles.)

2a. Who does the plowing, seeding, and milking? (the oldest Haskins boy)

INFERENTIAL QUESTIONS

1b. What is Council's "religion"? (helping those in need)

2b. In what sense is he a "common figure"? (Most children of farmers have to work hard.)

Other men, seeing the confidence of Council in the newcomer, had sold him tools on time; and as he was really an able farmer, he soon had round him many evidences of his care and thrift. At the advice of Council he had taken the farm for three years, with the privilege of re-renting or buying at the end of the term.

"It's a good bargain, an' y' want 'o nail it," said Council. "If you have any kind ov a crop, you c'n pay y'r debts, an' keep seed an' bread."

The new hope which now sprang up in the heart of Haskins and his wife grew great almost as a pain by the time the wide field of wheat began to wave and swirl in the winds of July. Day after day he would snatch a few moments after supper to go and look at it.

"Have ye seen the wheat t'-day, Nettie?" he asked one night as he rose from supper.

"No, Tim, I ain't had time."

"Well, take time now. Le's go look at it."

She threw an old hat on her head—Tommy's hat—and looking almost pretty in her thin, sad way, went out with her husband to the hedge.

"Ain't it grand, Nettie? Just look at it."

It was grand. Level, russet here and there, heavy-headed, wide as a lake, and full of multitudinous whispers and gleams of wealth, it stretched away before the gazers like the fabled field of the cloth of gold.[16]

"Oh, I think—I *hope* we'll have a good crop, Tim; and oh, how good the people have been to us!"

"Yes; I don't know where we'd be t'-day if it hadn't ben f'r Council and his wife."

"They're the best people in the world," said the little woman, with a great sob of gratitude.

"We'll be in the field on Monday, sure," said Haskins, gripping the rail on the fence as if already at the work of the harvest.

The harvest came, bounteous, glorious, but the winds came and blew it into tangles, and the rain matted it here and there close to the ground, increasing the work of gathering it threefold.

Oh, how they toiled in those glorious days! Clothing dripping with sweat, arms aching, filled with briers, fingers raw and bleeding, backs broken with the weight of heavy bundles, Haskins and his man toiled on. Tommy drove the harvester, while his father and a hired man bound on the machine. In this way they cut ten acres every day, and almost every night after supper, when the hand went to bed, Haskins returned to the field shocking the bound grain in the light of the moon. Many a night he worked till his anxious wife came out at ten o'clock to call him in to rest and lunch.

Realist idea: Middle- and lower-class people are often the subjects of Realistic fiction, and the writer takes their lives as seriously as the lives of the rich and powerful (p. 310).

16. **field . . . gold:** place in France where French King François I met the English King Henry VIII in 1520; a magnificent spectacle.

AT A GLANCE

- Haskins wins the respect of other farmers, who cheerfully do business with him.
- Haskins takes the farm for three years with the option to renew the lease or purchase.
- The abundant wheat harvest is glorious.

GUIDED READING

LITERAL QUESTIONS

1a. What grew "great almost as a pain"? (new hope)

2a. What does the wheat field resemble? ("the fabled field of the cloth of gold")

INFERENTIAL QUESTIONS

1b. Why would hope be painful? (After their former defeat, the Haskins rightfully fear failure.)

2b. Why do the gazers see it this way? (It is beautiful; gold stands for wealth; proceeds from the harvest may buy the farm.)

AT A GLANCE

- The Haskins' vivid memories of hunger and homelessness spur them on with their ferocious labor.
- After a year's time, Butler visits them and notes how his property has gained in value.

At the same time she cooked for the men, took care of the children, washed and ironed, milked the cows at night, made the butter, and sometimes fed the horses and watered them while her husband kept at the shocking.

No slave in the Roman galleys[17] could have toiled so frightfully and lived, for this man thought himself a free man, and that he was working for his wife and babes.

When he sank into his bed with a deep groan of relief, too tired to change his grimy, dripping clothing, he felt that he was getting nearer and nearer to a home of his own, and pushing the wolf of want a little farther from his door.

Character motivation (p. 339): Garland explains why Tim Haskins works so hard.

There is no despair so deep as the despair of a homeless man or woman. To roam the roads of the country or the streets of the city, to feel there is no rood of ground on which the feet can rest, to halt weary and hungry outside lighted windows and hear laughter and song within—these are the hungers and rebellions that drive men to crime and women to shame.

It was the memory of this homelessness, and the fear of its coming again, that spurred Timothy Haskins and Nettie, his wife, to such ferocious labor during that first year.

IV

" 'M, yes; 'm, yes; first rate," said Butler, as his eye took in the neat garden, the pigpen, and the well-filled barnyard. "You're gitt'n quite a stock around yeh. Done well, eh?"

Haskins was showing Butler around the place. He had not seen it for a year, having spent the year in Washington and Boston with Ashley, his brother-in-law, who had been elected to Congress.

"Yes, I've laid out a good deal of money durin' the last three years. I've paid out three hundred dollars f'r fencin'."

"Um—h'm! I see, I see," said Butler while Haskins went on:

"The kitchen there costs two hundred; the barn ain't cost much in money, but I've put a lot o' time on it. I've dug a new well, and I—".

"Yes, yes, I see. You've done well. Stock worth a thousand dollars," said Butler, picking his teeth with a straw.

"About that," said Haskins, modestly. "We begin to feel 's if we was gitt'n a home f'r ourselves; but we've worked hard. I tell you we begin to feel it, Mr. Butler, and we're goin' t' begin to ease up purty soon. We've been kind o' plannin' a trip back t' *her* folks after the fall plowin's done."

"*Eggs*-actly!" said Butler, who was evidently thinking of something else. "I suppose you've kind o' calc'lated on stayin' here three years more?"

---

17. **Roman galleys:** ancient ships propelled by slaves chained to rows of oars.

GUIDED READING

LITERAL QUESTIONS

1a. To what does Garland compare Haskins' labor? (the toil of a Roman galley slave)

2a. What does Butler ask when he first sees the place? ("Done well, eh?")

INFERENTIAL QUESTIONS

1b. Why does Haskins feel otherwise? (He labors, not for a despot, but for his land and family.)

2b. What conflict does the men's exchange suggest? (Each expects gain.)

"Well, yes. Fact is, I think I c'n buy the farm this fall, if you'll give me a reasonable show."

"Um—m! What do you call a reasonable show?"

"Well, say a quarter down and three years' time."

Butler looked at the huge stacks of wheat, which filled the yard, over which the chickens were fluttering and crawling, catching grasshoppers, and out of which the crickets were singing innumerably. He smiled in a peculiar way as he said, "Oh, I won't be hard on yeh. But what did you expect to pay f'r the place?"

Regionalist idea: Accurate descriptions of the physical environment are important in capturing "local color" (p. 311).

"Why, about what you offered it for before, two thousand, five hundred, or *possibly* three thousand dollars," he added quickly as he saw the owner shake his head.

"This farm is worth five thousand and five hundred dollars," said Butler, in a careless and decided voice.

"What!" almost shrieked the astounded Haskins. "What's this? Five thousand? Why that's double what you offered it for three years ago."

"Of course, and it's worth it. It was all run down then; now it's in good shape. You've laid out fifteen hundred dollars in improvements, according to your own story."

"But *you* had nothin' t' do about that. It's my work an' my money."

"You bet it was; but it's my land."

"But what's to pay me for all my—"

"Ain't you had the use of 'em?" replied Butler, smiling calmly into his face.

Haskins was like a man struck on the head with a sandbag; he couldn't think; he stammered as he tried to say: "But—I never'd git the use—You'd rob me! More'n that: you agreed—you promised that I could buy or rent at the end of three years at—"

"That's all right. But I didn't say I'd let you carry off the improvements, nor that I'd go on renting the farm at two-fifty. The land is doubled in value, it don't matter how; it don't enter into the question; an' now you can pay me five hundred dollars a year rent, or take it on your own terms at fifty-five hundred, or—git out."

He was turning away when Haskins, the sweat pouring from his face, fronted him, saying again:

"But *you've* done nothing to make it so. You hain't added a cent. I put it all there myself, expectin' to buy. I worked an' sweat to improve it. I was workin' for myself an' babes—"

"Well, why didn't you buy when I offered to sell? What y' kickin' about?"

"I'm kickin' about payin' you twice f'r my own things—my own fences, my own kitchen, my own garden."

Butler laughed. "You're too green t'eat, young feller. *Your* improvements! The law will sing another tune."

AT A GLANCE

- Haskins asks to buy, and Butler says improvements have doubled the value.
- When Haskins protests that the improvements are his own, Butler remains unmoved and says the law won't agree with Haskins.

GUIDED READING

LITERAL QUESTIONS

1a. Why does Butler double the price? (The improvements have doubled the property value.)

2a. When Haskins objects to paying for his own improvements, what does Butler say? ("The law will sing a different tune.")

INFERENTIAL QUESTIONS

1b. What does this demand reveal about Butler? (his dishonesty in profiting from others' misfortunes, labors, and dreams)

2b. What do you think he means by this? (He has powerful connections and unjust laws to support him.)

AT A GLANCE

Faced with losing all he has worked for or paying the thief, Haskins grabs a fork to kill him. But he sees his baby, stops, agrees to pay, runs Butler off his land, and collapses in defeat.

REFLECTING ON THE SELECTION

What extremes of human nature does this story portray? (the angelic goodness of the Councils and the manipulative greed of Butler)

"But I trusted your word."

"Never trust anybody, my friend. Besides, I didn't promise not to do this thing. Why, man, don't look at me like that. Don't take me for a thief. It's the law. The reg'lar thing. Everybody does it."

"I don't care if they do. It's stealin' jest the same. You take three thousand dollars of my money—the work o' my hands and my wife's." He broke down at this point. He was not a strong man mentally. He could face hardship, ceaseless toil, but he could not face the cold and sneering face of Butler.

"But I don't take it," said Butler, coolly. "All you've got to do is to go on jest as you've been a-doin', or give me a thousand dollars down, and a mortgage at ten per cent on the rest."

Haskins sat down blindly on a bundle of oats near by, and with staring eyes and drooping head went over the situation. He was under the lion's paw. He felt a horrible numbness in his heart and limbs. He was hid in a mist, and there was no path out.

Naturalist idea: In Naturalist fiction people are often caught within forces of society that are beyond their understanding and control (p. 311).

Butler walked about, looking at the huge stacks of grain, and pulling now and again a few handfuls out, shelling the heads in his hands and blowing the chaff away. He hummed a little tune as he did so. He had an accommodating air of waiting.

Haskins was in the midst of the terrible toil of the last year. He was walking again in the rain and the mud behind his plow; he felt the dust and dirt of the threshing. The ferocious husking time, with its cutting wind and biting, clinging snows, lay hard upon him. Then he thought of his wife, how she had cheerfully cooked and baked, without holiday and without rest.

"Well, what do you think of it?" inquired the cool, mocking, insinuating voice of Butler.

"I think you're a thief and a liar!" shouted Haskins, leaping up. "A blackhearted houn'!" Butler's smile maddened him; with a sudden leap he caught a fork in his hands, and whirled it in the air. "You'll never rob another man!" he grated through his teeth, a look of pitiless ferocity in his accusing eyes.

Butler shrank and quivered, expecting the blow; stood, held hypnotized by the eyes of the man he had a moment before despised—a man transformed into an avenging demon. But in the deadly hush between the lift of the weapon and its fall there came a gush of faint, childish laughter and then across the range of his vision, far away and dim, he saw the sunbright head of his baby girl, as with the pretty, tottering run of a two-year-old, she moved across the grass of the dooryard. His hands relaxed; the fork fell to the ground; his head lowered.

"Make out y'r deed an' mor'gage, an' git off'n my land, an' don't ye never cross my line again; if y' do, I'll kill ye."

Butler backed away from the man in wild haste, and climbing into his buggy with trembling limbs drove off down the road, leaving Haskins seated dumbly on the sunny piles of sheaves, his head sunk into his hands.

GUIDED READING

LITERAL QUESTIONS

1a. How does Garland describe Haskins' situation? (He is under the lion's paw.)

2a. What stops Haskins from killing Butler? (the sight of his baby)

INFERENTIAL QUESTIONS

1b. What do you think this expression means? (Trapped by a superior force, he cannot fight or flee.)

2b. Why do you think this stops him? (He would be imprisoned for the crime, leaving his dependents helpless.)

STUDY QUESTIONS

Recalling

1. According to the opening paragraph, under what conditions do the plowmen work all day? Whom does Stephen Council encounter as he picks his way home through the mud for dinner?
2. What natural disaster drove the Haskins family from Kansas?
3. Why does Stephen Council take Haskins to meet Jim Butler? How does Council attempt to outsmart Butler?
4. Who helps Tim Haskins work the farm? In what ways does Stephen Council give assistance?
5. When Butler sees the improvements that the Haskins family have made on the farm, what does he do?
6. What does Haskins do when he realizes that he is "under the lion's paw" (page 352)? What makes him abandon his violent impulses, and, consequently, what does he say and do?

Interpreting

7. What do the adjectives in the first four paragraphs of the story suggest about the realities of turn-of-the-century midwestern farming? What do the descriptions of the horse and geese help emphasize?
8. Why does Council help the Haskins family? Why does Butler help them?
9. In what struggle common in Naturalist literature (see page 311) is Haskins finally victorious? In what struggle is he the loser?

Extending

10. Can you identify with the characters of this story despite its Regionalism? In what way are the problems of turn-of-the-century midwestern farmers similar to many peoples' problems today?

VIEWPOINT

Robert E. Spiller, writing of Hamlin Garland's *Main-Travelled Roads* and its sequel, *Prairie Folks,* says that the stories

> tell of the unadorned hardships, lightened by occasional small pleasures and made meaningful by the power of nature, that fill the lives of the people of . . . the prairie.
>
> —*Literary History of the United States*

■ Find instances in "Under the Lion's Paw" of small pleasures that lighten the burden of the farmers. Do you agree that the power of nature makes the farmers' hardships more meaningful? Why or why not?

COMPOSITION

Writing About Literature and Its Period

■ Write a brief essay that begins with this statement: "'Under the Lion's Paw' typifies the literature of its period." List at least three reasons (consider the content, the style, and the tone of the story), and support them with quotations and specific details from the story. *For help with this assignment, refer to Lesson 10 in the Writing About Literature Handbook at the back of this book.*

Writing an Editorial

■ Many of the economic practices that Garland attacks were also criticized by the "muckraking" journalists of his day. Write a newspaper editorial in which you condemn a specific economic or social practice that you feel is unjust. Support your opinion with facts and examples, and end with a recommendation of how the situation should be remedied. You might examine editorials in a local newspaper for ideas. Be sure to balance the emotional appeal of your editorial with a clear, logical, and persuasive argument.

STUDY QUESTIONS

1. snow, muck; Tim Haskins
2. Grasshoppers had destroyed their crops.
3. rent farm; postpone payment until harvest, rent farm plowed
4. wife, son; seed, cows, shelter
5. doubles price for farm
6. goes to kill Butler; seeing his daughter, agrees to terms, head sinks into his hands
7.
   - demanding, grueling
   - Description of horses suggests that farmer must be like them: uncomplaining, patient.
   - Geese description suggests a freer world beyond the farmer's toil.
8. generosity; desire for profit
9. against nature; against society
10. Answers will vary, but students should identify with the desperation and determination of the family and with the Councils' generosity.

VIEWPOINT

- Pleasures: Council's relationship with horses, companionship and conversation over food, pride of bountiful harvest
- Some might think "bounteous, glorious" power of nature makes life meaningful; others may find the farmer's toil to harness nature dehumanizing.

COMPOSITION: GUIDELINES FOR EVALUATION

WRITING ABOUT LITERATURE AND ITS PERIOD

Objective

To prove Garland typifies literature of period

Guidelines for Evaluation

- suggested length: four paragraphs
- should begin with thesis statement
- should discuss Garland's Naturalist style
- should discuss tone of sympathy for farmers
- should cite specific supporting details

WRITING AN EDITORIAL

Objective

To take a stand and support it

Guidelines for Evaluation

- suggested length: two paragraphs
- should focus on a controversial issue, assume a clear position on controversy
- should use facts, examples, cogent reasoning
- should avoid overly emotional appeals
- should conclude with a logical solution

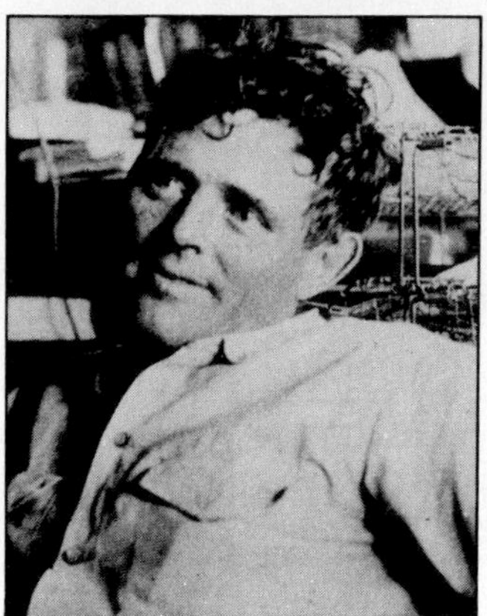

Jack London *1876–1916*

Few American writers knew working-class life as well as Jack London did, and few have written about it with London's immediacy. London's early years were spent in poverty. He had little formal education and worked at a series of odd jobs as he wandered about America and the rest of the world. Arrested for vagrancy near Buffalo, New York, London spent a month in jail. This was the turning point in his life.

London decided that he must have an education, and he worked hard to complete high school. He then attended the University of California for a few months but was lured away by the great Klondike Gold Rush of 1897–1898. Returning from Alaska empty-handed, London attempted to earn a living by setting his adventures down on paper. With the publication of *The Call of the Wild* in 1903, his fortunes changed dramatically: The struggling young writer suddenly became the highest-paid author in America. *The Sea Wolf* (1904) and *White Fang* (1906) were equally successful and, like *The Call of the Wild,* are still widely read today.

London's reading, and his sympathies with what he saw as an oppressed working class, made him an ardent believer in the necessity of social reform. Many of his books reflect his political ideas and deal with the struggle between opposing forces. Often London sets his conflicts in the great outdoors, where a human being struggles against the harsh laws of nature.

From his youth Jack London had learned that life is a struggle for survival; he never felt obliged to make life seem prettier or more romantic than he himself had found it. There have been many romantic tales of the Gold Rush in the Yukon, but "To Build a Fire" is not one of them. In this story, a lone man is pitted against a relentless Yukon winter. London's realism is sometimes quite grim, but it reflects his view of human life in an inhospitable universe.

■ Do human beings ever really win a battle against nature? What must we always consider when waging one?

Jack London

To Build a Fire

1 Day had broken cold and gray, exceedingly cold and gray, when the man turned aside from the main Yukon trail[1] and climbed the high earth-bank, where a dim and little-traveled trail led eastward through the fat spruce timberland. It was a steep bank, and he paused for breath at the top, excusing the act to himself by looking at his watch. It was nine o'clock. There was no sun nor hint of sun, though there was not
2 a cloud in the sky. It was a clear day, and yet there seemed an intangible pall over the face of things, a subtle gloom that made the day dark, and that was due to the absence of sun. This fact did not worry the man. He was used to the lack of sun. It had been days since he had seen the sun, and he knew that a few more days must pass before that cheerful orb, due south, would just peep above the skyline and dip immediately from view.

The man flung a look back along the way
3 he had come. The Yukon lay a mile wide and hidden under three feet of ice. On top of this ice were as many feet of snow. It was all pure white, rolling in gentle undulations where the ice jams of the freeze-up had formed. North and south, as far as his eye could see, it was unbroken white, save for a dark hairline that curved and twisted from around the spruce-covered island to the south, and that curved and twisted away into the north, where it disappeared behind another spruce-covered island. This dark hairline was the trail—the main trail—that led south five hundred miles to the Chilcoot Pass, Dyea,[2] and salt water; and that

1. **Yukon** [yo͞o′kon] **trail:** trail extending from southeastern Alaska through the Yukon territory of northwestern Canada and along the Yukon River through central Alaska to the Bering Sea.

2. **Dyea** [dī′a]: former town at the start of the trail.

AT A GLANCE

- At nine in the morning, toward the end of winter, a man makes his way along the Yukon trail.
- All around him stretches a vast, white expanse of ice and snow.

LITERARY OPTIONS

- conflict
- Naturalism
- setting

THEMATIC OPTIONS

- the power of nature
- pride
- instinct vs. intellect

1 PROTAGONIST

Here and throughout the story, the main character is simply "the man." In this setting, his identity is inconsequential; he is everyman.

2 NATURALISM

The description of the setting—particularly the "intangible pall over the face of things"—suggests nature's disinterest in the impending tragedy. The distancing of humanity from the natural world is a common characteristic of Naturalistic writing.

3 SETTING

The scene is vast, uniform, and untouched by civilization. The man's presence has no impact on it.

SELECTION FOR PRACTICE IN ACTIVE READING
(TCR 7, p. 65)

GUIDED READING

LITERAL QUESTION

1a. What excuse does the man make to himself as he stops for breath? (that he is checking the time)

INFERENTIAL QUESTION

1b. Why does he need an excuse? (He seems to be the sort of man who sticks to schedules, who does not approve of delay or weakness.)

AT A GLANCE

- The man is a newcomer or *chechaquo* to this land.
- His spittle crackles in the air, suggesting a temperature of seventy-five below zero.
- He plans to be back at his camp by six o'clock.
- He is accompanied by a large husky.

1 CONFLICT

Without imagination or instinct, the man cannot cope with the forces of nature, and so he is likely to be destroyed when he comes into conflict with them.

2 THEME

The power of nature—particularly when compared to human frailty—is a concept that is wholly alien to the man.

3 THEME

Because of his pride in his capacities, the man foolishly thinks that the temperature is inconsequential.

4 PLOT: EXPOSITION

This passage shows how unnecessary the trip was and how casual the man was about going out alone. Both facts tend to make the reader less sympathetic toward him.

5 POINT OF VIEW

The omniscient narrator gives the reader access to the dog's instinctive understanding of nature.

led north seventy miles to Dawson, and still on to the north a thousand miles to Nulato,[3] and finally to St. Michael on Bering Sea, a thousand miles and half a thousand more.

But all this—the mysterious, far-reaching hairline trail, the absence of sun from the sky, the tremendous cold, and the strangeness and weirdness of it all—made no impression on the man. It was not because he was long used to it. He was a newcomer in the land, a *checha-*
1 *quo,*[4] and this was his first winter. The trouble with him was that he was without imagination. He was quick and alert in the things of life, but only in the things, and not in the significances. Fifty degrees below zero meant eighty-odd degrees of frost. Such fact impressed him as being cold and uncomfortable, and that was all. It did
2 not lead him to meditate upon his frailty as a creature of temperature, and upon man's frailty in general, able only to live within certain narrow limits of heat and cold; and from there on it did not lead him to the conjectural field of immortality and man's place in the universe. Fifty degrees below zero stood for a bite of frost that hurt and that must be guarded against by the use of mittens, earflaps, warm moccasins, and thick socks. Fifty degrees below zero was to him just precisely fifty degrees below zero. That there should be anything more to it than that was a thought that never entered his head.

As he turned to go on, he spat speculatively. There was a sharp, explosive crackle that startled him. He spat again. And again, in the air, before it could fall to the snow, the spittle crackled. He knew that at fifty below spittle crackled on the snow, but this spittle
3 had crackled in the air. Undoubtedly it was colder than fifty below—how much colder he did not know. But the temperature did not matter. He was bound for the old claim on the left fork of Henderson Creek, where the boys were already. They had come over across the
4 divide from the Indian Creek country, while he had come the roundabout way to take a look at the possibilities of getting out logs in the spring from the islands in the Yukon. He would be in to camp by six o'clock; a bit after dark, it was true, but the boys would be there, a fire would be going, and a hot supper would be ready. As for lunch, he pressed his hand against the protruding bundle under his jacket. It was also under his shirt, wrapped up in a handkerchief and lying against the naked skin. It was the only way to keep the biscuits from freezing. He smiled agreeably to himself as he thought of those biscuits, each cut open and sopped in bacon grease, and each enclosing a generous slice of fried bacon.

He plunged in among the big spruce trees. The trail was faint. A foot of snow had fallen since the last sled had passed over, and he was glad he was without a sled, traveling light. In fact, he carried nothing but the lunch wrapped in the handkerchief. He was surprised, however, at the cold. It certainly was cold, he concluded, as he rubbed his numb nose and cheekbones with his mittened hand. He was a warm-whiskered man, but the hair on his face did not protect the high cheekbones and the eager nose that thrust itself aggressively into the frosty air.

At the man's heels trotted a dog, a big native husky, the proper wolf-dog, gray-coated and without any visible or temperamental dif-
5 ference from its brother, the wild wolf. The animal was depressed by the tremendous cold. It knew that it was no time for traveling. Its instinct told it a truer tale than was told to the man by the man's judgment. In reality, it was not merely colder than fifty below zero; it was colder than sixty below, than seventy below. It was seventy-five below zero. Since the freezing point is thirty-two above zero, it meant that one hundred and seven degrees of frost obtained. The dog did not know anything about thermometers. Possibly in its brain there was no sharp consciousness of a condition of very cold such as was in the man's brain. But the brute had its instinct. It experienced a vague

---

3. **Dawson** and **Nulato:** former goldmining centers in the Yukon.

4. ***chechaquo*** [chē chä′ kō]: In the Pacific Northwest, slang for "a newcomer."

GUIDED READING

LITERAL QUESTIONS

1a. How concerned is the man about the temperature? (not at all—it "did not matter")

2a. How does the dog feel about the cold? (It is depressed by the cold.)

INFERENTIAL QUESTIONS

1b. Why does he feel this way? (His lack of imagination and his pride blind him to the power of nature.)

2b. Why does it feel this way? (Instinct tells it of the dangers of being out in such severely cold weather.)

but menacing apprehension that subdued it and made it slink along at the man's heels, and that made it question eagerly every unwonted[5] movement of the man as if expecting him to go into camp or to seek shelter somewhere and build a fire. The dog had learned fire, and it wanted fire, or else to burrow under the snow and cuddle its warmth away from the air.

The frozen moisture of its breathing had settled on its fur in a fine powder of frost, and especially were its jowls, muzzle, and eyelashes whitened by its crystalled breath. The man's red beard and mustache were likewise frosted, but more solidly, the deposit taking the form of ice and increasing with every warm, moist breath he exhaled. Also, the man was chewing tobacco, and the muzzle of ice held his lips so rigidly that he was unable to clear his chin when he expelled the juice. The result was that a crystal beard of the color and solidity of amber was increasing its length on his chin. If he fell down it would shatter itself, like glass, into brittle fragments. But he did not mind the appendage. It was the penalty all tobacco
1 chewers paid in that country, and he had been out before in two cold snaps. They had not been so cold as this, he knew, but by the spirit thermometer[6] at Sixty Mile he knew they had been registered at fifty below and at fifty-five.

He held on through the level stretch of woods for several miles, crossed a wide flat, and dropped down a bank to the frozen bed of a small stream. This was Henderson Creek, and he knew he was ten miles from the forks. He looked at his watch. It was ten o'clock. He was making four miles an hour, and he calculated that he would arrive at the forks at half past twelve. He decided to celebrate that event by eating his lunch there.

The dog dropped in again at his heels, with a tail drooping discouragement, as the man swung along the creekbed. The furrow of the old sled trail was plainly visible, but a dozen inches of snow covered the marks of the last runners. In a month no man had come up or down that silent creek. The man held steadily
2 on. He was not much given to thinking, and just then particularly he had nothing to think about save that he would eat lunch at the forks and that at six o'clock he would be in camp with the boys. There was nobody to talk to; and, had there been, speech would have been impossible because of the ice muzzle on his mouth. So he continued monotonously to chew tobacco and to increase the length of his amber beard.

Once in a while the thought reiterated itself that it was very cold and that he had never experienced such cold. As he walked along he rubbed his cheekbones and nose with the back of his mittened hand. He did this automatically,
3 now and again changing hands. But rub as he would, the instant he stopped his cheekbones went numb, and the following instant the end of his nose went numb. He was sure to frost his cheeks; he knew that, and experienced a pang of regret that he had not devised a nose strap of the sort Bud wore in cold snaps. Such a strap passed across the cheeks, as well, and saved them. But it didn't matter much, after all. What were frosted cheeks? A bit painful, that was all; they were never serious.

Empty as the man's mind was of thoughts, he was keenly observant, and he noticed the changes in the creek, the curves and bends and timber jams, and always he sharply noted where he placed his feet. Once, coming around a bend, he shied abruptly, like a startled horse, curved away from the place where he had been walking, and retreated several paces back along the trail. The creek he knew was frozen clear to the bottom—no creek could contain
4 water in that arctic winter—but he knew also that there were springs that bubbled out from the hillsides and ran along under the snow and on top the ice of the creek. He knew that the coldest snaps never froze these springs, and he knew likewise their danger. They were traps. They hid pools of water under the snow that might be three inches deep, or three feet.

5. **unwonted** [un wôn'tid]: unusual.
6. **spirit thermometer:** thermometer that contains alcohol instead of mercury and is used in extreme cold.

AT A GLANCE

- The dog feels the need of warmth.
- The man and the dog turn to follow Henderson Creek.
- The man, his face now frostbitten, is on the alert for thin ice.

1 THEME

The passage indicates that the man is no novice to this type of environment. His refusal to learn from those experiences may lead the reader to withhold sympathy again.

2 CHARACTERIZATION

The man is aware only of his own immediate plans; he does not think about what he might learn from the environment or from the dog.

3 PLOT: RISING ACTION

Gradually, the man is freezing, yet he remains oblivious to the seriousness of his situation.

4 CONFLICT

The battle for survival is continuous. London's description of the underground springs suggests that nature is setting traps for the man.

GUIDED READING

LITERAL QUESTIONS

1a. As the man turns to follow the creek bed, how does the dog react? (Its tail drops in discouragement.)

2a. Which "traps" does the man fear? (springs that create pools of water under the snow)

INFERENTIAL QUESTIONS

1b. Why does it react this way? (It had hoped that the man would stop to build a fire.)

2b. Does this fear show any change in him? (It shows only that he is capable of responding to perils immediately facing him.)

AT A GLANCE

- The man thinks about the dangers of getting his feet wet.
- The man uses the dog to check the footing.
- At twelve-thirty, the man wants lunch but forgets to make a fire.
- The man's body reacts to the cold.

1 CHARACTERIZATION

The man thinks of getting his feet wet as a matter of delay, perhaps of trouble and danger; he refuses to acknowledge the grimmer possibility of death.

2 CHARACTERIZATION

For the man, the dog is just a tool, something he would use like a stick to test his footing.

3 THEME

Here the dog's instinct and the man's intellect concur for the first time in the story.

4 SETTING

In this world, the man is nothing; he does not even cast a shadow.

5 STYLE: REFRAIN

The man's unawareness is seen in his unimaginative refrain "it certainly was cold" (a line that appeared earlier in the story). Unlike the dog, however, the man does not know what to do about the cold.

Sometimes a skin of ice half an inch thick covered them, and in turn was covered by the snow. Sometimes there were alternate layers of water and ice skin, so that when one broke through he kept on breaking through for a while, sometimes wetting himself to the waist.

That was why he had shied in such panic. He had felt the give under his feet and heard
1 the crackle of a snow-hidden ice skin. And to get his feet wet in such a temperature meant trouble and danger. At the very least it meant delay, for he would be forced to stop and build a fire, and under its protection to bare his feet while he dried his socks and moccasins. He stood and studied the creek bed and its banks, and decided that the flow of water came from the right. He reflected a while, rubbing his nose and cheeks, then skirted to the left, stepping gingerly and testing the footing for each step. Once clear of the danger, he took a fresh chew of tobacco and swung along at his four-mile gait.

In the course of the next two hours he came upon several similar traps. Usually the snow above the hidden pools had a sunken, candied appearance that advertised the danger. Once again, however, he had a close call; and
2 once, suspecting danger, he compelled the dog to go on in front. The dog did not want to go. It hung back until the man shoved it forward, and then it went quickly across the white, unbroken surface. Suddenly it broke through, floundered to one side, and got away to firmer footing. It had wet its forefeet and legs, and almost immediately the water that clung to it
3 turned to ice. It made quick efforts to lick the ice off its legs, then dropped down in the snow and began to bite out the ice that had formed between the toes. This was a matter of instinct. To permit the ice to remain would mean sore feet. It did not know this, it merely obeyed the mysterious prompting that arose from the deep crypts of its being. But the man knew, having achieved a judgment on the subject, and he removed the mitten from his right hand and helped tear out the ice particles. He did not expose his fingers more than a minute, and was astonished at the swift numbness that smote them. It certainly was cold. He pulled on the mitten hastily, and beat the hand savagely across his chest.

At twelve o'clock the day was at its brightest. Yet the sun was too far south on its winter
4 journey to clear the horizon. The bulge of the earth intervened between it and Henderson Creek, where the man walked under a clear sky at noon and cast no shadow. At half past twelve, to the minute, he arrived at the forks of the creek. He was pleased at the speed he had made. If he kept it up, he would certainly be with the boys by six. He unbuttoned his jacket and shirt and drew forth his lunch. The action consumed no more than a quarter of a minute, yet in that brief moment the numbness laid hold of the exposed fingers. He did not put the mitten on, but instead struck the fingers a dozen sharp smashes against his leg. Then he sat down on a snow-covered log to eat. The sting that followed upon the striking of his fingers against his leg ceased so quickly that he was startled. He had had no chance to take a bite of biscuit. He struck the fingers repeatedly and returned them to the mitten, baring the other hand for the purpose of eating. He tried to take a mouthful, but the ice muzzle prevented. He had forgotten to build a fire and thaw out. He chuckled at his foolishness, and as he chuckled he noted the numbness creeping into the exposed fingers. Also, he noted that the stinging which had first come to his toes when he sat down was already passing away. He wondered whether the toes were warm or numb. He moved them inside the moccasins and decided that they were numb.

He pulled the mitten on hurriedly and stood up. He was a bit frightened. He stamped up and down until the stinging returned into
5 the feet. It certainly was cold, was his thought. That man from Sulphur Creek had spoken the truth when telling how cold it sometimes got in the country. And he had laughed at him at the time! That showed one must not be too sure of things. There was no mistake about it, it *was* cold. He strode up and down, stamping

GUIDED READING

LITERAL QUESTIONS

1a. When he suspects the danger of a hidden pool, what does the man get the dog to do? (He forces it to go in front.)

2a. What is it that makes the man chuckle when he stops for lunch? (He forgot to build a fire.)

INFERENTIAL QUESTIONS

1b. What does this action say about the man's relationship with the dog? (He has no feeling for the animal, no appreciation of what it knows.)

2b. Why does his chuckling seem odd? (His action suggests that he does not realize the gravity of his desperate situation.)

his feet and threshing his arms, until reassured by the returning warmth. Then he got out matches and proceeded to make a fire. From the undergrowth, where high water of the previous spring had lodged a supply of seasoned twigs, he got his firewood. Working carefully
1 from a small beginning, he soon had a roaring fire, over which he thawed the ice from his face and in the protection of which he ate his biscuits. For the moment the cold of space was outwitted. The dog took satisfaction in the fire, stretching out close enough for warmth and far enough away to escape being singed.

When the man had finished, he filled his pipe and took his comfortable time over a smoke. Then he pulled on his mittens, settled the earflaps of his cap firmly about his ears, and took the creek trail up the left fork. The dog was disappointed and yearned back toward
2 the fire. This man did not know cold. Possibly all the generations of his ancestry had been ignorant of cold, of real cold, of cold one hundred and seven degrees below freezing point. But the dog knew; all its ancestry knew, and it had inherited the knowledge. And it knew that it was not good to walk abroad in such fearful cold. It was the time to lie snug in a hole in the snow and wait for a curtain of cloud to be drawn across the face of outer space whence this cold came. On the other hand, there was no keen intimacy between the
3 dog and the man. The one was the toil slave of the other, and the only caresses it had ever received were the caresses of the whiplash and of harsh and menacing throat-sounds that threatened the whiplash. So the dog made no effort to communicate its apprehension to the man. It was not concerned in the welfare of the man; it was for its own sake that it yearned back toward the fire. But the man whistled, and spoke to it with the sound of whiplashes, and the dog swung in at the man's heel and followed after.

The man took a chew of tobacco and proceeded to start a new amber beard. Also, his moist breath quickly powdered with white his mustache, eyebrows, and lashes. There did not seem to be so many springs on the left fork of the Henderson, and for half an hour the man
4 saw no signs of any. And then it happened. At a place where there were no signs, where the soft, unbroken snow seemed to advertise solidity beneath, the man broke through. It was not deep. He wet himself halfway to the knees before he floundered out to the firm crust.

He was angry, and cursed his luck aloud. He had hoped to get into camp with the boys at six o'clock, and this would delay him an hour, for he would have to build a fire and dry out his footgear. This was imperative at that low temperature—he knew that much; and he turned aside to the bank, which he climbed. On top, tangled in the underbrush about the trunks of several small spruce trees, was a high-water deposit of dry firewood—sticks and twigs, principally, but also larger portions of seasoned branches and fine, dry, last-year's grasses. He threw down several large pieces on top of the snow. This served for a foundation and prevented the young flame from drowning itself in the snow it otherwise would melt. The flame he got by touching a match to a small shred of birch bark that he took from his pocket. This burned even more readily than paper. Placing it on the foundation, he fed the young flame with wisps of dry grass and with the tiniest dry twigs.

5 He worked slowly and carefully, keenly aware of his danger. Gradually, as the flame grew stronger, he increased the size of the twigs with which he fed it. He squatted in the snow, pulling the twigs out from their entanglement in the brush and feeding directly to the flame. He knew there must be no failure. When it is seventy-five below zero, a man must not fail in his first attempt to build a fire—that is, if his feet are wet. If his feet are dry, and he fails, he can run along the trail for half a mile and restore his circulation. But the circulation of wet and freezing feet cannot be restored by running when it is seventy-five below. No matter how fast he runs, the wet feet will freeze the harder.

All this the man knew. The old-timer on

AT A GLANCE

- The man builds a fire and eats his lunch.
- The man and the dog start out along the creek again.
- The man falls through and gets his feet and legs wet.
- Carefully, the man builds another fire.

1 THEME

Nature can be overcome only "for the moment"—only in a limited area and for a short time.

2 POINT OF VIEW

Once again the narrator enters the dog's mind, showing the difference between the dog's instinctive understanding of nature and the man's civilized failure to understand it fully.

3 CHARACTERIZATION

The insensitivity and blindness of the man toward nature are revealed in his treatment of the dog.

4 PLOT: RISING ACTION

Despite his caution, the man finds himself caught in one of nature's traps.

5 NATURALISM

As the man becomes aware of his dangerous situation, London chooses to focus on his specific actions rather than to probe his deepest feelings.

GUIDED READING

LITERAL QUESTIONS

1a. When the man falls through the ice, what does he blame? (his luck)

2a. As he builds his second fire, how does the man work? (slowly and carefully)

INFERENTIAL QUESTIONS

1b. What insight does this reaction offer about the man's shortsightedness? (By blaming luck, he can disassociate himself from any responsibility for his plight.)

2b. Is this approach in keeping with his character? (Working slowly and carefully is compatible with his rational approach to situations.)

AT A GLANCE

- The man is freezing as he works on the fire.
- The fire succeeds, and the man, feeling safe, prepares to remove his wet footgear.
- A load of snow from the tree above him falls on the fire and puts it out.

1 STYLE: IMAGERY

The narrator moves out into the space beyond the earth to create an image that shows nature's terrifying power.

2 THEME

So proud is the man of his "mannish" self-reliance that he nearly laughs at the advice that more seasoned travelers had offered him.

3 PLOT: RISING ACTION

The process of freezing is spreading, as nature inevitably takes hold of the man. The description of the numbness as a "lifeless" feeling alerts the reader to the probable outcome.

4 STYLE: SIMILE

By comparing the ice to iron and steel, London helps readers to feel the futility of the man's efforts.

5 CHARACTERIZATION

Despite his predicament, the man has tried to build the fire the easy way; he still fails to have respect for nature's power and capriciousness.

Sulphur Creek had told him about it the previous fall, and now he was appreciating the advice. Already all sensation had gone out of his feet. To build the fire he had been forced to remove his mittens, and the fingers had quickly gone numb. His pace of four miles an hour had kept his heart pumping blood to the surface of his body and to all the extremities. But the instant he stopped, the action of the pump eased
1 down. The cold of space smote the unprotected tip of the planet, and he, being on that unprotected tip, received the full force of the blow. The blood of his body recoiled before it. The blood was alive, like the dog, and like the dog it wanted to hide away and cover itself up from the fearful cold. So long as he walked four miles an hour, he pumped that blood, willy-nilly,[7] to the surface; but now it ebbed away and sank down into the recesses of his body. The extremities were the first to feel its absence. His wet feet froze the faster, and his exposed fingers numbed the faster, though they had not yet begun to freeze. Nose and cheeks were already freezing, while the skin of all his body chilled as it lost its blood.

But he was safe. Toes and nose and cheeks would be only touched by the frost, for the fire was beginning to burn with strength. He was feeding it with twigs the size of his finger. In another minute he would be able to feed it with branches the size of his wrist, and then he could remove his wet footgear, and, while it dried, he could keep his naked feet warm by the fire, rubbing them at first, of course, with snow. The fire was a success. He was safe. He remembered the advice of the old-timer on Sulphur Creek, and smiled. The old-timer had been very serious in laying down the law that
2 no man must travel alone in the Klondike[8] after fifty below. Well, here he was; he had had the accident; he was alone; and he had saved himself. Those old-timers were rather womanish, some of them, he thought. All a man had to do was to keep his head; and he was all right. Any man who was a man could travel alone. But it was surprising, the rapidity with which his cheeks and nose were freezing. And
3 he had not thought his fingers could go lifeless in so short a time. Lifeless they were, for he could scarcely make them move together to grip a twig, and they seemed remote from his body and from him. When he touched a twig, he had to look and see whether or not he had hold of it. The wires were pretty well down between him and his finger ends.

All of which counted for little. There was the fire, snapping and crackling and promising life with every dancing flame. He started to untie his moccasins. They were coated with ice;
4 the thick German socks were like sheaths of iron halfway to the knees; and the moccasin strings were like rods of steel all twisted and knotted as by some conflagration.[9] For a moment he tugged with his numb fingers, then, realizing the folly of it, he drew his sheath knife.

But before he could cut the strings, it happened. It was his own fault or, rather, his mis-
5 take. He should not have built the fire under the spruce tree. He should have built it in the open. But it had been easier to pull the twigs from the brush and drop them directly on the fire. Now the tree under which he had done this carried a weight of snow on its boughs. No wind had blown for weeks, and each bough was fully freighted. Each time he had pulled a twig he had communicated a slight agitation to the tree—an imperceptible agitation, so far as he was concerned, but an agitation sufficient to bring about the disaster. High up in the tree one bough capsized its load of snow. This fell on the boughs beneath, capsizing them. This process continued, spreading out and involving the whole tree. It grew like an avalanche, and it descended without warning upon the man and the fire, and the fire was blotted out! Where it had burned was a mantle of fresh and disordered snow.

The man was shocked. It was as though he

7. **willy-nilly:** inevitably.
8. **Klondike** [klon′dīk]: Yukon gold-mining region.
9. **conflagration:** big, destructive fire.

GUIDED READING

LITERAL QUESTIONS

1a. Which word does the man use to characterize some old-timers? *(womanish)*

2a. Why does the man build the fire under the spruce tree? (He wants to be close to the brush he uses to start the fire.)

INFERENTIAL QUESTIONS

1b. Why does he use this word? (He thinks that he understands the hazards of nature better than do the old-timers; he thinks they frighten too easily.)

2b. What do you predict will happen to the man as a result of this decision? (Students may be able to predict that the fact that the fire is extinguished will lead to the man's freezing to death.)

had just heard his own sentence of death. For a moment he sat and stared at the spot where the fire had been. Then he grew very calm. Perhaps the old-timer on Sulphur Creek was right. If he had only had a trailmate he would have been in no danger now. The trailmate
1 could have built the fire. Well, it was up to him to build the fire over again, and this second time there must be no failure. Even if he succeeded, he would most likely lose some toes. His feet must be badly frozen by now, and there would be some time before the second fire was ready.

Such were his thoughts, but he did not sit and think them. He was busy all the time they were passing through his mind. He made a new foundation for a fire, this time in the open, where no treacherous tree could blot it out. Next, he gathered dry grasses and tiny twigs from the high-water flotsam. He could not bring his fingers together to pull them out, but he was able to gather them by the handful. In this way he got many rotten twigs and bits of green moss that were undesirable, but it was the best he could do. He worked methodically, even collecting an armful of the larger branches to be used later when the fire gath-
2 ered strength. And all the while the dog sat and watched him, a certain yearning wistfulness in its eyes, for it looked upon him as the fire provider, and the fire was slow in coming.

When all was ready, the man reached in his pocket for a second piece of birch bark. He knew the bark was there, and, though he could not feel it with his fingers, he could hear its crisp rustling as he fumbled for it. Try as he would, he could not clutch hold of it. And all
3 the time, in his consciousness, was the knowledge that each instant his feet were freezing. This thought tended to put him in a panic, but he fought against it and kept calm. He pulled on his mittens with his teeth, and threshed his arms back and forth, beating his hands with all his might against his sides. He did this sitting down, and he stood up to do it; and all the while the dog sat in the snow, its wolf-brush of a tail curled around warmly over its forefeet, its sharp wolf ears pricked forward intently as it watched the man. And the man, as he beat and threshed with his arms and hands, felt a great surge of envy as he regarded the creature that was warm and secure in its natural covering.

After a time he was aware of the first faraway signals of sensation in his beaten fingers.
4 The faint tingling grew stronger till it evolved into a stinging ache that was excruciating, but which the man hailed with satisfaction. He stripped the mitten from his right hand and fetched forth the birch bark. The exposed fingers were quickly going numb again. Next he brought out his bunch of sulphur matches. But the tremendous cold had already driven the life out of his fingers. In his effort to separate one match from the others, the whole bunch fell in the snow. He tried to pick it out of the snow, but failed. The dead fingers could neither touch nor clutch. He was very careful. He drove the thought of his freezing feet, and nose, and cheeks, out of his mind, devoting his whole soul to the matches. He watched, using the sense of vision in place of touch, and when he saw his fingers on each side the bunch, he
5 closed them—that is, he willed to close them, for the wires were down, and the fingers did not obey. He pulled the mitten on the right hand, and beat it fiercely against his knee. Then, with both mittened hands, he scooped the bunch of matches, along with much snow, into his lap. Yet he was no better off.

After some manipulation he managed to get the bunch between the heels of his mittened hands. In this fashion he carried it to his mouth. The ice crackled and snapped when by a violent effort he opened his mouth. He drew the lower jaw in, curled the upper lip out of the way, and scraped the bunch with his upper teeth in order to separate a match. He succeeded in getting one, which he dropped on his lap. He was no better off. He could not pick it up. Then he devised a way. He picked it up in his teeth and scratched it on his leg. Twenty times he scratched before he succeeded in lighting it. As it flamed he held it

AT A GLANCE

- The man realizes that he must start another fire or die.
- He gathers what fuel he can away from any tree.
- His hands are too frozen to strike a match.
- Holding a match in his teeth, he strikes it on his leg.

1 CHARACTERIZATION

Despite everything, the man continues to believe he has control over his destiny.

2 RESPONSE JOURNAL

Students might trace the use of fire imagery in this story, either from London's view, the man's view, or the dog's view.

3 CONFLICT

The outer conflict—the struggle with frozen fingers to build a fire—has its inner counterpart as the man fights to remain calm.

4 NATURALISM

All romanticism about the rugged wilderness is gone in a world where pain is the only sign one has that one is still alive.

5 STYLE: IMPLIED METAPHOR

The narrator has previously used the phrase *the wires were down* to describe the man's inability to coax his hands to move. This naturalistic metaphor equates the man's body to an electrical system that has broken down because of the weather.

GUIDED READING

LITERAL QUESTIONS

1a. What does the man envy about the dog? (the warmth of its natural covering)

2a. How does the man react to the excruciating pain in his beaten fingers? (He finds it satisfying.)

INFERENTIAL QUESTIONS

1b. What might the man's envy of the dog's warm coat lead to? (Some students may predict that the man will try to kill the dog to get its fur.)

2b. Why does he have this reaction? (As long as his fingers hurt, they are not completely dead.)

AT A GLANCE

- Beginning to despair, the man lights all of his matches and burns his hands.
- His shivering hands scatter the lighted twigs, killing the fire.
- He calls to the dog, intending to kill it and put his freezing hands inside the carcass.

1 IRONY

Here the man's hands are ablaze as he feverishly attempts to light a fire to warm them.

2 SYMBOL

Again, but more explicitly, fire and life are linked.

3 CONFLICT

In nature, the strong survive by killing the weak. The man does not realize at this point that he is now probably weaker than the dog.

4 THEME

The dog's highly developed instincts are superior to the man's weakened intellect and undeveloped instincts. Therefore, the dog instinctively recognizes the naked threat that his master is too weak to hide.

with his teeth to the birch bark. But the burning brimstone went up his nostrils and into his lungs, causing him to cough spasmodically. The match fell into the snow and went out.

The oldtimer on Sulphur Creek was right, he thought in the moment of controlled despair that ensued: after fifty below, a man should travel with a partner. He beat his hands, but failed in exciting any sensation. Suddenly he bared both hands, removing the mittens with his teeth. He caught the whole bunch between the heels of his hands. His arm-muscles not being frozen enabled him to press the hand heels tightly against the matches. Then he scratched the bunch along his leg. It flared into flame, seventy sulphur matches at once! There was no wind to blow them out. He kept his head to one side to escape the strangling fumes, and held the blazing bunch to the birch
1 bark. As he so held it, he became aware of sensation in his hand. His flesh was burning. He could smell it. Deep down below the surface he could feel it. The sensation developed into pain that grew acute. And still he endured it, holding the flame of the matches clumsily to the bark that would not light readily because his own burning hands were in the way, absorbing most of the flame.

At last, when he could endure no more, he jerked his hands apart. The blazing matches fell sizzling into the snow, but the birch bark was alight. He began laying dry grasses and the tiniest twigs on the flame. He could not pick and choose, for he had to lift the fuel between the heels of his hands. Small pieces of rotten wood and green moss clung to the twigs, and he bit
2 them off as well as he could with his teeth. He cherished the flame carefully and awkwardly. It meant life, and it must not perish. The withdrawal of blood from the surface of his body now made him begin to shiver, and he grew more awkward. A large piece of green moss fell squarely on the little fire. He tried to poke it out with his fingers, but his shivering frame made him poke too far, and he disrupted the nucleus of the little fire, the burning grasses and tiny twigs separating and scattering. He tried to poke them together again, but in spite of the tenseness of the effort, his shivering got away with him, and the twigs were hopelessly scattered. Each twig gushed a puff of smoke and went out. The fire provider had failed. As he looked apathetically about him, his eyes chanced on the dog, sitting across the ruins of the fire from him, in the snow, making restless, hunching movements, slightly lifting one forefoot and then the other, shifting its weight back and forth on them with wistful eagerness.

The sight of the dog put a wild idea into his head. He remembered the tale of the man, caught in a blizzard, who killed a steer and crawled inside the carcass, and so was saved.
3 He would kill the dog and bury his hands in the warm body until the numbness went out of them. Then he could build another fire. He spoke to the dog, calling it to him; but in his voice was a strange note of fear that frightened the animal, who had never known the man to
4 speak in such way before. Something was the matter, and its suspicious nature sensed danger—it knew not what danger, but somewhere, somehow, in its brain arose an apprehension of the man. It flattened its ears down at the sound of the man's voice, and its restless, hunching movements and the liftings and shiftings of its forefeet became more pronounced; but it would not come to the man. He got on his hands and knees and crawled toward the dog. This unusual posture again excited suspicion, and the animal sidled mincingly away.

The man sat up in the snow for a moment and struggled for calmness. Then he pulled on his mittens, by means of his teeth, and got upon his feet. He glanced down at first in order to assure himself that he was really standing up, for the absence of sensation in his feet left him unrelated to the earth. His erect position in itself started to drive the webs of suspicion from the dog's mind; and when he spoke peremptorily,[10] with the sound of whiplashes in his voice, the dog rendered its customary allegiance and came to him. As it came

10. **peremptorily:** dictatorially.

GUIDED READING

LITERAL QUESTION

1a. As he looks at the dog, what plan occurs to the man? (He thinks that he can kill the dog and thaw his hands in its carcass.)

INFERENTIAL QUESTION

1b. How realistic is this plan? (It cannot succeed; his hands are not merely numbed—they have been frozen. Besides, the dog would probably be able to fight back against the weakened man. London himself calls the plan "a wild idea."

within reaching distance, the man lost his control. His arms flashed out to the dog, and he experienced genuine surprise when he discovered that his hands could not clutch, that there was neither bend nor feeling in the fingers. He had forgotten for the moment that they were frozen and that they were freezing more and more. All this happened quickly, and before the animal could get away, he encircled its body with his arms. He sat down in the snow, and in this fashion held the dog, while it snarled and whined and struggled.

1 But it was all he could do, hold its body encircled in his arms and sit there. He realized that he could not kill the dog. There was no way to do it. With his helpless hands he could neither draw nor hold his sheath knife nor throttle the animal. He released it, and it plunged wildly away, with tail between its legs, and still snarling. It halted forty feet away and surveyed him curiously, with ears sharply pricked forward. The man looked down at his hands in order to locate them, and found them hanging on the ends of his arms. It struck him as curious that one should have to use his eyes in order to find out where his hands were. He began threshing his arms back and forth, beating the mittened hands against his sides. He did this for five minutes, violently, and his heart pumped enough blood up to the surface to put a stop to his shivering. But no sensation
2 was aroused in the hands. He had an impression that they hung like weights on the ends of his arms, but when he tried to run the impression down, he could not find it.

A certain fear of death, dull and oppressive, came to him. This fear quickly became poignant as he realized that it was no longer a mere matter of freezing his fingers and toes, or
3 of losing his hands and feet, but that it was a matter of life and death with the chances against him. This threw him into a panic, and he turned and ran up the creekbed along the old, dim trail. The dog joined in behind and

AT A GLANCE

- The man attempts to kill the dog but realizes that he cannot.
- His hands no longer seem attached to his body.
- In a panic, he begins to run.

1 THEME

The man's incapacity to overcome the dog reinforces the idea that he is incapable of overcoming nature.

2 PLOT: FORESHADOWING

The narrator vividly suggests the dimming of the man's consciousness. The language here—"when he tried to run the impression down, he could not find it"—shows us how the man's confused mind stumbles, in contrast to his earlier self-possession.

3 CHARACTERIZATION

The man cannot stand the thought of death, and he tries to run away from it.

GUIDED READING

LITERAL QUESTION

1a. What does the man forget as he attempts to clutch the dog? (that his hands are frozen)

INFERENTIAL QUESTION

1b. How could he forget this fact? (His mind is beginning to shut down and is thus able to focus on only one thing at a time—in this case, killing the dog.)

AT A GLANCE

- The man thinks that he might be able to run to camp.
- The realization that the freezing is spreading makes him run frenetically and fall down.
- He decides to sleep his way to death.

1 THEME

The man's blind instinct to survive makes him deny the facts and imagine himself surviving the ordeal.

2 STYLE: ALLUSION

The reference to a winged Mercury strengthens the imagery of the running man whose legs no longer feel the earth. It also suggests that his mind is drifting further away from his physical circumstances.

3 BACKGROUND

A warm, comfortable, sleepy feeling is known to shortly precede death in one who is freezing. The man probably is aware of this fact, but he has not yet found its application to his situation.

4 THEME

The cold has the power to freeze everything, even the man's fears.

kept up with him. He ran blindly, without intention, in fear such as he had never known in his life. Slowly, as he plowed and floundered through the snow, he began to see things again—the banks of the creeks, the old timber jams, the leafless aspens, and the sky. The running made him feel better. He did not shiver.
1 Maybe, if he ran on, his feet would thaw out; and, anyway, if he ran far enough, he would reach camp and the boys. Without doubt he would lose some fingers and toes and some of his face; but the boys would take care of him, and save the rest of him when he got there. And at the same time there was another thought in his mind that said he would never get to the camp and the boys; that it was too many miles away, that the freezing had too great a start on him, and that he would soon be stiff and dead. This thought he kept in the background and refused to consider. Sometimes it pushed itself forward and demanded to be heard, but he thrust it back and strove to think of other things.

It struck him as curious that he could run at all on feet so frozen that he could not feel them when they struck the earth and took the
2 weight of his body. He seemed to himself to skim along above the surface, and to have no connection with the earth. Somewhere he had once seen a winged Mercury,[11] and he wondered if Mercury felt as he felt when skimming over the earth.

His theory of running until he reached camp and the boys had one flaw in it: he lacked the endurance. Several times he stumbled, and finally he tottered, crumpled up, and fell. When he tried to rise, he failed. He must sit and rest, he decided, and next time he
3 would merely walk and keep on going. As he sat and regained his breath, he noted that he was feeling quite warm and comfortable. He was not shivering, and it even seemed that a warm glow had come to his chest and trunk. And yet, when he touched his nose or cheeks, there was no sensation. Running would not thaw them out. Nor would it thaw out his hands and feet. Then the thought came to him that the frozen portions of his body must be extending. He tried to keep this thought down, to forget it, to think of something else; he was aware of the panicky feeling that it caused, and he was afraid of the panic. But the thought asserted itself, and persisted, until it produced a vision of his body totally frozen. This was too much, and he made another wild run along the trail. Once he slowed down to a walk, but the thought of the freezing extending itself made him run again.

And all the time the dog ran with him, at his heels. When he fell down a second time, it curled its tail over its forefeet and sat in front of him, facing him, curiously eager and intent. The warmth and security of the animal angered him, and he cursed it till it flattened down its ears appeasingly. This time the shivering came more quickly upon the man. He was losing in his battle with the frost. It was creeping into his body from all sides. The thought of it drove him on, but he ran no more than a hundred feet, when he staggered and pitched headlong. It was his last panic. When he had recovered his breath and control, he sat up and entertained in his mind the conception of meeting death with dignity. However, the conception did not come to him in such terms. His idea of it was that he had been making a fool of himself, running around like a chicken with its head cut off—such was the simile that oc-
4 curred to him. Well, he was bound to freeze anyway, and he might as well take it decently. With this newfound peace of mind came the first glimmerings of drowsiness. A good idea, he thought, to sleep off to death. It was like taking an anaesthetic.[12] Freezing was not so bad as people thought. There were lots worse ways to die.

He pictured the boys finding his body next day. Suddenly he found himself with them,

---

11. **Mercury:** in Roman mythology, messenger of the gods; considered to have winged feet.

12. **anaesthetic:** something that produces a loss of sensation.

GUIDED READING

LITERAL QUESTIONS

1a. What is the thought the man at first refuses to consider? ("that he would soon be stiff and dead")

2a. What is the man's "newfound peace of mind"? (accepting that he is going to freeze to death)

INFERENTIAL QUESTIONS

1b. Why does he reject this thought? (He is afraid to die and perhaps does not believe it can happen to him.)

2b. What has brought this feeling of peace? (Perhaps he has accepted that he has been the loser in this battle with nature.)

coming along the trail and looking for himself. And, still with them, he came around a turn in the trail and found himself lying in the snow. He did not belong with himself any more, for even then he was out of himself, standing with the boys and looking at himself in the snow. It certainly was cold, was his thought. When he got back to the States he could tell the folks what real cold was. He drifted on from this to a vision of the old-timer on Sulphur Creek. He could see him quite clearly, warm and comfortable, and smoking a pipe.

"You were right, old hoss; you were right," the man mumbled to the old-timer of Sulphur Creek.

Then the man drowsed off into what seemed to him the most comfortable and satisfying sleep he had ever known. The dog sat facing him and waiting. The brief day drew to a close in a long, slow twilight. There were no signs of a fire to be made, and, besides, never in the dog's experience had it known a man to sit like that in the snow and make no fire. As the twilight drew on, its eager yearning for the fire mastered it, and with a great lifting and shifting of forefeet, it whined softly, then flattened its ears down in anticipation of being chidden[13] by the man. But the man remained silent. Later, the dog whined loudly. And still later it crept close to the man and caught the scent of death. This made the animal bristle and back away. A little longer it delayed, howling under the stars that leaped and danced and shone brightly in the cold sky. Then it turned and trotted up the trail in the direction of the camp it knew, where were the other food providers and fire providers.

13. **chidden:** scolded.

STUDY QUESTIONS

Recalling

1. According to the third paragraph, what four things make no impression on the man as he navigates the wilderness? What is the "trouble" with the man?
2. What does the dog have that "tells" it a truer tale than the man's judgment (paragraph 6)?
3. Describe the "traps" that the man tries to avoid (page 357). Why does the man compel the dog to go in front on page 358?
4. The man builds his first fire after lunch. Why must he later build another fire?
5. When the man tries to build the second fire, his fires fail twice. What causes the first failure? The second?
6. What happens to the man at the end of the story? What happens to the dog?

Interpreting

7. Against what force does the man struggle in this story? What is the outcome of that struggle?
8. What two qualities of the dog and of the man contrast? What does the ending suggest about London's view of these qualities and their relationship to survival in the natural world?
9. Describe the mood or atmosphere of the story. What elements of Naturalism does it contain?

Extending

10. Do you think the man could have used his judgment and survived? What different decisions might he have made? What might he have done if he had not been lacking in imagination?

LITERARY FOCUS

Conflict

The **conflict** in a work of fiction is the battle that the main character must wage against an opposing force. Usually the events of the story are all related to the conflict, and the conflict is resolved in some way by the story's end.

10.
- Students might say that the man could have waited for cold to pass before starting the journey, or he might have sought shelter sooner.
- The man might have avoided the creek, carried better fuel, or built his fire in the open.

AT A GLANCE

- The man imagines himself with "the boys" as they find his body.
- The man falls asleep and dies.
- The dog waits for a while but then goes up the trail toward the camp.

1 IRONY

The refrain "it certainly was cold" now becomes more ironic, since the man is almost completely frozen.

2 THEME

The stars leap and dance; there is no mourning for the man. It is as if Nature is celebrating a victory.

REFLECTING ON THE STORY

Is the man any less a *chechaquo* ("newcomer") when he dies than when he started out? (Whether one thinks the man has learned any respect for Nature depends on how one interprets his dream statement to the old-timer: "You were right.")

STUDY QUESTIONS

1. trail, absence of sun, cold, strangeness; without imagination
2. instinct
3. springs under snow; test footing
4. dry clothes, warm feet after falling through ice into water
5. *first:* snow from tree overhead; *second:* smothers, scatters flames with frozen hands
6. falls asleep, freezes to death; trots off to cabin where the man's companions are waiting
7. overpowering cold; he loses
8. *man:* has reason, but ignores common sense, dies; *dog:* instinct warns of danger, survives; instinct superior to flawed reason
9. stark, grim; factual approach, natural forces beyond character's understanding, tone devoid of sentiment

LITERARY FOCUS

Possible answers:
conflict with nature: "The Outcasts of Poker Flat"; *conflict between two characters:* Harry and Deerslayer in *The Deerslayer; conflict between character and society:* Haskins in "Under the Lion's Paw"; *conflict between character and fate:* Ahab in *Moby-Dick; inner conflict:* Hooper in "The Minister's Black Veil"

VOCABULARY

1. (d) whispered
2. (d) recoiled
3. (c) went through
4. (b) lightened
5. (c) plod

COMPARING WRITERS

1. *Sylvia:* conflict with others; consciously chooses bird's life and solitude over stranger's friendship, grandmother's needs; *Mrs. Sommers:* internal conflict; impulsively chooses own needs over children's; *both:* faced with choice between personal desires and needs of others
2. *"Poker Flat":* greatest use of local color; rooted in California Gold Rush; *"White Heron":* regional color more subtle, less essential to story; except for dialect could have taken place elsewhere; *"Silk Stockings":* least use of local color; locale never specified
3. *both:* battle nature in way that affects lives; nature is malevolent; *London:* alone; very life at stake; *Garland:* farmers have support; *Emerson, Thoreau:* nature is ennobling and uplifting to spirit, never threatening

A battle with nature is a common conflict in literature, particularly Naturalist literature. Other common types are conflict between two characters; conflict between a character and the laws of society; conflict between a character and chance or fate; and inner conflict, in which a character struggles with personal weaknesses, illusions, or desires.

Thinking About Conflict

■ Consider the other stories you have read in this book. Find at least one example of each of the five kinds of conflict.

VOCABULARY

Vivid Action Words: Antonyms

A story about a man alone freezing to death seems an unlikely source for vivid verbs. Yet it is the masterful use of these words that gives this story much of its descriptive power. London shows us ice that "curved" and "twisted," a man who "stamped" and "strode," a dog that "whined" and "trotted."

A good way to understand exactly what a word means is to name its antonym, or opposite. The verbs in capitals are from "To Build a Fire." Choose the verb that is an antonym of each verb in capitals, *as it is used in this selection.*

1. CRACKLED: (a) popped (b) puffed (c) sparked (d) whispered
2. PLUNGED: (a) approached (b) entered (c) hung back (d) recoiled
3. SKIRTED: (a) circled (b) covered (c) went through (d) went back
4. FREIGHTED: (a) clear of (b) lightened (c) stiffened (d) strengthened
5. SKIM: (a) float (b) fly (c) plod (d) sink

COMPOSITION

Writing About a Quotation

■ The old-timer in "To Build a Fire" warns that "after fifty below, a man should travel with a partner." In a brief essay first explain the literal meaning of the warning. Then explain the deeper significance that the unheeded warning might have for the main character. Relate the quotation to the theme of the work. *For help with this assignment, refer to Lesson 5 in the Writing About Literature Handbook at the back of this book.*

Describing a Conflict

■ In a few paragraphs describe a struggle with nature that you or someone you know has experienced. Provide details to make the description vivid and build suspense by reminding the reader of the consequences of the struggle. Be sure to explain how the conflict was resolved.

COMPARING WRITERS

1. Both Sarah Orne Jewett, in "A White Heron," and Kate Chopin, in "A Pair of Silk Stockings," concentrate on their main characters' thoughts and feelings. In both stories the main character faces a certain choice and must make a decision. How are the choices facing the two characters different? How are they similar? How do the characters' decisions differ?
2. The writers in this unit do not use Regionalist techniques in the same way or to the same degree. Compare the use of local color in "The Outcasts of Poker Flat," "A White Heron," and "A Pair of Silk Stockings." Which story emphasizes local color the most? Which of the stories seem rooted in a particular time and place? Which one could perhaps have taken place somewhere else? Why?
3. Both the farmers in Garland's "Under the Lion's Paw" and the man in London's "To Build a Fire" battle nature. In what ways are their battles the same? How are they different? Compare the ideas about nature in these stories with the ideas about nature expressed by Emerson (pages 161–163) and Thoreau (pages 174–179).

COMPOSITION: GUIDELINES FOR EVALUATION

WRITING ABOUT A QUOTATION

Objective

To explain the significance of a quotation

Guidelines for Evaluation

- suggested length: three to four paragraphs
- should explain literal meaning of quotation
- should explain significance of quotation
- should show how quotation relates to theme

DESCRIBING A CONFLICT

Objective

To use details to describe conflict with nature

Guidelines for Evaluation

- suggested length: two to four paragraphs
- should relate familiar experience
- should describe setting, situation, resolution
- should use vivid words and details
- should build suspense by reminding reader of possible consequences of conflict

Stephen Crane *1871–1900*

Stephen Crane's amazing achievements within his short life—he died of tuberculosis at twenty-eight—show that he developed very early his extraordinary gift for writing. Crane left Syracuse University after only one semester, a period during which he spent more time playing baseball than studying. Yet during that semester he had already begun work on his first novel, *Maggie: A Girl of the Streets.*

After leaving Syracuse Crane moved to New York City and found work as a journalist. He was only twenty when he heard Hamlin Garland (page 340) lecture on Realism in fiction. Inspired, Crane resumed work on *Maggie,* a harsh, uncompromising picture of life among New York City's poor. The book was rejected by several editors, who felt the American public was not ready for so un-Romantic a tale. Apparently they were right: When in 1893 Crane borrowed money from his brother to have *Maggie* published, a few writers praised the book, but it did not sell.

Nevertheless, Crane began work on another novel. He called it *The Red Badge of Courage: An Episode of the American Civil War,* and it would prove to be his finest literary achievement. Hamlin Garland gave Crane the money to have the book typed; it was serialized in 1894 and published in book form one year later. *The Red Badge* was a resounding success and has become one of America's classic novels.

Most of Crane's other fiction and nonfiction is grounded in personal experience. His short story "The Blue Hotel" (1898) is set in the American West, which he visited in the course of his career as journalist; "The Open Boat" (1897) is based on his experience of being shipwrecked while traveling to Cuba. Crane also wrote some poetry, collected in two volumes—*The Black Riders* (1895) and *War Is Kind* (1899). These short, bitter poems reveal a man whose life had been filled with pain and hardship but who refused to shut his eyes to the grim truths he saw.

■ How does Crane's fictional account of the survivors of a shipwreck differ from a newspaper account of the same events?

AT A GLANCE

- Four men are in a small boat on a rough, windswept sea. They fear drowning.
- A cook, an oiler, and a correspondent are led by the captain, who is injured and dejected at losing his ship.

LITERARY OPTIONS

- conflict
- imagery
- point of view

THEMATIC OPTIONS

- nature's indifference to humanity
- challenge and endurance
- life and death

1 CHARACTERIZATION

The narrator refers to each man by occupation, suggesting that each label in itself says something about the man.

2 CHARACTERIZATION

The captain grieves over the loss of his ship and the men who died on it. He seems devoted to his responsibilities.

3 IMAGERY

Throughout, Crane uses images, similes, and metaphors to render experience precisely. Being seated upon a "bucking bronco" is an apt description of the plight of the shipwrecked men.

SELECTION FOR PRACTICE IN ACTIVE READING
(TCR 7, p. 71)

Stephen Crane

The Open Boat

A Tale Intended to Be After the Fact:
Being the Experience of Four Men
From the Sunk Steamer *Commodore.*

I

None of them knew the color of the sky. Their eyes glanced level, and were fastened upon the waves that swept toward them. These waves were of the hue of slate, save for the tops, which were of foaming white, and all of the men knew the colors of the sea. The horizon narrowed and widened, and dipped and rose, and at all times its edge was jagged with waves that seemed thrust up in points like rocks.

Many a man ought to have a bathtub larger than the boat which here rode upon the sea. These waves were most wrongfully and barbarously abrupt and tall, and each froth-top was a problem in small-boat navigation.

1 The cook squatted in the bottom, and looked with both eyes at the six inches of gunwale which separated him from the ocean. His sleeves were rolled over his fat forearms, and the two flaps of his unbuttoned vest dangled as he bent to bail out the boat. Often he said, "Gawd! that was a narrow clip." As he remarked it he invariably gazed eastward over the broken sea.

The oiler, steering with one of the two oars in the boat, sometimes raised himself suddenly to keep clear of water that swirled in over the stern. It was a thin little oar, and it seemed often ready to snap.

The correspondent, pulling at the other oar, watched the waves and wondered why he was there.

2 The injured captain, lying in the bow, was at this time buried in that profound dejection and indifference which comes, temporarily at least, to even the bravest and most enduring when, willy-nilly, the firm fails, the army loses, the ship goes down. The mind of the master of a vessel is rooted deep in the timbers of her, though he command for a day or a decade; and this captain had on him the stern impression of a scene in the grays of dawn of seven turned faces, and later a stump of a topmast with a white ball on it, that slashed to and fro at the waves, went low and lower, and down. Thereafter there was something strange in his voice. Although steady, it was deep with mourning, and of a quality beyond oration or tears.

"Keep 'er a little more south, Billie," said he.

"A little more south, sir," said the oiler in the stern.

3 A seat in this boat was not unlike a seat upon a bucking bronco, and, by the same token, a bronco is not much smaller. The craft pranced and reared and plunged like an animal. As each wave came, and she rose for it, she seemed like a horse making at a fence outrageously high. The manner of her scramble over these walls of water is a mystic thing, and, moreover, at the top of them were ordinarily these problems in white water, the foam racing down from the summit of each wave, requiring a new leap, and a leap from the air. Then, after scornfully bumping a crest, she would slide and race and splash down a long incline, and arrive bobbing and nodding in front of the next menace.

A singular disadvantage of the sea lies in the fact that, after successfully surmounting one wave, you discover that there is another behind it, just as important and just as nervously anxious to do something effective in the way of swamping boats. In a ten-foot dinghy one can get an idea of the resources of the sea in the line of waves that is not probable to the average experience, which is never at sea in a dinghy. As each slaty wall of water approached, it shut all else from the view of the men in the boat, and it was not difficult to imagine that this particular wave was the final outburst of the ocean, the last effort of the grim water. There was a terrible grace in the

GUIDED READING

LITERAL QUESTION

1a. According to the narrator, what lies beyond each successfully passed wave? (another wave that is just as important and just as dangerous)

INFERENTIAL QUESTION

1b. What kind of mood does such discussion create? (constantly increasing tension; possibly a sense of inescapable doom)

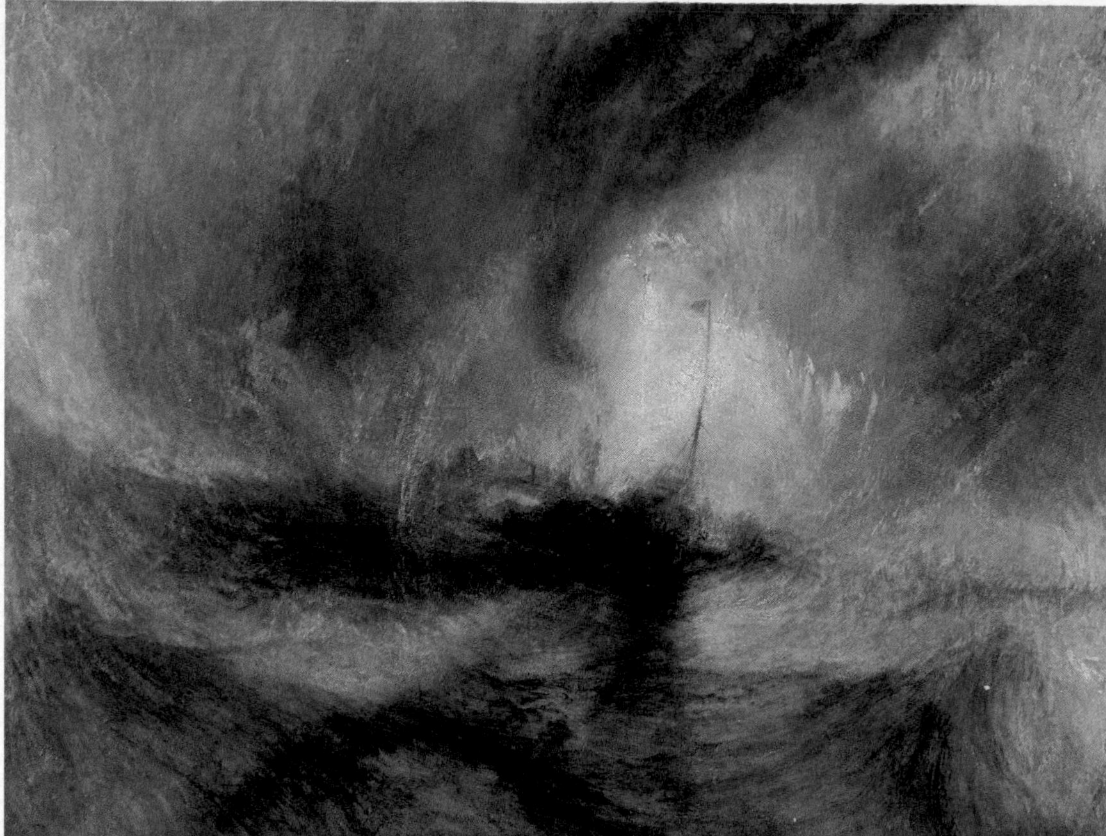

Tate Gallery, London

Snowstorm: Steamboat, J. M. W. Turner, 1842.

move of the waves, and they came in silence, save for the snarling of the crests.

1 In the wan light the faces of the men must have been gray. Their eyes must have glinted in strange ways as they gazed steadily astern. Viewed from a balcony, the whole thing would, doubtless, have been weirdly picturesque. But the men in the boat had no time to see it, and if they had had leisure, there were other things to occupy their minds. The sun swung steadily up the sky, and they knew it was broad day because the color of the sea changed from slate to emerald green streaked with amber lights, and the foam was like tumbling snow. The process of the breaking day was unknown to them. They were aware only of this effect upon the color of the waves that rolled toward them.

In disjointed sentences the cook and the correspondent argued as to the difference between a
2 lifesaving station and a house of refuge. The cook had said: "There's a house of refuge just north of the Mosquito Inlet Light, and as soon as they see us they'll come off in their boat and pick us up."

"As soon as who see us?" said the correspondent.

"The crew," said the cook.

"Houses of refuge don't have crews," said the correspondent. "As I understand them, they are

AT A GLANCE

- The sun moves higher in the sky.
- The cook and the correspondent disagree about the possibility of rescue.

1 POINT OF VIEW

Although using third-person narration, Crane tries to make his readers feel that they are in the boat rather than observing the action from outside.

2 PLOT: RISING ACTION

Throughout the story the men find reasons to continue hoping that they will be saved.

GUIDED READING

LITERAL QUESTION

1a. According to the narrator, why do the men not notice the picturesque quality of the seascape? ("There were other things to occupy their minds.")

INFERENTIAL QUESTION

1b. What concerns do you think preoccupy the men? (Possible answers: the danger of being swamped by the waves, the threat of starvation, the hope of rescue)

AT A GLANCE

- The men discuss the fact that the wind is pushing them towards the shore.
- They take turns rowing.

1 IMAGERY

The narrator paints a dual picture of the sea, one in which we can visualize both its beauty and its treachery. The observation that the sea was "probably splendid" suggests that we share the point of view of the men in the boat.

2 THEME

Nature, as represented by the gulls, watches the men indifferently.

3 STYLE: REPETITION

To capture the tedium of rowing, Crane repeats the word *rowed* and describes the slight variations in this monotonous routine.

only places where clothes and grub are stored for the benefit of shipwrecked people. They don't carry crews."

"Oh, yes, they do," said the cook.

"No, they don't," said the correspondent.

"Well, we're not there yet, anyhow," said the oiler in the stern.

"Well," said the cook, "perhaps it's not a house of refuge that I'm thinking of as being near Mosquito Inlet Light; perhaps it's a lifesaving station."

"We're not there yet," said the oiler in the stern.

II

As the boat bounced from the top of each wave the wind tore through the hair of the hatless men, and as the craft plopped her stern down
1 again the spray slashed past them. The crest of each of these waves was a hill, from the top of which the men surveyed for a moment a broad, tumultuous expanse, shining and wind-riven. It was probably splendid, it was probably glorious, this play of the free sea, wild with lights of emerald and white and amber.

"Bully good thing it's an onshore wind," said the cook. "If not, where would we be? Wouldn't have a show."

"That's right," said the correspondent.

The busy oiler nodded his assent.

Then the captain, in the bow, chuckled in a way that expressed humor, contempt, tragedy, all in one. "Do you think we've got much of a show now, boys?" said he.

Whereupon the three were silent, save for a trifle of hemming and hawing. To express any particular optimism at this time they felt to be childish and stupid, but they all doubtless possessed this sense of the situation in their minds. A young man thinks doggedly at such times. On the other hand, the ethics of their condition was decidedly against any open suggestion of hopelessness. So they were silent.

"Oh, well," said the captain, soothing his children, "we'll get ashore all right."

But there was that in his tone which made them think; so the oiler quoth, "Yes! if this wind holds."

The cook was bailing. "Yes! if we don't catch hell in the surf."

Canton-flannel gulls[1] flew near and far. Sometimes they sat down on the sea, near patches of brown seaweed that rolled over the waves with a movement like carpets on a line in a gale. The birds sat comfortably in groups, and they were
2 envied by some in the dinghy, for the wrath of the sea was no more to them than it was to a covey of prairie chickens a thousand miles inland. Often they came very close and stared at the men with black, beadlike eyes. At these times they were uncanny and sinister in their unblinking scrutiny, and the men hooted angrily at them, telling them to be gone. One came, and evidently decided to alight on the top of the captain's head. The bird flew parallel to the boat, and did not circle, but made short sidelong jumps in the air in chicken fashion. His black eyes were wistfully fixed upon the captain's head. "Ugly brute," said the oiler to the bird. "You look as if you were made with a jackknife." The cook and the correspondent swore darkly at the creature. The captain naturally wished to knock it away with the end of the heavy painter,[2] but he did not dare do it, because anything resembling an emphatic gesture would have capsized this freighted boat; and so, with his open hand, the captain gently and carefully waved the gull away. After it had been discouraged from the pursuit the captain breathed easier on account of his hair, and others breathed easier because the bird struck their minds at this time as being somehow gruesome and ominous.

3 In the meantime the oiler and the correspondent rowed; and also they rowed. They sat together in the same seat, and each rowed an oar. Then the oiler took both oars; then the correspondent took both oars; then the oiler; then the correspondent. They rowed and they rowed. The very ticklish part of the business was when the time came for the reclining one in the stern to take his turn at the oars. By the very last star of

1. **Canton-flannel gulls:** gulls whose feathers resemble Canton flannel, a strong cotton fabric that is soft on one side and ribbed on the other.

2. **painter:** rope used to tie a boat to a dock or wharf.

GUIDED READING

LITERAL QUESTIONS

1a. Which way is the wind blowing? (toward the shore)

2a. How do the birds sit on the water? (comfortably and in groups)

INFERENTIAL QUESTIONS

1b. Why is this detail important? (The wind may push the men toward land and safety.)

2b. How does their situation contrast with that of the men? (Although both are in groups, the birds are at home upon the water, whereas the men are in peril there.)

truth, it is easier to steal eggs from under a hen than it was to change seats in the dinghy. First
1 the man in the stern slid his hand along the thwart and moved with care, as if he were of Sèvres.[3] Then the man in the rowing seat slid his hand along the other thwart. It was all done with the most extraordinary care. As the two sidled past each other, the whole party kept watchful eyes on the coming wave, and the captain cried: "Look out, now! Steady, there!"

The brown mats of seaweed that appeared from time to time were like islands, bits of earth. They were traveling, apparently, neither one way nor the other. They were, to all intents, stationary. They informed the men in the boat that it was making progress slowly toward the land.

The captain, rearing cautiously in the bow after the dinghy soared on a great swell, said that he had seen the lighthouse at Mosquito Inlet. Presently the cook remarked that he had seen it. The correspondent was at the oars then, and for some reason he too wished to look at the lighthouse; but his back was toward the far shore, and the waves were important, and for some time he could not seize an opportunity to turn his head. But at last there came a wave more gentle than the others, and when at the crest of it he swiftly scoured the western horizon.

"See it?" said the captain.

"No," said the correspondent, slowly; "I didn't see anything."

"Look again," said the captain. He pointed. "It's exactly in that direction."

At the top of another wave the correspondent did as he was bid, and this time his eyes chanced on a small, still thing on the edge of the swaying horizon. It was precisely like the point of a pin. It took an anxious eye to find a lighthouse so tiny.

"Think we'll make it, Captain?"

"If this wind holds and the boat don't swamp, we can't do much else," said the captain.

2 The little boat, lifted by each towering sea and splashed viciously by the crests, made progress that in the absence of seaweed was not apparent to those in her. She seemed just a wee thing wallowing miraculously, top up, at the mercy of five oceans. Occasionally a great spread of water, like white flames, swarmed into her.

"Bail her, cook," said the captain, serenely.

"All right, Captain," said the cheerful cook.

III

3 It would be difficult to describe the subtle brotherhood of men that was here established on the seas. No one said that it was so. No one mentioned it. But it dwelt in the boat, and each man felt it warm him. They were a captain, an oiler, a cook, and a correspondent, and they were friends—friends in a more curiously iron-bound degree than may be common. The hurt captain, lying against the water jar in the bow, spoke always in a low voice and calmly; but he could never command a more ready and swiftly obedient crew than the motley three of the dinghy. It was more than a mere recognition of what was best for the common safety. There was surely in it a quality that was personal and heartfelt. And after this devotion to the commander of the boat, there was this comradeship, that the correspondent, for instance, who had been taught to be cynical of men, knew even at the time was the best experience of his life. But no one said that it was so. No one mentioned it.

"I wish we had a sail," remarked the captain. "We might try my overcoat on the end of an oar, and give you two boys a chance to rest." So the cook and the correspondent held the mast and spread wide the overcoat; the oiler steered; and the little boat made good way with her new rig. Sometimes the oiler had to scull sharply to keep a sea from breaking into the boat, but otherwise sailing was a success.

Meanwhile the lighthouse had been growing slowly larger. It had now almost assumed color, and appeared like a little gray shadow on the sky. The man at the oars could not be prevented from turning his head rather often to try for a glimpse of this little gray shadow.

At last, from the top of each wave, the men in the tossing boat could see land. Even as the lighthouse was an upright shadow on the sky, this land seemed but a long black shadow on the sea. It certainly was thinner than paper. "We must be

3. **Sèvres** [sev′rə]: fine porcelain made in Sèvres, France.

AT A GLANCE

- The boat is so small and unstable that the men must change seats very carefully.
- The captain sees the lighthouse.
- The men are warmed by the brotherhood of their ordeal.

1 VOCABULARY: CONNOTATION

The fragility of Sèvres porcelain suggests how easily the men's lives might be broken.

2 IMAGERY

The "viciousness" and "white flames" of the sea show no mercy toward the men. These images capture the moment-to-moment experience of the sea's savage power.

3 RESPONSE JOURNAL

Students might attempt to describe the "subtle brotherhood" of which Crane speaks.

GUIDED READING

LITERAL QUESTIONS

1a. What does the captain see when the boat rises on a "great swell"? (the lighthouse at Mosquito Inlet)

2a. By what do the men feel warmed? (a "subtle brotherhood")

INFERENTIAL QUESTIONS

1b. Why do the others want to see this sight? (The sight of the lighthouse means that they are approaching the shore, and this sight reassures them.)

2b. Why does this feeling encourage the men? (Each man is reminded that he is not alone.)

AT A GLANCE

- The wind dies down, and the men become discouraged, fatigued by rowing.

1 POINT OF VIEW

Moving into the minds of the oiler and correspondent, the narrator shows their reaction to the agony of rowing.

Sterling and Francine Clark Art Institute, Williamstown, MA

A Summer Squall, Winslow Homer, 1904.

about opposite New Smyrna," said the cook, who had coasted this shore often in schooners. "Captain, by the way, I believe they abandoned that lifesaving station there about a year ago."

"Did they?" said the captain.

The wind slowly died away. The cook and the correspondent were not now obliged to slave in order to hold high the oar; but the waves continued their old impetuous swooping at the dinghy, and the little craft, no longer under way, struggled woundily over them. The oiler or the correspondent took the oars again.

Shipwrecks are apropos of nothing. If men could only train for them and have them occur when the men had reached pink condition, there would be less drowning at sea. Of the four in the dinghy none had slept any time worth mentioning for two days and two nights previous to embarking in the dinghy, and in the excitement of clambering about the deck of a foundering ship they had also forgotten to eat heartily.

1 For these reasons, and for others, neither the oiler nor the correspondent was fond of rowing at this time. The correspondent wondered ingenuously how in the name of all that was sane could there be people who thought it amusing to

GUIDED READING

LITERAL QUESTION

1a. What does the narrator say are "apropos of nothing"? (shipwrecks)

INFERENTIAL QUESTION

1b. What do you think he means? (that it is virtually impossible to be well-prepared for a shipwreck)

row a boat. It was not an amusement; it was a diabolical punishment, and even a genius of mental aberrations could never conclude that it was anything but a horror to the muscles and a crime against the back. He mentioned to the boat in general how the amusement of rowing struck him, and the weary-faced oiler smiled in full sympathy. Previously to the foundering, by the way, the oiler had worked double watch in the engine room of the ship.

"Take her easy now, boys," said the captain. "Don't spend yourselves. If we have to run a surf you'll need all your strength, because we'll sure have to swim for it. Take your time."

1 Slowly the land arose from the sea. From a black line it became a line of black and a line of white—trees and sand. Finally the captain said that he could make out a house on the shore. "That's the house of refuge, sure," said the cook. "They'll see us before long, and come out after us."

The distant lighthouse reared high. "The keeper ought to be able to make us out now, if he's looking through a glass," said the captain. "He'll notify the lifesaving people."

"None of those other boats could have got ashore to give word of the wreck," said the oiler, in a low voice, "else the lifeboat would be out hunting us."

2 Slowly and beautifully the land loomed out of the sea. The wind came again. It had veered from the northeast to the southeast. Finally a new sound struck the ears of the men in the boat. It was the low thunder of the surf on the shore. "We'll never be able to make the lighthouse now," said the captain. "Swing her head a little more north, Billie."

"A little more north, sir," said the oiler.

Whereupon the little boat turned her nose once more down the wind, and all but the oarsman watched the shore grow. Under the influence of this expansion doubt and direful apprehension were leaving the minds of the men. The management of the boat was still most absorbing, but it could not prevent a quiet cheerfulness. In an hour, perhaps, they would be ashore.

Their backbones had become thoroughly used to balancing in the boat, and they now rode this wild colt of a dinghy like circus men. The correspondent thought that he had been drenched to the skin, but happening to feel in the top pocket of his coat, he found therein eight cigars. Four of them were soaked with sea water; four were perfectly scatheless. After a search,
3 somebody produced three dry matches; and thereupon the four waifs rode in their little boat and, with an assurance of an impending rescue shining in their eyes, puffed at the big cigars, and judged well and ill of all men. Everybody took a drink of water.

IV

"Cook," remarked the captain, "there don't seem to be any signs of life about your house of refuge."

"No," replied the cook. "Funny they don't see us!"

A broad stretch of lowly coast lay before the eyes of the men. It was of low dunes topped with dark vegetation. The roar of the surf was plain, and sometimes they could see the white lip of a
4 wave as it spun up the beach. A tiny house was blocked out black upon the sky. Southward, the slim lighthouse lifted its little gray length.

Tide, wind, and waves were swinging the dinghy northward. "Funny they don't see us," said the men.

The surf's roar was here dulled, but its tone was nevertheless thunderous and mighty. As the boat swam over the great rollers the men sat listening to this roar. "We'll swamp sure," said everybody.

It is fair to say here that there was not a lifesaving station within twenty miles in either direction; but the men did not know this fact, and in consequence they made dark and opprobrious[4] remarks concerning the eyesight of the nation's lifesavers. Four scowling men sat in the dinghy, and surpassed records in the invention of epithets.

---

4. **opprobrious** [ə prō′brē əs]: expressing disapproval.

AT A GLANCE

- Land becomes visible, and the men hear the sound of the surf.
- They turn the boat north.
- Feeling confident of rescue, the men celebrate by smoking cigars. Later, they realize that no one has seen them.

1 PLOT: RISING ACTION

The appearance of land is strong reason for the men's will to stiffen with the expectation of survival.

2 IMAGERY

The land looms "slowly" because the men would like to approach it more quickly; it looms "beautifully" because it means life to them.

3 CHARACTERIZATION

The smoking of the cigars shows the men's confidence in their imminent rescue.

4 THEME

The lighthouse, with its promise of rescue, lies to the south, but indifferent nature pushes them north.

GUIDED READING

LITERAL QUESTIONS

1a. What does the correspondent find in his coat? (some cigars)

2a. What fact do the men not know? (that there is no lifesaving station within twenty miles)

INFERENTIAL QUESTIONS

1b. What does his sharing of them say about the frame of mind of the men in the boat? (They are optimistic now that they have seen land.)

2b. What does this unknown fact suggest about the men's chances? (that they are even dimmer than the men realize)

AT A GLANCE

- The captain decides to turn the boat toward shore.
- The men exchange addresses in case they are not all saved.
- The oiler steers the boat back out to sea to avoid a strong surf, and the elements push the boat north and south.

1 THEME

The realization of their mortality and the fear of facing death trigger the bitterness that the men feel.

2 STYLE: REFRAIN

The almost poetic refrain of "If I am going to be drowned" will appear again in the story as the men reflect on their battle against nature.

3 THEME

Nature does not care when men die or how bravely they endure; rather, nature destroys and preserves life indifferently.

4 THEME

Some challenges require not a burst of bravery or strength but an ability to withstand pains that can slowly wear away the will.

"Funny they don't see us."

1 The lightheartedness of a former time had completely faded. To their sharpened minds it was easy to conjure pictures of all kinds of incompetency and blindness and, indeed, cowardice. There was the shore of the populous land, and it was bitter and bitter to them that from it came no sign.

"Well," said the captain, ultimately, "I suppose we'll have to make a try for ourselves. If we stay out here too long, we'll none of us have strength left to swim after the boat swamps."

And so the oiler, who was at the oars, turned the boat straight for the shore. There was a sudden tightening of muscles. There was some thinking.

"If we don't all get ashore," said the captain—"if we don't all get ashore, I suppose you fellows know where to send news of my finish?"

They then briefly exchanged some addresses and admonitions. As for the reflections of the
2 men, there was a great deal of rage in them. Perchance they might be formulated thus: "If I am going to be drowned—if I am going to be drowned—if I am going to be drowned, why, in the name of the seven mad gods who rule the sea,[5] was I allowed to come thus far and contemplate sand and trees? Was I brought here merely to have my nose dragged away as I was about to nibble the sacred cheese of life? It is preposterous! If this old ninny woman, Fate, cannot do better than this, she should be deprived of the management of men's fortunes. She is an old hen who knows not her intention. If she has decided to
3 drown me, why did she not do it in the beginning, and save me all this trouble? The whole affair is absurd. . . . But no; she cannot mean to drown me. She dare not drown me. She cannot drown me. Not after all this work!" Afterward the man might have had an impulse to shake his fist at the clouds. "Just you drown me, now, and then hear what I call you!"

The billows that came at this time were more formidable. They seemed always just about to break and roll over the little boat in a turmoil of foam. There was a preparatory and long growl in the speech of them. No mind unused to the sea would have concluded that the dinghy could ascend these sheer heights in time. The shore was still afar. The oiler was a wily surfman. "Boys," he said swiftly, "she won't live three minutes more, and we're too far out to swim. Shall I take her to sea again, Captain?"

"Yes; go ahead!" said the captain.

This oiler, by a series of quick miracles and fast and steady oarsmanship, turned the boat in the middle of the surf and took her safely to sea again.

There was a considerable silence as the boat bumped over the furrowed sea to deeper water. Then somebody in gloom spoke: "Well, anyhow, they must have seen us from the shore by now."

The gulls went in slanting flight up the wind toward the gray, desolate east. A squall, marked by dingy clouds, and clouds brick red, like smoke from a burning building, appeared from the southeast.

"What do you think of those lifesaving people? Ain't they peaches?"

"Funny they haven't seen us."

"Maybe they think we're out here for sport! Maybe they think we're fishin'. Maybe they think we're damned fools."

It was a long afternoon. A changed tide tried to force them southward, but wind and wave said northward. Far ahead, where coastline, sea, and sky formed their mighty angle, there were little dots which seemed to indicate a city on the shore.

"St. Augustine?"

The captain shook his head. "Too near Mosquito Inlet."

4 And the oiler rowed, and then the correspondent rowed; then the oiler rowed. It was a weary business. The human back can become the seat of more aches and pains than are registered in books for the composite anatomy of a regiment. It is a limited area, but it can become the theater of innumerable muscular conflicts, tangles, wrenches, knots, and other comforts.

"Did you ever like to row, Billie?" asked the correspondent.

---

5. **seven . . . sea:** probably refers to the Arctic, Antarctic, North and South Pacific, North and South Atlantic, and Indian oceans, each at the mercy of a deity.

GUIDED READING

LITERAL QUESTION

1a. What does the narrator describe as "a weary business"? (rowing)

INFERENTIAL QUESTION

1b. Why does the activity merit this description? (Not only is the physical labor wearying, but the frustration of exerting so much effort unsuccessfully is also draining emotionally.)

"No," said the oiler; "hang it!"

When one exchanged the rowing seat for a place in the bottom of the boat, he suffered a bodily depression that caused him to be careless of everything save an obligation to wiggle one finger. There was cold sea water swashing to and fro in the boat, and he lay in it. His head, pillowed on a thwart, was within an inch of the swirl of a wave crest, and sometimes a particularly obstreperous sea came inboard and drenched him once more. But these matters did not annoy him. It is almost certain that if the boat had capsized he would have tumbled comfortably out upon the ocean as if he felt sure that it was a great, soft mattress.

1 "Look! There's a man on the shore!"

"Where?"

"There! See 'im? See 'im?"

"Yes, sure! He's walking along."

"Now he's stopped. Look! He's facing us!"

"He's waving at us!"

"So he is! By thunder!"

"Ah, now we're all right! Now we're all right! There'll be a boat out here for us in half an hour."

"He's going on. He's running. He's going up to that house there."

The remote beach seemed lower than the sea, and it required a searching glance to discern the little black figure. The captain saw a floating stick, and they rowed to it. A bath towel was by some weird chance in the boat, and tying this on the stick, the captain waved it. The oarsman did not dare turn his head, so he was obliged to ask questions.

"What's he doing now?"

"He's standing still again. He's looking, I think. . . . There he goes again—toward the house. . . . Now he's stopped again."

"Is he waving at us?"

2 "No, not now; he was, though."

"Look! There comes another man!"

"He's running."

"Look at him go, would you!"

"Why, he's on a bicycle. Now he's met the other man. They're both waving at us. Look!"

"There comes something up the beach."

"What the devil is that thing?"

"Why, it looks like a boat."

"Why, certainly, it's a boat."

"No; it's on wheels."

"Yes, so it is. Well, that must be the lifeboat. They drag them along shore on a wagon."

"That's the lifeboat, sure."

"No, by———, it's—it's an omnibus."

"I tell you it's a lifeboat."

"It is not! It's an omnibus. I can see it plain. See? One of these big hotel omnibuses."

"By thunder, you're right. It's an omnibus, sure as fate. What do you suppose they are doing with an omnibus? Maybe they are going around collecting the life crew, hey?"

"That's it, likely. Look! There's a fellow waving a little black flag. He's standing on the steps of the omnibus. There come those other two fellows. Now they're all talking together. Look at the fellow with the flag. Maybe he ain't waving it!"

"That ain't a flag, is it? That's his coat. Why, certainly, that's his coat."

"So it is; it's his coat. He's taken it off and is waving it around his head. But would you look at him swing it!"

3 "Oh, say, there isn't any lifesaving station there. That's just a winter resort hotel omnibus that has brought over some of the boarders to see us drown."

"What's that idiot with the coat mean? What's he signaling, anyhow?"

"It looks as if he were trying to tell us to go north. There must be a life-saving station up there."

"No; he thinks we're fishing. Just giving us a merry hand. See? Ah, there, Willie!"

"Well, I wish I could make something out of those signals. What do you suppose he means?"

"He don't mean anything; he's just playing."

4 "Well, if he'd just signal us to try the surf again, or to go to sea and wait, or go north, or go south, or go to hell, there would be some reason in it. But look at him! He just stands there and keeps his coat revolving like a wheel. The ass!"

"There come more people."

"Now there's quite a mob. Look! Isn't that a boat?"

"Where? Oh, I see where you mean. No, that's no boat."

AT A GLANCE

- The men in the boat see a man on shore.
- The man on shore waves his coat in a circle, and the men in the boat cannot understand what he means.
- Because several people gather on shore, watching the men in the boat, the men expect to be saved soon.

1 PLOT: RISING ACTION

The appearance of a person on shore revives the men's hopes and rebuilds dramatic tension.

2 DIALOGUE

The unidentified exchanges capture the excitement of the men as well as their puzzlement as they attempt to figure out what is happening on shore.

3 IRONY

The people on shore apparently have gathered not to rescue the men but to watch them, unaware that the men in the boat are in desperate trouble.

4 CONFLICT

The men face not only the indifference of nature but also the blindness of those who might be able to save them.

GUIDED READING

LITERAL QUESTION

1a. What do the men see on shore? (a man looking at them)

INFERENTIAL QUESTION

1b. Why does this event make them think they will be all right? (They are confident that the man will recognize that they need help and that he will arrange for a rescue.)

AT A GLANCE

- The men keep hoping for help from land, but none comes.
- Night falls; the land disappears.
- The cook dreams of pie, but the oiler and correspondent do not want to talk about food.

1 STYLE: SIMILE

Crane's unusual comparison of the effect of the cold sea spray to that of a branding iron evokes the fear, the anger, and the pain of the men.

2 STYLE: METAPHOR

The image of nibbling cheese suggests human insignificance by comparing people to mice.

3 CHARACTERIZATION

Fittingly, the cook cannot help thinking and talking about food. Perhaps this fantasy is his way of dealing with the perils at hand.

4 IMAGERY

Crane's description captures the vastness and the beauty of the turbulent sea at night.

"That fellow is still waving his coat."

"He must think we like to see him do that. Why don't he quit it? It don't mean anything."

"I don't know. I think he is trying to make us go north. It must be that there's a lifesaving station there somewhere."

"Say, he ain't tired yet. Look at 'im wave!"

"Wonder how long he can keep that up. He's been revolving his coat ever since he caught sight of us. He's an idiot. Why aren't they getting men to bring a boat out? A fishing boat—one of those big yawls—could come out here all right. Why don't he do something?"

"Oh, it's all right now."

"They'll have a boat out here for us in less than no time, now that they've seen us."

A faint yellow tone came into the sky over the low land. The shadows on the sea slowly deepened. The wind bore coldness with it, and the men began to shiver.

"Holy smoke!" said one, allowing his voice to express his impious mood, "if we keep on monkeying out here! If we've got to flounder out here all night!"

"Oh, we'll never have to stay here all night! Don't you worry. They've seen us now, and it won't be long before they'll come chasing out after us."

1 The shore grew dusky. The man waving a coat blended gradually into this gloom, and it swallowed in the same manner the omnibus and the group of people. The spray, when it dashed uproariously over the side, made the voyagers shrink and swear like men who were being branded.

"I'd like to catch the chump who waved the coat. I feel like soaking him one, just for luck."

"Why? What did he do?"

"Oh, nothing, but then he seemed so damned cheerful."

In the meantime the oiler rowed, and then the correspondent rowed, and then the oiler rowed. Gray-faced and bowed forward, they mechanically, turn by turn, plied the leaden oars. The form of the lighthouse had vanished from the southern horizon, but finally a pale star appeared, just lifting from the sea. The streaked saffron in the west passed before the all-merging darkness, and the sea to the east was black. The land had vanished, and was expressed only by the low and drear thunder of the surf.

"If I am going to be drowned—if I am going to be drowned—if I am going to be drowned, why, in the name of the seven mad gods who rule the sea, was I allowed to come thus far and con-
2 template sand and trees? Was I brought here merely to have my nose dragged away as I was about to nibble the sacred cheese of life?"

The patient captain, drooped over the water jar, was sometimes obliged to speak to the oarsman.

"Keep her head up! Keep her head up!"

"Keep her head up, sir." The voices were weary and low.

This was surely a quiet evening. All save the oarsman lay heavily and listlessly in the boat's bottom. As for him, his eyes were just capable of noting the tall black waves that swept forward in a most sinister silence, save for an occasional subdued growl of a crest.

3 The cook's head was on a thwart, and he looked without interest at the water under his nose. He was deep in other scenes. Finally he spoke. "Billie," he murmured dreamfully, "what kind of pie do you like best?"

V

"Pie!" said the oiler and the correspondent, agitatedly. "Don't talk about those things, blast you!"

"Well," said the cook, "I was just thinking about ham sandwiches, and—"

4 A night on the sea in an open boat is a long night. As darkness settled finally, the shine of the light, lifting from the sea in the south, changed to full gold. On the northern horizon a new light appeared, a small bluish gleam on the edge of the waters. These two lights were the furniture of the world. Otherwise there was nothing but waves.

Two men huddled in the stern, and distances were so magnificent in the dinghy that the rower was enabled to keep his feet partly warm by

GUIDED READING

LITERAL QUESTIONS

1a. How does the weather change as sunset approaches? (The wind turns colder.)

2a. What appears after the lighthouse disappears? (a pale star)

INFERENTIAL QUESTIONS

1b. How might this change reflect the mood of the men? (It might indicate that although some men talk encouragingly, the general mood may be turning grimmer.)

2b. How might its appearance reflect the mood of the men? (It is pale, perhaps in reflection of their waning spirits; it is alone, as they seem to be—cut off from the rest of humanity.)

thrusting them under his companions. Their legs indeed extended far under the rowing seat until they touched the feet of the captain forward. Sometimes, despite the efforts of the tired oarsman, a wave came piling into the boat, an icy wave of the night, and the chilling water soaked them anew. They would twist their bodies for a moment and groan, and sleep the dead sleep once more, while the water in the boat gurgled about them as the craft rocked.

The plan of the oiler and the correspondent was for one to row until he lost the ability, and then arouse the other from his sea water couch in the bottom of the boat.

The oiler plied the oars until his head drooped forward and the overpowering sleep blinded him; and he rowed yet afterward. Then
1 he touched a man in the bottom of the boat, and called his name. "Will you spell me for a little while?" he said meekly.

"Sure, Billie," said the correspondent, awaking and dragging himself to a sitting position. They exchanged places carefully, and the oiler, cuddling down in the sea water at the cook's side, seemed to go to sleep instantly.

The particular violence of the sea had ceased. The waves came without snarling. The obligation of the man at the oars was to keep the boat headed so that the tilt of the rollers would not capsize her, and to preserve her from filling when the crests rushed past. The black waves were silent and hard to be seen in the darkness. Often one was almost upon the boat before the oarsman was aware.

In a low voice the correspondent addressed the captain. He was not sure that the captain was awake, although this iron man seemed to be always awake. "Captain, shall I keep her making for that light north, sir?"

The same steady voice answered him. "Yes. Keep it about two points off the port bow."

The cook had tied a life belt around himself in order to get even the warmth which this clumsy cork contrivance could donate, and he seemed almost stovelike when a rower, whose teeth invariably chattered wildly as soon as he ceased his labor, dropped down to sleep.

The correspondent, as he rowed, looked down at the two men sleeping under foot. The cook's arm was around the oiler's shoulders, and, with their fragmentary clothing and haggard faces, they were the babes of the sea—a grotesque rendering of the old babes in the wood.

2 Later he must have grown stupid at his work, for suddenly there was a growling of water, and a crest came with a roar and a swash into the boat, and it was a wonder that it did not set the cook afloat in his life belt. The cook continued to sleep, but the oiler sat up, blinking his eyes and shaking with the new cold.

"Oh, I'm awful sorry, Billie," said the correspondent, contritely.

"That's all right, old boy," said the oiler, and lay down again and was asleep.

Presently it seemed that even the captain dozed, and the correspondent thought that he was the one man afloat on all the oceans. The wind had a voice as it came over the waves, and it was sadder than the end.

3 There was a long, loud swishing astern of the boat, and a gleaming trail of phosphorescence, like blue flame, was furrowed on the black waters. It might have been made by a monstrous knife.

Then there came a stillness, while the correspondent breathed with the open mouth and looked at the sea.

Suddenly there was another swish and another long flash of bluish light, and this time it was alongside the boat, and might almost have been reached with an oar. The correspondent saw an enormous fin speed like a shadow through the water, hurling the crystaline spray and leaving the long glowing trail.

The correspondent looked over his shoulder at the captain. His face was hidden, and he seemed to be asleep. He looked at the babes of the sea. They certainly were asleep. So, being bereft of sympathy, he leaned a little way to one side and swore softly into the sea.

But the thing did not then leave the vicinity of the boat. Ahead or astern, on one side or the other, at intervals long or short, fled the long sparkling streak, and there was to be heard the

AT A GLANCE

- The men are so exhausted that they sleep soundly, despite the cold and the cramped conditions.
- While the others sleep, the oarsman tries to keep the boat from being swamped.
- The correspondent does not sleep. He sees the fin of a shark.

1 THEME

The question "Will you spell me for a little while?" occurs again and again, suggesting by its repetition the endurance needed to meet this exhausting challenge.

2 STYLE: ONOMATOPOEIA

Crane selects words *(growling, roar* and *swash)* that allow the reader to *hear* the menace besetting the open boat.

3 IMPRESSIONISM

Crane presents fragments of sound and color to convey the feeling of a terrible presence without identifying it as a shark.

GUIDED READING

LITERAL QUESTIONS

1a. How do the men react when icy water splashes into the boat? (They turn and groan; then they return to a deep sleep.)

2a. What makes the correspondent think that he is the "one man afloat on all the oceans"? (The other three in the boat seem to be sleeping.)

INFERENTIAL QUESTIONS

1b. What does this reaction suggest about them? (They are too exhausted—both physically and emotionally—to care about such a relatively small problem as discomfort.)

2b. How does this thought make the correspondent feel? (He seems to feel sad and lonely, as if he must face the challenge of the sea alone.)

AT A GLANCE

- The correspondent, watching the shark, wishes he were not alone.
- Crane describes one's response to the painful discovery that nature considers the individual unimportant.

1 IMAGERY

Crane's sight and sound images help the reader to conclude that the "thing" is actually a shark.

2 THEME

The refrain expresses the bitterness of these men as they face their mortality. As evidence that nature is indifferent to an individual's fate, the question in this refrain is never answered.

The Metropolitan Museum of Art, New York

Detail, *Northeaster,* Winslow Homer, 1895.

1 whiroo of the dark fin. The speed and power of the thing was greatly to be admired. It cut the water like a gigantic and keen projectile.

The presence of this biding thing did not affect the man with the same horror that it would if he had been a picnicker. He simply looked at the sea dully and swore in an undertone.

Nevertheless, it is true that he did not wish to be alone with the thing. He wished one of his companions to awake by chance and keep him company with it. But the captain hung motionless over the water jar, and the oiler and the cook in the bottom of the boat were plunged in slumber.

VI

2 "If I am going to be drowned—if I am going to be drowned—if I am going to be drowned, why, in the name of the seven mad gods who rule the sea, was I allowed to come thus far and contemplate sand and trees?"

During this dismal night, it may be remarked that a man would conclude that it was really the intention of the seven mad gods to drown him, despite the abominable injustice of it. For it was certainly an abominable injustice to drown a man who had worked so hard, so hard. The man felt it would be a crime most unnatural. Other people

GUIDED READING

LITERAL QUESTION

1a. How does the shark's presence affect the correspondent? (He is not horrified; he looks at it dully, with some anger.)

INFERENTIAL QUESTION

1b. Why do you think the correspondent is not horrified by the shark? (He has been facing death for several days.)

had drowned at sea since galleys swarmed with painted sails, but still—

When it occurs to a man that nature does not regard him as important, and that she feels she would not maim the universe by disposing of him, he at first wishes to throw bricks at the temple, and he hates deeply the fact that there are no bricks and no temples. Any visible expression of nature would surely be pelleted with his jeers.

Then, if there be no tangible thing to hoot, he feels, perhaps, the desire to confront a personification and indulge in pleas, bowed to one knee, and with hands supplicant, saying, "Yes, but I love myself."

A high cold star on a winter's night is the word he feels that she says to him. Thereafter he knows the pathos of his situation.

The men in the dinghy had not discussed these matters, but each had, no doubt, reflected upon them in silence and according to his mind. There was seldom any expression upon their faces save the general one of complete weariness. Speech was devoted to the business of the boat.

1 To chime the notes of his emotion, a verse mysteriously entered the correspondent's head. He had even forgotten that he had forgotten this verse, but it suddenly was in his mind.

> A soldier of the Legion lay dying in Algiers:
> There was a lack of woman's nursing, there
> was dearth of woman's tears;
> But a comrade stood beside him, and he took
> that comrade's hand,
> And he said, "I never more shall see my own,
> my native land."[6]

In his childhood the correspondent had been made acquainted with the fact that a soldier of the Legion lay dying in Algiers, but he had never regarded it as important. Myriads of his schoolfellows had informed him of the soldier's plight, but the dinning had naturally ended by making him perfectly indifferent. He had never considered it his affair that a soldier of the Legion lay dying in Algiers, nor had it appeared to him as a matter for sorrow. It was less to him than breaking of a pencil's point.

2 Now, however, it quaintly came to him as a human, living thing. It was no longer merely a picture of a few throes in the breast of a poet, meanwhile drinking tea and warming his feet at the grate; it was an actuality—stern, mournful, and fine.

The correspondent plainly saw the soldier. He lay on the sand with his feet out straight and still. While his pale left hand was upon his chest in an attempt to thwart the going of his life, the blood came between his fingers. In the far Algerian distance, a city of low square forms was set against a sky that was faint with the last sunset hues. The correspondent, plying the oars and dreaming of the slow and slower movements of the lips of the soldier, was moved by a profound and perfectly impersonal comprehension. He was sorry for the soldier of the Legion who lay dying in Algiers.

The thing which had followed the boat and waited had evidently grown bored at the delay. There was no longer to be heard the slash of the cutwater, and there was no longer the flame of the long trail. The light in the north still glimmered, but it was apparently no nearer to the boat. Sometimes the boom of the surf rang in the correspondent's ears, and he turned the craft seaward then and rowed harder. Southward, someone had evidently built a watch fire on the beach. It was too low and too far to be seen, but it made a shimmering, roseate reflection upon the bluff back of it, and this could be discerned from the boat. The wind came stronger, and sometimes a wave suddenly raged out like a mountain cat, and there was to be seen the sheen and sparkle of a broken crest.

3 The captain, in the bow, moved on his water jar and sat erect. "Pretty long night," he observed to the correspondent. He looked at the shore. "Those lifesaving people take their time."

"Did you see that shark playing around?"

"Yes, I saw him. He was a big fellow, all right."

6. **A soldier . . . native land:** verse compresses the first stanza of "Bingen on the Rhine" by Caroline Elizabeth Sarah Sheridan Norton (1808–1877).

AT A GLANCE

- The correspondent recalls a poem about a dying soldier. It has new meaning for him.
- The correspondent discovers that the captain has been awake and has seen the shark.

1 CHARACTERIZATION

The recollection of the poem suggests that the correspondent may be pondering his own death as snippets of his past become sharply focused.

2 CHARACTERIZATION

Because of his own plight, the correspondent learns compassion, as he begins to understand what a dying soldier might have felt.

3 CHARACTERIZATION

Despite appearances to the contrary, the captain is always alert and constantly observing.

GUIDED READING

LITERAL QUESTION

1a. In what way does the correspondent now see the dying soldier in Algiers? (He now sees him as being a real human being.)

INFERENTIAL QUESTION

1b. What might account for this change in attitude? (Sharing the experience of a struggle for life, the correspondent sees himself in the poem.)

AT A GLANCE

- The correspondent finally falls asleep.
- The cook tells the oarsmen to head out to sea.
- At daylight the captain decides that the men will soon be too weak to row and so they should head toward the beach.

1 IMAGERY

The vivid description and simile show how exhaustion has put the men in such a deep sleep that the battering by wind and sea cannot disturb them.

2 PLOT: RISING ACTION

No longer able to wait for help, the men must change their tactics and attempt to rescue themselves.

3 THEME

The prospect of one's death puts all of life, even the most seemingly insignificant elements, into a new perspective.

"Wish I had known you were awake."

Later the correspondent spoke into the bottom of the boat.

"Billie!" There was a slow and gradual disentanglement. "Billie, will you spell me?"

"Sure," said the oiler.

As soon as the correspondent touched the cold, comfortable sea water in the bottom of the boat and had huddled close to the cook's life belt he was deep in sleep, despite the fact that his teeth played all the popular airs. This sleep was so good to him that it was but a moment before he heard a voice call his name in a tone that demonstrated the last stages of exhaustion. "Will you spell me?"

"Sure, Billie."

The light in the north had mysteriously vanished, but the correspondent took his course from the wide-awake captain.

Later in the night they took the boat farther out to sea, and the captain directed the cook to take one oar at the stern and keep the boat facing the seas. He was to call out if he should hear the thunder of the surf. This plan enabled the oiler and the correspondent to get respite together. "We'll give those boys a chance to get into shape again," said the captain. They curled down and, after a few preliminary chatterings and trembles, slept once more the dead sleep. Neither knew they had bequeathed to the cook the company of another shark, or perhaps the same shark.

As the boat caroused on the waves, spray occasionally bumped over the side and gave them a fresh soaking, but this had no power to break
1 their repose. The ominous slash of the wind and the water affected them as it would have affected mummies.

"Boys," said the cook, with the notes of every reluctance in his voice, "she's drifted in pretty close. I guess one of you had better take her to sea again." The correspondent, aroused, heard the crash of the toppled crests.

As he was rowing, the captain gave him some whiskey and water, and this steadied the chills out of him. "If I ever get ashore and anybody shows me even a photograph of an oar—"

At last there was a short conversation.

"Billie! . . . Billie, will you spell me?"

"Sure," said the oiler.

VII

When the correspondent again opened his eyes, the sea and the sky were each of the gray hue of the dawning. Later, carmine and gold was painted upon the waters. The morning appeared finally, in its splendor, with a sky of pure blue, and the sunlight flamed on the tips of the waves.

On the distant dunes were set many little black cottages, and a tall white windmill reared above them. No man, nor dog, nor bicycle appeared on the beach. The cottages might have formed a deserted village.

2 The voyagers scanned the shore. A conference was held in the boat. "Well," said the captain, "if no help is coming, we might better try a run through the surf right away. If we stay out here much longer we will be too weak to do anything for ourselves at all." The others silently acquiesced in this reasoning. The boat was headed for the beach. The correspondent wondered if none ever ascended the tall wind tower, and if then they never looked seaward. This tower was a giant, standing with its back to the plight of the ants. It represented in a degree, to the correspondent, the serenity of nature amid the struggles of the individual—nature in the wind, and nature in the vision of men. She did not seem cruel to him then, nor beneficent, nor treacherous, nor wise. But she was indifferent, flatly indifferent. It is, perhaps, plausible that a man in this situation, impressed with the unconcern of the universe, should see the innumerable flaws of his life and have them taste wickedly in his mind and wish for another chance. A distinction between right and wrong seems absurdly clear to him, then, in this new ignorance of the
3 grave-edge, and he understands that if he were given another opportunity he would mend his conduct and his words, and be better and brighter during an introduction or at a tea.

"Now, boys," said the captain, "she is going to

GUIDED READING

LITERAL QUESTION

1a. How does the narrator describe nature at this moment? (as "indifferent, flatly indifferent")

INFERENTIAL QUESTION

1b. As the correspondent demonstrates, what is the result of such a view of nature? (Since there is nowhere to place blame, the circumstances of one's life become one's own responsibility. This acknowledgment makes the correspondent regret any conduct that was not admirable.)

swamp sure. All we can do is to work her in as far as possible, and then when she swamps, pile out and scramble for the beach. Keep cool now, and don't jump until she swamps sure."

The oiler took the oars. Over his shoulders he scanned the surf. "Captain," he said, "I think I'd better bring her about, and keep her head-on to the seas, and back her in."

"All right, Billie," said the captain. "Back her in." The oiler swung the boat then, and, seated in the stern, the cook and the correspondent were obliged to look over their shoulders to contemplate the lonely and indifferent shore.

The monstrous inshore rollers heaved the boat high until the men were again enabled to see the white sheets of water scudding up the slanted beach. "We won't get in very close," said the captain. Each time a man could wrest his attention from the rollers, he turned his glance toward the shore, and in the expression of the eyes during this contemplation there was a singular quality. The correspondent, observing the others, knew that they were not afraid, but the full meaning of their glances was shrouded.

1 As for himself, he was too tired to grapple fundamentally with the fact. He tried to coerce his mind into thinking of it, but the mind was dominated at this time by the muscles, and the muscles said they did not care. It merely occurred to him that if he should drown it would be a shame.

There were no hurried words, no pallor, no plain agitation. The men simply looked at the shore. "Now, remember to get well clear of the boat when you jump," said the captain.

Seaward the crest of a roller suddenly fell with a thunderous crash, and the long white comber came roaring down upon the boat.

"Steady now," said the captain. The men were silent. They turned their eyes from the shore to
2 the comber and waited. The boat slid up the incline, leaped at the furious top, bounced over it, and swung down the long back of the wave. Some water had been shipped, and the cook bailed it out.

But the next crest crashed also. The tumbling, boiling flood of white water caught the boat and whirled it almost perpendicular. Water swarmed in from all sides. The correspondent had his hands on the gunwale at this time, and when the water entered at that place he swiftly withdrew his fingers, as if he objected to wetting them.

The little boat, drunken with this weight of water, reeled and snuggled deeper into the sea.

"Bail her out, cook! Bail her out!" said the captain.

"All right, Captain," said the cook.

"Now, boys, the next one will do for us sure," said the oiler. "Mind to jump clear of the boat."

The third wave moved forward, huge, furious, implacable. It fairly swallowed the dinghy, and almost simultaneously the men tumbled into the sea. A piece of life belt had lain in the bottom of the boat, and as the correspondent went overboard he held this to his chest with his left hand.

The January water was icy, and he reflected immediately that it was colder than he had ex-
3 pected to find it off the coast of Florida. This appeared to his dazed mind as a fact important enough to be noted at the time. The coldness of the water was sad; it was tragic. This fact was somehow mixed and confused with his opinion of his own situation so that it seemed almost a proper reason for tears. The water was cold.

When he came to the surface he was conscious of little but the noisy water. Afterward he saw his companions in the sea. The oiler was ahead in the race. He was swimming strongly and rapidly. Off to the correspondent's left, the cook's great white and corked back bulged out of the water; and in the rear the captain was hanging with his one good hand to the keel of the overturned dinghy.

There is a certain immovable quality to a shore, and the correspondent wondered at it amid the confusion of the sea.

It seemed also very attractive; but the correspondent knew that it was a long journey, and he paddled leisurely. The piece of life preserver lay under him, and sometimes he whirled down the incline of a wave as if he were on a hand sled.

But finally he arrived at a place in the sea where travel was beset with difficulty. He did not

AT A GLANCE

- The men remain calm as the oiler backs the boat to the shore.
- The boat turns over, tumbling the men into the sea.
- When the correspondent surfaces, he sees the others swimming toward land.

1 CONFLICT

The struggle is no longer just the man against the sea; now the correspondent has to overcome his weary body too.

2 POINT OF VIEW

Moving in close to the action, Crane tries to put readers into the boat so that they too feel the rise of the boat on the wave.

3 POINT OF VIEW

Crane moves into the correspondent's mind to show the confusion of his thoughts as he spills into the water.

GUIDED READING

LITERAL QUESTIONS

1a. As the boat approaches the shore, are the men calm or do they panic? (They are calm.)

2a. What does the correspondent notice about the water when he falls into it? (It is icy.)

INFERENTIAL QUESTIONS

1b. Why do they feel this way? (They seem to be concentrating on what they need to do rather than on what might happen to them.)

2b. Why does this detail seem "tragic" to him? (His thoughts are slow and confused at this point; the coldness becomes a fact of great consequence.)

AT A GLANCE

- The oiler, cook, and captain swim toward the shore.
- The correspondent is trapped in a current.

pause swimming to inquire what manner of current had caught him, but there his progress ceased. The shore was set before him like a bit of scenery on a stage, and he looked at it, and understood with his eyes each detail of it.

As the cook passed, much farther to the left, the captain was calling to him, "Turn over on your back, cook! Turn over on your back and use the oar."

"All right, sir." The cook turned on his back, and, paddling with an oar, went ahead as if he were a canoe.

Presently the boat also passed to the left of the correspondent, with the captain clinging with one hand to the keel. He would have appeared like a man raising himself to look over a board fence if it were not for the extraordinary gymnastics of the boat. The correspondent marveled that the captain could still hold to it.

They passed on nearer to shore—the oiler, the cook, the captain—and following them went the water jar, bouncing gaily over the seas.

The correspondent remained in the grip of this strange new enemy, a current. The shore,

The Metropolitan Museum of Art, New York

The Sea, Jean Courbet (1819–1877).

GUIDED READING

LITERAL QUESTION

1a. What does the shore seem like, to the correspondent? ("a bit of scenery on a stage")

INFERENTIAL QUESTION

1b. Why do you think he feels this way? (It is both unreal and vivid to him—the refuge he has sought for so long.)

with its white slope of sand and its green bluff, topped with little silent cottages, was spread like a picture before him. It was very near to him then, but he was impressed as one who, in a gallery, looks at a scene from Brittany or Algiers.

1 He thought: "I am going to drown? Can it be possible? Can it be possible? Can it be possible?" Perhaps an individual must consider his own death to be the final phenomenon of nature.

But later a wave perhaps whirled him out of this small deadly current, for he found suddenly that he could again make progress toward the shore. Later still he was aware that the captain, clinging with one hand to the keel of the dinghy, had his face turned away from the shore and toward him, and was calling his name. "Come to the boat! Come to the boat!"

2 In his struggle to reach the captain and the boat, he reflected that when one gets properly wearied drowning must really be a comfortable arrangement—a cessation of hostilities accompanied by a large degree of relief; and he was glad of it, for the main thing in his mind for some moments had been horror of the temporary agony; he did not wish to be hurt.

Presently he saw a man running along the shore. He was undressing with most remarkable speed. Coat, trousers, shirt, everything flew magically off him.

"Come to the boat!" called the captain.

"All right, Captain." As the correspondent paddled, he saw the captain let himself down to bottom and leave the boat. Then the correspondent performed his one little marvel of the voyage.
3 A large wave caught him and flung him with ease and supreme speed completely over the boat and far beyond it. It struck him even then as an event in gymnastics and a true miracle of the sea. An overturned boat in the surf is not a plaything to a swimming man.

The correspondent arrived in water that reached only to his waist, but his condition did not enable him to stand for more than a moment. Each wave knocked him into a heap, and the undertow pulled at him.

Then he saw the man who had been running and undressing, and undressing and running, come bounding into the water. He dragged ashore the cook, and then waded toward the captain; but the captain waved him away and sent him to the correspondent. He was naked—naked as a tree in winter; but a halo was about his head, and he shone like a saint. He gave a strong pull, and a long drag, and a bully heave at the correspondent's hand. The correspondent, schooled in the minor formulas, said, "Thanks, old man." But suddenly the man cried, "What's that?" He pointed a swift finger. The correspondent said, "Go."

In the shallows, face downward, lay the oiler. His forehead touched sand that was periodically, between each wave, clear of the sea.

The correspondent did not know all that transpired afterward. When he achieved safe ground he fell, striking the sand with each particular part of his body. It was as if he had dropped from a roof, but the thud was grateful to him.

4 It seems that instantly the beach was populated with men with blankets, clothes, and flasks, and women with coffee pots and all the remedies sacred to their minds. The welcome of the land to the men from the sea was warm and generous; but a still and dripping shape was carried slowly up the beach, and the land's welcome for it could only be the different and sinister hospitality of the grave.

When it came night, the white waves paced to and fro in the moonlight, and the wind brought the sound of the great sea's voice to the men on shore, and they felt that they could then be interpreters.

AT A GLANCE

- A wave flings the correspondent safely over the boat. A man on shore pulls the cook and the correspondent to safety.
- The men feel that they now understand the sea's voice.

1 THEME

We understand our mortality intellectually, but we do not really believe in it; thus, death seems incredible when actually faced.

2 CONFLICT

The last challenge for the correspondent is to continue believing that the struggle to survive is worthwhile and to resist being lulled into accepting death's calm.

3 IMAGERY

The description of the correspondent's being thrown by the wave makes us feel as if we are watching something in slow motion.

4 THEME

The concern of the men and women on land for the men from the boat contrasts with the indifference of the sea.

REFLECTING ON THE STORY

Do you think the men in the boat are extraordinarily courageous, or are they ordinary people? (The men show courage in their endurance and in their compassion for one another, but students also may feel that the men acted as anyone would in such a situation.)

GUIDED READING

LITERAL QUESTION

1a. What do the men feel that they can interpret? (the voice of the sea)

INFERENTIAL QUESTION

1b. What might their interpretation be? (They would probably speak of the sea's grandeur, power, and—above all—its indifference.)

STUDY QUESTIONS

Recalling

1. Who are the characters in this story? Where are they? How did they get there?
2. How far are the men from shore? What prevents them from getting to the shore?
3. Describe what happens each time the men think their predicament has come to an end.
4. Why do the men finally decide to try to land the boat?

Interpreting

5. Give at least one example of the author's use of suspense in this story.
6. What words would you use to describe the mood of this story? Is the mood constant throughout the story, or does it change? Explain what you mean.
7. Did the experience in the boat change the correspondent's attitude toward other people? In what way?

Extending

8. Experience, even the vicarious experience of reading a story like this one, changes people. In what ways has reading "The Open Boat" changed or influenced your thinking?

LITERARY FOCUS

Three Elements of Fiction

Point of View

Point of view, as you know, is the relationship of the storyteller, or narrator, to the characters and actions of a story. In the **limited third-person point of view,** the narrator limits himself to revealing the thoughts of only one character. In the **omniscient third-person point of view,** the narrator is all-knowing. That is, the narrator not only reveals the thoughts of all the characters but also things that no one character could know.

Theme

The **theme** of a story is the main idea that the author communicates to the reader. It is usually some observation about life. A story may have an explicitly **stated theme** or an **implied theme** that is revealed gradually and indirectly as the story develops. Longer stories such as "The Open Boat" may have more than one theme.

Style

The **style** of a story is determined by the writer's choice of words and the way she or he puts the words together. Among the characteristic elements of Stephen Crane's style are his use of concrete and vivid words, strong images, figurative language, and the rhythm and alliteration in his sentences.

Thinking About Point of View, Theme, and Style

1. Which of the two points of view discussed above did Crane use in "The Open Boat"? Support your answer with references to the story.
2. One theme of "The Open Boat" could be a truth about people in crisis situations. Do you agree? If so, write a statement of such a theme. If not, write a statement of the theme you detect in "The Open Boat."
3. In analyzing Crane's style, some critics have noted the "snapshot quality" of his descriptions. Explain what you think they mean and give examples of descriptions with this quality from "The Open Boat."

VIEWPOINT

Critic Joseph Katz has pointed out a theme that recurs often in Crane's works—the insignificance of human beings in the universal scheme:

> Since the correspondent's viewpoint is most intimately revealed, his conclusion of nature's indifference dominates until the sacrificial death of the oiler . . . effectively redeems the significance of life.
>
> —*The Portable Stephen Crane*

■ Find at least two passages in "The Open Boat" that express the theme of nature's indifference to people. State your own ideas about the relationship of individuals to nature and the universe.

STUDY QUESTIONS

1. the captain of a ship, the cook, Billie (the oiler), the correspondent; in an open boat at sea; their ship, the steamer *Commodore,* sank

2. They are fairly close to the shore; rough surf might swamp boat, and they would drown.

3. First time, captain and oiler decide surf is too rough; second time, expected help from people on the beach does not come.

4. They conclude help won't come from shore, and they will be too weak to get themselves to shore if they wait longer.

5. by holding out possibility of safe arrival on shore and then withdrawing it; the threat of the shark that follows the boat; the current that prevents correspondent from reaching the shore

6. grim, fearful; changes from cheerful and hopeful when rescue seems assured to doubtful and despairing

7. yes; made him feel closer to other people

8. Possible answers: new insight into dangers of the sea; greater respect for/fear of forces of nature; increased appreciation for need to cooperate in crises

LITERARY FOCUS

1. both points of view used: *limited third-person point of view* (correspondent's thoughts) and *omniscient third-person point of view* ("It is fair to say here . . ."; "They then briefly exchanged . . .")

2. Possible answer: People need to cooperate to survive crises.

3. descriptions like photographs in clarity and detail; "These waves were of the hue of slate . . . thrust up in points like rocks"; "At last . . . thinner than paper"; "Southward, someone . . . discerned from the boat"; "The cook . . . as if he were a canoe."

VIEWPOINT

"If I am going to be drowned . . . after all this work!" and similar refrains; "When it occurs to a man . . ."; "The tower is a giant . . . flatly indifferent." Students' ideas will vary.

Sidney Lanier *1842–1881*

Sidney Lanier (lə nir′) grew up in the pre–Civil War South, but he greeted the new age of industrialism and scientific progress by writing some of the most advanced and daring poetry of his time.

Lanier was born in Macon, Georgia. At the outbreak of the Civil War, he enlisted in the Confederate Army as a private. Four months before the end of the war, he was captured by Union troops and sent to a federal prison, where he contracted the tuberculosis that would afflict him for the rest of his short life. His first published work, the novel *Tiger Lilies* (1867), was based on his Civil War experiences.

Lanier was primarily a poet and a musician. In fact, he played the flute well enough to join the Peabody Symphony Orchestra in Baltimore as first flutist. He sought to apply some of the rules of musical composition to the composition of poetry; his theories about the relationship of music to verse are contained in *The Science of English Verse* (1880).

■ What kind of relationship do you see between poetry and the popular music of today? Does Lanier's poetry share any of those similarities?

Sidney Lanier

Song of the Chattahoochee

  Out of the hills of Habersham,
  Down the valleys of Hall,[1]
I hurry amain[2] to reach the plain,
Run the rapid and leap the fall,
Split at the rock and together again,
Accept my bed, or narrow or wide,
And flee from folly on every side
With a lover's pain to attain the plain
  Far from the hills of Habersham,
  Far from the valleys of Hall.

  All down the hills of Habersham,
  All through the valleys of Hall,

1. **Habersham . . . Hall:** two mountainous counties in northern Georgia, through which the Chattahoochee River flows.
2. **amain** [ə mān′]: at full speed.

AT A GLANCE

- The poet traces the course of the Chattahoochee River in Georgia.
- *Stanza 1:* The river begins its rapid, shifting journey.

LITERARY OPTIONS

- sound and meaning
- personification
- structure

THEMATIC OPTIONS

- duty and destiny
- Nature

STRUCTURE

The first and last pair of lines in each ten-line stanza repeat the references to Habersham and Hall in a kind of refrain. The rhyme scheme of each stanza is as follows: *abcbcddcab.*

SPEAKER: PERSONIFICATION

The *I* who hurries is the Chattahoochee River (l. 3). Speaking as the river itself enables the poet to bring the topic to life for his readers.

INTERNAL RHYME

Some of the sense of lapping water is evoked by the sounds of the internal rhyming words, such as "amain"/"plain" (l. 3) and "pain"/"plain" (l. 8).

AT A GLANCE

- *Stanza 2:* The undergrowth tugs at the river.
- *Stanza 3:* The trees offer their shade.
- *Stanza 4:* The rocks entice the river.
- *Stanza 5:* Duty calls the river.

REGIONALISM

Naming the trees seen along the river creates an accurate description of the Georgia terrain (ll. 23–26).

ALLITERATION

The sound of the repeated hard c's supports the meaning by suggesting the hardness of the gems being described (l. 36).

MAIN IDEA

The downstream journey of the river is a duty-bound destiny (l. 44). The river must provide irrigation and power (l. 46).

REFLECTING ON THE POEM

In what ways does this river's journey parallel a person's life? (Students may point out that people face changing "scenery" as they grow older or that all people feel themselves pulled toward a distant goal or destiny.)

The rushes cried, *Abide, abide,*
The willful waterweeds held me thrall,
The laving[3] laurel turned my tide,
The ferns and the fondling grass said *Stay,*
The dewberry dipped for to work delay,
And the little reeds sighed, *Abide, abide,*
  Here in the hills of Habersham,
  Here in the valleys of Hall.

  High o'er the hills of Habersham,
  Veiling the valleys of Hall,
The hickory told me manifold
Fair tales of shade, the poplar tall
Wrought me her shadowy self to hold,
The chestnut, the oak, the walnut, the pine,
Overleaning, with flickering meaning and sign,
Said, *Pass not, so cold, these manifold*
  Deep shades of the hills of Habersham,
  These glades in the valleys of Hall.

  And oft in the hills of Habersham,
  And oft in the valleys of Hall,
The white quartz shone, and the smooth brook-stone
Did bar me of passage with friendly brawl,
And many a luminous jewel lone
— Crystals clear or a-cloud with mist
Ruby, garnet and amethyst —
Made lures with the lights of streaming stone
  In the clefts of the hills of Habersham,
  In the beds of the valleys of Hall.

  But oh, not the hills of Habersham,
  And oh, not the valleys of hall
Avail: I am fain[4] for to water the plain.
Downward the voices of Duty call —
Downward, to toil and be mixed with the main,[5]
The dry fields burn, and the mills are to turn,
And a myriad flowers mortally yearn,
And the lordly main from beyond the plain
  Calls o'er the hills of Habersham,
  Calls through the valleys of Hall.

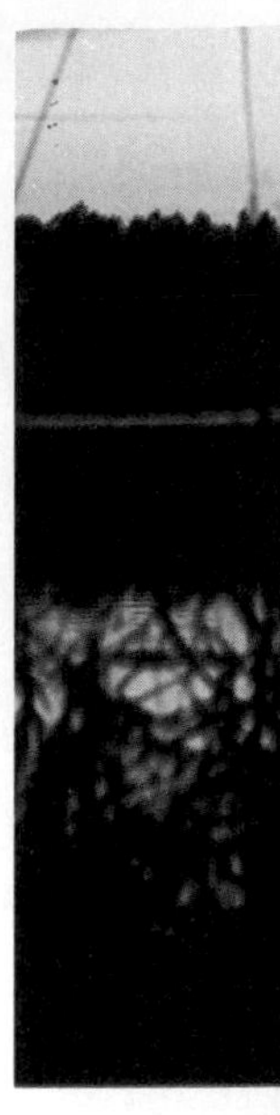

3. **laving:** washing up against.
4. **fain:** compelled by circumstances.
5. **main:** the open sea.

STUDY QUESTIONS

Recalling

1. Who is the speaker of this poem, according to the title?
2. According to the first stanza, to what does the river hurry? From what does it flee?
3. What do the ferns and grasses "say" to the river in the second stanza? What do the reeds "sigh"?
4. What "toil" must the river perform before it mixes with "the main," according to the last stanza? What calls the river in the last three lines?

Interpreting

5. To what two basic uses is the river put when it reaches the plain?
6. Basically, what lures the river to the hills of Habersham and the valleys of Hall?
7. What figurative device does the poet use in the title and throughout the poem? To what is the poet comparing the river?
8. On the figurative level what might the course of the river represent? "The folly on either side" (stanza 1)? The "duty" of the plain?
9. What do you think "the main" represents?
10. What poetic devices make the poem musical? How is the music related to the subject and the theme of the poem?

COMPOSITION

Writing About Sound and Meaning in Poetry

■ Lanier believed poetry should be as much like music as possible. Write a short composition describing the "music" you find in "The Song of the Chattahoochee." Begin by discussing the length of the lines and their regularity or irregularity. Then point out how the poet seems to be trying to reflect in sound the subject matter of the poem. Conclude with your opinion of the value of writing poetry in this way and your reasons for thinking as you do.

Writing an Extended Personification

■ In "Song of the Chattahoochee" Lanier personifies a river and has it speak for itself. Imagine that you are the wind, an ocean, a tree, or some other element of nature. Write a paragraph (or a poem, if you wish) in which you describe in detail your movements, thoughts, and sensations.

STUDY QUESTIONS

1. the Chattahoochee River
2. reach the plain; folly
3. stay; abide
4. water the plain, fields, flowers and turn mills; the sea
5. irrigation, power
6. natural beauty of hills, valley
7. personification; a human being with a destiny
8. person's lifetime; distractions from one's purpose in life; obligation to family, society
9. death or heaven
10. alliteration, internal rhyme, irregular rhythm; creates effect of rushing water or a ceaseless, determined progression

COMPOSITION: GUIDELINES FOR EVALUATION

WRITING ABOUT SOUND AND MEANING IN POETRY

Objective

To relate the sound of a poem to its meaning

Guidelines for Evaluation

- suggested length: four to six paragraphs
- should discuss irregular meter, regular pattern of beats in long and short lines
- should point out uses of poetic devices
- should conclude with statement of opinion

WRITING AN EXTENDED PERSONIFICATION

Objective

To use personification in a description

Guidelines for Evaluation

- suggested length: one paragraph or stanza
- should describe an element of nature that takes on human attributes
- should give details about movements, thoughts, and sensations
- should use precise, vivid verbs and adjectives

Edwin Arlington Robinson

1869–1935

Edwin Arlington Robinson was a New Englander who never forgot his regional tics. Born in Head Tide, a tiny village in Maine, Robinson grew up in Gardiner, Maine, on which he modeled Tilbury Town, the fictional setting for many of his most famous poems.

At twenty-eight Robinson moved to New York City, where he lived in semipoverty and wrote without much of a readership. His life was made somewhat easier in 1902 when President Theodore Roosevelt, an admirer of his work, appointed him to a post in the New York Custom House where Herman Melville had once been employed. However, Robinson's first real success did not come until 1910, with the publication of *The Town Down the River*. In time he was awarded three Pulitzer Prizes and found himself one of America's favorite poets.

In technique Robinson is a traditionalist whose tightly structured verse may, on first inspection, appear to be simpler than it really is. For if Robinson is traditional in style, he is daringly realistic in his subject matter. Most of his poems attempt to tell the "truth" about Tilbury Town. To a Realist like Robinson, that truth includes not only love and tranquillity, but also sadness, tragedy, frustration, and waste. The particular flavor of Robinson's best poems springs from his mixture of realism with irony and even humor. Richard Cory and Miniver Cheevy, two of Tilbury Town's most famous inhabitants, are keenly observed human beings, full of contradictions, living what Thoreau would have called "lives of quiet desperation."

■ Are most people what they seem to be on the surface?

Edwin Arlington Robinson

Richard Cory

Whenever Richard Cory went down town,
We people on the pavement looked at him:
He was a gentleman from sole to crown,
Clean favored, and imperially slim.

And he was always quietly arrayed,
And he was always human when he talked;
But still he fluttered pulses when he said,
"Good morning," and he glittered when he walked.

And he was rich—yes, richer than a king—
And admirably schooled in every grace:
In fine,[1] we thought that he was everything
To make us wish that we were in his place.

So on we worked, and waited for the light,
And went without the meat, and cursed the bread;
And Richard Cory, one calm summer night,
Went home and put a bullet through his head.

1. **In fine:** in brief.

STUDY QUESTIONS

Recalling

1. Which line in the poem identifies the speaker? Which lines tell you about the economic condition of the speaker?
2. What is Richard Cory "from sole to crown"? What effect does he have when he says "Good morning"?
3. What, "in fine," do the people think of Richard Cory (stanza 3)?
4. What is the "surprise" ending?

Interpreting

5. How are the "we" of the poem different from Richard Cory?
6. What do "crown" (line 3) and "imperially" (line 4) indicate about the speaker's impression of Richard Cory?
7. What effect does Cory's final action seem to have on everyone in Tilbury Town? What does Tilbury Town's reaction to Cory's life and death suggest about human understanding?

AT A GLANCE

- Richard Cory, rich and kingly, is much admired by the working class.
- One night Cory goes home and shoots himself.

LITERARY OPTIONS

- irony
- Naturalism

THEMATIC OPTIONS

- envy
- social classes

IMAGERY

The regal image of Cory in *stanza 1*—"sole to crown" and "imperially slim"—carries through the poem. In *stanza 2,* his appearance "fluttered pulses"; *stanza 3* announces his wealthiness. All of this leaves us unprepared for the poem's startling outcome.

IRONY

While the people who admire him so are struggling to live (ll. 13–14), Cory—who appears to have no difficulties in life—chooses to die by his own hand (l. 16).

NATURALISM

That the tragedy is presented without sentimentality suggests the inevitability of forces beyond any individual's control (l. 16).

REFLECTING ON THE POEM

Whose tragedy is greater—Cory's or those who lived to be like him? (Some students may feel that suicide is the worst possible end; others may argue that life is soured by misplaced admiration.)

STUDY QUESTIONS

1. second line; ll. 13–14
2. gentleman; flutters pulses
3. He is everything.
4. Cory commits suicide.
5. ordinary working people, poor folk who look to future for better times
6. thinks Cory has regal bearing
7. surprise; people usually wrong in their impressions

AT A GLANCE

Miniver Cheevy, an unhappy man, dreams of ancient and more glorious times.

LITERARY OPTIONS

- irony
- structure and meaning

THEMATIC OPTIONS

- dreams vs. action
- frustration and despair

IRONY

The word *grace* clashes with the image of "iron clothing" (ll. 23–24). That Miniver would find armor graceful underscores his unrealistic view of life.

MAIN IDEA AND REPETITION

The repetition of *thought* dramatizes Miniver's inability to act (ll. 27–28). The implication is that he thinks but never acts, as stressed again in *kept on thinking* (l. 30).

STRUCTURE

The short lines and stressed rhymes are typical of humorous verse, with the two-stress fourth line of each stanza at times acting as a dark punch line ("And he had reasons"). Thus, even the structure of the poem stands in ironic contrast to the tragedy represented by people like Miniver Cheevy.

REFLECTING ON THE POEM

Is Miniver Cheevy truly "fated" (l. 31) to the life he leads? (Some students might argue that he has chosen to indulge his fantasies; others might point out that all people must find some way to deal with the unpleasantries of modern life.)

Edwin Arlington Robinson

Miniver Cheevy

Miniver Cheevy, child of scorn,
  Grew lean while he assailed the seasons;
He wept that he was ever born,
  And he had reasons.

Miniver loved the days of old
  When swords were bright and steeds were prancing;
The vision of a warrior bold
  Would set him dancing.

Miniver sighed for what was not,
  And dreamed, and rested from his labors;
He dreamed of Thebes[1] and Camelot,[2]
  And Priam's[3] neighbors.

Miniver mourned the ripe renown
  That made so many a name so fragrant;
He mourned Romance, now on the town,[4]
  And Art, a vagrant.

Miniver loved the Medici,[5]
  Albeit[6] he had never seen one;
He would have sinned incessantly
  Could he have been one.

Miniver cursed the commonplace
  And eyed a khaki suit with loathing;
He missed the medieval grace
  Of iron clothing.

Miniver scorned the gold he sought,
  But sore annoyed was he without it;
Miniver thought, and thought, and thought,
  And thought about it.

Miniver Cheevy, born too late,
  Scratched his head and kept on thinking;
Miniver coughed, and called it fate,
  And kept on drinking.

1. **Thebes** [thēbz]: leading city-state of ancient Greece.
2. **Camelot:** legendary site in England of King Arthur's court and Round Table.
3. **Priam** [prī′əm]: King of Troy during the Trojan War.
4. **on the town:** on welfare.
5. **Medici** [med′i chē]: rich, powerful family of Florence, Italy, in the fourteenth, fifteenth, and sixteenth centuries.
6. **Albeit** [ôl bē′it]: although.

STUDY QUESTIONS

Recalling

1. For what does Cheevy sigh and mourn in the first five stanzas? What does Cheevy curse in the sixth stanza?
2. What are Cheevy's feelings about gold, according to the seventh stanza?
3. To what does Cheevy attribute his unhappiness in line 31? What does he keep on doing, according to the last line of the poem?

Interpreting

4. What do lines 9–10 reveal about Cheevy's character? Lines 17–18? Lines 25–26?
5. Basically, how does Cheevy see himself? How do we see him? What really causes his unhappiness?

Extending

6. Could Richard Cory and Miniver Cheevy be found only in a small Maine town at the turn of the century? Explain your answer.

LITERARY FOCUS

Irony

Irony is a contrast or a difference between the way things seem and the way they really are. In literature there are three kinds of irony. **Verbal irony** occurs when words that appear to be saying one thing are really saying something quite different. **Situational irony** occurs when what is expected to happen is not what actually comes to pass. **Dramatic irony** occurs when events that mean one thing to the characters mean something quite different to the reader.

Irony is often accompanied by a grim humor. There is an element of dark humor, for example, in the mistaken ideas that the townspeople have of Richard Cory, while Miniver Cheevy is almost comical in his hypocrisy and self-delusion.

Thinking About Irony

1. How is the use of the adjective "calm" in the next-to-last line of "Richard Cory" an example of verbal irony?
2. Explain the situational irony in "Richard Cory."
3. Tell why "Miniver Cheevy" is an example of dramatic irony.

COMPOSITION

Writing a Comparison/Contrast

■ Write a brief essay comparing and contrasting "Richard Cory" and "Miniver Cheevy." Begin with a statement of each poem's theme. Then show what the characters have in common and how they differ. Conclude by discussing the tone of each poem and the general impression each leaves with the reader. *For help with this assignment, refer to Lesson 2 in the Writing About Literature Handbook at the back of this book.*

Using Situational or Dramatic Irony

■ Write a character study in poem or paragraph form in which an ironic "surprise" ending throws new light on the character you are describing. For example, you might write about a person who seems popular but who is actually quite lonely, or about someone who seems kind but in the end proves false and calculating. The irony may be situational or dramatic.

STUDY QUESTIONS

1. ■ days of old
   ■ the commonplace
2. scorns it but is annoyed to be without it
3. fate; drinking
4. dreamer, unhappy with life; revels in imagination; scorns materialism but is avaricious
5. accident of fate; flighty drunk, unable to come to terms with reality; escapism
6. Students should see Cory and Cheevy as universal types.

LITERARY FOCUS

1. contrasts with violent desperation leading to suicide
2. Ending is ironic: Perceptions imply Cory should lead happy, full life.
3. Cheevy sees himself as a victim of fate. The reader knows his anguish is self-inflicted.

COMPOSITION: GUIDELINES FOR EVALUATION

WRITING A COMPARISON/CONTRAST

Objective

To compare and contrast Robinson's poems

Guidelines for Evaluation

- suggested length: four to six paragraphs
- should identify the themes of the poems
- should state that both characters are unhappy, unfulfilled men
- should contrast the characters
- should discuss the tone of each poem

USING SITUATIONAL OR DRAMATIC IRONY

Objective

To use irony to develop a character

Guidelines for Evaluation

- suggested length: two paragraphs, a few stanzas
- should carefully describe how the character seems to others or to self
- should set up a situation in which the character's true personality is revealed

Paul Laurence Dunbar *1872–1906*

Paul Laurence Dunbar was the first black American writer to make his living entirely by writing. Born in Dayton, Ohio, the son of former slaves, Dunbar became interested in writing verse when, as a child, he heard a poem by the English writer William Wordsworth. By the age of fourteen, Dunbar was reciting his own poems before school assemblies; in high school, the only black student in his class, he was editor in chief of the school newspaper.

Nevertheless, despite his school successes, Dunbar graduated into a world with few prospects for a poet. With the help of former schoolmates Orville and Wilbur Wright, he started a small newspaper for the black community, but the venture failed. Dunbar was forced to take a job as an elevator operator to support himself and his widowed mother.

In 1892 a former teacher arranged for Dunbar to read before the Western Association of Writers. His reading impressed the members so much that the poet soon found himself on the road to national recognition. His poetry collection *Majors and Minors* was published in 1895 to widespread critical acclaim, and *Lyrics of a Lowly Life* (1896) sold over twelve thousand copies.

Dunbar was a prolific writer, producing poems, stories, and novels. Many of his poems and stories are written in the dialect of the black community, but in "Douglass" Dunbar dispenses with dialect. To pay tribute to the black leader Frederick Douglass (1817?–1895), Dunbar adopts the grand language and formal speech of the sonnet.

■ What would you include in a written tribute to someone you admire? What does Dunbar include?

Paul Laurence Dunbar

Douglass

Ah, Douglass, we have fall'n on evil days,
  Such days as thou, not even thou didst know,
  When thee, the eyes of that harsh long ago
Saw, salient,[1] at the cross of devious ways,
And all the country heard thee with amaze.
  Not ended then, the passionate ebb and flow,
  The awful tide that battled to and fro;
We ride amid a tempest of dispraise.

Now, when the waves of swift dissension swarm,
  And Honor, the strong pilot, lieth stark,[2]
Oh, for thy voice high-sounding o'er the storm,
  For thy strong arm to guide the shivering bark,[3]
The blast-defying power of thy form,
  To give us comfort through the lonely dark.

---

1. **salient** [sāl′yənt]: standing out from the rest.
2. **stark:** stiff, as a corpse.
3. **bark:** sailing ship.

AT A GLANCE

- The poet notes that the struggles of his day are even harsher than those that Frederick Douglass knew.
- He wishes that Douglass were alive to speak for what is right and to guide his people.

LITERARY OPTIONS

- sonnet
- elegy

THEMATIC OPTIONS

- leadership
- loss

BACKGROUND

By the end of the nineteenth century, blacks found that the period of self-direction enjoyed during Reconstruction was over; oppression was to follow with the rise of organizations such as the Ku Klux Klan (l. 1).

SONNET

The octave describes the current crisis; the sestet proposes an idealistic solution. An extended metaphor of seafaring describes the problem and helps to connect the parts of the sonnet.

IMAGE PATTERN

The metaphor of the sea reaches its climax with this image of a small boat that lacks a leader strong enough to hold the rudder in the storm (l. 12).

REFLECTING ON THE POEM

What does the poet view as the greatest characteristic of Douglass? (Students might cite Dunbar's references to Douglass' eloquence as a speaker or to his leadership ability.)

STUDY QUESTIONS

1. They are worse.
2. amazement; high-sounding voice, strong arm, blast-defying power of his form
3. Storm at sea; image developed by reciting his qualities as leader/pilot and by implying that blacks are lost in a storm of controversy.
4. Douglass is being invoked as a universal symbol of leadership and the conscience of his people.
5. strength of character, high purpose, righteous anger

LITERARY FOCUS

- It is an Italian sonnet, divided into an octave and sestet with the rhyme scheme *abbaabba* in the octave and *cdcdcd* in the sestet.
- The sonnet form gives the poem a tight structure and formality that underscore the poet's seriousness.

COMPARING WRITERS

- Students should conclude that Lanier's "Song of the Chattahoochee" is the poem most rooted in the poet's native soil.
- Dunbar's "Douglass" includes historical facts.
- The two poems of Robinson's describe people who could be living almost anywhere.

STUDY QUESTIONS

Recalling

1. How do Dunbar's days compare to Douglass' earlier days, according to lines 1–3 and 6–8?
2. How had the country reacted to Douglass' insights, according to line 5? What three qualities of Douglass' does the speaker then call for in lines 11–14?

Interpreting

3. What image does the poem introduce in lines 6–8, and how is that image developed in lines 9–14?

Extending

4. Since Douglass was already dead when Dunbar wrote this poem, why do you think the poet calls upon him?
5. Which of Douglass' qualities or virtues suggested in this poem are evident from his autobiography on pages 240–243?

LITERARY FOCUS

The Sonnet

A **sonnet** is a lyric poem of fourteen lines written in **iambic pentameter**—five feet to a line, each foot made up of an unstressed syllable followed by a stressed one.

English sonnets, sometimes called **Shakespearean sonnets** (after the greatest poet to use them), have three quatrains (groups of four lines) followed by a rhymed couplet, with the rhyme scheme *abab cdcd efef gg.*

Italian sonnets, sometimes called **Petrarchan sonnets** (after the fourteenth-century Italian poet Francesco Petrarch), divide into a group of eight lines, or **octave,** followed by a group of six lines, or **sestet.** The octave has the rhyme scheme *abbaabba;* the sestet usually rhymes *cdcdee* or *cdecde.* The octave usually states a single thought, and the sestet usually expands upon that thought, contradicts it, or develops it in some other way.

Sonnets were immensely popular during the European Renaissance; poets wrote sonnet sequences, dozens of sonnets linked together by the same themes and often addressed to the same person. Sonnets usually dealt with lofty themes—love, faith, honor—and they enabled a poet to express deep emotions within conventional forms. They remained in fashion until the early nineteenth century. Some poets of our time use the sonnet form but often modify it to suit their own poetic needs.

Thinking About Sonnets

- Which type of sonnet is "Douglass"? Why? How does Dunbar's use of the sonnet form contribute to the effectiveness of his poem?

COMPARING WRITERS

- Sidney Lanier, Edwin Arlington Robinson, and Paul Laurence Dunbar had very different backgrounds, yet all three felt strongly about their roots and chose to express their feelings through poetry. Which of the poems in this section seems to you the most strongly rooted in the poet's native soil? Which poem includes historic facts? Which, despite regional settings, seem to be about human beings anywhere? Support your answers with evidence from the poems.

THE AMERICAN NOVEL

Unlike poetry and drama, novels are a relatively modern invention. A **novel** can best be defined as a book-length prose fiction. Early novels in English fall into three categories: the **picaresque novel,** a loose series of episodes recounting the adventures of wanderers and lovable rogues, often with a satiric aim; the **novel of sentiment,** a highly emotional tale of romance and tears that ends with a moral message; and the **gothic novel,** a tale of mystery and fear that includes elements of the supernatural as well as the romantic.

The earliest American novels also fell into these categories. Hugh Henry Brackenridge's *Modern Chivalry* (1792) is a picaresque adventure story that pokes fun at political problems during George Washington's presidency; Susanna Rowson's *Charlotte Temple* (1790) is a sentimental moral tale; and Charles Brockden Brown's *Wieland* (1798) and *Ormond* (1799) are tales of gothic horror that incidentally explore the psychological motivations of their characters.

It was not until the nineteenth century that America produced major novelists who are still widely read today. In 1823 James Fenimore Cooper (page 114) published the first of his Leatherstocking Tales, romantic adventures chronicling the exploits of Natty Bumppo, a noble frontiersman who became the model for the classic American hero. At about the same time William Gilmore Simms of South Carolina was writing similar Romantic adventure tales, earning for himself the nickname "the southern Cooper."

Another major novelist of the pre–Civil War period is Nathaniel Hawthorne (page 181), who published his masterpiece, *The Scarlet Letter,* in 1850. *The Scarlet Letter* is a tightly woven tale that explores the nature of sin; it is a work of complex symbolism and profound insights into its characters' minds and hearts. The nature of good and evil is also probed in *Moby-Dick* (1851), a tale of whales and whalers by Herman Melville (page 203). *Moby-Dick's* profound philosophical questioning and its almost Shakespearean language place it among the outstanding novels of the nineteenth century.

After confronting the realities of the Civil War, American novelists turned more and more toward Realistic fiction. In the works of Mark Twain (page 288), local color makes for true-to-life adventure, and Twain as a satirist never shirks from depicting the real world in all its folly. Twain's use of dialect and colloquial language had a strong impact on almost all American writers to follow him; novels with adolescent heroes like Twain's *Huckleberry Finn* (1884) appear again and again in American fiction.

CATHER FAULKNER

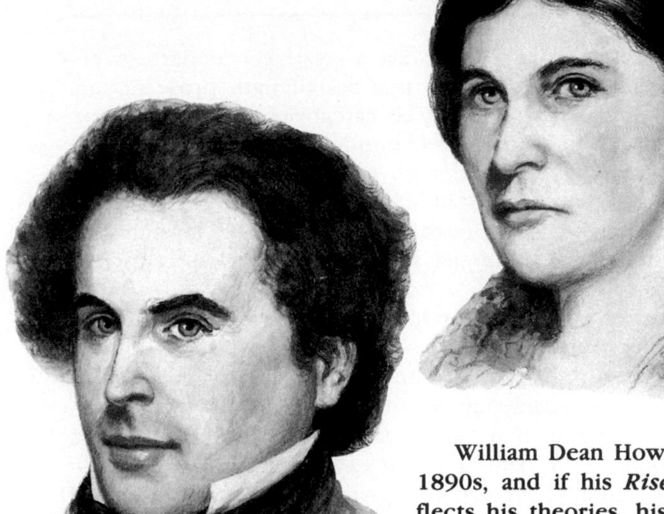

HAWTHORNE

MELVILLE

William Dean Howells set forth the principles of Realism in the 1890s, and if his *Rise of Silas Lapham* (1885) only partially reflects his theories, his ideas are masterfully realized in the novels of his friend Henry James. James explores the realities of society and the nature of the human mind in such works as *The American* (1877), *The Portrait of a Lady* (1881), and *The Turn of the Screw* (1898). His novel *The Ambassadors* (1903) is considered to be a masterpiece of **psychological realism,** writing that probes deeply into the complexities of characters' thoughts and motivations.

Realism is carried one step further in the Naturalistic novels of Stephen Crane (page 367), Theodore Dreiser, and Frank Norris. In the grim world of Dreiser's *Sister Carrie* (1900) and *An American Tragedy* (1925), characters are trapped by overwhelming forces that they cannot control or even understand. Norris' *McTeague* (1899) is a brutally frank portrait of greed, while *The Octopus* (1901) tells of the grim life of western ranchers battling the railroads.

Regionalism and Realism work hand in hand in the novels of Edith Wharton, which include *Ethan Frome* (1911), a portrait of New England farm life, and *The Age of Innocence* (1920). Ole Rolvaag's *Giants in the Earth* (1927) describes the life of Norwegian immigrants in South Dakota, while Willa Cather (page 513) offers a poetical portrait of the Nebraska frontier in *My Ántonia* (1918) and celebrates America's past in the equally lyrical *Death Comes for the Archbishop* (1927). Lyricism is also an element of Thomas Wolfe's autobiographical novel *Look Homeward, Angel* (1929), while Ellen Glasgow offers powerful pictures of the changing South in *Barren Ground* (1925) and *Vein of Iron* (1935).

Sinclair Lewis (page 483), the first American to win the Nobel Prize for Literature, was a sharp social critic, writing about small-town America in *Main Street* (1920), businessmen in *Babbitt*

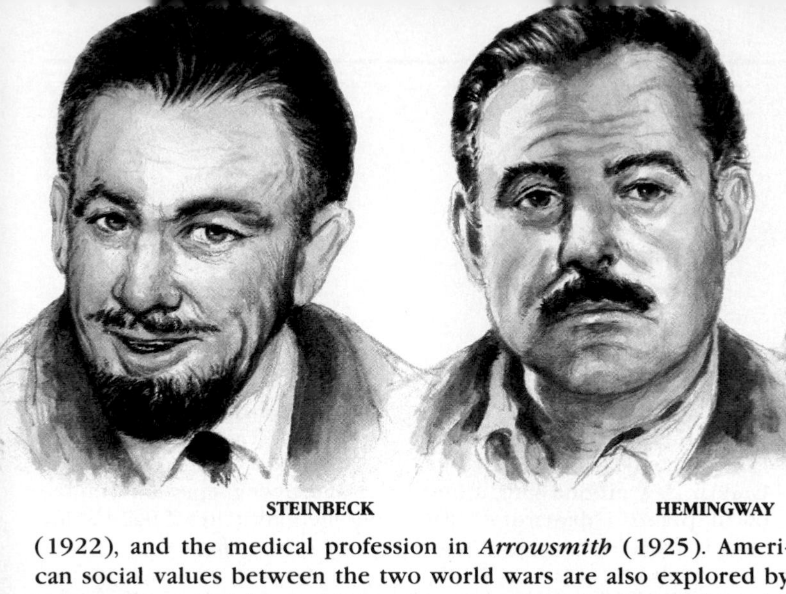

STEINBECK HEMINGWAY

(1922), and the medical profession in *Arrowsmith* (1925). American social values between the two world wars are also explored by F. Scott Fitzgerald (page 497) in *The Great Gatsby* (1925), by John Dos Passos in his trilogy *U.S.A.,* and by Nathanael West in *Day of the Locust* (1939).

TWAIN

JAMES

Probably the three most outstanding novelists of pre–World War II America are Ernest Hemingway (page 489), William Faulkner (page 638), and John Steinbeck (page 589). Hemingway further develops the American hero in such works as *A Farewell to Arms* (1929), a tale of love during World War I, and *For Whom the Bell Tolls* (1940), a story of an American who fights in the Spanish Civil War. Hemingway's detached, journalistic prose style has been much imitated. Faulkner writes lyrical "stream-of-consciousness" novels set in his native South, including *The Sound and the Fury* (1929), a portrait of a once aristocratic family, and *Light in August* (1932). Steinbeck draws warm, human portraits in such novels as *Of Mice and Men* (1937) and *The Grapes of Wrath* (1939), a saga of a dustbowl family driven to find a new life in California. Other important writers of fiction before World War II include Katherine Anne Porter (page 575), Eudora Welty (page 614), William Saroyan (page 795), and Thornton Wilder (page 668).

Novelists writing since World War II have turned more and more toward experimental fiction. Ralph Ellison's powerful novel *Invisible Man* (1952) is complex in its symbolism and its structure, while Joseph Heller explores World War II itself in his fragmentary dark comedy *Catch-22* (1961). Other postwar American novelists to achieve international recognition include Carson McCullers (page 661), John Updike (page 824), Bernard Malamud (page 786), Truman Capote (page 802), and Saul Bellow (page 865), who was awarded the Nobel Prize for Literature.

ACTIVE READING

The Emotional Imagination

You might assign this section after the class has read "The Outcasts of Poker Flat" and then review it after the class has completed the unit. Discuss with students how they should attune themselves to the nuances of language so that they can react emotionally as well as intellectually to literature. Point out that freeing our emotional imaginations involves a willing suspension of disbelief: We must give our imaginations over to the illusion, to the strangeness, of literature in the belief that there is something of ourselves to be found there.

ACTIVE READING

The Emotional Imagination

At the end of the first unit of this book (page 46), we talked about the need each reader has to bring an active imagination to literature. This is especially important as we read about the lives of people who lived in times and places different from our own. We called this the historical imagination. Yet there is another aspect of imaginative reading that we must learn to exercise as well—the *emotional imagination*.

It is true that we like to see people like ourselves mirrored in art. We take pleasure in seeing a familiar reality portrayed in a painting or in a story. Most literature, however, cannot limit itself to our reality.

Truly active reading means opening ourselves to ways of thinking, feeling, and seeing that are different from our own. We shut ourselves off from a great deal of pleasure and knowledge if we resist what is strange or unfamiliar. As we read, we need to give ourselves up to the language, reading slowly, carefully, allowing the language to guide us, to take us beyond ourselves and into the lives of characters different from ourselves—and into the minds of the writers, too.

For example, we may take two attitudes while reading Paul Laurence Dunbar's poem "Douglass" (page 393). We may stand apart from it, looking at what Dunbar said about Douglass and about the world that he, Dunbar, saw around him, a time of "dispraise," "dissension," and "lonely dark." Or we may exercise, while we read, a greater imagination, allowing ourselves to enter the spirit of a young black poet looking back upon a hero of an earlier time, crying out for the help that might come with Douglass' "high-sounding" voice and "blast-defying power." The "we" and "us" of the poem become all of us, black and white, male and female, as we read.

In the stories and poems in this unit, we are asked to become for a while a great many men and women. In Kate Chopin's "Pair of Silk Stockings" we imagine what it is like to feel restricted and to allow ourselves a few moments filled with the excitement of wider horizons. We share the frustrated anger and sense of injustice of a struggling midwestern farmer in Garland's "Under the Lion's Paw." Yet, paradoxically, what we often find as we read, giving ourselves up to "strange" experiences, is that after all there is something of ourselves in all of these characters. They are "what we might have been" or "what we might be."

The greatest challenge to our emotional imagination in this unit is Stephen Crane's "The Open Boat." Here we are asked to share the harrowing emotions of the four men, adrift in a dinghy, at the mercy of the elements.

As we live moment to moment with the men in "The Open Boat," we find ourselves moving with them from hopefulness to dread. We experience their sense of helplessness and outrage in the face of Nature's indifference to their fate. "Living with" these characters compels a recognition of the limits of our own power over natural forces.

Through our imagination, we can experience the intense emotion and insight of a life-and-death situation—without actually risking our lives.

Yet it is possible to deny ourselves so much wisdom, so much experience, by blocking our emotional imaginations as we read. By doing so we impoverish ourselves. Our emotional imaginations enable us to engage in the very lives of literary characters—an imaginative act that connects literature and the world of real people in which we live. How much wiser and richer we may be, and how much pleasure we may find in reading, if we are willing for an hour or two to enter—through language—the lives of others.

THE AMERICAN VOICE

Down to Earth

The writers of the Realist period in American literature often shocked their contemporaries. In our own time we still see them as breaking away from some long-standing American traditions.

The Realists and Naturalists no longer took comfort from the religious vision that had supported the Puritan writers. They did not share the sense of new possibilities that had fired the imaginations of the writers of the Revolution. They did not exult with the optimism of the Transcendentalists.

Instead, they brought their ideas and emotions out of the clouds and down to earth. They took long, hard looks at what living in the world was really like in their time—without flinching from the suffering, without explaining away or softening the *struggle* of being human.

London

There was no sun nor hint of sun, though there was not a cloud in the sky. It was a clear day, and yet there seemed an intangible pall over the face of things.

Garland

Haskins worked like a fiend, and his wife, like the heroic woman that she was, bore also uncomplainingly the most terrible burdens. They rose early and toiled without intermission till the darkness fell on the plain.

Robinson

So on we worked, and waited for the light.

Dunbar

Ah, Douglass, we have fall'n on evil days
Such days as thou, not even thou didst know.

Crane

If I am going to be drowned—if I am going to be drowned—if I am going to be drowned, why, in the name of the seven mad gods who rule the sea, was I allowed to come thus far and contemplate sand and trees? Was I brought here merely to have my nose dragged away as I was about to nibble the sacred cheese of life? It is preposterous! If this old ninny-woman, Fate, cannot do better than this, she should be deprived of the management of men's fortunes.

The writers in this unit reported what they saw: There were joys and times of happiness—but they were scattered within a world of struggle.

Key to Illustrations on Pages 308–309.

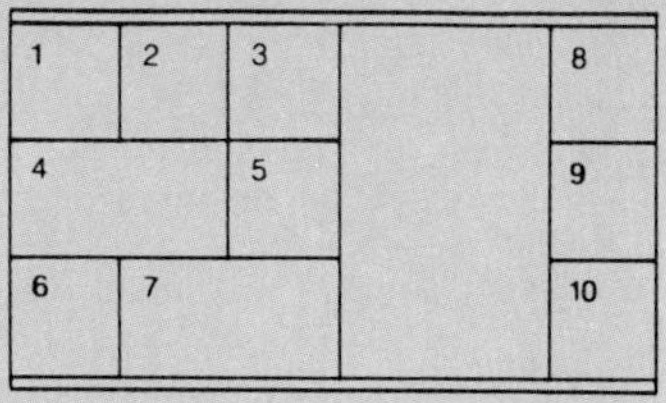

1	2	3		8
4		5		9
6	7			10

1. Paul Laurence Dunbar, detail of a postage stamp.
2. Alexander Graham Bell speaking at the opening of the New York–Chicago telephone circuit, 1892.
3. A Red Cross nurse tends a patient, from a calendar, 1899.
4. Wright brothers' first airplane flight at Kitty Hawk, North Carolina, December 17, 1903.
5. Stephen Crane, photographer unknown, c. 1895.
6. *Bret Harte,* John Pettie, 1884.
7. *The Wagon Boss,* Charles M. Russell, late nineteenth century.
8. Detail of *Country School,* Winslow Homer, 1871.
9. Sarah Orne Jewett, engraving.
10. Detail from *Northeaster,* Winslow Homer, 1895.

THE AMERICAN VOICE

Down to Earth

You might assign this section as a unit review. After students have read the section, ask them if they find anything shocking in the quotations here. Ask them to imagine what possibly could have shocked people ninety or more years ago when most of these selections were written. Elicit that many people then had a conception of literature as an elevated art in which certain topics and language were not tolerated.

Key to Illustrations appears on page 537.

NEW DIRECTIONS

1910–1930

The Era of Modernism

The English novelist Virginia Woolf once said that "on or about December 1910, human nature changed." Of course, human nature did not change, and Woolf knew it. What she meant was that the perception of human nature and of the human condition changed, and that the new perceptions were often expressed in startling and bewildering ways.

Life in the early twentieth century seemed suddenly different. New inventions allowed people to travel from place to place with a speed that was never before possible. The telephone, the radio, and the widespread availability of books, newspapers, and magazines all made people more aware of how others lived and thought. A person living in a remote village learned more about the variety and complexity of life on this planet than even a well-educated person living in a big city had known in the last century. The modern mind found this new knowledge exciting, but it was also bewildered by all the conflicting philosophies and ways of life.

The years from 1910 to 1930 are often called the Era of Modernism, for there seems to have been in both Europe and America a strong awareness of some sort of "break" with the past. Movements in all the arts overlapped and succeeded one another with amazing speed—Imagism, Cubism, Dadaism, Vorticism, and many others. The new

INTRODUCTION

After students have read the introduction to the unit, you might discuss the Modernist innovations covered in this section. To help students understand stream of consciousness, you might tell them that it means, in effect, writing things as they occur in a person's mind. You could ask student volunteers to provide a running narrative of their thoughts for a minute or so.

Modernist writers often wrote with fragments instead of whole entities. Discuss with students how the choice of subject matter has progressed in this book. Earlier writers described large themes and either allegorical characters or people of heroic stature. The Realists and Naturalists wrote about everyday life and working people. Modernists go one step further, often—like William Carlos Williams—writing about small pieces of everyday life or small pieces of a larger entity.

Key Ideas in This Period

- modernism
- complexity of modern life
- the outrage of war
- "stream of consciousness"
- the effects of modern psychology

Paris scene during the 1920s, when people often met at sidewalk cafés.

artists shared a desire to capture the complexity of modern life, to focus on the variety and confusion of the twentieth century by reshaping and sometimes discarding the ideas and habits of the nineteenth century. The Era of Modernism was indeed the era of the New.

The Lost Generation

The pivotal event of the Modernist era was World War I (1914–1918). Before the war the attitude toward the new century was one of great optimism. America was emerging from nineteenth-century isolation: The Spanish-American War and the opening of the Panama Canal made America a world power; millions of immigrants brought new ideas and ways of life to American shores. Improved communications and transportation made Europe and the East more accessible, and American artists were able to exchange views and share ideas with their colleagues abroad.

Many American writers of this period lived in Europe for part if not all of their lives. Ezra Pound went to London in 1908; Robert Frost visited England a few years later; Gertrude Stein settled in Paris; poet Langston Hughes and playwright Eugene O'Neill traveled the world as merchant seamen. In part because of their widening experience—and in part because of their extraordinary talents—Americans for the first time were in the vanguard of the arts: Pound and T. S. Eliot shaped the poetry of the Modernist era; Stein fostered the early careers of Pablo Picasso and other modern painters.

The European and American artistic communities drew closer together. Pound acted as the London representative of *Poetry: A Magazine of Verse,* an experimental publication begun in Chicago by Harriet Monroe in 1912. The Imagist poems that Pound sent back to Chicago had their effect on Carl Sandburg in the Midwest and Amy Lowell in New England, and in Chicago poets such as Sandburg, Edgar Lee Masters, and Vachel Lindsay now had an influential magazine in which their voices could be heard. O'Neill returned to New York City's Greenwich Village to see his experimental plays performed. Hughes became a leading figure in the burst of creativity called the Harlem Renaissance. Pound encouraged Frost, influenced John Crowe Ransom, and exchanged views with his old college friend William Carlos Williams. Hilda Doolittle published the first volume of Marianne Moore's poetry. Stein assisted Sherwood Anderson and the young Ernest Hemingway. Artists and writers taught one another, learned from one another, paid one another's bills, and helped one another bring new works before the public. The travelers came home from Europe and spread the Modernist message throughout America.

Those American writers who did not go abroad before the war visited Europe during and after the war. E. E. Cummings worked as an ambulance driver in World War I and was taken prisoner in France. Ernest Hemingway was wounded in action. Archibald MacLeish spent five years in Paris during the 1920s. Countee Cullen went there on a Guggenheim fellowship in 1928.

It was not simply going abroad, however, that made the greatest difference to Americans in Europe: It was the outrage of the war itself. World War I was the key event in early twentieth-century experience, an event that had a profound effect on the optimism that had preceded it. World War I was war on a scale that the world had never seen, war that destroyed a generation in Europe and led tens of thousands of Americans to early graves. To many, World War I was a tragic failure of old values, of old politics, of old ideas. Now more than ever people felt they must cast off the traditions of the nineteenth century; the need for change was deep, and the mood was often one of confusion and despair.

Gertrude Stein once told the young Ernest Hemingway, "You are all a lost generation," and the term has been used again and again to describe the people of the postwar years. It describes the Americans who remained in Paris as a colony of "expatriates," or exiles: Writers like Hemingway lived in semipoverty on the Left Bank of the river Seine and went to Gertrude Stein's salon as a safe refuge in stormy seas. It describes the Americans who returned to their native land with an intense awareness of living in an unfamiliar, changing world.

Yet, on the surface the mood in America during the 1920s did not seem desperate. Many Americans returned to their previous belief in isolation, their contempt for Europe reconfirmed by the war and the Treaty of Versailles that ended it. The open door was closed to immigrants, and America did not join the League of Nations, an association—later succeeded by the United Nations—established to promote peace. Instead Americans entered a decade of prosperity and exhibitionism that Prohibition, the legal ban against alcoholic beverages, did more to encourage than to curb. Fashions were extravagant; more and more automobiles crowded the roads; advertising flourished; and nearly every American home had a radio in it. Fads swept the nation: People danced the Charleston, and they sat upon flagpoles. In 1927 Charles Lindbergh piloted an airplane across the Atlantic and became everyone's hero.

Gertrude Stein in her Paris home, meeting place for writers and artists.

This was the Jazz Age, when New Orleans musicians moved "up the river" to Chicago, and the theaters of New York's Harlem pulsed with the music that had become a symbol of the times. These were the Roaring Twenties.

The roaring of the decade served to mask a quiet pain, the sense of loss that Gertrude Stein had observed in Paris. Carl Sandburg's poetic jazz rhythms might be hopeful, but Langston Hughes's are often bitter. F. Scott Fitzgerald portrays the Jazz Age as a generation of "the beautiful and damned," drowning in their pleasures. From England Eliot spoke of the "immense panorama of futility and anarchy which is contemporary history," and he gave a name to the modern world in the title of his most famous poem—*The Waste Land*.

The task of the Modernist writers was, however, not only to express the waste and futility they experienced. They took up the burden of attempting to make some sense of that experience.

Modernist Literature

When we speak of Modernist literature, we speak of a broad range of artists and movements all seeking, in varying degrees, to break with the style, form, and content of the nineteenth century. Old ways of seeing, old ways of making sense of experience, just did not seem to work anymore for twentieth-century writers. "Make it new" was the cry of Ezra Pound, and most other writers of the time worked vigorously and self-consciously to make their poems and plays and novels new and different.

Modern psychology had a profound impact on the literature of the early twentieth century, and most great Modernist writers were interested in the workings of the human mind. Ordinary discourse had always put thoughts in a linear, cause-and-effect order: "If this is true and that is true, then this must be true." Now came the recognition that the human mind does not always follow this straight-line pattern; we often think by leaping from associ-

Robie House, Chicago, Illinois, designed and built by Frank Lloyd Wright, 1910.

ation to association in what the psychologist William James called the "stream of consciousness."

Gertrude Stein, a pupil of James's, tried to capture this "stream" through such devices as repetition and run-on sentences. The greatest practitioner of the Modernist style, however, was the Irish novelist James Joyce, whose *Ulysses* (1922) is sometimes said to be the last novel ever written because it took prose narrative to its most extreme point. Joyce's influence was extraordinary, and although novels are of course still being written all over the world, they are written with a heightened awareness of the experiments of Joyce.

Modernists took risks as they wrote in new forms and styles. Eugene O'Neill uses a number of experimental devices to reveal the flow of his characters' thoughts on stage. Ernest Hemingway opens most of his stories in the middle of the "stream," revealing background information as it comes up naturally and not in the long expository sections standard in nineteenth-century fiction. In "The Love Song of J. Alfred Prufrock" T. S. Eliot attempts to duplicate the "stream" of Prufrock's thoughts in a dramatic monologue. The result is a series of fragments that the reader must piece together.

Modernist literature is often experimental in form and in content. Poetry usually discards the nineteenth-century traditions of meter and rhyme. Free verse is the tool of most Modernist poets, and even if a poem retains some rhymes, the poet rarely puts them in the usual places. The visual appearance of poetry is also a significant factor, another means of breaking with traditions. The poems of E. E. Cummings, for example, are noted for lowercase letters in strange places and words spaced oddly on a page. For his poems William Carlos Williams chooses everyday subjects that would seem highly unusual by nineteenth-century standards—a raid on the refrigerator, for instance, or a red wheelbarrow.

Modernist literature is often fragmentary, reflecting not only the "stream of consciousness" but the Modernist perception of the twentieth century as a jumble of conflicting ideas. Sometimes we are presented with only one fragment, the manner of presentation implying that there is no larger whole; the fragment "is what it is." This is true of Pound's and Doolittle's Imagist poetry, and of most of the poems of Gertrude Stein. It is also true of many poems by William Carlos Williams: In "This Is Just to Say," for example, Williams presents only a tiny piece of someone's life, but the poem is nevertheless satisfyingly complete; the fragment is enough.

Modernists often insist that their readers participate and draw their own conclusions. Direct statements of abstract ideas or emotions are usually avoided. The Modernist *shows* rather than *tells*. In Imagist poetry, for example, an image is used to capture an emotion; the poet does not tell us, "This is how I felt." In Hemingway's stories painful and moving experiences are coolly recounted by a detached narrator; the reader supplies the emotions and decides why the experiences are significant.

In the attempt to capture the bewilderment of modern life, Modernist literature is sometimes intentionally puzzling. We may sometimes miss the esoteric allusions in the poetry of Pound and Eliot, and we can never be sure why "so much depends" on Williams' red wheelbarrow. The point may be that the mystery itself is the "message." If there is something we do not know, we may not be meant to know it but rather to be puzzled by it and so to think about the mystery again and again.

The degrees to which writers of this period adapted Modernist techniques vary greatly. Some writers did take comfort in the pattern and discipline of nineteenth-century literary forms. Edna St. Vincent Millay, for example, continued to write sonnets; much of Robert Frost's poetry is traditionally rhymed and patterned. In content, however, these writers are part of the Modernist era: Their subject matter shows that they could not have been writing at any other time. In fact, one of the most fascinating aspects of Modernist literature is the way each individual writer comes to terms with the changes of the time. Each poet or novelist seems to ask, "What does being 'new' mean to me?" The responses of these creative individuals produced the great variety of Modernist literature.

American street scene during the 1920s, a time of progress and prosperity.

The Modernist Achievement

What did the Modernists accomplish? They took the first great steps in the search for a new art. They broke out of old forms and styles and generated new ones. They studied the elements of the past that could still be used and showed why the rest had to be put aside. Pound demonstrated the value of ancient Chinese literature; Eliot used the tradition of the English metaphysical poets of the seventeenth century. They and those who followed them used the past to create a new relationship with a new world. Wallace Stevens called this relationship "the supreme fiction," a way of living in the world, creating it anew every day, and being open to change even as the world itself changes. The Modernist achievement—in poetry, fiction, drama, in music and painting, in sculpture and architecture, in psychology and philosophy—lies largely in throwing open for us the doors of possibility.

TIME LINE

1910–1930 AMERICAN EVENTS

1910 First electric washing machines introduced

1911 Edith Wharton, *Ethan Frome*

Pulitzer Prizes established

Songwriter Irving Berlin, "Alexander's Ragtime Band"

1912 Harriet Monroe founds *Poetry: A Magazine of Verse*

Edna St. Vincent Millay, *Renascence and Other Poems*

1913 Henry Ford pioneers assembly line, producing 1,000 Model T automobiles a day

1914 Gertrude Stein, *Tender Buttons*

Robert Frost, *North of Boston*

1915 Edgar Lee Masters, *Spoon River Anthology*

1916 Norman Rockwell begins illustrating covers for *Saturday Evening Post*

Carl Sandburg, *Chicago Poems*

1917 U.S. declares war on Germany

Jeanette Rankin is first woman elected to House of Representatives

T. S. Eliot, *Prufrock and Other Observations*

WORLD EVENTS 1910–1930

1911 Antarctica: Norwegian explorer Roald Amundsen reaches South Pole

China: Manchu dynasty overthrown; republic established with Sun Yat-Sen as president

1912 Atlantic Ocean: *Titanic,* British ocean liner, sinks on its maiden voyage

England: George Bernard Shaw, *Pygmalion*

Sweden: Jim Thorpe, Native American, outstanding athlete at Olympic Games

1913 England: D. H. Lawrence, *Sons and Lovers*

Germany: Thomas Mann, *Death in Venice*

France: Premiere of *The Rite of Spring,* ballet by Russian composer Igor Stravinsky

1914 Beginning of World War I

Central America: Panama Canal opened

1915 Germany: Albert Einstein announces his general theory of relativity

1917 Russia: Revolution begins; Bolsheviks seize power

Switzerland: Carl Jung, *Psychology of the Unconscious*

France: Poet Paul Valéry, "La Jeune Parque"

1918 U.S. population: 103.5 million

Willa Cather, *My Ántonia*

1919 Sherwood Anderson, *Winesburg, Ohio*

1920 Women gain right to vote

Sinclair Lewis, *Main Street*

Beginning of Prohibition Era

Eugene O'Neill, *Beyond the Horizon*

1921 Marianne Moore, *Poems*

Rudolph Valentino stars in *The Sheik*

1922 T. S. Eliot, *The Waste Land*

Sinclair Lewis, *Babbitt*

William Carlos Williams, *Spring and All*

1923 E. E. Cummings, *tulips and chimneys*

Robert Frost, *New Hampshire*

Wallace Stevens, *Harmonium*

Time magazine first published

1924 George Gershwin, *Rhapsody in Blue*

Congress makes all native-born American Indians citizens

1925 Nellie Taylor Ross of Wyoming becomes first woman governor

F. Scott Fitzgerald, *The Great Gatsby*

The Gold Rush with Charlie Chaplin produced

Theodore Dreiser, *An American Tragedy*

1918 Worldwide influenza epidemic—approximately 20 million die by 1920

1919 France: Treaty of Versailles signed, ending World War I

1920 League of Nations established

1921 France: Pablo Picasso, *Three Musicians*

Ireland: W. B. Yeats, *Michael Robartes and the Dancer*

1922 Germany: Herman Hesse, *Siddhartha*

France: *Ulysses,* by Irish novelist James Joyce, published in Paris

Egypt: ancient tomb of Tutankhamen discovered

Italy: Benito Mussolini becomes dictator

1923 Germany: Adolph Hitler writes *Mein Kampf* while in jail

Germany: Arnold Schönberg composes *Piano Suite,* first work based on twelve-tone system

1924 Germany: Thomas Mann, *The Magic Mountain*

1925 Austria: *The Trial,* by Czech writer Franz Kafka, published after his death

England: Scot John Baird televises images of moving objects for first time

Austria: Composer Alban Berg, *Wozzeck,* an opera

American Events

1926 Ernest Hemingway, *The Sun Also Rises*

Langston Hughes, *The Weary Blues*

1927 *The Jazz Singer* with Al Jolson: first "talkie"

Charles Lindbergh makes first solo nonstop transatlantic flight

Babe Ruth hits sixty home runs for New York Yankees

Carl Sandburg, *The American Songbag*

1928 Stephen Vincent Benét, *John Brown's Body*

Anthropologist Margaret Mead, *Coming of Age in Samoa*

1929 William Faulkner, *The Sound and the Fury*

Ernest Hemingway, *A Farewell to Arms*

Stock Market crashes; beginning of Great Depression

1930 Grant Wood paints *American Gothic*

Sinclair Lewis first American to win Nobel Prize for Literature

World Events

1926 England: A. A. Milne, *Winnie the Pooh*

1927 Russia: Igor Pavlov, *Conditioned Reflexes*

England: Virginia Woolf, *To the Lighthouse*

1928 England: Sir Alexander Fleming discovers penicillin

Holland: Women participate in Olympics for first time

China: Chiang Kai-shek forms united government

France: Kellogg-Briand Pact signed, outlawing war

1929 Germany: Erich Maria Remarque, *All Quiet on the Western Front*

1932 Germany: Nazi party wins plurality in national election

India: Mahatma Gandhi leads protests against British rule

Ezra Pound *1885–1972*

Ezra Pound—whose expression "Make it new" served as a rallying cry for the writers of his time—was the driving force behind Modernist literature. For more than fifty years his restless mind busied itself seeking new discoveries and innovations in the art of poetry. Yet this self-styled "revolutionist" of the arts was also profoundly conservative, searching history for the "best" and most useful things he could find among the world's literature, religions, philosophies, and social systems.

Pound was born in a small town in Idaho, grew up in a suburb of Philadelphia, and after attending the University of Pennsylvania, left America for Europe, where he remained until 1945. His early years in London and Paris were a whirlwind of Modernist activity as he invented Imagism (see page 413) and worked hard at "modernizing" his own poetry. As the London representative of *Poetry* magazine, Pound helped nurture the careers of many new talents. He championed the Irish novelist James Joyce, became a close friend of T. S. Eliot, and influenced the prose of the young American novelist Ernest Hemingway.

After 1925 Pound made his home in Rapallo, Italy. Here he devoted his life to social-economic thought and to his long poem the *Cantos,* one of the most beautiful but puzzling poems ever written by a great poet.

In Italy Pound became an admirer of Benito Mussolini, and his idealistic but misplaced trust in that dictator had devastating consequences. During World War II he broadcast over the Italian radio, foolishly thinking that he was contributing to peace and to a better world society. After the war he was arrested and imprisoned by American troops in Pisa, an experience reflected in what is perhaps his greatest poetic achievement, *The Pisan Cantos.*

Judged mentally incapable of standing trial, Pound spent thirteen years in a hospital for the insane in Washington, D.C., where he continued to write some of his finest work. In 1958 he was allowed to return to his beloved Italy to live out a troubled old age.

The following poems are all from Pound's early years in London and Paris. "L'Art, 1910" ("Art, 1910") expresses his excitement for the "new" in painting and all the arts. "In a Station of the Metro" is a classic Imagist poem, presenting a quick, sharp image of people seen in the darkness of the Paris subway (the Metro). "Erat Hora" ("There Was an Hour") is Pound at his most lyrical, and "The River-Merchant's Wife" is a translation from the Chinese. All are written in the free verse that Pound worked hard to promote.

- Traditionally poetry has rhymed. Do you think rhyme is necessary in poetry? What does Pound think?

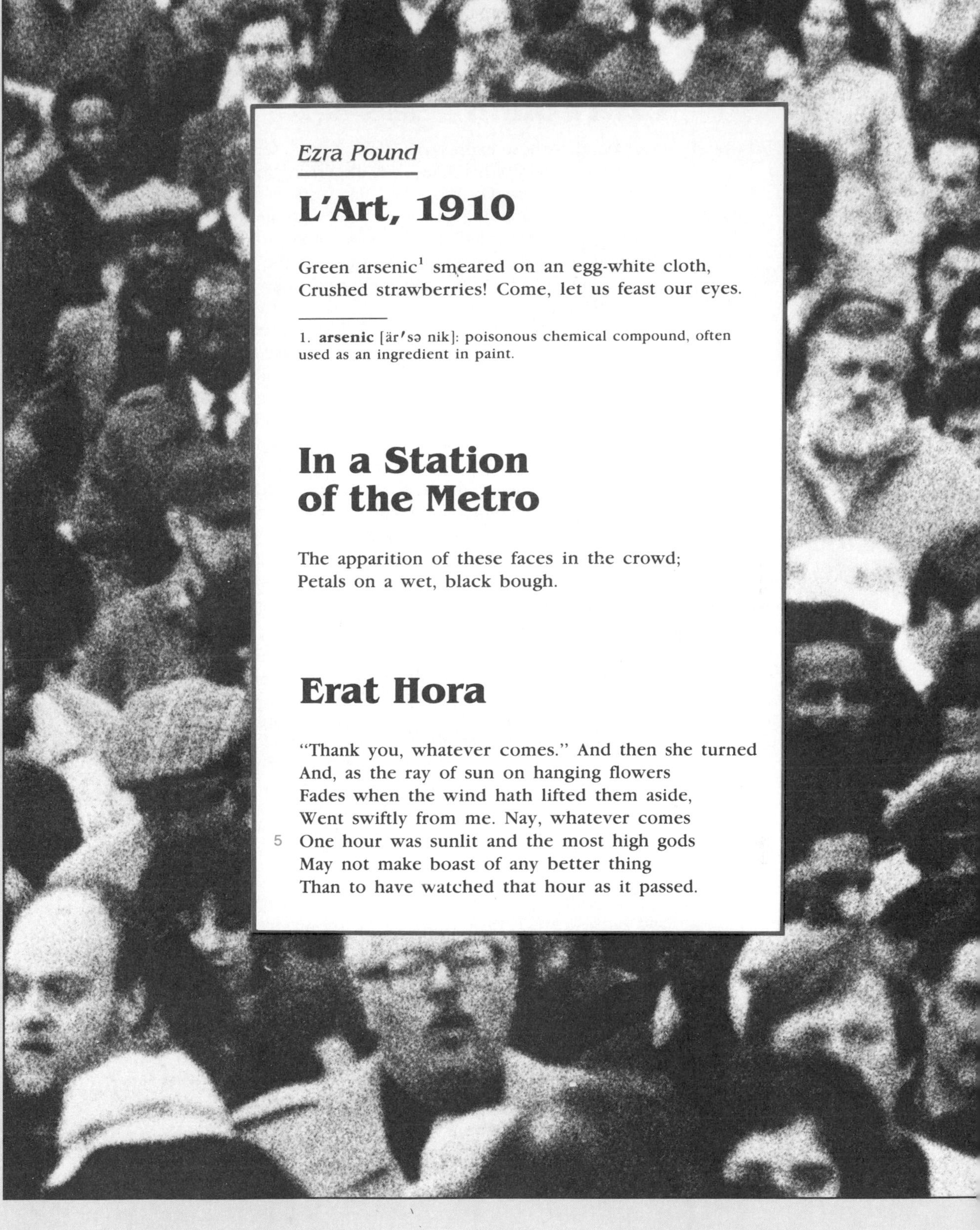

Ezra Pound

L'Art, 1910

Green arsenic[1] smeared on an egg-white cloth,
Crushed strawberries! Come, let us feast our eyes.

1. **arsenic** [är′sə nik]: poisonous chemical compound, often used as an ingredient in paint.

In a Station of the Metro

The apparition of these faces in the crowd;
Petals on a wet, black bough.

Erat Hora

"Thank you, whatever comes." And then she turned
And, as the ray of sun on hanging flowers
Fades when the wind hath lifted them aside,
Went swiftly from me. Nay, whatever comes
One hour was sunlit and the most high gods
May not make boast of any better thing
Than to have watched that hour as it passed.

LITERARY OPTIONS

- Imagism
- approximate rhyme

THEMATIC OPTIONS

- the nature of modern art
- people as objects
- memory

L'ART, 1910: IMAGERY

The poet uses three colors in his description. Two are the colors of foods; the third is the color of a poison. The combination, like modern art itself, is shocking.

IN A STATION OF THE METRO: RHYME

The approximate rhyme of "crowd" and "bough" helps to link the images that the poet presents. Like the rhyme the images themselves are not an exact match.

MAIN IDEA

Nothing is explained. This strategy is the main idea of Imagism—simply to offer images, without comment.

ERAT HORA: METAPHOR

The focus of the poem can be summarized in the statement "One hour was sunlit . . ." (l. 5). The poem is about love, but it is the picture of a frozen moment.

REFLECTING ON THE POEMS

In what ways do the first two poems differ from the third? What do all three poems have in common? (The first two poems seem like impromptu impersonal sketches, using unexpected language. "Erat Hora" is a more-developed poem about an emotion, using traditional language [*hath, Nay*]. Each of the three poems turns on a strong visual image.)

The River-Merchant's Wife: A Letter

While my hair was still cut straight across my forehead
I played about the front gate, pulling flowers.
You came by on bamboo stilts, playing horse,
You walked about my seat, playing with blue plums.
And we went on living in the village of Chokan:[1]
Two small people, without dislike or suspicion.

At fourteen I married My Lord you.
I never laughed, being bashful.
Lowering my head, I looked at the wall.
Called to, a thousand times, I never looked back.

At fifteen I stopped scowling,
I desired my dust to be mingled with yours
Forever and forever and forever.
Why should I climb the look out?

At sixteen you departed,
You went into far Ku-to-yen,[2] by the river of swirling eddies,
And you have been gone five months.
The monkeys make sorrowful noise overhead.

You dragged your feet when you went out.
By the gate now, the moss is grown, the different mosses,
Too deep to clear them away!
The leaves fall early this autumn, in wind.
The paired butterflies are already yellow with August
Over the grass in the West garden;
They hurt me. I grow older.
If you are coming down through the narrows of the river Kiang,[3]
Please let me know beforehand,
And I will come out to meet you
As far as Cho-fu-Sa.[4]

1. **Chokan** [chō′kän′]: suburb of Nanking, city in the People's Republic of China.
2. **Ku-to-yen** [ko͞o′tō′yen′]: island in the Yangtze Kiang [yäng′tsē kyang] River, largest river in China.
3. **river Kiang:** referring to the Yangtze Kiang River.
4. **Cho-fu-Sa** [chō′fo͞o′sä′]: beach along the Yangtze Kiang River, a few hundred miles above Nanking.

AT A GLANCE

In a letter to her husband, who has been away five months, a Chinese woman recounts her early marriage, her growing love for him, and her present loneliness.

LITERARY OPTIONS

- Imagism
- speaker

THEMATIC OPTIONS

- the growth of love
- loneliness

FORM

Because the poem takes the form of a letter from a Chinese wife to her husband, Pound can create an unusual mix of formal grace, matter-of-fact realism, understated intimacy, and deep feeling.

SPEAKER

The speaker is a young Chinese woman writing to her husband. Although she is only sixteen years old, she displays a surprising maturity as she considers the way in which her love has grown.

MAIN IDEA

The speaker does not express her loneliness directly. Instead, she mentions the "sorrowful" monkeys (l. 18) and refers to being hurt by the sight of "paired" butterflies (ll. 23–25).

IMAGERY

The speaker uses images from nature (deep moss, autumn leaves, "yellowed" butterflies) to suggest how long her husband has been away (ll. 19–24).

REFLECTING ON THE POEM

Summarize the speaker's change of attitude in her marriage. (At first a bashful and somewhat discontented bride, she soon learned to love her husband. She now grieves over his long absence and wants to be with him "forever and forever and forever" [l. 13].)

STUDY QUESTIONS

L'Art, 1910

1. art in 1910
2. mentions green, white, implies red; to feast our eyes
3. colorful, shocking painting; spontaneity; picks up on food connotations, demands sensory response
4. modern; because clashing colors and messy quality reflect breakdown of traditional forms
5. Answers will vary. Pound may be mocking the modern artist. The poison suggests this art is a kind of poison. On the other hand, arsenic is found in paint. He may be celebrating the shock of the new.
6. Answers will vary. Some might like the novelty; others may find it a mess.

In a Station of the Metro

1. Metro (subway) station
2. faces and petals on wet bough
3. no; juxtaposition of two images; images themselves and insight generated by juxtaposition
4. The word connotes dreams and spirits; something vaguely seen.

Erat Hora

1. fading of sun on flowers
2. sunlit
3. fond, probably in love; yes; one of best moments in life
4. the woman
5. indicates memory as content; value of experience and sadness of passing time
6.
- Answers will vary.
- Poems differ in their brevity, conciseness, juxtaposition of images, free verse.
- "L'Art, 1910," "Metro"; subject and language

The River-Merchant's Wife

1. letter; river-merchant's wife
2. fourteen; scowling, desired to be buried with husband; he left on journey
3. make sorrowful noise; hurt wife; grows older
4. travel out to meet him
5. loves him dearly; misses him
6. no; wife's sadness, loneliness
7. matter-of-fact; 5, 7, 9, 15, 22
8. Wife controls her feelings.

STUDY QUESTIONS

L'Art, 1910

Recalling

1. According to the title, what is being described?
2. What colors does the poem mention? What invitation does it include?

Interpreting

3. What does the combination of colors suggest about the physical appearance of the painting? What does "smeared" suggest? Why is "feast" especially well chosen?
4. Is the painting traditional or modern? Explain your opinion with examples from the poem.
5. Does Pound seem to like the painting? Can we be sure? Explain your opinion.

Extending

6. Do you think you would like the painting? Why or why not?

In a Station of the Metro

Recalling

1. Where does this poem take place?
2. What two images are juxtaposed, or placed next to each other, in the poem?

Interpreting

3. Does the poet supply you with any information about how you should think or feel about the poem? What does the poem consist of? What makes it "poetic"?
4. Why does the poet use the word *apparition* rather than *appearance?* (Consider the connotations of *apparition.*)

Erat Hora

Recalling

1. What simile describes the woman's departure?
2. What adjective describes the one hour that the speaker spent with the woman?

Interpreting

3. How does the speaker feel about the woman? Is he sorry that she leaves? What does he nevertheless feel about the hour they spent together?
4. Who probably speaks the words in quotation marks?
5. Explain how the poem's title relates to its content. What does the poem suggest about human experience and the passing of time?

Extending

6. What sharp images do this poem and the two preceding poems produce in your mind? How are the poems different from nineteenth-century poetry that you have read? Which two of these three poems by Pound are more radical departures? Explain your choice.

The River-Merchant's Wife

Recalling

1. What form does the poem take? Who is writing it?
2. At what age did the river-merchant's wife marry? What did she stop doing at fifteen, and what did she desire? What happened when the wife was sixteen?
3. What do the monkeys do in line 18? What do the butterflies do in line 25? What does the wife do in line 25?
4. If her husband tells her when he is coming through the narrows of the river Kiang, what will the wife do?

Interpreting

5. How have the wife's feelings for her husband changed since she married him? How does she feel about her husband's absence?
6. Is monkeys' chattering usually described as it is here? What do the negative descriptions of the monkeys and butterflies reflect?
7. Is the tone of this poem sentimental or matter-of-fact? Cite lines to support your answer.

Extending

8. How is the attitude of the wife in this poem different from the attitude expressed in nineteenth-century Romantic poetry that you have read? Compare this poem to Poe's "To Helen" or "Alone" (pages 132–133).

VIEWPOINT

Ezra Pound's own comment on "In a Station of the Metro" shows the poet at work:

> Three years ago in Paris I got out of a "metro" train at La Concorde, and saw suddenly a beautiful face, and then another and another, and then a beautiful child's face, and then another beautiful woman, and I tried all day to find words for what this had meant to me, and I could not find any words that seemed to me worthy, or as

lovely as that sudden emotion. And that evening, as I went home . . . I was still trying and I found, suddenly, the expression. I do not mean that I found words, but there came an equation . . . not in speech, but in little splotches of color. . . . That is to say, my experience in Paris should have gone into paint.

- What does Pound mean when he says that an "equation" can be a poetic experience? Do you think "In a Station of the Metro" would have made a good painting? Why or why not?

LITERARY FOCUS

Imagism

The literary movement **Imagism** was begun by Ezra Pound and a few friends who wanted to rid poetry of the "bad habits" that they felt nineteenth-century poets had fallen into: the use of too many words; the use of words no longer in actual speech; repetitious subject matter; and the use of tired poetic patterns, especially traditional stanzas and meters. The Imagists wanted "direct treatment of the 'thing' " and a rhythm like that of a musical phrase. Instead of having the poet tell us what we should be feeling, Pound and his colleagues wanted an image to produce the emotion, to "speak for itself."

In "In a Station of the Metro" Pound attempts to produce the emotion he felt when he disembarked into a Paris subway station and suddenly saw a number of faces in the dim light. To capture the emotion, Pound uses the image of petals on a wet, black bough. The image is not decoration: It is central to the poem's meaning. In fact, it *is* the poem's meaning.

Imagist poems are usually written in **free verse**—verse with no fixed rhythm—and are often quite short. They use one quick image to capture an emotion, to freeze one moment in time. Imagists took some of their inspiration from the highly disciplined Japanese verse form **haiku:** The first line of a haiku contains five syllables; the second line, seven; and the third line, five.

Imagism was a movement that came and went: Few pure Imagist poems were written after 1920. Nevertheless, the ideas of Imagism have had a great impact on modern poetry and on the way we read it.

Thinking About Imagism

- Why is "L'Art, 1910" an Imagist poem? What elements of Imagism does "Erat Hora" contain?

COMPOSITION

Writing About Poetry

- Although longer and more narrative than a pure Imagist poem, "The River-Merchant's Wife" uses many of the devices of Imagist poetry. In a brief essay discuss these devices and their relation to the poem's subject matter. First explain the meaning of the poem. Then consider the poem's use of (a) simple, direct language; (b) free verse; and (c) sharp images to convey emotions. *For help with this assignment, refer to Lesson 7 in the Writing About Literature Handbook at the back of this book.*

Writing an Imagist Poem

- Write your own Imagist poem of two to five lines. Use one central image to capture a mood or emotion. You might reexamine "In a Station of the Metro" before you begin. To begin, think of a scene that has interested you, and think of an object or action to which your scene can be compared. Write the poem by stating the relationship in simple terms. Read your poem aloud to decide where it can be broken into lines most naturally.

VIEWPOINT

- The "equation" itself is a kind of metaphor: This equals this.
- Answers will vary, although a poem that *is* an image would be easier to transform into a painting than a narrative poem would be.

LITERARY FOCUS

- "L'Art, 1910" is built upon a single image and does not state any feelings directly.
- "Erat Hora," although it discusses the speaker's emotions, is also built upon a single image.

COMPOSITION: GUIDELINES FOR EVALUATION

WRITING ABOUT POETRY

Objective

To show how elements of poem relate to subject

Guidelines for Evaluation

- suggested length: four to six paragraphs
- should discuss simple language as reflection of personality of speaker
- should see free verse as appropriate to poem
- should discuss images, which exclude sentimentality but convey intense emotion

WRITING AN IMAGIST POEM

Objective

To write a poem using Imagist techniques

Guidelines for Evaluation

- suggested length: two to five lines
- should juxtapose scene with image capturing mood or emotion of scene
- should suggest relationship between images
- should present one clear mood or emotion
- should suggest, not state, mood or emotion

T. S. Eliot *1888–1965*

Born into a prominent St. Louis family and educated at Harvard, Thomas Stearns Eliot first met Ezra Pound in England in 1914. The two men were outwardly different—Pound rough, wild, Bohemian; Eliot the image of a polite, conservatively dressed gentleman—yet together, both as critics and as poets, they did more than anyone else to revolutionize literary tastes in the twentieth century.

Eliot's long poem *The Waste Land*, which appeared in 1922, ranks with James Joyce's novel *Ulysses* as the greatest success of the Modernist movement in Anglo-American literature. It became instantly famous among literary people, many of whom thought that it spoke for the postwar generation in its suggestion that the twentieth century was a fragmented, emotionally and spiritually arid period. Few at the time saw the poem's deeply religious concerns, nor did they recognize that in defining the condition of the modern "waste land," Eliot was searching for something better.

The crisis marked by *The Waste Land* was resolved for Eliot when he became a devout member of the Church of England. In 1927 he described himself as "classicist in literature, royalist in politics, and Anglo-Catholic in religion"—a remarkable turnaround, for as a Modernist, Eliot was "supposed" to be none of these. His spiritual journey can be traced through his poetry from *Gerontion* (1919), *The Hollow Men* (1925), and *Ash Wednesday* (1930) to one of the most profound religious poems in English, *Four Quartets* (1943).

In his later years Eliot worked for a large British publishing house. He also wrote plays, many of them in verse, and contributed a substantial body of literary criticism. He was awarded the Nobel Prize for Literature in 1948. In the years that followed, Eliot achieved a personal happiness that at last matched the pleasure he derived from his public life as a leading man of letters.

"The Love Song of J. Alfred Prufrock" is an early poem but is marked by an assurance in phrasing that has made many of its lines almost proverbial in our century. It is a dramatic monologue spoken by one J. Alfred Prufrock, whose very name seems to combine the dignity and absurdity of his public and private selves. These two selves are probably the "you and I" of the first line—a person who outwardly is a "proper" member of the "best" society, but who inwardly is lost, lonely, and suffering, not unlike the poet himself at the time the poem was written.

■ Do people present one "face" to others while hiding another "face"? What reasons might Prufrock have for doing so?

T. S. Eliot

The Love Song of J. Alfred Prufrock

S'io credesse che mia risposta fosse
A persona che mai tornasse al mondo,
Questa fiamma staria senza piu scosse.
Ma perciocche giammai di questo fondo
Non torno vivo alcun, s'i'odo il vero,
Senza tema d'infamia ti rispondo.[1]

Let us go then, you and I,
When the evening is spread out against the sky
Like a patient etherized[2] upon a table;
Let us go, through certain half-deserted streets,
The muttering retreats
Of restless nights in one-night cheap hotels
And sawdust restaurants with oyster-shells:
Streets that follow like a tedious argument
Of insidious[3] intent
To lead you to an overwhelming question . . .
Oh, do not ask, "What is it?"
Let us go and make our visit.

In the room the women come and go
Talking of Michelangelo.[4]

The yellow fog that rubs its back upon the windowpanes,
The yellow smoke that rubs its muzzle on the windowpanes
Licked its tongue into the corners of the evening,
Lingered upon the pools that stand in drains,
Let fall upon its back the soot that falls from chimneys,
Slipped by the terrace, made a sudden leap,
And seeing that it was a soft October night,
Curled once about the house, and fell asleep.

---

1. ***S'io credesse . . . ti rispondo:*** "If I believed my reply were being made to one who would ever return to the world, this flame [his soul] would shake no more; but since, if what I hear is true, none ever did return alive from this depth, I answer you without fear of dishonor." One of the condemned spirits in Hell confesses his sins to the poet Dante in the *Inferno,* Chapter XXVII, lines 61–66. The spirit believed—wrongly—that Dante would be unable to return to the world from Hell.
2. **etherized** [ē′thə rīzd]: made insensitive to pain; anesthetized with ether, as before an operation.
3. **insidious** [in sid′ē əs]: waiting to entrap, or trick; deceitful.
4. **Michelangelo** [mi′kəl an′jə lō]: The great Italian artist Michelangelo Buonarroti [bwō nä rô′tē] (1475–1564).

AT A GLANCE

- Prufrock, the speaker, talks to himself on the way to a social occasion.
- He wants to ask someone a question but is afraid to think about such a confrontation.
- He creates a dreamlike atmosphere for himself by seeing the fog as an animal.

LITERARY OPTIONS

- dramatic monologue
- tone
- irony

THEMATIC OPTIONS

- passivity and disillusionment
- memory and time
- despair

DRAMATIC MONOLOGUE

The sentiments of this poem are expressed in the first person by Prufrock himself. The absence of commentary by Eliot adds to the sense of isolation that Prufrock reveals as the poem progresses.

SPEAKER

The "you and I" could refer to the duality in Prufrock's life—his bland social presence and his disturbed emotional state (l. 1).

TONE

Prufrock sets the melancholy yet ironic tone of the poem by describing the evening as a patient under anesthesia. Such an unexpected comparison alerts the reader that this poem will not be the usual sort of "love song" (ll. 2–3).

PERSONIFICATION

Prufrock describes the yellow fog as an animal that surrounds the house and then falls asleep (ll. 15–22). The "sleeping" fog recalls the comparison of the evening to an "etherized" patient (ll. 2–3).

GUIDED READING

LITERAL QUESTIONS

1a. Where do the streets in line 8 lead? (not to a physical place but to an "overwhelming question")

2a. How does Prufrock describe the fog in lines 15–22? (He likens it to an animal—perhaps a cat.)

INFERENTIAL QUESTIONS

1b. How does Prufrock feel about that question? (He wants to put it aside; he does not want to think about it.)

2b. Why might he choose such terms for his description? (Perhaps he unconsciously uses the dreamlike images to reflect his inability or reluctance to deal with reality.)

AT A GLANCE

- Prufrock tries to assure himself that there will be time to prepare for whatever social interaction he must face.
- He worries about what other people think of him.
- He worries about women in general and one woman in particular.

DRAMATIC MONOLOGUE

Prufrock consoles himself with thoughts of indecision (l. 32), daydreaming (l. 33), and retreat (l. 39).

MAIN IDEA

Prufrock is so worried about what others will think that he becomes unable to act (ll. 41, 44, and 56).

RESPONSE JOURNAL

Ask students to react to lines 43–44, discussing how too much concern about the opinions of others can be paralyzing.

IRONY

Although Prufrock seems to recognize that his life is utterly trivial, he also worries that *any* action, no matter how insignificant, will create some change and, hence, "disturb the universe."

And indeed there will be time
For the yellow smoke that slides along the street,
Rubbing its back upon the windowpanes;
There will be time, there will be time
To prepare a face to meet the faces that you meet;
There will be time to murder and create,
And time for all the works and days of hands
That lift and drop a question on your plate;
Time for you and time for me,
And time yet for a hundred indecisions,
And for a hundred visions and revisions,
Before the taking of a toast and tea.

In the room the women come and go
Talking of Michelangelo.

And indeed there will be time
To wonder, "Do I dare?" and, "Do I dare?"
Time to turn back and descend the stair,
With a bald spot in the middle of my hair—
(They will say: "How his hair is growing thin!")
My morning coat, my collar mounting firmly to the chin,
My necktie rich and modest, but asserted by a simple pin—
(They will say: "But how his arms and legs are thin!")
Do I dare
Disturb the universe?
In a minute there is time
For decisions and revisions which a minute will reverse.

For I have known them all already, known them all—
Have known the evenings, mornings, afternoons,
I have measured out my life with coffee spoons;
I know the voices dying with a dying fall
Beneath the music from a farther room.
So how should I presume?

And I have known the eyes already, known them all—
The eyes that fix you in a formulated phrase,
And when I am formulated, sprawling on a pin,
When I am pinned and wriggling on the wall,
Then how should I begin
To spit out all the butt-ends of my days and ways?
And how should I presume?

And I have known the arms already, known them all—
Arms that are braceleted and white and bare
(But in the lamplight, downed with light brown hair!)

GUIDED READING

LITERAL QUESTIONS

1a. How has Prufrock measured out his life? (with coffee spoons)

2a. What do women's eyes do to Prufrock? (They pin him to the wall.)

INFERENTIAL QUESTIONS

1b. What does this detail suggest about Prufrock's life? (It is trivial and predictable—nothing important or unexpected ever happens to him.)

2b. How does Prufrock's comment deepen the reader's understanding of his personality? (It shows that he is as terrified of women as he is of most other aspects of social interaction.)

Is it perfume from a dress
That makes me so digress?
Arms that lie along a table, or wrap about a shawl.
  And should I then presume?
  And how should I begin?

. . . . .

Shall I say, I have gone at dusk through narrow streets
And watched the smoke that rises from the pipes
Of lonely men in shirtsleeves, leaning out of windows? . . .

  I should have been a pair of ragged claws
Scuttling across the floors of silent seas.

. . . . .

And the afternoon, the evening, sleeps so peacefully!
Smoothed by long fingers,
Asleep . . . tired . . . or it malingers,[5]
Stretched on the floor, here beside you and me.
Should I, after tea and cakes and ices,
Have the strength to force the moment to its crisis?
But though I have wept and fasted, wept and prayed,
Though I have seen my head (grown slightly bald) brought in
    upon a platter,[6]
I am no prophet—and here's no great matter;
I have seen the moment of my greatness flicker,
And I have seen the eternal Footman[7] hold my coat, and snicker,
And in short, I was afraid.

  And would it have been worth it, after all,
After the cups, the marmalade, the tea,
Among the porcelain, among some talk of you and me,
Would it have been worthwhile,
To have bitten off the matter with a smile,
To have squeezed the universe into a ball
To roll it toward some overwhelming question,
To say: "I am Lazarus,[8] come from the dead,
Come back to tell you all, I shall tell you all"—
If one, settling a pillow by her head,
  Should say: "That is not what I meant at all.
  That is not it, at all."

---

5. **malingers** [mə ling′gərz]: pretends to be sick.
6. **head . . . platter:** The reference is to the prophet John the Baptist, whose head was delivered on a platter to Salome as a reward for her dancing (Matthew 14 : 1–11).
7. **eternal Footman:** Death.
8. **Lazarus** [laz′ə rəs]: The reference is to John 11:1–44, in which Jesus resurrected Lazarus from the dead.

AT A GLANCE

- Prufrock tries to think of a way to ask his question, which is probably a romantic overture of some kind.
- He realizes that he will not ask the question after all and wonders whether asking it would have made any difference.

IMAGERY

The images of lonely men and ragged claws (ll. 72–73) reveal Prufrock's anticipation of an unhappy but insignificant fate.

IMAGE PATTERN

In lines 75–78 the image of the sleeping afternoon/evening repeats the image of the "etherized" evening (ll. 2–3) and the "sleeping" fog (ll. 15–22). The suspension of time reflects Prufrock's suspension of meaningful action.

THEME

Compare the question that Prufrock poses in lines 79–80 with his answer in lines 84–86. That he did not ask the question for fear of failure and that he feels that his moment has passed deepen his contempt for himself.

ALLUSION

In the references to tearful prayer and fasting (l. 81), John the Baptist (ll. 82–83), and Lazarus (ll. 94–95), Prufrock ironically mocks his own real anguish. In contrast to these images of religious fervor and rebirth (Lazarus), Prufrock lacks the conviction to "force" even his little moment "to a crisis."

GUIDED READING

LITERAL QUESTIONS

1a. Did Prufrock "force the moment to its crisis," as he considers doing in line 80? Explain. (No; according to line 86 he "was afraid.")

2a. What does Prufrock fear that someone will say if he asks his "overwhelming question"? ("That is not what I meant at all./That is not it, at all.")

INFERENTIAL QUESTIONS

1b. For what do you think Prufrock has wept, fasted, and prayed? (courage, the ability to act, a sign of acceptance from the woman)

2b. What does this comment reveal about Prufrock? (He is so fearful of being misunderstood and rejected by the woman that he does not even attempt to approach her in a meaningful way.)

AT A GLANCE

- Prufrock again wonders whether asking his question would have mattered.
- He shakes off the rationalizations that he has been spinning for himself and admits that he is an unimportant and even foolish man.
- He concludes that nothing vital will ever happen to him.

DRAMATIC MONOLOGUE

Although the entire poem is one long monologue, the climax comes in lines 111–119. This portion is the only point at which Prufrock really asserts himself ("No!"). Sadly, the only matter about which he can assert himself is his own unimportance.

SYMBOL

The simple action of eating a peach (l. 122) symbolizes involvement in the vital experiences of life, even life apart from social interaction. Having failed to begin a romantic relationship, Prufrock must now ask himself if he dares to attempt even this lesser action.

THEME

By the end of the poem, Prufrock is completely disillusioned. He still finds himself attracted to tempting visions (ll. 126–128), but he also seems to realize that he is trapped in his own fear of life ("Till human voices wake us, and we drown").

REFLECTING ON THE POEM

Why might many people identify with Prufrock? (Students may suggest that everyone feels ineffectual, self-conscious, and timid at times.)

And would it have been worth it, after all,
Would it have been worthwhile,
After the sunsets and the dooryards and the sprinkled streets,
After the novels, after the teacups, after the skirts that trail
along the floor—
And this, and so much more?—
It is impossible to say just what I mean!
But as if a magic lantern[9] threw the nerves in patterns on
a screen:
Would it have been worthwhile
If one, settling a pillow or throwing off a shawl,
And turning toward the window, should say:
"That is not it at all,
That is not what I meant, at all."

. . . . .

No! I am not Prince Hamlet,[10] nor was meant to be;
Am an attendant lord, one that will do
To swell a progress,[11] start a scene or two,
Advise the prince; no doubt, an easy tool,
Deferential, glad to be of use,
Politic, cautious, and meticulous;
Full of high sentence,[12] but a bit obtuse;
At times, indeed, almost ridiculous—
Almost, at times, the Fool.

I grow old . . . I grow old . . .
I shall wear the bottoms of my trousers rolled.

Shall I part my hair behind? Do I dare to eat a peach?
I shall wear white flannel trousers, and walk upon the beach.
I have heard the mermaids singing, each to each.

I do not think that they will sing to me.

I have seen them riding seaward on the waves
Combing the white hair of the waves blown back
When the wind blows the water white and black.

We have lingered in the chambers of the sea
By sea-girls wreathed with seaweed red and brown
Till human voices wake us, and we drown.

9. **magic lantern:** machine for projecting images.
10. **Prince Hamlet:** tragic hero of Shakespeare's play *Hamlet.*
11. **to swell a progress:** take part in a royal procession.
12. **high sentence:** flowery, fancy speech full of proverbs and advice, like that of the old counselor Polonius in *Hamlet.*

GUIDED READING

LITERAL QUESTION

1a. What will wake Prufrock from his dreams of the sea? (human voices)

INFERENTIAL QUESTION

1b. Why does Prufrock state that "we drown" when the "human voices wake us"? (Safe—if melancholy—in the fantasy world of the mermaids, Prufrock seems to view a sudden confrontation with the real world of human voices as a killing—that is, paralyzing—blow to his spirit.)

STUDY QUESTIONS

Recalling

1. According to lines 1–14, what are "you and I" going out to "make"? To what do the streets lead? For what does Prufrock say there will be time in line 27? In lines 32–34?
2. According to lines 37–46, what would Prufrock "disturb" if he dared to ask his question? Why "in short" doesn't Prufrock "force the moment to its crisis" (lines 75–86)? What remark by someone "settling a pillow" would make asking the question not worthwhile (lines 87–98)?
3. After he fails to ask his question, who does Prufrock say he is and is not (lines 111–119)?
4. Whom has Prufrock heard singing, according to lines 124–131? What does he think these creatures will not do?

Interpreting

5. What do the opening quotation from Dante, the descriptions of the fog, and the simile in line 3 suggest about Prufrock's mood or feelings?
6. Reread lines 10–11, 45–46, 80, and 93–94. What do these lines suggest about Prufrock's opinion of the question he considers asking? What does the title suggest about the question? What is Prufrock trying to avoid when he keeps saying "there will be time" in lines 23–48?
7. Why would Prufrock think of himself as "you and I," or "we"? What do the following lines reveal about Prufrock's view of his life and his self-image: the opening quotation, lines 51, 73–74, 82, and 85?
8. How would Prufrock be like Lazarus if he asked the question? In not asking the question, why is he unlike Hamlet?
9. What do the images in lines 121–123 suggest about the future Prufrock foresees for himself? Is this future different from his past?
10. How are the mermaids unlike the women Prufrock visits? Why is it significant that Prufrock hears the mermaids? That they will not sing for him?

Extending

11. In what ways are we all like Prufrock some of the time? Why might a middle-aged person in particular identify with him?
12. Tell how this poem helps explain why the young Eliot called the modern world a "waste land" and why Gertrude Stein called the young generation who had fought in World War I a "lost generation."

VIEWPOINT

Although Prufrock says he is not Hamlet, the Eliot critic Grover Smith believes that

> Eliot's Prufrock is a tragic figure. . . . The plight of this hesitant, inhibited man, an aging dreamer trapped in decayed, shabby-genteel surroundings, aware of beauty and faced with sordidness, mirrors the plight of the sensitive in the presence of the dull.
>
> —*T. S. Eliot's Poetry and Plays*

■ What evidence supports Smith's view? What evidence suggests that Prufrock is not tragic but comic? Do you believe he is either one or the other? Explain.

LITERARY FOCUS

Dramatic Monologue

In plays we often encounter **monologues,** long speeches by one character that reveal his or her thoughts to the audience and to other characters. In a poem that is a **dramatic monologue,** we have, in a sense, the monologue without the rest of the play. The poet creates a character who does the talking and who, through speech, reveals something about his or her life and feelings. The poet who used dramatic monologue most often was the nineteenth-century English poet Robert Browning.

Eliot's "Love Song of J. Alfred Prufrock" is a dramatic monologue. Prufrock is not T. S. Eliot, although of course he has something of Eliot in him. He is a character created by Eliot, and he speaks directly to us. He tells us his thoughts in leaps and bounds, jumping from one image to another, just as a human mind does. As we listen to his monologue and make the connections that are not spelled out, we come to understand the essence of the man, the private self that Prufrock hides from acquaintances.

Thinking About Dramatic Monologue

■ In which of the poems by Ezra Pound does a character speak directly to us? What does this character reveal about himself or herself?

STUDY QUESTIONS

1. "our visit"; an overwhelming question; prepare face; hundred indecisions, visions, revisions
2. universe; fear; "That is not what I meant at all."
3. not Hamlet but attendant lord
4. mermaids; sing to him
5. depressed, feels lost
6. importance; question of love, marriage; avoid asking the question and being rejected
7. unable to reach decision; personality split; low self-esteem
8. disturb fixed lives of others; because Hamlet procrastinated but finally acted
9. lonely, stylish, ridiculous; no
10. vital, sensuous; retains sensitivity, passion; awaken desire but cannot satisfy it
11. Answers will vary. Students should note inner fears preventing action; middle-aged person may be more likely to feel has wasted life, little future, identify with Prufrock's images of self.
12. wasteland of emotion, energy; inescapably "lost" in it

VIEWPOINT

tragic nature: desperation, fear of asking, realization of self-condemnation; *comic nature:* discrepancy between problem and terror; *tragicomic:* problem not resolved in either disaster or happiness

LITERARY FOCUS

"River-Merchant's Wife"; married before she loved husband, now loves him, misses him

VOCABULARY

1. literally, backward looks; Prufrock spends his life looking back, fearing the future
2. to take before; focus on time; Prufrock is tentative, not one who aggressively takes anything ahead of time
3. from *mal,* evil; Prufrock takes something trivial, like pretending to be sick, and magnifies it into a vision of universal evil
4. from *defer,* originally to *bring down;* Prufrock has been brought down, defeated, made a mere attendant
5. from *metus,* fear; Prufrock's sensitivity and scrupulousness are the result of his fear of life

VOCABULARY

Word Origins and Overtones

Musical notes have overtones, reverberations that are part of the richness of the sound. Words, too, have overtones—the richness of meaning that comes from their origins and that is part of the "heritage" of the word.

In line 9 of "The Love Song of J. Alfred Prufrock," for example, Prufrock uses the word *insidious.* We may know that *insidious* means "secretly dangerous," but it is even more helpful to know that the word comes from Latin *in-* + *sedere,* "to lie in wait in order to ambush." Eliot has chosen the perfect word to suggest Prufrock's terror as he walks the streets.

Look up the origins of the following words in a dictionary, and tell how the origin of the word reflects its use by Eliot in "The Love Song of J. Alfred Prufrock:

1. revisions
2. presume
3. malingers
4. deferential
5. meticulous

COMPOSITION

Writing About Poetry

■ Although "The Love Song of J. Alfred Prufrock" is written in free verse, some sections have distinct rhythms, and there is a good deal of rhyme. In a brief essay discuss the use of rhyme and rhythm in the poem. First show how Eliot prevents his rhymes and rhythms from falling into a predictable pattern. Then explain how the lack of pattern relates to the tone and content of the poem. *For help with this assignment, refer to Lesson 7 in the Writing About Literature Handbook at the back of this book.*

Writing a Dramatic Monologue

■ Write a dramatic monologue in poetry or prose. Use the voice of the woman Prufrock loves or the voice of one of Prufrock's gentleman friends. Try to let the character's personality come through the monologue, and allow the character to include his or her impressions of Prufrock. You may begin by describing the character's first meeting with Prufrock.

COMPOSITION: GUIDELINES FOR EVALUATION

WRITING ABOUT POETRY

Objective

To relate the elements of a poem to its meaning

Guidelines for Evaluation

- suggested length: four to six paragraphs
- should identify some rhymes and their use
- should describe rhythms, lack of pattern
- should show how line length emphasizes meaning
- should make statement of how free verse of poem matches rambling of speaker's mind

WRITING A DRAMATIC MONOLOGUE

Objective

To write a dramatic monologue in prose or poem

Guidelines for Evaluation

- suggested length: four to seven paragraphs, ten to twenty lines
- should create distinctive voice
- should focus on single problem
- should evoke character solely through use of character's own words

William Carlos Williams *1883–1963*

Ezra Pound and T. S. Eliot left America because they thought that they could not thrive artistically in their native land. William Carlos Williams, who had been Pound's friend since college days, stayed home in New Jersey. He had an international background himself: His father was English; his mother, Puerto Rican. Williams wanted his poetry to be very American, made out of the American language, reflecting American sights and sounds and ways of life.

Williams was born in New Jersey and attended the University of Pennsylvania Medical School. He published his first volume of poetry in 1909, while still in college. These early poems were Romantic verses in the style of traditional nineteenth-century English poetry. When Williams sent Pound a copy of an early book of his verse, Pound wrote back from London with kindly but severe criticism: "Your book," he said, "would not attract even passing attention here. There are fine lines in it, but nowhere I think do you add anything to the poets you have used as models."

Within a few years, however, Williams found his own voice, and he was never again an imitator. He became a Modernist and initially an Imagist, but, unlike Pound and Eliot, he celebrated the world before his eyes and scorned allusions to history, religion, and ancient literature. Returning to New Jersey to raise a family and set up a medical practice, he fell in love with everyday American life. He wrote often of his patients and neighbors, working-class men and women in the industrialized section of New Jersey near the town of Paterson. His observations are contained in *Paterson* (1946–1958), a poem of epic length filled with delightful glimpses of urban American life. Another major work, *In the American Grain* (1925), explores the mythic greatness of famous Americans.

Williams' poetry is noted for its precision; in his best work he makes us think that a poem is just right—neither a word too few nor a word too many. His great gift is his ability to make poetry from the most ordinary objects and experiences. In the following poems he makes wonderful poetic moments out of the appearance of a wheelbarrow in the rain, peasants dancing, unusual behavior in a neighbor, a fire truck racing through the city, and a trip to the icebox.

- Can *any* object or experience be a subject for poetry? What does Williams say in his poems?

LITERARY OPTIONS

- free verse
- Imagism

THEMATIC OPTIONS

- art and the imagination
- love of life

THE RED WHEELBARROW: IMAGISM

The poet contrasts abstraction (*so much,* l. 1) with concrete objects (the red wheelbarrow, rain water, white chickens). He makes no comment upon the images, simply juxtaposing them and allowing them to speak to the reader for themselves.

THE DANCE: FREE VERSE

Although "The Dance" is written in free verse, the first and last lines are identical. This repetition takes the thought of the poem in a circle, much as the steps of the dance take the participants in a circle.

IMAGERY

The painting depicts a peasant fair. The poet's imagery is expressed in earthy vocabulary—*bellies* (l. 5), *hips* (l. 7), *butts* (l. 9), *shanks* (l. 10)—that matches the artist's feel for the subjects of his painting.

REFLECTING ON THE POEMS

What parts of life do these poems portray as most valuable? (the here and now, the beauty and vibrancy of ordinary things)

William Carlos Williams

The Red Wheelbarrow

so much depends
upon

a red wheel
barrow

glazed with rain
water

beside the white
chickens.

The Dance

In Breughel's[1] great picture, The Kermess,[2]
the dancers go round, they go round and
around, the squeal and the blare and the
tweedle of bagpipes, a bugle and fiddles
tipping their bellies (round as the thick-
sided glasses whose wash they impound[3])
their hips and their bellies off balance
to turn them. Kicking and rolling about
the Fair Grounds, swinging their butts, those
shanks must be sound to bear up under such
rollicking measures, prance as they dance
in Breughel's great picture, The Kermess.

1. **Breughel's** [bro͞o′gəlz]: referring to Pieter Brueghel the Elder (1522–1569), Flemish painter noted for his scenes of peasant life.
2. **The Kermess** [kur′mis]: Brueghel's 1568 painting of a peasant kermess, or fair.
3. **wash they impound:** liquid they drink.

Detail from *Peasant Dance,* Pieter Brueghel, c. 1568.

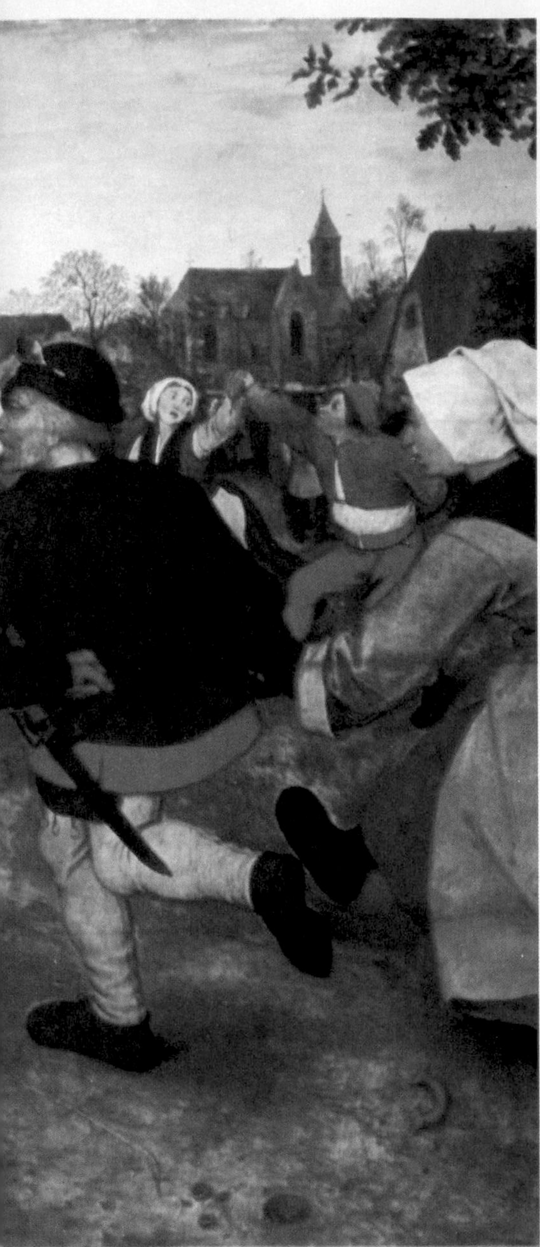

Kunsthistorisches Museum, Vienna

The Artist

Mr. T.
bareheaded
in a soiled undershirt
his hair standing out
on all sides
stood on his toes
heels together
arms gracefully
for the moment
curled above his head.
Then he whirled about
bounded
into the air
and with an *entrechat*[1]
perfectly achieved
completed the figure.
My mother
taken by surprise
where she sat
in her invalid's chair
was left speechless.
Bravo! she cried at last
and clapped her hands.
The man's wife
came from the kitchen:
What goes on here? she said.
But the show was over.

1. ***entrechat*** [än'trə shä']: in ballet, a leap in which dancers cross their legs or strike their heels together several times.

AT A GLANCE

- Mr. T., dressed in an undershirt, suddenly spins into the air in a ballet leap.
- The poet's invalid mother sees the leap and applauds.
- Mr. T.'s wife comes to see what is going on, but she has missed the event.

LITERARY OPTIONS

- form
- realism
- free verse

THEMATIC OPTIONS

- the universality of art
- the joy of the unexpected

THEME

The poet and his mother enjoy the performance, but the wife seems to have a different reaction (l. 26). The poet points out that art is everywhere but that you have to experience it personally to appreciate it.

REALISM

The poem begins (ll. 1–4) and ends (ll. 24–27) on notes of realism. The poet uses realistic details such as Mr. T.'s soiled undershirt and his wife's emergence from the kitchen to make the beauty of the leap quite surprising.

FORM

Notice how the form of the poem breaks the action into little parts, like small dance steps or turns. Williams playfully constructs the poem so that its phrases imitate their subject.

REFLECTING ON THE POEM

What does the poem's title reveal about the poet's view of Mr. T.? (It suggests that anyone who can create moments of beauty, as Mr. T. does, can be called an artist.)

LITERARY OPTIONS

- free verse
- Imagism

THEMATIC OPTIONS

- observations and sensations
- simple pleasures

THE GREAT FIGURE: SPEAKER

The speaker sees the figure *5* (l. 3), but no one else does (*unheeded,* l. 9). He is different, and his poem is different because it makes something remarkable of an item that most people would not notice.

IMAGISM

The poet provides striking details to recreate the rushing firetruck, but he focuses on the single image of the gold *5*. It is this detail that makes the experience memorable.

THIS IS JUST TO SAY: TONE

The tone of this poem is warmer than many of Williams' other poems because the poet is speaking to someone of whom he is fond. Despite its mundane topic, the poem sounds almost like a love letter.

REFLECTING ON THE POEMS

Why do you think that Williams has chosen such commonplace items—a firetruck and plums—as the subjects of poems? (Perhaps he is trying to show that everyone is surrounded by art, often in unexpected places.)

William Carlos Williams

The Great Figure

Among the rain
and lights
I saw the figure 5
in gold
on a red
firetruck
moving
tense
unheeded
to gong clangs
siren howls
and wheels rumbling
through the dark city.

This Is Just to Say

I have eaten
the plums
that were in
the icebox

and which
you were probably
saving
for breakfast

Forgive me
they were delicious
so sweet
and so cold

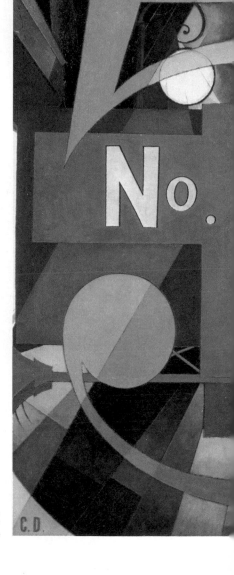

I Saw the Figure 5 in Gold,
Charles Demuth, 1928.

The Metropolitan Museum of Art

STUDY QUESTIONS

The Red Wheelbarrow

Recalling

1. What three items are mentioned in the poem? What does the first line tell us about them?

Interpreting

2. Why might the objects in the poem be very important? Can we be sure? Explain.
3. What elements of Imagism, described on page 413, does this poem exhibit? What elements of Modernist literature in general, described on pages 403–405, does the poem display?

The Dance

Recalling

1. In what direction do the dancers in Breughel's picture move?
2. What three words name the sounds of the bagpipes?

Interpreting

3. Is the music to which the people dance professional and melodious? Is their dancing professional? How do we know?
4. Identify six poetic devices that help the poet capture the dancing or its musical accompaniment.
5. What does the poet seem to admire about Breughel's painting?

Extending

6. Compare the painting by Breughel with the description in "The Dance." What visual details has the poet captured in words?

The Artist

Recalling

1. What is Mr. T. wearing? What does he do?
2. What does the speaker's mother say when she sees Mr. T.'s "performance"? What does Mr. T.'s wife say?

Interpreting

3. What is the contrast between the speaker's mother and Mr. T.'s wife? Between the speaker's mother and Mr. T.?
4. Besides the speaker's mother, who else appreciates "the show"? Explain.
5. Is it usual for Mr. T. to act as he does? How do we know? Who or what makes Mr. T. an artist?

STUDY QUESTIONS

The Red Wheelbarrow

1. red wheelbarrow, rainwater, chickens
2. juxtaposition in poet's vision, ordering power of imagination add to beauty, urgency, poignancy; no; seem ordinary, yet poet assures importance
3. images capture rather than explain emotions, free verse, everyday language, nontraditional subject matter; forces reader participation, reflects Modernist experimentation and break with past

The Dance

1. round and round
2. *squeal, blare, tweedle*
3. no, squeals, blares, tweedles; no; dancers kick, roll, prance
4. onomatopoeia, rhyme, rhythm, alliteration, repetition, simile
5. its energy and spirit
6. Poet has captured the kermess itself—prancing dancers, feasting, bagpipe player, general holiday feeling

The Artist

1. soiled undershirt; entrechat
2. "Bravo!"; "What goes on here?"
3. *mother:* appreciates performance; *wife:* walks out, disapproves; *mother:* invalid; *Mr. T.:* performs a dance for her
4. speaker; clear from description
5. no; mother is surprised; grace, spontaneity

The Great Figure

1. great
2. red fire truck; gold
3. tense, unheeded; dark city
4. The 5 is stationary, or "tense," on the fire truck, but the truck is moving.
5. importance of 5; most don't notice beauty of gold 5
6. ▪ all but poet
   ▪ No, poet draws attention to it.
7. ▪ found anywhere, fleeting quality;
   ▪ Modern machines have own beauty.
8. Answers will vary, but students should note that he finds beauty in unlikely images.

This Is Just to Say

1. plums; breakfast
2. not very; something extraordinary in an ordinary moment
3. tempting; enjoyment
4. unimportance of incident; poem mere note

LITERARY FOCUS

1. Broken groups of lines reach horizontally across the page; of varying length, each extends farther than the one preceding it. It reinforces motion and gesture.
2. word or phrase isolated on one line gains emphasis: *plums, icebox, saving, delicious, forgive me*

The Great Figure

Recalling

1. According to the title, what sort of figure is the figure *5*?
2. On what is the figure *5* printed? What color is it?
3. How is the figure *5* moving? Through what is it moving?

Interpreting

4. Explain how the figure *5* can literally be "moving tense."
5. Why is it significant that the figure *5* is "in gold"? That the city is "dark"?
6. By whom is the figure *5* "unheeded"? Is it really unheeded? Explain.
7. What does this poem suggest about beauty? About modern life?

Extending

8. Based on the poems by Williams that you have read, what generalization would you make about his subject matter? Do you find his poems "poetic"? Why or why not?

This Is Just to Say

Recalling

1. What has the speaker eaten? For what were these things probably being saved?

Interpreting

2. How important is the incident described in this poem? Why do you think Williams chose an incident of this sort for his poem?
3. What do the last four lines suggest about the objects being saved and the reason that the speaker expects to be forgiven?
4. What does the title have to do with the rest of the poem?

LITERARY FOCUS

Free Verse

T. S. Eliot once said that "free verse is a contradiction in terms." Eliot meant that a poet is never "free" to write down anything at all, break it into lines, and call it "verse," or poetry. There must be some reason for using **free verse**—verse with no fixed rhythm—some relationship between form and meaning.

Whitman (see page 260), Pound, and Eliot are all masters of free verse, and so is William Carlos Williams. In "The Red Wheelbarrow" Williams demonstrates how lines of free verse can be broken to direct the reader's attention to important words, images, or ideas. For example, he forces us to realize that the barrow indeed has a wheel by breaking up "wheelbarrow" on two lines:

a red wheel
barrow

Williams does the same with "rainwater," another familiar word we might rush over:

glazed with rain
water

Williams also keeps to a pattern when he breaks up his lines: A three-word line is followed by a one-word line to form a "stanza"; the "stanza" is repeated three times. Thus, while the poem has an irregular *rhythmic* pattern (the number of syllables in each line varies), it does have a strict *visual* pattern. We can see that Williams is writing "freely," but—as Eliot suggests—not as freely as we think at first.

Thinking About Free Verse

1. Describe the strict visual pattern of "The Artist." How is the pattern related to the poem's subject?
2. How do line breaks help emphasize thoughts and images in "This Is Just to Say" and "The Great Figure"?

COMPOSITION

Writing About Free Verse

■ Choose any one of Williams' poems, and write a brief analysis of the effects of the poet's use of free verse. First discuss the positions of specific words and the line breaks. Then describe the overall visual appearance of the poem. Consider how the arrangement of words on the page relates to the poem's content.

Writing Free Verse

■ Write a short free-verse poem in which the words form a visual pattern, as they do in "The Red Wheelbarrow" and "The Artist." Try to use the line breaks to emphasize important thoughts and images, as Williams does. If you wish, you might follow the model of "The Red Wheelbarrow": a three-word line followed by a one-word line repeated three times.

COMPOSITION: GUIDELINES FOR EVALUATION

WRITING ABOUT FREE VERSE

Objective

To analyze specific effects of free verse

Guidelines for Evaluation

- suggested length: four to six paragraphs
- should discuss positions of specific words and cite words emphasized by line breaks
- should note reasons for breaking lines
- should describe speech rhythms in free verse
- should describe appearance of poem, meaning

WRITING FREE VERSE

Objective

To write a poem using free verse

Guidelines for Evaluation

- suggested length: five to eight lines
- should use line breaks to emphasize words and images
- should suggest the rhythm of natural speech
- should possibly form a shape that has some relationship to the poem's content

H. D. (Hilda Doolittle) *1886–1961*

Hilda Doolittle, who signed her poetry H. D., was born in Bethlehem, Pennsylvania. As a student at Bryn Mawr College, she knew both Ezra Pound and William Carlos Williams, and she later renewed her acquaintance with Pound in London. One day, in the British Museum tearoom, she was showing some of her poems to Pound and to Richard Aldington, an English poet whom she later married. Pound took a blue pencil to the poems, deleting what he thought were unnecessary words—and Imagism was invented.

Pound sent three of Doolittle's poems to *Poetry* magazine, where they appeared over the name "H. D., Imagiste," and in time Doolittle became one of the leading Imagist poets. Her first collection of poetry, *Sea Garden,* was published in 1916; her *Collected Poems,* in 1925. In "Sea Rose" Doolittle rigorously avoids the sentimentality that usually accompanied the rose in poetry. In "Oread" she imagines herself a Greek mountain nymph experiencing the beauty of nature.

- What in nature do you find particularly beautiful? What excites H. D.'s admiration?

H. D.

Sea Rose

Rose, harsh rose,
marred and with stint of petals,
meager flower, thin,
sparse of leaf,

more precious
than a wet rose
single on a stem—
you are caught in the drift.

Stunted, with small leaf,
you are flung on the sand,
you are lifted
in the crisp sand
that drives in the wind.

Can the spice-rose
drip such acrid fragrance
hardened in a leaf?

AT A GLANCE

- The poet considers a battered sea rose.
- She wonders at the beauty of its fragrance.

LITERARY OPTIONS

- Imagism
- symbol

THEMATIC OPTIONS

- unexpected beauty
- hardship and survival

IMAGISM

The poet packs the first stanza with adjectives that create an unattractive image of the sea rose—*harsh, marred, meager, thin, sparse.*

FORM

Note how the form reinforces the idea: Lines 1–4 and 9–13 disparage and lines 5–8 and 14–16 exalt the sea rose. The poet lists its flaws and its wonders in alternating stanzas.

SYMBOL

By comparing the sea rose to a common rose (ll. 6–7 and 14), the poet hints that the sea rose is a symbol, just as the common rose is often used as a symbol. The sea rose may symbolize the value of sheer endurance in the face of hardship.

REFLECTING ON THE POEM

What might this poet think of more conventional beauty? (She might find it ordinary.)

LITERARY OPTIONS

- Imagism
- free verse

THEMATIC OPTIONS

- celebration of nature
- the power of the imagination

FREE VERSE

The irregularity of line lengths here might mimic the irregular terrain of the mountain.

IMAGISM

The poet never says that she admires nature. Nevertheless, she portrays it as such an oddly beautiful image—a sea of splashing trees—that her feelings are clear.

REFLECTING ON THE POEM

How does the sense of motion in this poem add to its main idea? (The idea of whirling, splashing pine trees creates a sense of energy surging through nature.)

STUDY QUESTIONS

Sea Rose

1. harsh, marred, with stint of petals, meager, thin, sparse of leaf
2. a single wet rose on a stem
3. flung upon sand, driven by wind; spice-rose
4. simply presents images, lets reader draw conclusions about comparison
5. survives on own in harsh world
6. Answers will vary. Students should see the rose as a symbol of a person, perhaps the poet.

Oread

1. the sea
2. the mountain on which she lives
3. the oread; exhilarated
4. Poem has single image, is in free verse and simple language; image conveys emotion.

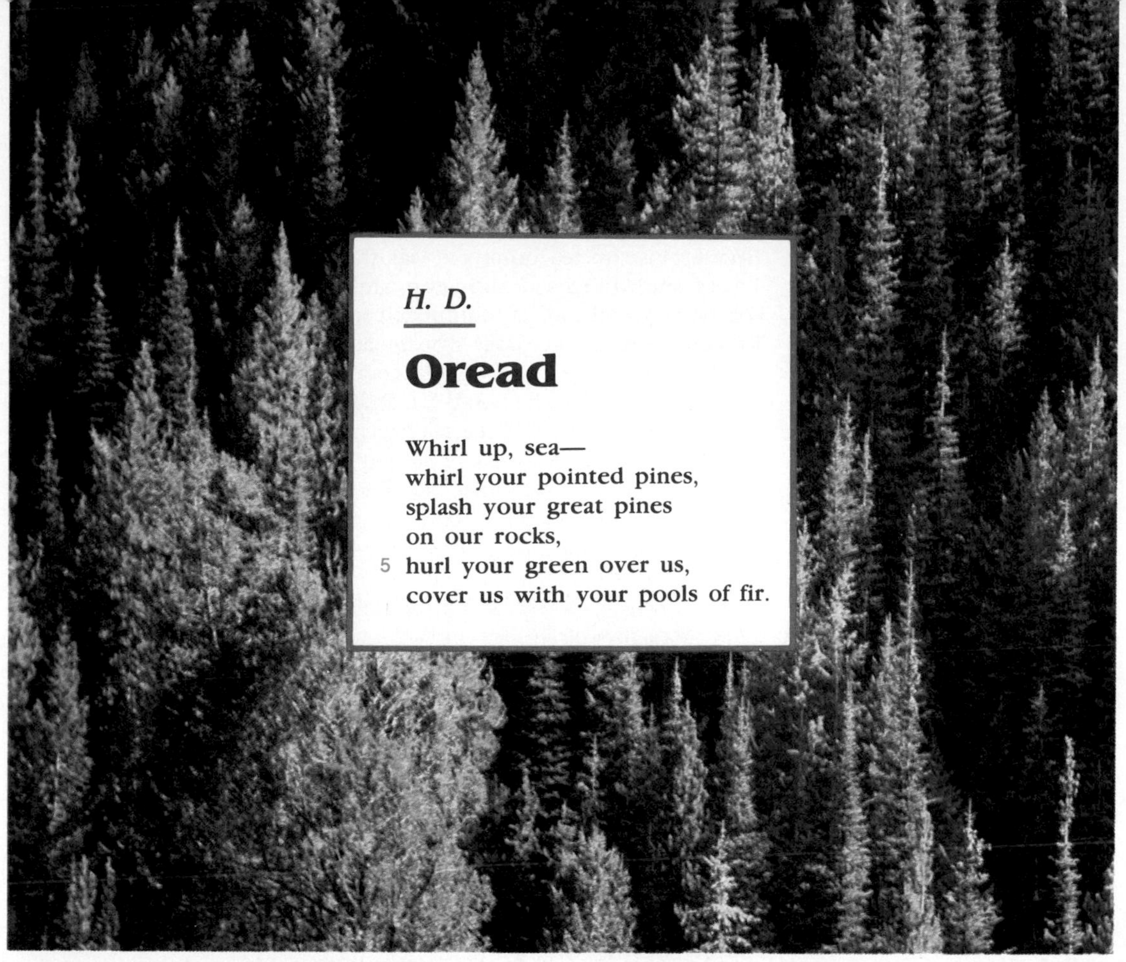

H. D.

Oread

Whirl up, sea—
whirl your pointed pines,
splash your great pines
on our rocks,
hurl your green over us,
cover us with your pools of fir.

STUDY QUESTIONS

Sea Rose

Recalling

1. What words and phrases describe the sea rose in lines 1–4?
2. What is the rose "more precious than"?
3. What happens to the sea rose in lines 9–13? To what rose is it compared in lines 14–15?

Interpreting

4. What elements of Imagism, as described on page 413, does this poem display?
5. What makes the sea rose more precious than the usual hothouse rose—that is, the "wet rose / single on a stem"?
6. In addition to a sea rose, what is this poem about?

Oread

Recalling

1. To whom or what is this poem addressed, according to the first line?

Interpreting

2. Since an oread is a *mountain* nymph, what is the "sea" in line 1?
3. Who is the speaker in this poem? How does the speaker seem to feel about being splashed by pines and green?
4. Why is this considered an Imagist poem (see page 413)?

Gertrude Stein *1874–1946*

Gertrude Stein is known as much for her influence on other artists as for her own contribution to literature. Wealthy, brilliant, and unconventional, Stein was a leading patron of Modernism and a good friend to the artists Pablo Picasso and Henri Matisse and the writers Ernest Hemingway and Sherwood Anderson.

Stein was born in Pennsylvania and grew up in Europe and California. As a student at Radcliffe, she met the psychologist William James and became interested in his theories about the workings of the human mind. She went on to study medicine at Johns Hopkins, but in 1902 abandoned her studies and abruptly moved to Paris, which became the capital of Modernism in all the arts. Here Stein was famous for her wit and hospitality; after World War I her home became the haven to which all American "expatriates" flocked. She returned only once to America, on a triumphant lecture tour in the early thirties, and after enduring the Nazi occupation of France, she died in 1946.

Stein was an early admirer of Picasso and Matisse—respected painters today, but considered shocking in their youth, when they broke with most of the conventions of the art world. Stein wanted her writing to be as revolutionary as the art she purchased and championed—and it was. Her first major work, *Three Lives* (1905), tries to present its characters' thinking patterns, but it still retains recognizable characters and a plot of sorts. With *The Making of Americans* (1925), plot and character disappear altogether, just as recognizable objects had begun to disappear from the paintings of the abstract artists.

Surprisingly, after these avant-garde ventures Stein showed herself capable of pleasing a wide audience: Her autobiography, published in 1933, was a great popular success. It is typical of the oddness and freshness of Stein's work that she called the book *The Autobiography of Alice B. Toklas,* naming it not for herself, but for her lifelong friend.

"I Am Rose" and "A Sound" are two short, experimental poems. The first, a bit like a nursery rhyme and a bit like Emily Dickinson, reminds us of Stein's famous utterance, "Rose is a rose is a rose is a rose." The second is from *Tender Buttons* (1914), a series of "portraits" of familiar objects rendered unfamiliar in an attempt to duplicate in words what the Cubists were doing in their paintings.

■ Usually language presents us with both sound and meaning. What happens when language becomes simply sound? Can the sound *be* the meaning? What does Stein think?

LITERARY OPTIONS

- repetition
- juxtaposition

THEMATIC OPTIONS

- personal identity
- the sound of language

"I AM ROSE": REPETITION

The first four words of each line have little connection with the rest of the line. The repetition of "I am a Rose" and the end rhymes give this poem its structure.

"I AM ROSE": MAIN IDEA

The main idea is the power of imagination to create an identity. The poet says that she is a rose, even though roses do not have eyes and do not sing.

"A SOUND": JUXTAPOSITION

Sounds and objects with no obvious connection are thrown together in this poem. The juxtaposition itself creates meaning.

REFLECTING ON THE POEMS

How do the ambiguous, "unpoetic" endings to the poems—*like anything* and *this is this*—reinforce Stein's ideas about art? (Both unconventional endings may suggest the Modernist principle that whatever the artist designates as art thereby becomes art.)

Gertrude Stein

I Am Rose

I am a Rose my eyes are bluc
I am a Rose and who are you
I am a Rose and when I sing
I am a Rose like anything

A Sound

Elephant beaten with candy and little pops and chews all bolts and reckless rats, this is this.

Chinese Restaurant, a Cubist painting by Max Weber, 1915.

STUDY QUESTIONS

I Am Rose

Recalling

1. According to the poem, when is the speaker most roselike?

Interpreting

2. Do you think this poem has a meaning? Why or why not?
3. What does this poem force the reader to do?
4. What sort of phrase is "like anything"? Are such phrases generally found in traditional nineteenth-century poetry? Explain your answer.
5. What elements of Modernism, as described on pages 403–405, does this poem display?

Extending

6. What might the roses in this poem and in H. D.'s "Sea Rose" (page 427) have in common? What might they have in common with Emerson's rhodora (page 169)? What does Emerson tell us about the rhodora that neither H. D. nor Stein tells us about her rose?

A Sound

Recalling

1. According to the title, what does this poem describe? What words in the poem seem to relate to the title?

Interpreting

2. Why do you think Stein does not tell us what the sound is? What does "this is this" imply?
3. What does this poem force the reader to do? What elements of Modernism, as described on pages 403–405, does it contain?

Extending

4. How is this poem like the painting in "L'Art, 1910"? Do you find Stein's poetry even more radical than Pound's? Why or why not?

VIEWPOINT

"A Sound" is from Stein's book *Tender Buttons.* Richard Bridgeman writes:

> For Gertrude Stein, *Tender Buttons* represented her full-scale break out of the prison of conventional form into the colorful realm of the sensitized imagination. But it did not signal an abandonment of control.
>
> —*Gertrude Stein in Pieces*

■ What makes "A Sound" unconventional? How does it express Stein's "sensitized imagination"? Do you agree that control has not been abandoned? Why or why not?

COMPARING WRITERS

■ Pound, Eliot, Williams, H. D., and Stein—all but one lived abroad for most of their lives, yet all helped revolutionize American poetry in the twentieth century. What did each of these writers have to say about modern life? How in his or her own way did each poet throw new light on the objects and phenomena of twentieth-century living?

STUDY QUESTIONS

I Am Rose

1. when she sings
2. Answers will vary. Some may see poem as meaningless nursery rhyme; others will see the analogy between the beauty of the rose and the poet's life or that everyday experiences mirror the rose's beauty.
3. help create meaning
4. colloquial, ambiguous; no
5. untraditional subject, experimental language, ambiguity
6. invented by poet's imagination; contain own reason for being; symbolize individuality, self-reliance

A Sound

1. a sound; *pops, chews*
2. Sound not literal, is aural impression created by words; that sound can exist without logical meaning.
3. create meaning; experimental language, free verse, visual arrangement, startling images
4. juxtaposes bizarre images, has jumble of words; probably yes, as it eliminates literal meaning

VIEWPOINT

juxtaposed images working on literal level and level of sound of words; expresses the energy and playfulness of poet's imagination; no, deliberately takes language into realm of music

COMPARING WRITERS

Pound: invented Imagism, inspired by Chinese culture; *Eliot:* characterized era, mixed dramatic poetry with stream-of-consciousness; *Williams:* found poetry in the everyday; *H. D.:* inspired by Greek culture, furthered Imagism; *Stein:* adviser to artists, took poetry beyond formal meaning into nonverbal world of painting, music

Carl Sandburg *1878–1967*

Although influenced by Pound and the Imagists, Carl Sandburg wanted to reach a wider audience—and he did. From the 1916 publication of *Chicago Poems* until his death in 1967, Sandburg was one of America's most popular and successful poets.

Sandburg was the son of Swedish immigrants who settled in Galesburg, Illinois. As a young man he fought in the Spanish-American War, traveled the country working a wide variety of jobs, and finally settled in Chicago. Here he found employment as a reporter and began to contribute to *Poetry* magazine.

From 1912 to 1925, Chicago was an exciting residence for a poet. It was home not only to the influential *Poetry* magazine but also to such notable writers as Theodore Dreiser, Sherwood Anderson, Vachel Lindsay, and Edgar Lee Masters. With the publication of *Chicago Poems,* Sandburg became one of Chicago's literary giants. Dubbed "the Bard of the Midwest," he soon wrote three more highly successful volumes of poetry, *Cornhuskers* (1918), *Smoke and Steel* (1920), and *Slabs of the Sunburnt West* (1922).

Sandburg was a great admirer of Walt Whitman and in his enthusiasm for America might be considered Whitman's successor. He also admired Abraham Lincoln, as Whitman had, and wrote what is considered the definitive Lincoln biography. He frequently lectured on the lives of Whitman and Lincoln, and he also performed folk songs throughout the United States—folk songs that he collected in *The American Songbag* (1927).

Sandburg won the Pulitzer Prize for his Lincoln biography in 1940 and for his *Complete Poems* in 1951. He was decorated by the King of Sweden, and he addressed a joint session of Congress on the 150th anniversary of Lincoln's birth. He continued to write through his final years on his farm in North Carolina.

If in such popular poems as "Fog" we can see the effect of the Imagists on Sandburg's poetry, the influence of Walt Whitman is even more marked. Sandburg's exuberant free verse is reminiscent of Whitman's style; his celebration of America reminds us of Whitman's themes. "Chicago," which originally appeared in *Poetry* magazine, is a catalogue of details describing the bustling city. "Jazz Fantasia" captures the sounds of the Jazz Age and displays Sandburg's fondness for American slang: A fantasia is a musical composition that does not follow a strict form. *The People, Yes,* a long poem published in 1936, is a declaration of faith in American workers and the American system.

■ If you were to choose images and details to celebrate America, what specific images would you select? What images does Sandburg select?

Carl Sandburg

from The People, Yes

The people will live on.
The learning and blundering people will live on.
They will be tricked and sold and again sold
And go back to the nourishing earth for rootholds,
The people so peculiar in renewal and comeback,
You can't laugh off their capacity to take it.
The mammoth[1] rests between his cyclonic dramas.

The people so often sleepy, weary, enigmatic,
is a vast huddle with many units saying:
"I earn my living.
I make enough to get by
and it takes all my time.
If I had more time
I could do more for myself
and maybe for others.
I could read and study
and talk things over
and find out about things.
It takes time.
I wish I had the time."

• • •

The people know the salt of the sea
and the strength of the winds
lashing the corners of the earth.
The people take the earth
as a tomb of rest and a cradle of hope.
Who else speaks for the Family of Man?
They are in tune and step
with constellations of universal law.

• • •

In the darkness with a great bundle of grief
the people march.
In the night, and overhead a shovel of stars for
keeps, the people march:
"Where to? what next?"

---

1. **mammoth** [mam′əth]: extinct prehistoric elephant; anything of enormous size and strength.

AT A GLANCE

- The poet feels that the masses of humanity—*the people*—draw their strength from contact with the earth.
- He asserts that, despite their mistakes, they will not only survive but triumph.

LITERARY OPTIONS

- free verse
- diction

THEMATIC OPTIONS

- the endurance of humanity
- inner resources

DICTION

The speaker mixes elevated diction *(cyclonic dramas)* with more colloquial speech *(You can't laugh off, for keeps)*. The effect is a democratic patchwork in which high thoughts and lowly experiences are sewn together.

FREE VERSE

Because the poet uses free verse, he can employ a variety of rhythms. In lines 10–20, the lines shorten noticeably to imitate everyday speech. This section contrasts the speaker's high aspirations for the people with the dulling weariness of the individual's daily routine.

REFLECTING ON THE POEM

Does the poet feel that humanity is doomed to repeat its mistakes? Explain. (The poet admits that mistakes have been made before and will be again. However, he seems to see mistakes as part of a learning process, and his view of the future is hopeful.)

AT A GLANCE

- The speaker catalogues Chicago's strengths and its weaknesses.
- He concludes that what makes Chicago special despite its problems is its tough pride and youthful vitality.

LITERARY OPTIONS

- personification
- imagery

THEMATIC OPTIONS

- pride in one's home
- the city as both good and evil

SPEAKER

The speaker is someone who knows the city (ll. 6–9). He loves the city, but he also admits its flaws. His directness encourages the reader to accept his views.

PERSONIFICATION

Note the rough language that the poet uses to personify Chicago in lines 1–5. It depicts the city as a young man with plenty of energy and coarse vitality.

IMAGERY

The images in this poem are drawn from the everyday life of the common worker. By themselves such details do not seem poetic at all, but together they create a powerful poetic impression.

REFLECTING ON THE POEM

Do you think that the poet could have the same feelings for any city besides Chicago? (Students might mention that if the poet considers youthful vitality to be the greatest characteristic of a city, he probably would be able to appreciate other cities with the same characteristic.)

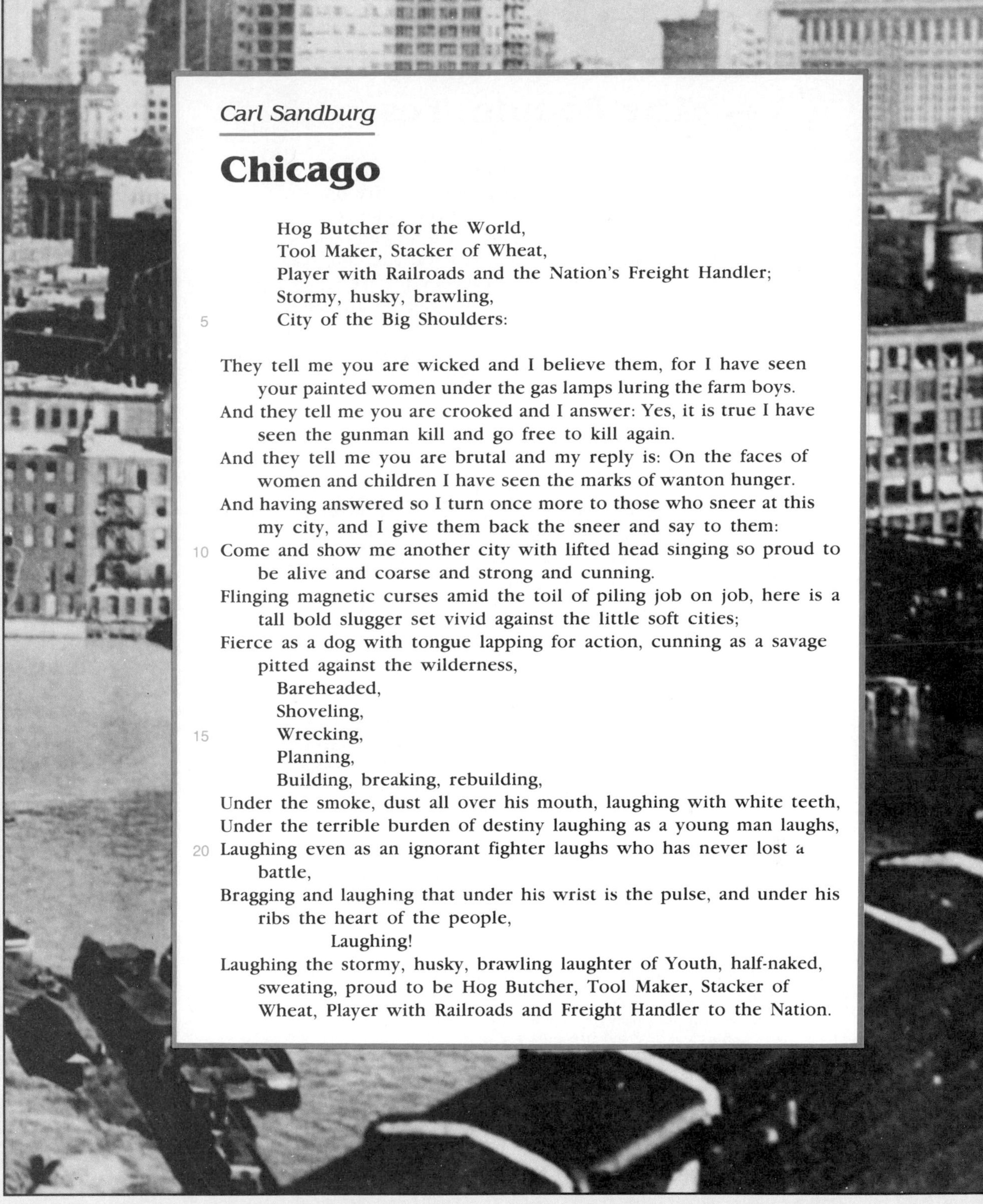

Carl Sandburg

Chicago

Hog Butcher for the World,
Tool Maker, Stacker of Wheat,
Player with Railroads and the Nation's Freight Handler;
Stormy, husky, brawling,
City of the Big Shoulders:

They tell me you are wicked and I believe them, for I have seen your painted women under the gas lamps luring the farm boys.
And they tell me you are crooked and I answer: Yes, it is true I have seen the gunman kill and go free to kill again.
And they tell me you are brutal and my reply is: On the faces of women and children I have seen the marks of wanton hunger.
And having answered so I turn once more to those who sneer at this my city, and I give them back the sneer and say to them:
Come and show me another city with lifted head singing so proud to be alive and coarse and strong and cunning.
Flinging magnetic curses amid the toil of piling job on job, here is a tall bold slugger set vivid against the little soft cities;
Fierce as a dog with tongue lapping for action, cunning as a savage pitted against the wilderness,
Bareheaded,
Shoveling,
Wrecking,
Planning,
Building, breaking, rebuilding,
Under the smoke, dust all over his mouth, laughing with white teeth,
Under the terrible burden of destiny laughing as a young man laughs,
Laughing even as an ignorant fighter laughs who has never lost a battle,
Bragging and laughing that under his wrist is the pulse, and under his ribs the heart of the people,
Laughing!
Laughing the stormy, husky, brawling laughter of Youth, half-naked, sweating, proud to be Hog Butcher, Tool Maker, Stacker of Wheat, Player with Railroads and Freight Handler to the Nation.

Jazz Fantasia

Drum on your drums, batter on your banjoes,
sob on the long cool winding saxophones.
Go to it, O jazzmen.

Sling your knuckles on the bottoms of the happy
tin pans, let your trombones ooze, and go husha-
husha-hush with the slippery sandpaper.

Moan like an autumn wind high in the lonesome treetops, moan soft
like you wanted somebody terrible, cry like a racing car slipping
away from a motorcycle cop, bang-bang! you jazzmen, bang
altogether drums, traps, banjoes, horns, tin cans—make two people
fight on the top of a stairway and scratch each other's eyes in a
clinch tumbling down the stairs.

Can the rough stuff . . . now a Mississippi steamboat pushes up the
night river with a hoo-hoo-hoo-oo . . . and the green lanterns calling
to the high soft stars . . . a red moon rides on the humps of the low
river hills . . . go to it, O jazzmen.

STUDY QUESTIONS

The People, Yes

Recalling

1. According to lines 1–8, what will the "learning and blundering" people do? In what are the people "so peculiar"? According to lines 8–20, what would the people do if they had more time? What do they wish?
2. According to lines 21–28, what do the people know? With what are they "in tune and step"?
3. According to lines 29–31, with what bundle do the people march? What do they ask?

Interpreting

4. Citing details to support your answer, tell what kind or class of people this poem is about. What aspects of "the people" are celebrated? (Consider especially lines 2, 5, 25, and the questions the people ask in the final line.)
5. Explain the "yes" in the poem's title.

Extending

6. This poem was written during the Great Depression of the 1930s. Explain how knowing this affects your interpretation of the poem.

Chicago

Recalling

1. What is Chicago called in the first three lines?
2. What three things do "they" tell the speaker in lines 6–8? What does the speaker say Chicago is like in line 10? In lines 13–17?
3. How does Chicago laugh in line 19? In line 20? What does it laugh in line 22?

AT A GLANCE

- The speaker celebrates the variety of sounds that jazz musicians can produce and the experiences their music can evoke.

LITERARY OPTIONS

- rhythm and onomatopoeia
- colloquial language

THEMATIC OPTIONS

- the expressiveness of music
- the vitality of modern life

RHYTHM

In lines 1–6 the poet's word choice and phrasing imitate the exciting, uneven rhythms of jazz.

ONOMATOPOEIA

The poet re-creates the sound of jazz by imitating the sounds of instruments (ll. 1–2 and 4–6) and by recalling a scene (l. 14) that could be duplicated in a jazz setting.

COLLOQUIAL LANGUAGE

The phrase *moan soft / like you wanted somebody terrible* (ll. 7–8) uses blunt, direct language that expresses powerful emotions.

REFLECTING ON THE POEM

How well does Sandburg capture the appeal of jazz in his poem? (Sandburg captures the powerful, earthy rhythms and unpredictable, haunting melodies of jazz by using irregular rhythms, colloquial language, and onomatopoeia.)

STUDY QUESTIONS

The People, Yes

1. live on; renewal, ability to come back; do more for selves, others; more time
2. salt of sea, strength of wind; constellations of universal law
3. grief; "Where to? what next?"
4. working; strength, courage
5. affirmation, faith in masses
6. Answers will vary. Students may see poet as empathizing with people's burdens.

Chicago

1. hog butcher, tool maker, wheat stacker, freight handler
2. Chicago: wicked, crooked, brutal; proud, coarse, strong, cunning; bareheaded, building, breaking
3. as young man; undefeated fighter; laughter of youth

4. energy, vitality; wickedness, harshness; part of same human energy making city great
5. sprawling free verse: suggests variety, lack of regularity, and surprises of the city; captures poet's enthusiasm
6. Answers will vary. Students should be able to make many comparisons between the poem and present urban life.

Jazz Fantasia

1. jazzmen
2. drums, banjos, saxophones, cymbals, trombones, horns
3. like an autumn wind, like they wanted someone "terrible"; like a racing car; like a Mississippi steamboat
4. free-flowing words; *go to it, somebody terrible, can the rough stuff;* often spoken by jazzmen, capture informality, freedom of music
5. love, sadness, dreaminess, aggression
6. from aggressive to dreamy mood
7. celebration, faith in energy and goodness; welcomes change, progress; Prufrock terrified of modern world, future

VIEWPOINT

- bursting with energy, freewheeling
- Thinking a poem should celebrate traditional ideas of beauty and cultural achievements, critics found the poem coarse.

LITERARY FOCUS

bang-bang, hoo-hoo-hoo-oo; make reading poem as personal as playing music

Interpreting

4. What does the poet like about Chicago? What negative aspects does he recognize? Explain how the good and bad are related.
5. In what ways does the form of the poem relate to its content?

Extending

6. What qualities of Sandburg's Chicago do you think are still reflected in urban life? Do you find big, bustling cities like Chicago as exciting as Sandburg does? Why or why not?

Jazz Fantasia

Recalling

1. According to lines 1–3, to whom is this poem addressed?
2. Identify at least five musical instruments named in this poem.
3. According to line 7, how should the musicians "moan"? How should they "cry"? According to line 8, like what boat should they sound?

Interpreting

4. What makes this poem a "fantasia"? Identify at least three words or phrases that are slang or ungrammatical. Why is the use of such words or phrases appropriate?
5. What human emotions and human situations does the poet feel jazz expresses?
6. Explain the transition, or change, that "Can the rough stuff" signals.

Extending

7. What would you say is Sandburg's attitude toward America and Americans, based on "Chicago" and this poem? What would you say is his attitude toward modern life and the whirlwind of changes that occurred at the beginning of this century? How are his attitude and his outlook different from J. Alfred Prufrock's (page 415)?

VIEWPOINT

In his biography of Sandburg, Professor Richard Crowder comments:

> Whether consciously or not, Sandburg sensed that the spirit of Chicago could not be expressed totally in the confines of the usual lyric verse. . . . "Chicago" unlocked both language, form, and subject matter in a way that some critics found distasteful, some puzzling, and some invigorating.
>
> —*Carl Sandburg*

■ How does Sandburg's free-verse form relate to the spirit of Chicago that he wishes to convey? Why do you think some critics in Sandburg's day might have found the language and subject matter of "Chicago" distasteful or puzzling?

LITERARY FOCUS

Jazz Rhythms and Onomatopoeia

When someone once asked him what jazz was, Louis Armstrong replied, "If you have to ask, you'll never know." Armstrong was one of many New Orleans artists who relocated in Chicago after 1919, making that city the center of jazz for a decade. And not just any decade—the twenties were the Jazz Age, when the originally black American music became music for all Americans and a symbol of the "roaring" times.

Jazz has a "feel" to it that cannot be well described in writing. If other music is usually *on* the beat, jazz is usually a bit *off* the beat, or *syncopated.* If the main aspect of most western music is its tune, the main feature of jazz is its rhythm. If most musicians follow their music to the note, jazz musicians do not: They *improvise.*

In "Jazz Fantasia" Sandburg not only wants to write about jazz, he wants to suggest something of its sound and rhythm:

> let your TROMbones OOZE, and go HUSHa-HUSHa-HUSH with the slippery SANDpaper.

The **onomatopoeia,** or use of words to imitate sounds, helps capture the rhythm: The stressed *hush-* followed by the unstressed *-a* and then repeated imitates the sandpaper's sound.

Thinking About Jazz Rhythms and Onomatopoeia

■ What other instances of onomatopoeia does "Jazz Fantasia" contain? How do they help capture jazz rhythms?

Edna St. Vincent Millay *1892–1950*

Edna St. Vincent Millay wrote of the rebellious spirit of her generation in the traditional language and style of Romantic poetry, and so achieved popularity with Modernist and Traditionalist alike.

Millay was born in Rockland, Maine, and educated at Vassar College. She began writing poetry in early youth; in fact, her popular poem *Renascence,* published when she was still at Vassar, had been written when she was in high school.

After college Millay headed straight for Greenwich Village, the section of New York City that had become the center for artists, intellectuals, and a Bohemian life style. The beautiful Edna Millay was a popular member of Greenwich Village society: She knew all sorts of people, acted in "experimental" theaters, and was the envy of hundreds of young Americans who read her poetry. Among her early volumes are *A Few Figs from Thistles* (1920), *Second April* (1921), and *The Harp-Weaver and Other Poems* (1923), for which she won the Pulitzer Prize.

Millay married in 1923 and lived the rest of her life on a farm in upstate New York. Nevertheless, she continued writing. During the Depression her poetry became more socially aware, and with the approach of World War II, she wrote many attacks on the Fascist regimes in Europe.

Most of Millay's poetry expresses personal joys and sorrows in sonnets and other strict verse forms. "Recuerdo," which means "I remember" in Spanish, dates from her Greenwich Village years. It is a melodious expression of the fun of being young and in love in the middle of New York City.

- Many poems record memories of special occasions in the poet's life. Do the special occasions have to be "big events" in order to bring forth special memories?

AT A GLANCE

- The poet recalls a special evening spent with a close companion.
- She tells of many of the adventures that they shared as they traveled around New York that night.

LITERARY OPTIONS

- rhyme and repetition
- metaphor

THEMATIC OPTIONS

- youthful memories
- simple pleasures
- loving generosity

RHYME AND REPETITION

The first two lines of each stanza are identical. The last four lines of each stanza change but are related through rhyme and content. The poet thus shows that memory, like the ferry, can move back and forth as it focuses upon specific details.

METAPHOR

That the sun was a "bucketful of gold" suggests the riches of love and the wealth of the evening's simple experiences (l. 12).

REFLECTING ON THE POEM

What is the strongest evidence in this poem to suggest that the poet loved this moment? (Students may mention that although the declaration of love is not stated directly, the repeated "we were very merry" and the catalog of pleasant details support the idea.)

STUDY QUESTIONS

1. went back and forth on the ferry
2. morning paper; fruit, money
3. speaker's companion
4. no; they were in a generous, happy mood; Since they were in their own private world, they were not interested in the paper's contents
5. underscores title; like the ferry, memory too moves back and forth
6. - sensitive, romantic, cares less for money than for memorable experiences
   - Experience and awareness are real wealth.

Edna St. Vincent Millay

Recuerdo

We were very tired, we were very merry—
We had gone back and forth all night on the ferry.
It was bare and bright, and smelled like a stable—
But we looked into a fire, we leaned across a table,
We lay on a hilltop underneath the moon;
And the whistles kept blowing, and the dawn came soon.

We were very tired, we were very merry—
We had gone back and forth all night on the ferry;
And you ate an apple, and I ate a pear,
From a dozen of each we had bought somewhere;
And the sky went wan, and the wind came cold,
And the sun rose dripping, a bucketful of gold.

We were very tired, we were very merry,
We had gone back and forth all night on the ferry.
We hailed, "Good morrow, mother!" to a shawl-covered head,
And bought a morning paper, which neither of us read;
And she wept, "God Bless you!" for the apples and pears,
And we gave her all our money but our subway fares.

STUDY QUESTIONS

Recalling

1. What did the speaker and her companion do all night?
2. What did the speaker and her companion buy from a "shawl-covered head"? What did they give to the woman?

Interpreting

3. Who is "you" in line 9? Describe the speaker's relationship with this person.
4. Did the appearance of the ferry (line 2) and the weather conditions (line 11) matter to the speaker and her companion? Explain. What is suggested by the purchase of a paper "which neither of us read" and by the gifts to the old woman?
5. Why are the repetitions in the poem appropriate to its content?
6. What qualities of the speaker's way of life encourage her generosity? What does line 12 suggest about the source of the poet's real wealth?

Edgar Lee Masters *1869–1950*

Edgar Lee Masters considered his midwestern childhood restrictive, but although he became a prosperous Chicago lawyer, his poetic imagination remained in the town where he had grown up. Masters was born in Garnett, Kansas, and spent most of his youth in southern Illinois, in the same rural area where Abraham Lincoln had spent his early years. In 1892 Masters moved to Chicago, where despite a thriving practice as a criminal lawyer, he began to contribute to *Poetry* magazine. Although he wrote a number of novels and plays, he is best remembered for *Spoon River Anthology* (1915), a poetic examination of small-town life in the Midwest.

In subject matter *Spoon River* bears a similarity to the Tilbury Town poems of Edwin Arlington Robinson. The people of Spoon River "speak" from their graves, summing up their lives.

■ As you listen to the characters speak, see if you can think of someone you know or have heard about who might be a good subject for a similar poem.

Edgar Lee Masters

Cassius Hueffer

They have chiseled on my stone the words:
"His life was gentle, and the elements so mixed in him
That nature might stand up and say to all the world,
This was a man."[1]
Those who knew me smile
As they read this empty rhetoric.

My epitaph[2] should have been:
"Life was not gentle to him,
And the elements so mixed in him
That he made warfare on life,
In the which he was slain."
While I lived I could not cope with slanderous tongues,
Now that I am dead I must submit to an epitaph
Graven by a fool!

1. **"His life . . . man"**: from Mark Antony's eulogy of Brutus in Shakespeare's *Julius Caesar* (Act V, Scene v, lines 73–75).
2. **epitaph** [ep′ ə taf]: inscription on a tombstone.

AT A GLANCE

Speaking from the grave, Cassius Hueffer considers the inappropriateness of his epitaph and bitterly suggests a more accurate summary of his life.

LITERARY OPTIONS

- irony
- dramatic monologue

THEMATIC OPTIONS

- illusion vs. reality
- misunderstanding

DRAMATIC MONOLOGUE

The speaker is a dead man commenting on his epitaph. As he speaks, he acknowledges the bitter irony of the epitaph's praise (ll. 5–6) and vents his anger about his life (ll. 12–14).

IRONY

The name *Cassius* opens the poem on an ironic note. The epitaph seen here was written for Brutus, "the noblest Roman of them all"—not for the envious, angry Cassius of the same play.

REFLECTING ON THE POEM

In what way does the kind epitaph represent yet another "slander" to Hueffer? (It describes a gentle man; Hueffer was angry and bitter.)

AT A GLANCE

Speaking from the grave, Lucinda Matlock recalls meeting her husband and many details of her life as a wife and mother. She concludes that the present generation is too soft.

LITERARY OPTIONS

- dramatic monologue
- tone

THEMATIC OPTIONS

- love of life
- survival of the strong

DRAMATIC MONOLOGUE

Lucinda directly states her philosophy of life in line 22. This unambiguous statement contrasts with the irony and indirection of most modern poetry.

TONE

The tone of this poem is forthright and objective. Lucinda states the important facts of her life without commenting on them until the final lines. She seems to feel that the facts of her full life are enough to prove her love of "Life."

REFLECTING ON THE POEM

Both Lucinda Matlock and Cassius Hueffer are characters in the *Spoon River Anthology*. What might Lucinda say to Cassius? (She would probably berate him for his cynicism and hatred of life. She might even tell him that he probably caused most of his own problems.)

Edgar Lee Masters

Lucinda Matlock

I went to the dances at Chandlerville,
And played snap-out[1] at Winchester.
One time we changed partners,
Driving home in the moonlight of middle June,
And then I found Davis.
We were married and lived together for seventy years,
Enjoying, working, raising the twelve children,
Eight of whom we lost
Ere I had reached the age of sixty.
I spun, I wove, I kept the house, I nursed the sick,
I made the garden, and for holiday
Rambled over the fields where sang the larks,
And by Spoon River gathering many a shell,
And many a flower and medicinal weed—
Shouting to the wooded hills, singing to the green valleys.
At ninety-six I had lived enough, that is all,
And passed to a sweet repose.
What is this I hear of sorrow and weariness,
Anger, discontent and drooping hopes?
Degenerate sons and daughters,
Life is too strong for you—
It takes life to love Life.

1. **snap-out:** game in which players hold hands in a long line and those at the end of the line are flung off when the leader makes a sudden turn.

STUDY QUESTIONS

Cassius Hueffer

Recalling

1. According to the epitaph on his grave, what was Hueffer's life?
2. According to Hueffer, how did "life" treat him?
3. What must Hueffer "submit to" now that he is dead, according to the last two lines?

Interpreting

4. Is the actual epitaph on Hueffer's grave a complimentary one? Why do people who knew Hueffer smile?
5. Does Hueffer blame himself for his unhappy life? Explain.
6. What does Hueffer's anger at the false epitaph reveal about his attitude during his life?

Extending

7. What do you think Lucinda Matlock would have told Hueffer? What might he have told her?

Lucinda Matlock

Recalling

1. How did Lucinda Matlock meet Davis? Who was Davis?
2. For how long did Lucinda Matlock live with her husband? How many children did they have? What happened to eight of them?
3. How old was Lucinda Matlock when she "had lived enough"?
4. What question does Lucinda Matlock ask? What does Lucinda Matlock say it takes "to love Life"?

Interpreting

5. What details of Lucinda Matlock's life would most people in the twentieth century find remarkable? Based on lines 6–9 and 10–17, does Lucinda Matlock think her life was remarkable?
6. Whom in particular is Lucinda Matlock addressing in this poem? Why does she address these people? What, basically, is she telling them?

Extending

7. Do you think Lucinda Matlock has a message for people today? Of what people from America's past does she remind you? Explain your answers.

COMPOSITION

Writing About Character

■ In a brief essay describe either Lucinda Matlock or Cassius Hueffer. Begin by stating what you believe were the person's significant characteristics, and then support your statement with details from the poem.

Writing an Epitaph

■ Write a poem in which a character you create speaks his or her own epitaph. Try to have your character clearly display some aspect of human nature; for example, he or she might be bitter, devout, ambitious, or hypocritical. Use free verse, as Masters does.

COMPARING WRITERS

■ Just as writers are often affected by the literary movements of their day, they are usually influenced by those who wrote before them. How is Sandburg reminiscent of Whitman? What aspects of traditional nineteenth-century poetry does Millay's poem exhibit? What do the poems of Edgar Lee Masters and Edwin Arlington Robinson have in common?

STUDY QUESTIONS

Cassius Hueffer

1. His life was gentle.
2. not gently
3. "an epitaph graven by a fool"
4. Yes; they know it is untrue.
5. in part; admits mixed elements in him, but mainly blames life
6. angry man, disliked hypocrisy, blamed world for his unhappiness
7. Answers will vary. Students should note that Matlock was satisfied with life, but Hueffer was not.

Lucinda Matlock

1. driving home after party; her husband
2. seventy years; twelve; died
3. ninety-six
4. "What is this I hear of sorrow . . .?"; life
5. long life, twelve children (eight dead), spinning; no
6. young people; to admonish them; meet life, live it with joy and spirit
7. Answers will vary. Students should note similarity of Matlock to pioneers and other independent and optimistic Americans.

COMPARING WRITERS

- Both share exuberance, embrace of life, love of America, belief in people, attempt to speak for nation; both catalogue world around them.
- traditional rhyme and meter, easily followed story, feelings and emotions clear
- Both write of small-town America, fictional town, private lives of characters; both use irony and realism.

COMPOSITION: GUIDELINES FOR EVALUATION

WRITING ABOUT CHARACTER

Objective

To identify a character's significant qualities

Guidelines for Evaluation

- suggested length: three to five paragraphs
- should state the character's significant characteristics
- should support statements with specific details

WRITING AN EPITAPH

Objective

To write a poetic epitaph

Guidelines for Evaluation

- suggested length: ten to twelve lines
- should reveal at least one defining characteristic of the speaker
- should suggest the reasons for the existence of that characteristic
- should use free verse but deliberate structure

Jean Toomer *1894–1967*

During the 1920s black literature flourished, particularly among writers in the Harlem section of New York City. This important flowering of black arts and letters became known as the Harlem Renaissance, and Jean Toomer was one of its most talented figures.

Toomer was born in Washington, D.C., and attended college in several parts of the United States. He then went to teach school in Georgia, where he absorbed the sights and sounds that went into *Cane* (1923). After settling in Harlem and contributing to a variety of literary journals, Toomer's interests turned to religion and philosophy, and he wrote a number of essays on these subjects. Like Melville, he was an almost forgotten writer for many years. His works were rediscovered in the 1960s.

Cane has since become one of the classics of black American literature. An unusual book, it combines prose sketches of black Southerners with poetry that expresses Toomer's feelings about identity and southern life. As a series of fragments meant to be brought together in the reader's mind, it resembles Eliot's *Waste Land* and Hemingway's *In Our Time* and reflects the Modernist experimentation of the period. In the following poem from *Cane,* Toomer captures the surprise of unseasonable weather in rural Georgia.

- How would we react if it were to snow in July? How much do we depend upon the predictability of nature's cycles? What startles Toomer in this poem?

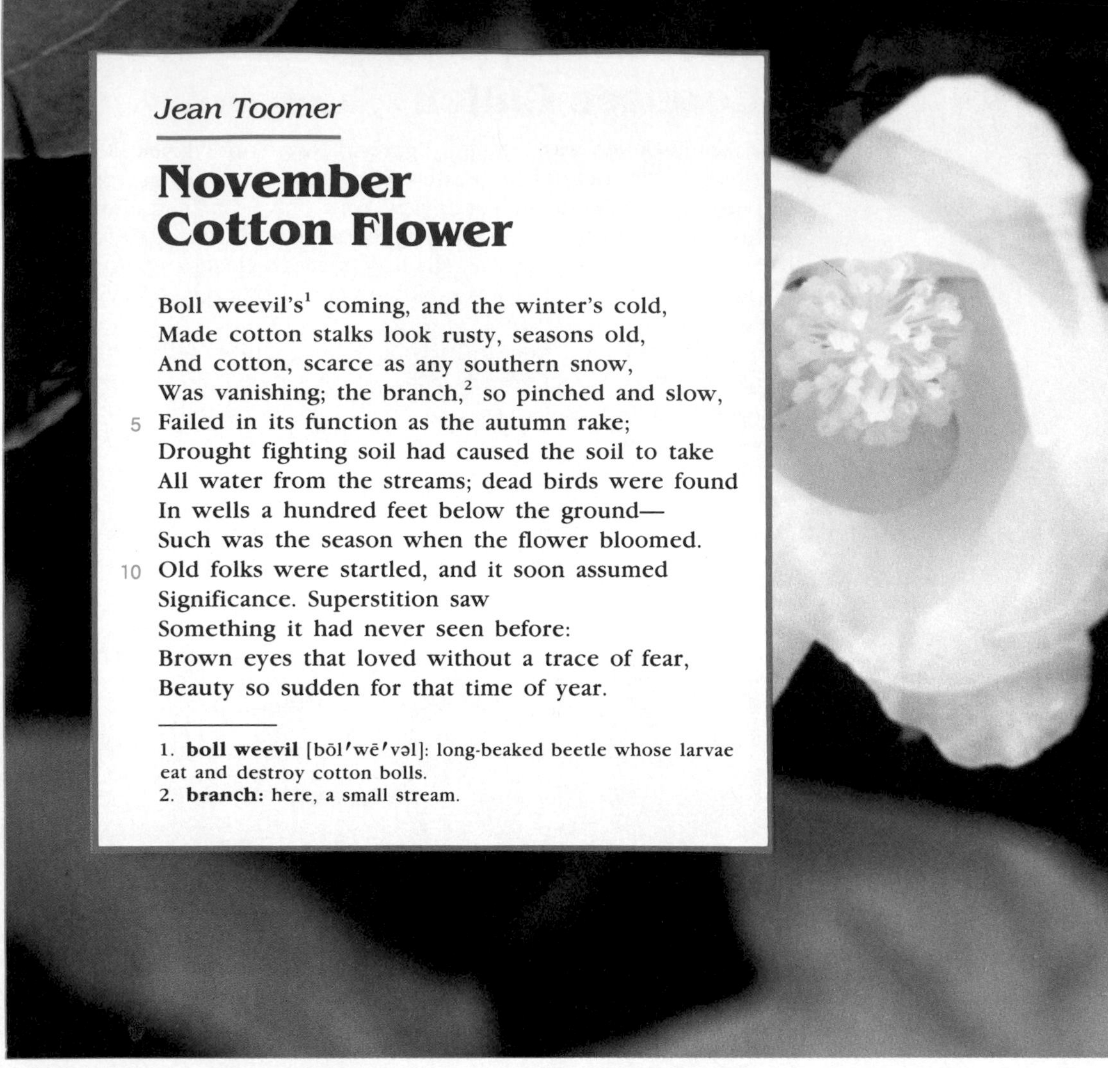

Jean Toomer

November Cotton Flower

Boll weevil's[1] coming, and the winter's cold,
Made cotton stalks look rusty, seasons old,
And cotton, scarce as any southern snow,
Was vanishing; the branch,[2] so pinched and slow,
Failed in its function as the autumn rake;
Drought fighting soil had caused the soil to take
All water from the streams; dead birds were found
In wells a hundred feet below the ground—
Such was the season when the flower bloomed.
Old folks were startled, and it soon assumed
Significance. Superstition saw
Something it had never seen before:
Brown eyes that loved without a trace of fear,
Beauty so sudden for that time of year.

1. **boll weevil** [bōl′wē′vəl]: long-beaked beetle whose larvae eat and destroy cotton bolls.
2. **branch:** here, a small stream.

STUDY QUESTIONS

Recalling

1. What two things, according to line 1, make the cotton stalks look rusty and old? What happens to the cotton in lines 3–4?
2. What event startles the "old folks," according to lines 9–11?
3. What does the poet say this unexpected event soon assumes?
4. What two things has "Superstition" never seen before?

Interpreting

5. In what season does this poem take place? What do the details of lines 1–8 imply about the human emotions this season usually arouses? What event makes this year different?
6. How does Toomer make the sudden bloom come as a surprise to the reader as well as to the people of Georgia?
7. Who is superstitious? What does the final couplet suggest about the effects of the sudden bloom on most human beings?

AT A GLANCE

- In the midst of a dying land, a cotton flower bloomed.
- Its appearance had a nearly supernatural effect on those who saw it.

LITERARY OPTIONS

- comparison and contrast
- sonnet

THEMATIC OPTIONS

- unexpected beauty
- rebirth

SONNET

The use of the sonnet form emphasizes the contrast in the poem. The octave focuses on the autumn drought, whereas the sestet focuses on the "sudden" beauty of the flower.

CONTRAST

Just as the two parts of the poem are set against each other, the bareness of the drought is set against the beauty of the flower—which the poet never actually describes.

REFLECTING ON THE POEM

Why might the blooming of a single flower in November evoke both joy and melancholy? (It might evoke joy because the flower seems to represent a rebirth of nature; it might evoke melancholy because the flower makes the wasteland around seem even more dead.)

STUDY QUESTIONS

1. boll weevils, winter's cold; vanishing
2. the blooming of the flower
3. significance
4. "brown eyes that loved without a trace of fear, / Beauty so sudden for that time of year"
5. late autumn; unhappiness, thoughts of decay and death; blooming of flower
6. follows details of drought
7. - old folks
   - Miracle of human love overcomes fear aroused by the flower's blooming.

Countee Cullen *1903–1946*

Countee Cullen was a central figure in New York's black literary circles at the time of the Harlem Renaissance. He began to publish poetry while still a student at New York University, and after getting his master's degree from Harvard, became an editor of *Opportunity,* an influential black journal. His first poetry collection, *Color,* was published in 1925 and was rapidly followed by *Copper Sun* and *The Ballad of the Brown Girl.*

In 1928 Cullen went to Paris on a Guggenheim fellowship. After his return he taught French in New York City public schools and continued to write and edit. In his later years he published two books for children, *The Lost Zoo* (1940) and *My Lives and How I Lost Them* (1942).

- Unlike the Modernists, Cullen retains the traditions of stanza, rhyme, and direct statement. Why do you think he does so?

Tombstones,
Jacob Lawrence, 1942.

Collection Whitney Museum of American Art

Countee Cullen

Any Human to Another

The ills I sorrow at
Not me alone
Like an arrow,
Pierce to the marrow,
Through the fat
And past the bone.

Your grief and mine
Must intertwine
Like sea and river,
Be fused and mingle,
Diverse yet single,
Forever and forever.

Let no man be so proud
And confident,
To think he is allowed
A little tent
Pitched in a meadow
Of sun and shadow
All his little own.

Joy may be shy, unique,
Friendly to a few,
Sorrow never scorned to speak
To any who
Were false or true.

Your every grief
Like a blade
Shining and unsheathed
Must strike me down.
Of bitter aloes[1] wreathed,
My sorrow must be laid
On your head like a crown.

---

1. **aloes** [al′ōz]: spiny plants of the lily family, native to South Africa. The medicinal juice of the plant has a very bitter taste.

STUDY QUESTIONS

Recalling

1. According to the title, who is speaking to whom?
2. What does the speaker not do alone, according to the first stanza? What two things must intertwine, according to the second stanza?
3. What is no one allowed, according to the third stanza?
4. According to the fourth stanza, what may joy be? To whom does sorrow never scorn to speak?

Interpreting

5. Restate the idea expressed in the third stanza without using figurative language.
6. Basically, why does the speaker feel we must share his sorrow? Precisely whose sorrow does he feel we must share?

Extending

7. Why is this a traditional poem by nineteenth-century standards? (See the explanation of Imagism on page 413 and of Modernism on pages 403–405.)

AT A GLANCE

The speaker points out that no one stands completely alone and that both joy and sorrow should be shared.

LITERARY OPTIONS

- simile
- personification

THEMATIC OPTIONS

- brotherhood
- coping with grief

SIMILE

Note how the use of simile develops the poet's vision of brotherhood. Sorrows that are felt by the individual alone are like an arrow (l. 3) or a blade (l. 26). However, when these sorrows are shared, they become an ennobling crown (ll. 30–31).

PERSONIFICATION

Cullen reverses the usual images of joy and sorrow, personifying joy as a withdrawn, quiet individual and sorrow as an open, sharing friend.

REFLECTING ON THE POEM

Why do you think the poet is so insistent that joy and sorrow be shared? (Perhaps he is intimating that the best way to cope with the harsh complexities of human experience is to seek the support of other people.)

STUDY QUESTIONS

1. any human to another
2. suffer sorrows; your grief and mine
3. a little tent of his own
4. shy, unique, friendly to a few; anyone
5. No one can live without others.
6. all people are brothers, sisters; his and everyone's
7. regular rhyme, meter; clearly states ideas, emotions; poet restating something old

Langston Hughes *1902–1967*

Langston Hughes was the most accomplished poet of the Harlem Renaissance. A true "Renaissance man," he wrote drama, fiction, popular songs, and movie screenplays; worked on anthologies and translations; and generously helped the careers of many younger writers. He is, however, best noted for his poetry.

Hughes was born in Missouri and went to high school in Cleveland, Ohio, where he began writing poetry for a school magazine. He went on to Columbia University in New York City but a year later left to go to sea. After traveling as a merchant seaman to Africa and Europe, he returned to America and continued writing poetry. His work appeared in a number of prominent black journals and in the chief anthology of the Harlem Renaissance, *The New Negro* (1925).

The poet Vachel Lindsay helped Hughes publish his first volume of poetry, *The Weary Blues* (1926). His literary reputation secure, Hughes decided to complete his formal education. After graduating from Lincoln University, he returned to New York City, where he continued to write and was active in the theater. His later books of poems include *The Dream Keeper* (1932), *Fields of Wonder* (1947), and *Montage of a Dream Deferred* (1951). He wrote two autobiographical volumes, *The Big Sea* (1940) and *I Wonder as I Wander* (1956).

Much of Hughes's best writing appeared in newspapers. Especially popular were the sketches he wrote for the Chicago *Defender* during the 1940s. These short tales chronicle the adventures of a character named Simple, whose innocent but shrewd observations of the world gave Hughes many opportunities for sharp satire and social criticism.

"Dream Variations" demonstrates how well Hughes had absorbed the international Modernist techniques and adapted them to his subject matter and to jazz and blues rhythms.

- How does Hughes blend the traditional and the modern in his poems?

Langston Hughes

Dream Variations

To fling my arms wide
In some place of the sun,
To whirl and to dance
Till the white day is done.
Then rest at cool evening
Beneath a tall tree
While night comes on gently,
    Dark like me—
That is my dream!

To fling my arms wide
In the face of the sun,
Dance! Whirl! Whirl!
Till the quick day is done.
Rest at pale evening . . .
A tall, slim tree . . .
Night coming tenderly
    Black like me.

STUDY QUESTIONS

Recalling

1. Where does the speaker want to fling his arms wide, according to the first stanza? According to the second stanza?
2. What is night called in line 8? In line 17?

Interpreting

3. What does the speaker associate with day and night?
4. What are the variations in the poem, as suggested by the title?
5. Which two lines make a slight shift in the poem's meter, or regular rhythm? Which line breaks the meter completely? What does the irregular rhythm of these lines suggest, or what effect does it seem to create?

COMPARING WRITERS

■ Toomer, Cullen, and Hughes all wrote of the experience of being black. What comments do their poems make about the black experience? What elements in their poems are also universal?

AT A GLANCE

The poet dreams of dancing in the sunlight and resting at evening.

LITERARY OPTIONS

- repetition
- imagery

THEMATIC OPTIONS

- dreams and ideals
- the black experience

REPETITION

The similarity of the first four lines of each stanza helps to tie the poem together.

IMAGERY

The poet links images of sunlight and the "white day" to action and images of darkness and "cool evening" to rest. He seems to rejoice in both aspects of his existence.

MAIN IDEA

The poet celebrates his blackness in this poem (ll. 7–8 and 16–17). In particular, he savors the "dark" and "black" night as it comes to him "gently" and "tenderly."

REFLECTING ON THE POEM

Does the poet seem to prefer day or night? (Students may note that although he creates positive images of the day, the fact that he identifies himself with the night suggests that he prefers night to day.)

STUDY QUESTIONS

1. some place of the sun; face of the sun
2. dark like me; black like me
3. day: dancing, sun, white; night: resting, coolness, black, himself
4. night-day, warmth-coolness, black-white
5. 8 and 17; 9; emphasizes them, suggests surprising and irregular movements of dreams

COMPARING WRITERS

Toomer: southern black agrarian, universal power of nature and love; *Cullen:* sorrow and suffering of racial injustice, burden of grief felt by everyone; *Hughes:* black and white experiences part of human experience

John Crowe Ransom *1888–1974*

John Crowe Ransom was one of the most influential critics of his time, as well as a poet in his own right. Born in Tennessee, Ransom first taught at Vanderbilt University, from which he had graduated before going on to Oxford University in England. At Vanderbilt, and later at Kenyon College in Ohio, Professor Ransom was at the center of an important circle of critics who brought about a revolution in the way we read literature.

Ransom's critical theories are contained in *The New Criticism* (1941), a work whose title gave a name to the revolution in critical thinking that Ransom helped lead. The New Critics give scrupulous attention to the *text* of a literary work, looking at what the text actually does instead of seeking its meaning in the author's biography or in ideas external to the work. In emphasizing that a literary work should "stand alone," the New Critics were obviously influenced by Pound and the Imagists (see page 413).

Ransom's background as professor and critic is apparent in his poetry: A self-conscious critical intelligence seems always to be looking over the poet's shoulder. His poems are noted for their craftsmanship and for their poised irony; they are extremely non-Romantic in tone but often formal in style.

In "Janet Waking" Ransom takes a subject that can easily lead to sentimentality—the death of a child's pet—and treats it in an unsentimental way. He achieves this lack of sentiment through a highly structured format and by shifting from childish to "adult" language, thereby distancing himself from the child's emotions with his characteristic aloofness.

- How does Ransom blend the intellectual and the emotional qualities of poetry?

John Crowe Ransom

Janet Waking

Beautifully Janet slept
Till it was deeply morning. She woke then
And thought about her dainty-feathered hen,
To see how it had kept.

One kiss she gave her mother.
Only a small one gave she to her daddy
Who would have kissed each curl of his
shining baby;
No kiss at all for her brother.

"Old Chucky, old Chucky!" she cried,
Running across the world upon the grass
To Chucky's house, and listening. But alas,
Her Chucky had died.

It was a transmogrifying[1] bee
Came droning down to Chucky's old bald head
And sat and put the poison. It scarcely bled,
But how exceedingly

And purply did the knot
Swell with the venom and communicate
Its rigor![2] Now the poor comb[3] stood
up straight
But Chucky did not.

So there was Janet
Kneeling on the wet grass, crying her
brown hen
(Translated[4] far beyond the daughters of men)
To rise and walk upon it.

And weeping fast as she had breath
Janet implored us, "Wake her from her sleep!"
And would not be instructed in how deep
Was the forgetful kingdom of death.

---

1. **transmogrifying** [trans mog′rə fī′ing]: transforming in a grotesque manner.
2. **rigor:** severity; here, referring to *rigor mortis,* the stiffening of body tissues after death.
3. **comb:** red, fleshy outgrowth on a chicken's head.
4. **translated:** transported.

STUDY QUESTIONS

Recalling

1. What does Janet think about when she wakes up? What does she discover?
2. What does Janet cry for the pet to do in the sixth stanza? What does she ask "us" in the last stanza? In what will she not be "instructed"?

Interpreting

3. Describe the tone of lines 19–20. What is the effect of these lines?
4. What is childish about Janet's actions in the second stanza? Is her reaction to Chucky's death equally childish? From what is Janet "waking"?

Extending

5. If you were Janet's parents, what would you do after providing the "instruction" in the last lines?

COMPOSITION

Writing About Poetry

■ In a brief essay analyze the structure of "Janet Waking." First describe the strict stanza form and rhyme scheme. Then discuss any breaks in meter and any slant rhymes that vary the strict form. Finally consider how the structure of the poem relates to its tone and content.

Writing a Narrative

■ Write a short narrative composition, or a poem if you wish, about an ordinary, everyday event. Describe the event in such a way, however, that it does not seem ordinary. Point out its causes and effects. Give details that bring out the drama or the suspense of the event. Conclude with a statement of the meaning of the event to those who experienced it.

AT A GLANCE

- Janet finds her pet hen killed by a bee sting.
- She begs her parents to help, but they can do nothing.

LITERARY OPTIONS

- rhyme
- diction

THEMATIC OPTIONS

- death
- innocence

RHYME SCHEME

The rhyme scheme *(abba)* ties each stanza together and creates a slight pause before each one's final line, making it a kind of punch line.

DICTION

The archaic phrases *gave she* (l. 6), *but alas* (l. 11), and *daughters of men* (l. 23) help create a double-edged tone, part ironic and part serious.

REFLECTING ON THE POEM

Is the poem essentially serious or humorous? Why? (Ransom's emphasis on the child's genuine grief and innocence keeps the core of the poem serious.)

STUDY QUESTIONS

1. her hen; dead hen
2. rise, walk; wake hen; death
3. ironic; wry humor
4. not kissing brother; yes, but not her grief; innocence
5. Answers might include comforting her.

COMPOSITION: GUIDELINES FOR EVALUATION

WRITING ABOUT POETRY

Objective

To analyze the structure of a poem

Guidelines for Evaluation

- suggested length: four to six paragraphs
- should identify stanza form, rhyme scheme, and irregular rhythm
- should discuss how contrast of irregular rhythm and regular stanza and rhyme duplicate the contrasts between Janet and adult

WRITING A NARRATIVE

Objective

To write a prose or poetic narrative

Guidelines for Evaluation

- suggested length: three to five paragraphs, eight to sixteen lines
- should find and describe the drama in an everyday event
- should conclude by summarizing the meaning of the event

Photograph © 1982 by Jill Krementz

Archibald MacLeish *1892–1982*

Archibald MacLeish attended Yale and the Harvard Law School, but he soon gave up law for literature. During the 1920s he spent five years in Paris, home to many American artists for whom experimentation was the order of the day. Two of his early volumes of poetry, *The Happy Marriage* (1924) and *Streets in the Moon* (1926), reflect the influence of Pound and Eliot.

When MacLeish returned to America, however, he departed from his Paris Modernism, seeking to reach a wider audience by making his poetry more accessible. He turned toward public speech, reciting his poetry before large gatherings and earning a reputation as a fine orator. He also held a series of important government posts during and after World War II. His *Collected Poems* appeared in 1950; in 1959 he won a Pulitzer Prize for *J. B., A Play in Verse,* a modern version of the biblical Book of Job.

In later years MacLeish taught rhetoric at Harvard and often appeared on television. Like Carl Sandburg and Robert Frost, he became one of America's best known and most revered poets. He was often called upon to write poems commemorating landmark American events.

- How do the final lines, "A poem should not mean / But be," sum up one of the chief doctrines of Imagism?

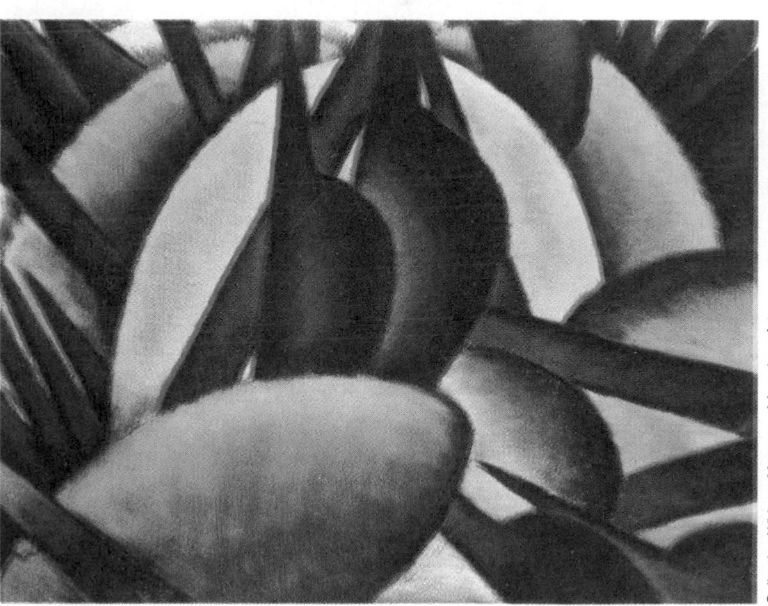

Plant Forms,
Arthur Dove, 1915.

Collection Whitney Museum of American Art

Archibald MacLeish

Ars Poetica

A poem should be palpable[1] and mute
As a globed fruit,

Dumb
As old medallions to the thumb,

Silent as the sleeve-worn stone
Of casement ledges where the moss
has grown—

A poem should be wordless
As the flight of birds.

A poem should be motionless in time
As the moon climbs,

Leaving, as the moon releases
Twig by twig the night-entangled trees,

Leaving, as the moon behind the winter leaves,
Memory by memory the mind—

A poem should be motionless in time
As the moon climbs.

A poem should be equal to:
Not true.

For all the history of grief
An empty doorway and a maple leaf.

For love
The leaning grasses and two lights
above the sea—

A poem should not mean
But be.

---

1. **palpable:** tangible; able to be touched and felt.

STUDY QUESTIONS

Recalling

1. What five adjectives in the first eight lines describe what a poem should be?
2. According to the second section, what should a poem be?
3. Rather than be "true," what should a poem be? Rather than "mean," what should it do?

Interpreting

4. How are the adjectives in lines 3, 5, and 7 related to "mute" in line 1? How can a poem be "palpable and mute"? What does "globed" suggest about the poem?
5. Is the statement in line 1 abstract or concrete? How does the simile in line 2 help explain it? Do lines 3–4, 5–6, and 7–8 follow the same logic?
6. What might line 9 mean? Why does the poet repeat lines 9–10 at the end of the second section?
7. What do lines 19–22 suggest a poet should do to capture "the history of grief" or "love"? What does MacLeish therefore mean in lines 17–18? Why would he single out "the history of grief" or "love"?
8. Explain in your own words the basic rule of Imagism stated in lines 23–24. Why is "Ars Poetica" *not* a pure Imagist poem?

VIEWPOINT

Archibald MacLeish was not the first poet to attempt to define his art; poets have done so throughout the centuries. In a 1923 article in the *Atlantic Monthly* Carl Sandburg said:

> poetry is the achievement of the synthesis
> of hyacinths and biscuits.
>
> —"Poetry Considered"

■ How is Sandburg's definition like MacLeish's in its *means* of conveying information? How is the "message" itself different? What are the implications of the word *biscuits*, and how do "biscuits" differ from the images MacLeish chooses?

AT A GLANCE

A poem should be "wordless" and "motionless" and needs no interpretation.

LITERARY OPTIONS

- metaphor
- simile

THEMATIC OPTIONS

- a definition of art
- sensation and experience

SIMILE

The first eight couplets (ll. 1–16) are all similes. While they are all different, they all involve vivid sensory experiences.

METAPHOR

The last four couplets use metaphors. The focus shifts from what a poem *resembles* to what it *is*.

REFLECTING ON THE POEM

What do you think MacLeish believes is the art of poetry? (Students may suggest that it is the capacity to create powerful images needing no explanation.)

STUDY QUESTIONS

1. *palpable, mute, dumb, silent, wordless*
2. motionless in time
3. "equal to"; "be"
4. synonyms; by containing a vivid image that speaks for itself instead of directly stating emotion; tactile, perfect whole
5. abstract; concretizes statement; yes
6. poem should create timeless image; to freeze motion, creating timeless image
7.
- use various images
- Poem should use imagery to create equivalents to emotions, not describe emotions directly.
- universal feelings

8.
- A poem should not tell what a poet means; it should incarnate the meaning.
- Poet states directly his ideas about poetry.

VIEWPOINT

- Both define poetry's meaning by using images or metaphors.
- *MacLeish*—poem should consist of image or series of images; *Sandburg*—poem must synthesize the mundane and the beautiful.
- Biscuits imply the commonplace and "unpoetic," in contrast to MacLeish's images.

Marianne Moore *1887–1972*

Marianne Moore is among the most delightful of American poets. Her witty, sharp, and strangely fascinating poems offer sparkling surfaces that quickly grasp her readers' attention and keep them alert.

Moore was born in Missouri, studied biology at Bryn Mawr College in Pennsylvania, and later moved to Brooklyn, New York. Her interest in science never left her, and it is apparent in both the subject matter and the precision of her verse. For a time she edited the influential New York literary journal *The Dial,* but she gained a large measure of popularity for a completely different reason: She was a passionate baseball fan.

In 1919 Moore sent some of her poetry to Ezra Pound, from whom she received much encouragement. She became widely admired by other poets, yet she herself was shy about publishing her work. Her first volume of poetry was published in England in 1921—without her knowledge and much to her annoyance—by H. D. and another admirer. Later volumes include *Observations* (1924) and *Selected Poems* (1935). Moore is also noted for her delightful translations of the French writer La Fontaine's *Fables* (1954).

Moore's poetry is refreshingly original; her vision is precise but rather eccentric. The brilliant and oblique surfaces of her poems are filled with observations of animals and nature, even as she cryptically tosses in mysterious quotations from her reading. Moore darts out with lines that move us immediately, but no sooner has her more direct self appeared than it disappears again, withdrawn behind her famous reticence.

"Poetry" is Moore's most frequently reprinted poem, a playful yet thoughtful reply to someone who seems to have told the poet that he or she did not "like" poetry. "Arthur Mitchell" describes the dancer and founder of the Dance Theater of Harlem, perhaps in his most famous role, that of Puck in Mendelssohn's ballet *A Midsummer Night's Dream.*

- Have you ever thought, "I don't like poetry?" Have you ever considered *why* you don't like it? Does Moore answer that question for you?

Marianne Moore

Poetry

I, too, dislike it: there are things that are important beyond all this fiddle.
Reading it, however, with a perfect contempt for it, one discovers in
it after all, a place for the genuine.
Hands that can grasp, eyes
that can dilate, hair that can rise
if it must, these things are important not because a

high-sounding interpretation can be put upon them but because they are
useful. When they become so derivative[1] as to become unintelligible,
the same thing may be said for all of us, that we
do not admire what
we cannot understand: the bat
holding on upside down or in quest of something to

eat, elephants pushing, a wild horse taking a roll, a tireless wolf under
a tree, the immovable critic twitching his skin like a horse that feels a flea, the baseball fan, the statistician—
nor is it valid
to discriminate against "business documents and

schoolbooks"; all these phenomena are important. One must make a distinction
however: when dragged into prominence by half poets, the result is not poetry,
nor till the poets among us can be
"literalists of
the imagination"—above
insolence and triviality and can present

for inspection, "imaginary gardens with real toads in them," shall we have
it. In the meantime, if you demand on the one hand,
the raw material of poetry in
all its rawness and
that which is on the other hand
genuine, you are interested in poetry.

1. **derivative:** arrived at through complex reasoning and deduction.

AT A GLANCE

The poet argues that poetry is valuable because it expresses what is genuine in life.

LITERARY OPTIONS

- imagery
- paradox

THEMATIC OPTIONS

- the nature of poetry
- "good" poetry vs. "bad" poetry

IMAGERY

The contrast between images such as "hair that can rise" (l. 5) and "high-sounding interpretation" (l. 7) suggests that poetry appeals to emotions, rather than the intellect.

INTERPRETATION

"Half poets" exploit startling images and unexpected language for their shock value, without connecting them to real human concerns (l. 19).

PARADOX

Moore's paradoxical image of poems as "'imaginary gardens with real toads in them'" (l. 24) sums up the idea that poems formulate rough human concerns within artful frameworks.

REFLECTING ON THE POEM

What does it mean to be "'literalists of the imagination'" (ll. 21–22)? (Students may suggest that it means to write imaginatively and yet express realities that can be understood in the heart of the reader.)

AT A GLANCE

- The poet compares the dancer Arthur Mitchell to a dragonfly, a jewel, and a peacock.
- His dancing makes abstract ideas come alive.

LITERARY OPTIONS

- rhyme
- imagery

THEMATIC OPTIONS

- skill as beauty
- the power of dance

IMAGERY

The images of this poem are fluid: *dragonfly / too rapid for the eye, jewels of mobility*, and *reveal / and veil a peacock-tail.* The dancer creates poetry in motion.

RHYME

Rhymes *(dragonfly / eye, virtuosity / mentality / mobility, veil / peacock-tail)* tie highly disparate images together, creating a unified portrait of the dancer.

VOCABULARY: WORD CHOICE

The choice of "contagious" to describe "gem" implies some emulation as well as admiration (l. 4).

REFLECTING ON THE POEM

In what sense is dance "poetry in motion"? (Like poetry dance expresses ideas through images. In dance the images move and change constantly.)

Marianne Moore

Arthur Mitchell

Slim dragonfly
too rapid for the eye
    to cage—
contagious gem of virtuosity—
make visible, mentality.
Your jewels of mobility

reveal
  and veil
    a peacock-tail.

Dancer Arthur Mitchell at home.

STUDY QUESTIONS

Poetry

Recalling

1. What does the poet call poetry in line 1? What does she say one discovers when reading poetry "with a perfect contempt for it"?
2. According to the poet, why are the things in lines 4–5 important? Why are they *not* important? When poems "become so derivative as to become unintelligible," what is our reaction?
3. What "distinction" must we make about poetry, according to lines 18–19? What would ideal poets be, according to lines 21–22, and what would they "present for inspection"?

Interpreting

4. What do lines 4–5 suggest about the elements that make good poetry "genuine"? What kind of poetry does Moore *dis*like?
5. What does Moore mean by "imaginary gardens with real toads in them"?
6. Why is the argument of the poem made more effective by the poet's pretending to agree with someone who dislikes poetry?

Arthur Mitchell

Recalling

1. For what is Mitchell "too rapid"? What sort of "gem" is he? What does he "make visible"?
2. What do Mitchell's "jewels of mobility" do?

Interpreting

3. What does "virtuosity" suggest about Mitchell's talents as a dancer?
4. In what way might Mitchell's art be "contagious"? What has it prompted in Moore?
5. What is a peacock's tail like when it opens? When it closes? What do the last three lines therefore imply about Mitchell's art?
6. In addition to Mitchell's art, what art does this poem seem to be about? What might the last three lines therefore imply?

VOCABULARY

Synonyms

A **synonym** is a word that has the same or nearly the same meaning as another word. *Joy* and *exaltation* are synonyms. The words in capital letters are from "Poetry." Choose the word that is nearest the meaning of each word in capitals, *as it is used in the selection.*

1. INSOLENCE: (a) pride (b) insomnia (c) privacy (d) insult
2. TRIVIALITY: (a) pot holder (b) temptation (c) something unimportant (d) surface
3. CONTEMPT: (a) relief (b) scorn (c) amazement (d) pity
4. PHENOMENA: (a) trifles (b) happenings (c) phantoms (d) eons
5. DISCRIMINATE: (a) let go (b) cheat (c) show anger (d) show preference

COMPARING WRITERS

■ For centuries poets have felt a need to keep defining, describing, and defending their art. Compare the definitions and the defenses of poetry in MacLeish's "Ars Poetica" and Moore's "Poetry." How do the poets differ in the images they use to define poetry? What does each say is the purpose of poetry? On what aspects of poetry do you think these two poets would agree?

STUDY QUESTIONS

Poetry

1. fiddle; a place for the genuine
2. usefulness; high-sounding interpretation can be applied; no longer admire
3. between real poetry and work of half-poets; literalists presenting imaginary gardens with real toads
4. creates visceral responses; trivial, lacking in imaginative impact
5. real subjects transformed into an imaginative reality
6. captures attention, luring reluctant reader into responsiveness

Arthur Mitchell

1. the eye; virtuosity; mentality
2. "reveal and veil the peacock-tail"
3. highly talented
4. inspires creative effort; a poem
5. multicolored; hides beauty; at times brilliant, at times mysterious and subtle
6. art that inspires; that all great art should reveal and conceal

VOCABULARY

1. (a) pride
2. (c) something unimportant
3. (b) scorn
4. (b) happenings
5. (d) show preference

COMPARING WRITERS

MacLeish: poem simply be; art for art's sake; *Moore:* raw, playful, genuine, earthy, engaged; *both:* needs no defense, needs continual redefinition

E. E. Cummings *1894–1962*

Edward Estlin Cummings, as a poet and as a painter, spent his artistic life in pursuit of one of the most American of goals—individuality. Cummings was born in Cambridge, Massachusetts, the son of a prominent New England clergyman. After graduating from Harvard, he served as an ambulance driver in World War I. He was held in a prison camp in France, an experience that resulted in his powerful book, *The Enormous Room* (1922). He lived briefly in Paris during the early twenties and upon returning to America settled in Greenwich Village, New York's artistic community. His career flourished, and he became one of Greenwich Village's most famous residents.

Both his poetry and his painting reflect Cummings' concern with the need to be independent in our modern age of technology. The first things we notice about his poems are the distinctive arrangements of the words on the page and the use of lowercase letters where earlier poets and more conventional writers use capitals. In fact, the poet liked to sign his work "e. e. cummings" and even had his name legally changed to this lowercase form. He also liked to play with words, to break them apart or use them in unusual ways.

The small letters, the unconventional syntax, and the unusual spacing of words were Cummings' way of expressing individuality and participating in what he called "The New Art." Yet beneath the unconventional Modernist surfaces, Cummings' poetry is a lyrical celebration of the most traditional of poetic subjects: the joy of living ("since feeling is first"), the wonders of nature ("r-p-o-p-h-e-s-s-a-g-r"), and love itself ("your little voice").

■ Can the placement of words on the page affect meaning? How can "searching" for the meaning become an enjoyable challenge?

E. E. Cummings

since feeling is first

since feeling is first
who pays any attention
to the syntax[1] of things
will never wholly kiss you;
wholly to be a fool
while Spring is in the world

my blood approves,
and kisses are a better fate
than wisdom
lady i swear by all flowers. Don't cry
—the best gesture of my brain is less than
your eyelids' flutter which says

we are for each other: then
laugh, leaning back in my arms
for life's not a paragraph

And death i think is no parenthesis

---

1. **syntax:** systematic arrangement.

r-p-o-p-h-e-s-s-a-g-r

r-p-o-p-h-e-s-s-a-g-r
who
a)s w(e loo)k
upnowgath
PPEGORHRASS
eringint(o-
aThe):l
eA
!p:
S a
(r
rIvInG .gRrEaPsPhOs)
to
rea(be)rran(com)gi(e)ngly
,grasshopper;

LITERARY OPTIONS

- analogy
- form

THEMATIC OPTIONS

- the enjoyment of life
- form and motion

"FEELING": ANALOGY

The poem builds on a complex analogy: Life is *not* like writing. Life has no "syntax" and no clear structure like a paragraph.

"r-p-o-p-h-e-s-s-a-g-r": FORM

Line 15 is the key to the poem's form. Once the reader sees that the subject is a grasshopper, the leap in lines 7–9 is clear. The rest of the poem suggests the course that the grasshopper takes as it jumps.

REFLECTING ON THE POEMS

What do you think is Cummings' purpose in ignoring traditional use of capitalization and punctuation? (Students may suggest that he wants to startle the reader into seeing his subjects—life and a grasshopper—in a new way. He is pushing the limits of language.)

AT A GLANCE

- The poet recalls a telephone call from his "dear girl."
- He remembers how dramatically he was moved by the sound of her voice.

LITERARY OPTIONS

- free verse
- personification
- hyperbole

THEMATIC OPTIONS

- the exhilaration of love
- the power of memory

FREE VERSE

The unexpected arrangement of lines suggests the speaker's wandering recollections, recalls his breathless excitement, and parallels his own ecstasy.

PERSONIFICATION

By attributing human characteristics to flowers (l. 3), flames (ll. 4–5), and the moon (l. 12), the speaker makes these natural objects extensions of his feelings.

HYPERBOLE AND MAIN IDEA

The variety and intensity of the speaker's emotions show that love can transform a small event into something quite spectacular.

REFLECTING ON THE POEM

Over what things does the voice of the "dear girl" have power? (Students might mention its power over the laws of nature, time, death, and the speaker himself.)

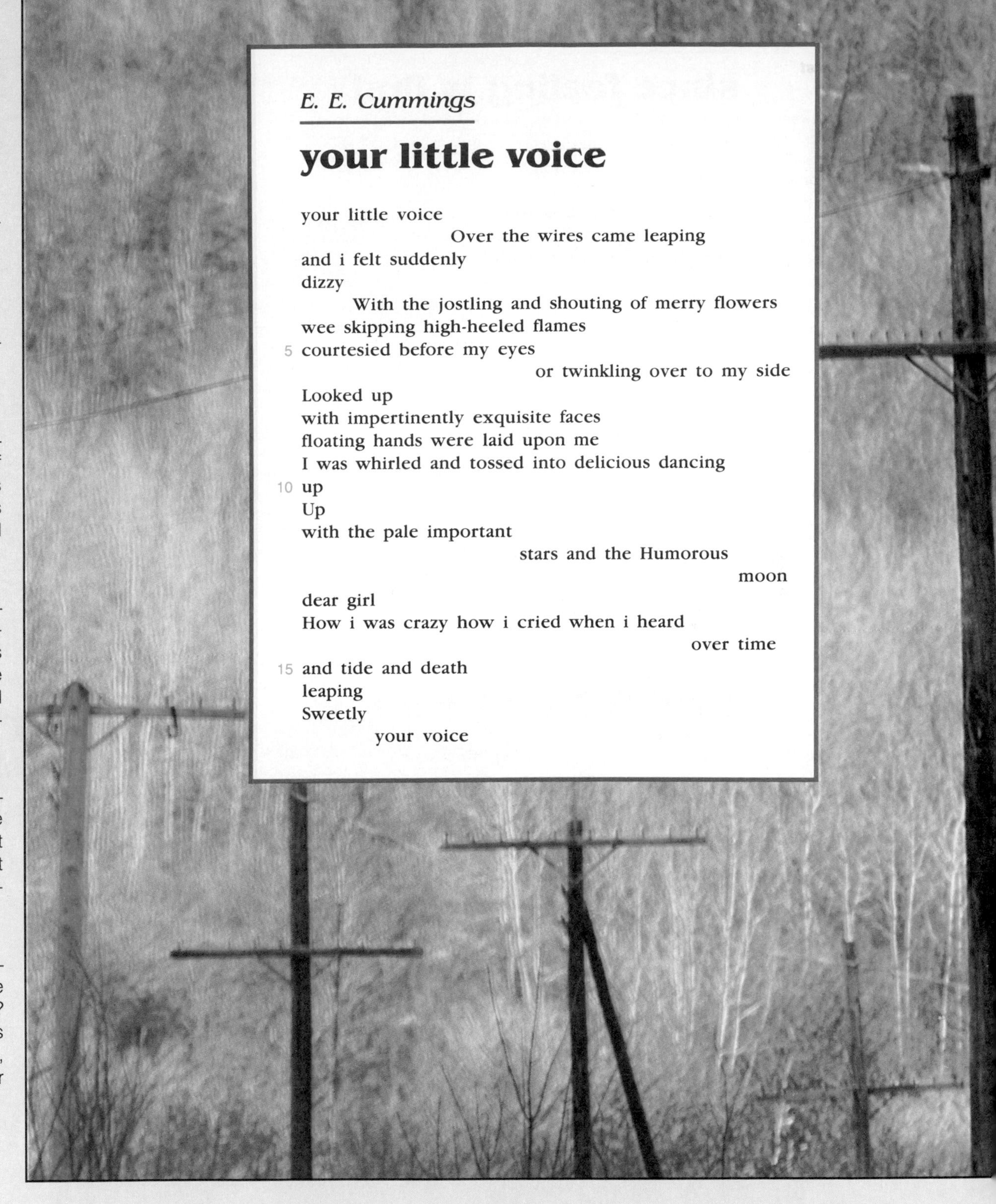

E. E. Cummings

your little voice

your little voice
Over the wires came leaping
and i felt suddenly
dizzy
With the jostling and shouting of merry flowers
wee skipping high-heeled flames
courtesied before my eyes
or twinkling over to my side
Looked up
with impertinently exquisite faces
floating hands were laid upon me
I was whirled and tossed into delicious dancing
up
Up
with the pale important
stars and the Humorous
moon
dear girl
How i was crazy how i cried when i heard
over time
and tide and death
leaping
Sweetly
your voice

STUDY QUESTIONS

since feeling is first

Recalling

1. What will a person "who pays attention to the syntax of things" never do?
2. Of what does the speaker's "blood" approve? What is a better fate than wisdom?
3. What is more than the "best gesture" of the speaker's brain? What does the flutter of the lady's eyelids say?
4. Why should the lady laugh?

Interpreting

5. With what is "syntax" contrasted? What does it represent? With what is "wisdom" contrasted? What is the relationship between the flutter of the lady's eyelids and "feeling"?
6. Basically, what is the speaker saying to the reader? To the lady?

r-p-o-p-h-e-s-s-a-g-r

Interpreting

1. How does the overall shape of the poem relate to its subject?
2. Why are the letters in the words jumbled?

your little voice

Recalling

1. Over what does the "dear girl's" voice come leaping in the first line? How does the speaker suddenly feel when the voice comes leaping?
2. Identify at least three images that the speaker associates with his dizziness.
3. Over what does the "dear girl's" little voice come leaping in the last five lines?

Interpreting

4. What ordinary experience of modern life does the poem make extraordinary?
5. How does the speaker feel about the "dear girl"?

Extending

6. What aspect of each of Cummings' poems makes it original and refreshing?

LITERARY FOCUS

The Shape of Poems

E. E. Cummings was among the first generation of poets who composed on the typewriter, and this instrument had a strong influence on his work. Poets composing on the typewriter found that they could visualize ways of spacing their lines and words that they would not have considered if their manuscripts were handwritten.

"r-p-o-p-h-e-s-s-a-g-r" is a classic example of a poem that is basically visual. It cannot be read aloud; its attempt is to capture, through word juggling, strange spacing, and surprising punctuation, the effect of a grasshopper gathering, leaping, and rearranging itself. The shape of the poem is a large part of its meaning.

In "The Artist" (page 423) William Carlos Williams also considers the shape of his poem on the printed page. The lines are divided into three groups of words of approximately the same lengths so that each line makes visual the dance step performed by Mr. T. with its final, abrupt end. The shape reflects the meaning.

Since playing with the shape of a poem was another means of breaking with the traditional conventions of stanza and meter, the practice became popular with many Modernist poets. As time passed, however, these visual games began to be less and less surprising.

Thinking About the Shape of Poems

■ How does the shape of "your little voice" reflect the content of the poem? Why does "up" appear as the only word on line 10 and line 11? Why is the second "up" capitalized?

COMPOSITION

Writing a Paraphrase

■ Rewrite the three poems by Cummings in prose paragraph form, using conventional English. Use correct punctuation, capitalization, and spellings, and add or change words for clarity where necessary. Conclude by telling what you think the poems gain and what they lose in paraphrases.

Writing a Poem with Shape

■ Choose an object or a creature that has a characteristic motion, and write a poem in which you capture that motion by playing with words and their visual appearance on the page, as "r-p-o-p-h-e-s-s-a-g-r" does. If a typewriter is unavailable, print your poem so that the spacing is clear. You might write about a basketball, a diver, a toaster, or a kangaroo.

STUDY QUESTIONS

since feeling is first

1. wholly kiss you
2. being a fool in spring; kisses
3. ■ eyelids' flutter
   ■ "We are for each other."
4. Life is not a paragraph, and death is not a parenthesis.
5. ■ feeling; imposed reason, order; kisses
   ■ Any action produces feeling, which is greater than thought.
6. asserting primacy of feeling; same thing plus "I love you"

r-p-o-p-h-e-s-s-a-g-r

1. reflects changing shape of grasshopper as it leaps
2. word-painting of action

your little voice

1. wires; dizzy
2. merry flowers, high-heeled flames, delicious dancing
3. "over time / and tide and death"
4. a telephone conversation
5. He loves her.
6. typography; transformation of ordinary experiences

LITERARY FOCUS

in lines and sentences deliberately broken up, suggesting confused and exhilarated emotions; to emphasize sensation of floating; suggests speaker is "up" to a greater degree

COMPOSITION: GUIDELINES FOR EVALUATION

WRITING A PARAPHRASE

Objective

To rewrite a poem using conventional prose

Guidelines for Evaluation

- suggested length: one paragraph per poem
- should use standard English sentences
- should comment on what each poem gains and loses in paraphrase

WRITING A POEM WITH SHAPE

Objective

To write a poem in which shape reflects content

Guidelines for Evaluation

- suggested length: four to fifteen lines
- should describe in words the movement of an object or a creature
- should experiment with spacing and line breaks to suggest visually the content of the poem

© Rollie McKenna

Wallace Stevens *1879–1955*

Stevens wrote, "The greatest poverty is not to live in a physical world." As a poet Stevens never stopped emphasizing the relationship between the concrete, physical world and the shaping power of the human imagination. He spent a lifetime putting into words the joy that comes from looking at "things as they are" and thinking about them.

Stevens was born in Pennsylvania and attended Harvard before moving to New York City, where he attended law school. In New York he mingled with other young writers, among them William Carlos Williams and Marianne Moore. His poems began to appear in magazines in 1914. Two years later Stevens and his wife moved to Hartford, Connecticut, where he worked as a lawyer; eventually he became vice-president of a large insurance company. He wrote his poetry on evenings and weekends, just as his friend Williams wrote after a busy day as a family doctor.

For most of his life Stevens drew a line, he said, between poetry and business. He kept his comfortable life quite uneventful, especially as compared to the lives of contemporary poets who fought in wars, sailed the oceans, and lived in Paris and Greenwich Village. On the other hand, his imaginative life was full: He wrote poems overflowing with ideas, striking images, and brilliant colors that moved him into the ranks of Pound, Eliot, and Frost as one of America's major poets.

Stevens' first volume, *Harmonium,* attracted little attention when it was published in 1923. So great, however, was his reputation among some poets and critics that *Harmonium* was republished in 1931. He did not publish again for more than a decade, but he then began to produce a lush and maturing body of work in *Ideas of Order* (1935), *The Man with the Blue Guitar* (1937), *Parts of a World* (1942), *Transport to Summer* (1947), and *The Auroras of Autumn* (1950). In his later years he began to break down the line between poetry and business, making some public appearances and receiving the honors of a younger generation who had grown up reading Stevens' verse and who had come to see him as a poetic "ancestor."

Living, as Stevens saw it, means to transform reality—what we experience "as and where we live"—by the power of the imagination. His early poems show the imagination in action, changing ordinary subjects into exotic, witty, and elegant lyrics. As he grew in poetic mastery, his poems became more philosophical, taking up the great subjects that Emerson, Whitman, and Dickinson also dealt with: nature, death, joy, the real and the ideal. He explored ways of thinking about reality so that we might find happiness within it, reconciling ourselves to the world we live in.

"The Load of Sugar Cane" offers a scene that would be an everyday experience to the unimaginative vision but one that becomes a bright and magical pleasure as Stevens presents and transforms it. "Anecdote of the Jar" also demonstrates the imagination at work, shaping the world around it.

- A poet looks at the ordinary and sees it in an unusual way. How does Stevens do that?

Wallace Stevens

The Load of Sugar Cane

The going of the glade boat[1]
Is like water flowing;

Like water flowing
Through the green saw grass,
Under the rainbows;

Under the rainbows
That are like birds,
Turning, bedizened,[2]

While the wind still whistles
As kildeer[3] do,

When they rise
At the red turban
Of the boatman.

---

1. **glade boat:** boat specially constructed for gliding through swampland.
2. **bedizened** [bi dī′ zənd]: brilliantly dressed or decorated.
3. **kildeer:** small wading birds with piercing cries.

AT A GLANCE

- The poet describes a swamp boat with sugar cane.
- He focuses on the motion and colors of the scene.

LITERARY OPTIONS

- Imagism
- simile

THEMATIC OPTIONS

- the universality of beauty
- the power of the imagination

IMAGISM

In true Imagistic spirit the poet turns the experience into a series of intense images.

SIMILE

The poet encloses one simile within another. The passage of the boat is like flowing water under the rainbows (ll. 1–6), but the rainbows are themselves like birds (ll. 7–13). He thereby suggests the way the imagination builds and builds again upon reality.

MAIN IDEA

The poem demonstrates how the ordinary beauty of the physical world can be intensified by the workings of the imagination.

REFLECTING ON THE POEM

How does the repetition of "under the rainbows" contribute to the appreciation of this poem? (Some may find that it transforms the swamp water into a kaleidoscope.)

AT A GLANCE

- The speaker sets a jar on a hill in Tennessee.
- The jar transforms the wilderness around it, but it itself remains lifeless.

LITERARY OPTIONS

- metaphor
- meter

THEMATIC OPTIONS

- artifice and nature
- the quest for order

METAPHOR

The poem is an extended metaphor. The jar represents the poet's imagination, and the hill is the world. Even as the jar transformed the Tennessee woods, so the imagination can transform any reality in the world.

METER

The simple iambic meter of the poem suggests a clear-cut comparison between human artifice (the jar) and the natural world (the hill).

REFLECTING ON THE POEM

In what sense is the jar positive? In what sense is it negative? (The jar's imposition of order is positive; its lifelessness seems negative.)

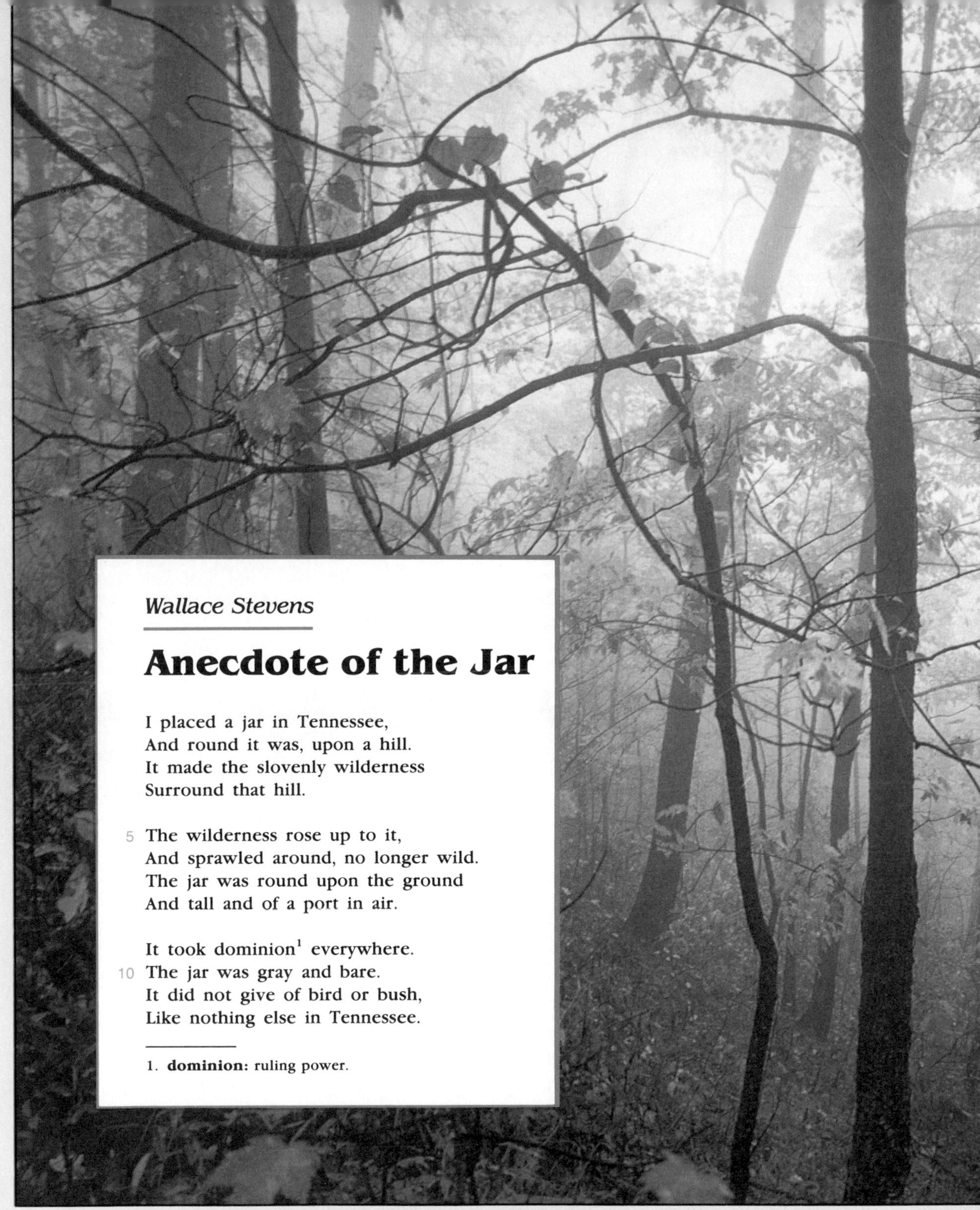

Wallace Stevens

Anecdote of the Jar

I placed a jar in Tennessee,
And round it was, upon a hill.
It made the slovenly wilderness
Surround that hill.

The wilderness rose up to it,
And sprawled around, no longer wild.
The jar was round upon the ground
And tall and of a port in air.

It took dominion[1] everywhere.
The jar was gray and bare.
It did not give of bird or bush,
Like nothing else in Tennessee.

1. **dominion:** ruling power.

STUDY QUESTIONS

The Load of Sugar Cane

Recalling

1. To what is the going of the glade boat likened?
2. Where does the water flow?
3. To what are the rainbows compared?
4. When do the birds turn? In what way does the wind whistle?
5. When do the kildeer whistle? At what do they rise?

Interpreting

6. Consider your answers for questions 1–5, and tell what the "events" in the poem form. That is, where does the poem begin; where does it move to in lines 2–5 and then in lines 6–10; where does the poem end?
7. What poetic devices contribute to the musical effect of this poem?

Anecdote of the Jar

Recalling

1. What shape is the jar? Where does the speaker place it?
2. According to the second stanza, what happens to the wilderness around the jar?
3. What does the jar "take" everywhere? Of what does it "not give"?

Interpreting

4. Explain in your own words the effect of the jar on the Tennessee wilderness. Does its effect seem positive in the first two stanzas? In the third? Why is *jar* an appropriate word?
5. How is a jar different from the wilderness? What might the jar represent?

Extending

6. Do you think ambiguity makes a poem more memorable? More effective? What do you think Marianne Moore (page 452) would have said about this poem?

VIEWPOINT

Lucy Beckett writes that the first lines of Stevens' "Anecdote of the Jar"

> define lightly but as well as any he ever wrote Stevens' hope for poetry, his belief that through it the slovenly wilderness of the modern world can be made, for however transient a time, to yield modern man something that will satisfy his need.
>
> —*Wallace Stevens*

■ Tell in your own words what need it is that the poem attempts to satisfy. Describe how poetry and all the arts attempt to meet that need.

COMPOSITION

Writing About Poetry

■ In a brief essay discuss the use of colors in "The Load of Sugar Cane." First describe the picture the poet tries to paint. Then tell how the colors blend and contrast. Conclude with a statement about the visual impression the poem leaves on the reader.

Writing a Description

■ Write a paragraph or a short poem describing an object or a scene. Use colors to give your reader a vivid impression of what you see. You may want to blend colors, contrast them, or even invent new names for some unusual colors.

STUDY QUESTIONS

The Load of Sugar Cane

1. like water flowing
2. through the green saw grass
3. birds turning, bedizened
4. while wind whistles; as kildeer
5. when rising; sight of red turban
6. ■ begins with the going of the boat and forms a circle of images that ends with the boatman
   ■ moves as boat moves, through saw grass, under rainbows which remind the poet of birds
   ■ Birds bring to mind the kildeer, rising at the color in the boatman's turban.
7. assonance, alliteration, repetition

Anecdote of the Jar

1. round; on a hill in Tennessee
2. It becomes no longer wild.
3. dominion; bird or bush
4. Jar creates positive order in wilderness; in third stanza effect is modified because it does not produce life; *jar* creates ambiguity: verb or simple word like the object.
5. made object, container; formal, ordered creation of culture
6. Answers will vary. Students should note deliberate ambiguity. Moore might have liked the way the poem puts an imaginary jar in the real wilderness.

VIEWPOINT

The jar as culture is the binding, humanizing force in our lives. Art strives to satisfy our need for order, our need to control the reality in which we live.

COMPOSITION: GUIDELINES FOR EVALUATION

WRITING ABOUT POETRY

Objective

To write about poetry

Guidelines for Evaluation

- suggested length: four to six paragraphs
- should offer general description of scene in poem
- should enumerate stated and implied colors
- should relate how colors blend within the slow-moving meter of the poem

WRITING A DESCRIPTION

Objective

To use color in writing

Guidelines for Evaluation

- suggested length: one paragraph or ten lines
- should describe an object or a scene using vivid colors
- should blend, compare, contrast, or invent colors

Robert Frost *1874–1963*

Robert Frost—a poet of dignity, simplicity, and ambiguity—has proved to be one of the most popular American poets of the twentieth century. A four-time winner of the Pulitzer Prize, Frost received special recognition by Congress in 1960 and the following January, at age eighty-six, had the honor of reciting at President John F. Kennedy's inauguration.

Frost was born in San Francisco but in early youth returned with his family to the area of the country with which he is closely associated—New England. His mother, who wrote poetry herself, introduced him to the works of the English Romantic writers, the New England Transcendentalists, and the poets of her native Scotland. After briefly attending Dartmouth and Harvard colleges and working as a journalist and a schoolteacher, Frost purchased a farm in New Hampshire. Here, between farm chores, he began his career as a poet.

Frost wrote not only of the natural world but also of his struggle to raise a family against a backdrop of financial hardship and of the bleak bouts of depression that would assail him all his life. In 1912, unable to get his poems published in America, he sold his farm and took his family to England.

In London Frost became acquainted with Ezra Pound and his associates, and he was able to publish his first volume, *A Boy's Will,* in 1913. Another volume, *North of Boston,* followed soon after. Through the influence of Pound and other critics, Frost became known on this side of the Atlantic, so that, by the time he returned to America in 1915, he was well on the road to fame.

Despite the debt of gratitude he owed Pound and the Modernists, Frost never subscribed to all the tenets of Modernism. To be sure, he was familiar with the ideas of William James and other modern psychologists, but he was equally familiar with the works of William Cullen Bryant, Ralph Waldo Emerson, and other nineteenth-century masters. In Frost's work we find traces of the Romantic love of nature that marked the literature of the nineteenth century coupled with a modern sense of irony. We find in Frost's poems some of Thoreau's love of isolation, Hawthorne's dark vision, Longfellow's traditional craftsmanship, Dickinson's dry humor, and Robinson's realistic characterization.

Eclectic in many ways, Frost is nevertheless able to achieve a quiet, reflective New England voice all his own. He speaks a common speech, unaffected, a modern Plain Style.

- If every poem is a voyage of discovery, how does Frost steer us on that voyage? What do we discover?

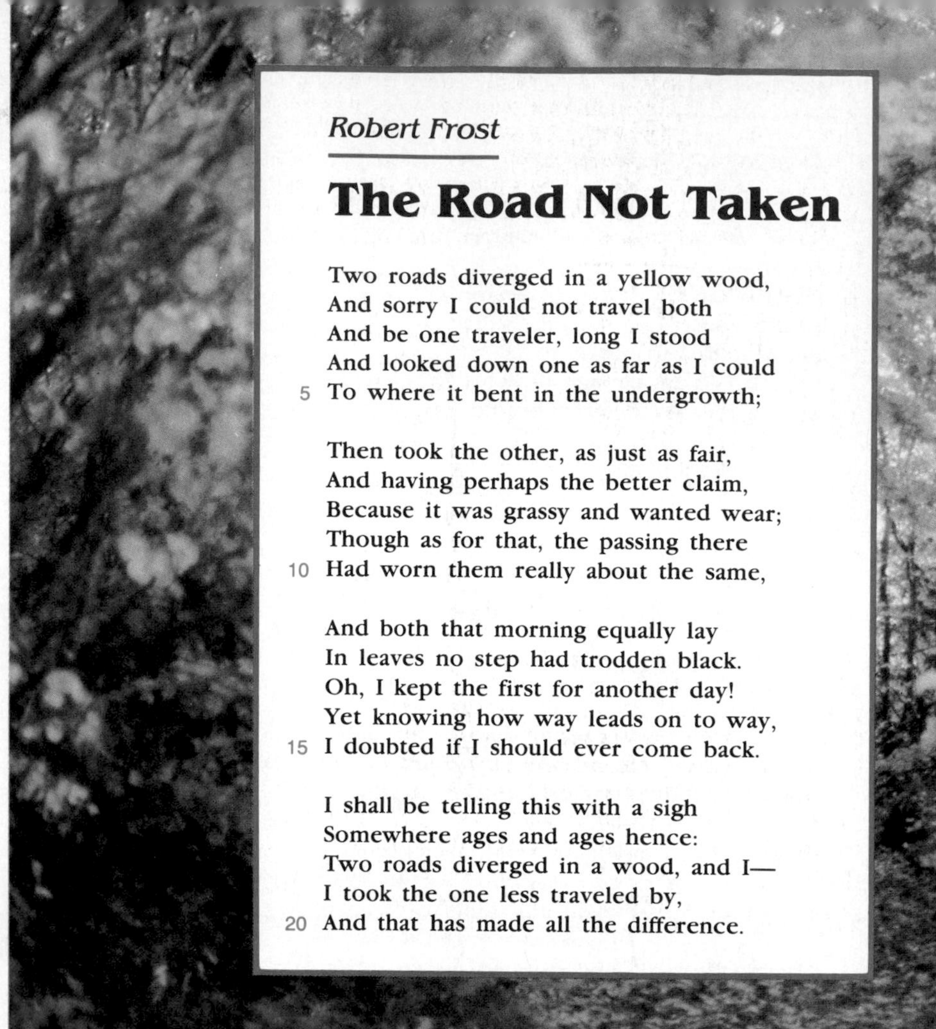

Robert Frost

The Road Not Taken

Two roads diverged in a yellow wood,
And sorry I could not travel both
And be one traveler, long I stood
And looked down one as far as I could
To where it bent in the undergrowth;

Then took the other, as just as fair,
And having perhaps the better claim,
Because it was grassy and wanted wear;
Though as for that, the passing there
Had worn them really about the same,

And both that morning equally lay
In leaves no step had trodden black.
Oh, I kept the first for another day!
Yet knowing how way leads on to way,
I doubted if I should ever come back.

I shall be telling this with a sigh
Somewhere ages and ages hence:
Two roads diverged in a wood, and I—
I took the one less traveled by,
And that has made all the difference.

STUDY QUESTIONS

Recalling

1. What diverged in the yellow wood? About what was the speaker sorry in the first stanza? Where does the speaker stand and look?
2. According to line 8, why did the second road have the better claim?
3. For what did the speaker "keep" the first road? What did he doubt?
4. How does the speaker think he will be telling this story "ages and ages hence"? What has "made all the difference"?

Interpreting

5. Considering lines 9–10 and 11–12, how different were the two roads? What is Frost therefore saying?
6. What might the roads represent? What does his choice indicate about the speaker?
7. Does the speaker think he made the wrong choice? Why or why not? How is his attitude related to the title?

Extending

8. Suggest other dilemmas comparable to the speaker's.

AT A GLANCE

- The poet comes to a fork in the road and chooses the path less worn. His choice made a difference in his life.

LITERARY OPTIONS

- rhyme
- symbol

THEMATIC OPTIONS

- the power of choice
- the mystery of the future

RHYME

The rhyme scheme—*abaab*—focuses the reader's attention on the last line of each stanza and, by extension, on the end of the poem.

SYMBOL

The road is a symbol for life. The fork is any choice, and the poet has chosen the unconventional. Yet he says that the difference is not in the road itself (ll. 8–12) but in how he feels about his choice.

REFLECTING ON THE POEM

Does the speaker feel that he made the "right" choice? (Ultimately the two roads seem equally "right"; the speaker simply knows that his choice made a difference.)

STUDY QUESTIONS

1. two roads; that he could not take both roads; looked down one
2. "it was grassy and wanted wear"
3. another day; that he would come back and take that road
4. with a sigh; that he took the less traveled road
5. One had been well traveled; the other, less so; neither had been traveled recently.
6. choices made about one's life; takes on challenges, chooses life of poet
7. There is ambiguity. The last line is an affirmation, but the title and sigh indicate doubts.
8. Answers will vary but could include marriage, professional choices, or any irrevocable decision.

LITERARY OPTIONS

- metaphor
- symbol
- sonnet

THEMATIC OPTIONS

- the power of love and hate
- isolation and loneliness

"FIRE AND ICE": METAPHOR

The poet metaphorically equates fire to desire and ice to hate. Either emotion is destructive enough to end the world.

"NIGHT": SYMBOL

The poet uses the night as a symbol for loneliness and isolation. He does not acknowledge the watchman (l. 5), nor does he respond to the cries from a distant street (l. 10).

"NIGHT": SONNET

Although the rhyme scheme is unconventional, this poem is a sonnet. However, it does not break into the traditional parts of a sonnet. Rather, it depicts variations on a single theme, loneliness.

REFLECTING ON THE POEMS

Imagine "Fire and Ice" as a kind of emotional thermometer. Where would you place the speaker of "Acquainted with the Night" on this thermometer? (The speaker seems equally detached from both desire and hate; he seems to be in some neutral zone.)

Robert Frost

Fire and Ice

Some say the world will end in fire,
Some say in ice.
From what I've tasted of desire
I hold with those who favor fire.
But if it had to perish twice,
I think I know enough of hate
To say that for destruction ice
Is also great
And would suffice.

Acquainted with the Night

I have been one acquainted with the night.
I have walked out in rain—and back in rain.
I have outwalked the furthest city light.

I have looked down the saddest city lane.
I have passed by the watchman on his beat
And dropped my eyes, unwilling to explain.

I have stood still and stopped the sound of feet
When far away an interrupted cry
Came over houses from another street,

But not to call me back or say good-by;
And further still at an unearthly height
One luminary clock against the sky

Proclaimed the time was neither wrong nor right.
I have been one acquainted with the night.

Nothing Gold Can Stay

Nature's first green is gold,
Her hardest hue to hold.
Her early leaf's a flower;
But only so an hour.
Then leaf subsides to leaf.
So Eden sank to grief,
So dawn goes down to day.
Nothing gold can stay.

STUDY QUESTIONS

Fire and Ice

Recalling

1. What are the two things "some say" the world will end in, according to the speaker?
2. What emotion does the speaker associate with each element that could end the world?

Interpreting

3. What does the poet suggest that the two emotions have in common?
4. What other kinds of destruction besides destruction of the world might the poem be about?
5. Is this poem written in free verse? Explain.

Acquainted with the Night

Recalling

1. When and where has the speaker walked in lines 1–3? What has he seen in line 4? What has he heard in lines 7–10?
2. What did the clock proclaim?

Interpreting

3. What is the night in this poem like? What does line 13 tell you about the speaker's mood on the night being described?
4. What might the speaker mean in a larger sense by "night"?
5. What effect or meaning does Frost achieve by repeating line 1 as line 14?

Extending

6. Compare the speaker of this poem with J. Alfred Prufrock (page 415).

Nothing Gold Can Stay

Recalling

1. According to the poem, what happens to "nature's first green"? To "her early leaf"? To Eden? To dawn?

Interpreting

2. To what might "green" and "gold" in line 1 refer?
3. What do Eden, dawn, and a flower have in common? What might "gold" therefore represent in the poem as a whole?
4. In light of your interpretation of "gold" in question 3, explain the possible meanings of the title and last line of this poem.

Extending

5. Do you agree with the ideas suggested in this poem? Why or why not?

LITERARY OPTIONS

- metaphor
- rhyme

THEMATIC OPTIONS

- the transience of beauty
- innocence and wisdom

METAPHOR

Nature's beauty is "gold" only in the brief preciousness of its life and in the lasting treasury of human memory.

ALLUSION

The poet stretches the meaning of the poem to include the innocence found and lost in Eden (l. 6). In this single line the poem moves from natural phenomena to the realm of morality and human experience.

RHYME

The poet uses rhyming couplets to outline his thoughts, creating an impression of simplicity and clarity.

REFLECTING ON THE POEM

Does this poem suggest that innocence is better than wisdom? (By metaphorically equating it to "gold," Frost implies that innocence is somehow more beautiful than wisdom.)

STUDY QUESTIONS

Fire and Ice

1. fire and ice
2. fire: desire; ice: hate
3. Both are destructive.
4. human personality, relations
5. no, regular iambic lines

Acquainted with the Night

1. in rain, past city limits; saddest city lane; cry
2. time neither wrong nor right
3. lonely, sad, rainy; feels outside society
4. darkness of soul, thirteenth hour when time stands still
5. reiterates implications of his journey: a return to start with no progress made
6. Both wander on gloomy nights, confused and besieged by doubts.

Nothing Gold Can Stay

1. hardest hue to hold; subsides; sank to grief; goes down to day
2. dawn
3. do not endure; ephemeral, precious nature of beauty
4. Beauty cannot last.
5. Answers will vary. Students might agree that beauty does not last.

Robert Frost

Stopping by Woods on a Snowy Evening

Whose woods these are I think I know.
His house is in the village, though;
He will not see me stopping here
To watch his woods fill up with snow.

My little horse must think it queer
To stop without a farmhouse near
Between the woods and frozen lake
The darkest evening of the year.

He gives his harness bells a shake
To ask if there is some mistake.
The only other sound's the sweep
Of easy wind and downy flake.

The woods are lovely, dark, and deep,
But I have promises to keep,
And miles to go before I sleep,
And miles to go before I sleep.

STUDY QUESTIONS

Recalling

1. Where does the owner of the woods live? What will he not see, according to the first stanza?
2. According to the speaker, what must the horse think? According to the second stanza, when is the event in the poem taking place?
3. According to the final stanza, what must the speaker do before he sleeps? What does the speaker say he must keep?

Interpreting

4. What causes the speaker to stop?
5. What do the owner and the horse have in common? How do they differ from the speaker?
6. Why does the speaker leave the woods? Does he regret leaving?
7. What might the incident in the woods represent? What might lines 15–16, especially "sleep," mean?
8. Describe the rhyme scheme of the poem. How is the poem "knit" to a close?

AT A GLANCE

- The speaker stops by the woods on a snowy evening.
- The woods attract the speaker, but he can stay no longer.

LITERARY OPTIONS

- rhyme
- symbol

THEMATIC OPTIONS

- solitude vs. society
- life and death

RHYME

The rhyme scheme is *aaba* / *bbcb* / *ccdc* / *dddd*. By locking the last few lines into the same rhyme and repeating the final two lines, the poet draws the reader to the most important idea in the poem: "And miles to go before I sleep."

MAIN IDEA

The main idea is found in lines 13–16. Although the woods may symbolize solitude, quiet, or even death, the poet has many things to do and many places to go before he can fully embrace this peaceful escape.

REFLECTING ON THE POEM

Why do you think this is a much-loved poem? (Students may see that it captures a modern person's need to find an unencumbered place. They also may find *And miles to go before I sleep* a very evocative line.)

STUDY QUESTIONS

1. village; speaker stopping
2. queer to stop; darkest evening of the year
3. go miles; promises
4. watch snow falling; stay within moment to forget commitments
5. do not take pleasure in stopping by the woods; more practical
6. has promises to keep; yes
7. impulse to rest from commitments; death, easing of heavy load
8.
   - *aaba bbcb ccdc dddd*
   - The poem is a chain-link form in which each stanza's third line hooks into the next stanza; the final repetition ends the use of hooks and reinforces the final line.

Desert Places

Snow falling and night falling fast, oh, fast
In a field I looked into going past,
And the ground almost covered smooth in snow,
But a few weeds and stubble showing last.

The woods around it have it—it is theirs.
All animals are smothered in their lairs.
I am too absent-spirited to count;
The loneliness includes me unawares.

And lonely as it is, that loneliness
Will be more lonely ere it will be less—
A blanker whiteness of benighted[1] snow
With no expression, nothing to express.

They cannot scare me with their empty spaces
Between stars—on stars where no human race is.
I have it in me so much nearer home
To scare myself with my own desert places.

1. **benighted:** surrounded by darkness.

STUDY QUESTIONS

Recalling

1. What does the speaker see in lines 1–4 of the poem?
2. What mood, created by the scene, affects the speaker, too, in lines 5–8?
3. Once in this mood, what does the speaker claim the future will bring, according to lines 9–12?
4. What does the speaker admit about the stars in lines 13–14?

Interpreting

5. Would you characterize the snow scene as a negative or a positive picture? Why?
6. How do you explain the jump to a discussion of stars in lines 13–14? How would you characterize the speaker of the poem?

Extending

7. How are the experiences described in this poem and in "Stopping by Woods on a Snowy Evening" alike? How are the moods created by these experiences different? How would Emerson (page 159) explain this difference?

AT A GLANCE

- The speaker feels the loneliness of a snowstorm.
- He finds that the loneliness within himself is the greatest "desert place" he knows.

LITERARY OPTIONS

- imagery
- repetition

THEMATIC OPTIONS

- the immensity of the universe
- the emptiness of a human soul

REPETITION

The repetition of *lonely* and *loneliness* reverberates throughout the poem.

IMAGERY

The build of images from a barren landscape to a barren cosmos prepares the reader to accept the enormity of the poet's conclusions about himself.

REFLECTING ON THE POEM

Which poem do you find more appealing—"Desert Places" or "Stopping by Woods on a Snowy Evening" (p. 468)? Explain your answer. (Most students probably will prefer the latter poem because of its simpler language and more memorable lines.)

STUDY QUESTIONS

1. snow falling, night falling, field, weeds, stubble
2. Thinking of animals smothered in lairs, he feels like a lonely outsider.
3. He will become more lonely.
4. will not be scared by the greater emptiness of stars where no humans live
5. Negative; animals are "smothered," words *lonely* and *loneliness* are repeated.
6.
- The speaker feels excluded from the human race and nature.
- frightened by unsheltering universe, partly responsible for own alienation

7.
- *Alike:* sense of isolation and loneliness, use of winter-night image
- *Different:* In "Stopping" the poet is drawn by the woods but continues on; in "Desert" the theme is of loneliness and despair.
- *Emerson:* important to be true to oneself, not to fear contradiction, to feel the changes of experience

AT A GLANCE

- The speaker notes that some force seems to undermine walls.
- Each spring he and his neighbor walk along the wall between their properties and replace the stones.

LITERARY OPTIONS

- blank verse
- symbol
- characterization

THEMATIC OPTIONS

- individualism vs. society
- reason vs. superstition

SPEAKER

The speaker's reasonableness and ability to observe the natural world are contrasted with his neighbor's response to the wall.

SYMBOL

The wall is a symbol for anything that separates people. This symbolic use of the wall is especially apparent as the neighbors walk along together, keeping the wall between them. They are worlds apart (ll. 12–15).

BLANK VERSE

The blank-verse lines do not rhyme, but they generally have a regular beat and consistent length. Blank verse enables Frost to create a conversational reflective tone.

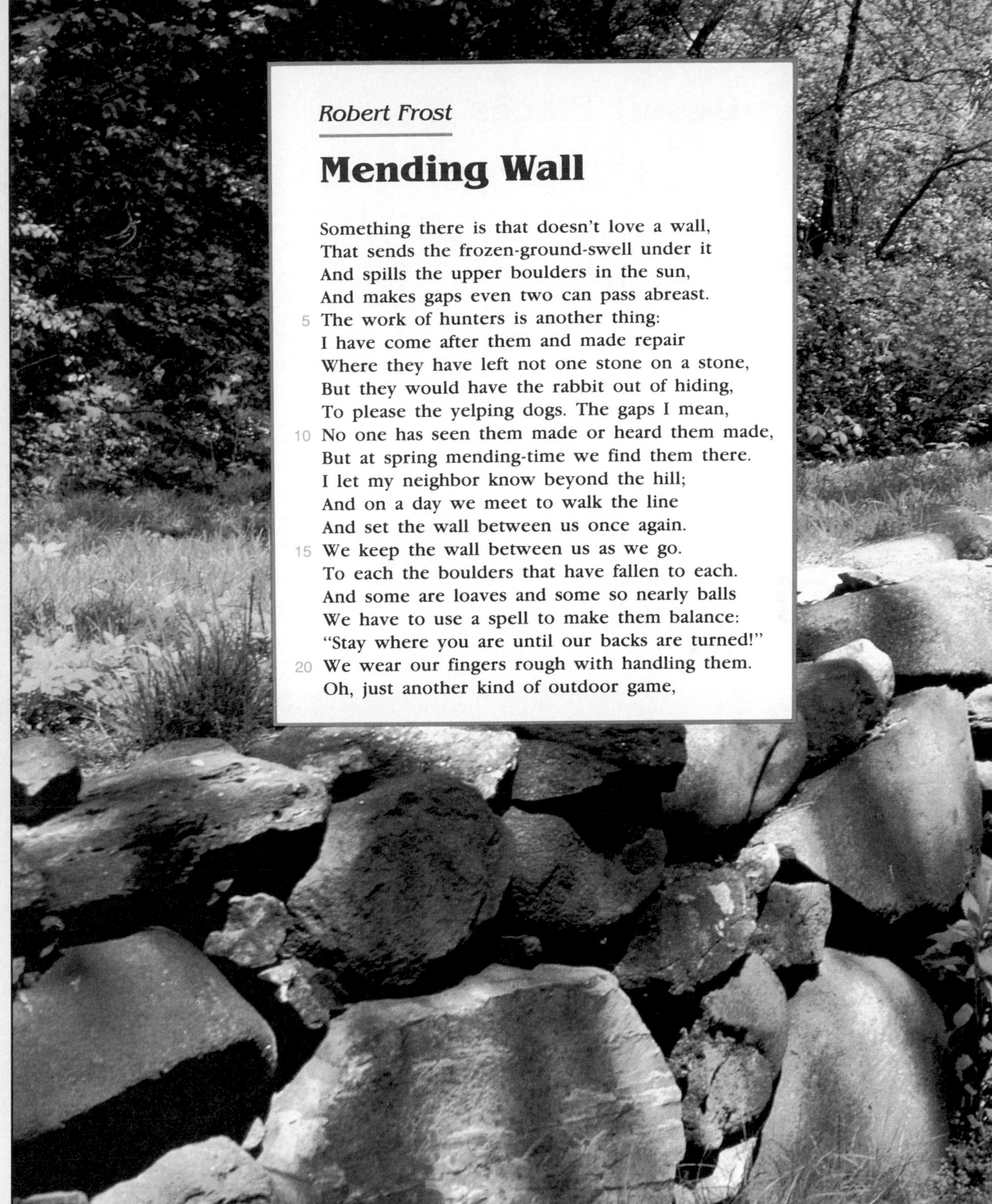

Robert Frost

Mending Wall

Something there is that doesn't love a wall,
That sends the frozen-ground-swell under it
And spills the upper boulders in the sun,
And makes gaps even two can pass abreast.
The work of hunters is another thing:
I have come after them and made repair
Where they have left not one stone on a stone,
But they would have the rabbit out of hiding,
To please the yelping dogs. The gaps I mean,
No one has seen them made or heard them made,
But at spring mending-time we find them there.
I let my neighbor know beyond the hill;
And on a day we meet to walk the line
And set the wall between us once again.
We keep the wall between us as we go.
To each the boulders that have fallen to each.
And some are loaves and some so nearly balls
We have to use a spell to make them balance:
"Stay where you are until our backs are turned!"
We wear our fingers rough with handling them.
Oh, just another kind of outdoor game,

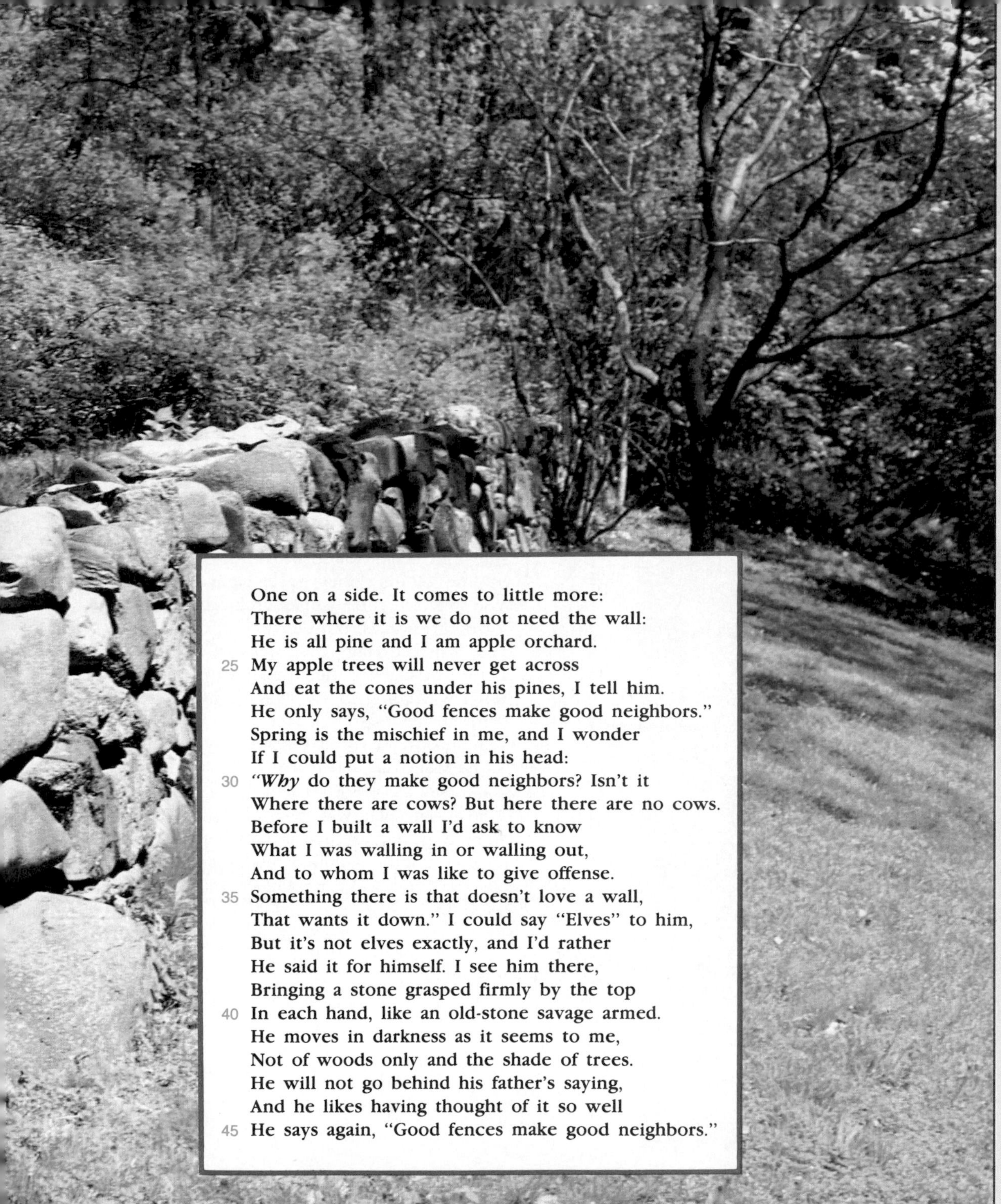

One on a side. It comes to little more:
There where it is we do not need the wall:
He is all pine and I am apple orchard.
My apple trees will never get across
And eat the cones under his pines, I tell him.
He only says, "Good fences make good neighbors."
Spring is the mischief in me, and I wonder
If I could put a notion in his head:
"*Why* do they make good neighbors? Isn't it
Where there are cows? But here there are no cows.
Before I built a wall I'd ask to know
What I was walling in or walling out,
And to whom I was like to give offense.
Something there is that doesn't love a wall,
That wants it down." I could say "Elves" to him,
But it's not elves exactly, and I'd rather
He said it for himself. I see him there,
Bringing a stone grasped firmly by the top
In each hand, like an old-stone savage armed.
He moves in darkness as it seems to me,
Not of woods only and the shade of trees.
He will not go behind his father's saying,
And he likes having thought of it so well
He says again, "Good fences make good neighbors."

AT A GLANCE

- The neighbor says, "Good fences make good neighbors."
- The neighbor cannot explain why; he just believes it, as his father did.

CHARACTERIZATION

The neighbor is described as a "savage" (l. 40). This description prepares the reader for the symbolic meaning of "darkness" in lines 41–42: ignorance, superstition, hostility.

RESPONSE JOURNAL

Have students flesh out the debate summed up in the lines *Something there is that does not love a wall* and *Good fences make good neighbors*.

MAIN IDEA

The speaker's awareness of nature's forces (ll. 1 and 35) contrasts with his neighbor's uncritical commitment to "good fences" (ll. 27 and 45). Perhaps that difference in perception explains why the neighbors are on different sides of the wall.

REFLECTING ON THE POEM

For what kind of person would the speaker probably agree that fences are necessary? (People like the neighbor—rather short-sighted and jealous of their privacy—probably need the fences for comfort.)

AT A GLANCE

- The speaker sees the bent birches draping themselves across the straighter trees.
- They are beautiful in ice storms, but they never recover.
- He would prefer that they were bent by a boy swinging in them.

LITERARY OPTIONS

- imagery
- main idea

THEMATIC OPTIONS

- oneness with nature
- escape from despair

IMAGERY

The sight and sounds of the birches being bedecked with and then stripped of ice are beautifully captured (ll. 7–13).

SIMILE

The simile of cascading hair provides a very accessible image, enabling the reader to visualize how the ice storm has permanently altered the birches (ll. 19–20).

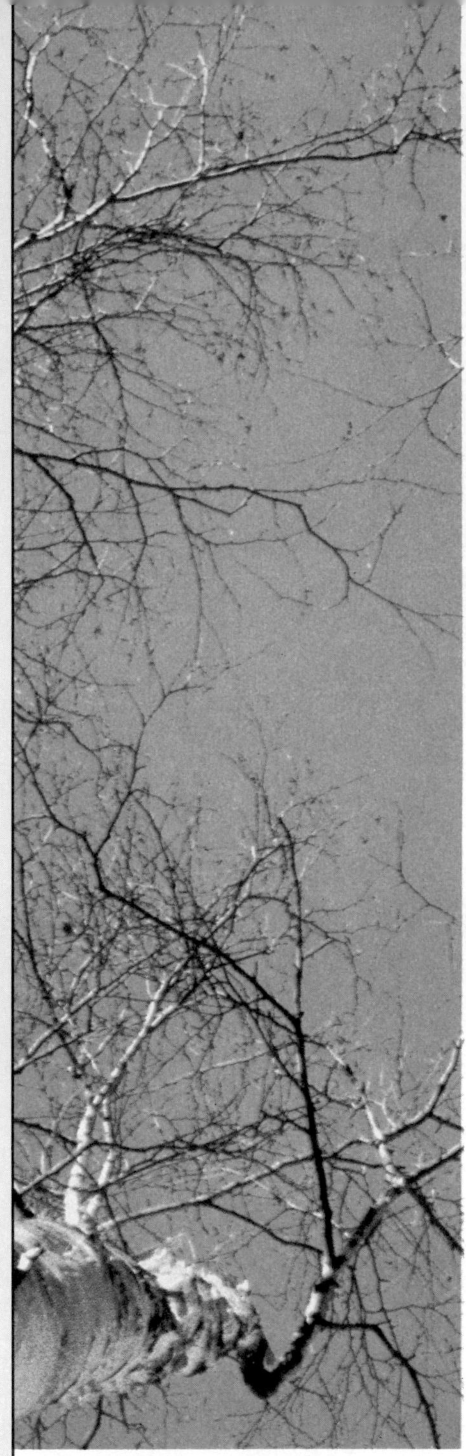

Robert Frost

Birches

When I see birches bend to left and right
Across the lines of straighter darker trees,
I like to think some boy's been swinging them.
But swinging doesn't bend them down to stay
As ice storms do. Often you must have seen them
Loaded with ice a sunny winter morning
After a rain. They click upon themselves
As the breeze rises, and turn many-colored
As the stir cracks and crazes their enamel.
Soon the sun's warmth makes them shed crystal shells
Shattering and avalanching on the snow crust—
Such heaps of broken glass to sweep away
You'd think the inner dome of heaven had fallen.
They are dragged to the withered bracken by the load,
And they seem not to break; though once they are bow
So low for long, they never right themselves:
You may see their trunks arching in the woods
Years afterwards, trailing their leaves on the ground
Like girls on hands and knees that throw their hair
Before them over their heads to dry in the sun.
But I was going to say when Truth broke in
With all her matter of fact about the ice storm,
I should prefer to have some boy bend them
As he went out and in to fetch the cows—
Some boy too far from town to learn baseball,
Whose only play was what he found himself,
Summer or winter, and could play alone.
One by one he subdued his father's trees

By riding them down over and over again
Until he took the stiffness out of them,
And not one but hung limp, not one was left
For him to conquer. He learned all there was
To learn about not launching out too soon
And so not carrying the tree away
Clear to the ground. He always kept his poise
To the top branches, climbing carefully
With the same pains you use to fill a cup
Up to the brim, and even above the brim.
Then he flung outward, feet first, with a swish,
Kicking his way down through the air to the ground.
So was I once myself a swinger of birches.
And so I dream of going back to be.
It's when I'm weary of considerations,
And life is too much like a pathless wood
Where your face burns and tickles with the cobwebs
Broken across it, and one eye is weeping
From a twig's having lashed across it open.
I'd like to get away from earth awhile
And then come back to it and begin over.
May no fate willfully misunderstand me
And half grant what I wish and snatch me away
Not to return. Earth's the right place for love:
I don't know where it's likely to go better.
I'd like to go by climbing a birch tree,
And climb black branches up a snow-white trunk
Toward heaven, till the tree could bear no more,
But dipped its top and set me down again.
That would be good both going and coming back.
One could do worse than be a swinger of birches.

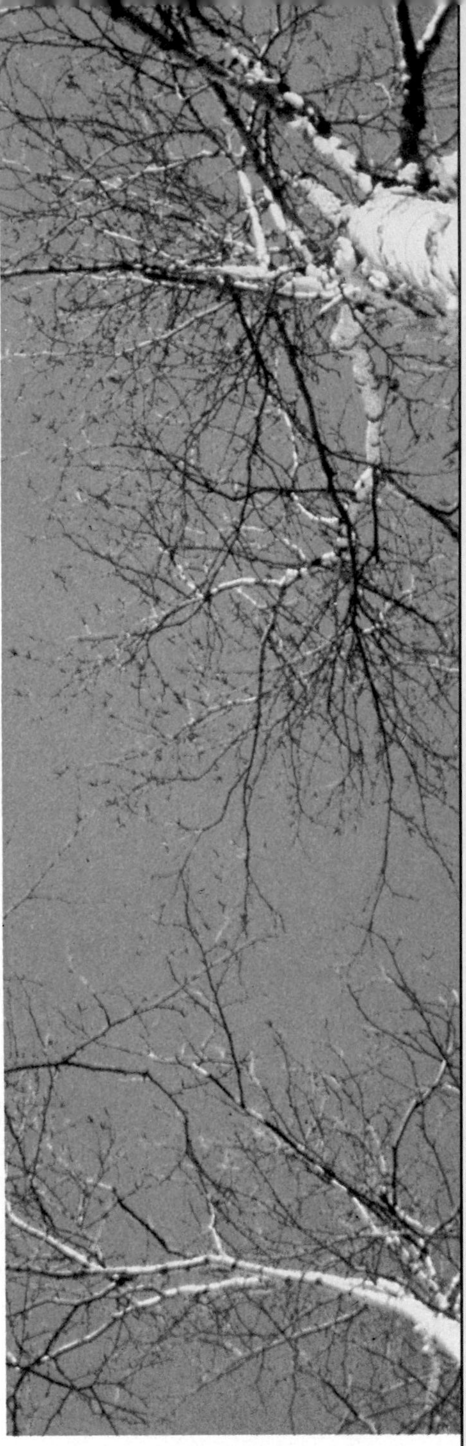

AT A GLANCE

- The speaker describes how boys bend birches by climbing them and then swinging down to earth.
- He says that he was once such a boy, and now, when difficulties come his way, he dreams of being one again.
- He would like to climb the tree toward heaven and then have it bow down and place him back on earth.

SIMILE

In keeping with the imagery of trees and nature, the poet compares life to a pathless wood (ll. 44–46).

MAIN IDEA

Swinging on the branches is a way of escaping life's psychological pressures (ll. 45–48), but just temporarily (ll. 50–51). For the poet, "Earth's the right place for love" (l. 52).

REFLECTING ON THE POEM

What does the poet mean when he says a person could "do worse than be a swinger of birches"? (Some students may suggest that the inability to experience childlike joy and the refusal to test one's limits are far worse.)

STUDY QUESTIONS

Mending Wall

1. wall continually falls down from frost; actions of hunters
2. each walks on own side replacing stones
3. divides pine and apple trees, which do not need a wall; no cows to keep in; "Good fences make good neighbors"
4. unthinking, lacks self-awareness
5. The speaker dislikes the wall and implies that nature is against it. He sees no reason for it, but he repairs it each year.

Birches

1. a swinging boy; ice storms
2. what he finds for himself in nature
3. returning to boyhood, being a "swinger of birches"; earth; take him seriously
4. heaven; set him down again
5. lonely, self-motivated; himself
6. When life gives me no rest or peace I would like to get away for a while; earth is the "right place for love."
7. learning the skill and discipline for living in world; forces of nature resist ascending beyond human capabilities
8.
   - allows thoughts and moods to be suggested by the natural world
   - *traditional:* standard rhyme schemes, stanza divisions, rhythmic patterns
   - *Romantic:* emphasis on nature and individual in content

VIEWPOINT

1.
   - the kind who shows the most unpleasant side of life and the kind who shows ordinary life
   - Answers will vary. He might have written less about nature and more about social or psychological problems.
2. Answers will vary. Students might agree that art gets to the core of life in its portrayal.

STUDY QUESTIONS

Mending Wall

Recalling

1. According to lines 1–9, what happens because "Something there is that doesn't love a wall"? What other kind of destruction to the wall, described in lines 5–9, is not as significant to the speaker?
2. Describe how the speaker and his neighbor go about fixing the wall at spring mending-time (lines 12–22).
3. According to the speaker in lines 24–36, why do he and his neighbor not need a wall? What does the neighbor say?

Interpreting

4. Describe the character of the neighbor as seen by the speaker.
5. Does the speaker definitely want the wall torn down? How do you know?

Birches

Recalling

1. According to lines 1–5, what does the speaker like to think has caused the birches to bend? What bends them "down to stay"?
2. According to lines 25–27, what is the "only play" of some boy "too far from town to learn baseball"?
3. Of what does the speaker dream, according to lines 41–42? From what would he like to get away for a while? What does he not want fate to do?
4. Toward what does the speaker want to climb? What does he want the tree to do when it can "bear no more"?

Interpreting

5. What sort of childhood does a boy who lives "too far from town to learn baseball" have? In describing the boy, whom is the speaker really describing?
6. Restate lines 43–48 in your own words, explaining why the speaker wants to get away from earth. According to lines 52–53, what is one reason he does *not* want to escape from earth?
7. What kinds of activities might swinging on birches represent? What might "could bear no more" signify?

Extending

8. What general statement, based on the poems you have read, can you make about Frost's relationship with nature? Explain how many of Frost's poems are traditional and Romantic in both form and content.

VIEWPOINT

Frost himself once wrote:

> There are two types of realist—the one who offers a good deal of dirt with his potato to show that it is a real one; and the one who is satisfied with the potato brushed clean. I'm inclined to be the second kind. . . . To me, the thing that art does for life is to strip it to form.
>
> —*Selected Prose of Robert Frost*

1. Explain in your own words the two types of realist Frost describes. How would Frost's poems be different if he were the first kind of realist?
2. Do you agree with Frost's statement about what art does? Why or why not?

LITERARY FOCUS

Tone

Tone in literature is the author's attitude. An author can demonstrate an attitude toward characters, toward subjects, and toward the reader.

Some tones are clearly defined and easy to notice, such as a humorous tone or an angry tone. Some tones are more complicated, reflecting a combination of emotions in the writer. An ironic tone, for example, can suggest that a writer is both sympathetic toward and critical of a character or a subject.

Tone is often crucial to understanding a poem or a story. It is sometimes necessary to read a passage several times, sometimes aloud, to try to hear the voice of the author and decide what tone is being conveyed. Mark Twain's stories, for example, convey much of their wry humor and irony only through the tone adopted by the author.

Robert Frost's tone undergoes many subtle changes from poem to poem. In "Birches" his tone seems serene and celebratory. In "Fire and Ice" he mixes his own brand of pessimism with a combination of objectivity and amusement.

Thinking About Tone

1. Describe in your own words the tone in any other of Frost's poems. Is the tone simple and clear, or does it seem to signal a combination of emotions in the poet?
2. Describe the tone in one poem by each of the following: Edwin Arlington Robinson (page 388), Ezra Pound (page 409), T. S. Eliot (page 414), and Wallace Stevens (page 460). Which tone seems most like the tone of a poem by Frost? Why?

COMPOSITION

Writing About Theme and Tone

■ Write a brief essay analyzing the relationship between the theme and the tone in one of Robert Frost's poems. Begin with a statement of the theme. Then describe the tone, and show how the tone supports or brings out the theme.

Writing a Description

■ Write a brief description in prose or poetry of some aspect of the natural world, using common speech as does Robert Frost. Keep your statements simple by reducing them to the clearest, most meaningful words that convey your ideas. You may choose to write about the weather, a storm, a season, or even the simplicity of the natural world itself.

COMPARING WRITERS

1. Try to find some common ground in Frost poems as different in content as "The Road Not Taken," "Stopping by Woods on a Snowy Evening," "Acquainted with the Night," "Mending Wall," and "Birches." As you answer, consider what these poems all seem to suggest about compromise and about moving on. Then compare Frost's message with the ideas of other poets of this period. Do any of the others also see the world as a confusing place?
2. Hughes, Ransom, MacLeish, Moore, Cummings, Stevens, and even Frost were all affected by the Imagists in one way or another. Which of their poems use modern free verse? Which poems make frequent use of images to capture emotions?

LITERARY FOCUS

1. Although Frost makes direct statements within a poem, a single emotional stance rarely rules the poem; ambiguity is always present to prevent the reader from making easy assumptions.
2. Students will probably find the Robinson poems, with their plain diction, irony, and understatement, most like Frost's.

COMPARING WRITERS

1. A common theme is compromise. The poet pauses on his journey; he regrets the road not taken; he wishes for a minute to be off the earth—but he stays here, completes his job, acknowledges commitments. Other poets find the world confusing, but their poems are involved with the world and people rather than with winter nights. The Imagists substitute fragments for things or people, but they too are celebrating something new.
2. The poems by Moore, Cummings, and Stevens are in free verse. Those poems and others all make frequent use of images to capture emotion.

COMPOSITION: GUIDELINES FOR EVALUATION

WRITING ABOUT THEME AND TONE

Objective

To analyze relationship between theme and tone

Guidelines for Evaluation

- suggested length: four to six paragraphs
- should identify the theme of the poem
- should cite the ambiguity of Frost's images within the plainness and simplicity of his diction

WRITING A DESCRIPTION

Objective

To describe an aspect of nature

Guidelines for Evaluation

- suggested length: one to two paragraphs, four to twelve lines
- should use concrete words with few adjectives and adverbs
- should use direct "common speech"

FICTION

Sherwood Anderson *1876–1941*

Sherwood Anderson's stories of American life reflect what he believed were the most important qualities for a modern writer: honesty, simplicity, and straightforwardness. Anderson grew up in Camden and Clyde, small Ohio towns much like the one he invented as the setting of his most famous work, *Winesburg, Ohio.* Camden and Clyde were prosperous farming communities, but the Anderson family did not prosper, and the young Anderson longed for the variety and opportunities of city life. He moved to Cleveland and later to Chicago, where he pursued an unsatisfying career in advertising. In 1912 he made a dramatic change in his life with his decision to write.

Anderson began to associate with Carl Sandburg, Theodore Dreiser, Edgar Lee Masters, and other writers living in Chicago. Influenced by the poems of Masters' *Spoon River Anthology,* Anderson began to record, in prose, his own feelings about life in small-town America. These tales of Winesburg were collected as a volume in 1919, and they made Anderson famous. He continued his explorations of small-town life in *The Triumph of the Egg* (1921), *Horses and Men* (1923), and *Death in the Woods and Other Stories* (1933), but he was never again as successful as he had been with the Winesburg stories.

Like Masters, Anderson did not believe that village life was the rose-colored picture that so many other writers painted. His characters are often lonely and isolated, dissatisfied with their world and frustrated in their attempts to find something better. Anderson treated them realistically, in the simple language that Gertrude Stein, his friend and champion, did much to encourage and that would, in turn, influence the styles of Ernest Hemingway and William Faulkner, two writers whose early careers Anderson helped nurture. "Sophistication" is typical of the Winesburg stories in its realism, its characters' honest longings, and its poetic evocation of the sights and sounds of turn-of-the-century life.

■ What does the word "sophistication" bring to mind? Do most of us want to be "sophisticated"? Why?

Sherwood Anderson

Sophistication

It was early evening of a day in the late fall and the Winesburg County Fair had brought crowds of country people into town. The day had been clear and the night came on warm and pleasant. On the Trunion Pike, where the road after it left town stretched away between berry fields now covered with dry brown leaves, the dust from passing wagons arose in clouds. Children, curled into little balls, slept on the straw scattered on wagon beds. Their hair was full of dust and their fingers black and sticky. The dust rolled away over the fields and the departing sun set it ablaze with colors.

1 In the main street of Winesburg crowds filled the stores and the sidewalks. Night came on, horses whinnied, the clerks in the stores ran madly about, children became lost and cried lustily, an American town worked terribly at the task of amusing itself.

Pushing his way through the crowds in Main Street, young George Willard concealed himself in the stairway leading to Doctor Reefy's office and looked at the people. With feverish eyes he watched the faces drifting past under the store lights. Thoughts kept coming into his head and he did not want to think. He stamped impatiently on the wooden steps and looked sharply about. "Well, is she going to stay with him all day? Have I done all this waiting for nothing?" he muttered.

2 George Willard, the Ohio village boy, was fast growing into manhood and new thoughts had been coming into his mind. All that day, amid the jam of people at the Fair, he had gone about feeling lonely. He was about to leave Winesburg to go away to some city where he hoped to get work on a city newspaper and he felt grown-up. The mood that had taken possession of him was a thing known to men and unknown to boys. He felt old and a little tired. Memories awoke in him. To his mind his new sense of maturity set him apart, made of him a half-tragic figure. He wanted someone to understand the feeling that had taken possession of him after his mother's death.

3 There is a time in the life of every boy when he for the first time takes the backward view of life. Perhaps that is the moment when he crosses the line into manhood. The boy is walking through the street of his town. He is thinking of the future and of the figure he will cut in the world. Ambitions and regrets awake within him. Suddenly something happens; he stops under a tree and waits as for a voice calling his name. Ghosts of old things creep into his consciousness; the voices outside of himself whisper a message concerning the limitations of life. From being quite sure of himself and his future he becomes not at all sure. If he be an imaginative boy a door is torn open and for the first time he looks out upon the world, seeing, as though they marched in procession before him, the countless figures of men who before his time have come out of nothingness into the world, lived their lives and again dis-
4 appeared into nothingness. The sadness of sophistication has come to the boy. With a little gasp he sees himself as merely a leaf blown by the wind through the streets of his village. He knows that in spite of all the stout[1] talk of his fellows he must live and die in uncertainty, a thing blown by the winds, a thing destined like corn to wilt in the sun. He shivers and looks eagerly about. The eighteen years he has lived seem but a moment, a breathing space in the long march of humanity. Already he hears death calling. With all his heart he wants to come close to some other human, touch someone with his hands, be touched by the hand of another. If he prefers that the other be a woman, that is because he believes that a

1. **stout:** tough.

AT A GLANCE

- Winesburg, Ohio, is crowded with people who have come for the fair.
- Eighteen-year-old George Willard is about to leave this town to find a newspaper job in the city.
- He reflects upon the realization that life is uncertain and that, like his mother, he will die someday.

LITERARY OPTIONS

- setting and mood
- internal conflict
- theme

THEMATIC OPTIONS

- adolescence and maturity
- loneliness and uncertainty
- sources of courage

1 SETTING

Anderson describes Winesburg in precise detail to emphasize the realism of the setting. He seals that description with a generalization about small-town America as he sees it.

2 CHARACTERIZATION

George (and later Helen) is largely revealed by what the narrator simply states about him, rather than by a description of his actions.

3 POINT OF VIEW

When the omniscient third-person narrator steps back to comment on life in general, the verbs shift from past tense to present tense.

4 STYLE: SIMILE

The image of the blowing leaf suggests the helplessness, randomness, and confusion that the characters find in their lives.

GUIDED READING

LITERAL QUESTIONS

1a. What does George plan to do when he leaves Winesburg? (find a job with a newspaper in the city)

2a. How old is George? (eighteen)

INFERENTIAL QUESTIONS

1b. Why must he leave Winesburg to accomplish his plan? (Apparently, the prospects of the city look more promising than do those of his small town.)

2b. What does being this age mean to him? (He feels that he is on the brink of manhood—mature, suddenly aware of the awful uncertainties of life.)

AT A GLANCE

- George thinks of Helen White and of how eager he is to tell her about the changes in him.
- Helen is experiencing similar feelings.
- Home from college for the fair, she spends the day with an instructor who impresses others but who strikes her as "pedantic."

1 THEME

The changes that George feels must be shared; he must reach outside of himself. He also may need to have his feelings validated.

2 CHARACTERIZATION

The narrator introduces Helen White, the other major character in the story. We see that Helen and George are traveling on parallel psychological tracks toward "sophistication" and, perhaps, toward each other.

Scene at a traditional American county fair, about 1910.

woman will be gentle, that she will understand. He wants, most of all, understanding.

When the moment of sophistication came to George Willard his mind turned to Helen White, the Winesburg banker's daughter. Always he had been conscious of the girl growing into womanhood as he grew into manhood. Once on a summer night when he was eighteen, he had walked with her on a country road and in her presence had given way to an impulse to boast, to make himself appear big and significant in her eyes. Now he wanted to see her for another purpose. He wanted to tell her of the new impulses that had come to him. He
1 had tried to make her think of him as a man when he knew nothing of manhood and now he wanted to be with her and to try to make her feel the change he believed had taken place in his nature.

As for Helen White, she also had come to a
2 period of change. What George felt, she in her young woman's way felt also. She was no longer a girl and hungered to reach into the grace and beauty of womanhood. She had come home from Cleveland, where she was attending college, to spend a day at the Fair. She also had begun to have memories. During the day she sat in the grandstand with a young man, one of the instructors from the college, who was a guest of her mother's. The young man was of a pedantic[2] turn of mind and she felt at once he would not do for her purpose. At the Fair she was glad to be seen in his company as he was well dressed and a stranger. She knew that the fact of his presence would create an impression. During the day she was

2. **pedantic:** scholarly but trivial.

GUIDED READING

LITERAL QUESTION

1a. What is it about the instructor that Helen does not like? (his pedantry)

INFERENTIAL QUESTION

1b. What does this complaint reveal about Helen? (She is lively and interested in more than mere book knowledge.)

happy, but when night came on she began to grow restless. She wanted to drive the instruc-
1 tor away, to get out of his presence. While they sat together in the grandstand and while the eyes of former schoolmates were upon them, she paid so much attention to her escort that he grew interested. "A scholar needs money. I should marry a woman with money," he mused.

Helen White was thinking of George Willard even as he wandered gloomily through the crowds thinking of her. She remembered the summer evening when they had walked together and wanted to walk with him again. She thought that the months she had spent in the city, the going to theaters and the seeing of great crowds wandering in lighted thoroughfares, had changed her profoundly. She wanted him to feel and be conscious of the change in her nature.

The summer evening together that had left its mark on the memory of both the young man and the woman had, when looked at quite
2 sensibly, been rather stupidly spent. They had walked out of town along a country road. Then they had stopped by a fence near a field of young corn and George had taken off his coat and let it hang on his arm. "Well, I've stayed here in Winesburg—yes—I've not yet gone away but I'm growing up," he had said. "I've been reading books and I've been thinking. I'm going to try to amount to something in life.

"Well," he explained, "that isn't the point. Perhaps I'd better quit talking."

The confused boy put his hand on the girl's arm. His voice trembled. The two started to walk back along the road toward town. In his desperation George boasted, "I'm going to be a big man, the biggest that ever lived here in
3 Winesburg," he declared. "I want you to do something, I don't know what. Perhaps it is none of my business. I want you to try to be different from other women. You see the point. It's none of my business, I tell you. I want you to be a beautiful woman. You see what I want."

The boy's voice failed and in silence the two came back into town and went along the street to Helen White's house. At the gate he tried to say something impressive. Speeches he had thought out came into his head, but they seemed utterly pointless. "I thought—I used to think—I had it in my mind you would marry Seth Richmond. Now I know you won't," was all he could find to say as she went through the gate and toward the door of her house.

On the warm fall evening as he stood in the stairway and looked at the crowd drifting through Main Street, George thought of the talk beside the field of young corn and was ashamed of the figure he had made of himself.
4 In the street the people surged up and down like cattle confined in a pen. Buggies and wagons almost filled the narrow thoroughfare. A band played and small boys raced along the sidewalk, diving between the legs of men. Young men with shining red faces walked awkwardly about with girls on their arms. In a room above one of the stores, where a dance was to be held, the fiddlers tuned their instruments. The broken sounds floated down through an open window and out across the murmur of voices and the loud blare of the horns of the band. The medley of songs got on young Willard's nerves. Everywhere, on all sides, the sense of crowding, moving life closed in about him. He wanted to run away by himself and think. "If she wants to stay with that fellow she may. Why should I care? What difference does it make to me?" he growled and went along Main Street and through Hern's Grocery into a side street.

George felt so utterly lonely and dejected that he wanted to weep but pride made him walk rapidly along, swinging his arms. He came to Wesley Moyer's livery barn[3] and stopped in the shadows to listen to a group of men who talked of a race Wesley's stallion, Tony Tip, had won at the Fair during the afternoon. A crowd had gathered in front of the barn and before the crowd walked Wesley, prancing up

---

3. **livery barn:** barn or stable from which horses and carriages can be hired.

AT A GLANCE

- Helen wants to get away from the instructor.
- She recalls a summer evening's walk and George's awkward expression of feeling for her.
- George is angry that Helen has spent the day with the instructor.
- Wanting to get away from the celebration in town, he walks to the livery barn.

1 CHARACTERIZATION

Helen cares enough about the impression that she makes upon her peers that she will feign interest in a man whom she does not like.

2 VOCABULARY: CONNOTATION

The word *stupidly* is used several times in the story. Each use suggests an ignorance of meanings and a sense of being swept along by enigmatic events.

3 INTERNAL CONFLICT

The confusion and yearning that George and Helen feel are evoked through George's stumbling speech.

4 SETTING

The congestion, noise, and awkwardness of the scene are described as an unpleasant counterpoint to George's contemplative mood.

GUIDED READING

LITERAL QUESTION

1a. On that summer evening what was the last thing that George had said? (that he knew that Helen would not marry Seth Richmond)

INFERENTIAL QUESTION

1b. What is the significance of this remark? (George probably hopes that Helen will marry him.)

AT A GLANCE

- Angered by Wesley Moyer's bragging, George decides to go to Helen's house.
- Helen, who is having a miserable time with the instructor, sneaks away to find George.
- They meet and go together to the Fair Ground.

1 STYLE: IRONY

The details of George's falling over the rubbish and of his torn pants provide an ironic commentary on the true extent of his sophistication, as does his almost childish repetition of "I'll walk right in . . . that's what I'll do."

2 VOCABULARY: DIALOGUE

The instructor's stuffy word choice and stilted sentence structure confirm the conclusion that Helen already has drawn about him. His diction contrasts sharply with that of George and Helen.

3 THEME

That George is described as "still saying words" just after Helen has noted "meaningless people saying words" reinforces Helen's sense of loneliness at this moment and may further comment on the depth of George's maturity.

4 SETTING

The present-tense description of the old grandstand suggests that these things still exist—if not in Winesburg, then in some other small town. The style here lends a universal and timeless quality to the description.

5 INTERNAL CONFLICT

The narrator extends the conflict that George and Helen feel. To consider things carefully and not to react impulsively is a battle that all young people must confront.

and down and boasting. He held a whip in his hand and kept tapping the ground. Little puffs of dust arose in the lamplight. "Quit your talking," Wesley exclaimed. "I wasn't afraid, I knew I had 'em beat all the time. I wasn't afraid."

Ordinarily George Willard would have been intensely interested in the boasting of Moyer, the horseman. Now it made him angry. He turned and hurried away along the street. "Old windbag," he sputtered. "Why does he want to be bragging? Why don't he shut up?"

1 George went into a vacant lot, and as he hurried alone, fell over a pile of rubbish. A nail protruding from an empty barrel tore his trousers. He sat down on the ground and swore. With a pin he mended the torn place and then arose and went on. "I'll go to Helen White's house, that's what I'll do. I'll walk right in. I'll say that I want to see her. I'll walk right in and sit down, that's what I'll do," he declared, climbing over a fence and beginning to run.

On the veranda of Banker White's house Helen was restless and distraught. The instructor sat between the mother and daughter. His talk wearied the girl. Although he had also been raised in an Ohio town, the instructor began to put on the airs of the city. He wanted to appear cosmopolitan.[4] "I like the chance you have given me to study the background out of which most of our girls come," he de-
2 clared. "It was good of you, Mrs. White, to have me down for the day." He turned to Helen and laughed. "Your life is still bound up with the life of this town?" he asked. "There are people here in whom you are interested?" To the girl his voice sounded pompous and heavy.

Helen arose and went into the house. At the door leading to a garden at the back she stopped and stood listening. Her mother began to talk. "There is no one here fit to associate with a girl of Helen's breeding," she said.

Helen ran down a flight of stairs at the back of the house and into the garden. In the darkness she stopped and stood trembling. It seemed to her that the world was full of meaningless people saying words. Afire with eagerness she ran through the garden gate and, turning a corner by the banker's barn, went into a little side street. "George! Where are you, George?" she cried, filled with nervous excitement. She stopped running, and leaned against
3 a tree to laugh hysterically. Along the dark little street came George Willard, still saying words. "I'm going to walk right into her house. I'll go right in and sit down," he declared as he came up to her. He stopped and stared stupidly. "Come on," he said and took hold of her hand. With hanging heads they walked away along the street under the trees. Dry leaves rustled underfoot. Now that he had found her George wondered what he had better do and say.

4 At the upper end of the Fair Ground, in Winesburg, there is a half-decayed old grandstand. It has never been painted and the boards are all warped out of shape. The Fair Ground stands on top of a low hill rising out of the valley of Wine Creek and from the grandstand one can see at night, over a cornfield, the lights of the town reflected against the sky.

George and Helen climbed the hill to the Fair Ground, coming by the path past Waterworks Pond. The feeling of loneliness and isolation that had come to the young man in the crowded streets of his town was both broken and intensified by the presence of Helen. What he felt was reflected in her.

5 In youth there are always two forces fighting in people. The warm unthinking little animal struggles against the thing that reflects and remembers, and the older, the more sophisticated thing had possession of George Willard. Sensing his mood, Helen walked beside him filled with respect. When they got to the grandstand they climbed up under the roof and sat down on one of the long bench-like seats.

There is something memorable in the experience to be had by going into a fairground

4. **cosmopolitan:** worldly; experienced.

GUIDED READING

LITERAL QUESTION

1a. How do George and Helen finally get together? (Helen flees her house to escape the pedantic instructor at the precise moment when George arrives at her house trying to work up the courage to speak to her.)

INFERENTIAL QUESTION

1b. What do you predict George and Helen will talk about? (They will probably try to express some of the thoughts that have been revealed so far. It is possible that they will reach some kind of understanding.)

that stands at the edge of a Middle Western town on a night after the annual fair has been
1 held. The sensation is one never to be forgotten. On all sides are ghosts, not of the dead, but of living people. Here, during the day just passed, have come the people pouring in from the town and the country around. Farmers with their wives and children and all the people from the hundreds of little frame houses have gathered within these board walls. Young girls have laughed and men with beards have talked of the affairs of their lives. The place has been filled to overflowing with life. It has itched and squirmed with life and now it is night and the life has all gone away. The silence is almost terrifying. One conceals oneself standing silently beside the trunk of a tree and what there is of a reflective tendency in his nature is intensified. One shudders at the thought of the meaninglessness of life while at the same instant, and if the people of the town are his people, one lives life so intensely that tears come into the eyes.

In the darkness under the roof of the grandstand, George Willard sat beside Helen White and felt very keenly his own insignificance in the scheme of existence. Now that he had come out of town where the presence of the people stirring about, busy with a multitude of affairs, had been so irritating, the irritation was
2 all gone. The presence of Helen renewed and refreshed him. It was as though her woman's hand was assisting him to make some minute readjustment of the machinery of his life. He began to think of the people in the town where he had always lived with something like reverence. He had reverence for Helen. He wanted to love and to be loved by her, but he did not want at the moment to be confused by her womanhood. In the darkness he took hold of her hand and when she crept close put a hand on her shoulder. A wind began to blow and he shivered. With all his strength he tried to hold and to understand the mood that had
3 come upon him. In that high place in the darkness the two oddly sensitive human atoms held each other tightly and waited. In the mind of
4 each was the same thought. "I have come to this lonely place and here is this other," was the substance of the thing felt.

In Winesburg the crowded day had run itself out into the long night of the late fall. Farm horses jogged away along lonely country roads pulling their portion of weary people. Clerks began to bring samples of goods in off the sidewalks and lock the doors of stores. In the Opera House a crowd had gathered to see a show and further down Main Street the fiddlers, their instruments tuned, sweated and worked to keep the feet of youth flying over a dance floor.

In the darkness in the grandstand Helen White and George Willard remained silent. Now and then the spell that held them was broken and they turned and tried in the dim light to see into each other's eyes. They kissed but that impulse did not last. At the upper end of the Fair Ground a half-dozen men worked over horses that had raced during the afternoon. The men had built a fire and were heating kettles of water. Only their legs could be seen as they passed back and forth in the light. When the wind blew, the little flames of the fire danced crazily about.

George and Helen arose and walked away into the darkness. They went along a path past a field of corn that had not yet been cut. The wind whispered among the dry corn blades. For a moment during the walk back into town the spell that held them was broken. When they had come to the crest of Waterworks Hill they stopped by a tree and George again put
5 his hands on the girl's shoulders. She embraced him eagerly and then again they drew quickly back from that impulse. They stopped kissing and stood a little apart. Mutual respect grew big in them. They were both embarrassed and to relieve their embarrassment dropped into the animalism of youth. They laughed and began to pull and haul at each other. In some way chastened and purified by the mood they had been in, they became, not man and woman, not boy and girl, but excited little animals.

AT A GLANCE

- George and Helen sit together in the dark at the grandstand; they kiss a few times.
- In the town the daytime mood of celebration now gives way to a more subdued atmosphere.
- At the Fair Ground George and Helen play together like "little animals."

1 MOOD

Anderson evokes a mood of mystery—the moment when one senses meaning in the everlasting flow of human life.

2 THEME

Here appears the clearest statement about the strength that George can draw from Helen. Even it, however, is tempered by George's desire not "to be confused by her womanhood."

3 VOCABULARY: CONNOTATION

Using the term *atoms* to describe George and Helen makes them representative of some cosmic force. It also depersonalizes them and makes them seem very small entities within that force.

4 THEME AND SETTING

The desire to touch and be touched is what motivates George and Helen. Their yearning to overcome loneliness can be satisfied only in a "lonely place."

5 INTERNAL CONFLICT

George and Helen struggle uncertainly to find the right expression for their feeling. Physical intimacy does not help them to cross the gulf of loneliness; instead, it just makes them self-conscious.

GUIDED READING

LITERAL QUESTIONS

1a. What is it about Helen that George fears could confuse him? (her womanhood)

2a. What do George and Helen do both times when the narrator says that "the spell" is broken? (They kiss.)

INFERENTIAL QUESTIONS

1b. Why would this characteristic confuse him? (Her sexuality would complicate the issue of his loneliness. It is the feeling that another human being understands him that George seeks.)

2b. What is this "spell"? (the haunting sense of shared loneliness expressed in the sentence "I have come to this lonely place and here is this other")

AT A GLANCE

George and Helen run down the hill together and walk on more subdued but somehow renewed in spirit.

REFLECTING ON THE STORY

Given what has already happened, what might Helen's action at the bottom of the hill signify? (perhaps a turning point in which she realizes that she has become a woman and is no longer entirely alone)

STUDY QUESTIONS

1. county fair; amusing itself
2. Helen White; boasted he would be the most important person from Winesburg; tell her of change in him
3. George Willard; change in her
4. in a side street; fairgrounds; sympathy; taken hold of the thing that makes mature life in the modern world possible
5. small, constricting
6. mature, able to reflect and remember; each other's company and growth; struggle to understand their lives and help one another grow up
7. knowledge of life's limitations; sharing of each other's lives
8.
   - We do not know what will happen to George and Helen.
   - Yes, it suggests much more life to come.
   - No, the lack of a traditional resolution reflects Modernist experimentation.
9. Answers will vary. *Positive:* Sophistication allows growth. *Negative:* It includes sadness.
10. Story implies that small towns restrict ambitions; opinions will vary on whether George found happiness.

It was so they went down the hill. In the darkness they played like two splendid young things in a young world. Once, running swiftly forward, Helen tripped George and he fell. He squirmed and shouted. Shaking with laughter, he rolled down the hill. Helen ran after him. For just a moment she stopped in the darkness. There is no way of knowing what woman's thoughts went through her mind but, when the bottom of the hill was reached and she came up to the boy, she took his arm and walked beside him in dignified silence. For some reason they could not have explained they had both got from their silent evening together the thing needed. Man or boy, woman or girl, they had for a moment taken hold of the thing that makes the mature life of men and women in the modern world possible.

STUDY QUESTIONS

Recalling

1. As the story opens, what event is being celebrated in Winesburg? At what does Winesburg work, according to the second paragraph?
2. For whom is George looking? What did he do when he walked with her down a country road "once on a summer night" (page 478)? What does he want to do now?
3. Of whom was Helen thinking "even as he wandered gloomily through the crowds thinking of her" (page 479)? What does Helen want to communicate about her nature (page 479)?
4. How do George and Helen finally meet? Where do they go? What is the "substance of the thing" they feel there (page 481)? According to the last paragraph, what have Helen and George done "for a moment"?

Interpreting

5. Briefly describe the kind of town Anderson creates as Winesburg, Ohio.
6. What do George and Helen have in common? What do they want to share? What does Anderson suggest about adolescents in general?
7. In the fifth paragraph, what does Anderson suggest is the "sadness of sophistication"? What does he later suggest is "the thing that makes the mature life of men and women in the modern world possible"?
8. What is inconclusive about the ending, or resolution, of the story? Does the inconclusive ending make the story more true to life? Does the story follow the standard short story format described in the Literary Focus on page 323? Explain your answers.
9. Looking at the story as a whole, does the title have a positive or negative connotation?

Extending

10. The twentieth century saw a tremendous shift in population as many young Americans left their rural communities for big cities. Does this story give you any insights into why they left? Do you think adolescents like George Willard were happy with the life they found in big cities? Explain.

COMPOSITION

Citing Evidence

■ In a brief essay illustrate with evidence from the story that George feels isolated from his community. You might proceed by tracing George's activities from the beginning to the end of the story. *For help with this assignment, refer to Lesson 3 in the Writing About Literature Handbook at the back of this book.*

Writing a Continuation of a Story

■ Write an additional page to the story of George and Helen. Follow one or both of the characters as they act upon the decision or discovery they make as Anderson ends the story. You may want to allow some time to pass, perhaps picking up the characters years later. Be sure to tie their lives to the character motivations in the story.

COMPOSITION: GUIDELINES FOR EVALUATION

CITING EVIDENCE

Objective

To cite evidence to support a statement

Guidelines for Evaluation

- suggested length: four to six paragraphs
- should make a statement describing George's isolation
- should cite details from the story
- should draw a conclusion based upon the evidence cited

WRITING A CONTINUATION OF A STORY

Objective

To continue a story

Guidelines for Evaluation

- suggested length: five to eight paragraphs
- should follow one or both characters as they act upon their new awareness
- should indicate the amount of time gone by
- should make clear connections between the existing story and the continuation

Sinclair Lewis *1885–1951*

Like Edgar Lee Masters and Sherwood Anderson, Sinclair Lewis wrote about the world of small-town America, a world that he too had found confining. Like Mark Twain, however, he looked with a satiric eye, and his dark humor and keen powers of observation made him one of the most popular novelists of the post–World War I era and the first American to receive the Nobel Prize for Literature.

Lewis was born in Sauk Centre, Minnesota, the son of a country doctor. His childhood was introspective and virtually friendless, and early in life he turned to writing as a means of escaping personal unhappiness. Lewis' early manhood was spent in various attempts to "find himself." He went to Yale but soon left. He lived briefly in a utopian community set up by the social critic Upton Sinclair; he traveled to Central America to seek work building the Panama Canal; he attempted to support himself as a writer in New York City. Eventually he completed his education at Yale and returned to New York, where he wrote industriously but with little financial success.

Everything changed in 1920 with *Main Street,* Lewis' fifth novel. A sharply observed satire, *Main Street* was a runaway best seller. Lewis' next novel, *Babbitt* (1922), was equally popular; in fact, the word *babbitt* has entered our language, synonymous with the type of conventional, conforming businessman the novel portrays. In 1930, after the publication of *Arrowsmith* (1925), *Elmer Gantry* (1927), and *Dodsworth* (1929), Lewis was awarded the Nobel Prize.

Like all great satirists, Lewis' intention was to liberate his readers from ideas that he found shallow and foolish. His hope was to reveal to Americans the foibles of their time and place, to hold up a mirror to the smug materialism that he saw around him, and, through laughter, to move Americans from the complacent attitudes into which they had fallen. His novels are often mercilessly hilarious, but in many he displays a deep sympathy for his characters. In "The Hack Driver" Lewis tells a tale of a "city slicker" on a rural errand.

■ Do people enjoy "making fools" out of one another? Does the hack driver in this story simply want to enjoy playing a trick?

AT A GLANCE

- The narrator introduces himself as recent law school graduate.
- He is disappointed at his lowly position with the large firm for which he delivers summonses.

LITERARY OPTIONS

- satire
- point of view
- irony

THEMATIC OPTIONS

- appearances vs. reality
- city vs. country
- youth and naiveté

1 POINT OF VIEW

The story is written in the first person. The narrator's main satirical target is his own youthful arrogance, naiveté, and superficiality.

2 STYLE: WORD CHOICE

The narrator's somewhat overblown language conveys his arrogance and contributes to the satirical tone of the story.

Sinclair Lewis

The Hack Driver

1 When I graduated from law school I suppose I was about as artificial and idiotic and ambitious as most youngsters. I wanted to climb, socially and financially. I wanted to be famous and dine at large houses with men who shuddered at the Common People who don't dress for dinner. You see, I hadn't learned that the only thing duller than a polite dinner is the conversation afterward, when the victims are digesting the dinner and accumulating enough strength to be able to play bridge. Oh, I was a fine young calf! I even planned a rich marriage. Imagine then how I felt when, after taking honors and becoming fifteenth assistant clerk in the magnificent law firm of Hodgins, Hodgins, Berkman and Taupe, I was set not at preparing briefs[1] but at serving summonses![2] Like a cheap private detective! Like a mangy sheriff's officer! They told me I had to begin that way and, holding my nose, I feebly went to work. I was kicked out of actresses' dressing rooms, and
2 from time to time I was righteously beaten by large and indignant litigants.[3] I came to know, and still more to hate, every dirty and shadowy corner of the city. I thought of fleeing to my

1. **briefs:** short reports summarizing the main point in a legal case.
2. **serving summonses:** delivering official orders to appear in court.
3. **litigants:** people involved in a lawsuit.

GUIDED READING

LITERAL QUESTION

1a. What is the narrator's job at Hodgins, Hodgins, Berkman, and Taupe? (He delivers summonses.)

INFERENTIAL QUESTION

1b. In what ways does this job contrast with the narrator's image of himself? (The narrator imagines himself being accepted as an equal by elegant, sophisticated people. Instead, he is treated worse than a servant would be, is "kicked out" of actresses' dressing rooms, and is even beaten up.)

home town, where I could at once become a
1 full-fledged attorney at law. I rejoiced one day when they sent me out forty miles or so to a town called New Mullion, to serve a summons on one Oliver Lutkins. This Lutkins had worked in the Northern Woods, and he knew the facts about a certain timberland boundary agreement. We needed him as a witness, and he had dodged service.

2 When I got off the train at New Mullion, my sudden affection for sweet and simple villages was dashed by the look of the place, with its mud-gushing streets and its rows of shops either paintless or daubed with a sour brown. Though it must have numbered eight or nine thousand inhabitants, New Mullion was as littered as a mining camp. There was one agreeable-looking man at the station—the expressman. He was a person of perhaps forty, red-faced, cheerful, thick; he wore his overalls and denim jumper as though they belonged to him, he was quite dirty and very friendly and you knew at once he liked people and slapped them on the back out of pure easy affection.

"I want," I told him, "to find a fellow named Oliver Lutkins."

"Him? I saw him 'round here 'twan't an hour ago. Hard fellow to catch, though—always chasing around on some phony business or other. Probably trying to get up a poker game in the back of Fritz Beinke's harness shop. I'll tell you, boy—Any hurry about locating Lutkins?"

"Yes. I want to catch the afternoon train back." I was as impressively secret as a stage detective.

3 "I'll tell you. I've got a hack. I'll get out the bone-shaker and we can drive around together and find Lutkins. I know most of the places he hangs out."

He was so frankly friendly, he so immediately took me into the circle of his affection, that I glowed with the warmth of it. I knew, of
4 course, that he was drumming up business, but his kindness was real, and if I had to pay hack fare in order to find my man, I was glad that the money would go to this good fellow. I got him down to two dollars an hour; he brought from his cottage, a block away, an object like a black piano box on wheels.

He didn't hold the door open, certainly he didn't say, "Ready, sir." I think he would have died before calling anybody "sir." When he gets to Heaven's gate he'll call St. Peter "Pete," and I imagine the good saint will like it. He remarked, "Well, young fellow, here's the handsome equipage,"[4] and his grin—well, it made me feel that I had always been his neighbor.
5 They're so ready to help a stranger, those villagers. He had already made it his own task to find Oliver Lutkins for me.

He said, and almost shyly: "I don't want to butt in on your private business, young fellow, but my guess is that you want to collect some money from Lutkins—he never pays anybody a cent; he still owes me six bits[5] on a poker game I was fool enough to get into. He ain't a bad sort of a Yahoo[6] but he just naturally hates to loosen up on a coin of the realm. So if you're trying to collect any money off him, we better kind of you might say creep up on him and surround him. If you go asking for him—anybody can tell you come from the city, with that trick Fedora[7] of yours—he'll suspect something and take a sneak. If you want me to, I'll go into Fritz Beinke's and ask for him, and you can keep out of sight behind me."

I loved him for it. By myself I might never have found Lutkins. Now, I was an army with reserves. In a burst I told the hack driver that I wanted to serve a summons on Lutkins; that the fellow had viciously refused to testify in a suit where his knowledge of a certain conversation would clear up everything. The driver listened earnestly—and I was still young enough to be grateful at being taken seriously

---

4. **equipage** [ek'wə pij]: fancy carriage.
5. **six bits:** *Bit* is a colloquial term for 12.5 cents; six bits is therefore 75 cents.
6. **Yahoo** [yä'hōō]: term for "man" deriving from brutish, manlike creatures in Jonathan Swift's *Gulliver's Travels.*
7. **Fedora** [fi dôr'ə]: Soft felt hat with a slightly curved brim.

AT A GLANCE

- The narrator goes to New Mullion to serve a summons on Oliver Lutkins.
- At the train station the expressman offers to help him.

1 PLOT: NARRATIVE HOOK

The narrator has a simple task—to serve a summons on Oliver Lutkins. His attempt to do so is what sets the story in motion.

2 SETTING

The appearance of the town clashes with the narrator's naive ideal of rustic charm.

3 VOCABULARY: SLANG

The expressman's use of slang (in particular, "bone-shaker") contributes to the humor of the story and to the effect he has on the narrator, who finds him a colorful character.

4 THEME

Accepting the expressman's apparent motives may turn out to be a naive misreading by the narrator. The narrator has already warned the reader about himself: He is "artificial and idiotic."

5 THEME

The narrator has definite notions about the differences between the city and the country. Here he states his stereotypical views about the generosity of country folk—but the reader already has been alerted to his general naiveté.

GUIDED READING

LITERAL QUESTIONS

1a. Whom does the narrator approach for assistance when he arrives in New Mullion? (the expressman)

2a. What reason does the expressman give for offering to help find Lutkins? (He says that questions from a stranger may cause Lutkins to hide.)

INFERENTIAL QUESTIONS

1b. Why does he ask this person? (The expressman appeals to the narrator's notion of what a fellow from the country should look like; the narrator expects to get help from such a person.)

2b. What other reasons might he have for being so helpful? (He may be curious, or he may want to hinder the search.)

AT A GLANCE

- Bill Magnuson (the expressman) and the narrator ask for Lutkins at several of the businesses in town, always finding themselves just a bit too late to catch him.
- Bill and the narrator picnic together.

1 PLOT: FORESHADOWING

Bill refers to Lutkins' skill at bluffing. The reader already has reason to suspect that Bill himself is bluffing.

2 DIALOGUE

The villagers' ironic and clever talk does not fit the stereotypical contrast between slow village people and snappy city folk.

3 RESPONSE JOURNAL

Ask students to comment upon what they expect the outcome of the story to be, given the details offered to this point.

4 POINT OF VIEW

The naive narrator believes himself slick enough to see through Bill's actions to his genuine motives.

by any man of forty. At the end he pounded my shoulder (very painfully) and chuckled: "Well, we'll spring a little surprise on Brer[8] Lutkins."

"Let's start, driver."

"Most folks around here call me Bill. Or Magnuson. William Magnuson, fancy carting and hauling."

"All right, Bill. Shall we tackle this harness shop—Beinke's?"

1 "Yes, jus' likely to be there as anywheres. Plays a lot of poker and a great hand at bluffing!" Bill seemed to admire Mr. Lutkins's ability as a scoundrel; I fancied that if he had been sheriff he would have caught Lutkins with fervor and hanged him with affection.

At the somewhat gloomy harness shop we descended and went in. The room was odorous with the smell of dressed leather. A scanty sort of a man, presumably Mr. Beinke, was selling a horse collar to a farmer.

"Seen Nolly Lutkins around today? Friend of his looking for him," said Bill, with treacherous heartliness.

Beinke looked past him at my shrinking alien self; he hesitated and owned: "Yuh, he was in here a little while ago. Guess he's gone over to the Swede's to get a shave."

2 "Well, if he comes in, tell him I'm looking for him. Might get up a little game of poker. I've heard tell that Lutkins plays these here immoral games of chance."

"Yuh, I believe he's known to sit in on Authors,[9]" Beinke growled.

We sought the barber shop of "the Swede." Bill was again good enough to take the lead, while I lurked at the door. He asked not only the Swede but two customers if they had seen Lutkins. The Swede decidedly had not; he raged: "I ain't seen him, and I don't want to, but if you find him you can just collect the dollar thirty-five he owes me." One of the customers thought he had seen Lutkins "hiking down Main Street, this side of the hotel."

"Well, then," Bill concluded, as we labored up into the hack, "his credit at the Swede's being ausgewent,[10] he's probably getting a scrape at Heinie Gray's. He's too darn lazy to shave himself."

3 At Gray's barber shop we missed Lutkins by only five minutes. He had just left—presumably for the poolroom. At the poolroom it appeared that he had merely bought a pack of cigarettes and gone on. Thus we pursued him, just behind him but never catching him, for an hour, till it was past one and I was hungry. Village born as I was, and in the city often lonely for good coarse country wit, I was so delighted by Bill's cynical opinions on the barbers and clergymen and doctors and draymen of New Mullion that I scarcely cared whether I found Lutkins or not.

"How about something to eat?" I suggested. "Let's go to a restaurant and I'll buy you a lunch."

"Well, ought to go home to the old woman. And I don't care much for these restaurants—ain't but four of 'em and they're all rotten. Tell you what we'll do. Like nice scenery? There's an elegant view from Wade's Hill. We'll get the old woman to put us up a lunch—she won't charge you but a half dollar, and it'd cost you that for a greasy feed at the cafe—and we'll go up there and have a Sunday-school picnic."

4 I knew that my friend Bill was not free from guile; I knew that his hospitality to the Young Fellow from the City was not altogether a matter of brotherly love. I was paying him for his time; in all I paid him for six hours (including the lunch hour) at what was then a terrific price. But he was no more dishonest than I, who charged the whole thing up to the Firm, and it would have been worth paying him myself to have his presence. His country serenity, his natural wisdom, was a refreshing bath to the city-twitching youngster. As we sat on the hilltop, looking across orchards and a creek which slipped among the willows, he talked of New Mullion, gave a whole gallery of portraits. He was cynical yet tender. Nothing had escaped him, yet there was nothing, no

8. **Brer** [brur]: southern dialect for "brother."
9. **Authors:** simple children's card game.

10. **ausgewent** [ous′ge went]: made-up, German-sounding word meaning "used up."

GUIDED READING

LITERAL QUESTIONS

1a. Where do the narrator and Bill look for Lutkins? (in a harness shop, two barber shops, a poolroom, and at some other unnamed stops)

2a. How does the narrator account for Bill's hospitality? (He suspects that Bill is mainly interested in the money he is being paid.)

INFERENTIAL QUESTIONS

1b. What does the search indicate about how well Bill knows Lutkins? (Since Bill knows all the places to look for Lutkins, he would seem to know him very well.)

2b. How else might such hospitality be explained? (It may be that Bill likes the narrator, or it may be that Bill is trying to keep the narrator from something.)

matter how ironically he laughed at it, which was beyond his understanding and forgiveness. In ruddy color he painted the rector's wife
1 who when she was most in debt most loudly gave the responses at which he called the "Episcopalopian church." He commented on the boys who came home from college in "ice cream pants," and on the lawyer who, after years of torrential argument with his wife, would put on either a linen collar or a necktie, but never both. He made them live. In that day I came to know New Mullion better than I did the city, and to love it better.

If Bill was ignorant of universities and of urban ways, yet much had he traveled in the
2 realm of jobs. He had worked on railroad section gangs, in harvest fields and contractors' camps, and from his adventures he had brought back a philosophy of simplicity and laughter. He strengthened me. Nowadays, thinking of Bill, I know what people mean (though I abominate the simpering phrase) when they yearn over "real he-men."

We left that placid place of orchards and resumed the search for Oliver Lutkins. We could not find him. At last Bill cornered a friend of Lutkins and made him admit that "he guessed Oliver'd gone out to his ma's farm, three miles north."

We drove out there, mighty with strategy.

"I know Oliver's ma. She's a terror. She's a cyclone," Bill sighed. "I took a trunk out for her once, and she pretty near took my hide off because I didn't treat it like it was a crate of eggs. She's somewheres about nine feet tall and four feet thick and quick's a cat, and she sure manhandles the Queen's English. I'll bet Oliver has heard that somebody's on his trail and he's sneaked out there to hide behind his ma's skirts. Well, we'll try bawling her out. But you
3 better let me do it, boy. You may be great at Latin and geography, but you ain't educated in cussing."

We drove into a poor farmyard; we were faced by an enormous and cheerful old woman. My guardian stockily stood before her and snarled, "Remember me? I'm Bill Magnuson, the expressman. I want to find your son Oliver. Friend of mine here from the city's got a present for him."

"I don't know anything about Oliver and I don't want to," she bellowed.

"Now you look here. We've stood for just about enough plenty nonsense. This young man is the attorney general's provost,[11] and we got legal right to search any and all premises for the person of one Oliver Lutkins."

4 Bill made it seem terrific, and the Amazon[12] seemed impressed. She retired into the kitchen and we followed. From the low old range, turned by years of heat into a dark silvery gray, she snatched a sadiron,[13] and she marched on us, clamoring, "You just search all you want to—providin' you don't mind getting burnt to a cinder!" She bellowed, she swelled, she laughed at our nervous retreat.

"Let's get out of this. She'll murder us," Bill groaned and, outside: "Did you see her grin? She was making fun of us. Can you beat that for nerve?"

I agreed that it was lese majesty.[14]

We did, however, make adequate search. The cottage had but one story. Bill went round it, peeking in at all the windows. We explored the barn and the stable; we were reasonably certain that Lutkins was not there. It was nearly time for me to catch the afternoon train, and Bill drove me to the station. On the way to the city I worried very little over my failure to find Lutkins. I was too absorbed in the thought of Bill Magnu-
5 son. Really, I considered returning to New Mullion to practice law. If I had found Bill so deeply and richly human might I not come to love the yet uncharted Fritz Beinke and the Swede barber and a hundred other slow-spoken, simple, wise neighbors? I saw a candid and happy life beyond the neat learnings of universities' law firms. I was excited, as one who has found a treasure.

But if I did not think much about Lutkins, the office did. I found them in a state next morning;

---

11. **provost** [prō′vəst]: official in charge.
12. **Amazon** [am′ə zon′]: here, a large, strong woman.
13. **sadiron** [sad′ī′ərn]: heavy iron for pressing clothes.
14. **lese majesty** [lēz′maj′is tē]: rude behavior toward someone, especially someone in authority, who should be treated with respect.

AT A GLANCE

- The narrator listens to Bill's talk about country people.
- The narrator and Bill go to the home of Lutkins' mother.
- She is a fearsome woman who chases them off.
- The narrator leaves town without having found Lutkins.

1 SATIRE

The narrator enjoys the fun Bill has satirizing the people of New Mullion, but he fails to notice that a lawyer is among those so satirized.

2 THEME

Much of Bill's charm comes from the variety and richness of his experiences, which appeal to the inexperienced youth.

3 IRONY

Apparently, the narrator's education has not prepared him for some aspects of his job.

4 CHARACTERIZATION

The use of the epithets *Amazon* and later *dragon* shows how strongly the narrator reacts to the mother. Perhaps this reaction is more a consequence of what Bill had said about her than of what he had actually observed.

5 POINT OF VIEW

The narrator's idealization of life in New Mullion reflects his naiveté, his city dweller's sentimentalization of the country, and his confusion of appearances and reality.

GUIDED READING

LITERAL QUESTIONS

1a. What does Bill tell the narrator about Lutkins' mother? (He describes her as fierce, aggressive, and dangerous.)

2a. How upset is the narrator over not finding Lutkins? (He is relatively unconcerned.)

INFERENTIAL QUESTIONS

1b. Why does he say these things? (He seems to be warning the narrator, but Bill may just want the narrator to be afraid of Lutkins' mother.)

2b. Why does the failure affect him this way? (He thinks that he has found a special place in New Mullion—an escape from the city life that has not been entirely to his liking.)

the suit was ready to come to trial; they had to
1 have Lutkins; I was a disgrace and a fool. That morning my eminent career almost came to an end. The Chief did everything but commit mayhem; he somewhat more than hinted that I would do well at ditchdigging. I was ordered back to New Mullion, and with me they sent an ex-lumbercamp clerk who knew Lutkins. I was rather sorry, because it would prevent my loafing again in the gorgeous indolence of Bill Magnuson.

When the train drew in at New Mullion, Bill was on the station platform, near his dray. What was curious was that the old dragon, Lutkins's mother, was there talking to him, and they were not quarreling but laughing.

From the car steps I pointed them out to the lumbercamp clerk, and in young hero worship I murmured: "There's a fine fellow, a real man."

"Meet him here yesterday?" asked the clerk.

"I spent the day with him."

"He help you hunt for Oliver Lutkins?"

"Yes, he helped me a lot."

"He must have! He's Lutkins himself!"

2 But what really hurt was that when I served the summons Lutkins and his mother laughed at me as though I were a bright boy of seven, and with loving solicitude they begged me to go to a neighbor's house and take a cup of coffee.

"I told 'em about you, and they're dying to have a look at you," said Lutkins joyfully. "They're about the only folks in town that missed seeing you yesterday."

STUDY QUESTIONS

Recalling

1. When he first graduated from law school, where did the narrator work? What was his "title," according to the opening paragraph?
2. Why did the narrator visit New Mullion?
3. What did the expressman at the station offer to do? What did he say his name was?
4. In what places did the hack driver and the narrator search for Oliver Lutkins? How did Lutkins' mother chase them from her farm?
5. Why was "the Chief" at the law firm angry with the narrator (page 488)?
6. With whom did the narrator return to New Mullion? What did the narrator discover on this second trip?

Interpreting

7. Why did the narrator like "Bill Magnuson"? What sort of character is Oliver Lutkins? Is Lutkins basically likable?
8. At the end of the story, why were Lutkins' neighbors "dying to have a look" at the young lawyer?
9. What sort of irony—verbal, situational, or dramatic—is the basis of this story? Are the narrator's evaluations of "Bill Magnuson" and of New Mullion humorous in retrospect? Which evaluation of New Mullion is especially inaccurate?

Extending

10. What other characters in this book or in films remind you of Oliver Lutkins, and why? Why do you think amusing tales of "country bumpkins" who outsmart "city slickers" have always been so popular in America?

VIEWPOINT

In introducing a collection of Lewis' short stories, his biographer Mark Schorer tells us:

> "The Hack Driver," . . . besides being an amusing comedy in its own right, expresses quite directly Lewis' own lifelong impulse to break out of the bondage of respectability.
>
> —Introduction to *I'm a Stranger Here Myself and Other Stories*

■ How might "The Hack Driver" express this "lifelong impulse" of Sinclair Lewis'? Which events or details in the story support Schorer's view?

AT A GLANCE

- The narrator is sent back to New Mullion, this time with someone who can recognize Lutkins.
- The narrator discovers that Bill Magnuson is actually Oliver Lutkins.

1 IRONY

The irony that the narrator would call his career "eminent" after having failed to complete a relatively unimportant task contributes to the effect the author desires.

2 SATIRE

The city slicker's veneer of self-esteem and awareness is stripped clean by the country folks, who have completely hoodwinked him.

REFLECTING ON THE STORY

Will this experience change the narrator's feelings about Lutkins and country life? (He may still feel that the person he spent the day with was worth knowing, or he may feel that he was cruelly treated by these country people.)

STUDY QUESTIONS

1. law firm; fifteenth assistant clerk
2. serve summons to Oliver Lutkins
3. take narrator in hack to find Lutkins; Bill Magnuson
4. harness shop, barber shop, pool hall, mother's farm; threatened them with a sadiron
5. suit ready to come to trial
6. clerk who knew Lutkins; that Bill Magnuson was Oliver Lutkins
7. agreeable-looking, friendly, warm, colorful; all of above, and practical joker; yes
8. see someone so gullible
9. situational; yes; came to know village better than city
10. Possible answer: Simon Wheeler; that people like irony of rustic cleverness winning over urban smugness

VIEWPOINT

narrator shown a fool; harsh treatment by superiors, natural attraction for warm personality of Lutkins

Ernest Hemingway *1899–1961*

Literature, for Ernest Hemingway, was "just writing as well as you can and finishing what you start." This simple understatement characterizes the style of the writer whom many now consider one of the masters of twentieth-century prose.

Hemingway was born in Oak Park, Illinois, began writing in high school, and later worked for a Kansas City newspaper. On family trips to the Michigan woods he was introduced to the outdoor adventures that would remain a part of his life and his writing. During World War I he served in the ambulance corps of the Italian army and was wounded in battle. The experiences of war and of being wounded were traumatic; Hemingway returns to them in one way or another in all his later writing.

After the war Hemingway went to Paris, then considered the literary capital of the world. Here, in an effort to perfect his craft, he read widely and sought the advice of more experienced writers. Gertrude Stein and Ezra Pound had a profound effect on his style: From Stein he learned to control sentence rhythms with plain words and repetition; from Pound, to use precise language, sharp images, and as few words as possible.

Hemingway's novel *The Sun Also Rises* (1926) brilliantly captures his years in Paris as one of the "lost generation"; his posthumous memoir *A Moveable Feast* (1964) contains vivid portraits of Pound, Stein, F. Scott Fitzgerald, and the other American artists who formed a colony of "expatriates" in those postwar years. His first major work, *In Our Time* (1925), is a series of thematically related stories that, in Modernist fashion, must be pieced together in the reader's mind. His other novels include *A Farewell to Arms* (1929), a love story set during World War I; *For Whom the Bell Tolls* (1940), an epic story set against the Spanish Civil War of the 1930s; and *The Old Man and the Sea* (1952), an allegorical tale of a fisherman off the coast of Cuba. In 1954 Hemingway received the Nobel Prize for Literature.

Like the author himself, the Hemingway hero lives a life of great adventure. Whether big-game hunting, deep-sea fishing, boxing, bullfighting, or soldiering, he displays what Hemingway called "grace under pressure." Yet this "tough-guy" image is in some ways a mask disguising an extremely sensitive nature. That sensitivity is apparent in his story "In Another Country," where the narrator reports with characteristic matter-of-factness events so sad and terrible that they need no comment.

■ Some situations are so sad that to put them into words is nearly impossible. How does Hemingway succeed in doing the impossible?

AT A GLANCE

- As the battles of World War I continue, the American narrator and his friends walk along Milan's chilly streets to the local hospital where they undergo therapy for war wounds.
- The treatment uses experimental machines.

LITERARY OPTIONS

- style
- symbolism
- tone

THEMATIC OPTIONS

- alienation and fragmentation
- detachment
- disillusionment

Model for Active Reading

In this selection, and in one selection in each unit, you will find notes in the right-hand margin that highlight parts of the selection. These notes point out important ideas of the literary period—in this case, Modernism—and draw your attention to literary elements and techniques covered in the Literary Focuses. Page numbers in the notes will refer you to more extensive discussions of these important ideas and elements.

Ernest Hemingway

In Another Country

In the fall the war[1] was always there, but we did not go to it any more. It was cold in the fall in Milan[2] and the dark came very early. Then the electric lights came on, and it was pleasant along the streets looking in the windows. There was much game hanging outside the shops, and the snow powdered in the fur of the foxes and the wind blew their tails. The deer hung stiff and heavy and empty, and small birds blew in the wind and the wind turned their feathers. It was a cold fall and the wind came down from the mountains.

Modernist idea: Instead of beginning with the *exposition* standard in traditional short stories (p. 323), Hemingway starts his story in the middle of the narrator's memory of the war (p. 404).

We were all at the hospital every afternoon, and there were different ways of walking across the town through the dusk to the hospital. Two of the ways were alongside canals, but they were long. Always, though, you crossed a bridge across a canal to enter the hospital. There was a choice of three bridges. On one of them a woman sold roasted chestnuts. It was warm, standing in front of her charcoal fire, and the chestnuts were warm afterward in your pocket. The hospital was very old and very beautiful, and you entered through a gate and walked across a courtyard and out a gate on the other side. There were usually funerals starting from the courtyard. Beyond the old hospital were the new brick pavilions, and there we met every afternoon and were all very polite and interested in what was the matter, and sat in the machines that were to make so much difference.

Point of view (p. 333): The story is told in the first person; the narrator uses the pronoun *I* and is limited to suggesting the attitudes and thoughts of other characters.

The doctor came up to the machine where I was sitting and said: "What did you like best to do before the war? Did you practice a sport?"

1. **the war:** World War I (1914–1918).
2. **Milan** [Mi lan′]: city in northern Italy.

GUIDED READING

LITERAL QUESTIONS

1a. What does the narrator not go to anymore? (the war)

2a. What does he do at the hospital? (meets others, sits at a machine)

INFERENTIAL QUESTIONS

1b. What does this information reveal about the narrator? (He is a former soldier.)

2b. What does this information tell you about his present situation? (He goes to the hospital for daily therapy, perhaps for a wound.)

I said: "Yes, football."

"Good," he said. "You will be able to play football again better than ever."

My knee did not bend and the leg dropped straight from the knee to the ankle without a calf, and the machine was to bend the knee and make it move as in riding a tricycle. But it did not bend yet, and instead the machine lurched when it came to the bending part. The doctor said: "That will all pass. You are a fortunate young man. You will play football again like a champion."

In the next machine was a major who had a little hand like a baby's. He winked at me when the doctor examined his hand, which was between two leather straps that bounced up and down and flapped the stiff fingers, and said: "And will I too play football, captain-doctor?" He had been a very great fencer, and before the war the greatest fencer in Italy.

The doctor went to his office in the back room and brought a photograph which showed a hand that had been withered almost as small as the major's, before it had taken a machine course, and after was a little larger. The major held the photograph with his good hand and looked at it very carefully. "A wound?" he asked.

"An industrial accident," the doctor said.

"Very interesting, very interesting," the major said, and handed it back to the doctor.

"You have confidence?"

"No," said the major.

There were three boys who came each day who were about the same age I was. They were all three from Milan, and one of them was to be a lawyer, and one was to be a painter, and one had intended to be a soldier, and after we were finished with the machines, sometimes we walked back together to the Café Cova, which was next door to the Scala.[3] We walked the short way through the communist quarter because we were four together. The people hated us because we were officers, and from a wineshop some one would call out, "A basso gli ufficiali!"[4] as we passed. Another boy who walked with us sometimes and made us five wore a black silk handkerchief across his face because he had no nose then and his face was to be rebuilt. He had gone out to the front from the military academy and been wounded within an hour after he had gone into the front line for the first time. They rebuilt his face, but he came from a very old family and they could never get the nose exactly right. He went to South America and worked in a bank. But this was a long time ago, and then we did not any of us know how it was going to be afterward. We only

Diction (p. 211): Hemingway chooses simple words to achieve a matter-of-fact tone.

Modernist idea: The author makes no direct statement about the tragedies of war but merely uses a verb tense *(was to be/had intended to be)* that forces his readers to draw their own conclusions (p. 404).

Tone (p. 474): Hemingway's characteristically matter-of-fact tone does not falter, even in reporting the most terrible facts.

3. **the Scala** [ska′lə]: famous opera house in Milan.
4. **"A basso gli ufficiali!"** [a ba′sō lyē o͞o fē cha′lē]: "Down with officers!"

AT A GLANCE

- The narrator is assured he will play football again one day. He notes an Italian major, once a fencing champion, who now has a hopelessly wounded hand; he sees a boy with no nose.
- Strolling with his Milanese friends, he sees that people hate them because they're officers.

GUIDED READING

LITERAL QUESTIONS

1a. Why is the major in a machine? (His hand is withered and useless.)

2a. In the communist quarter, what does someone shout? ("Down with officers!")

INFERENTIAL QUESTIONS

1b. How does his wound affect his life? (He is no longer a champion fencer.)

2b. Why might the officers feel disillusioned? (They were wounded in the war and are now reviled by the people whom they fought for.)

AT A GLANCE

Detached and disillusioned by war experiences, the narrator and his friends are held together by their daily meeting.

Scene in a Red Cross hospital, 1914.

knew then that there was always the war, but that we were not going to it any more.

We all had the same medals, except the boy with the black silk bandage across his face, and he had not been at the front long enough to get any medals. The tall boy with a very pale face who was to be a lawyer had been a lieutenant of Arditi[5] and had three medals of the sort we each had only one of. He had lived a very long time with death and was a little detached. We were all a little detached, and there was nothing that held us together except that we met every afternoon at the hospital. Although, as we walked to the Cova through the tough part of town, walking in the dark, with light and singing coming out of the wine-shops, and sometimes having to walk into the street when the men and women would crowd together on the sidewalk so that we would have had to jostle them to get by, we felt held together by there being something that had happened that they, the people who disliked us, did not understand.

Modernist idea: Detachment and disillusionment with warfare were common among the "lost generation" (p. 403).

5. **Arditi** [ar dē′tē]: corps of soldiers specially selected for dangerous operations.

GUIDED READING

LITERAL QUESTION

1a. What holds the officers together? (something that those who don't like them don't understand)

INFERENTIAL QUESTION

1b. What is this "something"? (They have lived with war and death and now feel detached and disillusioned.)

We ourselves all understood the Cova, where it was rich and warm and not too brightly lighted, and noisy and smoky at certain hours, and there were always girls at the tables and the illustrated papers on a rack on the wall. The girls at the Cova were very patriotic, and I found that the most patriotic people in Italy were the café girls—and I believe they are still patriotic.

The boys at first were very polite about my medals and asked me what I had done to get them. I showed them the papers, which were written in very beautiful language and full of *fratellanza* and *abnegazione,*[6] but which really said, with the adjectives removed, that I had been given the medals because I was an American. After that their manner changed a little toward me, although I was their friend against outsiders. I was a friend, but I was never really one of them after they had read the citations, because it had been different with them and they had done very different things to get their medals. I had been wounded, it was true; but we all knew that being wounded, after all, was really an accident. I was never ashamed of the ribbons, though, and sometimes, after the cocktail hour, I would imagine myself having done all the things they had done to get their medals; but walking home at night through the empty streets with the cold wind and all the shops closed, trying to keep near the street lights, I knew that I would never have done such things, and I was very much afraid to die, and often lay in bed at night by myself, afraid to die and wondering how I would be when I went back to the front again.

Round character (p. 323): The narrator is a complex, well-developed character whose thoughts, when we learn them, reveal conflicting emotions and attitudes.

The three with the medals were like hunting-hawks; and I was not a hawk, although I might seem a hawk to those who had never hunted; they, the three, knew better and so we drifted apart. But I stayed good friends with the boy who had been wounded his first day at the front, because he would never know now how he would have turned out; so he could never be accepted either, and I liked him because I thought perhaps he would not have turned out to be a hawk either.

The major, who had been the great fencer, did not believe in bravery, and spent much time while we sat in the machines correcting my grammar. He had complimented me on how I spoke Italian, and we talked together very easily. One day I had said that Italian seemed such an easy language to me that I could not take a great interest in it; everything was so easy to say. "Ah, yes," the major said. "Why, then, do you not take up the use of grammar?" So we took up the use of grammar, and soon Italian was such a difficult language that I was afraid to talk to him until I had the grammar straight in my mind.

Irony (p. 391): Both verbal and situational irony are abundant, but readers must perceive the irony on their own.

The major came very regularly to the hospital. I do not think

---

6. ***fratellanza*** [fra tāl an′za] **and** ***abnegazione*** [ab nā ga tzyō′nā]: Italian for "brotherhood" and "self-denial."

AT A GLANCE

- The narrator, who has received his medal simply because he is an American, feels excluded from the men who have truly earned theirs.
- The Italian major compliments the narrator on his Italian. The narrator studies grammar and becomes obsessed with perfecting it.

GUIDED READING

LITERAL QUESTION

1a. How does the major feel about bravery? (He doesn't believe in it.)

INFERENTIAL QUESTION

1b. Why is this attitude ironic? (His roles of champion fencer and officer probably demanded courage.)

AT A GLANCE

- While teaching the narrator Italian one day, the major bursts out in a tirade against marriage.
- He later apologizes, saying his wife has just died.

he ever missed a day, although I am sure he did not believe in the machines. There was a time when none of us believed in the machines, and one day the major said it was all nonsense. The machines were new then and it was we who were to prove them. It was an idiotic idea, he said, "a theory, like another." I had not learned my grammar, and he said I was a stupid impossible disgrace, and he was a fool to have bothered with me. He was a small man and he sat straight up in his chair with his right hand thrust into the machine and looked straight ahead at the wall while the straps thumped up and down with his fingers in them.

Symbolism (p. 190): The machines *are* machines in the story, but they also come to represent something else.

"What will you do when the war is over if it is over?" he asked me. "Speak grammatically!"

"I will go to the States."

"Are you married?"

"No, but I hope to be."

"The more of a fool you are," he said. He seemed very angry. "A man must not marry."

"Why, Signor Maggiore?"[7]

"Don't call me 'Signor Maggiore.' "

"Why must not a man marry?"

"He cannot marry. He cannot marry," he said angrily. "If he is to lose everything, he should not place himself in a position to lose that. He should not place himself in a position to lose. He should find things he cannot lose."

He spoke very angrily and bitterly, and looked straight ahead while he talked.

"But why should he necessarily lose it?"

"He'll lose it," the major said. He was looking at the wall. Then he looked down at the machine and jerked his little hand out from between the straps and slapped it hard against his thigh. "He'll lose it," he almost shouted. "Don't argue with me!" Then he called to the attendant who ran the machines. "Come and turn this thing off."

He went back into the other room for the light treatment and the massage. Then I heard him ask the doctor if he might use his telephone and he shut the door. When he came back into the room, I was sitting in another machine. He was wearing his cape and had his cap on, and he came directly toward my machine and put his arm on my shoulder.

"I am so sorry," he said, and patted me on the shoulder with his good hand. "I would not be rude. My wife has just died. You must forgive me."

"Oh—" I said, feeling sick for him. "I am *so* sorry."

7. **Signor Maggiore** [sēn yôr′ maj jō′rā]: Italian for "Mr. Major." In Italy it was a sign of respect to say *Signor* before an officer's rank.

GUIDED READING

LITERAL QUESTIONS

1a. How does the major feel about testing the machines? (He thinks it is idiotic.)

2a. What does the major learn on the telephone? (His wife has just died.)

INFERENTIAL QUESTIONS

1b. Why would he think that? (They cannot restore his hand or former life.)

2b. Why is he rude? (He had been trying to suppress his grief and despair.)

He stood there biting his lower lip. "It is very difficult," he said. "I cannot resign myself."

He looked straight past me and out through the window. Then he began to cry. "I am utterly unable to resign myself," he said and choked. And then crying, his head up looking at nothing, carrying himself straight and soldierly, with tears on both his cheeks and biting his lips, he walked past the machines and out the door.

The doctor told me that the major's wife, who was very young and whom he had not married until he was definitely invalided out of the war, had died of pneumonia. She had been sick only a few days. No one expected her to die. The major did not come to the hospital for three days. Then he came at the usual hour, wearing a black band on the sleeve of his uniform. When he came back, there were large framed photographs around the wall, of all sorts of wounds before and after they had been cured by the machines. In front of the machine the major used were three photographs of hands like his that were completely restored. I do not know where the doctor got them. I always understood we were the first to use the machines. The photographs did not make much difference to the major because he only looked out of the window.

Modernist idea: The lack of a traditional *climax* or *resolution* (p. 323) reflects the Modernist experimentation with standard forms and perception of the modern world as fragmentary and confusing (p. 404).

STUDY QUESTIONS

Recalling

1. Where does the narrator go every afternoon, according to the second paragraph?
2. What had the major been before the war, and in what part of the body has he been injured? When was the boy with the silk handkerchief injured? What had been the career plans of the three others who accompany the narrator to the cafe each afternoon?
3. According to the narrator, why do the three Italians change in their attitude toward him? What does the narrator say the "three with the medals" are like? Does the narrator feel he is like this?
4. Near the end of the story, what does the major say "a man must not" do? What has happened to the major's wife?
5. What do the pictures described in the last paragraph show? What does the narrator "not know" about these pictures? What has he "always understood"?

Interpreting

6. Why might the narrator feel different from the three boys from Milan? Why might he feel kinship with the boy with the silk handkerchief?
7. Why does the major tell the narrator not to marry?
8. How are the narrator's and the major's wounds more than merely physical injuries? Do the narrator and the major believe that the machines will work? What might the machines come to represent to the wounded soldiers by the story's end?
9. The story takes place in Italy, and the narrator is the only American. Is this the only reason for the title? Explain.

Extending

10. How does this story help explain the attitude of the "lost generation" after World War I? Do you think all the characters are "lost"? Why or why not?

AT A GLANCE

- The major exclaims, with infinite sadness, "I cannot resign myself."
- He stares hopelessly out the window.

REFLECTING ON THE STORY

In what sense is this story about loss? (The soldiers have lost their sense of purpose; they have all been wounded and so are diminished physically; the major has lost his wife and his hope.)

STUDY QUESTIONS

1. to the hospital
2. fencing champion, hand; his first hour at the front; lawyer, painter, soldier
3. that he received medals because he is American; hunting hawks; no
4. marry; has died
5. wounds before and after treatment; where they came from; that they were the first to use the machines
6. because he's American; wounded so early he did not develop as warrior
7. avoid pain, loss (his wife has died)
8. psychic scars, separate them from society; no; futility of healing resources of society
9. no—separation, alienation
10. pessimism, alienation of war: must face pain, wounds alone; narrator and major more "lost," but all scarred

VIEWPOINT

The hidden story is the alienation and despair that each character faces, symbolized by the machines. The narrator never confesses to these feelings, but the sense of the dimensions of the scarring, the levels which it has penetrated, is present nevertheless in the story.

LITERARY FOCUS

The rhythms of the sentences are abrupt, as if each statement must be closed to restrict excess emotion. The sentences are deliberately dull, after reflecting the blankness of the death they describe. The language of the narrator is almost colorless, as if all commitment and emotion has been taken out of him by the war. We sense the bitterness and pain in his own experience. The effect of this technique is to make us aware of *unspeakable* sadness.

VIEWPOINT

Hugh Kenner, an expert in modern literature, has remarked that Ernest Hemingway

> developed the knack of telling simultaneously an overt story and a hidden one.

■ Kenner suggests that the real center of a Hemingway story is not the direct statements on the "surface" of the story but the concerns that the writer communicates indirectly. How would you distinguish the "overt" story from the "hidden" one in "In Another Country"? What does the narrator never say that the reader nevertheless understands?

LITERARY FOCUS

Prose Style

Ernest Hemingway was as concerned about style as any poet would be. The simplicity of his prose is deceptive, for each word in carefully chosen and placed to create a rhythm that moves the reader along.

Reread the first paragraph of "In Another Country." Notice how the sentences get longer in the middle and how the last sentence is the shortest. There is a sense of conclusion to the last sentence, enhanced by the repetition of words from earlier sentences: "cold," "fall," "wind." The paragraph is circular: It returns us to the ideas with which it began. The repetition of *l* sounds makes it roll to its perfect conclusion. No word, no syllable, no sound is accidental or arbitrary.

At the same time, Hemingway's simple language mirrors the matter-of-fact point of view that he wishes to achieve. Hemingway writes in a **journalistic prose style,** observing from a detached point of view, presenting the facts as a journalist would and forcing the reader to draw the conclusions. When in the last paragraph of "In Another Country" the narrator tells us "I do not know where the doctor got them," we know he is implying with quiet irony that the pictures have been faked. Yet the sentence itself could have been written by a child. The simple language underscores Hemingway's desire to observe the facts without elaboration so that his readers are forced to draw the conclusions and perceive the irony for themselves.

Thinking About Prose Style

■ How do the sentence rhythms in the last paragraph reflect the finality of the death of the major's wife? How does the language underscore the narrator's matter-of-fact attitude toward the death? What do we conclude that the narrator never tells us?

COMPOSITION

Writing a Comparison/Contrast

■ Find a passage from "In Another Country" that illustrates the main characteristics of Hemingway's prose style. Then find a passage from another story in this volume that strikes you as very different in style. You might consider the stories of Poe, Crane, or Jewett. Make notes on word choice, sentence length, sound, and point of view in the two selections, and then arrange your notes in a logical order. Based on your notes, write a brief essay in which you compare and contrast the two prose styles. *For help with this assignment, refer to Lesson 2 in the Writing About Literature Handbook at the back of this book.*

Writing a Narrative

■ Choose an actual historical event, or invent a significant event. In a few paragraphs tell what happened using a detached, journalistic style similar to Ernest Hemingway's. Narrate the story of what happened in simple language; use dialogue if appropriate. Omit any direct statements about the significance of the event. Force your readers to draw their own conclusions by including hints about the event's importance.

COMPOSITION: GUIDELINES FOR EVALUATION

WRITING A COMPARISON/CONTRAST

Objective

To compare and contrast prose styles

Guidelines for Evaluation

- suggested length: four to six paragraphs
- should choose passages characteristic of an author or story
- should compare word choice, sentence length, sound, and point of view
- should make generalizations about the styles

WRITING A NARRATIVE

Objective

To write a narrative using a detached style

Guidelines for Evaluation

- suggested length: four to six paragraphs
- should focus on significant event
- should describe the event clearly, using simple language
- should omit direct statements about significance, allowing the reader to draw conclusions

F. Scott Fitzgerald *1896–1940*

When F. Scott Fitzgerald wrote "There are no second acts in American life," he might have been describing his own career. The spokesman of the Roaring Twenties, Fitzgerald achieved great success early in life but was unable to sustain that success into middle age. Burned out by personal and financial disasters, he died of a heart attack at forty-four.

Fitzgerald was born in St. Paul, Minnesota, into a family of little wealth but great social ambitions. After attending Princeton and serving as an officer in World War I, he settled in New York City, walking the streets in cardboard shoes and wondering where his next meal would come from. Such worries ended in 1920 with the publication of *This Side of Paradise.* The book was an overnight success, and Fitzgerald was able to marry Zelda Sayre, the southern belle with whom he had fallen in love, and to live glamorously in Europe and America.

Throughout the twenties Fitzgerald mingled with the rich and fashionable, maintaining a high style of living. When the frantic twenties ended in the great stock market crash of 1929, Fitzgerald's private life and lucrative career crashed also: His wife suffered a series of nervous breakdowns; his high-paying magazine market evaporated; and although he had made vast amounts of money, he found that he had spent it all. In a desperate attempt to pay for his wife's hospitalization, he spent his last years turning out undistinguished screenplays in Hollywood.

Yet Fitzgerald was also a serious artist, and he produced a body of work that captures the Jazz Age as only an insider could capture it. His masterpiece, *The Great Gatsby* (1925), is a vivid and moving portrait of Jazz Age characters whose talents and dignity are distorted by false values. His semiautobiographical short stories and novels *Tender Is the Night* (1934) and *The Last Tycoon* (1941) reflect a sharp awareness of the tragic attachment to wealth and "society" from which Fitzgerald, like his heroes, suffered.

Basil Lee, the hero of "He Thinks He's Wonderful," bears a striking resemblance to Fitzgerald as a teen-ager. Basil is viewed with Fitzgerald's characteristic blend of satire and sympathy.

■ Much of Fitzgerald's writing tends to be autobiographical. What might this story tell you about Fitzgerald as a teen-ager?

AT A GLANCE

- *Section 1:* Fifteen-year-old Basil Lee returns to Minnesota from an unhappy year of school in the East.
- On the train he encounters someone from home.

LITERARY OPTIONS

- characterization
- conflict
- satire

THEMATIC OPTIONS

- personal identity
- adolescence vs. maturity
- self-absorption vs. awareness of others

1 CHARACTERIZATION

Basil, appearing in a suit that does not fit, seems to be similarly askew emotionally.

2 CONFLICT

Basil's belief that everything is achievable through effort will inevitably lead to conflict because his expectations exceed what is humanly possible.

3 SETTING

The big city intimidates Basil, but it also appeals to his active imagination.

F. Scott Fitzgerald

He Thinks He's Wonderful

1

After the college board examinations in June, Basil Duke Lee and five other boys from St. Regis School boarded the train for the West. Two got out at Pittsburgh, one slanted south toward St. Louis and two stayed in Chicago; from then on Basil was alone. It was the first time in his life that he had ever felt the need of tranquillity, but now he took long breaths of it; for, though things had gone better toward the end, he had had an unhappy year at school.

He wore one of those extremely flat derbies[1] in vogue during the twelfth year of
1 the century, and a blue business suit become a little too short for his constantly lengthening body. Within he was by turns a disembodied spirit, almost unconscious of his person and moving in a mist of impressions and emotions, and a fiercely competitive individual trying desperately to control the rush of events that were the steps in his own evolution from child
2 to man. He believed that everything was a matter of effort—the current principle of American education—and his fantastic ambition was continually leading him to expect too much. He wanted to be a great athlete, popular, brilliant and always happy. During this year at school, where he had been punished for his "freshness," for fifteen years of thorough spoiling at home, he had grown uselessly introspective, and this interfered with that observation of others which is the beginning of wisdom. It was apparent that before he obtained much success in dealing with the world he would know that he'd been in a fight.

3 He spent the afternoon in Chicago, walking the streets and avoiding members of the underworld. He bought a detective story called "In the Dead of the Night," and at five o'clock recovered his suitcase from the station check room and boarded the Chicago, Milwaukee and St. Paul. Immediately he encountered a contemporary, also bound home from school.

1. **derbies:** stiff hats with round crowns and curved brims.

GUIDED READING

LITERAL QUESTION

1a. What does Basil expect of himself? (He wants every kind of success in abundance.)

INFERENTIAL QUESTION

1b. Why are these expectations likely to lead to an internal conflict? (No one can be fabulously successful at everything, and Basil will be disappointed.)

Margaret Torrence was fourteen; a serious girl, considered beautiful by a sort of tradition,
1 for she had been beautiful as a little girl. A year and a half before, after a breathless struggle, Basil had succeeded in kissing her on the forehead. They met now with extraordinary joy; for a moment each of them to the other represented home, the blue skies of the past, the summer afternoons ahead.

He sat with Margaret and her mother in the dining car that night. Margaret saw that he was no longer the ultraconfident boy of a year before; his brightness was subdued, and the air of consideration in his face—a mark of his recent discovery that others had wills as strong as his, and more power—appeared to Margaret as a charming sadness. The spell of peace after a struggle was still upon him. Margaret had always liked him—she was of the grave, conscientious type who sometimes loved him and whose love he could never return—and now she could scarcely wait to tell people how attractive he had grown.

After dinner they went back to the observation car and sat on the deserted rear platform while the train pulled them visibly westward between the dark wide farms. They talked of people they knew, of where they had gone for Easter vacation, of the plays they had seen in New York.

"Basil, we're going to get an automobile," she said, "and I'm going to learn to drive."

"That's fine." He wondered if his grandfather would let him drive the electric[2] sometimes this summer.

The light from inside the car fell on her young face, and he spoke impetuously, borne on by the rush of happiness that he was going home: "You know something? You know you're the prettiest girl in the city?"

At the moment when the remark blurred with the thrilling night in Margaret's heart, Mrs. Torrence appeared to fetch her to bed.

Basil sat alone on the platform for a while, scarcely realizing that she was gone, at peace with himself for another hour and content that everything should remain patternless and shapeless until tomorrow.

2

Fifteen is of all ages the most difficult to locate—to put one's fingers on and say, "That's the way I was." The melancholy Jacques[3] does not select it for mention, and all one can know is that somewhere between thirteen, boyhood's majority, and seventeen, when one is a sort of counterfeit young man, there is a time when youth fluctuates hourly between one world and another—pushed ceaselessly forward into unprecedented experiences and vainly trying to struggle back to the days when nothing had to
2 be paid for. Fortunately none of our contemporaries remember much more than we do of how we behaved in those days; nevertheless the curtain is about to be drawn aside for an inspection of Basil's madness that summer.

To begin with, Margaret Torrence, in one of those moods of idealism which overcome the most matter-of-fact girls, gave it as her rapt
3 opinion that Basil was wonderful. Having practised believing things all year at school, and having nothing much to believe at that moment, her friends accepted the fact. Basil suddenly became a legend. There were outbreaks of giggling when girls encountered him on the street, but he suspected nothing at all.

One night, when he had been home a week, he and Riply Buckner went on to an after dinner gathering on Imogene Bissel's veranda. As they came up the walk Margaret and two other girls suddenly clung together, whispered convulsively and pursued one another around the yard, uttering strange cries—an inexplicable business that ended only when Gladys Van Schellinger, tenderly and impressively accompanied by her mother's maid, arrived in a limousine.

---

2. **electric:** early type of automobile powered by an electric battery.

3. **the melancholy Jacques** [jā′kwēz]: a character in Shakespeare's *As You Like It* who philosophizes about the stages of life.

AT A GLANCE

- Margaret Torrence, the friend on the train, thinks that Basil has become attractive.
- *Section 2:* Margaret tells friends what she thinks of Basil; they begin to see him differently.

1 THEME

The awkward kiss reflects adolescent embarrassment and uncertainty.

2 POINT OF VIEW

The omniscient narrator has the perspective that Basil lacks.

3 SATIRE

The narrator pokes fun at the mindless way in which attitudes are adopted like fads by adolescents.

GUIDED READING

LITERAL QUESTION

1a. What does Basil tell Margaret on the train? (that she is pretty)

2a. How do Margaret and the other girls react when Basil arrives at Imogene's house? (They whisper to one another and run around the yard.)

INFERENTIAL QUESTION

1b. Why does he pay her this compliment? (Going home puts him in a good mood, and he feels like saying something nice.)

2b. How has Margaret caused this reaction? (Margaret's talk about Basil has made him a kind of celebrity.)

AT A GLANCE

- The teen-agers sing and play with romance vaguely in mind.
- While playing Truth, Margaret announces that her favorite boy is Basil.

1 THEME

The passage from adolescence to maturity is characterized by the change in the group's interests and in the feeling of suspense.

2 ATMOSPHERE

Fitzgerald uses fragments of idiomatic, adolescent talk and the popular song "Moonlight Bay" to capture the mood of a fondly remembered time.

3 THEME

Absorbed in himself, Basil's only response to Joe's good singing is to regret that he cannot sing as well.

4 BACKGROUND

In the game of Truth, the individual being questioned must tell the truth or forfeit a turn. In this passage the game of Truth imitates the adolescent struggle to create and try on an identity.

All of them were a little strange to one another. Those who had been East at school felt a certain superiority, which, however, was more than counterbalanced by the fact that romantic pairings and quarrels and jealousies and adventures, of which they were lamentably ignorant, had gone on while they had been away.

After the ice cream at nine they sat together on the warm stone steps in a quiet confusion that was halfway between childish teas-
1 ing and adolescent coquetry.[4] Last year the boys would have ridden their bicycles around the yard; now they had all begun to wait for something to happen.

They knew it was going to happen, the plainest girls, the shyest boys; they had begun to associate with others the romantic world of summer night that pressed deeply and sweetly on their senses. Their voices drifted in a sort of broken harmony in to Mrs. Bissel, who sat reading beside an open window.

2 "No, look out. You'll break it. Bay-zil!"
"Rip-lee!"
"Sure I did!"
Laughter.

"—on Moonlight Bay
We could hear their voices call—"

"Did you see—"
"Connie, don't—don't! You tickle. Look out!"
Laughter.
"Going to the lake tomorrow?"
"Going Friday."
"Elwood's home."
"Is Elwood home?"

"—you have broken my heart—"

"Look out now!"
"Look out!"

3 Basil sat beside Riply on the balustrade,[5] listening to Joe Gorman singing. It was one of the griefs of his life that he could not sing "so people could stand it," and he conceived a sudden admiration for Joe Gorman, reading into his personality the thrilling clearness of those sounds that moved so confidently through the dark air.

They evoked for Basil a more dazzling night than this, and other more remote and enchanted girls. He was sorry when the voice died away, and there was a rearranging of seats and a businesslike quiet—the ancient game of Truth had begun.

4 "What's your favorite color, Bill?"
"Green," supplies a friend.
"Sh-h-h! Let him alone."
Bill says, "Blue."
"What's your favorite girl's name?"
"Mary," says Bill.

"Mary Haupt! Bill's got a crush on Mary Haupt!"

She was a cross-eyed girl, a familiar personification of repulsiveness.

"Who would you rather kiss than anybody?"

Across the pause a snicker stabbed the darkness.

"My mother."

"No, but what girl?"

"Nobody."

"That's not fair. Forfeit! Come on, Margaret."

"Tell the truth, Margaret."

She told the truth and a moment later Basil looked down in surprise from his perch; he had just learned that he was her favorite boy.

"Oh, yes-s!" he exclaimed sceptically. "Oh, yes-s! How about Hubert Blair?"

He renewed a casual struggle with Riply Buckner and presently they both fell off the balustrade. The game became an inquisition into Gladys Van Schellinger's carefully chaperoned heart.

"What's your favorite sport?"

"Croquet."[6]

The admission was greeted by a mild titter.

"Favorite boy."

---

4. **coquetry** [kō′kə trē]: flirting.
5. **balustrade** [bal′əs trād′]: railing supported by posts.
6. **croquet** [krō kā′]: outdoor game in which mallets are used to drive a wooden ball through small hoops.

GUIDED READING

LITERAL QUESTION

1a. What truth does Margaret tell that surprises Basil? (that he is her favorite boy)

INFERENTIAL QUESTION

1b. Why does the revelation surprise him? (Although he had noticed her earlier attentiveness toward him, he does not understand its cause—her sensitivity to the change in him.)

"Thurston Kohler."

A murmur of disappointment.

"Who's he?"

"A boy in the East."

This was manifestly an evasion.

"Who's your favorite boy here?"

Gladys hesitated. "Basil," she said at length.

The faces turned up to the balustrade this
1 time were less teasing, less jocular. Basil depreciated the matter with "Oh, yes-s! Sure! Oh, yes-s!" But he had a pleasant feeling of recognition, a familiar delight.

Imogene Bissel, a dark little beauty and the most popular girl in their crowd, took Gladys' place. The interlocutors[7] were tired of gastronomic[8] preferences—the first question went straight to the point.

"Imogene, have you ever kissed a boy?"

"No." A cry of wild unbelief. "I have not!" she declared indignantly.

"Well, have you ever been kissed?"

Pink but tranquil, she nodded, adding, "I couldn't help it."

"Who by?"

"I won't tell."

"Oh-h-h! How about Hubert Blair?"

"What's your favorite book, Imogene?"

"Beverly of Graustark."

"Favorite girl?"

"Passion Johnson."

"Who's she?"

"Oh, just a girl at school."

Mrs. Bissel had fortunately left the window.

"Who's your favorite boy?"

2 Imogene answered steadily, "Basil Lee."

This time an impressed silence fell. Basil was not surprised—we are never surprised at our own popularity—but he knew that these were not those ineffable girls, made up out of books and faces momentarily encountered, whose voices he had heard for a moment in Joe Gorman's song. And when, presently, the first telephone rang inside, calling a daughter home, and the girls, chattering like birds, piled all together into Gladys Van Schellinger's limousine, he lingered back in the shadow so as not to seem to be showing off. Then, perhaps because he nourished a vague idea that if he got to know Joe Gorman very well he would get to sing like him, he approached him and asked him to go to Lambert's for a soda.

Joe Gorman was a tall boy with white eyebrows and a stolid face who had only recently become one of their "crowd." He did not like Basil, who, he considered, had been "stuck up" with him last year, but he was acquisitive of useful knowledge and he was momentarily overwhelmed by Basil's success with girls.

It was cheerful in Lambert's, with great moths batting aginst the screen door and languid couples in white dresses and suits spread about the little tables. Over their sodas, Joe proposed that Basil come home with him to spend the night; Basil's permission was obtained over the telephone.

Passing from the gleaming store into the darkness, Basil was submerged in an unreality in which he seemed to see himself from the outside, and the pleasant events of the evening began to take on fresh importance.

Disarmed by Joe's hospitality, he began to discuss the matter.

"That was a funny thing that happened tonight," he said, with a disparaging little laugh.

"What was?"

3 "Why, all those girls saying I was their favorite boy." The remark jarred on Joe. "It's a funny thing," went on Basil. "I was sort of unpopular at school for a while, because I was fresh,[9] I guess. But the thing must be that some boys are popular with boys and some are popular with girls."

He had put himself in Joe's hands, but he was unconscious of it; even Joe was only aware of a certain desire to change the subject.

"When I get my car," suggested Joe, up in his room, "we could take Imogene and Margaret and go for rides."

7. **interlocutors** [in'tər lok'yə tərz]: people participating in a conversation.
8. **gastronomic:** relating to food and fine eating.

9. **fresh:** unmannerly.

AT A GLANCE

- Gladys and Imogene also name Basil as their favorite boy.
- As party breaks up, Basil asks Joe Gorman to join him for a soda.
- Joe invites Basil to spend the night at his house.
- Basil begins to talk to Joe about why girls find him attractive.

1 CONFLICT

Basil does not know how to react to his unexpected popularity; his embarrassment competes with his pleasure.

2 POINT OF VIEW

The narrator both shows Basil's inflated sense of himself and expresses some sympathy for it by commenting that "we are never surprised at our own popularity."

3 THEME

Basil is struggling to determine exactly who he is and how he is connected to those around him. In the process, however, he distances himself from Joe.

GUIDED READING

LITERAL QUESTIONS

1a. Whom do all the girls say they like best? (Basil)

2a. What does Basil want to discuss with Joe? (his own new-found popularity with girls)

INFERENTIAL QUESTIONS

1b. Why do they say this? (Because of Margaret's influence, Basil has become something like a current fad.)

2b. Why does Basil's comment bother Joe? (It seems openly conceited and may also hurt Joe's feelings.)

AT A GLANCE

- Basil gives Joe advice about how to act and dress.
- Basil and Joe have a snack; then they go for a walk around the block in their pajamas.

1 CHARACTERIZATION

Basil's unasked-for and unnecessary advice shows the overbearing side of his personality.

2 IRONY

Given an unhappy year at school, Basil's statement that Joe would find school in the East beneficial is ironical.

3 CHARACTERIZATION

Joe's reaction to Basil's patronizing talk is shown by his actions—opening the door and trying to escape. Basil's insensitivity and self-absorption are also revealed.

4 THEME

Basil's actions seem inexplicable even to himself. He is struggling to forge himself into a single identity.

5 STYLE: IMAGERY

The picture of Joe and Basil slipping around as unsubstantial, ghostlike beings suggests their half-formed status: They are neither boys nor men.

"All right."

"You could have Imogene and I'd take Margaret, or anybody I wanted. Of course I know they don't like me as well as they do you."

"Sure they do. It's just because you haven't been in our crowd very long yet."

Joe was sensitive on that point and the remark did not please him. But Basil continued:
1 "You ought to be more polite to the older people if you want to be popular. You didn't say how do you do to Mrs. Bissel tonight."

"I'm hungry," said Joe quickly. "Let's go down to the pantry and get something to eat."

Clad only in their pajamas, they went downstairs. Principally to dissuade Basil from pursuing the subject, Joe began to sing in a low voice:

> "Oh, you beautiful doll,
> You great—big—"

But the evening, coming after the month of enforced humility at school, had been too much for Basil. He got a little awful. In the kitchen, under the impression that his advice had been asked, he broke out again:

"For instance, you oughtn't to wear those white ties. Nobody does that that goes East to school." Joe, a little red, turned around from the ice box and Basil felt a slight misgiving.
2 But he pursued with: "For instance, you ought to get your family to send you East to school. It'd be a great thing for you. Especially if you want to go East to college, you ought to first go East to school. They take it out of you."

Feeling that he had nothing special to be taken out of him, Joe found the implication distasteful. Nor did Basil appear to him at that moment to have been perfected by the process.

"Do you want cold chicken or cold ham?" They drew up chairs to the kitchen table. "Have some milk?"

"Thanks."

Intoxicated by the three full meals he had had since supper, Basil warmed to his subject. He built up Joe's life for him little by little, transformed him radiantly from what was little more than a Midwestern bumpkin[10] to an Easterner bursting with *savoir-faire*[11] and irresistible to girls. Going into the pantry to put away the milk, Joe paused by the open window for a breath of quiet air; Basil followed. "The thing is if a boy doesn't get it taken out of him at school, he gets it taken out of him at college," he was saying.

3 Moved by some desperate instinct, Joe opened the door and stepped out onto the back porch. Basil followed. The house abutted on the edge of the bluff occupied by the residential section, and the two boys stood silent for a moment, gazing at the scattered lights of the lower city. Before the mystery of the unknown human life coursing through the streets below, Basil felt the purport of his words grow thin and pale.

4 He wondered suddenly what he had said and why it had seemed important to him, and when Joe began to sing again softly, the quiet mood of the early evening, the side of him that was best, wisest and most enduring, stole over him once more. The flattery, the vanity, the fatuousness of the last hour moved off, and when he spoke it was almost in a whisper:

"Let's walk around the block."

The sidewalk was warm to their bare feet.
5 It was only midnight, but the square was deserted save for their whitish figures, inconspicuous against the starry darkness. They snorted with glee at their daring. Once a shadow, with loud human shoes, crossed the street far ahead, but the sound served only to increase their own unsubstantiality. Slipping quickly through the clearings made by gas lamps among the trees, they rounded the block, hurrying when they neared the Gorman house as though they had been really lost in a midsummer night's dream.

Up in Joe's room, they lay awake in the darkness.

---

10. **bumpkin:** awkward person.
11. ***savoir-faire*** [sav′wär fär′]: ability to behave appropriately in any situation.

GUIDED READING

LITERAL QUESTION

1a. What, according to Basil, is good about going to school in the East? (Eastern schools "take it out of you.")

2a. How does Basil change when, after the snack, he goes outside with Joe? (He begins to wonder why he had been talking so much.)

INFERENTIAL QUESTION

1b. What is this "it"? (Basil may be referring to youthful arrogance or freshness, or he may be making this statement just because it has been told to him.)

2b. Why does going outside have this effect on him? (He seems to sense that life goes on in the world apart from him. For a little while, at least, he stops concentrating on himself.)

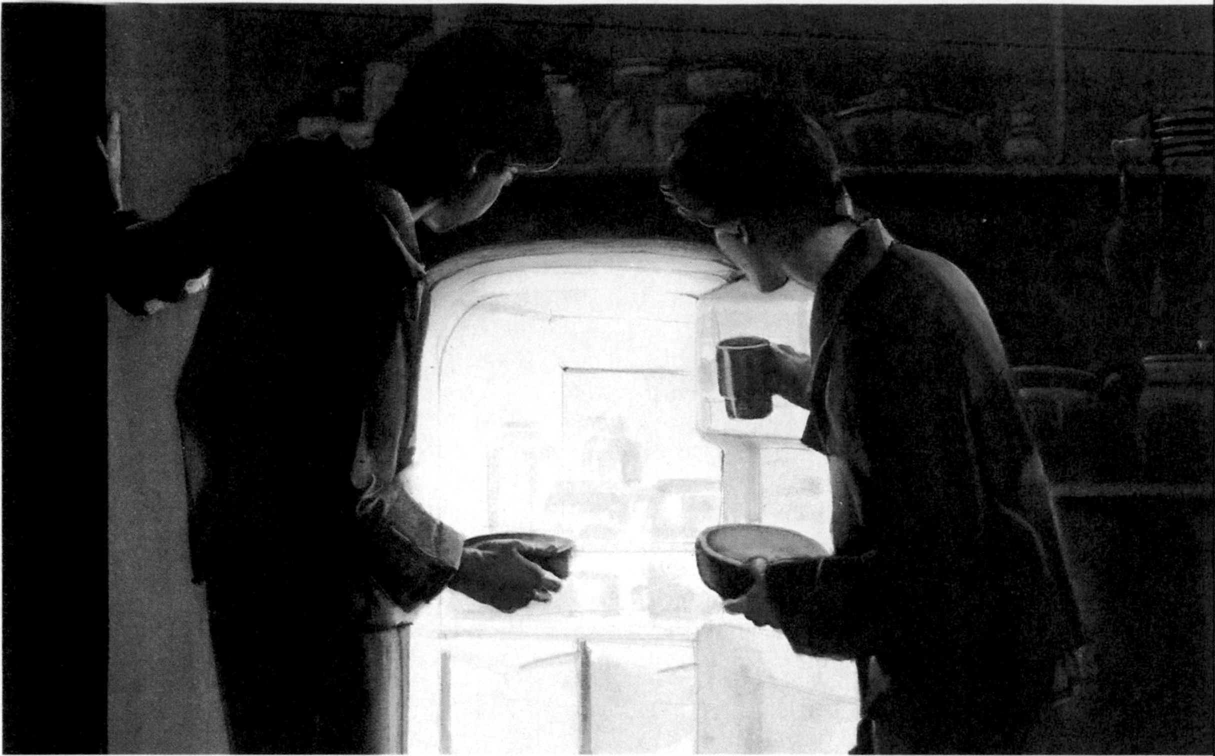

"I talked too much," Basil thought. "I probably sounded pretty bossy and maybe I made him sort of mad. But probably when we walked around the block he forgot everything I said."

Alas, Joe had forgotten nothing—except the advice by which Basil had intended him to profit.

1 "I never saw anybody as stuck up," he said to himself wrathfully. "He thinks he's wonderful. He thinks he's so darn popular with girls."

3

An element of vast importance had made its appearance with the summer; suddenly the
2 great thing in Basil's crowd was to own an automobile. Fun no longer seemed available save at great distances, at suburban lakes or remote country clubs. Walking downtown ceased to be a legitimate pastime. On the contrary, a single block from one youth's house to another's must be navigated in a car. Dependent groups formed around owners and they began to wield what was, to Basil at least, a disconcerting power.

On the morning of a dance at the lake he called up Riply Buckner.

"Hey, Rip, how you going out to Connie's tonight?"

"With Elwood Leaming."

"Has he got a lot of room?"

3 Riply seemed somewhat embarrassed. "Why, I don't think he has. You see, he's taking Margaret Torrence and I'm taking Imogene Bissel."

"Oh!"

Basil frowned. He should have arranged all this a week ago. After a moment he called up Joe Gorman.

AT A GLANCE

- Basil thinks that Joe will forget how talkative he had been, but Joe does not forget.
- *Section 3:* Basil discovers that his friends have made plans without consulting him.

1 CHARACTERIZATION

Basil's personality is revealed in the thoughts of his friends as well as through his own actions.

2 SYMBOL

Having a car is a mark of maturity; the bicycles of the previous summer are gone forever.

3 FORESHADOWING

Riply's embarrassment and the fact that the girls have dates hint that Basil has been deliberately cut out of their plans.

GUIDED READING

LITERAL QUESTION

1a. What does Basil learn from Riply? (that Riply and Elwood are going out with Imogene and Margaret)

INFERENTIAL QUESTION

1b. What does this information suggest about Basil's social status? (It seems to have fallen, perhaps because of his conversation with Joe.)

AT A GLANCE

- Basil arranges to ride to the party with Joe.
- He cuts himself while shaving.
- In the car he is ignored.
- He goes for a walk with Imogene but cannot talk of anything except himself.

1 SYMBOL

Like driving a car, shaving represents maturity. Basil's ineptitude at the task reinforces his lack of maturity.

2 SATIRE

Basil's efforts to make himself attractive end up making him look foolish.

3 VOCABULARY: CONNOTATION

The words *floated* and *wavered* evoke a dreamlike image—a fitting setting for party-goers of that uncertain, in-between age.

4 THEME

Absorbed in himself, Basil is unaware of Imogene's gesture. The narrator's comment—"If he had really cared for her he would have known"—leaves the reader with no doubt about Basil's need to be mature.

"Going to the Davies' tonight, Joe?"

"Why, yes."

"Have you got room in your car—I mean, could I go with you?"

"Why, yes, I suppose so."

There was a perceptible lack of warmth in his voice.

"Sure you got plenty of room?"

"Sure. We'll call for you quarter to eight."

1 Basil began preparations at five. For the second time in his life he shaved, completing the operation by cutting a short straight line under his nose. It bled profusely, but on the advice of Hilda, the maid, he finally stanched the flow with little pieces of toilet paper. Quite a number of pieces were necessary; so, in order to facilitate breathing, he trimmed it down with a
2 scissors, and with this somewhat awkward mustache of paper and gore clinging to his upper lip, wandered impatiently around the house.

At six he began working on it again, soaking off the tissue paper and dabbing at the persistently freshening crimson line. It dried at length, but when he rashly hailed his mother it opened once more and the tissue paper was called back into play.

At quarter to eight, dressed in blue coat and white flannels, he drew one last bar of powder across the blemish, dusted it carefully with his handkerchief and hurried out to Joe Gorman's car. Joe was driving in person, and in front with him were Lewis Crum and Hubert Blair. Basil got in the big rear seat alone and they drove without stopping out of the city onto the Black Bear Road, keeping their backs to him and talking in low voices together. He thought at first that they were going to pick up other boys; now he was shocked, and for a moment he considered getting out of the car, but this would imply that he was hurt. His spirit, and with it his face, hardened a little and he sat without speaking or being spoken to for the rest of the ride.

3 After half an hour the Davies' house, a huge rambling bungalow occupying a small peninsula in the lake, floated into sight. Lanterns outlined its shape and wavered in gleaming lines on the gold-and-rose colored water, and as they came near, the low notes of bass horns and drums were blown toward them from the lawn.

Inside Basil looked about for Imogene. There was a crowd around her seeking dances, but she saw Basil; his heart bounded at her quick intimate smile.

"You can have the fourth, Basil, and the eleventh and the second extra. . . . How did you hurt your lip?"

"Cut it shaving," he said hurriedly. "How about supper?"

"Well, I have to have supper with Riply because he brought me."

"No, you don't," Basil assured her.

"Yes, she does," insisted Riply, standing close at hand. "Why don't you get your own girl for supper?"

—but Basil had no girl, though he was as yet unaware of the fact.

After the fourth dance, Basil led Imogene down to the end of the pier, where they found seats in a motorboat.

"Now what?" she said.

He did not know. If he had really cared for
4 her he would have known. When her hand rested on his knee for a moment he did not notice it. Instead, he talked. He told her how he had pitched on the second baseball team at school and had once beaten the first in a five-inning game. He told her that the thing was that some boys were popular with boys and some boys were popular with girls—he, for instance, was popular with girls. In short, he unloaded himself.

At length, feeling that he had perhaps dwelt disproportionately on himself, he told her suddenly that she was his favorite girl.

Imogene sat there, sighing a little in the moonlight. In another boat, lost in the darkness beyond the pier, sat a party of four. Joe Gorman was singing:

"My little love—
—in honey man,
He sure has won my—"

GUIDED READING

LITERAL QUESTIONS

1a. What does Basil do for the second time in his life? (shave)

2a. How do Joe, Lewis, and Hubert treat Basil on the way to the party? (They ignore him.)

INFERENTIAL QUESTIONS

1b. Why does he think that this task is necessary? (He is trying to be as grown-up as possible.)

2b. Why do they treat him in this way? (Joe seems to have passed around the idea that Basil is stuck-up, and they are probably putting him in his place.)

"I thought you might want to know," said Basil to Imogene. "I thought maybe you thought I liked somebody else. The truth game didn't get around to me the other night."

"What?" asked Imogene vaguely. She had forgotten the other night, all nights except this, and she was thinking of the magic in Joe Gorman's voice. She had the next dance with him; he was going to teach her the words of a new
1 song. Basil was sort of peculiar, telling her all this stuff. He was good-looking and attractive and all that, but—she wanted the dance to be over. She wasn't having any fun.

The music began inside—"Everybody's Doing It," played with many little nervous jerks on the violins.

"Oh, listen!" she cried, sitting up and snapping her fingers. "Do you know how to rag?"[12]

"Listen, Imogene"—He half realized that something had slipped away—"let's sit out this dance—you can tell Joe you forgot."

She rose quickly. "Oh, no, I can't!"

2 Unwillingly Basil followed her inside. It had not gone well—he had talked too much again. He waited moodily for the eleventh dance so that he could behave differently. He believed now that he was in love with Imogene. His self-deception created a tightness in his throat, a counterfeit of longing and desire.

Before the eleventh dance he was aware that some party was being organized from which he was purposely excluded. There were whisperings and arguings among some of the boys, and unnatural silences when he came near. He heard Joe Gorman say to Riply Buckner, "We'll just be gone three days. If Gladys can't go, why don't you ask Connie? The chaperons'll—" he changed his sentence as he saw Basil—"and we'll all go to Smith's for ice cream soda."

Later, Basil took Riply Buckner aside but failed to elicit any information: Riply had not forgotten Basil's attempt to rob him of Imogene tonight.

"It wasn't about anything," he insisted. "We're
3 going to Smith's, honest. . . . How'd you cut your lip?"

"Cut it shaving."

When his dance with Imogene came she was even vaguer than before, exchanging mysterious communications with various girls as they moved around the room, locked in the convulsive grip of the Grizzly Bear.[13] He led her out to the boat again, but it was occupied, and they walked up and down the pier while
4 he tried to talk to her and she hummed:

"My little lov-in honey man—"

"Imogene, listen. What I wanted to ask you when we were on the boat before was about the night we played Truth. Did you really mean what you said?"

"Oh, what do you want to talk about that silly game for?"

It had reached her ears, not once but several times, that Basil thought he was wonderful—news that was flying about with as much volatility as the rumor of his graces two weeks
5 before. Imogene liked to agree with everyone—and she had agreed with several impassioned boys that Basil was terrible. And it was difficult not to dislike him for her own disloyalty.

But Basil thought that only ill luck ended the intermission before he could accomplish his purpose; though what he had wanted he had not known.

Finally, during the intermission, Margaret Torrence, whom he had neglected, told him the truth.

"Are you going on the touring party up to the St. Croix River?" she asked. She knew he was not.

"What party?"

"Joe Gorman got it up. I'm going with Elwood Leaming."

"No, I'm not going," he said gruffly. "I couldn't go."

"Oh!"

---

12. **rag:** type of dance popular in the early 1900s.

13. **Grizzly Bear:** popular dance of the period.

AT A GLANCE

- Basil wants Imogene to skip her dance with Joe, but she refuses.
- Basil realizes he is being excluded from party plans.
- Margaret tells Basil about the touring party, but Basil says that he "couldn't go."

1 CHARACTERIZATION

The narrator adds to the portrait of Basil by showing how his talking about himself is perceived by Imogene.

2 CONFLICT

Basil's desire to act less egotistic with Imogene and his need to believe he loves her show the conflict between his self-awareness and his self-absorption.

3 IRONY

Despite all of Basil's efforts to conceal it, nearly everyone asks about his cut lip. His attempt to seem grown-up has backfired.

4 CHARACTERIZATION

By humming the tune, Imogene shows that she is thinking about Joe and that she is finding Basil annoying.

5 THEME

Fitzgerald points out the fickleness of adolescence and the absurd ways in which people deal with their shortcomings.

GUIDED READING

LITERAL QUESTIONS

1a. When Basil becomes aware that a party is being planned without him, whom does he seek out? (Riply)

2a. Who finally tells Basil the truth about the touring party to the St. Croix River? (Margaret)

INFERENTIAL QUESTIONS

1b. Why does Riply deny everything? (Riply is angry with Basil for trying to get Imogene to skip her supper with him; he also may dislike Basil's conceited manner.)

2b. Why does Margaret tell him about the party? (Earlier in the story Margaret seemed to be genuinely fond of Basil, and she may be trying to hurt him for not paying much attention to her.)

AT A GLANCE

- Basil discovers that Joe has turned people against him.
- Bill Kampf invites Basil to spend a weekend with him and his popular cousin.
- Basil thinks that someday they will regret the way they have treated him.

1 POINT OF VIEW

The narrator looks through Basil's eyes to show that Basil automatically blames Joe rather than himself for his predicament.

2 CHARACTERIZATION

Basil's avoidance of people shows his embarrassment. However, even in this crisis he remains convinced of his own importance, believing that the mere sight of him would "diminish their pleasure."

3 IRONY

Basil's thoughts about his future prove the truth of what has been said about him.

4 ALLUSION

Fitzgerald makes a dim reference to Cupid and his arrows of love, adding the satiric touch that these arrows are from youthful sapling and are not to be taken too seriously.

5 READING SKILLS: INFERENCE

Five years from now, when she is twenty, her amorous adventures will have hardened her, but she is not yet brazen.

"I don't like Joe Gorman."

"I guess he doesn't like you much either."

"Why? What did he say?"

"Oh, nothing."

"But what? Tell me what he said."

After a minute she told him, as if reluctantly: "Well, he and Hubert Blair said you thought—you thought you were wonderful." Her heart misgave her.

But she remembered he had asked her for only one dance. "Joe said you told him that all the girls thought you were wonderful."

"I never said anything like that," said Basil indignantly, "never!"

1 He understood—Joe Gorman had done it all, taken advantage of Basil's talking too much—an affliction which his real friends had always allowed for—in order to ruin him. The world was suddenly compact of villainy. He decided to go home.

In the coat room he was accosted by Bill Kampf: "Hello, Basil, how did you hurt your lip?"

"Cut it shaving."

"Say, are you going to this party they're getting up next week?"

"No."

"Well, look, I've got a cousin from Chicago coming to stay with us and mother said I could have a boy out for the weekend. Her name is Minnie Bibble."

"Minnie Bibble?" repeated Basil, vaguely revolted.

"I thought maybe you were going to that party, too, but Riply Buckner said to ask you and I thought—"

"I've got to stay home," said Basil quickly.

"Oh, come on, Basil," he pursued. "It's only for two days, and she's a nice girl. You'd like her."

"I don't know," Basil considered. "I'll tell you what I'll do, Bill. I've got to get the street car home. I'll come out for the weekend if you'll take me over to Wildwood now in your car."

"Sure I will."

Basil walked out on the veranda and approached Connie Davies.

"Goodbye," he said. Try as he might, his voice was stiff and proud. "I had an awfully good time."

"I'm sorry you're leaving so early, Basil." But she said to herself: "He's too stuck up to have a good time. He thinks he's wonderful."

From the veranda he could hear Imogene's
2 laughter down at the end of the pier. Silently he went down the steps and along the walk to meet Bill Kampf, giving strollers a wide berth as though he felt the sight of him would diminish their pleasure.

It had been an awful night.

Ten minutes later Bill dropped him beside the waiting trolley. A few last picnickers sauntered aboard and the car bobbed and clanged through the night toward St. Paul.

Presently two young girls sitting opposite Basil began looking over at him and nudging each other, but he took no notice—he was thinking how sorry they would all be—Imogene and Margaret, Joe and Hubert and Riply.

3 "Look at him now!" they would say to themselves sorrowfully. "President of the United States at twenty-five! Oh, if we only hadn't been so bad to him that night!"

He thought he was wonderful!

4

Ermine Gilberte Labouisse Bibble was in exile. Her parents had brought her from New Orleans to Southampton[14] in May, hoping that the active outdoor life proper to a girl of fif-
4 teen would take her thoughts from love. But North or South, a storm of sapling arrows flew about her. She was "engaged" before the first of June.

Let it not be gathered from the foregoing
5 that the somewhat hard outlines of Miss Bibble at twenty had already begun to appear. She was of a radiant freshness; her head had reminded otherwise not illiterate young men of damp blue violets, pierced with blue windows that looked into a bright soul, with today's new roses showing through.

14. **Southampton:** resort town along the southern shore of Long Island in New York State.

GUIDED READING

LITERAL QUESTIONS

1a. What reason does Basil give Bill Kampf for his not going to Joe's weekend party? (He says that he has to stay home.)

2a. What does Connie think about Basil as he leaves her party? (She thinks that he is conceited.)

INFERENTIAL QUESTIONS

1b. Why does he lie? (He does not want to admit that he had been left out of the plans.)

2b. Why has she reached this conclusion? (Basil's behavior may have been a strong influence. Connie also has probably been influenced by the gossip about Basil.)

She was in exile. She was going to Glacier National Park[15] to forget. It was written[16] that in passage she would come to Basil as a sort of initiation, turning his eyes out from himself and giving him a first dazzling glimpse into the world of love.

She saw him first as a quiet handsome boy with an air of consideration in his face, which was the mark of his recent re-discovery that others had wills as strong as his, and more power. It appeared to Minnie—as a few months back it had appeared to Margaret Torrence, like a charming sadness. At dinner he was polite to Mrs. Kampf in a courteous way that he
1 had from his father, and he listened to Mr. Bibble's discussion of the word "Creole"[17] with such evident interest and appreciation that Mr. Bibble thought, "Now here's a young boy with something *to* him."

After dinner, Minnie, Basil and Bill rode into Black Bear village to the movies, and the slow diffusion of Minnie's charm and personality presently became the charm and personality of the affair itself.

2 It was thus that all Minnie's affairs for many years had a family likeness. She looked at Basil, a childish open look; then opened her eyes wider as if she had some sort of comic misgivings, and smiled—she smiled—

For all the candor of this smile, its effect, because of the special contours of Minnie's face and independent of her mood, was of sparkling invitation. Whenever it appeared Basil seemed to be suddenly inflated and borne upward, a little farther each time, only to be set down when the smile had reached a point where it must become a grin, and chose instead to melt away. It was like a drug. In a little while he wanted nothing except to watch it with a vast buoyant delight.

Then he wanted to see how close he could get to it.

There is a certain stage of an affair between young people when the presence of a third party is a stimulant. Before the second day had
3 well begun, before Minnie and Basil had progressed beyond the point of great gross compliments about each other's surpassing beauty and charm, both of them had begun to think about the time when they could get rid of their host, Bill Kampf.

In the late afternoon, when the first cool of the evening had come down and they were fresh and thin-feeling from swimming, they sat in a cushioned swing, piled high with pillows and shaded by the thick veranda vines; Basil put his arm around her and leaned toward her cheek and Minnie managed it that he touched her fresh lips instead. And he had always learned things quickly.

They sat there for an hour, while Bill's voice reached them, now from the pier, now from the hall above, now from the pagoda[18] at the end of the garden, and three saddled horses chafed their bits in the stable and all around them the bees worked faithfully among
4 the flowers. Then Minnie reached up to reality, and they allowed themselves to be found—

"Why, we were looking for you too."

And Basil, by simply waving his arms and wishing, floated miraculously upstairs to brush his hair for dinner.

5 "She certainly is a wonderful girl. Oh, gosh, she certainly is a wonderful girl!"

He mustn't lose his head. At dinner and afterward he listened with unwavering deferential attention while Mr. Bibble talked of the boll weevil.

"But I'm boring you. You children want to go off by yourselves."

"Not at all, Mr. Bibble. I was very interested—honestly."

"Well, you all go on and amuse yourselves. I didn't realize time was getting on. Nowadays it's so seldom you meet a young man with good manners and good common sense in his

---

15. **Glacier National Park:** national park in northwest Montana.
16. **written:** fated.
17. **"Creole"** [krē′ōl]: referring to the descendants of French and Spanish settlers in Louisiana.
18. **pagoda** [pə gō′də]: small summer house resembling a Far Eastern temple.

AT A GLANCE

- *Section 4:* Minnie finds Basil attractive, and her father considers him an intelligent young man.
- On the second afternoon Minnie and Basil sit in a swing and kiss.
- Basil decides that Minnie is wonderful.

1 SATIRE

Fitzgerald makes fun of the adult attitude that a young person who listens attentively to an older person's talk is showing intelligence and good judgment.

2 PARAPHRASING THIS PASSAGE

Many young men before and after Basil would, like Basil, find themselves caught up by Minnie's appearance, smile, and hollow congeniality.

3 SATIRE

Expressions such as "great gross compliments" and "surpassing beauty and charm" gently mock youthful awkwardness and ardor.

4 VOCABULARY: CONNOTATION

The use of the word *reality* suggests that the hour in the swing had the air of a dream or perhaps even an element of unreality about it.

5 PLOT: RISING ACTION

Basil's observations about Minnie's wonderfulness show that for the first time he is looking beyond himself.

GUIDED READING

LITERAL QUESTION

1a. What is Mr. Bibble's first impression of Basil? (that Basil has "something *to* him"—that he is intelligent)

2a. After their hour on the swing, what does Basil say to himself about Minnie? (that she is wonderful)

INFERENTIAL QUESTION

1b. On what is this impression based? (Because Basil listens to him when he talks, Mr. Bibble thinks that Basil has good sense.)

2b. How are Basil's feelings toward Minnie different from his feelings toward any other girl in the story? (For the first time Basil is thinking about the girl instead of thinking about himself.)

AT A GLANCE

- Basil and Minnie sit in a motorboat, talk, and kiss.
- Her father is planning to ask him to go with them to Glacier Park.
- As Mr. Bibble gives Basil a ride to the train station, Basil talks only about himself.

1 SETTING

The description of the scene on the lake supports the dreamy mood of romance.

2 THEME

Basil's preoccupation with himself is still leading him to think that others are as fascinated with him as he himself is.

3 IRONY

That Mr. Bibble is uninterested in what Basil has to say is shown by his reply, "Good!" when Basil says that he failed French.

4 POINT OF VIEW

The narrator allows readers to infer what Mr. Bibble is thinking from his action.

head, that an old man like me is likely to go along forever."

Bill walked down with Basil and Minnie to the end of the pier. "Hope we'll have a good sailing tomorrow. Say, I've got to drive over to the village and get somebody for my crew. Do you want to come along?"

"I reckon I'll sit here for a while and then go to bed," said Minnie.

"All right. You want to come, Basil?"

"Why—why, sure, if you want me, Bill."

"You'll have to sit on a sail I'm taking over to be mended."

"I don't want to crowd you."

"You won't crowd me. I'll go get the car."

When he had gone they looked at each other in despair. But he did not come back for an hour—something happened about the sail or the car that took a long time. There was only the threat, making everything more poignant and breathless, that at any minute he *would* be coming.

By and by they got into the motorboat and sat close together murmuring: "This fall—" "When you come to New Orleans—" "When I go to Yale year after next—" "When I come North to school—" "When I get back from Glacier Park—" "Kiss me once more." . . . "You're terrible. Do you know you're terrible? . . . You're absolutely terrible—"

1 The water lapped against the posts; sometimes the boat bumped gently on the pier; Basil undid one rope and pushed, so that they swung off and way from the pier, and became a little island in the night. . . .

Next morning, while he packed his bag, she opened the door of his room and stood beside him. Her face shone with excitement; her dress was starched and white.

"Basil, listen! I have to tell you: Father was talking after breakfast and he told Uncle George that he'd never met such a nice, quiet, level-headed boy as you, and Cousin Bill's got to tutor this month, so father asked Uncle George if he thought your family would let you go to Glacier Park with us for two weeks so I'd have some company." They took hands and danced excitedly around the room. "Don't say anything about it, because I reckon he'll have to write your mother and everything. Basil, isn't it wonderful?"

So when Basil left at eleven, there was no misery in their parting. Mr. Bibble, going into the village for a paper, was going to escort Basil to his train, and till the motorcar moved away the eyes of the two young people shone and there was a secret in their waving hands.

Basil sank back in the seat, replete with happiness. He relaxed—to have made a success of the visit was so nice. He loved her—he loved even her father sitting beside him, her father who was privileged to be so close to her, to fuddle[19] himself at that smile.

Mr. Bibble lit a cigar. "Nice weather," he said. "Nice climate up to the end of October."

"Wonderful," agreed Basil. "I miss October now that I go East to school."

"Getting ready for college?"

2 "Yes, sir; getting ready for Yale." A new pleasurable thought occurred to him. He hesitated, but he knew that Mr. Bibble, who liked him, would share his joy. "I took my preliminaries this spring and I just heard from them—I passed six out of seven."

"Good for you!"

Again Basil hesitated, then he continued: "I got A in ancient history and B in English history and English A. And I got C in algebra A and Latin A and B. I failed French A."

3 "Good!" said Mr. Bibble.

"I should have passed them all," went on Basil, "but I didn't study hard at first. I was the youngest boy in my class and I had a sort of swelled head about it."

4 It was well that Mr. Bibble should know he was taking no dullard to Glacier National Park. Mr. Bibble took a long puff of his cigar.

On second thought, Basil decided that his last remark didn't have the right ring and he amended it a little.

"It wasn't exactly a swelled head, but I never had to study very much, because in En-

19. **fuddle:** intoxicate.

GUIDED READING

LITERAL QUESTIONS

1a. Why does Mr. Bibble think of taking Basil to Glacier Park? (because he thinks that "nice, quiet, level-headed" Basil could keep his daughter company)

2a. As Mr. Bibble drives Basil to the train, what does Basil do? (talk about himself)

INFERENTIAL QUESTIONS

1b. When he extends this invitation, what does Mr. Bibble not know about Basil? (He is unaware that Basil is far from "quiet" and that Basil thinks that he is in love with Minnie.)

2b. Why is this course of action a mistake? (Mr. Bibble had come to think that Basil was "level-headed" because Basil was a good listener; besides, Basil already knows how others have reacted to such talk.)

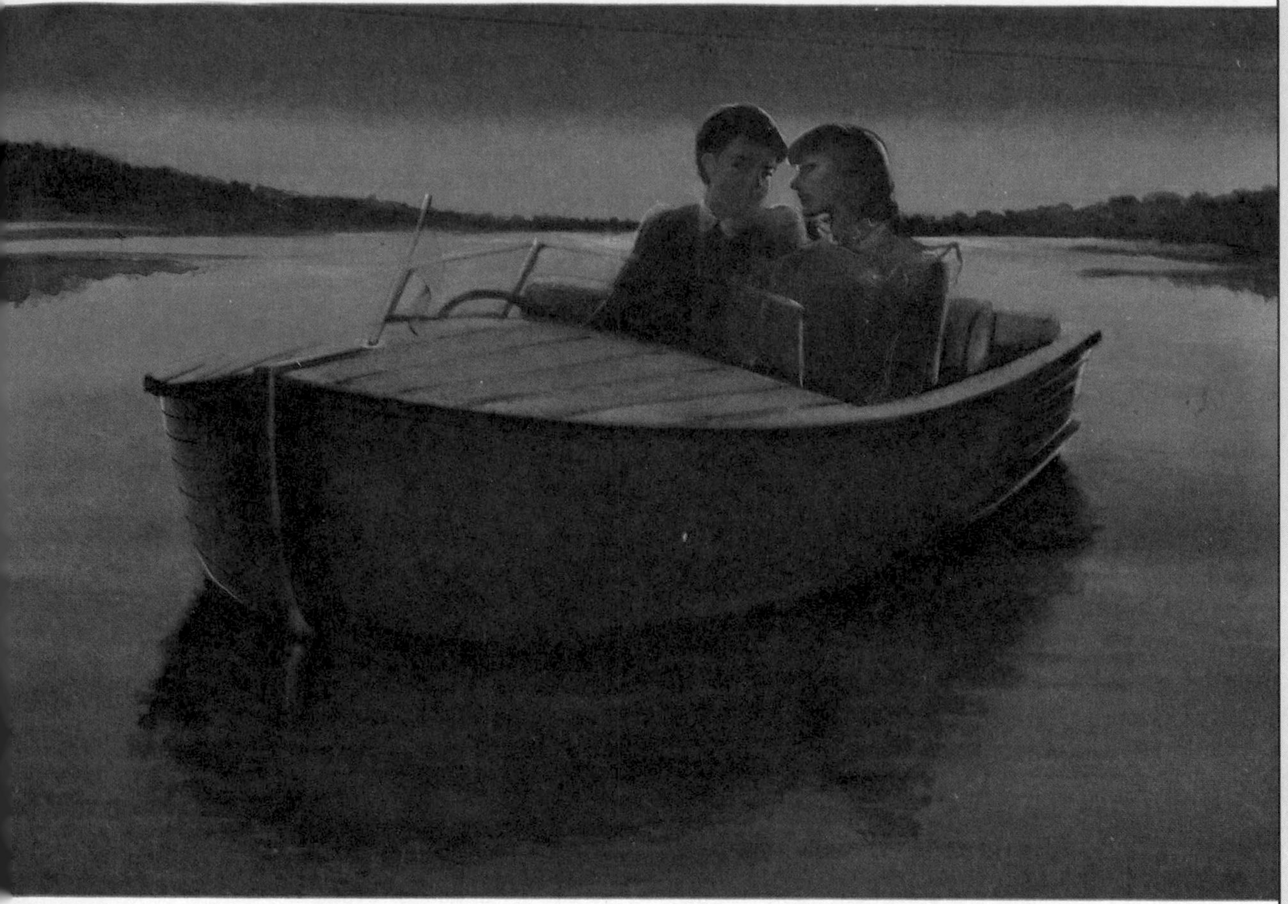

glish I'd usually read most of the books before,
and in history I'd read a lot too." He broke off
1 and tried again: "I mean, when you say swelled
head you think of a boy just going around with
his head swelled, sort of, saying, 'Oh, look how
much I know!' Well, I wasn't like that. I mean,
I didn't think I knew everything, but I was sort
of—"

As he searched for the elusive word, Mr. Bibble said, "H'm!" and pointed with his cigar at a spot in the lake.

"There's a boat," he said.

"Yes," agreed Basil. "I don't know much about sailing. I never cared for it. Of course I've been out a lot, just tending boards and all that, but most of the time you have to sit with nothing to do. I like football."

"H'm!" said Mr. Bibble. "When I was your age I was out in the Gulf in a catboat every day."

"I guess it's fun if you like it," conceded Basil.

"Happiest days of my life."

The station was in sight. It occurred to Basil that he should make one final friendly gesture.

"Your daughter certainly is an attractive girl,
2 Mr. Bibble," he said. "I usually get along with
girls all right, but I don't usually like them very
much. But I think your daughter is the most attractive girl I ever met." Then, as the car
stopped, a faint misgiving overtook him and he

AT A GLANCE

- Basil and Mr. Bibble disagree about the merits of sailing.
- Basil feels some misgiving after he tells Mr. Bibble that Minnie is the most attractive girl that he has ever met.

1 IRONY

The more Basil says about not having a swelled head, the more he shows his swell-headedness.

2 PLOT: CONFLICT

The only way Basil knows to make a good impression is to talk about himself. This time, however, he has a glimpse of his self-absorption.

GUIDED READING

LITERAL QUESTION

1a. What does Basil say that he does not much like? (sailing)

INFERENTIAL QUESTION

1b. What does Mr. Bibble think of this opinion? (Since Mr. Bibble says that he spent his happiest days in a catboat, he probably thinks that Basil is rather insensitive.)

AT A GLANCE

- Mr. Bibble decides not to take Basil to Glacier Park.
- Basil realizes that Minnie is gone and that he has again talked too much.
- Basil sees Imogene while he is driving his grandfather's electric car.

1 IRONY

Basil's attempts to make Mr. Bibble like him have had exactly the opposite effect.

2 STYLE: IMAGERY

The image of the electric chair dramatizes Basil's anxiety. He responds to each ring of the phone and doorbell as if it were a matter of life and death.

3 CHARACTERIZATION

Basil's poem reveals his fondness for sentimentality. It also shows that he is capable of thinking of someone other than himself.

4 THEME

Basil's self-absorption has cut him off from others. Rather than blame his misery on someone else, he now accepts responsibility.

5 SYMBOL

Being allowed to use the car is a mark of Basil's emerging maturity—a step "toward his unknown destiny."

was impelled to add with a disparaging little laugh, "Goodbye. I hope I didn't talk too much."

"Not at all," said Mr. Bibble. "Good luck to you. Goo'-bye."

A few minutes later, when Basil's train had pulled out, Mr. Bibble stood at the newsstand buying a paper and already drying his forehead against the hot July day.

1 "Yes, sir! That was a lesson not to do anything in a hurry," he was saying to himself vehemently. "Imagine listening to that fresh kid gabbling about himself all through Glacier Park! Thank the good Lord for that little ride!"

On his arrival home, Basil literally sat down and waited. Under no pretext would he leave the house save for short trips to the drug store for refreshments, whence he returned on a full
2 run. The sound of the telephone or the doorbell galvanized him into the rigidity of the electric chair.

That afternoon he composed a wondrous geographical poem, which he mailed to Minnie:

3 Of all the fair flowers of Paris
Of all the red roses of Rome,
Of all the deep tears of Vienna
The sadness wherever you roam,
I think of that night by the lakeside,
The beam of the moon and stars,
And the smell of an aching like perfume,
The tune of the Spanish guitars.

But Monday passed and most of Tuesday and no word came. Then, late in the afternoon of the second day, as he moved vaguely from room to room looking out of different windows into a barren lifeless street, Minnie called him on the phone.

"Yes?" His heart was beating wildly.

"Basil, we're going this afternoon."

"Going!" he repeated blankly.

"Oh, Basil, I'm so sorry. Father changed his mind about taking anybody West with us."

"Oh!"

"I'm so sorry, Basil."

"I probably couldn't have gone."

There was a moment's silence. Feeling her presence over the wire, he could scarcely breathe, much less speak.

"Basil, can you hear me?"

"Yes."

"We may come back this way. Anyhow, remember we're going to meet this winter in New York."

"Yes," he said, and he added suddenly: "Perhaps we won't ever meet again."

"Of course we will. They're calling me, Basil. I've got to go. Goodbye."

He sat down beside the telephone, wild with grief. The maid found him half an hour
4 later bowed over the kitchen table. He knew what had happened as well as if Minnie had told him. He had made the same old error, undone the behavior of three days in half an hour. It would have been no consolation if it had occurred to him that it was just as well. Somewhere on the trip he would have let go and things might have been worse—though perhaps not so sad. His only thought now was that she was gone.

He lay on his bed, baffled, mistaken, miserable but not beaten. Time after time, the same vitality that had led his spirit to a scourging made him able to shake off the blood like water not to forget, but to carry his wounds with him to new disasters and new atonements—toward his unknown destiny.

Two days later his mother told him that on condition of his keeping the batteries on charge, and washing it once a week, his grandfather had consented to let him use the elec-
5 tric whenever it was idle in the afternoon. Two hours later he was out in it, gliding along Crest Avenue at the maximum speed permitted by the gears and trying to lean back as if it were a Stutz Bearcat.[20] Imogene Bissel waved at him from in front of her house and he came to an uncertain stop.

"You've got a car!"

---

20. **Stutz Bearcat:** luxury car of the 1910s and 1920s, built very low to the ground.

GUIDED READING

LITERAL QUESTION

1a. What does Basil say when Minnie reminds him of their plan to meet in the winter in New York? (that they may never meet again)

2a. What does Basil gain permission to use? (his grandfather's electric car)

INFERENTIAL QUESTION

1b. What prompts his response? (He seems to realize that his weekend with Minnie was not reality and that in a short time the dream will fade.)

2b. How does Basil feel about this car? (Since he is out in the car two hours later, Basil is obviously very excited. Perhaps he sees the car as a step toward maturity.)

"It's grandfather's," he said modestly. "I thought you were up on that party at the St. Croix."

She shook her head. "Mother wouldn't let me go—only a few girls went. There was a big accident over in Minneapolis and mother won't even let me ride in a car unless there's someone over eighteen driving."

"Listen, Imogene, do you suppose your mother meant electrics?"

"Why, I never thought—I don't know. I could go and see."

"Tell your mother it won't go over twelve miles an hour," he called after her.

A minute later she ran joyfully down the walk. "I can go, Basil," she cried. "Mother never heard of any wrecks in an electric. What'll we do?"

1 "Anything," he said in a reckless voice. "I didn't mean that about this bus making only twelve miles an hour—it'll make fifteen. Listen, let's go down to Smith's and have a claret lemonade."

"Why, Basil Lee!"

STUDY QUESTIONS

Recalling

1. What opinion does Margaret spread about town when Basil returns from school (page 499)? What do Margaret, Gladys, and Imogene say about Basil when they play "Truth" (page 501)?
2. What does Basil tell Imogene at the dance at the lake (Section 3)? After Imogene abandons Basil to dance with Joe Gorman, what does Basil believe he feels for Imogene? What "truth" does Margaret tell Basil?
3. Where does Basil go when he is excluded from his friends' touring party? With whom does he now "fall in love"?
4. What does Basil expect Mr. Bibble to do? Does he do it? What are Mr. Bibble's last words about Basil (page 510)?
5. At the end of the story, what does Basil's grandfather let Basil use?

Interpreting

6. What makes Basil "think he's wonderful"? Why does he talk so much about himself? Does his outward confidence mask inner doubts? Explain.
7. Why does Margaret tell everyone that Basil is wonderful? Why do so many girls say that Basil is their "favorite boy"? Noting that their opinions change, what is Fitzgerald suggesting about adolescent behavior with these events?
8. How does Basil feel when Mr. Bibble fails to invite him to Glacier National Park? What does the ending of the story, in which Imogene goes for a ride with Basil, suggest about the depth of Basil's feelings?
9. Do you think Fitzgerald is making fun of Basil? Is he fond of Basil? Does he sympathize with Basil's problems? Explain.

Extending

10. Do you agree with any of Fitzgerald's observations about adolescence? Do you think Sherwood Anderson (page 476) or Mark Twain (page 288) would agree? Explain your opinion and give your reasons.

VIEWPOINT

Basil Lee appears in a series of stories by Fitzgerald, about which Jackson R. Bryer and John Kuehl write:

> Another recurrent motif or symbol is that of the automobile and the kind of romantic promise and social prestige its possession conveys.
>
> —Introduction to *The Basil and Josephine Stories*

■ Do you agree that in "He Thinks He's Wonderful" the automobile represents romance and social prestige? Why or why not? What other details of the story underscore Basil's romantic and social values?

AT A GLANCE

- Basil invites Imogene to go for a drive.
- Imogene happily accepts his offer.

1 THEME

Basil's growing confidence and sense of identity are shown by his decisiveness and his ability to focus on Imogene rather than on himself.

REFLECTING ON THE STORY

Was Basil actually conceited, or did he just seem to be so? (Students may see his talk about himself as a sign of particular pride or as a sign of general insecurity and uncertainty.)

STUDY QUESTIONS

1. that he is wonderful; that he is their favorite boy
2. that she is his favorite girl; thinks he likes her; about party from which he was excluded
3. Bill Kampf's house; Minnie Bibble
4. like him; no; "Imagine listening to that fresh kid gabbling about himself. . . !"
5. the electric car
6. girls' flattery and his own egoism; full of himself, eager to make impression; yes, but not strong ones
7. because they shared an intimate moment on the train; conformism; that they are fickle
8. wild with grief; fickle, shallow
9. both: shows us Basil's vanity and egoism, but also remembers the difficulties and awkwardness of adolescence
10.
    - Students might agree with some of Fitzgerald's observations.
    - Yes. Anderson's protagonist is older but at first displays similar awkwardness; Twain wrote of himself as a young fool and would find Basil the same.

VIEWPOINT

- Most students will probably see that the automobile represents prestige and romance.
- *Basil's romantic values:* view of himself as sophisticated, attraction to Minnie; *social values:* school, clothes, vacation

LITERARY FOCUS

- Direct characterization: "Within, he was by turns a disembodied spirit. . . . "
- Physical description: "He wore one of those extremely flat derbies."
- Action: "as he moved vaguely from room to room looking out of different windows."
- Thoughts: "It occurred to Basil that he should make one final friendly gesture."
- Speech: "You oughtn't to wear those white ties."
- Perceptions of others: "He thinks he's so darn popular with girls."

VOCABULARY

got a crush on, stuck up, and *a sort of swelled head*

LITERARY FOCUS

Characterization

Characterization refers to the personality of a character and the ways in which the writer creates and develops that personality. Characterization can be direct or indirect.

With **direct characterization** a writer directly states facts about a character's personality. Fitzgerald does this in the second paragraph of "He Thinks He's Wonderful" when he tells us, among other things, that Basil was "a mist of impressions and emotions" but also "a fiercely competitive person."

With **indirect characterization** a writer reveals a character's personality indirectly through descriptions of characters, their thoughts, words, and actions. A writer may indirectly reveal a character through physical description. When we learn that Basil is wearing a derby "in vogue" and a blue business suit, we recognize that he is a conformist who wants to impress others with his appearance; when we learn that the suit is "a little too short," we realize that he is awkward and not so impressive.

A second way of revealing character indirectly is through action. When Basil tries so hard to mask the cut he made shaving, we see again how concerned he is with his appearance.

We also learn about Basil from his thoughts. When Margaret tells Basil about the rumors Joe Gorman has been spreading, Fitzgerald shows us how upset and persecuted Basil feels by telling us (page 506) exactly what Basil is thinking.

A character may also be revealed through speech. Basil's final conversation with Mr. Bibble underscores his tendency to talk too much and helps explain why others find him conceited.

Finally, a character may be revealed through the perceptions of other characters. Mr. Bibble gives us one evaluation of Basil when he exclaims, "Imagine listening to that fresh kid gabbling about himself all through Glacier Park!"

Thinking About Characterization

- Find at least one more example of each of the six methods of characterization—direct and indirect—that help create the character of Basil Lee. Is Basil a round character (see page 323)? Explain.

VOCABULARY

Slang

Slang is very informal language that is not considered standard usage. Slang words are usually coined by groups of people who want to find new, fresh expressions or give new meanings to old expressions. Groups also coin words in order to give the members of the group a feeling of belonging to a special community of "insiders."

Some words in standard usage take on different meanings when they are used as slang. In "He Thinks He's Wonderful," for example, *freshness* describes a lovely, unspoiled girl. *Fresh,* when applied to Basil, however, is a slang word for impertinent or unmannerly.

- Find at least one other slang expression in the story. Tell what it means in standard English.

COMPOSITION

Writing About Character

- Choose one of the characters besides Basil in "He Thinks He's Wonderful" and, in a brief essay, examine the means by which he or she is characterized. Begin with a general statement about the character's personality. Then consider the various methods of characterization that Fitzgerald uses, citing examples from the story. Conclude by explaining whether the character is flat or round.

Writing a Description

- Write a paragraph in which you describe a popular literary or television character by using only *direct description* of that character's personality. Then, in a few paragraphs or a short story, capture the same character using any or all of the five methods of indirect characterization. Which of your efforts more effectively captures your character's personality, and why?

COMPOSITION: GUIDELINES FOR EVALUATION

WRITING ABOUT CHARACTER

Objective

To analyze methods of characterization

Guidelines for Evaluation

- suggested length: six to eight paragraphs
- should begin with a general statement about a character
- should discuss at least three methods of characterization, citing examples from story
- should say if character is flat or round

WRITING A DESCRIPTION

Objective

To write character descriptions

Guidelines for Evaluation

- suggested length: one; four to six paragraphs
- should present character clearly using only direct characterization
- should place the same character in a story or a passage of indirect characterization
- should comment on effectiveness of methods

Willa Cather *1873–1947*

Willa Cather's stories and novels breathe with the spirit of the American land. They also often present one of the most difficult subjects in fiction: the celebration of the life of a good person, a life "complete and beautiful."

Willa Cather was born in Virginia, but her family moved to a farm in Nebraska when she was ten years old. She began to write while still at the University of Nebraska, but later turned to editing, working first in Pittsburgh and then in New York City. In 1912 she turned her full attention to producing fiction.

The great prairie lands on which Cather spent her girlhood and the pioneering spirit of her Nebraska neighbors, many of them European immigrants, gave her material for much of her best writing. Unlike Sherwood Anderson and Sinclair Lewis, Cather loved the rural world of her youth. Her feeling for the land and its people was very deep; long after she had left Nebraska, she remembered it in such moving works as *O Pioneers!* (1913), *My Ántonia* (1918), and "Neighbor Rosicky" (1928). Other novels, such as *The Song of the Lark* (1915) and *Death Comes for the Archbishop* (1927), reveal her interest in the American Southwest, while *Shadows on the Rock* (1931), is a historical novel of seventeenth-century Quebec.

Cather's work is filled with bold strokes of the imagination and rises to moments of passionate intensity, but it never strives for oddness or eccentric effects. Cather's is a quiet art that disguises itself, so that the reader is more aware of the subject than of the technique. *Death Comes for the Archbishop,* for example, appears to be traditional in its beautiful recreation of the lives of two European priests in early New Mexico, but it is actually quite experimental in its loose construction and abandonment of a traditional plot.

In "Neighbor Rosicky" Cather celebrates a good person. The great Russian novelist Leo Tolstoy once declared that "Happy families are all alike"—implying that troubled lives and troubled people make better material for fiction. Yet in her portrait of Neighbor Rosicky, Cather demonstrates that happy families are not all alike. Rosicky is portrayed with such rich affection that he never becomes a type. He stands forth as an individual in harmony with himself, an individual who displays the human values that Willa Cather most admired.

■ Tolstoy once said that "Happy families are all alike." How is this family a contradiction of that statement?

AT A GLANCE

- *Section I:* Dr. Ed Burleigh diagnoses Rosicky as having a bad heart.
- Rosicky, a sixty-five-year-old farmer, does not look sick.

LITERARY OPTIONS

- theme
- characterization
- flashback

THEMATIC OPTIONS

- the rewards of a good life
- city life vs. country life
- the American dream

1 PLOT: EXPOSITION

Dialogue presents some of the essential information needed to appreciate the story.

2 CHARACTERIZATION

Details of his physical description (triangular eyelids, "ruddy color," and "ragged" hair) reveal Rosicky to be a curious man used to the outdoor life and not overly concerned about his appearance.

Willa Cather

Neighbor Rosicky

I

When Doctor Burleigh told neighbor Rosicky he had a bad heart, Rosicky protested.

"So? No, I guess my heart was always pretty good. I got a little asthma, maybe. Just a awful short breath when I was pitchin' hay last summer, dat's all."

"Well now, Rosicky, if you know more about it than I do, what did you come to me for? It's your heart that makes you short of
1 breath, I tell you. You're sixty-five years old, and you've always worked hard, and your heart's tired. You've got to be careful from now on, and you can't do heavy work any more. You've got five boys at home to do it for you."

The old farmer looked up at the Doctor with a gleam of amusement in his queer triangular-shaped eyes. His eyes were large and
2 lively, but the lids were caught up in the middle in a curious way, so that they formed a triangle. He did not look like a sick man. His brown face was creased but not wrinkled, he had a ruddy color in his smooth-shaven cheeks and in his lips, under his long brown moustache. His hair was thin and ragged around his ears, but very little gray. His forehead, naturally high and crossed by deep parallel lines, now ran all the way up to his pointed crown. Rosicky's face had the habit of looking interested—suggested a contented disposition and a reflective quality that was gay rather than grave. This gave him a certain detachment, the easy manner of an onlooker and observer.

GUIDED READING

LITERAL QUESTION

1a. What expression is in Rosicky's eyes as he looks up at Dr. Ed? (a gleam of amusement)

INFERENTIAL QUESTION

1b. What might Rosicky be thinking as he looks at the doctor? (He might think it amusing that after having to work hard all his life he is now told that he cannot do heavy work.)

"Well, I guess you ain't got no pills fur a bad heart, Doctor Ed. I guess the only thing is fur me to git me a new one."

Doctor Burleigh swung round in his desk-chair and frowned at the old farmer. "I think if I were you, I'd take a little care of the old one, Rosicky."

Rosicky shrugged. "Maybe I don't know how. I expect you mean fur me not to drink my coffee no more."

"I wouldn't, in your place. But you'll do as you choose about that. I've never yet been able to separate a Bohemian[1] from his coffee or his pipe. I've quit trying. But the sure thing is you've got to cut out farm work. You can feed the stock and do chores about the barn, but you can't do anything in the fields that makes you short of breath."

"How about shelling corn?"

"Of course not!"

Rosicky considered with puckered brows.

"I can't make my heart go no longer'n it wants to, can I, Doctor Ed?"

"I think it's good for five or six years yet, maybe more, if you'll take the strain off it. Sit around the house and help Mary. If I had a good wife like yours, I'd want to stay around the house."

His patient chuckled. "It ain't no place fur a man. I don't like no old man hanging round the kitchen too much. An' my wife, she's a awful hard worker her own self."

"That's it; you can help her a little. My Lord, Rosicky, you are one of the few men
1 I know who has a family he can get some comfort out of; happy dispositions, never quarrel among themselves, and they treat you right. I want to see you live a few years and enjoy them."

"Oh, they're good kids, all right," Rosicky assented.

The Doctor wrote him a prescription and asked him how his oldest son, Rudolph, who had married in the spring, was getting on. Rudolph had struck out for himself, on rented land. "And how's Polly? I was afraid Mary mightn't like an American daughter-in-law, but it seems to be working out all right."

2 "Yes, she's a fine girl. Dat widder[2] woman bring her daughters up very nice. Polly got lots of spunk, an' she got some style, too. Da's nice, for young folks to have some style." Rosicky inclined his head gallantly. His voice and his twinkly smile were an affectionate compliment to his daughter-in-law.

"It looks like a storm, and you'd better be getting home before it comes. In town in the car?" Doctor Burleigh rose.

3 "No, I'm in de wagon. When you got five boys, you ain't got much chance to ride round in de Ford. I ain't much for cars, noway."

"Well, it's a good road out to your place; but I don't want you bumping around in a wagon much. And never again on a hayrake, remember!"

Rosicky placed the Doctor's fee delicately behind the desk telephone, looking the other way, as if this were an absent-minded gesture. He put on his plush cap and his corduroy jacket with a sheepskin collar, and went out.

The Doctor picked up his stethoscope and frowned at it as if he were seriously annoyed with the instrument. He wished it had been telling tales about some other man's heart, some old man who didn't look the Doctor in the eye so knowingly, or hold out such a warm brown hand when he said goodbye. Doctor Burleigh had been a poor boy in the country before he went away to medical school; he had known Rosicky almost ever since he could remember, and he had a deep affection for Mrs. Rosicky.

4 Only last winter he had had such a good breakfast at Rosicky's, and that when he needed it. He had been out all night on a long, hard confinement[3] case at Tom Marshall's—a big rich farm where there was plenty of stock and plenty of feed and a great deal of expensive farm machinery of the newest model, and no comfort whatever. The woman had too many

1. **Bohemian** [bō hē′mē ən]: person from Bohemia, a region of western Czechoslovakia.

2. **widder:** Rosicky's pronunciation of *widow.*

3. **confinement:** childbirth.

AT A GLANCE

- Dr. Ed warns Rosicky to give up strenuous farm work.
- He asks about Rosicky's son Rudolph and Rudolph's new wife, Polly; Rosicky speaks highly of her.
- He wishes Rosicky were not ill and recalls a breakfast that he had at the Rosicky farm.

1 THEME

The good life is based on a happy family whose members care about one another and enjoy each other's company.

2 BACKGROUND

Rosicky's dialect identifies him as an immigrant. Willa Cather, herself, grew up among European immigrants in Nebraska, where her family had migrated in the 1880s.

3 CHARACTERIZATION

Rosicky's generosity shows in his willingness to let his boys use the family car. By saying he "ain't much for cars," he shows that he is not looking to be praised for his action.

4 FLASHBACK

This flashback and others throughout the story gradually piece together Rosicky's life and thereby explain his character.

GUIDED READING

LITERAL QUESTION

1a. What is Dr. Ed's advice? (that Rosicky should take life easy)

INFERENTIAL QUESTION

1b. Why does Rosicky not want to take the advice? (Rosicky enjoys the chores of farm life; he wants to live fully.)

AT A GLANCE

- Dr. Ed recalls how he turned down breakfast at the Marshalls' in order to join the Rosickys.
- They welcomed him warmly, and Mary Rosicky took obvious pride in him.

1 DESCRIPTION

The warm, homey atmosphere of the kitchen reflected the warmth and goodness of the family.

2 CHARACTERIZATION

This example of direct characterization shows Mary's pleasure in satisfying a basic need of those whom she loves. That her sons are listed along with the chickens and calves demonstrates Mary's love for all living things.

3 CHARACTERIZATION

Mary's inability to eat is an example of indirect characterization. This reaction shows her intense interest in those around her.

4 THEME

One element of the good life is genuine concern for other people, concern that is neither judgmental nor feigned.

children and too much work, and she was no manager. When the baby was born at last, and handed over to the assisting neighbor woman, and the mother was properly attended to, Burleigh refused any breakfast in that slovenly house, and drove his buggy—the snow was too deep for a car—eight miles to Anton Rosicky's place. He didn't know another farmhouse where a man could get such a warm welcome and such good strong coffee with rich cream. No wonder the old chap didn't want to give up his coffee!

He had driven in just when the boys had come back from the barn and were washing up
1 for breakfast. The long table, covered with a bright oilcloth, was set out with dishes waiting for them, and the warm kitchen was full of the smell of coffee and hot biscuit and sausage. Five big handsome boys, running from twenty to twelve, all with what Burleigh called natural good manners—they hadn't a bit of the painful self-consciousness he himself had to struggle with when he was a lad. One ran to put his horse away, another helped him off with his fur coat and hung it up, and Josephine, the youngest child and the only daughter, quickly set another place under her mother's direction.

2 With Mary, to feed creatures was the natural expression of affection—her chickens, the calves, her big hungry boys. It was a rare pleasure to feed a young man whom she seldom saw and of whom she was as proud as if he belonged to her. Some country housekeepers would have stopped to spread a white cloth over the oilcloth, to change the thick cups and plates for their best china, and the wooden-handled knives for plated ones. But not Mary.

"You must take us as you find us, Doctor Ed. I'd be glad to put out my good things for you if you was expected, but I'm glad to get you any way at all."

He knew she was glad—she threw back her head and spoke out as if she were announcing him to the whole prairie. Rosicky hadn't said anything at all; he merely smiled his twinkling smile, put some more coal on the fire, and went into his own room to pour the Doctor a little drink in a medicine glass. When they were all seated, he watched his wife's face from his end of the table and spoke to her in Czech. Then, with the instinct of politeness which seldom failed him, he turned to the Doctor and said slyly, "I was just tellin' her not to ask you no questions about Mrs. Marshall till you eat some breakfast. My wife, she's terrible fur to ask questions."

3 The boys laughed, and so did Mary. She watched the Doctor devour her biscuit and sausage, too much excited to eat anything herself. She drank her coffee and sat taking in everything about her visitor. She had known him when he was a poor country boy, and was boastfully proud of his success, always saying: "What do people go to Omaha for, to see a doctor, when we got the best one in the state right here?" If Mary liked people at all, she felt physical pleasure in the sight of them, personal exultation in any good fortune that came to them. Burleigh didn't know many women like that, but he knew she was like that.

When his hunger was satisfied, he did, of course, have to tell them about Mrs. Marshall, and he noticed what a friendly interest the boys took in the matter.

Rudolph, the oldest one (he was still living at home then), said: "The last time I was over there, she was lifting them big heavy milk cans, and I knew she oughtn't to be doing it."

"Yes, Rudolph told me about that when he come home, and I said it wasn't right," Mary
4 put in warmly. "It was all right for me to do them things up to the last, for I was terrible strong, but that woman's weakly. And do you think she'll be able to nurse it, Ed?" She sometimes forgot to give him the title she was so proud of. "And to think of your being up all night and then not able to get a decent breakfast! I don't know what's the matter with such people."

"Why, Mother," said one of the boys, "if Doctor Ed had got breakfast there, we wouldn't have him here. So you ought to be glad."

"He knows I'm glad to have him, John, any time. But I'm sorry for that poor woman, how

GUIDED READING

LITERAL QUESTIONS

1a. When Dr. Ed came for breakfast, did Mary use her good china or the everyday dishes? (everyday dishes)

2a. What did Rosicky say to Mary in Czech? (He said that she should not ask questions until the doctor has eaten.)

INFERENTIAL QUESTIONS

1b. What did her decision say about her feeling for Dr. Ed? (She treated him like one of her family.)

2b. Why did the boys and Mary laugh at what he said? (Rosicky's remark was playful teasing, not serious criticism.)

bad she'll feel the Doctor had to go away in the cold without his breakfast."

"I wish I'd been in practice when these were getting born." The doctor looked down the row of close-clipped heads. "I missed some good breakfasts by not being."

The boys began to laugh at their mother because she flushed so red, but she stood her ground and threw up her head. "I don't care, you wouldn't have got away from this house without breakfast. No doctor ever did. I'd have had something ready fixed that Anton could warm up for you."

The boys laughed harder than ever, and exclaimed at her: "I'll bet you would!" "She would, that!"

"Father, did you get breakfast for the doctor when we were born?"

"Yes, and he used to bring me my breakfast, too, mighty nice. I was always awful hungry!" Mary admitted with a guilty laugh.

While the boys were getting the Doctor's horse, he went to the window to examine the
1 house plants. "What do you do to your geraniums to keep them blooming all winter, Mary? I never pass this house that from the road I don't see your windows full of flowers."

She snapped off a dark red one, and a ruffled new green leaf, and put them in his buttonhole. "There, that looks better. You look too solemn for a young man, Ed. Why don't you git married? I'm worried about you. Settin' at breakfast, I looked at you real hard, and I seen you've got some gray hairs already."

"Oh, yes! They're coming. Maybe they'd come faster if I married."

"Don't talk so. You'll ruin your health eating at the hotel. I could send your wife a nice loaf of nut bread, if you only had one. I don't like to see a young man getting gray. I'll tell you something, Ed; you make some strong black tea and keep it handy in a bowl, and every morning just brush it into your hair, an' it'll keep the gray from showin' much. That's the way I do!"

Sometimes the Doctor heard the gossipers in the drugstore wondering why Rosicky didn't get on faster. He was industrious, and so were his boys, but they were rather free and easy, weren't pushers, and they didn't always show good judgment. They were comfortable, they were out of debt, but they didn't get much
2 ahead. Maybe, Doctor Burleigh reflected, people as generous and warmhearted and affectionate as the Rosickys never got ahead much; maybe you couldn't enjoy your life and put it into the bank, too.

II

When Rosicky left Doctor Burleigh's office he went into the farm implement store to light his pipe and put on his glasses and read over the list Mary had given him. Then he went into the general merchandise place next door and stood about until the pretty girl with the plucked eyebrows, who always waited on him, was free. Those eyebrows, two thin India-ink strokes, amused him, because he remembered how they used to be. Rosicky always prolonged his shopping by a little joking; the girl knew the old fellow admired her, and she liked to chaff[4] with him.

"Seems to me about every other week you buy ticking, Mr. Rosicky, and always the best quality," she remarked as she measured off the heavy bolt[5] with red stripes.

"You see, my wife is always makin' goose-fedder pillows, an' de thin stuff don't hold in dem little down fedders."

"You must have lots of pillows at your house."

"Sure. She makes quilts of dem, too. We sleeps easy. Now she's makin' a fedder quilt for my son's wife. You know Polly, that married
3 my Rudolph. How much my bill, Miss Pearl?"

"Eight eighty-five."

"Chust make it nine, and put in some candy fur de women."

"As usual. I never did see a man buy so

4. **chaff:** to tease and joke in a good-natured way.
5. **bolt:** roll of cloth of a specific length.

AT A GLANCE

- Conversation continued with a discussion of the breakfasts provided after the birth of Mary's babies and her advice that Dr. Ed marry.
- Back in the present the doctor discounts gossip about why the Rosickys are not "getting ahead."
- *Section II:* The story returns to Rosicky, who leaves the doctor's office and buys ticking and candy for his wife.

1 SYMBOL

The geraniums are a symbol of all living things that flourish in this household full of love.

2 THEME

The rewards of the good life are not measured in terms of dollars earned and saved; rather, they are directly related to the extent to which love can be experienced and expressed.

3 CHARACTERIZATION

The thoughtful gesture of buying candy for Mary shows that Rosicky is always thinking of his wife.

GUIDED READING

LITERAL QUESTION

1a. According to the drugstore gossip, why is Rosicky not getting ahead? (He is too free and easy, does not push enough, and lacks judgment.)

INFERENTIAL QUESTION

1b. Why would Rosicky disagree with this point of view? (He does not seem to feel that accumulating money is really "getting ahead"; living easily and comfortably are the keys to the good life.)

AT A GLANCE

- Rosicky drives by and admires the expensive High Prairie land.
- He sits and watches the snow fall peacefully on the graveyard near his land.
- Rosicky returns home, where Mary is waiting with his lunch.

1 THEME

Rosicky is not envious of the more expensive farms. He is happy with what he has. This fulfillment with one's life is part of the American dream.

2 DESCRIPTION

The picture of Rosicky's farm suggests the beauty and harmony of the simple life.

3 POINT OF VIEW

Because the story employs an omniscient third-person point of view, the reader is able to get into the heads of different characters. Here the reader sees the graveyard as Rosicky sees it—pleasant, quite appealing, and ironically full of life.

4 RESPONSE JOURNAL

Have students explain how they think Rosicky would define *embarrassment* and why it is a feeling that he rarely experiences. Have them cite examples from the story to support their thesis.

much candy for his wife. First thing you know, she'll be getting too fat."

"I'd like dat. I ain't much fur all dem slim women like what de style is now."

"That's one for me, I suppose, Mr. Bohunk!" Pearl sniffed and elevated her India-ink strokes.

When Rosicky went out to his wagon, it was beginning to snow—the first snow of the season, and he was glad to see it. He rattled out of town and along the highway through a wonderfully rich stretch of country, the finest farms in the county. He admired this High Prairie, as it was called, and always liked to drive through it. His own place lay in a rougher territory, where there was some clay in the soil
1 and it was not so productive. When he bought his land, he hadn't the money to buy on High Prairie; so he told his boys, when they grumbled, that if their land hadn't some clay in it, they wouldn't own it at all. All the same, he enjoyed looking at these fine farms, as he enjoyed looking at a prize bull.

After he had gone eight miles, he came to the graveyard, which lay just at the edge of his own hayland. There he stopped his horses and sat still on his wagon seat, looking about at the
2 snowfall. Over yonder on the hill he could see his own house, crouching low, with the clump of orchard behind and the windmill before, and all down the gentle hillslope the rows of pale gold cornstalks stood out against the white field. The snow was falling over the cornfield and the pasture and the hayland, steadily, with very little wind—a nice dry snow. The graveyard had only a light wire fence about it and was all overgrown with long red grass. The fine snow, settling into this red grass and upon the few little evergreens and the headstones, looked very pretty.

3 It was a nice graveyard, Rosicky reflected, sort of snug and homelike, not cramped or mournful—a big sweep all round it. A man could lie down in the long grass and see the complete arch of the sky over him, hear the wagons go by; in summer the mowing machine rattled right up to the wire fence. And it was so near home. Over there across the cornstalks his own roof and windmill looked so good to him that he promised himself to mind the Doctor and take care of himself. He was awful fond of his place, he admitted. He wasn't anxious to leave it. And it was a comfort to think that he would never have to go farther than the edge of his own hayfield. The snow, falling over his barnyard and the graveyard, seemed to draw things together like. And they were all old neighbors in the graveyard, most of them friends; there was nothing to feel awkward or
4 embarrassed about. Embarrassment was the most disagreeable feeling Rosicky knew. He didn't often have it—only with certain people whom he didn't understand at all.

Well, it was a nice snowstorm; a fine sight to see the snow falling so quietly and graciously over so much open country. On his cap and shoulders, on the horses' backs and manes, light, delicate, mysterious it fell; and with it a dry cool fragrance was released into the air. It meant rest for vegetation and men and beasts, for the ground itself; a season of long nights for sleep, leisurely breakfasts, peace by the fire. This and much more went through Rosicky's mind, but he merely told himself that winter was coming, clucked to his horses, and drove on.

When he reached home, John, the youngest boy, ran out to put away his team for him, and he met Mary coming up from the outside cellar with her apron full of carrots. They went into the house together. On the table, covered with oilcloth figured with clusters of blue grapes, a place was set, and he smelled hot coffeecake of some kind. Anton never lunched in town; he thought that extravagant, and anyhow he didn't like the food. So Mary always had something ready for him when he got home.

After he was settled in his chair, stirring his coffee in a big cup, Mary took out of the oven a pan of ***kolache***[6] stuffed with apricots, exam-

6. ***kolache*** [kō′lä chē]: buns made of sweet dough filled with jam or fruit.

GUIDED READING

LITERAL QUESTION

1a. What is it about Rosicky's land that makes it less productive than other land in the area? (His land has clay in the soil.)

2a. How does the graveyard look to Rosicky? ("snug and homelike"; a place filled with life)

INFERENTIAL QUESTION

1b. Why does he not resent not having better land? (The land is so important to him that he is glad to have any land at all.)

2b. What does this view of the graveyard say about Rosicky's concern about death? (Death is on his mind; but though he may not welcome it, neither does he fear it.)

ined them anxiously to see whether they had got too dry, put them beside his plate, and then sat down opposite him.

Rosicky asked her in Czech if she wasn't going to have any coffee.

She replied in English, as being somehow the right language for transacting business:
1 "Now what did Doctor Ed say, Anton? You tell me just what."

"He said I was to tell you some compliments, but I forgot 'em." Rosicky's eyes twinkled.

"About you, I mean. What did he say about your asthma?"

"He says I ain't got no asthma." Rosicky took one of the little rolls in his broad brown fingers. The thickened nail of his right thumb told the story of his past.

"Well, what is the matter? And don't try to put me off."

"He don't say nothing much, only I'm a little older, and my heart ain't so good like it used to be."

2 Mary started and brushed her hair back from her temples with both hands as if she were a little out of her mind. From the way she glared, she might have been in a rage with him.

"He says there's something the matter with your heart? Doctor Ed says so?"

"Now don't yell at me like I was a hog in de garden, Mary. You know I always did like to hear a woman talk soft. He didn't say anything de

AT A GLANCE

- Mary asks what the doctor told Rosicky.
- Rosicky at first avoids her question but then tells her about his bad heart.

1 DIALOGUE

The dialogue discloses how deeply this couple care for each other. Mary anxiously wants to know what the doctor said. Rosicky's answer shows both his concern for her and his lack of concern for himself.

2 CHARACTERIZATION

Mary's reaction to the implication of death in Rosicky's news is a blend of denial (hands to "her temples" squeezing out the thought) and anger ("in a rage with him" for daring to die and leave her). This reaction reveals her deep love for him.

GUIDED READING

LITERAL QUESTION

1a. What does Rosicky say at first when Mary asks what Dr. Ed said? (that he was supposed to relay some compliments but forgot them)

INFERENTIAL QUESTION

1b. Why does he not tell her Dr. Ed's diagnosis right away? (He is trying to make light of the situation so Mary will not take it so seriously.)

AT A GLANCE

- After Rosicky repeats Dr. Ed's advice, Mary studies her husband for signs of change.
- Mary reflects on the gentle city man she married and how the two of them share the same ideas about life.
- *Section III:* Mary talks to Dr. Ed and then cautions the boys to shield their father from hard work.

1 STYLE: FIGURES OF SPEECH

The simile draws on the imagery of farm life to describe Rosicky, suggesting his affinity for his lifestyle.

2 POINT OF VIEW

The omniscient narrator moves into Mary's mind to show Rosicky as Mary sees him after years of living together.

3 THEME

Central to Cather's portrait of the good life is that people share values leading to inner peace and fulfillment, not material success.

matter wid my heart, only it ain't so young like it used to be, an' he tell me not to pitch hay or run de corn-sheller."

Mary wanted to jump up, but she sat still. She admired the way he never under any circumstances raised his voice or spoke roughly. He was city-bred, and she was country-bred; she often said she wanted her boys to have their papa's nice ways.

"You never have no pain there, do you? It's your breathing and your stomach that's been wrong. I wouldn't believe nobody but Doctor Ed about it. I guess I'll go see him myself. Didn't he give you no advice?"

"Chust to take it easy like, an' stay round de house dis winter. I guess you got some carpenter work for me to do. I kin make some new shelves for you, and I want dis long time to build a closet in de boys' room and make dem two little fellers keep dere clo'es hung up."

Rosicky drank his coffee from time to time, while he considered. His moustache was of the soft long variety and came down over his mouth
1 like the teeth of a buggy-rake over a bundle of hay. Each time he put down his cup, he ran his blue handkerchief over his lips. When he took a drink of water, he managed very neatly with the back of his hand.

2 Mary sat watching him intently, trying to find any change in his face. It is hard to see anyone who has become like your own body to you. Yes, his hair had got thin, and his high forehead had deep lines running from left to right. But his neck, always clean shaved except in the busiest seasons, was not loose or baggy. It was burned a dark reddish brown, and there were deep creases in it, but it looked firm and full of blood. His cheeks had a good color. On either side of his mouth there was a half-moon down the length of his cheek, not wrinkles, but two lines that had come there from his habitual expression. He was shorter and broader than when she married him; his back had grown broad and curved, a good deal like the shell of an old turtle, and his arms and legs were short.

He was fifteen years older than Mary, but she had hardly ever thought about it before. He was her man, and the kind of man she liked. She was rough, and he was gentle—city-bred, as she al-
3 ways said. They had been shipmates on a rough voyage and had stood by each other in trying times. Life had gone well with them because, at bottom, they had the same ideas about life. They agreed, without discussion, as to what was most important and what was secondary. They didn't often exchange opinions, even in Czech—it was as if they had thought the same thought together. A good deal had to be sacrificed and thrown overboard in a hard life like theirs, and they had never disagreed as to the things that could go. It had been a hard life, and a soft life, too. There wasn't anything brutal in the short, broad-backed man with the three-cornered eyes and the forehead that went on to the top of his skull. He was a city man, a gentle man, and though he had married a rough farm girl, he had never touched her without gentleness.

They had been at one accord not to hurry through life, not to be always skimping and saving. They saw their neighbors buy more land and feed more stock than they did, without discontent. Once when the creamery agent came to the Rosickys to persuade them to sell him their cream, he told them how much money the Fasslers, their nearest neighbors, had made on their cream last year.

"Yes," said Mary, "and look at them Fassler children! Pale, pinched little things, they look like skimmed milk. I'd rather put some color into my children's faces than put money into the bank."

The agent shrugged and turned to Anton.

"I guess we'll do like she says," said Rosicky.

III

Mary very soon got into town to see Doctor Ed, and then she had a talk with her boys and set a guard over Rosicky. Even John, the youngest, had his father on his mind. If Rosicky went to throw hay down from the loft, one of the boys ran up the ladder and took the fork from him. He sometimes complained that

GUIDED READING

LITERAL QUESTION

1a. What is Mary's reply to the creamery agent's offer to buy the Rosickys' cream? (that she would rather give it to her children)

INFERENTIAL QUESTION

1b. Why does Rosicky go along with her? (Like Mary he does not consider monetary gain to be very important.)

though he was getting to be an old man, he wasn't an old woman yet.

That winter he stayed in the house in the afternoons and carpentered, or sat in the chair between the window full of plants and the wooden bench where the two pails of drinking water stood. This spot was called "Father's corner," though it was not a corner at all. He had a shelf there, where he kept his Bohemian papers and his pipes and tobacco, and his shears and needles and thread and tailor's thimble. Having been a tailor in his youth, he couldn't bear to see a woman patching at his clothes, or at the boys'. He liked tailoring, and always patched all the overalls and jackets and work-shirts. Occasionally he made over a pair of pants one of the older boys had outgrown, for the little fellow.

1 While he sewed, he let his mind run back over his life. He had a good deal to remember, really; life in three countries. The only part of his youth he didn't like to remember was the two years he had spent in London, in Cheapside,[7] working for a German tailor who was wretchedly poor. Those days, when he was nearly always hungry, when his clothes were dropping off him for dirt, and the sound of a strange language kept him in continual bewilderment, had left a sore spot in his mind that wouldn't bear touching.

He was twenty when he landed at Castle Garden[8] in New York, and he had a protector[9] who got him work in a tailor shop in Vesey Street, down near the Washington Market. He looked upon that part of his life as very happy. He became a good workman, he was industrious, and his wages were increased from time to time. He minded his own business and envied nobody's good fortune. He went to night school and learned to read English. He often did overtime work and was well paid for it, but somehow he never saved anything. He couldn't refuse a loan to a friend, and he was self-indulgent. He liked a good dinner, and a little went for beer, a little for tobacco; a good deal went to the girls. He often stood through an opera on Saturday nights; he could get standing room for a dollar. Those were the great days of opera in New York, and it gave a fellow something to think about for the rest of the week. Rosicky had a quick ear, and a childish love of all the stage splendor; the scenery,
2 the costumes, the ballet. He usually went with a chum, and after the performance they had beer and maybe some oysters somewhere. It was a fine life; for the first five years or so it satisfied him completely. He was never hungry or cold or dirty, and everything amused him: a fire, a dog fight, a parade, a storm, a ferry ride. He thought New York the finest, richest, friendliest city in the world.

Moreover, he had what he called a happy home life. Very near the tailor shop was a small furniture factory, where an old Austrian, Loeffler, employed a few skilled men and made unusual furniture, most of it to order, for the rich German housewives uptown. The top floor of Loeffler's five-story factory was a loft, where he kept his choice lumber and stored the odd pieces of furniture left on his hands. One of the young workmen he employed was a Czech,
3 and he and Rosicky became fast friends. They persuaded Loeffler to let them have a sleeping-room in one corner of the loft. They bought good beds and bedding and had their pick of the furniture kept up there. The loft was low-pitched, but light and airy, full of windows, and good-smelling by reason of the fine lumber put up there to season. Old Loeffler used to go down to the docks and buy wood from South America and the East from the sea captains. The young men were as foolish about their house as a bridal pair. Zichec, the young cabinetmaker, devised every sort of convenience, and Rosicky kept their clothes in order. At night and on Sundays, when the quiver of machinery underneath was still, it was the quietest place in the world, and on summer nights

7. **Cheapside:** working-class area in the East End of London.
8. **Castle Garden:** chief immigrant station of the United States between 1855 and 1890.
9. **protector:** friend or relative who helps a new immigrant.

AT A GLANCE

- Rosicky spends the winter doing carpentry and tailoring, a trade he learned in his youth.
- He recalls two miserable years he spent in London.
- He remembers coming to New York where he shared a loft over a furniture factory with another Czech immigrant.

1 FLASHBACK

In this long flashback Rosicky begins a series of reflections that fill in the most important events in his life.

2 SETTING

The active city life of Rosicky's youth provides a sharp contrast to his quiet country life.

3 THEME

The elements that made these days in New York happy were companionship and the sense of nature—fresh air and the smell of lumber. These would later be the same keys to his happiness in the country.

GUIDED READING

LITERAL QUESTION

1a. When he worked in New York how much of his pay did Rosicky save? (He never saved anything.)

INFERENTIAL QUESTION

1b. What does this tell you about Rosicky? (Even in his youth Rosicky never considered monetary gain important.)

AT A GLANCE

- Disillusionment with city life and fond memories of his grandparents' farm caused Rosicky to seek a position as a farm hand out west.
- He left the tailor shop and moved to Omaha.
- *Section IV:* Rosicky is a little worried about his son Rudolph.

1 THEME

Freedom and wide horizons can only be an illusion in the city; they are genuine only in the country.

2 SETTING

The description of the empty city creates a despairing mood, thus setting the stage for Rosicky's decision to act.

3 STYLE: FIGURES OF SPEECH

Comparing Rosicky to a tree with one taproot emphasizes his ties to the land. These ties are deep and refuse to be directed elsewhere.

4 PLOT: CONFLICT

Rosicky's worry about Rudolph provides one of the major problems of the story.

all the sea winds blew in. Zichec often practiced on his flute in the evening. They were both fond of music and went to the opera together. Rosicky thought he wanted to live like that forever.

But as the years passed, all alike, he began to get a little restless. When spring came round, he would begin to feel fretted, and he got to drinking. He was likely to drink too much of a Saturday night. On Sunday he was languid and heavy, getting over his spree. On Monday he plunged into work again. So he never had time to figure out what ailed him,
1 though he knew something did. When the grass turned green in Park Place, and the lilac hedge at the back of Trinity churchyard put out its blossoms, he was tormented by a longing to run away. That was why he drank too much; to get a temporary illusion of freedom and wide horizons.

Rosicky, the old Rosicky, could remember as if it were yesterday the day when the young Rosicky found out what was the matter with him. It was on a Fourth of July afternoon, and he was sitting in Park Place in the sun. The lower part of New York was empty. Wall
2 Street, Liberty Street, Broadway, all empty. So much stone and asphalt with nothing going on, so many empty windows. The emptiness was intense, like the stillness in a great factory when the machinery stops and the belts and bands cease running. It was too great a change, it took all the strength out of one. Those blank buildings, without the stream of life pouring through them, were like empty jails. It struck young Rosicky that this was the trouble with big cities; they built you in from the earth itself, cemented you away from any contact with the ground. You lived in an unnatural world, like the fish in an aquarium, who were probably much more comfortable than they ever were in the sea.

On that very day he began to think seriously about the articles he had read in the Bohemian papers, describing prosperous Czech farming communities in the West. He believed he would like to go out there as a farm hand; it was hardly possible that he could ever have land of his own. His people had always been workmen; his father and grandfather had worked in shops. His mother's parents had lived in the country, but they rented their farm and had a hard time to get along. Nobody in his family had ever owned any land—that belonged to a different station of life altogether. Anton's mother died when he was little, and he was sent into the country to her parents. He stayed with them until he was twelve, and formed those ties with the earth and the farm animals and growing things which are never made at all unless they are made early. After his grandfather died, he went back to live with his father and stepmother, but she was very hard on him, and his father helped him to get passage to London.

After that Fourth of July day in Park Place, the desire to return to the country never left him. To work on another man's farm would be all he asked; to see the sun rise and set and to plant things and watch them grow. He was a
3 very simple man. He was like a tree that has not many roots, but one taproot that goes down deep. He subscribed for a Bohemian paper printed in Chicago, then for one printed in Omaha. His mind got farther and farther west. He began to save a little money to buy his liberty. When he was thirty-five, there was a great meeting in New York of Bohemian athletic societies, and Rosicky left the tailor shop and went home with the Omaha delegates to try his fortune in another part of the world.

IV

Perhaps the fact that his own youth was well over before he began to have a family was one reason why Rosicky was so fond of his boys. He had almost a grandfather's indulgence
4 for them. He had never had to worry about any of them—except, just now, a little about Rudolph.

On Saturday night the boys always piled

GUIDED READING

LITERAL QUESTION

1a. What did the young Rosicky realize about city life one Fourth of July afternoon? (He suddenly saw the city as an empty, meaningless place.)

INFERENTIAL QUESTION

1b. Why does the old Rosicky remember this day so clearly? (It was a turning point—the day he decided to leave the city.)

into the Ford, took little Josephine, and went to town to the moving-picture show. One Saturday morning they were talking at the breakfast table about starting early that evening, so that they would have an hour or so to see the Christmas things in the stores before the show began. Rosicky looked down the table.

"I hope you boys ain't disappointed, but I want you to let me have de car tonight. Maybe some of you can go in with de neighbors."

Their faces fell. They worked hard all week, and they were still like children. A new jackknife or a box of candy pleased the older ones as much as the little fellow.

"If you and Mother are going to town," Frank said, "maybe you could take a couple of us along with you, anyway."

1 "No, I want to take de car down to Rudolph's, and let him an' Polly go in to de show. She don't git into town enough, an' I'm afraid she's gettin' lonesome, an' he can't afford no car yet."

That settled it. The boys were a good deal dashed. Their father took another piece of applecake and went on: "Maybe next Saturday night de two little fellers can go along wid dem."

"Oh, is Rudolph going to have the car every Saturday night?"

Rosicky did not reply at once; then he began to speak seriously: "Listen, boys; Polly ain't lookin' so good. I don't like to see nobody lookin' sad. It comes hard fur a town girl to be a farmer's wife. I don't want no trouble to start in Rudolph's family. When it starts, it ain't so easy to stop. An American girl don't git used to our ways all at once. I like to tell Polly she and Rudolph can have the car every Saturday night till after New Year's, if it's all right with you boys."

"Sure it's all right, Papa," Mary cut in. "And it's good you thought about that. Town girls is used to more than country girls. I lay awake nights, scared she'll make Rudolph discontented with the farm."

The boys put as good a face on it as they could. They surely looked forward to their Saturday nights in town. That evening Rosicky drove the car the half-mile down to Rudolph's new, bare little house.

2 Polly was in a short-sleeved gingham dress, clearing away the supper dishes. She was a trim, slim little thing, with blue eyes and shingled[10] yellow hair, and her eyebrows were reduced to a mere brush-stroke, like Miss Pearl's.

"Good evening, Mr. Rosicky. Rudolph's at the barn, I guess." She never called him father or Mary mother. She was sensitive about having married a foreigner. She never in the world would have done it if Rudolph hadn't been such a handsome, persuasive fellow and such a gallant lover. He graduated in her class in the high school in town, and their friendship began in the ninth grade.

Rosicky went in, though he wasn't exactly asked. "My boys ain't goin' to town tonight, an' I brought de car over fur you two to go in to de picture show."

3 Polly, carrying dishes to the sink, looked over her shoulder at him. "Thank you. But I'm late with my work tonight, and pretty tired. Maybe Rudolph would like to go in with you."

"Oh, I don't go to de shows! I'm too old-fashioned. You won't feel so tired after you ride in de air a ways. It's a nice clear night, an' it ain't cold. You go an' fix yourself up, Polly, an' I'll wash de dishes an' leave everything nice fur you."

Polly blushed and tossed her bob.[11] "I couldn't let you do that, Mr. Rosicky. I wouldn't think of it."

Rosicky said nothing. He found a bib apron on a nail behind the kitchen door. He slipped it over his head and then took Polly by her two elbows and pushed her gently toward the door of her own room. "I washed up de

---

10. **shingled:** woman's short haircut in which the hair over the nape of the neck is shaped close to the head.
11. **bob:** short hair.

AT A GLANCE

- Knowing Polly is unhappy, Rosicky decides to offer his car so she and Rudolph can go out on Saturday night.
- She is reluctant, but Rosicky insists and even offers to finish her kitchen chores.

1 PLOT: RISING ACTION

Rosicky's feeling that he needs to step into the situation shows how serious he thinks Polly's loneliness has become.

2 CHARACTERIZATION

The description of Polly shows her attention to the fashion of the city and suggests her city-bred nature.

3 VOCABULARY: LANGUAGE LEVEL

Polly's "proper" speech contrasts with Rosicky's dialect as a reminder of the differences both between city life and country life and between native-born Americans and immigrants.

GUIDED READING

LITERAL QUESTION

1a. What does Rosicky do when Polly says that she cannot go to the movies because she has too much work? (He puts on an apron and pushes Polly toward her bedroom.)

INFERENTIAL QUESTION

1b. What motivates his actions? (He believes that Polly really would like to go to town and feels it will help his son's marriage.)

AT A GLANCE

- When Polly asks Rosicky if he misses the city, he answers that city life is only for the rich.
- Rudolph and Polly go to town, and Rosicky cleans up.
- He hopes that Polly will not persuade Rudolph to leave their farm.

1 POINT OF VIEW

The omniscient narrator is now in Rudolph's mind. Thus the reader learns about a suppertime argument that suggests Rosicky's fears are justified.

2 RESPONSE JOURNAL

Have students write a letter from Polly to her younger sister. The letter should describe what Polly misses about her former life and how she views life on the farm.

3 SYMBOL

For Rosicky, a piece of land means freedom and the only way to choose one's destiny. To be a wage earner is to be subject to someone else's demands.

kitchen many times for my wife, when de babies was sick or somethin'. You go an' make yourself look nice. I like you to look prettier'n any of dem town girls when you go in. De young folks must have some fun, an' I'm goin' to look out fur you, Polly."

That kind, reassuring grip on her elbows, the old man's funny bright eyes, made Polly want to drop her head on his shoulder for a second. She restrained herself, but she lingered in his grasp at the door of her room, murmuring tearfully: "You always lived in the city when you were young, didn't you? Don't you ever get lonesome out here?"

As she turned round to him, her hand fell naturally into his, and he stood holding it and smiling into her face with his peculiar, knowing, indulgent smile without a shadow of reproach in it. "Dem big cities is all right fur de rich, but dey is terrible hard fur de poor."

"I don't know. Sometimes I think I'd like to take a chance. You lived in New York, didn't you?"

"An' London. Da's bigger still. I learned my trade dere. Here's Rudolph comin', you better hurry."

"Will you tell me about London some time?"

"Maybe. Only I ain't no talker, Polly. Run an' dress yourself up."

The bedroom door closed behind her, and Rudolph came in from the outside, looking
1 anxious. He had seen the car and was sorry any of his family should come just then. Supper hadn't been a very pleasant occasion. Halting in the doorway, he saw his father in a kitchen apron, carrying dishes to the sink. He flushed crimson and something flashed in his eye. Rosicky held up a warning finger.

"I brought de car over fur you an' Polly to go to de picture show, an' I made her let me finish here so you won't be late. You go put on a clean shirt, quick!"

"But don't the boys want the car, Father?"

"Not tonight dey don't." Rosicky fumbled under his apron and found his pants pocket. He took out a silver dollar and said in hurried whisper: "You go an' buy dat girl some ice cream an' candy tonight, like you was courtin'. She's awful good friends wid me."

Rudolph was very short of cash, but he took the money as if it hurt him. There had been a crop failure all over the county. He had more than once been sorry he'd married this year.

In a few minutes the young people came out, looking clean and a little stiff. Rosicky hurried them off, and then he took his own time with the dishes. He scoured the pots and pans and put away the milk and swept the kitchen. He put some coal in the stove and shut off the drafts, so the place would be warm for them when they got home late at night. Then he sat down and had a pipe and listened to the clock tick.

Generally speaking, marrying an American girl was certainly a risk. A Czech should marry a Czech. It was lucky that Polly was the daughter of a poor widow woman; Rudolph was proud, and if she had a prosperous family to throw up at him, they could never make it go. Polly was one of four sisters, and they all worked; one was bookkeeper in the bank, one taught music, and Polly and her younger sister had been clerks, like Miss Pearl. All four of them were musical, had pretty voices, and sang in the Methodist choir, which the eldest sister directed.

2 Polly missed the sociability of a store position. She missed the choir, and the company of her sisters. She didn't dislike housework, but she disliked so much of it. Rosicky was a little anxious about this pair. He was afraid Polly would grow so discontented that Rudy would quit the farm and take a factory job in Omaha. He had worked for a winter up there, two years ago, to get money to marry on. He had done very well, and they would always take
3 him back at the stockyards. But to Rosicky that meant the end of everything for his son. To be a landless man was to be a wage earner, a slave, all your life; to have nothing, to be nothing.

Rosicky thought he would come over and

GUIDED READING

LITERAL QUESTION

1a. How does Rudolph react to seeing his father in an apron at the kitchen sink? (He is angry.)

INFERENTIAL QUESTION

1b. Why does he react in this way? (He probably is angry at the thought that Polly would allow his father to do her chores in the kitchen.)

do a little carpentering for Polly after the New Year. He guessed she needed jollying. Rudolph was a serious sort of chap, serious in love and serious about his work.

Rosicky shook out his pipe and walked home across the fields. Ahead of him the lamplight shone from his kitchen windows. Suppose he were still in a tailor shop on Vesey Street,
1 with a bunch of pale, narrow-chested sons working on machines, all coming home tired and sullen to eat supper in a kitchen that was a parlor also; with another crowded, angry family quarreling just across the dumbwaiter[12] shaft, and squeaking pulleys at the windows where dirty washings hung on dirty lines above a court full of old brooms and mops and ashcans. . . .

He stopped by the windmill to look up at the frosty winter stars and draw a long breath before he went inside. That kitchen with the shining windows was dear to him; but the sleeping fields and bright stars and the noble darkness were dearer still.

V

On the day before Christmas the weather set in very cold; no snow, but a bitter, biting wind that whistled and sang over the flat land and lashed one's face like fine wires. There was baking going on in the Rosicky kitchen all day, and Rosicky sat inside, making over a coat that Albert had outgrown into an overcoat for John. Mary had a big red geranium in bloom for Christmas, and a row of Jerusalem cherry trees, full of berries. It was the first year she had ever grown these; Doctor Ed brought her the seeds from Omaha when he went to some
2 medical convention. They reminded Rosicky of plants he had seen in England; and all afternoon, as he stitched, he sat thinking about those two years in London, which his mind usually shrank from even after all this while.

He was a lad of eighteen when he dropped

12. **dumbwaiter:** small elevator used to send food, trash, etc., from one floor to another.

AT A GLANCE

- Rosicky imagines what his family might have been like if he had not left the city.
- *Section V:* On the day before Christmas Rosicky sits tailoring a coat for John and recalling his days in London.

1 STYLE: IMAGERY

This image of what city life might have meant for the family captures the depair of the poor in the city and externalizes Rosicky's fear of what could happen to his son.

2 FLASHBACK

For the second time in the story Rosicky recalls the low point of his life—his two years in London.

GUIDED READING

LITERAL QUESTION

1a. As Rosicky walks home, what does he imagine? (how his family might have turned out if he had stayed in the city)

INFERENTIAL QUESTION

1b. What might this mental image have to do with Rudolph and Polly? (Rosicky fears that what might have happened to him may yet happen to them.)

AT A GLANCE

- Rosicky recalls being stranded in London at the age of 18 and living in squalor with a poor tailor's family.
- At Christmas Eve dinner Rudolph talks about leaving farming.
- Mary begins a story about Rosicky and hard times.

1 CONTRAST

There is a sharp contrast between the cold despair of London and the warm fulfillment of Rosicky's present life.

2 SETTING

This description makes the reader feel the wretchedness and desperation of poverty. The entire passage shows why Cather herself thought that her greatest achievement was her sensitive portrayal of hard times written with a "gift of sympathy."

3 PLOT: CONFLICT

As farming becomes harder, the lure of the city becomes stronger for Rudolph. Rosicky's fears for his son are very real.

down into London, with no money and no connections except the address of a cousin who was supposed to be working at a confection-
1 er's. When he went to the pastry shop, however, he found that the cousin had gone to America. Anton tramped the streets for several days, sleeping in doorways and on the Embankment,[13] until he was in utter despair. He knew no English, and the sound of the strange language all about him confused him. By chance he met a poor German tailor who had learned his trade in Vienna,[14] and could speak a little Czech. This tailor, Lifschnitz, kept a repair shop in a Cheapside basement, underneath a cobbler. He didn't much need an apprentice, but he was sorry for the boy and took him in for no wages but his keep and what he could pick up. The pickings were supposed to be coppers given you when you took work home to a customer. But most of the customers called for their clothes themselves, and the coppers that came Anton's way were very few. He had, however, a place to sleep. The tailor's family lived upstairs in three rooms; a kitchen, a bedroom, where Lifschnitz and his wife and five children
2 slept, and a livingroom. Two corners of this living room were curtained off for lodgers; in one Rosicky slept on an old horsehair sofa, with a feather quilt to wrap himself in. The other corner was rented to a wretched, dirty boy, who was studying the violin. He actually practiced there. Rosicky was dirty, too. There was no way to be anything else. Mrs. Lifschnitz got the water she cooked and washed with from a pump in a brick court, four flights down. There were bugs in the place, and multitudes of fleas, though the poor woman did the best she could. Rosicky knew she often went empty to give another potato or a spoonful of dripping to the two hungry, sad-eyed boys who lodged with her. He used to think he would never get out of there, never get a clean shirt to his back again. What would he do, he wondered, when his clothes actually dropped to pieces and the worn cloth wouldn't hold patches any longer?

It was still early when the old farmer put aside his sewing and his recollections. The sky had been a dark gray all day, with not a gleam of sun, and the light failed at four o'clock. He went to shave and change his shirt while the turkey was roasting. Rudolph and Polly were coming over for supper.

After supper they sat round in the kitchen, and the younger boys were saying how sorry they were it hadn't snowed. Everybody was sorry. They wanted a deep snow that would lie long and keep the wheat warm, and leave the ground soaked when it melted.

"Yes, sir!" Rudolph broke out fiercely; "if we have another dry year like last year, there's going to be hard times in this country."

Rosicky filled his pipe. "You boys don't know what hard times is. You don't owe nobody, you got plenty to eat an' keep warm, an' plenty water to keep clean. When you got them, you can't have it very hard."

Rudolph frowned, opened and shut his big right hand, and dropped it clenched upon his
3 knee. "I've got to have a good deal more than that, Father, or I'll quit this farming gamble. I can always make good wages railroading, or at the packing house,[15] and be sure of my money."

"Maybe so," his father answered dryly.

Mary, who had just come in from the pantry and was wiping her hands on the roller towel, thought Rudy and his father were getting too serious. She brought her darning basket and sat down in the middle of the group.

"I ain't much afraid of hard times, Rudy," she said heartily. "We've had a plenty, but we've always come through. Your father wouldn't never take nothing very hard, not even hard times. I got a mind to tell you a story on him. Maybe you boys can't hardly remember the year we had that terrible hot wind, that burned everything up on the Fourth

13. **Embankment:** part of the north bank of the Thames River in London.

14. **Vienna** [vē en′ə]: capital city of Austria, near the Czechoslovakian border.

15. **packing house:** plant where meat is processed and packed.

GUIDED READING

LITERAL QUESTION

1a. What was life like for Rosicky in the Lifschnitz home? (miserable, dirty, wretched)

2a. Why does Rudolph say that he might leave farming? (He thinks that he can make more money in the city.)

INFERENTIAL QUESTION

1b. Why did he stay there? (Without family, friends, or a good job, he was trapped; he could not afford to go anywhere else.)

2b. What does Rosicky think of this attitude? (He probably would have to agree that the money might sometimes be better, but he would deny that life itself would be better.)

of July? All the corn an' the gardens. An' that was in the days when we didn't have alfalfa yet—I guess it wasn't invented.

"Well, that very day your father was out cultivatin' corn, and I was here in the kitchen makin' plum preserves. We had bushels of plums that year. I noticed it was terrible hot, but it's always hot in the kitchen when you're preservin', an' I was too busy with my plums to mind. Anton come in from the field about three o'clock, an' I asked him what was the matter.

" 'Nothin'," he says, 'but it's pretty hot, an' I think I won't work no more today.' He stood round for a few minutes, an' then he says:
1 'Ain't you near through? I want you should git up a nice supper for us tonight. It's Fourth of July.'

"I told him to git along, that I was right in the middle of preservin', but the plums would taste good on hot biscuit. 'I'm goin' to have fried chicken, too,' he says, and he went off an' killed a couple. You three oldest boys was little fellers, playin' round outside, real hot an' sweaty, an' your father took you to the horse tank down by the windmill an' took off your clothes an' put you in. Them two box elder trees was little then, but they made shade over the tank. Then he took off all his own clothes, an' got in with you. While he was playin' in the water with you, the Methodist preacher drove into our place to say how all the neighbors was goin' to meet at the schoolhouse that night, to pray for rain. He drove right to the windmill, of course, and there was your father and you three with no clothes on. I was in the kitchen door, an' I had to laugh, for the preacher acted like he ain't never seen a naked man before. He surely was embarrassed, an' your father couldn't git to his clothes; they was all hangin' up on the windmill to let the sweat dry out of 'em. So he laid in the tank where he was, an' put one of you boys on top of him to cover him up a little, an' talked to the preacher.

"When you got through playin' in the water, he put clean clothes on you and a clean shirt on himself, an' by that time I'd begun to get supper. He says: 'It's too hot in here to eat comfortable. Let's have a picnic in the orchard. We'll eat our supper behind the mulberry hedge, under them linden trees.'

"So he carried our supper down, an' a bottle of my wild grape wine, an' everything tasted good, I can tell you. The wind got cooler as the sun was goin' down, and it turned out pleasant, only I noticed how the leaves was curled up on the linden trees. That made me think, an' I asked your father if that hot wind all day hadn't been terrible hard on the gardens an' the corn.

" 'Corn,' he says, 'there ain't no corn.'

" 'What you talkin' about?' I said. 'Ain't we got forty acres?'

" 'We ain't got an ear,' he says, 'nor nobody else ain't got none. All the corn in this country was cooked by three o'clock today, like you'd roasted it in an oven.'

" 'You mean you won't get no crop at all?' I asked him. I couldn't believe it, after he'd worked so hard.

2 " 'No crop this year,' he says. 'That's why we're havin' a picnic. We might as well enjoy what we got.'

"An' that's how your father behaved, when all the neighbors was so discouraged they couldn't look you in the face. An' we enjoyed ourselves that year, poor as we was, an' our neighbors wasn't a bit better off for bein' miserable. Some of 'em grieved till they got poor digestions and couldn't relish what they did have."

The younger boys said they thought their
3 father had the best of it. But Rudolph was thinking that, all the same, the neighbors had managed to get ahead more, in the fifteen years since that time. There must be something wrong about his father's way of doing things. He wished he knew what was going on in the back of Polly's mind. He knew she liked his father, but he knew, too, that she was afraid of something. When his mother sent over coffee-cake or prune tarts or a loaf of fresh bread, Polly seemed to regard them with a certain

AT A GLANCE

- One Fourth of July Rosicky quit work to go swimming with the boys.
- Knowing that his corn crop had been destroyed, Rosicky urged his family to have a picnic to enjoy what they did have.
- As Mary's story ends, Rudolph's thoughts wander from doubts about his father's philosophy of life to concern about Polly.

1 INFERENCES

Rosicky's reaction to the disappointment of losing the corn may have something to do with the date. The Fourth of July marks his freedom from the city and may be his personal day of celebration.

2 THEME

The key to the good life—and happiness—lies not in events that happen to us but rather in how we deal with those events.

3 POINT OF VIEW

By entering Rudolph's mind, the narrator lets the reader see that Rudolph does not really understand his father's philosophy of life.

GUIDED READING

LITERAL QUESTION

1a. Why does Rosicky decide to have a picnic? (It is too hot to eat indoors, and he wants to celebrate the Fourth of July.)

INFERENTIAL QUESTION

1b. What does his decision say about Rosicky's attitude toward life's troubles? (He accepts what he cannot change and tries to enjoy life.)

AT A GLANCE

- Rosicky tells about one terrible Christmas in London when he had little money to buy food.
- Returning to the corner where he slept, he discovered a roast goose and ate half of it.
- Realizing that he had eaten the family's Christmas goose, a guilty Rosicky left the house with thoughts of suicide.

1 FLASHBACK

For the third time in the story, Rosicky goes back to the painful memory of his life in London.

2 TONE

Rosicky's dialect and simple manner of storytelling make his story all the more moving.

suspicion. When she observed to him that his brothers had nice manners, her tone implied that it was remarkable they should have. With his mother she was stiff and on her guard. Mary's hearty frankness and gusts of good humor irritated her. Polly was afraid of being unusual or conspicuous in any way, of being "ordinary," as she said!

When Mary had finished her story, Rosicky laid aside his pipe.

"You boys like me to tell you about some of dem hard times I been through in London?" Warmly encouraged, he sat rubbing his forehead along the deep creases. It was bothersome to tell a long story in English (he nearly always talked to the boys in Czech), but he wanted Polly to hear this one.

1 "Well, you know about dat tailor shop I worked in in London? I had one Christmas dere I ain't never forgot. Times was awful bad before Christmas; de boss ain't got much work, an' have it awful hard to pay his rent. It ain't so much fun, bein' poor in a big city like London, I'll say! All de windows is full of good t'ings to eat, an' all de pushcarts in de streets is full, an' you smell 'em all de time, an' you ain't got no money—not a damn bit. I didn't mind de cold so much, though I didn't have no overcoat, chust a short jacket I'd outgrowed so it wouldn't meet on me, an' my hands was chapped raw. But I always had a good appetite, like you all know, an' de sight of dem pork pies in de windows was awful fur me!

"Day before Christmas was terrible foggy dat year, an' dat fog gits into your bones and makes you all damp like. Mrs. Lifschnitz didn't give us nothin' but a little bread an' drippin' for supper, because she was savin' to try for to give us a good dinner on Christmas Day. After supper de boss say I can go an' enjoy myself, so I went into de streets to listen to de Christmas singers. Dey sing old songs an' make very nice music, an' I run round after dem a good ways, till I got awful hungry. I t'ink maybe if I go home, I can sleep till morning an' forgit my belly.

"I went into my corner real quiet, and roll up in my fedder quilt. But I ain't got my head down, till I smell somet'ing good. Seem like it git stronger an' stronger, an' I can't git to sleep noway. I can't understand dat smell. Dere was a gas light in a hall across de court, dat always shine in at my window a little. I got up an' look round. I got a little wooden box in my corner fur a stool, 'cause I ain't got no chair. I picks up dat box, and under it dere is a roast goose on a platter! I can't believe my eyes. I carry it to de window where de light comes in, an' touch it and smell it to find out, an' den I taste it to be sure. I say, I will eat chust one little bite of dat goose, so I can go to sleep, and tomorrow I won't eat none at all. But I tell you, boys, when I stop, one half of dat goose was gone!"

The narrator bowed his head, and the boys shouted. But little Josephine slipped behind his chair and kissed him on the neck beneath his ear.

"Poor little Papa, I don't want him to be hungry!"

"Da's long ago, child. I ain't never been hungry since I had your mudder to cook fur me."

"Go on and tell us the rest, please," said Polly.

"Well, when I come to realize what I done, of course, I felt terrible. I felt better in de
2 stomach, but very bad in de heart. I set on my bed wid dat platter on my knees, an' it all come to me; how hard dat poor woman save to buy dat goose, and how she get some neighbor to cook it dat got more fire, an' how she put it in my corner to keep it away from dem hungry children. Dey was a old carpet hung up to shut my corner off, an' de children wasn't allowed to go in dere. An' I know she put it in my corner because she trust me more'n she did de violin boy. I can't stand it to face her after I spoil de Christmas. So I put on my shoes and go out into de city. I tell myself I better throw myself in de river; but I guess I ain't dat kind of a boy.

"It was after twelve o'clock, an' terrible cold, an' I start out to walk about London all night. I walk along de river awhile, but dey

GUIDED READING

LITERAL QUESTION

1a. Whom in particular does Rosicky want to hear his story? (Polly)

INFERENTIAL QUESTION

1b. Why might he think it important for this person to hear his story? (He wants Polly to realize that city life has its hardships too.)

was lots of drunks all along; men, and women too. I chust move along to keep away from de police. I git onto de Strand, an' den over to
1 New Oxford Street, where dere was a big German restaurant on de ground floor, wid big windows all fixed up fine, an' I could see de people havin' parties inside. While I was lookin' in, two men and two ladies come out, laughin' and talkin' and feelin' happy about all dey been eatin' an' drinkin', and dey was speakin' Czech—not like de Austrians, but like de home folks talk it.

"I guess I went crazy, an' I done what I ain't never done before nor since. I went right up to dem gay people an' begun to beg dem: 'Fellow-countrymen, for God's sake give me money enough to buy a goose!'

"Dey laugh, of course, but de ladies speak awful kind to me, an' dey take me back into de restaurant and give me hot coffee and cakes, an' make me tell all about how I happened to come to London, an' what I was doin' dere. Dey take my name and where I work down on paper, an' both of dem ladies give me ten shillings.[16]

"De big market at Covent Garden ain't very far away, an' by dat time it was open. I go dere an' buy a big goose an' some pork pies, an' potatoes and onion, an' cakes an' oranges fur de children—all I could carry! When I git home, everybody is still asleep. I pile all I bought on de kitchen table, an' go in an' lay down on my bed, an' I ain't waken up till I hear dat woman scream when she come out into her kitchen. My goodness, but she was surprise! She laugh an' cry at de same time, an' hug me and waken all de children. She ain't stop fur no breakfast; she git de Christmas dinner ready dat morning, and we all sit down an' eat all we can hold. I ain't never seen dat violin boy have all he can hold before.

"Two three days after dat, de two men come to hunt me up, an' dey ask my boss, and he give me a good report an' tell dem I was a steady boy all right. One of dem Bohemians was very smart an' run a Bohemian newspaper in New York, an' de odder was a rich man, in de importing business, an' dey been traveling togedder. Dey told me how t'ings was easier in New York, an' offered to pay my passage when dey was goin' home soon on a boat. My boss say to me: 'You go. You ain't got no chance here, an' I like to see you git ahead, fur you always been a good boy to my woman, and fur dat fine Christmas dinner you give us all.' An' da's how I got to New York."

That night when Rudolph and Polly, arm in arm, were running home across the fields with the bitter wind at their backs, his heart leaped for joy when she said she thought they might have his family come over for supper on New Year's Eve. "Let's get up a nice supper, and not let your mother help at all; make her be company for once."

"That would be lovely of you, Polly," he said humbly. He was a very simple, modest boy, and he, too, felt vaguely that Polly and her sisters were more experienced and worldly than his people.

VI

The winter turned out badly for farmers. It was bitterly cold, and after the first light snows before Christmas there was no snow at all—
2 and no rain. March was as bitter as February. On those days when the wind fairly punished the country, Rosicky sat by his window. In the fall he and the boys had put in a big wheat planting, and now the seed had frozen in the ground. All that land would have to be
3 ploughed up and planted over again, planted in corn. It had happened before, but he was younger then, and he never worried about what had to be. He was sure of himself and of Mary; he knew they could bear what they had to bear, that they would always pull through somehow. But he was not so sure about the young ones, and he felt troubled because Rudolph and Polly were having such a hard start.

Sitting beside his flowering window while

16. **shillings:** In the British monetary system before 1971, the shilling was a coin worth 1/20 of a pound. Ten shillings would have been a fairly generous gift at the time the story takes place.

AT A GLANCE

- Rosicky begged money from two Czech couples and bought Christmas dinner for the Lifschnitz family.
- Shortly thereafter, the same benefactors paid his passage to New York.
- *Section VI:* Rosicky worries about how the hard winter will affect his children, especially Rudolph.

1 CONTRAST

The atmosphere of the German restaurant contrasts sharply with that of the poor house where Rosicky lives. The city is a happy place for those who can afford it, but it is a terrible place for the poor.

2 STYLE: PERSONIFICATION

The elements of nature seem to decide deliberately and maliciously to make existence hard for the farmer.

3 PLOT: CONFLICT

The constant struggle that farmers must face may be more than Rudolph and Polly are willing to accept—or so Rosicky fears.

GUIDED READING

LITERAL QUESTIONS

1a. Whom did the young Rosicky ask for help in London? (people he heard speaking Czech)

2a. How much money did each of the women give Rosicky? (ten shillings)

INFERENTIAL QUESTIONS

1b. Why did he turn to these people? (The fact that they spoke his language established a tie between them.)

2b. How much of that did he probably spend on Christmas dinner? Explain your answer. (He probably spent all of it, buying as much as he could to expiate his guilt.)

AT A GLANCE

- Rosicky hopes that his boys will work the land after he is gone.
- He thinks about what a terrible place the city is for good, honest people and is grateful for his country life.
- Spring arrives, warm but dry.

1 BACKGROUND

The 1880s—the decade when Rosicky would have been in his twenties—were marked by bloody labor disputes that pitted the "robber barons" of industry against the newly organized labor unions. Certainly these violent times colored Rosicky's view of city life and of "wage earners."

2 CONTRAST

The city, by its very nature, brings people too close together and magnifies misery; the country, on the other hand, permits the space that people need in order to live well.

3 SETTING

The setting of this story—the summer heat that burns, the winter wind that freezes, and now the dusty spring—is always changing. The farmer must deal with the challenges that each new season brings.

the panes rattled and the wind blew in under the door, Rosicky gave himself to reflection as he had not done since those Sundays in the loft of the furniture factory in New York, long ago. Then he was trying to find what he wanted in life for himself; now he was trying to find what he wanted for his boys, and why it was he so hungered to feel sure they would be here, working this very land, after he was gone.

They would have to work hard on the farm, and probably they would never do much more than make a living. But if he could think of them as staying here on the land, he wouldn't have to fear any great unkindness for them. Hardships, certainly; it was a hardship to have the wheat freeze in the ground when seed was so high; and to have to sell your stock because you had no feed. But there would be other years when everything came along right, and
1 you caught up. And what you had was your own. You didn't have to choose between bosses and strikers, and go wrong either way. You didn't have to do with dishonest and cruel people. They were the only things in his experience he had found terrifying and horrible; the look in the eyes of a dishonest and crafty man, of a scheming and rapacious[17] woman.

2 In the country, if you had a mean neighbor, you could keep off his land and make him keep off yours. But in the city, all the foulness and misery and brutality of your neighbors was part of your life. The worst things he had come upon in his journey through the world were human—depraved and poisonous specimens of man. To this day he could recall certain terrible faces in the London streets. There were mean people everywhere, to be sure, even in their own country town here. But they weren't tempered, hardened, sharpened, like the treacherous people in cities who live by grinding or cheating or poisoning their fellow men. He had helped to bury two of his fellow workmen in the tailoring trade, and he was distrustful of the organized industries that see one out of the world in big cities. Here, if you were sick, you had Doctor Ed to look after you; and if you died, fat Mr. Haycock, the kindest man in the world, buried you.

It seemed to Rosicky that for good, honest boys like his, the worst they could do on the farm was better than the best they would be likely to do in the city. If he'd had a mean boy, now, one who was crooked and sharp and tried to put anything over on his brothers, then town would be the place for him. But he had no such boy. As for Rudolph, the discontented one, he would give the shirt off his back to anyone who touched his heart. What Rosicky really hoped for his boys was that they could get through the world without ever knowing much about the cruelty of human beings. "Their mother and me ain't prepared them for that," he sometimes said to himself.

These thoughts brought him back to a grateful consideration of his own case. What an escape he had had, to be sure! He, too, in his time, had had to take money for repair work from the hand of a hungry child who let it go so wistfully; because it was money due his boss. And now, in all these years, he had never had to take a cent from anyone in bitter need—never had to look at the face of a woman become like a wolf's from struggle and famine. When he thought of these things, Rosicky would put on his cap and jacket and slip down to the barn and give his workhorses a little extra oats, letting them eat it out of his hand in their slobbery fashion. It was his way of expressing what he felt, and made him chuckle with pleasure.

The spring came warm, with blue skies—
3 but dry, dry as a bone. The boys began ploughing up the wheat fields to plant them over in corn. Rosicky would stand at the fence corner and watch them, and the earth was so dry it blew up in clouds of brown dust that hid the horses and the sulky plough and the driver. It was a bad outlook.

The big alfalfa field that lay between the home place and Rudolph's came up green, but Rosicky was worried because during that open

17. **rapacious** [rə pā′shəs]: greedy.

GUIDED READING

LITERAL QUESTION

1a. What is it that Rosicky and Mary have not prepared their boys for? (the cruelty of which people are capable)

INFERENTIAL QUESTION

1b. Why has such preparation not been part of the boys' education? (Rosicky probably would prefer that his children never learn what he has learned about the dark side of humanity in the city.)

windy winter a great many Russian thistle plants had blown in there and lodged. He kept asking the boys to rake them out; he was afraid their seed would root and "take the alfalfa." Rudolph said that was nonsense. The boys were working so hard planting corn, their father felt he couldn't insist about the thistles, but he set great store by that big alfalfa field. It was a feed you could depend on—and there was some deeper reason, vague, but strong.
1 The peculiar green of that clover woke early memories in old Rosicky, went back to something in his childhood in the old world. When he was a little boy, he had played in fields of that strong blue-green color.

One morning, when Rudolph had gone to town in the car, leaving a work team idle in his barn, Rosicky went over to his son's place, put the horses to the buggy rake, and set about quietly raking up those thistles. He behaved with guilty caution, and rather enjoyed stealing a march on Doctor Ed, who was just then taking his first vacation in seven years of practice and was attending a clinic in Chicago. Rosicky got the thistles raked up, but did not stop to burn them. That would take some time, and his breath was pretty short, so he thought he had better get the horses back to the barn.

He got them into the barn and to their stalls, but the pain had come on so sharp in his chest that he didn't try to take the harness off. He started for the house, bending lower with every step. The cramp in his chest was shutting him up like a jackknife. When he reached the windmill, he swayed and caught at the ladder. He saw Polly coming down the hill, running with the swiftness of a slim greyhound. In a flash she had her shoulder under his armpit.

2 "Lean on me, Father, hard! Don't be afraid. We can get to the house all right."

Somehow they did, though Rosicky became blind with pain; he could keep on his legs, but he couldn't steer his course. The next thing he was conscious of was lying on Polly's bed, and Polly bending over him wringing out bath towels in hot water and putting them on his chest. She stopped only to throw coal into the stove,

AT A GLANCE

- Rosicky rakes out the thistles in the alfalfa field next to Rudolph's farm.
- As he finishes the job and gets the horses into the barn, he has a heart attack.
- Polly finds him and helps him into the house.

1 STYLE: IMAGERY

The image of the blue-green alfalfa field where Rosicky played as a boy is important because it was at that time of his life when he first learned to love the land.

2 CHARACTERIZATION

This is the first time that Polly calls Rosicky *Father.* The crisis is bringing out her true loving nature and marks a change in attitude toward her husband's family.

GUIDED READING

LITERAL QUESTION

1a. What is it that brings on Rosicky's heart attack? (raking thistles from the alfalfa field)

INFERENTIAL QUESTION

1b. Why does he work despite Dr. Ed's warning? (He wants to help his boys, he enjoys the work, and the alfalfa field is very important to him.)

AT A GLANCE

- Polly cares for Rosicky until he begins to come out of the crisis.
- She confides in Rosicky that she is pregnant.
- She realizes how much Rosicky loves her, and she loves him in return.

1 PLOT: CLIMAX

The two threads of the story—Rosicky's ailing heart and his fear that Polly will take his son from the farm—meet when the attack comes and Polly shows her true quality.

2 CHARACTERIZATION

Rosicky's capacity to love is the key to his character.

3 SYMBOL

Rosicky's hand is a symbol of his love and joy of life. It is through this hand that Polly understands and accepts his philosophy of life.

1 and she kept the teakettle and the black pot going. She put these hot applications on him for nearly an hour, she told him afterwards, and all that time he was drawn up stiff and blue, with the sweat pouring off him.

As the pain gradually loosed its grip, the stiffness went out of his jaws, the black circles round his eyes disappeared, and a little of his natural color came back. When his daughter-in-law buttoned his shirt over his chest at last, he sighed.

"Da's fine, de way I feel now, Polly. It was a awful bad spell, an' I was so sorry it all come on you like it did."

Polly was flushed and excited. "Is the pain really gone? Can I leave you long enough to telephone over to your place?"

Rosicky's eyelids fluttered. "Don't telephone, Polly. It ain't no use to scare my wife. It's nice and quiet here, an' if I ain't too much trouble to you, just let me lay still till I feel like myself. I ain't got no pain now. It's nice here."

Polly bent over him and wiped the moisture from his face. "Oh, I'm so glad it's over!" she broke out impulsively. "It just broke my heart to see you suffer so, Father."

Rosicky motioned her to sit down on the chair where the teakettle had been, and looked up at her with that lively affectionate gleam in his eyes. "You was awful good to me, I won't never forgit dat. I hate it to be sick on you like dis. Down at de barn I say to myself, dat young girl ain't had much experience in sickness, I don't want to scare her, an' maybe she's got a baby comin' or somet'ing."

Polly took his hand. He was looking at her so intently and affectionately and confidingly; his eyes seemed to caress her face, to regard it with pleasure. She frowned with her funny streaks of eyebrows, and then smiled back at him.

"I guess maybe there is something of that kind going to happen. But I haven't told anyone yet, not my mother or Rudolph. You'll be the first to know."

His hand pressed hers. She noticed that it was warm again. The twinkle in his yellow-brown eyes seemed to come nearer.

"I like mighty well to see dat little child, Polly," was all he said. Then he closed his eyes and lay half-smiling. But Polly sat still, thinking hard. She had a sudden feeling that nobody in the world, not her mother, not Rudolph, or anyone, really loved her as much as old Rosicky did. It perplexed her. She sat frowning
2 and trying to puzzle it out. It was as if Rosicky had a special gift for loving people, something that was like an ear for music or an eye for color. It was quiet, unobtrusive; it was merely there. You saw it in his eyes—perhaps that was why they were merry. You felt it in his hands, too. After he dropped off to sleep, she sat holding his warm, broad, flexible brown hand. She had never seen another in the least like it. She wondered if it wasn't a kind of gypsy hand, it was so alive and quick and light in its communications—very strange in a farmer. Nearly all the farmers she knew had huge lumps of fists, like mauls, or they were knotty and bony and uncomfortable-looking, with stiff fingers. But Rosicky's was like quicksilver,[18] flexible, muscular, about the color of a pale cigar, with deep, deep creases across the palm. It wasn't nervous, it wasn't a stupid lump; it was a warm brown human hand, with some cleverness in it, a great deal of generosity, and something else which Polly could only call "gypsy-like"—something nimble and lively and sure, in the way that animals are.

Polly remembered that hour long after-
3 wards; it had been like an awakening to her. It seemed to her that she had never learned so much about life from anything as from old Rosicky's hand. It brought her to herself; it communicated some direct and untranslatable message.

When she heard Rudolph coming in the car, she ran out to meet him.

"Oh, Rudy, your father's been awful sick!

---

18. **quicksilver:** fluid and moving, like mercury.

GUIDED READING

LITERAL QUESTIONS

1a. What is it Rosicky tells Polly that he will never forget? (the way she took care of him during his heart attack)

2a. What does Polly think that Rosicky's hand communicated to her? (some direct and untranslatable message)

INFERENTIAL QUESTIONS

1b. Why will he never forget? (He now knows that Polly has a good heart and will make his son happy; he has peace of mind.)

2b. What do you think Polly has learned from Rosicky's hand? (She probably has come to the realization that Rosicky's values are the ones that lead to true happiness in life.)

He raked up those thistles he's been worrying about, and afterwards he could hardly get to the house. He suffered so I was afraid he was going to die."

Rudolph jumped to the ground. "Where is he now?"

"On the bed. He's asleep. I was terribly scared, because, you know, I'm so fond of your father." She slipped her arm through his and they went into the house. That afternoon they took Rosicky home and put him to bed, though he protested that he was quite well again.

The next morning he got up and dressed and sat down to breakfast with his family. He told Mary that his coffee tasted better than usual to him, and he warned the boys not to bear any tales to Doctor Ed when he got home. After breakfast he sat down by his window to do some patching and asked Mary to thread several needles for him before she went to feed her chickens—her eyes were better than his, and her hands steadier. He lit his pipe and took up John's overalls. Mary had been watching him anxiously all morning, and as she went out of the door with her bucket of scraps, she saw that he was smiling. He was thinking, indeed, about Polly, and how he might never have known what a tender heart she had if he hadn't got sick over there. Girls nowadays didn't wear their heart on their sleeve. But
1 now he knew Polly would make a fine woman after the foolishness wore off. Either a woman had that sweetness at her heart or she hadn't. You couldn't always tell by the look of them; but if they had that, everything came out right in the end.

After he had taken a few stitches, the cramp began in his chest, like yesterday. He put his pipe cautiously down on the windowsill and bent over to ease the pull. No use—he had better try to get to his bed if he could. He rose and groped his way across the familiar floor, which was rising and falling like the deck of a ship. At the door he fell. When Mary came in, she found him lying there, and the moment she touched him she knew that he was gone.

Doctor Ed was away when Rosicky died, and for the first few weeks after he got home he was hard driven. Every day he said to himself that he must get out to see that family that had lost their father. One soft, warm moonlight night in early summer he started for the farm. His mind was on other things, and not until his road ran by the graveyard did he realize that Rosicky wasn't over there on the hill where the red lamplight shone, but here, in the moonlight. He stopped his car, shut off the engine, and sat there for a while.

A sudden hush had fallen on his soul. Everything here seemed strangely moving and significant, though signifying what, he did not know. Close by the wire fence stood Rosicky's mowing machine, where one of the boys had been cutting hay that afternoon; his own work-horses had been going up and down there. The
2 new-cut hay perfumed all the night air. The moonlight silvered the long, billowy grass that grew over the graves and hid the fence; the few little evergreens stood out black in it, like shadows in a pool. The sky was very blue and soft, the stars rather faint because the moon was full.

For the first time it struck Doctor Ed that this was really a beautiful graveyard. He thought of city cemeteries, acres of shrubbery and heavy stone, so arranged and lonely and unlike anything in the living world. Cities of the dead, indeed; cities of the forgotten, of the "put away." But this was open and free, this little square of long grass which the wind forever stirred. Nothing but the sky overhead, and the many-colored fields running on until they met
3 that sky. The horses worked here in summer; the neighbors passed on their way to town; and over yonder, in the cornfield, Rosicky's own cattle would be eating fodder as winter came on. Nothing could be more undeathlike than this place; nothing could be more right for a man who had helped to do the work of great cities and had always longed for the open country and had got to it at last. Rosicky's life seemed to him complete and beautiful.

AT A GLANCE

- Polly and Rudolph take Rosicky home.
- The next day as Rosicky sits and sews, he thinks about how Polly's true sweet nature was revealed by the tender care she took of him.
- Rosicky has another attack and dies.
- Sitting by the cemetery several weeks later, Dr. Ed reflects on Rosicky's "complete and beautiful" life.

1 PLOT: RESOLUTION

Rosicky now knows that Polly will not take Rudolph away from the farm. He can die in peace.

2 STYLE: IMAGERY

The images at the graveyard suggest beauty and life rather than grief and death.

3 THEME

The sights witnessed by Dr. Ed demonstrate that Rosicky's life was part of a life force nourished by the land. Such a force never ends, not even in death.

REFLECTING ON THE STORY

Was Rosicky's wisdom and happiness the result of something born in him or the result of his experience? (Some students may feel that his inborn temperament set Rosicky apart; others may suggest that the experiences of his youth taught him about the good life and where to find it.)

GUIDED READING

LITERAL QUESTIONS

1a. Just before he dies, what does Rosicky decide about Polly? (that she will be all right, is a "fine woman")

2a. How is the graveyard where Rosicky is buried different from a city cemetery? (It is a beautiful place, open, and free; a place where his neighbors and animals amble by.)

INFERENTIAL QUESTIONS

1b. Why does this give him comfort? (If Polly is all right, she will be a good wife to Rudolph and not make him leave the farm.)

2b. Why is this a fitting place for Rosicky? (He loved the land, its freedom, and the good things that come from it.)

STUDY QUESTIONS

1. bad heart; heavy work
2. had same ideas about life; seem to have same thoughts together
3. Rosicky's son, daughter-in-law; afraid they will give up on farming
4. boys will continue to work the land; the city
5. raking thistle plants; Polly
6. Rosicky; to cities of the dead; "open and free"
7. Rosicky believes in enjoying life; will not scrimp, save
8. Mr. and Mrs. Rosicky—close and loving; Polly and Rudolph—nervous and formal; caring for Rosicky softens manner
9. own boss, control own destiny; closeness to nature, independence
10. happiness, peace of mind; sees that Rudolph and Polly get a good start
11. ▪ Anderson—stifling; Cather—nourishing; Master's "Lucinda Matlock" like Rosicky, but Cassius Heuffer represents meanness.
    ▪ unnatural place to live
    ▪ Answers will vary. Students might agree in part.

VIEWPOINT

remove thistles, grow corn, plant wheat in drought; confidence at Fourth of July picnic; believes in land, willing to work hard for living

LITERARY FOCUS

1. ▪ land nourishes life full of love, kindness; death part of nature and its pain mitigated by full, loving life
   ▪ city—people live to make money, get ahead, not to love
   ▪ American dream—fulfillment, not material success

STUDY QUESTIONS

Recalling

1. According to the opening paragraph, what is Doctor Ed's diagnosis of Anton Rosicky? What does the doctor say Rosicky must stop doing?
2. According to page 520, why had life gone well for Rosicky and his wife? Why do they not often exchange opinions?
3. Who are Rudolph and Polly, and what is Rosicky afraid will happen to them, according to page 523?
4. For what does Rosicky "hunger to feel sure" (page 530)? Where does he not want his children to live?
5. How does Rosicky bring on his first heart attack? Who helps him to recover?
6. Who is buried in the graveyard when Doctor Ed stops there near the end of the story? To what does the doctor compare the graveyard? How does he describe the graveyard?

Interpreting

7. Basically, why is the Rosicky farm adequate but not prosperous?
8. Describe the relationship between Mr. and Mrs. Rosicky. How is their relationship different from the relationship between Rudolph and Polly when we first meet them? What changes do we see in Polly in the course of the story?
9. Why is land so important to Rosicky? What are some of the positive values he equates with living off the land?
10. What has Rosicky achieved in his lifetime? What has he achieved in the course of this story—that is, from the time Doctor Ed tells him he has heart trouble until the time of his death?

Extending

11. How is Cather's attitude toward rural life different from that of Sherwood Anderson (page 476) or Edgar Lee Masters (page 439)? What attitude does Cather project about city life? Do you agree, and why?

VIEWPOINT

The literary critic Granville Hicks once wrote:

> From the first, it is clear, the one theme that seemed to Miss Cather worth writing about was heroic idealism, the joyous struggle against nature sustained by a confidence in the ultimate beneficence of that nature against which it fought.
>
> —"The Case Against Willa Cather"

■ Where in the story does Rosicky struggle against nature? Where does he display confidence that nature is ultimately "beneficent," or kind? In what ways is the immigrant hero of "Neighbor Rosicky" like the Puritans and pioneers of early America?

LITERARY FOCUS

Theme

A work of fiction always tells us a story—about people, where they lived, what they thought, what adventures they encountered. In "Neighbor Rosicky," for example, we become interested in Rosicky and his whole family. We are interested in Rosicky's health, in his farm, in how the marriage of Rudolph and Polly will work out, and so on.

Yet the "story" is only half the story: The other half is its meaning, its ideas, the significance the author gives it. The main idea of a story is its **theme.**

When we state a theme, we are only indicating our own sense of what gives the story importance or meaning. We are not "summing up" the story itself or reducing it to some commonplace thought. For example, if we were merely to say that "Neighbor Rosicky" shows that "if you lead a good life, you may die content," we would be leaving out everything that makes the story interesting.

We must also recognize that there is no one theme to the exclusion of all others. A complex story like "Neighbor Rosicky" has many themes. It is not only about the life and death of a good man; it is also about rural life as opposed to city life and about the fulfillment of the American dream in the lives of pioneers and immigrants. Exactly what we decide is the theme will often depend on our own perceptions, on what *we* think is important in the world.

Thinking About Theme

1. State in your own words what "Neighbor Rosicky" has to say about life and death, about rural versus city life, and about the American dream.

2. What other themes do you find in the story? What, for example, does the story say about love and marriage? About family and neighbors? Why is the title significant?

VOCABULARY

Sentence Completions

Each of the following sentences contains a blank with four possible words for completing the sentence. The words are from "Neighbor Rosicky." Choose the word that completes each sentence correctly, using the word *as it is used in the selection.*

1. We keep shovels, axes, a plow, and other ____ in the shed in the backyard.
   (a) implements (c) dispositions
   (b) resources (d) trifles
2. The log split in half with the last blow of the ____ on the wedge.
   (a) broom (c) saw
   (b) drill (d) maul
3. The clerk cut three yards from the ____ of silk.
   (a) ream (c) bolt
   (b) ticking (d) loom
4. His classmates loved to ____ him about the pretty girl.
   (a) renounce (c) chastise
   (b) chaff (d) reproach

COMPOSITION

Writing About Theme

■ Choose one story or poem you have read in this book, and tell what you think is its theme. Write an essay in which you begin by stating the theme. Then show how the author illuminates this theme through characterization, setting, events, point of view, and tone. *For help with this assignment, refer to Lesson 6 in the Writing About Literature Handbook.*

Writing About Character

■ Some of the characters you have encountered in this unit are unhappy or confused about their lives. Choose one of these characters—Cassius Hueffer (page 439), Basil Lee (page 498), George Willard, or Helen White (page 477), for example—and show how he or she might have benefited from an encounter with Anton Rosicky, as Polly did. Describe the encounter in the first person, in the form of a diary entry written by the character you choose, or in the third person, in short story form.

COMPARING WRITERS

■ One effect of the Modernist movement was to encourage writers to demand more participation from their audiences. In what ways does each of the stories in this unit involve you in the lives and thoughts of its characters?

2. ■ love, marriage from trust, closeness
■ close family works together, is considerate
■ Rosicky is the definitive "good neighbor."

VOCABULARY

1. (a) implements
2. (d) maul
3. (c) bolt
4. (b) chaff

COMPARING WRITERS

Each story reveals one or more characters learning. Hemingway is most oblique, avoiding direct statements and requiring readers to participate fully.

COMPOSITION: GUIDELINES FOR EVALUATION

WRITING ABOUT THEME

Objective

To analyze the theme of a story

Guidelines for Evaluation

- suggested length: four to eight paragraphs
- should identify theme of selection
- should cite examples of characterization, setting, plot, point of view, and tone

WRITING ABOUT CHARACTER

Objective

To describe one character's reaction to another

Guidelines for Evaluation

- suggested length: five to fifteen paragraphs
- should describe an encounter between Rosicky and another character in this book
- should show how one character can affect another's thoughts or attitudes

ACTIVE READING

Making Inferences

After the students have read this page, tell them that making inferences is a basic thinking skill that they use without even knowing it. Much of our everyday discourse requires making inferences.

ACTIVE READING

Making Inferences

The words *imply* and *infer* are sometimes confused. To *imply* something is to suggest without stating it directly. For example, a person who asks, "Are you going to be using the car tonight?" is usually implying, "I'd like to use the car." To *infer* is to "draw out" a meaning or a suggestion that is not stated directly; the person who is asked if he or she is going to be using the car *infers* that the person asking wants to use it.

A speaker or an author can *imply;* a listener or a reader can *infer.* Both of these processes are at work, or should be at work, in much modern literature. When a writer and a reader are both participating in these actions with attention and imagination, the experience of literature can be its most creative and satisfying.

Of course not everything in literature demands that we make inferences. Often things are what they are, and statements can be taken for just what they say. When someone once asked Ezra Pound what the frogs "meant" in one of his poems, Pound replied that sometimes "frogs is frogs." When Doctor Ed, at the end of "Neighbor Rosicky," says that Rosicky's life was "complete and beautiful," Willa Cather would like us to infer nothing beyond that simple and sublime statement, complete in itself, and see Rosicky's life as the doctor and Cather herself see it.

Yet the selections in this unit often do demand that we make inferences. Marianne Moore's "Poetry" (page 453), for example, begins, "I, too, dislike it." It becomes clear, however, by the time we have finished the poem, that Moore wants us to infer that in fact she *does* like poetry—only, of course, when it is "genuine."

In "The Road Not Taken" (page 465) we soon infer that the poem is about more than a walk Robert Frost once took in the woods. The poet implies that the roads in the wood are in some sense "the roads of life" when he tells us that he will be "telling this with a sigh" at some time in the future and says that his choice of road has made "all the difference." The clues are so strong that we know we must make some inferences about these "roads."

Hemingway's "In Another Country" forces us to make many inferences. When the gentle Italian major suddenly acts strangely, speaking "angrily and bitterly" and telling the narrator that a man "cannot marry," it is at first impossible to infer the major's motives. However, by the end of the story we can infer that the major knew his wife to be in great danger of dying and that he loves his wife so much that the thought of losing her is more than he can bear.

Making inferences is a vital part of reading literature. An author can imply a great deal in a story or a poem, but if we do not infer from what is there and participate as we read, we leave the experience of literature incomplete.

THE AMERICAN VOICE

"Make It New"

When Ezra Pound said, "Make it new," he expressed what so many American artists felt. The twentieth century, so vastly different from what had come before it, presented a whole world that had to be re-seen, re-evaluated, and re-imagined. The writers in this unit built into their poems and stories the surprise of the new, the shock of the new. It inspired some to celebrate; it left some with confusion and a sense of loss. Their works contained unusual images, desperate questions, and experiments in reordering the world. "What now would make sense?" they asked. "How should we face the future?" These artists reshaped literature to try to arrive at new relationships between people and the *new* New World.

Eliot
Do I dare
Disturb the universe? . . .

Williams
Then he whirled about
bounded
into the air
and with an entrechat
perfectly achieved
completed the figure. . . .
What goes on here? she said.

Stein
. . . this is this.

MacLeish
A poem should be wordless
As the flight of birds.

Stevens
I placed a jar in Tennessee,
And round it was, upon a hill.
It made the slovenly wilderness
Surround that hill.

Anderson
Man or boy, woman or girl, they had for a moment taken hold of the thing that makes the mature life of men and women in the modern world possible.

Hemingway
He stood there biting his lower lip. "It is very difficult," he said. "I cannot resign myself."

Fitzgerald
. . . not to forget, but to carry his wounds with him to new disasters and new atonements—toward his unknown destiny.

Whether the modern age inspired them or dispirited them, the writers grouped here affirmed the power of the imagination. The act of writing itself was a way of ordering a disordered time and place, an authentic source of delight. Through literature life still offered meaning, beauty, and a measure of joy.

Key to Illustrations on Pages 400–401.

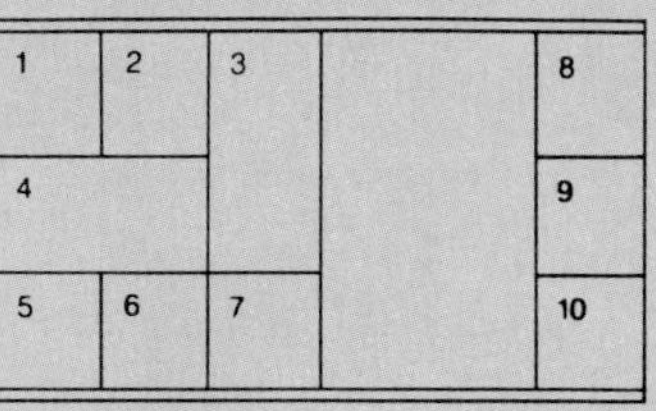

1. Detail of *American Gothic,* Grant Wood, 1930.
2. United States Army poster, World War I.
3. Detail of *Allies Day,* Childe Hassam, 1917.
4. Detail of *Morning News,* Francis Luis Mora, 1912.
5. Detail of *Gertrude Stein,* Pablo Picasso, 1906.
6. Lamp, designed by Louis Tiffany, c. 1910.
7. F. Scott Fitzgerald, photographer unknown.
8. Robert Frost, photograph by Tom Hollyman.
9. *I Saw the Figure 5 in Gold,* Charles Demuth, 1928.
10. Ernest Hemingway, photograph by John Bryson.

THE AMERICAN VOICE

"Make It New"
In conjunction with this page, remind the students of the discussion of Modernism in the introduction to the unit. By now they should be able to place Pound's exhortation in a historical context of change and dislocation. You could have them read through the quotations in this section and identify what makes them new: Eliot's stream of consciousness and Prufrock's anxiety, Williams' broken rhythms and discovery of art in common places, Stein's stream of consciousness and sound experiments, Stevens' emphasis on the power of imagination, and the emphasis in fiction on forging a new identity in a new world.

Photograph © 1982 by Jill Krementz

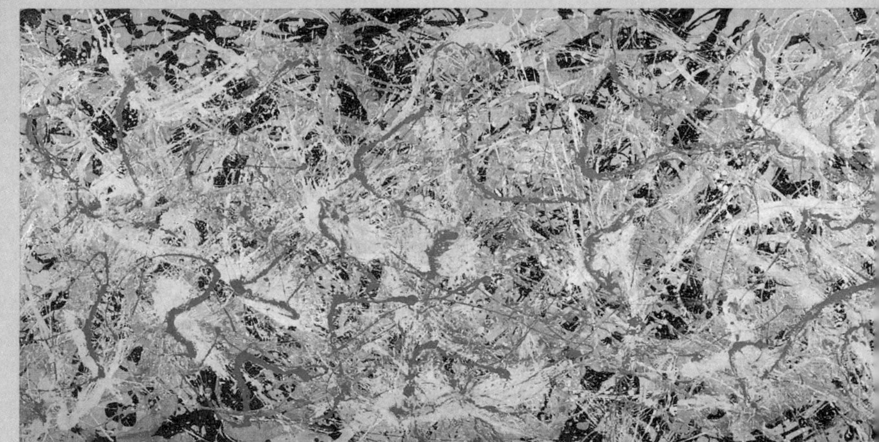

Key to Illustrations appears on page 755.

MIDCENTURY VOICES

1930–1960

The Great Depression

The vibrant, experimental, roaring 1920s ended with a bang—the great stock market crash of 1929. Not only the United States but all the industrial nations of the world found themselves suddenly cast into a disastrous economic depression. The collapse of Wall Street meant terrible times: Businesses failed; factories closed down. Millions of Americans found themselves out of work, their homes or farms lost, their hopes abandoned.

As the Great Depression deepened, the cities of America could no longer be celebrated as Carl Sandburg had celebrated Chicago (page 434)—laughing as a "fighter laughs who has never lost a battle." The American landscape saw armies of wandering men and women searching for jobs. Soup kitchens and bread lines were a constant reminder of how many Americans were forced to accept the charity of others.

The poverty and despair of the 1930s brought forth a new attitude toward government and society. President Franklin Roosevelt called for a "New Deal" for the American people, and his administrations began many programs of direct and indirect assistance to those who had lost not only their jobs but faith in their own future. Americans confronted a decade of self-doubt that was all the more shocking because of the vivid decade that had preceded it.

INTRODUCTION

After having students read the introduction, you might focus discussion on the following:

- Ask students what they know of recent economic conditions. Can they remember "bad times"? What made them bad? What happened to improve the economy or make it worse?
- Students might be surprised to find out that the government paid artists and writers to work during the Depression. Ask them how artists and writers make their living now. Do they think most writers are able to support themselves from their writing?
- Remind students that the Depression and World War II kept the country in a state of crisis for sixteen years. Ask them to speculate what the reaction of Americans was to the end of the war and to the return of economic prosperity. (They should realize that after such a prolonged period of crisis most people were very interested in setting down roots, buying homes, raising families, and building careers.)

Key Ideas in This Period

- the effects of the Great Depression and World War II
- the individual
- nostalgia
- public and private experience
- nature in the Atomic Age

American photographers like Walker Evans documented the country's struggle through the 1930s.

The Literature of Crisis

In the world of literature, as in all the arts, a period of great freedom and experimentation came to an end with the Depression. Many of the great artists of the early twentieth century had years to live and some of their greatest works still to produce—painters such as Pablo Picasso, composers such as Igor Stravinsky and Arnold Schoenberg, and writers such as Pound, Eliot, Yeats, Stevens, and Joyce. Yet these artists had done their shocking work, their influential work, in the first decades of the century.

The next generation, the writers in this unit, absorbed the lessons of the Modernists: They grew up in an atmosphere of Modernism and incorporated into their own work the discoveries and experiments, the new styles and forms, of Modernism. Yet they also witnessed the hard lessons of a nation's poverty and suffering. These writers—striving for both artistic excellence *and* social commitment—produced what critic Alfred Kazin has called the literature of crisis.

In order to put these writers to work, the federal government, through such agencies as the Works Progress Administration, commissioned books, pamphlets, brochures, and other writing of a largely documentary nature. This literature was intended not only to give writers a chance to make a living but also to put America on record for itself, to remind it of its greatness in a time of trouble. This documentary literature included descriptions and histories of American places—landmarks, towns, cities, and rivers. Writers prepared a detailed guidebook for each state. Writers also collaborated with photographers such as Margaret Bourke-White and Dorothea Lange to produce journalistic and photographic records of the ways America lived. The greatest of these documents is *Let Us Now Praise Famous Men*—a study of Alabama sharecroppers—by writer James Agee and photographer Walker Evans.

The major fiction writers of the time produced novels closely tied to the lives of ordinary people, literature in which style and experiment stepped aside in favor of human stories told with emotion and social commitment. These were the kind of books produced by John Steinbeck, John Dos Passos, and James T. Farrell. Dos Passos' trilogy *U.S.A.* (completed 1936) used journalistic techniques and a style imitating newsreels to tell an episodic story of social unrest and the decline of individuality. The undoubted masterpiece of this type of novel is Steinbeck's *Grapes of Wrath* (1939), the gripping story of the Joads, Oklahoma farmers driven by poverty to find a new natural paradise in California. Ma Joad's outcry sums up the sense of the times: "We ain' gonna die out. People is goin' on—changin' a little, maybe, but goin' right on."

In contrast to the documentary and Realist writers of the time, two novelists combined a feeling for the people with a continued reliance on the American Romantic tradition. Thomas Wolfe's novels—including *Of Time and the River* (1935) and *You Can't Go Home Again* (1940)—are highly autobiographical, lyrical journeys into the artist's own self. William Faulkner's large, complex novels are Romantic in another sense: They create a whole world of their own. *The Sound and the Fury* (1929), *Absalom, Absalom!* (1936), and *The Hamlet* (1940) are among the Faulkner novels that detail the decline of southern aristocratic families and the rise of the opportunistic people who replace them. In a style often demanding, often a kind of modern gothic, Faulkner's novels raise his characters to mythic proportions. Modern and Romantic, both Wolfe and Faulkner reflect a profound understanding of the common people and of their time and place. In a time of social crisis, they emphasized the individual.

Postwar America

During the 1930s Americans watched the rise of Fascism in Europe, as Mussolini came to power in Italy, Hitler in Germany, and Franco in Spain. They watched Russia labor under the dictatorship of Stalin. In 1939 they watched World War II break out and Europe once again become an enormous battleground.

Many Americans had long felt free of Europe's troubles. In the modern world, however, every country is tied to every other country through economics, trade, political alliances, or beliefs and principles. In a time of rapid transportation and communication, in the age of modern warfare, Americans could not remain uninvolved. Democracy itself seemed threatened, as the world appeared to be falling to fascist expansion. After the attack at Pearl Harbor on December 7, 1941, Americans entered the war, suffered through it, and helped to win the most devastating conflict the world had ever seen.

The effect of World War II on American culture and literature, however, was quite different from the effect of World War I. After World War I Americans had abandoned their old beliefs and optimism and threw themselves headlong into whatever was new and exciting, breaking boundaries and establishing forms. After World War II Americans did not seem as disillusioned, as much a "lost generation," as they had been during the 1920s. There were crises of course—for example, the anti-Communist McCarthy hearings and the Cold War with the Soviet Union. Overall, however, the country entered a period of prosperity, growth, and a generally contented peacefulness. The greatest reason for anxiety seemed to sink beneath the surface of daily life: With the development of atomic warfare, the world, it was clear, would never be quite the same again.

Four Darks in Red, Mark Rothko, 1958.

Postwar Literature

Some postwar literature directly confronts the events of the time. Randall Jarrell's "Death of the Ball Turret Gunner" recalls the violence of aerial warfare. W. H. Auden's "Unknown Citizen" portrays an individual dwarfed by the State. Yet much of the literature seems to respond *indirectly* to its own time, turning away as if in self-protection. Thornton Wilder's *Our Town,* which seems the most peaceful and untroubled of works, was already, at its first production in 1938, a nostalgic celebration of a world that had vanished. In Steinbeck's "Leader of the People" and in James Agee's "Knoxville: Summer, 1915" we find a nostalgia for vanished worlds. In Walter Van Tilburg Clark's "Portable Phonograph" the world looks longingly back to a time before its most destructive war. Faulkner's "Bear" takes its characters back to an almost mythological past.

The literature of 1930–1960 is so varied that it is difficult to make generalizations about it. Indeed, generalizations about periods of literature are always dangerous and must be taken only as indications of tendencies. Yet we do notice in postwar writing a trend toward poems and stories that celebrate private experiences, memories of childhood (as in Theodore Roethke), or moments of private happiness (as in Sylvia Plath's "Blackberrying" and Jack Kerouac's "Alone on a Mountaintop"). Literature reflects the world in which it is created—even if that reflection is a withdrawal from public concerns into private experience.

TIME LINE

1930–1960 AMERICAN EVENTS

1930 Katherine Anne Porter, *Flowering Judas and Other Stories*

1931 Empire State Building, 102 stories, completed

1932 William Faulkner, *Light in August*

Amelia Earhart first woman to fly solo across Atlantic Ocean

1933 Congress passes anti-Depression acts, founds National Recovery Administration (NRA), and begins many public works projects

1934 Clarinetist Benny Goodman organizes band and becomes "King of Swing"

1935 George and Ira Gershwin, opera *Porgy and Bess*

1936 Jesse Owens, black American track star, wins four Olympic gold medals in Berlin

1937 John Dos Passos, *U.S.A.*

1938 Thornton Wilder, *Our Town*

Orson Welles's radio broadcast *Invasion from Mars* causes panic

1939 John Steinbeck, *The Grapes of Wrath*

1940 Richard Wright, *Native Son*

Carson McCullers, *The Heart Is a Lonely Hunter*

Thomas Wolfe, *You Can't Go Home Again*

1941 U.S. enters World War II

Eudora Welty, *A Curtain of Green and Other Stories*

WORLD EVENTS 1930–1960

1930 Worldwide economic depression

1932 England: Aldous Huxley, *Brave New World*

1933 Germany: Adolf Hitler appointed chancellor

Ireland: W. B. Yeats, *Collected Poems*

1934 Germany: Engineer Werner von Braun launches two experimental rockets

1936 Spain: Civil War begins

1937 France: Spaniard Pablo Picasso paints *Guernica*

1938 England: Graham Greene, *Brighton Rock*

Hungary: Lajos Biro invents ballpoint pen

1939 France: Irish novelist James Joyce, *Finnegans Wake*

Beginning of World War II

1942 William Faulkner, "The Bear"

1944 Tennessee Williams, *The Glass Menagerie*

1945 Frank Lloyd Wright designs Guggenheim Museum

John Steinbeck, *The Red Pony*

1946 Benjamin Spock, M.D., *Baby and Child Care*

1948 W. H. Auden, *The Age of Anxiety*

Delmore Schwartz, *In Dreams Begin Responsibilities*

Transistor invented

1949 William Faulkner wins Nobel Prize for Literature

Arthur Miller, *Death of a Salesman*

1950 Jackson Pollock paints *Lavender Mist,* first "drip" painting

1951 Marianne Moore, *Collected Poems*

UNIVAC, first mass-produced computer

1952 Ernest Hemingway, *The Old Man and the Sea*

Ralph Ellison, *Invisible Man*

1942 France: Albert Camus, *The Stranger*

1943 France: Oceanographer Jacques Cousteau invents aqualung

1944 France: Jean-Paul Sartre, *No Exit*

1945 Japan: Atomic bombs dropped on Hiroshima and Nagasaki

England: George Orwell, *Animal Farm*

1946 Greece: Nikos Kazantzakis, *Zorba the Greek*

1947 Holland: *Diary of a Young Girl,* by Anne Frank, discovered and published

1948 Israel established by United Nations

South Africa: Alan Paton, *Cry the Beloved Country*

1949 China: Communists, led by Mao Zedung, defeat Nationalists; establish People's Republic

England: George Orwell, *Nineteen Eighty-Four*

1950 Korea: War begins between North and South Korea

Japan: Akira Kurosawa's film *Rashomon* gains world renown

1952 Albert Schweitzer, German humanitarian and physician, receives Nobel Peace Prize

Wales: Dylan Thomas, *Collected Poems*

Ireland: Samuel Beckett, *Waiting for Godot*

	AMERICAN EVENTS		WORLD EVENTS
1953	Theodore Roethke, *The Waking*	1953	Tibet: Edmund Hillary of New Zealand and Tenzing Norgay of Nepal climb Mount Everest
	Arthur Miller, *The Crucible*		
		1954	England: William Golding, *The Lord of the Flies*
1955	Elizabeth Bishop, *North and South—A Cold Spring*		
1956	John F. Kennedy, *Profiles in Courage*	1956	Sweden: Filmmaker Ingmar Bergman, *The Seventh Seal*
1957	Leonard Bernstein and Stephen Sondheim, *West Side Story*	1957	U.S.S.R.: *Sputnik I,* first satellite, launched
1958	First commercial copying machine is produced	1958	U.S.S.R.: Boris Pasternak, *Dr. Zhivago*
1959	Alaska and Hawaii become forty-ninth and fiftieth states	1959	Germany: Günter Grass, *The Tin Drum*
	Robert Lowell, *Life Studies*		France: Eugene Ionesco, *Rhinoceros*
1960	Jack Kerouac, *Lonesome Traveler*	1960	England: Playwright Harold Pinter, *The Caretaker*
	Gwendolyn Brooks, *The Bean Eaters*		

W. H. Auden *1907–1973*

Wystan Hugh Auden was one of the master craftsmen of English verse. In many ways he wrote against the grain of Modernism, basing his poems upon a wide knowledge of traditional meters and forms. His poems are not afraid of sentiment or nostalgia, but they characteristically surprise us with reminders of realities.

Auden was born an Englishman, and it was as an English poet that he made a dazzling, youthful reputation. After 1939, however, he lived mostly in America, becoming an American citizen in 1946.

The English Auden made a reputation for himself while still an undergraduate at Oxford University. His first volume, *Poems,* appeared in 1930. Throughout the thirties he continued to amaze the reading public with his brash verses that reflected an interest in science, industrial landscapes, and modern psychology. With such comrades as novelist Christopher Isherwood and poet Stephen Spender, he plunged into politics. He saw Nazi Germany at first hand, and he worked with the Republican side against the Fascists in Spain.

In 1939 he began a new life and freed himself from the restrictions of Europe. He came to New York, where he produced some of his finest works. In America he felt a revival of his Christianity, which grew stronger as he grew older. He taught at Swarthmore College during World War II, and in 1948 he won the Pulitzer Prize for *The Age of Anxiety,* a long poem that uses Old English alliterations as it follows the lives of four people through a postwar world of uncertainty and isolation. His other major volumes are *Nones* (1951), *The Shield of Achilles* (1955), and *Homage to Clio* (1960). A prolific and versatile writer, Auden also collaborated with the great modern composer Igor Stravinsky on an opera, *The Rake's Progress,* in addition to producing lively literary criticism.

In his later years Auden lived in a house he bought in Kirchstetten, Austria. He died in Vienna in 1973 and was buried near his beloved house. On his memorial plaque in London's Westminster Abbey are words from the poem he wrote in memory of the Irish poet W. B. Yeats—"In the prison of his days / Teach the free man how to praise"—words that sum up his own life as well.

Auden's poems are marked by exquisite craft, wise observation of history, and trust in the value of art. Like "The Unknown Citizen" they can sharply describe the relationships between people and the governments they create. Like "If I Could Tell You" they can brim with a deeply moving human sympathy.

■ During this period many Americans were uncertain of the future. How does Auden capture that uncertainty in his poetry?

W. H. Auden

If I Could Tell You

Time will say nothing but I told you so,
Time only knows the price we have to pay;
If I could tell you I would let you know.

If we should weep when clowns put on their show,
If we should stumble when musicians play,
Time will say nothing but I told you so.

There are no fortunes to be told, although,
Because I love you more than I can say,
If I could tell you I would let you know.

The winds must come from somewhere when they blow,
There must be reasons why the leaves decay;
Time will say nothing but I told you so.

Perhaps the roses really want to grow,
The vision seriously intends to stay;
If I could tell you I would let you know.

Suppose the lions all get up and go,
And all the brooks and soldiers run away;
Will Time say nothing but I told you so?
If I could tell you I would let you know.

STUDY QUESTIONS

Recalling

1. According to the poem, what is the only thing that time will say? What would the speaker do if he could? Why would he do this, according to the third stanza?
2. What does the fourth stanza say about the winds and the leaves? What does the fifth stanza say about the roses and the vision?

Interpreting

3. What seems to be the relationship between the speaker and the person he addresses? Which images in the poem suggest this relationship?
4. What does the speaker fear will happen to the roses and the vision? What does he therefore fear will happen to his relationship with the person he addresses? Is he certain about the future?
5. Might this poem be about more than the relationship between the speaker and the person he addresses? Explain.

Extending

6. In what ways is this poem reminiscent of poetry of previous centuries? (Consider both the form and content of the poem.) In what way is it a "modern" poem? (Consider the tone, or attitude, of the poet.)

AT A GLANCE

- The speaker tells his love that he cannot predict the future or guarantee that their love will endure.
- He states that the only lesson that time can teach is "I told you so."

LITERARY OPTIONS

- villanelle
- imagery

THEMATIC OPTIONS

- impermanence
- romantic love

SPEAKER

The speaker's reflections about the inscrutability of time seem to respond to a lover's question about the future (ll. 1–3).

IMAGERY

The speaker underscores the transient quality of human experience with the images of blowing wind and decaying leaves (ll. 10–11).

VILLANELLE

The strict nineteen-line form and insistent dual rhyme scheme of the villanelle provide an ironic contrast to the speaker's assertion that there is no predictability or order in the universe.

REFLECTING ON THE POEM

Do you think it appropriate to call this a love poem? Why or why not? (Students who find the term appropriate may cite the speaker's suggestion that love may endure; those who disagree may cite the speaker's "no promise" attitude.)

STUDY QUESTIONS

1. "I told you so"; "let you know"; "I love you more than I can say"
2. "winds must come from somewhere," "must be reasons" for leaves' decay; roses may "want to grow," vision may intend to stay
3. love; line 8 is explicit
4. decay, leave; end; no
5. yes; about transience of all things, pain felt in holding on to what may be lost
6. love poem, adherence to strict form; world as filled with uncertainty, impermanence

The Unknown Citizen

(To JS/07/M/378
This Marble Monument
Is Erected by the State)

He was found by the Bureau of Statistics to be
One against whom there was no official complaint,
And all the reports on his conduct agree
That, in the modern sense of an old-fashioned word, he was a saint,
For in everything he did he served the Greater Community.
Except for the War till the day he retired
He worked in a factory and never got fired,
But satisfied his employers, Fudge Motors Inc.
Yet he wasn't a scab[1] or odd in his views,
For his Union reports that he paid his dues,
(Our report on his Union shows it was sound)
And our Social Psychology workers found
That he was popular with his mates and liked a drink.
The Press are convinced that he bought a paper every day
And that his reactions to advertisements were normal in every way.
Policies taken out in his name prove that he was fully insured,
And his Health-card shows he was once in hospital but left it cured.
Both Producers Research and High-Grade Living declare
He was fully sensible to the advantages of the Installment Plan
And had everything necessary to the Modern Man,
A phonograph, a radio, a car and a frigidaire.
Our researchers into Public Opinion are content
That he held the proper opinions for the time of year;
When there was peace, he was for peace; when there was war, he
went.
He was married and added five children to the population,
Which our Eugenist[2] says was the right number for a parent of his
generation,
And our teachers report that he never interfered with their
education.
Was he free? Was he happy? The question is absurd:
Had anything been wrong, we should certainly have heard.

---

1. **scab:** worker who refuses to strike or replaces a striker.
2. **Eugenist** [ū jen′ist]: specialist in eugenics, the movement to improve inherited traits in humans.

AT A GLANCE

- The State erects a monument in praise of an unknown citizen who was a model of conformity.
- The State declares that the citizen must have been free and happy because if anything had been wrong, it would have known.

LITERARY OPTIONS

- satire
- rhyme

THEMATIC OPTIONS

- governmental dehumanization
- the constraints of conformity

SATIRE

Using such an "old-fashioned," morally charged word as *saint* to convey the degree of conformity satirizes a system of government under which conformity is more important than personality (ll. 3–5).

RHYME

Notice how the speaker uses simple, jingoistic rhyming couplets to prate about the virtues of the unknown citizen (ll. 14–17).

MAIN IDEA

The wooden response to the simple poignant questions "Was he free? Was he happy?" conveys an authoritarian government's deafness to issues of human dignity and personal freedom (l. 28).

REFLECTING ON THE POEM

The poem reports a roster of facts known about the citizen; yet the title calls him "unknown." What overall impact does the poem's satiric tone have on its meaning? (It helps to illustrate how pompous and self-serving bureaucratic systems can become.)

STUDY QUESTIONS

1. a marble monument; the State
2. "modern sense": there were no complaints against him, "he served the Greater Community"
3. Union, Social Psychology workers, Press, Producers Research, High-Grade Living, Eugenist; Fudge Motors Inc.
4. "Was he free? Was he happy?"; had anything been wrong, the State would have heard
5. paternalistic, bureaucratic, impersonal; to exalt the nameless, faceless, statistically normal worker-citizen
6. served community, good worker, popular, good consumer, held correct opinions, had correct number of children; no, poet satirizes such ideals
7. State contends citizens are free, happy, but does not understand conditions for happiness, such as individuality
8. blind conformity, unthinking acceptance of expectations of state, impersonal bureaucracies existing only to perpetuate themselves
9. reducing names to numbers, need for people to feel they fit in; students might agree with many of the poet's opinions

VIEWPOINT

- "Unknown Citizen": mind—satire of modern state; heart—siding with individual
- "If I Could . . .": heart—theme; mind—construction

LITERARY FOCUS

1. Government should humanely serve society, and the people should actively serve the government.
2. Answers will vary. Satires may not bring immediate change, but may initiate political action; repressive regimes fear satire, as political action is threat to status quo; South Africa and the Soviet Union have both silenced satirists.

STUDY QUESTIONS

Recalling

1. According to the inscription under the title, on what does this poem appear? Who has erected it?
2. According to lines 1–5, in what sense was the unknown citizen a "saint"?
3. Identify at least four organizations or groups of people who have passed positive judgments on the unknown citizen. Except for the war, where did the unknown citizen work until he retired (line 7)?
4. What questions are asked in the last two lines of the poem? According to the poem, why are these questions absurd?

Interpreting

5. What kind of "State," or government, has erected this monument? Why would a government erect a public monument to an "unknown citizen"?
6. Describe at least four ways in which the unknown citizen was found to be "ideal." Does the *poet* find such behavior ideal?
7. What is ironic about the last two lines of the poem?
8. Basically, what is this poem criticizing?

Extending

9. What aspects of the modern world does this poem make you think about? Do you agree with the poet's opinion of everything he criticizes? Why or why not?

VIEWPOINT

Hayden Carruth, a critic of Auden, has written:

> Auden was a profoundly emotional writer, and I fail to see how any reader can miss that quality in his writing, that force, that humility, even when the knowledge is specialized—Auden was fond of scientific writing and by no means unschooled in it—and the thought is complex or quirky. For me, the poet who shows me his mind as well as his heart . . . is always more interesting than the one who shows me his heart alone.

■ Where in Auden's poems do you find the poet "showing his mind"? Where do you find him "showing his heart"?

LITERARY FOCUS

Satire

Auden's "Unknown Citizen" is a popular modern satire. **Satire** is a kind of writing that holds up someone or something to ridicule or serious criticism. It is an attitude, not a form. Satirists see something they think is wrong with another person, with a group of people, with an institution, or with society at large. They attempt to correct the follies or errors of the world by holding those errors up for inspection in a way that allows us to laugh at them.

Some satires are gentle, poking good-natured fun; others are harsh, attacking serious evils. In either case, satire is a public art: It intends to make society better by showing the excesses and imbalances of human nature. It assumes that there is a rational norm of behavior, and it makes us laugh, even if that laughter is bitter, at departures from the norm.

Auden's "Unknown Citizen" is a serious poem with bitter overtones, although we may not see at first how serious it is. Auden pushes his vision of the modern bureaucratic state to an extreme, hoping that his comic excess will make each of us realize that we, too, are in danger of becoming "unknown citizens."

Thinking About Satire

1. How would you describe the norm of a good government and a good society that Auden wants to bring about?
2. Do you think satires are really effective in bringing about changes in the world? Why or why not?

© Rollie McKenna

Theodore Roethke *1908–1963*

Theodore Roethke was a much loved and honored poet during his lifetime, winning the Pulitzer Prize, the National Book Award, and the Bollingen Prize. However, many of his poems have received a higher honor than any official prize can bestow: They have become favorite poems with many readers.

Roethke fashioned his poems from intense memories of his childhood and boyhood in Michigan. His father and grandfather were florists, and Roethke grew up in a world of flowers, plants, and large commercial greenhouses. Images of growth and decay can be found in all of his books, including *Open House* (1941), *The Lost Son* (1948), *The Waking* (1953), and *Words for the Wind* (1958).

Roethke's poems are closely observed lyrics. He details the processes of the natural world and, like Emerson and Whitman, almost mystically identifies with nature: "In my veins, in my bones I feel it." In the free verse of "Big Wind" he recaptures a struggle to keep his flowers alive as a great storm lashes his greenhouse. Like Auden, Roethke was also a master of the stricter forms of poetry, and in "The Waking" he puts some thoroughly modern ideas into a thoroughly old-fashioned form.

■ Can the form that a poem takes add meaning to its words? How does a poet accomplish meaning through form?

AT A GLANCE

- When a violent storm occurs, the poet and his father work to save a greenhouse and its roses.
- As a storm-tossed ship sails into calm waters, so the greenhouse survives when calm morning breaks.

LITERARY OPTIONS

- metaphor
- free verse

THEMATIC OPTIONS

- human ingenuity
- the power of nature

FREE VERSE

The form of the poem, as the speaker describes the storm and the roses, expands and contracts in line-length and meter (ll. 17–20).

METAPHOR

In comparing the storm-buffeted greenhouse to a boat on a stormy sea, the poet establishes a controlling image that dramatizes the power of nature and the heroism of endurance (ll. 21–25).

MAIN IDEA

The greenhouse, dignified and intact in the morning, offers testimony that human ingenuity can triumph over natural disasters (ll. 26–33).

REFLECTING ON THE POEM

In what way does the poem's form complement its subject matter? (The natural-sounding free verse mirrors the natural processes taking place during the storm.)

Theodore Roethke

Big Wind

Where were the greenhouses going,
Lunging into the lashing
Wind driving water
So far down the river
All the faucets stopped?—
So we drained the manure machine
For the steam plant,
Pumping the stale mixture
Into the rusty boilers,
Watching the pressure gauge
Waver over to red,
As the seams hissed
And the live steam
Drove to the far
End of the rose-house,
Where the worst wind was,
Creaking the cypress window frames,
Cracking so much thin glass
We stayed all night,
Stuffing the holes with burlap;
But she rode it out,
That old rose-house,
She hove[1] into the teeth of it,
The core and pith[2] of that ugly storm,
Ploughing with her stiff prow,
Bucking into the wind-waves
That broke over the whole of her,
Flailing her sides with spray,
Flinging long strings of wet across the rooftop,
Finally veering, wearing themselves out, merely
Whistling thinly under the wind-vents;
She sailed until the calm morning,
Carrying her full cargo of roses.

1. **hove:** heaved.
2. **pith:** vital force.

The Waking

I wake to sleep, and take my waking slow.
I feel my fate in what I cannot fear.
I learn by going where I have to go.

We think by feeling. What is there to know?
I hear my being dance from ear to ear.
I wake to sleep, and take my waking slow.

Of those so close beside me, which are you?
God bless the Ground! I shall walk softly there,
And learn by going where I have to go.

Light takes the Tree; but who can tell us how?
The lowly worm climbs up a winding stair;
I wake to sleep, and take my waking slow.

Great Nature has another thing to do
To you and me; so take the lively air,
And, lovely, learn by going where to go.

This shaking keeps me steady. I should know.
What falls away is always. And is near.
I wake to sleep, and take my waking slow.
I learn by going where I have to go.

STUDY QUESTIONS

Big Wind

Recalling

1. What question does the first line ask? What are the greenhouses doing in lines 2–3?
2. What do the speaker and his companion do in lines 6–9? What is the pressure gauge for the boilers doing?
3. What outcome does the speaker report in lines 20–21? In lines 32–33?

Interpreting

4. What is the controlling image (see page 34) in this poem?
5. What might the storm have done to the greenhouses and the roses?
6. Who or what saved the rose-house? What could have happened to the speaker and his companions?
7. How does the speaker seem to feel about the old rose-house? What more general message might there be in the rose-house's endurance?

Extending

8. What do you think a Naturalist writer like Jack London (page 354) or Stephen Crane (page 367) might have said about this poem? What qualities of the poem reflect the tradition of American nature poetry? What qualities are especially modern?

AT A GLANCE

- The speaker wakes to "sleep" and thinks "by feeling."
- On our journey to death, he says, we are experiencing life.
- Nature teaches us that we should live life to the fullest even as we learn from it.

LITERARY OPTIONS

- villanelle
- paradox

THEMATIC OPTIONS

- life and death
- knowledge and self-awareness

PARADOX

By using paradoxical sensory images that reverse traditional expectations (thinking by feeling; hearing a dance; waking to sleep), Roethke suggests that one must suspend habitual systems of belief to appreciate the fullness of life (ll. 4–6).

VILLANELLE

In altering the expected refrain slightly (substituting *and* for *I*), the speaker mirrors the idea of process expressed in the poem and reinforces the importance of learning from life (l. 9).

REFLECTING ON THE POEM

In what way does the villanelle form contribute to the poem's main idea? (It reinforces the idea of union and harmony; it reflects a natural progression and continuity.)

STUDY QUESTIONS

Big Wind

1. where greenhouses are going; lunging into lashing wind
2. drain manure machine, pump mixture into boilers; wavers over to the red
3. greenhouse rode out storm; sailed until calm morning with full cargo of roses
4. greenhouse as ship in a storm
5. destroyed them
6. human ingenuity, hard work; hurt in an explosion
7. affection, pride; ingenuity triumphs, beauty endures
8. less optimistic about overcoming nature; subject, love for roses; descriptions, form

The Waking

1. sleep; what he cannot fear; by going where he has to; by feeling
2. his being dance; has another thing to do; take lively air, learn by going where to go
3. living from day to day; death; lead us all to death
4. experience life as deeply as possible while he has it
5. live life fully; poet will die only after living life fully, having learned all he can
6. *Roethke:* affirms life, derives strength from nature; *Prufrock:* alienated from nature, unable to live life fully

LITERARY FOCUS

1. first refrain is statement until final stanza, then question; second refrain, *I learn by going,* becomes *And learn by going* in third stanza and *And, lovely, learn* in fifth
2. meditative, comes back full circle to starting point

The Waking

Recalling

1. According to the poem, to what does the speaker wake? In what does he feel his fate (line 2)? How does he learn? How does he think we all think (line 4)?
2. What does the speaker hear in line 5? What does he say about nature in line 13? What advice does he give in lines 14–15?

Interpreting

3. What might the speaker mean by the waking? By the sleeping? What is "another thing" that nature has to do "to you and me," in addition to the waking described in stanzas 1–4?
4. Why would the speaker "take his waking slow"?
5. Explain the advice we are given in line 14. How is it related to the refrain "I learn by going where I have to go"?

Extending

6. In what ways is the attitude toward life expressed in this poem different from the attitude expressed in Eliot's "Love Song of J. Alfred Prufrock" on page 415?

LITERARY FOCUS

The Villanelle

W. H. Auden's "If I Could Tell You" (page 546) and Theodore Roethke's "Waking" are written in the strict form known as the villanelle. A **villanelle** is a poem of nineteen lines divided into five tercets (three-line stanzas) and a final quatrain, using only two rhymes throughout. It was a favorite verse form of French poets four hundred years ago, and some modern poets such as Auden, Roethke, and the Welsh poet Dylan Thomas have accepted its challenge in our century.

The most unusual characteristic of the villanelle is its use of refrains, or repeated lines. The first line of the poem becomes the final line of the second and fourth stanzas, and the third line becomes the final line of the third and fifth stanzas. Both refrains are brought together in the final two lines.

While Auden and Roethke adhere to the demands of the villanelle, they also vary the form slightly to avoid stiffness. Both poets vary their refrains. Auden keeps his two rhymes pure: All the lines rhyme with "so" and "pay." Roethke, however, uses some slant rhymes: "Slow" is made to rhyme with "you" and "how"; "fear" is made to rhyme with "there," "stair," and "air."

Why would modern poets choose to write in so limited and demanding a form as the villanelle? We may suggest two answers. First, good poets are skilled in a craft and sometimes they want to challenge themselves. The Irish poet W. B. Yeats wrote of the "fascination of what's difficult," and clearly Auden and Roethke were fascinated with the sheer difficulty of the villanelle. The poem gives pleasure to both poet and reader when the form "comes out right." Second, the circling form of the villanelle can be a reflection of the subject matter of the poem: It suggests, for example, the circling and repeating questions about life asked in Auden's "If I Could Tell You."

Thinking About the Villanelle

1. How does Auden vary the refrain in "If I Could Tell You"? How does Roethke vary the refrain in "The Waking"?
2. Why is the villanelle form appropriate to the subject of Roethke's "Waking"?

COMPOSITION

Writing About a Quotation

■ In a brief essay explain the importance of Roethke's refrain, "I learn by going where I have to go." Begin by telling precisely what the line means. Then discuss how the line adds to the meaning of other lines in the poem. Conclude with your own reflections on the value of what the poem says. *For help with this assignment, refer to Lesson 5 in the Writing About Literature Handbook at the back of this book.*

Writing a Villanelle

■ After studying Auden's and Roethke's villanelles, try writing one of your own. Think of it as an exercise in craft, a puzzle to be solved. You may want to begin by choosing the rhymes you want to use and then planning the final words of all your lines. Then "fill in" each line, keeping in mind that although Auden and Roethke have used five beats in each line (pentameter), you need not.

COMPOSITION: GUIDELINES FOR EVALUATION

WRITING ABOUT A QUOTATION

Objective

To analyze a line of poetry

Guidelines for Evaluation

- suggested length: three to five paragraphs
- should state literal meaning of line
- should explain the resonant power of line, especially used as refrain
- should evaluate the essential connection poet makes between life and death

WRITING A VILLANELLE

Objective

To write a villanelle

Guidelines for Evaluation

- suggested length: nineteen lines
- should be nineteen lines long
- should have five three-line stanzas and one four-line stanza
- should use alternating refrains
- should use two rhymes throughout

Photograph © 1982 by Jill Krementz

Robert Lowell *1917–1977*

Robert Lowell was born into one of the oldest and most distinguished of Boston families: Two well-known American poets, James Russell Lowell (page 221) and Amy Lowell, were among his ancestors. Yet from an early age Lowell turned away from the comfortable life, writing poetry that seemed haunted by a sense of the past, by a mysterious burden of guilt, by an urgent and inescapable seriousness.

The need to perform a symbolic art made Lowell leave the East, with all its reminders of the past, and attend college in Ohio, where he studied under the poet John Crowe Ransom (page 448). Immensely talented and thoughtful, Lowell achieved early success as a poet, winning the Pulitzer Prize for *Lord Weary's Castle* (1946) before he was thirty. In that book and in *The Mills of the Kavanaughs* (1951) he examined his own world-weariness in verse that is highly crafted, heavy, and dense with symbols. In this style, he seemed to have achieved a permanent reputation.

In mid-life, however, Lowell suddenly and drastically changed his style. He had discovered the poetry of some younger Americans, in particular Allen Ginsberg, who were writing in a much more open and direct style. Lowell's own poetry, the poetry that had brought him such early fame, no longer pleased him. It sounded to his ears "willfully difficult," with a "stiff, humorless, and even impenetrable surface." He began working on a new sort of poetry that has come to be called confessional poetry.

In these **confessional poems** Lowell began to speak with a sometimes embarrassing openness and frankness about his own life. He broke radically with the dominant critical tradition of his generation, a tradition that taught that we are never to think of the "I" in a poem as the actual person of the poet himself. In Lowell's later poems the "I" is clearly to be taken as Robert Lowell himself. The volume in which Lowell's new, personal poems appeared was *Life Studies* (1959), and it became immensely influential, giving rise to a group of talented confessional poets that included John Berryman, Sylvia Plath, and Anne Sexton. Following their example, lesser poets all over America began to write poems about "I"—talky poems that recounted their personal problems, few of which were as interesting as the spiritual quest of Robert Lowell.

"Hawthorne" is typical of Lowell in many ways. It is personal yet it deals with the past. Carefully crafted yet casual, it offers a portrait of an artist in search of the sources of art.

■ Can a poet be concerned with capturing the past and still write a "personal" poem? How does Lowell reveal the personal?

AT A GLANCE

- The poet pictures Hawthorne at work in Salem's Customs House.
- He speaks of how Hawthorne's shyness belies the fire of his imagination.
- Hawthorne broods over a common object, trying unsuccessfully to extract some universal truth from it.

LITERARY OPTIONS

- imagery
- tone

THEMATIC OPTIONS

- the value of the past
- art vs. commerce

IMAGERY

Lowell draws concrete, direct visual pictures from common experience (flat, unvaried surface; yellow drain; unhealthy hair) to convey how nonnourishing and uninspiring he finds contemplation of the past (ll. 3–6).

TONE

The speaker's exhortations to study his images of the Fireside Poets and Hawthorne reinforce his personal tone and reflect the urgency that infuses his attempt to understand the creative process that distinguished Hawthorne (ll. 23–31).

MAIN IDEA

The final image of eyes disturbed by meditating on the conjunction of insignificance and truth suggests Lowell's belief that the past, however elusive or incomprehensible, provides a rich source of inspiration (ll. 39–42).

REFLECTING ON THE POEM

How would you describe Lowell's attitude toward the creative process? (It seems to be a mysterious process, with both destructive and transformational powers.)

Robert Lowell

Hawthorne

Follow its lazy main street lounging
from the alms house to Gallows Hill[1]
along a flat, unvaried surface
covered with wooden houses
aged by yellow drain
like the unhealthy hair of an old dog.
You'll walk to no purpose
in Hawthorne's Salem.

I cannot resilver the smudged plate.[2]

I drop to Hawthorne, the customs officer,[3]
measuring coal and mostly trying to keep warm—
to the stunted black schooner,
the dismal South-end dock,
the wharf-piles with their fungus of ice.
On State Street[4]
a steeple with a glowing dial-clock
measures the weary hours,
the merciless march of professional feet.

Even this shy distrustful ego
sometimes walked on top of the blazing roof,
and felt those flashes
that char the discharged cells of the brain.

Look at the faces—
Longfellow, Lowell, Holmes and Whittier![5]
Study the grizzled silver of their beards.
Hawthorne's picture,
however, has a blond mustache
and golden General Custer scalp.[6]
He looks like a Civil War officer.
He shines in the firelight. His hard
survivor's smile is touched with fire.

Leave him alone for a moment or two,
and you'll see him with his head
bent down, brooding, brooding,
eyes fixed on some chip,
some stone, some common plant,
the commonest thing,
as if it were the clue.
The disturbed eyes rise,
furtive, foiled, dissatisfied
from meditation on the true
and insignificant.

---

1. **Gallows Hill:** site in Salem, Massachusetts, where people who were believed to be witches were hanged.
2. **resilver . . . plate:** referring to early photographs, which were taken on a metal plate coated with silver.
3. **customs officer:** Hawthorne worked as a customs officer in Salem and Boston.
4. **State Street:** main street in Boston's business district.
5. **Longfellow . . . Whittier!:** Fireside Poets, who lived in New England.
6. **golden . . . scalp:** referring to the long blond hair of George Armstrong Custer (1839–1876), who served as a general in the Civil War and was later killed by the Sioux and Cheyenne in the Battle of Little Big Horn.

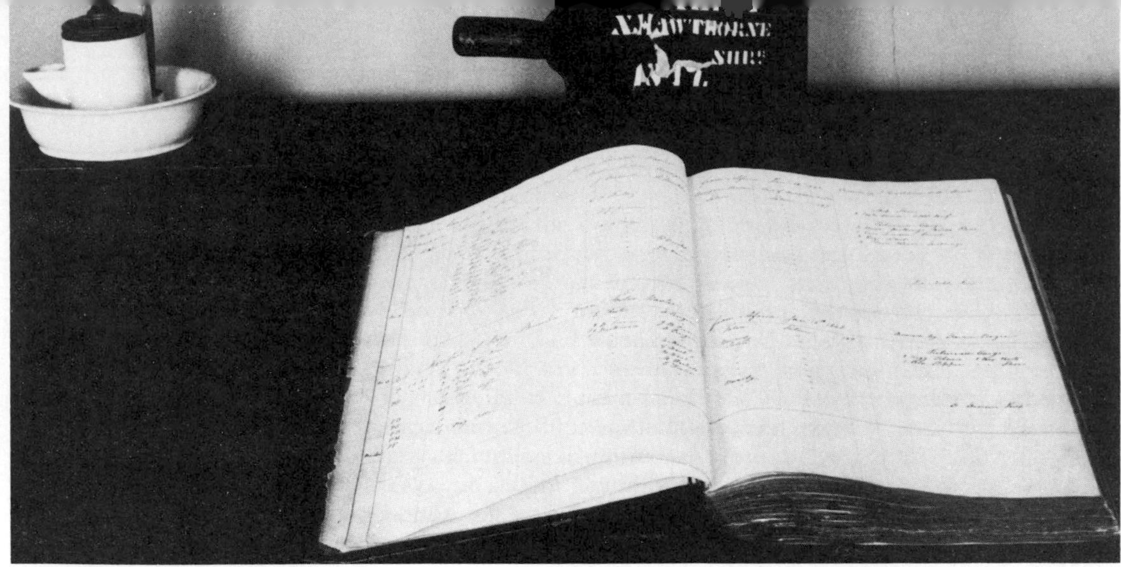

STUDY QUESTIONS

Recalling

1. According to lines 1–8, if "you" follow the lazy main street of Hawthorne's Salem, how will you walk? What can the speaker not do, according to line 9?
2. What description is given of Hawthorne's duties as a customs officer? How is Hawthorne described in line 19? What does the speaker say Hawthorne sometimes did and felt?
3. With what four other New England writers is Hawthorne contrasted in lines 23–31? What does Hawthorne's picture show in contrast to the other writers' grizzled beards?
4. According to lines 32–42, how will "you" see Hawthorne if you "leave him alone for a moment or two"? On what do his eyes seem to be fixed? What makes them "furtive, foiled, dissatisfied"?

Interpreting

5. What is the speaker trying to find as he walks the streets of Hawthorne's Salem? What does line 9 suggest?
6. What aspects of Hawthorne's job as a customs officer are captured in lines 10–11? What aspect of Hawthorne is captured in lines 20–22?
7. Why is it significant that Hawthorne does *not* have a grizzled beard, as the other New England writers do?
8. What qualities does the speaker seem to admire in Hawthorne?

Extending

9. What are some of the things you might learn about a writer and his work by visiting the places where he lived and learning about his jobs and background? Why do you think another writer—such as Robert Lowell—might be especially interested in paying such a visit?

COMPOSITION

Writing About a Work and Its Author

■ Write a brief essay telling what light Lowell's "Hawthorne" throws on Hawthorne's story "The Minister's Black Veil" (page 182). Discuss Lowell's claim that Hawthorne looked for meaning in "the commonest thing," and tell how that search for meaning relates to the story. Why might Hawthorne, after having written the story, appear to Lowell "foiled, dissatisfied"?

Writing About the Past

■ Write a short composition or a poem in which you take a close look at some event or person in America's past and tell what that event or person means to you. Describe your subject fully in its own time and place. Then indicate why it is still important and valuable to you.

STUDY QUESTIONS

1. to no purpose; resilver the smudged photographic plate
2. measures coal, tries to keep warm; a "shy distrustful ego"; "sometimes walked on top of the blazing roof,/and felt those flashes/that char the discharged cells of the brain"
3. Longfellow, Lowell, Holmes, Whittier; blond moustache, "golden General Custer scalp"
4. head bent, brooding; "some chip/some stone . . . the commonest thing"; meditation on the true and insignificant
5. sense of who Hawthorne was, how he lived and dealt with artistic conflicts; speaker cannot recapture past and derive understanding from it
6. comfortlessness, lack of creativity; creativity
7. face conveys youth, vitality, Custer-like tendency toward daring
8. perseverance among "merciless march of professional feet," creativity, smile, mind
9. sources of inspiration, aspects of private life; sense of kinship from reading or emulating person's work; visit strengthens bond, furthers understanding, contributes to own artistic growth

COMPOSITION: GUIDELINES FOR EVALUATION

WRITING ABOUT A WORK AND ITS AUTHOR

Objective

To write about a work and its author

Guidelines for Evaluation

- suggested length: three to six paragraphs
- should relate Lowell's claim to the black veil
- should explain story's search for meaning and why Hawthorne might have been dissatisfied after writing it

WRITING ABOUT THE PAST

Objective

To write about the past

Guidelines for Evaluation

- suggested length: two paragraphs or stanzas
- should describe the person or event within a historical context
- should explain the significance of the subject for the writer

AT A GLANCE

- The speaker focuses on the sound of a cracked record.
- He describes the power of the conscious mind.

LITERARY OPTIONS

- repetition
- free verse

THEMATIC OPTIONS

- the limitations of intelligence
- the crisis of modern life

REPETITION

The repetition of *and repeats* and *long enough* evoke both the mechanical sound of a broken record and the loss of meaning that occurs when the mind becomes fixated upon a single idea (ll. 3–4).

FREE VERSE

Wide variations in line length, long run-on lines, and abrupt changes in thought help to convey the dissonant, jarring quality of modern life (ll. 6–9).

MAIN IDEA

Fearing suggests that the world, like a broken record, has a fatal flaw, incomprehensible to the powers of reason, that places continuity, harmony, and assurance out of reach (ll. 9–12).

REFLECTING ON THE POEM

What does the title suggest about the meaning of the poem? (The allusion to the musical tradition of the blues suggests that the poem deals with the pain of the human condition.)

Kenneth Fearing *1902–1961*

Kenneth Fearing was both a poet and a novelist, but he made his living by writing articles for magazines. Like Auden, he wrote several verse satires of contemporary life, including *Dead Reckoning* (1938) and *Stranger at Coney Island* (1949).

Fearing liked to fill his poems with common American speech, slang, clichés, urban landscapes, and images drawn from objects Americans use in their everyday life. With such "unpoetic" materials he created compassionate portraits of people who often seem buried beneath trivial objects, unclear thoughts, and abused language.

■ As you read this poem, can you hear the cracks in the record?

Kenneth Fearing

Cracked Record Blues

If you watch it long enough you can see the clock move,
If you try hard enough you can hold a little water in the palm of
    your hand,
If you listen once or twice you know it's not the needle, or the tune,
    but a crack in the record when sometimes a phonograph falters
    and repeats, and repeats, and repeats, and repeats—

And if you think about it long enough, long enough, long enough,
    long enough then everything is simple and you can understand
    the times,
You can see for yourself that the Hudson[1] still flows, that the seasons
    change as ever, that love is always love,
Words still have a meaning, still clear and still the same;
You can count upon your fingers that two plus two still equals, still
    equals, still equals, still equals—
There is nothing in this world that should bother the mind.

Because the mind is a common sense affair filled with common sense
    answers to common sense facts,
It can add up, can add up, can add up, can add up earthquakes and
    subtract them from fires,
It can bisect an atom or analyze the planets—
All it has to do is to, do is to, do is to, do is to start at the beginning
    and continue to the end.

1. **Hudson:** Hudson River in New York.

STUDY QUESTIONS

Recalling

1. According to line 3, what will we know if we listen once or twice? According to line 4, what can we understand if we think about it long enough?
2. According to lines 9–11, why is there "nothing in this world" that should bother the mind? What are the three things the mind can do? According to the last line, what must the mind do to perform these three things?

Interpreting

3. Considering the parallel structure of lines 3 and 4, determine what the poet is equating with the cracked record.
4. To what aspect of modern life do lines 10 and 11 refer? What do the things in these lines have in common with a phonograph record? How is the last line of the poem related to a phonograph record?
5. Does the poet really believe that "everything is simple" and that the mind can understand everything if it starts at the beginning and continues to the end? What does the crack in the record suggest?
6. How does the poem's sound echo its sense?

Extending

7. What are some of the things in modern life that this poem makes you think about? What specific things are suggested by lines 10 and 11, for example?

STUDY QUESTIONS

1. it is not needle or tune, but crack in record; the times
2. it "is a common sense affair filled with common sense answers to common sense facts"; add up earthquakes and subtract them from fires, bisect an atom, analyze the planets; be allowed to start at the beginning and continue to the end
3. tendency of human mind to falter, remain confused
4. scientific knowledge, inquiry into great and small things; scientific advances, like record, have uncontrollable imperfections that flaw them
5. no; no easy progression from beginning to end; human mind itself is flawed
6. sounds get stuck and repeat themselves, imitating implied description of human mind
7. nuclear energy, atomic weapons; contrast between humankind's vast potential and "crack" preventing us from channeling this potential for useful purposes

AT A GLANCE

- The speaker catches a large fish.
- The fish, battered and homely, had not fought its capture.
- The speaker examines her catch in detail.

LITERARY OPTIONS

- description
- imagery

THEMATIC OPTIONS

- harmony with nature
- private experience

DESCRIPTION

The speaker's personal tone and camera-clear description have a cinematic quality: The reader sees events unfold as in a film (ll. 1–4).

VOCABULARY: WORD CHOICE

By modifying *weight* with *grunting*, the poet creates a dramatic sensory image for the hanging fish (l. 7).

IMAGERY

The attention that the poet gives to listing the seemingly unattractive physical details about the fish reflects the highly personal nature of the moment. The comparison of several features to wallpaper and roses reveals the transforming power of the imagination (ll. 10–17).

Elizabeth Bishop *1911–1980*

Elizabeth Bishop's verse is warm and personal, with an elegance that reflects the personality and reputation of the poet herself. Bishop was born in Massachusetts, grew up in Nova Scotia, Canada, and attended Vassar College. She took inspiration from the poems of Marianne Moore (page 452), particularly Moore's meticulous observation of nature. Bishop traveled a great deal during her life, and themes of home and exile are often to be found in her poems. For sixteen years she lived in Brazil, before returning to her native Massachusetts in the later part of her life. She received many honors, including the Pulitzer Prize and National Book Award.

■ You have probably heard "At that moment, I knew the truth." What is the moment and what is the truth for Elizabeth Bishop?

Elizabeth Bishop

The Fish

I caught a tremendous fish
and held him beside the boat
half out of water, with my hook
fast in a corner of his mouth.
He didn't fight.
He hadn't fought at all.
He hung a grunting weight,
battered and venerable
and homely. Here and there
his brown skin hung in strips
like ancient wallpaper,
and its pattern of darker brown
was like wallpaper:
shapes like full-blown roses
stained and lost through age.
He was speckled with barnacles,[1]
fine rosettes[2] of lime,
and infested
with tiny white sea-lice,

1. **barnacles** [bär′nə kəlz]: small saltwater shellfish that attach themselves to underwater objects and other animals.
2. **rosettes** [rō zets′]: rose-shaped patterns.

and underneath two or three
rags of green weed hung down.
While his gills were breathing in
the terrible oxygen
—the frightening gills,
fresh and crisp with blood,
that can cut so badly—
I thought of the coarse white flesh
packed in like feathers,
the big bones and the little bones,
the dramatic reds and blacks
of his shiny entrails,[3]
and the pink swim-bladder[4]
like a big peony.
I looked into his eyes
which were far larger than mine
but shallower, and yellowed,
the irises backed and packed
with tarnished tinfoil
seen through the lenses
of old scratched isinglass.[5]
They shifted a little, but not
to return my stare.
—It was more like the tipping
of an object toward the light.
I admired his sullen face,
the mechanism of his jaw,
and then I saw
that from his lower lip
—if you could call it a lip—
grim, wet, and weaponlike,
hung five old pieces of fish line,
or four and a wire leader[6]
with the swivel still attached,
with all their five big hooks
grown firmly in his mouth.
A green line, frayed at the end
where he broke it, two heavier lines,
and a fine black thread
still crimped from the strain and snap

3. **entrails:** inner organs.
4. **swim-bladder:** gas-filled sac in most bony fishes that enables them to maintain or change depth in water.
5. **isinglass** [ī'zin glas']: thin sheets of transparent mica, a crystallized mineral.
6. **leader:** short piece of line used to attach a hook to fish line.

when it broke and he got away.
Like medals with their ribbons
frayed and wavering,
a five-haired beard of wisdom
trailing from his aching jaw.
I stared and stared
and victory filled up
the little rented boat,
from the pool of bilge[7]
where oil had spread a rainbow
around the rusted engine
to the bailer[8] rusted orange,
the sun-cracked thwarts,[9]
the oarlocks on their strings,
the gunnels[10]—until everything
was rainbow, rainbow, rainbow!
And I let the fish go.

7. **bilge** [bilj]: dirty, stagnant water that collects in the bottom of a boat.
8. **bailer:** device for removing water from a boat.
9. **thwarts:** seats for rowers.
10. **gunnels:** upper edges of the sides of a boat.

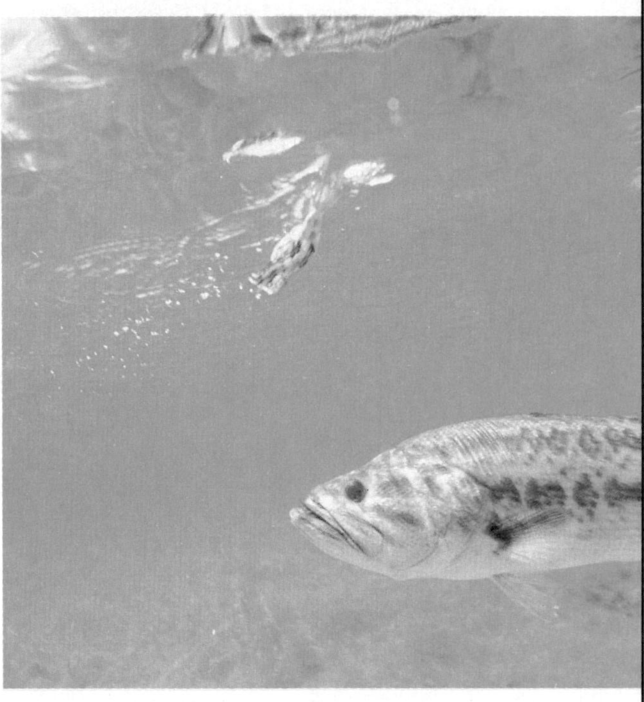

AT A GLANCE

- As the speaker continues to examine the fish, she notes five old fishhooks in its mouth.
- She senses an air of victory about this fish.
- In her rusty boat a rainbow spreads in the bilge and suddenly she decides to let the fish go.

ASSONANCE AND CONSONANCE

The introduction of assonance *(backed and packed)* and consonance *(tarnished tinfoil; scratched isinglass)* intensify the description of the fish's eyes (ll. 37–40).

IMAGERY

In transforming the fishhooks into a simile with human dimension *(Like medals with their ribbons)*, and attributing human feeling *(aching jaw)* to the fish, the speaker shows a growing empathy with the creature (ll. 61–64).

MAIN IDEA

Through the fish's struggles for survival and subsequent victories, the speaker sees mirrored her own personal victories (ll. 65–67).

REFLECTING ON THE POEM

In what way does the image of the rainbow clarify the speaker's sense of revelation? (It conveys a sense of excitement and wonder in her awareness of universal harmony.)

STUDY QUESTIONS

1. a tremendous fish; it does not fight at all
2. battered, venerable, homely; like ancient wallpaper; terrible oxygen
3. five fish hooks with broken lines; medals; beard of wisdom
4. victory; rainbow; lets fish go
5. won five struggles to stay alive; did not struggle this time
6. precise, with undercurrent of emotion; deadly to fish
7. rational vs. emotional responses to nature; acts from emotion, lets fish go; has taken on a personality of its own by winning five battles to survive
8. Students might say environmental concerns.

VOCABULARY

1. c—wounded : cut
2. a—impressive : holy
3. b—dandruff : scalp
4. d—saturated : soaked
5. b—fish : mammal

STUDY QUESTIONS

Recalling

1. What does the speaker catch? What does line 6 report about the difficulty of catching it?
2. What three adjectives describe the fish in lines 8–9? What simile describes its skin? What are its gills breathing, according to line 23?
3. After studying the fish's eyes and face, what does the speaker see hanging from its lower "lip"? With what does she compare these things in line 61? In line 63?
4. What does the speaker say fills the little rented boat in line 66? What does everything become, according to line 75? What does the speaker then do?

Interpreting

5. What do the five hooks with their broken lines indicate about the fish? How do they contrast with the information in lines 5–6?
6. Is the description of the fish basically emotional, or is it precise and scientific? Why does the poet call the oxygen "terrible"?
7. What conflict within the speaker might your answers to question 6 reflect? What is the outcome of that conflict? Why does the speaker let the fish go?

Extending

8. What other "conflicts" or dilemmas of modern life does this poem make you think about?

VOCABULARY

Analogies

Analogies are comparisons that point out relationships between items. Analogy items on vocabulary tests are usually written as two pairs of words. The words in the first pair are related to each other in the same way as those in the second pair: for example,

HOT : COLD : : BRIGHT : DARK.

The first word in capitals in each of the following analogies is from "The Fish." Complete the analogies by choosing the pair of words that is related in the same way as the pair in capital letters.

1. BATTERED : BRUISED : :
   (a) beaten : rubbed (c) wounded : cut
   (b) scorched : flame (d) wrecked : injured
2. VENERABLE : SAINTLY : :
   (a) impressive : holy (c) ancient : modern
   (b) novel : new (d) animal : human
3. BARNACLES : OYSTERS : :
   (a) rocks : crabs (c) unwanted : wanted
   (b) dandruff : scalp (d) rotten : fresh
4. INFESTED : FILLED : :
   (a) ruinous : lucrative (c) permeable : porous
   (b) poisoned : cured (d) saturated : soaked
5. GILLS : LUNGS : :
   (a) water : land (c) oxygen : air
   (b) fish : mammal (d) before : after

Randall Jarrell *1914–1965*

Tennessee-born Randall Jarrell was one of the most versatile writers of his generation: poet, teacher, translator, novelist, essayist, and highly respected literary critic.

Jarrell's interest in literature was stimulated by the poet-critic John Crowe Ransom (page 448), who was teaching at Tennessee's Vanderbilt University, where Jarrell went to college. Jarrell too became a teacher, a profession he loved: He once said that even if he were rich enough not to have to work, he would want to go on teaching. His books of poetry include *Losses* (1948) and *The Woman at the Washington Zoo* (1960).

The only interruption to Jarrell's life as teacher-critic-poet came during World War II, when he served in the Army Air Force. His war experiences provided him with some of his best poems, such as the memorable "Death of the Ball Turret Gunner," for which Jarrell himself provided this note:

> A ball turret was a plexiglass sphere set into the belly of a B-17 or B-24, and inhabited by two .50 caliber machine-guns and one man, a short small man. When this gunner tracked with his machine-guns a fighter attacking his bomber from below, he revolved with the turret; hunched upside-down in his little sphere, he looked like the fetus in the womb. The fighters which attacked him were armed with cannon firing explosive shells. The hose was a steam hose.

- How does this poem find poetic imagery in death and war?

Randall Jarrell

The Death of the Ball Turret Gunner

From my mother's sleep I fell into the State,
And I hunched in its belly till my wet fur froze.
Six miles from earth, loosed from its dream of life,
I woke to black flak[1] and the nightmare fighters.
When I died they washed me out of the turret with a hose.

1. **flak:** anti-aircraft fire.

LITERARY OPTIONS

- tone
- imagery

THEMATIC OPTIONS

- a soldier's vulnerability in war
- governmental dehumanization

TONE

The voice of the dead gunner gives a haunting, elegiac tone to the account of his brief life and death (l. 1).

IMAGERY

Stark physical images *(belly; wet fur)* contrast sharply with the elegiac tone and evoke the poignancy of a life cut short (l. 2).

REFLECTING ON THE POEM

Do you think that this is an effective antiwar poem? Why or why not? (Some students may point to its revelation of the human cost of war as evidence of its effectiveness; others may feel that the case discussed is too specific to have a broad interpretation.)

AT A GLANCE

- The speaker affirms the productivity of her grandmothers.
- The past remains alive in her grandmothers' memories.
- The speaker wonders why she is not like them.

LITERARY OPTIONS

- lyric poem
- repetition

THEMATIC OPTIONS

- the nourishment of the past
- isolation in the modern world

LYRIC POEM

The simple language, sparse use of modifiers, and reliance on strong and direct verbs impart a stateliness and grace to the meditative lines (ll. 1–5).

REPETITION

The full context of meaning for the word *strong* (l. 6) develops through the repetition of *My grandmothers* and the *They* clauses.

REFLECTING ON THE POEM

What do you think the speaker gains from the past? (a sense of her place in history; pride; poetic stimulation) What is she unable to recover? (the harmony with the world that her grandmothers felt)

Photograph © 1982 by Jill Krementz

Margaret Walker *born 1915*

Margaret Walker's work is aimed at bringing to the attention of readers the strengths and trials of black Americans. Born in Birmingham, Alabama, where her father was a Methodist preacher, Walker gained success with her first book, *For My People,* winning the Yale Younger Poets prize in 1942. She studied at Northwestern University and the University of Iowa and then embarked upon a life of writing and teaching. For many years she taught at Jackson State College in Mississippi.

■ How does the past affect the present? How does Walker show us that influence?

Margaret Walker

Lineage

My grandmothers were strong.
They followed plows and bent to toil.
They moved through fields sowing seed.
They touched earth and grain grew.
They were full of sturdiness and singing.
My grandmothers were strong.

My grandmothers are full of memories
Smelling of soap and onions and wet clay
With veins rolling roughly over quick hands
They have many clean words to say.
My grandmothers were strong.
Why am I not as they?

Gwendolyn Brooks *born 1917*

The first black writer to win a Pulitzer Prize (for *Annie Allen* in 1950), Gwendolyn Brooks is recognized as one of America's most steadily productive and distinguished poets. Brooks grew up in Chicago, where she has spent most of her life and where she often sets her poems. She began writing poetry that was quite formal and traditional, but in her later work she often adopted free verse and more open forms. Her later work also became more outspoken as she turned to problems of social and racial justice. Her volumes include *A Street in Bronzeville* (1945) and *The Bean Eaters* (1960).

■ In what ways do we try to preserve the past? How does the speaker in this poem compare himself to people of the past?

Gwendolyn Brooks

Strong Men, Riding Horses

Lester after the Western

Strong Men, riding horses. In the West
On a range five hundred miles. A Thousand. Reaching
From dawn to sunset. Rested blue to orange.
From hope to crying. Except that Strong Men are
Desert-eyed. Except that Strong Men are
Pasted to stars already. Have their cars
Beneath them. Rentless, too. Too broad of chest
To shrink when the Rough Man hails. Too flailing
To redirect the Challenger, when the challenge
Nicks; slams; buttonholes. Too saddled.

I am not like that. I pay rent, am addled
By illegible landlords, run, if robbers call.

What mannerisms I present, employ,
Are camouflage, and what my mouths remark
To word-wall off that broadness of the dark
Is pitiful.
I am not brave at all.

AT A GLANCE

- The speaker, Lester, thinks about the strength, rootlessness, and bravery of cowboys.
- He compares himself to movie cowboys and finds himself inferior to them.

LITERARY OPTIONS

- mood
- main idea

THEMATIC OPTIONS

- the end of the cowboy era
- the crisis of urban life

MOOD

Lester's cinematic vision of the cowboys contains larger-than-life types who emanate power and generate high drama (ll. 1–3).

IRONY

The ironic juxtaposition of *addled* with *saddled*, along with the shrunken two-line stanza, suggests a rueful sense of loss of a supposedly golden past (ll. 10–12).

MAIN IDEA

Lester's frank, outspoken confession dramatically illustrates the modern urban person's sense of insignificance and inadequacy (l. 17).

REFLECTING ON THE POEM

What does Brooks's use of the speaker Lester add to the power of her poem? (As a downtrodden urban male, Lester contrasts more sharply with the cowboys than the poet—a female—would.)

STUDY QUESTIONS *(Jarrell)*

Recalling

1. Into what did the ball turret gunner fall? From what was he loosed? To what did he wake?
2. What happened when he died?

Interpreting

3. Why is it significant that the gunner falls where he falls in line 1?
4. What does the poem suggest about war?

Extending

5. Does the ball turret gunner have anything in common with the unknown citizen in Auden's poem on page 547? Why or why not?

STUDY QUESTIONS *(Walker)*

Recalling

1. What were the speaker's "grandmothers," according to line 1? What happened when they touched earth?
2. What are the speaker's grandmothers now, according to line 7?
3. What does the speaker ask in the final line?

Interpreting

4. State in your own words the qualities that the speaker seems to admire in her grandmothers. What does she mean by "grandmothers"?
5. What does the last line imply about the speaker's wishes?
6. Describe the diction, or word choice, in the poem. How is it related to the poem's content?

Extending

7. How would you answer the speaker's final question? Do you agree that modern Americans are not as strong as their ancestors? What are some of the things we have today that our "grandmothers" might have desired?

STUDY QUESTIONS *(Brooks)*

Recalling

1. What sort of men are riding horses in the West, according to line 1? For what are these men "too broad of chest"?
2. According to lines 11–12, how is the speaker unlike the strong men of the West? What are his "mannerisms," according to line 14? What adjective describes the remarks he makes to "word-wall off that broadness of the dark"?
3. What does the speaker conclude about himself in the final line?

Interpreting

4. What characters from American life is this poem about? What do "broad of chest," "desert-eyed," and "rentless" suggest about these characters?
5. What do "camouflage" and "word-wall" suggest about the speaker's methods of "fighting"? How would these methods differ from the fighting methods of a traditional western hero?
6. What two things does the speaker find wrong with the strong men? (Consider the fact that they are "desert-eyed" and "rentless" and that they are "*too* broad of chest.") What one quality does he particularly envy? (Consider the last two lines of the poem.)

Extending

7. What aspects of modern civilization does this poem make you think about? What are the rewards of being "civilized"? What might we envy about the less "civilized" heroes of the American West?

VOCABULARY *(Brooks)*

Compound Words

When Gwendolyn Brooks creates the compound word *word-wall,* she is doing what English speakers have been doing for centuries: putting old words together to describe something new. For example, *landlord,* another compound Brooks uses, was originally used by medieval farmers to describe the *lord,* or nobleman, who owned the *land* they farmed.

Using a dictionary, explain the origins of each of the following compound words, as well as the current meaning or meanings.

1. aboveboard
2. aftermath
3. barnstorm
4. bigwig
5. turtleneck
6. catercorner
7. crestfallen
8. foolscap
9. pinafore
10. turnpike

STUDY QUESTIONS

Jarrell

1. the state; earth's dream of life; black flak, nightmare fighters
2. washed out of turret with hose
3. impersonal, indifferent government controls destiny
4. impersonal, dehumanizing, gruesome
5. both victims of a state indifferent to their humanity

Walker

1. strong; grain grew
2. "full of memories," old
3. "Why am I not as they?"
4. strength, hard work, sturdiness, joy; her forbears
5. wishes she were stronger, more like her ancestors
6. words simple, direct, evoking rural simplicity, oneness with land; portrait of speaker's grandmothers: simple, rural
7. "Grandmothers" might have desired modern conveniences.

Brooks

1. strong; to shrink when Rough Man hails
2. pays rent, addled by landlords, runs from robbers; camouflage; pitiful
3. "I am not brave at all."
4. cowboys; proud, rugged, individualistic, rootless
5. hides feelings, swaggers and bluffs way out of fights; fists rather than words
6. loners, drifters; bravery
7. Students might discuss problems of urban dwellers.

VOCABULARY

1. ABOVEBOARD: originally "above the table"; now "without dishonesty or concealment"
2. AFTERMATH: originally *after* + *math,* meaning "a second crop"; now "any result"
3. BARNSTORM: originally "to go about countryside performing plays"; now "to tour giving airplane rides, showing stunt flying"
4. BIGWIG: in eighteenth century a wig-wearing magistrate; now "an important person"
5. TURTLENECK: suggested by folded appearance of turtle's neck; "garment with high, snugly fitting turndown collar"
6. CATERCORNER: originally "having corners," from French *quatre* (four); now "diagonally"
7. CRESTFALLEN: originally "rooster that has lost a fight"; now "humbled"
8. FOOLSCAP: originally "sheet of paper with watermark of fool's head"; now "a size of paper measuring 13 inches by 16 inches"
9. PINAFORE: from *pin* + *afore,* "pinned in front"; now "woman's sleeveless overgarment"
10. TURNPIKE: originally Middle English *turnpyke,* "turnstile-like barrier across a toll road"; now "a toll road"

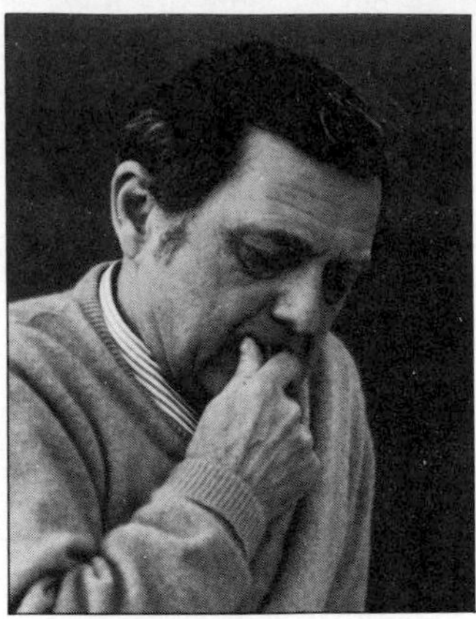

Reed Whittemore *born 1919*

Reed Whittemore, though best known for his lyric poems, has also written stories and essays, taught English in college, and co-edited one of America's "little magazines," *Furioso,* from 1939 to 1953. His books include *Heroes and Heroines* (1946), *An American Takes a Walk* (1956), and *The Boy from Iowa* (1962).

"The Fall of the House of Usher" is a good example of the importance of tone in a work of literature. Whittemore retells the story of Edgar Allan Poe's famous gothic tale (page 135).

■ An author's tone shapes our reaction to literature. What reaction is Whittemore seeking in this poem?

Reed Whittemore

The Fall of the House of Usher

It was a big boxy wreck of a house
Owned by a classmate of mine named Rod Usher,
Who lived in the thing with his twin sister.
He was a louse and she was a souse.

While I was visiting them one wet summer, she died.
We buried her,
Or rather we stuck her in a back room for a bit, meaning to
bury her
When the graveyard dried.

But the weather got wetter.
One night we were both waked by a twister,
Plus a screeching and howling outside that turned out to be sister
Up and dying again, making it hard for Rod to forget her.

He didn't. He and she died in a heap, and I left quick,
Which was lucky since the house fell in right after,

Like a ton of brick.

AT A GLANCE

- The speaker visits the house of Rod Usher and his twin sister.
- The sister dies; the other two wait for the graveyard to dry before they bury her.
- The sister returns to life and claims Rod; the speaker flees just before the Ushers' house falls in.

LITERARY OPTIONS

- parody
- diction

THEMATIC OPTIONS

- the importance of tone
- the flattery of imitation

VOCABULARY: DICTION

The speaker's unadorned, colloquial language establishes a flippant tone at odds with the supernatural events (ll. 1–4).

PARODY

The jarring contrast between Poe's elaborate, highly detailed account and this abrupt, matter-of-fact report sharpens the sense of parody and satirizes Poe's narrative tone and perspective (ll. 5–8).

RHYME

The use of internal rhyme *(weather/wetter; we were/twister)* humorously evokes the sound of the storm and recalls Poe's use of onomatopoeia for suspense.

REFLECTING ON THE POEM

In what way does the poem flatter Edgar Allan Poe? (by imitating his plot, even though by parody)

STUDY QUESTIONS

1. "big boxy wreck"; Rod Usher and his twin sister
2. dies; "in a back room for a bit"
3. a twister and the sister; die "in a heap"; leaves "quick"
4. "like a ton of brick"
5. ▪ Whittemore tersely reports the plot, using unadorned, colloquial language; Poe uses florid words, rich imagery, and formal language.
   ▪ *Whittemore:* simpler style, humor; *Poe:* horror
6. flippant; create humorous, lighthearted effect rather than terror
7. cliché; usually describes something overly large and heavy; it is ponderous and silly
8. yes; the poem is a backhanded compliment, criticizing excess of style but acknowledging Poe's popularity and ability to create terrifying effects through language

LITERARY FOCUS

Answers will vary. Lines 4, 7, 10–11, and 15 are likely favorites; *boxy wreck of a house, stuck her in a back room,* and similar informal expressions

STUDY QUESTIONS

Recalling

1. How is the House of Usher described in line 1? Who is living in "the thing," according to lines 2–3?
2. What happens to the sister "one wet summer"? Where do "Rod" and the narrator "stick" the sister?
3. What wakes "Rod" and the narrator one night? What happens to "Rod" and his sister in line 13? What does the narrator do?
4. According to line 15, how does the House of Usher "fall in"?

Interpreting

5. How is the diction, or word choice, of this poem different from that in Poe's "Fall of the House of Usher"? How is the poet's overall style different from that of Poe?
6. What is the tone, or writer's attitude, in this poem? How do style, diction, and rhyme contribute to that tone?
7. What sort of phrase is the last line of the poem? When is this phrase usually used? What comment about Poe's story does this phrase seem to make?

Extending

8. Could any masterpiece—a play by Shakespeare, for example—be made to sound funny if presented in a shorthand version of the plot alone? In what way does this poem pay a compliment to Poe?

LITERARY FOCUS

Parody

Parody is humorous imitation. A writer can parody another writer's plot, characters, setting, theme, or style, usually by means of exaggeration.

Parody is almost as old as literature itself. It seems that as soon as people began writing, there was someone ready to make fun of what they had written. One of the oldest parodies is *The Clouds,* a comedy by the Greek playwright Aristophanes. It pokes fun at the thinking of the great philosopher Socrates. In another play, *The Frogs,* Aristophanes mocks the styles of two of the greatest writers of all time, the Greek tragedians Sophocles and Euripides.

We should not assume, however, that a parodist hates or even dislikes the author being parodied. In a sense, parody is a form of tribute. It is impossible or pointless to parody an unknown writer or a mediocre writer. Every good writer has mannerisms, and those mannerisms are what make the writer's style unique. Cooper, Emerson, Thoreau, Whitman, Twain, Eliot, Hemingway, Fitzgerald—all have been the subject of parodies.

"The Fall of the House of Usher" by Reed Whittemore does not parody Poe's style: Poe's narrator, as you may recall, speaks in a most elaborate English, and if there is any joke on style in this poem, it is a joke on the inarticulateness of much modern American speech. Whittemore's parody is actually aimed at Poe's plot, and indeed Poe skirts the absurd in his famous story. It is an "unbelievable" story, made great by Poe's style, which wraps the tale in a language that makes it not only believable but unforgettable.

Whittemore's parody, therefore, allows us to laugh at the absurd aspects of "The Fall of the House of Usher" at the same time that our admiration for Poe is enhanced. After all, if Poe's story were not a *great* story, Whittemore would never have written his parody.

Thinking About Parody

■ Which lines in Whittemore's poem do you think are the funniest? Which expressions contrast most vividly with Poe's original words?

Photograph © 1982 by Jill Krementz

Richard Wilbur *born 1921*

Richard Wilbur has established himself as a poet working steadily within the traditional forms and approaches of English poetry. His poems are elegant without calling attention to themselves. They are thoughtful, fresh, and carefully crafted.

Wilbur was born in New York City but has lived most of his adult life in New England. He has taught at several New England colleges. His first volume, *The Beautiful Changes* (1947), won him the solid recognition that has increased with *Things of This World* (1956), *Advice to a Prophet* (1961), *Walking to Sleep* (1969), and *The Mind-Reader* (1976). He has also produced superb verse translations of the French dramatist Molière and written essays that have been collected as *Responses* (1976).

Wilbur is a master of stanza forms, as he shows in "Year's End." He adopts an unusual but effective rhyme scheme and then maintains it gracefully for the length of the poem. Like Robert Frost, an early master of Wilbur's, he likes to work against the challenge of a form rather than in free verse. (Frost has said that, to him, writing free verse was like playing tennis without a net.) "Year's End" is typical of Wilbur's meditative lyrics: not flashy, not a confession of the author's personal problems, but simply deriving pleasure from its moving images and its imaginative use of language. The shape of the poem is a common one in Romantic and post-Romantic poetry: We see the speaker walking in a landscape, and we overhear the thoughts that the landscape produces within him.

■ Pictures and words often cause us to think and feel. What thoughts and feelings does this landscape bring forth in Wilbur?

AT A GLANCE

- While contemplating the landscape on a snowy New Year's Eve, the speaker reflects upon leaves frozen in the lake, fern fossils in rocks, and mammoths preserved in ice.
- He remembers how the people of Pompeii were frozen in the middle of action.
- Sudden ends of time give us pause; we do not know when our ends will come.

LITERARY OPTIONS

- tone
- rhyme

THEMATIC OPTIONS

- death in the midst of life
- the process of time

TONE

The speaker creates a nostalgic, meditative tone by focusing on what eyes see now and have seen in the past (ll. 7–8).

PERSONIFICATION

The personification of ferns ("laid their fragile cheeks") heightens a sense of appreciation of life, death, and the sudden end of time (ll. 13–14).

RHYME

The regular rhyme scheme and consistent iambic pentameter complement the continuity reflected in frozen or fossilized once-living things (ll. 13–18).

MAIN IDEA

In referring to the fossilized remains at Pompeii, Wilbur provides a powerful picture that also is a reminder of how fleeting life can be (ll. 19–24).

REFLECTING ON THE POEM

How would you describe Wilbur's attitude toward nature? (He views it as providing valuable lessons rather than comfort.)

Richard Wilbur

Year's End

Now winter downs[1] the dying of the year,
And night is all a settlement of snow;
From the soft street the rooms of houses show
A gathered light, a shapen[2] atmosphere,
Like frozen-over lakes whose ice is thin
And still allows some stirring down within.

I've known the wind by water banks to shake
The late leaves down, which frozen where they fell
And held in ice as dancers in a spell
Fluttered all winter long into a lake;
Graved[3] on the dark in gestures of descent,
They seemed their own most perfect monument.

There was perfection in the death of ferns
Which laid their fragile cheeks against the stone
A million years. Great mammoths overthrown
Composedly have made their long sojourns,
Like palaces of patience, in the gray
And changeless lands of ice. And at Pompeii[4]

The little dog lay curled and did not rise
But slept the deeper as the ashes rose
And found the people incomplete, and froze
The random hands, the loose unready eyes
Of men expecting yet another sun
To do the shapely thing they had not done.

These sudden ends of time must give us pause.
We fray[5] into the future, rarely wrought[6]
Save in the tapestries of afterthought.
More time, more time. Barrages of applause
Come muffled from a buried radio.
The New-year bells are wrangling with the snow.

1. **downs:** covers in white, as with feathers ("down").
2. **shapen:** shaped.
3. **graved:** engraved.
4. **Pompeii** [pom pā′]: city of ancient Rome, partly preserved in lava from a volcanic eruption that destroyed it in A.D. 79
5. **fray:** battle; here, also unravel.
6. **wrought:** shaped.

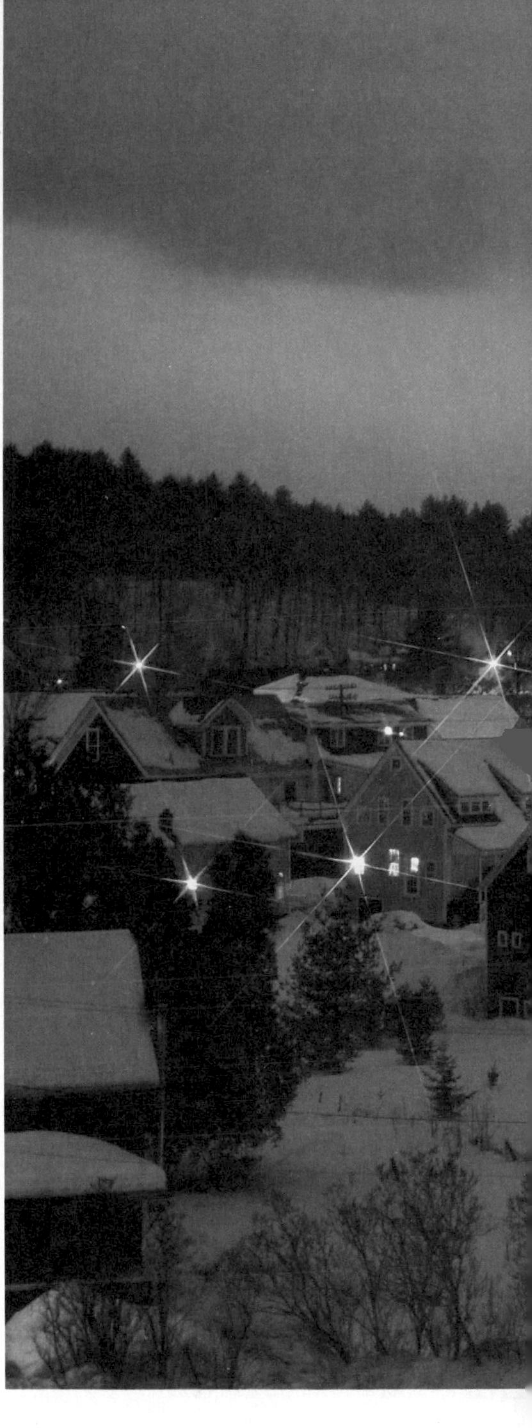

STUDY QUESTIONS

Recalling

1. According to the title, when does this poem take place? What does winter "down" in the first stanza?
2. In the second stanza what happens to the leaves where they fall? With what are the leaves held in ice compared?
3. What perfection does the poet note in lines 13–15? With what does he compare great mammoths in the gray and changeless lands of ice?
4. What do the ashes find in the fourth stanza? What did the people frozen by the ashes in Pompeii expect, according to lines 23–24?
5. What must give us pause, according to line 25? What is "wrangling with the snow" in the last line?

Interpreting

6. What do the frozen leaves, the fern fossils, the mammoths, and the dog and people of Pompeii have in common? What do the "perfect monument" of the frozen leaves, the "perfection" of the fern fossils, and the description of the mammoths suggest about the poet's view of these things?
7. According to the poet, did the people of Pompeii achieve perfection before they died? Did they expect to? When do lines 26–27 suggest that human beings become perfectly "shaped"?
8. What human attitude toward life do the bells of the new year represent, and why are the bells "wrangling" with the snow? Does the poet suggest that the bells will win the "wrangle"? Explain.
9. What aspect of our own lives does the poet suggest we think about when we pause to consider "these sudden ends of time"?

Extending

10. What are some of the thoughts you have had on New Year's Eve? Do you find the last day of the year happy, sad, or both? Why do you suppose so many people throughout the world celebrate in some way on their respective new years?

STUDY QUESTIONS

1. "year's end" (New Year's Eve); "the dying of the year"
2. frozen in the lake; "dancers in a spell"
3. death of ferns; "palaces of patience"
4. "the people incomplete"; "yet another sun/To do the shapely thing they had not done"
5. "These sudden ends of time"; "the New-year bells"
6. preserved as they were at moment of death; these "perfect" things had fulfilled their purpose
7. no; yes; "rarely," "save in the tapestries of afterthought"
8.
- The bells represent the human effort to control time. By wrangling with the snow, a symbol for death, they affirm the human determination to survive.
- Yes; unless the entire race is destroyed, "barrages of applause" will guarantee our future.

9. We cannot be certain of the future; therefore, we should do "the shapely thing" now.
10.
- Students' answers will vary according to experience.
- Some new year celebrations have religious significance; others contain cultural rituals. All indicate that human beings are aware of the future.

© Rollie McKenna

Sylvia Plath *1932–1963*

Sylvia Plath was born in Boston and published her first poems and fiction when she was only seventeen. Her interest in writing continued while she was a student at Smith College. Plath's poetry and her autobiographical novel, *The Bell Jar,* show, however, that she lived an intense and often troubled inner life.

She graduated from Smith in 1955 with highest honors and won a scholarship to Cambridge University in England. There she met and married Ted Hughes, who was to become one of the leading British poets of his generation. Plath and Hughes lived in America for a while but then returned to England, where she wrote most of the poems for which she is best known.

Plath was influenced by her friend Robert Lowell (page 553), whose *Life Studies* (1959) had begun a fashion for "confessional" poetry. Plath adopted the confessional mode, writing, she said, at "top speed, as one might write an urgent letter." These late poems, published by her husband after her death, appeared in the volume *Ariel* (1965). In recent years, interest in Plath's life has occasioned the publication of most of the poems she left in manuscript, as well as her letters and diaries.

Most of Plath's poems are deeply personal, but they do not all record her sufferings. "Blackberrying," though with a violent undercurrent, is in the tradition of Romantic nature poetry that began in America with William Cullen Bryant.

■ In what ways can an experience with nature reflect our innermost thoughts and fears? How does Plath reveal her thoughts and fears in "Blackberrying?"

Sylvia Plath

Blackberrying

Nobody in the lane, and nothing, nothing but blackberries,
Blackberries on either side, though on the right mainly,
A blackberry alley, going down in hooks, and a sea
Somewhere at the end of it, heaving. Blackberries
Big as the ball of my thumb, and dumb as eyes
Ebon[1] in the hedges, fat
With blue-red juices. These they squander on my fingers.
I had not asked for such a blood sisterhood; they must love me.
They accommodate themselves to my milkbottle, flattening their
sides.

Overhead go the choughs[2] in black, cacophonous[3] flocks—
Bits of burnt paper wheeling in a blown sky.
Theirs is the only voice, protesting, protesting.
I do not think the sea will appear at all.
The high, green meadows are glowing, as if lit from within.
I come to one bush of berries so ripe it is a bush of flies,
Hanging their blue-green bellies and their wing panes in a Chinese
screen.[4]
The honey-feast of the berries has stunned them; they believe in
heaven.
One more hook, and the berries and bushes end.

The only thing to come now is the sea.
From between two hills a sudden wind funnels at me,
Slapping its phantom laundry in my face.
These hills are too green and sweet to have tasted salt.
I follow the sheep path between them. A last hook brings me
To the hills' northern face, and the face is orange rock
That looks out on nothing, nothing but a great space
Of white and pewter[5] lights, and a din like silversmiths
Beating and beating at an intractable metal.

---

1. **Ebon** [eb′ən]: black.
2. **choughs** [chufs]: birds with glossy black feathers and red legs and beak.
3. **cacophonous** [kə kof′ə nəs]: harsh sounding.
4. **Chinese screen:** folding screen of wood and silk, covered with scenes painted in brilliant colors.
5. **pewter** [pū′tər]: dull, silvery-gray.

AT A GLANCE

- The speaker is in a lane filled with ripe blackberries, which she picks.
- As birds fly overhead she thinks the sea may not appear at the end of the lane.
- She walks on and, beyond the hills, sees a great space of light, which is the sea.

LITERARY OPTIONS

- imagery
- assonance/consonance

THEMATIC OPTIONS

- the power of nature
- the value of private experience

IMAGERY

The three-dimensional images appeal to sight *(a blackberry alley, heaving sea)* and touch *(squander on my fingers)* (ll. 3–7).

ASSONANCE/CONSONANCE

The use of assonance (the sounds of *o*) and consonance (*c*, *ck*, and *b*) to convey how the birds look and sound captures the richness and immediacy of seeing the birds (ll. 10–11).

PERSONIFICATION

The highly personal image of the laundry slapping the speaker's face reflects belief in nature's awesome power to confront the individual with the underlying harmony and wrenchingly dissonant aspects of human experience (ll. 20–21).

REFLECTING ON THE POEM

What makes Plath's view of nature particularly modern? (She sees joy and harmony in the natural world but feels like a wondering spectator, rather than one in harmony with nature.)

© Rollie McKenna

Anne Sexton *1928–1972*

Like Sylvia Plath, Anne Sexton was a student of Robert Lowell's. She studied poetry with Lowell at Boston University, and most of her poems are written in the "confessional" mode, recording some of life's most painful experiences—such as the loss of loved ones and the breakdown of relationships—with a raw directness. Sexton once said that poetry should be a "shock to the senses. It should almost hurt." Certainly the material of her poetry is the life of a woman who felt a great deal of hurt in her life.

Sexton was born in Newton, Massachusetts. For a while, she taught high school, and later she taught at Boston University. Her life was troubled with recurring mental illness, a struggle that forms the basis for some of her finest poems. Her books include *To Bedlam and Part Way Back* (1960), *All My Pretty Ones* (1962), *Live or Die* (for which she won the Pulitzer Prize in 1967), *Love Poems* (1969), and *The Book of Folly* (1972).

"What's That" is a beautifully mysterious poem, filled with delicate expression and hidden anxiety. If we are never sure exactly what the "it" is that is the subject of the poem, we are sure that it is a reality different from that represented by the cars going by on the street.

■ In what ways can memories be mysterious? In sharing Sexton's memories with her, can we determine what the mysterious "it" might be?

Model for Active Reading

In this selection, and in one selection in each unit, you will find notes in the right-hand margin that highlight parts of the selection. These notes point out important ideas of the period—in this case, postwar ideas—and draw your attention to literary elements and techniques covered in the Literary Focuses. Page numbers in the notes will refer you to more extensive discussions of these important ideas and elements.

Anne Sexton

What's That

Before it came inside
I had watched it from my kitchen window,
watched it swell like a new balloon,
watched it slump and then divide,
like something I know I know—
a broken pear or two halves of the moon,
or round white plates floating nowhere
or fat hands waving in the summer air
until they fold together like a fist or a knee.
After that it came to my door. Now it lives here.
And of course: it is a soft sound, soft as a seal's ear,
that was caught between a shape and a shape and then
returned to me.

You know how parents call
from sweet beaches anywhere, *come in come in,*
and how you sank under water to put out
the sound, or how one of them touched in the hall
at night: the rustle and the skin
you couldn't know, but heard, the stout
slap of tides and the dog snoring. It's here
now, caught back from time in my adult year—
the image we did forget: the cranking shells on our feet
or the swing of the spoon in soup. It is as real
as splinters stuck in your ear. The noise we steal
is half a bell. And outside cars whisk by on the
suburban street

and are there and are true.
What else is this, this intricate shape of air?
calling me, calling you.

Free verse (p. 426): The poem does not employ a regular rhythm, or meter.

Rhyme scheme (p. 170): Despite the irregular rhythm, a strict pattern of rhymes in the first stanza is repeated in the second.

Postwar idea: Many midcentury poets deal with intimate personal experiences (p. 541).

Diction and tone (p. 211 and p. 474): Twentieth-century American poets often use contractions and colloquial English, achieving an informal tone.

Postwar idea: Many midcentury writers have more questions than they have answers (p. 541).

AT A GLANCE

- The speaker saw *it* (unidentified) before it came inside. Now *it* lives here.
- She recounts childhood moments at the beach with her parents.
- The outside world has material reality; *it* has an intricate reality of another sort.

LITERARY OPTIONS

- free verse
- tone

THEMATIC OPTIONS

- appearance and reality
- the unconscious

REFLECTING ON THE POEM

In what way is this poem like a dream? (in its changeability, its combination of vivid images and mystery, in its intensity)

STUDY QUESTIONS (PLATH)

1. only blackberries; sea; juices; blackberries must love her
2. sea; berries and bushes end
3. sudden wind; too green to be near sea; hill's face; nothing but great space and a din
4. personal, exhilarating encounter with nature
5. that sea will never appear; yes; yes
6. *nothing, nothing but;* stresses emptiness of sea
7. nature exhilarating, but temporary

LITERARY FOCUS (PLATH)

- sound: lines 10, 12, 17–26; taste: lines 17, 22; touch: lines 7, 9, 20–21
- Sensory images allow reader to share poet's experiences and emotional reactions.

STUDY QUESTIONS (SEXTON)

1. kitchen window; "like a new balloon"; "something I know I know": broken pear, halves of moon, round white plates
2. came to door; in house
3. parents calling, sinking underwater, snoring dog; forgotten image, from time; splinters in ear
4. there and true; "What else is this, this intricate shape of air? / calling me, calling you"
5. visual, aural images; never named, merely compared
6. mundane reality; shifting, intangible reality of memory
7. uncertain herself
8. everyone haunted by memories
9. Answers will vary. Students should see vividness of childhood memories described.

STUDY QUESTIONS *(Plath)*

Recalling

1. What is in the lane, according to line 1? To what do they go down "in hooks"? What do they "squander" on the speaker's fingers? What does she conclude in line 8?
2. In line 13 what does the speaker not think will appear? What happens in line 18?
3. What funnels at the speaker in line 20? What does the poet decide about the hills in line 22? To what has the last "hook" brought her in line 24? On what does the orange rock "look out"?

Interpreting

4. What sort of experience is the speaker's encounter with the blackberries?
5. What does the speaker think will never happen? Does it happen? Is this ironic?
6. What words in line 25 have we heard earlier in the poem? Explain how the repetition relates to the poem's irony.
7. What does the poem suggest about human emotions or emotional experiences?

LITERARY FOCUS *(Plath)*

Imagery

We cannot read "Blackberrying" without sensing its intense feeling. It is a highly emotional poem, and as we read, word by word, line by line, we share the poet's emotional adventure.

Yet notice how seldom, if ever, the poet tells us *directly* what she is feeling. Rather, she makes the *images* project the feeling. She does not tell us *about* the experience: She recreates it for us, largely through the imagery, so that we may experience it ourselves.

Most of the imagery in this poem is visual, made of vivid pictures. These are not just any paths, but paths that twist like a series of "hooks," forcing us to see this particular landscape. "Green meadows" is in itself not a remarkable image, but it becomes one when described as "glowing, as if lit from within." The image tells us, indirectly, that the poet, too, must be somehow "lit from within" as she shares, becomes a part of, this landscape.

Thinking About Imagery

- Identify the images of sound, taste, and touch in "Blackberrying." Tell what each contributes to an understanding of the poet's emotions.

STUDY QUESTIONS *(Sexton)*

Recalling

1. From where did the poet watch "it" before it came inside? How did it swell? Like what did it slump and then divide?
2. What happened after the poet watched it, according to line 10? Where does it now live?
3. Identify three images the poet remembers in lines 13–19. According to lines 20–21, what is here *now,* and from what was it caught back? To what is it compared in lines 22–23?
4. According to line 25, what are the cars whisking by on the suburban street? With what question does the poem end?

Interpreting

5. How does the poem communicate the reality of "it"? How does the poem communicate the vagueness of "it"?
6. What do the cars on the street represent? With what are they contrasted?
7. Why does the poet never explain precisely what "it" is?
8. Explain what the final question may mean.

Extending

9. Have you ever had an experience similar to the one described in this poem—an experience of *déjà vu,* for example? Discuss how the poet captures that experience in this poem.

COMPARING WRITERS

The concern with the problems of society at large that marked much of the literature of the Great Depression and the World War II years gave way, in the fifties, to more personal concerns. Nevertheless, in writing about themselves, modern writers also express attitudes and problems of modern life that we all share.

1. Which of the poems you have read in this unit exhibit primarily social concerns? What are their concerns?
2. Which of the poems in this unit deal with highly personal feelings or experiences? What are some of the modern attitudes or dilemmas they reflect?
3. Which of the poems suggest that modern Americans can learn something from America's past? What values do they suggest can be learned from the past?

COMPARING WRITERS

1. *"Unknown Citizen":* conformity, bureaucracy, materialism; *"Cracked Record Blues":* mind's shortcomings in complex society; *"Ball Turret Gunner":* war, state, and individuals; *"Lineage," "Strong Men":* loss of positive character traits in adaptation to modern society
2. "If I Could Tell You," "Big Wind," "The Waking," "The Fish," "Blackberrying," "What's That"; celebration of personal emotions; uncertainty
3. *"Hawthorne":* inspiration; *"Lineage":* strength, simplicity; *"Strong Men":* positive and negative values in brave, strong, rootless cowboy

FICTION

Katherine Anne Porter *1890–1980*

Katherine Anne Porter wrote very little in the course of a long lifetime. Yet almost everything she wrote was so polished, so well-crafted, that she is considered among the finest of American prose writers.

Porter was born in Indian Creek, Texas, and her family had roots in the Old South. Many of her stories reflect her adolescent life in the Southwest and the family tales she heard when a girl. She worked on newspapers and then lived, for a significant period of her youth, in Mexico, which she called "my familiar country." Some of her most famous tales have a Mexican background. In later years Porter taught in American universities.

Porter excelled in the short story and novella, forms that reflect her talent for concentration and discipline. Her first book, which included "The Jilting of Granny Weatherall," was *Flowering Judas,* published in 1930. Her other major works were *Noon Wine* (1937), *Pale Horse, Pale Rider* (1939), *The Leaning Tower* (1944), and the novel *Ship of Fools* (1962).

Porter writes often of the passing of the old order and of the confusion and guilt that accompany change. However, she deals with these large subjects in very confined forms. In "The Jilting of Granny Weatherall" every phrase that runs through Granny's mind counts toward the total effect. The story's disjointed "stream-of-consciousness" style, still experimental at the time it was written, reflects the Modernist break with traditional narrative, a break that Porter saw in the works of James Joyce, Virginia Woolf, and Ernest Hemingway.

■ Porter wanted to "discover and understand human motives and feelings." How does she share her discovery and understanding of Granny in this story?

AT A GLANCE

- Granny is sick in bed, and Dr. Harry tries to examine her.
- She denies she is sick even though she is dying.

LITERARY OPTIONS

- stream of consciousness
- flashback
- point of view

THEMATIC OPTIONS

- pride vs. love
- memory and time
- loss and recovery

1 POINT OF VIEW

Two third-person narrative voices are juxtaposed. One sounds more educated; the other uses Granny's diction ("The brat . . . breeches.")

2 STYLE

Vivid images and a simile ("like a cushion") express Granny's feelings more intensely.

3 WORD CHOICE

Porter writes with precision and economy: a single word, *marvel,* underscores Dr. Harry's placating attitude and genuine admiration.

4 THEME

Granny's statement affirms her advanced age and reveals an accumulated store of memories.

Katherine Anne Porter

The Jilting of Granny Weatherall

1 She flicked her wrist neatly out of Doctor Harry's pudgy careful fingers and pulled the sheet up to her chin. The brat ought to be in knee breeches. Doctoring around the country with spectacles on his nose! "Get along now, take your schoolbooks and go. There's nothing wrong with me."

2 Doctor Harry spread a warm paw like a cushion on her forehead where the forked green vein danced and made her eyelids twitch. "Now, now, be a good girl, and we'll have you up in no time."

"That's no way to speak to a woman nearly eighty years old just because she's down. I'd have you respect your elders, young man."

"Well, Missy, excuse me." Doctor Harry pat-
3 ted her cheek. "But I've got to warn you, haven't I? You're a marvel, but you must be careful or you're going to be good and sorry."

4 "Don't tell me what I'm going to be. I'm on my feet now, morally speaking. It's Cornelia. I had to go to bed to get rid of her."

Her bones felt loose, and floated around in her skin, and Doctor Harry floated like a balloon around the foot of the bed. He floated and pulled down his waistcoat and swung his glasses on a cord. "Well, stay where you are, it certainly can't hurt you."

"Get along and doctor your sick," said Granny Weatherall. "Leave a well woman alone. I'll call for you when I want you. . . . Where were you forty years ago when I pulled through milk leg[1] and double pneumonia? You weren't even born. Don't let Cornelia lead you on," she shouted, because Doctor Harry ap-

1. **milk leg:** painful swelling of the leg, usually as a result of infection during childbirth.

GUIDED READING

LITERAL QUESTION

1a. How does Granny feel physically? (Her bones feel loose and float around in her skin.)

INFERENTIAL QUESTION

1b. Why do you think Granny denies that she is seriously ill? (She is a strong and independent woman who likes to take charge of her own life.)

peared to float up to the ceiling and out. "I pay my own bills, and I don't throw my money away on nonsense!"

She meant to wave goodbye, but it was too
1 much trouble. Her eyes closed of themselves, it was like a dark curtain drawn around the bed. The pillow rose and floated under her, pleasant as a hammock in a light wind. She listened to the leaves rustling outside the window. No, somebody was swishing newspapers: no, Cornelia and Doctor Harry were whispering together. She leaped broad awake, thinking they whispered in her ear.

"She was never like this, *never* like this!" "Well, what can we expect?" "Yes, eighty years old. . . ."

2 Well, and what if she was? She still had ears. It was like Cornelia to whisper around doors. She always kept things secret in such a public way. She was always being tactful and kind. Cornelia was dutiful; that was the trouble with her. Dutiful and good: "So good and dutiful," said Granny, "that I'd like to spank her." She saw herself spanking Cornelia and making a fine job of it.

"What'd you say, Mother?"

Granny felt her face tying up in hard knots.

"Can't a body think, I'd like to know?"

"I thought you might want something."

"I do. I want a lot of things. First off, go away and don't whisper."

3 She lay and drowsed, hoping in her sleep that the children would keep out and let her rest a minute. It had been a long day. Not that she was tired. It was always pleasant to snatch a minute now and then. There was always so much to be done, let me see: tomorrow.

Tomorrow was far away and there was nothing to trouble about. Things were finished somehow when the time came; thank God there was always a little margin over for peace: then a person could spread out the plan of life and tuck in the edges orderly. It was good to have everything clean and folded away, with the hair brushes and tonic bottles sitting straight on the white embroidered linen: the day started without fuss and the pantry shelves laid out with rows of jelly glasses and brown jugs and white stone-china jars with blue whirligigs[2] and words painted on them: coffee, tea, sugar, ginger, cinnamon, allspice: and the
4 bronze clock with the lion on top nicely dusted off. The dust that lion could collect in twenty-four hours! The box in the attic with all those letters tied up, well, she'd have to go through that tomorrow. All those letters—George's letters and John's letters and her letters to them both—lying around for the children to find afterwards made her uneasy. Yes, that would be tomorrow's business. No use to let them know how silly she had been once.

5 While she was rummaging around she found death in her mind and it felt clammy and unfamiliar. She had spent so much time preparing for death there was no need for bringing it up again. Let it take care of itself now. When she was sixty she had felt very old, finished, and went around making farewell trips to see her children and grandchildren, with a secret in her mind: This is the very last of your mother, children! Then she made her will and came down with a long fever. That was all just a notion like a lot of other things, but it was lucky too, for she had once for all got over the idea of dying for a long time. Now she couldn't be worried. She hoped she had better sense now. Her father had lived to be one hundred and two years old and had drunk a noggin of strong hot toddy on his last birthday. He told the reporters it was his daily habit, and he owed his long life to that. He had made quite a scandal and was very pleased about it. She believed she'd just plague Cornelia a little.

"Cornelia! Cornelia!" No footsteps, but a sudden hand on her cheek. "Bless you, where have you been?"

"Here, Mother."

"Well, Cornelia, I want a noggin of hot toddy."

---

2. **whirligigs:** circular patterns; swirls.

AT A GLANCE

- Granny becomes angry when Cornelia whispers about her.
- Granny surrenders to memories of herself as a young mother.
- She acknowledges the idea of death but pushes it away.

1 FIGURATIVE LANGUAGE

Comparisons to dark curtains and a floating hammock suggest Granny's tentative connection to the present.

2 CHARACTERIZATION

Granny is frustrated with the loss of her physical powers.

3 SETTING

There are two settings in this story: Granny's bedroom and Granny's mind.

4 STREAM OF CONSCIOUSNESS

The interior monologue illustrates how Granny processes and connects images from the past and present.

5 THEME

Routine household chores contrast with death's imminence. Its presence jars both Granny and the readers.

GUIDED READING

LITERAL QUESTIONS

1a. Why does Granny think she is angry with Cornelia? (She thinks Cornelia is rude to whisper about her and is too dutiful.)

2a. What words does the narrator use to describe the thought of death? (*clammy* and *unfamiliar*)

INFERENTIAL QUESTIONS

1b. Can you think of other reasons why Granny might be angry with Cornelia? (She feels a loss of control over her life. Cornelia's concern forces her to confront her illness.)

2b. How can you explain the use of these words in view of the fact that she "couldn't be worried" about death? (She believes that having thought about death, she has put it in its proper place.)

AT A GLANCE

- Granny is annoyed because Cornelia thinks of her as old.
- She reviews her past achievements and thinks about her husband, John. She fears he won't recognize her.

1 POINT OF VIEW

The shift of Granny's interior thought ("Wait, wait, Cornelia . . .") shows the intensity of her pride.

2 IMAGERY

The strong, simple image *hard pull* suggests both how difficult her earlier life was and how directly she dealt with adversity.

3 CHARACTERIZATION

Granny desires to be physically active and to impose order on her world.

4 FORESHADOWING

The image of the rising fog here begins a series of images (*smoke, clouds, light*) that prefigure Granny's death.

5 FIGURATIVE LANGUAGE

The comparison of the children to calves at twilight creates a picture as vivid and poignant as Granny's memories.

"Are you cold, darling?"

"I'm chilly, Cornelia. Lying in bed stops the circulation. I must have told you that a thousand times."

Well, she could just hear Cornelia telling her husband that Mother was getting a little childish and they'd have to humor her. The thing that most annoyed her was that Cornelia thought she was deaf, dumb, and blind. Little hasty glances and tiny gestures tossed around her and over her head saying, "Don't cross her, let her have her way, she's eighty years old," and she sitting there as if she lived in a thin
1 glass cage. Sometimes Granny almost made up her mind to pack up and move back to her own house where nobody could remind her every minute that she was old. Wait, wait, Cornelia, till your own children whisper behind your back!

In her day she had kept a better house and had got more work done. She wasn't too old yet for Lydia to be driving eighty miles for advice when one of the children jumped the track, and Jimmy still dropped in and talked things over: "Now, Mammy, you've a good business head, I want to know what you think of this? . . ." Old. Cornelia couldn't change the furniture around without asking. Little things, little things! They had been so sweet when they were little. Granny wished the old
2 days were back again with the children young and everything to be done over. It had been a hard pull, but not too much for her. When she thought of all the food she had cooked, and all the clothes she had cut and sewed, and all the gardens she had made—well, the children showed it. There they were, made out of her, and they couldn't get away from that. Sometimes she wanted to see John again and point to them and say, Well, I didn't do so badly, did I? But that would have to wait. That was for tomorrow. She used to think of him as a man, but now all the children were older than their father, and he would be a child beside her if she saw him now. It seemed strange and there was something wrong in the idea. Why, he couldn't possibly recognize her. She had fenced in a hundred acres once, digging the post holes herself and clamping the wires with just a boy to help. That changed a woman. John would be looking for a young woman with the peaked Spanish comb in her hair and the painted fan. Digging post holes changed a woman. Riding country roads in the winter when women had their babies was another thing: sitting up nights with sick horses and sick children and hardly ever losing one. John, I hardly ever lost one of them! John would see that in a minute, that would be something he could understand, she wouldn't have to explain anything!

3 It made her feel like rolling up her sleeves and putting the whole place to rights again. No matter if Cornelia was determined to be everywhere at once, there were a great many things left undone on this place. She would start tomorrow and do them. It was good to be strong enough for everything, even if all you made melted and changed and slipped under your hands, so that by the time you finished you almost forgot what you were working for. What was it I set out to do? she asked herself in-
4 tently, but she could not remember. A fog rose over the valley, she saw it marching across the creek swallowing the trees and moving up the hill like an army of ghosts. Soon it would be at the near edge of the orchard, and then it was time to go in and light the lamps. Come in, children, don't stay out in the night air.

5 Lighting the lamps had been beautiful. The children huddled up to her and breathed like little calves waiting at the bars in the twilight. Their eyes followed the match and watched the flame rise and settle in a blue curve, then they moved away from her. The lamp was lit, they didn't have to be scared and hang on to Mother any more. Never, never, never more. God, for all my life I thank Thee. Without Thee, my God, I could never have done it. Hail, Mary, full of grace.[3]

I want you to pick all the fruit this year and see that nothing is wasted. There's always

3. **Hail . . . grace:** beginning of a Roman Catholic prayer to the Virgin Mary.

GUIDED READING

LITERAL QUESTIONS

1a. When does Granny plan to tell John how well she has done with her children? (tomorrow)

2a. What accomplishments made Granny proud? (cooking, sewing, gardening, raising her children)

INFERENTIAL QUESTIONS

1b. Why isn't Granny ready to tell John now? (She isn't ready to die; also, she doesn't want her work to be over.)

2b. How do you think this feeling might contribute to her injured pride? (She believes she has done very well and has difficulty accepting a situation in which she cannot take charge and exercise control.)

1 someone who can use it. Don't let good things rot for want of using. You waste life when you waste good food. Don't let things get lost. It's bitter to lose things. Now, don't let me get to thinking, not when I am tired and taking a little nap before supper. . . .

The pillow rose about her shoulders and pressed against her heart and the memory was being squeezed out of it: oh, push down the pillow, somebody: it would smother her if she
2 tried to hold it. Such a fresh breeze blowing and such a green day with no threats in it. But he had not come, just the same. What does a woman do when she has put on the white veil and set out the white cake for a man and he doesn't come? She tried to remember. No, I swear he never harmed me but in that. He never harmed me but in that . . . and what if he did? There was the day, the day, but a whirl of dark smoke rose and covered it, crept up and over into the bright field where everything was planted so carefully in orderly rows. That was hell, she knew hell when she saw it. For sixty years she had prayed against remembering him and against losing her soul in the deep pit of hell, and now the two things were min-
3 gled in one and the thought of him was a smoky cloud from hell that moved and crept in her head when she had just got rid of Doctor Harry and was trying to rest a minute. Wounded vanity, Ellen, said a sharp voice in the top of her mind. Don't let your wounded vanity get the upper hand of you. Plenty of girls get jilted. You were jilted, weren't you? Then stand up to it. Her eyelids wavered and let in streamers of blue-gray light like tissue paper over her eyes. She must get up and pull the shades down or she'd never sleep. She was in bed again and the shades were not down. How could that happen? Better turn over, hide from the light, sleeping in the light gave you nightmares. "Mother, how do you feel now?" and a stinging wetness on her forehead. But I don't like having my face washed in cold water!

Hapsy? George? Lydia? Jimmy? No, Cornelia, and her features were swollen and full of little puddles. "They're coming, darling, they'll all be here soon." Go wash your face, child, you look funny.

Instead of obeying, Cornelia knelt down and put her head on the pillow. She seemed to be talking but there was no sound. "Well, are you tongue-tied? Whose birthday is it? Are you going to have a party?"

Cornelia's mouth moved urgently in strange shapes. "Don't do that, you bother me, daughter."

"Oh, no, Mother. Oh, no. . . ."

Nonsense. It was strange about children. They disputed your every word. "No what, Cornelia?"

4 "Here's Doctor Harry."

"I won't see that boy again. He just left five minutes ago."

"That was this morning, Mother. It's night now. Here's the nurse."

"This is Doctor Harry, Mrs. Weatherall. I never saw you look so young and happy!"

"Ah, I'll never be young again—but I'd be happy if they'd let me lie in peace and get rested."

She thought she spoke up loudly, but no one answered. A warm weight on her forehead, a warm bracelet on her wrist, and a breeze went on whispering, trying to tell her something. A shuffle of leaves in the everlasting hand of God. He blew on them and they danced and rattled. "Mother, don't mind, we're going to give you a little hypodermic." "Look here, daughter, how do ants get in this bed? I saw sugar ants yesterday." Did you send for Hapsy too?

It was Hapsy she really wanted. She had to go a long way back through a great many rooms to find Hapsy standing with a baby on her arm. She seemed to herself to be Hapsy also, and the baby on Hapsy's arm was Hapsy and himself and herself, all at once, and there was no surprise in the meeting. Then Hapsy melted from within and turned flimsy as gray gauze and the baby was a gauzy shadow, and Hapsy came up close and said, " thought you'd never come," and looked at her very searchingly and said, "You haven't changed a

AT A GLANCE

- Granny remembers the day she was jilted many years ago.
- Dr. Harry pays an evening visit. Granny is unaware that time has passed.
- Granny remembers Hapsy, her dead child.

1 CHARACTERIZATION

Granny's admonition clarifies her need for order and expresses her own anger about the various losses she has experienced.

2 FLASHBACK

Granny's stream-of-consciousness account of the jilting suggests an intense memory that resists suppression.

3 IMAGERY

Mingled images—"dark smoke" (recalling her first lover) and "cloud from hell" (evoking death)—suggest that she sees her past jilting and approaching death as breaches of universal order.

4 PLOT: RISING ACTION

Granny grows increasingly confused about the passing of time as her death draws nearer. Dr. Harry's second visit heightens the tension.

GUIDED READING

LITERAL QUESTIONS

1a. What specific memory does the pillow squeeze out of Granny's mind? (the day she was jilted)

2a. Who is Hapsy? (Granny's dead daughter)

INFERENTIAL QUESTIONS

1b. How do you think Granny's memory of the jilting has affected her life? (She has tried to repress the memory, but it has hung over her life like a dark cloud shadowing all the bright things she has gained.)

2b. What does Granny's encounter with Hapsy suggest about the power of memory? (Granny has lost Hapsy to death but can bring her back to life in her memory.)

AT A GLANCE

- Granny wants to see George, the man who jilted her.
- Granny feels that something is still missing.
- Father Connolly gives her the last rites.
- Memories of the jilting and of Hapsy become interwoven with the present.

1 STREAM OF CONSCIOUSNESS

The narrator gives us direct access to Granny's thoughts. She seems to measure her whole life against the jilting; she realizes that something basic is still missing.

2 PLOT: RISING ACTION

Cornelia's intrusion into Granny's thoughts brings us back to focus on Granny's impending death.

3 CHARACTERIZATION

Granny's belief that she can arrange her spiritual salvation suggests her pride and her inability to relinquish control.

4 FLASHBACK

Porter's tactile images (*bottom dropped, blind, sweating, nothing underfoot*) suggest that Granny's loss of control was momentary. Nevertheless, when she put her life back together, she felt that something was missing.

5 FORESHADOWING

The image of the rising shadows in long angles and the gleaming, tall black dresser prefigure Granny's death.

bit!" They leaned forward to kiss, when Cornelia began whispering from a long way off, "Oh, is there anything you want to tell me? Is there anything I can do for you?"

Yes, she had changed her mind after sixty years and she would like to see George. I want you to find George. Find him and be sure to tell him I forgot him. I want him to know I had my husband just the same and my children and my house like any other woman. A good house too and a good husband that I loved and fine children out of him. Better than I hoped
1 for even. Tell him I was given back everything he took away and more. Oh, no, oh, no, there was something else besides the house and the man and the children. Oh, surely they were not all? What was it? Something not given back. . . . Her breath crowded down under her ribs and grew into a monstrous frightening shape with cutting edges; it bored up into her head, and the agony was unbelievable: Yes, John, get the doctor now, no more talk, my time has come.

When this one was born it should be the last. The last. It should have been born first, for it was the one she had truly wanted. Everything came in good time. Nothing left out, left over. She was strong, in three days she would
2 be as well as ever. Better. A woman needed milk in her to have her full health.

"Mother, do you hear me?"

"I've been telling you—"

"Mother, Father Connolly's here."

"I went to Holy Communion only last week. Tell him I'm not so sinful as all that."

"Father just wants to speak to you."

He could speak as much as he pleased. It was like him to drop in and inquire about her soul as if it were a teething baby, and then stay on for a cup of tea and a round of cards and gossip. He always had a funny story of some sort, usually about an Irishman who made his little mistakes and confessed them, and the point lay in some absurd thing he would blurt out in the confessional showing his struggles between native piety and original sin. Granny felt easy about her soul. Cornelia, where are your manners? Give Father Connolly a chair.
3 She had her secret comfortable understanding with a few favorite saints who cleared a straight road to God for her. All as surely signed and sealed as the papers for the new Forty Acres. Forever . . . heirs and assigns[4] for-
4 ever. Since the day the wedding cake was not cut, but thrown out and wasted. The whole bottom dropped out of the world, and there she was blind and sweating with nothing under feet and the walls falling away. His hand had caught her under the breast, she had not fallen, there was the freshly polished floor with the green rug on it, just as before. He had cursed like a sailor's parrot and said, "I'll kill him for you." Don't lay a hand on him, for my sake leave something to God. "Now, Ellen, you must believe what I tell you. . . ."

So there was nothing, nothing to worry about any more, except sometimes in the night one of the children screamed in a nightmare, and they both hustled out shaking and hunting for the matches and calling, "There, wait a minute, here we are!" John, get the doctor now, Hapsy's time has come. But there was Hapsy standing by the bed in a white cap. "Cornelia, tell Hapsy to take off her cap. I can't see her plain."

Her eyes opened very wide and the room stood out like a picture she had seen some-
5 where. Dark colors with the shadows rising towards the ceiling in long angles. The tall black dresser gleamed with nothing on it but John's picture, enlarged from a little one, with John's eyes very black when they should have been blue. You never saw him, so how do you know how he looked? But the man insisted the copy was perfect, it was very rich and handsome. For a picture, yes, but it's not my husband. The table by the bed had a linen cover and a candle and a crucifix. The light was blue from Cornelia's silk lampshades. No sort of light at all, just frippery.[5] You had to live forty years with kerosene lamps to appreciate honest elec-

4. **assigns:** people to whom property is legally transferred.

5. **frippery:** showy, useless display of elegance.

GUIDED READING

LITERAL QUESTION

1a. What thought occurs to Granny that causes her unbelievable agony? ("something was not given back")

INFERENTIAL QUESTION

1b. What do you think the "something not given back" might be? (Granny's innocence; her belief in the orderly, harmonious universe; her assumptions about her own power and her ability to control life)

tricity. She felt very strong and she saw Doctor Harry with a rosy nimbus[6] around him.

"You look like a saint, Doctor Harry, and I vow that's as near as you'll ever come to it."

"She's saying something."

"I heard you, Cornelia. What's all this carrying-on?"

"Father Connolly's saying—"

Cornelia's voice staggered and bumped like a cart in a bad road. It rounded corners and turned back again and arrived nowhere. Granny stepped up in the cart very lightly and reached for the reins, but a man sat beside her and she
1 knew him by his hands, driving the cart. She did not look in his face, for she knew without seeing, but looked instead down the road where the trees leaned over and bowed to each other and a thousand birds were singing a Mass. She felt like singing too, but she put her hand in the bosom of her dress and pulled out a rosary, and Father Connolly murmured Latin in a very solemn voice and tickled her feet.[7] Will you stop that nonsense? I'm a married woman. What if he did run away and leave me to face the priest by myself? I found another a whole world better. I wouldn't have exchanged my husband for anybody except Saint Michael[8] himself, and you may tell him that for me with a thank-you in the bargain.

Light flashed on her closed eyelids, and a deep roaring shook her. Cornelia, is that lightning? I hear thunder. There's going to be a storm. Close all the windows. Call the children in. . . . "Mother, here we are, all of us." "Is that you, Hapsy?" "Oh, no, I'm Lydia. We drove as fast as we could." Their faces drifted above her, drifted away. The rosary fell out of her hands and Lydia put it back. Jimmy tried to help, their hands fumbled together, and Granny closed two fingers around Jimmy's thumb. Beads wouldn't do, it must be something alive. She was so amazed her thoughts ran round and round. So, my dear Lord, this is my death and I wasn't even thinking about it. My children have come to see me die. But I can't, it's not
2 time. Oh, I always hated surprises. I wanted to give Cornelia the amethyst[9] set—Cornelia, you're to have the amethyst set, but Hapsy's to wear it when she wants, and, Doctor Harry, do shut up. Nobody sent for you. Oh, my dear Lord, do wait a minute. I meant to do something about the Forty Acres, Jimmy doesn't need it and Lydia will later on, with that worthless husband of hers. I meant to finish the altar cloth and send six bottles of wine to Sister Borgia for her dyspepsia.[10] I want to send six bottles of wine to Sister Borgia, Father Connolly, now don't let me forget.

Cornelia's voice made short turns and tilted over and crashed. "Oh, Mother, oh, Mother, oh, Mother. . . ."

"I'm not going, Cornelia. I'm taken by surprise. I can't go."

You'll see Hapsy again. What about her? "I thought you'd never come." Granny made a long journey outward, looking for Hapsy. What if I don't find her? What then? Her heart sank down and down, there was no bottom to death, she couldn't come to the end of it. The blue light from Cornelia's lampshade drew into a tiny point in the center of her brain, it flickered and winked like an eye, quietly it fluttered and dwindled. Granny lay curled down within herself, amazed and watchful, staring at the point of light that was herself; her body was now only a deeper mass of shadow in an endless darkness and this darkness would curl around the light and swallow it up. God, give a sign!

For the second time there was no sign. Again no bridegroom and the priest in the house. She could not remember any other sorrow because this grief wiped them all away. Oh, no, there's nothing more cruel than this—I'll never forgive it. She stretched herself with a deep breath and blew out the light.

6. **nimbus:** halo.
7. **murmured . . . feet:** administered last rites, including prayers and applying holy oil to the feet.
8. **Saint Michael:** an archangel.
9. **amethyst** [am'ə thist]: purple or violet quartz, used in jewelry.
10. **dyspepsia** [dis pep'shə]: indigestion.

AT A GLANCE

- Granny receives the last rites and asks God for a sign that she is saved. There is no response.
- The children gather around her bed, and she realizes that she is dying.
- Granny dies.

1 FIGURATIVE LANGUAGE

The cart, the faceless driver, bowing trees, and singing birds provide a metaphorical description of Granny's passage from life to death.

2 THEME

Granny's focus on undone chores underscores her desperate need to deny death and to retain control.

REFLECTING ON THE STORY

What is the one grief that Granny can never forgive? (that having worked and sacrificed, she is not given any guarantees of salvation)

GUIDED READING

LITERAL QUESTIONS

1a. Why does Granny say she can't die now? (She says it's not her time, and she doesn't like surprises.)

2a. What image symbolizes Granny's waning life? (the blue light from Cornelia's lampshade)

INFERENTIAL QUESTIONS

1b. Why do you think Granny always hated surprises? (Granny likes to take charge and impose order. Surprises, like the jilting, show the limits of her control and a breakdown of order.)

2b. What significance do you think there might be to Granny's blowing out the light herself? (True to character, she chooses to die rather than linger in a world over which she has lost control.)

STUDY QUESTIONS

1. get rid of Cornelia; tomorrow; death; clammy, unfamiliar
2. her children; her husband; with Cornelia
3. Children had been sweet; it was hard; she didn't do too badly.
4. jilting by George; that she had a family, forgot him; something not given back
5. a sign; is jilted; grief
6. ■ Granny dies.
   ■ light
   ■ unprepared, does not expect to die
7. hard, but full; weathered all hardships; firm, caring
8. that she has not forgotten him; innocence, love, or her soul
9. of grace or salvation; absence of sign from God with jilting
10. ■ one hardship she hasn't come to terms with
    ■ By God: Anger and pride deprive her of salvation.
11. ■ has courage, competence, expects difficult life, does not admit defeat
    ■ Granny denies death, while Dickinson accepted it.
    ■ Modern world of doubt: Death may lead to despair, annihilation.

VIEWPOINT

1. pride; Christ (See Matt. 25:1–13.)
2. Answers will vary. Many students will probably find this a valid interpretation.

STUDY QUESTIONS

Recalling

1. Why does Granny Weatherall tell Doctor Harry she has taken to her bed (paragraph 5)? For what day does Granny make plans soon after Doctor Harry leaves? What does she "find" while "rummaging around" in her mind? How does it feel to her?
2. Who are Cornelia, Lydia, and Jimmy? Who was John? With whom does Granny now live?
3. Identify three thoughts that Granny has about her earlier years as a housewife and mother.
4. As she looks back on her long life, which event does Granny recall with particular anger? According to page 580, what does Granny want George to know? What does she conclude about the things she was "given back"?
5. What does Granny ask of God in the next-to-last paragraph? What happens "for the second time"? Why can Granny not remember any other sorrow, according to the last paragraph?

Interpreting

6. What happens in the last sentence of the story? With what image is life equated in this sentence and elsewhere in the story? What does Granny's attitude toward the doctor and the priest suggest about her attitude toward death?
7. What sort of life did Granny live? How is her life related to her surname? What sort of wife and mother does she seem to have been?
8. What is ironic in Granny's thought about George: "Find him and be sure to tell him I forgot him"? What might the "something not given back" on page 580 be?
9. What sort of sign might Granny want from God? What are the two "cruelties" that Granny confuses in the final paragraph?
10. Why does the jilting come back to Granny so frequently as she faces death? What is the real "jilting of Granny Weatherall"?

Extending

11. In what way is Granny's attitude toward life like that of traditional nineteenth-century pioneers? In what way is her attitude toward death different from attitudes expressed in the nineteenth century—those of Emily Dickinson, for example? How might this difference in attitude reflect modern times?

VIEWPOINT

In introducing a collection of short stories that contains "The Jilting of Granny Weatherall," Calvin Skaggs offers this analysis:

> Porter shows us a woman so scarred by her early romantic wound that she has suppressed her emotional needs. By dedicating herself to work—to raising a family and ripping a prosperous farm from the frontier—she has avoided recognizing the scar tissue that surrounds, and deadens, her life. . . . But at the moment of her death she recognizes the darkness to which her inability to forgive that first jilting has doomed her. Too late she sees that she has been jilted again, this time by the bridegroom who judges the essential nature and quality of a life.
>
> —Introduction to *The American Short Story,* Vol. 2

1. According to this analysis, what is Granny's tragic flaw, the characteristic of her personality that brings her to a tragic end? Whom does Skaggs believe is the "second bridegroom"?
2. Do you agree with this analysis of Granny's character? Why or why not?

LITERARY FOCUS

Stream of Consciousness and Flashback

In the twentieth century, with its great interest in psychology, storytellers often abandon the chronological, straight-line narrative that dominated literature for centuries. If, for example, Granny Weatherall's story were told in chronological time sequence, we would read first about her jilting, then about her marriage and the birth of her children, then about the time when she moved to Cornelia's house, and finally about the days just before her death. Clock time works that way, but the mind and the memory work differently. In our century writers began to represent the way time happens in our minds. This kind of writing is often called the **stream of consciousness,** from a phrase by the American psychologist William James.

Most of our thoughts do not come to us in complete sentences. During very few minutes in any given day do we think logically. Most of what goes on in our minds is a series of thoughts and images that switch rapidly back and forth between the present, the past, and the future, as things and ideas remind us of other things and ideas. Your own stream of consciousness is not hard for *you* to interpret because you are *in* it. For others, however, much of it would make no sense.

In some ways stream-of-consciousness writing is truer to reality than writing that suggests more orderly thinking. Yet such stream-of-consciousness fiction can also be difficult to read. In "The Jilting of Granny Weatherall" we, the readers, have to retell the story, as it were, in chronological order. We have to do some imaginative work to reorder the events, but our reward is great: We gain the illusion of being present to the private thoughts of Granny Weatherall. Porter gives us enough clues that allow us to recreate the story, and the result is an experience that we could not have had if the story had been written any other way.

One of Porter's techniques is drawn from movie making—the **flashback,** an interruption in the narrative to show an event that happened earlier. We take this technique so for granted as a narrative method in movies that we hardly notice it. A character may be reminded of something from the past, and suddenly the whole story shifts back into the past; we see something that happened earlier, and then we just as suddenly find ourselves in the present again. In this story, in the very first paragraph, we find a flashback, as Granny remembers Doctor Harry when she knew him as a little boy. Porter uses the flashback to help create the stream of consciousness.

Thinking About Stream of Consciousness and Flashback

1. Why is the stream of consciousness especially appropriate in "The Jilting of Granny Weatherall," given the story's subject matter?
2. Give another example of flashback from "The Jilting of Granny Weatherall."

COMPOSITION

Writing About Stream of Consciousness

■ Choose three or four incidents in the life of Granny Weatherall, and write about them as if you were telling the story in the traditional way. Place the events in chronological order, and use an objective third-person point of view. When you have finished, discuss what has been gained or lost by the method that Katherine Anne Porter uses.

Writing in the Stream-of-Consciousness Manner

■ Putting yourself in the place of one of the other characters in "The Jilting of Granny Weatherall," write a stream-of-consciousness account of what might be going on in your mind as Granny Weatherall is dying. Show how the present and past reality mix and how one thought or image suggests another.

LITERARY FOCUS

1. Stream of consciousness helps Porter illustrate how the mind of a dying person works. Flashbacks show how Granny juxtaposes present and past.

2. Examples:
- She thinks of how she used to keep house.
- She remembers being sick when she was forty.
- She remembers digging post holes and working on the farm.
- She remembers the children when they were young.

COMPOSITION: GUIDELINES FOR EVALUATION

WRITING ABOUT STREAM OF CONSCIOUSNESS

Objective

To analyze stream of consciousness

Guidelines for Evaluation

- suggested length: six to eight paragraphs
- should retell a portion of the story in a traditional narrative manner
- should identify advantages and disadvantages of stream of consciousness in this story

WRITING STREAM OF CONSCIOUSNESS

Objective

To write in the stream-of-consciousness manner

Guidelines for Evaluation

- suggested length: four to six paragraphs
- should be in the first person
- should "see" events as chosen character does
- should move between the present and the past
- should use free association

Photograph © 1982 by Jill Krementz

Jerome Weidman *born 1913*

When Jerome Weidman, who was born in New York, graduated from high school, he did not intend to be a writer. The time was the height of the Great Depression, and for Weidman "there was only one problem, and that was to eat." During the 1930s, while attending college and then law school at night, he worked as a clerk in New York City's garment district for eleven dollars a week. Reading was his pastime, and as a challenge to himself he wrote a short story based on an anecdote that he had overheard. A magazine accepted the story, and he got ten dollars for his efforts. A contest encouraged him to begin his first novel, and although it did not win the contest, the novel, *I Can Get It for You Wholesale,* was published in 1937. Weidman became a full-time writer.

Along with other novels and numerous collections of short stories, Weidman has written plays, including the musical *Fiorello!* (1960), for which he shared the Pulitzer Prize. *I Can Get It for You Wholesale,* based on the novel, was produced on Broadway in 1962. Weidman has also written several screenplays.

"My Father Sits in the Dark," from a short story collection of the same name, shows Weidman's simple and straightforward way of writing. He bases his entire story on an **anecdote,** a short account of an interesting event in someone's life. Like an old photograph, his story captures a lost time and a feeling for his father that a boy cannot forget.

■ In this anecdote from his childhood, Weidman reveals an understanding that he reached about his father. As you read, can you predict what that understanding will be?

Jerome Weidman

My Father Sits in the Dark

My father has a peculiar habit. He is fond of sitting in the dark, alone. Sometimes I come home very late. The house is dark. I let myself in quietly because I do not want to disturb my
1 mother. She is a light sleeper. I tiptoe into my room and undress in the dark. I go to the kitchen for a drink of water. My bare feet make no noise. I step into the room and almost trip over my father. He is sitting in a kitchen chair, in his pajamas, smoking his pipe.

"Hello, Pop," I say.

"Hello, son."

"Why don't you go to bed, Pa?"

"I will," he says.

But he remains there. Long after I am asleep I feel sure that he is still sitting there, smoking.

Many times I am reading in my room. I hear my mother get the house ready for the night. I hear my kid brother go to bed. I hear my sister come in. I hear her do things with jars and combs until she, too, is quiet. I know she has gone to sleep. In a little while I hear my mother say good night to my father. I continue to read. Soon I become thirsty. (I drink a lot of water.) I go to the kitchen for a drink. Again I almost stumble across my father. Many times it startles me. I forget about him. And there he is—smoking, sitting, thinking.

"Why don't you go to bed, Pop?"

"I will, son."

But he doesn't. He just sits there and smokes and thinks. It worries me. I can't un-
2 derstand it. What can he be thinking about? Once I asked him.

"What are you thinking about, Pa?"

"Nothing," he said.

Once I left him there and went to bed. I awoke several hours later. I was thirsty. I went to the kitchen. There he was. His pipe was out. But he sat there, staring into a corner of the kitchen. After a moment I became accustomed to the darkness. I took my drink. He still sat and stared. His eyes did not blink. I thought he was not even aware of me. I was afraid.

"Why don't you go to bed, Pop?"

"I will, son," he said. "Don't wait up for me."

"But," I said, "you've been sitting here for hours. What's wrong? What are you thinking about?"

"Nothing, son," he said. "Nothing. It's just restful. That's all."

3 The way he said it was convincing. He did not seem worried. His voice was even and pleasant. It always is. But I could not understand it. How could it be restful to sit alone in an uncomfortable chair far into the night, in darkness?

What can it be?

I review all the possibilities. It can't be money. I know that. We haven't much, but when he is worried about money he makes no secret of it. It can't be his health. He is not reticent about that either. It can't be the health of anyone in the family. We are a bit short on money, but we are long on health. (Knock wood, my mother would say.) What can it be? I am afraid I do not know. But that does not stop me from worrying.

Maybe he is thinking of his brothers in the old country. Or of his mother and two stepmothers. Or of his father. But they are all dead. And he would not brood about them like that. I say brood, but it is not really true. He does not brood. He does not even seem to be thinking. He looks too peaceful, too, well not contented, just too peaceful, to be brooding. Perhaps it is as he says. Perhaps it is restful. But it does not seem possible. It worries me.

4 If I only knew what he thinks about. If I only knew that he thinks at all. I might not be able to help him. He might not even need help. It may be as he says. It may be restful.

AT A GLANCE

- The young man is distressed by his father's habit of sitting alone in the dark.
- His father assures him that nothing is wrong.
- The young man persists in trying to understand his father's behavior.

LITERARY OPTIONS

- characterization
- tone

THEMATIC OPTIONS

- family ties
- the value of the past

1 POINT OF VIEW

Note how the first-person narrator's limited view intensifies the mystery: The reader, like the son, must struggle to understand.

2 CHARACTERIZATION

As a result of the father's natural reticence in conversation with his son, as well as the absence of any physical description of the father, he emerges as an inscrutable and shadowy figure.

3 TONE

The narrator's language, direct but formal, and his use of the present tense establish a thoughtful, reflective tone.

4 CONFLICT

The son's determination to find a way to penetrate his father's thought shapes the gentle conflict of the story.

GUIDED READING

LITERAL QUESTION

1a. Whom does the boy believe his father may be thinking about? (his two brothers in the old country; his mother and two stepmothers; his own father)

INFERENTIAL QUESTION

1b. What can you infer about the father's past from the references to the old country? (that he had close family ties that now live only in his memory)

AT A GLANCE

- The son notes his father's good mental and physical health but still worries.
- The son once again confronts his father; the father reassures him but discloses nothing.
- The son turns on the kitchen light, alarming his father.

1 CHARACTERIZATION

The young man's sensitivity and determination emerge from his struggle to understand more about his father.

2 TONE

The concerned son's series of simple questions imbue the narrative with urgency.

3 SETTING

The auditory details of the night-time setting (the ticking clock, humming auto, and swishing papers) intensify the sense of darkness and immediacy.

But at least I would not worry about it.

Why does he just sit there, in the dark? Is his mind failing? No, it can't be. He is only fifty-three. And he is just as keen-witted as ever. In fact, he is the same in every respect.
1 He still likes beet soup. He still reads the second section of the *Times* first. He still wears wing collars. He still believes that Debs[1] could have saved the country and that T.R.[2] was a tool of the moneyed interests. He is the same in every way. He does not even look older than he did five years ago. Everybody remarks about that. Well-preserved, they say. But he sits in the dark, alone, smoking, staring straight ahead of him, unblinking, into the small hours of the night.

If it is as he says, if it is restful, I will let it go at that. But suppose it is not. Suppose it is
2 something I cannot fathom. Perhaps he needs help. Why doesn't he speak? Why doesn't he frown or laugh or cry? Why doesn't he do something? Why does he just sit there?

Finally I become angry. Maybe it is just my unsatisfied curiosity. Maybe I *am* a bit worried. Anyway, I become angry.

"Is something wrong, Pop?"

"Nothing, son. Nothing at all."

But this time I am determined not to be put off. I am angry.

"Then why do you sit here all alone, thinking, till late?"

"It's restful, son. I like it."

I am getting nowhere. Tomorrow he will be sitting there again. I will be puzzled. I will be worried. I will not stop now. I am angry.

"Well, what do you *think* about, Pa? Why do you just sit here? What's worrying you? What do you think about?"

"Nothing's worrying me, son. I'm all right. It's just restful. That's all. Go to bed, son."

My anger has left me. But the feeling of worry is still there. I must get an answer. It seems so silly. Why doesn't he tell me? I have a funny feeling that unless I get an answer I will go crazy. I am insistent.

"But what do you *think* about, Pa? What is it?"

"Nothing, son. Just things in general. Nothing special. Just things."

I can get no answer.

It is very late. The street is quiet and the house is dark. I climb the steps softly, skipping the ones that creak. I let myself in with my key and tiptoe into my room. I remove my clothes and remember that I am thirsty. In my bare feet I walk to the kitchen. Before I reach it I know he is there.

I can see the deeper darkness of his hunched shape. He is sitting in the same chair, his elbows on his knees, his cold pipe in his teeth, his unblinking eyes staring straight ahead. He does not seem to know I am there. He did not hear me come in. I stand quietly in the doorway and watch him.

Everything is quiet, but the night is full of little sounds. As I stand there motionless I be-
3 gin to notice them. The ticking of the alarm clock on the icebox. The low hum of an automobile passing many blocks away. The swish of papers moved along the street by the breeze. A whispering rise and fall of sound, like low breathing. It is strangely pleasant.

The dryness in my throat reminds me. I step briskly into the kitchen.

"Hello, Pop," I say.

"Hello, son," he says. His voice is low and dreamlike. He does not change his position or shift his gaze.

I cannot find the faucet. The dim shadow of light that comes through the window from the street lamp only makes the room seem darker. I reach for the short chain in the center of the room. I snap on the light.

He straightens up with a jerk, as though he has been struck. "What's the matter, Pop?" I ask.

"Nothing," he says. "I don't like the light."

"What's the matter with the light?" I say. "What's wrong?"

1. **Debs:** Eugene Victor Debs (1855–1926), labor leader and Socialist candidate for President.
2. **T.R.:** Theodore Roosevelt (1858–1919), President of the United States (1901–1909).

GUIDED READING

LITERAL QUESTIONS

1a. What reason does the father give to explain his habit? (He says that it is restful.)

2a. How does the father react when the boy turns on the light? (as if he had been struck)

INFERENTIAL QUESTIONS

1b. Why does the son not accept his father's explanation? (He finds the response inadequate; he wants to know what his father thinks about.)

2b. Why do you think that the father reacts in this way? (The darkness helps him get lost in his thoughts; the light brings him back to reality.)

"Nothing," he says. "I don't like the light."

I snap the light off. I drink my water slowly. I must take it easy, I say to myself. I must get to the bottom of this.

"Why don't you go to bed? Why do you sit here so late in the dark?"

"It's nice," he says. "I can't get used to lights. We didn't have lights when I was a boy in Europe."

My heart skips a beat and I catch my breath
1 happily. I begin to think I understand. I remember the stories of his boyhood in Austria. I see the wide-beamed *kretchma,*[3] with my grandfather behind the bar. It is late, the customers are gone, and he is dozing. I see the bed of glowing coals, the last of the roaring fire. The room is already dark, and growing darker. I see a small boy, crouched on a pile of twigs at one side of the huge fireplace, his starry gaze fixed on the dull remains of the dead flames. The boy is my father.

2 I remember the pleasure of those few moments while I stoop quietly in the doorway watching him.

"You mean there's nothing wrong? You just sit in the dark because you like it, Pop?" I find it hard to keep my voice from rising in a happy shout.

"Sure," he says. "I can't think with the light on."

I set my glass down and turn to go back to my room. "Good night, Pop," I say.

"Good night," he says.

Then I remember. I turn back. "What do you think about, Pop?" I ask.

His voice seems to come from far away. It is quiet and even again. "Nothing," he says softly. "Nothing special."

3. ***kretchma*** [krech′mə]: tavern.

AT A GLANCE

- The father explains that there were no lights in the old country.
- The son gets an image of his father as a boy sitting in front of the dying embers of a fire in the grandfather's tavern in Austria.
- The son finally understands his father's habit.

1 PLOT: RESOLUTION

The son's worries about his father come to an end as he realizes that his father's habit is rooted in the past.

2 THEME

The ability of the past to nourish those in the present is effectively conveyed in the narrator's memory of himself as a boy looking at a father who, in turn, held loving memories of his own father.

REFLECTING ON THE STORY

What does the father's comment that he cannot think with the light on suggest about him? (It reflects his desire to escape from the present and nourish himself with warm memories of his past.)

STUDY QUESTIONS

1. sitting alone in the dark
2. what his father is thinking about; "nothing"
3. "It is restful"; money, health, family in the old country, it is peaceful, father's mind failing
4. "we didn't have lights when I was a boy in Europe"; father as a boy in front of dying coals of fire in grandfather's empty tavern in Austria
5. pleasure, happiness; what his father thinks about; "nothing"
6. seems to be behavior of one who is troubled; father resists attempts to communicate; explanation alleviates concern for father's well-being
7. close, has enjoyed listening to stories of father's childhood; had been foremost concern, but he learns something more valuable
8. yes; scene pictured by son; remembering boyhood, security and warmth, sounds of night, simple way of life now gone forever

STUDY QUESTIONS

Recalling

1. What is the "peculiar habit" of the narrator's father?
2. What does the narrator wish to know in the tenth paragraph? What does his father answer when he asks?
3. What is the father's first explanation for his habit? What are four "possibilities" that the narrator reviews in trying to understand why his father sits alone in darkness?
4. What is the father's explanation of his dislike for lights? What scene does the narrator picture when he hears this explanation?
5. Once the narrator understands his father's dislike for lights, what does he feel? What question does he almost forget to ask? When he asks it, what does his father reply?

Interpreting

6. Why is the narrator puzzled, bothered, and finally angered by his father's behavior? Why is he so happy near the story's end?
7. What does the narrator's ability to picture his father's life in Austria suggest about the narrator's relationship with his father? Why is it ironic that he almost forgets to ask what his father is thinking?
8. By the story's end, do we have an idea about what the father might be thinking? If so, what might it be, and what gives us a clue?

COMPOSITION

Writing a Comparison/Contrast

■ In this story the inner life of a character is revealed through the eyes of another character. Compare and contrast the father here with Granny Weatherall, a character who reveals her own inner life, in Katherine Anne Porter's "Jilting of Granny Weatherall" (page 576). Begin by telling what each character reveals. Then suggest what each character holds back. Conclude with your own opinion of the emotional effect of the two stories. *For help with this assignment, refer to Lesson 2 in the Writing About Literature Handbook at the back of this book.*

Writing an Anecdote

■ In recounting an interesting event in someone's life, an anecdote often illuminates that person's character in some way. Write an anecdote about a person you know well, or if you prefer, about a character you have invented. Reveal in the anecdote something important about the subject's life or character.

COMPOSITION: GUIDELINES FOR EVALUATION

WRITING A COMPARISON/CONTRAST

Objective

To compare and contrast two characters

Guidelines for Evaluation

- suggested length: five to six paragraphs
- should show that Porter's character reveals many details of life, while Weidman's does not
- should explain Granny's concealing bitterness
- should explain that father shows he is at peace
- should assess emotional effect of each story

WRITING AN ANECDOTE

Objective

To write an anecdote revealing a character trait

Guidelines for Evaluation

- suggested length: one to three paragraphs
- should recount an interesting event in a person's life
- should show how the event reveals a character trait

John Steinbeck *1902–1968*

Often during his long career John Steinbeck enjoyed a rare combination of enormous popularity and serious critical acclaim. His great work, *The Grapes of Wrath* (1939), is among the most famous and widely read novels of this century. In its epic depiction of one dispossessed Oklahoma family's migration to California in search of a new life, it remains one of the most powerfully moving books written about the Great Depression.

John Steinbeck was born in Salinas, California, where much of his fiction is set. His varied early experiences helped shape him as a writer. When he was unable to complete his college studies at Stanford University, he worked his way to New York City on a cattle boat, hoping to get his early writing published. Failing this, he worked briefly as a newspaper reporter and then returned to California, where he continued to write while taking an assortment of jobs, including fruit picker, surveyor, caretaker on an estate, mason's assistant, and chemist's assistant. During World War II he returned to journalism, serving as a war correspondent in Italy.

Steinbeck wrote a great deal. In the two decades after 1932, he produced sixteen long works of fiction, which vary widely in length, form, and subject. *In Dubious Battle* (1936) concerns the plight of exploited migrant laborers; *Of Mice and Men* (1937) tells of the tragic friendship of two migrant workers; *Cannery Row* (1945) and *Sweet Thursday* (1954) are lighter works, full of local color and gentle humor; *The Pearl* (1947) is a retelling of a Mexican folk tale; and *Travels with Charley* (1962) is an account of the author's journey across America in a pickup truck with his poodle, Charley.

Steinbeck's novels and stories usually offer a strong sense of social justice, a heightened sensitivity to the colors and textures of the American landscape, and a compelling plot. His characters are memorable, perhaps the finest elements in his writing: people from different races and occupations, people who have lived, authentic people who seem to step right off the page. The main character of "The Leader of the People" is such a man: not in tune with his time, immersed in his memories, yet embodying an entire segment of American history.

■ Do times make people, or do people make the times? Is Grandfather a product of his times, or a victim of the past?

AT A GLANCE

- Billy Buck, a ranch hand, rakes the remains of an old haystack.
- Jody, a little boy, comes out of the house.
- They talk about the hay.

LITERARY OPTIONS

- characterization
- point of view

THEMATIC OPTIONS

- the vanished frontier
- family ties

1 SETTING

The physical details, the visual imagery of land, house, and sky, and the focus on sound help create a realistic setting.

2 CHARACTERIZATION

Jody's deliberate scuffing of his shoes is the natural gesture of a little boy whose energy and independence are at odds with social constraints.

John Steinbeck

The Leader of the People

On Saturday afternoon Billy Buck, the ranch
hand, raked together the last of the old year's
haystack and pitched small forkfuls over the
wire fence to a few mildly interested cattle.
1 High in the air small clouds like puffs of cannon smoke were driven eastward by the March
wind. The wind could be heard whishing in
the brush on the ridge crests, but no breath of
it penetrated down into the ranch cup.

The little boy, Jody, emerged from the
house eating a thick piece of buttered bread.
He saw Billy working on the last of the hay-
2 stack. Jody tramped down scuffing his shoes in
a way he had been told was destructive to
good shoe leather. A flock of white pigeons
flew out of the black cypress tree as Jody
passed, and circled the tree and landed again.
A half-grown tortoise-shell cat leaped from the
bunkhouse porch, galloped on stiff legs across
the road, whirled and galloped back again. Jody
picked up a stone to help the game along, but
he was too late, for the cat was under the
porch before the stone could be discharged.
He threw the stone into the cypress tree and
started the white pigeons on another whirling
flight.

Arriving at the used-up haystack, the boy leaned against the barbed wire fence. "Will that be all of it, do you think?" he asked.

The middle-aged ranch hand stopped his careful raking and stuck his fork into the ground. He took off his black hat and smoothed down his hair. "Nothing left of it that isn't soggy from ground moisture," he said. He replaced his hat and rubbed his dry leathery hands together.

GUIDED READING

LITERAL QUESTION

1a. What does Jody pick up to help the cat's game along? (a stone to make the pigeons fly)

INFERENTIAL QUESTION

1b. What does Jody's action suggest about his character? (He is playful and mischievous, and he likes excitement.)

1 "Ought to be plenty mice," Jody suggested.

"Lousy with them," said Billy. "Just crawling with mice."

"Well, maybe, when you get all through, I could call the dogs and hunt the mice."

"Sure, I guess you could," said Billy Buck. He lifted a forkful of the damp ground-hay and threw it into the air. Instantly three mice leaped out and burrowed frantically under the hay again.

Jody sighed with satisfaction. Those plump, sleek, arrogant mice were doomed. For eight months they had lived and multiplied in the
2 haystack. They had been immune from cats, from traps, from poison, and from Jody. They had grown smug in their security, overbearing, and fat. Now the time of disaster had come; they would not survive another day.

Billy looked up at the top of the hills that surrounded the ranch. "Maybe you better ask your father before you do it," he suggested.

"Well, where is he? I'll ask him now."

"He rode up to the ridge ranch after dinner. He'll be back pretty soon."

Jody slumped against the fence post. "I don't think he'd care."

3 As Billy went back to his work he said ominously, "You'd better ask him anyway. You know how he is."

Jody did know. His father, Carl Tiflin, insisted upon giving permission for anything that was done on the ranch, whether it was important or not. Jody sagged farther against the post until he was sitting on the ground. He looked up at the little puffs of wind-driven cloud. "Is it like to rain, Billy?"

"It might. The wind's good for it, but not strong enough."

"Well, I hope it don't rain until after I kill those mice."

Jody turned back and looked at the side-hill where the road from the outside world came down. The hill was washed with lean March sunshine. Silver thistles, blue lupins,[1] and a few poppies bloomed among the sage bushes. Halfway up the hill Jody could see Doubletree Mutt, the black dog, digging in a squirrel hole. He paddled for a while and then paused to kick bursts of dirt out between his hind legs, and he dug with an earnestness which belied the knowledge he must have had that no dog had ever caught a squirrel by digging in a hole.

Suddenly, while Jody watched, the black dog stiffened and backed out of the hole and looked up the hill toward the cleft in the ridge where the road came through. Jody looked up too. For a moment Carl Tiflin on horseback stood out against the pale sky and then he moved down the road toward the house. He carried something white in his hand.

The boy started to his feet. "He's got a letter," Jody cried. He trotted away toward the ranch house, for the letter would probably be read aloud and he wanted to be there. He reached the house before his father did, and ran in. He heard Carl dismount from his creaking saddle and slap the horse on the side to send it to the barn where Billy would unsaddle it and turn it out.

Jody ran into the kitchen. "We got a letter!" he cried.

His mother looked up from a pan of beans. "Who has?"

"Father has. I saw it in his hand."

Carl strode into the kitchen then, and Jody's mother asked, "Who's the letter from, Carl?"

He frowned quickly. "How did you know there was a letter?"

She nodded her head in the boy's direction. "Big-Britches Jody told me."

Jody was embarrassed.

4 His father looked down at him contemptuously. "He *is* getting to be a Big-Britches," Carl said. "He's minding everybody's business but his own. Got his big nose into everything."

Mrs. Tiflin relented a little. "Well, he hasn't enough to keep him busy. Who's the letter from?"

Carl still frowned on Jody. "I'll keep him busy if he isn't careful." He held out a sealed letter. "I guess it's from your father."

Mrs. Tiflin took a hairpin from her head and

1. **lupins** [lo͞o′ pinz]: plants with hand shaped leaves and variously colored flowers.

AT A GLANCE

- When Jody plans a mouse hunt, Billy warns him to get his father's permission.
- Carl Tiflin rides home with a letter from his wife's father.
- He is annoyed when he learns that Jody has told Mrs. Tiflin about the letter.

1 VOCABULARY: DIALECT

Billy's slang expression *lousy with them* reflects his California ranch background and adds a realistic, colorful dimension to the dialogue.

2 POINT OF VIEW

The omniscient narrator's informed perspective affords a sophisticated view of Jody's boyish thoughts and feelings.

3 CHARACTERIZATION

The dialogue between Billy and Jody offers a preview of Carl Tiflin's authoritarian, no-nonsense personality.

4 CHARACTERIZATION

The fact that Carl is contemptuous of his son for such a minor infraction reinforces the impression of Carl given in the dialogue between Billy and Jody.

GUIDED READING

LITERAL QUESTIONS

1a. What does Jody ask when Billy looks up at the clouds? (whether it will rain)

2a. What name does Mrs. Tiflin call Jody in front of Carl? ("Big-Britches Jody")

INFERENTIAL QUESTIONS

1b. What can you conclude about Billy from Jody's question? (He is at home in the outdoors and is considered an authority on the weather.)

2b. What does this name suggest about the way that Jody's mother sees him? (She thinks that he is too forward and presumptuous for a little boy.)

AT A GLANCE

- Mrs. Tiflin reads the letter and announces her father's imminent arrival.
- Carl is upset because he finds the older man's stories repetitious and tedious.
- Mrs. Tiflin defends her father.
- Jody hurries with his chores and volunteers to go to meet Grandfather.

1 DIALOGUE

Note how, through the dialogue, Carl's impatience, his wife's defensive attitude, and Jody's delight project three distinct impressions of Grandfather.

2 THEME

Mrs. Tiflin's loving defense of her father alludes to the frontier spirit and to its later warning after the settlement of the nation.

3 DESCRIPTION

The careful attention to detail and description draws a realistic, contemporary picture of life on the ranch.

slit open the flap. Her lips pursed judiciously. Jody saw her eyes snap back and forth over the lines. "He says," she translated, "he says he's going to drive out Saturday to stay for a little while. Why, this is Saturday. The letter must have been delayed." She looked at the postmark. "This was mailed day before yesterday. It should have been here yesterday." She looked up questioningly at her husband, and then her face darkened angrily. "Now what have you got that look on you for? He doesn't come often."

Carl turned his eyes away from her anger. He could be stern with her most of the time, but when occasionally her temper arose, he could not combat it.

"What's the matter with you?" she demanded again.

In his explanation there was a tone of apology Jody himself might have used. "It's just that he talks," Carl said lamely. "Just talks."

"Well, what of it? You talk yourself."

1 "Sure I do. But your father only talks about one thing."

"Indians!" Jody broke in excitedly. "Indians and crossing the plains!"

Carl turned fiercely on him. "You get out, Mr. Big-Britches! Go on, now! Get out!"

Jody went miserably out the back door and closed the screen with elaborate quietness. Under the kitchen window his shamed, downcast eyes fell upon a curiously shaped stone, a stone of such fascination that he squatted down and picked it up and turned it over in his hands.

The voices came clearly to him through the open kitchen window. "Jody's right," he heard his father say. "Just Indians and crossing the plains. I've heard that story about how the horses got driven off about a thousand times. He just goes on and on, and he never changes a word in the things he tells."

When Mrs. Tiflin answered her tone was so changed that Jody, outside the window, looked up from his study of the stone. Her voice had become soft and explanatory. Jody knew how her face would have changed to match the tone. She said quietly, "Look at it this way, Carl. That was the big thing in my father's life. He led a wagon train clear across the plains to the coast, and when it was finished, his life was done. It was a big thing to do, but it didn't last
2 long enough. Look!" she continued, "it's as though he was born to do that, and after he finished it, there wasn't anything more for him to do but think about it and talk about it. If there'd been any farther west to go, he'd have gone. He's told me so himself. But at last there was the ocean. He lives right by the ocean where he had to stop."

She had caught Carl, caught him and entangled him in her soft tone.

"I've seen him," he agreed quietly. "He goes down and stares off west over the ocean." His voice sharpened a little. "And then he goes up to the Horseshoe Club in Pacific Grove,[2] and he tells people how the Indians drove off the horses."

She tried to catch him again. "Well, it's everything to him. You might be patient with him and pretend to listen."

Carl turned impatiently away. "Well, if it gets too bad, I can always go down to the bunkhouse and sit with Billy," he said irritably. He walked through the house and slammed the front door after him.

Jody ran to his chores. He dumped the grain to the chickens without chasing any of them. He gathered the eggs from the nests. He trotted into the house with the wood and interlaced it so carefully in the woodbox that
3 two armloads seemed to fill it to overflowing.

His mother had finished the beans by now. She stirred up the fire and brushed off the stove top with a turkey wing. Jody peered cautiously at her to see whether any rancor toward him remained. "Is he coming today?" Jody asked.

"That's what his letter said."

"Maybe I better walk up the road to meet him."

Mrs. Tiflin clanged the stove lid shut. "That would be nice," she said. "He'd probably like to be met."

2. **Pacific Grove:** town on central California coast.

GUIDED READING

LITERAL QUESTIONS

1a. Why is Carl upset about Grandfather's visit? (He thinks that Grandfather talks too much about the past.)

2a. Where does Grandfather live? (right by the Pacific Ocean)

INFERENTIAL QUESTIONS

1b. What do you think makes Carl so impatient with Grandfather? (He is too down-to-earth to appreciate what Grandfather represents.)

2b. What do you think the ocean represents to Grandfather? (the literal end of the frontier, an unbridgeable gap between the past and the present)

"I guess I'll just do it then."

1 Outside, Jody whistled shrilly to the dogs. "Come on up the hill," he commanded. The two dogs waved their tails and ran ahead. Along the roadside the sage had tender new tips. Jody tore off some pieces and rubbed them on his hands until the air was filled with the sharp wild smell. With a rush the dogs leaped from the road and yapped into the brush after a rabbit. That was the last Jody saw of them, for when they failed to catch the rabbit, they went back home.

Jody plodded on up the hill toward the ridge top. When he reached the little cleft where the road came through, the afternoon wind struck him and blew up his hair and ruf-
2 fled his shirt. He looked down on the little hills and ridges below and then out at the huge green Salinas Valley.[3] He could see the white town of Salinas far out in the flat and the flash of its windows under the waning sun. Directly below him, in an oak tree, a crow congress had convened. The tree was black with crows all cawing at once.

Then Jody's eyes followed the wagon road down from the ridge where he stood, and lost it behind a hill, and picked it up again on the
3 other side. On that distant stretch he saw a cart slowly pulled by a bay horse. It disappeared behind the hill. Jody sat down on the ground and watched the place where the cart would reappear again. The wind sang on the hilltops and the puffball clouds hurried eastward.

Then the cart came into sight and stopped. A man dressed in black dismounted from the seat and walked to the horse's head. Although it was so far away, Jody knew he had unhooked the checkrein, for the horse's head dropped forward. The horse moved on, and the man walked slowly up the hill beside it. Jody gave a glad cry and ran down the road toward them. The squirrels bumped along off the road, and a road runner flirted its tail and raced over the edge of the hill and sailed out like a glider.

Jody tried to leap into the middle of his shadow at every step. A stone rolled under his foot and he went down. Around a little bend he raced, and there, a short distance ahead, were his grandfather and the cart. The boy dropped from his unseemly running and approached at a dignified walk.

The horse plodded stumble-footed up the hill and the old man walked beside it. In the lowering sun their giant shadows flickered darkly behind them. The grandfather was dressed in a black broadcloth suit and he wore kid congress gaiters[4] and a black tie on a short, hard collar. He carried his black slouch hat[5] in his hand. His white beard was cropped close and his white eyebrows overhung his eyes like mustaches. The blue eyes were sternly merry. About the whole face and figure there was a granite dignity, so that every motion seemed an impossible thing. Once at rest, it seemed the old man would be stone, would never move again. His steps were slow and certain. Once made, no step could ever be retraced; once headed in a direction, the path would never bend nor the pace increase nor slow.

When Jody appeared around the bend, Grandfather waved his hat slowly in welcome, and he called, "Why, Jody! Come down to meet me, have you?"

4 Jody sidled near and turned and matched his step to the old man's step and stiffened his body and dragged his heels a little. "Yes, sir," he said. "We got your letter only today."

"Should have been here yesterday," said Grandfather. "It certainly should. How are all the folks?"

"They're fine, sir." He hesitated and then suggested shyly. "Would you like to come on a mouse hunt tomorrow, sir?"

"Mouse hunt, Jody?" Grandfather chuckled. "Have the people of this generation come down to hunting mice? They aren't very strong,

---

3. **Salinas** [sə lēn′əs] **Valley:** agricultural area in California south of San Francisco.

4. **kid congress gaiters:** old-fashioned ankle-high shoes made from the soft skin of a young goat, with an elastic insert on each side.

5. **slouch hat:** hat with a drooping brim.

AT A GLANCE

- Jody watches Grandfather arrive.
- Jody runs down the hill to meet the dignified elderly man.
- Jody invites Grandfather to join his mouse hunt.

1 DESCRIPTION

The emphasis on action and sensory detail (a shrill whistle, the smell of sage) adds a three-dimensional realism to the narrative.

2 SETTING

Jody's view of the rich California farming valley and the town of Salinas evokes the vastness and grandeur of the landscape and the determined spirit that civilized it.

3 PERSPECTIVE

With clarity and power, Steinbeck's cinematically realistic style draws attention to the relationship between character and landscape; the reader views the story as if it were projected on a giant screen.

4 CHARACTERIZATION

Jody respects his grandfather; and by imitating him, Jody shows that he has chosen him as a role model.

GUIDED READING

LITERAL QUESTIONS

1a. After running down the hill, what does Jody do as he nears Grandfather? (slows and approaches Grandfather at a dignified walk)

2a. Which two words describe Grandfather's steps? (*slow* and *certain*)

INFERENTIAL QUESTIONS

1b. What does Jody's change in pace suggest about his feelings for his grandfather? (He loves and admires him and wants to be like him.)

2b. What does his style of walking suggest about his character? (He has a strong sense of purpose; he seems set in his ways and sure of himself.)

AT A GLANCE

- Grandfather talks with Jody about the mouse hunt, how Jody has grown, and a pig who died on the ranch.
- Carl, Billy, and Mrs. Tiflin gather at the house to greet Grandfather.
- The family and Billy eat dinner.

1 RESPONSE JOURNAL

Ask students to comment upon Grandfather's view of this aspect of the history of the West, based upon the comparison that he suggests to Jody.

2 CHARACTERIZATION

Jody's perception of Grandfather's kindness and respect for personal feelings shows new dimensions of the old man's character.

3 PLOT: RISING ACTION

The gathering of the family and Billy, each of whom has a different view of Grandfather and the frontier past, sharpens the sense of drama and impending conflict.

the new people, but I hardly thought mice would be game for them."

"No, sir. It's just play. The haystack's gone. I'm going to drive out the mice to the dogs. And you can watch, or even beat the hay a little."

The stern, merry eyes turned down on him. "I see. You don't eat them, then. You haven't come to that yet."

Jody explained, "The dogs eat them, sir. It wouldn't be much like hunting Indians, I guess."

1 "No, not much—but then later, when the troops were hunting Indians and shooting children and burning teepees, it wasn't much different from your mouse hunt."

They topped the rise and started down into the ranch cup, and they lost the sun from their shoulders. "You've grown," Grandfather said. "Nearly an inch, I should say."

"More," Jody boasted. "Where they mark me on the door, I'm up more than an inch since Thanksgiving even."

Grandfather's rich throaty voice said, "Maybe you're getting too much water and turning to pith and stalk. Wait until you head out, and then we'll see."

2 Jody looked quickly into the old man's face to see whether his feelings should be hurt, but there was no will to injure, no punishing nor putting-in-your-place light in the keen blue eyes. "We might kill a pig," Jody suggested.

"Oh, no! I couldn't let you do that. You're just humoring me. It isn't the time and you know it."

"You know Riley, the big boar, sir?"

"Yes, I remember Riley well."

"Well, Riley ate a hole into that same haystack, and it fell down on him and smothered him."

"Pigs do that when they can," said Grandfather.

"Riley was a nice pig, for a boar, sir. I rode him sometimes, and he didn't mind."

A door slammed at the house below them, and they saw Jody's mother standing on the porch waving her apron in welcome. And they saw Carl Tiflin walking up from the barn to be at the house for the arrival.

The sun had disappeared from the hills by now. The blue smoke from the house chimney hung in flat layers in the purpling ranch cup. The puffball clouds, dropped by the falling wind, hung listlessly in the sky.

Billy Buck came out of the bunkhouse and flung a wash basin of soapy water on the ground. He had been shaving in midweek, for Billy held Grandfather in reverence, and Grandfather said that Billy was one of the few men of the new generation who had not gone soft. Although Billy was in middle age, Grandfather considered him a boy. Now Billy was hurrying toward the house too.

3 When Jody and Grandfather arrived, the three were waiting for them in front of the yard gate.

Carl said, "Hello, sir. We've been looking for you."

Mrs. Tiflin kissed Grandfather on the side of his beard and stood still while his big hand patted her shoulder. Billy shook hands solemnly, grinning under his straw mustache. "I'll put up your horse," said Billy, and he led the rig away.

Grandfather watched him go, and then, turning back to the group, he said as he had said a hundred times before, "There's a good boy. I knew his father, old Mule-tail Buck. I never knew why they called him Mule-tail except he packed mules."

Mrs. Tiflin turned and led the way into the house. "How long are you going to stay, Father? Your letter didn't say."

"Well, I don't know. I thought I'd stay about two weeks. But I never stay as long as I think I'm going to."

In a short while they were sitting at the white oilcloth table eating their supper. The lamp with the tin reflector hung over the table. Outside the dining-room windows the big moths battered softly against the glass.

Grandfather cut his steak into tiny pieces and chewed slowly. "I'm hungry," he said,

GUIDED READING

LITERAL QUESTION

1a. How does Billy feel about Grandfather? (He reveres him.)

INFERENTIAL QUESTION

1b. How does the admiration of a character such as Billy affect the reader's view of Grandfather? (It suggests that Grandfather is worthy of respect.)

"Driving out here got my appetite up. It's like when we were crossing. We all got so hungry every night we could hardly wait to let the meat get done. I could eat about five pounds of buffalo meat every night."

"It's moving around does it," said Billy. "My father was a government packer. I helped him when I was a kid. Just the two of us could about clean up a deer's ham."[6]

"I knew your father, Billy," said Grandfather. "A fine man he was. They called him Mule-tail Buck. I don't know why except he packed mules."

"That was it," Billy agreed. "He packed mules."

Grandfather put down his knife and fork and looked around the table. "I remember one time we ran out of meat—" His voice dropped to a curious low singsong, dropped into a tonal groove the story had worn for itself. "There was no buffalo, no antelope, not even rabbits. The hunters couldn't even shoot a coyote. That was the time for the leader to be on the watch. I was the leader, and I kept my eyes open. Know why? Well, just the minute the people began to get hungry they'd start slaughtering
1 the team oxen. Do you believe that? I've heard of parties that just ate up their draft cattle. Started from the middle and worked toward the ends. Finally they'd eat the lead pair, and then the wheelers.[7] The leader of a party had to keep them from doing that."

In some manner a big moth got into the room and circled the hanging kerosene lamp. Billy got up and tried to clap it between his hands. Carl struck with a cupped palm and caught the moth and broke it. He walked to the window and dropped it out.

2 "As I was saying," Grandfather began again, but Carl interrupted him. "You'd better eat some more meat. All the rest of us are ready for our pudding."

Jody saw a flash of anger in his mother's eyes. Grandfather picked up his knife and fork.

6. **ham:** hind leg.

7. **wheelers:** cattle harnessed nearest the wheels of a vehicle.

AT A GLANCE

- During dinner Grandfather tells about leading wagon trains out west.
- When Carl interrupts him and tells him to finish eating, Mrs. Tiflin becomes angry.

1 VOCABULARY: DICTION

Grandfather's references to draft cattle, the lead pair, and the wheelers evoke the frontier past and add realism to his own narrative as well as to the larger one.

2 CONFLICT

Carl's rude, patronizing interruption, followed by Mrs. Tiflin's anger, intensifies the sense of conflict and builds dramatic tension.

GUIDED READING

LITERAL QUESTION

1a. According to Grandfather, what did the people do when they got hungry and there were no wild animals to shoot? (They killed the team oxen and the cattle.)

INFERENTIAL QUESTION

1b. What does this detail suggest about what it was like to travel west? (It shows how dangerous and difficult the journey was.)

AT A GLANCE

- After supper Grandfather begins one of his stories.
- Carl says that they have heard it before, but Grandfather, urged on by Jody, tells the story.
- Billy leaves, and Carl tries to turn the conversation by talking about the dry weather.

1 CHARACTERIZATION

Jody's perception of the predictable physical changes that occur as Grandfather stares into the fire provides a graphic, moving picture of how Grandfather surrenders present time to the past.

2 THEME

Jody's compassionate, brave act suggests that all people are faced with choices that permit them to act upon what is best or worst in their natures.

3 POINT OF VIEW

Steinbeck uses the omniscient narrator like the lens of a camera to show images that encompass all the immediate action.

"I'm pretty hungry, all right," he said. "I'll tell you about that later."

When supper was over, when the family and Billy Buck sat in front of the fireplace in the other room, Jody anxiously watched Grand-
1 father. He saw the signs he knew. The bearded head leaned forward; the eyes lost their sternness and looked wonderingly into the fire; the big lean fingers laced themselves on the black knees. "I wonder," he began, "I just wonder whether I ever told you how those thieving Piutes[8] drove off thirty-five of our horses."

"I think you did," Carl interrupted. "Wasn't it just before you went up into the Tahoe[9] country?"

Grandfather turned quickly toward his son-in-law. "That's right. I guess I must have told you that story."

"Lots of times," Carl said cruelly, and he avoided his wife's eyes. But he felt the angry eyes on him, and he said, "Course I'd like to hear it again."

Grandfather looked back at the fire. His fin-
2 gers unlaced and laced again. Jody knew how he felt, how his insides were collapsed and empty. Hadn't Jody been called a Big-Britches that very afternoon? He arose to heroism and opened himself to the term Big-Britches again. "Tell about Indians," he said softly.

Grandfather's eyes grew stern again. "Boys always want to hear about Indians. It was a job for men, but boys want to hear about it. Well, let's see. Did I ever tell you how I wanted each wagon to carry a long iron plate?

Everyone but Jody remained silent. Jody said, "No. You didn't."

"Well, when the Indians attacked, we always put the wagons in a circle and fought from between the wheels. I thought that if every wagon carried a long plate with rifle holes, the men could stand the plates on the outside of the wheels when the wagons were in the circle and they would be protected. It would save lives and that would make up for the extra weight of the iron. But of course the party wouldn't do it. No party had done it before and they couldn't see why they should go to the expense. They lived to regret it, too."

3 Jody looked at his mother and knew from her expression that she was not listening at all. Carl picked at a callus on his thumb and Billy Buck watched a spider crawling up the wall.

Grandfather's tone dropped into its narrative groove again. Jody knew in advance exactly what words would fall. The story droned on, speeded up for the attack, grew sad over the wounds, struck a dirge at the burials on the great plains. Jody sat quietly watching Grandfather. The stern blue eyes were detached. He looked as though he were not very interested in the story himself.

When it was finished, when the pause had been politely respected as the frontier of the story, Billy Buck stood up and stretched and hitched his trousers. "I guess I'll turn in," he said. Then he faced Grandfather. "I've got an old powder horn and a cap and ball pistol down to the bunkhouse. Did I ever show them to you?"

Grandfather nodded slowly. "Yes, I think you did, Billy. Reminds me of a pistol I had when I was leading the people across." Billy stood politely until the little story was done, and then he said, "Good night," and went out of the house.

Carl Tiflin tried to turn the conversation then. "How's the country between here and Monterey?[10] I've heard it's pretty dry."

"It is dry," said Grandfather. "There's not a drop of water in the Laguna Seca.[11] But it's a long pull from '87. The whole country was powder then, and in '61 I believe all the coyotes starved to death. We had fifteen inches of rain this year."

"Yes, but it all came too early. We could do with some now." Carl's eyes fell on Jody. "Hadn't you better be getting to bed?"

8. **Piutes** [pī'ūts]: Indians of the southwestern United States.
9. **Tahoe** [tä'hō]: mountainous area between California and Nevada.
10. **Monterey** [män'tə rā']: city in central California.
11. **Laguna Seca:** Spanish for "dry lagoon."

GUIDED READING

LITERAL QUESTIONS

1a. How does Grandfather look while he is telling his story? (as though he were not very interested himself)

2a. What does Grandfather say when Jody asks him to tell about Indians? ("It was a job for men, but boys want to hear about it.")

INFERENTIAL QUESTIONS

1b. What does Grandfather's detachment from his story suggest? (He is repeating the story mechanically and is unable to recapture the feelings of the past.)

2b. Why would boys have enjoyed hearing about Indians? (because the stories dealt with bold actions and the idea of achieving manhood)

Jody stood up obediently. "Can I kill the mice in the old haystack, sir?"

"Mice? Oh! Sure, kill them all off. Billy said there isn't any good hay left."

Jody exchanged a secret and satisfying look with Grandfather. "I'll kill every one tomorrow," he promised.

Jody lay in his bed and thought of the impossible world of Indians and buffaloes, a
1 world that had ceased to be forever. He wished he could have been living in the heroic time, but he knew he was not of heroic timber. No one living now, save possibly Billy Buck, was worthy to do the things that had been done. A race of giants had lived then, fearless men, men of a staunchness unknown in this day. Jody thought of the wide plains and of the wagons moving across like centipedes. He thought of Grandfather on a huge white horse, marshaling the people. Across his mind marched the great phantoms, and they marched off the earth and they were gone.

He came back to the ranch for a moment,
2 then. He heard the dull rushing sound that space and silence make. He heard one of the dogs, out in the doghouse, scratching a flea and bumping his elbow against the floor with every stroke. Then the wind arose again and the black cypress groaned and Jody went to sleep.

He was up half an hour before the triangle sounded for breakfast. His mother was rattling the stove to make the flames roar when Jody went through the kitchen. "You're up early," she said. "Where are you going?"

"Out to get a good stick. We're going to kill the mice today."

"Who is 'we'?"

"Why, Grandfather and I."

"So you've got him in it. You always like to have someone in with you in case there's blame to share."

"I'll be right back," said Jody. "I just want to have a good stick ready for after breakfast."

He closed the screen door after him and went out into the cool blue morning. The birds were noisy in the dawn and the ranch cats came down from the hill like blunt snakes. They had been hunting gophers in the dark, and although the four cats were full of gopher meat, they sat in a semicircle at the back door and mewed piteously for milk. Doubletree Mutt and Smasher moved sniffing along the edge of the brush, performing the duty with rigid ceremony, but when Jody whistled, their heads jerked up and their tails waved. They plunged down to him, wriggling their skins and yawning. Jody patted their heads seriously and
3 moved on to the weathered scrap pile. He selected an old broom handle and a short piece of inch-square scrap wood. From his pocket he took a shoelace and tied the ends of the sticks loosely together to make a flail. He whistled his new weapon through the air and struck the ground experimentally, while the dogs leaped aside and whined with apprehension.

Jody turned and started down past the house toward the old haystack ground to look over the field of slaughter, but Billy Buck, sitting patiently on the back steps, called to him, "You better come back. It's only a couple of minutes till breakfast."

Jody changed his course and moved toward the house. He leaned his flail against the steps. "That's to drive the mice out," he said. "I'll bet they're fat, I'll bet they don't know what's going to happen to them today."

"No, nor you either," Billy remarked philosophically, "nor me, nor anyone."

Jody was staggered by this thought. He knew it was true. His imagination twitched away from the mouse hunt. Then his mother came out on the back porch and struck the triangle, and all thoughts fell in a heap.

Grandfather hadn't appeared at the table when they sat down. Billy nodded at his empty chair. "He's all right? He isn't sick?"

"He takes a long time to dress," said Mrs. Tiflin. "He combs his whiskers and rubs up his shoes and brushes his clothes."

Carl scattered sugar on his mush. "A man that's led a wagon train across the plains has got to be pretty careful how he dresses."

Mrs. Tiflin turned on him. "Don't do that,

AT A GLANCE

- In bed Jody mourns the loss of the frontier.
- The next morning Jody prepares a weapon for the mouse hunt.
- Everyone but Grandfather gathers at the table for breakfast.

1 THEME

Influenced by Grandfather's stories, Jody's vision of the American frontier is tinged with sadness and a deep sense of loss because the country no longer accommodates such challenges.

2 POINT OF VIEW

The omniscient narrator's articulate expression of Jody's thoughts and impressions shifts the focus from the past to the present.

3 DESCRIPTION

The careful attention to physical detail and the emphasis on sensory impressions contribute realism.

GUIDED READING

LITERAL QUESTIONS

1a. When does Jody wish he could have lived? ("in the heroic time")

2a. What does Carl say to explain why Grandfather is late for breakfast? (that a man who has led a wagon train needs to be careful about how he dresses)

INFERENTIAL QUESTIONS

1b. What does Jody's wish suggest about life in the present? (It fails to offer the same possibility for heroism, bravery, or adventure.)

2b. What does Carl's comment show about his feelings about Grandfather? (He has little respect for him; he is annoyed by the old man's perpetuating the past.)

AT A GLANCE

- When Grandfather overhears Carl say that the frontier days should be forgotten, Carl apologizes in shame.
- Grandfather, upset that Carl might be right, stays home while Jody goes on the mouse hunt.
- Jody returns early, and Grandfather explains why he feels bad.

1 PLOT: CLIMAX

Grandfather's overhearing Carl is the turning point of the story. Grandfather must come to grips with the past, and Carl is forced to face the consequences of his insensitive behavior.

2 CHARACTERIZATION

Carl's surprisingly contrite behavior demonstrates a softer, more sensitive aspect of his character.

3 STYLE: DESCRIPTION

The appeal to the senses of sight, sound, smell, and touch enhances the realism and immediacy of the setting.

4 THEME

Grandfather values the power to evoke the frontier spirit and animate people with a wondrous sense of it.

Carl! Please don't!" There was more of threat than of request in her tone. And the threat irritated Carl.

"Well, how many times do I have to listen to the story of the iron plates, and the thirty-five horses? That time's done. Why can't he forget it, now it's done?" He grew angrier while he talked and his voice rose. "Why does he have to tell them over and over? He came across the plains. All right! Now it's finished. Nobody wants to hear about it over and over."

The door into the kitchen closed softly. The four at the table sat frozen. Carl laid his mush spoon on the table and touched his chin with his fingers.

Then the kitchen door opened and Grandfather walked in. His mouth smiled tightly and his eyes squinted. "Good morning," he said, and he sat down and looked at his mush dish.

1 Carl could not leave it there. "Did—did you hear what I said?"

Grandfather jerked a little nod.

"I don't know what got into me, sir. I didn't mean it. I was just being funny."

Jody glanced in shame at his mother, and he saw that she was looking at Carl, and that she wasn't breathing. It was an awful thing that he was doing. He was tearing himself to pieces to talk like that. It was a terrible thing to him to retract a word, but to retract it in shame was infinitely worse.

Grandfather looked sidewise. "I'm trying to get right side up," he said gently. "I'm not being mad. I don't mind what you said, but it might be true, and I would mind that."

2 "It isn't true," said Carl. "I'm not feeling well this morning. I'm sorry I said it."

"Don't be sorry, Carl. An old man doesn't see things sometimes. Maybe you're right. The crossing is finished. Maybe it should be forgotten, now it's done."

Carl got up from the table. "I've had enough to eat. I'm going to work. Take your time, Billy!" He walked quickly out of the dining room. Billy gulped the rest of his food and followed soon after. But Jody could not leave his chair.

"Won't you tell any more stories?" Jody asked.

"Why, sure I'll tell them, but only when—I'm sure people want to hear them."

"I like to hear them, sir."

"Oh! Of course you do, but you're a little boy. It was a job for men, but only little boys like to hear about it."

Jody got up from his place. "I'll wait outside for you, sir. I've got a good stick for those mice."

He waited by the gate until the old man came out on the porch. "Let's go down and kill the mice now," Jody called.

"I think I'll just sit in the sun, Jody. You go kill the mice."

"You can use my stick if you like."

"No, I'll just sit here a while."

Jody turned disconsolately away and walked down toward the old haystack. He tried to whip up his enthusiasm with thoughts of the fat juicy mice. He beat the ground with his flail. The dogs coaxed and whined about him, but he could not go. Back at the house he could see Grandfather sitting on the porch, looking small and thin and black.

Jody gave up and went to sit on the steps at the old man's feet.

"Back already? Did you kill the mice?"

"No, sir. I'll kill them some other day."

3 The morning flies buzzed close to the ground and the ants dashed about in front of the steps. The heavy smell of sage slipped down the hill. The porch boards grew warm in the sunshine.

Jody hardly knew when Grandfather started to talk. "I shouldn't stay here, feeling the way I do." He examined his strong old hands. "I feel as though the crossing wasn't worth doing." His eyes moved up the sidehill and stopped on a motionless hawk perched on a
4 dead limb. "I tell those old stories, but they're not what I want to tell. I only know how I want people to feel when I tell them.

"It wasn't Indians that were important, nor adventures, nor even getting out here. It was a whole bunch of people made into one big

GUIDED READING

LITERAL QUESTIONS

1a. In the eyes of Jody's mother, what does Carl do that tears him to pieces? (He takes back, in shame, something that he has just said.)

2a. What does Grandfather mind about what Carl says about the past? (that it may be true that the past is over and nobody wants to hear about it)

INFERENTIAL QUESTIONS

1b. In what way is Carl's apology a noble or heroic action? (He puts someone else's feelings above his own.)

2b. What would Carl's being right about the past suggest about Grandfather's life? (that what Grandfather did served no larger purpose and that his importance, like the past, is over)

crawling beast. And I was the head. It was
1 westering[12] and westering. Every man wanted something for himself, but the big beast that was all of them wanted only westering. I was the leader, but if I hadn't been there, someone else would have been the head. The thing had to have a head.

"Under the little bushes the shadows were black at white noonday. When we saw the mountains at last, we cried—all of us. But it wasn't getting here that mattered, it was movement and westering.

"We carried life out here and set it down the way those ants carry eggs. And I was the leader. The westering was as big as God, and the slow steps that made the movement piled up and piled up until the continent was crossed.

"Then we came down to the sea, and it was done." He stopped and wiped his eyes until the rims were red. "That's what I should be telling instead of stories."

When Jody spoke, Grandfather started and looked down at him. "Maybe I could lead the people some day," Jody said.

12. **westering:** moving west.

The old man smiled. "There's no place to go. There's the ocean to stop you. There's a line of old men along the shore hating the ocean because it stopped them."

"In boats I might, sir."

"No place to go, Jody. Every place is taken. But that's not the worst—no, not the worst. Westering has died out of the people. Westering isn't a hunger any more. It's all done. Your father is right. It is finished." He laced his fingers on his knee and looked at them.

2 Jody felt very sad. "If you'd like a glass of lemonade I could make it for you."

Grandfather was about to refuse, and then he saw Jody's face. "That would be nice," he said. "Yes, it would be nice to drink lemonade."

Jody ran into the kitchen where his mother was wiping the last of the breakfast dishes. "Can I have a lemon to make a lemonade for Grandfather?"

His mother mimicked—"And another lemon to make a lemonade for you."

"No, ma'am. I don't want one."

"Jody! You're sick!" Then she stopped suddenly. "Take a lemon out of the cooler," she said softly. "Here, I'll reach the squeezer down to you."

AT A GLANCE

- Grandfather describes the feelings of the frontier days.
- He says that the westering spirit has died out.
- Jody makes Grandfather a glass of lemonade.

1 FIGURATIVE LANGUAGE: METAPHOR

Comparing the long procession of wagon trains to a big beast conveys the enormous, elemental energy that drove settlers on their quests.

2 CHARACTERIZATION

Grandfather matches Jody's sensitivity and love by accepting the boy's offer to make him lemonade. He understands Jody's need to make him feel better.

REFLECTING ON THE STORY

Would you conclude that Steinbeck feels "westering" is indeed extinct? (No; Jody has the values and goals that make similar achievements possible.)

GUIDED READING

LITERAL QUESTION

1a. What does Grandfather say when Jody asks if he, Jody, could lead the people someday? (that there is no longer any place to take them and that the ocean will stop him)

INFERENTIAL QUESTION

1b. What does Grandfather's comment suggest about his own sense of purpose? (that it died with the past)

STUDY QUESTIONS

1. comes out of house, scuffs shoes, throws stone at pigeons; kill mice
2. Grandfather talks too much; Indians, crossing plains; that was the big thing in his life
3. blue, "sternly merry"; granite dignity; slow, certain
4. mouse hunt; will to injure
5. no one wants to hear stories; must retract words in shame; tell stories without being asked
6. no; abandon hunt, sit with him
7. many people "made into one big crawling beast. And I was the head"; life; "There's no place to go."
8. solid, dignified, purposeful; idealistic, pragmatic, proud to be leader; no
9. cares for him, welcomes his company; moved by his grief and dignity, feels closer to him
10. *beginning:* restless, bored, selfish desire to kill mice; *end:* interested in Grandfather, selfless, caring; mouse hunting childish compared with selfless giving
11. people lost pioneering spirit, life dull, not grand; Great Depression: personal survival foremost, not adventure

VIEWPOINT

realizes essential truth of his life, the times, accepts knowledge with dignity; Jody changes from restless, aggressive boy to wiser, more compassionate one

STUDY QUESTIONS

Recalling

1. What are Jody's first three actions in the story? Now that most of the good hay is gone, what project does Jody decide to undertake?
2. What is Carl Tiflin's "lame" reason for not being pleased to learn of his father-in-law's plans to visit? According to Jody and his father, what does Jody's grandfather talk about all the time? Why does he talk about it, according to Mrs. Tiflin?
3. How are Grandfather's eyes described when Jody goes out to meet him? What is there "about his old face and figure"? What sort of steps does he take?
4. In what adventure does Jody invite his grandfather to participate? When, in his first conversation with Grandfather, Jody wonders if the old man has insulted him, what does he *not* detect in Grandfather's eyes?
5. What does Grandfather overhear his son-in-law saying about him the next morning? Why does Jody consider his father's apology "a terrible thing" for him? What does Grandfather decide he will not do anymore?
6. Does Grandfather join Jody on the mouse hunt? What does Jody decide to do after seeing Grandfather on the porch "looking small and thin and black"?
7. In his final conversation with Jody, what does Grandfather say was important about his adventures leading the wagon train? What does he say the wagon train carried out west? How does he answer when Jody says that he might "lead the people some day"?

Interpreting

8. What does the initial description of Grandfather reveal about his character and personality? What do the final paragraphs of the story suggest about his ideals and spirit? Does Carl Tiflin share his ideals?
9. What do Jody's reaction to the news of his grandfather's visit and his behavior in greeting his grandfather reveal about his feelings toward the old man? How do his feelings deepen by the story's end?
10. How do Jody's last actions in the story differ from his first? Why does he lose interest in his mouse-hunting project?

Extending

11. What, basically, is Grandfather's evaluation of "modern" life in the final paragraphs? Why would such an evaluation be particularly understandable in a story written during the Great Depression?

VIEWPOINT

Joseph Warren Beach, in noting Steinbeck's faith in human nature, writes:

> He is one who feels strongly on the subject of man's essential dignity of spirit and his unexhausted possibilities for modification and improvement.
>
> —*American Fiction 1920–1940*

■ In what sense is Grandfather's dignity maintained at the end of "The Leader of the People" despite the fact that his spirit seems broken? Which other characters modify their behavior in the story, and why are their changes improvements?

LITERARY FOCUS

Characterization

John Steinbeck is considered a master at creating believable, compelling, and memorable characters in his short stories and novels. To do so, he uses many methods of characterization (see page 512), both direct and indirect.

Consider, for example, his characterization of Grandfather. Steinbeck makes a direct statement by referring to him in the title as "the leader of the people." He presents a detailed physical description when Jody sees him, first from a distance, and then closer up. He tells what Carl Tiflin, Mrs. Tiflin, and Billy Buck all think of him. He shows him in action after his arrival. And, in the end, he lets Grandfather speak for himself and reveal his innermost thoughts. As a consequence of this subtle and varied characterization, we not only become familiar with Grandfather but in the end come to appreciate, sympathize with, and perhaps even admire him.

Steinbeck also gives us indirect information about Grandfather by creating a foil for him in the character of Carl Tiflin. A **foil** is a character who, through contrast, underscores the characteristics of another character. Carl Tiflin is almost the exact opposite of Grandfather: He is a practical man living in the present, abrupt, sometimes even unkind. As we note the differences between Grandfather and his son-in-law, we understand Grandfather's character better and appreciate those virtues that Carl Tiflin lacks.

Thinking About Characterization

1. Look closely at another character in "The Leader of the People." What methods of characterization does Steinbeck use in creating and developing the character? Does the character seem as well-developed as Grandfather? Why or why not?
2. What other character foils have you encountered in your reading, and in what way are they foils? For example, how is Hurry Harry a foil for Cooper's Deerslayer (page 115)?

VOCABULARY

Antonyms

Antonyms are words that have opposite or nearly opposite meanings. The following words in capitals are from "The Leader of the People." Choose the word that is an antonym of each word in capitals, *as the word is used in this selection.* Write the number of each item and the letter of your choice on a separate sheet.

1. IMMUNE: (a) witty (b) serious (c) vulnerable (d) resistant
2. RETRACT: (a) annoy (b) admit (c) survive (d) lessen
3. BELIED: (a) confirmed (b) denied (c) contradicted (d) behaved
4. DISCONSOLATELY: (a) madly (b) immensely (c) eagerly (d) sorrowfully
5. OVERBEARING: (a) meek (b) fond (c) domineering (d) exhausted

COMPOSITION

Analyzing Theme Through Character

■ The theme of a story is often revealed through character—what a character thinks, says, does, or represents. Write an essay in which you analyze the theme of "The Leader of the People" by looking at its characters. Begin with a statement of the theme in your own words. Then support your statement with examples from what characters in the story do and say. Conclude with examples from the grandfather's final long speech. *For help with this assignment, refer to Lesson 6 in the Writing About Literature Handbook at the back of this book.*

Creating a Character Foil

■ Choose one of the characters who appear in this book—Granny Weatherall (page 576) perhaps, or Roderick Usher (page 135)—and make a list of his or her strengths and weaknesses. Then, in a second column, list qualities that contrast with the strengths and weaknesses you have listed. From your second list write a short portrait of a character who is a foil for the character you chose. In creating your foil, you may wish to examine the six methods of characterization described in the Literary Focus on page 512.

LITERARY FOCUS

1. Jody: dynamic character developed through action, but also through dialogue and by revealing his thoughts; only Jody: other characters are static
2. narrator of "The Hack Driver" plays city slicker in contrast to Lutkin, the country rube; Hurry Harry is undisciplined, boastful, ignoble in contrast to noble Deerslayer

VOCABULARY

1. IMMUNE (c) vulnerable
2. RETRACT (b) admit
3. BELIED (a) confirmed
4. DISCONSOLATELY (c) eagerly
5. OVERBEARING (a) meek

COMPOSITION: GUIDELINES FOR EVALUATION

ANALYZING THEME THROUGH CHARACTER

Objective

To show how characters are used to reveal theme

Guidelines for Evaluation

- suggested length: six to eight paragraphs
- should state theme of story
- should cite examples of Grandfather's, Jody's, and Carl's words, thoughts, and actions and explain how they relate to the theme
- should cite Grandfather's long speech

CREATING A CHARACTER FOIL

Objective

To create a character foil

Guidelines for Evaluation

- suggested length: three to four paragraphs
- should describe a character that is a foil for another character
- should show understanding of first character
- should vary methods of characterization: direct statement, description, action, speech

Thomas Wolfe *1900–1938*

Almost everything about Thomas Wolfe was larger than life. He was six feet five inches tall, powerfully built, with dark, intense eyes, untidy black hair, and a wide mouth. He was enormously energetic, and he possessed the gift of total recall. He had a tremendous appetite for sensory and physical experience, which he once admitted was an "intemperate excess, an almost insane hunger." As a writer, Wolfe worked with uncontrollable, maniacal drive: He did not so much compose his stories and novels as pour them out in endless waves of images, descriptions, and remembrances. It is not surprising that his published work is uneven: Amid long stretches of unpolished writing, there appear passages of extraordinary beauty, clarity, and lyrical power.

Wolfe grew up in North Carolina. His father was a stonecutter, gifted with a vast and well-stocked memory and a love of poetry as well. Wolfe was first determined to become a playwright, but his efforts were largely ignored, and he soon turned to fiction. In 1924 he began teaching English to make a living, and in the same year started what was to become his famous first novel, *Look Homeward, Angel.* The novel was a success, and it also marked the beginning of his fruitful association with the great editor Maxwell Perkins, who had helped Wolfe shape his massive manuscripts into finished work. Both *Of Time and the River,* his second novel, and *From Death to Morning,* a collection of short stories, appeared in 1935. Three years later, Wolfe died after he had begun work on his fourth novel.

"The Far and the Near" exemplifies Wolfe's gifts as a writer: his strong sense of place, his ability to render sensory perception persuasively, and his profound awareness of the fragility of human experience.

■ Is it possible to get too near to the truth? Should some things be seen *only* from far away?

Stone City, Iowa, Grant Wood, 1930.

Thomas Wolfe

The Far and the Near

1 On the outskirts of a little town upon a rise of land that swept back from the railway there was a tidy little cottage of white boards, trimmed vividly with green blinds. To one side of the house there was a garden neatly patterned with plots of growing vegetables, and an arbor[1] for the grapes which ripened late in August. Before the house there were three mighty oaks which sheltered it in their clean and massive shade in summer, and to the other side there was a border of gay flowers. The whole place had an air of tidiness, thrift, and modest comfort.

Every day, a few minutes after two o'clock in the afternoon, the limited express between the two cities passed this spot. At that moment the great train, having halted for a breathing space at the town nearby, was beginning to lengthen evenly into its stroke, but it had not yet reached the full drive of its terrific speed.
2 It swung into view deliberately, swept past with a powerful swaying motion of the engine, a low smooth rumble of its heavy cars upon pressed steel, and then it vanished in the cut. For a moment the progress of the engine could be marked by heavy bellowing puffs of smoke that burst at spaced intervals above the edges of the meadow grass, and finally nothing could be heard but the solid clacking tempo of the wheels receding into the drowsy stillness of the afternoon.

Every day for more than twenty years, as the train approached this house, the engineer had blown on the whistle, and every day, as
3 soon as she heard this signal, a woman had appeared on the back porch of the little house and waved to him. At first she had a small child clinging to her skirts, and now this child had grown to full womanhood, and every day she, too, came with her mother to the porch and waved.

The engineer had grown old and gray in service. He had driven his great train, loaded with its weight of lives, across the land ten
4 thousand times. His own children had grown up and married, and four times he had seen before him on the tracks the ghastly dot of tragedy converging like a cannon ball to its eclipse of horror at the boiler head[2]—a light spring wagon filled with children, with its clustered row of small stunned faces; a cheap automobile

1. **arbor:** open-work lattice structure, usually shady and covered with vines.

2. **boiler head:** front section of a steam locomotive.

GUIDED READING

LITERAL QUESTIONS

1a. What stands to one side of the house? (a neatly patterned vegetable garden and a grape arbor)

2a. What has the engineer seen in front of him four times on the track? (people about to be struck by his engine)

INFERENTIAL QUESTIONS

1b. What do these details suggest about the inhabitants of the house? (that they are productive and nurturing)

2b. What can you infer about the engineer's life from this information? (that it has been difficult; marked by tragedy, guilt, and grief)

AT A GLANCE

- Daily at two o'clock, a train passes a small, tidy cottage.
- For years, when the engineer has blown his whistle, a woman and her daughter have come to the porch and waved.
- The engineer has seen four tragic accidents on the track.

LITERARY OPTIONS

- description
- point of view

THEMATIC OPTIONS

- the importance of perspective
- the value of the past

1 SETTING

The absence of physical or geographical details about the town contrasts with the vivid details used to describe the house, suggesting that this story could happen any time, in any home.

2 DESCRIPTION

The sensuous, lyrical style develops from attention to sensory details (especially sounds, as in *low smooth rumble*) and from the power of the long, majestic, descriptive sentences.

3 CHARACTERIZATION

The absence of specific descriptive details establishes the woman and child as flat characters rather than as fully realized, three-dimensional human beings.

4 POINT OF VIEW

The third-person narrator's broad, mature perspective and poetic use of language give the engineer's impressions cohesion and dignity.

AT A GLANCE

- The engineer has known joy, grief, danger and hard work.
- Because the vision of the two women has meant so much to him, he goes to visit them when he retires.
- The town, the house, and the woman who answers the door seem disquietingly different.

1 STYLE: REPETITION/ PARALLELISM

Wolfe uses repetition *(he had seen them)* and parallel structure to intensify the effect that the women have on the engineer's imagination.

2 THEME

The confusion and perplexity that the engineer feels develop from the new, more intimate perspective with which he views the streets and the question that it poses about his past perceptions.

3 POINT OF VIEW

The voice of the third-person narrator conveys the immediacy of the engineer's feelings while adding perspective to his experiences.

stalled upon the tracks, set with the wooden figures of people paralyzed with fear; a battered hobo walking by the rail, too deaf and old to hear the whistle's warning; and a form flung past his window with a scream—all this the man had seen and known. He had known all the grief, the joy, the peril, and the labor such a man could know; he had grown seamed and weathered in his loyal service, and now, schooled by the qualities of faith and courage and humbleness that attended his labor, he had grown old, and had the grandeur and the wisdom these men have.

But no matter what peril or tragedy he had known, the vision of the little house and the women waving to him with a brave free motion of the arm had become fixed in the mind of the engineer as something beautiful and enduring, something beyond all change and ruin, and something that would always be the same, no matter what mishap, grief, or error might break the iron schedule of his days.

The sight of the little house and of these two women gave him the most extraordinary
1 happiness he had ever known. He had seen them in a thousand lights, a hundred weathers. He had seen them through the harsh bare light of wintry gray across the brown and frosted stubble of earth, and he had seen them again in the green luring sorcery of April.

He felt for them and for the little house in which they lived such tenderness as a man might feel for his own children, and at length the picture of their lives was carved so sharply in his heart that he felt that he knew their lives completely, to every hour and moment of the day, and he resolved that one day, when his years of service should be ended, he would go and find these people and speak at last with them whose lives had been so wrought[3] into his own.

That day came. At last the engineer stepped from a train onto the station platform of the town where these two women lived. His years upon the rail had ended. He was a pensioned servant of his company, with no more work to do. The engineer walked slowly through the station and out into the streets of the town. Everything was as strange to him as if he had never seen this town before. As he walked on, his sense of bewilderment and confusion grew.
2 Could this be the town he had passed ten thousand times? Were these the same houses he had seen so often from the high windows of his cab? It was all as unfamiliar, as disquieting as a city in a dream, and the perplexity of his spirit increased as he went on.

Presently the houses thinned into the straggling outposts of the town, and the street faded into a country road—the one on which the women lived. And the man plodded on slowly in the heat and dust. At length he stood before the house he sought. He knew at once that he had found the proper place. He saw the lordly oaks before the house, the flower beds, the garden, and the arbor, and farther off, the glint of rails.

Yes, this was the house he sought, the place he had passed so many times, the destination
3 he had longed for with such happiness. But now that he had found it, now that he was here, why did his hand falter on the gate; why had the town, the road, the earth, the very entrance to this place he loved turned unfamiliar as the landscape of some ugly dream? Why did he now feel this sense of confusion, doubt, and hopelessness?

At length he entered by the gate, walked slowly up the path and in a moment more had mounted three short steps that led up to the porch, and was knocking at the door. Presently he heard steps in the hall, the door was opened, and a woman stood facing him.

And instantly, with a sense of bitter loss and grief, he was sorry he had come. He knew at once that the woman who stood there looking at him with a mistrustful eye was the same woman who had waved to him so many thousand times. But her face was harsh and pinched and meager; the flesh sagged wearily in sallow[4]

3. **wrought:** formed; shaped.

4. **sallow:** sickly, yellowish.

GUIDED READING

LITERAL QUESTIONS

1a. What had become fixed in the engineer's mind as something beyond change? (his vision of the house and the two women waving)

2a. What causes the engineer to feel a sense of loss and grief? (the mistrusting eye and harsh, pinched face of the woman)

INFERENTIAL QUESTIONS

1b. What do you think has made it possible for the engineer to believe that the house and women would never change? (He sees them only from a distance and keeps them alive in his imagination.)

2b. What does the engineer lose with bitterness? (the sustaining power of his former view)

folds, and the small eyes peered at him with timid suspicion and uneasy doubt. All the brave freedom, the warmth, and the affection that he had read into her gesture vanished in the moment that he saw her and heard her unfriendly tongue.

And now his own voice sounded unreal and ghastly to him as he tried to explain his presence, to tell her who he was and the reason he had come. But he faltered on, fighting stubbornly against the horror of regret, confusion, disbelief that surged up in his spirit, drowning all his former joy and making his act of hope and tenderness seem shameful to him.

At length the woman invited him almost unwillingly into the house, and called her daughter in a harsh shrill voice. Then, for a brief agony of time, the man sat in an ugly little parlor, and he tried to talk while the two women stared at him with a dull, bewildered hostility, a sullen, timorous restraint.

And finally, stammering a crude farewell, he departed. He walked away down the path and then along the road toward town, and suddenly
1 he knew that he was an old man. His heart, which had been brave and confident when he looked along the familiar vista of the rails, was now sick with doubt and horror as it saw the strange and unsuspected visage of an earth which had always been within a stone's throw of him, and which he had never seen or known. And he knew that all the magic of that bright lost way, the vista of that shining line, the imagined corner of that small good universe of hope's desire, was gone forever, could never be got back again.

STUDY QUESTIONS

Recalling

1. What words and phrases describe the little cottage in the opening paragraph? Whom does the engineer see every day for more than twenty years when his train passes the little cottage?
2. What has the engineer known in his twenty years of service with the railroad, according to the fourth paragraph? According to the fifth paragraph, what "vision" counteracts each peril or tragedy he has known? What does he resolve in the seventh paragraph?
3. When the engineer at last visits the little cottage, what sort of woman stands looking at him? What vanishes in the moment he sees her and hears her unfriendly tongue? How does the woman invite him into the cottage, according to the next-to-last paragraph?
4. What does the engineer know about himself as he leaves the cottage in the final paragraph?

Interpreting

5. What did the engineer's mind do to the little cottage and its inhabitants for all the years he saw them?
6. Why might the engineer have placed so much importance on his vision? Why would he feel old after his vision is destroyed?
7. What is the significance of the story's title?

Extending

8. Do you think the engineer should have visited the cottage? In his place, would you have done so? Explain your answers.

COMPOSITION

Writing a Comparison/Contrast

■ Compare and contrast the engineer's vision of the little house and its inhabitants, seen every day from his passing train, with his actual closeup encounter with them after his years of service on the train are over. In what ways does the reality fall short of the vision?

Writing an Advertisement

■ Suppose the little house were for sale. Write an ad appealing to the tastes of someone like the engineer, someone who has worked hard all his life and is now seeking to purchase a retirement home with his savings. Use vivid language and persuasive adjectives.

AT A GLANCE

- The women turn out to be suspicious and unwelcoming.
- The engineer has an awkward visit with the women.
- He leaves the house, feeling that a magic part of his life has been lost forever.

1 THEME

The value of the past and the engineer's sense of self both diminish when he realizes that his perceptions were flawed by the limitations of his perspective.

REFLECTING ON THE STORY

How do setting and characterization contribute to the meaning of the story? (generalized setting and representational characters suggest universal need to see enduring value in the world)

STUDY QUESTIONS

1. tidy, of white boards, mighty oaks; woman and her daughter
2. grief, joy, peril; house, women; to visit them
3. mistrustful, face harsh, flesh sags; brave freedom, warmth, affection he had read into her; almost unwillingly
4. he is old, magic of world he saw from cab is gone forever
5. romanticized them
6. symbol of security, domestic tranquility; much of what he saw, thought is false; no longer has goals, purpose
7. *from afar:* house and women beautiful; *up close:* ugly
8. two possibilities: better off facing truth, should have visited cottage sooner; should have stayed away, kept idealized vision

COMPOSITION: GUIDELINES FOR EVALUATION

WRITING A COMPARISON/CONTRAST

Objective

To compare and contrast an illusion with reality

Guidelines for Evaluation

- suggested length: tnree to five paragraphs
- should contrast the two visions
- should contrast woman from afar and close up
- should show that reality contradicts vision
- should contrast elation with disillusionment
- should say reality sustains less than illusion

WRITING AN ADVERTISEMENT

Objective

To write an advertisement for a house

Guidelines for Evaluation

- suggested length: one paragraph
- should give a physical description of the house that agrees with that in the story
- should use vivid and persuasive language
- should address an audience of people like the engineer

AT A GLANCE

- In his mind the narrator is watching a movie that takes place on Sunday, June 12, 1909.
- In the movie the narrator's father walks down the streets of Brooklyn on his way to court the narrator's mother.

LITERARY OPTIONS

- point of view
- characterization

THEMATIC OPTIONS

- personal responsibility
- reality vs. fantasy

1 SETTING

By imagining himself in a movie theater watching a silent film, the narrator establishes two time frames simultaneously: the present, when he views the faded, poor-quality movie; and the past, which is shown in that movie.

2 POINT OF VIEW

The frame story allows the narrator to share the feelings he has in the present and then offer, like the running commentary on a sound track, his special perspective on the main characters (his parents) in the film.

© Rollie McKenna

Delmore Schwartz *1913–1966*

Delmore Schwartz was born in Brooklyn, New York. He attended the University of Wisconsin, New York University, and Harvard. He later taught at several universities, including Harvard, Princeton, and the University of Chicago, and he served as editor for the important periodicals *Partisan Review* and *The New Republic.*

Schwartz was primarily a poet and a literary critic, but he also wrote short stories and plays. In 1960 he was awarded the prestigious Bollingen Prize for poetry for his collection *Summer Knowledge.*

"In Dreams Begin Responsibilities" is the title story of Schwartz's first important book, published in 1938.

■ When do we become adults? Does that moment involve responsibility? How does this character realize what becoming an adult means?

Delmore Schwartz

In Dreams Begin Responsibilities

I

I think it is the year 1909. I feel as if I were in a motion picture theater, the long arm of light crossing the darkness and spinning, my
1 eyes fixed on the screen. This is a silent picture as if an old Biograph[1] one, in which the actors are dressed in ridiculously old-fashioned clothes, and one flash succeeds another with sudden jumps. The actors too seem to jump about and walk too fast. The shots themselves are full of dots and rays, as if it were raining when the picture was photographed. The light is bad.

It is Sunday afternoon, June 12th, 1909, and my father is walking down the quiet streets of Brooklyn on his way to visit my mother. His clothes are newly pressed and his tie is too
2 tight in his high collar. He jingles the coins in his pockets, thinking of the witty things he will say. I feel as if I had by now relaxed entirely in the soft darkness of the theater; the organist peals out the obvious and approximate emotions on which the audience rocks unknowingly. I am anonymous, and I have forgotten myself. It is always so when one goes to the movies, it is, as they say, a drug.

My father walks from street to street of trees, lawns and houses, once in a while coming to an avenue on which a streetcar skates and gnaws, slowly progressing. The conductor, who has a handlebar mustache, helps a young lady wearing a hat like a bowl with feathers on to the car. She lifts her long skirts slightly as she mounts the steps. He leisurely makes change and rings his bell. It is obviously Sunday, for everyone is wearing Sunday clothes,

1. **Biograph:** company that produced films in the early 1900s.

GUIDED READING

LITERAL QUESTION

1a. How does the narrator describe the visual quality of the film he is watching? (The actors seem to jump and walk too fast; the shots are full of dots and rays; the light is bad.)

INFERENTIAL QUESTION

1b. What does the poor visual quality suggest about the nature of memory? (Memory is faulty; it cannot recall the past as it actually happened.)

and the streetcar's noises emphasize the quiet of the holiday. Is not Brooklyn the City of Churches? The shops are closed and their shades drawn, but for an occasional stationery store or drugstore with great green balls in the window.

My father has chosen to take this long walk because he likes to walk and think. He thinks about himself in the future and so arrives at the place he is to visit in a state of mild exaltation. He pays no attention to the houses he is passing, in which the Sunday dinner is being eaten, nor to the many trees which patrol each street, now coming to their full leafage and the time when they will room the whole street in cool shadow. An occasional carriage passes, the horse's hooves falling like stones in the quiet afternoon, and once in a while an automobile, looking like an enormous upholstered sofa, puffs and passes.

1 My father thinks of my mother, of how nice it will be to introduce her to his family. But he is not yet sure that he wants to marry her, and once in a while he becomes panicky about the bond already established. He reassures himself by thinking of the big men he admires who are married: William Randolph Hearst,[2] and William Howard Taft, who has just become President of the United States.

My father arrives at my mother's house. He has come too early and so is suddenly embar-
2 rassed. My aunt, my mother's sister, answers the loud bell with her napkin in her hand, for the family is still at dinner. As my father enters, my grandfather rises from the table and shakes hands with him. My mother has run upstairs to tidy herself. My grandmother asks my father if he has had dinner, and tells him that Rose will be downstairs soon. My grandfather opens the conversation by remarking on the mild June weather. My father sits uncomfortably near the table, holding his hat in his hand. My grandmother tells my aunt to take my father's hat. My uncle, twelve years old, runs into the house, his hair tousled. He shouts a greeting to my father, who has often given him a nickel, and then runs upstairs. It is evident that the respect in which my father is held in this household is tempered by a good deal of mirth. He is impressive, yet he is very awkward.

II

Finally my mother comes downstairs, all dressed up, and my father being engaged in conversation with my grandfather becomes uneasy, not knowing whether to greet my mother or continue the conversation. He gets up from the chair clumsily and says "hello" gruffly. My grandfather watches, examining their congruence,[3] such as it is, with a critical eye, and meanwhile rubbing his bearded cheek roughly, as he always does when he reflects. He is worried; he is afraid that my father will not make a good husband for his oldest daughter. At this
3 point something happens to the film, just as my father is saying something funny to my mother; I am awakened to myself and my unhappiness just as my interest was rising. The audience begins to clap impatiently. Then the trouble is cared for but the film has been returned to a portion just shown, and once more I see my grandfather rubbing his bearded cheek and pondering my father's character. It is difficult to get back into the picture once more and forget myself, but as my mother giggles at my father's words, the darkness drowns me.

My father and mother depart from the house, my father shaking hands with my mother once more, out of some unknown uneasiness. I stir uneasily also, slouched in the hard chair of the theater. Where is the older uncle, my mother's older brother? He is studying in his bedroom upstairs, studying for his final examination at the College of the City of New York, having been dead of rapid pneumonia for the last twenty-one years. My mother and father walk down the same quiet streets once more. My mother is holding my father's

2. **William Randolph Hearst:** publisher of newspapers and magazines in the United States (1863–1951).

3. **congruence** [kong′gro͞o əns]: match; appropriateness.

AT A GLANCE

- After debating with himself about the advisability of marriage, the father arrives early and the mother's family is at dinner.
- The grandfather is unsure that the father will make a good husband.
- The father and mother leave the house.

1 POINT OF VIEW

The narrator's special knowledge of his parents' history gives him at times the broad, informed perspective of an omniscient narrator.

2 DESCRIPTION

The narrator uses short sentences to approximate the jump cuts of silent film; however, he illuminates the images with clear, simple language and careful observation of physical detail.

3 POINT OF VIEW

The narrator's sudden self-awareness and references to an unidentified unhappiness suggest that his observations are filtered through a highly personal perspective.

GUIDED READING

LITERAL QUESTION

1a. How does the narrator's father reassure himself about getting married? (by thinking about married men whom he admires)

INFERENTIAL QUESTION

1b. What do the father's thoughts about Hearst and Taft suggest about his own goals? (He wants to be successful, wealthy, and powerful.)

AT A GLANCE

- The mother discusses a book that she is reading, and the father judges its characters.
- The couple take a streetcar to Coney Island.
- The father is confident, bragging about how much money he has made; the narrator weeps.

1 CHARACTERIZATION

The narrator's observations on his father's pompous, judgmental nature grow from the motivation that he ascribes to his father.

2 CHARACTERIZATION

From the same personal perspective that colors his view of his father, the narrator portrays the serious self-importance and self-consciousness that he imagines to have occupied his mother's thoughts.

arm and telling him of the novel which she has been reading; and my father utters judgments of the characters as the plot is made clear to
1 him. This is a habit which he very much enjoys, for he feels the utmost superiority and confidence when he approves and condemns the behavior of other people. At times he feels moved to utter a brief "Ugh"—whenever the story becomes what he would call sugary. This tribute is paid to his manliness. My mother feels satisfied by the interest which she has awakened; she is showing my father how intelligent she is, and how interesting.

They reach the avenue, and the streetcar leisurely arrives. They are going to Coney Island[4] this afternoon, although my mother
2 considers that such pleasures are inferior. She has made up her mind to indulge only in a walk on the boardwalk and a pleasant dinner, avoiding the riotous amusements as being beneath the dignity of so dignified a couple.

My father tells my mother how much money he has made in the past week, exaggerating an amount which need not have been exaggerated. But my father has always felt that actualities somehow fall short. Suddenly I begin to weep. The determined old lady who sits

4. **Coney Island:** amusement park and beach in Brooklyn, N.Y.

GUIDED READING

LITERAL QUESTION

1a. At what point does the narrator suddenly begin to weep? (after mentioning his father's habit of exaggerating reality)

INFERENTIAL QUESTION

1b. What might cause the narrator to weep? (perhaps a feeling that he may have disappointed his father or that his father was never satisfied with the reality of life)

next to me in the theater is annoyed and looks at me with an angry face, and being intimi-
1 dated, I stop. I drag out my handkerchief and dry my face, licking the drop which has fallen near my lips. Meanwhile I have missed something, for here are my mother and father alighting at the last stop, Coney Island.

III

They walk toward the boardwalk, and my father commands my mother to inhale the pungent air from the sea. They both breathe in deeply, both of them laughing as they do so. They have in common a great interest in health, although my father is strong and husky, my mother frail. Their minds are full of theories of what is good to eat and not good to eat, and sometimes they engage in heated discussions of the subject, the whole matter ending in my father's announcement, made with a scornful bluster, that you have to die sooner or later anyway. On the boardwalk's flagpole, the American flag is pulsing in an intermittent wind from the sea.

My father and mother go to the rail of the boardwalk and look down on the beach where a good many bathers are casually walking about. A few are in the surf. A peanut whistle pierces the air with its pleasant and active whine, and my father goes to buy peanuts. My mother remains at the rail and stares at the ocean. The ocean seems merry to her; it pointedly sparkles and again and again the pony waves are released. She notices the children digging in the wet sand, and the bathing costumes of the girls who are her own age. My father returns with the peanuts. Overhead the sun's lightning strikes and strikes, but neither of them are at all aware of it. The boardwalk is full of people dressed in their Sunday clothes and idly strolling. The tide does not reach as far as the boardwalk, and the strollers would feel no danger if it did. My mother and father lean on the rail of the boardwalk and absently stare at the ocean. The ocean is becoming rough; the waves come in slowly, tugging strength from far back. The moment before
2 they somersault, the moment when they arch their backs so beautifully, showing green and white veins amid the black, that moment is intolerable. They finally crack, dashing fiercely upon the sand, actually driving, full force downward, against the sand, bouncing upward and forward, and at last petering out into a small stream which races up the beach and then is recalled. My parents gaze absentmindedly at the ocean, scarcely interested in its harshness. The sun overhead does not disturb
3 them. But I stare at the terrible sun which breaks up sight, and the fatal, merciless, passionate ocean, I forget my parents. I stare fascinated and finally, shocked by the indifference of my father and mother, I burst out weeping once more. The old lady next to me pats me on the shoulder and says "There, there, all of this is only a movie, young man, only a movie," but I look up once more at the terrifying sun and the terrifying ocean, and being unable to control my tears, I get up and go to the men's room, stumbling over the feet of the other people seated in my row.

IV

When I return, feeling as if I had awakened in the morning sick for lack of sleep, several hours have apparently passed and my parents are riding on the merry-go-round. My father is on a black horse, my mother on a white one, and they seem to be making an eternal circuit for the single purpose of snatching the nickel rings[5] which are attached to the arm of one of the posts. A hand-organ is playing; it is one with the ceaseless circling of the merry-go-round.

For a moment it seems that they will never get off the merry-go-round because it will never stop. I feel like one who looks down on the avenue from the fiftieth story of a building. But at length they do get off; even the music of the hand-organ has ceased for a moment. My father has acquired ten rings, my mother only

---

5. **nickel rings:** A nickel ring could be exchanged for a free ride.

AT A GLANCE

- The couple walk along the boardwalk at Coney Island.
- The narrator, shocked by his parents' indifference to the harsh sea and sun, weeps again and goes to the men's room.
- The narrator returns and sees his parents on a merry-go-round.

1 POINT OF VIEW

As the narrator watches his parents' involvement intensify, his present personal responses become increasingly vivid and sensory.

2 STYLE: FIGURES OF SPEECH

The personification of the waves underscores the significance of the ocean to the narrator.

3 POINT OF VIEW

The narrator's awareness of the consequences of his parents' union charges his observations with emotional intensity.

GUIDED READING

LITERAL QUESTIONS

1a. Which adjectives does the narrator use to describe the sun and the ocean? *(terrible, fatal, merciless, passionate)*

2a. What does the old woman say to comfort the narrator when he starts to weep again? *(. . . this is only a movie.)*

INFERENTIAL QUESTIONS

1b. What do you think the sun and the ocean represent to the narrator? (life, the process of time, uncontrollable events)

2b. Why do you think the narrator is not comforted by the woman's words? (He believes that the movie projects a reality that will endure after the movie's images fade.)

AT A GLANCE

- The couple go to a good restaurant for dinner and the father proposes marriage.
- When the mother accepts, the narrator gets up from his seat and yells at the screen that nothing good will come of the marriage.
- The couple go to a photographer who has trouble getting a good picture.

1 CHARACTERIZATION

Through an "omniscient" intrusion into his father's thoughts, the narrator indicates his own view of his father's self-absorption and self-deception.

2 STYLE: REPETITION

The narrator's repetition of the word *then,* like the rising crescendo of the waltz in the background, conveys the impetuous, urgent rush of emotion that leads the father to propose marriage.

3 THEME

The narrator's shout dramatizes the gap between the idealistic dreams of love, security, and comfort that motivated his parents to marry and the actual consequences of their action.

two, although it was my mother who really wanted them.

They walk on along the boardwalk as the afternoon descends by imperceptible degrees into the incredible violet of dusk. Everything fades into a relaxed glow, even the ceaseless murmuring from the beach, and the revolutions of the merry-go-round. They look for a place to have dinner. My father suggests the best one on the boardwalk and my mother demurs,[6] in accordance with her principles.

However they do go to the best place, asking for a table near the window, so that they can look out on the boardwalk and the mobile ocean. My father feels omnipotent as he places a quarter in the waiter's hand as he asks for a table. The place is crowded and here too there is music, this time from a kind of string trio. My father orders dinner with a fine confidence.

As the dinner is eaten, my father tells of his plans for the future, and my mother shows with expressive face how interested she is, and
1 how impressed. My father becomes exultant. He is lifted up by the waltz that is being played, and his own future begins to intoxicate him. My father tells my mother that he is going to expand his business, for there is a great deal of money to be made. He wants to settle down. After all, he is twenty-nine, he has lived by himself since he was thirteen, he is making more and more money, and he is envious of his married friends when he visits them in the cozy security of their homes, surrounded, it seems, by the calm domestic pleasures, and by
2 delightful children, and then, as the waltz reaches the moment when all the dancers swing madly, then, then with awful daring, then he asks my mother to marry him, although awkwardly enough and puzzled, even in his excitement, at how he had arrived at the proposal, and she, to make the whole business worse, begins to cry, and my father looks nervously about, not knowing at all what to do now, and my mother says: "It's all I've wanted from the moment I saw you," sobbing, and he finds all of this very difficult, scarcely to his taste, scarcely as he had thought it would be, on his long walks over Brooklyn Bridge in the
3 revery of a fine cigar, and it was then that I stood up in the theater and shouted: "Don't do it. It's not too late to change your minds, both of you. Nothing good will come of it, only remorse, hatred, scandal, and two children whose characters are monstrous." The whole audience turned to look at me, annoyed, the usher came hurrying down the aisle flashing his searchlight, and the old lady next to me tugged me down into my seat, saying: "Be quiet. You'll be put out, and you paid thirty-five cents to come in." And so I shut my eyes because I could not bear to see what was happening. I sat there quietly.

V

But after awhile I begin to take brief glimpses, and at length I watch again with thirsty interest, like a child who wants to maintain his sulk although offered the bribe of candy. My parents are now having their picture taken in a photographer's booth along the boardwalk. The place is shadowed in the mauve light which is apparently necessary. The camera is set to the side on its tripod and looks like a Martian man. The photographer is instructing my parents in how to pose. My father has his arm over my mother's shoulder, and both of them smile emphatically. The photographer brings my mother a bouquet of flowers to hold in her hand but she holds it at the wrong angle. Then the photographer covers himself with the black cloth which drapes the camera and all that one sees of him is one protruding arm and his hand which clutches the rubber ball which he will squeeze when the picture is finally taken. But he is not satisfied with their appearance. He feels with certainty that somehow there is something wrong in their pose. Again and again he issues from his hidden place with new directions. Each suggestion merely makes matters worse. My father is becoming impatient. They try a seated pose. The photographer explains that he has pride,

6. **demurs** [di murz′]: objects.

GUIDED READING

LITERAL QUESTIONS

1a. How does the father react to the mother's emotional response to the marriage proposal? (He is uncomfortable; her reaction is not what he expected.)

2a. To what does the narrator compare his interest in watching the movie again? (to a child bribed with candy)

INFERENTIAL QUESTIONS

1b. What does his reaction suggest about his expectations of married life? (The reality probably will differ from his fantasy and will not suit his taste.)

2b. What bribe do you think the movie offers the narrator? (an understanding of the past, which will help him cope with the present)

he is not interested in all of this for the money, he wants to make beautiful pictures. My father says: "Hurry up, will you? We haven't got all night." But the photographer only scurries about apologetically, and issues new
1 directions. The photographer charms me. I approve of him with all my heart, for I know just how he feels, and as he criticizes each revised pose according to some unknown idea of rightness, I become quite hopeful. But then my father says angrily: "Come on, you've had enough time, we're not going to wait any longer." And the photographer, sighing unhappily, goes back under his black covering, holds out his hand, says: "One, two, three, Now!", and the picture is taken, with my father's smile turned to a grimace and my mother's bright and false. It takes a few minutes for the picture to be developed and as my parents sit in the curious light they become quite depressed.

VI

2 They have passed a fortune teller's booth, and my mother wishes to go in, but my father does not. They begin to argue about it. My mother becomes stubborn, my father once more impatient, and then they begin to quarrel, and what my father would like to do is walk off and leave my mother there, but he knows that that would never do. My mother

AT A GLANCE

- The photographer keeps reposing the couple to make a more perfect picture.
- The father finally forces the photographer to take an imperfect picture.
- The mother wants to consult a fortune teller; the father refuses.

1 THEME

The narrator's hope that the photographer will match his parents' pose to "some unknown idea of rightness" reflects his larger yearning: that reality can somehow be made to conform to an idealized view of life.

2 CHARACTERIZATION

The mother's desire to consult a fortune teller, like her sobbing response to the proposal, suggests a sentimentality at odds with the father's practicality.

GUIDED READING

LITERAL QUESTION

1a. How do the couple's smiles appear in the finished picture? (The father's smile is a grimace; the mother's smile is forced and unnatural.)

INFERENTIAL QUESTION

1b. In what sense does their appearance here foreshadow their future together? (It suggests that the father will be unhappy and that the mother's seeming happiness will cover her true feelings.)

AT A GLANCE

- The father consents to see the fortune teller; then he changes his mind and leaves.
- When the narrator again jumps up and begins to shout, the usher drags him to the lobby.
- The narrator wakes up on his twenty-first birthday.

1 CHARACTERIZATION

The narrator is a dynamic character who undergoes a change during the story. At first objecting to his parents' union and his resultant life, he now accepts both as a reality that must be faced.

2 THEME

In acknowledging the movie as his own dream, the narrator shifts and broadens his perspective. He accepts the past as an integral part of his personal history and accepts responsibility for his own life.

REFLECTING ON THE STORY

What role does the past play in helping the narrator to understand his present circumstances? (It gives him historical perspective; it makes him see that people must accept responsibility.)

STUDY QUESTIONS

1. watching a silent movie; his mother's house; June 12, 1909
2. Coney Island; her intelligence; exaggerates
3. "Sun's lightning"; ocean; no, fascinated
4. riding merry-go-round; demurs; best restaurant
5. future; to marry him; *It's all I've wanted from the moment I saw you; Don't do it*
6. entering fortune teller's booth; strides out; holds back mother; *What are they doing?*
7. *What are* you *doing*?; "the bleak winter morning of my twenty-first birthday"

refuses to budge. She is near to tears, but she feels an uncontrollable desire to hear what the palm-reader will say. My father consents angrily, and they both go into a booth which is in a way like the photographer's, since it is draped in black cloth and its light is shadowed. The place is too warm, and my father keeps saying this is all nonsense, pointing to the crystal ball on the table. The fortune teller, a fat, short woman, garbed in what is supposed to be Oriental robes, comes into the room from the back and greets them, speaking with an accent. But suddenly my father feels that the whole thing is intolerable; he tugs at my mother's arm, but my mother refuses to budge. And then, in terrible anger, my father lets go of my mother's arm and strides out, leaving my mother stunned. She moves to go after my father, but the fortune teller holds her arm tightly and begs her not to do so, and I in my seat am shocked more than can ever be said, for I feel as if I were walking a tightrope a hundred feet over a circus audience and suddenly the rope is showing signs of breaking, and I get up from my seat and begin to shout once more the first words I can think of to communicate my terrible fear and once more the usher comes hurrying down the aisle flashing his searchlight, and the old lady pleads with me, and the shocked audience has turned
1 to stare at me, and I keep shouting: "What are they doing? Don't they know what they are doing? Why doesn't my mother go after my father? If she does not do that, what will she do? Doesn't my father know what he is doing?" But the usher has seized my arm and is dragging me away, and as he does so, he says: "What are *you* doing? Don't you know that you can't do whatever you want to do? Why should a young man like you, with your whole life before you, get hysterical like this? Why don't you *think* of what you're doing? You can't act like this even if other people aren't around! You will be sorry if you do not do what you should do, you can't carry on like this, it is not right, you will find that out soon enough, everything you do matters too much," and he said that drag-
2 ging me through the lobby of the theater into the cold light, and I woke up into the bleak winter morning of my twenty-first birthday, the windowsill shining with its lip of snow, and the morning already begun.

STUDY QUESTIONS

Recalling

1. What does the narrator imagine himself to be doing in the opening paragraphs? Where is his father going? When does this incident take place?
2. Where does the father take the mother in section II? What does the mother feel she has shown by interesting him in her conversation? What does the father do when he tells her how much money he made that week?
3. As the couple go to the rail of the boardwalk in section III, what "strikes overhead" that they scarcely notice? In what "harsh" scene are they scarcely interested? Is the narrator equally uninterested in these things?
4. What are the couple doing in the opening paragraphs of section IV? How does the mother react when the father suggests they eat at the best restaurant on the boardwalk? Where do the couple eat?
5. What plans does the father discuss as they dine? What does he ask the mother? What does the mother say as she begins sobbing? What does the narrator stand up and shout?
6. About what do the couple quarrel in section VI? What does the father do when he decides the "whole thing" is intolerable? What does the fortune teller do? What does the narrator shout?
7. What does the "usher" say to the narrator as he drags him from the "theater"? To what does the narrator awaken in the final paragraph?

Interpreting

8. In general, what characteristics do the father and mother seem to have? Do we find anything positive or touching about their day's outing? If so, what? How does the title apply to both the father and the mother?
9. What do the glaring sun, the ominous ocean, and the fortune teller's staying hand all foreshadow, or predict? Why do the couple fail to notice the sun and ocean? Why does the narrator notice?
10. Where in the story does the narrator's negative view of his parents' marriage change for the positive?
11. What do the usher's remarks and the fact that the narrator awakens to his twenty-first birthday suggest has happened to the narrator at the story's end? Why is it impossible for the narrator to be against his parents' marriage any longer? How does the title apply to the narrator?

Extending

12. What does the fact that the narrator imagines events so crucial to his life as the plot of a *movie* suggest to you about the significance of the mass media in the twentieth century? What effect do you think movies and television shows have had on Americans' perceptions, on their views of themselves and the world?

LITERARY FOCUS

Point of View: The Frame Story

The **point of view** of a work of fiction is the position from which the characters and action are seen by the author. One special means of creating point of view is to use a **frame story,** a story in which another story takes place. The author begins with one story and one character or set of characters. Then, *within that story,* the author introduces another story and another character or set of characters. Frequently a character in the frame story narrates the story it contains.

The frame story of "In Dreams Begin Responsibilities" involves a narrator who imagines that he is in a movie theater watching a film about his own parents. The story of his parents, which unfolds in the film that the narrator describes, is the story within the story.

One advantage of the frame story is that it provides a writer with a kind of double voice: Both the frame story and the inner story can express the theme. Each story can comment on the other and can thus reinforce and deepen the overall meaning. For example, at the end of Schwartz's story, the narrator awakens from a dream and realizes *from his dream* that life will not always be just as he wants it, that "everything you do matters too much."

Thinking About the Frame Story

■ Several times in the story the narrator interrupts the movie to weep or to shout at the screen. At these moments the frame story and the inner story converge. How do these moments help to clarify the theme of the story?

COMPOSITION

Analyzing the Title of a Story

■ Write an essay in which you discuss the title in terms of its significance to the whole story. Consider the kinds of "dreams" that occur in the story. What are the "responsibilities" that the author is concerned with?

Writing a Story Within a Story

■ Using the structure of "In Dreams Begin Responsibilities" as a model, write a short story within a story. Begin with a character watching a movie. Then allow the character to become "involved" in the movie in some way. Feel free to invent an ending different from the kind Schwartz uses.

8. shy, awkward, try to do what they think they should; grave dignity; both look to future with dreams of happiness for which they will have to bear responsibilities
9. trouble: reality is misery; involved with selves; views scene with perspective of future
10. during scene at fortune teller's booth when woman stops mother
11. accepted responsibility for himself; as son, his existence depends on it; realizes through dream that he is responsible for what he will become
12. Mass media pervade modern life; movies and TV have helped Americans confuse reality with illusion.

LITERARY FOCUS

The narrator comments directly on his parents' actions at these times. At first he holds them responsible for his situation as well as their own. At the story's end, he recognizes that he must take responsibility for what he is.

COMPOSITION: GUIDELINES FOR EVALUATION

ANALYZING THE TITLE OF A STORY

Objective

To explain the significance of a story's title

Guidelines for Evaluation

- suggested length: three to five paragraphs
- should consider dreams of father, mother, and narrator
- should discuss responsibilities of narrator and his parents
- should explain that title expresses theme

WRITING A STORY WITHIN A STORY

Objective

To write a frame story

Guidelines for Evaluation

- suggested length: six to ten paragraphs
- should use frame-story technique
- should parallel structure of Schwartz's story
- should relate events of inner story to frame
- should develop a single theme

Photograph © 1982 by Jill Krementz

Eudora Welty *born 1909*

Eudora Welty has lived virtually all of her life in Jackson, Mississippi, where she was born. She was educated at the Mississippi State College for Women and at the University of Wisconsin. Early in her career she studied advertising copywriting and worked as a government publicity agent. During World War II she was briefly a staff member of the *New York Times Book Review,* for which she wrote reviews of battlefield reports from North Africa under the pseudonym "Michael Ravenna."

She is best known for her short stories, which have appeared in several collections, including *A Curtain of Green* (1941), *The Wide Net* (1943), and *Thirteen Stories* (1965). She has also written several novels, including *Delta Wedding* (1946), *The Ponder Heart* (1954), and *The Optimist's Daughter* (1972), for which she was awarded the Pulitzer Prize. She is the author of a children's book, *The Shoe Bird* (1964), and of a collection of photographs of Mississippi, *One Time, One Place* (1971).

With grace and gentle humor, an eye for the eccentric and for telling details, and a wonderful ear for language and dialogue, Eudora Welty has in her fiction traced and defined a broad range of southern experience. Yet by doing so, she has also touched the universal. "A Worn Path" concerns an old woman's labored journey, but, as the author herself notes, it is also about "the deep-grained habit of love."

■ How much should people sacrifice for someone they love? How does Phoenix Jackson answer that question?

Eudora Welty

A Worn Path

It was December—a bright frozen day in the early morning. Far out in the country there was an old Negro woman with her head tied in a red rag, coming along a path through the pinewoods. Her name was Phoenix Jackson. She was very old and small and she walked slowly in the dark pine shadows, moving a little from side to side in her steps, with the balanced heaviness and lightness of a pendulum in
1 a grandfather clock. She carried a thin, small cane made from an umbrella, and with this she kept tapping the frozen earth in front of her. This made a grave and persistent noise in the still air, that seemed meditative like the chirping of a solitary little bird.

She wore a dark striped dress reaching down to her shoe tops, and an equally long apron of bleached sugar sacks, with a full pocket: all neat and tidy, but every time she took a step she might have fallen over her shoelaces, which dragged from her unlaced shoes. She looked straight ahead. Her eyes
2 were blue with age. Her skin had a pattern all its own of numberless branching wrinkles and as though a whole little tree stood in the middle of her forehead, but a golden color ran underneath, and the two knobs of her cheeks were illumined by a yellow burning under the dark. Under the red rag her hair came down on her neck in the frailest of ringlets, still black, and with an odor like copper.

Now and then there was a quivering in the thicket. Old Phoenix said, "Out of my way, all you foxes, owls, beetles, jack rabbits, coons and wild animals! . . . Keep out from under these feet, little bobwhites. . . . Keep the big wild hogs out of my path. Don't let none of those come running my direction. I got a long way." Under her small black-freckled hand her cane, limber as a buggy whip, would switch at the brush as if to rouse up any hiding things.

On she went. The woods were deep and still. The sun made the pine needles almost too bright to look at, up where the wind rocked. The cones dropped as light as feathers. Down in the hollow was the mourning dove—it was not too late for him.

3 The path ran up a hill. "Seem like there is chains about my feet, time I get this far," she said, in the voice of argument old people keep to use with themselves. "Something always take a hold of me on this hill—pleads I should stay."

After she got to the top she turned and gave a full, severe look behind her where she had come. "Up through pines," she said at length. "Now down through oaks."

Her eyes opened their widest, and she started down gently. But before she got to the bottom of the hill a bush caught her dress.

Her fingers were busy and intent, but her skirts were full and long, so that before she could pull them free in one place they were caught in another. It was not possible to allow the dress to tear. "I in the thorny bush," she said. "Thorns, you doing your appointed work. Never want to let folks pass, no sir. Old eyes thought you was a pretty little *green* bush."

Finally, trembling all over, she stood free, and after a moment dared to stoop for her cane.

"Sun so high!" she cried, leaning back and looking, while the thick tears went over her eyes. "The time getting all gone here."

At the foot of this hill was a place where a log was laid across the creek.

"Now comes the trial," said Phoenix.

Putting her right foot out, she mounted the log and shut her eyes. Lifting her skirt, leveling her cane fiercely before her, like a festival figure in some parade, she began to march across. Then she opened her eyes and she was safe on the other side.

"I wasn't as old as I thought," she said.

AT A GLANCE

- On a cold December morning an old black woman, Phoenix Jackson, begins a journey through the woods.
- She talks to the animals, telling them to give way.
- She struggles up a hill, disentangles herself from briars, and negotiates a log across a creek.

LITERARY OPTIONS

- allegory
- characterization

THEMATIC OPTIONS

- the endurance of love
- the power of faith

1 ALLUSION

The description *solitary little bird* reinforces the allusion to the mythical bird, emblem of immortality.

2 STYLE: IMAGERY

The striking sensory images of colors and scents charge the realism of rich physical details with emotion.

3 ALLEGORY

Phoenix's reflections on the difficulty of her walk, her survey of the distance already covered, and the challenges that await her add a mythic dimension to her literal journey.

GUIDED READING

LITERAL QUESTIONS

1a. To whom does Phoenix talk when she hears quivering in the thicket? (the animals in the woods)

2a. What does Phoenix say after she crosses the log in the creek? (that she isn't as old as she had thought)

INFERENTIAL QUESTIONS

1b. What does this behavior suggest about her character? (She is in touch with and at home in the natural world.)

2b. What do her remarks imply about how she views her journey? (She sees it as a test of her strength and determination.)

AT A GLANCE

- Phoenix rests and thinks that she sees a boy giving her a slice of cake.
- She crawls under a barbed-wire fence.
- When she crosses a field of dead corn, she thinks that she sees a ghost.

1 STYLE: FIGURES OF SPEECH

Phoenix's coping with her trials "like a baby" suggests that she embodies a sense of time that embraces death and rebirth.

2 ALLEGORY

Reference to the "maze" that she must traverse evokes the struggles of Theseus in the labyrinth at Knossos and imputes a mythic quality to her journey.

But she sat down to rest. She spread her skirts on the bank around her and folded her hands over her knees. Up above her was a tree in a pearly cloud of mistletoe. She did not dare to close her eyes, and when a little boy brought her a plate with a slice of marble-cake on it she spoke to him. "That would be acceptable," she said. But when she went to take it there was just her own hand in the air.

So she left that tree, and had to go through
1 a barbed-wire fence. There she had to creep and crawl, spreading her knees and stretching her fingers like a baby trying to climb the steps. But she talked loudly to herself: she could not let her dress be torn now, so late in the day, and she could not pay for having her arm or her leg sawed off if she got caught fast where she was.

At last she was safe through the fence and risen up out in the clearing. Big dead trees, like black men with one arm, were standing in the purple stalks of the withered cotton field. There sat a buzzard.

"Who you watching?"

In the furrow she made her way along.

"Glad this not the season for bulls," she said, looking sideways, "and the good Lord made his snakes to curl up and sleep in the winter. A pleasure I don't see no two-headed snake coming around that tree, where it come once. It took a while to get by him, back in the summer."

2 She passed through the old cotton and went into a field of dead corn. It whispered and shook and was taller than her head. "Through the maze now," she said, for there was no path.

Then there was something tall, black, and skinny there, moving before her.

At first she took it for a man. It could have been a man dancing in the field. But she stood still and listened, and it did not make a sound. It was silent as a ghost.

"Ghost," she said sharply, "who be you the ghost of? For I have heard of nary death close by."

GUIDED READING

LITERAL QUESTION

1a. When Phoenix sees something tall, black, and skinny in the cornfield, what does she think that it is? (a man; then a ghost)

INFERENTIAL QUESTION

1b. What does Phoenix's response to seeing a ghost suggest about her? (that she believes in ghosts and is not frightened by them)

But there was no answer—only the ragged dancing in the wind.

She shut her eyes, reached out her hand, and touched a sleeve. She found a coat and inside that an emptiness, cold as ice.

1 "You scarecrow," she said. Her face lighted. "I ought to be shut up for good," she said with laughter. "My senses is gone. I too old. I the oldest people I ever know. Dance, old scarecrow," she said, "while I dancing with you."

She kicked her foot over the furrow, and with mouth drawn down, shook her head once or twice in a little strutting way. Some husks blew down and whirled in streamers about her skirts.

Then she went on, parting her way from side to side with the cane, through the whispering field. At last she came to the end, to a wagon track where the silver grass blew between the red ruts. The quail were walking around like pullets, seeming all dainty and unseen.

"Walk pretty," she said. "This the easy place. This the easy going."

2 She followed the track, swaying through the quiet bare fields, through the little strings of trees silver in their dead leaves, past cabins silver from weather, with the doors and windows boarded shut, all like old women under a spell sitting there. "I walking in their sleep," she said, nodding her head vigorously.

In a ravine she went where a spring was silently flowing through a hollow log. Old Phoenix bent and drank. "Sweet-gum[1] makes the water sweet," she said, and drank more. "Nobody know who made this well, for it was here when I was born."

The track crossed a swampy part where the moss hung as white as lace from every limb. "Sleep on, alligators, and blow your bubbles." Then the track went into the road.

Deep, deep the road went down between the high green-colored banks. Overhead the live-oaks met, and it was as dark as a cave.

3 A black dog with a lolling tongue came up out of the weeds by the ditch. She was meditating, and not ready, and when he came at her she only hit him a little with her cane. Over she went in the ditch, like a little puff of milkweed.[2]

Down there, her senses drifted away. A dream visited her, and she reached her hand up, but nothing reached down and gave her a pull. So she lay there and presently went to talking. "Old woman," she said to herself, "that black dog come up out of the weeds to stall you off, and now there he sitting on his fine tail, smiling at you."

A white man finally came along and found her—a hunter, a young man, with his dog on a chain.

"Well, Granny!" he laughed. "What are you doing there?"

"Lying on my back like a June bug waiting to be turned over, mister," she said, reaching up her hand.

He lifted her up, gave her a swing in the air, and set her down. "Anything broken, Granny?"

"No sir, them old dead weeds is springy enough," said Phoenix, when she had got her breath. "I thank you for your trouble."

"Where do you live, Granny?" he asked, while the two dogs were growling at each other.

"Away back yonder, sir, behind the ridge. You can't even see it from here."

"On your way home?"

"No sir, I going to town."

"Why, that's too far! That's as far as I walk when I come out myself, and I get something for my trouble." He patted the stuffed bag he carried, and there hung down a little closed claw. It was one of the bobwhites, with its beak hooked bitterly to show it was dead. "Now you go on home, Granny!"

"I bound to go to town, mister," said Phoenix. "The time come around."

---

1. **Sweet-gum:** fragrant juice from sweet-gum trees.

2. **milkweed:** plant with milky juice and feathery seeds.

AT A GLANCE

- Phoenix realizes that the "ghost" is a scarecrow and continues on, enjoying an easy part of her walk.
- A black dog alarms her, and she falls into a ditch.
- A hunter rescues her and tries to convince her to turn back.

1 CHARACTERIZATION

Phoenix's ability to laugh at herself and take pleasure in the scarecrow reflects an acceptance of human frailty and vulnerability. Her reference to her extreme age, like her name, suggests the rigor of her spirit.

2 STYLE: IMAGERY

Vivid sensory images that emphasize sound and color ("quiet bare fields," silver trees and cabins) and the use of simile ("like old women") animate the landscape.

3 ALLEGORY

Phoenix's encounter with the black dog and her fall into the ditch suggest Aeneas's encounter with Cerberus, the watchdog at the entrance to Hades.

GUIDED READING

LITERAL QUESTIONS

1a. What does Phoenix do when she gets to the spring by the hollow log? (She drinks the water.)

2a. What does Phoenix tell the hunter when he asks her what she was doing in the ditch? (She responds that she is lying on her back "like a bug waiting to be turned over.")

INFERENTIAL QUESTIONS

1b. What does her action suggest about her relationship to the natural world? (Nature is her friend; it gives her sustenance.)

2b. What does her reply suggest about her character? (that she knows her own limitations and has a great deal of faith)

AT A GLANCE

- When Phoenix sees a nickel fall from the hunter's pocket, she distracts him and picks it up.
- When she finally reaches her destination, Natchez, the town is busy with Christmas shoppers.
- She asks a woman to tie her shoelaces.

1 RESPONSE JOURNAL

Have students discuss the different levels at which it might be true that there is "no telling" Phoenix's age.

2 CHARACTERIZATION

Phoenix's calm response to the hunter's pointing his gun at her dramatically portrays her bravery and dignity; her assumption that she deserves punishment for keeping the nickel adds a note of pathos.

3 THEME

The reference to Christmas underscores the allegorical level of the story, reinforcing the power of love to transform experience and the importance of faith.

4 VOCABULARY: REGIONALISM

There is a strong regional flavor to Phoenix's speech.

He gave another laugh, filling the whole landscape. "I know you old colored people! Wouldn't miss going to town to see Santa Claus!"

But something held old Phoenix very still. The deep lines in her face went into a fierce and different radiation. Without warning, she had seen with her own eyes a flashing nickel fall out of the man's pocket onto the ground.

1 "How old are you, Granny?" he was saying.

"There is no telling, mister," she said, "no telling."

Then she gave a little cry and clapped her hands and said, "Git on away from here, dog! Look! Look at that dog!" She laughed as if in admiration. "He ain't scared of nobody. He a big black dog." She whispered, "Sic him!"

"Watch me get rid of that cur," said the man. "Sic him, Pete! Sic him!"

Phoenix heard the dogs fighting, and heard the man running and throwing sticks. She even heard a gunshot. But she was slowly bending forward by that time, further and further forward, the lids stretched down over her eyes, as if she were doing this in her sleep. Her chin was lowered almost to her knees. The yellow palm of her hand came out from the fold of her apron. Her fingers slid down and along the ground under the piece of money with the grace and care they would have in lifting an egg from under a setting hen. Then she slowly straightened up, she stood erect, and the nickel was in her apron pocket. A bird flew by. Her lips moved. "God watching me the whole time. I come to stealing."

The man came back, and his own dog panted about them. "Well, I scared him off that time," he said, and then he laughed and lifted his gun and pointed it at Phoenix.

She stood straight and faced him.

2 "Doesn't the gun scare you?" he said, still pointing it.

"No, sir, I seen plenty go off closer by, in my day, and for less than what I done," she said, holding utterly still.

He smiled, and shouldered the gun. "Well, Granny," he said, "you must be a hundred years old, and scared of nothing. I'd give you a dime if I had any money with me. But you take my advice and stay home, and nothing will happen to you."

"I bound to go on my way, mister," said Phoenix. She inclined her head in the red rag. Then they went in different directions, but she could hear the gun shooting again and again over the hill.

She walked on. The shadows hung from the oak trees to the road like curtains. Then she smelled woodsmoke, and smelled the river, and she saw a steeple and the cabins on their steep steps. Dozens of little black children whirled around her. There ahead was Natchez[3] shining. Bells were ringing. She walked on.

3 In the paved city it was Christmas time. There were red and green electric lights strung and crisscrossed everywhere, and all turned on in the daytime. Old Phoenix would have been lost if she had not distrusted her eyesight and depended on her feet to know where to take her.

She paused quietly on the sidewalk where people were passing by. A lady came along in the crowd, carrying an armful of red-, green- and silver-wrapped presents; she gave off perfume like the red roses in hot summer, and Phoenix stopped her.

"Please, missy, will you lace up my shoe?" She held up her foot.

"What do you want, Grandma?"

"See my shoe," said Phoenix. "Do all right for out in the country, but wouldn't look right to go in a big building."

"Stand still then, Grandma," said the lady. She put her packages down on the sidewalk beside her and laced and tied both shoes tightly.

4 "Can't lace 'em with a cane," said Phoenix. "Thank you, missy. I doesn't mind asking a nice lady to tie up my shoe, when I gets out on the street."

Moving slowly and from side to side, she

3. **Natchez:** town in southern Mississippi.

GUIDED READING

LITERAL QUESTION

1a. Who ties Phoenix's shoelaces? (a woman with an armful of Christmas presents)

INFERENTIAL QUESTION

1b. What does this incident suggest about Welty's views about human relationships? (that regardless of background or status, all people need and depend on each other)

went into the big building, and into a tower of
1 steps, where she walked up and around and around until her feet knew to stop.

She entered a door, and there she saw nailed up on the wall the document that had been stamped with the gold seal and framed in the gold frame, which matched the dream that was hung up in her head.

"Here I be," she said. There was a fixed and ceremonial stiffness over her body.

"A charity case, I suppose," said an attendant who sat at the desk before her.

But Phoenix only looked above her head. There was sweat on her face, the wrinkles in her skin shone like a bright net.

2 "Speak up, Grandma," the woman said. "What's your name? We must have your history, you know. Have you been here before? What seems to be the trouble with you?"

Old Phoenix only gave a twitch to her face as if a fly were bothering her.

"Are you deaf?" cried the attendant.

But then the nurse came in.

"Oh, that's just old Aunt Phoenix," she said. "She doesn't come for herself—she has a little grandson. She makes these trips just as regular as clockwork. She lives away back off the Old Natchez Trace."[4] She bent down. "Well, Aunt Phoenix, why don't you just take a seat? We won't keep you standing after your long trip." She pointed.

The old woman sat down, bolt upright in the chair.

"Now, how is the boy?" asked the nurse.

Old Phoenix did not speak.

3 "I said, how is the boy?"

But Phoenix only waited and stared straight ahead, her face very solemn and withdrawn into rigidity.

"Is his throat any better?" asked the nurse. "Aunt Phoenix, don't you hear me? Is your grandson's throat any better since the last time you came for the medicine?"

---

4. **Old Natchez Trace:** road between Natchez and Nashville, Tennessee, used in the early 1800s.

AT A GLANCE

- Phoenix enters the hospital and goes to the doctor's office.
- The nurse explains that Phoenix comes regularly to get medicine for her grandson's throat.
- Phoenix does not answer any questions put to her by the nurse.

1 ALLEGORY

Phoenix's feet's "knowing" where to stop and her attention to a document on the wall suggest that her actions are guided by a spiritual force that will assure the success of her mission.

2 CONTRAST

The attendant's gruff treatment of Phoenix, as well as her disdain for charity cases, contrasts sharply with the attitude of the woman shopper who tied Phoenix's shoelace.

3 PLOT: CLIMAX

Welty heightens the drama of Phoenix's forgetfulness by focusing on her demeanor, while contrasting her lack of response with the nurse's ongoing speech.

GUIDED READING

LITERAL QUESTION

1a. According to the nurse, why does Phoenix come to the hospital regularly? (to get medicine for her grandson)

INFERENTIAL QUESTION

1b. What does this information suggest about the nature of her journey? (that it is motivated by love)

AT A GLANCE

- The nurse explains that the grandson had swallowed lye a few years before.
- Phoenix describes how her grandson endures his suffering.
- When the attendant gives Phoenix a nickel, Phoenix leaves to buy her grandson a paper windmill.

1 CHARACTERIZATION

Phoenix's plea to be forgiven for her lapse of memory reflects not only her inherent dignity but also her wisdom in knowing that the spirit is strong even if the body is weak.

2 VOCABULARY: DICTION

Phoenix's uneducated syntax and grammar and simple, direct sentences portray a moving, highly evocative image of her grandson's affliction.

3 ALLUSION

The paper windmill that Phoenix will hold straight up in front of her, like a talisman or a sacred symbol, reflects her belief in the power of faith to overcome earthly tribulations.

REFLECTING ON THE STORY

How do the references to Christmas, a time of giving, reinforce the larger meaning of the story? (They underscore the transformational power of love and faith.)

With her hands on her knees, the old woman waited, silent, erect and motionless, just as if she were in armor.

"You mustn't take up our time this way, Aunt Phoenix," the nurse said. "Tell us quickly about your grandson, and get it over. He isn't dead, is he?"

At last there came a flicker and then a flame of comprehension across her face, and she spoke.

"My grandson. It was my memory had left me. There I sat and forgot why I made my long trip."

"Forgot?" The nurse frowned. "After you came so far?"

Then Phoenix was like an old woman begging a dignified forgiveness for waking up
1 frightened in the night. "I never did go to school, I was too old at the Surrender,"[5] she said in a soft voice. "I'm an old woman without an education. It was my memory fail me. My little grandson, he is just the same, and I forgot it in the coming."

"Throat never heals, does it?" said the nurse, speaking in a loud, sure voice to old Phoenix. By now she had a card with something written on it, a little list. "Yes. Swallowed lye. When was it?—January—two, three years ago—"

2 Phoenix spoke unasked now. "No, missy, he not dead, he just the same. Every little while his throat begin to close up again, and he not able to swallow. He not get his breath. He not able to help himself. So the time come around, and I go on another trip for the soothing medicine."

"All right. The doctor said as long as you came to get it, you could have it," said the nurse. "But it's an obstinate case."

"My little grandson, he sit up there in the house all wrapped up, waiting by himself," Phoenix went on. "We is the only two left in the world. He suffer and it don't seem to put him back at all. He got a sweet look. He going to last. He wear a little patch quilt and peep out holding his mouth open like a little bird. I remembers so plain now. I not going to forget him again, no, the whole enduring time. I could tell him from all the others in creation."

"All right." The nurse was trying to hush her now. She brought her a bottle of medicine. "Charity," she said, making a check mark in a book.

Old Phoenix held the bottle close to her eyes, and then carefully put it into her pocket.

"I thank you," she said.

"It's Christmas time, Grandma," said the attendant. "Could I give you a few pennies out of my purse?"

"Five pennies is a nickel," said Phoenix stiffly.

"Here's a nickel," said the attendant.

Phoenix rose carefully and held out her hand. She received the nickel and then fished the other nickel out of her pocket and laid it beside the new one. She stared at her palm closely, with her head on one side.

Then she gave a tap with her cane on the floor.

"This is what come to me to do," she said.
3 "I going to the store and buy my child a little windmill they sells, made out of paper. He going to find it hard to believe there such a thing in the world. I'll march myself back where he waiting, holding it straight up in this hand."

She lifted her free hand, gave a little nod, turned around, and walked out of the doctor's office. Then her slow step began on the stairs, going down.

---

5. **the Surrender:** surrender of the Confederate army at the end of the Civil War on April 9, 1865.

GUIDED READING

LITERAL QUESTION

1a. Which question from the nurse gets Phoenix to talk again? (*He isn't dead, is he?*)

INFERENTIAL QUESTION

1b. What does her answer—which continues through several paragraphs—reveal about her view of life? (She seems to feel that although life can be a struggle, it has moments of sweetness and beauty that make the struggle worthwhile.)

STUDY QUESTIONS

Recalling

1. What details in the first two paragraphs describe Phoenix Jackson?
2. Identify at least two obstacles Phoenix encounters on her journey. What does she see when she closes her eyes after sitting down to rest from her arduous crossing of the creek?
3. What does the hunter who rescues Phoenix from the ditch drop from his pocket during their conversation? What does Phoenix do to divert his attention? What does she say after she puts her acquisition in her apron pocket?
4. To what town is Phoenix going? What holiday is being celebrated?
5. What explanation does Phoenix give for her inability to answer the questions posed by the attendant and the nurse? Why does Phoenix come to Natchez regularly? What happened to her grandson two or three years ago?
6. What does the attendant give Phoenix? What does Phoenix decide to do with the money she has acquired?

Interpreting

7. What do the many difficulties of Phoenix's journey suggest about its importance? What motivates Phoenix's expedition to Natchez?
8. What sort of person is Phoenix Jackson? What do her thoughts after she picks up the hunter's nickel suggest about the importance she places on a nickel? What does her decision about how to spend the money reveal about her character?
9. What might be the significance of the story's being set at Christmas time?
10. In what sense is the title of the story literal? In what sense is Phoenix's love for her grandson itself "a worn path"?

Extending

11. Does this story satisfy the requirements of Regional literature, as defined by Hamlin Garland on page 311? Does it go beyond the regional to the universal as all great Regionalist works do? Defend your answers.

VIEWPOINT

Commenting on the ways in which a short story differs from a novel, Eudora Welty has said:

> A short story is confined to one mood, to which everything in the story pertains. Characters, setting, time, events, are all subject to the mood. And you can try more ephemeral, more fleeting things in a story—you can work more by suggestion—than in a novel. Less is resolved, more is suggested, perhaps.
>
> —*Writers at Work: The Paris Review Interviews*

■ Would you agree that "A Worn Path" is "confined to one mood"? How would you describe that mood? What do you think the story suggests about Phoenix's brave journey?

VOCABULARY

Biblical and Mythological Allusions

The name Phoenix refers to a miraculous bird of Egyptian and Greek mythology that, after living for five hundred years, supposedly built itself a great funeral pyre, died in the flames, and arose from the ashes to live again. Welty's use of the name suggests the durability of her main character.

What would the following names suggest about a character? Use a dictionary to find the biblical or mythological allusions each makes.

1. Cassandra
2. Minerva
3. Penelope
4. Orpheus
5. Demeter
6. Thalia
7. Job
8. Cain
9. Ishmael
10. Freya

COMPOSITION

Writing a Comparison/Contrast

■ Briefly compare and contrast the theme of this story with that of John Steinbeck's "Leader of the People" (page 590). Begin with a comparison of the journeys each describes. Then contrast the importance of the journeys to the people in the stories. Conclude with a statement about the heroism each exemplifies. *For help with this assignment, refer to Lesson 2 in the Writing About Literature Handbook at the back of this book.*

Describing a Character

■ Welty characterizes Phoenix through physical description and description of her movements. Invent a character engaged in a particular action. Describe the action with details that characterize the performer of the action.

STUDY QUESTIONS

1. old, small, wears red rag, and so on
2. hill, thorns; boy with cake
3. nickel; talks to dog; "God watching me the whole time."
4. Natchez; Christmas
5. memory left her; for grandson's medicine; swallowed lye
6. nickel; buy paper windmill
7. epic journey, quest; love, faith
8. strong, wise, loving; knows she may be punished for her sin; self-sacrificing
9. journey is act of faith
10. journey made many times; love is deep and abiding
11. yes, unique to South; yes, mythic nature yields universality

VIEWPOINT

yes; pervading love; love is a powerful force that has worn a path across time

VOCABULARY

1. (Greek: seer none believed) one whose warnings are disregarded
2. (Roman: goddess of wisdom) a wise, inventive woman
3. (Ulysses' faithful wife) a faithful woman
4. (Greek: musician with magical powers) accomplished musician
5. (Greek: goddess of agriculture, marriage) woman with gift for growing things; good wife
6. (Greek: muse of comedy) amusing woman skilled in the arts
7. (Bible: man who suffered without losing faith in God) one who endures suffering
8. (Genesis: killed his brother Abel) a fratricide
9. (Genesis: son of Abraham and Hagar) an outcast
10. (Norse: goddess of love, beauty) beautiful, fair woman

COMPOSITION: GUIDELINES FOR EVALUATION

WRITING A COMPARISON / CONTRAST

Objective

To compare and contrast two characters' journeys

Guidelines for Evaluation

- suggested length: three to five paragraphs
- should note similarities in hardships
- should note symbolic quality of both journeys
- should note his trip was his life; battled nature
- should note she repeats her spiritual journey
- should say he is tragic, she is heroic

DESCRIBING A CHARACTER

Objective

To describe a character through action

Guidelines for Evaluation

- suggested length: one to two paragraphs
- should use vivid, descriptive words and details that describe gesture and movement
- should have a total effect of revealing the character's personality

Walter Van Tilburg Clark *1909–1971*

A literary descendant of Bret Harte (page 315), Walter Van Tilburg Clark also wrote about the American West—its tough character, frontier towns, rugged landscapes, and rigorous climate. He used these materials, however, only as a point of departure for his short stories and novels; generally he moved on to broader philosophical issues.

The most famous example is his novel *The Ox-Bow Incident* (1940). On the one hand, it is a tale of cowboys, cattle rustling, and a lynching; on the other hand, it is an imaginative and compelling examination of the nature and meaning of justice and of humanity's responsibility in the fair dispensation of it.

Clark was born in East Orland, Maine, but grew up largely in Reno, Nevada. He returned to New England to attend graduate school at the University of Vermont. For ten years, during which he wrote and published his first two novels and several short stories, he also taught English and dramatics and coached athletics in public schools in Cazenovia, New York.

In 1945, following the publication of his second novel, *The City of Trembling Leaves,* Clark gave up teaching and with his family moved to New Mexico and later to Nevada, California, and Montana to concentrate on his writing. *The Track of the Cat* (1949), again set in the West, tells of the hunt by three brothers for a vicious black panther. *The Watchful Gods and Other Stories* appeared in 1950.

Clark's many interests included geology and Indian lore. Among his most serious concerns—as "The Portable Phonograph" makes evident—were natural conservation and the future survival of the human race.

■ Clark's concern with the survival of the human race led him to writing this short story. What does he foresee for us and why does he believe as he does?

Walter Van Tilburg Clark

The Portable Phonograph

The red sunset, with narrow, black cloud strips like threats across it, lay on the curved horizon of the prairie. The air was still and cold, and in it settled the mute darkness and greater cold of night. High in the air there was wind, for through the veil of the dusk, the clouds could be seen gliding rapidly south and changing shapes. A queer sensation of torment, of two-sided, unpredictable nature, arose from the stillness of the earth air beneath the violence of the upper air. Out of the sunset,
1 through the dead, matted grass and isolated weed stalks of the prairie, crept the narrow and deeply rutted remains of a road. In the road, in places, there were crusts of shallow, brittle ice. There were little islands of an old oiled pavement in the road too, but most of it was mud, now frozen rigid. The frozen mud still bore the toothed impress of great tanks, and a wanderer on the neighboring undulations might have stumbled, in this light, into large, partially filled-in and weed-grown cavities, their banks channeled and beginning to spread into badlands. These pits were such as might have been made by falling meteors, but they were not. They were the scars of gigantic bombs, their rawness already made a little natural by rain, seed, and time. Along the road there were rakish remnants of fence. There was also, just visible, one portion of tangled and multiple barbed wire still erect, behind which
2 was a shelving[1] ditch with small caves, now very quiet and empty, at intervals in its back wall. Otherwise there was no structure or remnant of a structure visible over the dome of the darkling[2] earth, but only, in sheltered hollows, the darker shadows of young trees trying again.

Under the wuthering[3] arch of the high wind, a V of wild geese fled south. The rush of their pinions[4] sounded briefly, and the faint, plaintive notes of their expeditionary talk. Then they left a still greater vacancy. There was the smell and expectation of snow, as there is likely to be when the wild geese fly south. From the remote distance, toward the red sky, came faintly the protracted howl and quick yap-yap of a prairie wolf.

3 North of the road, perhaps a hundred yards, lay the parallel and deeply entrenched course of a small creek, lined with leafless alders and willows. The creek was already silent under ice. Into the bank above it was dug a sort of cell, with a single opening like the mouth of a mine tunnel. Within the cell there was a little red of fire, which showed dully through the opening, like a reflection or a deception of the imagination. The light came from the chary[5] burning of four blocks of poorly aged peat, which gave off a petty warmth and much acrid smoke. But the precious remnants of wood, old fence posts and timbers from the long-deserted dugouts, had to be saved for the real cold, for the time when a man's breath blew white, the moisture in his nostrils stiffened at once when he stepped out, and the expansive blizzards paraded for days over the vast open, swirling and settling and thickening till the dawn of the cleared day when the sky was a thin blue-green and the terrible cold, in which a man could not live for three hours unwarmed, lay over the uniformly drifted swell of the plain.

Around the smoldering peat four men were seated cross-legged. Behind them, traversed by their shadows, was the earth bench, with two old and dirty army blankets, where the owner

1. **shelving:** sloping.
2. **darkling:** growing dark; deeply shadowed.
3. **wuthering:** blowing with a dull roar.
4. **pinions:** wings.
5. **chary** [chār′ē]: sparing; careful.

AT A GLANCE

- At sunset the prairie shows scars of a deadly holocaust.
- Fragments of fence and small caves are the only visible structures.
- Four men sit around a small fire in a cell dug into the bank of a frozen creek.

LITERARY OPTIONS

- symbolism
- style
- mood

THEMATIC OPTIONS

- art and imagination
- mistrust and aggression
- the dangers of modern technology

1 SETTING

Reinforced by the absence of chronological data, Clark's description conveys an image of the prairie that paradoxically evokes both the dawn and the death of civilization.

2 SYMBOLISM

Human destructiveness contrasts with nature's innate creativity, as reflected in the "young trees trying again."

3 MOOD

Clark's richly detailed description of the still, lifeless landscape *(leafless trees, silent creek)* adds vivid dimension to the bleak setting and conveys a prevailing mood of stasis and destruction.

GUIDED READING

LITERAL QUESTION

1a. What caused the large, weed-covered cavities that scar the prairie? (bombs)

INFERENTIAL QUESTION

1b. Based on the evidence of the bomb craters, what can you infer about the nature of the holocaust? (It was caused by war.)

AT A GLANCE

- The host, Dr. Jenkins, rewraps four books that he saved.
- Dr. Jenkins offers to play his phonograph and generously offers to use a steel needle instead of a thorn.

1 CHARACTERIZATION

Dr. Jenkins' physical descriptions (long gray beard and hair; "gnarled" brows and cheekbones; "big hands") evoke images of the imposing biblical figures painted during the Renaissance and underscore the religious aspect of his role.

2 POSTWAR IDEA

The reference to "a race of mechanical fools" reflects the Atomic Age's fear of technology's destructiveness.

3 THEME

Dr. Jenkins' generosity, kindled by the wisdom of *The Tempest* and the established sense of brotherhood, demonstrates the power of beauty and art to bridge the differences between humans.

4 SYMBOLISM

The packed floor of the earth cell is an ironically primitive backdrop for the technological marvel of the portable phonograph. Together they dramatize the achievements of the human race and the consequences of human folly.

of the cell slept. In a niche in the opposite wall were a few tin utensils which caught the glint of the coals. The host was rewrapping in a piece of daubed burlap four fine, leather-bound books. He worked slowly and very carefully, and at last tied the bundle securely with a piece of grass-woven cord. The other three looked intently upon the process, as if a great significance lay in it. As the host tied the cord,
1 he spoke. He was an old man, his long, matted beard and hair gray to nearly white. The shadows made his brows and cheekbones appear gnarled, his eyes and cheeks deeply sunken. His big hands, rough with frost and swollen by rheumatism, were awkward but gentle at their task. He was like a prehistoric priest performing a fateful ceremonial rite. Also his voice had in it a suitable quality of deep, reverent despair, yet perhaps at the moment, a sharpness of selfish satisfaction. "When I perceived what was happening," he said, "I told myself, 'It is the end. I cannot take much; I will take these.'

"Perhaps I was impractical," he continued. "But for myself, I do not regret, and what do
2 we know of those who will come after us? We are the doddering remnant of a race of mechanical fools. I have saved what I love; the soul of what was good in us is here; perhaps the new ones will make a strong enough beginning not to fall behind when they become clever."

He rose with slow pain and placed the wrapped volumes in the niche with his utensils. The others watched him with the same ritualistic gaze.

"Shakespeare, the Bible, *Moby-Dick*, the *Divine Comedy*,"[6] one of them said softly. "You might have done worse, much worse."

"You will have a little soul left until you die," said another harshly. "That is more than is true of us. My brain becomes thick, like my hands." He held the big, battered hands, with their black nails, in the glow to be seen.

"I want paper to write on," he said. "And there is none."

The fourth man said nothing. He sat in the shadow farthest from the fire, and sometimes his body jerked in its rags from the cold. Although he was still young, he was sick and coughed often. Writing implied a greater future than he now felt able to consider.

The old man seated himself laboriously, and reached out, groaning at the movement, to put another block of peat on the fire. With bowed heads and averted eyes, his three guests acknowledged his magnanimity.

"We thank you, Doctor Jenkins, for the reading," said the man who had named the books.

They seemed then to be waiting for some-
3 thing. Doctor Jenkins understood, but was loath[7] to comply. In an ordinary moment he would have said nothing. But the words of *The Tempest*,[8] which he had been reading, and the religious attention of the three, made this an unusual occasion.

"You wish to hear the phonograph," he said grudgingly.

The two middle-aged men stared into the fire, unable to formulate and expose the enormity of their desire.

The young man, however, said anxiously, between suppressed coughs, "Oh, please," like an excited child.

The old man rose again in his difficult way,
4 and went to the back of the cell. He returned and placed tenderly upon the packed floor, where the firelight might fall upon it, an old portable phonograph in a black case. He smoothed the top with his hand, and then opened it. The lovely green-felt-covered disc became visible.

"I have been using thorns as needles," he said. "But tonight, because we have a musician among us"—he bent his head to the young man, almost invisible in the shadow—"I will use a steel needle. There are only three left."

The two middle-aged men stared at him in speechless adoration. The one with the big

6. ***Moby-Dick*, the *Divine Comedy*:** Herman Melville's great novel and Dante's poetic masterpiece.

7. **loath** [lōth]: reluctant.

8. ***The Tempest*:** play by Shakespeare, which takes place on an isolated island.

GUIDED READING

LITERAL QUESTION

1a. What few books does Dr. Jenkins save? (Shakespeare; the Bible; *Moby-Dick; The Divine Comedy*)

INFERENTIAL QUESTION

1b. Why might Dr. Jenkins believe that these books represent the goodness in the human soul? (They represent the power of imagination and art, span the wisdom of the ages, and express our ability to find meaning and purpose in life on earth.)

hands, who wanted to write, moved his lips, but the whisper was not audible.

"Oh, don't!" cried the young man, as if he were hurt. "The thorns will do beautifully."

"No," the old man said. "I have become ac-
1 customed to the thorns, but they are not really good. For you, my young friend, we will have good music tonight.

"After all," he added generously, and beginning to wind the phonograph, which creaked, "they can't last forever."

"No, nor we," the man who needed to write said harshly. "The needle, by all means."

"Oh, thanks," said the young man. "Thanks," he said again in a low, excited voice, and then stifled his coughing with a bowed head.

"The records, though," said the old man when he had finished winding, "are a different matter. Already they are very worn. I do not play them more than once a week. One, once a week, that is what I allow myself.

"More than a week I cannot stand it; not to hear them," he apologized.

2 "No, how could you?" cried the young man. "And with them here like this."

"A man can stand anything," said the man who wanted to write, in his harsh, antagonistic voice.

"Please, the music," said the young man.

"Only the one," said the old man. "In the long run, we will remember more that way."

He had a dozen records with luxuriant gold and red seals. Even in that light the others could see that the threads of the records were becoming worn. Slowly he read out the titles, and the tremendous, dead names of the composers and the artists and the orchestras. The three worked upon the names in their minds, carefully. It was difficult to select from such a wealth what they would at once most like to remember. Finally, the man who wanted to write named Gershwin's[9] "New York."

"Oh, no!" cried the sick young man, and then could say nothing more because he had to cough. The others understood him, and the harsh man withdrew his selection and waited for the musician to choose.

3 The musician begged Doctor Jenkins to read the titles again, very slowly, so that he could remember the sounds. While they were read, he lay back against the wall, his eyes closed, his thin, horny hand pulling at his light beard, and listened to the voices and the orchestras and the single instruments in his mind.

---

9. **Gershwin's:** referring to George Gershwin (1898–1937), American composer.

AT A GLANCE

- Over protests Dr. Jenkins insists on using the needle. He plays the records only once a week because they are wearing out.
- He reads the labels of a dozen records and asks the group to choose only one. They allow the sick musician to choose.

1 DIALOGUE

Note how Clark uses dialogue to heighten tension during the rising action as well as to dramatize the conflict between Dr. Jenkins' generosity and the cynicism of the man who needed to write.

2 MOOD

Both the desperate intensity of the musician and the cold pessimism of the would-be writer reinforce the sense of desolation and irretrievable loss that pervade the cell.

3 THEME

The musician's ability to surrender his consciousness to memory and imagination poignantly demonstrate the power of art and imagination to transform ordinary experience.

GUIDED READING

LITERAL QUESTIONS

1a. Why does Dr. Jenkins play his records only once a week? (They are wearing out.)

2a. Whom does the group allow to choose the music they will hear? (the sick musician)

INFERENTIAL QUESTIONS

1b. What might you infer about Clark's views on art based on the point he makes about the worn records? (The most enduring form of artistic expression lies in its power to ennoble the human spirit.)

2b. What do you think is the significance of their allowing the musician to choose the music? (They think he will die soon, and so they are being generous to him.)

AT A GLANCE

- The group debate the merits of Shelley and *Moby-Dick.*
- They listen to the record, a Debussy nocturne, thank Dr. Jenkins, and leave the cell.
- Suspecting trouble, Dr. Jenkins prepares for bed.

1 PARAPHRASING THE PASSAGE

The would-be writer is suggesting that the harshness and stark conflict of *Moby-Dick* suit the bleak postwar environment in which they live. Shelley's poetry, he implies, is too ethereal.

2 CLIMAX

The religious terminology *(rose to their knees, an attitude of worship)* suggests the group's emotional intensity as they prepare to listen to the music.

3 STYLE

Note how the "swelling and ebbing" of the coordinated clauses and use of alliteration with the long *o* and *l* approximate the rhythm and the power of the music.

When the reading was done, he spoke despairingly. "I have forgotten," he complained; "I cannot hear them clearly.

"There are things missing," he explained.

"I know," said Doctor Jenkins. "I thought
1 that I knew all of Shelley[10] by heart. I should have brought Shelley."

"That's more soul than we can use," said the harsh man. "*Moby-Dick* is better.

"We can understand that," he emphasized.

The Doctor nodded.

"Still," said the man who had admired the books, "we need the absolute if we are to keep a grasp on anything.

"Anything but these sticks and peat clods and rabbit snares," he said bitterly.

"Shelley desired an ultimate absolute," said the harsh man. "It's too much," he said. "It's no good; no earthly good."

The musician selected a Debussy[11] nocturne. The others considered and approved.
2 They rose to their knees to watch the Doctor prepare for the playing, so that they appeared to be actually in an attitude of worship. The peat glow showed the thinness of their bearded faces, and the deep lines in them, and revealed the condition of their garments. The other two continued to kneel as the old man carefully lowered the needle onto the spinning disc, but the musician suddenly drew back against the wall again, with his knees up, and buried his face in his hands.

At the first notes of the piano, the listeners were startled. They stared at each other. Even the musician lifted his head in amazement, but then quickly bowed it again, strainingly, as if he were suffering from a pain he might not be able to endure. They were all listening deeply, without movement. The wet, blue-green notes tinkled forth from the old machine, and were individual, delectable presences in the cell. The individual, delectable presences swept into a sudden tide of unbearably beautiful disso-
3 nance, and then continued fully the swelling and ebbing of that tide, the dissonant inpourings, and the resolutions, and the diminishments, and the little, quiet wavelets of interlude lapping between. Every sound was piercing and singularly sweet. In all the men except the musician, there occurred rapid sequences of tragically heightened recollection. He heard nothing but what was there. At the final, whispering disappearance, but moving quietly so that the others would not hear him and look at him, he let his head fall back in agony, as if it were drawn there by the hair, and clenched the fingers of one hand over his teeth. He sat that way while the others were silent, and until they began to breathe again normally. His drawn-up legs were trembling violently.

Quickly Doctor Jenkins lifted the needle off, to save it and not to spoil the recollection with scraping. When he had stopped the whirling of the sacred disc, he courteously left the phonograph open and by the fire, in sight.

The others, however, understood. The musician rose last, but then abruptly, and went quickly out at the door without saying anything. The others stopped at the door and gave their thanks in low voices. The Doctor nodded magnificently.

"Come again," he invited, "in a week. We will have the 'New York.' "

When the two had gone together, out toward the rimed[12] road, he stood in the entrance, peering and listening. At first, there was only the resonant boom of the wind overhead, and then far over the dome of the dead, dark plain, the wolf cry lamenting. In the rifts of clouds, the Doctor saw four stars flying. It impressed the Doctor that one of them had just been obscured by the beginning of a flying cloud at the very moment he heard what he had been listening for, a sound of suppressed coughing. It was not nearby, however. He believed that down against the pale alders he could see the moving shadow.

With nervous hands he lowered the piece of canvas which served as his door, and pegged

10. **Shelley:** Percy Bysshe Shelley (1792–1822), English poet.
11. **Debussy** [deb′yoo sē′]: Claude Debussy (1862–1918), French composer.

12. **rimed:** frosty.

GUIDED READING

LITERAL QUESTION

1a. What sound does Dr. Jenkins hear after the group leaves? (the sound of the musician's cough)

INFERENTIAL QUESTION

1b. What do you think is happening? (The sick musician may be lingering outside Dr. Jenkins' dwelling, perhaps hoping to steal the phonograph.)

it at the bottom. Then quickly and quietly, looking at the piece of canvas frequently, he slipped the records into the case, snapped the lid shut, and carried the phonograph to his couch. There, pausing to stare at the canvas and listen, he dug earth from the wall and disclosed a piece of board. Behind this there was a deep hole in the wall into which he put the phonograph. After a moment's consideration, he went over and reached down his bundle of books and inserted it also. Then, guardedly, he once more sealed up the hole with the board and the earth. He also changed his blankets, and the grass-stuffed sack which served as a pillow, so that he could lie facing the entrance. After carefully placing two more blocks of peat upon the fire, he stood for a long time watching the stretched canvas, but it seemed to billow naturally with the first gusts of a lowering
1 wind. At last he prayed, and got in under his blankets, and closed his smoke-smarting eyes. On the inside of the bed, next the wall, he could feel with his hand the comfortable piece of lead pipe.

STUDY QUESTIONS

Recalling

1. Identify five details in the first paragraph that help capture a bleak and desolate landscape. What are the pits that "might have been made by falling meteors" but were not?
2. To whom is the host, Doctor Jenkins, compared in the fourth paragraph? What does he say in the fourth and fifth paragraphs?
3. When the characters are introduced, what activity has just concluded? What important activity follows?
4. Describe the physical reaction that the musician has as he listens to the Debussy nocturne.
5. After his visitors have left, what does Doctor Jenkins do "with nervous hands"? Where does he put the phonograph, the records, and the books? What does he face when he lies down to sleep, and what does he feel with his hand?

Interpreting

6. What cataclysmic event has occurred that left these four men "the doddering remnant of a race of mechanical fools"? In using the term "mechanical fools," what does Doctor Jenkins suggest has caused this event?
7. Briefly describe the feelings the four men have for the books, the phonograph, and the records. What is suggested by the depiction of their activities in terms of ritual or religious ceremony?
8. Why does Doctor Jenkins hide the phonograph, records, and books after his guests leave? What is suggested by his feeling for the "comfortable piece of lead pipe"?
9. What is the irony of Doctor Jenkins' final action? What does the story suggest is the true cause of violence and destruction?

Extending

10. Do you agree with the suggestions about human nature made in this story? Why or why not?

COMPOSITION

Analyzing a Symbol

■ The portable phonograph is clearly the central symbol in Clark's story. Write an essay in which you analyze its significance. Begin by telling what it means to the characters in the story. Then tell what it means to you. *For help with this assignment, refer to Lesson 5 in the Writing About Literature Handbook at the back of this book.*

Creating a Time Capsule

■ A time capsule is designed to be found and opened by future generations. Make a list of ten things you would preserve if you had to create a time capsule to protect objects against a disaster. Write a sentence for each object, telling why your think it should be preserved and defining its value for people in the future.

AT A GLANCE

- Dr. Jenkins hides the phonograph and the books.
- He prays, then goes to bed, holding a piece of lead pipe.

1 THEME

Dr. Jenkins' paradoxical actions in praying and arming himself with a lead pipe vividly portray the conflict between the desire for spiritual enlightenment and the pursuit of pure self-interest.

REFLECTING ON THE STORY

What does the phonograph symbolize in the story? (Answers will vary: the power of art to uplift us spiritually; the union of art and technology.)

STUDY QUESTIONS

1. *clouds, cold, darkness, ice, mud;* bomb craters
2. ■ prehistoric priest
   ■ When he saw the end coming, he took books; he hopes future generations will not "fall behind."
3. reading *The Tempest;* playing record
4. He lifts head, bows it, lets head fall back while he clenches fingers over teeth.
5. lowers canvas; hole; canvas door, lead pipe
6. total war; overreliance on technology
7. ■ reverence, awe
   ■ Art is spiritually ennobling.
8. suspects young musician covets them; prepared to kill to protect treasures
9. willingness to destroy civilization to save it; jealousy, avarice
10. Answers will vary. Pessimists will agree, citing leaders calling for more weapons to avert war; optimists will disagree, saying humanity can save itself through influence of art, religion, love.

COMPOSITION: GUIDELINES FOR EVALUATION

ANALYZING A SYMBOL

Objective

To explain the significance of a symbol

Guidelines for Evaluation

- suggested length: two to four paragraphs
- should explain characters view phonograph as symbol of lost beauty, culture
- should note irony of its mechanical form
- should draw conclusions by explaining what the symbol means to the writer

CREATING A TIME CAPSULE

Objective

To develop a list according to a criterion

Guidelines for Evaluation

- suggested length: ten items
- should identify ten items according to criterion, i.e., "significant in my life"
- should use sentences to identify criterion and define item's value for people of future
- should use a consistent format for each item

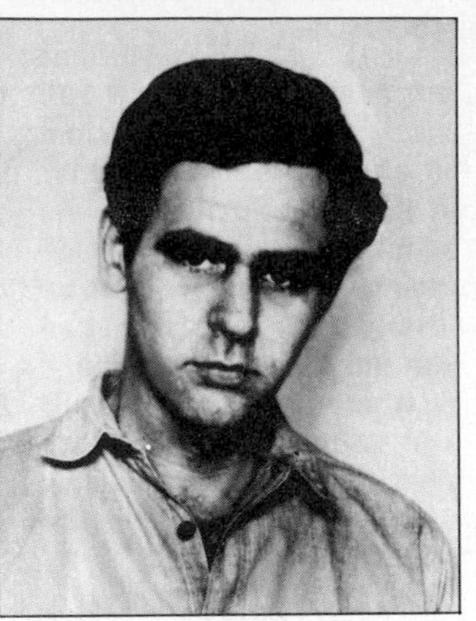

James Agee *1909–1955*

James Agee was a poet, novelist, and screen writer. This lyrical and sensitive stylist was also one of the most incisive and influential American film critics of the 1930s and 1940s.

Agee was born in Knoxville, Tennessee, and grew up in the Cumberland Mountain region. During vacations from school he worked in wheat fields in Kansas and Nebraska. From this background he developed a strong attachment to the land, which provided a source for much of his later writing.

At Harvard, where he attended college, Agee wrote poetry and was editor of the Harvard *Advocate. Permit Me Voyage* (1934), a collection of verse, contained a foreword by the poet Archibald MacLeish (page 450), who praised Agee for his "delicate and perceptive ear."

In the summer of 1936, on a joint assignment for *Fortune* magazine, Agee and the great photographer Walker Evans lived for several weeks among sharecroppers in Alabama. Deeply affected by what he saw, he wrote a passionate and poetic commentary intended to accompany Evans' evocative photographs of the sharecroppers' life. Although the article never appeared in the magazine, both text and photographs were published in book form in 1941, as *Let Us Now Praise Famous Men.*

After 1948 Agee concentrated on writing for films, and his best scripts were *The African Queen* (1951) and *The Night of the Hunter* (1955). He also wrote a novella, *The Morning Watch* (1951), and a novel, *A Death in the Family* (1957), which was awarded the Pulitzer Prize. Agee's film criticism is collected in *Agee on Film* (1958).

Like Thomas Wolfe, James Agee was often Romantic and even undisciplined in his writing, allowing his works to take on their own shapes as they grew, without forms imposed by the author. Yet, as MacLeish noted, Agee possessed a true poet's ear and a remarkable sense of rhythm. He had a sharply perceptive eye for detail. All of these qualities give his finest prose the lyrical beauty of poetry. "Knoxville: Summer, 1915" is a perfect example of Agee's achievement—a remembrance of childhood, rich in sensory impressions and nostalgic feeling. Written in 1947, it was later added as an introduction to his masterpiece, *A Death in the Family.*

■ Since we cannot relive childhood, many writers try to recapture it. What do you know about Agee's childhood when you finish reading this remembrance?

James Agee

Knoxville: Summer, 1915

1 We are talking now of summer evenings in Knoxville, Tennessee, in the time that I lived there so successfully disguised to myself as a child. It was a little bit mixed sort of block, fairly solidly lower middle class, with one or two juts apiece on either side of that. The houses corresponded: middle-sized gracefully fretted[1] wood houses built in the late nineties and early nineteen hundreds, with small front and side and more spacious back yards, and
2 trees in the yards, and porches. These were softwooded trees, poplars, tulip trees, cottonwoods. There were fences around one or two of the houses, but mainly the yards ran into each other with only now and then a low hedge that wasn't doing very well. There were few good friends among the grown people, and they were not poor enough for the other sort of intimate acquaintance, but everyone nodded and spoke, and even might talk short times, trivially, and at the two extremes of the general or the particular, and ordinarily nextdoor neighbors talked quite a bit when they happened to run into each other, and never paid calls. The men were mostly small businessmen, one or two very modestly executives, one or two worked with their hands, most of them clerical, and most of them between thirty and forty-five.

But it is of these evenings I speak.

Supper was at six and was over by half past. There was still daylight, shining softly and with
3 a tarnish, like the lining of a shell; and the carbon lamps[2] lifted at the corners were on in the light, and the locusts were started, and the fire flies were out, and a few frogs were flopping in the dewy grass, by the time the fathers and the children came out. The children ran out first hell bent and yelling those names by which they were known; then the fathers sank out leisurely in crossed suspenders, their collars removed and their necks looking tall and shy. The mothers stayed back in the kitchen washing and drying, putting things away, recrossing their traceless footsteps like the lifetime journeys of bees, measuring out the dry cocoa for breakfast. When they came out they had taken off their aprons and their skirts were dampened and they sat in rockers on their porches quietly.

It is not of the games children play in the evening that I want to speak now, it is of a contemporaneous atmosphere that has little to do with them: that of the fathers of families, each in his space of lawn, his shirt fishlike pale in the unnatural light and his face nearly anon-
4 ymous, hosing their lawns. The hoses were attached at spiggots that stood out of the brick foundations of the houses. The nozzles were variously set but usually so there was a long sweet stream of spray, the nozzle wet in the hand, the water trickling the right forearm and the peeled-back cuff, and the water whishing out a long loose and low-curved cone, and so gentle a sound. First an insane noise of violence in the nozzle, then the still irregular sound of adjustment, then the smoothing into steadiness and a pitch as accurately tuned to the size and style of stream as any violin. So many qualities of sound out of one hose: so many choral differences out of those several hoses that were in earshot. Out of any one hose, the almost dead silence of the release, and the short still arch of the separate big drops, silent as a held breath, and the only noise the flattering noise on leaves and the slapped grass at the fall of each big drop. That, and the intense hiss with the intense stream; that, and that same intensity not growing less but growing more quiet and delicate with the

1. **fretted:** having ornamental borders of symmetrically arranged vertical and horizontal straight lines.
2. **carbon lamps:** lamps with carbon filaments.

AT A GLANCE

- The narrator describes summer evenings in Knoxville in 1915.
- After supper the children run out to play and the fathers appear.
- Each father gets out his hose and waters the lawn.

LITERARY OPTIONS

- style: imagery
- point of view

THEMATIC OPTIONS

- the quest for self-identity
- childhood memories

1 POINT OF VIEW

The first-person narrator's inclusion of the reader ("We are talking now") and reference to a specific recollected time and place invite the reader to participate in a nostalgic vision of childhood.

2 SETTING

The use of specific physical detail (kinds of trees; number of fences) establishes a clear, vivid picture of the block the narrator lived on as a child.

3 STYLE: IMAGERY

The figurative comparison between the quality of the daylight and the lining of a shell and the evocative power that develops from the accumulation of sensory impressions (sound of the locusts; sight of the fireflies; feel of the grass) infuse the description with a lyric, poetic dimension.

4 STYLE: REPETITION

The repetition of the consonant sound *s* evokes the sound that hoses make, thus intensifying the reader's participation in the narrator's memory.

GUIDED READING

LITERAL QUESTIONS

1a. What kinds of jobs do the men of the block have? (They are small businessmen, modest executives, laborers, clerks.)

2a. What aspect of his childhood memories does the narrator specify as the focus of his interest? (the contemporaneous atmosphere created by the fathers watering their lawns)

INFERENTIAL QUESTIONS

1b. Why do you think Agee supplies this kind of detail about the men? (It gives his evocation of the past more dimension and clarity.)

2b. Why do you think the memory has so much importance to the narrator? (because the initial experience stimulated his sensory perceptions)

AT A GLANCE

- The nozzles make a whole chorus of sounds echoed by the sounds of the locusts and the crickets.
- After the men stop watering, people sit on their porches and listen to the night sounds.

1 STYLE: FIGURES OF SPEECH

The detailed description shapes the simile into a prosaic, rather than poetic, expression of experience.

2 STYLE: IMAGERY

Agee's focus on sensory impression (*damp of dew, green-black smear of smell, cold silver noise*) infuses the narrative with an intensely lyrical dimension that reinforces the beauty of his nostalgic recollections.

3 POINT OF VIEW

The narrator's shift of tense from the past to the present indicates his total surrender to memory and increases the reader's appreciation by intensifying the immediacy of the narrator's childhood memories.

turn of the nozzle, up to that extreme tender whisper when the water was just a wide bell of film. Chiefly, though, the hoses were set much alike, in a compromise between distance and tenderness of spray (and quite surely a sense of art behind this compromise, and a quiet deep joy, too real to recognize itself), and the sounds therefore were pitched much alike; pointed by the snorting start of a new hose; decorated by some man playful with the nozzle; left empty, like God by the sparrow's fall, when any single one of them desists: and all, though near alike, of various pitch; and in this unison. These sweet pale streamings in the light lift out their pallors and their voices all together, mothers hushing their children, the hushing unnaturally prolonged, the men gentle and silent and each snail-like withdrawn into the quietude of what he singly is doing, and gentle happy and peaceful, tasting the mean[3] goodness of their living like the last of their suppers in their mouths; while the locusts carry on this noise of hoses on their much higher and sharper key. The noise of the locust is dry, and it seems not to be rasped or vibrated but urged from him as if through a small orifice by a breath that can never give out. Also there is never one locust but an illusion of at least a thousand. The noise of each
1 locust is pitched in some classic locust range out of which none of them varies more than two full tones: and yet you seem to hear each locust discrete from all the rest, and there is a long, slow, pulse in their noise, like the scarcely defined arch of a long and high set bridge. They are all around in every tree, so that the noise seems to come from nowhere and everywhere at once, from the whole shell heaven, shivering in your flesh and teasing your eardrums, the boldest of all the sounds of night. And yet it is habitual to summer nights, and is of the great order of noises, like the noises of the sea and of the blood her precocious grandchild, which you realize you are hearing only when you catch yourself listening. Meantime from low in the dark, just outside the swaying horizons of the hoses, conveying
2 always grass in the damp of dew and its strong green-black smear of smell, the regular yet spaced noises of the crickets, each a sweet cold silver noise three-noted, like the slipping each time of three matched links of a small chain.

But the men by now, one by one, have silenced their hoses and drained and coiled them. Now only two, and now only one, is left, and you see only ghostlike shirt with the sleeve garters,[4] and sober mystery of his mild face like the lifted face of large cattle enquiring of your presence in a pitchdark pool of meadow; and now he too is gone; and it has become that time of evening when people sit on their porches, rocking gently and talking gently and watching the street and the standing up into their sphere of possession of the trees,
3 of birds hung havens, hangars. People go by; things go by. A horse, drawing a buggy, breaking his hollow iron music on the asphalt; a loud auto; a quiet auto; people in pairs, not in a hurry, scuffling, switching their weight of aestival[5] body, talking casually, the taste hovering over them of vanilla, strawberry, pasteboard and starched milk, the image upon them of lovers and horsemen, squared with clowns in hueless amber. A streetcar raising its iron moan; stopping, belling and starting; stertorous;[6] rousing and raising again its iron increasing moan and swimming its gold windows and straw seats on past and past and past, the bleak spark crackling and cursing above it like a small malignant spirit set to dog its tracks; the iron whine rises on rising speed; still risen, faints; halts; the faint stinging bell; rises again, still fainter, fainting, lifting, lifts, faints forgone: forgotten. Now is the night one blue dew.

Now is the night one blue dew, my father has
drained, he has coiled the hose.

---

3. **mean:** humble.

4. **sleeve garters:** elastic bands worn over shirt sleeves to regulate their length.
5. **aestival** [es′tə vəl]: relating to summer.
6. **stertorous:** loud, raspy.

GUIDED READING

LITERAL QUESTIONS

1a. What do the men taste "like the last of the suppers in their mouths"? (the goodness of their lives)

2a. What sounds does the narrator recollect as people sit on their porches talking? (a horse and buggy, cars, people talking, a streetcar)

INFERENTIAL QUESTIONS

1b. What does this simile suggest about the narrator's view of the past? (He sees the past as nurturing.)

2b. What impact do these details have on the reader's ability to visualize the evening? (The details all clarify and color his description, making it easy to visualize what the night was like.)

A scene in Knoxville, Tennessee, c. 1915.

Low on the length of lawns, a frailing[7] of fire who breathes.
Content, silver, like peeps of light, each cricket makes his comment over and over in the drowned grass.
A cold toad thumpily flounders.
Within the edges of damp shadows of side yards are hovering children nearly sick with joy of fear, who watch the unguarding of a telephone pole.
Around white carbon corner lamps bugs of all sizes are lifted elliptic, solar systems. Big hardshells bruise themselves, assailant: he is fallen on his back, legs squiggling.
Parents on porches: rock and rock: From damp strings morning glories: hang their ancient faces.
The dry and exalted noise of the locusts from all the air at once enchants my eardrums.

On the rough wet grass of the back yard my father and mother have spread quilts. We all lie there, my mother, my father, my uncle, my aunt, and I too am lying there. First we were sitting up, then one of us lay down, and then we all lay down, on our stomachs, or on our sides, or on our backs, and they have kept on talking. They are not talking much, and the talk is quiet, of nothing in particular, of noth-
1 ing at all in particular, of nothing at all. The stars are wide and alive, they seem each like a smile of great sweetness, and they seem very near. All my people are larger bodies than mine, quiet, with voices gentle and meaningless like the voices of sleeping birds. One is an artist, he is living at home. One is a musician, she is living at home. One is my mother who is good to me. One is my father who is good to me. By some chance, here they are, all on this earth; and who shall ever tell the sorrow of being on this earth, lying, on quilts, on the grass, in a summer evening, among the sounds of night. May God bless my people, my uncle, my aunt, my mother, my good father, oh, remember them kindly in their time of trouble; and in the hour of their taking away.

2 After a little I am taken in and put to bed. Sleep, soft smiling, draws me unto her: and those receive me, who quietly treat me, as one familiar and well-beloved in that home: but will not, oh, will not, not now, not ever; but will not ever tell me who I am.

7. **frailing:** delicate light.

AT A GLANCE

- The narrator offers a poem that recapitulates his prose memories of the summer evening.
- In the back yard he lies on a quilt with his family.
- Later he is taken to bed and falls asleep.
- He laments that memories of his family can never tell him who he is.

1 STYLE: IMAGERY

The images are ones of tranquility and benevolence.

2 POINT OF VIEW

The narrator's adult perspective on his childhood helps him appreciate the security and love that nurtured him but also confronts him with his separateness and need to determine his own identity.

REFLECTING ON THE STORY

What does the last line of the story suggest about the narrator's motivation for remembering the summer evenings? (He is in search of a sense of himself and hopes the past will help him.)

GUIDED READING

LITERAL QUESTION

1a. To whom does the narrator offer a blessing? (his aunt, uncle, mother and father)

INFERENTIAL QUESTION

1b. How does he feel about these people? (He loves them very much.)

STUDY QUESTIONS

1. subject: summer evenings; setting: Knoxville, Tennessee, when the narrator lived there as a child
2. children playing, water coming out of nozzles, locusts, crickets, a horse and buggy, an auto, people talking; children, fathers, mothers
3. narrator, parents, aunt, uncle; nothing in particular; asks God to bless his people in their time of trouble and in the hour of taking away
4. Memories can never tell him who he is.
5. lush, poetic; poetic prose
6. security, emotional richness; love, trust; tranquil tone, prayer, declaration that he was "well-beloved"
7. It suggests that he has had to leave home to seek his own way and that he misses the security and comfort of childhood; memories cannot restore lost innocence or help the adult define his identity.
8. Students might echo Milton's opinion: "The childhood shows the man / As morning shows the day." Students might point out the influences of community, school, society, heredity, and chance.

STUDY QUESTIONS

Recalling

1. According to the opening paragraph, what are the narrator's subject and setting (time *and* place)?
2. Name at least three sounds of the summer evening that the narrator describes. What three "categories" of people are described in the third paragraph?
3. Who lies on the quilts in the next-to-last paragraph? Of what do they speak? What prayer does the narrator offer at the end of the paragraph?
4. What is the narrator's closing thought?

Interpreting

5. Briefly describe the style in which this story is written. Why is the poem in the middle of the story less of an interruption than it would be in many other prose narratives?
6. What particular qualities of the life pictured here emerge by the story's end? What seems to be the narrator's attitude toward his family? Give details to support your answer.
7. What does the final paragraph suggest about the narrator's reasons for remembering his childhood in such detail? What does it suggest such memories can never do to the narrator's satisfaction?

Extending

8. To what extent do you think our childhood environment determines who we are? What other factors do you think are important in determining our personalities? Discuss.

COMPOSITION

Writing a Comparison/Contrast

■ Write a short essay comparing the poetic style of "Knoxville: Summer, 1915" to the spare style of Hemingway's "In Another Country" (page 490). Begin by describing the author's purpose in each selection. Then explain how each author's style relates to his purpose, giving examples from the selection to support your descriptions of each author's style. Conclude with your own opinion of the total effect of each of the styles on the reader. *For help with this assignment, refer to Lesson 2 in the Writing About Literature Handbook at the back of this book.*

Writing an Evocative Remembrance

■ Remember an experience or a place that still gives you a special feeling when you think of it. Describe your recollection as imaginatively and as clearly as you can. Include details that evoke sensory impressions, such as particular sounds, sights, and smells.

COMPOSITION: GUIDELINES FOR EVALUATION

WRITING A COMPARISON/CONTRAST

Objective

To compare and contrast two stories

Guidelines for Evaluation

- suggested length: six to eight paragraphs
- should describe Hemingway's and Agee's purposes and styles
- should explain the effect of each style

WRITING AN EVOCATIVE REMEMBRANCE

Objective

To recollect a place or experience vividly

Guidelines for Evaluation

- suggested length: one to three paragraphs
- should clearly identify the experience or place being recollected
- should use sensory language
- should have a single mood or emotional effect

Elizabeth Enright *1909–1968*

Elizabeth Enright began her career as an illustrator of children's books. She wrote several stories to accompany her illustrations and later stopped illustrating in order to concentrate on writing.

Enright was born in Oak Park, Illinois, but lived most of her life in New York City. Her parents were professional artists, her mother an illustrator, her father a political cartoonist; her uncle was the famous architect Frank Lloyd Wright. As a child in this "environment of paint brushes and India ink and water colors and drawing boards," Elizabeth Enright enjoyed imitating her parents. By her own account, she drew all over telephone books, blackboards, sidewalks, her mother's best writing paper, and, when no other medium was available, on her own bare knees.

She studied art in New York and Paris, and after several years as an illustrator for magazines, she published her first book, *Kintu: A Congo Adventure* (1955), for which she supplied the text as well. *Borrowed Summer and Other Stories* (1946) contains her first writing for adults. It was followed by *The Moment Before the Rain* (1955), *The Riddle of the Fly and Other Stories* (1959), and *Doublefields: Memories and Stories* (1966).

One critic noted that Enright's best stories are "seen through the disabused [undeceived] eyes of women." The main character in "The Signature" is a good example of such a woman. In detailing her quest for identity—a common quest in post–World War II fiction—Enright also makes some strong comments about the possible future identities of us all.

■ Why do we need to have a sense of identity? What happens when we have none? How can we find our identity?

AT A GLANCE

- A woman walks along a street of an unfamiliar city, not knowing her name or anything about her past.
- In her purse she finds strange currency marked with an abstraction of a human eye.

LITERARY OPTIONS

- setting
- tone
- point of view

THEMATIC OPTIONS

- the search for identity
- the dehumanization of modern life
- the value of the past

1 TONE

The narrator's detached but detailed observations suggest that she views the street from a comprehensive distance, as if in a dream, and create an eerie, foreboding undertone.

2 SETTING

The environment assumes an actively menacing, adversarial role as it misleads and reverses the narrator's expectations.

3 POINT OF VIEW

The narrator's flat, objective, detailed physical observations ("I looked at my hands") seem to develop from her lack of both memory and sense of personal history.

4 SYMBOL

The diamond shape takes on a symbolic dimension, reflecting both the narrator's frustrated search for identity and the ominous, totalitarian sense that characterizes the city.

Elizabeth Enright

The Signature

1 The street was wide and sloped gently upward ahead of me. It was paved with hard-baked dust almost white in the early-afternoon light, dry as clay and decked with bits of refuse. On either side the wooden houses stood blind to the street, all their shutters closed. The one- and two-story buildings—some of them set back a little; there was no sidewalk—had door yards with dusted grass and bushes, but many of them stood flush to the road itself with nothing but a powdered weed or two for grace. All of the houses had an old, foreign look, and all were unpainted, weather-scoured to the same pale color, except for the eaves of some which had been trimmed with wooden zigzags and painted long ago, like the crude, faded shutters, in tones of blue or red.

2 The sky was blanched with light, fronded with cirrus,[1] unemphatic; just such a sky as one finds near the sea, and this, in addition to the scoured, dry, enduring look of the town, persuaded me that an ocean or harbor must be somewhere near at hand. But when I came up over the rise of the road, I could find no furred line of blue at any horizon. All I could see was the great town—no, it was a city—spread far and wide, low lying, sun bleached, and unknown to me. And this was only one more thing that was unknown to me, for not
3 only was I ignorant of the name of the city, but I was ignorant of my own name, and of my own life, and nothing that I seized on could offer me a clue. I looked at my hands: they were the hands of a middle-aged women, coarsening at the joints, faintly blotched. On the third finger of the left hand there was a golden wedding ring, but who had put it there I could not guess. My body in the dark dress, my dust-chalked shoes were also strangers to me, and I was frightened and felt that I had been frightened for a long time, so long that the feeling had become habitual—something that I could live with, in a pinch, or, more properly, something that until this moment I had felt that I could live with. But now I was in terror of my puzzle.

I had the conviction that if I could once see my own face, I would remember who and what I was, and why I was in this place. I searched for a pane of glass to give me my reflection, but every window was shuttered fast. It was a season of drought, too, and there was not so much as a puddle to look into; in my pocket there was no mirror and my purse contained only a few bills of a currency unknown to me. I took the bills out and looked at them; they were old and used and the blue numerals and characters engraved on them were also of a sort I had never seen before, or could not remember having seen. In the center of each bill, where ordinarily one finds the pictures of a statesman or a monarch, there was instead an angular, spare symbol: a laterally elongated diamond shape with a heavy vertical line drawn through it at the center, rather like an abstraction of the human eye. As I resumed my walking I was aware of an impression that I had seen this symbol recently and often, in other places, and at the very moment I was thinking this I came upon it again, drawn in chalk on the side of a house. After that, watching for it, I saw it several times: marked in the dirt of the road, marked on the shutters, carved on the railing of a fence.

4 It was this figure, this eye-diamond, which reminded me, by its persistence, that the eye of another person can be a little mirror, and now with a feeling of excitement, of possible hope, I began walking faster, in search of a face.

From time to time I had passed other peo-

1. **fronded . . . cirrus:** having high, wispy clouds resembling fern leaves ("fronds").

GUIDED READING

LITERAL QUESTIONS

1a. What does the narrator notice about the shutters on the houses? (They are all closed.)

2a. Where does the narrator see the mark of the eye-diamond? (on currency; "in the dirt of the road"; on shutters; carved on a fence)

INFERENTIAL QUESTIONS

1b. How do the shutters contribute to the mood of the day? (The fact that they are all closed during the day seems unfriendly and ominous.)

2b. What do you think the persistence of the eye-diamond suggests about its meaning? (that it is a governmental insignia or a religious symbol)

1 ple, men and women, in the street. Their dark, anonymous clothes were like the clothes of Italian peasants, but the language they spoke was not Italian, nor did it resemble any language I had ever heard, and many of their faces had a fair Northern color. I noticed when I met these people that the answering looks they gave me, while attentive, were neither inimical[2] nor friendly. They looked at me with that certain privilege shared by kings and children, as if they possessed the right to judge, while being ignorant of, or exempt from, accepting judgment in return. There is no answer to this look and appeal is difficult, for one is already in a defensive position. Still, I had tried to appeal to them; several times I had addressed the passers-by hoping that one of them might understand me and tell me where I was, but no
2 one could or would. They shook their heads or lifted their empty hands, and while they did not appear hostile, neither did they smile in answer to my pleading smiles. After they had passed I thought it strange that I never heard a whisper or a laugh or any added animation in their talk. It was apparently a matter of complete indifference to them that they had been approached in the street by a stranger speaking a strange language.

Knowing these things I thought that it might be difficult to accomplish my purpose, and indeed this proved to be the case. The next people I met were three women walking together; two were young and one was middle-aged. I approached the taller of the young women, for her eyes were on a level with my own, and looking steadily into them and coming close, I spoke to her.

"Can you tell me where I am?" I said to her. "Can you understand what I am saying?"

The words were a device, I expected no answer and got none of any sort. As I drew close she looked down at the ground; she would not meet my gaze. A little smile moved the corners of her lips, and she stepped aside. When I turned to her companions they also looked away, smiling. This expression on other faces might have been called embarrassment, but not on theirs. The smile they shared seemed noncommittal, secretive, knowledgeable in a way that I could not fathom, and afterward I thought it curious that they had shown no surprise.

3 For a long time after that I met no one at all. I met no cat, no dog, no cabbage butterfly; not even an ant on the packed, bald dust of the road, and finally rejecting its ugliness and light I turned to the left along another street, narrower and as graceless, and walked by the same monotony of weather-beaten houses. After a few minutes I heard a sound that halted me and I stood listening. Somewhere not far away I heard children's voices. Though their words were foreign they spoke also in the common tongue of children everywhere: voices high, eruptive, excited, sparked with the universal jokes, chants, quarrels of play; and here, listening to them, my memory stirred for the first time—a memory of memory, in fact. For whatever it was that nearly illuminated consciousness was not the memory itself, but a remnant of light which glowed on the periphery of the obstacle before it: a penumbra.

4 Where are the children, I thought; where are they! With great urgency and longing I set out in the direction of their voices, determined to find them and in doing so to find something of myself. Their voices chattered, skipped, squabbled like the voices of sparrows, never far away, but though I turned and hunted and listened and pursued I could not find them. I never found them, and after a while I could not hear them either. The ghostly light of memory faded and was extinguished, and my despair rose up in darkness to take its place.

The next person I met was a man, young and dark-browed, and when I confronted him and asked my questions, it was without hope. I knew he would not meet my look, or let his eyes show me my longed-for, dreaded face. Yet here I was wrong; he stood before me without speaking, but the gaze with which he answered mine was so intense and undeviating that it

---

2. **inimical:** hostile.

AT A GLANCE

- The woman sees people dressed in dark clothes and speaking a foreign language.
- No one understands her questions; they do not meet her eyes.
- She hears children's voices but cannot find them.

1 POINT OF VIEW

The first-person narration intensifies the reader's appreciation of the narrator's growing frustration: Like the narrator the reader struggles to make sense of the events as they occur.

2 SETTING

The indifference of the people and the absence of any animation in their talk suggest something unnatural about the city and its inhabitants and strengthen the eerie, ominous overtones that pervade the story.

3 TONE

The repetition of the word *no* and the simple, detailed catalogue of living creatures she does not see in the city add a note of desperation to her calm, objective observations.

4 THEME

The narrator's urgent need to find the children reflects her frustrated desire to regain her own past and a sense of her own identity.

GUIDED READING

LITERAL QUESTIONS

1a. What happens when the narrator tries to stare into the eyes of another woman? (The woman won't meet her gaze.)

2a. What does the narrator feel as her memory fades? (despair)

INFERENTIAL QUESTIONS

1b. What does this incident suggest about the narrator's search for her identity in the eyes of a city inhabitant? (that the city dwellers cannot or will not give her a sense of self)

2b. What does the narrator's despair when her memory fades suggest? (Memory is our link to the past; the past gives us a sense of who we are.)

AT A GLANCE

- The city is silent. The woman hears the sound of stakes being driven into the ground.
- When the stars come out they, too, are unfamiliar.
- She finds trees and a large stone house in a public garden.

1 RISING ACTION

Dramatic tension builds as the narrator waits for the natural world to confirm what she thinks she knows with unshakable conviction.

2 THEME

The anguish of the narrator's search for self is intensified when the natural world, a traditional expression of underlying order and meaning, fails to confirm her most basic convictions.

3 SETTING

The narrator's fear that the trees will elude her—as the children have—reflects the adversarial, antagonistic relationship she experiences between herself and her environment.

4 MODERN IDEA

The sense of a frightening, unfamiliar universe and the fear of self-discovery characterize a common view of life in a technological society.

was I who dropped my eyes and stepped aside. I could not look, and soon I heard him going on his way.

1 I had been walking a long time, and the light was changing; the sun was low and full in my face. West, I said to myself; at least I know west, and I know that I am a woman, and that that is the sun. When the stars come out I will know those, too, and perhaps they will tell me something else.

After a while I sat down on a wooden step to rest. I was struck by the silence of the city around me, and I realized this was because it was a city of walkers who walked on dust instead of on pavements. I remembered that I had seen no mark of a wheel on any road, and that nothing had moved in the sky all day except for a few birds in flight.

A breath of dry wind crept along the dust at my feet, and, far away, a noise of knocking started, a sound of stakes being driven into the ground with a wooden mallet. Desolate, reiterated, it sounded as though somewhere in the city they were preparing a gallows or a barricade. Too tired and dispirited to move I sat there listening to the double knock-and-echo of each blow. A few people passed me on their way home, each of them giving me the glance of casual appraisal I had seen so often. Doors opened and doors closed, the sun went down, and soon the street was still again and the knocking stopped. Where would I sleep that night, or find a meal? I neither knew nor cared.

One by one the stars came out on the deepening sky, perfect, still, as if they were really what they seemed to be—calm ornaments for hope, promises of stillness and forever.

2 I looked for Venus, then Polaris,[3] then for Mars. I could not find them, and as the stars grew in number, coming imperceptibly into their light, I saw with slow-growing shock that these were not the stars I knew. The messages of this night sky were written in a language of constellations I had never seen or dreamed. I stared up at the brand-new Catherine wheels,[4] insignias, and fiery thorn crowns on the sky, and I do not think that I was really surprised when I spied at the zenith, small but bright, a constellation shaped like an elongated diamond, like the glittering abstraction of a human eye. . . .

It was just at this moment, before I could marshal or identify my thoughts in the face of such a development, that I heard a sound of trees, wind in the leaves of trees, and I realized, irrelevantly it seemed, that in all my walking in this city—how many hours, how many days?—I had not seen a single tree, and the sound of their presence was as welcome as the sound of rain is after a siege of drought. As
3 I stood up it occurred to me that neither had I seen one child among all the strangers I had met, that though I had heard the children I had not been able to find them, and now to all the other fears was added the fear that the trees, too, would magically elude me.

The street was dark, though light was glimmering through the cracks of the closed shutters. What was left of sunset, green as water, lay on the western horizon. Yet was it really western? In a sky of new stars, was it not pos-
4 sible and in fact probable that what I had believed to be the sun was not really Sun at all? Then what were the compass points, what were the easts and wests of this city? And what would I find when once I found myself?

I heard the beckoning of trees again and as if they were the clue to sanity, I ran along the street in the direction of their sound. I turned a corner, and there, ah yes, there were the trees: a grove of tall, dry, paper-murmuring trees that grew in a little park or public garden where people were walking together or sitting on the dusty grass. At the center of this park or garden there was a great house of stone, the first stone building I had seen all day. It was lighted from top to bottom; the lights of its long windows twittered in gold among the

3. **Polaris:** North Star.

4. **Catherine wheels:** wheels with projecting spikes used in fireworks.

GUIDED READING

LITERAL QUESTIONS

1a. What does the narrator think is being prepared when she hears the sounds of stakes being hit with a mallet? ("a gallows or a barricade")

2a. What does the narrator see when she stares up at the zenith of the night sky? ("a constellation shaped like an elongated diamond")

INFERENTIAL QUESTIONS

1b. What do the images of the gallows and barricade convey about how the narrator views her search for self? (They suggest that she believes her search will end in a destructive outcome.)

2b. What does the appearance of the eye-diamond even in the sky suggest about it? (that it invades every aspect of human existence)

small leaves of the trees, and a door stood open at the head of a flight of steps.

I passed many people on the path, but now I did not look at them or ask them questions. I knew that there was nothing they could do for me. I walked straight to the steps and up them and through the door into the lighted house. It was empty, as I had expected, a great empty ringing house, but there was a splendor about it, even in its emptiness, as if those who had left it—and left it recently—had been creatures of joy, better than people and gayer than gods. But they, whoever they were, had gone. My footsteps sounded on the barren floor, and the talk of the loiterers outside, the foreign talk, came in the windows clearly on the night air.

The mirror was at the end of the hall. I walked toward it with my fists closed, and my heart walked, too, heavily in my chest. I watched the woman's figure in the dark dress and the knees moving forward. When I was close to it, I saw, low in the right-hand corner of the mirror, the scratched small outline of the eye-diamond, a signature, carved on the surface of the glass by whom, and in what cold
1 spirit of raillery?[5] Lifting my head, I looked at
my own face. I leaned forward and looked
closely at my face, and I remembered everything. I remembered everything. And I knew
the name of the city I would never leave, and,
alas, I understood the language of its citizens.

5. **raillery:** taunting; teasing.

STUDY QUESTIONS

Recalling

1. How are the houses of the city described in the opening paragraph?
2. Of what things is the narrator ignorant, according to the second paragraph? What emotion does she feel? What "conviction" does she have in the third paragraph?
3. What does the narrator see on the currency in her purse? Where else does she see this sign in the third paragraph? Of what does the sign remind her?
4. How do the people on the street react when the narrator addresses them? How does the young, dark-browed man react, and why does the narrator drop her eyes and step aside?
5. What does the narrator think the knocking noises that she hears might be?
6. What does the narrator find at the end of the hall? What "signature" is on it? What happens when she looks into it? What does she know at the end of the story?

Interpreting

7. What do the shuttered windows, the passersby, the absence of children, and the knocking sounds all suggest about the world in which the narrator finds herself?
8. In what way is the eye-diamond unlike a usual signature?
9. Identify the kind of world in which the narrator finds herself. What does the final sentence suggest about her feelings?

Extending

10. How might this story be an allegory about the modern world?

COMPOSITION

Analyzing the Total Effect of a Story

■ Write a short essay analyzing the total effect of "The Signature." Begin with a statement about the overall impact of the story. Then explain how the author uses the following literary elements to achieve this effect: plot, character, setting, point of view, and tone. *For help with this assignment, refer to Lesson 8 in the Writing About Literature Handbook at the back of this book.*

Creating a Futuristic Setting

■ Write a brief description of what you think the future will be like in the place where you live. You may want to organize your description by concentrating on the sensory elements of a setting: sight, sound, smell, taste, and touch.

AT A GLANCE

- The narrator enters the house, which is empty.
- She finds a mirror that bears the eye-diamond symbol.
- She looks at herself and remembers everything.

1 CLIMAX

The terrible epiphany of understanding that the narrator experiences when she looks in the mirror remains unexplained to the reader. Nevertheless, the narrator's small but telling "alas" reveals that her discovery causes her pain.

REFLECTING ON THE STORY

What elements in the story suggest that it is a parable about totalitarianism? (the dark uniformity of the people's clothes; their passivity; the ubiquitous, anonymous eye-diamond)

STUDY QUESTIONS

1. one or two stories, shuttered, flush to road, unpainted, foreign
2. city's name, own name, own life; fear; seeing her face will restore her memory
3. elongated diamond with vertical line drawn through it; side of a house, dirt in road, shutters, fence railing; human eye
4. indifferent; looks at her with intense, unwavering gaze
5. building of gallows or barricade
6. mirror; eye-diamond; remembers everything; name of city she would never leave, language of its citizens
7. joyless, frightened society
8. signature usually mark of identity; reader never told what eye-diamond identifies
9. possibly repressive police state; would like to escape city, but realizes she is a citizen herself and is trapped
10. lost bearings (strange stars), vision (line across eye), soul and sense of community (shuttered houses), creativity and fecundity (absence of children)

COMPOSITION: GUIDELINES FOR EVALUATION

ANALYZING A STORY'S TOTAL EFFECT

Objective

To analyze a short story's elements

Guidelines for Evaluation

- suggested length: six to eight paragraphs
- should contain thesis statement on impact
- should discuss mysterious quality of plot
- should discuss narrator's state of mind, fears
- should show setting, point of view, tone

CREATING A FUTURISTIC SETTING

Objective

To describe a place/time with sensory details

Guidelines for Evaluation

- suggested length: three to five paragraphs
- should describe a place in the future
- should use sensory imagery
- should appeal to the five senses

William Faulkner *1897–1962*

William Faulkner created in literature a cosmos of his own, an entire world apart. Yoknapatawpha County was the name of his imagined landscape, and he proudly claimed to be its "Sole Owner and Proprietor." He populated it with a broad spectrum of remarkable characters—farmers, hunters, aristocrats, businessmen, former black slaves, dispossessed Indians, and several generations of whole families moving on different levels of southern society. He set his characters in country he knew well and against a background of history he profoundly understood. One of the greatest of American writers, Faulkner created a kind of mythical kingdom that exists simultaneously in the past and in the present.

William Faulkner spent most of his life in Oxford, Mississippi. His family was proud of its southern heritage, especially proud of a great-grandfather, Colonel William Clark Falkner, who had served with distinction in the Confederate Army, later built railroads, and had even written a popular Romantic novel, *The White Rose of Memphis.* When Faulkner was in third grade, he was asked what he wanted to do when he grew up. His prompt reply: "I want to be a writer like my great-granddaddy."

Faulkner's early experiences were varied. He loved to read, was curious about foreign literature, and even taught himself French. In 1918 he enlisted as a student flyer in the Royal Canadian Air Force but returned to Oxford a year later to attend the University of Mississippi. By then he had begun to write seriously, though his earliest efforts were in poetry.

In 1924, hoping to find work in journalism, Faulkner went to New Orleans, where he became friends with the prominent novelist and short story writer Sherwood Anderson (page 476). In that year his first book, a collection of verse entitled *The Marble Faun,* was published, but sales were poor. On Anderson's advice, Faulkner wrote his first novel, set in the South and called *Soldier's Pay.* With Anderson's recommendation, the novel was published.

After a brief stay in Europe, Faulkner returned to Oxford, where for the next few years he worked as a carpenter, house painter, deckhand, even as a golf professional—and wrote feverishly, mostly at night. He turned out poems and stories, a second novel, *Mosquitoes* (1927), and a third, *Flags in the Dust* (1927)—the first of his novels to be set in Yoknapatawpha County. Nevertheless, publishers ignored him, and, convinced that his work would never again appear in print, he decided abruptly to stop worrying about publication. "One day I seemed to shut a door," he remembered, "between me and all publishers' addresses and book lists. I said to myself, Now I can write."

At this point Faulkner embarked on what was to become his major phase, producing several books now considered to be among the greatest American novels. From 1929 to 1942, he completed two collections of stories, a second volume of poetry, and ten novels, including *The Sound and the Fury* (1929), *As I Lay Dying* (1930), *Light in August* (1932), *Absalom, Absalom!* (1936), and *The Unvanquished* (1938). Still, in spite of his great productivity, the respect of other writers, and the genuine appreciation of a handful of critics, he remained virtually unknown to the general reading public.

The complexity of Faulkner's writing style contributed to his continued obscurity. Faulkner's works are full of repetition, inconsistent punctuation, long and puzzling sentences, flashbacks, and multiple points of view. He often wrote in the stream-of-consciousness mode (see page 582). To further complicate matters, the consciousness he presented was sometimes that of a child, an idiot, or a person on the edge of madness. But as readers now understand, the difficulty of the style was in keeping with the complexity of the subject. For it was part of Faulkner's aim to represent in the consciousness of his characters the tangled interrelationships between the modern American present and the historical past.

By 1945, although his work was admired abroad—in France, especially—all seventeen of Faulkner's books had gone out of print. The great change came in 1946 with the publication of *The Portable Faulkner,* a selection of his works edited by the sympathetic critic Malcolm Cowley. A remarkable renewal of interest in Faulkner took place, as if suddenly people understood what they had not seen before. Critics began to reassess him, readers took a second look at what copies of his works they could find, and his publisher began reprinting his books. In 1950 Faulkner's *Collected Stories* won the National Book Award, and Faulkner himself was awarded the Nobel Prize.

Yoknapatawpha County stands as a grand allegory about the real American South in history. But beyond that, it is an evocation of the tremendous variety of human experience and the struggle of the human spirit everywhere. In his Nobel Prize Acceptance Speech (see page 652), Faulkner urged all writers to concern themselves above all with "the old universal truths . . . courage and honor and hope and pride and compassion and pity and sacrifice. . . ."

■ What are "old universal truths?" How does the young boy discover "truth" when he is stalking a bear?

AT A GLANCE

- A ten-year-old boy goes on a hunting trip with his father, Major de Spain, and General Compson.
- The boy has heard about the bear for as long as he can remember.
- The bear, mythically strong and powerful, represents the past untamed wilderness.

LITERARY OPTIONS

- symbol
- style
- theme

THEMATIC OPTIONS

- the passage to adulthood
- the value of life
- the power of nature

1 SYMBOL

The bear, an actual "shaggy tremendous shape," impervious to both the assaults and constraints of society, assumes a mythic stature by virtue of his longevity and power.

2 THEME

The inherent conflict between the claims of society and the unbound wilderness shapes the boy's struggle as he experiences the passage to manhood.

3 STYLE: SENTENCE STRUCTURE

The repetition of the words *not* and *not even* and parallel sentence units help Faulkner convey this boy's sense that the yearly hunting ritual embraces a meaning that transcends its literal, objective significance.

William Faulkner

The Bear

He was ten. But it had already begun, long before that day when at last he wrote his age in two figures and he saw for the first time the camp where his father and Major de Spain and old General Compson and the others spent two weeks each November and two weeks again each June. He had already inherited then, without ever having seen it, the tremendous bear with one trap-ruined foot which, in an area almost a hundred miles deep, had earned for itself a name, a definite designation like a living man.

He had listened to it for years: the long legend of corncribs rifled, of shotes[1] and grown pigs and even calves carried bodily into the woods and devoured, of traps and deadfalls[2] overthrown and dogs mangled and slain, and shotgun and even rifle charges delivered at
1 point-blank range and with no more effect than so many peas blown through a tube by a boy—a corridor of wreckage and destruction beginning back before he was born, through which sped, not fast but rather with the ruthless and irresistible deliberation of a locomotive, the shaggy tremendous shape.

It ran in his knowledge before he ever saw it. It looked and towered in his dreams before he even saw the unaxed woods where it left its crooked print, shaggy, huge, red-eyed, not malevolent but just big—too big for the dogs which tried to bay[3] it, for the horses which tried to ride it down, for the men and the bullets they fired into it, too big for the very country which was its constricting scope. He seemed to see it entire with a child's complete divination before he ever laid eyes on either—the doomed wilderness whose edges were being constantly and punily gnawed at by men with axes and plows who feared it because it was wilderness, men myriad and nameless even to one another in the land where the old bear had earned a name, through which ran not even a mortal animal but an anachronism,[4] in-
2 domitable and invincible, out of an old dead time, a phantom, epitome and apotheosis[5] of the old wild life at which the puny humans swarmed and hacked in a fury of abhorrence and fear, like pygmies about the ankles of a drowsing elephant; the old bear solitary, indomitable and alone, widowered, childless and absolved of mortality—old Priam[6] reft of his old wife and having outlived all his sons.

Until he was ten, each November he would watch the wagon containing the dogs and the bedding and food and guns and his father and Tennie's Jim, the Negro, and Sam Fathers, the Indian, son of a slave woman and a Chickasaw[7] chief, depart on the road to town, to Jefferson, where Major de Spain and the others would
3 join them. To the boy, at seven and eight and nine, they were not going into the Big Bottom to hunt bear and deer, but to keep yearly rendezvous with the bear which they did not even intend to kill. Two weeks later they would return, with no trophy, no head and skin. He had not expected it. He had not even been afraid it would be in the wagon. He believed that even after he was ten and his father would let him go too, for those two November weeks, he would merely make another one, along with his father and Major de Spain and General Compson and the others, the dogs which feared to bay it and the rifles and shotguns

1. **shotes:** young pigs.
2. **deadfalls:** traps that drop heavy weights on prey.
3. **bay:** bark at and chase in an attempt to corner.

4. **anachronism** [ə nak'rə niz'əm]: something that seems to exist out of its proper time.
5. **epitome** [i pit'ə mē] . . . **apotheosis** [ə poth'ē ō'sis]: most typical and most ideal.
6. **Priam** [prī'əm]: last king of Troy during Trojan War. His wife and sons were killed when the Greeks invaded.
7. **Chickasaw:** tribe of Indians originally from northern Mississippi and parts of Tennessee.

GUIDED READING

LITERAL QUESTIONS

1a. What runs in the boy's "knowledge" before he ever sees it? (the bear)

2a. To which mythical character is the bear compared? (Priam, the last king of Troy)

INFERENTIAL QUESTIONS

1b. What effect do you think the passage of time has on the boy's perception of the bear? (It makes the bear both familiar and increasingly powerful.)

2b. In what way does this allusion contribute to the existing image of the bear? (It humanizes the bear and endows him with a doomed, tragic dimension.)

1 which failed even to bleed it, in the yearly pageant of the old bear's furious immortality.

Then he heard the dogs. It was in the second week of his first time in the camp. He stood with Sam Fathers against a big oak beside the faint crossing where they had stood each dawn for nine days now, hearing the dogs. He had heard them once before, one morning last week—a murmur, sourceless, echoing through the wet woods, swelling presently into separate voices which he could recognize and call by name. He had raised and cocked the gun as Sam told him and stood motionless again while the uproar, the invisible course, swept up and past and faded; it seemed to him that he could actually see the deer, the buck, blond, smoke-colored, elongated with speed, fleeing, vanishing, the woods, the gray solitude, still ringing even when the cries of the dogs had died away.

"Now let the hammers down," Sam said.

"You knew they were not coming here too," he said.

"Yes," Sam said, "I want you to learn how to do when you didn't shoot. It's after the chance for the bear or the deer has done already come and gone that men and dogs get killed."

"Anyway," he said, "it was just a deer."

Then on the tenth morning he heard the dogs again. And he readied the too-long, too-heavy gun as Sam had taught him, before Sam
2 even spoke. But this time it was no deer, no ringing chorus of dogs running strong on a free scent, but a moiling[8] yapping an octave too high, with something more than indecision and even abjectness in it, not even moving very fast, taking a long time to pass completely out of hearing, leaving even then somewhere in the air that echo, thin, slightly hysterical, abject, almost grieving, with no sense of a fleeing, unseen, smoke-colored, grass-eating shape ahead of it, and Sam, who had taught him first of all to cock the gun and take position where he could see everywhere and then never move again, had himself moved up beside him; he could hear Sam breathing at his shoulder and he could see the arched curve of the old man's inhaling nostrils.

"Hah," Sam said. "Not even running. Walking."

"Old Ben!" the boy said. "But up here!" he cried. "Way up here!"

3 "He do it every year," Sam said. "Once. Maybe to see who in camp this time, if he can shoot or not. Whether we got the dog yet that can bay and hold him. He'll take them to the river, then he'll send them back home. We may as well go back, too; see how they look when they come back to camp."

When they reached the camp the hounds were already there, ten of them crouching back under the kitchen, the boy and Sam squatting to peer back into the obscurity where they huddled, quiet, the eyes luminous, glowing at them and vanishing, and no sound, only that effluvium[9] of something more than dog, stronger than dog and not just animal, just beast, because still there had been nothing in front of that abject and almost painful yapping save the solitude, the wilderness, so that when the eleventh hound came in at noon and with all the others watching—even old Uncle Ash,
4 who called himself first a cook—Sam daubed the tattered ear and the raked shoulder with turpentine and axle grease, to the boy it was still no living creature, but the wilderness which, leaning for the moment down, had patted lightly once the hound's temerity.

"Just like a man," Sam said. "Just like folks. Put off as long as she could having to be brave, knowing all the time that sooner or later she would have to be brave once to keep on living with herself, and knowing all the time beforehand what was going to happen to her when she done it."

That afternoon, himself on the one-eyed wagon mule which did not mind the smell of blood nor, as they told him, of bear, and with Sam on the other one, they rode for more than three hours through the rapid, shortening win-

8. **moiling:** confused.

9. **effluvium** [i flo͞o′vē əm]: disagreeable odor.

AT A GLANCE

- In the second week the dogs bark at deer.
- Sam Fathers teaches the boy about hunting.
- On the tenth morning the bear, unseen, comes to look the camp over. The bear injures one of the dogs.

1 VOCABULARY: WORD CHOICE

Note how the word *pageant* evokes the sense of an event with deep historical dimensions. It reinforces the spiritual significance of the hunt and its moral implications in the evolution of the boy's consciousness.

2 SYMBOL

The jarring, frightened, remorseful yapping of the dogs reinforces the symbolic dimension of the bear's innate power.

3 VOCABULARY: DIALECT

Sam's syntax and grammar reinforce the regional tone of the story while underscoring, in their lack of complexity and sophistication, his closeness to the natural rather than the civilized world.

4 SETTING

In ascribing human powers to the wilderness, Faulkner endows the literal setting with an energy and vitality that charge the narration.

GUIDED READING

LITERAL QUESTIONS

1a. Whom does the boy stand with as he waits for the dogs to catch the bear's scent? (Sam Fathers)

2a. According to Sam, why does the eleventh dog go after the bear? (to be brave once so that she can live with herself)

INFERENTIAL QUESTIONS

1b. What significance can you infer from Sam's name? (In teaching the boy how to hunt, Sam becomes his spiritual father.)

2b. What do Sam's comments suggest about the nature of bravery? (Bravery means taking action even when you know the consequences may be painful.)

AT A GLANCE

- Sam and the boy see the bear's footprint.
- The boy says he will shoot the bear the next day. Sam warns the boy that the bear might attack him.
- The next day they go even deeper into the wilderness.

1 SETTING

The absence of a path or trail and the unfamiliarity of the country reflect, on a literal level, the mythical and spiritual progress of the boy's initiation.

2 SYMBOL

The symbolic implications of the bear's innate wildness and power are broadened by the boy's perception of its ultimate mortality.

3 STYLE: SENTENCE STRUCTURE

The accumulation of modifying, parallel clauses and the repetition of the words *which* and *and* reinforce the boy's discomfort with the gun and help convey his feelings of unpreparedness for his hunt.

4 THEME

The boy's reflections on the timeless, unaltered wilderness reveal a heightened consciousness and a mature realization that humans can never possess nature.

1 ter day. They followed no path, no trail even that he could see; almost at once they were in a country which he had never seen before. Then he knew why Sam had made him ride the mule which would not spook. The sound one stopped short and tried to whirl and bolt even as Sam got down, blowing its breath, jerking and wrenching at the rein while Sam held it, coaxing it forward with his voice, since he could not risk tying it, drawing it forward while the boy got down from the marred one.

Then, standing beside Sam in the gloom of the dying afternoon, he looked down at the rotted overturned log, gutted and scored with claw marks and, in the wet earth beside it, the print of the enormous warped two-toed foot. He knew now what he had smelled when he peered under the kitchen where the dogs hud-
2 dled. He realized for the first time that the bear which had run in his listening and loomed in his dreams since before he could remember to the contrary, and which, therefore, must have existed in the listening and dreams of his father and Major de Spain and even old General Compson, too, before they began to remember in their turn, was a mortal animal, and that if they had departed for the camp each November without any actual hope of bringing its trophy back, it was not because it could not be slain, but because so far they had had no actual hope to.

"Tomorrow," he said.

"We'll try tomorrow," Sam said. "We ain't got the dog yet."

"We've got eleven. They ran him this morning."

"It won't need but one," Sam said. "He ain't here. Maybe he ain't nowhere. The only other way will be for him to run by accident over somebody that has a gun."

"That wouldn't be me," the boy said. "It will be Walter or Major or—"

"It might," Sam said. "You watch close in the morning. Because he's smart. That's how come he has lived this long. If he gets hemmed up and has to pick out somebody to run over, he will pick out you."

"How?" the boy said. "How will he know—" He ceased. "You mean he already knows me, that I ain't never been here before, ain't had time to find out yet whether I—" He ceased again, looking at Sam, the old man whose face revealed nothing until it smiled. He said humbly, not even amazed, "It was me he was watching. I don't reckon he did need to come but once."

The next morning they left the camp three hours before daylight. They rode this time because it was too far to walk, even the dogs in the wagon; again the first gray light found him in a place which he had never seen before, where Sam had placed him and told him to stay and
3 then departed. With the gun which was too big for him, which did not even belong to him, but to Major de Spain, and which he had fired only once—at a stump on the first day, to learn the recoil and how to reload it—he stood against a gum tree beside a little bayou[10] whose black still water crept without movement out of a canebrake[11] and crossed a small clearing and into cane again, where, invisible, a bird—the big woodpecker called Lord-to-God by Negroes—clattered at a dead limb.

It was a stand like any other, dissimilar only in incidentals to the one where he had stood each morning for ten days; a territory new to him, yet no less familiar than that other one which, after almost two weeks, he had come to
4 believe he knew a little—the same solitude, the same loneliness through which human beings had merely passed without altering it, leaving no mark, no scar, which looked exactly as it must have looked when the first ancestor of Sam Fathers' Chickasaw predecessors crept into it and looked about, club or stone ax or bone arrow drawn and poised; different only because, squatting at the edge of the kitchen, he smelled the hounds huddled and cringing beneath it and saw the raked ear and shoulder of the one who, Sam said, had had to be brave once in order to live with herself, and saw yesterday in the earth beside the gutted log the print of the living foot.

---

10. **bayou** [bī′ o͞o]: marshy inlet of a lake or river.
11. **canebrake:** dense growth of cane plants.

GUIDED READING

LITERAL QUESTIONS

1a. What does the boy find near the overturned log? (the bear's footprint)

2a. Whom does the boy realize the bear was watching in camp? (him)

INFERENTIAL QUESTIONS

1b. What do you think the boy feels when he sees the footprint? (fear)

2b. How do you think the boy's realization affects his pursuit of the bear? (It makes the pursuit more personal and more challenging.)

He heard no dogs at all. He never did hear them. He only heard the drumming of the woodpecker stop short off and knew that the bear was
1 looking at him. He never saw it. He did not know whether it was in front of him or behind him. He did not move, holding the useless gun, which he had not even had warning to cock and which even now he did not cock, tasting in his saliva that taint as of brass which he knew now because he had smelled it when he peered under the kitchen at the huddled dogs.

Then it was gone. As abruptly as it had ceased, the woodpecker's dry, monotonous clatter set up again, and after a while he even believed he could hear the dogs—a murmur, scarce a sound even, which he had probably been hearing for some time before he even remarked it, drifting into hearing and then out again, dying away. They came nowhere near him. If it was a bear they ran, it was another bear. It was Sam himself who came out of the cane and crossed the bayou, followed by the injured bitch of yesterday. She was almost at heel, like a bird dog, making no sound. She came and crouched against his leg, trembling, staring off into the cane.

"I didn't see him," he said. "I didn't, Sam!"

"I know it," Sam said. "He done the looking. You didn't hear him neither, did you?"

"No," the boy said. "I—"

2 "He's smart," Sam said. "Too smart." He looked down at the hound, trembling faintly and steadily against the boy's knee. From the raked shoulder a few drops of fresh blood oozed and clung. "Too big. We ain't got the dog yet. But maybe someday. Maybe not next time. But someday."

So I must see him, he thought. *I must look at him.* Otherwise, it seemed to him that it

AT A GLANCE

- The boy feels but does not see the bear looking at him.
- The boy talks with Sam about his encounter.
- Sam says they don't have the right dog to run the bear yet.

1 PLOT: RISING ACTION

The boy's fear, once he sees the bear as a real, tangible aspect of nature, increases the story's dramatic tension and heightens the boy's inner conflict.

2 CHARACTERIZATION

Sam's innate understanding of the bear and his underlying optimism reflect the instincts that set him apart from the other hunters and reinforce his union with the natural world.

GUIDED READING

LITERAL QUESTION

1a. After the bear leaves, what sound begins as abruptly as it stopped? (the woodpecker's clatter)

INFERENTIAL QUESTION

1b. What does this detail suggest about the nature of the wilderness? (In the wild, all aspects of nature affect one another.)

AT A GLANCE

- The boy decides he must see the bear.
- In June, the next year, the boy returns to the camp with the same companions. He pretends to hunt squirrels.
- Sam tells the boy he hasn't looked for the bear in the right way.

1 THEME

The boy's determination to face the bear, and thus to confront his own primitive instincts, shapes the vision of manhood he wishes to achieve.

2 SETTING

Faulkner's detailed description of the older hunters' behavior and the relationships that exist between blacks and whites in camp underscore the story's regional tone.

3 STYLE

The rich physical details convey not only a strong visual image of the landscape but also the boy's pleasure in and reverence for the natural world.

4 SYMBOL

Sam, part black, part Indian, lives on the fringes of society and so is free of social conditioning. He symbolizes the strength and innate wisdom of the man in harmony with the natural universe.

would go on like this forever, as it had gone on with his father and Major de Spain, who was older than his father, and even with old General Compson, who had been old enough to be a brigade commander in 1865. Otherwise, it would go on so forever, next time and next time, after and after and after. It seemed to him that he could see the two of them, himself and the bear, shadowy in the limbo from which time emerged, becoming time; the old bear absolved of mortality and himself partak-
1 ing, sharing a little of it, enough of it. And he knew now what he had smelled in the huddled dogs and tasted in his saliva. He recognized fear. *So I will have to see him,* he thought, without dread or even hope. *I will have to look at him.*

It was in June of the next year. He was eleven. They were in camp again, celebrating Major de Spain's and General Compson's birthdays. Although the one had been born in September and the other in the depth of winter and in another decade, they had met for two weeks to fish and shoot squirrels and turkey and run coons and wildcats with the dogs at
2 night. That is, he and Boon Hoggenbeck and the Negroes fished and shot squirrels and ran the coons and cats, because the proved hunters, not only Major de Spain and old General Compson, who spent those two weeks sitting in a rocking chair before a tremendous iron pot of Brunswick stew, stirring and tasting, with old Ash to quarrel with about how he was making it and Tennie's Jim to pour whisky from the demijohn[12] into the tin dipper from which he drank it, but even the boy's father and Walter Ewell, who were still young enough, scorned such, other than shooting the wild gobblers with pistols for wagers on their marksmanship.

Or, that is, his father and the others believed he was hunting squirrels. Until the third day he thought that Sam Fathers believed that too. Each morning he would leave the camp right after breakfast. He had his own gun now, a Christmas present. He went back to the tree beside the little bayou where he had stood that morning. Using the compass which old General Compson had given him, he ranged from that point; he was teaching himself to be a better-than-fair woodsman without knowing he was doing it. On the second day he even found the gutted log where he had first seen the crooked print. It was almost completely crumbled now, healing with unbelievable speed, a passionate and almost visible relinquishment, back into the earth from which the tree had grown.

He ranged the summer woods now, green with gloom; if anything, actually dimmer than
3 in November's gray dissolution, where, even at noon, the sun fell only in intermittent dappling upon the earth, which never completely dried out and which crawled with snakes—moccasins and water snakes and rattlers, themselves the color of the dappled gloom, so that he would not always see them until they moved, returning later and later, first day, second day, passing in the twilight of the third evening the little log pen enclosing the log stable where Sam was putting up the horses for the night.

"You ain't looked right yet," Sam said.

He stopped. For a moment he didn't answer. Then he said peacefully, in a peaceful rushing burst as when a boy's miniature dam in a little brook gives way, "All right. But how? I went to the bayou. I even found that log again. I—"

"I reckon that was all right. Likely he's been watching you. You never saw his foot?"

"I," the boy said—"I didn't—I never thought—"

4 "It's the gun," Sam said. He stood beside the fence, motionless—the old man, the Indian, in the battered faded overalls and the frayed five-cent straw hat which in the Negro's race had been the badge of his enslavement and was now the regalia of his freedom. The camp—the clearing, the house, the barn and its tiny lot with which Major de Spain in his turn had scratched punily and evanescently at the wilderness—faded in the dusk, back into the im-

12. **demijohn:** large wicker-covered bottle with a narrow neck and handle.

GUIDED READING

LITERAL QUESTIONS

1a. What do the boy's father and the others believe the boy is hunting during his second visit to the camp? (squirrels)

2a. What does the boy get as a Christmas present? (his own gun)

INFERENTIAL QUESTIONS

1b. Why do you think the boy tries to mislead the others? (He sees his pursuit of the bear as a private, personal challenge.)

2b. What do you think is the significance of the gift? (It reflects society's acknowledgment of the boy's growing maturity.)

memorial darkness of the woods. *The gun,* the boy thought. *The gun.*

1 "Be scared," Sam said. "You can't help that. But don't be afraid. Ain't nothing in the woods going to hurt you unless you corner it, or it smells that you are afraid. A bear or a deer, too, has got to be scared of a coward the same as a brave man has got to be."

The gun, the boy thought.

"You will have to choose," Sam said.

He left the camp before daylight, long before Uncle Ash would wake in his quilts on the kitchen floor and start the fire for breakfast. He had only the compass and a stick for snakes. He could go almost a mile before he would begin to need the compass. He sat on a log, the invisible compass in his invisible hand, while the secret night sounds, fallen still at his movements, scurried again and then ceased for good, and the owls ceased and gave over to the waking of day birds, and he could see the compass. Then he went fast yet still quietly; he was becoming better and better as a woodsman, still without having yet realized it.

He jumped a doe and a fawn at sunrise, walked them out of the bed, close enough to see them—the crash of undergrowth, the white scut,[13] the fawn scudding behind her faster than he had believed it could run. He was hunting right, upwind, as Sam had taught him; not that it mattered now. He had left the gun; of his own will and relinquishment he had ac-
2 cepted not a gambit, not a choice, but a condition in which not only the bear's heretofore inviolable anonymity but all the old rules and balances of hunter and hunted had been abrogated.[14] He would not even be afraid, not even in the moment when the fear would take him completely—blood, skin, bowels, bones, memory from the long time before it became his memory—all save that thin, clear, quenchless, immortal lucidity which alone differed him from this bear and from all the other bear and deer he would ever kill in the humility and pride of his skill and endurance, to which Sam had spoken when he leaned in the twilight on the lot fence yesterday.

By noon he was far beyond the little bayou, farther into the new and alien country than he had ever been. He was traveling now not only by the compass but by the old, heavy, biscuit-thick silver watch which had belonged to his grandfather. When he stopped at last, it was for the first time since he had risen from the log at dawn when he could see the compass. It was far enough. He had left the camp nine hours ago; nine hours from now, dark would have already been an hour old. But he didn't think that. He thought, *All right. Yes. But what?* and stood for a moment, alien and small in the green and topless solitude, answering his own question before it had formed and ceased.
3 It was the watch, the compass, the stick—the three lifeless mechanicals with which for nine hours he had fended the wilderness off; he hung the watch and compass carefully on a bush and leaned the stick beside them and relinquished completely to it.

He had not been going very fast for the last two or three hours. He went no faster now, since distance would not matter even if he could have gone fast. And he was trying to keep a bearing on the tree where he had left the compass, trying to complete a circle which would bring him back to it or at least intersect itself, since direction would not matter now ei-
4 ther. But the tree was not there, and he did as Sam had schooled him—made the next circle in the opposite direction, so that the two patterns would bisect somewhere, but crossing no print of his own feet, finding the tree at last, but in the wrong place—no bush, no compass, no watch—and the tree not even the tree, because there was a down log beside it and he did what Sam Fathers had told him was the next thing and the last.

As he sat down on the log he saw the crooked print—the warped, tremendous, two-toed indentation which, even as he watched it, filled with water. As he looked up, the wilderness coalesced, solidified—the glade, the tree

---

13. **scut:** short, stumpy tail.
14. **abrogated** [ab′rə gā′tid]: abolished.

AT A GLANCE

- Sam encourages the boy to be scared but not afraid.
- The boy leaves camp early the next day to search for the bear without his gun.
- After hours in the wilderness, the boy leaves his compass, watch, and stick and goes on.
- He finds the bear's footprint.

1 THEME

Sam's advice to the boy—to embrace his fear but not to act on it—clarifies the importance of achieving true maturity through an unquestioned acceptance of the natural world.

2 STYLE: REPETITION

The series of negative choruses that precede the positive clauses ("not a . . . but a") prolong the resolution of meaning and charge the narrative with a driving, oratorical power.

3 SYMBOL

The boy surrenders to the wilderness and rejects misleading social precepts when he relinquishes the watch, compass, and stick, which represent humanity's attempt to overcome time and space.

4 SETTING

On the literal level the boy's loss of bearings in the once-familiar wilderness remind us of his underlying human vulnerability.

GUIDED READING

LITERAL QUESTIONS

1a. What is the boy becoming better at without realizing it? (being a woodsman)

2a. What does the boy do with the watch, compass, and stick? (He hangs the watch and compass on a tree and places the stick beside it.)

INFERENTIAL QUESTIONS

1b. What do you think the boy's increasing skill signifies? (his growing harmony with the natural world and his progress toward maturity)

2b. Why do you think he relinquishes the watch, compass, and stick? (He realizes he must meet the bear armed only with his natural, primitive instincts.)

AT A GLANCE

- The boy sees the bear.
- During the next three years the boy becomes a skilled hunter.
- At fourteen he sees the bear again.

1 STYLE

Faulkner's use of profuse descriptive verbs and adjectives (*emerge / appear; immobile, solid, fixed*) and balancing of negatives against positives (*not as big as / but as big as*) help him convey nuances of feeling and perception.

2 CHARACTERIZATION

The boy's skill as a woodsman and his familiarity with the wilderness suggest a wisdom based on respect for and harmony with the natural world.

3 BACKGROUND

Faulkner believes that true maturity can be achieved only if we confront the natural creature buried deep inside of us.

he sought, the bush, the watch and the compass glinting where a ray of sunlight touched
1 them. Then he saw the bear. It did not emerge, appear; it was just there, immobile, solid, fixed in the hot dappling of the green and windless noon, not as big as he had dreamed it, but as big as he had expected it, bigger, dimensionless against the dappled obscurity, looking at him where he sat quietly on the log and looked back at it.

Then it moved. It made no sound. It did not hurry. It crossed the glade, walking for an instant into the full glare of the sun; when it reached the other side it stopped again and looked back at him across one shoulder while his quiet breathing inhaled and exhaled three times.

Then it was gone. It didn't walk into the woods, the undergrowth. It faded, sank back into the wilderness as he had watched a fish, a huge old bass, sink and vanish back into the dark depths of its pool without even any movement of its fins.

He thought, *It will be next fall.* But it was not next fall, nor the next nor the next. He was fourteen then. He had killed his buck, and Sam Fathers had marked his face with the hot blood, and in the next year he killed a bear.
2 But even before that accolade he had become as competent in the woods as many grown men with the same experience; by his fourteenth year he was a better woodsman than most grown men with more. There was no territory within thirty miles of the camp that he did not know—bayou, ridge, brake, landmark tree and path. He could have led anyone to any point in it without deviation, and brought them out again. He knew game trails that even Sam Fathers did not know; in his thirteenth year he found a buck's bedding place, and unbeknown to his father he borrowed Walter Ewell's rifle and lay in wait at dawn and killed the buck when it walked back to the bed, as Sam had told him how the old Chickasaw fathers did.

But not the old bear, although by now he knew its footprint better than he did his own, and not only the crooked one. He could see any one of the three sound ones and distinguish it from any other, and not only by its size. There were other bears within those thirty miles which left tracks almost as large,
3 but this was more than that. If Sam Fathers had been his mentor and the backyard rabbits and squirrels at home his kindergarten, then the wilderness the old bear ran was his college, the old male bear itself, so long unwifed and childless as to have become its own ungendered progenitor,[15] was his alma mater. But he never saw it.

He could find the crooked print now almost whenever he liked, fifteen or ten or five miles, or sometimes nearer the camp than that. Twice while on stand during the three years he heard the dogs strike its trail by accident; on the second time they jumped it seemingly, the voices high, abject, almost human in hysteria, as on that first morning two years ago. But not the bear itself. He would remember that noon three years ago, the glade, himself and the bear fixed during that moment in the windless and dappled blaze, and it would seem to him that it had never happened, that he had dreamed that too. But it had happened. They had looked at each other, they had emerged from the wilderness old as earth, synchronized to that instant by something more than the blood that moved the flesh and bones which bore them, and touched, pledged something, affirmed something more lasting than the frail web of bones and flesh which any accident could obliterate.

Then he saw it again. Because of the very fact that he thought of nothing else, he had forgotten to look for it. He was still-hunting with Walter Ewell's rifle. He saw it cross the end of a long blowdown, a corridor where a tornado had swept, rushing through rather than over the tangle of trunks and branches as a locomotive would have, faster than he had ever believed it could move, almost as fast as a deer even, because a deer would have spent most of

15. **ungendered progenitor:** its own parent; not born of any other.

GUIDED READING

LITERAL QUESTIONS

1a. What does the bear do when it reaches the other side of the glade? (It stops and looks at the boy across one shoulder.)

2a. What can the boy find routinely when he is fourteen? (the bear's footprint)

INFERENTIAL QUESTIONS

1b. What do the bear's actions suggest about the nature of the relationship between the bear and the boy? (that the two have a special destiny to fulfill)

2b. What can you infer about the boy's character from his new ability? (He is in touch with his primitive instincts.)

that time in the air, faster than he could bring the rifle sights up to it, so that he believed the reason he never let off the shot was that he was still behind it, had never caught up with it. And now he knew what had been wrong during all the three years. He sat on a log, shaking and trembling as if he had never seen the woods before nor anything that ran them, wondering with incredulous amazement how he could have forgotten the very thing which Sam Fathers had told him and which the bear itself had proved the next day and had now returned after three years to reaffirm.

And he now knew what Sam Fathers had meant about the right dog, a dog in which size would mean less than nothing. So when he returned alone in April—school was out then, so that the sons of farmers could help with the land's planting, and at last his father had granted him permission, on his promise to be back in four days—he had the dog. It was his own, a mongrel of the sort called by Negroes a fyce, a ratter, itself not much bigger than a rat and possessing that bravery which had long since stopped being courage and had become foolhardiness.

1 It did not take four days. Alone again, he found the trail on the first morning. It was not a stalk; it was an ambush. He timed the meeting almost as if it were an appointment with a human being. Himself holding the fyce muffled in a feed sack and Sam Fathers with two of the hounds on a piece of plowline rope, they lay down wind of the trail at dawn of the second morning. They were so close that the bear turned without even running, as if in surprised amazement at the shrill and frantic uproar of the released fyce, turning at bay against the trunk of a tree, on its hind feet; it seemed to the boy that it would never stop rising, taller

AT A GLANCE

- The bear moves too fast for the boy to shoot him. The boy realizes he has forgotten Sam's advice about hunting dogs.
- The next April he returns alone with Sam and a new, "foolhardy" dog.
- They find the bear's trail on the first morning.

1 PLOT: RISING ACTION

As the action rises towards the climax, the boy demythologizes the bear and approaches the experience in a thoroughly practical manner.

GUIDED READING

LITERAL QUESTION

1a. What kind of bravery does the boy's dog show? (foolhardy)

INFERENTIAL QUESTION

1b. What kind of bravery do you think might be viewed as foolhardy? (bravery that risks the needless loss of life)

AT A GLANCE

- The boy has a clear shot at the bear but doesn't take it. He throws away the gun to rescue the dog.
- He doesn't give his father a reason for not shooting the bear.
- His father reads to him from a poem.

1 CLIMAX

Faulkner's direct, sensory language underscores the stark reality of the bear and the hunt.

2 THEME

The boy's perception of the unalterable patterns of nature reflect Faulkner's concern with the illusory and ultimately destructive consequences of possession.

3 STYLE

Faulkner's repetition of the word *and,* the accumulation of concrete nouns and strong verbs, and the balancing of positives against negatives convey the urgency of the boy's consciousness as he struggles to understand the hunt.

and taller, and even the two hounds seemed to take a sort of desperate and despairing courage from the fyce, following it as it went in.

Then he realized that the fyce was actually not going to stop. He flung, threw the gun away, and ran; when he overtook and grasped the frantically pinwheeling little dog, it seemed to him that he was directly under the bear.

1 He could smell it, strong and hot and rank. Sprawling, he looked up to where it loomed and towered over him like a cloudburst and colored like a thunderclap, quite familiar, peacefully and even lucidly familiar, until he remembered: This was the way he had used to dream about it. Then it was gone. He didn't see it go. He knelt, holding the frantic fyce with both hands, hearing the abased wailing of the hounds drawing farther and farther away, until Sam came up. He carried the gun. He laid it down quietly beside the boy and stood looking down at him.

"You've done seed him twice now with a gun in your hands," he said. "This time you couldn't have missed him."

The boy rose. He still held the fyce. Even in his arms and clear of the ground, it yapped frantically, straining and surging after the fading uproar of the two hounds like a tangle of wire springs. He was panting a little, but he was neither shaking nor trembling now.

"Neither could you!" he said. "You had the gun! Neither did you!"

"And you didn't shoot," his father said. "How close were you?"

"I don't know, sir," he said. "There was a big wood tick inside his right hind leg. I saw that. But I didn't have the gun then."

"But you didn't shoot when you had the gun," his father said. "Why?"

But he didn't answer, and his father didn't wait for him to, rising and crossing the room, across the pelt of the bear which the boy had killed two years ago and the larger one which his father had killed before he was born, to the bookcase beneath the mounted head of the boy's first buck. It was the room which his father called the office, from which all the plantation business was transacted; in it for the fourteen years of his life he had heard the best of all talking. Major de Spain would be there and sometimes old General Compson, and Walter Ewell and Boon Hoggenbeck and Sam Fathers and Tennie's Jim, too, because they, too, were hunters, knew the woods and what ran them.

He would hear it, not talking himself but
2 listening—the wilderness, the big woods, bigger and older than any recorded document of white man fatuous enough to believe he had bought any fragment of it or Indian ruthless enough to pretend that any fragment of it had been his to convey. It was of the men, not white nor black nor red, but men, hunters with the will and hardihood to endure and the humility and skill to survive, and the dogs and the bear and deer juxtaposed and reliefed against it, ordered and compelled by and within the wilderness in the ancient and unremitting contest by the ancient and immitigable rules which voided all regrets and brooked no quarter, the voices quiet and weighty and deliberate for retrospection and recollection and exact remembering, while he squatted in the blazing firelight as Tennie's Jim squatted, who stirred only to put more wood on the fire and to pass the bottle from one glass to another. Because the bottle was always present, so that after a while it seemed to him that
3 those fierce instants of heart and brain and courage and wiliness and speed were concentrated and distilled into that brown liquor which not women, not boys and children, but only hunters drank, drinking not of the blood they had spilled but some condensation of the wild immortal spirit, drinking it moderately, humbly even, not with the pagan's base hope of acquiring thereby the virtues of cunning and strength and speed, but in salute to them.

His father returned with the book and sat down again and opened it. "Listen," he said. He read the five stanzas aloud, his voice quiet and deliberate in the room where there was no fire now because it was already spring. Then he looked up. The boy watched him. "All right,"

GUIDED READING

LITERAL QUESTIONS

1a. What does the boy say to Sam after Sam points out that the boy couldn't have missed shooting the bear? ("Neither could you!")

2a. What does his father do when the boy doesn't explain why he didn't shoot the bear? (reads from a book of poetry)

INFERENTIAL QUESTIONS

1b. What does the similarity in response suggest about Sam and the boy's relationship? (They share the same basic values.)

2b. What do you think the boy's father is trying to accomplish when he reads the poem? (help the boy understand the significance of his refusal to shoot)

his father said. "Listen." He read again, but only the second stanza this time, to the end of it, the last two lines, and closed the book and put it on the table beside him. " 'She cannot fade, though thou hast not thy bliss, for ever wilt thou love, and she be fair,' "[16] he said.

"He's talking about a girl," the boy said.

1 "He had to talk about something," his father said. Then he said, "He was talking about truth. Truth doesn't change. Truth is one thing. It covers all things which touch the heart—honor and pride and pity and justice and courage and love. Do you see now?"

He didn't know. Somehow it was simpler than that. There was an old bear, fierce and ruthless, not merely just to stay alive, but with the fierce pride of liberty and freedom, proud enough of that liberty and freedom to see it threatened without fear or even alarm; nay, who at times even seemed deliberately to put that freedom and liberty in jeopardy in order to savor them, to remind his old strong bones and flesh to keep supple and quick to defend and preserve them. There was an old man, son of a Negro slave and an Indian king, inheritor on the one side of the long chronicle of a people who had learned humility through suffering, and pride through the endurance which survived the suffering and injustice, and on the
2 other side, the chronicle of a people even longer in the land than the first, yet who no longer existed in the land at all save in the solitary brotherhood of an old Negro's alien blood and the wild and invincible spirit of an old bear. There was a boy who wished to learn humility and pride in order to become skillful and worthy in the woods, who suddenly found himself becoming so skillful so rapidly that he feared he would never become worthy because he had not learned humility and pride, although he had tried to, until one day and as suddenly he discovered that an old man who could not have defined either had led him, as though by the hand, to that point where an old bear and a little mongrel dog showed him that, by possessing one thing other, he would possess them both.

And a little dog, nameless and mongrel and many-fathered, grown, yet weighing less than six pounds, saying as if to itself, "I can't be dangerous, because there's nothing much smaller than I am; I can't be fierce, because they would call it just noise; I can't be humble, because I'm already too close to the ground to genuflect;[17] I can't be proud, because I wouldn't be near enough to it for anyone to know who
3 was casting that shadow, and I don't even know that I'm not going to heaven, because they have already decided that I don't possess an immortal soul. So all I can be is brave. But it's all right. I can be that, even if they still call it just noise."

That was all. It was simple, much simpler than somebody talking in a book about a youth and a girl he would never need to grieve over, because he could never approach any nearer her and would never have to get any farther away. He had heard about a bear, and finally got big enough to trail it, and he trailed it four years and at last met it with a gun in his hands and he didn't shoot. Because a little dog—But he could have shot long before the little dog covered the twenty yards to where the bear waited, and Sam Fathers could have shot at any time during that interminable minute while Old Ben stood on his hind feet over them. He stopped. His father was watching him gravely across the spring-rife twilight of the room; when he spoke, his words were as quiet as the twilight, too, not loud, because they did not need to be because they would last, "Courage, and honor, and pride," his father said, "and
4 pity, and love of justice and of liberty. They all touch the heart, and what the heart holds to becomes truth, as far as we know truth. Do you see now?"

Sam, and Old Ben, and Nip, he thought. And himself too. He had been all right too. His father had said so. "Yes, sir," he said.

---

16. **" 'She . . . fair' ":** from Keats's "Ode on a Grecian Urn."

17. **genuflect** [jen′yo͞o flekt]: bend the knee as in worship or respect.

AT A GLANCE

- The boy's father repeats lines from Keats's "Ode on a Grecian Urn." He tells the boy the poem is about truth.
- The boy realizes he was right not to kill the bear.

1 THEME

Note how the father's explanation of Keats's poem clarifies the moral precepts the boy embraces as he passes into manhood.

2 SYMBOL

As the boy gains greater understanding of the true nature of manhood, the symbolic dimensions of both Sam and the bear unite into a deep appreciation of the underlying unity between man and nature.

3 THEME

In personifying the dog and in attributing human motivation to its courage, Faulkner dramatically expresses his deep conviction that we can be truly brave only when we perceive our true place in nature.

4 PLOT: RESOLUTION

The boy's mature awareness of the brotherhood that exists between himself, Sam, the bear, and the dog resolves his earlier conflicts and embraces a sense of manhood that respects all living things.

REFLECTING ON THE STORY

In what ways does the yearly hunt provide an appropriate arena for the boy to test his manhood? (The hunt approximates the condition of natural existence, allowing the boy to discover his innate resources.)

GUIDED READING

LITERAL QUESTIONS

1a. According to the boy's father, what does truth cover? (all things that touch the heart)

2a. How does the boy believe he can gain humility and pride? ("by possessing one thing other")

INFERENTIAL QUESTIONS

1b. What kind of truth do you think the father is talking about? (inner truth; spiritual understanding)

2b. What do you think the boy sees as "the one thing other" that he needs to possess? (Answers may vary: pity, compassion, respect for liberty, a sense of brotherhood with all living things.)

STUDY QUESTIONS

1. stories about bear; dogs, men, horses, the country itself
2. son of slave woman and Chickasaw chief; comes to camp to see who is there, if they can shoot, if they have a dog that can bay him; put off being brave, but knew it had to, to live with itself
3. bear's footprint; bear is mortal, can be killed; the boy
4. see bear; leaves behind gun and abandons watch, compass, stick; yes
5. as woodsman; small ratter; gun; shoot the bear
6. fierce, ruthless with fierce pride of liberty and freedom; pride and humility; truth, honor, pride, pity, justice, courage, love
7. no; could kill bear
8. woods, nature; bear's terms
9. nature; nature can be killed by rapacious actions of people
10. little dog; all aware of their place in nature
11. to value living things; bear's pride of liberty and freedom
12.
    - view of nature, connection between humans and nature
    - characters and tone are southern
    - individual against wilderness; coming of age; frontier; as proving ground for courage
    - Modernist juxtaposition of images and ideas
13. Answers will vary. Students should note that inner truth is different from objective reality.

VIEWPOINT

The bear represents nature's timelessness. He is not immortal, but his survival is a celebration of nature and of people's ability to comprehend this awesome truth.

STUDY QUESTIONS

Recalling

1. According to the opening paragraphs, to what has the boy listened for years? For what is the bear "too big" (paragraph 3)?
2. What is Sam Father's ancestry? According to Sam, what does the bear do every year? How did the dog with the injured ear behave "just like folks"?
3. When the boy rides the one-eyed mule to a country he never saw before, what does he see in the wet earth? What does he realize for the first time? According to Sam, whom will the bear "pick out" if he must "run over" somebody?
4. During the next outing, what does the boy decide he must do so that it will not "go on like this forever"? Then, the following June, what does he leave behind and what three "lifeless mechanicals" does he abandon during his search for the bear? Does he see the bear?
5. When the boy is fourteen, in what way is he now better than most grown men? What kind of dog does he bring with him for the final hunt? What does he throw away as he runs after the dog and bear? What do both the boy and Sam fail to do?
6. How does the boy evaluate the bear on page 649? To what does he realize Sam led him? What values does the boy's father talk about in the next-to-last paragraph?

Interpreting

7. Is the boy a threat to the bear the first time he accompanies the others on the hunt? How does he change in this respect by the time of the final hunt?
8. In abandoning his "mechanical devices" on Sam's advice, of what is the boy becoming a part? On what terms is he now challenging the bear?
9. What might the bear represent? On this symbolic level, why is it significant that the bear is "mortal"?
10. Who or what is the "Nip" mentioned in the last paragraph? What do the bear, Nip, and even Sam have in common?
11. What might be the "one thing other" that the boy has learned from the dog and the bear? In failing to shoot the bear, for what things is the boy showing respect?
12. What elements of Romanticism does this story contain? Of Regionalism? With what common American themes does it deal? Why is it nevertheless a story that could not have been written in the nineteenth century?

Extending

13. Do you agree with the father's definition of truth that he provides in his last words? Why or why not?

VIEWPOINT

The critic Cleanth Brooks has commented that Faulkner's love for nature

> is certainly powerful and deep-seated, and on occasion it rises up into great rhapsodic hymns that celebrate the power and continuity of nature, finally changeless through all its apparent changes.
>
> —*William Faulkner: The Yoknapatawpha Country*

■ How would you apply this statement to "The Bear"? How can the story be regarded as a celebration of the permanence and power and changelessness of nature?

LITERARY FOCUS

Symbol and Theme

A **symbol** in a literary work is anything that has a meaning in itself and that also represents or suggests something larger than itself, such as an idea, a quality, a belief, or a value. The unifying symbol in this story is the great bear itself—a "shaggy tremendous shape." The bear is an actual bear, and much of the story is concerned with the process by which the boy, every year a better hunter, develops the skills needed not only to hunt the bear but merely to *see* the elusive animal. Yet, as Faulkner's descriptions suggest, the bear symbolizes, or represents, very much more. For example, it is

> an anachronism, indomitable and invincible, out of an old dead time, a phantom, epitome and apotheosis of the old wild life at which the puny humans swarmed and hacked in a fury of abhorrence and fear.

Sentences like this show how a writer can use a symbol to reveal a theme. Ageless carrier of "the old wild life," the bear, in Faulkner's vision, is one of the forces of nature from which all life springs and which humanity with the abuses of civilization, increasingly threatens.

Thinking About Symbol and Theme

■ Find two other passages in "The Bear" that illustrate the bear's symbolic function. Explain the symbolism, and then comment on its relation to the story's themes.

VOCABULARY

Sentence Completions

Each of the following sentences contains a blank with four possible words for completing the sentence. The words are from "The Bear." Choose the word that completes each sentence correctly, using the word *as it is used in this selection.* Write the number of each item and the letter of your choice on a separate sheet.

1. Two pieces of the puzzle were ____.
   (a) moiling (c) juxtaposed
   (b) ungendered (d) intermittent
2. The presence of an automobile was a deliberate ____ in the eighteenth-century setting of the play.
   (a) anachronism (c) epitome
   (b) apotheosis (d) lucidity
3. The crown and scepter are part of the queen's ____.
   (a) material (c) effluvium
   (b) regalia (d) canebrake
4. The new play received ____ from all the critics.
   (a) designations (c) relinquishments
   (b) predecessors (d) accolades
5. The various factions ____ to form a new political party.
   (a) marred (c) reaffirmed
   (b) coalesced (d) synchronized

COMPOSITION

Analyzing the Total Effect of a Story

■ Write an essay in which you analyze the total effect of this story. What is the impact of the story? How does the author use the following literary elements to achieve this effect: setting, character, plot, point of view, tone, symbol, and theme? *For help with this assignment, refer to Lesson 8 in the Writing About Literature Handbook at the back of this book.*

Writing Diary Entries

■ Suppose the boy in "The Bear" had been keeping a diary of his hunting experiences. Write the entries that he might have written after each outing in his pursuit of the bear. Or, if you prefer, write only the entry he might have written after his final outing and his conversation with his father. Include details about the hunt and also the boy's thoughts and feelings. You may add your own details to those already in the story.

COMPARING WRITERS

The contrasting concerns for society at large and for the individual in particular are evident in the varied themes and settings of the stories in this unit. Nevertheless, social and personal concerns are not always mutually exclusive.

1. Describe the character growth or personal learning experience that occurs in Schwartz's "In Dreams Begin Responsibilities," Steinbeck's "Leader of the People," and Faulkner's "Bear." What do these stories have to say about modern society in general or about modern America's relationship to the past?
2. What are some of the positive personal values suggested by Welty's "Worn Path," Weidman's "My Father Sits in the Dark," and Agee's "Knoxville: Summer, 1915"?
3. What do the main characters of "The Jilting of Granny Weatherall" and "The Far and the Near" have in common? Why could neither of these characters have appeared in nineteenth-century literature?
4. What social concerns are expressed in "The Portable Phonograph" and "The Signature"? Which of these stories also expresses a common personal concern of postwar literature, and what is that concern? Which has concerns similar to those expressed in Auden's poem "The Unknown Citizen" (page 547)?

LITERARY FOCUS

- "It ran in his knowledge before he ever saw it . . ."; bear an archetypal being, beyond nature
- "It did not emerge . . . dimensionless against the dappled obscurity . . ."; bear represents nature as passive, pervasive

VOCABULARY

1. (c) juxtaposed
2. (a) anachronism
3. (b) regalia
4. (d) accolades
5. (b) coalesced

COMPARING WRITERS

1.
   - *Schwartz:* Narrator learns to accept past, responsibility; society unstable, insecure.
   - *Steinbeck:* Jody learns compassion, loses restless aggressiveness; Grandfather comes to terms with present; strengths of people in past mistakenly no longer valued.
   - *Faulkner:* Boy becomes adult, learns pride, humility, courage, honor; people destroy wilderness containing important lessons.
2. *Welty:* love, family, faith; *Weidman:* love, family, sense of roots, respect for others' inner needs; *Agee:* love, family, roots
3. old people who have let a single idea dominate their lives; *Weatherall:* memory of jilting deprives her of richness of life; *engineer:* illusion colors view of life, disillusionment taints memories; experiences typical of modern literature
4. power of society and government over lives of individuals; "Phonograph": nuclear holocaust; "Signature," "Citizen": conformity, lack of individual identity, totalitarian state

COMPOSITION: GUIDELINES FOR EVALUATION

ANALYZING THE TOTAL EFFECT OF A STORY

Objective

To explain the effect of a story's elements

Guidelines for Evaluation

- suggested length: eight to ten paragraphs
- should note coming of age and conflict
- should discuss characters, plot
- should discuss bear as symbol of nature
- should note two intertwined themes

WRITING DIARY ENTRIES

Objective

To view the story from the boy's perspective

Guidelines for Evaluation

- suggested length: two to six paragraphs
- should relate events from the story
- should give information beyond that in the story
- should tell how boy feels about events
- should use a first-person point of view

AT A GLANCE

- Faulkner warns young writers that the fear of the nuclear age has made them forget human values.
- He affirms the endurance of the human spirit and urges writers to help guide humanity on the right path.

LITERARY OPTIONS

- style
- persuasion

THEMATIC OPTIONS

- the enduring human spirit
- the writer's social responsibilities

1 PERSUASION: AUDIENCE

Faulkner underscores the writer's critical role in society.

2 STYLE: REPETITION

Repetition of the word *teach* reinforces Faulkner's belief in the enduring value of universal truths.

3 PERSUASION

Faulkner reinforces his goal of establishing a clear and viable choice between fear and hope, extinction and affirmation.

REFLECTING ON THE SELECTION

Do you agree or disagree with Faulkner's premise that writers have a social responsibility? (Answers will vary: Yes, because literature influences society; no, because writers should be free to write what they please.)

NONFICTION

William Faulkner

Nobel Prize Acceptance Speech

I feel that this award was not made to me as a man but to my work—a life's work in the agony and sweat of the human spirit, not for glory and least of all for profit, but to create out of the materials of the human spirit something which did not exist before. So this award is only mine in trust. It will not be difficult to find a dedication for the money part of it commensurate with the purpose and significance of
1 its origin. But I would like to do the same with the acclaim too, by using this moment as a pinnacle from which I might be listened to by the young men and women already dedicated to the same anguish and travail, among whom is already that one who will some day stand here where I am standing.

Our tragedy today is a general and universal physical fear so long sustained by now that we can even bear it. There are no longer problems of the spirit. There is only the question: when will I be blown up? Because of this, the young man or woman writing today has forgotten the problems of the human heart in conflict with itself which alone can make good writing because only that is worth writing about, worth the agony and the sweat.

2 He must learn them again. He must teach himself that the basest of all things is to be afraid; and, teaching himself that, forget it forever, leaving no room in his workshop for anything but the old verities and truths of the heart, the old universal truths lacking which any story is ephemeral and doomed—love and honor and pity and pride and compassion and sacrifice. Until he does so he labors under a curse. He writes not of love but of lust, of defeats in which nobody loses anything of value, of victories without hope and worst of all without pity or compassion. His griefs grieve on no universal bones, leaving no scars. He writes not of the heart but of the glands.

Until he relearns these things he will write as though he stood among and watched the end of man. I decline to accept the end of man. It is easy enough to say that man is immortal simply because he will endure; that when the last ding-dong of doom has clanged and faded from the last worthless rock hanging tideless in the last red and dying evening, that even then there will still be one more sound: that of his puny inexhaustible voice, still talking. I refuse to accept this. I believe that man will not merely endure: he will prevail. He is immortal, not because he alone among creatures has an inexhaustible voice, but because he has a soul, a spirit capable of compassion and sacrifice and endurance. The poet's, the writer's, duty is to write about these things. It
3 is his privilege to help man endure by lifting his heart, by reminding him of the courage and honor and hope and pride and compassion and pity and sacrifice which have been the glory of his past. The poet's voice need not merely be the record of man, it can be one of the props, the pillars to help him endure and prevail.

GUIDED READING

LITERAL QUESTIONS

1a. What question does Faulkner believe overwhelms problems of the human spirit? ("When will I be blown up?")

2a. Why does Faulkner think that humanity will prevail? (because of its soul)

INFERENTIAL QUESTIONS

1b. What do Faulkner's remarks about this question suggest about the nature of the nuclear age? (We have lost our sense of human values in the face of awesome technological advances.)

2b. How do you think Faulkner's vision of human destiny affects his writing? (It gives his work a sense of passionate affirmation.)

STUDY QUESTIONS

Recalling

1. To whom does Faulkner address this speech, according to the first paragraph?
2. What, according to Faulkner, is the emotion that is today's tragedy? What question overrides everything else?
3. What does Faulkner say are "the old universal truths" lacking which any story is "ephemeral and doomed"?
4. What does Faulkner "decline to accept" in the fourth paragraph? Why does he believe humanity is immortal? What does he say of the poet's voice in his final sentence?

Interpreting

5. Explain in your own words the distinction Faulkner makes between valuable writing and writing that lacks value.
6. In order to determine Faulkner's purpose in this speech, discuss whether he really wants writers to *forget* the question in his second paragraph. What does his last sentence imply? In what things does he believe young writers must have faith?

Extending

7. Of which works that you have read in this unit and the two preceding units do you think Faulkner would approve, and why? Of which works do you think he would disapprove, and why? How do Faulkner's ideas differ from the ideas expressed in "The Portable Phonograph" on page 623?

COMPOSITION

Analyzing an Author's Purpose

■ Faulkner's speech is directed at a particular audience: all writers, present and future. He has a particular purpose as well. In an essay, analyze his purpose—what he is trying to say, what he is trying to do. Begin by stating his purpose. Then support your statement by citing the various techniques he uses to achieve his purpose—for example, imagery, use of repetition, and statements of opinion. *For help with this assignment, refer to Lesson 4 in the Writing About Literature Handbook at the back of this book.*

Expressing an Opinion Persuasively

■ Do you agree that humanity "will not merely endure" but will "prevail"? Express either your agreement or your disagreement with Faulkner's view. In either case, support your opinion with examples, details, facts, and well-chosen images.

STUDY QUESTIONS

1. "young men and women already dedicated to the same anguish and travail" as his
2. "a general and universal physical fear"; "When will I be blown up?"
3. love, honor, pity, pride, compassion, sacrifice
4. the end of humanity; because human beings have souls; can help humanity endure, prevail
5. Valuable writing deals with the basic truths of love, honor, pride, pity, compassion, and sacrifice. Writing of little value deals with fear and doom.
6.
   - not forget question, but cease being afraid
   - Writers play an important role in the survival of the species.
   - themselves; the nobility of the human soul
7.
   - Answers will vary. He would approve of works showing belief in basic human values, importance of nature, possibility of survival and growth in the future.
   - "Phonograph" assumes mistrust, jealousy, and other negative emotions predominate; it does not demonstrate the triumph of love, honor, pity, pride, compassion, and sacrifice.

COMPOSITION: GUIDELINES FOR EVALUATION

ANALYZING AN AUTHOR'S PURPOSE

Objective

To explain how an author achieves his purpose

Guidelines for Evaluation

- suggested length: four to six paragraphs
- should note purpose is to state importance of writer's faith in man as necessary to survival
- should discuss Faulkner's use of imagery, repetition, and statements of opinion
- should cite specific examples from the speech

EXPRESSING AN OPINION PERSUASIVELY

Objective

To write persuasively

Guidelines for Evaluation

- suggested length: three to five paragraphs
- should state the writer's opinion
- should use persuasive techniques, particularly examples, facts, details, and images
- should be logical and well thought out
- should have an appropriate conclusion

Jack Kerouac *1922–1969*

Jack Kerouac was born in Lowell, Massachusetts, where, he said, he "roamed fields and riverbanks by day and night, wrote little novels in my room, first novel written at age eleven." After serving in the Navy and as a merchant seaman, and having decided to be a "lonesome traveler," he roamed the United States and Mexico, working at an assortment of jobs, including railroad brakeman and forest ranger.

Out of his various experiences and wanderings Kerouac wrote his popular novel *On the Road* (1957), which celebrated the freedom and vigorous life of the American "traveler." The novel was a sensation, and Kerouac became the most famous of the writers and artists known as the Beat Generation. The Beats, Kerouac said, took their name from the fact that they were weary ("beat") of the ordinary, dull routine of American life. They were nonconformists who searched for the unusual, the special experience that would bring all the threads of life together in one ecstatic moment. It has also been suggested that they took their name from their search for an earthly "*beat*itude," or holiness.

On the Road was Kerouac's first attempt to write in what he called a "visual American form"—a "spontaneous prose" that would capture the vitality and impulsiveness of experience. *On the Road* does suggest that spontaneity, despite the fact that it is a highly-crafted work and was rewritten several times. Kerouac's outlook on life has been described as "an affirmative attitude in which wonder and delight take the largest place." His later books, however, never matched the success of *On the Road.*

"Alone on a Mountaintop," from Kerouac's *Lonesome Traveler*, is one of his best attempts at describing his quest. It records the wonder and delight, and the fear and serenity, of his experience as a fire lookout in northwest Washington in 1956.

■ How many different paths can there be to "finding ourselves"? Which path led Kerouac to his discovery?

Jack Kerouac

from Lonesome Traveler

Alone on a Mountaintop

I was a fire lookout and after two nights of trying to sleep in the boom and slap of the Forest Service floats,[1] they came for me one rainy morning—a powerful tugboat lashed to a large corral float bearing four mules and three horses, my own groceries, feed, batteries and equipment. The muleskinner's[2] name was Andy and he wore the same old floppy cowboy hat he'd worn in Wyoming twenty years ago. "Well, boy, now we're gonna put you away where we can't reach ya—you better get ready."

"It's just what I want, Andy, be alone for three solid months nobody to bother me."

"It's what you're sayin' now but you'll change your tune after a week."

1 I didn't believe him. I was looking forward to an experience men seldom earn in this modern world: complete and comfortable solitude in the wilderness, day and night, sixty-three days and nights to be exact. We had no idea how much snow had fallen on my mountain during the winter and Andy said: "If there didn't it means you gotta hike two miles down that hard trail every day or every other day with two buckets, boy. I ain't envyin' you—I been back there. And one day it's gonna be hot and you're about ready to broil, and bugs you can't even count 'em, and next day a li'l' ole summer blizzard come hit you around the corner of Hozomeen[3] which sits right there near Canada in your back yard and you won't be able to stick logs fast enough in that potbelly stove of yours." But I had a full rucksack loaded with turtleneck sweaters and warm shirts and pants and long wool socks bought on the Seattle waterfront, and gloves and an earmuff cap, and lots of instant soup and coffee in my grub list.

2 "Shoulda brought yourself a quart of brandy, boy," says Andy shaking his head as the tug pushed our corral float up Ross Lake through the log gate and around to the left dead north underneath the immense rain shroud of Sourdough Mountain and Ruby Mountain.

"Where's Desolation Peak?" I asked, meaning my own mountain (*A mountain to be kept forever,* I'd dreamed all that spring) (O lonesome traveler!)

"You ain't gonna see it today till we're practically on top it and by that time you'll be so soakin' wet you won't care."

Assistant Ranger Marty Gohlke of Marblemount Ranger Station was with us too, also giving me tips and instructions. Nobody seemed to envy Desolation Peak except me. After two hours pushing through the storming waves of the long rainy lake with dreary misty timber rising steeply on both sides and the mules and horses chomping on their feedbags patient in the downpour, we arrived at the foot of Desolation Trail and the tugman (who'd been providing us with good hot coffee in the pilot cabin) eased her over and settled the float against a steep muddy slope full of bushes and
3 fallen trees. The muleskinner whacked the first mule and she lurched ahead with her double-sided pack of batteries and canned goods, hit the mud with forehoofs, scrambled, slipped, almost fell back in the lake and finally gave one mighty heave and went skittering out of sight in the fog to wait on the trail for the other mules and her master. We all got off, cut the barge loose, waved to the tug man, mounted our horses and started up a sad and dripping party in heavy rain.

1. **floats:** raftlike platforms.
2. **muleskinner:** mule driver.
3. **Hozomeen:** Mt. Hozomeen.

AT A GLANCE

- The author travels by tugboat with a muleskinner (Andy) and a ranger (Marty) to the base of Desolation Peak, where he will work at a fire lookout.
- They reach the mountain and ascend with pack mules.

LITERARY OPTIONS

- narration
- description

THEMATIC OPTIONS

- the values of personal experience
- self-reliance
- the power of nature

1 THEME

Kerouac's pleasurable expectation of spending time alone in the wilderness reflects his concern with the critical, nurturing value of private experience.

2 NARRATION

Kerouac's use of dialogue creates a narrative framework, adding color and humor, heightening dramatic interest, and conveying a sharper, more fully realized sense of his experiences.

3 DESCRIPTION

The abundance of sensory details that convey oral, tactile, and visual impressions give the reader a strong sense of what the scene looked, sounded, and felt like.

GUIDED READING

LITERAL QUESTION

1a. What does Kerouac tell Andy when Andy announces that they are going to put him where they can't reach him? (that he wants to be alone for three months with no one to bother him)

INFERENTIAL QUESTION

1b. Why do you think Kerouac might want to be alone? (to learn more about himself)

AT A GLANCE

- The three men have a hard climb up the mountain in the rain. They reach alpine meadows covered with blue and red flowers.
- When they reach the timber line, it begins to snow.
- The lookout shack is dirty and damp.

1 NARRATION

The chronological ordering of events reinforces the narrative tone of the essay and heightens dramatic interest by presenting Kerouac's experiences as a story.

2 DESCRIPTION

Kerouac's lush, figurative language (*powdered meadow; drenching mists, tiny-budded flowers*) and emphasis on color and pattern create a strong image of the landscape that captures the vivid flow of his impressions.

3 CHARACTERIZATION

Andy and Marty are experienced in the wild. By contrast, Kerouac's attempts to make himself more comfortable suggest both his city origins and his lack of experience with the natural elements.

1 At first the trail, always steeply rising, was so dense with shrubbery we kept getting shower after shower from overhead and against our out-saddled knees. The trail was deep with round rocks that kept causing the animals to slip. At one point a great fallen tree made it impossible to go on until Old Andy and Marty went ahead with axes and cleared a short cut around the tree, sweating and cursing and hacking as I watched the animals. By-and-by they were ready but the mules were afraid of the rough steepness of the short cut and had
2 to be prodded through with sticks. Soon the trail reached alpine meadows powdered with blue lupine everywhere in the drenching mists, and with little red poppies, tiny-budded flowers as delicate as designs on a small Japanese teacup. Now the trail zigzagged widely back and forth up the high meadow. Soon we saw the vast foggy heap of a rock-cliff face above and Andy yelled "Soon's we get up high as that we're almost there but that's another two thousand feet though you think you could reach up and touch it!"

3 I unfolded my nylon poncho and draped it over my head, and, drying a little, or, rather, ceasing to drip, I walked alongside the horse to warm my blood and began to feel better. But the other boys just rode along with their heads bowed in the rain. As for altitude all I could tell was from some occasional frightening spots on the trail where we could look down on distant treetops.

The alpine meadow reached to timber line[4] and suddenly a great wind blew shafts of sleet on us. "Gettin' near the top now!" yelled Andy—and suddenly there was snow on the trail, the horses were chumping through a foot of slush and mud, and to the left and right everything was blinding white in the gray fog. "About five and a half thousand feet right now" said Andy rolling a cigarette as he rode in the rain.

We went down, then up another spell, down again, a slow gradual climb, and then Andy yelled "There she is!" and up ahead in the mountaintop gloom I saw a little shadowy peaked shack standing alone on the top of the world and gulped with fear:

"This my home all summer? And *this* is summer?"

The inside of the shack was even more miserable, damp and dirty, leftover groceries and magazines torn to shreds by rats and mice, the floor muddy, the windows impenetrable. But hardy Old Andy who'd been through this kind of thing all his life got a roaring fire crackling in the potbelly stove and had me lay out a pot

4. **timber line:** point beyond which trees cannot grow.

GUIDED READING

LITERAL QUESTIONS

1a. What do Andy and Marty do when the trail is blocked by a fallen tree? (They clear a short cut around the tree with axes.)

2a. What happens when the group reaches the timber line? (It begins to sleet and snow.)

INFERENTIAL QUESTIONS

1b. What do their actions suggest about their characters? (They are tough, strong, and self-reliant.)

2b. What does the sudden change in weather suggest about the kind of experience Kerouac is likely to have on the mountaintop? (It will be intense, full of surprises, and a test of his fortitude and resilience.)

Photographs of the Desolation Peak lookout station and North Cascades National Park, Washington.

of water with almost half a can of coffee in it saying "Coffee ain't no good 'less it's *strong!*" and pretty soon the coffee was boiling a nice brown aromatic foam and we got our cups out and drank deep.

1 Meanwhile I'd gone out on the roof with Marty and removed the bucket from the chimney and put up the weather pole with the anemometer[5] and done a few other chores—when we came back in Andy was frying Spam and eggs in a huge pan and it was almost like a party. Outside, the patient animals chomped on their supper bags and were glad to rest by the old corral fence built of logs by some Desolation lookout of the Thirties.

Darkness came, incomprehensible.

In the gray morning after they'd slept in sleeping bags on the floor and I on the only bunk in my mummy bag, Andy and Marty left,
2 laughing, saying, "Well, whatayou think now hey? We been here twelve hours and you still ain't been able to see more than twelve feet!"

"By gosh that's right, what am I going to do for watching fires?"

"Don't worry boy, these clouds'll roll away and you'll be able to see a hunnerd miles in every direction."

I didn't believe it and I felt miserable and spent the day trying to clean up the shack or pacing twenty careful feet each way in my "yard" (the ends of which appeared to be sheer drops into silent gorges), and I went to
3 bed early. About bedtime I saw my first star, briefly, then giant phantom clouds billowed all around me and the star was gone. But in that instant I thought I'd seen a mile-down maw[6] of grayblack lake where Andy and Marty were back in the Forest Service boat which had met them at noon.

In the middle of the night I woke up suddenly and my hair was standing on end—I saw a huge black shadow in my window. Then I saw that it had a star above it, and realized that this was Mt. Hozomeen (8080 feet) looking in my window from miles away near Canada. I
4 got up from the forlorn bunk with the mice scattering underneath and went outside and gasped to see black mountain shapes gianting all around, and not only that but the billowing curtains of the northern lights shifting behind the clouds. It was a little too much for a city boy—the fear that the Abominable Snowman might be breathing behind me in the dark sent me back to bed where I buried my head inside my sleeping bag.

But in the morning—Sunday, July sixth—I

5. **anemometer:** instrument for measuring wind speed.

6. **maw:** gaping, dark opening.

AT A GLANCE

- The men eat dinner in a party atmosphere.
- In the morning, Andy and Marty leave. Depressed by the heavy cloud cover, the author cleans the shack.
- He feels a city boy's fear of nature.

1 THEME

Kerouac's description of how the men transform the grim and dreary atmosphere into a party mood by dealing directly and efficiently with the real circumstances reflects the value and importance of self-reliance.

2 NARRATION

Note how the dialogue adds important descriptive information as well as dramatic interest.

3 MOOD

Kerouac's figurative descriptions (*giant phantom clouds; mile-down maw of grayblack lake*) convey both a clear image of what he sees and a vivid sense of the wonder and strangeness he feels.

4 VOCABULARY: WORD INVENTION

Kerouac creates his own verb, *gianting*, to convey the unique reality of his perception of the mountains.

GUIDED READING

LITERAL QUESTION

1a. How does Kerouac respond when he wakes up in the middle of the night and sees the shadow of the mountains? (He is frightened and buries his head inside his sleeping bag.)

INFERENTIAL QUESTION

1b. What do you think frightens him? (his awe of nature's power; his sense of aloneness)

AT A GLANCE

- The next day, the sky clears and the clouds vanish.
- The author enjoys the beauty of the landscape.
- He describes a fire he sees from his lookout.
- He details his daily routine.

1 DESCRIPTION

Note how the sensory details Kerouac provides (*marshmallow cover; warm sunshine; drowsy warm doorstep*) underscore the personal, private nature of his experience.

2 NARRATION

This detailed sequence of events reinforces the narrative framework of the essay and adds both dramatic interest and intensity.

3 CHARACTERIZATION

Kerouac's description of his daily routine reflects the pleasure he takes in his solitude and self sufficiency as well as his underlying competence and resourcefulness.

1 was amazed and overjoyed to see a clear blue sunny sky and down below, like a radiant pure snow sea, the clouds making a marshmallow cover for all the world and all the lake while I abided in warm sunshine among hundreds of miles of snow-white peaks. I brewed coffee and sang and drank a cup on my drowsy warm doorstep.

At noon the clouds vanished and the lake appeared below, beautiful beyond belief, a perfect blue pool twenty five miles long and more, and the creeks like toy creeks and the timber green and fresh everywhere below and even the joyous little unfolding liquid tracks of vacationists' fishingboats on the lake and in the lagoons. A perfect afternoon of sun, and behind the shack I discovered a snowfield big enough to provide me with buckets of cold water till late September.

My job was to watch for fires. One night a terrific lightning storm made a dry run across the Mt. Baker National Forest without any rainfall. When I saw that ominous black cloud
2 flashing wrathfully toward me I shut off the radio and laid the aerial on the ground and waited for the worst. Hiss! hiss! said the wind, bringing dust and lightning nearer. Tick! said the lightning rod, receiving a strand of electricity from a strike on nearby Skagit Peak. Hiss! tick! and in my bed I felt the earth move. Fifteen miles to the south, just east of Ruby Peak and somewhere near Panther Creek, a large fire raged, a huge orange spot. At ten o'clock lightning hit it again and it flared up dangerously.

I was supposed to note the general area of lightning strikes. By midnight I'd been staring so intently out the dark window I got hallucinations of fires everywhere, three of them right in Lightning Creek, phosphorescent orange verticals of ghost fire that seemed to come and go.

In the morning, there at 177° 16′ where I'd seen the big fire was a strange brown patch in the snowy rock showing where the fire had raged and sputtered out in the all-night rain that followed the lightning. But the result of this storm was disastrous fifteen miles away at McAllister Creek where a great blaze had outlasted the rain and exploded the following afternoon in a cloud that could be seen from Seattle. I felt sorry for the fellows who had to fight these fires, the smoke-jumpers who parachuted down on them out of planes and the trail crews who hiked to them, climbing and scrambling over slippery rocks and scree slopes,[7] arriving sweaty and exhausted only to face the wall of heat when they got there. As a lookout I had it pretty easy and only had to concentrate on reporting the exact location (by instrument findings) of every blaze I detected.

3 Most days, though, it was the routine that occupied me. Up at seven or so every day, a pot of coffee brought to a boil over a handful of burning twigs, I'd go out in the alpine yard with a cup of coffee hooked in my thumb and leisurely make my wind speed and wind direction and temperature and moisture readings—then, after chopping wood, I'd use the two-way radio and report to the relay station on Sourdough. At 10 A.M. I usually got hungry for breakfast, and I'd make delicious pancakes, eating them at my little table that was decorated with bouquets of mountain lupine and sprigs of fir.

Early in the afternoon was the usual time for my kick of the day, instant chocolate pudding with hot coffee. Around two or three I'd lie on my back on the meadowside and watch the clouds float by, or pick blueberries and eat them right there. The radio was on loud enough to hear any calls for Desolation.

Then at sunset I'd roust up my supper out of cans of yams and Spam and peas, or sometimes just pea soup with corn muffins baked on top of the wood stove in aluminum foil. Then I'd go out to that precipitous snow slope and shovel my two pails of snow for the water tub and gather an armful of fallen firewood from the hillside like the proverbial Old Woman of Japan. For the chipmunks and conies[8] I put pans of leftovers under the shack, in the mid-

---

7. **scree slopes:** slopes covered with loose, sliding rock fragments.
8. **conies:** rabbits.

GUIDED READING

LITERAL QUESTIONS

1a. What does Kerouac discover behind the shack? (a snowfield to provide him with fresh water)

2a. How does Kerouac spend his afternoons? (lying on his back watching clouds; picking blueberries)

INFERENTIAL QUESTIONS

1b. What does his discovery suggest about our relationship to the natural world? (We can sustain ourselves in the natural world without society's conveniences.)

2b. What does the description suggest about how Kerouac spent much of his time on the mountain? (He concentrated on enjoying the natural world.)

dle of the night I could hear them clanking around. The rat would scramble down from the attic and eat some too.

1 Sometimes I'd yell questions at the rocks and trees, and across gorges, or yodel—"What is the meaning of the void?" The answer was perfect silence, so I knew.

Before bedtime I'd read by kerosene lamp whatever books were in the shack. It's amazing how people in solitary hunger after books. After poring over every word of a medical tome, and the synopsized versions of Shakespeare's plays by Charles and Mary Lamb,[9] I climbed up in the little attic and put together torn cowboy pocket books and magazines the mice had ravaged—I also played stud poker with three imaginary players.

Around bedtime I'd bring a cup of milk almost to a boil with a tablespoon of honey in it, and drink that for my lamby[10] nightcap, then I'd curl up in my sleeping bag.

2 No man should go through life without once experiencing healthy, even bored solitude in the wilderness, finding himself depending solely on himself and thereby learning his true and hidden strength. Learning, for instance, to eat when he's hungry and sleep when he's sleepy.

Also around bedtime was my singing time. I'd pace up and down the well-worn path in the dust of my rock singing all the show tunes I could remember, at the top of my voice too, with nobody to hear except the deer and the bear.

In the red dusk, the mountains were symphonies in pink snow—Jack Mountain, Three Fools Peak, Freezeout Peak, Golden Horn, Mt. Terror, Mt. Fury, Mt. Despair, Crooked Thumb Peak, Mt. Challenger and the incomparable Mt. Baker bigger than the world in the distance—and my own little Jackass Ridge that completed the Ridge of Desolation. Pink snow and the clouds all distant and frilly like ancient remote cities of Buddhaland splendor, and the wind working incessantly—whish, whish—booming, at times rattling my shack.

For supper I made chop suey and baked some biscuits and put the leftovers in a pan for deer that came in the moonlit night and nibbled like big strange cows of peace—long-antlered buck and does and babies too—as I meditated in the alpine grass facing the magic moon-laned lake. And I could see firs reflected in the moonlit lake five thousand feet below, upside down, pointing to infinity.

And all the insects ceased in honor of the moon.

Sixty-three sunsets I saw revolve on that
3 perpendicular hill—mad raging sunsets pouring in sea foams of cloud through unimaginable crags like the crags you grayly drew in pencil as a child, with every rose-tint of hope beyond, making you feel just like them, brilliant and bleak beyond words.

Cold mornings with clouds billowing out of Lightning Gorge like smoke from a giant fire but the lake cerulean[11] as ever.

August comes in with a blast that shakes your house and augurs[12] little Augusticity—then that snowy-air and woodsmoke feeling—then the snow comes sweeping your way from Canada, and the wind rises and dark low clouds rush up as out of a forge. Suddenly a green-rose rainbow appears right on your ridge with steamy clouds all around and an orange sun turmoiling . . .

What is a rainbow,
Lord?—a hoop
For the lowly

. . . and you go out and suddenly your shadow is ringed by the rainbow as you walk on the hilltop, a lovely-haloed mystery making you want to pray.

A blade of grass jiggling in the winds of infinity, anchored to a rock, and for your own poor gentle flesh no answer.

Your oil lamp burning in infinity.

---

9. **Charles and Mary Lamb:** English Romantic authors of *Tales from Shakespeare.*
10. **lamby:** innocent.

11. **cerulean** [sə ro͞o′lē ən]: sky-blue.
12. **augurs** [ô′gərz]: foretells.

AT A GLANCE

- The author describes his evening routine.
- He affirms the importance of solitude in the wilderness.
- He describes the beauty of the landscape, the sunsets, and the change in seasons.

1 POSTWAR IDEA

The question Kerouac poses about the meaning of the world reflects a dominant theme in post-World War II literature—the struggle to extract an underlying sense of meaning in the universe.

2 PURPOSE

In this assertion Kerouac explains his decision to stay alone on a mountaintop for three months.

3 DESCRIPTION

Kerouac's vivid, figurative description of the natural world (*raging sunsets; rose-tint of hope*) conveys the transcendental nature of his experience.

REFLECTING ON THE SELECTION

Why is the burning oil lamp a fitting image with which to close the essay? (It symbolizes his solitude, smallness, spiritual growth, and affirmation of life.)

GUIDED READING

LITERAL QUESTIONS

1a. What does Kerouac do around bedtime? (prepare himself a cup of milk with honey)

2a. What does the shadow ringed by a rainbow make Kerouac want to do? (pray)

INFERENTIAL QUESTIONS

1b. What does this activity suggest about the kind of pleasures Kerouac enjoys? (They are simple, innocent, and childlike.)

2b. What can you infer about Kerouac's attitude toward nature from his response to the rainbow? (He is spiritually uplifted by his experience of the natural world.)

STUDY QUESTIONS

1. He was a fire lookout.
2. ■ "This is my home all summer? And *this* is summer?"
   ■ Mt. Hozomeen
   ■ amazement, joy
3. ■ gets up, makes coffee, takes readings, chops wood, reports to relay station, has breakfast, eats in afternoon, relaxes in meadow, has supper, shovels snow, gathers wood, puts out leftovers, reads, drinks hot milk and honey, goes to sleep
   ■ snowfield
   ■ "What is the meaning of the void?"
   ■ silence
4. experience healthy, even bored solitude in wilderness; true and hidden strength
5. like crags: brilliant, bleak; "hoop" for the lowly
6. oil lamp
7. Answers will vary; possible answers: trip up, adjusting to solitude, unpleasant conditions, boredom.
8. simple pleasures; spiritually, learning own strength, feeling closer to life and nature; symbol of self, life
9. ■ Romanticism: love of nature, focus on self
   ■ Transcendentalism: metaphysical connection with nature, concern with self-reliance
   ■ Twentieth-century: references to Zen and show tunes; informality of language, characterization, and narrative voice
10. Answers will vary. Students should see both as strong individualists with antiauthoritarian bias. The nonconformism matched the ideals and rebelliousness of youth at that time.

VOCABULARY

1. (b) loneliness : solitude
2. (a) shawl : jacket
3. (b) volume : capacity
4. (d) impervious : penetrate
5. (c) steep : incline

STUDY QUESTIONS

Recalling

1. For what reasons was the author "alone on a mountaintop"?
2. What were the author's first remarks when he saw the shack in which he was to live? What "huge black shadow" frightened him when he woke up on his first night and found the fog had cleared? What were his emotions upon seeing the view in the morning?
3. Summarize the author's usual daily routine described on page 658. What provided him with water? What questions did he sometimes yell at the rocks and trees? What was the answer?
4. What does the author say no one should go through life without doing (page 659)? What does he say a person learns from this experience?
5. What does the author say he felt when he watched the sunsets on the crags? How does his "poem" describe the sudden rainbow?
6. What is burning in infinity, according to the closing sentence?

Interpreting

7. What was difficult about Kerouac's summer on the mountain?
8. What did Kerouac learn to appreciate as a result of his experience? In what way did he grow? What is the significance of the oil lamp in the closing sentence?
9. What elements of Romanticism does Kerouac's narrative contain? Of Transcendentalism? What makes the narrative a distinct product of the twentieth century?

Extending

10. Why do you think both Jack Kerouac and Henry David Thoreau (page 172) were so popular with American youth of the 1950s and 1960s?

VOCABULARY

Analogies

Analogies are comparisons that point out relationships between items. Analogy items on vocabulary tests are usually written as two pairs of words. The words in the first pair are related to each other in the same way as those in the second pair: for example, SHORT : TALL : : SMALL : LARGE.

The first word in capitals in each of the following analogies is from "Alone on a Mountaintop." Complete the analogies by choosing the pair of words that is related in the same way as the pair in capital letters.

1. DESOLATION : ISOLATION : :
   (a) desperation : emptiness
   (b) loneliness : solitude
   (c) fire : slaughter
   (d) loss : misery
2. PONCHO : COAT : :
   (a) shawl : jacket
   (b) boots : galoshes
   (c) frock : dress
   (d) leather : rubber
3. ALTITUDE : HEIGHT : :
   (a) attitude : affection
   (b) volume : capacity
   (c) amplitude : amplifier
   (d) rectitude : law
4. IMPENETRABLE : PIERCE : :
   (a) unclear : unknown
   (b) spoiled : ruin
   (c) unhurt : wound
   (d) impervious : penetrate
5. PRECIPITOUS : SLOPE : :
   (a) angular : rectangle
   (b) mountainous : hilly
   (c) steep : incline
   (d) rocky : cliff

COMPOSITION

Analyzing an Author's Purpose

■ Write an essay analyzing Kerouac's purpose in "Alone on a Mountaintop." Begin by summarizing the main ideas of the work. Then tell how the author's tone suggests his attitude and the attitude he wants his reader to share. Be sure to cite any devices the author uses to achieve his purpose. *For help with this assignment, refer to Lesson 4 in the Writing About Literature Handbook at the back of this book.*

Writing a Description

■ Write a brief description of a natural scene or of some aspect of nature you have experienced. Make your description as vivid and vigorous as you can. Feel free to use some of Kerouac's descriptive techniques, such as colloquial speech, onomatopoeia, and imagery.

COMPOSITION: GUIDELINES FOR EVALUATION

ANALYZING AN AUTHOR'S PURPOSE

Objective

To explain the author's purpose in an essay

Guidelines for Evaluation

- suggested length: three to five paragraphs
- should state the main idea, that solitude is spiritually enriching
- should describe tone, relate it to purpose
- should identify literary techniques used and show how they help achieve purpose

WRITING A DESCRIPTION

Objective

To write a description of nature

Guidelines for Evaluation

- suggested length: one to three paragraphs
- should describe a natural setting
- should use vivid language
- should use details, other literary devices
- should communicate sensory information
- should have a unified effect

Carson McCullers *1917–1967*

Individuality, selfhood, the fragile human personality—these are Carson McCullers' concerns. Her sensitive and sometimes disturbing novels and stories follow the lives of people trying desperately to gain and keep a hold on an indifferent world.

Carson McCullers was born in Columbus, Georgia. She was an accomplished musician, and her first ambitions directed her to New York City to study music. Her family sold an heirloom to provide her with the money to study at the Juilliard School of Music; unfortunately, however, all the money was lost on the subway.

She began working at various day jobs while taking writing courses at night at Columbia University. One of her teachers there spotted her talent and helped her publish her first short story. Her best known works are *The Heart Is a Lonely Hunter* (1940), *The Member of the Wedding* (1946), and *The Ballad of the Sad Cafe* (1951). *The Member of the Wedding*—the story of a sensitive teen-ager on the eve of her brother's wedding—was turned into a successful play by McCullers herself in 1950.

From the age of twenty-nine, McCullers was paralyzed on her left side, and this condition severely hampered her ability to work continuously. One of her books, *Clock Without Hands* (1961), took ten years to complete; she finished it by typing one page each day with one hand for a year.

An abiding concern in Carson McCullers' writing is loneliness. In this selection from *The Mortgaged Heart,* she suggests a path away from unwanted solitude and toward true belonging.

■ How can we conquer the loneliness that we all feel at times? What does McCullers advise us to do?

AT A GLANCE

- The quest for identity from birth to death is the cause of loneliness.
- After finding an identity, we seek to belong to something. Love gives us that sense of belonging.
- Americans are individualists; Europeans are made secure by class loyalties.

LITERARY OPTIONS

- the essay
- purpose
- repetition

THEMATIC OPTIONS

- the search for identity
- the power of love
- the value of self-knowledge

1 PURPOSE

McCullers clearly identifies her purpose and immediately establishes the perspective from which she will examine the question.

2 ESSAY

In developing her thesis and by observing her subjects objectively, McCullers presents an organized, structured argument that makes a rational appeal to the reader.

3 MAIN IDEA

McCullers' dispassionate reflections on the conflict between the quest for identity and the need to belong convey the anguish of the modern world's preoccupation with self-definition.

4 TONE

McCullers' direct, concrete language and calm, reasoned approach to her emotionally charged subject establish a calm, dignified tone that lends strength and conviction to her thesis.

Carson McCullers

from The Mortgaged Heart

This city, New York—consider the people in it, the eight million of us. An English friend of mine, when asked why he lived in New York City, said that he liked it here because he could be so alone. While it was my friend's desire to be alone, the aloneness of many Americans who live in cities is an involuntary and
1 fearful thing. It has been said that loneliness is the great American malady. What is the nature of this loneliness? It would seem essentially to be a quest for identity.

To the spectator, the amateur philosopher, no motive among the complex ricochets of our desires and rejections seems stronger or more enduring than the will of the individual to claim his identity and belong. From infancy to death, the human being is obsessed by these dual motives. During our first weeks of life, the
2 question of identity shares urgency with the need for milk. The baby reaches for his toes, then explores the bars of his crib; again and again he compares the difference between his own body and the objects around him, and in the wavering, infant eyes there comes a pristine wonder.

Consciousness of self is the first abstract problem that the human being solves. Indeed, it is this self-consciousness that removes us from lower animals. This primitive grasp of identity develops with constantly shifting emphasis through all our years. Perhaps maturity is simply the history of those mutations that reveal to the individual the relation between himself and the world in which he finds himself.

3 After the first establishment of identity there comes the imperative need to lose this new-found sense of separateness and to belong to something larger and more powerful than the weak, lonely self. The sense of moral isolation is intolerable to us.

In *The Member of the Wedding*[1] the lovely twelve-year-old girl, Frankie Addams, articulates this universal need: "The trouble with me is that for a long time I have just been an *I* person. All people belong to a *We* except me. Not to belong to a *We* makes you too lonesome."

Love is the bridge that leads from the *I* sense to the *We,* and there is a paradox about personal love. Love of another individual opens a new relation between the personality and the world. The lover responds in a new way to nature and may even write poetry. Love is affirmation; it motivates the *yes* responses and the sense of wider communication. Love casts out fear, and in the security of this togetherness we find contentment, courage. We no longer fear the age-old haunting questions: "Who am I?" "Why am I?" "Where am I going?"—and having cast out fear, we can be honest and charitable.

4 For fear is a primary source of evil. And when the question "Who am I?" recurs and is unanswered, then fear and frustration project a negative attitude. The bewildered soul can answer only: "Since I do not understand 'Who I am,' I only know what I am *not*." The corollary of this emotional incertitude is snobbism, intolerance and racial hate. The xenophobic[2] individual can only reject and destroy, as the xenophobic nation inevitably makes war.

The loneliness of Americans does not have its source in xenophobia; as a nation we are an outgoing people, reaching always for immediate contacts, further experience. But we tend to seek out things as individuals, alone. The European, secure in his family ties and rigid class loyalties, knows little of the moral loneliness

1. ***The Member of the Wedding:*** novel and play by Carson McCullers.
2. **xenophobic** [zē′nō fō′bik]: afraid of strangers and foreigners.

GUIDED READING

LITERAL QUESTIONS

1a. Why does McCullers' friend live in New York City? (because he likes to be alone)

2a. In McCullers' view how do Americans tend to seek out things? ("as individuals, alone")

INFERENTIAL QUESTIONS

1b. Why do you think it might be easy to be alone in the midst of eight million people? (You become part of a mass, anonymous.)

2b. In what way do you think individualism reinforces loneliness? (As an individual you don't rely on traditional systems of values or thought that link you to a larger, universal meaning.)

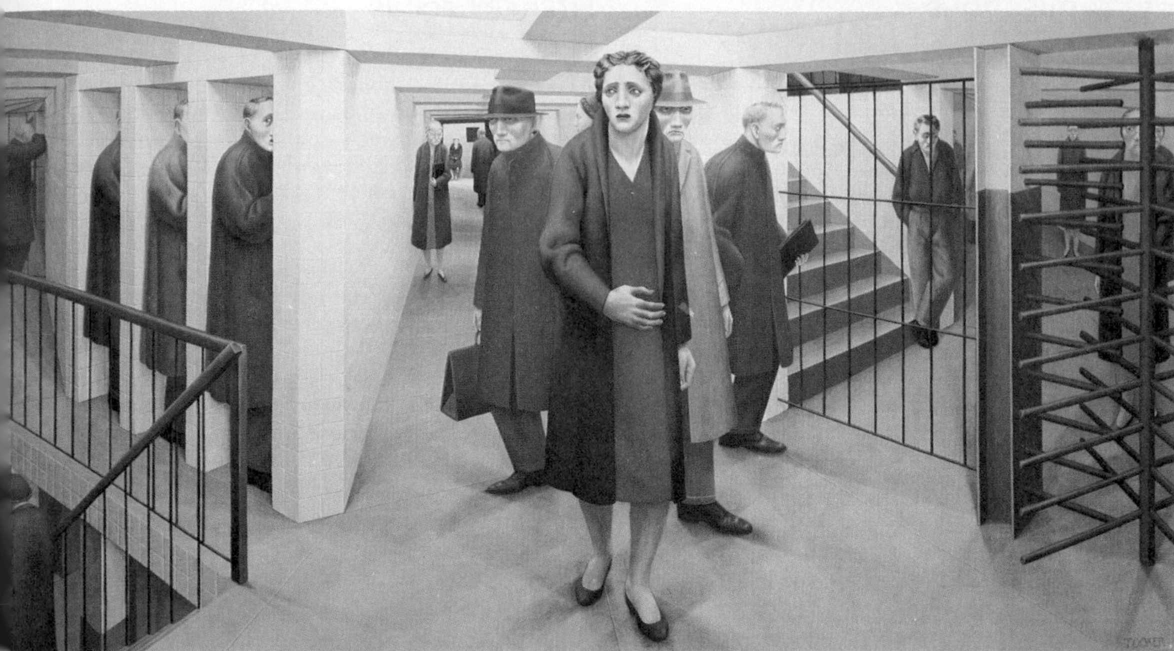

The Subway, George Tooker, 1950.

that is native to us Americans. While the European artists tend to form groups or aesthetic schools, the American artist is the eternal maverick[3]—not only from society in the way of all creative minds, but within the orbit of his own art.

1 Thoreau took to the woods to seek the ultimate meaning of his life. His creed was simplicity and his *modus vivendi*[4] the deliberate stripping of external life to the Spartan necessities in order that his inward life could freely flourish. His objective, as he put it, was to back the world into a corner. And in that way did he discover "What a man thinks of himself, that it is which determines, or rather indicates, his fate."

On the other hand, Thomas Wolfe turned to the city, and in his wanderings around New York he continued his frenetic[5] and lifelong search for the lost brother, the magic door. He too backed the world into a corner, and as he passed among the city's millions, returning their stares, he experienced "That silent meeting [that] is the summary of all the meetings of men's lives."

2 Whether in the pastoral joys of country life or in the labyrinthine city, we Americans are always seeking. We wander, question. But the answer waits in each separate heart—the answer of our own identity and the way by which we can master loneliness and feel that at last we belong.

---

3. **maverick:** nonconformist; loner.
4. ***modus vivendi*** [mō′dəs vi ven′dī]: Latin for "manner of living."
5. **frenetic:** frenzied.

AT A GLANCE

- The American artist is a nonconformist.
- Thoreau sought self-knowledge in the wilderness. Thomas Wolfe looked for self-knowledge in the city.
- We each find our identity in our "separate heart."

1 ESSAY

McCullers cites Thoreau, an acknowledged authority on the subject of American individualism, rather than personal references, to develop her argument about the quest for identity.

2 REPETITION

The use of parallel sentence structure *(Whether in/or in)* and verb repetition add dramatic momentum, power, and resonance to McCullers' poignant observation of our inherent separateness.

REFLECTING ON THE SELECTION

Do you think there is a conflict between the quest for identity and the need to belong? (Answers will vary: Yes, because you give up part of yourself to belong; no, because belonging reinforces your identity.)

GUIDED READING

LITERAL QUESTION

1a. What did Thomas Wolfe search for in New York City? ("the lost brother, the magic door")

INFERENTIAL QUESTION

1b. What do you think he expected to find in the "lost brother" or through the "magic door"? (a sense of himself; self-knowledge)

STUDY QUESTIONS

1. quest for identity; claim one's identity, to belong
2. love; fear of questions about our identity
3. no; seek out things alone; more secure in family and class ties
4. seeking, wandering, questioning; answer of our own identity
5. ▪ need to know who we are, need to belong to something other than self
   ▪ Love banishes loneliness, loneliness causes fear.
6. individualism; no—end of loneliness found in individual
7. neither; answer in each heart
8. Answers will vary. Students should support or counter arguments.

LITERARY FOCUS

1. Loneliness is great American malady; people need to claim identity, belong; consciousness of self is first problem to solve; next challenge is to find something to belong to; love is bridge to belonging; fear from questions is source of evil; American loneliness stems from individualism; American artists sought ultimate meaning of life; Americans seek answers to identity, which waits in each separate heart.
2. "went down and up another spell," "Up at seven or so"; first person, speaks directly to reader, quotes informal dialogue, everyday objects

COMPARING WRITERS

1. write about seeking one's identity; Kerouac: time of solitude in wilderness; McCullers: look into own heart for answer to identity
2. ▪ Kerouac: spiritual richness in solitude; loneliness from being out of touch with self, surroundings
   ▪ McCullers: combined need to establish individual identity, to belong to something larger than oneself

STUDY QUESTIONS

Recalling

1. How does McCullers define the nature of loneliness in her first paragraph? What are the "dual motives" of human beings, according to the second paragraph?
2. According to the sixth paragraph, what helps us make the bridge from "I" to "We"? What sort of fear does this emotion cast out?
3. Does McCullers feel that Americans are xenophobic? What do they nevertheless tend to do, according to the eighth paragraph? In what way are Europeans different?
4. According to McCullers' final paragraph, what are Americans always doing? What does she say can be discovered "in each separate heart"?

Interpreting

5. Explain in your own words McCullers' explanation of the cause of loneliness. What does her essay suggest is the relationship between loneliness and both love and fear?
6. What common American characteristic does McCullers suggest is the cause of American loneliness? Is McCullers suggesting that European loyalties are preferable? Consider her final paragraph in answering the second question, and explain your answer.
7. Does McCullers suggest that the city is preferable to the country—or vice versa—as the place to discover identity and solve the problem of loneliness? What does her final paragraph suggest in this regard, and why?

Extending

8. Choose one of the following ideas from McCullers' essay, and explain why you agree or disagree:
   a. Once a human being is conscious of his or her separateness, he or she has the need to lose this separateness and to belong to something larger and more powerful.
   b. Love helps cast out the fear that arises from the questions asked in the search for identity.
   c. Fear is a primary source of evil, and is caused by bewilderment at the questions asked in the search for identity.
   d. Americans are outgoing but tend to seek things as individuals, alone.

LITERARY FOCUS

The Essay

An **essay** is a moderately brief nonfiction work that deals with a particular topic. The form dates back to the French philosopher Montaigne (1533–1592), and the word *essay* comes from the French *essai,* which means "an attempt."

Essays may be classified as formal or informal. A **formal essay** is a carefully structured attempt to instruct or persuade. It has a serious tone, presents its argument logically, and generally refrains from personal references. An **informal essay** is an attempt to entertain the reader while exploring a topic. Its tone is light, its structure somewhat sprawling, and it may make personal references. In fact, informal essays are sometimes called **personal essays.**

McCullers' analysis of loneliness is an example of a formal essay. It is carefully structured, moving from point to point in logical order, reasonable, and clear. On the other hand, Jack Kerouac looks at isolation from a highly personal viewpoint. His essay is sprawling and anecdotal, creating a self-portrait and expressing a personal vision.

Thinking About the Essay

1. Outline the logic of Carson McCullers' formal essay. What are the main points she tries to persuade the reader to share?
2. Find at least two examples of informal language in Kerouac's "Alone on a Mountaintop." What other means does Kerouac employ to achieve the light tone of an informal essay?

COMPARING WRITERS

1. In his "Nobel Prize Acceptance Speech," William Faulkner discusses the fear he perceives in the modern world. How do Jack Kerouac and Carson McCullers address the problem Faulkner brings up?
2. Both Carson McCullers and Jack Kerouac seem to think that there are advantages and disadvantages to being alone. Compare the two writers' views on "aloneness."
3. McCullers' essay suggests that identity and the need to belong are common problems of modern Americans. Which selections that you have read in this unit also address these problems? What solutions do they suggest?

3. ▪ Auden, Walker, Brooks, Plath, Weidman, Steinbeck, Wolfe, Schwartz, Agee, Enright, and Faulkner all deal with identity and belonging.
   ▪ Walker, Enright: no solutions, only questions; Weidman: mutual understanding; Agee: solace in family ties, no sense of identity; Schwartz: identity achieved painfully, through taking responsibility for what we are and will be; Faulkner: identity comes through initiation into adulthood and through acquisition of pride, honor, and other virtues

DRAMA

Drama consists of stories that are written to be performed for an audience. The dramatist, or playwright, writes two things: **dialogue** that the actors speak and **stage directions** that give instructions to the various people involved in putting on the play, including the actors. The actual "putting on" of the play is called **staging,** and it involves scenery, costumes, lighting, and props—movable articles like chairs or books—as well as the activities of the actors.

Drama as a form of literature dates back to the ancient Greeks and seems to have had its origins in religious ritual. The Greeks classified drama in two categories: tragedy and comedy. A **tragedy** is a play in which the main character comes to an unhappy end. A **comedy,** on the other hand, has a happy ending. Classical Greek tragedies generally involve a **protagonist,** or main character, who cuts a noble figure except for one tragic flaw that brings about his or her ruin. Usually the protagonist has one or more **antagonists**—rivals or opponents—and invariably there is a **chorus,** a group of players who narrate portions of the play and comment upon the action. Greek comedies are humorous and frequently satirical—in fact, the Greek comic playwright Aristophanes is considered the father of satire.

The Greek philosopher Aristotle defined the principles of drama as he saw them, and his ideas were adopted and adapted by classical Roman playwrights and by the great dramatists of Elizabethan England in the sixteenth and early seventeenth centuries. Classical and Elizabethan dramas were generally written in verse, and the masterpieces of the great Elizabethan playwright William Shakespeare (1564–1616) are known as much for their powerful poetry as their perceptive insights into the human heart. Shakespeare's tragedies generally follow the pattern of Greek tragedies, but most of his comedies are lighthearted romances, quite different from the biting satires of Aristophanes.

The theater audience in Elizabethan times was a motley crew: Public theaters were open to people from all ranks of English society. However, by the end of the seventeenth century, the public theaters in London had all but disappeared, and plays were performed in private theaters attended chiefly by the wealthy classes. This period saw the birth of the **comedy of manners,** a realistic and often satirical look at life in sophisticated society. This kind of play owes much of its existence to the works of the French playwright Molière (1622–1673). The comedy of manners remained a popular form throughout the eighteenth century, though English audiences of the period also enjoyed **sentimental comedies,** unrealistic tales that contain romance and tears and that usually offer a moral message.

With the Romantic movement—a movement that spurred some of the world's greatest poetry and prose—drama declined, and a rather inferior form of play, the melodrama, was born. **Melodramas** are highly emotional plays with little concern for developing convincing motivation for their characters. They were extremely popular in the nineteenth century until the influence of Realism was felt upon the stage. With Realism came the great plays of Anton Chekhov (1860–1904), a Russian, and of Henrik Ibsen (1828–1906), a Norwegian, who explore social issues and give audiences a "slice of life" as it is lived. Psychological realism came to the stage as **Expressionism,** a movement in drama that is concerned with the inner realities of characters' minds. Early Expressionist dramas are best exemplified in the plays of Sweden's Johan August Strindberg (1849–1912).

The plays of Ibsen and Strindberg have had a profound impact on all subsequent drama worldwide, for twentieth-century drama often deals with external and internal realities. Also in twentieth-century drama we see an end to the classical distinctions between tragedy and comedy. To be sure, the terms are still used, but more and more the devices of each are blended within one work, and we refer to any serious modern play as a drama.

American Drama

Up until the twentieth century American drama made little impact on American literature as a whole. The reasons for the lack of American drama are understandable: Theaters such as the elitist European ones of the eighteenth century would not flourish in America, at that time an infant democracy, and the melodrama of the nineteenth century would not attract serious American writers. There were, of course, some American plays of literary interest written before 1900: Royall Tyler's *The Contrast* (1787), America's first comedy, and the nineteenth-century verse tragedies of George Henry Boker are considered to be of literary merit. However, it was not until Realism and Expressionism began to appear on the stage that serious American writers turned to drama.

In the beginning of the twentieth century, so-called little theaters sprang up throughout the United States, theaters that encouraged serious playwrights because they were willing to produce original works by unknown talents. The first American dramatist to achieve an international reputation, Eugene O'Neill (1888–1953), began his career as a writer for the Provincetown Players, a "little theater" company begun in Provincetown, Massachusetts.

The plays of Eugene O'Neill reflect his New England background and Irish American heritage and display the Realism and interest in modern psychology characteristic of Ibsen and Strindberg. O'Neill's plays also reflect the Modernist experimentation of the early twentieth century: In *Strange Interlude* (1928) characters' thoughts are heard by the audience, and in *The Great God Brown* (1926) characters don and remove masks while they are speaking. Among O'Neill's other famous plays are *Mourning Becomes Electra* (1931), *The Ice Man Cometh* (1946), and *Long Day's Journey into Night* (1956), a semiautobiographical drama produced after the playwright's death.

Led by O'Neill, American drama flourished between the two world wars. Elmer Rice wrote a portrait of tenement life called *Street Scene* (1929); Clifford Odets explored serious social problems in *Awake and Sing!* (1935) and *Waiting for Lefty* (1935). Maxwell Anderson wrote plays in verse, and George S. Kaufman and Moss Hart entertained audiences with their witty satires.

The twenties and thirties also saw the development of a strictly American form, the **musical comedy,** which reached its peak after World War II in the works of Rodgers and Hammerstein, Lerner and Loewe, Leonard Bernstein, and Stephen Sondheim. Major American dramatists since World War II include Tennessee Williams *(The Glass Menagerie, A Streetcar Named Desire)*; William Inge *(Picnic, The Dark at the Top of the Stairs)*; Arthur Miller *(Death of a Salesman, The Crucible)*; and Edward Albee *(Who's Afraid of Virginia Woolf?)*.

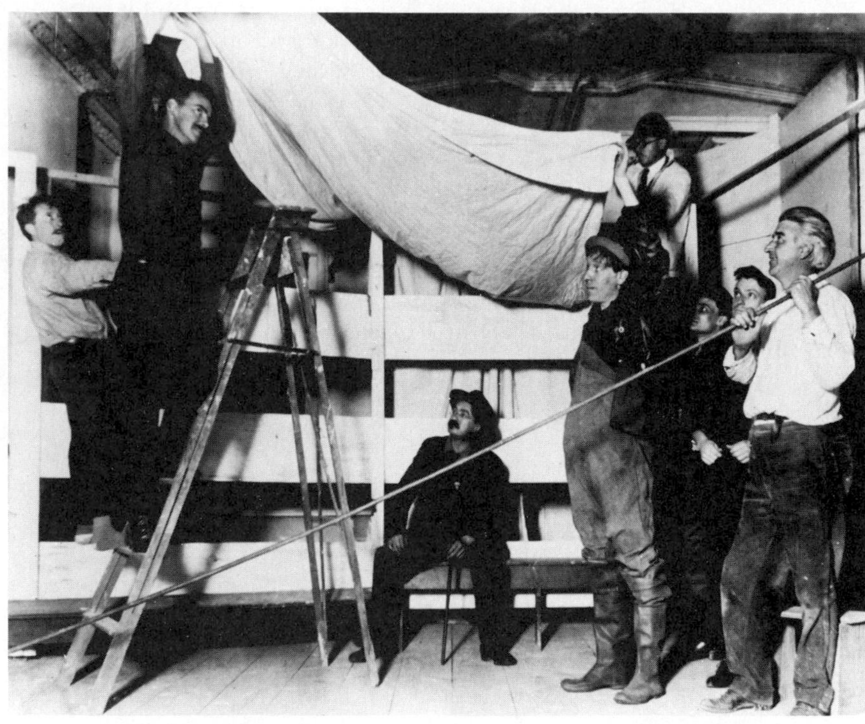

Eugene O'Neill (on ladder, holding cloth) and others preparing for the first production of O'Neill's *Bound East for Cardiff*, Provincetown Playhouse, 1916.

Thornton Wilder *1897–1975*

In 1927 Thornton Wilder was teaching French to high school students in New Jersey. That year he published a novel, his second, that he presumed would attract little more notice than had his first one. The new novel was set in Peru several centuries ago, in a time and place that would have seemed to hold little interest for Americans caught up in the exploits of Babe Ruth and Charles Lindbergh. Yet *The Bridge of San Luis Rey* proved to be an enormous success, winning the Pulitzer Prize and remaining one of the most popular American novels.

Born in Madison, Wisconsin, Wilder spent part of his youth in China, where his father was consul general. He went to Oberlin College and Yale and then studied in Rome for a year before taking up his duties as French instructor and housemaster at Lawrenceville Academy near Princeton, New Jersey. The unexpected success of his second novel brought Wilder a substantial income, and he was no longer obliged to teach for a living. Yet he continued to do so a while longer, and with great success, first at the University of Chicago and then at Harvard.

He also continued to write novels, six in the course of his lifetime, and he managed what few other novelists have been able to do: He became a successful playwright. Since his childhood Wilder had been fascinated by the theater. Accordingly, in his late thirties, this well-established novelist turned seriously to writing plays. One was a deceptively simple drama of New England village life that appeared on Broadway in 1938. That play, *Our Town,* would prove to be even more popular than his novel of colonial Peru. Wilder's other plays include *The Long Christmas Dinner* (1931) and *The Skin of Our Teeth* (1942). He was awarded the first National Medal for Literature in 1965.

■ Do you see any importance in the ordinary experiences of life? What point does Wilder make about these experiences in *Our Town*?

Introducing Our Town

It has been said that not a day has passed since its original performance that *Our Town* has not been staged by some group, somewhere in America. It remains a favorite partly because of the ease with which it can be staged: no curtain, no scenery, scarcely any props beyond a few pieces of furniture and a couple of ladders. Such staging is a strong break with dramatic traditions. Yet, seeing the play, audiences soon adjust to the almost empty stage. Imagination helps us convert a wooden plank into a drugstore counter and picture above the bare floorboards the hollyhocks of Mrs. Gibbs's garden.

If Wilder's untraditional staging intrigues audiences, so does his use of one traditional device, the chorus. In classical Greek drama the chorus was a group of people who introduced the action of the play and commented on events as they progressed. By Shakespeare's day the role of chorus was acted by one person, but Realistic drama generally abandoned the chorus entirely, finding choral interruptions awkward and unrealistic. Wilder reintroduces the role of chorus with the character of the Stage Manager. In theater productions a stage manager is a person who remains behind the scenes, taking charge of the staff and seeing to changes in scenery, props, and other aspects of the play's staging. In *Our Town,* however, the Stage Manager is a character who appears on the stage as the audience is seated and immediately establishes himself as the narrator and interpreter of the events they are about to see.

Those events cannot be labeled as either comic or tragic. *Our Town* offers a rich mix of human emotions; it is simply a drama. At times it is Realistic in its depiction of everyday life as it was lived in turn-of-the-century New England. More frequently, it goes beyond Realism into the realm of Expressionism, taking us deep into the perceptions and emotions of its characters. It remains a favorite because of the warmly nostalgic view it offers of what people like to believe was a simple, appealing age. Yet most of all it retains its popularity because it speaks, with hope and love, of the burdens and blessings of being human, while reminding us of the infinite value of the ordinary and the everyday.

Thornton Wilder

Our Town

CHARACTERS *(in the order of their appearance)*

STAGE MANAGER
DR. GIBBS
JOE CROWELL
HOWIE NEWSOME
MRS. GIBBS
MRS. WEBB
GEORGE GIBBS
REBECCA GIBBS
WALLY WEBB
EMILY WEBB
PROFESSOR WILLARD
MR. WEBB
WOMAN IN THE BALCONY
MAN IN THE AUDITORIUM
LADY IN THE BOX
SIMON STIMSON
MRS. SOAMES
CONSTABLE WARREN
SI CROWELL
THREE BASEBALL PLAYERS
SAM CRAIG
JOE STODDARD

The entire play takes place in Grover's Corners, New Hampshire.

ACT 1

[No curtain.
No scenery.
The audience, arriving, sees an empty stage in half-light.
Presently the STAGE MANAGER, *hat on and pipe in mouth, enters and begins placing a table and three chairs downstage left, and a table and three chairs downstage right. He also places a low bench at the corner of what will be the Webb house, left.*
"Left" and "right" are from the point of view of the actor facing the audience. "Up" is toward the back wall.
As the house lights go down he has finished setting the stage and leaning against the right proscenium[1] *pillar watches the late arrivals in the audience.*
When the auditorium is in complete darkness he speaks.]

1 **STAGE MANAGER.** This play is called "Our Town." It was written by Thornton Wilder; produced and directed by A. . . . (or: produced by A. . . .; directed by B. . . .). In it you will see Miss C. . . .; Miss D. . . .; Miss E. . . .; and Mr. F. . . .; Mr. G. . . .; Mr.
2 H. . . .; and many others. The name of the town is Grover's Corners, New Hampshire—just across the Massachusetts line: latitude 42 degrees 40 minutes; longitude 70 degrees 37 minutes. The First Act shows a day in our town. The day is May 7, 1901. The time is just before dawn.

[A rooster crows.]

The sky is beginning to show some streaks of light over in the East there, behind our mount'in. The morning star always gets wonderful bright the minute before it has to go—doesn't it?

[He stares at it for a moment, then goes upstage.]

Well, I'd better show you how our town lies. Up here—

[That is: parallel with the back wall.]

is Main Street. Way back there is the railway station; tracks go that way. Polish Town's across the tracks, and some Canuck[2] families.

[Toward the left.]

Over there is the Congregational Church; across the street's the Presbyterian.
Methodist and Unitarian are over there.
Baptist is down in the holla' by the river.
Catholic Church is over beyond the tracks.
Here's the Town Hall and Post Office combined; jail's in the basement.
Bryan[3] once made a speech from these very steps here.
Along here's a row of stores. Hitching posts and horse blocks in front of them. First automobile's going to come along in about five years—belonged to Banker Cartwright, our richest citizen . . . lives in the big white house up on the hill.
3 Here's the grocery store and here's Mr. Morgan's drugstore. Most everybody in town manages to look into those two stores once a day. Public School's over yonder. High School's still farther over. Quarter of nine mornings, noontimes, and three o'clock afternoons, the hull[4] town can hear the yelling and screaming from those schoolyards.

[He approaches the table and chairs downstage right.]

This is our doctor's house—Doc Gibbs'. This is the back door.

[Two arched trellises, covered with vines and flowers, are pushed out, one by each proscenium pillar.]

---

1. **proscenium** [prō sē′nē əm]: part of a stage in front of the curtain.
2. **Canuck** [kə nuk′]: slang for French-Canadian.
3. **Bryan:** William Jennings Bryan (1860–1925), U.S. statesman and orator.
4. **hull:** New England dialect pronunciation of "whole."

AT A GLANCE

- The Stage Manager enters, introduces the characters, and states the setting.
- He describes the town of Grover's Corners, New Hampshire.
- He points out the Gibbs house.

LITERARY OPTIONS

- characterization
- theme

THEMATIC OPTIONS

- endless cycles of life and death
- the order of the universe
- the marvel of ordinary life

1 POINT OF VIEW

The Stage Manager's entrance and first speech are a clue to his function. He stands outside the play like an omniscient narrator in a short story.

2 SETTING

The play opens in the town of Grover's Corners at the height of spring in the first year of the twentieth century. It is just before dawn. The details of setting suggest that it is time for beginnings.

3 DETAILS

The details form a picture of a stereotypical turn-of-the-century town in rural America.

GUIDED READING

LITERAL QUESTIONS

1a. According to the Stage Manager, what does the first act show? (a day in his town)

2a. How soon does he expect the first automobile to come along? (in about five years)

INFERENTIAL QUESTIONS

1b. Do you think that this will be an ordinary day, or an unusual one? Explain your answer. (It probably will be ordinary. There is no indication that anything unusual is likely to happen in Grover's Corners.)

2b. What does this comment suggest about the Stage Manager? (He knows the future as well as the past.)

AT A GLANCE

- Dr. Gibbs is coming home after delivering twins.
- Mrs. Gibbs begins to make breakfast, as does Mrs. Webb.
- Dr. Gibbs encounters Joe Crowell, Jr., delivering papers.

1 INFERENCES

The names in the cemetery suggest that the town has not changed much in over 200 years.

2 STYLE: DIALECT

The Stage Manager speaks in a comfortable, colloquial dialect, as do the inhabitants of the town.

3 THEME

Mrs. Gibbs' encapsulated life and the story of her with her forebears appear part of a larger order, a natural cycle of life and death.

There's some scenery for those who think they have to have scenery.
This is Mrs. Gibbs' garden. Corn . . . peas . . . beans . . . hollyhocks . . . heliotrope . . . and a lot of burdock.

[*Crosses the stage.*]

In those days our newspaper come out twice a week—the Grover's Corners *Sentinel*—and this is Editor Webb's house.
And this is Mrs. Webb's garden.
Just like Mrs. Gibbs', only it's got a lot of sunflowers, too.

[*He looks upward, center stage.*]

Right here . . . 's a big butternut tree.

[*He returns to his place by the right proscenium pillar and looks at the audience for a minute.*]

Nice town, y'know what I mean?
Nobody very remarkable ever come out of it, s'far as we know.
1 The earliest tombstones in the cemetery up there on the mountain say 1670–1680—they're Grovers and Cartwrights and Gibbses and Herseys—same names as are around here now.
Well, as I said: it's about dawn.
The only lights on in town are in a cottage over by the tracks where a Polish mother's just had twins. And in the Joe Crowell house, where Joe Junior's getting up so as to deliver the paper. And in the depot, where Shorty Hawkins is gettin' ready to flag the 5:45 for Boston.

[*A train whistle is heard. The* STAGE MANAGER *takes out his watch and nods.*]

Naturally, out in the country—all around—there've been lights on for some time, what with milkin's and so on. But town people sleep late.
So—another day's begun.
2 There's Doc Gibbs comin' down Main Street now, comin' back from that baby case. And here's his wife comin' downstairs to get breakfast.

[MRS. GIBBS, *a plump, pleasant woman in the middle thirties, comes "downstairs" right. She pulls up an imaginary window shade in her kitchen and starts to make a fire in her stove.*]

Doc Gibbs died in 1930. The new hospital's named after him.
Mrs. Gibbs died first—long time ago, in fact. She went out to visit her daughter, Rebecca, who married an insurance man in Canton, Ohio, and died there—pneumonia—but her
3 body was brought back here. She's up in the cemetery there now—in with a whole mess of Gibbses and Herseys—she was Julia Hersey 'fore she married Doc Gibbs in the Congregational Church over there.
In our town we like to know the facts about everybody.
There's Mrs. Webb, coming downstairs to get her breakfast, too.
—That's Doc Gibbs. Got that call at half past one this morning.
And there comes Joe Crowell, Jr., delivering Mr. Webb's *Sentinel.*

[DR. GIBBS *has been coming along Main Street from the left. At the point where he would turn to approach his house, he stops, sets down his—imaginary—black bag, takes off his hat, and rubs his face with fatigue, using an enormous handkerchief.*
MRS. WEBB, *a thin, serious, crisp woman, has entered her kitchen, left, tying on an apron. She goes through the motions of putting wood into a stove, lighting it, and preparing breakfast.*
Suddenly, JOE CROWELL, JR., *eleven, starts down Main Street from the right, hurling imaginary newspapers into doorways.*]

JOE CROWELL, JR. Morning, Doc Gibbs.

DR. GIBBS. Morning, Joe.

JOE CROWELL, JR. Somebody been sick, Doc?

DR. GIBBS. No. Just some twins born over in Polish Town.

GUIDED READING

LITERAL QUESTIONS

1a. What is Mrs. Webb's garden like? (very like Mrs. Gibbs')

2a. What finally happened to Dr. Gibbs? (He died in 1930.)

INFERENTIAL QUESTIONS

1b. What does this fact suggest about the people in the town? (Fundamentally they are very much alike.)

2b. What purpose does this information serve? (It suggests that the audience is looking back on a vanished time; it awakens a recognition that these events are fleeting.)

JOE CROWELL, JR. Do you want your paper now?

1 **DR. GIBBS.** Yes, I'll take it. Anything serious goin' on in the world since Wednesday?

JOE CROWELL, JR. Yessir. My schoolteacher, Miss Foster, 's getting married to a fella over in Concord.

DR. GIBBS. I declare. How do you boys feel about that?

JOE CROWELL, JR. Well, of course, it's none of my business—but I think if a person starts out to be a teacher, she ought to stay one.

DR. GIBBS. How's your knee, Joe?

JOE CROWELL, JR. Fine, Doc, I never think about it at all. Only like you said, it always tells me when it's going to rain.

DR. GIBBS. What's it telling you today? Goin' to rain?

JOE CROWELL, JR. No, sir.

DR. GIBBS. Sure?

JOE CROWELL, JR. Yessir.

DR. GIBBS. Knee ever make a mistake?

JOE CROWELL, JR. No, sir.

[JOE *goes off.* DR. GIBBS *stands reading his paper.*]

STAGE MANAGER. Want to tell you something about that boy Joe Crowell there. Joe was awful bright—graduated from high school here, head of his class. So he got a scholarship to Massachusetts Tech. Graduated head of his class there, too. It was all wrote up in the Bos-
2 ton paper at the time. Goin' to be a great engineer, Joe was. But the war[5] broke out and he died in France. All that education for nothing.

HOWIE NEWSOME. [*Off left.*] Giddap, Bessie! What's the matter with you today?

STAGE MANAGER. Here comes Howie Newsome, deliverin' the milk.

5. **war:** World War I (1914–1918).

[HOWIE NEWSOME, *about thirty, in overalls, comes along Main Street from the left,*
3 *walking beside an invisible horse and wagon and carrying an imaginary rack with milk bottles. The sound of clinking milk bottles is heard. He leaves some bottles at* MRS. WEBB'S *trellis, then, crossing the stage to* MRS. GIBBS', *he stops center to talk to* DR. GIBBS.]

HOWIE NEWSOME. Morning, Doc.

DR. GIBBS. Morning, Howie.

HOWIE NEWSOME. Somebody sick?

DR. GIBBS. Pair of twins over to Mrs. Goruslawski's.

HOWIE NEWSOME. Twins, eh? This town's gettin' bigger every year.

DR. GIBBS. Goin' to rain, Howie?

HOWIE NEWSOME. No, no. Fine day—that'll burn through. Come on, Bessie.

DR. GIBBS. Hello Bessie.

[*He strokes the horse, which has remained up center.*]

How old is she, Howie?

HOWIE NEWSOME. Going on seventeen. Bessie's all mixed up about the route ever since the Lockharts stopped takin' their quart of milk every day. She wants to leave 'em a quart just the same—keeps scolding me the hull trip.

[*He reaches* MRS. GIBBS' *back door. She is waiting for him.*]

MRS. GIBBS. Good morning, Howie.

HOWIE NEWSOME. Morning, Mrs. Gibbs. Doc's just comin' down the street.

MRS. GIBBS. Is he? Seems like you're late today.

HOWIE NEWSOME. Yes. Somep'n went wrong with the separator.[6] Don't know what 'twas. [*He passes* DR. GIBBS *up center.*] Doc!

6. **separator:** device for separating cream from milk.

AT A GLANCE

- Doc Gibbs chats with Joe Crowell, Jr.
- He chats next with Howie Newsome, the milkman.
- Howie delivers milk to Mrs. Gibbs, who is at her back door.

1 DIALOGUE

The colloquial vocabulary and sentence structure capture the rhythms of natural speech.

2 THEME

The Stage Manager's revelation about Joe's fate reminds the audience of the cycles of life, growth, and death.

3 STAGING

The lack of stage props such as Joe's newspapers and Howie's milk bottles allows the audience to use its imagination and become more involved with the play.

GUIDED READING

LITERAL QUESTIONS

1a. What serious thing does Joe Crowell, Jr., say is going on in the world? (His teacher is getting married.)

2a. What finally happened to Joe Crowell, Jr.? (He was killed during World War I in France.)

INFERENTIAL QUESTIONS

1b. What does this news suggest about the seriousness of events in people's lives? (The things that happen to us seem the most serious.)

2b. What does this information suggest? (that life can be short and fragile)

AT A GLANCE

- Mrs. Gibbs and Mrs. Webb call to wake their children.
- Mrs. Gibbs worries that Dr. Gibbs does not get enough rest.
- She complains to him about their son, George.

1 DIALOGUE

The busy dialogue reflects the fact that, as in real life, many things go on almost simultaneously.

2 CHARACTERIZATION

Mrs. Gibbs' fussing, although somewhat fretful, shows her concern for her husband.

DR. GIBBS. Howie!

MRS. GIBBS. [*Calling upstairs.*] Children! Children! Time to get up.

1 **HOWIE NEWSOME.** Come on, Bessie! [*He goes off right.*]

MRS. GIBBS. George! Rebecca!

[DR. GIBBS *arrives at his back door and passes through the trellis into his house.*]

MRS. GIBBS. Everything all right, Frank?

DR. GIBBS. Yes. I declare—easy as kittens.

MRS. GIBBS. Bacon'll be ready in a minute. Set down and drink your coffee. You can catch a couple hours' sleep this morning, can't you?

DR. GIBBS. Hm! . . . Mrs. Wentworth's coming at eleven. Guess I know what it's about, too. Her stummick ain't what it ought to be.

2 **MRS. GIBBS.** All told, you won't get more'n three hours' sleep. Frank Gibbs, I don't know what's goin' to become of you. I do wish I could get you to go away someplace and take a rest. I think it would do you good.

MRS. WEBB. Emileeee! Time to get up! Wally! Seven o'clock!

MRS. GIBBS. I declare, you got to speak to George. Seems like something's come over him lately. He's no help to me at all. I can't even get him to cut me some wood.

DR. GIBBS.

[*Washing and drying his hands at the sink.* MRS. GIBBS *is busy at the stove.*]

Is he sassy to you?

MRS. GIBBS. No. He just whines! All he thinks about is that baseball—George! Rebecca! You'll be late for school.

GUIDED READING

LITERAL QUESTION

1a. What does Mrs. Gibbs say that her husband will have to do? (speak to George)

INFERENTIAL QUESTION

1b. What does she hope will be accomplished by his action? (She probably hopes that he will talk George out of his daydreaming and persuade him to be more helpful with household chores.)

DR. GIBBS. M-m-m . . .

MRS. GIBBS. George!

DR. GIBBS. George, look sharp!

GEORGE'S VOICE. Yes, Pa!

DR. GIBBS. [*As he goes off the stage.*] Don't you hear your mother calling you? I guess I'll go upstairs and get forty winks.

MRS. WEBB. Walleee! Emileee! You'll be late for school! Walleee! You wash yourself good or I'll come up and do it myself.

REBECCA GIBBS' VOICE. Ma! What dress shall I wear?

MRS. GIBBS. Don't make a noise. Your father's been out all night and needs his sleep. I washed and ironed the blue gingham for you special.

REBECCA. Ma, I hate that dress.

MRS. GIBBS. Oh, hush-up-with-you.

REBECCA. Every day I go to school dressed like a sick turkey.

MRS. GIBBS. Now, Rebecca, you always look *very* nice.

REBECCA. Mama, George's throwing soap at me.

MRS. GIBBS. I'll come and slap the both of you,—that's what I'll do.

[*A factory whistle sounds.*
The CHILDREN *dash in and take their places at the tables.*
Right, GEORGE, *about sixteen, and* REBECCA, *eleven. Left,* EMILY *and* WALLY, *same ages. They carry strapped schoolbooks.*]

1 **STAGE MANAGER.** We've got a factory in our town too—hear it? Makes blankets. Cartwrights own it and it brung 'em a fortune.

MRS. WEBB. Children! Now I won't have it. Breakfast is just as good as any other meal and I won't have you gobbling like wolves. It'll stunt your growth—that's a fact. Put away your book, Wally.

WALLY. Aw, Ma! By ten o'clock I got to know all about Canada.

MRS. WEBB. You know the rule's well as I do—no books at table. As for me, I'd rather have my children healthy than bright.

EMILY. I'm both, Mama: you know I am. I'm the brightest girl in school for my age. I have a wonderful memory.

2 **MRS. WEBB.** Eat your breakfast.

WALLY. I'm bright, too, when I'm looking at my stamp collection.

MRS. GIBBS. I'll speak to your father about it when he's rested. Seems to me twenty-five cents a week's enough for a boy your age. I declare I don't know how you spend it all.

GEORGE. Aw, Ma—I gotta lotta things to buy.

MRS. GIBBS. Strawberry phosphates[7]—that's what you spend it on.

GEORGE. I don't see how Rebecca comes to have so much money. She has more'n a dollar.

REBECCA. [*Spoon in mouth, dreamily.*] I've been saving it up gradual.

MRS. GIBBS. Well, dear, I think it's a good thing to spend some every now and then.

REBECCA. Mama, do you know what I love most in the world—do you? Money.

MRS. GIBBS. Eat your breakfast.

THE CHILDREN. Mama, there's first bell. I gotta hurry. I don't want any more. I gotta hurry.

[*The* CHILDREN *rise, seize their books and dash out through the trellises. They meet, down center, and chattering, walk to Main Street, then turn left.*
The STAGE MANAGER *goes off, unobtrusively, right.*]

MRS. WEBB. Walk fast, but you don't have to run. Wally, pull up your pants at the knee. Stand up straight, Emily.

7. **phosphates:** soft drinks of soda water and syrup.

AT A GLANCE

- After Dr. Gibbs goes off to bed, Rebecca Gibbs complains about her dress for school.
- Mrs. Webb tells Wally Webb to put his book away and eat his breakfast.
- George debates with his mother about a raise in allowance, while Rebecca states that she saves her money.
- The children rush off to school.

1 POINT OF VIEW

Functioning as an omniscient observer, the Stage Manager can interrupt the action for a digression whenever he chooses.

2 READING SKILLS: COMPARISONS

The counterpoint between the Gibbs and Webb families emphasizes the ways in which families are similar.

GUIDED READING

LITERAL QUESTIONS

1a. How does Emily Webb characterize herself to her mother? ("I'm the brightest girl in school for my age. I have a wonderful memory.")

2a. What is Mrs. Gibbs' response to Rebecca's announcement that she loves money best? ("Eat your breakfast.")

INFERENTIAL QUESTIONS

1b. What does her description reveal about her? (She is very impressed with herself.)

2b. What does her answer reveal about her? (She is sensible and does not take her children's outlandish statements too seriously.)

AT A GLANCE

- While Mrs. Gibbs is feeding her chickens, she sees Mrs. Webb stringing beans.
- Mrs. Gibbs says that a secondhand-furniture dealer has offered a good price for her grandmother's highboy.
- She confesses that she would sell the highboy if she could convince her husband to use the money for a trip.

1 DIALOGUE

The dialogue exemplifies the everyday small talk of ordinary people.

2 STYLE: DIALECT

The colloquial language captures Mrs. Gibbs' breathless excitement.

3 CHARACTERIZATION

Mrs. Gibbs reveals the romantic side of her character through her dream to see Paris.

MRS. GIBBS. Tell Miss Foster I send her my best congratulations—can you remember that?

REBECCA. Yes, Ma.

MRS. GIBBS. You look real nice, Rebecca. Pick up your feet.

ALL. Good-bye.

[MRS. GIBBS *fills her apron with food for the chickens and comes down to the footlights.*]

MRS. GIBBS. Here, chick, chick, chick.
No, go away, you. Go away.
Here, chick, chick, chick.
What the matter with *you?* Fight, fight, fight—that's all you do.
Hm . . . *you* don't belong to me. Where'd you come from? [*She shakes her apron.*] Oh, don't be so scared. Nobody's going to hurt you.

[MRS. WEBB *is sitting on the bench by her trellis, stringing beans.*]

1 Good morning, Myrtle. How's your cold?

MRS. WEBB. Well, I still get that tickling feeling in my throat. I told Charles I didn't know as I'd go to choir practice tonight. Wouldn't be any use.

MRS. GIBBS. Have you tried singing over your voice?

MRS. WEBB. Yes, but somehow I can't do that and stay on the key. While I'm resting myself I thought I'd string some of these beans.

MRS. GIBBS.

[*Rolling up her sleeves as she crosses the stage for a chat.*]

Let me help you. Beans have been good this year.

MRS. WEBB. I've decided to put up forty quarts if it kills me. The children say they hate 'em, but I notice they're able to get 'em down all winter.

[*Pause. Brief sound of chickens cackling.*]

MRS. GIBBS. Now, Myrtle. I've got to tell you something, because if I don't tell somebody I'll burst.

MRS. WEBB. Why, Julia Gibbs!

MRS. GIBBS. Here, give me some more of those beans. Myrtle, did one of those secondhand-furniture men from Boston come to see you last Friday?

MRS. WEBB. No-o.

2 **MRS. GIBBS.** Well, he called on me. First I thought he was a patient wantin' to see Dr. Gibbs. 'N he wormed his way into my parlor, and, Myrtle Webb, he offered me three hundred and fifty dollars for Grandmother Wentworth's highboy, as I'm sitting here!

MRS. WEBB. Why, Julia Gibbs!

MRS. GIBBS. He did! That old thing! Why, it was so big I didn't know where to put it and I almost give it to Cousin Hester Wilcox.

MRS. WEBB. Well, you're going to take it, aren't you?

MRS. GIBBS. I don't know.

MRS. WEBB. You don't know—three hundred and fifty dollars! What's come over you?

MRS. GIBBS. Well, if I could get the Doctor to take the money and go away someplace on a
3 real trip, I'd sell it like that.—Y'know, Myrtle, it's been the dream of my life to see Paris, France.—Oh, I don't know. It sounds crazy, I suppose, but for years I've been promising myself that if we ever had the chance—

MRS. WEBB. How does the Doctor feel about it?

MRS. GIBBS. Well, I did beat about the bush a little and said that if I got a legacy—that's the way I put it—I'd make him take me somewhere.

MRS. WEBB. M-m-m . . . What did he say?

MRS. GIBBS. You know how he is. I haven't heard a serious word out of him since I've known him. No, he said, it might make him dis-

GUIDED READING

LITERAL QUESTION

1a. What has been the dream of Mrs. Gibbs' life? (to see Paris)

INFERENTIAL QUESTION

1b. What does this dream reveal about her? (She is a romantic at heart.)

contented with Grover's Corners to go traipsin' about Europe; better let well enough alone, he says. Every two years he makes a trip to the battlefields of the Civil War and that's enough treat for anybody, he says.

MRS. WEBB. Well, Mr. Webb just *admires* the way Dr. Gibbs knows everything about the Civil War. Mr. Webb's a good mind to give up Napoleon and move over to the Civil War, only Dr. Gibbs being one of the greatest experts in the country just makes him despair.

MRS. GIBBS. It's a fact! Dr. Gibbs is never so happy as when he's at Antietam or Gettysburg.[8] The times I've walked over those hills, Myrtle, stopping at every bush and pacing it all out, like we were going to buy it.

MRS. WEBB. Well, if that secondhand man's really serious about buyin' it, Julia, you sell it. And then you'll get to see Paris, all right. Just keep droppin' hints from time to time—that's how I got to see the Atlantic Ocean, y'know.

MRS. GIBBS. Oh, I'm sorry I mentioned it. Only it seems to me that once in your life before you die you ought to see a country where they don't talk in English and don't even want to.

[*The* STAGE MANAGER *enters briskly from the right. He tips his hat to the ladies, who nod their heads.*]

STAGE MANAGER. Thank you, ladies. Thank you very much.

[MRS. GIBBS *and* MRS. WEBB *gather up their things, return into their homes and disappear.*]

1 Now we're going to skip a few hours.
But first we want a little more information about the town, kind of a scientific account, you might say.
So I've asked Professor Willard of our State University to sketch in a few details of our past history here.

8. **Antietam** [an tē′təm] . . . **Gettysburg:** Civil war battle sites.

Is Professor Willard here?

[PROFESSOR WILLARD, *a rural savant, pince-nez*[9] *on a wide satin ribbon, enters from the right with some notes in his hand.*]

May I introduce Professor Willard of our State University.
A few brief notes, thank you, Professor—unfortunately our time is limited.

2 **PROFESSOR WILLARD.** Grover's Corners . . . let me see . . . Grover's Corners lies on the old Pleistocene[10] granite of the Appalachian range. I may say it's some of the oldest land in the world. We're very proud of that. A shelf of Devonian basalt crosses it with vestiges of Mesozoic[11] shale, and some sandstone outcroppings; but that's all more recent: two hundred, three hundred million years old.
Some highly interesting fossils have been found . . . I may say: unique fossils . . . two miles out of town, in Silas Peckham's cow pasture. They can be seen at the museum in our University at any time—that is, at any reasonable time. Shall I read some of Professor Gruber's notes on the meteorological situation—mean precipitation, et cetera?

STAGE MANAGER. Afraid we won't have time for that, Professor. We might have a few words on the history of man here.

3 **PROFESSOR WILLARD.** Yes . . . anthropological data: Early Amerindian[12] stock. Cotahatchee[13] tribes . . . no evidence before the tenth century of this era . . . hm . . . now entirely disappeared . . . possible traces in three families.
Migration toward the end of the seventeenth century of English brachycephalic[14] blue-eyed

9. **pince-nez** [pans′nā′]: eyeglasses without temples, held on the nose by a spring.
10. **Pleistocene** [plīs′tə sēn′]: geological era in which granite was formed.
11. **Devonian** [də vō′nē ən] . . . **Mesozoic** [mes′ə zō′ik]: other geological eras.
12. **Amerindian** [am′ə rin′dē ən]: American Indian.
13. **Cotahatchee** [kō′te ha′chē]: Amerindian tribe.
14. **brachycephalic** [brak′i sə fal′ik]: having a short or broad head.

AT A GLANCE

- Mrs. Gibbs says that her husband, a Civil War expert, prefers visiting battlefields to visiting Europe.
- After Mrs. Webb encourages her to try to change Dr. Gibbs' mind, Mrs. Gibbs confesses her desire to see a foreign country before she dies.
- The Stage Manager introduces Professor Willard, who lectures on the local geology and anthropology.

1 POINT OF VIEW

The Stage Manager returns the focus to the town, placing it in a grand geological and historical perspective.

2 THEME

Against the backdrop of geological time, the events in Grover's Corners can be viewed as a tiny part of a vast scheme.

3 THEME

The appearance and disappearance of human habitation on the spot suggest the cycles of life that are part of the history of humankind.

GUIDED READING

LITERAL QUESTIONS

1a. How did Mrs. Webb get to see the Atlantic Ocean? (by dropping hints to her husband)

2a. What does Mrs. Gibbs say that she thinks people should do once in their lives? (see a country whose inhabitants don't speak English and don't even want to)

INFERENTIAL QUESTIONS

1b. What does this information suggest about the roles of women and men at the time? (Women often found it necessary to achieve their goals by indirection.)

2b. Why might she feel this way? (Mrs. Gibbs recognizes that there is a world beyond Grover's Corners, and she would like to experience it.)

AT A GLANCE

- The professor gives population statistics.
- The Stage Manager introduces Mr. Webb, the newspaper editor.
- Webb provides town demographics and takes questions from the audience about the town.

1 DETAILS

Mr. Webb relates details about the town in a concise, informative style as befits a good editor.

2 STEREOTYPE

Mr. Webb reinforces the idea that Grover's Corners is a stereotypical American town.

3 NARRATOR

As a means of imparting more information about the town, the Stage Manager invites "the audience" to ask questions of Mr. Webb. The function of the Stage Manager throughout the play shows that *Our Town* is by no means a conventional play.

stock . . . for the most part. Since then some Slav and Mediterranean—

STAGE MANAGER. And the population, Professor Willard?

PROFESSOR WILLARD. Within the town limits: 2,640.

STAGE MANAGER. Just a moment, Professor. [*He whispers into the professor's ear.*]

PROFESSOR WILLARD. Oh, yes, indeed? The population, *at the moment,* is 2,642. The Postal District brings in 507 more, making a total of 3,149. Mortality and birth rates: constant. By MacPherson's gauge: 6.032.

STAGE MANAGER. Thank you very much, Professor. We're all very much obliged to you, I'm sure.

PROFESSOR WILLARD. Not at all, sir; not at all.

STAGE MANAGER. This way, Professor, and thank you again.

[*Exit* PROFESSOR WILLARD.]

Now the political and social report: Editor Webb. Oh, Mr. Webb?

[MRS. WEBB *appears at her back door.*]

MRS. WEBB. He'll be here in a minute. . . . He just cut his hand while he was eatin' an apple.

STAGE MANAGER. Thank you, Mrs. Webb.

MRS. WEBB. Charles! Everybody's waitin'. [*Exit* MRS. WEBB.]

STAGE MANAGER. Mr. Webb is Publisher and Editor of the Grover's Corners *Sentinel.* That's our local paper, y'know.

[MR. WEBB *enters from his house, pulling on his coat. His finger is bound in a handkerchief.*]

MR. WEBB. Well . . . I don't have to tell you that we're run here by a Board of Selectmen.[15]—All males vote at the age of twenty-
1 one. Women vote indirect. We're lower middle class: sprinkling of professional men . . . ten per cent illiterate laborers. Politically, we're eighty-six per cent Republicans; six per cent Democrats; four per cent Socialists; rest, indifferent.

Religiously, we're eighty-five per cent Protestants; twelve per cent Catholics; rest, indifferent.

STAGE MANAGER. Have you any comments, Mr. Webb?

2 **MR. WEBB.** Very ordinary town, if you ask me. Little better behaved than most. Probably a lot duller.

But our young people here seem to like it well enough. Ninety percent of 'em graduating from high school settle down right here to live—even when they've been away to college.

3 **STAGE MANAGER.** Now, is there anyone in the audience who would like to ask Editor Webb anything about the town?

WOMAN IN THE BALCONY. Is there much drinking in Grover's Corners?

MR. WEBB. Well, ma'am, I wouldn't know what you'd call *much.* Satiddy nights the farmhands meet down in Ellery Greenough's stable and holler some. We've got one or two town drunks, but they're always having remorses every time an evangelist comes to town. No, ma'am, I'd say likker ain't a regular thing in the home here, except in the medicine chest. Right good for snake bite, y'know—always was.

BELLIGERENT MAN AT BACK OF AUDITORIUM. Is there no one in town aware of—

STAGE MANAGER. Come forward, will you, where we can all hear you. What were you saying?

BELLIGERENT MAN. Is there no one in town aware of social injustice and industrial inequality?

MR. WEBB. Oh, yes, everybody is—somethin' terrible. Seems like they spend most of their time talking about who's rich and who's poor.

BELLIGERENT MAN. Then why don't they do

15. **Board of Selectmen:** elected town officials.

GUIDED READING

LITERAL QUESTIONS

1a. According to Mr. Webb, how do women in Grover's Corners vote? ("indirect")

2a. What percentage of Grover's Corners' young people settle down there? (ninety percent)

INFERENTIAL QUESTIONS

1b. What does he mean? (Not having the vote themselves, they supposedly can influence their husbands' votes.)

2b. What probably accounts for this statistic? (The town seems a good place to live—warm, neighborly, and unpretentious. The young people apparently recognize this attraction.)

something about it? [*He withdraws without waiting for an answer.*]

MR. WEBB. Well, I dunno. . . . I guess we're all hunting like everybody else for a way the diligent and sensible can rise to the top and the lazy and quarrelsome can sink to the bottom. But it ain't easy to find. Meanwhile, we do all we can to help those that can't help themselves and those that can we leave alone. Are there any other questions?

LADY IN A BOX. Oh, Mr. Webb? Mr. Webb, is there any culture or love of beauty in Grover's Corners?

MR. WEBB. Well, ma'am, there ain't much—not in the sense you mean. Come to think of it, there's some girls that play the piano at High School Commencement; but they ain't happy about it. No, ma'am, there isn't much culture; but maybe this is the place to tell you that we've got a lot of pleasures of a kind here: we like the sun comin' up over the mountain in the morning, and we all notice a good deal about the birds. We pay a lot of attention to them. And we watch the change of the seasons; yes, everybody knows about them. But those other things—you're right, ma'am—there ain't much. *Robinson Crusoe* and the Bible; and Handel's "Largo," we all know that; and Whistler's "Mother"[16]—those are just about as far as we go.

LADY IN A BOX. So I thought. Thank you, Mr. Webb.

STAGE MANAGER. Thank you, Mr. Webb.

[MR. WEBB *retires.*]

1 Now, we'll go back to the town. It's early afternoon. All 2,642 have had their dinners and all the dishes have been washed.

16. **Robinson Crusoe . . . "Mother":** *Robinson Crusoe* is a novel by the English writer Daniel Defoe (1660?–1731). Handel's "Largo" is a musical composition by German-born composer George Frederick Handel (1685–1759). Whistler's "Mother" refers to "Arrangement in Gray and Black: Portrait of the Artist's Mother" by American painter James McNeil Whistler (1834–1903).

[MR. WEBB, *having removed his coat, returns and starts pushing a lawn mower to and fro beside his house.*]

2 There's an early-afternoon calm in our town: a buzzin' and a hummin' from the school buildings; only a few buggies on Main Street—the horses dozing at the hitching posts; you all remember what it's like. Doc Gibbs is in his office, tapping people and making them say "ah." Mr. Webb's cuttin' his lawn over there; one man in ten thinks it's a privilege to push his own lawn mower.

No, sir. It's later than I thought. There are the children coming home from school already.

[*Shrill girls' voices are heard, off left.* EMILY *comes along Main Street, carrying some books. There are some signs that she is imagining herself to be a lady of startling elegance.*]

EMILY. I *can't,* Lois. I've got to go home and help my mother. I *promised.*

3 **MR. WEBB.** Emily, walk simply. Who do you think you are today?

EMILY. Papa, you're terrible. One minute you tell me to stand up straight and the next minute you call me names. I just don't listen to you. [*She gives him an abrupt kiss.*]

MR. WEBB. Golly, I never got a kiss from such a great lady before.

[*He goes out of sight.* EMILY *leans over and picks some flowers by the gate of her house.* GEORGE GIBBS *comes careening down Main Street. He is throwing a ball up to dizzying heights, and waiting to catch it again. This sometimes requires his taking six steps backward. He bumps into an* OLD LADY *invisible to us.*]

GEORGE. Excuse me, Mrs. Forrest.

STAGE MANAGER. [*As* MRS. FORREST.] Go out and play in the fields, young man. You got no business playing baseball on Main Street.

AT A GLANCE

- Mr. Webb describes the town's social awareness.
- He says that there is not much culture, but there is a love of natural beauty.
- Emily Webb, arriving home from school, banters with her father.

1 BACKGROUND

New Englanders of 1901 always ate *dinner* at noon. The evening meal was *supper*.

2 DESCRIPTION

The Stage Manager's description of early afternoon in his town is one of small-town somnolence.

3 CHARACTERIZATION

Emily's airs are part of growing up. She is trying out different personae to find out who she will be. At heart, though, she is a loving daughter to both her parents.

GUIDED READING

LITERAL QUESTION

1a. According to Mr. Webb, is there much culture in Grover's Corners? (no)

INFERENTIAL QUESTION

1b. How does the lady's definition of culture differ from one that Mr. Webb might give? (She limits it to the arts; he sees the town in a broader cultural context that includes appreciation of natural beauty.)

AT A GLANCE

- George compliments Emily on her intelligence and asks her for help with his homework.
- He tells her his prospects: his uncle is offering him a farm and a house.
- Emily asks her mother whether she is pretty.

1 FORESHADOWING

George's awareness of Emily's head as she studies reveals his admiration for her and hints that their relationship will grow closer as they mature.

2 POINT OF VIEW

Here the audience learns something about George through direct experience with the character rather than through the Stage Manager. Because the audience does not learn things only through the narrator, his function differs somewhat from that of an omniscient narrator in a short story.

GEORGE. Awfully sorry, Mrs. Forrest. Hello, Emily.

EMILY. H'lo.

GEORGE. You made a fine speech in class.

EMILY. Well . . . I was really ready to make a speech about the Monroe Doctrine, but at the last minute Miss Corcoran made me talk about the Louisiana Purchase instead. I worked an awful long time on both of them.

1 **GEORGE.** Gee, it's funny, Emily. From my window up there I can just see your head nights when you're doing your homework over in your room.

EMILY. Why, can you?

GEORGE. You certainly do stick to it, Emily. I don't see how you can sit still that long. I guess you like school.

EMILY. Well, I always feel it's something you have to go through.

GEORGE. Yeah.

EMILY. I don't mind it really. It passes the time.

GEORGE. Yeah. Emily, what do you think? We might work out a kinda telegraph from your window to mine; and once in a while you could give me a kinda hint or two about one of those algebra problems. I don't mean the answers, Emily, of course not . . . just some little hint . . .

EMILY. Oh, I think *hints* are allowed. So—ah—if you get stuck, George, you whistle to me; and I'll give you some hints.

GEORGE. Emily, you're just naturally bright, I guess.

EMILY. I figure that it's just the way a person's born.

2 **GEORGE.** Yeah. But, you see, I want to be a farmer, and my Uncle Luke says whenever I'm ready I can come over and work on his farm and if I'm any good I can just gradually have it.

EMILY. You mean the house and everything?

[Enter MRS. WEBB *with a large bowl and sits on the bench by her trellis.]*

GEORGE. Yeah. Well, thanks . . . I better be getting out to the baseball field. Thanks for the talk, Emily. Good afternoon, Mrs. Webb.

MRS. WEBB. Good afternoon, George.

GEORGE. So long, Emily.

EMILY. So long, George.

MRS. WEBB. Emily, come and help me string these beans for the winter. George Gibbs let himself have a real conversation, didn't he? Why, he's growing up. How old would George be?

EMILY. I don't know.

MRS. WEBB. Let's see. He must be almost sixteen.

EMILY. Mama, I made a speech in class today and I was very good.

MRS. WEBB. You must recite it to your father at supper. What was it about?

EMILY. The Louisiana Purchase. It was like silk off a spool. I'm going to make speeches all my life.—Mama, are these big enough?

MRS. WEBB. Try and get them a little bigger if you can.

EMILY. Mama, will you answer me a question, serious?

MRS. WEBB. Seriously, dear—not serious.

EMILY. Seriously—will you?

MRS. WEBB. Of course, I will.

EMILY. Mama, am I good looking?

MRS. WEBB. Yes, of course you are. All my children have got good features; I'd be ashamed if they hadn't.

EMILY. Oh, Mama, that's not what I mean. What I mean is: am I *pretty?*

MRS. WEBB. I've already told you, yes. Now

GUIDED READING

LITERAL QUESTION

1a. How does Mrs. Webb answer Emily's "serious" question? ("Yes, of course you are good looking.")

INFERENTIAL QUESTION

1b. Why is Emily not satisfied with the answer? (Emily is really asking something else—whether she is attractive to the opposite sex, not merely whether she has good features.)

that's enough of that. You have a nice young pretty face. I never heard of such foolishness.

EMILY. Oh, Mama, you never tell us the truth about anything.

MRS. WEBB. I *am* telling you the truth.

EMILY. Mama, were *you* pretty?

MRS. WEBB. Yes, I was, if I do say it. I was the prettiest girl in town next to Mamie Cartwright.

EMILY. But, Mama, you've got to say *some*thing about me. Am I pretty enough . . . to get anybody . . . to get people interested in me?

MRS. WEBB. Emily, you make me tired. Now stop it. You're pretty enough for all normal purposes. Come along now and bring that bowl with you.

EMILY. Oh, Mama, you're no help at all.

STAGE MANAGER. Thank you. Thank you! That'll do. We'll have to interrupt again here. Thank you, Mrs. Webb; thank you, Emily.

[MRS. WEBB *and* EMILY *withdraw.*]

There are some more things we want to explore about this town.

[*He comes to the center of the stage. During the following speech the lights gradually dim to darkness, leaving only a spot on him.*]

I think this is a good time to tell you that the Cartwright interests have just begun building a new bank in Grover's Corners—had to go to Vermont for the marble, sorry to say. And they've asked a friend of mine what they should put in the cornerstone for people to dig up . . . a thousand years from now. . . . Of course, they've put in a copy of the *New York Times* and a copy of Mr. Webb's *Sentinel*. . . . We're kind of interested in this because some scientific fellas have found a way of painting all that reading matter with a glue—a silicate glue—that'll make it keep a thousand—two thousand years.

1 We're putting in a Bible . . . and the Constitution of the United States—and a copy of William Shakespeare's plays. What do you say, folks? What do you think?

Y'know—Babylon[17] once had two million people in it, and all we know about 'em is the names of the kings and some copies of wheat contracts . . . and contracts for the sale of
2 slaves. Yet every night all those families sat down to supper, and the father came home from his work, and the smoke went up the chimney—same as here. And even in Greece and Rome, all we know about the *real* life of the people is what we can piece together out of the joking poems and the comedies they wrote for the theatre back then.

So I'm going to have a copy of this play put in the cornerstone and the people a thousand years from now'll know a few simple facts about us—more than the Treaty of Versailles[18] and the Lindbergh flight.[19] See what I mean?

So—people a thousand years from now—this is the way we were in the provinces north of New York at the beginning of the twentieth
3 century. This is the way we were: in our growing up and in our marrying and in our living and in our dying.

[*A choir partially concealed in the orchestra pit has begun singing "Blessed Be the Tie That Binds."*

SIMON STIMSON *stands directing them.*

Two ladders have been pushed onto the stage; they serve as indication of the second story in the Gibbs and Webb houses. GEORGE *and* EMILY *mount them, and apply themselves to their schoolwork.*

DR. GIBBS *has entered and is seated in his kitchen reading.*]

Well!—good deal of time's gone by. It's evening.

---

17. **Babylon** [bab′ə lən]: ancient city famous for luxury and wickedness.
18. **Treaty of Versailles** [vər sī′]: treaty ending World War I (1919).
19. **Lindbergh flight:** first nonstop solo transatlantic flight (1927) by U.S. aviator Charles A. Lindbergh.

AT A GLANCE

- Emily wants to know if she is pretty enough to attract boys.
- Mrs. Webb assures Emily that she is "pretty enough for all normal purposes."
- The Stage Manager explains that a copy of this play will go in a time capsule so that future generations will know what life was really like in a small New England town in 1901.

1 RESPONSE JOURNAL

Have students respond to the Stage Manager's question about what should be placed in the time capsule.

2 THEME

Life has been going on for ordinary people in much the same way for untold centuries. The Stage Manager implies that *real* life is not what is found in the history books, but what can be seen in this play.

3 THEME

The play shows that life is an endless cycle of birth, growth, and death.

GUIDED READING

LITERAL QUESTION

1a. What kind of help does Emily say that her mother is? (no help at all)

INFERENTIAL QUESTION

1b. What did Emily probably want her mother to say? (that she is pretty enough to attract any boy)

AT A GLANCE

- Choir practice is going on.
- Emily gives George a hint on his math homework.
- Dr. Gibbs talks to George about helping his mother more.

1 MOOD

The peaceful activities of evening create a mood of gentleness and calm.

2 CHARACTERIZATION

Emily's sensory awareness shows her to be a sensitive person.

3 THEME

The "same music" reiterates the idea of the cycles of life, in which weddings are a prominent feature.

1 You can hear choir practice going on in the Congregational Church.
The children are at home doing their schoolwork.
The day's running down like a tired clock.

SIMON STIMSON. Now look here, everybody. Music come into the world to give pleasure.—Softer! Softer! Get it out of your heads that music's only good when it's loud. You leave loudness to the Methodists. You couldn't beat 'em, even if you wanted to. Now again. Tenors!

GEORGE. Hsst! Emily!

EMILY. Hello.

GEORGE. Hello!

EMILY. I can't work at all. The moonlight's so *terrible.*

GEORGE. Emily, did you get the third problem?

EMILY. Which?

GEORGE. The *third?*

EMILY. Why, yes, George—that's the easiest of them all.

GEORGE. I don't see it. Emily, can you give me a hint?

EMILY. I'll tell you one thing: the answer's in yards.

GEORGE. ! ! ! In yards? How do you mean?

EMILY. In *square* yards.

GEORGE. Oh . . . in square yards.

EMILY. Yes, George, don't you see?

GEORGE. Yeah.

EMILY. In square yards of *wallpaper.*

GEORGE. Wallpaper—oh, I see. Thanks a lot, Emily.

2 EMILY. You're welcome. My, isn't the moonlight *terrible?* And choir practice going on. I think if you hold your breath you can hear the train all the way to Contoocook. Hear it?

GEORGE. M-m-m—What do you know!

EMILY. Well, I guess I better go back and try to work.

GEORGE. Good night, Emily. And thanks.

EMILY. Good night, George.

SIMON STIMSON. Before I forget it: how many of you will be able to come in Tuesday afternoon and sing at Fred Hersey's wedding?—show your
3 hands. That'll be fine; that'll be right nice. We'll do the same music we did for Jane Trowbridge's last month.
Now we'll do: "Art Thou Weary; Art Thou Languid?" It's a question, ladies and gentlemen, make it talk. Ready.

DR. GIBBS. Oh, George, can you come down a minute?

GEORGE. Yes, Pa. [*He descends the ladder.*]

DR. GIBBS. Make yourself comfortable, George; I'll only keep you a minute. George, how old are you?

GEORGE. I? I'm sixteen, almost seventeen.

DR. GIBBS. What do you want to do after school's over?

GEORGE. Why, you know, Pa. I want to be a farmer on Uncle Luke's farm.

DR. GIBBS. You'll be willing, will you, to get up early and milk and feed the stock . . . and you'll be able to hoe and hay all day?

GEORGE. Sure, I will. What are you . . . what do you mean, Pa?

DR. GIBBS. Well, George, while I was in my office today I heard a funny sound . . . and what do you think it was? It was your mother chopping wood. There you see your mother—getting up early; cooking meals all day long; washing and ironing—and still she has to go out in the back yard and chop wood. I suppose she just got tired of asking you. She just gave up and decided it was easier to do it herself. And you eat her meals, and put on the clothes she keeps nice for you, and you run off and play baseball,—like she's some hired girl we keep around the house but that we don't like very

GUIDED READING

LITERAL QUESTIONS

1a. How does Emily describe the moonlight? ("terrible")

2a. What "funny sounds" did Dr. Gibbs hear? (Mrs. Gibbs chopping wood)

INFERENTIAL QUESTIONS

1b. What does this description suggest about the moonlight? (It must be a very bright, clear night of the sort that evokes wonder.)

2b. Why does he call it "funny"? (He should not have been hearing his wife chopping wood; George should have been doing it.)

1 much. Well, I knew all I had to do was call your attention to it. Here's a handkerchief, son. George, I've decided to raise your spending money twenty-five cents a week. Not, of course, for chopping wood for your mother, because that's a present you give her, but because you're getting older—and I imagine there are lots of things you must find to do with it.

GEORGE. Thanks, Pa.

DR. GIBBS. Let's see—tomorrow's your payday. You can count on it—Hmm. Probably Rebecca'll feel she ought to have some more too.
2 Wonder what could have happened to your mother. Choir practice never was as late as this before.

GEORGE. It's only half past eight, Pa.

DR. GIBBS. I don't know why she's in that old choir. She hasn't any more voice than an old crow. . . . Traipsin' around the streets at this hour of the night . . . Just about time you retired, don't you think?

GEORGE. Yes, Pa.

[GEORGE *mounts to his place on the ladder. Laughter and good nights can be heard on stage left and presently* MRS. GIBBS, MRS. SOAMES *and* MRS. WEBB *come down Main Street. When they arrive at the corner of the stage they stop.*]

MRS. SOAMES. Good night, Martha. Good night, Mr. Foster.

MRS. WEBB. I'll tell Mr. Webb; I *know* he'll want to put it in the paper.

MRS. GIBBS. My, it's late!

MRS. SOAMES. Good night, Irma.

MRS. GIBBS. Real nice choir practice, wa'n't it? Myrtle Webb! Look at the moon, will you! Tsk-tsk-tsk. Potato weather, for sure.

[*They are silent a moment, gazing up at the moon.*]

MRS. SOAMES. Naturally I didn't want to say a word about it in front of those others, but now we're alone—really, it's the worst scandal that ever was in this town!

AT A GLANCE

- George takes his father's talk to heart, and Dr. Gibbs raises his allowance.
- Dr. Gibbs frets over his wife's lateness from choir practice.
- The women stop to chat on their way home.

1 CHARACTERIZATION

George is moved to tears after his father points out the boy's lack of consideration for his mother. George is sometimes thoughtless but is not deliberately unkind.

2 CHARACTERIZATION

Dr. Gibbs' fretting over his wife's absence shows his concern for her welfare but also his desire to have her at home, where—in his opinion—she belongs. In this, he is typical of turn-of-the-century husbands.

GUIDED READING

LITERAL QUESTION

1a. How does Dr. Gibbs refer to the choir? ("that old choir")

INFERENTIAL QUESTION

1b. Why does he feel as he does about it? (He seems to resent that it takes Mrs. Gibbs away from the house.)

AT A GLANCE

- The women discuss Simon Stimson's drinking.
- Dr. and Mrs. Gibbs discuss Stimson and then Mrs. Gibbs revives the subject of going away on vacation.
- Dr. Gibbs grumbles that people locking their doors shows they are becoming citified.

1 CHARACTERIZATION

Mrs. Webb's willingness to defend Stimson shows that she is a kind person who will not speak ill of her neighbors.

2 STEREOTYPE

Mrs. Gibbs is a stereotype of the turn-of-the-century wife. Instead of stating her wishes directly, she tries to convince her husband that what she wants is what *he* wants.

3 VOCABULARY: CONNOTATION

Citified connotes artificiality and affectation. *Burgle* suggests a small-time kind of theft. Dr. Gibbs' disdain for city ways comes out in his choice of words.

MRS. GIBBS. What?

MRS. SOAMES. Simon Stimson!

MRS. GIBBS. Now, Louella!

MRS. SOAMES. But, Julia! To have the organist of a church *drink* and *drunk* year after year. You know he was drunk tonight.

MRS. GIBBS. Now, Louella! We all know about Mr. Stimson, and we all know about the troubles he's been through, and Dr. Ferguson knows too, and if Dr. Ferguson keeps him on there in his job the only thing the rest of us can do is just not to notice it.

MRS. SOAMES. *Not to notice it!* But it's getting worse.

1 **MRS. WEBB.** No, it isn't, Louella. It's getting better. I've been in that choir twice as long as you have. It doesn't happen anywhere near so often. . . . My, I hate to go to bed on a night like this. I better hurry. Those children'll be sitting up till all hours. Good night, Louella.

[*They all exchange good nights. She hurries downstage, enters her house and disappears.*]

MRS. GIBBS. Can you get home safe, Louella?

MRS. SOAMES. It's as bright as day. I can see Mr. Soames scowling at the window now. You'd think we'd been to a dance the way the menfolk carry on.

[*More good nights.* MRS. GIBBS *arrives at her home and passes through the trellis into the kitchen.*]

MRS. GIBBS. Well, we had a real good time.

DR. GIBBS. You're late enough.

MRS. GIBBS. Why, Frank, it ain't any later'n usual.

DR. GIBBS. And you stopping at the corner to gossip with a lot of hens.

MRS. GIBBS. Now, Frank, don't be grouchy. Come out and smell the heliotrope in the moonlight. [*They stroll out arm in arm along the footlights.*] Isn't that wonderful? What did you do all the time I was away?

DR. GIBBS. Oh, I read—as usual. What were the girls gossiping about tonight?

MRS. GIBBS. Well, believe me, Frank—there is something to gossip about.

DR. GIBBS. Hmm! Simon Stimson far gone, was he?

MRS. GIBBS. Worst I've ever seen him. How'll that end, Frank? Dr. Ferguson can't forgive him forever.

DR. GIBBS. I guess I know more about Simon Stimson's affairs than anybody in this town. Some people ain't made for small-town life. I don't know how that'll end; but there's nothing we can do but just leave it alone. Come, get in.

MRS. GIBBS. No, not yet . . . Frank, I'm worried about you.

DR. GIBBS. What are you worried about?

2 **MRS. GIBBS.** I think it's my duty to make plans for you to get a real rest and change. And if I get a legacy, well, I'm going to insist on it.

DR. GIBBS. Now, Julia, there's no sense in going over that again.

MRS. GIBBS. Frank, you're just *unreasonable*!

DR. GIBBS. [*Starting into the house.*] Come on, Julia, it's getting late. First thing you know you'll catch cold. I gave George a piece of my mind tonight. I reckon you'll have your wood chopped for a while anyway. No, no, start getting upstairs.

MRS. GIBBS. Oh, dear. There's always so many things to pick up, seems like. You know, Frank, Mrs. Fairchild always locks her front door every night. All those people up that part of town do.

3 **DR. GIBBS.** [*Blowing out the lamp.*] They're all getting citified, that's the trouble with them. They haven't got nothing fit to burgle and everybody knows it.

GUIDED READING

LITERAL QUESTIONS

1a. How does Dr. Gibbs explain Simon Stimson's behavior? ("Some people ain't made for small-town life.")

2a. What does he tell Mrs. Gibbs that he did about George? (gave George a piece of his mind)

INFERENTIAL QUESTIONS

1b. What does this explanation suggest about Stimson? (He probably is disappointed and frustrated with the life he leads.)

2b. Is that description accurate? Why might he have used that wording? (No; Dr. Gibbs treated George gently but probably likes to be seen as a stern head of his family.)

[*They disappear.*
REBECCA *climbs up the ladder beside* GEORGE.]

GEORGE. Get out, Rebecca. There's only room for one at this window. You're always spoiling everything.

REBECCA. Well, let me look just a minute.

GEORGE. Use your own window.

REBECCA. I did, but there's no moon there. . . . George, do you know what I think, do you? I think maybe the moon's getting nearer and nearer and there'll be a big 'splosion.

GEORGE. Rebecca, you don't know anything. If the moon were getting nearer, the guys that sit up all night with telescopes would see it first and they'd tell about it, and it'd be in all the newspapers.

1 **REBECCA.** George, is the moon shining on South America, Canada and half the whole world?

GEORGE. Well—prob'ly is.

[*The* STAGE MANAGER *strolls on.*
Pause. The sound of crickets is heard.]

STAGE MANAGER. Nine thirty. Most of the lights are out. No, there's Constable Warren trying a few doors on Main Street. And here comes Editor Webb, after putting his newspaper to bed.

[MR. WARREN, *an elderly policeman, comes along Main Street from the right,* MR. WEBB *from the left.*]

MR. WEBB. Good evening, Bill.

CONSTABLE WARREN. Evenin', Mr. Webb.

MR. WEBB. Quite a moon!

CONSTABLE WARREN. Yepp.

MR. WEBB. All quiet tonight?

CONSTABLE WARREN. Simon Stimson is rollin' around a little. Just saw his wife movin' out to hunt for him so I looked the other way—there he is now.

[SIMON STIMSON *comes down Main Street from the left, only a trace of unsteadiness in his walk.*]

MR. WEBB. Good evening, Simon . . . Town seems to have settled down for the night pretty well. . . .

[SIMON STIMSON *comes up to him and pauses a moment and stares at him, swaying slightly.*]

2 Good evening . . . Yes, most of the town's settled down for the night, Simon. . . . I guess we better do the same. Can I walk along a ways with you?

[SIMON STIMSON *continues on his way without a word and disappears at the right.*]

Good night.

CONSTABLE WARREN. I don't know how that's goin' to end, Mr. Webb.

3 **MR. WEBB.** Well, he's seen a peck of trouble, one thing after another. . . . Oh, Bill . . . if you see my boy smoking cigarettes, just give him a word, will you? He thinks a lot of you, Bill.

CONSTABLE WARREN. I don't think he smokes no cigarettes, Mr. Webb. Leastways, not more'n two or three a year.

MR. WEBB. Hm . . . I hope not. Well, good night, Bill.

CONSTABLE WARREN. Good night, Mr. Webb. [*Exit.*]

MR. WEBB. Who's that up there? Is that you, Myrtle?

EMILY. No, it's me, Papa.

MR. WEBB. Why aren't you in bed?

EMILY. I don't know. I just can't sleep yet, Papa. The moonlight's so *won*-derful. And the smell of Mrs. Gibbs' heliotrope. Can you smell it?

MR. WEBB. Hm . . . Yes. Haven't any troubles on your mind, have you, Emily?

EMILY. *Troubles,* Papa? *No.*

AT A GLANCE

- Rebecca joins George at his window and they talk about the moon.
- Mr. Webb talks to Constable Warren about Stimson, who soon appears at the scene obviously drunk.
- Mr. Webb, having failed in an attempt to escort Stimson home, goes home himself and chats with Emily.

1 THEME

Rebecca's question suggests a concern with the individual's place in the universe.

2 CHARACTERIZATION

Mr. Webb's innate graciousness and tact are apparent in his treatment of Simon Stimson.

3 READING SKILLS: COMPARISONS

Mr. Webb's explanation of Stimson's drinking problem is that he has had a lot of troubles. This contrasts with Dr. Gibbs' view that Stimson is not made for small-town life.

GUIDED READING

LITERAL QUESTION

1a. What does Mr. Webb say to Constable Warren about Simon Stimson? ("Well, he's seen a peck of trouble.")

INFERENTIAL QUESTION

1b. What attitudes does this answer reflect? (compassion and a nonjudgmental spirit)

AT A GLANCE

- Mr. Webb wishes Emily good night.
- Rebecca tells George about a letter Jane Crofut got with an unusual address.
- The Stage Manager ends the act.

1 THEME

The perspective of the address suggests the place of the individual in an orderly universe.

REFLECTING ON ACT 1

How would you describe Grover's Corners and its people? (Students may suggest that the town is simple, quiet, and almost idyllic; its people seem good, honest, hard-working, and thoughtful. Their ordinary problems and concerns make them seem real.)

STUDY QUESTIONS

1. before dawn, May 7, 1901, in Grover's Corners, New Hampshire; no scenery
2.
   - Dr. Gibbs dies in 1930, new hospital named for him; Mrs. Gibbs dies earlier in Ohio
   - wins scholarship to MIT and graduates, but is killed in France in World War I
   - wants to travel to Paris
   - *Geology:* town lies on Pleistocene granite, shelf of Devonian basalt crosses it with Mesozoic shale
   - *Anthropology:* Cotahatchee tribe in tenth century, English from seventeenth century, later some Slav and Mediterranean stock
   - ordinary, well-behaved, dull

MR. WEBB. Well, enjoy yourself, but don't let your mother catch you. Good night, Emily.

EMILY. Good night, Papa.

[MR. WEBB *crosses into the house, whistling "Blessed Be the Tie That Binds" and disappears.*]

REBECCA. I never told you about that letter Jane Crofut got from her minister when she was sick. He wrote Jane a letter and on the envelope the address was like this: It said: Jane Crofut; The Crofut Farm; Grover's Corners; Sutton County; New Hampshire; United States of America.

GEORGE. What's funny about that?

1 **REBECCA.** But listen, it's not finished: the United States of America; Continent of North America; Western Hemisphere; the Earth; the Solar System; the Universe; the Mind of God—that's what it said on the envelope.

GEORGE. What do you know!

REBECCA. And the postman brought it just the same.

GEORGE. What do you know!

STAGE MANAGER. That's the end of the First Act, friends. You can go and smoke now, those that smoke.

STUDY QUESTIONS

Recalling

1. According to the Stage Manager, when does the action of the play begin, and where does the play take place? According to the stage directions, what sort of scenery does it have?
2. In Act 1 what do we learn about the following? (a) the futures of Dr. and Mrs. Gibbs, (b) Joe Crowell's future, (c) Mrs. Gibbs's dreams, (d) the geology and anthropology of Grover's Corners, (e) Editor Webb's opinion of Grover's Corners.
3. What is Emily Webb imagining herself to be as she walks home from school, according to page 679? What is George Gibbs doing as he races down Main Street? What does Emily promise George she will do? What "serious" question does Emily ask her mother?
4. Where does the Stage Manager plan to put a copy of *Our Town* "for people to dig up a thousand years from now"? What does he say the play will tell them?
5. What is Doc Gibbs's explanation for Simon Stimson's problems, according to page 684? What is his explanation for the fact that some people in town have taken to locking their front doors at night?
6. Why does Rebecca come to her brother's room in the final scenes of Act 1? What question does she ask? What does Rebecca tell her brother about Jane Crofut's letter?

Interpreting

7. What sort of relationship does the Stage Manager set up with the audience? Is he a character living in 1901 America? Explain. What seems to be the Stage Manager's attitude toward the deaths of Doc and Mrs. Gibbs and of Joe Crowell?
8. What sort of town is Grover's Corners? What sort of people are the Gibbs and Webb families? Briefly characterize Emily and George.
9. What does the play seem to be suggesting no longer exists? What mood or attitude does this suggestion evoke in the audience?
10. What does the address described by Rebecca in the last scene do to Grover's Corners and its inhabitants? What does the "Our" in the play's title suggest?
11. Why might Wilder specifically request settings with so little scenery?

Extending

12. What aspects of life in Grover's Corners do you think are gone forever in most places in America? What aspects remain a part of life as lived in America now?

3. lady of elegance; throwing ball; give homework hints; if she is good-looking
4. cornerstone of bank; how ordinary people lived in 1901
5. not made for small-town life; people "getting citified"
6. look at moon; where else it shines; curious address
7. informal; seemingly, but knows future; matter-of-fact
8. small, peaceful; ordinary, close, middle-class; *Emily:* bright, friendly, introspective; *George:* eager, energetic, earnest
9. innocence, small-town isolation; nostalgia
10. part of cosmic order; town is our common past—ideal and imagined
11. forces audience to imagine ideal small town; modernist structure, involves audience both actually and intellectually
12. Possible answers: isolation from social and political problems, innocence about larger world, sense of security; strong family ties, community traditions, everyday rewards, and problems of living and dying

ACT 2

[The tables and chairs of the two kitchens are still on the stage.
The ladders and the small bench have been withdrawn.
The STAGE MANAGER *has been at his accustomed place watching the audience return to its seats.]*

STAGE MANAGER. Three years have gone by.
Yes, the sun's come up over a thousand times.
Summers and winters have cracked the mountains a little bit more and the rains have brought down some of the dirt.
1 Some babies that weren't even born before have begun talking regular sentences already; and a number of people who thought they were right young and spry have noticed that they can't bound up a flight of stairs like they used to, without their heart fluttering a little.
All that can happen in a thousand days.
Nature's been pushing and contriving in other ways, too: a number of young people fell in love and got married.
Yes, the mountain got bit away a few fractions of an inch; millions of gallons of water went by the mill; and here and there a new home was set up under a roof.
Almost everybody in the world gets married—you know what I mean? In our town there aren't hardly any exceptions. Most everybody in the world climbs into their graves married.
The First Act was called the Daily Life. This act is called Love and Marriage. There's another act coming after this: I reckon you can guess what that's about.

So:
It's three years later. It's 1904.
It's July 7th, just after High School Commencement. That's the time most of our young people jump up and get married.
Soon as they've passed their last examinations in solid geometry and Cicero's Orations,[1] looks like they suddenly feel themselves fit to be married.
It's early morning. Only this time it's been raining. It's been pouring and thundering.
Mrs. Gibbs' garden, and Mrs. Webb's here: drenched.
2 All those bean poles and pea vines: drenched.
All yesterday over there on Main Street, the rain looked like curtains being blown along.
Hm . . . it may begin again any minute.
There! You can hear the 5:45 for Boston.

*[*MRS. GIBBS *and* MRS. WEBB *enter their kitchens and start the day as in the First Act.]*

And there's Mrs. Gibbs and Mrs. Webb come down to make breakfast, just as though it were an ordinary day. I don't have to point out to the women in my audience that those ladies they see before them, both of those ladies cooked three meals a day—one of 'em for twenty years, the other for forty—and no summer vacation. They brought up two children apiece, washed, cleaned the house—and *never a nervous breakdown.*
It's like what one of those Middle West poets said: You've got to love life to have life, and you've got to have life to love life[2]. . . . It's what they call a vicious circle.

HOWIE NEWSOME. *[Off stage left.]* Giddap, Bessie!

3 **STAGE MANAGER.** Here comes Howie Newsome delivering the milk. And there's Si Crowell delivering the papers like his brother before him.

*[*SI CROWELL *has entered hurling imaginary newspapers into doorways;* HOWIE NEWSOME *has come along Main Street with Bessie.]*

SI CROWELL. Morning, Howie.

HOWIE NEWSOME. Morning, Si. Anything in the papers I ought to know?

---

1. **Cicero's** [sis′ə rōz′] **Orations:** speeches made by the Roman orator and statesman Cicero (106–43 B.C.).

2. **You've . . . life:** Edgar Lee Masters' poem "Lucinda Matlock" (page 440) actually reads "It takes life to love life."

AT A GLANCE

- The Stage Manager recapitulates the intervening three years and introduces the second act as "Love and Marriage."
- Mrs. Gibbs and Mrs. Webb prepare breakfast in their kitchens.
- Howie Newsome comes with milk; Si Crowell with papers.

LITERARY OPTIONS

- theme
- conflict

THEMATIC OPTIONS

- endless cycles of life
- the search for perfection
- the individual's place in the universe

1 THEME

The Stage Manager's comments remind the viewer of the inexorable march of time and of the cycle of life.

2 STYLE: IMAGERY

In the absence of scenery, the simile stimulates visualization; the train whistle, auditory imaging.

3 STYLE: STRUCTURE

The beginning of the day parallels the beginning of the day in the first act.

GUIDED READING

LITERAL QUESTIONS

1a. What does the Stage Manager say almost everyone in the world does? (gets married)

2a. What lines does he attribute to a Midwestern poet? ("You've got to love life to have life, and you've got to have life to love life.")

INFERENTIAL QUESTIONS

1b. What does this comment suggest about the institution of marriage? (It is a universal human need.)

2b. What does his version of the lines mean? (The more you put into life, the more you can get out of it; the fuller life is, the happier most people are.)

AT A GLANCE

- Si Crowell, the constable, and Howie discuss George's impending marriage and retirement from local baseball.
- Howie delivers milk to Mrs. Gibbs and Mrs. Webb.
- The Gibbses talk about George's coming marriage.

1 STYLE: STRUCTURE

Si's attitude toward marriage parallels his brother Joe's in the first act. The importance of marriage is beyond the grasp of young boys, of whom the Crowells are representative.

2 THEME

Constable Warren's perspective shows the continuing cycle of life.

3 INFERENCES

Dr. Gibbs' comment about the groom not having much to shave intimates that he believes George is too young to get married.

SI CROWELL. Nothing much, except we're losing about the best baseball pitcher Grover's Corners ever had—George Gibbs.

HOWIE NEWSOME. Reckon he is.

SI CROWELL. He could hit and run bases, too.

HOWIE NEWSOME. Yep. Mighty fine ball player. Whoa! Bessie! I guess I can stop and talk if I've a mind to!

1 **SI CROWELL.** I don't see how he could give up a thing like that just to get married. Would you, Howie?

HOWIE NEWSOME. Can't tell, Si. Never had no talent that way.

[CONSTABLE WARREN *enters. They exchange good mornings.*]

You're up early, Bill.

CONSTABLE WARREN. Seein' if there's anything I can do to prevent a flood. River's been risin' all night.

HOWIE NEWSOME. Si Crowell's all worked up here about George Gibbs' retiring from baseball.

2 **CONSTABLE WARREN.** Yes, sir; that's the way it goes. Back in '84 we had a player, Si—even George Gibbs couldn't touch him. Name of Hank Todd. Went down to Maine and become a parson. Wonderful ball player.—Howie, how does the weather look to you?

HOWIE NEWSOME. Oh, 'tain't bad. Think maybe it'll clear up for good.

[CONSTABLE WARREN *and* SI CROWELL *continue on their way.*

HOWIE NEWSOME *brings the milk first to* MRS. GIBBS' house. She meets him by the trellis.]

MRS. GIBBS. Good morning, Howie. Do you think it's going to rain again?

HOWIE NEWSOME. Morning, Mrs. Gibbs. It rained so heavy, I think maybe it'll clear up.

MRS. GIBBS. Certainly hope it will.

HOWIE NEWSOME. How much did you want today?

MRS. GIBBS. I'm going to have a houseful of relations, Howie. Looks to me like I'll need three-a-milk and two-a-cream.

HOWIE NEWSOME. My wife says to tell you we both hope they'll be very happy, Mrs. Gibbs. Know they *will.*

MRS. GIBBS. Thanks a lot, Howie. Tell your wife I hope she gits there to the wedding.

HOWIE NEWSOME. Yes, she'll be there; she'll be there if she kin. [HOWIE NEWSOME *crosses to* MRS. WEBB'S house.] Morning, Mrs. Webb.

MRS. WEBB. Oh, good morning, Mr. Newsome. I told you four quarts of milk, but I hope you can spare me another.

HOWIE NEWSOME. Yes'm . . . and the two of cream.

MRS. WEBB. Will it start raining again, Mr. Newsome?

HOWIE NEWSOME. Well. Just sayin' to Mrs. Gibbs as how it may lighten up. Mrs. Newsome told me to tell you as how we hope they'll both be very happy, Mrs. Webb. Know they *will.*

MRS. WEBB. Thank you, and thank Mrs. Newsome and we're counting on seeing you at the wedding.

HOWIE NEWSOME. Yes, Mrs. Webb. We hope to git there. Couldn't miss that. Come on, Bessie.

[*Exit* HOWIE NEWSOME.

DR. GIBBS *descends in shirt sleeves, and sits down at his breakfast table.*]

DR. GIBBS. Well, Ma the day has come. You're losin' one of your chicks.

MRS. GIBBS. Frank Gibbs, don't you say another word. I feel like crying every minute. Sit down and drink your coffee.

3 **DR. GIBBS.** The groom's up shaving himself—only there ain't an awful lot to shave. Whistling and singing, like he's glad to leave us. Every

GUIDED READING

LITERAL QUESTIONS

1a. What is Constable Warren's response when he hears that Si is upset about George Gibbs' retiring from baseball? ("that's the way it goes")

2a. What message does Howie carry from his wife to Mrs. Gibbs and Mrs. Webb? ("We hope they'll be very happy.")

INFERENTIAL QUESTIONS

1b. What does Constable Warren's response imply? (There have been fine baseball players before George Gibbs and there will probably be fine ones after.)

2b. To whom is he referring, and why? (He is referring to George and Emily; they are getting married.)

now and then he says "I do" to the mirror, but it don't sound convincing to me.

MRS. GIBBS. I declare, Frank, I don't know how he'll get along. I've arranged his clothes and seen to it he's put warm things on—Frank! they're too *young.* Emily won't think of such things. He'll catch his death of cold within a week.

DR. GIBBS. I was remembering my wedding morning, Julia.

MRS. GIBBS. Now don't start that, Frank Gibbs.

1 **DR. GIBBS.** I was the scaredest young fella in the State of New Hampshire. I thought I'd make a mistake for sure. And when I saw you comin' down that aisle I thought you were the prettiest girl I'd ever seen, but the only trouble was that I'd never seen you before. There I was in the Congregational Church marryin' a total stranger.

MRS. GIBBS. And how do you think I felt! Frank, weddings are perfectly awful things. Farces—that's what they are! [*She puts a plate before him.*] Here, I've made something for you.

DR. GIBBS. Why, Julia Hersey—French toast!

MRS. GIBBS. 'Tain't hard to make and I had to do *some*thing.

[*Pause.* DR. GIBBS *pours on the syrup.*]

DR. GIBBS. How'd you sleep last night, Julia?

MRS. GIBBS. Well, I heard a lot of the hours struck off.

2 **DR. GIBBS.** Ye-e-s! I get a shock every time I think of George setting out to be a family man—that great gangling thing! I tell you Julia, there's nothing so terrifying in the world as a *son.* The relation of father and son is the darndest, awkwardest—

MRS. GIBBS. Well, mother and daughter's no picnic, let me tell you.

DR. GIBBS. They'll have a lot of troubles, I suppose, but that's none of our business. Everybody has a right to their own troubles.

MRS. GIBBS. [*At the table, drinking her coffee, meditatively.*] Yes . . . people are meant to go through life two by two. 'Tain't natural to be lonesome.

[*Pause.* DR. GIBBS *starts laughing.*]

DR. GIBBS. Julia, do you know one of the things I was scared of when I married you?

MRS. GIBBS. Oh, go along with you!

DR. GIBBS. I was afraid we wouldn't have material for conversation more'n'd last us a few weeks. [*Both laugh.*] I was afraid we'd run out and eat our meals in silence, that's a fact.—Well, you and I been conversing for twenty years now without any noticeable barren spells.

MRS. GIBBS. Well—good weather, bad weather—'tain't very choice, but I always find something to say. [*She goes to the foot of the stairs.*] Did you hear Rebecca stirring around upstairs?

DR. GIBBS. No. Only day of the year Rebecca hasn't been managing everybody's business up there. She's hiding in her room. I got the impression she's crying.

MRS. GIBBS. Lord's sakes! This has got to stop. Rebecca! Rebecca! Come and get your breakfast.

[GEORGE *comes rattling down the stairs, very brisk.*]

GEORGE. Good morning, everybody. Only five more hours to live.

[*Makes the gesture of cutting his throat, and a loud "k-k-k," and starts through the trellis.*]

MRS. GIBBS. George Gibbs, where are you going?

GEORGE. Just stepping across the grass to see my girl.

3 **MRS. GIBBS.** Now, George! You put on your overshoes. It's raining torrents. You don't go out of this house without you're prepared for it.

AT A GLANCE

- Mrs. Gibbs worries because of the couple's youth.
- As Dr. Gibbs recalls his wedding day, they talk about the difficulties of being parents.
- When George states his intention to go see Emily, his mother orders him to put on overshoes first.

1 THEME

Dr. Gibbs' remembrances of his own wedding day illustrate that marriage is one of the cycles of life—first the father got married, and now the son.

2 DIALOGUE

The dialogue between Mr. and Mrs. Gibbs expresses the natural tensions between children and parents, youth and age.

3 CHARACTERIZATION

Even though George is about to get married, Mrs. Gibbs still views him as her little boy.

GUIDED READING

LITERAL QUESTIONS

1a. What does Dr. Gibbs say that everyone has a right to? (their own troubles)

2a. What does Mrs. Gibbs warn George to do before he goes out? (put on his overshoes)

INFERENTIAL QUESTIONS

1b. What does he mean by this statement? (People have a right to experience life for themselves without undue interference even from those who love them.)

2b. What does this warning suggest about their relationship? (She always will feel protective toward him.)

AT A GLANCE

- Reluctantly, George puts on his overshoes.
- Mrs. Webb tells him that he can't see Emily before their wedding, and she goes upstairs to see that Emily doesn't come down.
- He has an awkward conversation with Mr. Webb about marriage.

1 CHARACTERIZATION

George, about to be married, asserts his independence; Mrs. Gibbs asserts her parental prerogative.

2 THEME

The "millions" recall the life cycle of which George is a part. Grover's Corners is a traditional place in which lives follow traditional patterns.

3 STAGE DIRECTIONS

The stage directions indicate that the conversation between George and Mr. Webb is very awkward.

GEORGE. Aw, Ma. It's just a *step!*

MRS. GIBBS. George! You'll catch your death of cold and cough all through the service.

DR. GIBBS. George, do as your mother tells you! [DR. GIBBS *goes upstairs.*]

[GEORGE *returns reluctantly to the kitchen and pantomimes putting on overshoes.*]

1 MRS. GIBBS. From tomorrow on you can kill yourself in all weathers, but while you're in my house you'll live wisely, thank you. Maybe Mrs. Webb isn't used to callers at seven in the morning. Here, take a cup of coffee first.

GEORGE. Be back in a minute. [*He crosses the stage, leaping over the puddles.*] Good morning, Mother Webb.

MRS. WEBB. Goodness! You frightened me! Now, George, you can come in a minute out of the wet, but you know I can't ask you in.

GEORGE. Why not—?

MRS. WEBB. George, you know's well as I do: the groom can't see his bride on his wedding day, not until he sees her in church.

GEORGE. Aw!—that's just a superstition. Good morning, Mr. Webb. [*Enter* MR. WEBB.]

MR. WEBB. Good morning, George.

GEORGE. Mr. Webb, you don't believe in that superstition, do you?

MR. WEBB. There's a lot of common sense in some superstitions, George. [*He sits at the table, facing right.*]

2 MRS. WEBB. Millions have folla'd it, George, and you don't want to be the first to fly in the face of custom.

GEORGE. How is Emily?

MRS. WEBB. She hasn't waked up yet. I haven't heard a sound out of her.

GEORGE. Emily's *asleep!!!*

MRS. WEBB. No wonder! We were up 'till all hours, sewing and packing. Now I'll tell you what I'll do; you set down here a minute with Mr. Webb and drink this cup of coffee; and I'll go upstairs and see she doesn't come down and surprise you. There's some bacon, too; but don't be long about it.

[*Exit* MRS. WEBB.
3 *Embarrassed silence.*
MR. WEBB *dunks doughnuts in his coffee.*
More silence.]

MR. WEBB. [*Suddenly and loudly.*] Well, George, how are you?

GEORGE. [*Startled, choking over his coffee.*] Oh, fine, I'm fine. [*Pause.*] Mr. Webb, what sense could there be in a superstition like that?

MR. WEBB. Well, you see—on her wedding morning a girl's head's apt to be full of . . . clothes and one thing and another. Don't you think that's probably it?

GEORGE. Ye-e-s. I never thought of that.

MR. WEBB. A girl's apt to be a mite nervous on her wedding day. [*Pause.*]

GEORGE. I wish a fellow could get married without all that marching up and down.

MR. WEBB. Every man that's ever lived has felt that way about it, George; but it hasn't been any use. It's the womenfolk who've built up weddings, my boy. For a while now the women have it all their own. A man looks pretty small at a wedding, George. All those good women standing shoulder to shoulder making sure that the knot's tied in a mighty public way.

GEORGE. But . . . you *believe* in it, don't you, Mr. Webb?

MR. WEBB. [*With alacrity.*] Oh, yes; *oh, yes.* Don't you misunderstand me, my boy. Marriage is a wonderful thing—wonderful thing. And don't you forget that, George.

GEORGE. No, sir. Mr. Webb, how old were you when you got married?

GUIDED READING

LITERAL QUESTION

1a. What does Mr. Webb say about some superstitions? ("There's a lot of common sense in some . . .")

INFERENTIAL QUESTION

1b. In what sense might he be correct? (Customs often grow for a good reason, even though that reason may be obscured by time.)

MR. WEBB. Well, you see: I'd been to college and I'd taken a little time to get settled. But Mrs. Webb—she wasn't much older than what Emily is. Oh, age hasn't much to do with it, George—not compared with . . . uh . . . other things.

GEORGE. What were you going to say, Mr. Webb?

MR. WEBB. Oh, I don't know. Was I going to say something? [*Pause.*] George, I was thinking the other night of some advice my father gave me when I got married. Charles, he said, Charles, start out early showing who's boss, he said. Best thing to do is to give an order, even if it don't make sense; just so she'll learn to obey. And he said: if anything about your wife irritates you—her conversation, or anything—just get up and leave the house. That'll make it clear to her, he said. And, oh, yes! he said never, *never* let your wife know how much money you have, never.

GEORGE. Well, Mr. Webb . . . I don't think I could . . .

1 **MR. WEBB.** So I took the opposite of my father's advice and I've been happy ever since. And let that be a lesson to you, George, never to ask advice on personal matters. George, are you going to raise chickens on your farm?

GEORGE. What?

MR. WEBB. Are you going to raise chickens on your farm?

GEORGE. Uncle Luke's never been much interested, but I thought—

2 **MR. WEBB.** A book came into my office the other day, George, on the Philo System of raising chickens. I want you to read it. I'm thinking of beginning in a small way in the back yard, and I'm going to put an incubator in the cellar—

[*Enter* MRS. WEBB.]

MRS. WEBB. Charles, are you talking about that old incubator again? I thought you two'd be talking about things worth while.

MR. WEBB. [*Bitingly.*] Well, Myrtle, if you want to give the boy some good advice, I'll go upstairs and leave you alone with him.

MRS. WEBB. [*Pulling* GEORGE *up.*] George, Emily's got to come downstairs and eat her breakfast. She sends you her love but she doesn't want to lay eyes on you. Good-bye.

GEORGE. Good-bye.

[GEORGE *crosses the stage to his own home, bewildered and crestfallen. He slowly dodges a puddle and disappears into his house.*]

MR. WEBB. Myrtle, I guess you don't know about that older superstition.

MRS. WEBB. What do you mean, Charles?

MR. WEBB. Since the cave men: no bridegroom should see his father-in-law on the day of the wedding, or near it. Now remember that. [*Both leave the stage.*]

STAGE MANAGER. Thank you very much, Mr. and Mrs. Webb. Now I have to interrupt again here. You see, we want to know how all this began—this wedding, this plan to spend a lifetime together. I'm awfully interested in how big things like that begin.
3 You know how it is: you're twenty-one or twenty-two and you make some decisions; then whisssh! you're seventy: you've been a lawyer for fifty years, and that white-haired lady at your side has eaten over fifty thousand meals with you.
How do such things begin?
George and Emily are going to show you now the conversation they had when they first knew that . . . that . . . as the saying goes . . . they were meant for one another.
But before they do it I want you to try and remember what it was like to have been very young.
And particularly the days when you were first

AT A GLANCE

- Mr. Webb shares his own father's poor advice on marriage with George as a lesson not to ask advice on personal matters.
- Mrs. Webb sends George home.
- The Stage Manager talks about how people decide to marry.

1 STYLE: HUMOR

The unexpected ending to Mr. Webb's story provides humor, as does his *non sequitur* about chickens.

2 CHARACTERIZATION

Uncomfortable with the elemental subject of marriage, Mr. Webb finds a neutral topic.

3 THEME

The Stage Manager's capsule version of life is a reminder of how quickly it goes by.

GUIDED READING

LITERAL QUESTIONS

1a. What lesson does Mr. Webb tell George to learn? ("never to ask advice on personal matters")

2a. In what does the Stage Manager say that he is awfully interested? (how big things like weddings begin)

INFERENTIAL QUESTIONS

1b. How does his anecdote illustrate the lesson? (The advice he got was negative and outdated: he would have been most unwise to have followed it.)

2b. In what way is this topic a "big thing"? (A wedding is a major life change for the participants.)

AT A GLANCE

- The Stage Manager sets the stage for a flashback to George and Emily's junior year in high school.
- Emily tells George that he has become conceited.
- George sees her point and thanks her for telling him.

1 FLASHBACK

By establishing the scene as a flashback, the author ensures that the audience will understand its significance.

2 CONFLICT

When Emily begins to criticize George it appears to be the beginning of a conflict. The conflict, however, never materializes.

3 CONFLICT

George's receptive reaction to Emily's criticism cuts off the possibility of an external conflict.

in love; when you were like a person sleep-walking, and you didn't quite see the street you were in, and didn't quite hear everything that was said to you. You're just a little bit crazy. Will you remember that, please?
Now they'll be coming out of high school at three o'clock. George has just been elected President of the Junior Class, and as it's June, that means he'll be President of the Senior Class all next year. And Emily's just been elected Secretary and Treasurer.
I don't have to tell you how important that is.

[*He places a board across the backs of two chairs, which he takes from those at the Gibbs family's table. He brings two high stools from the wings and places them behind the board. Persons sitting on the stools will be facing the audience. This is the counter of Mr. Morgan's drugstore. The sounds of young people's voices are heard off left.*]

1 Yepp—there they are coming down Main Street now.

[EMILY, *carrying an armful of—imaginary—schoolbooks, comes along Main Street from the left.*]

EMILY. I can't, Louise. I've got to go home. Good-bye. Oh, Ernestine! Ernestine! Can you come over tonight and do Latin? Isn't that Cicero the worst thing—! Tell your mother you *have* to. G'bye. G'bye, Helen. G'bye, Fred.

[GEORGE, *also carrying books, catches up with her.*]

GEORGE. Can I carry your books home for you, Emily?

EMILY. [*Cooly.*] Why . . . uh . . . Thank you. It isn't far. [*She gives them to him.*]

GEORGE. Excuse me a minute, Emily. Say, Bob, if I'm a little late, start practice anyway. And give Herb some long high ones.

EMILY. Good-bye, Lizzy.

GEORGE. Good-bye, Lizzy. I'm awfully glad you were elected, too, Emily.

EMILY. Thank you.

[*They have been standing on Main Street, almost against the back wall. They take the first steps toward the audience when* GEORGE *stops and says:*]

GEORGE. Emily, why are you mad at me?

EMILY. I'm not mad at you.

GEORGE. You've been treating me so funny lately.

EMILY. Well, since you ask me, I might as well say it right out, George—[*She catches sight of a teacher passing.*] Good-bye, Miss Corcoran.

GEORGE. Good-bye, Miss Corcoran. Wha—what is it?

2 **EMILY.** [*Not scoldingly; finding it difficult to say.*] I don't like the whole change that's come over you in the last year. I'm sorry if that hurts your feelings, but I've got to—tell the truth and shame the devil.

GEORGE. A *change?* Wha—what do you mean?

EMILY. Well, up to a year ago I used to like you a lot. And I used to watch you as you did everything . . . because we'd been friends so long . . . and then you began spending all your time at *baseball* . . . and you never stopped to speak to anybody any more. Not even to your own family you didn't . . . and, George, it's a fact, you've got awful conceited and stuck-up, and all the girls say so. They may not say so to your face, but that's what they say about you behind your back, and it hurts me to hear them say it, but I've got to agree with them a little. I'm sorry if it hurts your feelings . . . but I can't be sorry I said it.

3 **GEORGE.** I . . . I'm glad you said it, Emily. I never thought that such a thing was happening to me. I guess it's hard for a fella not to have faults creep into his character.

[*They take a step or two in silence, then stand still in misery.*]

EMILY. I always expect a man to be perfect and I think he should be.

GUIDED READING

LITERAL QUESTIONS

1a. What does the Stage Manager ask the audience to remember? (what it was like to be in love)

2a. What does Emily tell George that people are saying about him? (that he has become conceited and stuck-up)

INFERENTIAL QUESTIONS

1b. Why is it important for the audience to follow his instruction? (It will help them to understand the next scene and what the characters are feeling.)

2b. What does George's response suggest? (He takes her opinion seriously and respects her.)

GEORGE. Oh . . . I don't think it's possible to be perfect, Emily.

1 **EMILY.** Well, my *father* is, and as far as I can see *your* father is. There's no reason on earth why you shouldn't be, too.

GEORGE. Well, I feel it's the other way round. That men aren't naturally good; but girls are.

EMILY. Well, you might as well know right now that I'm not perfect. It's not as easy for a girl to be perfect as a man, because we girls are more—more—nervous. Now I'm sorry I said all that about you. I don't know what made me say it.

GEORGE. Emily—

EMILY. Now I can see it's not the truth at all. And I suddenly feel that it isn't important, anyway.

GEORGE. Emily . . . would you like an ice-cream soda, or something, before you go home?

EMILY. Well, thank you. . . . I would.

[They advance toward the audience and make an abrupt right turn, opening the door of Morgan's drugstore. Under strong emotion, EMILY *keeps her face down.* GEORGE *speaks to some passers-by.]*

GEORGE. Hello, Stew—how are you? Good afternoon, Mrs. Slocum.

2 *[The* STAGE MANAGER, *wearing spectacles and assuming the role of* MR. MORGAN, *enters abruptly from the right and stands between the audience and the counter of his soda fountain.]*

STAGE MANAGER. Hello, George. Hello, Emily.
3 What'll you have? Why, Emily Webb—what you been crying about?

GEORGE. *[He gropes for an explanation.]* She . . . she just got an awful scare, Mr. Morgan. She almost got run over by that hardware store wagon. Everybody says that Tom Huckins drives like a crazy man.

STAGE MANAGER. *[Drawing a drink of water.]* Well now! You take a drink of water, Emily. You look all shook up. I tell you, you've got to look both ways before you cross Main Street these days. Gets worse every year. What'll you have?

EMILY. I'll have a strawberry phosphate, thank you, Mr. Morgan.

GEORGE. No, no, Emily. Have an ice-cream soda with me. Two strawberry ice-cream sodas, Mr. Morgan.

STAGE MANAGER. *[Working the faucets.]* Two strawberry ice-cream sodas, yes sir. Yes, sir. There are a hundred and twenty-five horses in Grover's Corners this minute I'm talking to you. State Inspector was in here yesterday. And now they're bringing in these auto-mo-biles,
4 the best thing to do is to just stay home. Why, I can remember when a dog could go to sleep all day in the middle of Main Street and nothing come along to disturb him. *[He sets the imaginary glasses before them.]* There they are. Enjoy 'em. *[He sees a customer, right.]* Yes, Mrs. Ellis. What can I do for you? *[He goes out right.]*

EMILY. They're so expensive.

GEORGE. No, no—don't you think of that. We're celebrating our election. And then do you know what else I'm celebrating?

EMILY. N-no.

GEORGE. I'm celebrating because I've got a friend who tells me all the things that ought to be told me.

EMILY. George, *please* don't think of that. I don't know why I said it. It's not true. You're—

GEORGE. No, Emily, you stick to it. I'm glad you spoke to me like you did. But you'll *see*: I'm going to change so quick—you bet I'm going to change. And, Emily, I want to ask you a favor.

EMILY. What?

GEORGE. Emily, if I go away to State Agriculture

AT A GLANCE

- Emily tells George that she expects a man to be perfect but admits that she is not perfect.
- When Emily apologizes to George, he takes her for a soda.

1 THEME

The couple expect in each other what they know is impossible in themselves; yet the yearning for perfection and belief in perfectibility are real and universal.

2 POINT OF VIEW

The Stage Manager's function as an omniscient narrator of sorts has been unconventional throughout the play. Here he assumes the role of one of the characters.

3 CONFLICT

Emily experiences an internal conflict. She has deep feelings for George, but instead of stating these she has criticized him.

4 THEME

The developments in transportation within Mr. Morgan's lifetime suggest the continuous march of progress, even though many fundamentals of the human condition remain constant.

GUIDED READING

LITERAL QUESTIONS

1a. For what is Emily sorry? (for saying that George has become conceited and stuck-up)

2a. How does George explain Emily's tears to Mr. Morgan? ("She almost got run over by that hardware store wagon.")

INFERENTIAL QUESTIONS

1b. Why does she apologize? (George's receptive reaction and her feelings for him make her sorry to have criticized him.)

2b. Why does he lie? (He wants to protect Emily and himself from the embarrassment that disclosing their personal conversation would cause.)

AT A GLANCE

- George asks Emily to write to him at college and she agrees.
- She fears he will lose interest in the town, but he assures her he never will.
- He expresses doubts about going to college at all.

1 THEME

Emily puts Grover's Corners in a larger perspective, suggesting that we are part of something larger than ourselves.

2 CONFLICT

George weighs the benefits of college against the possibility of drifting apart from Emily and Grover's Corners.

College next year, will you write me a letter once in a while?

EMILY. I certainly will. I certainly will, George . . .

[*Pause. They start sipping the sodas through the straws.*]

It certainly seems like being away three years you'd get out of touch with things. Maybe letters from Grover's Corners wouldn't be so in-
1 teresting after a while. Grover's Corners isn't a very important place when you think of all— New Hampshire; but I think it's a very nice town.

GEORGE. The day wouldn't come when I wouldn't want to know everything that's happening here. I know *that's* true, Emily.

EMILY. Well, I'll try to make my letters interesting. [*Pause.*]

GEORGE. Y'know, Emily, whenever I meet a farmer I ask him if he thinks it's important to go to Agriculture School to be a good farmer.

EMILY. Why, George—

GEORGE. Yeah, and some of them say that it's even a waste of time. You can get all those things, anyway, out of the pamphlets the government sends out. And Uncle Luke's getting old—he's about ready for me to start in taking over his farm tomorrow, if I could.

EMILY. My!

2 **GEORGE.** And, like you say, being gone all that time . . . in other places and meeting other people . . . Gosh, if anything like that can happen I don't want to go away. I guess new people aren't any better than old ones. I'll bet they almost never are. Emily . . . I feel that you're as good a friend as I've got. I don't need to go and meet the people in other towns.

EMILY. But, George, maybe it's very important for you to go and learn all that about—cattle

GUIDED READING

LITERAL QUESTION

1a. What does George say that he does not need to do? (go and meet the people in other towns)

INFERENTIAL QUESTION

1b. What feeling underlies this statement? (He is afraid to risk losing Emily.)

judging and soils and those things. . . . Of course, I don't know.

1 **GEORGE.** [*After a pause, very seriously.*] Emily, I'm going to make up my mind right now. I won't go. I'll tell Pa about it tonight.

EMILY. Why, George, I don't see why you have to decide right now. It's a whole year away.

GEORGE. Emily, I'm glad you spoke to me about that . . . that fault in my character. What you said was right; but there was *one* thing wrong in it, and that was when you said that for a year I wasn't noticing people, and . . . you, for instance. Why, you say you were watching me when I did everything . . . I was doing the same about you all the time. Why, sure—I always thought about you as one of the chief people I thought about. I always made sure where you were sitting on the bleachers, and who you were with, and for three days now I've been trying to walk home with you; but something's always got in the way. Yesterday I was standing over against the wall waiting for you, and you walked home with *Miss Corcoran.*

EMILY. George! . . . Life's awful funny! How could I have known that? Why, I thought—

GEORGE. Listen, Emily, I'm going to tell you why I'm not going to Agriculture School. I think that once you've found a person that you're very fond of . . . I mean a person who's fond of you, too, and likes you enough to be interested in your character . . . Well, I think that's just as important as college is, and even more so. That's what I think.

EMILY. I think it's awfully important, too.

GEORGE. Emily.

EMILY. Y-yes, George.

2 **GEORGE.** Emily, if I *do* improve and make a big change . . . would you be . . . I mean: *could* you be . . .

EMILY. I . . . I am now; I always have been.

GEORGE. [*Pause.*] So I guess this is an important talk we've been having.

EMILY. Yes . . . yes.

GEORGE. [*Takes a deep breath and straightens his back.*] Wait just a minute and I'll walk you home.

[*With mounting alarm he digs into his pockets for the money.*
The STAGE MANAGER *enters, right.*
GEORGE, *deeply embarrassed, but direct, says to him:*]

Mr. Morgan, I'll have to go home and get the money to pay you for this. It'll only take me a minute.

STAGE MANAGER. [*Pretending to be affronted.*] What's that? George Gibbs, do you mean to tell me—!

GEORGE. Yes, but I had reasons, Mr. Morgan. Look, here's my gold watch to keep until I come back with the money.

STAGE MANAGER. That's all right. Keep your watch. I'll trust you.

GEORGE. I'll be back in five minutes.

STAGE MANAGER. I'll trust you ten years, George—not a day over. Got all over your shock, Emily?

EMILY. Yes, thank you, Mr. Morgan. It was nothing.

GEORGE. [*Taking up the books from the counter.*] I'm ready.

[*They walk in grave silence across the stage and pass through the trellis at the Webbs' back door and disappear.*
The STAGE MANAGER *watches them go out, then turns to the audience, removing his spectacles.*]

3 **STAGE MANAGER.** Well—[*He claps his hands as a signal.*] Now we're ready to get on with the wedding.

[*He stands waiting while the set is prepared for the next scene.*

AT A GLANCE

- George decides not to go away to college.
- He confesses to Emily how much she means to him.
- Emily implies that she feels the same about him, and they leave the drugstore.

1 PLOT: CLIMAX

George's decision to remain at home—and marry Emily—is a turning point in his relationship with Emily.

2 CHARACTERIZATION

Emily and George are so close and know each other so well that both know their love is declared even though the word is not used.

3 FLASHBACK

The intrusion of the Stage Manager signals the end of the flashback. It suggests that nothing critical happened from that time until the day of the wedding.

GUIDED READING

LITERAL QUESTIONS

1a. What does George say he is glad that Emily told him about? (the fault in his character)

2a. What kind of talk does he say that they have been having? (important)

INFERENTIAL QUESTIONS

1b. Why is he glad? (He learned that she cared about him; he had been looking for an opportunity to talk with her.)

2b. Why does he think so? (The two have agreed, though not in so many words, to get married.)

AT A GLANCE

- The stage is set for the wedding and the Stage Manager says he will play the minister.
- Nature, he says, is interested in both quantity and quality.
- As the wedding is about to take place, Mrs. Webb fears that Emily is unprepared for married life.

1 THEME

Nature is striving toward perfection.

2 THEME

By suggesting that the dead still are interested in the living, the Stage Manager both reminds the audience of the cycles of life and hints at action to come in Act 3.

3 POINT OF VIEW

In a short story the omniscient narrator is able to get inside the minds of the characters. Here this is accomplished by letting the character tell the audience what is on her mind. Mrs. Webb expresses the sadness that accompanies change, even when the change is positive.

STAGEHANDS *remove the chairs, tables and trellises from the Gibbs and Webb houses.*
They arrange the pews for the church in the center of the stage. The congregation will sit facing the back wall. The aisle of the church starts at the center of the back wall and comes toward the audience.
A small platform is placed against the back wall on which the STAGE MANAGER *will stand later, playing the minister. The image of a stained-glass window is cast from a lantern slide upon the back wall.*
When all is ready the STAGE MANAGER *strolls to the center of the stage, down front, and, musingly, addresses the audience.*]

There are a lot of things to be said about a wedding; there are a lot of thoughts that go on during a wedding.
We can't get them all into one wedding, naturally, and especially not into a wedding at Grover's Corners, where they're awfully plain and short.
In this wedding I play the minister. That gives me the right to say a few more things about it.
For a while now, the play gets pretty serious.
Y'see, some churches say that marriage is a sacrament. I don't quite know what that means, but I can guess. Like Mrs. Gibbs said a few minutes ago: People were made to live two-by-two.

This is a good wedding, but people are so put together that even at a good wedding there's a lot of confusion way down deep in people's minds and we thought that that ought to be in our play, too.
The real hero of this scene isn't on the stage at all, and you know who that is. It's like what
1 one of those European fellas said: every child born into the world is nature's attempt to make a perfect human being. Well, we've seen nature pushing and contriving for some time now. We all know that nature's interested in quantity; but I think she's interested in quality, too—that's why I'm in the ministry.
2 And don't forget all the other witnesses at this wedding—the ancestors. Millions of them. Most of them set out to live two-by-two, also. Millions of them.
Well, that's all my sermon. 'Twan't very long, anyway.

[*The organ starts playing Handel's "Largo."*
The congregation streams into the church and sits in silence.
Church bells are heard.
MRS. GIBBS *sits in the front row, the first seat on the aisle, the right section; next to her are* REBECCA *and* DR. GIBBS. *Across the aisle* MRS. WEBB, WALLY *and* MR. WEBB. *A small choir takes its place, facing the audience under the stained-glass window.*
MRS. WEBB, *on the way to her place, turns back and speaks to the audience.*]

3 **MRS. WEBB.** I don't know why on earth I should be crying. I suppose there's nothing to cry about. It came over me at breakfast this morning; there was Emily eating her breakfast as she's done for seventeen years and now she's going off to eat it in someone else's house. I suppose that's it.
And Emily! She suddenly said: I can't eat another mouthful, and she put her head down on the table and *she* cried.

[*She starts toward her seat in the church, but turns back and adds:*]

Oh, I've got to say it: you know, there's something downright cruel about sending our girls out into marriage this way.
I hope some of her girl friends have told her a thing or two. It's cruel, I know, but I couldn't bring myself to say anything. I went into it blind as a bat myself.

[*In half-amused exasperation.*]

The whole world's wrong, that's what's the matter. There they come.

[*She hurries to her place in the pew.*
GEORGE *starts to come down the right aisle of the theatre, through the audience.*
Suddenly THREE MEMBERS *of his baseball team appear by the right proscenium pillar*

GUIDED READING

LITERAL QUESTIONS

1a. Who does the Stage Manager say is not on the stage? ("the real hero of this scene")

2a. Who are the "other witnesses" that the Stage Manager says not to forget? (ancestors)

INFERENTIAL QUESTIONS

1b. Whom does he mean? (God or nature)

2b. What is the purpose of this reminder? (It brings the focus back to the theme of the individual as part of a larger order.)

and start whistling and catcalling to him. They are dressed for the ball field.]

THE BASEBALL PLAYERS. Eh, George, George! Hast—yaow! Look at him, fellas—he looks scared to death. Yaow! George, don't look so innocent, you old geezer. We know what you're thinking. Don't disgrace the team, big boy. Whoo-oo-oo.

STAGE MANAGER. All right! All right! That'll do. That's enough of that.

[*Smiling, he pushes them off the stage. They lean back to shout a few more catcalls.*]

1 There used to be an awful lot of that kind of thing at weddings in the old days—Rome, and later. We're more civilized now—so they say.

[*The choir starts singing "Love Divine, All Love Excelling—."* GEORGE *has reached the stage. He stares at the congregation a moment, then takes a few steps of withdrawal, toward the right proscenium pillar. His mother, from the front row, seems to have felt his confusion. She leaves her seat and comes down the aisle quickly to him.*]

2 **MRS. GIBBS.** George! George! What's the matter?

GEORGE. Ma, I don't want to grow old. Why's everybody pushing me so?

MRS. GIBBS. Why, George . . . you wanted it.

GEORGE. No, Ma, listen to me—

MRS. GIBBS. No, no, George—you're a man now.

GEORGE. Listen, Ma—for the last time I ask you . . . All I want to do is to be a fella—

MRS. GIBBS. George! If anyone should hear you! Now stop. Why, I'm ashamed of you!

GEORGE. [*He comes to himself and looks over the scene.*] What? Where's Emily?

MRS. GIBBS. [*Relieved.*] George! You gave me such a turn.

GEORGE. Cheer up, Ma. I'm getting married.

MRS. GIBBS. Let me catch my breath a minute.

GEORGE. [*Comforting her.*] Now, Ma, you save Thursday nights. Emily and I are coming over to dinner every Thursday night . . . you'll see. Ma, what are you crying for? Come on; we've got to get ready for this.

[MRS. GIBBS, *mastering her emotion, fixes his tie and whispers to him.*
In the meantime, EMILY, *in white and wearing her wedding veil, has come through the audience and mounted onto the stage. She too draws back, frightened, when she sees the congregation in the church. The choir begins: "Blessed Be the Tie That Binds."*]

EMILY. I never felt so alone in my whole life. And George over there, looking so . . .! I *hate* him. I wish I were dead. Papa! Papa!

MR. WEBB.

[*Leaves his seat in the pews and comes toward her anxiously.*]

Emily! Emily! Now don't get upset. . . .

3 **EMILY.** But Papa—I don't want to get married. . . .

MR. WEBB. Sh—sh—Emily. Everything's all right.

EMILY. Why can't I stay for a while just as I am? Let's go away—

MR. WEBB. No, no, Emily. Now stop and think a minute.

EMILY. Don't you remember that you used to say—all the time you used to say—all the time: that I was *your* girl! There must be lots of places we can go to. I'll work for you. I could keep house.

MR. WEBB. Sh . . . You mustn't think of such things. You're just nervous, Emily. [*He turns and calls.*] George! George! Will you come here a minute? [*He leads her toward* GEORGE.] Why you're marrying the best young fellow in the world. George is a fine fellow.

EMILY. But Papa—

AT A GLANCE

- George, having doubts about the marriage, tells his mother he does not want to grow old.
- She tells him that he is a man now, and he recovers to comfort her.
- After Emily expresses her fears to her father, he calls George to steady her.

1 THEME

The Stage Manager reminds viewers that they are part of a great, ongoing cycle. His ironic comment at the end suggests that human nature does not change much through time.

2 CONFLICT

In giving way to his inner fears, George expresses universal doubts. He wants Emily but does not want what marriage implies: responsibilities, aging, and eventual death.

3 COMPARISONS

Emily's doubts and fears are very similar to George's. Like Mrs. Gibbs, Mr. Webb recognizes that these universal fears are natural and that they will pass.

GUIDED READING

LITERAL QUESTIONS

1a. What does George say that everybody is doing to him? (pushing him)

2a. What does Emily say that she feels about George when she sees him? (She hates him.)

INFERENTIAL QUESTIONS

1b. Why does he feel this way? (He is frightened of the inevitability of manhood, so feels propelled by forces he cannot control.)

2b. What may have inspired this feeling? (Marriage to George symbolizes the end of the safety and comfort of childhood.)

AT A GLANCE

- The young couple affirm their love, and the wedding proceeds.
- Mrs. Soames' chatter about the wedding drowns out much of the clergyman's words.

1 DIALOGUE

This simple dialogue expresses a universal human longing.

2 STEREOTYPE

Mrs. Soames represents the stereotypical wedding guest. Her comments are superficial but express the hopes of humankind for every couple.

[MRS. GIBBS *returns unobtrusively to her seat.*
MR. WEBB *has one arm around his daughter.*
He places his hand on GEORGE*'s shoulder.*]

MR. WEBB. I'm giving away my daughter, George. Do you think you can take care of her?

1 **GEORGE.** Mr. Webb, I want to . . . I want to try. Emily, I'm going to do my best. I love you, Emily. I need you.

EMILY. Well, if you love me, help me. All I want is someone to love me.

GEORGE. I will, Emily. Emily, I'll try.

EMILY. And I mean for *ever.* Do you hear? For ever and ever.

[*They fall into each other's arms.*
The March from Lohengrin[3] *is heard.*
The STAGE MANAGER, *as* CLERGYMAN, *stands on the box, up center.*]

MR. WEBB. Come, they're waiting for us. Now you know it'll be all right. Come, quick.

[GEORGE *slips away and takes his place beside the* STAGE MANAGER-CLERGYMAN.
EMILY *proceeds up the aisle on her father's arm.*]

STAGE MANAGER. Do you, George, take this woman, Emily, to be your wedded wife, to have . . .

[MRS. SOAMES *has been sitting in the last row of the congregation.*
She now turns to her neighbors and speaks in a shrill voice. Her chatter drowns out the rest of the clergyman's words.]

2 **MRS. SOAMES.** Perfectly lovely wedding! Loveliest wedding I ever saw. Oh, I do love a good wedding, don't you? Doesn't she make a lovely bride?

GEORGE. I do.

STAGE MANAGER. Do you, Emily, take this man, George, to be your wedded husband—

[*Again his further words are covered by those of* MRS. SOAMES.]

MRS. SOAMES. Don't know *when* I've seen such a lovely wedding. But I always cry. Don't know why it is, but I always cry. I just like to see young people happy, don't you? Oh, I think it's lovely.

[*The ring.*
The kiss.
The stage is suddenly arrested into silent tableau.
The STAGE MANAGER, *his eyes on the distance, as though to himself:*]

3. ***March . . .* Lohengrin** [lō′ən grin′]: wedding march from the opera *Lohengrin* by German composer Richard Wagner (1813–1883); often called "Here Comes the Bride."

GUIDED READING

LITERAL QUESTIONS

1a. What does Emily say is all she wants, and for how long does she want it? (someone to love her for ever and ever)

2a. What kind of wedding does Mrs. Soames say that it is? (lovely)

INFERENTIAL QUESTIONS

1b. Why does she emphasize the time factor? (She wants to be sure that George's love is one thing in her life that will never change.)

2b. Why, then, does Mrs. Soames cry? (She feels the deep emotion that accompanies an occasion that is both solemn and happy.)

STAGE MANAGER. I've married over two hundred couples in my day.
Do I believe in it?
I don't know.
1 M. . . . marries N. . . . millions of them.
The cottage, the go-cart, the Sunday-afternoon drives in the Ford, the first rheumatism, the grandchildren, the second rheumatism, the deathbed, the reading of the will—

[*He now looks at the audience for the first time, with a warm smile that removes any sense of cynicism from the next line.*]

Once in a thousand times it's interesting.
—Well, let's have Mendelssohn's "Wedding March"![4]

[*The organ picks up the March.*
The BRIDE *and* GROOM *come down the aisle, radiant, but trying to be very dignified.*]

2 **MRS. SOAMES.** Aren't they a lovely couple? Oh, I've never been to such a nice wedding. I'm sure they'll be happy. I always say: *happiness,* that's the great thing! The important thing is to be happy.

[*The* BRIDE *and* GROOM *reach the steps leading into the audience. A bright light is thrown upon them. They descend into the auditorium and run up the aisle joyously.*]

STAGE MANAGER. That's all the Second Act, folks. Ten minutes' intermission.

CURTAIN

4. **Mendelssohn's** [mend'əl sənz] **"Wedding March":** popular recessional march from the ballet *A Midsummer Night's Dream* by German composer Felix Mendelssohn (1809–1847).

STUDY QUESTIONS

Recalling

1. How much time has passed between Acts 1 and 2? What does the Stage Manager say Act 1 is called? Act 2? What does he say about Act 3?
2. What does the Stage Manager say happens just after high school commencement?
3. What scene do Emily and George replay after George leaves the Webb house? In that scene what does Emily tell George he has become? What does he decide he is not going to do, and why?
4. Who marries the couple? What does he say about the "real hero" of the scene (page 696)? About "every child"?
5. What protest does George make to his mother just before the wedding? What does Emily protest to her father?

Interpreting

6. Why might Wilder show us the morning of the wedding before he shows us Emily and George becoming engaged?
7. In the engagement scene do Emily and George actually declare their love for each other in so many words? What does your answer suggest about their relationship?
8. Are Emily's prenuptial misgivings similar to George's? What seems to cause the misgivings of each?
9. Who is the Stage Manager suggesting is the "real hero" of the wedding? (Consider what he says about every child born.)
10. Do we know what the third act will be about, as the Stage Manager suggests? If so, what? (Consider the information the Stage Manager wanted to preserve by putting the play into a "time capsule" in Act 1.)
11. In quoting Lucinda Matlock (page 687), what is the Stage Manager suggesting about the people who live in Grover's Corners?

Extending

12. At the wedding Mrs. Soames exclaims, "The important thing is to be happy." Do you agree? Think of lives, from your reading or experience, that you admire. What besides happiness might be equally important?

AT A GLANCE

- The Stage Manager sums up the events of married life.
- As the bride and groom come down the aisle, Mrs. Soames says happiness is "the great thing."
- The Stage Manager ends the second act.

1 THEME

Life is short and goes by quickly in myriad ordinary, everyday occurrences.

2 RESPONSE JOURNAL

Ask students to explain why they believe that Wilder's view does or does not agree with that of Mrs. Soames—namely, "The important thing is to be happy."

REFLECTING ON ACT 2

How are the wedding and its participants symbolic? (Students may suggest that each character represents typical people in that situation.)

STUDY QUESTIONS

1. three years; Daily Life; Love and Marriage; "I reckon you can guess what that's about."
2. Most young people marry.
3. scene in which they first knew they were meant for each other; conceited; go to college, because having found a person he cares for is more important
4. Stage Manager; not on stage; nature's attempt to make a perfect human being
5. being pushed to grow up; does not want to marry, hates George, does not want change
6. tells us marriage is inevitable; focuses our attention on cause–effect relationships
7. no; feel no need to state love because they see marriage as inevitable; are so close that they know their love is declared even though the word is not used
8. Yes. Each feels young and unready to take on responsibility; wishes to stay young and be protected; fears aging and death.
9. God or nature is the real hero.
10. yes; death
11. They are simple people living simple lives as fully and as well as they know how.
12. Students might say the need for love, understanding, achievement, excitement, challenge, etc.

AT A GLANCE

- The Stage Manager enumerates nine years of change in Grover's Corners.
- He presents the graveyard and points out the old markers.
- He indicates the newer graves of Mrs. Gibbs, Wally Webb, Mrs. Soames, Mr. Stimson.

LITERARY OPTIONS

- flashback
- repetition

THEMATIC OPTIONS

- the eternal quality of the individual
- lack of awareness of life

1 MOOD

The Stage Manager's description of the graveyard suggests spaciousness and timeless strength. It creates a mood of tranquility.

2 TONE

The Stage Manager's tone is matter-of-fact as he mentions the deaths that have occurred among the characters. He accepts these events as natural and expected.

3 VOCABULARY: CONNOTATION

A *fit* is a sudden burst of activity or disturbance that passes away. The surprising use of it as a synonym for *life* suggests both life's turbulence and transience.

ACT 3

[During the intermission the audience has seen the STAGEHANDS *arranging the stage. On the right-hand side, a little right of the center, ten or twelve ordinary chairs have been placed in three openly spaced rows facing the audience. These are graves in the cemetery.*
Toward the end of the intermission the ACTORS *enter and take their places. The front row contains: toward the center of the stage, an empty chair; then* MRS. GIBBS; SIMON STIMSON.
The second row contains, among others, MRS. SOAMES.
The third row has WALLY WEBB.
The dead do not turn their heads or their eyes to right or left, but they sit in a quiet without stiffness. When they speak their tone is matter-of-fact, without sentimentality and, above all, without lugubriousness.

The STAGE MANAGER *takes his accustomed place and waits for the house lights to go down.*]

STAGE MANAGER. This time nine years have gone by, friends—summer, 1913.
Gradual changes in Grover's Corners. Horses are getting rarer.
Farmers coming into town in Fords.
Everybody locks their house doors now at night. Ain't been any burglars in town yet, but everybody's heard about 'em.
You'd be surprised, though—on the whole, things don't change much around here. This is certainly an important part of Grover's Cor-
1 ners. It's on a hilltop—a windy hilltop—lots of sky, lots of clouds—often lots of sun and moon and stars. You come up here, on a fine afternoon and you can see range on range of hills—awful blue they are—up there by Lake Sunapee and Lake Winnipesaukee . . . and way up, if you've got a glass, you can see the White Mountains and Mt. Washington—where North Conway and Conway is. And, of course, our favorite mountain, Mt. Monadnock, 's right here—and all these towns that lie around it: Jaffrey, 'n East Jaffrey, 'n Peterborough, 'n Dublin; and [*Then pointing down in the audience.*] there, quite a ways down, is Grover's Corners.
Yes, beautiful spot up here. Mountain laurel and lilacs. I often wonder why people like to be buried in Woodlawn and Brooklyn when they might pass the same time up here in New Hampshire. Over there—[*Pointing to stage left.*] are the old stones—1670, 1680. Strong-minded people that come a long way to be independent. Summer people walk around there laughing at the funny words on the tombstones . . . it don't do any harm. And genealogists come up from Boston—get paid by city people for looking up their ancestors. They want to make sure they're Daughters of the American Revolution[1] and of the *Mayflower*. . . . Well, I guess that don't do any harm, either. Wherever you come near the human race, there's layers and layers of nonsense. . . .

Over there are some Civil War veterans. Iron flags on their graves . . . New Hampshire boys . . . had a notion that the Union ought to be kept together, though they'd never seen more than fifty miles of it themselves. All they knew was the name, friends—the United States of America. The United States of America. And they went and died about it.
This here is the new part of the cemetery.
2 Here's your friend Mrs. Gibbs. 'N let me see—Here's Mr. Stimson, organist at the Congregational Church. And Mrs. Soames who enjoyed the wedding so—you remember? Oh, and a lot of others. And Editor Webb's boy, Wallace, whose appendix burst while he was on a Boy Scout trip to Crawford Notch.
Yes, an awful lot of sorrow has sort of quieted down up here. People just wild with grief have brought their relatives up to this hill. We all know how it is . . . and then time . . . and sunny days . . . and rainy days . . . 'n snow
3 . . . We're all glad they're in a beautiful place and we're coming up here ourselves when our fit's over.

1. **Daughters . . . Revolution:** society of women whose ancestors fought in the American Revolution.

GUIDED READING

LITERAL QUESTION

1a. What does the Stage Manager say has happened to sorrow in this place? (It has "quieted down.")

INFERENTIAL QUESTION

1b. What might cause this change? (Time and the peace and serenity of the place eventually cause sorrow to fade.)

Now there are some things we all know, but we don't take'm out and look at'm very often.
1 We all know that *something* is eternal. And it ain't houses and it ain't names, and it ain't earth, and it ain't even the stars . . . everybody knows in their bones that *something* is eternal, and that something has to do with human beings. All the greatest people ever lived have been telling us that for five thousand years and yet you'd be surprised how people are always losing hold of it. There's something way down deep that's eternal about every human being. [*Pause.*]
2 You know as well as I do that the dead don't stay interested in us living people for very long. Gradually, gradually, they lose hold of the earth . . . and the ambitions they had . . . and the pleasures they had . . . and the things they suffered . . . and the people they loved.
They get weaned away from earth—that's the way I put it—weaned away.
And they stay here while the earth part of 'em burns away, burns out; and all that time they slowly get indifferent to what's goin' on in Grover's Corners. They're waitin'. They're waitin' for something that they feel is comin'. Something important, and great. Aren't they waitin' for the eternal part in them to come out clear?
Some of the things they're going to say maybe'll hurt your feelings—but that's the way it is: mother 'n daughter . . . husband 'n wife . . . enemy 'n enemy . . . money 'n miser . . . all those terribly important things kind of grow pale around here. And what's left when memory's gone, and your identity, Mrs. Smith?

[*He looks at the audience a minute, then turns to the stage.*]

Well! There are some *living* people. There's Joe Stoddard, our undertaker, supervising a new-made grave. And here comes a Grover's Corners boy, that left town to go out West.

[JOE STODDARD *has hovered about in the background.* SAM CRAIG *enters left, wiping his forehead from the exertion. He carries an umbrella and strolls front.*]

SAM CRAIG. Good afternoon, Joe Stoddard.

JOE STODDARD. Good afternoon, good afternoon. Let me see now: do I know you?

SAM CRAIG. I'm Sam Craig.

JOE STODDARD. Gracious sakes' alive! Of all people! I should'a knowed you'd be back for the funeral. You've been away a long time Sam.

SAM CRAIG. Yes, I've been away over twelve years. I'm in business out in Buffalo now, Joe. But I was in the East when I got news of my cousin's death, so I thought I'd combine things a little and come and see the old home. You look well.

JOE STODDARD. Yes, yes, can't complain. Very sad, our journey today, Samuel.

SAM CRAIG. Yes.

JOE STODDARD. Yes, yes. I always say I hate to supervise when a young person is taken. They'll be here in a few minutes now. I had to come here early today—my son's supervisin' at the home.

SAM CRAIG. [*Reading stones.*] Old Farmer McCarty, I used to do chores for him—after school. He had the lumbago.

JOE STODDARD. Yes, we brought Farmer McCarty here a number of years ago now.

3 **SAM CRAIG.** [*Staring at* MRS. GIBBS' knees.] Why, this is my Aunt Julia . . . I'd forgotten that she'd . . . of course, of course.

JOE STODDARD. Yes, Doc Gibbs lost his wife two-three years ago . . . about this time. And today's another pretty bad blow for him, too.

MRS. GIBBS. [*To* SIMON STIMSON: *in an even voice.*] That's my sister Carey's boy, Sam . . . Sam Craig.

SIMON STIMSON. I'm always uncomfortable when *they're* around.

MRS. GIBBS. Simon.

SAM CRAIG. Do they choose their own verses much, Joe?

AT A GLANCE

- The Stage Manager says that there is something eternal in everyone.
- While Joe Stoddard is preparing a grave, Sam Craig arrives, saying that he has come for his cousin's funeral.
- Mrs. Gibbs recognizes Sam as her sister's son.

1 THEME

The "eternal" is unknown and undefined, but the sense of it persists through the ages.

2 IRONY

The Stage Manager imputes to the dead the forgetfulness usually attributed to the living.

3 SUSPENSE

The discussion between Joe and Sam hints at the death of a character important to Dr. Gibbs, without revealing who it is.

GUIDED READING

LITERAL QUESTION

1a. What does Joe say that today will be for Dr. Gibbs? ("another pretty bad blow")

INFERENTIAL QUESTION

1b. What does this probably mean? (Dr. Gibbs must have lost someone else important to him, probably another member of his family.)

AT A GLANCE

- Sam Craig learns that his cousin died in childbirth.
- The funeral procession arrives.
- Mrs. Gibbs says that the dead person is Emily, and Mrs. Soames reminisces about her.

1 IRONY

Simon Stimson's carefully chosen message to the living has had little lasting effect; in death, as in life, Stimson has been misunderstood.

2 THEME

In a detached manner, Mrs. Soames remembers the positive and negative aspects of life.

JOE STODDARD. No . . . not usual. Mostly the bereaved pick a verse.

SAM CRAIG. Doesn't sound like Aunt Julia. There aren't many of those Hersey sisters left now. Let me see: where are . . . I wanted to look at my father's and mother's . . .

JOE STODDARD. Over there with the Craigs . . . Avenue F.

SAM CRAIG. [*Reading* SIMON STIMSON's *epitaph.*] He was organist at church, wasn't he? Hm, drank a lot, we used to say.

JOE STODDARD. Nobody was supposed to know about it. He'd seen a peck of trouble. [*Behind his hand.*] Took his own life, y'know?

SAM CRAIG. Oh, did he?

JOE STODDARD. Hung himself in the attic. They tried to hush it up, but of course it got around. He chose his own epytaph. You can see it there. It ain't a verse exactly.

1 **SAM CRAIG.** Why, it's just some notes of music—what is it?

JOE STODDARD. Oh, I wouldn't know. It was wrote up in the Boston papers at the time.

SAM CRAIG. Joe, what did she die of?

JOE STODDARD. Who?

SAM CRAIG. My cousin.

JOE STODDARD. Oh, didn't you know? Had some trouble bringing a baby into the world. 'Twas her second, though. There's a little boy 'bout four years old.

SAM CRAIG. [*Opening his umbrella.*] The grave's going to be over there?

JOE STODDARD. Yes, there ain't much more room over here among the Gibbses, so they're opening up a whole new Gibbs section over by Avenue B. You'll excuse me now. I see they're comin'.

[*From left to center, at the back of the stage, comes a procession.* FOUR MEN *carry a casket, invisible to us. All the rest are under umbrellas. One can vaguely see:* DR. GIBBS, GEORGE, *the* WEBBS, *etc. They gather about a grave in the back center of the stage, a little to the left of center.*]

MRS. SOAMES. Who is it, Julia?

MRS. GIBBS. [*Without raising her eyes.*] My daughter-in-law, Emily Webb.

MRS. SOAMES. [*A little surprised, but no emotion.*] Well, I declare! The road up here must have been awful muddy. What did she die of, Julia?

MRS. GIBBS. In childbirth.

2 **MRS. SOAMES.** Childbirth. [*Almost with a laugh.*] I'd forgotten all about that. My, wasn't life awful—[*With a sigh.*] and wonderful.

SIMON STIMSON. [*With a sideways glance.*] Wonderful, was it?

MRS. GIBBS. Simon! Now, remember!

MRS. SOAMES. I remember Emily's wedding. Wasn't it a lovely wedding! And I remember her reading the class poem at Graduation Exercises. Emily was one of the brightest girls ever graduated from High School. I've heard Principal Wilkins say so time after time. I called on them at their new farm, just before I died. Perfectly beautiful farm.

A WOMAN FROM AMONG THE DEAD. It's on the same road we lived on.

A MAN AMONG THE DEAD. Yepp, right smart farm.

[*They subside. The group by the grave starts singing "Blessed Be the Tie That Binds."*]

A WOMAN AMONG THE DEAD. I always liked that hymn. I was hopin' they'd sing a hymn.

[*Pause. Suddenly* EMILY *appears from among the umbrellas. She is wearing a white dress. Her hair is down her back and tied by a white ribbon like a little girl. She comes slowly, gazing wonderingly at the dead, a little dazed.*

She stops halfway and smiles faintly. After looking at the mourners for a moment, she

GUIDED READING

LITERAL QUESTIONS

1a. What was Simon Stimson's epitaph? (some notes of music)

2a. What words does Mrs. Soames use to describe life? ("awful—and wonderful")

INFERENTIAL QUESTIONS

1b. Why might he have chosen such an epitaph for himself? (He had been a musician, and music is a way of communicating.)

2b. What does she mean? (Life is a mixture of sorrow and joy.)

walks slowly to a vacant chair beside MRS. GIBBS *and sits down.*]

EMILY. [*To them all, quietly, smiling.*] Hello.

MRS. SOAMES. Hello, Emily.

A MAN AMONG THE DEAD. Hello, M's Gibbs.

EMILY. [*Warmly.*] Hello, Mother Gibbs.

MRS. GIBBS. Emily.

EMILY. Hello. [*With surprise.*] It's raining. [*Her eyes drift back to the funeral company.*]

MRS. GIBBS. Yes . . . They'll be gone soon, dear. Just rest yourself.

EMILY. It seems thousands and thousands of years since I . . . Papa remembered that that was my favorite hymn.
Oh, I wish I'd been here a long time. I don't like being new here. How do you do, Mr. Stimson?

SIMON STIMSON. How do you do, Emily.

[EMILY *continues to look about her with a wondering smile; as though to shut out from her mind the thought of the funeral company she starts speaking to* MRS. GIBBS *with a touch of nervousness.*]

1 **EMILY.** Mother Gibbs, George and I have made that farm into just the best place you ever saw. We thought of you all the time. We wanted to show you the new barn and a great long cement drinking fountain for the stock. We bought that out of the money you left us.

MRS. GIBBS. I did?

EMILY. Don't you remember, Mother Gibbs—the legacy you left us? Why, it was over three hundred and fifty dollars.

MRS. GIBBS. Yes, yes, Emily.

EMILY. Well, there's a patent device on the drinking fountain so that it never overflows, Mother Gibbs, and it never sinks below a certain mark they have there. It's fine.

[*Her voice trails off and her eyes return to the funeral group.*]

It won't be the same to George without me, but it's a lovely farm.

[*Suddenly she looks directly at Mrs. Gibbs.*]

2 Live people don't understand, do they?

MRS. GIBBS. No, dear—not very much.

EMILY. They're sort of shut up in little boxes, aren't they? I feel as though I knew them last a thousand years ago . . . My boy is spending the day at Mrs. Carter's. [*She sees* MR. CARTER *among the dead.*] Oh, Mr. Carter, my little boy is spending the day at your house.

MR. CARTER. Is he?

EMILY. Yes, he loves it there.—Mother Gibbs, we have a Ford, too. Never gives any trouble. I don't drive, though. Mother Gibbs, when does this feeling go away? Of being . . . one of *them?* How long does it . . . ?

MRS. GIBBS. Sh! dear. Just wait and be patient.

EMILY. [*With a sigh.*] I know. Look, they're finished. They're going.

MRS. GIBBS. Sh—.

[*The umbrellas leave the stage.* DR. GIBBS *has come over to his wife's grave and stands before it a moment.* EMILY *looks up at his face.* MRS. GIBBS *does not raise her eyes.*]

EMILY. Look! Father Gibbs is bringing some of my flowers to you. He looks just like George,
3 doesn't he? Oh, Mother Gibbs, I never realized before how troubled and how . . . how in the dark live persons are. Look at him. I loved him so. From morning till night, that's all they are—troubled.

[DR. GIBBS *goes off.*]

THE DEAD. Little cooler than it was. Yes, that rain's cooled it off a little. Those northeast winds always do the same thing, don't they? If it isn't a rain, it's a three-day blow.

[*A patient calm falls on the stage. The* STAGE MANAGER *appears at his proscenium pillar, smoking.* EMILY *sits up abruptly with an idea.*]

AT A GLANCE

- Emily appears among the dead.
- She tells Mrs. Gibbs how George and she improved their farm.
- She wonders how long it takes to stop feeling like one of the living and notices how troubled live persons are.

1 CHARACTERIZATION

Enthusiasm and energy show Emily's youth in regard both to her worldly life and to her experience with death. She is more "alive" than the other dead, who have grown acclimated to waiting.

2 THEME

Emily begins to see the limited awareness with which most people live their lives.

3 THEME

Emily's new perspective enables her to see how the troubles and cares of life prevent people from understanding and appreciating their lives.

GUIDED READING

LITERAL QUESTIONS

1a. What did Mrs. Gibbs leave to Emily and George? (a legacy of more than three hundred fifty dollars)

2a. What does Emily realize about the living? (They are troubled and "in the dark.")

INFERENTIAL QUESTIONS

1b. Why does Mrs. Gibbs not remember this event? (It is one of the now unimportant details of life that have slipped from her memory.)

2b. What prompts this realization? (She sees Dr. Gibbs still grieving for his wife.)

AT A GLANCE

- Emily realizes that she can go back and live days over again.
- The dead advise her not to do so, but she insists, saying that she will choose a happy day.
- The Stage Manager warns her that she will watch herself living it and see the thing the living never know.

1 POINT OF VIEW

Again, the Stage Manager is seen as an omniscient character. Not only can he speak with certainty about the future, but he can converse with the dead.

2 FORESHADOWING

The Stage Manager's warning foreshadows that Emily's experience among the living will not be a happy one.

EMILY. But, Mother Gibbs, one can go back; one can go back there again . . . into living. I feel it. I know it. Why just then for a moment I was thinking about . . . about the farm . . . and for a minute I *was* there, and my baby was on my lap as plain as day.

MRS. GIBBS. Yes, of course you can.

EMILY. I can go back there and live all those days over again . . . why not?

MRS. GIBBS. All I can say is, Emily, don't.

EMILY. [*She appeals urgently to the* STAGE MANAGER.] But it's true, isn't it? I can go and live . . . back there . . . again.

1 **STAGE MANAGER.** Yes, some have tried—but they soon come back here.

MRS. GIBBS. Don't do it, Emily.

MRS. SOAMES. Emily, don't. It's not what you think it'd be.

EMILY. But I won't live over a sad day. I'll choose a happy one—I'll choose the day I first knew that I loved George. Why should that be painful?

[THEY *are silent. Her question turns to the* STAGE MANAGER.]

2 **STAGE MANAGER.** You not only live it; but you watch yourself living it.

EMILY. Yes?

STAGE MANAGER. And as you watch it, you see the thing that they—down there—never know.

GUIDED READING

LITERAL QUESTION

1a. According to the Stage Manager, what happens when someone relives a day? ("You not only live it; but you watch yourself living it.")

INFERENTIAL QUESTION

1b. Why, then, might Emily's wish be inadvisable? (She would notice things that she had not seen before but would be unable to change them.)

You see the future. You know what's going to happen afterwards.

EMILY. But is that—painful? Why?

MRS. GIBBS. That's not the only reason why you shouldn't do it, Emily. When you've been here longer you'll see that our life here is to forget all that, and think only of what's ahead, and be ready for what's ahead. When you've been here longer you'll understand.

EMILY. [*Softly.*] But, Mother Gibbs, how can I *ever* forget that life? It's all I know. It's all I had.

MRS. SOAMES. Oh, Emily. It isn't wise. Really, it isn't.

EMILY. But it's a thing I must know for myself. I'll choose a happy day, anyway.

MRS. GIBBS. *No!* At least, choose an unimportant day. Choose the least important day in your life. It will be important enough.

EMILY. [*To herself.*] Then it can't be since I was married; or since the baby was born. [*To the stage manager, eagerly.*] I can choose a birthday at least, can't I? I choose my twelfth birthday.

STAGE MANAGER. All right. February 11th, 1899. A Tuesday. Do you want any special time of day?

EMILY. Oh, I want the whole day.

1 **STAGE MANAGER.** We'll begin at dawn. You remember it had been snowing for several days; but it had stopped the night before, and they had begun clearing the roads. The sun's coming up.

EMILY. [*With a cry; rising.*] There's Main Street . . . why, that's Mr. Morgan's drugstore before he changed it! . . . And there's the livery stable.

[*The stage at no time in this act has been very dark; but now the left half of the stage gradually becomes very bright—the brightness of a crisp winter morning.*
EMILY *walks toward Main Street.*]

STAGE MANAGER. Yes, it's 1899. This is fourteen years ago.

EMILY. Oh, that's the town I knew as a little girl. And, *look,* there's the old white fence that used to be around our house. Oh, I'd forgotten that! Oh, I love it so! Are they inside?

STAGE MANAGER. Yes, your mother'll be coming downstairs in a minute to make breakfast.

EMILY. [*Softly.*] Will she?

STAGE MANAGER. And you remember: your father had been away for several days; he came back on the early-morning train.

EMILY. No . . .?

STAGE MANAGER. He'd been back to his college to make a speech—in western New York, at Clinton.

EMILY. Look! There's Howie Newsome. There's our policeman. But he's *dead;* he *died.*

[*The voices of* HOWIE NEWSOME, CONSTABLE WARREN *and* JOE CROWELL, JR., *are heard at the left of the stage.* EMILY *listens in delight.*]

HOWIE NEWSOME. Whoa, Bessie!—Bessie! 'Morning, Bill.

CONSTABLE WARREN. Morning, Howie.

HOWIE NEWSOME. You're up early.

CONSTABLE WARREN. Been rescuin' a party; darn near froze to death, down by Polish Town thar. Got drunk and lay out in the snowdrifts. Thought he was in bed when I shook'm.

EMILY. Why, there's Joe Crowell . . .

2 **JOE CROWELL.** Good morning, Mr. Warren. 'Morning, Howie.

[MRS. WEBB *has appeared in her kitchen, but* EMILY *does not see her until she calls.*]

MRS. WEBB. Chil-*dren!* Wally! Emily! . . . Time to get up.

EMILY. Mama, I'm here! Oh! how young Mama

AT A GLANCE

- Mrs. Gibbs tells Emily that the dead must forget the past and think only of what is ahead.
- After Mrs. Gibbs' warning to choose an unimportant day, Emily decides to relive her twelfth birthday.
- As the day begins Emily sees Howie, the Constable, Joe Crowell, and her mother as they were in 1899.

1 FLASHBACK

The flashback is unusual because Emily both observes it and participates in it.

2 REPETITION

Here the dawn routine of Acts 1 and 2 is repeated. This shows how things remain constant and also how they change. The routine differs slightly each time the scene occurs.

GUIDED READING

LITERAL QUESTIONS

1a. What does the Stage Manager tell Emily she will be able to see while she is reliving a day? (the future)

2a. What day does she choose to relive? (her twelfth birthday)

INFERENTIAL QUESTIONS

1b. Why might her perspective prove painful? (She will see the future but will have no power to change it.)

2b. Why does she select that day? (She thinks that it must have been "unimportant" and therefore safe.)

AT A GLANCE

- Howie delivers milk to Mrs. Webb and they discuss the cold.
- Arriving home from a trip to his old college, Mr. Webb first chats with the Constable and then with his wife.
- Emily marvels at how young her parents look and then goes into the kitchen to see her mother.

1 DIALOGUE

This small talk is very similar to the conversations at the beginning of Acts 1 and 2.

2 THEME

Mrs. Webb's comment illustrates how we take life for granted.

3 CHARACTERIZATION

Emily now looks at life from a new perspective. She wants to appreciate all the small joys of life she took for granted while she was alive.

looks! I didn't know Mama was ever that young.

MRS. WEBB. You can come and dress by the kitchen fire, if you like; but hurry.

[HOWIE NEWSOME *has entered along Main Street and brings the milk to* MRS. WEBB'S *door.*]

1 Good morning, Mr. Newsome. Whhhh—it's cold.

HOWIE NEWSOME. Ten below by my barn, Mrs. Webb.

MRS. WEBB. Think of it! Keep yourself wrapped up. [*She takes her bottles in, shuddering.*]

EMILY. [*With an effort.*] Mama, I can't find my blue hair ribbon anywhere.

MRS. WEBB. Just open your eyes, dear, that's all. I laid it out for you special—on the dresser, there. If it were a snake it would bite you.

EMILY. Yes, yes . . .

[*She puts her hand on her heart.* MR. WEBB *comes along Main Street, where he meets* CONSTABLE WARREN. *Their movements and voices are increasingly lively in the sharp air.*]

MR. WEBB. Good morning, Bill.

CONSTABLE WARREN. Good morning, Mr. Webb. You're up early.

MR. WEBB. Yes, just been back to my old college in New York State. Been any trouble here?

CONSTABLE WARREN. Well, I was called up this mornin' to rescue a Polish fella—darn near froze to death he was.

MR. WEBB. We must get it in the paper.

CONSTABLE WARREN. 'Twan't much.

EMILY. [*Whispers.*] Papa.

[MR. WEBB *shakes the snow off his feet and enters his house.*
CONSTABLE WARREN *goes off, right.*]

MR. WEBB. Good morning, Mother.

MRS. WEBB. How did it go, Charles?

MR. WEBB. Oh, fine, I guess. I told'm a few things. Everything all right here?

2 MRS. WEBB. Yes—can't think of anything that's happened, special. Been right cold. Howie Newsome says it's ten below over to his barn.

MR. WEBB. Yes, well, it's colder than that at Hamilton College. Students' ears are falling off. It ain't Christian. Paper have any mistakes in it?

MRS. WEBB. None that I noticed. Coffee's ready when you want it.

[*He starts upstairs.*]

Charles! Don't forget; it's Emily's birthday. Did you remember to get her something?

MR. WEBB. [*Patting his pocket.*] Yes, I've got something here. [*Calling up the stairs.*] Where's my girl? Where's my birthday girl? [*He goes off left.*]

MRS. WEBB. Don't interrupt her now, Charles. You can see her at breakfast. She's slow enough as it is. Hurry up, children! It's seven o'clock. Now, I don't want to call you again.

EMILY. [*Softly, more in wonder than in grief.*] I can't bear it. They're so young and beautiful. Why did they ever have to get old? Mama, I'm
3 here. I'm grown up. I love you all, everything. I can't look at everything hard enough.

[*She looks questioningly at the* STAGE MANAGER, *saying or suggesting: "Can I go in?" He nods briefly. She crosses to the inner door to the kitchen, left of her mother, and as though entering the room, says, suggesting the voice of a girl of twelve.*]

Good morning, Mama.

MRS. WEBB.

[*Crossing to embrace and kiss her; in her characteristic matter-of-fact manner.*]

Well, now, dear, a very happy birthday to my

GUIDED READING

LITERAL QUESTIONS

1a. How does Mrs. Webb answer Mr. Webb's question about what has happened in his absence? ("can't think of anything that's happened, special")

2a. What does Emily say that she "can't bear"? (Seeing how young and beautiful her parents are.)

INFERENTIAL QUESTIONS

1b. What does this conversation signify? (Mrs. Webb, like the others, is unaware that life itself is special.)

2b. What prompts this reaction? (She knows that they, like everyone else, must grow older, experience sadness, and die. Such knowledge is painful to her.)

girl and many happy returns. There are some surprises waiting for you on the kitchen table.

EMILY. Oh, Mama, you *shouldn't* have.

1 [*She throws an anguished glance at the* STAGE MANAGER.]

I can't—I can't.

MRS. WEBB. [*Facing the audience, over her stove.*] But birthday or no birthday, I want you to eat your breakfast good and slow. I want you to grow up and be a good strong girl.

That in the blue paper is from your Aunt Carrie; and I reckon you can guess who brought the postcard album. I found it on the doorstep when I brought in the milk—George Gibbs . . . must have come over in the cold pretty early . . . right nice of him.

EMILY. [*To herself.*] Oh, George! I'd forgotten that. . . .

MRS. WEBB. Chew that bacon good and slow. It'll help keep you warm on a cold day.

2 **EMILY.** [*With mounting urgency.*] Oh, Mama, just look at me one minute as though you really saw me. Mama, fourteen years have gone by. I'm dead. You're a grandmother, Mama. I married George Gibbs, Mama. Wally's dead,

AT A GLANCE

- Mrs. Webb shows Emily her presents and points out a postcard album from George.
- Emily tries to get her mother to see her as she is now.

1 STAGE DIRECTIONS

This underscores how painful this experience is for Emily.

2 THEME

Emily's plea to her mother emphasizes the importance of recognizing the value of each moment of life.

GUIDED READING

LITERAL QUESTION

1a. What does Emily say that she had forgotten? (that George had left her a birthday gift)

INFERENTIAL QUESTION

1b. What does the forgetfulness suggest about Emily? (Like most people Emily has taken certain things for granted; now that she is dead she realizes how important the small events in her life were.)

AT A GLANCE

- Emily begs her mother to take the time to appreciate the moment, but neither Mrs. Webb nor Mr. Webb can hear her.
- Unable to continue, Emily bids goodbye to the small pleasures of life, and returns to the hilltop.
- Mrs. Gibbs takes exception to Simon Stimson's assertion that life was just ignorance and blindness.

1 CONFLICT

Emily's pain arises because the happiness of the day was never fully realized by all concerned. The poignancy overwhelms the pleasure.

2 RESPONSE JOURNAL

Have students offer their thoughts about what Mrs. Gibbs might say was the "truth" of being alive.

3 SYMBOL

The star, on which the dead fix their attention, is a symbol of eternity, constancy, and the beauty of the universe.

too. Mama, his appendix burst on a camping trip to North Conway. We felt just terrible about it—don't you remember? But, just for a moment now we're all together. Mama, just for a moment we're happy. *Let's look at one another.*

MRS. WEBB. That in the yellow paper is something I found in the attic among your grandmother's things. You're old enough to wear it now, and I thought you'd like it.

EMILY. And this is from you. Why, Mama, it's just lovely and it's just what I wanted. It's beautiful!

[*She flings her arms around her mother's neck. Her mother goes on with her cooking, but is pleased.*]

MRS. WEBB. Well, I hoped you'd like it. Hunted all over. Your Aunt Norah couldn't find one in Concord, so I had to send all the way to Boston. [*Laughing.*] Wally has something for you, too. He made it at manual-training class and he's very proud of it. Be sure you make a big fuss about it. Your father has a surprise for you, too; don't know what it is myself. Sh—here he comes.

MR. WEBB. [*Off stage.*] Where's my girl? Where's my birthday girl?

1 **EMILY.** [*In a loud voice to the* STAGE MANAGER.] I can't. I can't go on. It goes so fast. We don't have time to look at one another.

[*She breaks down sobbing.*
The lights dim on the left half of the stage. MRS. WEBB *disappears.*]

I didn't realize. So all that was going on and we never noticed. Take me back—up the hill—to my grave. But first: Wait! One more look. Good-bye, Good-bye, world. Good-bye, Grover's Corners . . . Mama and Papa. Good-bye to clocks ticking . . . and Mama's sunflowers. And food and coffee. And new-ironed dresses and hot baths . . . and sleeping and waking up. Oh, earth, you're too wonderful for anybody to realize you.

[*She looks toward the* STAGE MANAGER *and asks abruptly, through her tears:*]

Do any human beings ever realize life while they live it?—every, every minute?

STAGE MANAGER. No. [*Pause.*] The saints and poets, maybe—they do some.

EMILY. I'm ready to go back.

[*She returns to her chair beside* MRS. GIBBS. *Pause.*]

MRS. GIBBS. Were you happy?

EMILY. No . . . I should have listened to you. That's all human beings are! Just blind people.

MRS. GIBBS. Look, it's clearing up. The stars are coming out.

EMILY. Oh, Mr. Stimson, I should have listened to them.

SIMON STIMSON. [*With mounting violence; bitingly.*] Yes, now you know. Now you know! That's what it was to be alive. To move about in a cloud of ignorance; to go up and down trampling on the feelings of those . . . of those about you. To spend and waste time as though you had a million years. To be always at the mercy of one self-centered passion, or another. Now you know—that's the happy existence you wanted to go back to. Ignorance and blindness.

2 **MRS. GIBBS.** [*Spiritedly.*] Simon Stimson, that ain't the whole truth and you know it. Emily, look at that star. I forget its name.

A MAN AMONG THE DEAD. My boy Joel was a sailor—knew 'em all. He'd set on the porch evenings and tell 'em all by name. Yes, sir, wonderful!

3 **ANOTHER MAN AMONG THE DEAD.** A star's mighty good company.

A WOMAN AMONG THE DEAD. Yes. Yes, 'tis.

SIMON STIMSON. Here's one of *them* coming.

THE DEAD. That's funny. 'Tain't no time for one of them to be here. Goodness sakes.

GUIDED READING

LITERAL QUESTION

1a. According to Simon Stimson, what is the condition of living? (ignorance and blindness)

INFERENTIAL QUESTION

1b. Does his opinion find any support in the play? Explain your answer. (Although the play points out human blindness to the value of the moment, it does so without the bitterness that colors Simon's opinion.)

EMILY. Mother Gibbs, it's George.

MRS. GIBBS. Sh, dear. Just rest yourself.

EMILY. It's George.

[GEORGE *enters from the left, and slowly comes toward them.*]

A MAN FROM AMONG THE DEAD. And my boy, Joel, who knew the stars—he used to say it took millions of years for that speck o' light to git to the earth. Don't seem like a body could believe it, but that's what he used to say—millions of years.

[GEORGE *sinks to his knees then falls full length at* EMILY'S *feet.*]

A WOMAN AMONG THE DEAD. Goodness! That ain't no way to behave!

MRS. SOAMES. He ought to be home.

EMILY. Mother Gibbs?

MRS. GIBBS. Yes, Emily?

EMILY. They don't understand, do they?

MRS. GIBBS. No, dear. They don't understand.

[*The* STAGE MANAGER *appears at the right, one hand on a dark curtain which he slowly draws across the scene.*
In the distance a clock is heard striking the hour very faintly.]

STAGE MANAGER. Most everybody's asleep in Grover's Corners. There are a few lights on: Shorty Hawkins, down at the depot, has just watched the Albany train go by. And at the livery stable somebody's setting up late and talking. Yes, it's clearing up. There are the stars—doing their old, old crisscross journeys in the sky. Scholars haven't settled the matter yet, but they seem to think there are no living beings
1 up there. Just chalk . . . or fire. Only this one is straining away, straining away all the time to make something of itself. The strain's so bad that every sixteen hours everybody lies down and gets a rest. [*He winds his watch.*] Hm. . . . Eleven o'clock in Grover's Corners. You get a good rest, too. Good night.

THE END

STUDY QUESTIONS

Recalling

1. How much time has elapsed between Acts 2 and 3? Which characters that we have met before are "buried" in the cemetery where Act 3 opens?
2. In his opening speech what does the Stage Manager say all the greatest people have been telling us, though some people forget? What does he ask "Mrs. Smith" near the end of this monologue?
3. How did Emily die? What warnings does Mrs. Gibbs give Emily when Emily expresses the desire to return among the living? What day does Emily choose to relive?
4. What does Emily ask her mother to do "with mounting urgency" on page 707? What does she tell the Stage Manager she did not realize? What does she ask him about human beings? What does he answer?
5. What living person comes to the cemetery near the end of the play? What is Emily's final remark to Mrs. Gibbs?
6. What does the Stage Manager say about the stars in his final speech? What does he say about "this one"?

Interpreting

7. Who is the "Mrs. Smith" that the Stage Manager addresses on page 701? What might the answer to his question be?
8. Why has revisiting a happy, seemingly innocuous day in her life been painful for Emily? What human blindness and failure does she notice?

AT A GLANCE

- George comes to the cemetery and lies on Emily's grave.
- The dead talk about his lack of understanding.
- The Stage Manager comments on the human striving for perfection and bids the audience good night.

1 THEME

The earth and its people strive toward perfection, trying to do better with each succeeding generation.

RESPONDING TO ACT 3

What theme is emphasized by Emily's return to her twelfth birthday? (Students may suggest that Emily's return to the past demonstrates how little most people appreciate what is happening around them while it is going on.)

STUDY QUESTIONS

1. nine years; Mrs. Gibbs, Simon Stimson, Mrs. Soames, Wally Webb
2. something eternal about every human; "And what's left when your memory's gone and your identity, Mrs. Smith?"
3. in childbirth; warnings: not to go back, watch yourself living life, see the future, choose unimportant day; her twelfth birthday
4. look at her; how much goes on that we don't notice; if anyone ever realizes life while living; no, possibly saints and poets
5. George falls on Emily's grave; "They don't understand, do they?"
6. unlikely that there are any living beings "up there"; is straining away all the time to make something of itself
7. anyone in audience; "Nothing but your soul"
8. realizes how little awareness people have of each other; people do not appreciate themselves, each other, or the joys of everyday life.

9. the earth; no, despite faults, it tries to make something of itself; effort is positive
10. everyday life, other people, life itself; rooted people with sense of connection with past, future; slow-changing, in touch with what is basic, universal
11. Interested students should name writers in universal themes and basic questions about life, i.e., Faulkner.

VIEWPOINT

- drunkenness, war, early death from illness or in childbirth, suicide
- life in all its dimensions, not overly idealized or overly sordid
- past no more perfect than present

LITERARY FOCUS

Thinking About Characters in Drama

1. - young man might address older man by name
   - middle-aged man might use younger man's name when answering
   - older man might reveal where he has been in response to a question
   - young man might say, "I must go. I'll miss my train."
2. - *advantages:* gives overview of characters' lives; tells about past and future; distances us by making play seem illusion; draws us in by addressing us directly
   - *disadvantage:* technique might be found overly artificial

9. To which "star" is the Stage Manager referring when he speaks of "this one" in his final speech? Is his view of this "star" negative? Explain.
10. What are some of the things this play teaches us to appreciate? Why might Wilder have chosen Grover's Corners, a regional setting, for themes that are basically universal themes?

Extending

11. When Emily asks the Stage Manager if human beings ever realize life while they live it, he replies, "The saints and poets, maybe—they do some." Based on your own reading, who are some of the poets or other writers that you think come closest to realizing life fully? Justify your answers.

VIEWPOINT

Richard Goldstone, a biographer of Thornton Wilder, acknowledges that *Our Town*

> is not directly relevant to current social conditions, but neither was it relevant in 1938 [when first produced]. No one in Grover's Corners is addicted to anything stronger than coffee; no one seems to sustain any disease worse than whooping cough; crime seems unknown. . . . The village life described by Wilder, however, although it avoids the depiction of the mean, petty, ugly, and sordid, is no sentimental idyll. . . .
>
> —*Thornton Wilder: An Intimate Portrait*

■ Which specific unpleasant and distressing aspects of life are represented in the play? Why are they included? What do they contribute to the total effect of the play?

LITERARY FOCUS

Characters in Drama

The writer of a conventional play must create his characters differently from a novelist or short story writer. A playwright cannot comment directly on the characters; all that we know of them must come through what they say and do on stage and from what other characters on stage say about them. Moreover, what is said must seem natural. The **exposition** (explaining what the situation is when the play begins, what the relationships are among the characters, even what their names are) must arise naturally from what is said and done on stage.

Or at least it must in a conventional play. *Our Town,* however, is by no means conventional. Not only are scenery and props virtually abandoned; the stage manager, who ordinarily would be out of sight—having done his work before the audience arrives—is here allowed to remain and direct matters, much as the narrator of a novel might direct, explain, and comment on the action that he or she is describing. Thus, the Stage Manager in *Our Town* functions partly as a chorus to react to and evaluate what is happening. Even so, the various scenes from which he removes himself resemble scenes in more conventional plays, where characters reveal themselves solely through their speech and actions.

Thinking About Characters in Drama

1. Imagine Act 1 without the Stage Manager. As the play opens, two people, one middle-aged, one young, appear on stage. In what possible ways might we learn the name of the middle-aged man? Of the young man? How might we find out where the older man has been? How would we learn where the young man is going?
2. What, in your opinion, are the advantages and disadvantages of using a "chorus" or narrator in a drama, as Wilder does in *Our Town?*

Theme in Drama

Like other kinds of fiction, plays present specific *subjects* out of which general *themes* develop—themes that may relate to all of us. The specific subject of *Our Town* is life as lived by certain people in Grover's Corners, New Hampshire, in the early part of the twentieth century. But out of that specific subject grow themes that relate to lives lived at other times and places.

Some of those themes are suggested by the Stage Manager. Early in Act 2, for example, he remarks that "Nature's been pushing and contriving," moving the universe forward as though to create something better than what has preceded. "Every child born into the world," he says later, "is nature's attempt to make a perfect human being." Nature is interested, he believes, in progress toward perfection. Meanwhile, life goes on in its cyclical way, routines of birth, marriage, and death repeated over and over again.

Such general ideas, applicable to all of us but growing out of the specific events shown on stage, are what constitute the themes of the play.

Thinking About Theme in Drama

1. If an idea about change (and lack of change) is one of the themes of *Our Town,* what are some of the other themes? Consider, for example, the themes suggested by Jane Crofut's letter, by the attitudes of "the dead," by Emily's statements and pleas when she relives her twelfth birthday, and by the Stage Manager's closing remarks.
2. Do you think the play has one theme that dominates? Which one is it, and why?

Action in Drama

The conventional play moves from **exposition** (the explanation of the situation when the curtain goes up), through **rising action** (which generally involves **complication**—things going wrong or moving differently from the expected way) to a **climax** and through **falling action** to **resolution** (the unraveling or explanation of the plot). In a conventional play the protagonist, or main character, is the focal point of the action, providing a single center of attention for the play.

Our Town, however, as we have seen, is not conventional. The Stage Manager provides much of the exposition. In general, there are no complications, no climax, no effort at suspense. The purpose of the play is not to surprise or mystify or startle. Rather, it is to reveal and understand. Because an underlying theme of *Our Town* concerns the cyclical nature of life—the repeated routines by means of which our lives are led—the very structure of the play stresses repetition, as its action stresses what is ordinary and expected.

Thinking About Action in Drama

1. The action that opens Act 3 does contain some suspense, some withholding of crucial information that awakens our curiosity. What information is withheld?
2. Without using the standard devices for creating suspense, how does Wilder keep our interest focused on the action of the play?
3. Does *Our Town* have a protagonist? In what sense is the entire town the protagonist?

VOCABULARY

Antonyms

Antonyms are words that have opposite or nearly opposite meanings. The following words in capitals are from *Our Town.* Choose the word that is an antonym of each word in capitals, *as the word is used in the selection.* Write the number of each item and the letter of your choice on a separate sheet.

1. UNOBTRUSIVELY: (a) quietly (b) ominously (c) unmentionably (d) conspicuously
2. DILIGENT: (a) lazy (b) sensible (c) powerful (d) glamorous
3. SAVANT: (a) teacher (b) leader (c) ignoramus (d) philosopher
4. AFFRONTED: (a) restive (b) bereaved (c) discontented (d) mollified
5. LUGUBRIOUSNESS: (a) sorrow (b) delight (c) pride (d) monotony

COMPOSITION

Applying a Statement to a Work of Literature

■ Write a brief essay in defense of this statement: "*Our Town* presents a full and accurate picture of life as it is really lived, including what is truly important and leaving out only what is not important." Make sure you cite specific details from the play. *For help with this assignment, refer to Lesson 9 in the Writing About Literature Handbook at the back of this book.*

Writing a Dialogue

■ Try your hand at creating characters dramatically—that is, through nothing but dialogue and stage directions. Begin by writing a brief stage direction describing the setting in which your characters will find themselves. Then write a short dialogue between two or more characters. The dialogue should reveal their names, backgrounds, and something of their characteristics or attitudes. Within your dialogue include brief stage directions for actors, telling them how to move or sound when they perform your dialogue.

Thinking About Theme in Drama

1. There is order in the universe; there is something eternal in everyone, death is not an ending; people are not aware of life while they live it; we are part of something larger than ourselves, something which is straining for perfection.
2. Answers will vary. Students should see a connection between: paradox of stasis and change; endless cycles of life and death; particular as symbol for the universal.

Thinking About Action in Drama

1. identity of deceased
2. Stage Manager confides in us; characters nice people; flashbacks, interruptions, chorus of the dead all sustain interest
3. No. George and Emily are the focus of some action, but they are not protagonists; all the individuals, living and dead, are part of the town, which takes on an identity of its own.

VOCABULARY

1. (d) conspicuously
2. (a) lazy
3. (c) ignoramus
4. (d) mollified
5. (b) delight

COMPOSITION: GUIDELINES FOR EVALUATION

APPLYING A STATEMENT TO A WORK OF LITERATURE

Objective

To analyze the strengths of *Our Town*

Guidelines for Evaluation

- suggested length: three to six paragraphs
- should tell how life is realistically portrayed
- should tell which important aspects of life are included and which unimportant aspects are not included

WRITING A DIALOGUE

Objective

To create characters dramatically

Guidelines for Evaluation

- suggested length: 300 words
- should describe setting with stage directions
- should reveal characters through dialogue
- should capture patterns of spoken language
- should use stage directions

Tennessee Williams *1911–1983*

Tennessee Williams was christened Thomas Lanier Williams. In 1939 he began writing under the pen name Tennessee, the name of the state in which his father was born. After he graduated from college in 1938, several plays he wrote were produced by amateur theater groups. *Battle of Angels* (1940) was the first play by Williams to be professionally produced; however, it closed during its pre-Broadway tryout. This was not the case with *The Glass Menagerie,* which brought him recognition and success after it opened in 1945 and played for 561 performances on Broadway. A second successful drama, *A Streetcar Named Desire* (1948), ran for 855 performances. Williams won the New York Drama Critics Award for both these plays. The latter also received the Pulitzer Prize for drama, as did *Cat on a Hot Tin Roof* (1955).

In *The Glass Menagerie,* as in the best of his other plays, Williams gives a compassionate portrayal of sensitive and vulnerable characters striving to retain some vestiges of human dignity and self-esteem in a harsh and indifferent world.

■ As you are reading *The Glass Menagerie,* be aware of your reactions to Amanda Wingfield. Notice her negative traits as well as her positive ones. Decide how you finally feel about this unusual character, and why you feel as you do.

Tennessee Williams

The Glass Menagerie

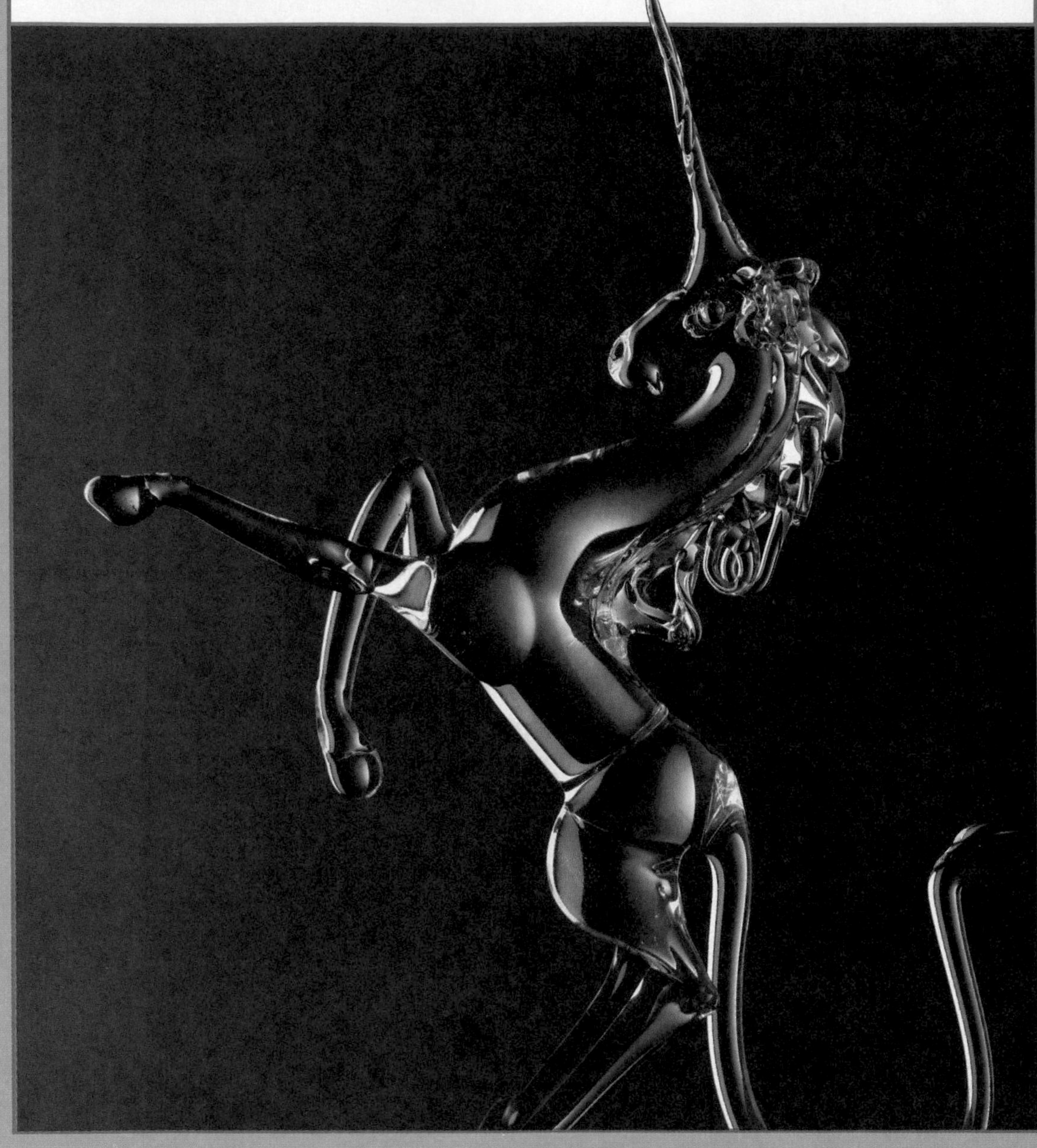

AT A GLANCE

- *Scene 1:* Stage directions describe the neighborhood of the Wingfield apartment.
- Williams explains that the scene is memory and is thus nonrealistic.
- The apartment features a collection of glass animals and a portrait of the father.
- Tom enters dressed as a merchant sailor.

LITERARY OPTIONS

- staging
- characterization
- symbol

THEMATIC OPTIONS

- illusion vs. reality
- coping with adversity
- parents and children

1 SYMBOL

The fire escape is a symbol for all those residing in this claustrophobic setting who are afflicted by the "fires of human desperation."

2 VOCABULARY: CONNOTATION

The words *dark, murky, tangled,* and *sinister* suggest the hopelessness and desperation of the setting.

3 STAGING

The presence of gauze curtains makes the audience feel that they are watching something dreamlike. By creating an unreal setting, Williams is, in fact, aiming for a reality that transcends mere physical appearances.

ACT I

Scene 1.

[The Wingfield apartment is in the rear of the building, one of those vast hivelike conglomerations of cellular living units that flower as warty growths in overcrowded urban centers of lower middle-class population and are symptomatic of the impulse of this largest and fundamentally enslaved section of American society to avoid fluidity and differentiation and to exist and function as one interfused
1 *mass of automatism. The apartment faces an alley and is entered by a fire escape, a structure whose name is a touch of accidental poetic truth, for all of these huge buildings are always burning with the slow and implacable fires of human desperation. The fire escape is included in the set—that is, the landing of it and steps descending from it. (Note that the stage-left alley may be entirely omitted, since it is never used except for* TOM*'s first entrance, which can take place stage right.) The scene is memory and is therefore nonrealistic. Memory takes a lot of poetic license. It omits some details, others are exaggerated, according to the emotional value of the articles it touches, for memory is seated predominantly in the heart. The interior is therefore rather dim and poetic.*

[Cue 1. As soon as the house lights dim, dance hall music heard onstage right. Old popular music of, say, 1915–1920 period. This continues until TOM *is at fire-escape landing, having lighted cigarette, and begins speaking.*

[At the rise of the house curtain, the audience is faced with the dark, grim rear wall of the Wingfield tenement. (The stage set proper is screened out by a gauze curtain, which suggests the front part, outside, of the building.) This building, which runs parallel to the footlights,
2 *is flanked on both sides by dark, narrow alleys which run into murky canyons of tangled clotheslines, garbage cans and the sinister latticework of neighboring fire escapes. (The alleys are actually in darkness, and the objects just mentioned are not visible.) It is up and down these side alleys that exterior entrances and exits are made, during the play. At the end of* TOM*'s opening commentary, the dark tenement wall slowly reveals (by means of a transparency) the interior of the ground-floor*
3 *Wingfield apartment. (Gauze curtain, which suggests front part of building, rises on the interior set.) Downstage is the living room, which also serves as a sleeping room for* LAURA*, the day bed unfolding to make her bed. Just above this is a small stool or table on which is a telephone. Upstage, center, and divided by a wide arch or second proscenium with transparent faded portieres (or second curtain; "second curtain" is actually the inner gauze curtain between the living room and the dining room, which is upstage of it), is the dining room. In an old-fashioned whatnot[1] in the living room are seen scores of transparent glass animals. A blown-up photograph of the father hangs on the wall of the living room, facing the audience, to the left of the archway. It is the face of a very handsome young man in a doughboy's First World War cap.[2] He is gallantly smiling, ineluctably smiling, as if to say, "I will be smiling forever." (Note that all that is essential in connection with dance hall is that the window be shown lighting lower part of alley. It is not necessary to show any considerable part of dance hall.) The audience hears and sees the opening scene in the dining room through both the transparent fourth wall (this is the gauze curtain which suggests outside of building) of the building and the transparent gauze portieres of the dining room arch. It is during this revealing scene that the fourth wall slowly ascends, out of sight. This transparent exterior wall is not brought down again until the very end of the play, during* TOM*'s final speech. The narrator is an undisguised convention of the play. He takes whatever license with dramatic convention as is convenient to his purposes.*

*[*TOM *enters dressed as a merchant sailor from*

1. **whatnot:** shelves for small, decorative objects.
2. **doughboy's . . . cap:** hat worn by U.S. soldiers during World War I.

GUIDED READING

LITERAL QUESTIONS

1a. What makes the scene nonrealistic? (memory)

2a. Whose picture is on the wall? (that of Mr. Wingfield, Tom's father)

INFERENTIAL QUESTIONS

1b. What can you infer about when the play takes place? (The play will take place in the past.)

2b. Why is this character shown in a picture? (He will probably be important to the plot.)

*alley, stage left (i.e., stage right if left alley is omitted), and strolls across the front of the stage to the fire escape. (*TOM *may lean against grillwork of this as he lights cigarette.) There he stops and lights a cigarette. He addresses the audience.*]

1 **TOM.** I have tricks in my pocket—I have things up my sleeve—but I am the opposite of the stage magician. He gives you illusion that has the appearance of truth. I give you truth in the pleasant disguise of illusion. I take you back to an alley in St. Louis. The time that quaint period when the huge middle class of America was matriculating from a school for the blind. Their eyes had failed them, or they had failed their eyes, and so they were having their fingers pressed forcibly down
2 on the fiery Braille alphabet of a dissolving economy.—In Spain there was revolution.—Here there was only shouting and confusion and labor disturbances, sometimes violent, in otherwise peaceful cities such as Cleveland—Chicago—Detroit. . . . That is the social background of this play. . . . The play is memory. [*Music cue 2.*] Being a memory play, it is dimly lighted, it is sentimental, it is not realistic.—In memory everything seems to happen to music.—That explains the fiddle in the wings. I am the narrator of the play, and also a character in it. The other characters in the play are my mother, Amanda, my sister, Laura, and a gentleman caller who appears in the final scenes. He is the most realistic character in the play, being an emissary from a world that we were somehow set apart from.—But having a poet's weakness for symbols, I am using this character as a symbol—as the long-delayed but always expected something that we live for.—There is a fifth character who doesn't appear other than in a photograph hanging on the wall. When you see the picture of this grinning gentleman, please remember this is our father who left us a long time ago. He was a telephone man who fell in love with long distance—so he gave up his job with the telephone company and skipped the light fantastic out of town. . . . The last we heard of him was a picture postcard from the Pacific coast of Mexico, con-
3 taining a message of two words—"Hello—Good-by!" and no address. [*Lights up in dining room.* TOM *exits right. He goes off downstage, takes off his sailor overcoat and skull-fitting knitted cap and remains offstage by dining room right door for his entrance cue.* AMANDA*'s voice becomes audible through the portieres—i.e., gauze curtains separating dining room from living room.* AMANDA *and* LAURA *are seated at a drop-leaf table.* AMANDA *is sitting in center chair and* LAURA *in left chair. Eating is indicated by gestures without food or utensils.* AMANDA *faces the audience. The interior of the dining room has lit up softly and through the scrim—gauze curtains—we see* AMANDA *and* LAURA *seated at the table in the upstage area.*]

AMANDA. You know, Laura, I had the funniest experience in church last Sunday. The church was crowded except for one pew way down front and in that was just one little woman. I smiled very sweetly at her and said, "Excuse me, would you mind if I shared this pew?" "I certainly would," she said, "this space is rented." Do you know that is the first time that I ever knew that the Lord rented space. [*Dining room gauze curtains open automatically.*] These northern Episcopalians! I can understand the southern Episcopalians, but these northern ones, no. [TOM *enters dining room right, slips over to table and sits in chair right.*] Honey, don't push your food with your fingers. If you have to push your food with something, the thing to use is a crust of bread. You must chew your food. Animals have secretions in their stomachs which enable them to digest their food without mastication, but human beings must chew their food before they swal-
4 low it down, and chew, chew. Oh, eat leisurely. Eat leisurely. A well-cooked meal has many delicate flavors that have to be held in the mouth for appreciation, not just gulped down. Oh, chew, chew—chew! [*At this point the scrim curtain—if the director decides to use it—the one suggesting exterior wall, rises here and does not come down again until just before the end of the play.*] Don't you want to give your salivary glands a chance to function?

AT A GLANCE

- Tom, the narrator, establishes the setting, St. Louis during the Depression, and introduces the other characters—his mother Amanda, his sister Laura, and a gentleman caller.
- Tom removes his sailor's outfit to become a character in the play.
- Amanda tells Laura about her experience in church and cautions Tom to chew his food.

1 THEME

Tom's statement prepares the audience for Williams' belief that reality can be found in the symbolic aspects of objects rather than in their mere appearances.

2 SETTING

The remembered events of the play took place during the Great Depression, a time of confusion and unrest—both for America as a nation and for the members of the Wingfield family.

3 POINT OF VIEW

The small change in costume turns Tom from the 1940s narrator of events to the 1930s participant in the events.

4 CHARACTERIZATION

Even though her children are grown, Amanda offers her silly admonitions as if they were still small.

GUIDED READING

LITERAL QUESTIONS

1a. According to Tom, where will the gentleman caller come from? (a world from which the Wingfields are set apart)

2a. According to the stage directions, how is eating indicated? (by gestures only, without food or utensils)

INFERENTIAL QUESTIONS

1b. What kind of world does the gentleman caller probably come from? (the real world, as opposed to the illusionary world of the Wingfields)

2b. Why is this appropriate for this play? (It is a memory play; it is not supposed to be realistic.)

AT A GLANCE

- Tom rebels against Amanda's advice on how to eat.
- Amanda goes to get the coffee, telling Laura to keep herself fresh for gentlemen callers.
- Amanda recalls receiving seventeen gentlemen callers one Sunday afternoon in her youth.

1 CONFLICT

Amanda is struggling against reality. She wants Laura to have gentlemen callers so desperately that she can ignore effortlessly Laura's clear statement that she is not expecting any callers.

2 CHARACTERIZATION

Although she has heard the story time after time, Laura is sensitive to her mother's feelings and will listen to it again.

3 THEME

Amanda lives among the memories of her youth; they seem more real to her than her current surroundings.

4 CHARACTERIZATION

Amanda is a self-confident individual. She says that as a girl she was not only pretty and graceful, but she also possessed a quick wit and the ability to converse easily.

TOM. Mother, I haven't enjoyed one bite of my dinner because of your constant directions on how to eat it. It's you that makes me hurry through my meals with your hawklike attention to every bite I take. It's disgusting—all this discussion of animals' secretion—salivary glands—mastication! [*Comes down to armchair in living room right, lights cigarette.*]

AMANDA. Temperament like a Metropolitan star! You're not excused from this table.

TOM. I'm getting a cigarette.

AMANDA. You smoke too much.

LAURA. [*Rising.*] Mother, I'll bring in the coffee.

AMANDA. No, no, no, no. You sit down. I'm going to be the colored boy today and you're going to be the lady.

LAURA. I'm already up.

AMANDA. Resume your seat. Resume your seat. You keep yourself fresh and pretty for the gentlemen callers. [LAURA *sits.*]

1 LAURA. I'm not expecting any gentlemen callers.

AMANDA. [*Who has been gathering dishes from table and loading them on tray.*] Well, the nice thing about them is they come when they're least expected. Why, I remember one Sunday afternoon in Blue Mountain when your mother was a girl. . . . [*Goes out for coffee, upstage right.*]

TOM. I know what's coming now! [LAURA *rises.*]

2 LAURA. Yes. But let her tell it. [*Crosses to left of daybed, sits.*]

TOM. Again?

LAURA. She loves to tell it.

AMANDA. [*Entering from right in dining room and coming down into living room with tray*
3 *and coffee.*] I remember one Sunday afternoon in Blue Mountain when your mother was a girl she received—seventeen—gentlemen callers! [AMANDA *crosses to* TOM *at armchair right, gives him coffee, and crosses center.* LAURA *comes to her, takes cup, resumes her place on left of daybed.* AMANDA *puts tray on small table right of daybed, sits right on daybed. Inner curtain closes, light dims out.*] Why, sometimes there weren't chairs enough to accommodate them all and we had to send the colored boy over to the parish house to fetch the folding chairs.

TOM. How did you entertain all those gentlemen callers? [TOM *finally sits in armchair right.*]

AMANDA. I happened to understand the art of conversation!

TOM. I bet you could talk!

AMANDA. Well, I could. All the girls in my day could, I tell you.

TOM. Yes?

AMANDA. They knew how to entertain their gen-
4 tlemen callers. It wasn't enough for a girl to be possessed of a pretty face and a graceful figure—although I wasn't slighted in either respect. She also needed to have a nimble wit and a tongue to meet all occasions.

TOM. What did you talk about?

AMANDA. Why, we'd talk about things of importance going on in the world! Never anything common or coarse or vulgar. My callers were gentlemen—all! Some of the most prominent men on the Mississippi Delta—planters and sons of planters! There was young Champ Laughlin. [*Music cue 3.*] He later became vice president of the Delta Planters' Bank. And Hadley Stevenson; he was drowned in Moon Lake.—My goodness, he certainly left his widow well provided for—a hundred and fifty thousand dollars in government bonds. And the Cutrere Brothers—Wesley and Bates. Bates was one of my own bright particular beaus! But he got in a quarrel with that wild Wainwright boy and they shot it out on the floor of Moon Lake Casino. Bates was shot through the stomach. He died in the ambulance on his way to Memphis. He certainly left his widow well provided for, too—eight or ten

GUIDED READING

LITERAL QUESTIONS

1a. What is Amanda's reason for wanting Laura to stay fresh and pretty? (She wants Laura ready to meet gentlemen callers.)

2a. What special event does Amanda remember happening one Sunday in Blue Mountain? (She received seventeen gentlemen callers.)

INFERENTIAL QUESTIONS

1b. What does this reason say about Amanda's expectations for Laura? (Amanda expects Laura to meet an appropriate young man and to marry.)

2b. What does this suggest about Amanda? (Either she was very popular or she is exaggerating.)

thousand acres, no less. He never loved that woman; she just caught him on the rebound. My picture was found on him the night he died. Oh and that boy, that boy that every girl in the Delta was setting her cap for! That beautiful [*Music fades out.*] brilliant young Fitzhugh boy from Greene County!

1 **TOM.** What did he leave his widow?

AMANDA. He never married! What's the matter with you—you talk as though all my old admirers had turned up their toes to the daisies!

TOM. Isn't this the first you've mentioned that still survives?

AMANDA. He made an awful lot of money. He went North to Wall Street and made a fortune. He had the Midas touch—everything that boy touched just turned to gold! [*Gets up.*] And I could have been Mrs. J. Duncan Fitzhugh—mind you! [*Crosses left center.*] But—what did I do?—I just went out of my way and picked your father! [*Looks at picture on left wall. Goes to small table right of daybed for tray.*]

LAURA. [*Rises from daybed.*] Mother, let me clear the table.

AMANDA. [*Crossing left for* LAURA*'s cup, then crossing right for* TOM*'s.*] No, dear, you go in front and study your typewriter chart. Or practice your shorthand a little. Stay fresh and pretty! It's almost time for our gentlemen callers to start arriving. How many do you suppose we're going to entertain this afternoon? [TOM *opens curtains between dining room and living room for her. These close behind her, and she exits into kitchen right.* TOM *stands upstage center in living room.*]

LAURA. [*To* AMANDA, *offstage.*] I don't believe we're going to receive any, Mother.

2 **AMANDA.** [*Offstage.*] Not any? Not one? Why, you must be joking! Not one gentleman caller? What's the matter? Has there been a flood or a tornado?

LAURA. [*Crossing to typing table.*] It isn't a flood. It's not a tornado, Mother. I'm just not popular like you were in Blue Mountain. Mother's afraid
3 that I'm going to be an old maid. [*Music cue 4. Lights dim out.* TOM *exits upstage center in blackout.* LAURA *crosses to menagerie stage right.*]

ACT I

Scene 2. *The same. Lights dim up on living room.*

[LAURA *discovered by menagerie, polishing glass. Crosses to phonograph, play record. She times this business so as to put needle on record as music cue 4 ends. Enter* AMANDA *down alley right. Rattles key in lock.* LAURA *crosses guiltily to typewriter and types.* (*Small typewriter table with typewriter on it is still on stage in living room left.*) AMANDA *comes into room right closing door. Crosses to armchair, putting hat, purse and gloves on it. Something has happened to* AMANDA. *It is written in her face: a look that is grim and hopeless and a little absurd. She has on one of those cheap or imitation velvety-looking cloth coats with imitation fur collar. Her hat is five or six years old, one of those dreadful cloche hats that were worn in the late twenties, and she is clasping an*
4 *enormous black patent-leather pocketbook with nickel clasps and initials. This is her full-dress outfit, the one she usually wears to the DAR.*[3] *She purses her lips, opens her eyes very wide, rolls them upward and shakes her head. Seeing her mother's expression,* LAURA *touches her lips with a nervous gesture.*]

LAURA. Hello, Mother, I was just. . . .

AMANDA. I know. You were just practicing your typing, I suppose. [*Behind chair right.*]

LAURA. Yes.

---

3. **DAR:** meeting of the Daughters of the American Revolution, an organization of women descended from Americans who fought in or gave aid to the American Revolution.

AT A GLANCE

- Amanda recalls the fine marriage that she might have made.
- Laura knows that Amanda fears that Laura will never marry.
- *Scene 2:* Laura is seen polishing her glass menagerie and playing records.
- Laura hears her mother enter and sits down at the typewriter.

1 DIALOGUE

Amanda and Tom's parrying reveals both the antagonism and the affection that exist between them.

2 THEME

Amanda's main tool for coping with disappointment is denial; to accept that there will be no gentlemen callers would destroy an illusion.

3 STAGING

In actual productions of the play, the music cue refers to circus music. It is played as if it were some distance away; thus, it is simultaneously the lightest and saddest of music.

4 CHARACTERIZATION

Amanda's affiliation with the Daughters of the American Revolution gives her an outward sign of social prestige and reinforces her belief that she is of finer stock than those around her.

GUIDED READING

LITERAL QUESTIONS

1a. What does Tom ask after Amanda mentions Duncan Fitzhugh? ("What did he leave his widow?")

2a. What does Laura say that her mother fears? (Amanda fears that Laura will never marry.)

INFERENTIAL QUESTIONS

1b. Why does he ask this question? (Amanda's other beaus all died and left their widows well provided for. Since Amanda dwells on this fact, Tom teases her by expressing surprise that one of her beaus is still alive.)

2b. What does Laura seem to think of her mother's fear? (She seems to share it.)

AT A GLANCE

- Amanda confronts Laura with her discovery that Laura has not been attending business college.
- When she asks Laura where she has been going every day, Laura replies that she has been walking.

1 CHARACTERIZATION

Amanda's roundabout approach to what is bothering her shows her tendency to dramatize her feelings.

2 PLOT: COMPLICATION

When Amanda discovers that Laura has not been attending typing class, she is stripped of the illusion that Laura will become independent.

3 CHARACTERIZATION

Amanda tries to use her basic response to things she does not like—she denies the truth.

4 CHARACTERIZATION

Laura's excessive shyness prevents her from learning a skill that will make her independent.

AMANDA. Deception, deception, deception!

LAURA. [*Shakily.*] How was the DAR meeting, Mother?

AMANDA. [*Crosses to* LAURA.] DAR meeting!

LAURA. Didn't you go to the DAR meeting, Mother?

1 AMANDA. [*Faintly, almost inaudibly.*] No, I didn't go to any DAR meeting. [*Then more forcibly.*] I didn't have the strength—I didn't have the courage. I just wanted to find a hole in the ground and crawl in it and stay there the rest of my entire life. [*Tears typing charts, throws them on floor.*]

LAURA. [*Faintly.*] Why did you do that, Mother?

AMANDA. [*Sits on right end of daybed.*] Why? Why? How old are you, Laura?

LAURA. Mother, you know my age.

AMANDA. I was under the impression that you were an adult, but evidently I was very much mistaken. [*She stares at* LAURA.]

LAURA. Please don't stare at me, Mother! [AMANDA *closes her eyes and lowers her head. Pause.*]

AMANDA. What are we going to do? What is going to become of us? What is the future? [*Pause.*]

LAURA. Has something happened, Mother? Mother, has something happened?

AMANDA. I'll be all right in a minute. I'm just bewildered—by life. . . .

LAURA. Mother, I wish that you would tell me what's happened!

AMANDA. I went to the DAR this afternoon, as you know; I was to be inducted as an officer. I stopped off at Rubicam's Business College to tell them about your cold and to ask how you were progressing down there.

LAURA. Oh. . . .

AMANDA. Yes, oh—oh—oh. I went straight to your typing instructor and introduced myself as
2 your mother. She didn't even know who you were. Wingfield, she said? We don't have any such scholar enrolled in this school. I assured her she did. I said my daughter Laura's been coming to classes since early January. "Well, I don't know," she said, "unless you mean that terribly shy little girl who dropped out of school after a
3 few days' attendance?" No, I said, I don't mean that one. I mean my daughter, Laura, who's been coming here every single day for the past six weeks! "Excuse me," she said. And she took down the attendance book and there was your name, unmistakable, printed, and all the dates you'd been absent. I still told her she was wrong. I still said, "No, there must have been some mistake! There must have been some mix-up in the records!" "No," she said, "I remember her per-
4 fectly now. She was so shy and her hands trembled so that her fingers couldn't touch the right keys! When we gave a speed test—she just broke down completely—was sick at the stomach and had to be carried to the washroom! After that she never came back. We telephoned the house every single day and never got any answer." [*Rises from daybed, crosses right center.*] That was while I was working all day long down at that department store, I suppose, demonstrating those—— [*With hands indicates brassiere.*] Oh! I felt so weak I couldn't stand up! [*Sits in armchair.*] I had to sit down while they got me a glass of water! [LAURA *crosses up to phonograph.*] Fifty dollars' tuition. I don't care about the money so much, but all my hopes for any kind of future for you—gone up the spout, just gone up the spout like that. [LAURA *winds phonograph up.*] Oh, don't *do* that, Laura!—Don't play that Victrola!

LAURA. Oh! [*Stops phonograph, crosses to typing table, sits.*]

AMANDA. What have you been doing every day when you've gone out of the house pretending that you were going to business college?

LAURA. I've just been going out walking.

AMANDA. That's not true!

GUIDED READING

LITERAL QUESTION

1a. What is it that has so upset Amanda? (her discovery that Laura had not been going to typing class)

INFERENTIAL QUESTION

1b. Why has the truth upset her? (Her plans for Laura have been undone; she is forced to face reality.)

LAURA. Yes, it is, Mother, I just went walking.

AMANDA. Walking? Walking? In winter? Deliberately courting pneumonia in that light coat? Where did you walk to, Laura?

LAURA. All sorts of places—mostly in the park.

AMANDA. Even after you'd started catching that cold?

LAURA. It was the lesser of two evils, Mother. I couldn't go back. I threw up on the floor!

AMANDA. From half-past seven till after five every day you mean to tell me you walked around in the park, because you wanted to make me think that you were still going to Rubicam's Business College?

LAURA. Oh, Mother, it wasn't as bad as it sounds. I went inside places to get warmed up.

AMANDA. Inside where?

LAURA. I went in the art museum and the bird houses at the zoo. I visited the penguins every day! Sometimes I did without lunch and went to
1 the movies. Lately I've been spending most of my afternoons in the jewel box, that big glass house[4] where they raise the tropical flowers.

AMANDA. You did all that to deceive me, just for deception! Why? Why? Why? Why?

2 **LAURA.** Mother, when you're disappointed, you get that awful suffering look on your face, like the picture of Jesus' mother in the museum! [*Rises.*]

AMANDA. Hush!

LAURA. [*Crosses right to menagerie.*] I couldn't face it. I couldn't. [*Music cue 5.*]

AMANDA. [*Rising from daybed.*] So what are we going to do now, honey, the rest of our lives? Just sit down in this house and watch the parades go by? Amuse ourselves with the glass menagerie? Eternally play those worn-out records your fa-
3 ther left us as a painful reminder of him? [*Slams phonograph lid.*] We can't have a business career. [*End music cue 5.*] No, we can't do that—that just gives us indigestion. [*Around right of daybed.*] What is there left for us now but dependency all our lives? I tell you, Laura, I know so well what happens to unmarried women who aren't prepared to occupy a position in life.
4 [*Crosses left, sits on daybed.*] I've seen such pitiful cases in the South—barely tolerated spinsters living on some brother's wife or a sister's husband—tucked away in some mouse trap of a room—encouraged by one in-law to go on and visit the next in-law—little birdlike women—without any nest—eating the crust of humility all their lives! Is that the future that we've mapped out for ourselves? I swear I don't see any other alternative. And I don't think that's a very pleasant alternative. Of course—some girls *do* marry. My goodness, Laura, haven't you ever liked some boy?

LAURA. Yes, Mother, I liked one once.

AMANDA. You did?

LAURA. I came across his picture a while ago.

AMANDA. He gave you his picture, too? [*Rises from daybed, crosses to chair right.*]

LAURA. No, it's in the yearbook.

AMANDA. [*Sits in armchair.*] Oh—a high school boy.

LAURA. Yes. His name was Jim. [*Kneeling on floor, gets yearbook from under menagerie.*] Here he is in *The Pirates of Penzance.*

AMANDA. [*Absently.*] The what?

LAURA. The operetta the senior class put on. He had a wonderful voice. We sat across the aisle from each other Mondays, Wednesdays and Fridays in the auditorium. Here he is with a silver cup for debating! See his grin?

AMANDA. So he had a grin, too! [*Looks at picture of father on wall behind phonograph. Hands yearbook back.*]

4. **big glass house:** greenhouse at the St. Louis Zoo.

AT A GLANCE

- Laura tells her mother where she has spent her days—the park, the zoo, and the movies.
- Amanda paints an unattractive picture of Laura's future if she does not marry or have a vocation.
- Laura says that there was a boy whom she once liked named Jim.

1 SYMBOL

The glass house and its delicate flowers, like the glass menagerie itself, suggest the fragility of Laura.

2 CHARACTERIZATION

Laura shows great concern for her mother's feelings. She does not want to shatter Amanda's illusions.

3 STAGING

The gesture of slamming the lid shows Amanda's anger not only at Laura's deception but also at the husband who left her with two children and those old records.

4 IRONY

Despite her railing against spinsterhood, Amanda is practically unmarried herself, having only a picture of a husband.

GUIDED READING

LITERAL QUESTIONS

1a. How has Laura been spending her afternoons? (at the art museum, the zoo, the movies, the place where they grow tropical flowers)

2a. Who is the boy Laura liked once? (Jim, a boy from high school)

INFERENTIAL QUESTIONS

1b. Why has she spent her time like this? (Being shy, she has chosen activities that do not involve other people.)

2b. How did he probably feel about Laura? (Her memories seem to be of Jim at a distance, suggesting that he did not much notice her.)

AT A GLANCE

- When Laura expresses fear she will not get married because she is crippled, Amanda tells her not to use that word.
- *Scene 3:* As narrator, Tom explains that his mother is more determined than every to find a gentleman caller for Laura.
- In order to get extra money for her campaign to find Laura a beau, Amanda is trying to sell magazine subscriptions by phone.

1 THEME

People living in a world of illusion do not want to face reality even if it is staring them in the face.

2 VOCABULARY: CONNOTATION

For Amanda being "charming" is like having a charm that protects and sees one over life's rough spots.

3 POINT OF VIEW

Tom once again acts as the narrator. He is something like the omniscient narrator in the short story in that he comments on the action and sets the scene. However, most of what we learn about the characters is from direct experience rather than what Tom says.

4 STYLE: IMAGERY

With the words "haunted" and "specter," Williams conjures up an image of a ghostly caller who lives with the Wingfields much as Mr. Wingfield does.

LAURA. He used to call me—Blue Roses.

AMANDA. Blue Roses? What did he call you a silly name like that for?

LAURA. [*Still kneeling.*] When I had that attack of pleurosis—he asked me what was the matter when I came back. I said pleurosis—he thought that I said "Blue Roses." So that's what he always called me after that. Whenever he saw me, he'd holler, "Hello, Blue Roses!" I didn't care for the girl that he went out with. Emily Meisenbach. Oh, Emily was the best-dressed girl at Soldan. But she never struck me as being sincere. . . . I read in a newspaper once that they were engaged. [*Puts yearbook back on a shelf of glass menagerie.*] That's a long time ago—they're probably married by now.

AMANDA. That's all right, honey, that's all right. It doesn't matter. Little girls who aren't cut out for business careers sometimes end up married to very nice young men. And I'm just going to see that you do that, too!

LAURA. But Mother——

AMANDA. What is it now?

1 LAURA. I'm—crippled!

AMANDA. Don't say that word! [*Rises, crosses to center stage. Turns to* LAURA.] How many times have I told you never to say that word! You're not crippled, you've just got a slight defect. [LAURA *rises.*] If you lived in the days when I was a girl and they had long graceful skirts sweeping the ground, it might have been considered an
2 asset. When you've got a slight disadvantage like that, you've just got to cultivate something else to take its place. You have to cultivate charm—or vivacity—or *charm!* [*Spotlight on photograph. Then dim out.*] That's the only thing your father had plenty of—charm! [AMANDA *sits on daybed.* LAURA *crosses to armchair and sits. Music cue 6. Blackout.*]

ACT I

Scene 3. *The same.*

[*Lights up again but only on right alley and fire-escape landing, rest of the stage dark. (Typewriter table and typewriter have been taken*
3 *offstage.) Enter* TOM, *again wearing merchant sailor overcoat and knitted cap, in alley right. As music cue 6 ends,* TOM *begins to speak.*]

TOM. [*Leans against grill of fire escape, smoking.*] After the fiasco at Rubicam's Business College, the idea of getting a gentleman caller for my sister Laura began to play a more and more important part in my mother's calculations. It became an obsession. Like some archetype of the
4 universal unconscious,[5] the image of the gentleman caller haunted our small apartment. An evening at home rarely passed without some allusion to this image, this specter, this hope. . . . And even when he wasn't mentioned, his presence hung in my mother's preoccupied look and in my sister's frightened, apologetic manner. It hung like a sentence passed upon the Wingfields! But my mother was a woman of action as well as words. [*Music cue 7.*] She began to take logical steps in the planned direction. Late that winter and in the early spring—realizing that extra money would be needed to properly feather the nest and plume the bird—she began a vigorous campaign on the telephone, roping in subscribers to one of those magazines for matrons called *The Homemaker's Companion,* the type of journal that features the serialized sublimations of ladies of letters who think in terms of delicate cuplike breasts, slim, tapering waists, rich creamy thighs, eyes like wood smoke in autumn, fingers that soothe and caress like soft, soft strains of music. Bodies as powerful as Etruscan sculpture. [*He exits down right into wings. Light in alley right is blacked out, and a head spot falls on* AMANDA, *at phone in living room. Music cue 7 ends as* TOM *stops speaking.*]

5. **archetype . . . unconscious:** theory that unconscious memories pass down to us from our ancestors; developed by Swiss psychiatrist Carl G. Jung (1875–1961).

GUIDED READING

LITERAL QUESTIONS

1a. What is it that Laura thinks will keep her from being married? (the fact that she is crippled)

2a. What does Amanda do to make extra money? (She sells magazine subscriptions.)

INFERENTIAL QUESTIONS

1b. Why does Amanda not share this point of view? (Amanda wants Laura to be married and does not want to consider the possibility that anything will stand in the way of her wishes.)

2b. Why does she need the money? (She thinks that if she can make both the apartment and Laura look a little nicer, then Laura will have a better chance of having a serious gentleman caller.)

AMANDA. Ida Scott? [*During this speech* TOM *enters dining room upstage right unseen by audience, not wearing overcoat or hat. There is an unlighted reading lamp on table. Sits at center of dining room table with writing materials.*] This is Amanda Wingfield. We missed you at the
1 DAR last Monday. Oh, first I want to know how's your sinus condition? You're just a Christian martyr. That's what you are. You're just a Christian martyr. Well, I was just going through my little red book, and I saw that your subscription to the *Companion* is about to expire just when that wonderful new serial by Bessie Mae Harper is starting. It's the first thing she's written since "Honeymoon for Three." Now, that was unusual, wasn't it? Why, Ida, this one is even lovelier. It's all about the horsy set on Long Island and a debutante is thrown from her horse while taking him over the jumps at the—regatta. Her spine—her spine is injured. That's what the horse did—he stepped on her. Now, there is only one surgeon in the entire world that can keep her from being completely paralyzed, and that's the man she's engaged to be married to and he's tall and he's blond and he's handsome. That's unusual, too, huh? Oh, he's not perfect. Of course he has a weakness. He has the most terrible weakness in the entire world. He just drinks too much. What? Oh, no, Honey, don't let them burn. You go take a look in the oven and I'll hold on. . . . Why, that woman! Do you know what she did? She hung up on me. [*Dining room and living room lights dim in. Reading lamp lights up at same time.*]

LAURA. Oh, Mother, Mother, Tom's trying to write. [*Rises from armchair where she was left at curtain of previous scene, goes to curtain between dining room and living room, which is already open.*]

AMANDA. Oh! So he is. So he is. [*Crosses from phone, goes to dining room and up to* TOM.]

TOM. [*At table.*] Now what are you up to?

2 AMANDA. I'm trying to save your eyesight. [*Business with lamp.*] You've only got one pair of eyes and you've got to take care of them. Oh, I know that Milton[6] was blind, but that's not what made him a genius.

TOM. Mother, will you please go away and let me finish my writing?

AMANDA. [*Squares his shoulders.*] Why can't you sit up straight? So your shoulders don't stick through like sparrows' wings?

TOM. Mother, please go busy yourself with something else. I'm trying to write.

AMANDA. [*Business with* TOM.] Now, I've seen a
3 medical chart, and I know what that position does to your internal organs. You sit up and I'll show you. Your stomach presses against your lungs, and your lungs press against your heart, and that poor little heart gets discouraged because it hasn't got any room left to go on beating for you.

TOM. What in hell . . . ! [*Inner curtains between living room and dining room close. Lights dim down in dining room.* LAURA *crosses, stands center of curtains in living room listening to following scene between* TOM *and* AMANDA.]

4 AMANDA. Don't you talk to me like that——

TOM. —am I supposed to do?

AMANDA. What's the matter with you? Have you gone out of your senses?

TOM. Yes, I have. You've driven me out of them.

AMANDA. What is the matter with you lately, you big—big—idiot?

TOM. Look, Mother—I haven't got a thing, not a single thing left in this house that I can call my own.

AMANDA. Lower your voice!

TOM. Yesterday you confiscated my books. You had the nerve to——

AMANDA. I did. I took that horrible novel back to the library—that awful book by that insane Mr.

---

6. **Milton:** John Milton (1608–1674), English poet.

AT A GLANCE

- Amanda calls Ida Scott to sell her a magazine subscription.
- When Ida hangs up on her, Amanda turns her attention to Tom, who is trying to write.
- Tom resents her interference and an argument ensues.

1 DIALECT

Amanda's rambling manner of speech and southern dialect suit her effusive character.

2 THEME

Amanda's attempt to be protective and Tom's rebuff of her attempt are typical of many parent-child relations.

3 HUMOR

Amanda tries to be authoritative and ends up sounding ridiculous because she really does not know what she is talking about.

4 CONTRAST

Unlike Laura, Tom rebels against his mother's attempts to control his life.

GUIDED READING

LITERAL QUESTIONS

1a. What does the woman to whom Amanda is talking on the phone do? (She hangs up.)

2a. What is Tom trying to do when Amanda disturbs him? (to write)

INFERENTIAL QUESTIONS

1b. Why does the woman do this to Amanda? (Amanda is the sort of person who cannot recognize that, far from charming people, she aggrevates them.)

2b. What might this activity symbolize for Tom? (a means of temporarily escaping from his environment)

Lawrence.[7] I cannot control the output of a diseased mind or people who cater to them, but I won't allow such filth in my house. No, no, no, no, no!

TOM. House, house! Who pays the rent on the house, who makes a slave of himself to——!

AMANDA. Don't you dare talk to me like that! [LAURA *crosses downstage left to back of armchair.*]

TOM. No, *I* mustn't say anything! *I've* just got to keep quiet and let you do all the talking.

AMANDA. Let me tell you something!

TOM. I don't want to hear any more.

AMANDA. You will hear more——[LAURA *crosses to phonograph.*]

TOM. [*Crossing through curtains between dining room and living room. Goes upstage of door right where, in a dark spot, there is supposedly a closet.*] Well, I'm not going to listen. I'm going out. [*Gets out coat.*]

AMANDA. [*Coming through curtains into living room, stands center stage.*] You are going to listen to me, Tom Wingfield. I'm tired of your impudence.—And another thing—I'm right at the end of my patience!

TOM. [*Putting overcoat on back of armchair and*
1 *crossing back to* AMANDA.] What do you think I'm at the end of, Mother? Aren't I supposed to have any patience to reach the end of? I know, I know. It seems unimportant to you, what I'm *doing*—what I'm trying to do—having a difference between them! You don't think that.

AMANDA. I think you're doing things that you're ashamed of, and that's why you act like this. [TOM *crosses to daybed and sits.*] I don't believe that you go every night to the movies. Nobody goes to the movies night after night. Nobody in their right mind goes to the movies as often as you pretend to. People don't go to the movies at nearly midnight and movies don't let out at two A.M. Come in stumbling, muttering to yourself like a maniac. You get three hours' sleep and then go to work. Oh, I can picture the way you're doing down there. Moping, doping, because you're in no condition.

TOM. That's true—that's very, very true. I'm in no condition!

AMANDA. How dare you jeopardize your job? Jeopardize our security? How do you think we'd manage——? [*Sits armchair right.*]

TOM. Look, Mother, do you think I'm *crazy* about the *warehouse?* You think I'm in love with the Continental Shoemakers? You think I want to spend fifty-five years of my life down there in that—*celotex*[8] *interior!* with *fluorescent*
2 *tubes?!* Honest to God, I'd rather somebody picked up a crowbar and battered out my brains—than go back mornings! But I *go!* Sure, every time you come in yelling that bloody *Rise and Shine!* Rise and shine!! I think how lucky dead people are! But I get up. [*Rises from daybed.*] I *go!* For sixty-five dollars a month I give up all that I dream of doing and being *ever!* And you say that is all I think of. Oh, God! Why, Mother, if self
3 is all I ever thought of, Mother, *I'd* be where *he* is—*GONE!* [*Crosses to get overcoat on back of armchair.*] As far as the system of transportation reaches! [AMANDA *rises, crosses to him and grabs his arm.*] Please don't grab at me, Mother!

AMANDA. [*Following him.*] I'm not grabbing at you. I want to know where you're going now.

TOM. [*Taking overcoat and starts crossing to door right.*] I'm going to the movies!

AMANDA. [*Crosses center.*] I don't believe that lie!

TOM. [*Crosses back to* AMANDA.] No? Well, you're right. For once in your life you're right. I'm not going to the movies. I'm going to opium dens!

---

7. **Mr. Lawrence:** D. H. Lawrence (1885–1930), English novelist and poet.

8. **celotex:** trademark for composition board made of sugar cane residue; used for insulation.

AT A GLANCE

- Tom reminds Amanda that he pays the rent.
- She complains about Tom's staying out late every night.
- He answers that he hates his job, but he still goes every morning.
- He gets ready to leave, but she grabs his arm and demands to know where he is going.

1 CHARACTERIZATION

Tom suggests that Amanda is so self-involved that she does not consider her children's feelings even though she makes an outward appearance at concern.

2 CHARACTERIZATION

Despite his resentment, Tom is aware of and acts on his responsibility, making up for the long-gone father.

3 THEME

One way to cope with life's problems—the method chosen by Tom's father—is to run away.

GUIDED READING

LITERAL QUESTIONS

1a. How does Tom feel about his job at Continental Shoemakers? (He hates it.)

2a. When Amanda tells Tom that he is lying, where does he tell her that he is going? (to opium dens)

INFERENTIAL QUESTIONS

1b. Why does he continue working there? (He feels responsible for his sister and mother. Also, the play is set during the Depression, and Tom does not have much choice in jobs.)

2b. Why does he tell such an obvious lie? (Tom is angry at Amanda and wants to shock her into leaving him alone.)

AT A GLANCE

- Tom sarcastically tells Amanda he is a member of a criminal gang and that his enemies will one day blow up the apartment.
- Unable to get his coat on, he hurls it across the room in frustration, breaking one of Laura's glass animals.
- *Scene 4:* Tom returns drunk from the movies.

1 CHARACTERIZATION

Tom ends his outburst with an attack on one of Amanda's most cherished memories. His caustic remark shows how resentful and angry he feels toward his mother.

2 STAGING

Tom's difficulties with his coat reflect how trapped he feels by his situation.

3 SYMBOL

Tom's response to his breaking part of Laura's menagerie shows how significant he feels the glass animals are to her. Perhaps he realizes that she is as fragile as the shattered glass.

4 STAGING

The movie-ticket stubs show the audience where Tom has been; the great quantity of them reminds the audience of Tom's desperate need to escape. The empty bottle shows Tom has also chosen another form of escape.

Yes, Mother, opium dens, dens of vice and criminals' hangouts, Mother. I've joined the Hogan gang. I'm a hired assassin, I carry a Tommy gun in a violin case! I run a string of cathouses in the valley! They call me Killer, Killer Wingfield, I'm really leading a double life. By day I'm a simple, honest warehouse worker, but at night I'm a dynamic czar of the underworld. Why, I go to gambling casinos and spin away a fortune on the roulette table! I wear a patch over one eye and a false moustache, sometimes I wear green whiskers. On those occasions they call me—El Diablo![9] Oh, I could tell you things to make you sleepless! My enemies plan to dynamite this place some night! Some night they're going to blow us all sky high. And will I be glad! Will I be
1 happy! And so will you be. You'll go up—up—over Blue Mountain on a broomstick! With seventeen gentlemen callers. You ugly babbling old witch! [*He goes through a series of violent, clumsy movements, seizing his overcoat, lunging to right door, pulling it fiercely open. The women watch him, aghast. His arm catches in*
2 *the sleeve of the coat as he struggles to pull it on. For a moment he is pinioned by the bulky garment. With an outraged groan he tears the coat off again, splitting the shoulder of it, and hurls it across the room. It strikes against the shelf of* LAURA*'s glass collection; there is a tinkle of shattering glass.* LAURA *cries out as if wounded.*]

LAURA. My glass!—menagerie. . . . [*She covers her face and turns away. Music cue 8 through to end of scene.*]

AMANDA. [*In an awful voice.*] I'll never speak to you again as long as you live unless you apologize to me! [AMANDA *exits through living room curtains.* TOM *is left with* LAURA. *He stares at her*
3 *stupidly for a moment. Then he crosses to shelf holding glass menagerie. Drops awkwardly on his knees to collect fallen glass, glancing at* LAURA *as if he would speak, but couldn't. Blackout.* TOM, AMANDA, *and* LAURA *exit in blackout.*]

9. **El Diablo** [el dē äb′ lō]: Spanish for "the devil."

ACT I

Scene 4. *The interior is dark. Faint light in alley right. A deep-voiced bell in a church is tolling the hour of five as the scene commences.*

[TOM *appears at the top of right alley. After each solemn boom of the bell in the tower he shakes a little toy noisemaker or rattle as if to express the tiny spasm of man in contrast to the sustained power and dignity of the Almighty. This and the unsteadiness of his advance make it evident that he has been drinking. As he climbs the few steps to the fire-escape landing, light steals up inside.* LAURA *appears in nightdress, entering living room from left door of dining room, observing* TOM*'s*
4 *empty bed (daybed) in the living room.* TOM *fishes in his pockets for door key, removing a motley assortment of articles in the search, including a perfect shower of movie-ticket stubs and an empty bottle. At last he finds the key, but just as he is about to insert it, it slips from his fingers. He strikes a match and crouches below the aoor.*]

TOM. [*Bitterly.*] One crack—and it falls through! [LAURA *opens door right.*][10]

LAURA. Tom! Tom, what are you doing?

TOM. Looking for a door key.

LAURA. Where have you been all this time?

TOM. I have been to the movies.

LAURA. All this time at the movies?

TOM. There was a very long program. There was a Garbo picture and a Mickey Mouse and a travelogue and a newsreel and a preview of coming attractions. And there was an organ solo and a collection for the milk fund—simultaneously—which ended up in a terrible fight between a fat lady and an usher!

LAURA. [*Innocently.*] Did you have to stay through everything?

10. **Laura . . . right:** next few speeches spoken on fire-escape landing.

GUIDED READING

LITERAL QUESTIONS

1a. What is Tom doing as Scene 3 ends? (picking up pieces of the fallen glass)

2a. What stage direction accompanies Laura's question asking if Tom had to stay out all evening? ("Innocently.")

INFERENTIAL QUESTIONS

1b. What feelings prompt his action? (Tom is not angry at Laura; he knows how much the menagerie means to her, and he feels guilty for having damaged it.)

2b. What does this reveal about Laura? (She naively believes her brother even though it is obvious that he has not been at the movies all this time.)

TOM. Of course! And, oh, I forgot! There was a big stage show! The headliner on this stage show was Malvolio the Magician. He performed wonderful tricks, many of them, such as pouring water back and forth between pitchers. First it turned to wine and then it turned to beer and then it turned to whiskey. I know it was whiskey it finally turned into because he needed somebody to come up out of the audience to help him, and I came up—both shows! It was Kentucky straight bourbon. A very generous fellow, he gave souvenirs. [*He pulls from his back pocket a shimmering rainbow-colored scarf.*] He gave me this. This is his magic scarf. You can have it, Laura. You wave it over a canary cage and you get a bowl of gold fish. You wave it over the gold-fish bowl and they fly away canaries. . . .
1 But the wonderfullest trick of all was the coffin trick. We nailed him into a coffin and he got out of the coffin without removing one nail. [*They enter.*] There is a trick that would come in handy for me—get me out of this two-by-four situation! [*Flops onto daybed and starts removing shoes.*]

LAURA. Tom—shhh!

TOM. What're you shushing me for?

LAURA. You'll wake up Mother.

TOM. Goody goody! Pay 'er back for all those "Rise an' Shines." [*Lies down groaning.*] You
2 know it don't take much intelligence to get yourself into a nailed-up coffin, Laura. But who in hell ever got himself out of one without removing one nail? [*As if in answer, the father's grinning photograph lights up.* LAURA *exits upstage left. Lights fade except for blue glow in dining room. Pause after lights fade, then clock chimes six times. This is followed by the alarm clock. Dim in forestage.*]

ACT I

Scene 5. *Scene is the same.*

[*Immediately following. The church bell is heard striking six. At the sixth stroke the alarm clock goes off in* AMANDA*'s room offstage right of dining room and after a few moments we hear her calling, "Rise and shine! Rise and shine! Laura, go tell your brother to rise and shine!"*]

TOM. [*Sitting up slowly in daybed.*] I'll rise—but I won't shine. [*The light increases.*]

AMANDA. [*Offstage.*] Laura, tell your brother his coffee is ready. [LAURA, *fully dressed, a cape over her shoulders, slips into living room.* TOM *is still in bed, covered with blanket, having taken off only shoes and coat.*]

LAURA. Tom!—It's nearly seven. Don't make Mother nervous. [*He stares at her stupidly. Be-*
3 *seechingly.*] Tom, speak to Mother this morning. Make up with her, apologize, speak to her!

TOM. [*Putting on shoes.*] She won't to me. It's her that started not speaking.

LAURA. If you just say you're sorry she'll start speaking.

TOM. Her not speaking—is that such a tragedy?

LAURA. Please—please!

AMANDA. [*Calling offstage right from kitchen.*] Laura, are you going to do what I asked you to do, or do I have to get dressed and go out myself?

LAURA. Going, going—soon as I get on my coat! [*She rises and crosses to door right.*] Butter and what else? [*To* AMANDA.]

AMANDA. [*Offstage.*] Just butter. Tell them to charge it.

LAURA. Mother, they make such faces when I do that.

AMANDA. [*Offstage.*] Sticks and stones can break our bones, but the expression on Mr. Garfinkel's face won't harm us! Tell your brother his coffee is getting cold.

LAURA. [*At door right.*] Do what I asked you, will you, will you, Tom? [*He looks sullenly away.*]

AMANDA. Laura, go now or just don't go at all!

LAURA. [*Rushing out right.*] Going—going! [*A second later she cries out. Falls on fire-escape*

AT A GLANCE

- Tom tells Laura he saw a magician who escaped from a nailed-up coffin.
- *Scene 5:* In the morning Amanda, not speaking to Tom, tells Laura to tell him coffee is ready.
- Laura asks Tom to make up with Amanda.
- Rushing out to buy some butter for Amanda, Laura falls on the fire escape.

1 THEME

Magic presents the illusion of escape, but it cannot help a responsible person escape from life's demands.

2 STAGING

Lighting the photograph represents a cynically humorous answer to the question of how one can escape from life's constraints—one can simply walk away.

3 CHARACTERIZATION

As sensitive as she is, Laura cannot stand the tension between her mother and brother. She knows that Amanda wants the ice to be broken but that her pride prevents her from doing so.

GUIDED READING

LITERAL QUESTION

1a. What does Tom say would come in handy for him? (the magic trick of escaping from a nailed-up coffin)

INFERENTIAL QUESTION

1b. What does this comment reveal about his feelings? (He feels trapped and suffocated by having to work at a job he hates to support his mother and sister.)

AT A GLANCE

- Laura recovers and goes on her way.
- Tom apologizes to Amanda.
- She makes him promise not to become a drunkard.
- She nags him about breakfast.

1 CHARACTERIZATION

Tom's sensitivity to his sister's fall reveals how fond and aware of her he really is.

2 STAGING

The goings-on with the hot coffee and the awkwardness of Tom and Amanda create a humorous picture of two people desiring, yet resisting, reconciliation.

3 CHARACTERIZATION

Amanda is filled with self-pity, feeling that all the sacrifices that she has made for her children are totally unappreciated.

4 CHARACTERIZATION

Amanda's sobbing self-pity changes quickly to an enthusiastic expression of pride in her children. This pride shows how her children have helped to ease the "everlasting regret" of her own experience.

1 *landing.* TOM *springs up and crosses to door right.* AMANDA *rushes anxiously in from dining room, puts dishes on dining room table.* TOM *opens door right.*]

TOM. Laura?

LAURA. I'm all right. I slipped, but I'm all right. [*Goes up right alley, out of sight.*]

AMANDA. [*On fire escape.*] I tell you if anybody falls down and breaks a leg on those fire-escape steps, the landlord ought to be sued for every cent he——[*Sees* TOM.] Who are you? [*Leaves fire-escape landing, crosses to dining room and returns with bowls, coffee cup, cream, etc. Puts them on small table right of daybed, crosses to armchair, sits. Counts three. Music cue 9. As* TOM *reenters right, listlessly for his coffee, she turns her back to him, as she sits in armchair. The light on her face with its aged but childish features is cruelly sharp, satirical as a Daumier*[11] *print.* TOM *glances sheepishly but sullenly at her averted figure and sits on daybed next to the food. The coffee is scalding hot, he sips it and gasps and spits it back in the cup. At*
2 *his gasp,* AMANDA *catches her breath and half turns. Then catches herself and turns away.* TOM *blows on his coffee, glancing sidewise at his mother. She clears her throat.* TOM *clears his. He starts to rise. Sinks back down again, scratches his head, clears his throat again.* AMANDA *coughs.* TOM *raises his cup in both hands to blow on it, his eyes staring over the rim of it at his mother for several moments. Then he slowly sets the cup down and awkwardly and hesitantly rises from daybed.*]

TOM. [*Hoarsely.*] I'm sorry, Mother. I'm sorry for all those things I said. I didn't mean it. I apologize.

3 **AMANDA.** [*Sobbingly.*] My devotion has made me a witch and so I make myself hateful to my children!

11. **Daumier** [dō myā′]: Honoré Daumier (1808–1879), French painter and caricaturist.

TOM. No, you don't.

AMANDA. I worry so much, I don't sleep, it makes me nervous!

TOM. [*Gently.*] I understand that.

AMANDA. You know I've had to put up a solitary battle all these years. But you're my right hand bower! Now don't fail me. Don't fall down.

TOM. [*Gently.*] I try, Mother.

4 **AMANDA.** [*With great enthusiasm.*] That's all right! You just keep on trying and you're bound to succeed. Why, you're—you're just full of natural endowments! Both my children are—they're very precious children and I've got an awful lot to be thankful for; you just must promise me one thing. [*Music cue 9 stops.*]

TOM. What is it, Mother?

AMANDA. Promise me you're never going to become a drunkard!

TOM. I promise, Mother. I won't ever become a drunkard, Mother.

AMANDA. That's what frightened me so, that you'd be drinking! Eat a bowl of Purina.[12]

TOM. Just coffee, Mother.

AMANDA. Shredded wheat biscuit?

TOM. No, no, Mother, just coffee.

AMANDA. You can't put in a day's work on an empty stomach. You've got ten minutes—don't gulp! Drinking too-hot liquids makes cancer of the stomach. . . . Put cream in.

TOM. No, thank you.

AMANDA. To cool it.

TOM. No! No, thank you, I want it black.

AMANDA. I know, but it's not good for you. We have to do all that we can to build ourselves up. In these trying times we live in, all that we have to cling to is—each other. . . . That's why it's so

12. **Purina:** cooked cereal.

GUIDED READING

LITERAL QUESTIONS

1a. After the goings-on with the hot coffee, what does Tom say to Amanda? (that he is sorry)

2a. What does Amanda say she has had to put up all these years? (a solitary battle)

INFERENTIAL QUESTIONS

1b. Why does he speak to her? (Tom may want to break the tension between him and his mother, or he may be motivated to apologize for Laura's sake.)

2b. To what is she referring? (having to raise two children without a husband)

important to——Tom, I—I sent out your sister so I could discuss something with you. If you hadn't spoken I would have spoken to you. [*Sits down.*]

TOM. [*Gently.*] What is it, Mother, that you want to discuss?

AMANDA. Laura! [TOM *puts his cup down slowly. Music cue 10.*]

TOM. —Oh.—Laura. . . .

AMANDA. [*Touching his sleeve.*] You know how Laura is. So quiet but—still water runs deep! She notices things and I think she—broods about them. [TOM *looks up.*] A few days ago I came in and she was crying.

TOM. What about?

AMANDA. You.

TOM. Me?

1 AMANDA. She has an idea that you're not happy here. [*Music cue 10 stops.*]

TOM. What gave her that idea?

AMANDA. What gives her any idea? However, you do act strangely. [TOM *slaps cup down on small table.*] I—I'm not criticizing, understand that! I know your ambitions do not lie in the warehouse, that like everybody in the whole wide world—you've had to—make sacrifices, but—
2 Tom—Tom—life's not easy, it calls for—Spartan endurance! There's so many things in my heart that I cannot describe to you! I've never told you but I—loved your father. . . .

TOM. [*Gently.*] I know that, Mother.

AMANDA. And you—when I see you taking after his ways! Staying out late—and—well, you had been drinking the night you were in that—terrifying condition! Laura says that you hate the apartment and that you go out nights to get away from it! Is that true, Tom?

TOM. No. You say there's so much in your heart that you can't describe to me. That's true of me, too. There's so much in my heart that I can't describe to you! So let's respect each other's——

AMANDA. But, why—why, Tom—are you so restless? Where do you go to, nights?

TOM. I—go to the movies.

AMANDA. Why do you go to the movies so much, Tom?

TOM. I go to the movies because—I like adventure. Adventure is something I don't have much of at work, so I go to the movies.

AMANDA. But, Tom, you go to the movies entirely too much!

TOM. I like a lot of adventure. [AMANDA *looks baffled, then hurt. As the familiar inquisition resumes he becomes hard and impatient again.* AMANDA *slips back into her querulous attitude toward him.*]

AMANDA. Most young men find adventure in their careers.

TOM. Then most young men are not employed in a warehouse.

AMANDA. The world is full of young men employed in warehouses and offices and factories.

TOM. Do all of them find adventure in their careers?

AMANDA. They do or they do without it! Not everybody has a craze for adventure.

TOM. Man is by instinct a lover, a hunter, a fighter, and none of those instincts are given much play at the warehouse!

3 AMANDA. Man is by instinct! Don't quote instinct to me! Instinct is something that people have got away from! It belongs to animals! Christian adults don't want it!

TOM. What do Christian adults want, then, Mother?

AMANDA. Superior things! Things of the mind and the spirit! Only animals have to satisfy instincts! Surely your aims are somewhat higher than theirs! Than monkeys—pigs——

AT A GLANCE

- Amanda tells Tom that Laura thinks he is unhappy.
- Amanda asks if Tom goes out at nights to get away from the apartment; he denies it, but says there is much in his heart he cannot describe.
- He says that he goes to movies for adventure, but Amanda cannot understand this.

1 IRONY

Considering Tom's outburst in Scene 3, Laura would have to be deaf and blind not to recognize Tom's profound unhappiness.

2 THEME

Amanda opens up to Tom and discusses her true feelings. This is a change from the usual superficiality that exists between the mother and son.

3 CHARACTERIZATION

Amanda shuns what she considers base and coarse in life. She feels instinct belongs to the animals, while humans want superior things "of the mind and the spirit."

GUIDED READING

LITERAL QUESTIONS

1a. What does Amanda say that she wants to talk to Tom about? (Laura)

2a. What does Tom say that he wants more of in his life? (adventure)

INFERENTIAL QUESTIONS

1b. What does she really seem to want to talk about? (Tom's unhappiness with living at home)

2b. Why does Amanda object to this statement? (To Amanda a desire for adventure probably sounds like a desire to leave, and she depends upon Tom's income.)

AT A GLANCE

- Amanda tells Tom about her fears for Laura.
- Amanda knows he wants to join the merchant marine, but she wants him to stay at home until his sister is married.

1 FORESHADOWING

The letter that Amanda saw and the garb that Tom wears as narrator point rather clearly to how Tom will deal with his situation.

2 CHARACTERIZATION

Amanda, a manipulative character, uses the strongest arguments at her disposal to persuade Tom to find a husband for Laura. She tempts him with freedom and plays on his deep feelings for Laura.

TOM. I reckon they're not.

AMANDA. You're joking. However, that isn't what I wanted to discuss.

TOM. [*Rising.*] I haven't much time.

AMANDA. [*Pushing his shoulders.*] Sit down.

TOM. You want me to punch in red at the warehouse, Mother?

AMANDA. You have five minutes. I want to talk about Laura.

TOM. All right! What about Laura?

AMANDA. We have to be making some plans and provisions for her. She's older than you, two years, and nothing has happened. She just drifts along doing nothing. It frightens me terribly how she just drifts along.

TOM. I guess she's the type that people call home girls.

AMANDA. There's no such type, and if there is, it's a pity! That is unless the home is hers, with a husband!

TOM. What?

AMANDA. [*Crossing downstage right to armchair.*] Oh, I can see the handwriting on the wall as plain as I see the nose in front of my face! It's terrifying! More and more you remind me of your father! He was out all [*Sits in armchair.*]
1 hours without explanation!—Then left! Good-by! And me with the bag to hold. I saw that letter you got from the merchant marine. I know what you're dreaming of. I'm not standing here blindfolded. Very well, then. Then do it! But not till there's somebody to take your place.

TOM. What do you mean?

AMANDA. I mean that as soon as Laura has got somebody to take care of her, married, a home of
2 her own, independent—why, then you'll be free to go wherever you please, [*Rises, crosses to* TOM.] on land, on sea, whichever way the wind blows you! But until that time you've got to look out for your sister. [*Crosses right behind armchair.*] I don't say me because I'm old and don't matter! I say for your sister because she's young and dependent. I put her in business college—a dismal failure! Frightened her so it made her sick at the stomach. I took her over to the Young People's League at the church. Another fiasco. She spoke to nobody, nobody spoke to her. [*Sits in armchair.*] Now all she does is fool with those pieces of glass and play those worn-out records. What kind of a life is that for a girl to lead?

TOM. What can I do about it?

AMANDA. Overcome selfishness! Self, self, self is

GUIDED READING

LITERAL QUESTIONS

1a. What reason does Amanda give for not telling Tom he has to look out for her? (She is old and does not matter.)

2a. What does Amanda say Tom must overcome? (selfishness)

INFERENTIAL QUESTIONS

1b. Why does she say this? (She probably knows Tom would not stay just to take care of her, but he would feel a responsibility to look out for Laura.)

2b. Why is this ironic? (Amanda is basically a selfish person herself, but does not see it.)

all that you ever think of! [TOM *springs up and crosses right to get his coat and put it on. It is ugly and bulky. He pulls on a cap with earmuffs.*] Where is your muffler? Put your wool muffler on! [*He snatches it angrily from the hook and tosses it around his neck and pulls both ends tight.*] Tom! I haven't said what I had in mind to ask you.

TOM. I'm too late to——

AMANDA. [*Catching his arm—very importunately. Then shyly.*] Down at the warehouse, aren't there some—nice young men?

TOM. No!

AMANDA. There must be—some. . . .

TOM. Mother——[*Gesture.*]

AMANDA. Find out one that's clean-living—doesn't drink and—ask him out for Sister!

TOM. What?

1 **AMANDA.** For Sister! To meet! Get acquainted!

TOM. [*Stamping to door right.*] Oh, my go-osh!

AMANDA. Will you? [*He opens door. Imploringly.*] Will you? [*He starts out.*] Will you? Will you, dear? [TOM *exits up alley right.* AMANDA *is on fire-escape landing.*]

TOM. [*Calling back.*] Yes!

AMANDA. [*Reentering right and crossing to
2 phone. Music cue 11.*] Ella Cartwright? Ella, this is Amanda Wingfield. First, first, how's that kidney trouble? Oh, it has? It has come back? Well, you're just a Christian martyr, you're just a Christian martyr. I was noticing in my little red book that your subscription to the *Companion* has run out just when that wonderful new serial by Bessie Mae Harper was starting. It's all about the horsy set on Long Island. Oh, you have? You have read it? Well, how do you think it turns out? Oh, no. Bessie Mae Harper never lets you down. Oh, of course, we have to have complications. You have to have complications—oh, you can't have a story without them—but Bessie Mae Harper always leaves you with such an uplift——What's the matter, Ella? You sound so mad. Oh, because
3 it's seven o'clock in the morning. Oh, Ella, I forgot that you never got up until nine. I forgot that anybody in the world was allowed to sleep as late as that. I can't say any more than I'm sorry, can I? Oh, you will? You're going to take that subscription from me anyhow? Well, bless you, Ella, bless you, bless you, bless you. [*Music cue 11 fades into music cue 11A, dance music, and continues into next scene. Dim out lights. Music cue 11A.*]

ACT I

Scene 6. ***The same.—Only right alley lighted, with dim light.***

TOM. [*Enters downstage right and stands as before, leaning against grillwork, with cigarette, wearing merchant sailor coat and cap.*] Across the alley was the Paradise Dance Hall. Evenings in spring they'd open all the doors and windows and the music would come outside. Sometimes
4 they'd turn out all the lights except for a large glass sphere that hung from the ceiling. It would turn slowly about and filter the dusk with delicate rainbow colors. Then the orchestra would play a waltz or a tango, something that had a slow and sensuous rhythm. The young couples would come outside, to the relative privacy of the alley. You could see them kissing behind ash pits and telephone poles. This was the compensation for lives that passed like mine, without change or adventure. Changes and adventure, however, were imminent this year. They were waiting around the corner for all these dancing kids. Suspended in the mist over Berchtesgaden,[13] caught in the folds of Chamberlain's umbrella——In Spain there was Guernica![14] Here there was only

---

13. **Berchtesgaden** [bärkʜ′ tes gä′dən]: Hitler's mountain retreat, where he was visited by British Prime Minister Neville Chamberlain in 1938. Chamberlain agreed to Hitler's annexation of Czechoslovakia in exchange for a pledge of peace. Hitler broke this pledge, bringing war.
14. **Guernica** [ger nē′kä]: town in northern Spain held by democratic forces in the Spanish Civil War and bombed by the Germans in 1937 to support the Spanish Fascists.

AT A GLANCE

- Tom agrees to bring someone home to meet Laura.
- Amanda continues with her magazine sales.
- *Scene 6:* Tom, again as narrator, describes the Paradise Dance Hall across the alley.

1 PLOT: RISING ACTION

Amanda's plea for Tom to find a gentleman caller sets into motion the events of Act II.

2 CHARACTERIZATION

Amanda's warmth is ritualistic and perfunctory—a means to an end.

3 IRONY

After charging Tom with thinking only of himself, it is ironic that Amanda would begin her telephone sales at seven in the morning, giving no thought to the people whom she is calling.

4 SYMBOL

The glass sphere with its rainbow colors is similar to Laura's glass menagerie: something beautiful that can be easily broken.

GUIDED READING

LITERAL QUESTIONS

1a. What does Amanda want Tom to do? (find a gentleman caller for Laura)

2a. What is across the alley from the Wingfield apartment? (the Paradise Dance Hall)

INFERENTIAL QUESTIONS

1b. How does Tom feel about the request? (He seems to agree to it only so that Amanda will stop nagging him.)

2b. Why does Tom call this place a "compensation"? (Places like the dance hall—and the movies—provide a substitute for real adventure; these dancing kids would soon find "adventure" in World War II.)

AT A GLANCE

- Out on the fire escape, Amanda asks Tom to talk about wishing.
- He says that he has invited a gentleman caller for Laura and that the gentleman has accepted.

1 CHARACTERIZATION

Amanda constantly suggests ways for Tom to improve himself. Her suggestions, however, do not take into account his desires, only her own desires for him.

2 THEME

Amanda depends on wishes. She seems to believe that her wishes can somehow alter reality. Her life is an illusion; it is not based in the real world.

3 PLOT: RISING ACTION

Amanda's wish has been granted: She will get the gentleman caller she has sought for Laura.

hot swing music and liquor, dance halls, bars, and movies, and sex that hung in the gloom like a chandelier and flooded the world with brief, deceptive rainbows. . . . While these unsuspecting kids danced to "Dear One, the World is Waiting for the Sunrise." All the world was really waiting for bombardments. [*Music cue 11A stops. Dim in dining room: faint glow.* AMANDA *is seen in dining room.*]

AMANDA. Tom, where are you?

TOM. [*Standing as before.*] I came out to smoke. [*Exit right into the wings, where he again changes coats and leaves hat.*]

AMANDA. [TOM *reenters and stands on fire-escape landing, smoking. He opens door for* AMANDA, *who sits on hassock on landing.*] Oh, you smoke too much. A pack a day at fifteen cents a pack. How much would that be in a month? Thirty
1 times fifteen? It wouldn't be very much. Well, it would be enough to help toward a night school course in accounting at the Washington U.! Wouldn't that be lovely?

TOM. I'd rather smoke.

AMANDA. I know! That's the tragedy of you. This fire-escape landing is a poor excuse for the porch we used to have. What are you looking at?

TOM. The moon.

2 **AMANDA.** Is there a moon this evening?

TOM. It's rising over Garfinkel's Delicatessen.

AMANDA. Oh! So it is! Such a little silver slipper of a moon. Have you made a wish on it?

TOM. Um-mm.

AMANDA. What did you wish?

TOM. That's a secret.

AMANDA. All right, I won't tell you what I wished, either. I can keep a secret, too. I can be just as mysterious as you.

TOM. I bet I can guess what you wished.

AMANDA. Why, is my head transparent?

TOM. You're not a sphinx.

AMANDA. No, I don't have secrets. I'll tell you what I wished for on the moon. Success and happiness for my precious children. I wish for that whenever there's a moon, and when there isn't a moon, I wish for it, too.

TOM. I thought perhaps you wished for a gentleman caller.

AMANDA. Why do you say that?

TOM. Don't you remember asking me to fetch one?

AMANDA. I remember suggesting that it would be nice for your sister if you brought home some nice young man from the warehouse. I think that I've made that suggestion more than once.

TOM. Yes, you have made it repeatedly.

AMANDA. Well?

3 **TOM.** We are going to have one.

AMANDA. *What?*

TOM. A gentleman caller!

AMANDA. You mean you have asked some nice young man to come over? [*Rising from stool, facing* TOM.]

TOM. I've asked him to dinner.

AMANDA. You really did?

TOM. I did.

AMANDA. And did he—accept?

TOM. He did!

AMANDA. He did?

TOM. He did.

AMANDA. Well, isn't that lovely!

TOM. I thought that you would be pleased.

AMANDA. It's definite, then?

GUIDED READING

LITERAL QUESTION

1a. When Tom says that he invited a gentleman caller, does Amanda seem to believe him, or does she doubt him? (She seems to doubt him.)

INFERENTIAL QUESTION

1b. Why does she react in this way? (She may think that Tom is teasing her.)

TOM. Oh, very definite.

AMANDA. How soon?

TOM. Pretty soon.

AMANDA. How soon?

TOM. Quite soon.

AMANDA. How soon?

TOM. Very, very soon.

AMANDA. Every time I want to know anything you start going on like that.

TOM. What do you want to know?

AMANDA. Go ahead and guess. Go ahead and guess.

TOM. All right, I'll guess. You want to know when the gentleman caller's coming—he's coming tomorrow.

AMANDA. Tomorrow? Oh, no, I can't do anything about tomorrow. I can't do anything about tomorrow.

TOM. Why not?

AMANDA. That doesn't give me any time.

TOM. Time for what?

AMANDA. Time for preparations. Oh, you should have phoned me the minute you asked him—the minute he accepted!

TOM. You don't have to make any fuss.

AMANDA. Of course I have to make a fuss! I can't have a man coming into a place that's all sloppy. It's got to be thrown together properly. I certainly have to do some fast thinking by tomorrow night, too.

TOM. I don't see why you have to think at all.

AMANDA. That's because you just don't know. [*Enter living room, crosses to center stage. Dim in living room.*] You just don't know, that's all. We can't have a gentleman caller coming into a pigsty! Now, let's see. Oh, I've got those three pieces of wedding silver left. I'll polish that up. I wonder how that old lace tablecloth is holding
1 up all these years? We can't wear anything. We haven't got it. We haven't got anything to wear. We haven't got it. [*Goes back to door right.*]

TOM. Mother! This boy is no one to make a fuss over.

AMANDA. [*Crossing to center.*] I don't know how you can say that when this is the first gentleman caller your little sister's ever had! I think it's pathetic that that little girl has never had a single gentleman caller! Come on inside! Come on inside!

TOM. What for?

AMANDA. I want to ask you a few things.

TOM. [*From doorway right.*] If you're going to make a fuss, I'll call the whole thing off. I'll call the boy up and tell him not to come.

AMANDA. No! You mustn't ever do that. People hate broken engagements. They have no place to go. Come on inside. Come on inside. Will you come inside when I ask you to come inside? Sit down. [TOM *comes into living room.*]

TOM. Any particular place you want me to sit?

AMANDA. Oh! Sit anywhere. [TOM *sits in armchair right.*] Look! What am I going to do about that? [*Looking at daybed.*] Did you ever see anything look so sad? I know, I'll get a bright piece of cre-
2 tonne.[15] That won't cost much. And I made payments on a floor lamp. So I'll have that sent out! And I can put a bright cover on the chair. I wish I had time to paper the walls. What's his name?

TOM. His name is O'Connor.

AMANDA. O'Connor—he's Irish and tomorrow's
3 Friday—that means fish. Well, that's all right, I'll make a salmon loaf and some mayonnaise dressing for it. Where did you meet him? [*Crosses to daybed and sits.*]

---

15. **cretonne** [krē'ton]: strong, printed cotton fabric used for draperies and slipcovers.

AT A GLANCE

- Tom informs Amanda that the caller is coming to dinner tomorrow.
- She worries that she does not have enough time to get the apartment and Laura properly prepared for the caller.

1 STYLE: SENTENCE STRUCTURE

The short sentences and repetitions suggest that Amanda is in a dither as she faces the realization of her long-awaited dream.

2 CHARACTERIZATION

Amanda is the type of person who makes others uncomfortable because she tries too hard: papering the walls for this occasion is completely inappropriate.

3 BACKGROUND

Amanda assumes that the gentleman caller is a Roman Catholic because his last name is Irish. At the time Catholics traditionally observed meatless Fridays.

GUIDED READING

LITERAL QUESTION

1a. What is Amanda's complaint about the caller who is coming tomorrow? (She does not have time to get ready for him.)

INFERENTIAL QUESTION

1b. Why does Tom disagree with Amanda's point of view? (He sees the dinner as a casual event, not the first step in a campaign toward matrimony.)

AT A GLANCE

- Amanda is concerned that the caller, James O'Connor, might drink.
- She asks about Jim's job and income.
- She lectures Tom on the necessity of planning for the future.

1 **VOCABULARY: CONNOTATION**

"Poor" suggests Tom's pity for his acquaintance, who is going to be beset by Amanda.

2 **RESPONSE JOURNAL**

Students might comment upon how this exchange shows mother and son at cross-purposes.

3 **IRONY**

Eager to make the best of things, Amanda calls one of the lower positions in any company (shipping clerk) "fairly important."

4 **CHARACTERIZATION**

In decrying Tom's lack of purpose, Amanda alludes to the "everlasting regret" of her own life.

TOM. At the warehouse, of course. Where else would I meet him?

AMANDA. Well, I don't know. Does he drink?

TOM. What made you ask me that?

AMANDA. Because your father did.

TOM. Now, don't get started on that!

AMANDA. He drinks, then.

TOM. No, not that I know of.

AMANDA. You have to find out. There's nothing I want less for my daughter than a man who drinks.

1 **TOM.** Aren't you being a little bit premature? After all, poor Mr. O'Connor hasn't even appeared on the scene yet.

AMANDA. But he will tomorrow. To meet your sister. And what do I know about his character? [*Rises and crosses to* TOM *who is still in armchair, smooths his hair.*]

TOM. [*Submitting grimly.*] Now what are you up to?

AMANDA. I always did hate that cowlick. I never could understand why it won't sit down by itself.

2 **TOM.** Mother, I want to tell you something and I mean it sincerely right straight from my heart. There's a lot of boys who meet girls which they don't marry!

AMANDA. You know you always had me worried because you could never stick to a subject. [*Crosses to daybed.*] What I want to know is what's his position at the warehouse?

TOM. He's a shipping clerk.

3 **AMANDA.** Oh! Shipping clerk! Well, that's fairly important. That's where you'd be if you had more get-up. How much does he earn? [*Sits on daybed.*]

TOM. I have no way of knowing that for sure. I judge his salary to be approximately eighty-five dollars a month.

AMANDA. Eighty-five dollars? Well, that's not princely.

TOM. It's twenty dollars more than I make.

AMANDA. I know that. Oh, how well I know that! How well I know that! Eighty-five dollars a month. No. It can't be done. A family man can never get by on eighty-five dollars a month.

TOM. Mother, Mr. O'Connor is not a family man.

AMANDA. Well, he might be some time in the future, mightn't he?

TOM. Oh, I see. . . . Plans and provisions.

4 **AMANDA.** You are the only young man that I know of who ignores the fact that the future becomes the present, the present the past, and the past turns into everlasting regret if you don't plan for it.

TOM. I will think that over and see what I can make of it!

AMANDA. Don't be supercilious with your mother! Tell me some more about this.—What do you call him? Mr. O'Connor, Mr. O'Connor. He must have another name besides Mr.——?

TOM. His full name is James D. O'Connor. The D. is for Delaney.

AMANDA. Delaney? Irish on both sides and he doesn't drink?

TOM. [*Rises from armchair.*] Shall I call him up and ask him? [*Starts toward phone.*]

AMANDA. [*Crossing to phone.*] No!

TOM. I'll call him up and tell him you want to know if he drinks. [*Picks up phone.*]

AMANDA. [*Taking phone away from him.*] No, you can't do that. You have to be discreet about that subject. When I was a girl in Blue Mountain if it was [TOM *sits on right of daybed.*] suspected that a young man was drinking and any girl was receiving his attentions—if any girl *was* receiving his attentions, she'd go to the minister of his church and ask about his character—or her fa-

GUIDED READING

LITERAL QUESTION

1a. According to Amanda, for what is eighty-five dollars a month too little money? (raising a family)

INFERENTIAL QUESTION

1b. What makes her think of this expense? (Her intention is to see Laura married to the first caller that comes along.)

ther, if her father was living, then it was his duty to go to the minister of his church and ask about

1 his character, and that's how young girls in Blue Mountain were kept from making tragic mistakes. [*Picture dims in and out.*]

TOM. How come you made such a tragic one?

AMANDA. Oh, I don't know how he did it, but that face fooled everybody. All he had to do was grin and the world was bewitched. [*Behind daybed,*

2 *crosses to armchair.*] I don't know of anything more tragic than a young girl just putting herself at the mercy of a handsome appearance, and I hope Mr. O'Connor is *not* too good-looking.

TOM. As a matter of fact he isn't. His face is covered with freckles and he has a very large nose.

AMANDA. He's not right-down homely?

TOM. No. I wouldn't say rightdown—homely—medium homely, I'd say.

AMANDA. Well, if a girl had any sense she'd look for character in a man anyhow.

TOM. That's what I've always said, Mother.

AMANDA. You've always said it—you've always said it! How could you've always said it when you never even thought about it?

TOM. Aw, don't be so suspicious of me.

AMANDA. I am. I'm suspicious of every word that comes out of your mouth, when you talk to me, but I want to know about this young man. Is he up and coming?

TOM. Yes. I really do think he goes in for self-improvement.

AMANDA. What makes you think it?

TOM. He goes to night school.

AMANDA. Well, what does he do there at night school?

TOM. He's studying radio engineering and public speaking.

AMANDA. Oh! Public speaking! Oh, that shows, that shows that he intends to be an executive some day—and radio engineering. Well, that's coming . . . huh?

TOM. I think it's here.

AMANDA. Well, those are all very illuminating facts. [*Crosses to back of armchair.*] Facts that every mother should know about any young man calling on her daughter, seriously or not.

TOM. Just one little warning, Mother. I didn't tell him anything about Laura. I didn't let on we had dark ulterior motives. I just said, "How about coming home to dinner some time?" and he said, "Fine," and that was the whole conversation.

AMANDA. I bet it was, too. I tell you, sometimes you can be as eloquent as an oyster. However, when he sees how pretty and sweet that child is, he's going to be, well, he's going to be very glad he was asked over here to have some dinner. [*Sits in armchair.*]

TOM. Mother, just one thing. You won't expect too much of Laura, will you?

AMANDA. I don't know what you mean. [TOM *crosses slowly to* AMANDA. *He stands for a moment, looking at her. Then—*]

3 **TOM.** Well, Laura seems all those things to you and me because she's ours and we love her. We don't even notice she's crippled any more.

AMANDA. Don't use that word.

TOM. Mother, you have to face the facts; she is, and that's not all.

AMANDA. What do you mean "that's not all"? [TOM *kneels by her chair.*]

TOM. Mother—you know that Laura is very different from other girls.

AMANDA. Yes, I do know that, and I think that difference is all in her favor, too.

TOM. Not quite all—in the eyes of others—strangers—she's terribly shy. She lives in a world of her own and those things make her seem a little peculiar to people outside the house.

AMANDA. Don't use that word peculiar.

AT A GLANCE

- Tom describes Jim as "medium homely" and cites his attendance in night school as a sign of interest in self-improvement.
- Tom explains that he invited Jim to dinner without mentioning Laura.
- Tom brings up the disturbing facts that Laura is crippled and a little peculiar.

1 STAGING

The flickering picture of Mr. Wingfield is a visual reminder of Amanda's "tragic mistake."

2 CHARACTERIZATION

Amanda sees herself as someone who was manipulated by a deceiver. In reality she probably was at least partly responsible.

3 CONFLICT

Amanda is still struggling to shut out reality. Tom states simple facts about Laura, but Amanda refuses to acknowledge them.

GUIDED READING

LITERAL QUESTIONS

1a. What does Amanda describe as the most tragic thing that can happen to a young girl? (falling in love with a handsome face)

2a. What has Tom not told the gentleman caller? (that he has an unmarried sister)

INFERENTIAL QUESTIONS

1b. What in Amanda's past causes her to have this opinion? (She feels that she herself was deceived by the handsome face of Mr. Wingfield.)

2b. Why has Tom not mentioned this detail? (He may have been embarrassed, or he may not have wanted to scare the young man off.)

AT A GLANCE

- Tom states that Laura lives in a world of little glass animals.
- Amanda calls Laura out to wish on the moon for happiness.

1 THEME

Laura copes with the disappointments in her life by retreating into the past, symbolized by her records, and into the private world of her menagerie.

REFLECTING ON ACT I

How is each member of the Wingfield family trapped? (Students might mention economic constraints or might talk about Amanda's imaginative construction of her past, Laura's shyness, and Tom's sense of responsibility.)

STUDY QUESTIONS

1. Amanda, Laura, and Tom Wingfield; Amanda is the mother of Laura and Tom.
2. Tom; functions as narrator and takes part in action of play; stage directions indicate that, as narrator, he dresses as merchant sailor and changes before participating in action
3. deserted his family
4. Laura not attending business college; fears that, being crippled and withdrawn, Laura will not marry, and will not be able to support herself
5. hates his job at the warehouse but feels he must stay there to support Amanda and Laura
6. a collection of glass animals that Laura keeps
7. a man that Tom works with and whom he has invited to dinner
8. during the Depression, just before World War II; Tom's first speech as narrator; Tom's narration at the beginning of Scene 6
9. Answers will vary; most will see words as sincere expression of Amanda's hopes.
10. Predictions will vary but should be based on evidence in Act I.
11. Possible answers: encourage her to see more people; invite her to go places and do things; find ways to help her be more self-confident.

TOM. You have to face the facts.—She is.

AMANDA. I don't know in what way she's peculiar. [*Music cue 12, till curtain.* TOM *pauses a moment for music, then—*]

1 **TOM.** Mother, Laura lives in a world of little glass animals. She plays old phonograph records—and—that's about all——[TOM *rises slowly, goes quietly out the door right, leaving it open, and exits slowly up the alley.* AMANDA *rises, goes on to fire-escape landing right, looks at moon.*]

AMANDA. Laura! Laura! [LAURA *answers from kitchen right.*]

LAURA. Yes, Mother.

AMANDA. Let those dishes go and come in front! [LAURA *appears with dish towel. Gaily.*] Laura, come here and make a wish on the moon!

LAURA. [*Entering from kitchen right and comes down to fire-escape landing.*] Moon—moon?

AMANDA. A little silver slipper of a moon. Look over your left shoulder, Laura, and make a wish! [LAURA *looks faintly puzzled as if called out of sleep.* AMANDA *seizes her shoulders and turns her at an angle on the fire-escape landing.*] Now! Now, darling, wish!

LAURA. What shall I wish for, Mother?

AMANDA. [*Her voice trembling and her eyes suddenly filling with tears.*] Happiness! And just a little bit of good fortune! [*The stage dims out.*]

CURTAIN

STUDY QUESTIONS

Recalling

1. What three characters appear on the stage during Act I? How are they related to one another?
2. Which character plays a double role? How do the stage directions make it clear which role this character is playing?
3. What has happened to Tom and Laura's father?
4. At the beginning of Scene 2, what discovery has upset Amanda? Why is she so concerned about Laura?
5. What accounts for Tom's unhappiness?
6. What does the title of this play refer to?
7. Who is James D. O'Connor?

Interpreting

8. When does the play take place? What clues let you know this?
9. What is your reaction to what Amanda says is her secret wish: "Success and happiness for my precious children"? Why?
10. What do you predict will happen in the next act? Give reasons for your predictions.

Extending

11. If you knew someone like Laura, what would you do to help her?

ACT II

***Scene 7.** The same.*

[Inner curtains closed between dining room and living room. Interiors of both rooms are dark as
1 *at beginning of play.* TOM *has on the same jacket and cap as at first. Same dance hall music as cue 1, fading as* TOM *begins.]*

TOM. *[Discovered leaning against grill on fire-escape landing, as before, and smoking.]* And so the following evening I brought Jim home to dinner. I had known Jim slightly in high school. In high school, Jim was a hero. He had tremendous Irish good nature and vitality with the scrubbed and polished look of white chinaware. He seemed to move in a continual spotlight. He was a star in basketball, captain of the debating club, president of the senior class and the glee club, and he sang the male lead in the annual light opera. He was forever running or bounding, never just walking. He seemed always just at the point of defeating the law of gravity. He was shooting with such velocity through his adolescence that you would just logically expect him to arrive at nothing short of the White House by the time he was thirty. But Jim apparently ran into more interference after his graduation from high school because his speed had definitely slowed. And so, at this particular time in our lives he was holding a job that wasn't much better than mine. He was the only one at the warehouse with whom I was on friendly terms. I was valuable to Jim as someone who could remember his former glory, who had seen him win basketball games and the silver cup in debating. He knew of my secret practice of retiring to a cabinet of the washroom to work on poems whenever business was slack in the warehouse. He called me Shakespeare. And while the other boys in the warehouse regarded me with suspicious hostility, Jim took a humorous attitude toward me. Gradually his attitude began to affect the other boys and their hostility wore off. And so, after a time they began to smile at me too, as people smile at some oddly fashioned dog that trots across their path at some distance. I knew that Jim and Laura had known each other in high school because I had heard my sister Laura speak admiringly of Jim's voice. I didn't know if Jim would remember her or not. Because in high school Laura had been as unobtrusive as Jim had been astonishing. And, if he did remember Laura, it was not as my sister, for when I asked him home to dinner, he smiled and said, "You know, a funny thing, Shakespeare, I never thought of you as having folks!" Well, he was about to discover that I did. . . . *[Music cue 13.* TOM *exits stage right. Interior living room lights dim in.* AMANDA *is sitting on small table right of daybed sewing on hem on* LAURA*'s dress.* LAURA *stands facing the door right.* AMANDA *has worked like a Turk in*
2 *preparation for the gentleman caller. The results are astonishing. The new floor lamp with its rose silk shade is in place, right of living room next to wall, a colored paper lantern conceals the broken light fixture in the ceiling, chintz covers are on chairs and sofa, a pair of new sofa pillows make their initial appearance.* LAURA *stands in the middle of room with lifted arms while* AMANDA *crouches before her, adjusting the hem of the new dress, devout and ritualistic. The dress is colored and designed by*
3 *memory. The arrangement of* LAURA*'s hair is changed, it is softer and more becoming. A fragile, unearthly prettiness has come out in* LAURA*; she is like a piece of translucent glass touched by light, given a momentary radiance, not actual, not lasting.* AMANDA, *still seated, is sewing* LAURA*'s dress.* LAURA *is standing right of* AMANDA.*]*

AMANDA. Why are you trembling so, Laura?

LAURA. Mother, you've made me so nervous!

AMANDA. Why, how have I made you nervous?

LAURA. By all this fuss! You make it seem so important.

AMANDA. I don't understand you at all, honey. Every time I try to do anything for you that's the least bit different you just seem to set yourself against it. Now take a look at yourself. *[*LAURA *starts for door right.]* No, wait! Wait just a minute—I forgot something. *[Picks two powder puffs from daybed.]*

AT A GLANCE

- *Scene 7:* Tom, as narrator, describes Jim's great success in high school activities.
- Jim likes Tom because Tom remembers Jim's "former glory."
- Tom doubts that Jim would remember Laura, who was terribly shy even in high school.
- Amanda has done an astonishing job fixing up both the apartment and Laura, but all the fuss makes Laura nervous.

LITERARY OPTIONS

- symbol
- characterization
- theme

THEMATIC OPTIONS

- the fragility of dreams
- illusion vs. reality
- coping with adversity

1 POINT OF VIEW

The story, told through the eyes of Tom as he looks back on events, is more poignant because his narrator's role gives Tom the necessary distance from these events.

2 STAGING

The changed look of the apartment shows how appearances can deceive.

3 SYMBOL

Throughout the play glass and its fragile beauty are linked to the equally fragile Laura.

GUIDED READING

LITERAL QUESTIONS

1a. How does Tom characterize the Jim that he knew in high school? (talented, popular, and energetic)

2a. How did Jim's attitude toward Tom affect the way in which the other warehouse workers treated Tom? (Their hostility wore off.)

INFERENTIAL QUESTIONS

1b. If these qualities have not changed, does Jim seem an appropriate match for Laura? (Jim's vitality probably would clash with Laura's fear of life; they seem mismatched.)

2b. Why did Jim's attitude have this effect? (The warehouse workers must have respected Jim.)

AT A GLANCE

- Amanda tries to get Laura to pad out her dress.
- Amanda changes into a girlish frock and recalls the days when she was young, attended balls, and had admirers.

1 CHARACTERIZATION

Amanda's vanity shows in her reluctance to accept that the years have caused a change in the way her weight is distributed.

2 VOCABULARY: CONNOTATION

"Girlish" is a reminder that Amanda is in a sense trapped in her youth, having never really matured.

3 THEME

One way to cope with an unpleasant present is to live in a real (or imagined) past.

4 STAGING

Amanda's conferring of the flowers on Laura shows how she is attempting to re-create the past, as she remembers it, in Laura's present life.

LAURA. What is it?

AMANDA. A couple of improvements. [*Business with powder puffs.*] When I was a girl we had round little lacy things like that and we called them "Gay Deceivers."

LAURA. I won't wear them!

AMANDA. Of course you'll wear them.

LAURA. Why should I?

AMANDA. Well, to tell you the truth, honey, you're just a little bit flat-chested.

LAURA. You make it seem like we were setting a trap.

AMANDA. We are. All pretty girls are a trap and men expect them to be traps. Now look at yourself in that glass. [LAURA *crosses right. Looks at mirror, invisible to audience, which is in darkness upstage right of right door.*] See? You look just like an angel on a postcard. Isn't that lovely? Now you just wait. I'm going to dress myself up. You're going to be astonished at your mother's appearance. [*End of music cue leads into dance music, which then leads into music cue 14, a few lines below, at stage direction.* AMANDA *exits through curtains upstage off left in dining room.* LAURA *looks in mirror for a moment. Removes "Gay Deceivers," hides them under mattress of daybed. Sits on small table right of daybed for a moment, goes out to fire-escape landing, listens to dance music, until* AMANDA*'s*
1 *entrance.* AMANDA, *offstage.*] I found an old dress in the trunk. But what do you know? I had to do a lot to it but it broke my heart when I had to let it out. Now, Laura, just look at your mother. Oh, no! Laura, come look at me now! [*Enters dining room left door. Comes down through living room curtain to living room center. Music cue 14.*]

2 LAURA. [*Reenters from fire-escape landing. Sits on left arm of armchair.*] Oh, Mother, how lovely! [AMANDA *wears a girlish frock. She carries a bunch of jonquils.*]

AMANDA. [*Standing center, holding flowers.*] It used to be. It used to be. It had a lot of flowers on it, but they got awful tired so I had to take them all off. I led the cotillion[16] in this dress years ago. I won the cake walk[17] twice at Sunset Hill, and I wore it to the Governor's Ball in Jackson. You should have seen your mother. You should have seen your mother how she just sashayed around [*Crossing around left of daybed back to center.*] the ballroom, just like that. I had it on the day I met your father. I had malaria fever, too. The change of climate from east Tennessee to the Delta—weakened my resistance. Not enough to be dangerous, just enough to make me restless and giddy. Oh, it was lovely. Invitations poured in from all over. My mother said, "You can't go any place because you have a fever. You have to stay in bed." I said I wouldn't and I took qui-
3 nine[18] and kept on going and going. Dances every evening and long rides in the country in the afternoon and picnics. That country—that country—so lovely—so lovely in May, all lacy with dogwood and simply flooded with jonquils. My mother said, "You can't bring any more jonquils in this house." I said, "I will," and I kept on bringing them in anyhow. Whenever I saw them I said, "Wait a minute, I see jonquils," and I'd make my gentlemen callers get out of the carriage and help me gather some. To tell you the truth, Laura, it got to be a kind of joke. "Look out," they'd say, "here comes that girl and we'll have to spend the afternoon picking jonquils." My mother said, "You can't bring any more jonquils in the house, there aren't any more vases to hold them." "That's quite all right," I said, "I can hold some myself." Malaria fever, your father and
4 jonquils. [AMANDA *puts jonquils in* LAURA*'s lap and goes out onto fire-escape landing. Music cue 14 stops. Thunder heard.*] I hope they get here before it starts to rain. I gave your brother a little extra change so he and Mr. O'Connor could take the service car home. [LAURA *puts flowers on armchair right, and crosses to door right.*]

LAURA. Mother!

16. **cotillion:** elaborate ballroom dance.
17. **cake walk:** strutting ballroom dance developed from a southern black competitive dance.
18. **quinine:** drug commonly used to treat malaria.

GUIDED READING

LITERAL QUESTIONS

1a. What does Amanda want Laura to do to her dress? (pad it)

2a. How does Amanda dress for the evening? (in a girlish frock, an old dress from her trunk)

INFERENTIAL QUESTIONS

1b. Why does Laura object to the suggestion? (Laura is shy and does not want to attract attention to herself; besides, she does not approve of the deceptiveness.)

2b. Why is this apparel inappropriate? (Aside from probably being out of fashion and too fancy for the occasion, the dress is the gown of a young girl.)

AMANDA. What's the matter now? [*Reentering room.*]

LAURA. What did you say his name was?

AMANDA. O'Connor. Why?

LAURA. What is his first name?

AMANDA. [*Crosses to armchair right.*] I don't remember——Oh, yes, I do too—it was—Jim! [*Picks up flowers.*]

LAURA. Oh, Mother, not Jim O'Connor!

AMANDA. Yes, that was it, it was Jim! I've never known a Jim that wasn't nice. [*Crosses left behind daybed, puts flowers in vase.*]

LAURA. Are you sure his name was Jim O'Connor?

AMANDA. Why, sure I'm sure. Why?

LAURA. Is he the one that Tom used to know in high school?

AMANDA. He didn't say so. I think he just got to know him—[*Sits on daybed.*] at the warehouse.

LAURA. There was a Jim O'Connor we both knew in high school. If that is the one that Tom is bringing home to dinner—— Oh, Mother, you'd have to excuse me, I wouldn't come to the table!

AMANDA. What's this now? What sort of silly talk is this?

1 LAURA. You asked me once if I'd ever liked a boy. Don't you remember I showed you this boy's picture?

AMANDA. You mean the boy in the yearbook?

LAURA. Yes, that boy.

AMANDA. Laura, Laura, were you in love with that boy?

LAURA. [*Crosses to right of armchair.*] I don't know, Mother. All I know is that I couldn't sit at the table if it was him.

AMANDA. [*Rises, crosses left and walks up left of daybed.*] It won't be him! It isn't the least bit likely. But whether it is or not, you will come to the table—you will not be excused.

LAURA. I'll have to be, Mother.

AMANDA. [*Behind daybed.*] I don't intend to humor your silliness, Laura. I've had too much from you and your brother, both. So just sit down and compose yourself till they come. Tom has forgotten his key, so you'll *have* to let them in when they arrive.

LAURA. Oh, Mother—*you* answer the door! [*Sits in chair right.*]

AMANDA. How can I when I haven't even finished making the mayonnaise dressing for the salmon?

LAURA. Oh, Mother, please answer the door, don't make me do it! [*Thunder heard offstage.*]

AMANDA. Honey, do be reasonable! What's all this fuss about—just one gentleman caller—that's all—just one! [*Exits through living room curtains.* TOM *and* JIM *enter alley right, climb fire-escape steps to landing and wait outside of*

2 *closed door. Hearing them approach,* LAURA *rises with a panicky gesture. She retreats to living room curtains. The doorbell rings.* LAURA *catches her breath and touches her throat. More thunder heard offstage.*]

AMANDA. [*Offstage.*] Laura, sweetheart, the door!

LAURA. Mother, please, you go to the door! [*Starts for door right, then back.*]

AMANDA. [*Offstage, in a fierce whisper.*] What is the matter with you, you silly thing? [*Enters through living room curtains, and stands by daybed.*]

LAURA. Please you answer it, please.

AMANDA. Why have you chosen this moment to lose your mind? You go to that door.

3 LAURA. I can't.

AMANDA. Why can't you?

LAURA. Because I'm sick. [*Crosses to left end of daybed and sits.*]

AMANDA. You're sick! Am I sick? You and your brother have me puzzled to death. You can never act like normal children. Will you give me one

AT A GLANCE

- Laura realizes that the caller is probably the boy she loved in high school.
- She tells Amanda that if it is he, she will not come to dinner.
- When Tom and Jim arrive, Amanda tries to get Laura to answer the door, but Laura claims to be sick.

1 PLOT: RISING ACTION

Laura discovers that the young man who will call on them is the great love of her life.

2 CHARACTERIZATION

Laura's reaction to the doorbell epitomizes her inability to face up to and deal with life.

3 THEME

One way to avoid dealing with life's challenges is to come up with reasons that excuse one from having to act.

GUIDED READING

LITERAL QUESTIONS

1a. What does Laura discover about the caller? (He is the boy she loved in high school.)

2a. When the doorbell rings, what does Amanda want Laura to do? (to open the door)

INFERENTIAL QUESTIONS

1b. Why does this discovery undo her? (She is too frightened of life to face her dreams when they turn into reality.)

2b. Why is this action so important to Amanda? (She is anxious for Laura to make an immediate and favorable impression upon the caller.)

AT A GLANCE

- Laura opens the door to let the young men in, but soon she retreats into the next room.
- Jim encourages Tom to take a course in public speaking to gain social poise.

1 CHARACTERIZATION

Jim displays a certain earthiness and a sense of humor.

2 THEME

Jim tries to overcome the adversity in his life by pursuing courses that he believes will lead to great success.

3 THEME

Jim's "social poise" (like Amanda's "charm") is a matter of appearance rather than substance.

good reason why you should be afraid to open a door? You go to that door. Laura Wingfield, you march straight to that door!

LAURA. [*Crosses to door right.*] Yes, Mother.

AMANDA. [*Stopping* LAURA.] I've got to put courage in you, honey, for living. [*Exits through living room curtains, and exits right into kitchen.* LAURA *opens door.* TOM *and* JIM *enter.* LAURA *remains hidden in hall behind door.*]

TOM. Laura—[LAURA *crosses center.*] this is Jim. Jim, this is my sister Laura.

JIM. I didn't know that Shakespeare had a sister! How are you, Laura?

LAURA. [*Retreating stiff and trembling. Shakes hands.*] How—how do you do?

JIM. Well, I'm okay! Your hand's *cold,* Laura! [TOM *puts hat on phone table.*]

LAURA. Yes, well—I've been playing the Victrola. . . .

1 **JIM.** Must have been playing classical music on it. You ought to play a little hot swing music to warm you up. [LAURA *crosses to phonograph.* TOM *crosses up to* LAURA. LAURA *starts phonograph—looks at* JIM. *Exits through living room curtains and goes offstage left.*]

JIM. What's the matter?

TOM. Oh—Laura? Laura is—is terribly shy. [*Crosses and sits on daybed.*]

JIM. [*Crosses downstage center.*] Shy, huh? Do you know it's unusual to meet a shy girl nowadays? I don't believe you ever mentioned you had a sister?

TOM. Well, now you know I have one. You want a piece of the paper?

JIM. [*Crosses to* TOM.] Uh-huh.

TOM. Comics?

JIM. Comics? Sports! [*Takes paper. Crosses, sits in chair right.*] I see that Dizzy Dean[19] is on his bad behavior.

TOM. [*Starts to door right. Goes out.*] Really?

JIM. Yeah. Where are *you* going? [*As* TOM *reaches steps right of fire-escape landing.*]

TOM. [*Calling from fire-escape landing.*] Out on the terrace to smoke.

JIM. [*Rises, leaving newspaper in armchair, goes over to turn off Victrola. Crosses right. Exits to fire-escape landing.*] You know, Shakespeare—I'm going to sell you a bill of goods!

TOM. What goods?

JIM. A course I'm taking.

TOM. What course?

2 **JIM.** A course in public speaking! You know you and me, we're not the warehouse type.

TOM. Thanks—that's good news. What has public speaking got to do with it?

JIM. It fits you for—executive positions!

TOM. Oh.

JIM. I tell you it's done a helluva lot for me.

TOM. In what respect?

JIM. In all respects. Ask yourself: What's the difference between you and me and the guys in the office down front? Brains?—No!—Ability?—No! Then what? Primarily, it amounts to just one single thing——

TOM. What is that one thing?

3 **JIM.** Social poise! The ability to square up to somebody and hold your own on any social level!

AMANDA. [*Offstage.*] Tom?

TOM. Yes, Mother?

AMANDA. Is that you and Mr. O'Connor?

---

19. **Dizzy Dean:** flamboyant National League pitcher who played for Chicago and St. Louis in the 1930s.

GUIDED READING

LITERAL QUESTIONS

1a. What does Amanda say she must put into Laura? (courage for living)

2a. In which course does Jim try to interest Tom? (public speaking)

INFERENTIAL QUESTIONS

1b. What does this comment reveal about Amanda? (Although her methods may not always be productive, she understands Laura's emotional shortcomings and genuinely wants to help her.)

2b. How much has the course seemed to help Jim? (His personality is outgoing, but he has not obtained a better position.)

TOM. Yes, Mother.

AMANDA. Make yourselves comfortable.

TOM. We will.

AMANDA. Ask Mr. O'Connor if he would like to wash his hands?

JIM. No, thanks, ma'am—I took care of that down at the warehouse. Tom?

TOM. Huh?

JIM. Mr. Mendoza was speaking to me about you.

TOM. Favorably?

JIM. What do you think?

TOM. Well——

JIM. You're going to be out of a job if you don't wake up.

TOM. I'm waking up——

JIM. Yeah, but you show no signs.

1 **TOM.** The signs are interior. I'm just about to make a change. I'm right at the point of committing myself to a future that doesn't include the warehouse or Mr. Mendoza, or even a night school course in public speaking.

JIM. Now what are you gassing about?

TOM. I'm tired of the movies.

JIM. The movies!

TOM. Yes, movies! Look at them. [*He waves his hands.*] All of those glamorous people—having adventures—hogging it all, gobbling the whole thing up! You know what happens? People go to
2 the *movies* instead of *moving.* Hollywood characters are supposed to have all the adventures for everybody in America, while everybody in America sits in a dark room and watches them having it! Yes, until there's a war. That's when adventure becomes available to the masses! Everyone's dish, not only Gable's![20] Then the people in the dark room come out of the dark room to have some adventure themselves—goody—goody! It's our turn now to go to the South Sea Islands—to make a safari—to be exotic, far off. . . ! But I'm not patient. I don't want to wait till then. I'm tired of the movies and I'm about to move!

JIM. [*Incredulously.*] Move?

TOM. Yes.

JIM. When?

TOM. Soon!

JIM. Where? Where?

TOM. I'm starting to boil inside. I know I seem dreamy, but inside—well, I'm boiling! Whenever I pick up a shoe I shudder a little, thinking how short life is and what I am doing!—Whatever that means, I know it doesn't mean shoes—except as something to wear on a traveler's feet! [*Gets card from inside coat pocket.*] Look!

JIM. What?

TOM. I'm a member.

JIM. [*Reading.*] The Union of Merchant Seamen.

TOM. I paid my dues this month, instead of the electric light bill.

3 **JIM.** You'll regret it when they turn off the lights.

TOM. I won't be here.

JIM. Yeah, but how about your mother?

TOM. I'm like my father. The bastard son of a bastard. See how he grins? And he's been absent going on sixteen years.

JIM. You're just talking, you drip. How does your mother feel about it?

TOM. Sh! Here comes Mother! Mother's not acquainted with my plans!

AMANDA. [*Offstage.*] Tom!

TOM. Yes, Mother?

AMANDA. [*Offstage.*] Where are you all?

20. **Gable:** Clark Gable (1901–1960), popular romantic star in American films.

AT A GLANCE

- Jim warns Tom that Tom's job is in danger.
- Tom tells Jim that he is about to make a move.
- He has used the money for the electric bill to pay his dues in the Union of Merchant Seamen.
- Tom tells Jim not to mention his plans in front of his mother.

1 THEME

Tom realizes that genuine change comes by responding to the promptings from within, not by acting to satisfy the expectations of others.

2 THEME

According to Tom, people are all too willing to settle for the appearance of adventure rather than experiencing the real thing.

3 SYMBOL

Light is associated with hopes and dreams (the light of the glass sphere at the dance hall and the light through Laura's glass animals); when the lights go out, the dreams die with them.

GUIDED READING

LITERAL QUESTIONS

1a. What has Tom done with the money for the electric bill? (paid his dues in the Union of Merchant Seamen)

2a. What does Tom reply when Jim asks how his mother feels about his plans? (She does not know about them.)

INFERENTIAL QUESTIONS

1b. What is his plan? (to join the union and then get on a ship and leave home)

2b. What does this suggest about Tom? (He is afraid to tell her because he knows how she will react.)

AT A GLANCE

- Amanda greets Jim cordially, turning on her southern charm.
- Amanda describes Laura as quite domestic, saying she herself could never cook anything.
- Amanda refers briefly to her vanished husband.

1 CHARACTERIZATION

The youthful southern vivacity that Amanda affects is a facade, one that fools Amanda more than anyone else.

2 DIALECT

Amanda so lives her role that her southern dialect becomes more pronounced, as evidenced by her *fo'*.

3 THEME

For Amanda the pretense of Laura's domesticity is a way of creating the right appearance.

4 ALLUSION

Amanda's twist of "Man proposes, God disposes" shows how trivial and humorous she can be.

TOM. On the terrace, Mother.

AMANDA. [*Enters through living room curtain and stands center.*] Why don't you come in? [*They start inside. She advances to them.* TOM *is distinctly shocked at her appearance. Even* JIM
1 *blinks a little. He is making his first contact with girlish southern vivacity and in spite of the night school course in public speaking is somewhat thrown off the beam by the unexpected outlay of social charm. Certain responses are attempted by* JIM *but are swept aside by* AMANDA'*s gay laughter and chatter.* TOM *is embarrassed but after the first shock* JIM *reacts very warmly. Grins and chuckles, is altogether won over.* TOM *and* JIM *come in, leaving door open.*]

TOM. Mother, you look so pretty.

AMANDA. You know, that's the first compliment you ever paid me. I wish you'd look pleasant when you're about to say something pleasant, so I could expect it. Mr. O'Connor? [JIM *crosses to* AMANDA.]

JIM. How do you do?

AMANDA. Well, well, well, so this is Mr. O'Connor? Introduction's entirely unnecessary. I've heard so much about you from my boy. I finally said to him, "Tom, good gracious, why don't you bring this paragon to supper finally? I'd like to meet this nice young man at the warehouse! Instead of just hearing you sing his praises so much?" I don't know why my son is so stand-offish—that's not southern behavior. Let's sit down. [TOM *closes door, crosses upstage right, stands.* JIM *and* AMANDA *sit on daybed,* JIM, *right,* AMANDA *left.*] Let's sit down, and I think we could stand a little more air in here. Tom, leave the door open. I felt a nice fresh breeze a moment ago. Where has it gone to? Mmmm, so warm already! And not quite summer, even. We're going to burn up when summer really gets started. However, we're
2 having—we're having a very light supper. I think light things are better fo'—for this time of year. The same as light clothes are. Light clothes and light food are what warm weather calls fo'. You know our blood gets so thick during th' winter—it takes a while fo' us to adjust ou'selves—when the season changes. . . . It's come so quick this year. I wasn't prepared. All of a sudden—Heavens! Already summer!—I ran to the trunk an'—pulled out this light dress—terribly old! Historical almost! But feels so good—so good and cool, why, y' know——

TOM. Mother, how about our supper?

3 AMANDA. [*Rises, crosses right to* TOM.] Honey, you go ask Sister if supper is ready! You know that Sister is in full charge of supper. Tell her you hungry boys are waiting for it. [TOM *exits through curtains and offstage left.* AMANDA *turns to* JIM.] Have you met Laura?

JIM. Well, she came to the door.

AMANDA. She let you in?

JIM. Yes, ma'am.

AMANDA. [*Crossing to armchair and sitting.*] She's very pretty.

JIM. Oh, yes, ma'am.

AMANDA. It's rare for a girl as sweet an' pretty as Laura to be domestic! But Laura is, thank heavens, not only pretty but also very domestic. I'm not at all. I never was a bit. I never could make a thing but angel food cake. Well, in the South we had so many servants. Gone, gone, gone. All vestige of gracious living! Gone completely! I wasn't prepared for what the future brought me. All of my gentlemen callers were sons of planters and so of course I assumed that I would be married to one and raise my family on a large piece of land
4 with plenty of servants. But man proposes—and woman accepts the proposal!—To vary that old, old saying a little bit—I married no planter! I married a man who worked for the telephone company!—That gallantly smiling gentleman over there! [*Points to picture.*] A telephone man who—fell in love with long distance!—Now he travels and I don't even know where!—But what am I going on for about my—tribulations? Tell me yours—I hope you don't have any! Tom?

TOM. [*Reenters through living room curtains from offstage left.*] Yes, Mother.

GUIDED READING

LITERAL QUESTIONS

1a. How does Tom react to his mother's appearance? (He is shocked.)

2a. What quality of Laura's does Amanda say is rare in one so pretty? (She is domestic.)

INFERENTIAL QUESTIONS

1b. Why does he react in this way? (Her dress is totally inappropriate; she tries to make herself appear as the person she still believes herself to be.)

2b. Why does Amanda stress this quality in talking about Laura? (She wants to impress Jim with Laura's qualifications for marriage.)

AMANDA. What about that supper?

TOM. Why, supper is on the table. [*Inner curtains between living room and dining room open. Lights dim up in dining room, dim out in living room.*]

AMANDA. Oh, so it is. [*Rises, crosses up to table center in dining room and chair center.*] How lovely. Where is Laura?

TOM. [*Going to chair left and standing.*] Laura is not feeling too well and thinks maybe she'd better not come to the table.

AMANDA. Laura!

LAURA. [*Offstage. Faintly.*] Yes, Mother? [TOM *gestures re:* JIM.]

AMANDA. Mr. O'Connor. [JIM *crosses upstage left to table and to chair left and stands.*]

JIM. Thank you, ma'am.

AMANDA. Laura, we can't say grace till you come to the table.

LAURA. [*Enters upstage left, obviously quite*
1 *faint, lips trembling, eyes wide and staring. Moves unsteadily toward dining room table.*] Oh, Mother, I'm so sorry. [TOM *catches her as she feels faint. He takes her to daybed in living room.*]

AMANDA. [*As* LAURA *lies down.*] Why, Laura, you are sick, darling! Laura—rest on the sofa. Well! [*To* JIM.] Standing over the hot stove made her ill!—I told her that it was just too warm this evening, but—— [*To* TOM.] Is Laura all right now?

2 TOM. She's better, Mother. [*Sits in chair left in dining room. Thunder offstage.*]

AMANDA. [*Returning to dining room and sitting at table, as* JIM *does.*] My goodness, I suppose we're going to have a little rain! Tom, you say grace.

TOM. What?

AMANDA. What do we generally do before we have something to eat? We say grace, don't we?

TOM. For these and all thy mercies—God's holy name be praised. [*Lights dim out. Music cue 15.*]

AT A GLANCE

- Tom says that supper is ready, but Laura is too ill to come to the table.
- Amanda insists that she come; she does, but feels faint and falls into Tom's arms.
- Tom places Laura on the daybed and is imposed upon by Amanda to say grace.

1 CHARACTERIZATION

To avoid the anxiety of the situation, Laura has actually made herself sick.

2 STAGING

The thunder reflects the turmoil and strong emotions of the characters.

GUIDED READING

LITERAL QUESTION

1a. What is Tom's response when Amanda asks him to say grace? ("What?")

INFERENTIAL QUESTION

1b. What does this response indicate? (The family usually does not say grace.)

AT A GLANCE

- *Scene 8:* The lights go out just after dinner.
- Jim looks to see if the cause of the blackout is in the fuse box.
- Amanda discovers that Tom did not pay the electric bill.

1 SYMBOL

Light has been associated with hopes and dreams. In this scene Jim toasts the "old South" (represented by Amanda), and all the lights go out. Perhaps the blackout portends the end of Amanda's dreams.

2 IRONY

Amanda's reference to the mysteriousness of the universe bears a truth that the audience appreciates much better than she does.

3 CHARACTERIZATION

With her goal clearly in mind, Amanda is adaptable. She will not let a little thing like the lack of electricity spoil her plans; she is determined.

ACT II

***Scene 8.** The same. A half hour later. Dinner is coming to an end in dining room.*

[AMANDA, TOM *and* JIM *sitting at table as at end of last scene. Lights dim up in both rooms, and music cue 15 ends.*]

AMANDA. [*Laughing, as* JIM *laughs too.*] You know, Mr. O'Connor, I haven't had such a pleasant evening in a very long time.

1 JIM. [*Rises.*] Well, Mrs. Wingfield, let me give you a toast. Here's to the old South.

AMANDA. The old South. [*Blackout in both rooms.*]

JIM. Hey, Mr. Light Bulb!

AMANDA. Where was Moses when the lights went out? Do you know the answer to that one, Mr. O'Connor?

JIM. No, ma'am, what's the answer to that one?

AMANDA. Well, I heard one answer, but it wasn't very nice. I thought you might know another one.

JIM. No, ma'am.

AMANDA. It's lucky I put those candles on the table. I just put them on for ornamentation, but it's nice when they prove useful, too.

JIM. Yes, ma'am.

AMANDA. Now, if one of you gentlemen can provide me with a match we can have some illumination.

JIM. [*Lighting candles. Dim in glow for candles.*] I can, ma'am.

AMANDA. Thank you.

JIM. [*Crosses back to right of dining room table.*] Not at all, ma'am.

AMANDA. I guess it must be a burned-out fuse. Mr. O'Connor, do you know anything about a burned-out fuse?

JIM. I know a little about them, ma'am, but where's the fuse box?

AMANDA. Must you know that, too? Well, it's in the kitchen. [JIM *exits right into kitchen.*] Be careful. It's dark. Don't stumble over anything. [*Sound of crash offstage.*] Oh, my goodness, wouldn't it be awful if we lost him! Are you all right, Mr. O'Connor?

JIM. [*Offstage.*] Yes, ma'am, I'm all right.

2 AMANDA. You know, electricity is a very mysterious thing. The whole universe is mysterious to me. Wasn't it Benjamin Franklin who tied a key to a kite? I'd like to have seen that—he might have looked mighty silly. Some people say that science clears up all the mysteries for us. In my opinion they just keep on adding more. Haven't you found it yet?

JIM. [*Reenters right.*] Yes, ma'am. I found it all right, but them fuses look okay to me. [*Sits as before.*]

AMANDA. Tom.

TOM. Yes, Mother?

AMANDA. That light bill I gave you several days ago. The one I got the notice about?

TOM. Oh—yeah. You mean last month's bill?

AMANDA. You didn't neglect it by any chance?

TOM. Well, I——

AMANDA. You did! I might have known it!

JIM. Oh, maybe Shakespeare wrote a poem on that light bill, Mrs. Wingfield?

AMANDA. Maybe he did, too. I might have known better than to trust him with it! There's such a high price for negligence in this world today.

JIM. Maybe the poem will win a ten-dollar prize.

3 AMANDA. We'll just have to spend the rest of the evening in the nineteenth century, before Mr. Edison found that Mazda lamp!

JIM. Candle light is my favorite kind of light.

GUIDED READING

LITERAL QUESTION

1a. What does Amanda say about Jim after she hears the crash? ("Wouldn't it be awful if we lost him!")

INFERENTIAL QUESTION

1b. To what is she referring? (losing him literally because of an accident and losing him as a suitor for Laura)

AMANDA. That shows you're romantic! But that's no excuse for Tom. However, I think it was very nice of them to let us finish our dinner before they plunged us into everlasting darkness. Tom, as a penalty for your carelessness you can help me with the dishes.

JIM. [*Rising.* TOM *rises.*] Can I be of some help, ma'am?

AMANDA. [*Rising.*] Oh, no, I couldn't allow that.

JIM. Well, I ought to be good for *something.*

AMANDA. What did I hear?

JIM. I just said, "I ought to be good for something."

AMANDA. That's what I thought you said. Well, Laura's all by her lonesome out front. Maybe you'd like to keep her company. I can give you this lovely old candelabrum for light. [JIM *takes candles.*] It used to be on the altar at the Church of the Heavenly Rest, but it was melted a little out of shape when the church burned down. The church was struck by lightning one spring, and Gypsy Jones who was holding a revival meeting in the village, said that the church was struck by lightning because the Episcopalians had started to have card parties right in the church.

1 JIM. Is that so, ma'am?

AMANDA. I never say anything that isn't so.

JIM. I beg your pardon.

AMANDA. [*Pouring wine into glass—hands it to* JIM.] I'd like Laura to have a little dandelion wine. Do you think you can hold them both?

JIM. I can try, ma'am.

AMANDA. [*Exits upstage right into kitchen.*] Now, Tom, you get into your apron.

2 TOM. Yes, Mother. [*Follows* AMANDA. JIM *looks around, puts wine glass down, takes swig from wine decanter, replaces it with thud, takes wine glass—enters living room. Inner curtains close as dining room dims out.* LAURA *sits up nervously as* JIM *enters. Her speech at first is low and breathless from the almost intolerable strain of being alone with a stranger. In her speeches in this scene, before* JIM*'s warmth overcomes her paralyzing shyness,* LAURA*'s voice is thin and breathless as though she has just run up a steep flight of stairs.*]

JIM. [*Entering holding candelabra with lighted candles in one hand and glass of wine in other, and stands.*] How are you feeling now? Any better? [JIM*'s attitude is gently humorous. In playing this scene it should be stressed that while the incident is apparently unimportant, it is to* LAURA *the climax of her secret life.*]

LAURA. Yes, thank you.

JIM. [*Gives her glass of wine.*] Oh, here, this is for you. It's a little dandelion wine.

LAURA. Thank you.

JIM. [*Crosses center.*] Well, drink it—but don't get drunk. [*He laughs heartily.*] Say, where'll I put the candles?

LAURA. Oh, anywhere. . . .

JIM. Oh, how about right here on the floor? You got any objections?

LAURA. No.

JIM. I'll just spread a newspaper under it to catch the drippings. [*Gets newspaper from armchair. Puts candelabra down on floor center.*] I like to sit on the floor. [*Sits on floor.*] Mind if I do?

3 LAURA. Oh, no.

JIM. Would you give me a pillow?

LAURA. What?

JIM. A pillow!

LAURA. Oh. . . . [*Puts wine glass on telephone table, hands him pillow, sits left on daybed.*]

JIM. How about you? Don't you like to sit on the floor?

LAURA. Oh, yes.

JIM. Well, why don't you?

LAURA. I—will.

AT A GLANCE

- Amanda asks Jim to keep Laura company in the living room.
- Jim takes Laura a glass of wine.

1 CHARACTERIZATION

Amanda's sensitivity comes out in the way she mistakes a conversational "is that so?" for a questioning of her veracity. Ironically, she usually twists the truth for effect.

2 STAGING

Jim's surreptitious drinking from the wine decanter tends to confirm Amanda's fear that the gentleman caller drinks.

3 STYLE: SENTENCE STRUCTURE

The painful brevity of Laura's lines shows her stiff discomfort.

GUIDED READING

LITERAL QUESTIONS

1a. What does Amanda ask Jim to do? (entertain Laura in the living room)

2a. How do the stage directions describe the meaning of Laura's scene with Jim? (It is the "climax of her secret life.")

INFERENTIAL QUESTIONS

1b. What does Amanda expect will happen? (She is hoping for romance to blossom.)

2b. Why does it have this meaning? (Laura probably has often imagined such a meeting.)

AT A GLANCE

- Jim and Laura sit on the floor, and Jim gets her to sit closer.
- Jim recalls the Century of Progress world's fair.
- Laura reminds Jim that they knew each other in high school.

1 IRONY

Laura's romantic dream has come to pass, and the love of her life is sitting next to her by candlelight—talking about chewing gum.

2 STAGING

Laura's taking of the gum is a step toward feeling more relaxed. It is after this point that she initiates conversation.

3 CHARACTERIZATION

Jim's easy manner and warmth help put Laura at ease.

JIM. Take a pillow! [*Throws pillow as she sits on floor.*] I can't see you sitting way over there. [*Sits on floor again.*]

LAURA. I can—see you.

JIM. Yeah, but that's not fair. I'm right here in the limelight. [LAURA *moves a little closer to him.*] Good! Now I can see you! Are you comfortable?

LAURA. Yes. Thank you.

JIM. So am I. I'm comfortable as a cow! Say, would you care for a piece of chewing gum? [*Offers gum.*]

LAURA. No, thank you.

1 JIM. I think that I will indulge. [*Musingly unwraps it and holds it up.*] Gee, think of the fortune made by the guy that invented the first piece of chewing gum! It's amazing, huh? Do you know that the Wrigley[21] Building is one of the sights of Chicago?—I saw it summer before last at the Century of Progress.[22]—Did you take in the Century of Progress?

LAURA. No, I didn't.

JIM. Well, it was a wonderful exposition, believe me. You know what impressed me most? The Hall of Science. Gives you an idea of what the future will be like in America. Oh, it's more wonderful than the present time is! Say, your brother tells me you're shy. Is that right, Laura?

LAURA. I—don't know.

JIM. I judge you to be an old-fashioned type of girl. Oh, I think that's a wonderful type to be. I hope you don't think I'm being too personal—do you?

LAURA. Mr. O'Connor?

JIM. Huh?

2 LAURA. I believe I *will* take a piece of gum, if you don't mind. [JIM *peels gum—gets on knees, hands it to* LAURA. *She breaks off a tiny piece.* JIM *looks at what remains, puts it in his mouth, and sits again.*] Mr. O'Connor, have you—kept up with your singing?

JIM. Singing? Me?

LAURA. Yes. I remember what a beautiful voice you had.

JIM. You heard me sing?

LAURA. Oh, yes! Very often. . . . I—don't suppose—you remember me—at all?

JIM. [*Smiling doubtfully.*] You know, as a matter of fact I did have an idea I'd seen you before. Do you know it seemed almost like I was about to remember your name. But the name I was about to remember—wasn't a name! So I stopped myself before I said it.

LAURA. Wasn't it—Blue Roses?

3 JIM. [*Grinning.*] Blue Roses! Oh, my gosh, yes—Blue Roses! You know, I didn't connect you with high school somehow or other. But that's where it was, it was high school. Gosh, I didn't even know you were Shakespeare's sister! Gee, I'm sorry.

LAURA. I didn't expect you to.—You—barely knew me!

JIM. But, we did have a speaking acquaintance.

LAURA. Yes, we—spoke to each other.

JIM. Say, didn't we have a class in something together?

LAURA. Yes, we did.

JIM. What class was that?

LAURA. It was—singing—chorus!

JIM. Aw!

LAURA. I sat across the aisle from you in the auditorium. Mondays, Wednesdays and Fridays.

JIM. Oh, yeah! I remember now—you're the one who always came in late.

LAURA. Yes, it was so hard for me, getting upstairs.

21. **Wrigley:** large manufacturer of chewing gum.
22. **Century of Progress:** name for Chicago World's Fair, 1933–1934.

GUIDED READING

LITERAL QUESTIONS

1a. What does Jim say that Laura's brother has told him? (that Laura is shy)

2a. Laura asks Jim if he has kept up with something. What was it? (his singing)

INFERENTIAL QUESTIONS

1b. How do Laura's responses bear out this assessment in the early stages of their conversation? (She gives brief, hesitant answers to everything Jim says; she seems unable to hold up her end of the conversation.)

2b. Why is this information important to her memory of Jim? (One of the reasons for Laura's affection for Jim was his beautiful singing voice.)

I had that brace on my leg then—it clumped so loud!

1 JIM. I never heard any clumping.

LAURA. [*Wincing at recollection.*] To me it sounded like—thunder!

JIM. I never even noticed.

LAURA. Everybody was seated before I came in. I had to walk in front of all those people. My seat was in the back row. I had to go clumping up the aisle with everyone watching!

JIM. Oh, gee, you shouldn't have been self-conscious.

LAURA. I know, but I was. It was always such a relief when the singing started.

JIM. I remember now. And I used to call you Blue Roses. How did I ever get started calling you a name like that?

2 LAURA. I was out of school a little while with pleurosis. When I came back you asked me what was the matter. I said I had pleurosis and you thought I said Blue Roses. So that's what you always called me after that!

JIM. I hope you didn't mind?

LAURA. Oh, no—I liked it. You see, I wasn't acquainted with many—people. . . .

JIM. Yeah. I remember you sort of stuck by yourself.

LAURA. I never did have much luck at making friends.

JIM. Well, I don't see why you wouldn't.

LAURA. Well, I started out badly.

JIM. You mean being——?

LAURA. Well, yes, it—sort of—stood between me. . . .

JIM. You shouldn't have let it!

LAURA. I know, but it did, and I——

JIM. You mean you were shy with people!

LAURA. I tried not to be but never could——

JIM. Overcome it?

LAURA. No, I—never could!

JIM. Yeah. I guess being shy is something you have to work out of kind of gradually.

LAURA. Yes—I guess it——

JIM. Takes time!

LAURA. Yes. . . .

JIM. Say, you know something, Laura? [*Rises to sit on daybed right.*] People are not so dreadful when you know them. That's what you have to
3 remember! And everybody has problems, not just you but practically everybody has problems. You think of yourself as being the only one who is disappointed. But just look around you and what do you see—a lot of people just as disappointed as you are. You take me, for instance. Boy, when I left high school I thought I'd be a lot further along at this time than I am now. Say, you remember that wonderful write-up I had in *The Torch?*

LAURA. Yes, I do! [*She gets yearbook from under pillow left of daybed.*]

JIM. Said I was bound to succeed in anything I went into! Holy Jeez! *The Torch!* [*She opens book, shows it to him and sits next to him on daybed.*]

LAURA. Here you are in *The Pirates of Penzance!*

JIM. *The Pirates!* "Oh, better far to live and die under the brave black flag I fly!" I sang the lead in that operetta.

LAURA. So beautifully!

JIM. Aw. . . .

LAURA. Yes, yes—beautifully—beautifully!

JIM. You heard me then, huh?

LAURA. I heard you all three times!

JIM. No!

LAURA. Yes.

AT A GLANCE

- When Laura recalls being embarrassed "clumping" into choir with the brace on her leg, Jim tells her that she should not have been so self-conscious.
- She brings out the high school yearbook with a picture of him in *The Pirates of Penzance*.
- She tells him that she attended all three performances.

1 IRONY

Her brace—the only feature Laura thought anyone would notice about her—went unnoticed; her handicap was more emotional than physical.

2 STYLE: SENTENCE STRUCTURE

Laura is now relaxed in Jim's company, as evidenced by the long, fluid sentence structure.

3 THEME

Jim shows a common-sense approach to life. Everyone has problems to face; nobody should be so self-involved as to think his or her problem is unique.

GUIDED READING

LITERAL QUESTIONS

1a. At what did Laura never have much luck? (making friends)

2a. What did Laura see three times? (Jim's performance in *The Pirates of Penzance*)

INFERENTIAL QUESTIONS

1b. What has stood in her way? (She has thought of herself as crippled and has felt ashamed, so she never gave people a chance to know her.)

2b. Why did she see it three times? (She was in love with Jim and probably wanted to take every opportunity to see him.)

AT A GLANCE

- Laura tells Jim she wanted to ask him to sign her program, but was too shy.
- She reminds him about his popularity in high school, and he signs her program.
- Laura says that she dropped out of high school after getting bad grades.
- When Jim asks her what she has been doing since high school, she mentions the course in business college.

1 THEME

Success, like dreams, can be fleeting: Jim's apparent popularity has not lasted.

2 PLOT: RISING ACTION

Laura, believing Jim was engaged to Emily, now has reason to hope as she hears Jim is no longer interested in Emily.

3 SYMBOL

Laura is like glass, for her inward glow can be easily seen. As she struggles to hide this surge of emotion, she turns to her glass menagerie for comfort.

JIM. You mean all three performances?

LAURA. Yes!

JIM. What for?

LAURA. I—wanted to ask you to—autograph my program. [*Takes program from book.*]

JIM. Why didn't you ask me?

LAURA. You were always surrounded by your own friends so much that I never had a chance.

JIM. Aw, you should have just come right up and said, "Here is my ——"

LAURA. Well, I—thought you might think I was——

JIM. Thought I might think you was—what?

LAURA. Oh——

1 JIM. [*With reflective relish.*] Oh! Yeah, I was beleaguered by females in those days.

LAURA. You were terribly popular!

JIM. Yeah. . . .

LAURA. You had such a—friendly way——

JIM. Oh, I was spoiled in high school.

LAURA. Everybody liked you!

JIM. Including you?

LAURA. I—why, yes, I—I did, too. . . .

JIM. Give me that program, Laura. [*She does so, and he signs it.*] There you are—better late than never!

LAURA. My—what a—surprise!

JIM. My signature's not worth very much right now. But maybe some day—it will increase in value! You know, being disappointed is one thing and being discouraged is something else. Well, I may be disappointed but I am not discouraged. Say, you finished high school?

LAURA. I made bad grades in my final examinations.

JIM. You mean you dropped out?

LAURA. [*Rises.*] I didn't go back. [*Crosses right to menagerie.* JIM *lights cigarette still sitting on daybed.* LAURA *puts yearbook under menagerie. Rises, picks up unicorn—small glass object—her back to* JIM. *When she touches unicorn, music cue 16A begins.*] How is—Emily Meisenbach getting along?

JIM. That kraut head!

LAURA. Why do you call her that?

JIM. Because that's what she was.

2 LAURA. You're not still—going with her?

JIM. Oh, I never even see her.

LAURA. It said in the personal section that you were—engaged!

JIM. Uh-huh. I know, but I wasn't impressed by that—propaganda!

LAURA. It wasn't—the truth?

JIM. It was only true in Emily's optimistic opinion!

3 LAURA. Oh. . . . [*Turns right of* JIM. JIM *lights a cigarette and leans indolently back on his elbows smiling at* LAURA *with a warmth and charm which lights her inwardly with altar candles. She remains by the glass menagerie table and turns in her hands a piece of glass to cover her tumult. Cut music 16A.*]

JIM. What have you done since high school? Huh?

LAURA. What?

JIM. I said what have you done since high school?

LAURA. Nothing much.

JIM. You must have been doing something all this time.

LAURA. Yes.

JIM. Well, then, such as what?

LAURA. I took a business course at business college. . . .

JIM. You did? How did that work out?

GUIDED READING

LITERAL QUESTIONS

1a. Which girl does Laura ask Jim about? (Emily Meisenbach)

2a. What does Jim say is the current status of his relationship with Emily? ("I never even see her.")

INFERENTIAL QUESTIONS

1b. Why does Laura mention this girl? (Having read in the newspaper that Jim was engaged to Emily, Laura is trying to find out if he is attached.)

2b. What implications must Laura see in this remark? (It must create a spark of hope in her. She is still attracted to him, and if he is no longer seeing Emily, Laura must see him as available.)

LAURA. [*Turns back to* JIM.] Well, not very—well. . . . I had to drop out, it gave me—indigestion. . . .

JIM. [*Laughs gently.*] What are you doing now?

LAURA. I don't do anything—much. . . . Oh, please don't think I sit around doing nothing! My glass collection takes a good deal of time. Glass is something you have to take good care of.

JIM. What did you say—about glass?

1 LAURA. [*She clears her throat and turns away again, acutely shy.*] Collection, I said—I have one.

JIM. [*Puts out cigarette. Abruptly.*] Say! You know what I judge to be the trouble with you? [*Rises from daybed and crosses right.*] Inferiority complex! You know what that is? That's what they call it when a fellow low-rates himself! Oh, I understand it because I had it, too. Uh-huh! Only my case was not as aggravated as yours seems to be. I had it until I took up public speaking and developed my voice, and learned that I had an aptitude for science. Do you know that until that time I never thought of myself as being outstanding in any way whatsoever!

LAURA. Oh, my!

JIM. Now I've never made a regular study of it—[*Sits in armchair right.*] mind you, but I have a friend who says I can analyze people better than doctors that make a profession of it. I don't claim that's necessarily true, but I can sure guess a person's psychology. Excuse me, Laura. [*Takes out gum.*] I always take it out when the flavor is
2 gone. I'll just wrap it in a piece of paper. [*Tears a piece of paper off the newspaper under the candelabrum, wraps gum in it, crosses to daybed, looks to see if* LAURA *is watching. She isn't. Crosses around daybed.*] I know how it is when you get it stuck on a shoe. [*Throws gum under daybed, crosses around left of daybed. Crosses right to* LAURA.] Yep—that's what I judge to be your principal trouble. A lack of confidence in yourself as a person. Now I'm basing that fact on a number of your remarks and on certain observations I've made. For instance, that clumping you thought was so awful in high school. You say that you dreaded to go upstairs? You see what you did? You dropped out of school, you gave up an education all because of a little clump, which as far as I can see is practically nonexistent! Oh, a little physical defect is all you have. It's hardly noticeable even! Magnified a thousand times by your imagination! You know what my strong advice to you is? You've got to think of yourself as *superior* in some way! [*Crosses left to small table right of daybed. Sits.* LAURA *sits in armchair.*]

LAURA. In what way would I think?

JIM. Why, man alive, Laura! Look around you a little and what do you see? A world full of common people! All of 'em born and all of 'em going to die! Now, which of them has one-tenth of your strong points! Or mine! Or anybody else's for that matter? You see, everybody excels in some
3 one thing. Well—some in many! You take me, for instance. My interest happens to lie in electrodynamics. I'm taking a course in radio engineering at night school, on top of a fairly responsible job at the warehouse. I'm taking that course *and* studying public speaking.

LAURA. Ohhhh. My!

JIM. Because I believe in the future of television! I want to be ready to go right up along with it. [*Rises, crosses right.*] I'm planning to get in on the ground floor. Oh, I've already made the right connections. All that remains now is for the industry itself to get under way—full steam! You know, *knowledge*—ZSZZppp! *Money*—Zzzzzzpp! *POWER!* Wham! That's the cycle democracy is built on! [*Pause.*] I guess you think I think a lot of myself!

LAURA. No—o-o-o, I don't.

JIM. [*Kneels at armchair right.*] Well, now how about you? Isn't there some one thing that you take more interest in than anything else?

LAURA. Oh—yes. . . .

JIM. Well, then, such as what?

AT A GLANCE

- Laura says she keeps busy with her glass collection.
- Jim decides that she has an inferiority complex.
- He tells her that she ought to take more pride in herself and find something that interests her.

1 CHARACTERIZATION

Laura's shyness causes her once again to become meek as she talks about her glass collection. Jim, not realizing that she is talking about the most important thing in her life, abruptly changes the subject.

2 STAGING

How Jim handles the used gum shows that his concern for others is more appearance than substance.

3 CHARACTERIZATION

Jim starts to show Laura that she is in some way superior, but he soon turns to a recital of his own achievements.

GUIDED READING

LITERAL QUESTIONS

1a. According to Jim, what is the trouble with Laura? (She has an inferiority complex.)

2a. According to Jim, how should Laura thinks of herself? ("as superior in some way")

INFERENTIAL QUESTIONS

1b. What leads him to this conclusion? (Not finishing high school, not having a job, and being so shy prove to Jim that Laura does not think much of herself.)

2b. How is this advice supposed to help her? (Jim seems to think that if Laura concentrates on a strength of hers, she will become less timid.)

AT A GLANCE

- Laura shows Jim the pride of her glass menagerie—her unicorn.
- Upon hearing the music from the dance hall, Jim persuades Laura to dance with him.

1 SYMBOL

The unicorn represents Laura's personality—her uniqueness, separateness, and vulnerability. The fact that she trusts Jim with it symbolizes that she has completely opened herself up to Jim.

2 VOCABULARY: CONNOTATION

Jim is wrong to think that unicorns ever existed, but the word "extinct" suggests a disappearance or loss that aptly fits Laura, someone who no longer has a place in the realities of the modern world.

3 CONTRAST

Unlike Laura, Jim is not made out of glass. He is able to face life's adversities head on. He is a member of the real world, while Laura's world is one of illusion.

LAURA. Well, I do—as I said—have my—glass collection. . . . [*Music cue 16A.*]

JIM. Oh, you do. What kind of glass is it?

LAURA. [*Takes glass ornament off shelf.*] Little articles of it, ornaments mostly. Most of them are little animals made out of glass, the tiniest little animals in the world. Mother calls them the glass menagerie! Here's an example of one, if you'd like to see it! This is one of the oldest, it's nearly thirteen. [*Hands it to* JIM.] Oh, be careful—if you breathe, it breaks! [*The bell solo should begin here. This is last part of cue 16A and should play to end of record.*]

JIM. I'd better not take it. I'm pretty clumsy with things.

1 **LAURA.** Go on, I trust you with him! [JIM *takes horse.*] There—you're holding him gently! Hold him over the light, he loves the light! [JIM *holds horse up to light.*] See how the light shines through him?

JIM. It sure does shine!

LAURA. I shouldn't be partial, but he is my favorite one.

JIM. Say, what kind of a thing is this one supposed to be?

LAURA. Haven't you noticed the single horn on his forehead?

JIM. Oh, a unicorn, huh?

LAURA. Mmmm-hmmmmm!

2 **JIM.** Unicorns, aren't they extinct in the modern world?

LAURA. I know!

JIM. Poor little fellow must feel kind of lonesome.

LAURA. Well, if he does he doesn't complain about it. He stays on a shelf with some horses that don't have horns and they all seem to get along nicely together.

JIM. They do. Say, where will I put him?

LAURA. Put him on the table. [JIM *crosses to small table right of daybed, puts unicorn on it.*] They all like a change of scenery once in a while!

JIM. [*Center, facing upstage, stretching arms.*] They do. [*Music cue 16B: dance music.*] Hey! Look how big my shadow is when I stretch.

LAURA. [*Crossing to left of daybed.*] Oh, oh, yes—it stretched across the ceiling!

JIM. [*Crosses to door right, exits, leaving door open, and stands on fire-escape landing. Sings to music.* (*Popular record of day for dance hall.*) *When* JIM *opens door, music swells.*] It's stopped raining. Where does the music come from?

LAURA. From the Paradise Dance Hall across the alley.

JIM. [*Reentering room, closing door right, crosses to* LAURA.] How about cutting the rug a little, Miss Wingfield? Or is your program filled up? Let me take a look at it. [*Crosses back center stage. Music, in dance hall, goes into a waltz. Business here with imaginary dance-program card.*] Oh, say! Every dance is taken! I'll just scratch some of them out. Ahhhh, a waltz! [*Crosses to* LAURA.]

LAURA. I—can't dance!

JIM. There you go with that inferiority stuff!

LAURA. I've never danced in my life!

JIM. Come on, try!

3 **LAURA.** Oh, but I'd step on you!

JIM. Well, I'm not made out of glass.

LAURA. How—how do we start?

JIM. You hold your arms out a little.

LAURA. Like this?

JIM. A little bit higher. [*Takes* LAURA *in arms.*] That's right. Now don't tighten up, that's the principal thing about it—just relax.

LAURA. It's hard not to.

JIM. Okay.

LAURA. I'm afraid you can't budge me.

GUIDED READING

LITERAL QUESTIONS

1a. Which is Laura's favorite glass animal? (the unicorn)

2a. What does Jim tell Laura is the principal thing about dancing? (not to tighten up—to relax)

INFERENTIAL QUESTIONS

1b. Why is this probably her favorite? (It is the oldest, and its uniqueness probably reminds Laura of herself.)

2b. Why is this difficult for her? (She is doubly nervous—she has never danced before, and she is with the love of her life.)

JIM. [*Dances around left of daybed slowly.*] What do you bet I can't?

LAURA. Goodness, yes, you can!

JIM. Let yourself go, now, Laura, just let yourself go.

LAURA. I'm——

JIM. Come on!

LAURA. Trying!

JIM. Not so stiff now—easy does it!

LAURA. I know, but I'm——!

JIM. Come on! Loosen your backbone a little! [*When they get to upstage corner of daybed—so that the audience will not see him lift her—*JIM*'s arm tightens around her waist and he swings her around center stage with her feet off floor about three complete turns before they hit the small table right of daybed. Music swells as* JIM *lifts her.*] There we go! [JIM *knocks glass horse off table. Music fades.*]

1 LAURA. Oh, it doesn't matter——

JIM. [*Picks horse up.*] We knocked the little glass horse over.

LAURA. Yes.

JIM. [*Hands unicorn to* LAURA.] Is he broken?

LAURA. Now he's just like all the other horses.

JIM. You mean he lost his——?

LAURA. He's lost his horn. It doesn't matter. Maybe it's a blessing in disguise.

JIM. Gee, I bet you'll never forgive me. I bet that was your favorite piece of glass.

LAURA. Oh, I don't have favorites—[*Pause.*] much. It's no tragedy. Glass breaks so easily. No matter how careful you are. The traffic jars the shelves and things fall off them.

JIM. Still I'm awfully sorry that I was the cause of it.

LAURA. I'll just imagine he had an operation. The horn was removed to make him feel less—

2 freakish! [*Crosses left, sits on small table.*] Now he will feel more at home with the other horses, the ones who don't have horns. . . .

JIM. [*Sits on arm of armchair right, faces* LAURA.] I'm glad to see that you have a sense of humor. You know—you're—different than anybody else I know? [*Music cue 17.*] Do you mind me telling you that? I mean it. You make me feel sort of—I don't know how to say it! I'm usually pretty good at expressing things, but—this is something I don't know how to say! Did anybody ever tell you that you were pretty? [*Rises, crosses to* LAURA.] Well, you are! And in a different way from
3 anyone else. And all the nicer because of the difference. Oh, boy, I wish that you were my sister. I'd teach you to have confidence in yourself. Being different is nothing to be ashamed of. Because other people aren't such wonderful people. They're a hundred times one thousand.

AT A GLANCE

- Jim twirls Laura around; they bump into the table, causing the unicorn's horn to be broken off.
- She tells him not to feel bad; now the unicorn will be just like the other horses.
- He tells her she is pretty, in a different way from anyone else.

1 CHARACTERIZATION

Laura's calm response to the breaking of her favorite glass animal shows that the relationship she thinks is developing with Jim has become more important to her than her glass collection, making it very important indeed.

2 SYMBOL

Laura's identity with the unicorn is strengthened by her implication that "he" has felt "freakish" because of the horn, just as she has felt freakish because of her handicap.

3 FORESHADOWING

Jim's wishing that Laura were his sister strongly hints at the nature of his feelings for her and at how their relationship is likely to end.

GUIDED READING

LITERAL QUESTION

1a. How does Laura feel the unicorn's losing his horn will affect his relationship with the horses? (He will feel more at home with them.)

INFERENTIAL QUESTION

1b. In what way does this parallel Laura's feelings? (Her relationship with Jim is beginning to make her feel more like other people.)

AT A GLANCE

- Jim kisses Laura, but then tells her he is going steady with a girl named Betty.
- Laura gives Jim the unicorn as a souvenir of the evening.
- Amanda enters with lemonade.

1 CHARACTERIZATION

That "blue" is wrong for roses but right for Laura underscores how different she is—even in Jim's eyes.

2 PLOT: CLIMAX

The kiss is the high point of the romance, and it seems to promise the fulfillment of Laura's dreams.

3 THEME

Dreams are fragile and can be shattered in an instant; a new bit of information can change what seemed full of promise into something pathetically hopeless.

4 SYMBOL

Wounded by the encounter, Laura no longer wants to keep what has come to be a symbol of her shattered dreams.

You're one times one! They walk all over the earth. You just stay here. They're as common
1 as—weeds, but—you, well you're—*Blue Roses!*

LAURA. But blue is—wrong for—roses. . . .

JIM. It's right for you!—You're pretty!

LAURA. In what respect am I pretty?

JIM. In all respects—your eyes—your hair. Your hands are pretty! You think I'm saying this because I'm invited to dinner and have to be nice. Oh, I could do that! I could say lots of things without being sincere. But I'm talking to you sincerely. I happened to notice you had this inferiority complex that keeps you from feeling comfortable with people. Somebody ought to build your confidence up—way up! and make you proud instead of shy and turning away and—
2 blushing——[JIM *lifts* LAURA *up on small table; on way up.*] Somebody—ought to—[*Lifts her down.*] somebody ought to—kiss you, Laura! [*They kiss.* JIM *releases her and turns slowly away, crossing a little downstage right. Then, quietly, to himself, as music ends.*] Gee, I shouldn't have done that—that was way off the beam. [*Gives way downstage right. Turns to* LAURA. LAURA *sits on small table.*] Would you care for a cigarette? You don't smoke, do you? How about a mint? Peppermint—Live-Saver? My pocket's a regular drug store. . . . Laura, you know, if I had a sister like you, I'd do the same thing as Tom. I'd bring fellows home to meet you. Maybe I shouldn't be saying this. That may not have been the idea in having me over. But what if it was? There's nothing wrong with that.—The only trouble is that in my case—I'm not in a position to——I can't ask for your number and say I'll phone. I can't call up next weekend—ask for a date. I thought I had better explain the situation in case you—misunderstood and I hurt your feelings. . . .

3 LAURA. [*Faintly.*] You—won't—call again?

JIM. [*Crossing to right of daybed, and sitting.*] No, I can't. You see, I've—got strings on me. Laura, I've—been going steady! I go out all the time with a girl named Betty. Oh, she's a nice quiet home girl like you, and Catholic and Irish, and in a great many ways we—get along fine. I met her last summer on a moonlight boat trip up the river to Alton, on the *Majestic.* Well—right away from the start it was—love! Oh, boy, being in love has made a new man of me! The power of love is pretty tremendous! Love is something that—changes the whole world. It happened that Betty's aunt took sick and she got a wire and had to go to Centralia. So naturally when Tom asked me to dinner—naturally I accepted the invitation, not knowing—I mean—not knowing.
4 I wish that you would—say something. [LAURA *gives* JIM *unicorn.*] What are you doing that for? You mean you want me to have him? What for?

LAURA. A—souvenir. [*She crosses right to menagerie.* JIM *rises.*]

AMANDA. [*Offstage.*] I'm coming, children. [*She enters into dining room from kitchen right.*] I thought you'd like some liquid refreshment. [*Puts tray on small table. Lifts a glass.*] Mr. O'Connor, have you heard that song about lemonade? It's

"Lemonade, lemonade,
Made in the shade and stirred with a spade—
And then it's good enough for any old maid!"

JIM. No, ma'am, I never heard it.

AMANDA. Why are you so serious, honey? [*To* LAURA.]

JIM. Well, we were having a serious conversation.

AMANDA. I don't understand modern young people. When I was a girl I was gay about everything.

JIM. You haven't changed a bit, Mrs. Wingfield.

AMANDA. I suppose it's the gaiety of the occasion that has rejuvenated me. Well, here's to the gaiety of the occasion! [*Spills lemonade on dress.*] Oooo! I baptized myself. [*Puts glass on small table right of daybed.*] I found some cherries in the kitchen, and I put one in each glass.

JIM. You shouldn't have gone to all that trouble, ma'am.

GUIDED READING

LITERAL QUESTIONS

1a. What does Jim do that he later regrets? (kisses Laura)

2a. What does Laura give Jim? (her unicorn)

INFERENTIAL QUESTIONS

1b. Why does he do this? (He finds her attractive and wants to build her confidence.)

2b. Why does she give it to him? (Having had her hopes raised and then dashed, she may not want it reminding her of Jim.)

AMANDA. It was no trouble at all. Didn't you hear us cutting up in the kitchen? I was so outdone with Tom for not bringing you over sooner, but now you've found your way I want you to come all the time—not just once in a while—but all the time. Oh, I think I'll go back in that kitchen. [*Starts to exit upstage center.*]

JIM. Oh, no, ma'am, please don't go, ma'am. As a matter of fact, I've got to be going.

AMANDA. Oh, Mr. O'Connor, it's only the shank of the evening! [JIM *and* AMANDA *stand upstage center.*]

JIM. Well, you know how it is.

AMANDA. You mean you're a young working man and have to keep workingmen's hours?

JIM. Yes, ma'am.

AMANDA. Well, we'll let you off early this time, but only on the condition that you stay later next time, much later——What's the best night for you? Saturday?

JIM. Well, as a matter of fact, I have a couple of time clocks to punch, Mrs. Wingfield, one in the morning and another one at night!

AMANDA. Oh, isn't that nice, you're so ambitious! You work at night, too?

JIM. No, ma'am, not work but—Betty!

AMANDA. [*Crosses left below daybed.*] Betty? Who's Betty?

1 **JIM.** Oh, just a girl. The girl I go steady with!

AMANDA. You mean it's serious? [*Crosses downstage left.*]

JIM. Oh, yes, ma'am. We're going to be married the second Sunday in June.

AMANDA. [*Sits on daybed.*] Tom didn't say anything at all about your going to be married.

JIM. Well, the cat's not out of the bag at the warehouse yet. [*Picks up hat from telephone table.*] You know how they are. They call you Romeo and stuff like that.—It's been a wonderful evening, Mrs. Wingfield. I guess this is what they mean by southern hospitality.

AMANDA. It was nothing. Nothing at all.

JIM. I hope it don't seem like I'm rushing off. But I promised Betty I'd pick her up at the Wabash depot an' by the time I get my jalopy down there her train'll be in. Some women are pretty upset if you keep them waiting.

2 **AMANDA.** Yes, I know all about the tyranny of women! Well, good-by, Mr. O'Connor. [AMANDA *puts out hand.* JIM *takes it.*] I wish you happiness—and good fortune. You wish him that, too, don't you, Laura?

LAURA. Yes, I do, Mother.

JIM. [*Crosses left to* LAURA.] Good-by, Laura. I'll always treasure that souvenir. And don't you forget the good advice I gave you. So long, Shakespeare! [*Upstage center.*] Thanks, again, ladies.—Good night! [*He grins and ducks jauntily out right.*]

3 **AMANDA.** [*Faintly.*] Well, well, well. Things have a way of turning out so badly——[LAURA *crosses to phonograph, puts on record.*] I don't believe that I would play the Victrola. Well, well—well, our gentleman caller was engaged to be married! Tom!

TOM. [*Offstage.*] Yes, Mother?

AMANDA. Come out here. I want to tell you something very funny.

TOM. [*Entering through right kitchen door to dining room and into living room, through curtains, downstage center.*] Has the gentleman caller gotten away already?

AMANDA. The gentleman caller made a very early departure. That was a nice joke you played on us, too!

TOM. How do you mean?

AMANDA. You didn't mention that he was engaged to be married.

TOM. Jim? Engaged?

AT A GLANCE

- Amanda asks Jim to come again.
- He tells her about his engagement and leaves.
- She accuses Tom of playing a joke on them.

1 THEME

With Jim's confession, Amanda's dream of finding a husband for Laura is suddenly crushed.

2 CHARACTERIZATION

Now that Jim is no longer seen as a young man who may be trapped, Amanda's southern vivacity disappears.

3 THEME

When your dreams are based on illusions, they are bound to turn out badly.

GUIDED READING

LITERAL QUESTIONS

1a. Jim tells Amanda that he is kept busy in the evenings; what keeps him busy? (Betty)

2a. What does Amanda think Tom did? (played a joke on her and Laura)

INFERENTIAL QUESTIONS

1b. How does this probably make Amanda feel? (disappointed, angry, frustrated)

2b. Why would she think this? (She feels that Tom is always rebelling against her and teasing her; she probably feels that this is his way of getting back at her.)

AT A GLANCE

- Amanda and Tom fight over Jim, and Tom leaves.
- Tom, as the narrator, explains that he never went home again.
- Now wherever he goes, Tom is haunted by his memory of Laura.

1 IRONY

Amanda does not realize that it is she who lives in a dream and manufactures illusions.

2 PLOT: RESOLUTION

Tom's conflict with his mother and her world of illusion ends with his departure. Amanda and Laura will probably continue living in their dream world.

3 SYMBOL

Pieces of glass and the light that shines through them bring back the fragility of Laura and the broken pieces of her dreams.

REFLECTING ON THE PLAY

Why is happiness always out of reach for the Wingfields? (Some students may suggest that the Wingfields trap themselves in their memories and dreams; others may think that they are victims of circumstance.)

AMANDA. That's what he just informed us.

TOM. I'll be jiggered! I didn't know.

AMANDA. That seems very peculiar.

TOM. What's peculiar about it?

AMANDA. Didn't you tell me he was your best friend down at the warehouse?

TOM. He is, but how did I know?

AMANDA. It seems very peculiar you didn't know your best friend was engaged to be married!

TOM. The warehouse is the place where I work, not where I know things about people!

1 **AMANDA.** You don't know things anywhere! You live in a dream; you manufacture illusions! [TOM *starts for right door.*] Where are you going? Where are you going? Where are you going?

TOM. I'm going to the movies.

AMANDA. [*Rises, crosses up to* TOM.] That's right, now that you've had us make such fools of ourselves. The effort, the preparations, all the expense! The new floor lamp, the rug, the clothes for Laura! All for what? To entertain some other girl's fiancé! Go to the movies, go! Don't think about us, a mother deserted, an unmarried sister who's crippled and has no job! Don't let anything interfere with your selfish pleasure! Just go, go, go—to the movies!

2 **TOM.** All right, I will, and the more you shout at me about my selfish pleasures, the quicker I'll go, and I won't go to the movies either. [*Gets hat from phone table, slams door right, and exits up alley right.*]

AMANDA. [*Crosses up to fire-escape landing, yelling.*] Go, then! Then go to the moon—you selfish dreamer! [*Music cue 18. Interior light dims out. Reenters living room, slamming right door.* TOM*'s closing speech is timed with the interior pantomime. The interior scene is played as though viewed through soundproof glass, behind outer scrim curtain.* AMANDA, *standing, appears to be making a comforting speech to* LAURA *who is huddled on right side of daybed. Now that we cannot hear the mother's speech, her silliness is gone and she has dignity and tragic beauty.* LAURA*'s hair hides her face until at the end of the speech she lifts it to smile at her mother.* AMANDA*'s gestures are slow and graceful, almost dancelike, as she comforts her daughter.* TOM, *who has meantime put on, as before, the jacket and cap, enters downstage right from offstage, and again comes to fire-escape landing, stands as he speaks. Meantime lights are upon* AMANDA *and* LAURA, *but are dim.*]

TOM. I didn't go to the moon. I went much farther. For time is the longest distance between two places. . . . I left St. Louis. I descended these steps of this fire escape for the last time and followed, from then on, in my father's footsteps, attempting to find in motion what was lost in space. . . . I traveled around a great deal. The cities swept about me like dead leaves, leaves that were brightly colored but torn away from the branches. I would have stopped, but I was pursued by something. It always came upon me unawares, taking me altogether by surprise. Perhaps it was a familiar bit of music. Perhaps it was only a piece of transparent glass. . . . Perhaps I am walking along a street at night, in some strange city, before I have found companions, and I pass the lighted window of a shop where perfume is
3 sold. The window is filled with pieces of colored glass, tiny transparent bottles in delicate colors, like bits of a shattered rainbow. Then all at once my sister touches my shoulder. I turn around and look into her eyes. . . . Oh, Laura, Laura, I tried to leave you behind me, but I am more faithful than I intended to be! I reach for a cigarette, I cross the street, I run into a movie or a bar. I buy a drink, I speak to the nearest stranger—anything that can blow your candles out!—for nowadays the world is lit by lightning! Blow out your candles, Laura. . . . [LAURA *blows out candles still burning in candelabrum and the whole interior is blacked out.*] And so—good-by! [*Exits up alley right. Music continues to the end.*]

CURTAIN

GUIDED READING

LITERAL QUESTIONS

1a. For what does Amanda blame Tom? (for not knowing that Jim is engaged)

2a. At first, where does Tom say he is going? (to the movies)

INFERENTIAL QUESTIONS

1b. Why does she blame Tom? (She always seems to need to blame someone for the way things turn out.)

2b. Why does he change his mind? (Amanda makes him so angry that he decides the time has come to become a merchant seaman, as he secretly has planned.)

STUDY QUESTIONS

Recalling

1. What has happened to the Wingfield living room since the end of Act I?
2. Why is Laura so nervous about meeting Jim O'Connor?
3. What plan does Tom reveal to Jim while Amanda and Laura are in the kitchen?
4. Explain how Laura's behavior changes from the time Jim comes to her in the living room after dinner to the time the glass unicorn is broken.
5. What prevents Jim from seeing more of Laura?
6. Why does Tom leave angrily after Jim's departure? Where does Tom go?

Interpreting

7. How would you describe Amanda's behavior with Jim? Why do you think she acts this way?
8. Do you think Jim might have become seriously interested in Laura if he were not already engaged? Why or why not?
9. What do you think will happen to Laura in the future?

Extending

10. Tom tells Jim, "People go to the *movies* instead of moving." Do you think this statement is true of Americans today? Why or why not?

VIEWPOINT

In one edition of *The Glass Menagerie,* the list of characters that precedes the text of the play describes Amanda Wingfield as follows:

> There is much to admire in Amanda Wingfield, and as much to love and pity as there is to laugh at. Certainly she has endurance and a kind of heroism, and though her foolishness makes her unwittingly cruel at times, there is tenderness in her slight person.
>
> —*Masterpieces of the Drama*

■ Do you agree with this analysis? If so, choose a few of the traits mentioned in the quotation, and find words and actions of Amanda's in the play that reveal these traits. If you do not agree, write your own analysis of Amanda's character.

LITERARY FOCUS

The Narrator in Drama

Tom functions in two capacities in this play—as the **narrator** who is outside the action of the play and as one of the characters who is closely involved in the action of the play. As the narrator Tom establishes a link between the audience and the characters and action in the play. Through his monologues Tom sets the time of the play, provides background, introduces and comments on the characters, and interprets the events of the plot.

Thinking About the Narrator in Drama

■ In his review of the opening of *The Glass Menagerie* on Broadway, critic Lewis Nichols stated that the part of the narrator in the play "probably is not essential." Would you be able to understand and appreciate *The Glass Menagerie* if Tom did not function as a narrator? Why or why not?

COMPOSITION

Applying a Statement to a Work of Literature

■ In a short essay defend or challenge this statement: "In *The Glass Menagerie,* Tennessee Williams makes it clear that people have within themselves the key to the prisons in which they are locked." *For help with this assignment, refer to Lesson 9 in the Writing About Literature Handbook at the back of this book.*

Writing a Scene for a Play

■ Imagine a different outcome of the scene in which Jim comes to dinner: he becomes romantically interested in Laura and the two decide to see more of each other. Write a scene depicting the events that lead to this outcome. Use dialogue, stage directions, and, if you wish, a monologue by Tom as the narrator.

COMPARING PLAYS

■ Compare and contrast the views of Americans and American life as portrayed in *Our Town* and *The Glass Menagerie.* Begin with a paragraph stating your intention. In another paragraph describe American people and life as seen by Wilder. In a third paragraph compare and contrast Wilder's views with the views presented by Williams. In a final paragraph state how each view resembles or differs from your own.

STUDY QUESTIONS

1. new floor lamp, paper lantern hides broken light fixture, chintz covers
2. She has loved him secretly.
3. tells Jim that he has joined Union of Merchant Seamen
4. at first very nervous, hardly able to talk; gradually opens up, talks to Jim about high school, shows her "glass menagerie," dances
5. He is engaged.
6. Amanda thinks he knew Jim was engaged, accuses him of making fools of them; probably to join Merchant Marine
7. coquettish, vivacious, gay; trying to make a good impression so that he will become interested in Laura
8. Answers will vary. Although Jim's words to Laura, his kind treatment of her, and his kissing her all indicate this possibility, the two are also very unlike.
9. Possible answers: will retreat to her isolated world; may come further out of herself.
10. Answers will vary; statement may be updated by substituting *television* for *movies.*

VIEWPOINT

aspects of Amanda's character given in quotation: much to love and pity, much to laugh at, endurance, a kind of heroism, foolishness, unwitting cruelty

LITERARY FOCUS

Possible answer: Tom as narrator not really necessary; most of information he gives repeated in the play proper; however, he makes it easier for audience to follow and interpret actions.

COMPARING PLAYS

Wilder's view: optimistic; people triumphant in struggles; American life wholesome; *Williams' view:* pessimistic, people fail but are nevertheless admirable; American life full of conflicts

COMPOSITION: GUIDELINES FOR EVALUATION

APPLYING A STATEMENT TO A WORK OF LITERATURE

Objective

To prove or disprove a possible theme

Guidelines for Evaluation

- suggested length: four paragraphs
- should begin with thesis statement and continue with brief summary of play or general statement of theme
- should justify opinion with citations

WRITING A SCENE FOR A PLAY

Objective

To write one scene for a play

Guidelines for Evaluation

- suggested length: student's choice
- should be in play format
- should include dialogue and stage directions
- may include a narrator's part

ACTIVE READING

Beyond the Surface

You might assign this page after the class has read Auden's "Unknown Citizen" and discuss with them how they should read beyond the surface by making inferences—that is, by drawing conclusions from verifiable facts. Throughout the unit encourage students to read beyond the surface by first ascertaining the facts and then by making inferences that can be supported by the facts and careful reasoning.

ACTIVE READING

Beyond the Surface

We sometimes hear people say that when they read literature they look for "hidden meanings." Yet no writer wants to *hide* his or her meanings from us. Writers want to *reveal* their meanings. Nevertheless, they seldom tell us directly what a poem or a story means.

Literature is an art of implication. It wants to surprise us, to make us participate in the experience it offers. Often it deals with the questions, the enigmas, the mysteries of our existence. No, writers do not want to hide anything from us, yet they do expect our cooperation. They expect us *to go beyond the surface.*

Look again at the poems by W. H. Auden that open this unit (page 546). In both of them, Auden expects us to go beyond the surface, to open ourselves to suggestions. In one of the poems the refrain, "If I could tell you I would let you know," may make us think: *Life is filled with mysteries and wonders, experiences we cannot fully explain.* The poet suggests that he is in love but wondering about, worrying about, what will become of this love. The poem is about uncertainty, and it asks us to share its mixture of delight and sorrow.

In "The Unknown Citizen" we look beyond the surface to see that Auden is not the speaker of the poem. He is not part of the government that seems so "concerned" for the citizen, nor does he *like* a government that judges people by statistics and reports. By the end of the poem, we know that that government would never have heard whether or not the Unknown Citizen felt free or happy. But what has happened to us as readers? We have *joined* the poet in his experience. How much less powerful these poems would be if Auden had merely *stated* his meanings!

Prose, too, asks us to look beyond the surface. In Katherine Anne Porter's "Jilting of Granny Weatherall," the point of the story is that Granny has never forgotten or forgiven the man who jilted her many years before. Her long and seemingly successful life has always been troubled by that memory. Porter's story is more moving because she allows us to watch that thought troubling Granny's mind, rising, receding, and rising to the surface again. The real action of the story is just a bit beyond Granny's consciousness. As readers beyond the surface, we gain a finer experience by not having the point spelled out for us.

Years after *Our Town* had become famous, Thornton Wilder commented that the key words in the play are "hundreds," "thousands," and "millions." He did not make this direct comment within the play itself but rather left it to his audiences to sense the meaning and emotion those words convey. As we read or watch *Our Town*, we may not say to ourselves, "Ah, there are some key words!" Yet surely we find that our experience includes the meanings Wilder intended. *Our Town* is not a realistic picture of life in a New Hampshire village. Rather, it is a meditation upon the mystery of the individual life measured against the joys and griefs of all those who have lived.

As readers we do not always see the full implications of a work of literature. That is why we study literature, discuss it, write about it: to discover what is beyond the surface. Our discussions, whether spoken or written, are attempts to share our enthusiasms and puzzlements. For literature is not only communication between writer and reader; it is communication within a community of readers, too. Each member of that community may see or feel slightly different possibilities in a story or play or poem. By sharing our thoughts, each of us comes to have a larger experience of literature and of life.

THE AMERICAN VOICE

A Usable Past

One critic has said that Americans have spent much of their time and imagination on a quest for a usable past. The years from 1930 to 1960 seem to have been spent largely in that search. The shock of the Great Depression and the cataclysm of World War II forced many Americans to think twice about what part of the American tradition was still meaningful to them. Many of the authors in this unit reveal a desire to look back at the past—whether in its personal or public aspects—and draw strength, ideas, or at least some kind of lesson from it.

Walker
My grandmothers were strong.
Why am I not as they?

Wilbur
There was perfection in the death of ferns
Which laid their fragile cheeks against the stone
A million years. . . .

Porter
Since the day the wedding cake was not cut, but thrown out and wasted. The whole bottom dropped out of the world. . . .

Weidman
I begin to think I understand. I remember the stories of his boyhood in Austria.

Steinbeck
Jody lay in his bed and thought of the impossible world of Indians and buffaloes, a world that had ceased to be forever.

Clark
I have saved what I love; the soul of what was good in us is here; perhaps the new ones will make a strong enough beginning not to fall behind when they become clever.

Agee
We are talking now of summer evenings in Knoxville, Tennessee, in the time that I lived there so successfully disguised to myself as a child.

Faulkner
. . . not even a mortal animal but an anachronism, indomitable and invincible, out of an old dead time, a phantom, epitome and apotheosis of the old wild life.

The writers in this unit stepped back into the past to see what they could retrieve. Some found inspiring models for living. Others discovered that the past can never be exactly repeated, that in a new time new heroes and new definitions of heroism must be created.

Key to Illustrations on Pages 538–539.

1	2			8
3	4	5		9
6	7			10

1. Detail from *Room in New York,* Edward Hopper, 1932.
2. Clothes for the needy during the Depression, photographer unknown.
3. Costume designs by Patricia Zipprodt for a production of Thornton Wilder's *Our Town.*
4. Amelia Earhart, first woman to fly solo across the Atlantic Ocean (1932), postage stamp, 1963.
5. John Steinbeck, drawing by Alexis Oussenko.
6. Eudora Welty, photograph by Jill Krementz.
7. *Number 27,* Jackson Pollock, 1950.
8. Thornton Wilder, photographer unknown, 1933.
9. Guggenheim Museum in New York City, designed by Frank Lloyd Wright, 1943.
10. Celebrating the end of World War II, photographer unknown, 1945.

A Usable Past

After the class has read this page, discuss how events so changed the world in these three decades of crisis that many mid-century writers looked to the past for guidance. In reviewing the quotations, ask students to decide whether the authors view the past as a source of personal strength (Walker, Clark, Faulkner), of ideas for the present (Wilbur), or of some kind of lesson (Porter, Weidman, Steinbeck, Agee).

Photograph © 1982 by Jill Krementz

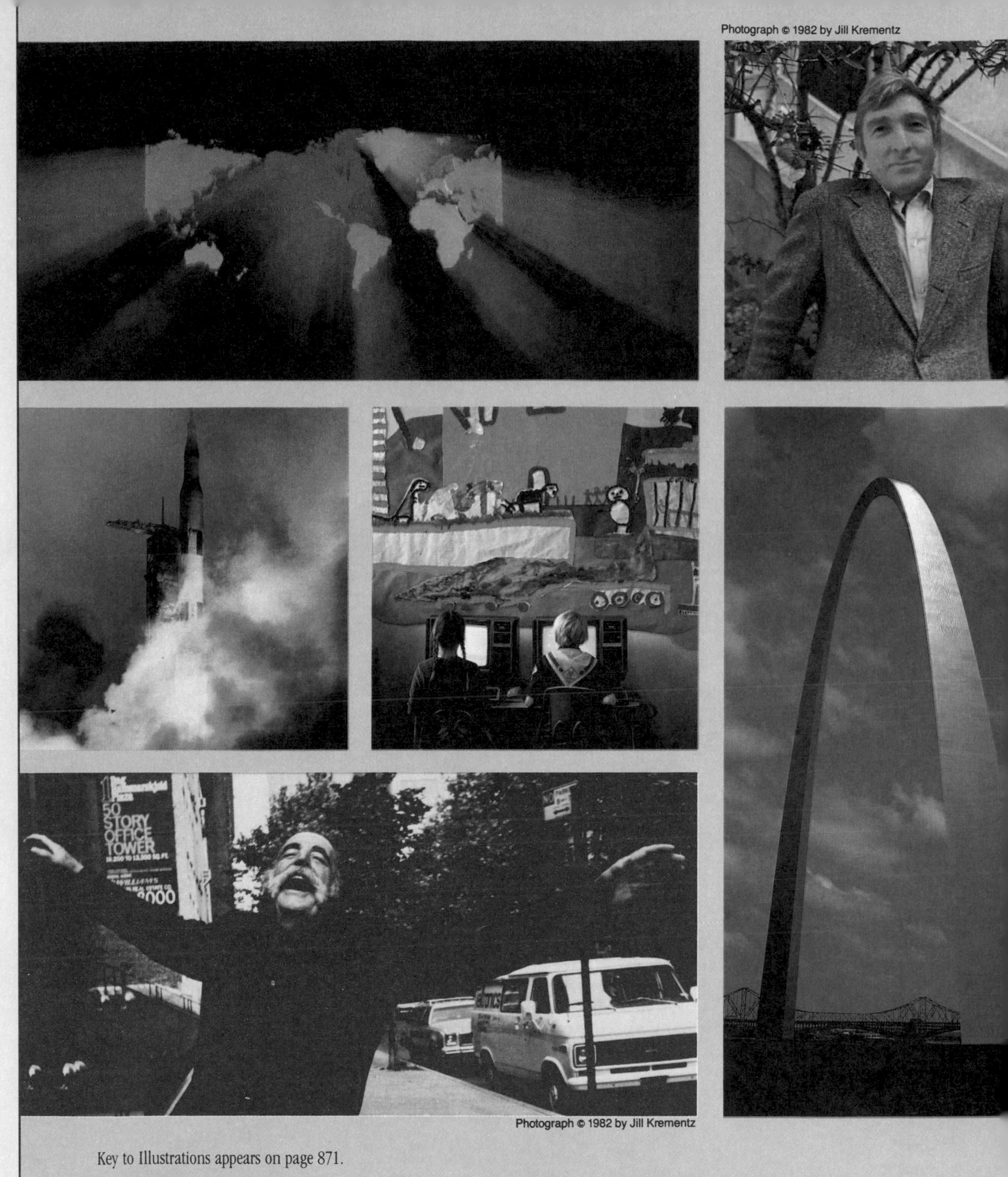

Photograph © 1982 by Jill Krementz

Key to Illustrations appears on page 871.

IN OUR TIME

1960–Present

The Contemporary Experience

What is it that makes the contemporary experience—the time of *our* lives—different from the past? Many historians feel that the time we ourselves live through is the most difficult to describe. Nevertheless, we produce hundreds of books each year trying to explain what it means to be a contemporary American.

The 1960s were a turbulent time in America, perhaps in reaction to the more placid 1950s. Young people in particular felt that they had to make their voices heard. They took strong, sometimes violent, stands on political matters such as American involvement in Vietnam and social matters such as the rights of black Americans and the changing role of women in American society. Many Americans searched for "peace," forming new communities in an effort to redefine the ways people might live together in the contemporary world. These efforts often involved reaching back into the past to revitalize old values and adapt them to new problems and new attitudes. Once again Americans seemed to be face to face with a New World.

As America moved into the 1970s, many of the attitudes of the sixties were absorbed into daily life while others were rejected. In the seventies Americans seemed to become more aware of their material welfare than they had been in the previous decade. The Space Age had arrived. Computers began af-

Photograph © 1982 by Jill Krementz

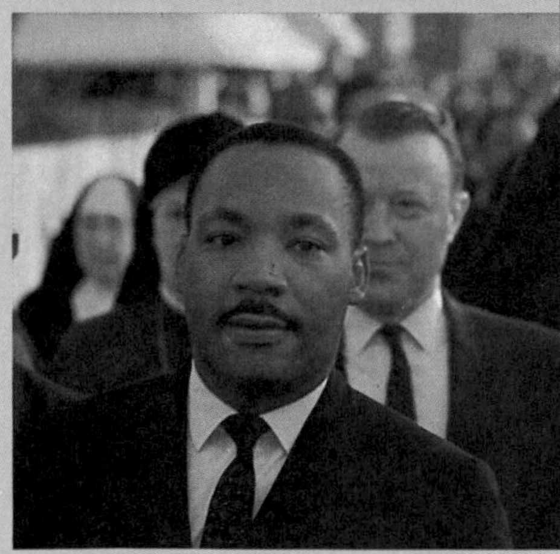

INTRODUCTION

After students have read the introduction to the unit, you might ask them what they know of John F. Kennedy, Martin Luther King, Jr., the Vietnam War, the sixties, the civil rights movement, and the women's movement. Discuss how advances in technology and the computer age have changed our lives. Also discuss the changes from the sixties that have been absorbed into our culture. Students might cite new ideas about male and female roles as well as new industries and careers resulting from developments in electronics and aerospace technology.

You might ask students if they are surprised that there have been no major movements in literature since Modernism. What does that say about our time and about Modernism? Discuss how "modern" Modernism was in its time, how it anticipated and provoked many of the changes in the way we see the world.

As our lives have become more complicated, many people have grown more self-absorbed. Literature, therefore, has focused on the small concerns of the self and the significance of the minor events in human life.

Key Ideas in This Period

- traditionalism and modernism
- the effects of technology
- authenticity
- the individual
- the contemporary American experience

fecting everyone to a greater and greater degree each year. World and national economic problems beset almost everyone, and some of the ideals of the sixties found themselves transformed by the hard facts of making a living in the seventies.

Through the 1980s and beyond, we continue to balance American ideals and realities, to look closely at our goals and our achievements. Americans have created a new sense of the possible without giving up the American dream.

Contemporary Literature

Surprisingly, the literature of our time is fundamentally traditional, but the traditions it follows are the traditions of Modernism. Modernism is our heritage, the extraordinary efforts and accomplishments of the writers and artists of the early decades of our century. There have been no major movements in literature since that time, only refinements, restatements, all building on the shoulders of our giants—Pound, Eliot, Frost, Stevens, Hemingway, Faulkner.

Modernism has given us forms and techniques that we have not yet exhausted. Even literature that calls itself postmodern is dependent upon the Modernist tradition. Modern free verse with its irregular rhythms, its use of association instead of direct statement, and its breakdown of standard forms still intrigues our poets. The stream-of-consciousness technique in prose, the creation of prose poems, the imitation of storytelling techniques taken from movies, continue to be exciting when used by our contemporary novelists.

Drawing by Ziegler, *New Yorker* magazine, 1983.

"Whither goeth literature, Emily, there also must I go."

Some of our writers still seem experimental; some try to incorporate Modernist techniques into more conventional forms. However, to a certain extent, we have become so used to the "modern" style of writing and expression that we often hardly notice it. Literature is following the path taken by modern music: The "outrageous" harmonies that seemed so new in early twentieth-century music are now a part of our everyday sounds on television, in movies, and in popular songs.

Technology has greatly affected our time, of course. The paperback revolution has made more books available to more people than ever before in history. Television, computers, and word processors have changed the ways we absorb information, the way writers write, the way all of us read and organize our thoughts. Although our time appears to many people to be an age of *images*—pictures on screens—many others realize that for the subtleties of communication we are still vitally dependent upon *words.*

The following selections can only begin to display the great variety of writing taking place in our time. Our poets are still consolidating the treasures of Modernism; many of the poems written in our time seem as if they could have been written in the 1920s. Our prose writers are trying to find ways of telling stories that will be both "new" and accessible to most people. The invention, for example, of the form called the nonfiction novel tries to do just that.

Earlier in this century, people talked about the "death of the novel," but the talk was premature. In addition to those writers represented in the following pages, there are many other American writers who have created exciting fiction in our time—among them John Cheever, Isaac Bashevis Singer, Donald Barthelme, Robert Coover, Norman Mailer, and William Gass.

Authenticity

The poet T. S. Eliot said that when it comes to the literature of one's own time, it is impossible to know who the great writers are. Eliot thought we can say

Detail from *Summer Rental, Number 2,* Robert Rauschenberg, 1960.

whether or not we feel that a work of contemporary literature is *authentic.* Yet it is the future, or time, that decides who the classic writers will be.

Only in time is there that sifting process in which some writers are forgotten and others remembered. In American literature we can see how impossible it was for men and women of the nineteenth century to know which writers we in the twentieth century would think great or interesting. In the nineteenth century almost everyone knew that Emerson was great and would become a classic, but few suspected the degree of esteem in which we would come to hold his young friend Thoreau. Emily Dickinson was unknown then, and Herman Melville was forgotten.

One thing, however, is certain. The great writers survive because they are *authentic.* A writer may be sincere but may simply not be in touch with what is truly important to his or her time. A writer may intend to write well, but only *mastery* of the art of writing will allow what is genuine, what is authentic, to be fully expressed. We are continually judging the writers of our time, and authenticity—the full expression of the genuine—is our best guide.

We find in the writers of our own time a familiar American reality. A father and son flying a kite together, a mother and son riding bikes, someone driving a car to town to mail a letter, a baseball player, a man with a flower on his fire escape—these are more familiar to us than Melville's whaling voyage, Cooper's frontiersman, or Taylor's spinning wheel. Yet what is important is the use our contemporaries make of their material, the transformation they make of the everyday into the universal, the authenticity of the experience they offer.

Whatever the greatness or popularity of the writers of our time, they share one quality: freedom of style and content. They take as their material any and every aspect of American experience. They are the heirs of Poe and Hawthorne, of Whitman and Dickinson, of Mark Twain and Willa Cather and Ernest Hemingway and Gertrude Stein. An American writer today can *choose* his or her literary ancestors according to need or taste. An American writer writes as he or she chooses, using traditional or experimental styles or combining the best of both.

No schools or movements dominate the American writing scene today. Our artists are heirs to the entire American past. We have our contemporary Romantics, our Realists and Naturalists, our Regionalists, our Traditionalists, our Modernists. We can enjoy them all, as long as what they write is authentic, as long as it speaks to our hearts and minds, as long as it gives us pleasure and insight.

With the help of American writers like these, we try to understand our time. For that is one of the main uses of literature—to find the language that makes sense of our experience.

TIME LINE

1960–Present AMERICAN EVENTS

1960 John Updike, *Rabbit, Run*

1961 President John Kennedy establishes Peace Corps

Joseph Heller, *Catch–22*

1962 John Steinbeck wins Nobel Prize for Literature

Rachel Carson's *Silent Spring* sparks environmental reform movement

1963 President John Kennedy assassinated

Martin Luther King, Jr., "I Have a Dream" speech

Bernard Malamud, *Idiots First*

1964 Saul Bellow, *Herzog*

Ralph Ellison, *Shadow and Act*

Martin Luther King, Jr., wins Nobel Peace Prize

1965 *Ariel*, poems of Sylvia Plath, published posthumously

John Berryman, 77 *Dream Songs*

1967 Stanley Kubrick directs *2001: A Space Odyssey*

U.S. population: 200 million

1968 Martin Luther King, Jr., assassinated

Robert F. Kennedy assassinated

WORLD EVENTS 1960–Present

1960 Africa: Many national independence movements begin

1961 U.S. and U.S.S.R. make first manned space flights

East Germany: Communists build Berlin Wall

1962 World population: 1.6 billion

Cuba: U.S. blockade forces removal of Soviet missiles

1963 U.S.S.R.: Valentina Tereshkova, first female cosmonaut

1965 England: Harold Pinter, *The Homecoming*

1966 India: Indira Gandhi becomes Prime Minister

1967 South Africa: Dr. Christiaan Barnard performs first heart transplant

1968 U.S.S.R. invades Czechoslovakia

U.S.S.R.: Novelist Alexander Solzhenitsyn, *Cancer Ward*

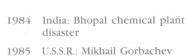

	American Events		World Events
1969	Neil Armstrong and Edwin Aldrin, first men to walk on moon	1969	Israel: Golda Meir becomes Prime Minister
	N. Scott Momaday, *The Way to Rainy Mountain*		
	Robert Penn Warren, *Audubon: A Vision*		
1971	Voting age lowered from 21 to 18	1971	Switzerland: Women gain right to vote
1972	Engineer Robert Moog patents synthesizer, electronic musical instrument		
1973	Vietnam War ends	1973	World oil and energy crisis
1976	John Ashbery, *Self-Portrait in a Convex Mirror*	1976	China: Earthquake kills 655,000 people
	Saul Bellow wins Nobel Prize for Literature		
		1979	Iran: Ayatollah Khomeini overthrows Shah; fifty Americans taken hostage
			U.S.S.R. invades Afghanistan
			England: Trinidad-born novelist V. S. Naipaul, *A Bend in the River*
1981	First flight of space shuttle	1981	Poland: Independent trade union, Solidarity, suppressed
	Inauguration of Ronald Reagan leads to shift in domestic and foreign policies		
	Mark Helprin, *Ellis Island*		
1982	World's first permanent artificial heart transplant		
1984	Personal computers and cable television enter more and more American homes	1984	India: Bhopal chemical plant disaster
1985	Five unpublished Hemingway stories are found	1985	U.S.S.R.: Mikhail Gorbachev named Party Secretary
1986	*Challenger* explosion		
1987	Stock market plunge	1987	U.S.S.R. and China: Continuing increase of openness toward the West

POETRY

Robert Penn Warren *born 1905*

One of the most respected American men of letters, Robert Penn Warren has succeeded in almost every form of literature. He has written poetry, stories, novels, plays, criticism, and biography. In addition, he collaborated with critic Cleanth Brooks on two of the most influential textbooks for teaching literature, *Understanding Poetry* and *Understanding Fiction*.

During the first part of his life, Warren, who was born in Kentucky, lived, went to college, and taught in the South. Indeed, the South with all of its traditions is one of Warren's great subjects. During the 1920s he was a member of the group of southern poets called the Fugitives, writers who contributed to *The Fugitive* magazine and who wrote with a strong sense of their own region. These writers included John Crowe Ransom (page 448) and Allen Tate. In 1930 Warren joined several other southern writers to produce a book called *I'll Take My Stand,* celebrating agrarian, or rural, values in the face of the modern industrial world. He was also one of the founding editors of the *Southern Review* in 1935. Beyond working as a writer and editor, Warren pursued an outstanding career as a teacher. Among his novels, *All the King's Men* (1946)—a powerful story of southern politics—is considered a modern classic. He has won almost every major literary prize in America, including the Pulitzer Prize (once for fiction and twice for poetry) and the National Book Award.

Warren began writing poetry in his teens and has always written poetry while at the same time working in other forms of literature. His volume *Selected Poems: New and Old, 1923–1966* shows his steady dedication to the art. In his later years he has concentrated on poetry, publishing *Incarnation* (1968), *Audubon* (1969), *Or Else* (1974), and other volumes. His poetry reflects a profound love and understanding of his region; he is closely tied to the American land. Often narrative and usually deeply personal, sometimes even rather mystical, his poetry is nevertheless simple and unaffected.

Warren's *Audubon* illustrates a style of modern writing that began with Ezra Pound's *Cantos,* poetry that includes fragments of actual historical documents. Warren's poem is a tribute to John James Audubon (1785–1851), the great American naturalist and painter, who traveled through America studying and painting the birds and other animals native to this continent. Audubon's masterpiece is the huge volume of colored engravings called *Birds of America* (1827–1838).

■ What other examples do you know of historical figures who have become subjects for poems? Why are they good subjects?

from Audubon: A Vision

He walked in the world. Knew the lust of the eye.

Wrote: "Ever since a Boy I have had an astonishing desire
to see Much of the World and particularly
to acquire a true knowledge of the Birds of North
America."

He dreamed of hunting with Boone,[1] from imagination
painted his portrait.
He proved that the buzzard does not scent its repast,
but sights it.
He looked in the eye of the wounded white-headed eagle.

Wrote: ". . . the Noble Fellow looked at his Ennemies
with a Contemptible Eye."

At dusk he stood on a bluff, and the bellowing of buffalo
Was like distant ocean. He saw
Bones whiten the plain in the hot daylight.

He saw the Indian, and felt the splendor of God.

Wrote: ". . . for there I see the Man Naked from his
hand and yet free from acquired Sorrow."

Below the salt,[2] in rich houses, he sat, and knew insult.
In the lobbies and couloirs[3] of greatness he dangled,
And was not unacquainted with contumely.[4]

Wrote: "My Lovely Miss Pirrie of Oackley Passed by Me
this Morning, but did not remember how beautifull
I had rendered her face once by Painting it
at her Request with Pastelles."

Wrote: ". . . but thanks to My humble talents I can run
the gantlet[5] throu this World without her help."

Pileated Woodpecker, John James Audubon.

1. **Boone:** Daniel Boone (1734–1820), U.S. frontiersman.
2. **Below the salt:** in a less honored position. Guests were once seated at the upper or lower part of the table with a bowl of salt in the middle; honored guests were above the salt.
3. **couloirs** [kōōl wärz′]: corridors.
4. **contumely** [kon′too mə lē]: rudeness.
5. **run the gantlet** [gônt′lit]: here, to carry on while being criticized or opposed from all sides.

AT A GLANCE

- The speaker describes how Audubon explored and was excited by nature, especially the birds of North America.
- Audubon was also impressed by the buffalo and the Indian.
- He was uncomfortable in social settings, where he was often treated rudely.

LITERARY OPTIONS

- dramatic poem
- imagery

THEMATIC OPTIONS

- frontier and civilization
- freedom and position

DRAMATIC POEM

Warren's words are interspersed with the actual writings of Audubon. The result is that there are two speakers—Warren, whose grand phrasing glorifies Audubon, and Audubon himself, whose simplicity of style nevertheless supports Warren's view of him.

ALLUSION

"Lust of the eye" is a biblical naming of the sin of loving the world too much (I John 2:16). Rather than a sin, Warren considers it a virtue in its application to his subject (l. 1).

IMAGERY

"Wounded white-headed eagle" (l. 7) and "bellowing of buffalo" (l. 10) dramatize how civilization ravaged the frontier. *Bones whiten* (l. 12) completes this image of destruction.

AT A GLANCE

- Audubon lived independently for most of his life.
- In later years he did enter into society, but he was no longer creative.
- When he died he was still dreaming of wilderness and birds.

VOCABULARY: CONNOTATION

The word *fat* could connote the fat of the land (with its implied exploitation of nature) or the indulgence of Fat Tuesday, the last day of Mardi Gras (with its implied belittlement of society) (l. 27).

RESPONSE JOURNAL

Have students define what Audubon would have considered "humbug" (l. 29).

MAIN IDEA

That the brushes of the painter are now dry refers to Warren's contention that Audubon's creative juices stopped flowing once he entered proper society (ll. 37–39).

REFLECTING ON THE POEM

Why did Audubon love the world as he did? (Students might mention the abundance of natural beauty and the prospect of learning about new frontiers.)

Meadowlark, John James Audubon.

And ran it, and ran undistracted by promise of ease,
Nor even the kind condescension of Daniel Webster.[6]

Wrote: ". . . would give me a fat place was I willing to
have one; but I love indepenn and piece more
than humbug and money."

And proved same, but in the end, entered
On honor. Far, over the ocean, in the silken salons,[7]
With hair worn long like a hunter's, eyes shining,
He whistled the birdcalls of his distant forest.

Wrote: ". . . in my sleep I continually dream of birds."

And in the end, entered into his earned house,
And slept in a bed, and with Lucy.[8]

But the fiddle
Soon lay on the shelf untouched, the mouthpiece
Of the flute was dry, and his brushes.

His mind
Was darkened, and his last joy
Was in the lullaby they sang him, in Spanish, at sunset.

He died, and was mourned, who had loved the world.

Who had written: ". . . a world which though wicked
enough in all conscience is *perhaps* as
good as worlds unknown."

---

6. **Daniel Webster:** U.S. orator and statesman (1792–1852) who served in the House of Representatives, in the Senate, and as Secretary of State.
7. **Far . . . salons:** referring to Audubon's art exhibitions in Great Britain.
8. **Lucy:** Lucy Bakewell, Audubon's wife.

STUDY QUESTIONS

Recalling

1. According to line 1, what did Audubon know? According to line 4, what did he wish "particularly to acquire"?
2. With whom did Audubon dream of hunting (lines 5–7)? What did he prove about the buzzard? In what eye did he look?
3. What did Audubon hear at dusk as he stood on the bluff? What did he see in the hot daylight? What did he feel when he saw the Indian (line 13)?
4. According to line 16, what did Audubon know when he sat below the salt in "rich houses"? What is Miss Pirrie's behavior an example of, according to line 18?
5. Why, according to lines 27–29, did Audubon refuse Daniel Webster's offer of a "fat place" to live? What happened to Audubon soon after he settled in his "earned house"? At the end of the poem, what words does Audubon use to describe the world?

Interpreting

6. What does "lust of the eye" suggest about Audubon's interest in nature? What do the allusions to Boone and the Indian suggest?
7. Was Audubon well-educated? Did he contribute to the science of ornithology? Explain your answers.
8. What does the image of the bones whitening on the plain imply about the buffalo, and what does "wounded" imply about the bald eagle? What does the poem suggest Audubon had in common with these animals?
9. What does Audubon seem to represent for the poet? What would insults and rudeness to Audubon therefore represent? What would Audubon's death signify?

Extending

10. What other heroes whom you have read about in this book have qualities in common with those of Audubon as Warren portrays him? What other works of literature are concerned with themes similar to those of this poem?

VIEWPOINT

Warren has made an interesting comment on his own work, which applies to the spirit in which he wrote this poem, *Audubon: A Vision:*

> Once you are engaged by a subject, are in your book, have your idea, you may or may not want to do some investigating. But you ought to do it in the same spirit in which you'd take a walk in the evening air to think things over.

■ The documentary material in *Audubon* clearly shows that Warren researched this work. His comment, however, tells us that he began with his fascination for Audubon. The research, the documentation, came later. Name two subjects (writers, literary works, or movements) in this book that have fascinated you and that you would find especially interesting to research. Try to explain your fascination.

COMPOSITION

Citing Evidence

■ Using your school and local libraries, research a writer, literary work, or literary movement that you have read about in this book. Write a composition incorporating your research. First make a clear thesis statement about one aspect of your subject. Then support your statement with information, quotations, and interpretations beyond those in this book. Cite your sources and include suggestions for further reading for those who want to go into the subject more deeply. *For help with this assignment, refer to Lesson 3 in the Writing About Literature Handbook at the back of this book.*

Writing a Poem with Documents

■ Write a poem that includes fragments of actual speech and documents side by side with your own verse. You might work with material from newspapers, magazines, biographies, or autobiographies. A volume of letters or a journal can supply material for such a historical-poetic work. Arrange your fragments and quotations so that the whole has an original shape.

STUDY QUESTIONS

1. "lust of the eye"; "true knowledge of the birds of North America"
2. Daniel Boone; does not scent its food, but sights it; "wounded white-headed eagle"
3. bellowing buffalo; "bones whiten the plain"; "splendor of God"
4. "insult"; "contumely," or rudeness
5. loved "indepenn and piece more than humbug and money"; fiddle and flute were untouched, and his brushes were dry; wicked in conscience, *perhaps* as good as worlds unknown
6. passionate interest in nature; admired frontier wilderness
7. from quotations, no; yes, proved that the buzzard *sights* rather than *scents* its prey
8. near extinction because of man; also hurt by civilization
9. pioneer spirit, love of nature; civilization's failure to appreciate wilderness; defeat of pioneer spirit
10. Answers will vary. Students might mention Grandfather in "Leader of the People" or Natty in *Deerslayer*.

VIEWPOINT

Answers will vary depending on students' interests.

COMPOSITION: GUIDELINES FOR EVALUATION

CITING EVIDENCE

Objective

To research a topic and write about it

Guidelines for Evaluation

- suggested length: eight to ten paragraphs
- should state a thesis
- should use facts gathered from research to support the thesis statement
- should cite sources for the facts

WRITING A POEM WITH DOCUMENTS

Objective

To write a poem with quotations from documents

Guidelines for Evaluation

- suggested length: twelve to eighteen lines
- should contain original material
- should contain material from documentary sources
- should integrate both types of material

AT A GLANCE

- The speaker remembers how his father got up early on Sundays and got the fire going.
- The speaker did not get up until the house was warm and his shoes were shined.
- The speaker did not appreciate all the things his father did at the time.

LITERARY OPTIONS

- imagery
- tone

THEMATIC OPTIONS

- parental love and sacrifice
- memory and regret

IMAGERY

"Cold" can be felt, but Hayden creates other ways for the reader to experience the cold. It can be seen—*blueblack* (l. 2)—and it can be heard—*splintering, breaking* (l. 6).

TONE

"No one ever thanked him" (l. 5) is first stated matter-of-factly. At the end of the poem, however, the poet twice asks "What did I know?" (l. 13), indicating his feeling of regret for having been indifferent to his father.

REFLECTING ON THE POEM

What could be the significance of the title of the poem? (Some students may say that Sunday is a day of rest for everyone but parents; others may say that *winter* suggests the cold response that the father received.)

Robert Hayden *1913–1980*

Like so many contemporary poets, Robert Hayden was a college teacher for most of his adult life. After taking a graduate degree from the University of Michigan (his native state), he taught for many years at Fisk University in Nashville, Tennessee, and then returned as a professor to Michigan. He also worked as a poetry editor, as a publisher, and as the editor of a collection of Afro-American literature.

Hayden's first book of poems, *Heart-Shape in the Dust,* was published in 1940. It was followed by many others, including *A Ballad of Remembrance* (1962) and *Angle of Ascent: New and Selected Poems* (1975). "Those Winter Sundays" draws sympathy and compassion from a memory of childhood.

■ During what experiences do we realize a parent's love?

Robert Hayden

Those Winter Sundays

**Sundays too my father got up early
and put his clothes on in the blueblack cold,
then with cracked hands that ached
from labor in the weekday weather made
banked fires blaze. No one ever thanked him.**

**I'd wake and hear the cold splintering, breaking.
When the rooms were warm, he'd call,
and slowly I would rise and dress,
fearing the chronic angers of that house,**

**Speaking indifferently to him,
who had driven out the cold
and polished my good shoes as well.
What did I know, what did I know
of love's austere and lonely offices?**

William Stafford *born 1914*

William Stafford is a poet with a strong sense of place, and his place is the American Midwest and West. A native of Kansas, in his youth he worked for the United States Forest Service, on farms, and in organizations promoting world peace. He has been a college teacher at several schools, mostly at Lewis and Clark College in Oregon.

The poet Louis Simpson has said that "if ever this country is to have a sense of itself, it will be through work like Stafford's." The qualities of Stafford's work that prompt such praise are its simplicity, its modern plain style, and its ability to make a song and a metaphor out of a common domestic experience.

■ Why do some parents have difficulty in "letting go?" Do some bonds always remain?

William Stafford

Father and Son

No sound—a spell—on, on out
where the wind went, our kite sent back
its thrill along the string that
sagged but sang and said, "I'm here!
I'm here!"—till broke somewhere,
gone years ago, but sailed forever clear
of earth. I hold—whatever tugs
the other end—I hold that string.

AT A GLANCE

- The speaker recalls flying a kite with his father.
- The kite pulled his hand, the string broke, and the kite sailed away.
- He continues to hold on to the string, still feeling the kite's tug.

LITERARY OPTIONS

- metaphor
- speaker

THEMATIC OPTIONS

- father and son
- enduring love

SPEAKER

The initial lines capture a child's excitement in sharing something with his father, whereas the last lines reveal an adult's quiet but genuine affection for such a man (ll. 1–4, 7–8).

METAPHOR

Flying a kite is a metaphor for the love between a father and son. Even as the string breaks and the kite sails away, so can the speaker feel the "tug" of his father, years after the man has died (ll. 5–8).

REFLECTING ON THE POEM

Is the son's memory of his father basically happy or basically sad? (It seems basically happy, particularly through the image of a soaring kite that rejoices in its existence.)

AT A GLANCE

- The speaker leaves a book of poems he is reading to "climb a slight rise of grass."
- He watches some ants, listens to some grasshoppers, and hears a cricket sing.

LITERARY OPTIONS

- structure
- imagery

THEMATIC OPTIONS

- reality and imitation
- appreciating nature

STRUCTURE

The poet uses short sentences to describe what he does and long sentences to describe what the insects do. The structure focuses the reader's attention upon nature, not upon the poet.

IMAGERY

The sensitive images created in lines 5–6, 8–10, and 12–13 make the reader feel that he is seeing nature in such an intimate way that he becomes a part of the scene.

REFLECTING ON THE POEM

In what way does this modern poet echo the sentiments of the Romantic era? (Students might suggest that, like many Romantic writers, he finds the natural world a solace and refuge.)

James Wright *1927–1980*

James Wright has been called a poet of extraordinary compassion, one of the most life-affirming poets of our time. Born in Martins Ferry, Ohio, in 1927, Wright studied at Kenyon College and was influenced and encouraged by the poet John Crowe Ransom (page 448). His first volume of verse was published in the distinguished Yale Series of Younger Poets, devoted to publishing first volumes of poetry. After that volume, *The Green Wall* (1957), Wright continued to perfect his gift for lyric with *Saint Judas* (1959), *The Branch Will Not Break* (1963), *Shall We Gather at the River* (1968), and *Collected Poems* (1971). Like so many contemporary poets, Wright has supported himself as a university teacher. In fact, the predominance of the teacher-poet has become one of the most marked characteristics of the contemporary poetry scene.

Wright's poem "Depressed by a Book of Bad Poetry" displays the same directness, the almost transparent language, used by William Stafford (page 767) and Robert Bly (page 778).

■ How can poetry be poetry without "sounding like poetry"? Does this poem "sound like poetry"? Why is it poetry?

James Wright

Depressed by a Book of Bad Poetry, I Walk Toward an Unused Pasture and Invite the Insects to Join Me

Relieved, I let the book fall behind a stone.
I climb a slight rise of grass.
I do not want to disturb the ants
Who are walking single file up the fence post,
Carrying small white petals,
Casting shadows so frail that I can see through them.
I close my eyes for a moment, and listen.
The old grasshoppers
Are tired, they leap heavily now,
Their thighs are burdened.
I want to hear them, they have clear sounds to make.
Then lovely, far off, a dark cricket begins
In the maple trees.

STUDY QUESTIONS *(Hayden)*

Recalling

1. What did the speaker's father do on winter Sundays? In what terms are the father's hands described? With what observation does the first stanza close?
2. Why, according to the second stanza, did the speaker rise and dress slowly? How did he speak to his father, according to line 10?
3. What question does the speaker ask?

Interpreting

4. What is suggested by the "too" in the first line? What did the father do on other days?
5. What does line 9 suggest about the household described in this poem? What do line 14 and the father's activities suggest?
6. What does the speaker seem to regret?

Extending

7. What do you think Emily in *Our Town* (page 670) would have told the people in this household?

STUDY QUESTIONS *(Stafford)*

Recalling

1. What are the father and son doing in the first five lines? What does their kite send back along the string in line 3? What message does it send back in lines 5–7?
2. What happened to the kite, according to lines 5–7? What does the speaker still hold?

Interpreting

3. Is the speaker the father or the son? What might their "kite" be? What does "I'm here! I'm here!" suggest?
4. What is suggested by the kite's being broken? By the speaker's still holding onto the string? What else might tug at the other end?

STUDY QUESTIONS *(Wright)*

Recalling

1. What has depressed the speaker? Toward what does he walk? Whom or what does he invite to join him?
2. Whom or what does the speaker not want to disturb?
3. What adjectives describe the grasshoppers? What sort of sounds does the speaker say they make?
4. What adjectives describe the cricket? What does the cricket do?

Interpreting

5. In general terms, what gives the speaker solace, or comfort, after reading the bad poetry? Why is it appropriate that much of his solace comes from *sounds?*
6. What does this poem suggest about art and its relationship to nature?

COMPARING WRITERS

■ "Depressed by a Book of Bad Poetry" belongs to the long tradition of English and American nature poetry. In that tradition the troubled poet goes to the purity of nature to find healing or renewal. Compare the attitude toward nature in Wright's poem to the attitude toward nature in the excerpt from Robert Penn Warren's *Audubon* (page 763), in William Cullen Bryant's "Thanatopsis" (page 120), and in Walt Whitman's "When I Heard the Learn'd Astronomer" (page 268). Which of the poems seems to you the most moving? Which takes the most important questions as its subject? What generalizations can you make about the language of contemporary poetry as contrasted with the language of earlier American Romantic poetry?

STUDY QUESTIONS

Hayden

1. got up early, dressed, started a fire; cracked, aching; "No one ever thanked him"
2. fear of house's "chronic angers"; "indifferently"
3. "What did I know of love's austere and lonely offices?"
4. father rose early even on Sunday, a supposed day of rest; everything he did on Sunday, and then he worked
5. tense, angry, love rarely expressed; father showed love by caring for physical needs, child did not understand
6. did not show more love and appreciation to his father
7. appreciate life while living it, truly see each other

Stafford

1. flying kite; "thrill"; tug
2. sailed clear of earth; string
3. son; their love; recognition and reassurance of that love
4. speaker has grown up; holds on to love; responsibilities

Wright

1. book of bad poetry; unused pasture; insects
2. the ants
3. *old, tired, burdened; clear*
4. *lovely, far off, dark; sing*
5. nature; sound of bad poetry erased by insects' sounds
6. need to hear sounds of nature, discern efforts of smallest creatures before writing

Comparing Writers

- To Wright nature is benign, beautiful, and comforting. To Warren also it is beautiful, but it contains violence and death. Bryant finds it comforting because it reflects the spiritual world. Bryant and Whitman, like Wright, reject the academic explication of nature for direct observation.
- The students' experiences will determine which poems they find most moving.
- Contemporary poetry uses words and images that are more concrete and less ornate than the language of American Romantic poetry.

Photograph © 1982 by Jill Krementz

John Ashbery *born 1927*

One of the most brilliant and experimental of contemporary poets, John Ashbery seems always in search of a new definition of poetry. He blends a visionary, sometimes highly abstract style with the most ordinary of everyday objects and events. His subjects and tones shift with great speed—just as our minds move instantaneously from one thing to another.

John Ashbery was born in Rochester, New York, and after attending Harvard and Columbia universities, received a Fulbright scholarship that took him to France. He remained in France for almost ten years, and his poetry is deeply influenced by modern French poetry and important French literary criticism. In fact, Ashbery is often considered the leading American poet to reflect the most recent critical thinking about the direction poetry is taking in our time.

In Paris Ashbery became an art critic, a profession that he continued when he returned to New York in 1965. His close association with the "action painters" in New York is usually thought to be another influence on his writing. Action painting is abstract, and it is about the act of painting itself. In the same way, Ashbery's poems are often about the *act* of writing a poem, not about a completed meaning that a poem hands over to us.

Ashbery began publishing poems in 1956 with the volume *Some Trees.* His other books include *The Tennis Court Oath* (1962), *Self-Portrait in a Convex Mirror* (1975), *Houseboat Days* (1977), and *Paradoxes and Oxymorons* (1968), from which the following poem is taken. Ashbery once said that his poems "might be considered to be a snapshot of whatever is going on in my mind at the time," and indeed his poems are often impossible to understand if we try to get from them some meaning that can be expressed in prose. They are, however, a kind of elegant fun for the reader who can relax and allow them to happen, allow their brilliant images and playful shifting of voices to have their own way.

"Paradoxes and Oxymorons" is a poem that plays a trick upon "you" (the reader), but it is a trick designed to make a serious point. It makes us stop and stare at the eternal "paradoxes and oxymorons" at the center of writing and reading poetry. A **paradox** is an apparent contradiction. An **oxymoron** is a bringing together of contradictory things within a phrase such as *brilliant darkness.* In simple language that sounds *almost* as if we could follow its argument on a "plain level," this poem turns itself inside out as it makes us wonder where the meaning comes from in any poem.

■ Where does the meaning come from in this poem? From the poet? From the poem? From us?

John Ashbery

Paradoxes and Oxymorons

This poem is concerned with language on a very plain level.
Look at it talking to you. You look out a window
Or pretend to fidget. You have it but you don't have it.
You miss it, it misses you. You miss each other.

The poem is sad because it wants to be yours, and cannot.
What's a plain level? It is that and other things,
Bringing a system of them into play. Play?
Well, actually, yes, but I consider play to be

A deeper outside thing, a dreamed role-pattern,
As in the division of grace these long August days
Without proof. Open-ended. And before you know
It gets lost in the steam and chatter of typewriters.

It has been played once more. I think you exist only
To tease me into doing it, on your level, and then you aren't there
Or have adopted a different attitude. And the poem
Has set me softly down beside you. The poem is you.

Collection Whitney Museum of American Art

Summer Rental, Number 2,
Robert Rauschenberg, 1960.

AT A GLANCE

- The poem talks to the reader even though the reader sometimes misses its meaning.
- A poem is many things, but it is also the reader.

LITERARY OPTIONS

- modern style
- paradoxes and oxymorons

THEMATIC OPTIONS

- the relationship between poet and reader
- effective communication

MODERN STYLE

The poet may use plain language (denotation), but the effect of his particular choice of words on the individual reader (connotation) is both personal and idiosyncratic (ll. 3–4).

PARADOX

The poem itself is a paradox. The poet believes that it is the reader's (l. 5), yet he knows that it has a meaning of its own (ll. 2–3) that the reader may not accept (ll. 14–15).

OXYMORON

"Open-ended" (l. 11) and "deeper outside" (l. 9) are oxymorons that capture the poet's understanding of poetry quite aptly.

REFLECTING ON THE POEM

Based on your reading of this poem, do you think that it is more important to know what the poet intended or to respond freely to the poet's words? (Some students may decide on a balance between the two.)

STUDY QUESTIONS

1. language on a plain level; "talking to you"; "You have it but you don't have it."
2. wants to be yours, cannot; "What's a plain level?"
3. exist to tease poet into doing it, on your level, then you aren't there; set poet down beside you; poem is you
4. yes; reader
5. you have it but don't; elusive meaning, discrepancy between intended and interpreted meaning
6. communicates poet's thoughts, becomes part of reader, who completes it with own interpretation; poem exists apart from reader with intended meaning but also is part of reader, who has given own interpretation
7. poem shows poems never deal with language on a plain level, even when using plain language; exists on two levels: literal and suggested
8. Answers will vary. Students should see importance of text but say that each reader brings something to a poem.

VIEWPOINT

Answers will vary. Students should see that in a poem like Ashbery's the structure becomes the subject.

STUDY QUESTIONS

Recalling

1. According to line 1, with what is this poem concerned? What is it doing in line 2? According to line 3, do you "have" the poem?
2. Why, according to stanza 2, is the poem "sad"? What question is asked in line 6?
3. What does the speaker say about your reasons for existing in stanza 4? According to lines 15–16, what has the poem done? What is it?

Interpreting

4. Is the speaker in this poem speaking to you as a poet? Who is "you" in this poem?
5. What paradox, or apparent contradiction, is expressed in line 3? What might this paradox suggest about poetry?
6. What do the last two lines suggest about the effects of a poem on its readers? In what way are these suggestions paradoxical?
7. Why is line 1 paradoxical? What does the paradox suggest about all good poetry?

Extending

8. Which do you think is more important to a poem—the poet's meaning or the reader's interpretation? Discuss.

VIEWPOINT

The critic Denis Donoghue has commented on Ashbery's intention as a poet:

> I assume that Mr. Ashbery's concern is to give the process of the mind as it moves through . . . reflections, not merely the results of reflection. It is an extreme version of the common distinction between "a mind speaking" and "what is being said."

■ What are the advantages of a poet showing his mind at work—"a mind speaking"? What can we learn as we watch the process of a poem in the making? Tell in your own words what this kind of process poem reveals about "what is being said" in any poem at any time.

LITERARY FOCUS

Modern Style

Style in literature—especially modern literature—is one of the most difficult literary elements to discuss. We talk about "a writer's style," but when we have to describe that style precisely, we find that it is hard to do. We use words like *lyrical, dignified, ornate, journalistic, comic, satiric,* or even simpler but less helpful words like *dull, vivid, simple,* or *complex.* We can say that **style** is a writer's own characteristic way of writing, including virtually all the ways words are used: diction, syntax, sentence length, imagery, rhythm. As with all terms that have so many ways of being used, we should be careful when we use the term *style.* One useful distinction, however, can be kept in mind: the distinction between the style of a period and the style of an individual author.

In the world of contemporary poetry, there is no single "style of the period." Some writers use "plain" speech, not far from ordinary conversation or prose. Others use highly unusual, extraordinary speech, language that attempts to express what "ordinary" language cannot express. Some writers use short, clipped sentences; others use long, complicated constructions with many subordinate clauses and modifying phrases.

Some poets today are highly literal; they say exactly what they mean, neither more nor less. Some are highly metaphorical, requiring us to penetrate complex constructions of images. Some are objective, trying to eliminate as far as possible the personality of the poet behind the poem. Some are subjective, believing that there is nothing more important than the outpouring of their own feelings.

For most of us, poems in the modern "plain" style are the most attractive poems on first reading. Marianne Moore, in her famous poem "Poetry" (page 453), admits that "we / do not admire what / we cannot understand." Yet we would be soon bored if we understood everything at once or easily. In "Paradoxes and Oxymorons" John Ashbery makes fun of the idea of reading on a "plain level." As he demonstrates in the poem itself, the question of where "meaning" comes from is never a "plain" question. There are no unusual words in Ashbery's poem. The sentences seem short and clear as we read them one by one. Yet as we attempt to follow the argument, to fit the sentences together, we see that this poem is hardly written in a "plain" style like that of Robert Hayden's "Those Winter Sundays" (page 766) or James Wright's "Depressed by a Book of Bad Poetry" (page 768).

The modern philosopher Ludwig Wittgenstein believed that "what we cannot speak about we must pass over in silence." Poets, however, resist that silence. When the style of a modern poem turns away from simple statements, it is attempting to speak about things that cannot be spoken about in "ordinary" language. It is attempting to make meaning, to find meaning, for experience. The style—perhaps we should say the *styles* of modern poetry, whether direct or indirect, plain or fantastic—tries to be adequate to whatever experience is the subject of a poem. At times, perhaps, something that looks like a "plain level" will do. Yet when it will not do, the poets of our time devise other styles, for, as an art, poetry refuses to pass over any of our wide-ranging human experience in silence.

Thinking About Modern Style

■ Choose any poem in this book written in the twentieth century. Describe in your own words the style of the poem. Be as specific as possible, referring to the poem's diction, sentence structure, imagery, and rhythm. Most important, tell whether you think the style is adequate to the poet's experience. In other words, does the poem "work"?

VOCABULARY

Words from Greek

In the Golden Age of Greece, oratory and rhetoric, or the art of using words effectively, were highly developed arts. Greek has given us many words for figures of speech and literary elements. The title of Ashbery's poem comes from two Greek words for figures of speech.

In Greek the root *para* means "beside" or "beyond"; *doxa* means "belief." A paradox, therefore, seems beyond belief—something incredible or self-contradictory but true if you think twice about it. In Greek the root *oxy* means "sharp" or "acute," and *moron* means "foolish." An oxymoron, then, is a figure of speech that combines two ideas or words in a way that seems particularly unreasonable, such as *cruel kindness* or *wise fool.*

By using your dictionary, find out the root meanings in Greek of the following literary terms.

1. metaphor
2. irony
3. drama
4. epic
5. hyperbole
6. analogy
7. protagonist

COMPOSITION

Developing a Thesis Statement

■ Write a short composition in which you develop a thesis about some aspect of modern literature. You may want to write about style or subject matter or free verse or the modern use of any literary technique. First state your thesis in clear, concise terms. Then support the thesis with several examples drawn from selections you have read in this book. *For help with this assignment, refer to Lesson 1 in the Writing About Literature Handbook at the back of this book.*

Writing About Writing

■ Write a short composition or poem about your own act of writing. Let the reader see your "mind at work." Let the process of writing itself be your subject, and do not hesitate to experiment with new ways of expressing yourself.

LITERARY FOCUS

Answers will vary. Students should include all elements adding up to a poet's style and relate the style to the content.

VOCABULARY

1. *meta,* "over"; *pherein,* "to carry"; to carry over
2. *eironeia,* "dissembler in speech"
3. *drama,* a deed or action
4. *epos,* "a word, speech, tale, song, epic"
5. *hyper,* "over, beyond"; *ballein,* "to throw"; to throw beyond
6. *ana,* "according to"; *logos,* "ratio, relation"
7. *protos,* "first"; *agonistes,* "actor"; first actor

COMPOSITION: GUIDELINES FOR EVALUATION

DEVELOPING A THESIS STATEMENT

Objective

To develop a thesis about modern literature

Guidelines for Evaluation

- suggested length: 3–5 paragraphs
- should state a thesis about modern literature
- should support the thesis with specific examples from selections in the textbook

WRITING ABOUT WRITING

Objective

To write about the process of writing

Guidelines for Evaluation

- suggested length: 2–4 paragraphs, 14–18 lines
- should describe the process of writing
- should focus on the writer's personal approach
- should use experimental techniques to communicate the mental processes of writing

© by Jill Krementz.

Adrienne Rich *born 1929*

The poems of Adrienne Rich almost always reflect her characteristic attitude toward change. She affirms that the greatest changes in society, the large-scale changes in the way we all live and think about each other, are determined and directed by changes in the minds of *individuals.*

Adrienne Rich grew up in Baltimore, Maryland, and attended Radcliffe College in Cambridge, Massachusetts. She had begun writing poetry years before her graduation, and in the same year that she graduated from college her first volume appeared in the Yale Series of Younger Poets (1951). The poet who selected her volume for this distinction was the great W. H. Auden (page 573).

Rich's early work was neat, crafted, polished, as the title of her second volume, *The Diamond Cutters* (1955), suggests. In the early 1960s, however, Rich abandoned the style that had brought her early success. Like Robert Lowell, whose "confessional" poetry so influenced his contemporaries, Rich began to write in a freer style, talking directly about her own deepest experiences. Women readers have felt especially close to Rich, who speaks in her poems about the meaning and experience of being a woman in this century. Her later works include *Snapshots of a Daughter-in-Law* (1963), *Leaflets* (1969), *The Will to Change* (1971), and *Diving into the Wreck* (1973).

In "The Observer" Rich remembers a woman scientist who lived alone in Africa among gorillas. She compares her own life with the life she imagines for the scientist who "observes" the gorillas, far from the stress of "civilization."

■ Why do we often imagine our lives as being different if we were in a different country or a different time? Why would there be a difference?

Adrienne Rich

The Observer

Completely protected on all sides
by volcanoes
a woman, darkhaired, in stained jeans
sleeps in central Africa.
In her dreams, her notebooks, still
private as maiden diaries,
the mountain gorillas move through their life term;
their gentleness survives
observation. Six bands of them
inhabit, with her, the wooded highland.
When I lay me down to sleep
unsheltered by any natural guardians
from the panicky life-cycle of my tribe
I wake in the old cellblock
observing the daily executions,
rehearsing the laws
I cannot subscribe to,
envying the pale gorilla-scented dawn
she wakes into, the stream where she washes her hair,
the camera-flash of her quiet
eye.

AT A GLANCE

- The poet describes a woman scientist living in central Africa among six bands of gorillas.
- She then describes her own feelings about living in civilized society.
- She envies the woman in Africa.

LITERARY OPTIONS

- irony
- metaphor

THEMATIC OPTIONS

- civilization vs. nature
- perception

IRONY

Volcanoes suggest terrifyingly destructive eruptions. Nevertheless, the poet chooses them (ll. 1–2) to convey a feeling of security and serenity.

METAPHOR

Equating "the old cellblock" (l. 14) and "executions" (l. 15) with civilized society and its members shows how strongly the poet feels about being trapped in such a society and its rituals.

MAIN IDEA

The poet contrasts the tameness of the uncivilized world to the wildness of the civilized world and finds the former preferable (ll. 11–21).

REFLECTING ON THE POEM

Is the poet being an objective "observer" as she describes the two worlds? (Some students may feel that the poem should not be interpreted literally.)

Alicia Ostriker *born 1937*

Alicia Ostriker was born in New York City, and attended college and graduate school at Brandeis University in Massachusetts and the University of Wisconsin. She is an authority on the work of the English Romantic poet, William Blake. Her volumes of poetry include *Songs* (1969), *Once More Out of Darkness* (1974), and *The Mother/Child Poems* (1980). Ostriker teaches at Rutgers University in New Jersey and lives in Princeton with her husband and three children.

"His Speed and Strength," with its mythological references and its delicate similes, demonstrates how a poem may arise from our ordinary lives.

■ How does Ostriker create a memorable moment from an everyday event?

Alicia Ostriker

His Speed and Strength

His speed and strength, which is the strength of ten
years, races me home from the pool.
First I am ahead, Niké,[1] on my bicycle,
no hands, and the *Times* crossword tucked in my rack,
then he is ahead, the Green Hornet,[2]
buzzing up Witherspoon,
flashing around the corner to Nassau Street.

At noon sharp he demonstrated his neat
one-and-a-half flips off the board:
Oh, brave. Did you see me, he wanted to know.
And I doing my backstroke laps was Juno
Oceanus,[3] then for a while I watched some black
and white boys wrestling and joking, teammates, wet
plums and peaches touching each other as if

it is not necessary to make hate,
as if Whitman was right and there is no death.[4]
A big wind at our backs, it is lovely, the maple boughs
ride up and down like ships. Do you mind
if I take off, he says. I'll catch you later,
see you. I shout and wave, as he peels
away, pedalling hard, rocket and pilot.

---

1. **Niké** [nī′kē]: in Greek mythology, goddess of victory, usually depicted with wings.
2. **Green Hornet:** radio, television, and comic book hero.
3. **Juno Oceanus** [jo͞o′nō ō sē′ə nəs]: here, queen of the ocean. In Roman mythology Juno was queen of the gods.
4. **Whitman . . . death:** See "Song of Myself" (page 261).

AT A GLANCE

- A mother and her son race home from the pool on bicycles.
- Earlier at the pool the son showed his diving skill, and she watched black and white boys playing without hate or awareness of death.
- She waves to him as he races ahead.

LITERARY OPTIONS

- allusion
- setting

THEMATIC OPTIONS

- parental pride
- the innocence of youth

ALLUSION

Some of the metaphors used (ll. 3, 5, 11–12) are also allusions. The heroic figures reinforce the strength of the parent-child bond and support the poet's proud tone.

SETTING

The "*Times* crossword" (l. 4), the "pool" (l. 2), and the "maple boughs" (l. 17) suggest a reasonably affluent suburban setting. However, the bond of the human relationship transcends all distinctions of class.

MAIN IDEA

An everyday experience is transformed into a paean. The poem rejoices in the beauty of the proud bond between mother and son; it also glories in youth's triumph over hate and death.

REFLECTING ON THE POEM

Do you think that the son sees himself as a "rocket and pilot" (l. 21), or is he so only in his mother's eyes? (Students may recall being ten years old and thinking of themselves in a similar way.)

LITERARY OPTIONS

- imagery
- lyric poem

THEMATIC OPTIONS

- moments of peace
- mystery in commonplace experiences

IMAGERY

Feeling the "cold iron" (l. 3) and being in the midst of "swirls of snow" (l. 2) are sensory images that show how aware the poet is of his immediate surroundings.

LYRIC POEM

The poet uses very simple language to reveal how much he loves the peaceful feeling (l. 4). He wants to indulge this feeling, even at the expense of not meeting his responsibility (l. 5).

REFLECTING ON THE POEM

How does the speaker respond to the "deserted" street? (Its "privacy" provides him with the opportunity to experience great peace.)

Robert Bly *born 1926*

Born in Minnesota, where he still lives, Robert Bly has devoted his life to poetry with an almost exclusive attention. In addition to producing several volumes of poetry—including *Silence in the Snowy Fields, Light Around the Body,* and *Sleepers Joining Hands*—he has edited poetry anthologies and published superb translations of Swedish and Spanish poets, including Pablo Neruda and Federico García Lorca.

Known for his famous poetry readings, Bly does much more than *read* his poems. He *performs* them, often using masks and costumes, different voices, and gestures and dance movements. His effort is to revive poetry as an excitement, an experience that goes far beyond words on the printed page. Understandably, the songs, chants, and rituals of primitive peoples—for whom poetry was a performance—have influenced him enormously.

Bly's poems, like "Driving to Town Late to Mail a Letter," are often extremely simple, suggesting magic and mystery behind the most common American experience. Few people other than Bly, or his poetic ancestor, William Carlos Williams (page 421), would have thought to make a poem out of what most people think of as a chore or errand.

■ How can mailing a letter be a poetic experience?

Robert Bly

Driving to Town Late to Mail a Letter

It is a cold and snowy night. The main street is deserted.
The only things moving are swirls of snow.
As I lift the mailbox door, I feel its cold iron.
There is a privacy I love in this snowy night.
Driving around, I will waste more time.

STUDY QUESTIONS *(Rich)*

Recalling

1. What protects the woman in Africa? In what terms are her notebooks described?
2. From what is the speaker unsheltered when she sleeps? In what does she waken?
3. Into what does the woman in Africa waken? What emotion does the speaker feel toward the woman in Africa?

Interpreting

4. Where does the speaker live? How does she feel about this world?
5. What does the speaker seem to envy about the woman in Africa?

Extending

6. Do you think it is common or unusual to want to change places with another? Why?

COMPOSITION *(Rich)*

Writing About Literature and Its Period

■ "The Observer" tells of two ways of life in the modern world. Write a composition explaining what is typically modern about the speaker's experience. First identify the characteristics of modern experience reflected in Rich's poem. Then describe in your own words the advantages and disadvantages of the life of the scientist in the poem. Conclude by telling what aspects of modern life are *not* described in the poem. *For help with this assignment, refer to Lesson 10 in the Writing About Literature Handbook at the back of this book.*

Writing About a Place

■ Write a short composition about a place in which you think a friend would like to live. Describe the place in detail, telling how the friend would live and what the friend would do there. Most important, tell, as Rich does in "The Observer," how the place would give definition and meaning to a life and a career.

STUDY QUESTIONS *(Ostriker)*

Recalling

1. What sort of strength does the speaker's son have, according to lines 1–2? With whom does the speaker compare her son when he races ahead on his bicycle?
2. What did the son do "at noon sharp"? What did he want to know?
3. Whom does the speaker say she felt like as she did backstroke laps in the pool? Afterward, what did she watch for a while? How does the speaker say the "wet plums and peaches" touched each other (lines 14–16)?
4. With what adjective does the speaker describe riding past the maple trees with the wind at her back? What does she do as her son "peels away" on his bicycle?

Interpreting

5. What is the speaker's attitude toward her son? Toward the day's outing? What does the title suggest is the relationship between the speaker's son and her attitude toward the day's outing?
6. What do lines 15–16 suggest the speaker has almost been able to forget during the day's outing? In what way is her son's appreciation of the outing different from hers?
7. What attitude toward youth does this poem project? Is it Romantic or Transcendentalist in any way? Explain.

Extending

8. Do you agree with the suggestions this poem makes about youth? Why or why not?

STUDY QUESTIONS *(Bly)*

Recalling

1. According to the title, what is the speaker doing?
2. What does the speaker love about "this snowy night"? What does he say he will do?

Interpreting

3. Is there a paradox, or discrepancy, between the activity indicated in the title and the final statement of the poem? If so, what is it?
4. Why does the speaker seem to want to continue driving around? What might he be avoiding? What sort of conflict does the poem suggest?

Extending

5. In what way is the conflict in this poem like that of the speaker in "Stopping by Woods on a Snowy Evening" (page 468)? What sort of reactions do snowy nights inspire in people?

STUDY QUESTIONS

Rich

1. volcanoes; private as diaries
2. natural guardians; old cell-block
3. pale gorilla-scented dawn; envy
4. urban setting; dislikes it
5. envies safety, peacefulness, simplicity, closeness to nature
6. Answers will vary. Envy is common, but many people would not actually change places.

Ostriker

1. ten years; Green Hornet
2. neat dive; if mother saw him
3. Juno Oceanus; boys wrestling; "as if it is not necessary to make hate," "no death"
4. lovely; shouts, waves
5. admiration, love; joy, celebration; appreciation of son makes outing joyous
6. grim realities of hate, death; enjoys, but does not see larger importance to day
7. ■ celebratory
   ■ yes; reference to Whitman implies death part of life; image of boy conveys Romantic idea of perfectability
8. Answers will vary. Poet ignores problems of youth, idealizes it.

Bly

1. driving to town late at night to mail a letter
2. the privacy; drive around, waste more time
3. yes; title implies purpose, final statement suggests wasting time
4. at peace; work; doing vs. being
5. ■ *Forst:* desire to stay vs. need to continue journey; *Bly:* demands on time vs. desire to waste it
   ■ Answers will vary. Students might say peace, awe.

COMPOSITION: GUIDELINES FOR EVALUATION

WRITING ABOUT LITERATURE AND ITS PERIOD

Objective

To write about a poem in terms of context

Guidelines for Evaluation

- suggested length: four to seven paragraphs
- should identify aspects of modern life in poem
- should cite specific examples from the poem
- should give opinion on positive and negative aspects of living apart from civilization

WRITING ABOUT A PLACE

Objective

To write about a place

Guidelines for Evaluation

- suggested length: four to six paragraphs
- should describe place in detail
- should tell what life in place would be like
- should state how place would give shape and meaning to person's life

Simon J. Ortiz *born 1941*

Simon J. Ortiz was born in New Mexico, where his ancestors, people of the Acoma Pueblo tribe, lived for hundreds of years. He was educated at the University of New Mexico, where he is now a professor, and at the Writers School of the University of Iowa. Ortiz has lived most of his life in the Southwest and has dedicated himself to education, particularly to the education of Native Americans.

In his poetry Ortiz continues the long storytelling traditions of his people. When asked why he writes, Ortiz once replied: "Because Indians always tell a story. The only way to continue is to tell a story. . . . Your children will not survive unless you tell something about them—how they were born, how they came to this certain place, how they continue."

The people of Acoma Pueblo are famous for their pottery, a craft with an unbroken tradition going back to the Anasazi people who lived in New Mexico over a thousand years ago, and beyond the Anasazi into prehistory.

■ Would you like to learn a craft passed down in a family for generations? What could be the value of the learning itself?

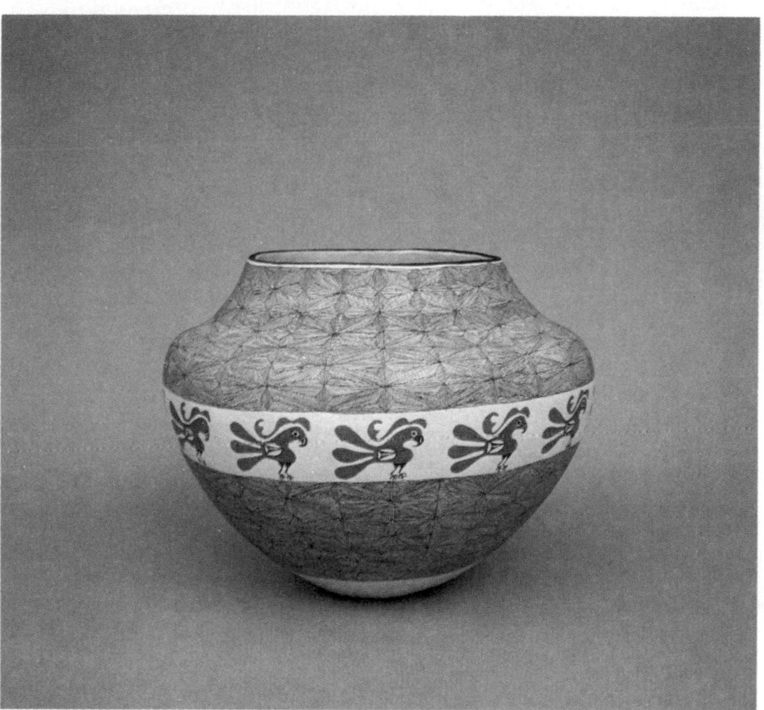

Acoma pottery,
by Marie and Joann Chino,
1982.

Simon J. Ortiz

from My Mother and My Sisters

My oldest sister wears thick glasses
because she can't see very well.
She makes beautifully formed pottery.
That's the thing about making dhyuuni;[1]
it has to do more with a sense of touching
than with seeing because fingers
have to know the texture of clay
and how the pottery is formed from lines
of shale strata and earth movements.
The pottery she makes is thinwalled
and has a fragile but definite balance.
In other words, her pottery has a true ring
when it is tapped with a finger knuckle.

Here, you try it;
you'll know what I mean.

The design that my mother is painting
onto the bowl is done with a yucca[2] stem brush.
My other sister says, "Our mother,
she can always tell when someone else has used
a brush that she is working with," because
she has chewed it and made it into her own way.
She paints with movements whose origin
has only to do with years of knowing
just the right consistency of paint,
the tensile vibrancy of the yucca stem,
and the design that things are supposed to have.

She can always tell.

---

1. **dhyuuni** [dē hyo͞o′nē]: "pottery" in Keresan [ker′ə sən], language of the Acoma Pueblo Indians.
2. **yucca** [yuk′ə]: flowering desert plant, with a woody stem and stiff sword-shaped leaves.

STUDY QUESTIONS

Recalling

1. According to lines 1–13, why does the speaker's oldest sister wear thick glasses? Why can she nevertheless make beautifully formed pottery?
2. What "test" indicates the definite balance of the pottery? What does the speaker ask us to do in lines 14–15?
3. What does the other sister say about her mother's brush in lines 16–26? What does the speaker say about the mother's movements as she paints?

Interpreting

4. What do lines 23 and 26 suggest about the nature of Pueblo pottery making? What does line 21 suggest? What attitude toward the mother's talent do the speaker and the other daughter share?
5. Briefly describe the language in which this poem is written. Is it "poetic"? Is it precise? In light of your answers, state the probable purpose of this poem, the reason the poet has written it.
6. What is the effect of lines 14–15 on the reader?

Extending

7. Why do you think so many people in modern America find it important to pass down traditional arts and customs from generation to generation? How might their practices be related to Carson McCullers' description of the loneliness of modern Americans on page 662?

AT A GLANCE

- The poet's sister cannot see well, but she makes beautiful pottery.
- His mother paints designs on his sister's pottery with yucca brushes that she has made her own by chewing them.
- She paints with ease, having years of experience.

LITERARY OPTIONS

- speaker
- symbol

THEMATIC OPTIONS

- the value of tradition
- cultural continuity

SPEAKER

The speaker's intensely personal tone is reflected in the conversational quality of the poem. For example, when the speaker asks the reader to "try it" (l. 14), it seems as if the two are in actual conversation.

SYMBOL

Pottery making is a symbol for all the traditional cultural arts. The mother symbolizes how an art is transmitted to the next generation (ll. 22–26).

REFLECTING ON THE POEM

According to the poet, how important is tradition to an individual? (Some students may conclude that tradition gives an individual a sense of having roots in a particular culture.)

STUDY QUESTIONS

1. cannot see well; more to do with touch than with sight
2. "true ring" when tapped; tape pottery "with a finger knuckle"
3. can tell when someone else has used it, has made it into her own; from years of experience
4. ancient tradition, art; individual dimension in traditional forms; respect, admire
5. conversational, not poetic or precise; preserve customs, traditions, sense of cultural continuity, as through pottery
6. draw reader into poem
7. Answers will vary. Traditional arts part of collective and individual identities, give people a sense of roots.

AT A GLANCE

When the speaker proves a geometric theorem, her house expands, leaving the speaker in the open.

LITERARY OPTIONS

- symbol
- imagery

THEMATIC OPTIONS

- intellectual accomplishment
- growth and change

SYMBOL

The house is a concrete representation of the angles, points, lines, and planes of geometry; it also represents the enclosure of the mind (l. 1).

IMAGERY

The light—knowledge—that pours through the windows of the house changes them into butterflies. The metamorphosis suggests the soaring of inspiration (l. 7).

REFLECTING ON THE POEM

The topic of a moment of sudden insight is common in poetry. What, then, makes this poem so unusual? (Students may suggest that poems of insight usually are inspired by romantic love or the beauty of nature. It is unusual to be inspired by mathematics.)

Rita Dove *born 1952*

The poetry of Rita Dove is known for its lively imagery and rhythms as well as its interesting intellectual slant. Born in Akron, Ohio, Dove graduated *summa cum laude* from Miami University and later from the University of Iowa Writers' Workshop. Both a Fulbright/Hays and a Guggenheim fellow and once writer-in-residence at Tuskegee Institute, she now teaches in the English Department at Arizona State University. Volumes of her poetry include *The Yellow House on the Corner* (1980), *Museum* (1983), and *Thomas and Beulah* (1985), for which she received the Pulitzer Prize for poetry in 1987.

■ Can you remember an instance in your life when an intellectual activity caused you intense emotion?

Rita Dove

Geometry

I prove a theorem and the house expands:
the windows jerk free to hover near the ceiling,
the ceiling floats away with a sigh.

As the walls clear themselves of everything
but transparency, the scent of carnations
leaves with them. I am out in the open

and above the windows have hinged into butterflies,
sunlight glinting where they've intersected.
They are going to some point true and unproven.

Diana Chang *born 1934*

Like so many poets of modern America, Diana Chang brings to her work the experience of another language and another culture. Diana Chang was born in New York, grew up in China until the end of World War II, then returned to the United States to attend Barnard College, from which she graduated in 1955. Her poetry and novels often reflect her background. *The Frontiers of Love* (1956), for example, is set in wartime Shanghai, where Chang herself lived. Her other novels include *The Only Game in Town* and *Eye to Eye.* Chang also edited *The American Pen,* the magazine of the international writers' association, P. E. N.

"Most Satisfied by Snow" is written in the spare style of the oriental poetry that was so appealing to the early Imagists (see page 413).

■ In this poem what does Diana Chang "show" about the natural world and about herself?

Diana Chang

Most Satisfied by Snow

Against my windows,
fog knows
what to do, too

Spaces pervade
us, as well

But occupied by snow,
I see

Matter
matters

I, too,
flowering

AT A GLANCE

- From her window the speaker sees fog and snow.
- She realizes that "matter matters" and thinks of herself as "flowering."

LITERARY OPTIONS

- Imagism
- imagery

THEMATIC OPTIONS

- self-realization
- the power of nature

IMAGISM

In true Imagist spirit the lines of this poem are very economical, providing a sharply focused picture with no excesses.

IMAGERY

The images of fog, snow, and spaces form the basis of the poem. However, the image of something flowering in the snow (ll. 6, 11) is incongruous and consequently very dramatic.

ASSONANCE

The connection of the speaker with the natural world is reinforced through assonance. Three *o* sounds appear in *fog knows / what to do, too* (ll. 2–3); those same sounds appear in *occupied, snow,* and *too* (ll. 6, 10).

REFLECTING ON THE POEM

According to the speaker, what is so satisfying about snow? (Students might suggest that even snow can produce something beautiful and fruitful in the mind of the observer.)

AT A GLANCE

- The poet says that she and Emily Dickinson belong both to yesterday and to today.
- They are both creators of new and unique things.

LITERARY OPTIONS

- metaphor
- imagery

THEMATIC OPTIONS

- the artistic tradition
- past and present

IMAGERY

The statement *day is anchored to wait for its hour* (ll. 3–4) creates the image of time standing still in the past. *That hour when what is unborn begins to throb* (ll. 6–8) creates the image of time being dynamic in the present.

METAPHOR

The poet sees artists as "cultivators" (l. 9), "weavers" (l. 10), and "migrant workers" (ll. 11–12). She does not choose metaphors that suggest elitism; rather, her metaphors focus upon the laboring class.

RESPONSE JOURNAL

Have students describe what they think might be the content of the "floating gardens" (ll. 13–14).

REFLECTING ON THE POEM

In what sense is art timeless? (Students may see the relationship between past and present artists. Some may realize that great art can be appreciated regardless of when it was created.)

Lucha Corpi *born 1945*

Lucha Corpi is part of the great renaissance in Latin American and South American literature that is now taking place and being felt in the United States. Lucha Corpi was born in Veracruz, Mexico. She came to California when she was nineteen and studied at the University of California at Berkeley and San Francisco State University. Corpi, who has held a fellowship in creative writing from the National Endowment for the Arts, now lives and teaches English in Oakland, California. Her poems have appeared in literary magazines and anthologies, and in a collection, *Fireflight* (1976).

"Emily Dickinson" is from Lucha Corpi's collection *Palabras de Mediodia (Noon Words).* Written originally in Spanish, the collection has been translated into English by Catherine Rodriguez-Nieto.

■ Why do we sometimes see ourselves better by comparing ourselves to others? What does Corpi reveal about herself through her comparison?

Lucha Corpi

Emily Dickinson

Like you, I belong to yesterday,
to the bays where
day is anchored to
wait for its hour.

Like me, you belong to today,
the progression of that hour
when what is unborn
begins to throb.

We are cultivators of
the unsayable, weavers
of singulars,[1] migrant
workers in search of
floating gardens[2] as yet
unsown, as yet unharvested.

---

1. **weavers of singulars:** in Spanish, *singulares* means "unique things," or "creations."
2. **floating gardens:** probably a reference to the floating gardens of Xochimilco (hō chē mēl′kō) in Mexico City.

STUDY QUESTIONS *(Dove)*

Recalling

1. According to the first stanza, when does the house expand? What hovers? What floats away?
2. Where is the speaker at the end of the second stanza?
3. In the last stanza what do the windows become? Where are the transformed windows going?

Interpreting

4. How does completing a geometry problem make the speaker feel? Support your answer with examples.
5. How might this poem be viewed as an extended metaphor? What possible larger meanings for "house" do you think the poet intends?
6. Examine Dove's imagery. Which images suggest height? light? openness? freedom? How do these images relate to the speaker's reaction to her mathematical accomplishment?
7. What is the relationship between the poem's first and last lines? How are they similar? different? What does the stated destination of the last line add to the emotion of the poem?

Extending

8. What are some of the benefits that mental exploration, or investigation, and actual travel have in common? Explain your answer.

STUDY QUESTIONS *(Chang)*

Recalling

1. What does the speaker state the fog against her windows "knows"? What does she observe about people in lines 4–5?
2. What does the speaker see because she is "occupied by snow"? What does she observe about herself in line 11?

Interpreting

3. With what aspect of the weather does the speaker associate the "spaces" human beings? What might these "spaces" be?
4. With what aspect of the weather does the speaker associate the "matter" of human beings? What does the title therefore suggest about her attitude toward this "matter"? What do lines 10–11 suggest the "matter" of human beings might do?
5. In what sense are the "windows" in line 1 literal? In what sense are they figurative?
6. State the meaning of this poem in your own words. What aspects of the poem seem Romantic? What aspects seem Imagist (page 413)?

Extending

7. How is the image of the snow in this poem different in its connotations from the snow imagery of Robert Frost (page 468)?

STUDY QUESTIONS *(Corpi)*

Recalling

1. In what way is the speaker like Emily Dickinson, according to line 1? According to line 5?
2. What sort of "cultivator" does the speaker call herself and Emily Dickinson? What sort of "migrant workers" are they?

Interpreting

3. What do the images in lines 1–8 suggest about Dickinson's and the speaker's poetry? That is, in what sense do they belong to "yesterday"? Why do they belong to "today"?
4. What does this poem imply about art in general? About Emily Dickinson's art in particular?

VOCABULARY *(Corpi)*

Words from Spanish

Many words we use in modern American English have crossed over from the Spanish language. Use a dictionary to explain the meanings and etymology, or word history, of each of the following words.

1. arroyo	5. cordovan	9. iguana
2. bonanza	6. mantilla	10. canyon
3. tornado	7. puma	11. tango
4. castanet	8. plaza	12. siesta

COMPARING WRITERS

■ Lucha Corpi says that she and Emily Dickinson are "cultivators of the unsayable." How does this phrase apply to the other poets on pages 762–783? Choose any four poets from those pages, and describe in your own words the central theme, the "unsayable" idea or emotion, that each is trying to express. Tell what it is that makes each theme difficult or impossible to express. Compare the writers, and demonstrate with examples which poet, in your opinion, succeeds best in saying the "unsayable."

STUDY QUESTIONS

Dove

1. when the speaker proves a theorem; the windows; the ceiling
2. out in the open
3. butterflies; to some point true and unproven
4. Exhilarated, free—house expands, ceiling floats away.
5. "House" might stand for "mind," "understanding."
6. *height*—windows hover, ceiling floats away, the windows have hinged into butterflies; *light*—walls become transparent, the open, glinting sunlight; *openness*—ceiling floats away; *freedom*—all images cumulatively; express the speaker's delight, self-expansion, and freedom
7. The last is the result of the first; it adds to the poem's sense of openness, freedom.
8. *Possible answers:* personal growth, excitement, novelty, challenge

Chang

1. what to do; pervaded by spaces
2. matter matters; she flowers
3. fog; undefined potentials
4. snow; satisfying; flower
5. looking out window at fog; poet's eyes
6. People have untapped potential they can realize; *Romantic:* idea of perfectibility, imagery from nature; *Imagist:* imagery and spare style
7. *Frost:* peace, death; *Chang:* life-enhancing, strive not rest

Corpi

1. she belongs to yesterday; Dickinson belongs to today
2. "of the unsayable"; in search of unsown floating gardens
3. rooted in past, speak to unborn
4. rooted in tradition, timeless; it is universal

COMPARING WRITERS

Students should cite tendency of poems in this unit to have clear, descriptive diction but elusive thoughts or themes.

VOCABULARY

1. from Latin *arrugia,* "shaft," "pit"; dry gulley, rivulet
2. "fair weather", "prosperity"; rich vein in mine, wealth
3. *tornar,* "to turn"; violent wind
4. *castañeta,* "chestnut"; pieces of wood used to beat time to music
5. cordoban; leather originally made in Córdoba, Spain
6. a woman's veil or scarf
7. mountain lion found in Americas
8. public square, market place
9. *iwana;* large tropical lizard
10. *cañén,* "tube, funnel"; narrow valley between high cliffs
11. dance with long, gliding steps
12. Latin *sexta hora,* "sixth hour," noon; brief rest after noon meal

FICTION

Photograph © 1982 by Jill Krementz

Bernard Malamud *1914–1986*

In accepting the National Book Award in 1959 for *The Magic Barrel,* a collection of stories, Bernard Malamud said: "I am quite tired of the colossally deceitful devaluation of man in this day. . . . The devaluation exists because [humanity] accepts it without protest." Malamud's fiction protests that devaluation. Though he understands the pressures of history and society on the individual, Malamud always keeps his faith in the ability of the human spirit to endure and overcome.

Bernard Malamud was born in Brooklyn, New York; his parents were Russian immigrants. He graduated from City College of New York and Columbia University, and while teaching evening classes he began writing short stories, which appeared in *Harper's Bazaar, Partisan Review, Commentary,* and other magazines. Malamud has continued a career as both a teacher and a novelist, winning wide recognition for such books as *The Assistant* (1957), *Idiots First* (1963), and *Dubin's Lives* (1979). His novel of injustice in czarist Russia, *The Fixer* (1966), won both the National Book Award and the Pulitzer Prize.

Malamud's fiction portrays the struggles, defeats, and triumphs of ordinary people—shopkeepers, pawnbrokers, tenement dwellers. He uses the experience of Jewish people as an allegory for all of human experience: His characters are often pursued by a sense of injustice, burdened with grief, and strengthened by their own persistent clinging to life. They are intensely aware of the past while trying to make a life for themselves in the modern world. Malamud's protagonists seek a kind of nobility; they strive to maintain their beliefs and principles while coming to terms with the realities and compromises of living. The mixture of victory and defeat in their lives gives Malamud's work its tragicomic character.

Malamud's style is artfully simple. His language captures the essence of American Yiddish, mainly through its syntax but also in its vocabulary. His stories contain a robust humor, striking contrasts, a strong sense of compassion, and a complete understanding of his characters and their way of life. He writes of the Jewish experience, he said, "because I know it."

"The First Seven Years" is representative of Malamud's folklike style and of his ability to create believable characters. Like so many of his stories, it has the quality of a realistic fairy tale. It is both a down-to-earth story of real people and a fable with a message.

■ Think of the fables you have heard. What messages have they imparted?

Bernard Malamud

The First Seven Years

1 Feld, the shoemaker, was annoyed that his helper, Sobel, was so insensitive to his reverie that he wouldn't for a minute cease his fanatic pounding at the other bench. He gave him a look, but Sobel's bald head was bent over the last[1] as he worked and he didn't notice. The shoemaker shrugged and continued to peer through the partly frosted window at the near-sighted haze of falling February snow. Neither the shifting white blur outside, nor the sudden deep remembrance of the snowy Polish village where he had wasted his youth could turn his thoughts from Max the college boy, (a constant visitor in the mind since early that morning when Feld saw him trudging through the snow-drifts on his way to school) whom he so much respected because of the sacrifices he had made throughout the years—in winter or direst heat—to further his education. An old wish returned to haunt the shoemaker: that he had had a son instead of a daughter, but this blew away in the snow for Feld, if anything, was a practical man. Yet he could not help but contrast the diligence of the boy, who was a peddler's son, with Miriam's unconcern for an education. True, she was always with a book in her hand, yet when the opportunity arose for a college education, she had said no she would rather find a job. He had begged her to go, pointing out how many fathers could not afford to send their children to college, but she said
2 she wanted to be independent. As for education, what was it, she asked, but books, which Sobel, who diligently read the classics, would as usual advise her on. Her answer greatly grieved her father.

A figure emerged from the snow and the door opened. At the counter the man withdrew from a wet paper bag a pair of battered shoes for repair. Who he was the shoemaker for a moment had no idea, then his heart trembled as he realized, before he had thoroughly discerned the face, that Max himself was standing there, embarrassedly explaining what he wanted done to his old shoes. Though Feld listened eagerly, he couldn't hear a word, for the opportunity that had burst upon him was deafening.

He couldn't exactly recall when the thought had occurred to him, because it was clear he had more than once considered suggesting to the boy that he go out with Miriam. But he had not dared speak, for if Max said no, how would he face him again? Or suppose Miriam, who harped so often on independence, blew up in anger and shouted at him for his meddling? Still, the chance was too good to let by: all it meant was an introduction. They might long ago have become friends had they happened to meet somewhere, therefore was it not his duty—an obligation—to bring them together, nothing more, a harmless connivance to replace an accidental encounter in the subway,
3 let's say, or a mutual friend's introduction in the street? Just let him once see and talk to her and he would for sure be interested. As for Miriam, what possible harm for a working girl in an office, who met only loud-mouthed salesmen and illiterate shipping clerks, to make the acquaintance of a fine scholarly boy? Maybe he would awaken in her a desire to go to college; if not—the shoemaker's mind at last came to grips with the truth—let her marry an educated man and live a better life.

When Max finished describing what he wanted done to his shoes, Feld marked them, both with enormous holes in the soles which he pretended not to notice, with large white-chalk x's, and the rubber heels, thinned to the nails, he marked with o's, though it troubled him he might have mixed up the letters. Max

1. **last:** foot-shaped block on which shoes are made or repaired.

AT A GLANCE

- Feld, a shoemaker, is disappointed that his daughter, Miriam, does not want to go to college.
- He admires Max, a young man who is going to college.
- When Max comes in to have his shoes repaired, Feld thinks about getting Max and Miriam together.

LITERARY OPTIONS

- revelation
- point of view
- irony

THEMATIC OPTIONS

- spiritual vs. material needs
- the power of love
- the meaning of knowledge

1 IRONY

Feld is unhappily sensitive to the noise that his helper makes while he works. The irony is that Sobel would make no noise if he loafed. Feld's reaction becomes even more ironic considering that later events will expose his own lack of sensitivity.

2 CHARACTERIZATION

Sobel may be merely a helper, but he is well read, self-educated and an influence in Miriam's life.

3 MOTIVATION

So anxious is he about his daughter's future that Feld is willing to assume the role of matchmaker, a role usually fulfilled by a woman.

GUIDED READING

LITERAL QUESTIONS

1a. What is Feld's old wish? (to have a son)

2a. Who comes into the store? (Max)

INFERENTIAL QUESTIONS

1b. Why does Feld think of his old wish? (His daughter is not interested in an education as he presumes a son would have been.)

2b. Why does Feld not hear what Max says? (He is preoccupied with the thought of how to get Max and Miriam together.)

AT A GLANCE

- Feld takes Max aside and tries to arrange a date between him and Miriam.
- Max asks to see a picture of Miriam and Feld complies.
- Max agrees to meet Miriam.

1 CHARACTERIZATION

The description of Max's appearance is entirely negative. His appearance has no effect on Feld because he is only concerned with the fact that Max is educated.

2 IRONY

Max is described as a person who does not care about his own appearance. Nevertheless, he wants to see a picture of Miriam before he will consider asking her out.

inquired the price, and the shoemaker cleared his throat and asked the boy, above Sobel's insistent hammering, would he please step through the side door there into the hall. Though surprised, Max did as the shoemaker requested, and Feld went in after him. For a minute they were both silent, because Sobel had stopped banging, and it seemed they understood neither was to say anything until the noise began again. When it did, loudly, the shoemaker quickly told Max why he had asked to talk to him.

"Ever since you went to high school," he said, in the dimly-lit hallway, "I watched you in the morning go to the subway to school, and I said always to myself, this is a fine boy that he wants so much an education."

1 "Thanks," Max said, nervously alert. He was tall and grotesquely thin, with sharply cut features, particularly a beak-like nose. He was wearing a loose, long slushy overcoat that hung down to his ankles, looking like a rug draped over his bony shoulders, and a soggy, old brown hat, as battered as the shoes he had brought in.

"I am a business man," the shoemaker abruptly said to conceal his embarrassment, "so I will explain you right away why I talk to you. I have a girl, my daughter Miriam—she is nineteen—a very nice girl and also so pretty that everybody looks on her when she passes by in the street. She is smart, always with a book, and I thought to myself that a boy like you, an educated boy—I thought maybe you will be interested sometime to meet a girl like this." He laughed a bit when he had finished and was tempted to say more but had the good sense not to.

Max stared down like a hawk. For an uncomfortable second he was silent, then he asked, "Did you say nineteen?"

"Yes."

2 "Would it be all right to inquire if you have a picture of her?"

"Just a minute." The shoemaker went into the store and hastily returned with a snapshot that Max held up to the light.

"She's all right," he said.

Feld waited.

"And is she sensible—not the flighty kind?"

"She is very sensible."

After another short pause, Max said it was okay with him if he met her.

"Here is my telephone," said the shoe-

GUIDED READING

LITERAL QUESTIONS

1a. What does Feld want to talk to Max about? (Miriam, his daughter)

2a. What does Max say after seeing the picture of Miriam? (*She's all right.*)

INFERENTIAL QUESTIONS

1b. Why do you think that Feld wants to go into the hall to talk to Max? (He is embarrassed, perhaps because he knows that he is meddling in Miriam's life.)

2b. How does Feld feel about Max's response? (He is so preoccupied with making the arrangement that he ignores Max's attitude.)

maker, hurriedly handing him a slip of paper. "Call her up. She comes home from work six o'clock."

Max folded the paper and tucked it away into his worn leather wallet.

"About the shoes," he said. "How much did you say they will cost me?"

"Don't worry about the price."

"I just like to have an idea."

"A dollar—dollar fifty. A dollar fifty," the shoemaker said.

At once he felt bad, for he usually charged two twenty-five for this kind of job. Either he should have asked the regular price or done the work for nothing.

1 Later, as he entered the store, he was startled by a violent clanging and looked up to see Sobel pounding with all his might upon the naked last. It broke, the iron striking the floor and jumping with a thump against the wall, but before the enraged shoemaker could cry out, the assistant had torn his hat and coat from the hook and rushed out into the snow.

So Feld, who had looked forward to anticipating how it would go with his daughter and Max, instead had a great worry on his mind. Without his temperamental helper he was a lost man, especially since it was years now that he had carried the store alone. The shoemaker had for an age suffered from a heart condition that threatened collapse if he dared exert himself. Five years ago, after an attack, it had appeared as though he would have either to sacrifice his business upon the auction block and live on a pittance thereafter, or put himself at the mercy of some unscrupulous employee who would in the end probably ruin him. But just at the moment of his darkest despair, this Polish refugee, Sobel, appeared one night from the street and begged for work. He was a stocky man, poorly dressed, with a bald head that had once been blond, a severely plain face and soft blue eyes prone to tears over the sad books he read, a young man but old—no one would have guessed thirty. Though he confessed he knew nothing of shoemaking, he said he was apt and would work for a very little if Feld taught him the trade. Thinking that with, after all, a landsman,[2] he would have less to fear than from a complete stranger, Feld took him on and within six weeks the refugee rebuilt as good a shoe as he, and not long thereafter expertly ran the business for the thoroughly relieved shoemaker.

2 Feld could trust him with anything and did, frequently going home after an hour or two at the store, leaving all the money in the till, knowing Sobel would guard every cent of it. The amazing thing was that he demanded so little. His wants were few; in money he wasn't interested—in nothing but books, it seemed—which he one by one lent to Miriam, together with his profuse, queer written comments, manufactured during his lonely rooming house evenings, thick pads of commentary which the shoemaker peered at and twitched his shoulders over as his daughter, from her fourteenth year, read page by sanctified page, as if the word of God were inscribed on them. To protect Sobel, Feld himself had to see that he received more than he asked for. Yet his conscience bothered him for not insisting that the assistant accept a better wage than he was getting, though Feld had honestly told him he could earn a handsome salary if he worked elsewhere, or maybe opened a place of his own. But the assistant answered, somewhat ungraciously, that he was not interested in going elsewhere, and though Feld frequently asked himself what keeps him here? why does he
3 stay? he finally answered it that the man, no doubt because of his terrible experiences as a refugee, was afraid of the world.

After the incident with the broken last, angered by Sobel's behavior, the shoemaker decided to let him stew for a week in the rooming house, although his own strength was taxed dangerously and the business suffered. However, after several sharp nagging warnings from both his wife and daughter, he went finally in search of Sobel, as he had once before, quite

2. **landsman:** fellow countryman.

AT A GLANCE

- Sobel becomes very upset, breaks the last, and leaves.
- Feld's business suffers, for he depended upon Sobel.
- Honest, hard-working, and studious, Sobel had stayed in Feld's employ despite the chances of better work elsewhere.

1 CHARACTERIZATION

Sobel's violent reaction reveals his strong emotions about Feld's matchmaking.

2 REVELATION

Whereas Feld does become aware of Sobel's loyalty, at this point he cannot fathom that somehow his loyalty could be related to Miriam's presence. This revelation comes later in the story.

3 POINT OF VIEW

The story is written in limited third-person from the viewpoint of Feld. From Feld's perspective it is easier to view Sobel as an unfortunate victim rather than as a serious suitor for his daughter.

GUIDED READING

LITERAL QUESTION

1a. What does Sobel do? (breaks the last and angrily departs)

INFERENTIAL QUESTION

1b. Why does Sobel act this way? (He is probably upset about Feld's matchmaking because he cares for Miriam.)

AT A GLANCE

- Sobel pretends not to be home when Feld goes to talk to him, so Feld hires another helper.
- Max takes Miriam out on a date.
- Under questioning from Feld, Miriam says that the date was all right and that Max has asked her out again.

1 REVELATION

Feld's decision suggests that he subconsciously senses that something is going on between Sobel and Miriam. Instead of admitting his fears, he attributes his decision not to see Sobel to the cold and his fatigue.

2 BACKGROUND

For decades young people in America considered a date on Saturday night a special occasion. It was a clear indication that the young man and young woman thought highly of each other.

3 CHARACTERIZATION

Miriam's response shows that she is angered and upset by her father's meddling.

recently, when over some fancied slight—Feld had merely asked him not to give Miriam so many books to read because her eyes were strained and red—the assistant had left the place in a huff, an incident which, as usual, came to nothing for he had returned after the shoemaker had talked to him, and taken his seat at the bench. But this time, after Feld had plodded through the snow to Sobel's house—he had thought of sending Miriam but the idea became repugnant to him—the burly landlady at the door informed him in a nasal voice that Sobel was not at home, and though Feld knew this was a nasty lie, for where had the refugee
1 to go? still for some reason he was not completely sure of—it may have been the cold and his fatigue—he decided not to insist on seeing him. Instead he went home and hired a new helper.

Having settled the matter, though not entirely to his satisfaction, for he had much more to do than before, and so, for example, could no longer lie late in bed mornings because he had to get up to open the store for the new assistant, a speechless, dark man with an irritating rasp as he worked, whom he would not trust with the key as he had Sobel. Furthermore, this one, though able to do a fair repair job, knew nothing of grades of leather or prices, so Feld had to make his own purchases; and every night at closing time it was necessary to count the money in the till and lock up. However, he was not dissatisfied, for he lived much in his thoughts of Max and Miriam. The college boy had called her, and they had arranged a meeting for this coming Friday
2 night. The shoemaker would personally have preferred Saturday, which he felt would make it a date of the first magnitude, but he learned Friday was Miriam's choice, so he said nothing. The day of the week did not matter. What mattered was the aftermath. Would they like each other and want to be friends? He sighed at all the time that would have to go by before he knew for sure. Often he was tempted to talk to Miriam about the boy, to ask whether she thought she would like his type—he had told
3 her only that he considered Max a nice boy and had suggested he call her—but the one time he tried she snapped at him—justly—how should she know?

At last Friday came. Feld was not feeling particularly well so he stayed in bed, and Mrs. Feld thought it better to remain in the bedroom with him when Max called. Miriam received the boy, and her parents could hear their voices, his throaty one, as they talked. Just before leaving, Miriam brought Max to the bedroom door and he stood there a minute, a tall, slightly hunched figure wearing a thick, droopy suit, and apparently at ease as he greeted the shoemaker and his wife, which was surely a good sign. And Miriam, although she had worked all day, looked fresh and pretty. She was a large-framed girl with a well-shaped body, and she had a fine open face and soft hair. They made, Feld thought, a first-class couple.

Miriam returned after 11:30. Her mother was already asleep, but the shoemaker got out of bed and after locating his bathrobe went into the kitchen, where Miriam, to his surprise, sat at the table, reading.

"So where did you go?" Feld asked pleasantly.

"For a walk," she said, not looking up.

"I advised him," Feld said, clearing his throat, "he shouldn't spend so much money."

"I didn't care."

The shoemaker boiled up some water for tea and sat down at the table with a cupful and a thick slice of lemon.

"So how," he sighed after a sip, "did you enjoy?"

"It was all right."

He was silent. She must have sensed his disappointment, for she added, "You can't really tell much the first time."

"You will see him again?"

Turning a page, she said that Max had asked for another date.

"For when?"

"Saturday."

"So what did you say?"

GUIDED READING

LITERAL QUESTIONS

1a. How does Feld "settle the matter"? (He hires a new helper to replace Sobel.)

2a. Where does Max take Miriam on their date? (for a walk)

INFERENTIAL QUESTIONS

1b. Is the settlement a good one? (Probably not. The new helper is nowhere as good as Sobel.)

2b. How do you think Feld feels about this? (Feld is probably embarrassed at Max's being so cheap. Because he does not want Miriam to understand the truth, he takes the blame.)

"What did I say?" she asked, delaying for a moment—"I said yes."

Afterwards she inquired about Sobel, and Feld, without exactly knowing why, said the assistant had got another job. Miriam said nothing more and began to read. The shoemaker's conscience did not trouble him; he was satisfied with the Saturday date.

During the week, by placing here and there a deft question, he managed to get from Miriam some information about Max. It surprised him to learn that the boy was not studying to be either a doctor or lawyer but was taking a business course leading to a degree in accountancy. Feld was a little disappointed because he thought of accountants as bookkeepers and would have preferred "a higher profession."
1 However, it was not long before he had investigated the subject and discovered that Certified Public Accountants were highly respected people, so he was thoroughly content as Saturday approached. But because Saturday was a busy day, he was much in the store and therefore did not see Max when he came to call for Miriam. From his wife he learned there had been nothing especially revealing about their meeting. Max had rung the bell and Miriam had got her coat and left with him—nothing
2 more. Feld did not probe, for his wife was not particularly observant. Instead, he waited up for Miriam with a newspaper on his lap, which he scarcely looked at so lost was he in thinking of the future. He awoke to find her in the room with him, tiredly removing her hat. Greeting her, he was suddenly inexplicably afraid to ask anything about the evening. But since she volunteered nothing he was at last forced to inquire how she had enjoyed herself. Miriam began something noncommittal but apparently changed her mind, for she said after a minute, "I was bored."

When Feld had sufficiently recovered from his anguished disappointment to ask why, she answered without hesitation, "Because he's nothing more than a materialist."

"What means this word?"

"He has no soul. He's only interested in things."

He considered her statement for a long time but then asked, "Will you see him again?"

"He didn't ask."

"Suppose he will ask you?"

"I won't see him."

He did not argue; however, as the days went by he hoped increasingly she would change her mind. He wished the boy would

AT A GLANCE

- Feld learns that Max is studying to be an accountant.
- Miriam goes out with Max again on Saturday night.
- When Feld presses her for information, she says that Max is a materialist and she will not see him again.

1 CHARACTERIZATION

Feld does not approve of accounting until he finds that other people respect the profession. His rapid change of heart shows how important appearances are to Feld.

2 IRONY

Feld thinks that he is more observant than his wife. It never occurs to him that there may have been nothing to observe and that his ideas about Max and Miriam are illusions, not true observations.

GUIDED READING

LITERAL QUESTION

1a. What does Feld do when Miriam calls Max a materialist? (He asks her if she will see him again.)

INFERENTIAL QUESTION

1b. Do you think that Feld is more like Max or more like Miriam? (At this point he seems more like Max, a materialist.)

AT A GLANCE

- Max does not see Miriam again, but does come in for his shoes.
- Feld has a heart attack when he finds that his new helper is a thief.
- Feld asks Sobel to come back, but he refuses.
- Sobel tells Feld that he loves Miriam and that she was the only reason he had stayed with Feld for five years.

1 THEME

Sobel recognizes the value of knowledge for its own sake, a concept Feld cannot comprehend.

2 PLOT: CLIMAX

This dramatic exchange brings the story to its most intense moment. By declaring openly his love for Miriam, Sobel has shattered what is left of Feld's illusions.

3 REVELATION

Sobel's declaration of love forces Feld to acknowledge what he has always known. He can no longer deny reality.

telephone, because he was sure there was more to him than Miriam, with her inexperienced eye, could discern. But Max didn't call. As a matter of fact he took a different route to school, no longer passing the shoemaker's store, and Feld was deeply hurt.

Then one afternoon Max came in and asked for his shoes. The shoemaker took them down from the shelf where he had placed them, apart from the other pairs. He had done the work himself and the soles and heels were well built and firm. The shoes had been highly polished and somehow looked better than new. Max's Adam's apple went up once when he saw them, and his eyes had little lights in them.

"How much?" he asked, without directly looking at the shoemaker.

"Like I told you before," Feld answered sadly. "One dollar fifty cents."

Max handed him two crumpled bills and received in return a newly-minted silver half dollar.

He left. Miriam had not been mentioned. That night the shoemaker discovered that his new assistant had been all the while stealing from him, and he suffered a heart attack.

Though the attack was very mild, he lay in bed for three weeks. Miriam spoke of going for Sobel, but sick as he was Feld rose in wrath against the idea. Yet in his heart he knew there was no other way, and the first weary day back in the shop thoroughly convinced him, so that night after supper he dragged himself to Sobel's rooming house.

He toiled up the stairs, though he knew it was bad for him, and at the top knocked at the door. Sobel opened it and the shoemaker entered. The room was a small, poor one, with a single window facing the street. It contained a narrow cot, a low table and several stacks of books piled haphazardly around on the floor along the wall, which made him think how queer Sobel was, to be uneducated and read so much. He had once asked him, Sobel, why you read so much? and the assistant could not answer him. Did you ever study in a college someplace? he had asked, but Sobel shook his
1 head. He read, he said, to know. But to know what, the shoemaker demanded, and to know, why? Sobel never explained, which proved he read much because he was queer.

Feld sat down to recover his breath. The assistant was resting on his bed with his heavy back to the wall. His shirt and trousers were clean, and his stubby fingers, away from the shoemaker's bench, were strangely pallid. His face was thin and pale, as if he had been shut in this room since the day he had bolted from the store.

"So when you will come back to work?" Feld asked him.

To his surprise, Sobel burst out, "Never."

Jumping up, he strode over to the window that looked out upon the miserable street. "Why should I come back?" he cried.

"I will raise your wages."

"Who cares for your wages!"

The shoemaker, knowing he didn't care, was at a loss what else to say.

"What do you want from me, Sobel?"

"Nothing."

"I always treated you like you was my son."

Sobel vehemently denied it. "So why you look for strange boys in the street they should go out with Miriam? Why you don't think of me?"

The shoemaker's hands and feet turned freezing cold. His voice became so hoarse he couldn't speak. At last he cleared his throat and croaked, "So what has my daughter got to do with a shoemaker thirty-five years old who works for me?"

2 "Why do you think I worked so long for you?" Sobel cried out. "For the stingy wages I sacrificed five years of my life so you could have to eat and drink and where to sleep?"

"Then for what?" shouted the shoemaker.

"For Miriam," he blurted—"for her."

The shoemaker, after a time, managed to say, "I pay wages in cash, Sobel," and lapsed into silence. Though he was seething with ex-
3 citement, his mind was coldly clear, and he
had to admit to himself he had sensed all along
that Sobel felt this way. He had never so much

GUIDED READING

LITERAL QUESTIONS

1a. Why does Feld think that Sobel is queer? (because he reads so much and has no education)

2a. What does Feld say when Sobel says that he has worked "for Miriam"? (I pay wages in cash.)

INFERENTIAL QUESTIONS

1b. What does this conclusion reveal about Feld? (He does not appreciate wisdom in itself.)

2b. What does Feld mean? (He does not like the idea that Sobel has worked for him just to be near Miriam.)

as thought it consciously, but he had felt it and was afraid.

"Miriam knows?" he muttered hoarsely.

"She knows."

"You told her?"

"No."

"Then how does she know?"

"How does she know?" Sobel said, "because she knows. She knows who I am and what is in my heart."

1 Feld had a sudden insight. In some devious way, with his books and commentary, Sobel had given Miriam to understand that he loved her. The shoemaker felt a terrible anger at him for his deceit.

"Sobel, you are crazy," he said bitterly. "She will never marry a man so old and ugly like you."

Sobel turned black with rage. He cursed the shoemaker, but then, though he trembled to hold it in, his eyes filled with tears and he broke into deep sobs. With his back to Feld, he stood at the window, fists clenched, and his shoulders shook with his choked sobbing.

Watching him, the shoemaker's anger diminished. His teeth were on edge with pity for the man, and his eyes grew moist. How strange and sad that a refugee, a grown man, bald and old with his miseries, who had by the skin of his teeth escaped Hitler's incinerators,[3] should fall in love, when he had got to America, with a girl less than half his age. Day after day, for five years he had sat at his bench, cutting and hammering away, waiting for the girl to become a woman, unable to ease his heart with speech, knowing no protest but desperation.

"Ugly I didn't mean," he said half aloud.

Then he realized that what he had called ugly was not Sobel but Miriam's life if she married him. He felt for his daughter a strange and gripping sorrow, as if she were already Sobel's bride, the wife, after all, of a shoemaker, and had in her life no more than her mother had had. And all his dreams for her—why he had slaved and destroyed his heart with anxiety and labor—all these dreams of a better life were dead.

The room was quiet. Sobel was standing by the window reading, and it was curious that when he read he looked young.

"She is only nineteen," Feld said brokenly.
2 "This is too young yet to get married. Don't ask her for two years more, till she is twenty-one, then you can talk to her."

Sobel didn't answer. Feld rose and left. He went slowly down the stairs but once outside, though it was an icy night and the crisp falling snow whitened the street, he walked with a stronger stride.

But the next morning, when the shoemaker arrived, heavy-hearted, to open the store, he saw he needn't have come, for his assistant was already seated at the last, pounding leather for his love.

3. **Hitler's incinerators:** During World War II in Europe, the Nazis, under the dictatorship of Adolf Hitler (1889–1945), operated concentration camps in which millions of Jews were killed.

STUDY QUESTIONS

Recalling

1. According to the first paragraph, why does Feld, the shoemaker, respect Max? What does Miriam say about books and education? From whom does she get advice on her reading?
2. About what does Feld speak privately to Max when Max comes into the store with a pair of shoes? What startles Feld when he returns to the store after his conversation with Max?
3. For what reason did Sobel leave the shop in a huff once before? What does Feld do this time when Sobel does not return to work?

AT A GLANCE

- Feld tells Sobel that Miriam will never marry him, but then feels sorry for Sobel.
- He tells Sobel to wait until Miriam is twenty-one before talking to her about marriage.
- Sobel comes back to work.

1 IRONY

It is ironic that Feld would deem Sobel deceitful. In fact, Sobel's actions are very open and very much in keeping with his character.

2 ALLUSION

Jacob of the Old Testament had to work an additional seven years before he could marry Laban's daughter Rachel. Perhaps Sobel can expect a similar fate.

REFLECTING ON THE STORY

Why do you think that Malamud chose "pounding leather for love" as the story's last words? (Some students might think Sobel will have to "pound" for years before his love is realized.)

STUDY QUESTIONS

1. sacrifices for education; "What is education, but books?"; Sobel
2. having Max meet Miriam; Sobel clanging on the "naked last"
3. asked not to give Miriam so many books; goes to his house, turns back before seeing him, hires another assistant

4. He is a materialist; no
5. new assistant stealing from him; Sobel
6. love for Miriam; she would never marry a man like Sobel; wait until she is twenty-one before asking to marry; with a stronger stride
7. prestige, a good living, respect; knowledge, books; respect, prestige, a good job
8. Max is materialistic, Sobel an idealist; Sobel has sacrificed more, is better educated
9. yes, has good intentions; yes, wants material possessions to spare loved ones from hardship; yes, recognizes Sobel's devotion
10. Answers will vary. Students might say Sobel would be a better husband because he shares Miriam's values. She will marry Sobel because he is determined.

VIEWPOINT

- attempt to match Miriam and Max fails, but leads to new understanding of those important to him
- needs for love, spiritual fulfillment are "most human needs"
- need for better material life for Miriam remains unsatisfied

LITERARY FOCUS

1. when he finds Sobel has worked for Miriam, and she is aware of his love; realizes there is more to Sobel than he thought, can provide Miriam with love and understanding
2. Answers will vary. Because we see Sobel through Feld's eyes, we do not know his feelings. He may have gained understanding of Feld and practical world he has ignored; finally speaks of his love, asks to marry Miriam

4. What does Miriam say about Max after their second date? Is she interested in seeing him again?
5. What causes Feld's heart attack? After he recovers, whom does he go to see?
6. Why has Sobel worked for so many years for a low wage? What does Feld say "bitterly" when Sobel confesses his plans and dreams? What does Feld then finally tell Sobel, and how does Feld walk when he leaves Sobel?

Interpreting

7. What does being educated seem to mean to Feld? To Miriam? To Max?
8. Compare Max and Sobel. Why is it ironic that Feld admires Max because of the sacrifice he has made to further his education and does not admire Sobel?
9. Is Feld a sympathetic character? Is he materialistic? Does he change by the story's end? Explain your answers.

Extending

10. Who do you think would make a better husband for Miriam, Sobel or Max? Do you think Miriam will marry Sobel when she is twenty-one? Explain your answers.

VIEWPOINT

In discussing Malamud's concerns, Sidney Richman writes:

> Throughout his fiction, the theme of victory through defeat is constant; for it is only when his needs remain unsatisfied that Malamud's hero can recognize the form of his most human needs.
>
> —*Bernard Malamud*

■ Explain how Feld the shoemaker achieves "victory through defeat." What are the "most human needs" that he recognizes at the end of the story? What needs will "remain unsatisfied"?

LITERARY FOCUS

Revelation and Epiphany

Most modern stories do not follow the old-fashioned rules for stories: They do not end with a neat resolution of the hero's problems, tying up all the loose ends in a clearly comic or tragic conclusion. Instead, they often focus on a moment of **revelation,** a point at which a character comes to see something with a deep understanding. The character may achieve self-knowledge or a deeper knowledge of another character; relationships between characters may become clear; the meaning and implications of an event may take shape.

The moment of revelation was an important literary technique for the influential Irish novelist James Joyce. Joyce called such a moment an **epiphany** (a "showing forth"), a sudden flash of recognition in which the essential truth about something is perceived. Many modern fiction writers have used the epiphany to give a new kind of structure to their stories.

Thinking About Revelation and Epiphany

1. Identify the moment of revelation for Feld in "The First Seven Years." Describe in your own words the insight he gains.
2. Does Sobel also have an epiphany? Support your opinion with quotations from the story.

COMPOSITION

Developing a Thesis Statement

■ Write a brief composition stating and developing a thesis statement about "The First Seven Years." First make a clear thesis statement by completing this sentence: "Both Feld and the reader of the story come to understand that. . . ." Then support your statement with quotations from the text and with your own experience as a reader. *For help with this assignment, refer to Lesson 1 in the Writing About Literature Handbook at the back of this book.*

Writing About a Concept

■ A concept is usually difficult to write about because it is not concrete. Nevertheless, writers of fiction do succeed in making concepts come alive through characters. Write a brief story or narrative poem in which you try to convey the meaning of a concept, such as *loyalty, respect, success,* or *love.* You may want to create a dramatic scene, allowing two or more characters to embody different attitudes toward the concept. Have the actions and words of the characters reveal the meaning of the concept. Do not *tell* your readers what you mean; *show* them.

COMPOSITION: GUIDELINES FOR EVALUATION

DEVELOPING A THESIS STATEMENT

Objective

To develop and support a thesis statement

Guidelines for Evaluation

- suggested length: four to six paragraphs
- should open with a thesis about the story
- should use quotations from the story to support the thesis
- should use student's own experience to support the thesis

WRITING ABOUT A CONCEPT

Objective

To present a concept indirectly

Guidelines for Evaluation

- suggested length: seven to ten paragraphs, sixteen to twenty-four lines
- should present ideas through character development and dramatic confrontation
- should make a statement about an abstraction without stating it directly

Photograph © 1982 by Jill Krementz

William Saroyan *1908–1981*

William Saroyan enjoyed an emotional, even sentimental attachment to America. He set much of his fiction in uniquely American locales—the local grocery store, the telegraph office, the small-town neighborhood. Fiercely antimaterialistic, he championed the humble, imprudent, plain yet poetic people who would never be rich or famous, or ever be sorry about it.

Born of Armenian immigrant parents in Fresno, California, Saroyan lived in an orphanage for a few years just after his father's death. He sold papers when he was eight, and while in high school he worked as a telegraph messenger. Later he held jobs in a law office, a grocery, a vineyard, and a post office. From 1942 to 1945, after becoming a famous writer, he served in the United States Army.

Saroyan's literary career began with short stories, and he had more than five hundred of these published. He also wrote a few plays, one of which—*The Time of Your Life* (1939)—won the Pulitzer Prize (though Saroyan declined the award). In addition, he wrote movie screenplays, including the one for *The Human Comedy,* which he later rewrote as a novel.

When some reviewers criticized him for excessive optimism, Saroyan replied: "Out of ignorance and desperation, poverty and pain, . . . emerge intelligence and grace, humor and resignation, decency and integrity." His characters are warmly human and lovable, and he treats them with sympathy and gentle humor. His style achieves a sense of spontaneity, as if he were telling a story to a neighbor over a backyard fence. His language is simple, natural, and familiar, full of colloquial American idioms.

"There Was a Young Lady of Perth" is a fondly remembered tale of a young writer's first attempts to compose a limerick. A **limerick** is a humorous five-line poem in which the first, second, and fifth lines rhyme and have the rhythm ˘ ′ ˘ ˘ ′ ˘ ˘ ′. The third and fourth lines rhyme with each other and have rhythm ˘ ˘ ′ ˘ ˘ ′. The narrator of the story suggests that in a limerick "somebody from somewhere tried to do something and as a result something unexpected happened." As Saroyan's tale progresses, we realize that this is not only the pattern of a limerick but also the pattern of the story itself.

■ This story, like a limerick, reveals "something unexpected" that happens. Are we in any way prepared for the unexpected?

AT A GLANCE

- The narrator recalls when he sold the first issue of *Liberty* magazine as a boy.
- The magazine had an article about George M. Cohan and a limerick contest.

LITERARY OPTIONS

- humor
- point of view
- characterization

THEMATIC OPTIONS

- obsessive perseverance
- the role of the artist
- family values

1 HUMOR

The differences in these sums are so great that clearly the author is using these numbers for comic effect; exaggeration is an important device used in writing humor.

2 POINT OF VIEW

This is a first-person narration. Here the narrator gives a clue that he is a writer. If he remembers, then he writes what actually happened. If not, he must invent something or do research.

George M. Cohan, from a "Great Americans" advertisement.

William Saroyan

There Was a Young Lady of Perth

I sold the first issue of *Liberty* magazine. In it was the beginning of the memoirs of George M. Cohan, and a limerick contest, for which
1 the first prize was an enormous sum of money. Was it five thousand dollars, fifty thousand, or five hundred thousand? In any case, it was enough to make me stop and think about there having been a young lady of Perth.

Now, of course, I'm not unaware that most people don't remember the first issue of *Liberty* magazine, if in fact they remember the second. How could they? The magazine saw the light of day when I was not much more than eleven or twelve, or thirteen or fourteen.

Did I sell it, or did I buy it? Did I make a profit of two and a half cents, or did I throw away a nickel? Memory fails me, and while it's not as bad as if a bank had failed me, it's bad
2 enough, because I *deal* in memory. And when memory fails me, I'm in trouble. I have either got to invent, or I have got to do research.

I can invent fair to middling, feeling an awful liar all the while, but I can't do research worth a bottle cap. I forget what I'm looking for and wind up with six or seven other things that I can't use. I don't mind inventing if there is a little aesthetic truth in it, as we say in the profession—"versimilitude," I once heard one writer say, but I can't vouch for either the spelling or the aptness. *Very similar* would have to be the words I would use, because I can spell those words and believe I know what they mean.

George M. Cohan happened to be a man I admired even more than I admired Benjamin Franklin, who was quite simply one of the truly

GUIDED READING

LITERAL QUESTION

1a. What does the narrator say fails him? (memory)

INFERENTIAL QUESTION

1b. Why do you think the narrator mentions this? (He uses it for comic effect, going off on a humorous digression about memory and writing.)

great cutups in my life, as of course (later on, and in a different way) George M. Cohan was. I knew Ben had put up a kite and taken a chance on electrocution in order to invent electricity, and I knew he had written a boy's story called *The Autobiography of,* but the thing I liked about him was his easygoing way of getting to be a great man. Finally, they sent him to Paris as the ambassador, and he *enchanted* the French, in their own words.

And so, in that first issue of *Liberty* magazine I was eager to find out how George M. Cohan had begun his life, because George, the Yankee Doodle Dandy, was still alive and kicking. I thought it would be interesting to find out his secret of success, in case someday our paths were to cross. There was no such chance with Ben Franklin, of course.

Was the year 1924? If so, Ben had been dead for some time, and George M. was surely not much more than thirty. Or might it have been forty? Thirty or forty, he was certainly at the height of his fame, writing plays, singing, dancing, and being an all-round American Boy, born on Independence Day. They made a movie about him, but I presumed they had done it for money, so I never saw it.

The world was different then, whether it was 1924, or a couple of years earlier, or a couple later. It was just plain different. It wasn't necessarily better, and in all probability it was worse, but an American Boy had a chance in those days, on his own, unsponsored, so to say. All he needed was willingness, wit, and vitality, and so it was great to be an American, to be under voting age, to be unknown, to have the challenge there night and day, still unmet.

1 *Liberty* magazine had a fine editorial policy, although I have forgotten precisely what it was. In the name of something, somebody meant to be an American Boy, and to make money. I envied him, although I didn't know his name. He was back of the whole thing, though, and the arrival of his magazine into my life an event of some importance.

After work, I examined the magazine from cover to cover to find out what it came to, and then I read George M. Cohan's contribution, which I found fascinating, because he was swift, confident, and talented. He was born backstage, and as soon as he could walk he went out and wowed 'em, singing, dancing, and telling jokes.

The photographs of George and his beautiful sister and his handsome father and mother were an inspiration, but in those days the the-
2 ater wasn't my line, and so if I was to get started in the business of making my fame and fortune, out of the pages of *Liberty* magazine, it would have to be by winning the limerick contest, by making something out of the fact that there *was* a young lady of Perth, if in fact that was what it was, as it probably wasn't, although it was certainly the equivalent of it.

The trouble was I didn't know anything about limericks, but *Liberty* magazine gave a brief history of them, how they had originated in a place called Limerick, and the magazine also gave three or four illustrations of perfect ones. These were incredibly clever, apt, wise, and witty. Somebody from somewhere tried to do something and as a result something unexpected happened. In a way, that was a little like the story of my life up to that time, and now it was time for a change. Instead of being the subject of a limerick, I wanted to be a
3 writer of one, I wanted to be the writer of the greatest limerick of all time, because that would mean that I would win the contest, I would win the money, and people would say, "There goes the American Boy who wrote the limerick."

I couldn't think of a second line, though. There was a young lady of Perth; who she was or what she was up to, I couldn't guess.

I kept it in mind, though. I had the first line, supplied by the magazine, and all I needed next was a second line that was so extraordinary that the rest of the lines of the limerick would fall into place and sound like perfection itself. The words that rhymed with Perth were "worth," "mirth," "birth," "dearth," "girth," and, of course, "earth"—all good usable words. There *was* an earth, there *was* a birth, there were mirth and worth and the oth-

AT A GLANCE

- The narrator admired Benjamin Franklin and George M. Cohan.
- He remembers how the limerick contest excited him as a way to get recognition.
- If he could just think of a perfect second line, he could win.

1 IRONY

Here humor comes out of irony. The narrator forgets what the editorial policy of the magazine was, but he remembers that it was "fine."

2 TONE

Besides being humorous the simple, informal narration portrays a personal, intimate tone.

3 CHARACTERIZATION

As a boy the narrator felt the important things in life were success, popularity, and money.

GUIDED READING

LITERAL QUESTION

1a. What experience did the narrator have with limericks when he decided to enter the contest? (none)

INFERENTIAL QUESTION

1b. What does this tell you about him? (He was not afraid to take on a challenge.)

AT A GLANCE

- At first the narrator's family are also interested in the contest, but they soon lose interest.
- The narrator decides to have "stick-to-itiveness" and stay in the contest.
- The winning limerick comes to him when his head hits the pavement after a bike accident.

1 THEME

The speaker has a close family. They all become involved in his project, and they share their experiences.

2 THEME

The speaker means to win the contest by perseverance because he thinks that is the key to greatness.

3 VOCABULARY: DICTION

The use of five words to describe dropping out of the contest shows how much the contest meant to the narrator and adds to the comic tone through exaggeration.

4 HUMOR

The detail about the narrator's cap would be important if it had protected his head from the fall. However, since the cap had fallen off before his head hit the pavement, its inclusion in the narration has a humorous effect.

ers, and so all I really needed to do was rattle them together and throw them out like dice, for a natural. With my conscious mind, the mind that was supposed to be equal to such a challenge, equal to thought, I had little luck. "There was a young lady of Perth who didn't know what she was worth," for instance, just wasn't right.

And so I slept on it, or, to be a little more exact, it slept on me. The young lady of Perth was here, there, and everywhere, but the limerick remained incomplete, and I woke up in the morning knowing I had been in a fight and hadn't won.

That first issue of *Liberty* magazine passed
1 from me to my brother, who also took an interest in the limerick contest, and then to my sisters, so that before the second issue of the magazine came out everybody in my family was at work trying to win fame and fortune as a limerick writer. We weren't good at it, though. I don't know who fell out first, but I know it wasn't me. I think it was my brother, who tended to be cynical about contests in general, and about theories of how easy it is to rise in the world. He said it just wasn't an overnight proposition. A man of thirteen, he believed, was a little less likely to be invited to Washington to discuss educational reform with President Harding than a man of sixteen, for instance. But a man of sixteen was less likely than a man of nineteen, and our neighborhood was pretty well stocked with nineteen-year-old American Boys who knew a thing or two about educational reform—throw out teachers who had remained stupid after considerable schooling. That was the basic educational reform principle of the neighborhood.

I noticed with regret my brother's scorn for the limerick-writing contest, and I made up my mind to be different. I made up my mind to
2 have stick-to-itiveness, because I had heard that everybody who had ever amounted to anything had had stick-to-itiveness. I reasoned that if *they* had had it, and had *needed* it, and had won through to success on *account* of it, I was going to have it, too. Every evening when I got home from work I checked with the other contestants, only to discover, after two or three such checks, that everybody had given up. I also discovered that my persistence, or stick-to-itiveness, was being taken for a nuisance.

Somebody said, "To heck with the young lady of Perth. This is Fresno."

3 This amounted to nothing better than the waving of the white flag, surrender, armistice, failure, humiliation. I was flabbergasted and more determined than ever to win the contest.

There was time, the deadline was still ten or eleven days off, and I felt confident that long before the required midnight postmark of the final day I would have my limerick neatly written and on its way to *Liberty* magazine in—wherever it was. I don't believe it was in New York, or in Chicago, either. I just don't remember where it was, but it was somewhere, and this place could be reached by train mail in a matter of six or seven days. There was no airmail in those days.

One afternoon the chain on my bike broke while I was sprinting, and I was sent over the handle bars onto the pavement. Something was always happening to my bike. It wasn't holding up, but nobody ever said, "They don't make them the way they used to." The wire spokes of the wheel were always loosening, and while I had a spoke tightener, as every practical-minded messenger had, whenever I tightened a couple of loose spokes I noticed that the alignment of the wheel became unbalanced. You had to be an expert even in a thing like that.

4 The dive was on my head, which was at least a little protected by the blue cap of Postal Telegraph, or at any rate would have been had the cap not fallen off just before my head struck the pavement, when I needed it most.

It was quite a jolt, but, as always, I hoped there had been no witnesses, for I despised having accidents, and I resented help and sympathy.

The minute my head hit the pavement the whole winning limerick came to me, and I was

GUIDED READING

LITERAL QUESTIONS

1a. What kind of people had "stick-to-itiveness," according to the narrator? (everybody who had ever amounted to anything)

2a. What did the narrator hope after the accident? (that there had been no witnesses)

INFERENTIAL QUESTIONS

1b. What did those people probably have that the narrator did not? (talent and experience in their fields)

2b. What does this tell you about him? (He was very self-conscious as a boy.)

stunned by the brilliance and rightness of it, the simplicity and inevitability of it, and by the fact that it had taken a foolish accident to bring the thing around. I was all set to begin committing it to memory before I forgot it when an elderly lady of Fresno hurried up and asked, as a mother or a grandmother might, "Are you all right?"

"Yes, ma'am, it's nothing, thank you." All quickly said, so she would be satisfied and move along, but no, she wanted to chat.

"Are you sure? Here, let me help you up."

Well, then I realized I was still flat on my back, so I leaped to my feet, picked up the fallen bike, and began to unwheel the chain, which had become entangled around the hub.

1 There was no getting away from her, or rather no getting her away from me. On and on she chatted, and of course my upbringing compelled me to answer every question respectfully.

At last I was able to walk away with my bike. It was time to commit the limerick to memory, but all I could remember was the first line again. The thing was lost.

I was still so mad that evening when I got home that my brother couldn't help noticing.

"What's the matter with you?"

"Lousy chain broke again."

I didn't want to tell him about the limerick because I was afraid he wouldn't believe me, and a younger brother hates not being believed. I'd *had* that whole limerick right after I had dived, and it was the winning one, too. I'd had it, and then that nice old lady of Fresno had come up and had made me forget it. My brother examined my head and told me there was a bump there. I told him I *knew* there was a bump there. He wasn't really satisfied with my reason for being mad, and little by little he won me over to a full confession. I was astonished that he *didn't* disbelieve me. On the contrary, he was sure that I *had* had the winning limerick and had lost it.

"The thing to do," he said, "is to get it back."

"How?"

"The same way."

"Sprint and break the chain and dive on my head? Nothing doing."

"That's how it came to you. That's how you'll get it back. If you want something badly enough, you've got to pay the price for it."

2 "It was an accident," I said. "I'm not going to have an accident on purpose. I don't think it's possible in the first place, and even if it were, even if I *had* another accident, how do I know what kind of limerick I'd get out of it? It might not be the winner at all."

"Suit yourself," my brother said.

3 Now, it never occurred to me that he was having fun, and I kept thinking about his suggestion. After supper we went out to the back yard, where our wheels were. I looked at mine, with the chain as good as new again, repaired by Frank the Portuguese bike man, from whom we had bought our bikes, secondhand, and after a moment I got on the bike real slow and easy and rode out across the empty lot adjoining our back yard, and then out onto the sidewalk of San Benito Avenue, and then out onto the pavement of M Street, and there I began to sprint. My brother came running after me, shouting, "For goodness sake, I was only kidding, don't do it, you'll kill yourself."

Well, the fact is I really hadn't *meant* to do it, I had only meant to sprint, racing, going as fast as I could go, as a kind of test of the fates. The chain was strong, and it just wasn't likely to break—unless the fates wanted me to take another dive, get back the winning limerick, and be on my way to fame and fortune. I heard my brother. The memory of what it was I had a lot of—stick-to-itiveness—came back to me, and I decided I *would* do my best to make that repaired chain snap and break, after all. I raced three blocks to Ventura Avenue without luck; the chain was as strong as ever. My brother rode up on his wheel and said, "Now, look, if you really think that that's the way to get the lost limerick back, I'll do everything I can to help you."

"How?"

AT A GLANCE

- The persistent assistance of an old woman makes the narrator forget the lines.
- When his older brother facetiously suggests that he re-create the accident to remember the limerick, he takes off on his bike.
- At first his brother tries to stop him, but then the older boy says he will help.

1 CHARACTERIZATION

The narrator's respect for his elders keeps him from getting on with his mission.

2 PARADOX

The construction of "accident on purpose" is paradoxical and very humorous.

3 POINT OF VIEW

The story is told from the point of view of the narrator as a young boy but with the hindsight of the narrator as a mature writer. As a child he thought his brother was serious; as an adult he knows he was teasing.

GUIDED READING

LITERAL QUESTIONS

1a. Does the speaker think his brother believes his story about the limerick? (Yes. He says he was astonished that his brother did not disbelieve it.)

2a. What does the narrator's brother do right after the narrator takes off on his bike? (tries to stop him)

INFERENTIAL QUESTIONS

1b. Does the brother believe the speaker? (Probably not. His suggestion about re-creating the accident shows that he is probably just teasing his brother.)

2b. What does this show about the relationship between the two brothers? (Although his older brother might tease the narrator, he really loves him.)

AT A GLANCE

- The narrator's brother suggests that he drop the narrator on his head.
- They are distracted by a handball game.
- The family spends a pleasant evening.
- The narrator sends in the best limerick he can think of and loses the contest.

1 **STYLE: IMAGERY**

The image of the brewery as a "Bavarian red-brick castle" shows that it was a special place for the narrator and the other children.

2 **THEME**

Family warmth and simple joys are the important things in life.

3 **CONFLICT**

The speaker experiences the pull of perseverance against the joys of family life.

"I'll hold you about two feet above the pavement—that's enough—and drop you. It's safer that way."

We were riding back on M Street in any
1 case, so we rode on up to the Rainier Brewery, a kind of Bavarian red-brick castle entangled in railroad tracks and company roads, and we rode around the brewery, closed now, finished for the day, and we discussed the problem. After a while we dismounted and sat on the steps of the brewery to discuss procedure a little further and to make sure that nobody was around. The coast was clear and procedure had been agreed upon, when Eddie Imirian and Johnny Suni came up, bouncing an old tennis ball. My brother and I were challenged to a game of handball against the brewery wall. We won 21 to 18, and then it was dark, but Eddie and Johnny wanted another game, so we played in the dark and won 21 to 12.

When we reached our house, the boys sat with us on our front porch steps and talked about school. It looked as if they never wanted to go home, but finally they did, and my brother said, "Well, how about it?"

"The tar on San Benito Avenue isn't hard enough," I said.

"Want to try the sidewalk?"

"It's *harder* than the pavement I hit."

"Whatever you say."

Well, we were both pretty tired, but it seemed to me this was a matter of stick-to-itiveness if I ever saw one, so I quickly said, "Let's try her."

My brother was holding me around the knees, about two feet over the sidewalk, and was all set to drop me on my head when my mother came out on the front porch with a pitcher of tahn on a tray. "Oh-oh," my brother said.

Well, it was now or never, so I said, "Let go."

Now, I was all set to get back the winning limerick, but my brother didn't let go.

"Why are you holding your brother that way?" my mother said.

"Just exercise," my brother said. "We take turns."

He let me down, and I took him around the knees and held him precisely as he had held me. For a moment I thought of dropping *him*, without plan, but I thought better of it and didn't.

"Come and drink tahn," my mother said.

I let him down and we went up onto the porch and drank two big glasses each of the best drink in the world. Put two cups of yogurt in a pitcher, add four or five cups of cold water, stir, and drink.

Well, the drink was great, because it helped you to know how alive you were, and what a privilege it was.

One of my sisters began to play *Dardanella* on the piano, and the other began to sing. My brother and I listened and looked around at where we were, and then up at the sky, full of
2 stars. It was kind of silly, in a way, living in a house like that, nothing to it really, a few boards and a little wallpaper, and us, in a whole neighborhood like that, but what could you do? The tahn was great. The air was full of something that made you know you were alive, and the sky seemed a lot like something almost as good as money in the bank.

Pretty soon my sisters came out on the porch. We all sat around and talked and told
3 jokes and laughed. I liked it, but I kept feeling I was losing my stick-to-itiveness, and that was the one thing I couldn't afford to lose. After about an hour we went inside to close up for the night.

My brother dropped me headfirst onto my bed, but all I did was bounce. The winning limerick didn't come back. And then I dropped him, and all *he* did was bounce.

I did my best with my conscious mind, and sent in a limerick, and lost.

I read every installment of George M. Cohan's life, and I envied him. I read the winning limerick, too. It didn't come to very much.

About forty years later I reached Perth,

GUIDED READING

LITERAL QUESTIONS

1a. What reason does the narrator's brother give to his mother for holding his brother around the knees? (He says they are doing it for exercise.)

2a. What did the speaker do with his sisters? (They sat around and talked and told jokes and laughed.)

INFERENTIAL QUESTIONS

1b. Why does he say this? (He knows how angry she would be if he told her the truth.)

2b. What does this tell you about the members of this family? (They are closely knit, seem to get along well, and enjoy each other's company. Family time seems to take high priority.)

which is on the west coast of Australia. It seemed like a nice place, something like Fresno. I saw the young lady of Perth in person. I saw her six or seven *hundred* times, as a matter of fact. I *spoke* to her six or seven times. She replied in a nice Australian accent. There was nothing suitable for a limerick in her.

She was just a nice girl.

In 1939 I met George M. Cohan in the offices of a theater in New York. He was a gentle, kindly fellow with a touch of sorrow in his eyes.

Liberty magazine changed hands a couple of times, and then gave up the ghost.

I forgot all about limericks. Also, stick-to-itiveness.

1 I decided that *don't-stick-to-itiveness* is a pretty usable philosophy, too, especially for a writer.

STUDY QUESTIONS

Recalling

1. About how old was the narrator when the first issue of *Liberty* magazine came out? Why was he interested in reading about George M. Cohan, according to the sixth paragraph?
2. In about what year did the incident take place? How was the world different then?
3. For what reasons did the narrator want to be the writer of "the greatest limerick of all time"? What kept him working on the limerick contest when others in his family gave up?
4. What happened to generate the "winning limerick" in the narrator's mind? What caused him to "lose" it?
5. What did the narrator feel he was losing when he and his family "sat around and talked and joked and laughed" on the porch? What did he decide about this loss, according to the final paragraph?
6. What does the narrator report about Perth and George M. Cohan in the last section?

Interpreting

7. What does the story suggest is at the root of the narrator's "stick-to-itiveness"? What does his admiration for Franklin (page 56) and George M. Cohan have to do with it?
8. Briefly describe the narrator as an adult. Why is it significant that he has been to Perth and met George M. Cohan? In saying that "the world" was different in 1924, what does he suggest about himself?
9. What sort of scene is the scene on the porch? How might it help explain the narrator's comment in his final paragraph? What does the story suggest might be more important than "stick-to-itiveness," especially to a writer?

Extending

10. Do you agree with the narrator's view of "stick-to-itiveness," or perseverance? How would you define success?

COMPOSITION

Writing About a Narrator

■ A story that uses a first-person narrator, as "There Was a Young Lady of Perth" does, challenges the reader. After all, the narrator may be forgetting something important or deliberately not telling the whole story or slanting the interpretation of what happened. Write a composition about Saroyan's narrator. What elements in the story persuade you to believe everything the narrator says? What elements give you some doubt? Cite specific passages that show why you do or do not accept the narrator's version of the story.

Writing a Limerick

■ Complete the limerick beginning "There was a young lady of Perth," or write one with your own opening line. Remember the source of the humor in a limerick is usually situational irony: When someone tries to do something, something unexpected happens.

AT A GLANCE

- The narrator meets young ladies in Perth and Cohan in New York, and he puts these encounters in perspective.
- He decides that "don't-stick-to-itiveness" is a usable philosophy.

1 CHARACTERIZATION

The narrator is a dynamic character. He has changed his opinion about the importance of stick-to-itiveness.

REFLECTING ON THE STORY

What does the author seem to be saying about writing in this story? (You do not become a writer just by persistence. You must be open to what is happening around you.)

STUDY QUESTIONS

1. between eleven and fourteen; find Cohan's secret of success
2. 1924; because boy had chance to succeed on his own
3. win contest, money, fame; stick-to-itiveness
4. bicycle accident, fell on head; interference of old lady
5. stick-to-itiveness; *"don't-stick-to-itiveness* is a pretty usable philosophy"
6. Perth: has seen young lady, spoken to her, found nothing suitable for a limerick in her; Cohan: "a gentle, kindly fellow . . . sorrow in his eyes"
7. idealized image of American boy; success through persistence
8. urbane, successful, easygoing; show success; has changed
9. warm family scene; warmth and love preferable to stick-to-itiveness; that writer must be open, understand human relations
10. Answers will vary. Possible answer: yes; finding joy in everyday life.

COMPOSITION: GUIDELINES FOR EVALUATION

WRITING ABOUT A NARRATOR

Objective

To analyze character of a first-person narrator

Guidelines for Evaluation

- suggested length: three to six paragraphs
- should comment on narrator's reliability
- should find places persuading reader to believe narrator; show where narrator may be inaccurate or deliberately lying
- should give specific examples

WRITING A LIMERICK

Objective

To write a limerick

Guidelines for Evaluation

- suggested length: five lines
- should adhere to limerick form
- should achieve humor through situational irony

Photograph © 1982 by Jill Krementz

Truman Capote *1924–1986*

Almost all of Truman Capote's works focus directly or indirectly on the theme of innocence. His fiction poses problems and asks questions, blurring the boundaries between innocence and ignorance, innocence and guilt, innocence and maturity.

Truman Capote was born in New Orleans, Louisiana, but attended schools in New York and Connecticut. He worked for the *New Yorker* magazine, first as a cataloguer of cartoons, later as a writer. Capote's first novel *(Other Voices, Other Rooms)* was published in 1948. He followed that with other successful novels, among them *The Grass Harp* (1951), *Breakfast at Tiffany's* (1958), and a "nonfiction novel," *In Cold Blood* (1966). A writer who has tried many different media, Capote has also produced stage plays, nonfiction, television plays, and movie scripts.

Capote's skill as a fiction writer has won him many awards. Twice he was given the O. Henry Memorial Award for a short story (in 1943 for "Miriam" and in 1946 for "Shut a Final Door"). He won the National Institute of Arts and Letters creative writing award in 1959 and the Mystery Writers of America Edgar Award (named for Edgar Allan Poe) in 1966 for *In Cold Blood.* Capote also received an Emmy Award in 1967 for the television adaption of his short story "A Christmas Memory."

In Cold Blood presents an insightful look into a violent crime, but Capote is equally adept at comedy, mystery, and delicate stories of sensitive human relationships. His style is pure, the result of much rewriting. Close attention to meaningful detail, an ear for dialogue, and a facility for creating fresh metaphors give his writing a crisp realism. An adept storyteller, Capote weaves a compassionate understanding of character into intriguing, often suspenseful plots.

"Miriam," one of Capote's most popular stories, is a combination of suspense and compassionate characterization. Its mystery is more than a matter of plot: It is the mystery of human emotions.

■ What does the name "Miriam" suggest to you? Does the name itself suggest something mysterious?

Truman Capote

Miriam

For several years Mrs. H. T. Miller had lived alone in a pleasant apartment (two rooms with kitchenette) in a remodeled brownstone[1] near the East River. She was a widow: Mr. H. T. Miller had left a reasonable amount of insur-
1 ance. Her interests were narrow, she had no friends to speak of, and she rarely journeyed farther than the corner grocery. The other people in the house never seemed to notice her: her clothes were matter of fact, her hair iron-gray, clipped, and casually waved; she did not use cosmetics, her features were plain and inconspicuous, and on her last birthday she was sixty-one. Her activities were seldom spontaneous: she kept the two rooms immaculate, smoked an occasional cigarette, prepared her own meals, and tended a canary.

Then she met Miriam. It was snowing that night. Mrs. Miller had finished drying the supper dishes and was thumbing through an afternoon paper when she saw an advertisement of a picture playing at a neighborhood theater. The title sounded good, so she struggled into her beaver coat, laced her galoshes, and left
2 the apartment, leaving one light burning in the foyer—she found nothing more disturbing than a sensation of darkness.

The snow was fine, falling gently, not yet making an impression on the pavement. The wind from the river cut only at street crossings. Mrs. Miller hurried, her head bowed, oblivious as a mole burrowing a blind path. She stopped at a drugstore and bought a package of peppermints.

A long line stretched in front of the box office; she took her place at the end. There would be (a tired voice groaned) a short wait for all seats. Mrs. Miller rummaged in her
3 leather handbag till she collected exactly the correct change for admission. The line seemed to be taking its own time and, looking around for some distraction, she suddenly became conscious of a little girl standing under the edge of the marquee.

Her hair was the longest and strangest Mrs. Miller had ever seen: absolutely silver-white, like an albino's. It flowed waist-length in smooth, loose lines. She was thin and fragilely constructed. There was a simple, special elegance in the way she stood with her thumbs in the pockets of a tailored plum velvet coat.

Mrs. Miller felt oddly excited, and when the little girl glanced toward her, she smiled warmly. The little girl walked over and said, "Would you care to do me a favor?"

"I'd be glad to, if I can," said Mrs. Miller.

"Oh, it's quite easy. I merely want you to buy a ticket for me; they won't let me in otherwise. Here, I have the money." And gracefully she handed Mrs. Miller two dimes and a nickel.

They went into the theater together. An usherette directed them to a lounge; in twenty minutes the picture would be over.

4 "I feel just like a genuine criminal," said Mrs. Miller gaily, as she sat down. "I mean that sort of thing's against the law, isn't it? I do hope I haven't done the wrong thing. Your mother knows where you are, dear? I mean she does, doesn't she?"

The little girl said nothing. She unbuttoned her coat and folded it across her lap. Her dress underneath was prim and dark blue. A gold chain dangled about her neck and her fingers, sensitive and musical-looking, toyed with it. Examining her more attentively, Mrs. Miller decided the truly distinctive feature was not her hair, but her eyes; they were hazel, steady, lacking any childlike quality whatsoever and, because of their size, seemed to consume her small face.

Mrs. Miller offered a peppermint. "What's your name, dear?"

"Miriam," she said, as though, in some cu-

1. **brownstone:** house with brown stone facade.

AT A GLANCE

- Mrs. Miller goes to a movie where a little girl named Miriam asks her to buy a ticket.
- Mrs. Miller does, and after they go in she looks at Miriam closely and sees that she is a strange child.

LITERARY OPTIONS

- suspense and foreshadowing
- characterization
- conflict

THEMATIC OPTIONS

- appearance and reality
- modern life
- loneliness

1 THEME

We see from the very beginning that Mrs. Miller is a solitary woman in New York City. She may be lonely, although she does not seem to acknowledge her deepest feelings.

2 SUSPENSE

Though Mrs. Miller seems competent and secure, it now emerges that she fears the dark. Her character is more ambiguous than it first appeared and the story more mysterious.

3 CHARACTERIZATION

By layering details the author creates a full picture of Mrs. Miller: She is orderly and does not like surprises. That she collects "exactly the correct change" is very much in character.

4 CHARACTERIZATION

Mrs. Miller is not the sort to break the law, yet she seems to enjoy the idea. She is acting out of character.

GUIDED READING

LITERAL QUESTIONS

1a. Where does Mrs. Miller live? (in an apartment)

2a. What does Miriam want her to do? (buy a ticket for her at the movies)

INFERENTIAL QUESTIONS

1b. What is her life like? (orderly, predictable, dull, probably lonely and boring)

2b. Why do you think Mrs. Miller buys Miriam's ticket? (Mrs. Miller seems to be fascinated by the child, who may represent a break from her solitary, routine existence.)

AT A GLANCE

- Mrs. Miller is surprised at Miriam's name, since her own name is Miriam.
- Snow falls for a week, and Mrs. Miller loses track of time.

1 SUSPENSE

This discovery is the first of many odd coincidences in this story. They add to the effect of mystery, as if some departure from reality is taking place.

2 DIALOGUE

This whole conversation is like a fencing match. Neither Miriam will really talk to the other. Mrs. Miller says things that do not require answers, and Miriam gives her replies no one would expect.

3 STYLE: METAPHOR

The metaphor of the snow as a curtain concealing secrets also applies to Miriam. She reveals almost nothing about herself, and she is wrapped in a cloak of mystery as strange and impenetrable as her snowlike white hair.

1 rious way, it were information already familiar.

"Why, isn't that funny? My name's Miriam too. And it's not a terribly common name either. Now, don't tell me your last name's Miller!"

"Just Miriam."

"But isn't that funny?"

"Moderately," said Miriam, and rolled the peppermint on her tongue.

Mrs. Miller flushed and shifted uncomfortably. "You have such a large vocabulary for such a little girl."

2 "Do I?"

"Well, yes," said Mrs. Miller, hastily changing the topic to: "Do you like the movies?"

"I really wouldn't know," said Miriam. "I've never been before."

Women began filling the lounge; the rumble of the newsreel[2] bombs exploded in the distance. Mrs. Miller rose, tucking her purse under her arm. "I guess I'd better be running now if I want to get a seat," she said. "It was nice to have met you."

Miriam nodded ever so slightly.

It snowed all week. Wheels and footsteps moved soundlessly on the street, as if the busi-
3 ness of living continued secretly behind a pale but impenetrable curtain. In the falling quiet there was no sky or earth, only snow lifting in the wind, frosting the window glass, chilling the rooms, deadening and hushing the city. At all hours it was necessary to keep a lamp lighted, and Mrs. Miller lost track of the days: Friday was no different from Saturday and on Sunday she went to the grocery: closed, of course.

That evening she scrambled eggs and fixed a bowl of tomato soup. Then, after putting on a flannel robe and cold-creaming her face, she

2. **newsreel:** short motion picture of current events.

GUIDED READING

LITERAL QUESTION

1a. What happens after the movie? (It snows all week.)

INFERENTIAL QUESTION

1b. In what way might Mrs. Miller's behavior be somewhat strange during this time? (She keeps a light on at all times, and she loses track of what day it is.)

propped herself up in bed with a hot-water bottle under her feet. She was reading the *Times* when the doorbell rang. At first she thought it must be a mistake and whoever it was would go away. But it rang and rang and settled to a persistent buzz. She looked at the
1 clock: a little after eleven; it did not seem possible, she was always asleep by ten.

Climbing out of bed, she trotted barefoot across the living room. "I'm coming; please be patient." The latch was caught; she turned it this way and that way and the bell never paused an instant. "Stop it!" she cried. The bolt gave way and she opened the door an inch. "What in heaven's name?"

"Hello," said Miriam.

"Oh . . . why, hello," said Mrs. Miller, stepping hesitantly into the hall. "You're that little girl."

"I thought you'd never answer, but I kept my finger on the button; I knew you were home. Aren't you glad to see me?"

Mrs. Miller did not know what to say. Miriam, she saw, wore the same plum velvet coat and now she had also a beret to match; her white hair was braided in two shining plaits and looped at the ends with enormous white ribbons.

"Since I've waited so long, you could at least let me in," she said.

"It's awfully late."

Miriam regarded her blankly. "What difference does that make? Let me in. It's cold out here and I have on a silk dress." Then, with a gentle gesture, she urged Mrs. Miller aside and passed into the apartment.

She dropped her coat and beret on a chair. She was indeed wearing a silk dress. White silk. White silk in February. The skirt was beautifully pleated and the sleeves long; it made a faint rustle as she strolled about the room. "I like your place," she said. "I like the rug; blue's my favorite color." She touched a paper rose in a vase on the coffee table. "Imitation," she commented wanly. "How sad. Aren't imitations sad?" She seated herself on the sofa, daintily spreading her skirt.

"What do you want?" asked Mrs. Miller.

"Sit down," said Miriam. "It makes me nervous to see people stand."

2 Mrs. Miller sank to a hassock. "What do you want?" she repeated.

"You know, I don't think you're glad I came."

For a second time Mrs. Miller was without an answer; her hand motioned vaguely. Miriam giggled and pressed back on a mound of chintz[3] pillows. Mrs. Miller observed that the girl was less pale than she remembered; her cheeks were flushed.

"How did you know where I lived?"

Miriam frowned. "That's no question at all. What's your name? What's mine?"

"But I'm not listed in the phone book."

"Oh, let's talk about something else."

Mrs. Miller said, "Your mother must be insane to let a child like you wander around at all hours of the night . . . and in such ridiculous clothes. She must be out of her mind."

Miriam got up and moved to a corner where a covered bird cage hung from a ceiling chain. She peeked beneath the cover. "It's a canary," she said. "Would you mind if I woke him? I'd like to hear him sing."

"Leave Tommy alone," said Mrs. Miller anxiously. "Don't you dare wake him."

"Certainly," said Miriam. "But I don't see why I can't hear him sing." And then, "Have you anything to eat? I'm starving! Even milk and a jam sandwich would be fine."

"Look," said Mrs. Miller, arising from the hassock, "look, if I made some nice sandwiches will you be a good child and run along home? It's past midnight, I'm sure."

"It's snowing," reproached Miriam. "And cold and dark."

3 "Well, you shouldn't have come here to begin with," said Mrs. Miller, struggling to control her voice. "I can't help the weather. If you want anything to eat you'll have to promise to leave."

---

3. **chintz** [chints]: colorful, patterned, cotton fabric, usually glazed.

AT A GLANCE

- After a week of snow Miriam shows up at Mrs. Miller's door late at night, dressed in white silk.
- Mrs. Miller wants her to leave but says she will give the child some food if she promises to go soon.

1 CHARACTERIZATION

Mrs. Miller is changing. She lives by habit, but she is not following her habits this evening.

2 CONFLICT

Mrs. Miller plainly does not want Miriam around, but she cannot find the courage to get rid of her.

3 CHARACTERIZATION

Mrs. Miller tries to regain control by appearing angry and indifferent. But she falls back on a bribe, and Miriam is really in control.

GUIDED READING

LITERAL QUESTIONS

1a. What does Mrs. Miller say when Miriam asks if she is glad to see her? (She has no answer.)

2a. What kind of dress is Miriam wearing? (She is wearing a white silk dress.)

INFERENTIAL QUESTIONS

1b. Do you think Mrs. Miller is glad to see Miriam? (Answers will vary. Her behavior is ambiguous; she is both lonely and suspicious.)

2b. What might be unusual about Miriam's dress? (It sounds like a wedding dress, odd on a little girl, and not appropriate winter wear. Also, its luxuriousness shows that she is not an urchin.)

AT A GLANCE

- Mrs. Miller goes to make her some food, and when she returns, Miriam is looking at her jewelry.
- She helps herself to a cameo.
- Mrs. Miller realizes how alone she is.
- Miriam asks for a kiss, but when Mrs. Miller refuses, Miriam breaks her vase.

1 SUSPENSE

The situation seems to be completely beyond Mrs. Miller's control: She is being manipulated by a strange child, and the canary is singing at the wrong time. Neither Mrs. Miller nor the reader knows what to expect of Miriam.

2 THEME

Mrs. Miller never realized how lonely she was, but the presence of a strange other has forced her to acknowledge this fact about her life.

3 CHARACTERIZATION

There is something foreboding about the contradictions in Miriam's personality. She is described as sweet and childlike, wanting a kiss, and then as violent. The phrase *slyly innocent* captures this dichotomy.

Miriam brushed a braid against her cheek. Her eyes were thoughtful, as if weighing the proposition. She turned toward the bird cage. "Very well," she said, "I promise."

1 *How old is she? Ten? Eleven?* Mrs. Miller, in the kitchen, unsealed a jar of strawberry preserves and cut four slices of bread. She poured a glass of milk and paused to light a cigarette. *And why has she come?* Her hand shook as she held the match, fascinated, till it burned her finger. The canary was singing—singing as he did in the morning and at no other time. "Miriam," she called, "Miriam, I told you not to disturb Tommy." There was no answer. She called again; all she heard was the canary. She inhaled the cigarette and discovered she had lighted the cork-tip end and . . . oh, really, she mustn't lose her temper.

She carried the food in on a tray and set it on the coffee table. She saw first that the bird cage still wore its night cover. And Tommy was singing. It gave her a queer sensation. And no one was in the room. Mrs. Miller went through an alcove leading to her bedroom; at the door she caught her breath.

"What are you doing?" she asked.

Miriam glanced up, and in her eyes there was a look that was not ordinary. She was standing by the bureau, a jewel case opened before her. For a minute she studied Mrs. Miller, forcing their eyes to meet, and she smiled. "There's nothing good here," she said. "But I like this." Her hand held a cameo brooch. "It's charming."

"Suppose—perhaps you'd better put it back," said Mrs. Miller, feeling suddenly the need of some support. She leaned against the doorframe; her head was unbearably heavy; a pressure weighted the rhythm of her heartbeat. The light seemed to flutter defectively. "Please, child—a gift from my husband. . . ."

"But it's beautiful and I want it," said Miriam. *"Give it to me."*

2 As she stood, striving to shape a sentence which would somehow save the brooch, it came to Mrs. Miller there was no one to whom she might turn; she was alone; a fact that had not been among her thoughts for a long time. Its sheer emphasis was stunning. But here in her own room in the hushed snow city were evidences she could not ignore or, she knew with startling clarity, resist.

Miriam ate ravenously, and when the sandwiches and milk were gone, her fingers made cobweb movements over the plate, gathering crumbs. The cameo gleamed on her blouse, the blond profile like a trick reflection of its wearer. "That was very nice," she sighed, "though now an almond cake or a cherry would be ideal. Sweets are lovely, don't you think?"

Mrs. Miller was perched precariously on the hassock, smoking a cigarette. Her hair net had slipped lopsided and loose strands straggled down her face. Her eyes were stupidly concentrated on nothing, and her cheeks were mottled in red patches, as though a fierce slap had left permanent marks.

"Is there a candy . . . a cake?"

Mrs. Miller tapped ash on the rug. Her head swayed slightly as she tried to focus her eyes. "You promised to leave if I made the sandwiches," she said.

"Dear me, did I?"

"It was a promise and I'm tired and I don't feel well at all."

"Mustn't fret," said Miriam. "I'm only teasing."

She picked up her coat, slung it over her arm, and arranged her beret in front of a mirror. Presently she bent close to Mrs. Miller and whispered, "Kiss me good night."

"Please . . . I'd rather not," said Mrs. Miller.

3 Miriam lifted a shoulder, arched an eyebrow. "As you like," she said, and went directly to the coffee table, seized the vase containing the paper roses, carried it to where the hard surface of the floor lay bare, and hurled it downward. Glass sprayed in all directions and she stamped her foot on the bouquet.

Then slowly she walked to the door, but before closing it she looked back at Mrs. Miller with a slyly innocent curiosity.

Mrs. Miller spent the next day in bed, rising once to feed the canary and drink a cup of tea;

GUIDED READING

LITERAL QUESTIONS

1a. How did Mrs. Miller light her cigarette? (She lit the wrong end.)

2a. What does Miriam do with the paper roses? (She stamps them on the floor under her feet.)

INFERENTIAL QUESTIONS

1b. What does the episode with the cigarette tell you about Mrs. Miller? (She is losing control.)

2b. Does this action reveal anything about Miriam? (She becomes violent over trivial matters. She hates artificial and cheap things. She is curious, observant, and very sinister.)

she took her temperature and had none, yet her dreams were feverishly agitated; their unbalanced mood lingered even as she lay staring
1 wide-eyed at the ceiling. One dream threaded through the others like an elusively mysterious theme in a complicated symphony, and the scenes it depicted were sharply outlined, as though sketched by a hand of gifted intensity: a small girl, wearing a bridal gown and a wreath of leaves, led a gray procession down a mountain path, and among them there was unusual silence till a woman at the rear asked, "Where is she taking us?" "No one knows," said an old man marching in front. "But isn't she pretty?" volunteered a third voice. "Isn't she like a frost flower—so shining and white?"

Tuesday morning she woke up feeling better; harsh slats of sunlight, slanting through Venetian blinds, shed a disrupting light on her unwholesome fancies. She opened the window to discover a thawed, mild-as-spring day; a sweep of clean new clouds crumpled against a vastly blue, out-of-season sky; and across the low line of rooftops she could see the river and smoke curving from tugboat stacks in a warm wind. A great silver truck plowed the snow-banked street, its machine sound humming on the air.

After straightening the apartment, she went to the grocer's, cashed a check, and continued to Schrafft's, where she ate breakfast and chatted happily with the waitress. Oh, it was a wonderful day . . . more like a holiday . . . and it would be so foolish to go home.

She boarded a Lexington Avenue bus and rode up to Eighty-sixth Street; it was here that she had decided to do a little shopping.

2 She had no idea what she wanted or needed, but she idled along, intent only upon the passers-by, brisk and preoccupied, who gave her a disturbing sense of separateness.

It was while waiting at the corner of Third Avenue that she saw the man: an old man, bowlegged and stooped under an armload of bulging packages; he wore a shabby brown coat and a checkered cap. Suddenly she realized they were exchanging a smile; there was nothing friendly about this smile, it was merely two cold flickers of recognition. But she was certain she had never seen him before.

He was standing next to an el[4] pillar, and as she crossed the street he turned and followed. He kept quite close; from the corner of her eye she watched his reflection wavering on the shopwindows.

Then in the middle of the block she stopped and faced him. He stopped also and cocked his head, grinning. But what could she say? Do? Here, in broad daylight, on Eighty-sixth Street? It was useless and, despising her own helplessness, she quickened her steps.

Now Second Avenue is a dismal street, made from scraps and ends; part cobblestone, part asphalt, part cement; and its atmosphere of desertion is permanent. Mrs. Miller walked five blocks without meeting anyone, and all the while the steady crunch of his footfalls in the snow stayed near. And when she came to a florist's shop, the sound was still with her. She hurried inside and watched through the glass door as the old man passed; he kept his eyes straight ahead and didn't slow his pace, but he did one strange, telling thing: he tipped his cap.

"Six white ones, did you say?" asked the florist. "Yes," she told him, "white roses."

3 From there she went to a glassware store and selected a vase, presumably a replacement for the one Miriam had broken, though the price was intolerable and the vase itself (she thought) grotesquely vulgar. But a series of unaccountable purchases had begun, as if by prearranged plan—a plan of which she had not the least knowledge or control.

She bought a bag of glazed cherries, and at a place called the Knickerbocker Bakery she paid forty cents for six almond cakes.

Within the last hour the weather had turned cold again; like blurred lenses, winter clouds cast a shade over the sun, and the skel-

4. **el:** elevated railroad.

AT A GLANCE

- Mrs. Miller has a strange dream, and when she wakes it is a lovely day.
- She goes shopping and encounters a strange old man.
- She buys white roses, a new vase, and the sweets she knows that Miriam likes.

1 FORESHADOWING

The dream is clearly about Miriam, and the effect of the dream is eerie, like Miriam herself.

2 THEME

Mrs. Miller is beginning to sense her loneliness. She sees herself as separate, even in the midst of a crowd.

3 SUSPENSE

The things that Mrs. Miller is buying are the things that Miriam asked for. The ambiguity of these events, which foreshadow Miriam's return, creates suspense.

GUIDED READING

LITERAL QUESTION

1a. What does Mrs. Miller buy at the florist? (She buys six white roses.)

INFERENTIAL QUESTION

1b. Why do you think she buys the roses? (Either subconsciously or mysteriously, she probably has bought the flowers for Miriam. The roses are white, like Miriam's hair. Also, the girl's comments made it clear that she despises *paper* flowers.)

AT A GLANCE

- Miriam comes back, telling Mrs. Miller that she has come to stay.
- Mrs. Miller goes to the neighbor's apartment in a panic to ask for help in getting rid of Miriam.

1 FORESHADOWING

The reader, as well as Mrs. Miller, knows that it is Miriam at the door.

2 CHARACTERIZATION

The reason is ambiguous, but it is clear that Mrs. Miller has managed to repress her deepest emotions and unresolved feelings.

3 DIALOGUE

The use of conversational language and run-on speech seems a shock after Mrs. Miller's surrealistic encounters with Miriam.

eton of an early dusk colored the sky; a damp mist mixed with the wind and the voices of a few children who romped high on mountains of gutter snow seemed lonely and cheerless. Soon the first flake fell, and when Mrs. Miller reached the brownstone house, snow was falling in a swift screen and foot tracks vanished as they were printed.

The white roses were arranged decoratively in the vase. The glazed cherries shone on a ceramic plate. The almond cakes, dusted with sugar, awaited a hand. The canary fluttered on its swing and picked at a bar of seed.

1 At precisely five the doorbell rang. Mrs. Miller *knew* who it was. The hem of her house coat trailed as she crossed the floor. "Is that you?" she called.

"Naturally," said Miriam, the word resounding shrilly from the hall. "Open this door."

"Go away," said Mrs. Miller.

"Please hurry—I have a heavy package."

"Go away," said Mrs. Miller. She returned to the living room, lighted a cigarette, sat down and calmly listened to the buzzer; on and on and on. "You might as well leave. I have no intention of letting you in."

Shortly the bell stopped. For possibly ten minutes Mrs. Miller did not move. Then, hearing no sound, she concluded Miriam had gone. She tiptoed to the door and opened it a sliver; Miriam was half reclining atop a cardboard box with a beautiful French doll cradled in her arms.

"Really, I thought you were never coming," she said peevishly. "Here, help me get this in, it's awfully heavy."

It was not spell-like compulsion that Mrs. Miller felt, but rather a curious passivity; she brought in the box, Miriam the doll. Miriam curled up on the sofa, not troubling to remove her coat or beret, and watched disinterestedly as Mrs. Miller dropped the box and stood trembling, trying to catch her breath.

"Thank you," she said. In the daylight she looked pinched and drawn, her hair less luminous. The French doll she was loving wore an exquisite powdered wig and its idiot glass eyes sought solace in Miriam's. "I have a surprise," she continued. "Look into my box."

Kneeling, Mrs. Miller parted the flaps and lifted out another doll; then a blue dress which she recalled as the one Miriam had worn that first night at the theater; and of the remainder she said, "It's all clothes. Why?"

"Because I've come to live with you," said Miriam, twisting a cherry stem. "Wasn't it nice of you to buy me the cherries—"

"But you can't! Go away—go away and leave me alone!"

"—and the roses and the almond cakes? How really wonderfully generous. You know, these cherries are delicious. The last place I lived was with an old man; he was terribly poor and we never had good things to eat. But I think I'll be happy here." She paused to snuggle her doll closer. "Now, if you'll just show
2 me where to put my things . . . ."

Mrs. Miller's face dissolved into a mask of ugly red lines; she began to cry, and it was an unnatural, tearless sort of weeping, as though, not having wept for a long time, she had forgotten how. Carefully she edged backward till she touched the door.

She fumbled through the hall and down the stairs to a landing below. She pounded frantically on the door of the first apartment she came to; a short, redheaded man answered and
3 she pushed past him. "Say, what is this?" he said. "Anything wrong, lover?" asked a young woman who appeared from the kitchen, drying her hands. And it was to her that Mrs. Miller turned.

"Listen," she cried, "I'm ashamed behaving this way, but—well, I'm Mrs. H. T. Miller and I live upstairs and"—she pressed her hands over her face—"it sounds so absurd. . . ."

The woman guided her to a chair, while the man excitedly rattled pocket change. "Yeah?"

"I live upstairs and there's a little girl visiting me, and I suppose that I'm afraid of her. She won't leave and I can't make her and—she's going to do something terrible. She's al-

GUIDED READING

LITERAL QUESTION

1a. What did Mrs. Miller feel when she opened the door a sliver? (She felt a curious passivity.)

INFERENTIAL QUESTION

1b. What does this feeling tell you about Mrs. Miller? (She is not acting out of compulsion, and yet she does not seem to have the power to resist. It is as if she is an observer of her own life.)

ready stolen my cameo, but she's about to do something worse—something terrible!"

The man asked, "Is she a relative, huh?"

Mrs. Miller shook her head. "I don't know who she is. Her name's Miriam, but I don't know for certain who she is."

"You gotta calm down, honey," said the woman, stroking Mrs. Miller's arm. "Harry here'll tend to this kid. Go on, lover." And Mrs. Miller said, "The door's open—5A."

After the man left, the woman brought a towel and bathed Mrs. Miller's face. "You're very kind," Mrs. Miller said. "I'm sorry to act like such a fool, only this wicked child. . . ."

"Sure, honey," consoled the woman. "Now, you better take it easy."

Mrs. Miller rested her head in the crook of her arm; she was quiet enough to be asleep. The woman turned a radio dial; a piano and a husky voice filled the silence and the woman, tapping her foot, kept excellent time. "Maybe we oughta go up too," she said.

"I don't want to see her again. I don't want to be anywhere near her."

"Uh huh, but what you shoulda done, you shoulda called a cop."

Presently they heard the man on the stairs. He strode into the room frowning and scratching the back of his neck. "Nobody there," he said, honestly embarrassed. "She musta beat it."

1 "Harry, you're a jerk," announced the woman. "We been sitting here the whole time and we woulda seen . . ." She stopped abruptly, for the man's glance was sharp.

"I looked all over," he said, "and there just ain't nobody there. Nobody, understand?"

"Tell me," said Mrs. Miller, rising, "tell me, did you see a large box? Or a doll?"

"No, ma'am, I didn't."

And the woman, as if delivering a verdict, said, "Well, for cryinoutloud. . . ."

Mrs. Miller entered her apartment softly; she walked to the center of the room and stood quite still. No, in a sense it had not changed: the roses, the cakes, and the cherries were in place. But this was an empty room, emptier than if the furnishings and familiars were not present, lifeless and petrified as a funeral parlor. The sofa loomed before her with a new strangeness: its vacancy had a meaning that would have been less penetrating and terrible had Miriam been curled on it. She gazed fixedly at the space where she remembered setting the box and for a moment the hassock spun desperately. And she looked through the window; surely the river was real, surely snow was falling. But then one could not be certain witness to anything: Miriam, so vividly *there* . . . and yet, where was she? Where, where?

As though moving in a dream, she sank to a chair. The room was losing shape; it was dark and getting darker and there was nothing to be done about it; she could not lift her hand to
2 light a lamp.

Suddenly, closing her eyes, she felt an upward surge, like a diver emerging from some deeper, greener depth. In times of terror or immense distress there are moments when the mind waits, as though for a revelation, while a skein of calm is woven over thought; it is like sleep, or a supernatural trance; and during this lull one is aware of a force of quiet reasoning:
3 well, what if she had never really known a girl named Miriam? That she had been foolishly frightened on the street? In the end, like everything else, it was of no importance. For the only thing she had lost to Miriam was her identity, but now she knew she had found again the person who lived in this room, who cooked her own meals, who owned a canary, who was someone she could trust and believe in: Mrs. H. T. Miller.

Listening in contentment, she became aware of a double sound: a bureau drawer opening and closing; she seemed to hear it long after completion—opening and closing.
4 Then gradually the harshness of it was replaced by the murmur of a silk dress and this, delicately faint, was moving nearer and swelling in intensity till the walls trembled with the vibration and the room was caving under a wave of whispers. Mrs. Miller stiffened and opened her eyes to a dull, direct stare.

"Hello," said Miriam.

AT A GLANCE

- The neighbor goes up to look for Miriam, but nobody is there.
- Mrs. Miller goes back to her room and thinks that she only imagined the child.
- Just when she relaxes with that idea, Miriam reappears.

1 CONFLICT

The neighbor thinks Harry did not look carefully, but Harry's sharp glance is a signal to her. Harry thinks Mrs. Miller is crazy, but he does not want to say it.

2 FIGURATIVE LANGUAGE

The image of a diver emerging from the depths suggests waking up from a nightmare or coming out of a trance. The author wants to create a sense of relief here to set up the reversal in the last line of the story.

3 CHARACTERIZATION

Mrs. Miller returns to the businesslike character of the story's beginning. For this brief flash she is her old self once again.

4 FIGURATIVE LANGUAGE

The ebb and flow of the imagery parallels the emotional upheaval Mrs. Miller is feeling. Contentment is disrupted by harshness, a murmur becomes a wave. She goes from feeling soothed to feeling stiff. The author sets the scene for the ending of the story.

REFLECTING ON THE STORY

Why do you think Mrs. Miller is both attracted to Miriam and afraid of her? (She is attracted because Miriam fills a void in her life. But she is afraid because she knows or at least suspects that Miriam may be a figment of her own imagination—an indication that Mrs. Miller may be losing her grip on reality.)

GUIDED READING

LITERAL QUESTION

1a. When Mrs. Miller returns to her room, what does it remind her of? (a funeral parlor)

INFERENTIAL QUESTION

1b. Why do you think the emptiness bothers her? (She is terribly lonely. If Miriam is an illusion, then Mrs. Miller's loneliness is reality.)

STUDY QUESTIONS

1. well-off widow, narrow interests, clean apartment, no friends, seldom far from home, seldom spontaneous; at movies
2. long, silver hair, same name as Mrs. Miller; white silk; likes apartment, blue favorite color, imitations sad, wants to hear canary sing, asks for milk and sandwich, demands brooch; breaks vase
3. girl in bridal gown leading gray procession down mountain
4. stooped, bowlegged, shabby, old; unaccountable purchases: roses, vase, cherries, almond cakes
5. rings bell, waits; nothing; they would have seen her go
6. her identity; her identity
7. eats sandwiches, breaks vase, takes brooch; looks, name, finding Mrs. Miller, disappearance, reappearance; Miriam will take over
8. self-sufficient, self-contained, lonely; surprise, annoyance, fear; things Miriam asked for; she expected, prepared for her
9. old man she lived with; no
10. Possible answer: She is more alive because of contact.
11. Answers will vary. The dream could be foreshadowing; no; draw own conclusions
12. Answers will vary. Students might note lack of strong sense of identity.

LITERARY FOCUS

1. ■ Who is Miriam? Where does she come from? Is she real?
   ■ answers to these questions
2. Miriam's unusual manner, speech, dress; same name as Mrs. Miller; having never been to movies; old man; unaccountable purchases
3. momentarily relaxed; we believe that nightmare is over

STUDY QUESTIONS

Recalling

1. What does the opening paragraph tell us about Mrs. Miller's living conditions, interests, and activities? How does she meet Miriam?
2. What is unusual about Miriam's appearance and her name? What kind of dress does Miriam wear on her first visit to Mrs. Miller's apartment? What comments and requests does she make? What does she do when Mrs. Miller will not kiss her good night?
3. What dream does Mrs. Miller have?
4. Describe the man whom Mrs. Miller encounters on her shopping trip. What purchases does she make on her trip?
5. Explain how Miriam gains access to Mrs. Miller's apartment at five o'clock. What does Mrs. Miller's neighbor discover when he goes up to Mrs. Miller's apartment? According to his girlfriend, why would it have been impossible for anyone to have "beat it"?
6. According to the final paragraphs, what had Mrs. Miller "lost" to Miriam? What has she found again when Miriam departs?

Interpreting

7. What evidence suggests that Miriam is real? That she is a figment of Mrs. Miller's imagination? What do the last two paragraphs imply about Mrs. Miller's future relationship with the girl?
8. Describe the kind of life Mrs. Miller led before meeting Miriam, and explain what might prompt her initial kindness to the girl. Explain the relevance of the things Mrs. Miller purchases on her shopping trip. Why is her reluctance to open the door for Miriam ironic?
9. What might be the relationship between Miriam and the old man whom Mrs. Miller encounters on the street? Can we be sure?
10. Has Miriam's appearance had any positive effects on Mrs. Miller? Explain.
11. Interpret Mrs. Miller's dream and the general significance Miriam might have in her life. Is there one interpretation to this story? What does the story force the reader to do?

Extending

12. Despite its ambiguity and elements of fantasy, what does this story suggest to you about people and the way they behave?

LITERARY FOCUS

Suspense and Foreshadowing

Suspense is that quality in a story that makes us uncertain or tense about the outcome of events. As readers, we want to know what will happen next and if a character will be saved or lost, happy or unhappy.

There are two types of suspense. In the first and most common we do not know the outcome of events, and the suspense is a matter of plot—*what* will happen. In the second type the outcome is inevitable: We know the plot, but the suspense is a matter of the author's style and characterizations—*how* things will happen.

Many different elements help to create suspense. Characters may not possess some important information: Will they learn the truth? Characters may not possess some important object: Will they obtain it? Writers sometimes increase suspense by the use of **foreshadowing**—presenting events or characters in such a way as to hint at what is going to happen to them.

Thinking About Suspense and Foreshadowing

1. What questions draw us into "Miriam"? What information is withheld from us?
2. Find examples of foreshadowing in the story.
3. What happens to the tension in the story when Miriam leaves the apartment? Why?

COMPOSITION

Writing About Theme

■ Write a brief composition on the theme of "Miriam." Before writing, review the plot, and list the major events. Determine the significance of each major event, and look for the development of a theme. State the theme clearly. Then, using examples from the story, show how the theme is revealed through characterization, setting, plot, point of view, and tone. *For help with this assignment, refer to Lesson 6 in the Writing About Literature Handbook at the back of this book.*

Narrating a Scene

■ Narrate a scene in which unexplainable events occur to an ordinary person. First present the person, as Capote does in the first paragraph of "Miriam." Then begin the action, first with normal activity. Gradually introduce events that baffle the character and the reader.

COMPOSITION: GUIDELINES FOR EVALUATION

WRITING ABOUT THEME

Objective

To write about theme

Guidelines for Evaluation

- suggested length: five to six paragraphs
- should state the theme of the story
- should state importance of each major event
- should show how the theme is developed
- should cite examples from the story

NARRATING A SCENE

Objective

To write an eerie story

Guidelines for Evaluation

- suggested length: five to nine paragraphs
- should describe a character
- should show the character engaged in normal activities
- should show the character coping with strange and unexplained events

A. C. Greene *born 1923*

A. C. Greene has been writing about Texas since he joined the staff of his hometown newspaper, the *Abilene Reporter-News*, in 1948. He has taught and headed the department of journalism at Hardin-Simmons University, the University of Texas at Austin, and Southern Methodist University while also perfecting his craft as a columnist, editor, television producer, and news commentator. The titles of some of Greene's books show where his heart and interests lie: *Living Texas: A Gathering of Experiences* (1970), *Growing Up in Texas* (1972), *Views in Texas* (1974), and *The Book of Dallas* (1976).

■ Two of the characters in "The Girl at Cabe Ranch" both love and hate the dry ranch country that is the story's setting. What do they hate about it? What do they find to love?

A. C. Greene

The Girl at Cabe Ranch

The road turned into a puzzle of trails going off left and right. I asked the boy, Harris, if he knew which was which and he shook his head, yes.

The woman at the Chamber of Commerce back in Toller said Harris knew the country better than anybody except Uncle Bartlett, whoever that was.

"I don't see how you can tell these ruts apart," I said to the boy as we bounced along in the pickup.

"Just know 'em," he said.

1 I had picked a bad day in a bad month in a bad season to make the trip. Fifteenth of July. It couldn't have been hotter and it couldn't have been drier. One of the ranchers in Toller said if it rained now all the cows would die from fright. Why had Uncle Sam picked such places for western history, or why had I picked western history as my field when there are so many more timely and relevant disciplines?

After the Chamber of Commerce woman recommended him I found Harris and we made a deal. He said we'd better go in his old pickup truck, the roads might be a little hard on my Chrysler. I thought about the Chrysler now, parked at the courthouse square, its air conditioner doing me no good.

We went north out of Toller on the state high-
2 way, across a wide, hot mesquite[1] prairie. The tires on the concrete highway sounded to me like sizzling flesh and went bumpity-bump, bumpity-bump as they hit the tar-filled joints. The sound took the place of the conversation I wasn't having with Harris.

---

1. **mesquite** [mes kēt′]: small, thorny tree that grows in desert regions of the southwestern United States.

AT A GLANCE

- The narrator, a historian, has hired a young man named Harris to take him to his destination.
- They are traveling in Harris's pickup truck on a hot, dry July 15.

LITERARY OPTIONS

- setting
- characterization

THEMATIC OPTIONS

- attachment to home
- security vs. adventure

1 SETTING

The hot, dry, empty Texas ranchland has drawn the narrator back. It has dominated his life, by influencing his choice of professions; it also dominates the other characters' lives.

2 STYLE: FIGURES OF SPEECH

The simile comparing the sound of the tires to sizzling flesh underscores how hot and dry the weather is.

GUIDED READING

LITERAL QUESTION

1a. What does the narrator say is his field of work? (western history)

INFERENTIAL QUESTION

1b. What can you infer about his destination? (He is going to visit a historical site.)

AT A GLANCE

- The narrator discusses the Cabes with Harris and thinks how he was born less than fifty miles from the Cabe ranch.
- He thinks about how he left this part of the country twenty-five years ago.
- He mistakes the foreman's house for the Cabe house; Harris drives on.

1 CHARACTERIZATION

The description—especially the comparison to the famous picture—reflects the young man's intensity.

2 STYLE: DESCRIPTION

The description emphasizes the spare, monochromatic, monotonous nature of the landscape.

3 THEME

The narrator's contentment arises from his sense of being at home after a long absence.

4 CHARACTERIZATION

Harris's appearance suggests that he takes pride in the way he looks.

The ranch road turned off the highway ten miles out of town, and now we had driven another five or so over Cabe ranch land.

"I don't see any cattle," I said.

1 The boy didn't answer but kept glaring down the road like that old picture of the heroic railroad engineer in a storm you used to see.

I hadn't been told the boy's full name. Just Harris. Something Harris or Harris Something; the woman at the Chamber of Commerce didn't say and neither did Harris.

He looked to be about twenty. He might have been a little older. The older I get the less I can tell ages, especially younger ages.

"Any of the Cabes live out here?" I asked.

"Mart Cabe does," he said.

"I don't think I'd want to live out here, even if I owned it all," I said.

"He doesn't own it all. He's got two brothers own part of it."

"Well, I wouldn't want to live on it if I had ten brothers."

"He's just got two."

I told myself I had asked for that comeback, but I knew Harris hadn't meant it as a retort. There was no need for me to be so damned contemptuous of this country. It was mine, too, or I was its. I was born less than fifty miles from the Cabe ranch.

But something had gone different in me, and where boys like Harris whoever-he-was had taken up 4H clubs and horses, I'd taken up history and books. Pretty soon they couldn't understand me and my history books, and I didn't try to understand them and their horses. So I left. That had been a long time ago. Twenty-five years ago, at least. A long time to be away and come back.

The sun was shining from all directions. The
2 ground was red and dusty, the grass was brown and dusty; but then, "brown is the natural condition of the grass," an old emigrants' guide once said of this country.

The land rolled away in hills which fell into breaks and draws. You could see for miles. It was all rocks and grass and red clay dirt and the only trees were mesquite bushes, seldom taller than a man—and the ranchers killed even those because they kept the brown grass from growing.

3 But I found myself settling into an excited sort of contentment as I rode with the boy, letting him pick out the way from among these twisting, all-alike trails. I breathed deep, feeling the hot, dry air going down into my lungs. The air is the best thing about that country, to me.

The boy was wearing an old Stetson Double X with the wings folded up rodeo style. When I was a boy a rancher wouldn't have been caught dead wearing his Stetson that way. Television even
4 tells the cowboys how to dress. Harris was nice looking, neat around the neck, and his hair clean. He had to have some pride to keep his hair washed, working on the ranches away from everybody like he did.

"Is that the Cabe house over there?" I pointed to a gray, wooden structure, needing paint, with a lone tree beside it.

"That's the Mulkeys'. Mr. Mulkey's the foreman." The boy looked over at the Mulkey house. "The Cabe house is a lot nicer."

We drove around the gray house. A television aerial rose above it and a red Ford was parked in the carport. With a few neighbors and a coat of paint the whole scene would have fit neatly in a suburb. A woman waved at us.

"We going to stop?" I asked as the boy slowed down.

"Not unless you want to," he said.

I laughed. "You're the boss, Harris. You're taking me where we're going."

We didn't stop. The road, if you want to call it that, circled the house and went into a big pasture behind it. We came out of the pasture through a cattle guard, then dropped down the side of a hill and were alone again. Hot it was, but magnificent it was, too. You could turn in any direction and see no trace of the hand of man—except for our pickup truck.

About two miles from the foreman's house the ruts parted like railroad tracks at a switch. One set went right, through a tall gate with a sign on it: Horsetail Ranch. We took that one.

"The name sounds like a dude ranch," I commented as we started down this new branch of

GUIDED READING

LITERAL QUESTIONS

1a. How long has the narrator been away? (twenty-five years)

2a. According to the narrator, what is the best thing about the country? (the air)

INFERENTIAL QUESTIONS

1b. Why has he stayed away so long? (He probably feels he does not belong there.)

2b. What does this comment suggest about his relationship to his former home? (He still appreciates things about it and takes nourishment from it.)

the road. Once again my humor failed to reach Harris.

"Horsetail's a big outfit. The Cabes've got land all the way into Young County."

1 Sometimes I would lose all traces of the road as the entire landscape turned into a brown panorama. Here and there another set of tracks would spill off, disappearing into the grass like a ship's wake. Then we came to a level stretch and I could see tall, green trees about a mile ahead.

"That must be the river," I said, more or less to myself.

"That's the Clear Fork," the boy said. "It runs all year."

"Is it drinkable?"

"Reckon so. I've done it enough. Gets gyppy when it's low. Drains from the gyp[2] beds out on the Plains." He paused, then asked, "You thirsty?"

Before I could answer he said, "We'll stop by the house and get a drink. They've got a good well."

The Cabe ranch house surprised me. I was prepared for something like the foreman's house or possibly something huge and Victorian out of a western movie. It was neither. It had age and dignity and that unexpected beauty one finds now and then left from the frontier. It was tall
2 and stood high off the ground. It was built of rock, old and carefully masoned. A square cupola surmounted the roof, and there were six tall, slender chimneys, three on the east, three on the west, standing in rows. A white, wooden fence was around the yard and four lines of old, big trees outlined the rectangle of land where the house stood.

"That is tremendous," I said in admiration.

Harris drove the pickup to the back door and honked the horn, then got out. "We'll go in," he said.

An old brown hound yelped and barked at us from inside the fence as we walked up to the gate. The boy leaned over and unlatched the gate from the inside and said something to the old hound. He waited to snap the latch on the gate after I went through as though I wouldn't know how.

We walked up to the big, deep porch along the back side of the house. The door opened and a blond-headed girl came out, looked at me, then at the boy.

"Hello," she said.

"Hello, Sid," he said back. "How about some water?"

She looked at me without answering him.

"Oh. This is Dr. Powell." He made a motion toward me.

"I'm Sidonie Cabe," she said, deciding to hold out her hand. It wasn't hard and dry like some country hands are from work and weather. But then, it wasn't soft and moist either.

3 She was a good-looking girl. About eighteen, I guessed. She had on shorts, and her long, slim legs were brown. She was barefoot and her toenails were painted bright red. It looked freshly done.

"Come in," she said. "Mother and Sis are over at the Fultons'. I'm here by myself."

"Where's your dad?" the boy asked.

---

2. **gyp** [jip]: short for the mineral gypsum.

AT A GLANCE

- They take the road to the Cabe ranch house and stop at the house for a drink of water.
- Harris introduces the narrator, Dr. Powell, to Sidonie Cabe, an attractive eighteen-year-old.
- Sid tells them she is home alone.

1 STYLE: FIGURES OF SPEECH

The simile comparing the disappearing road to a ship's wake suggests that the land has much of the same vastness and emptiness as an ocean.

2 SYMBOL

The strength and beauty of the house in the vast grassland is a concrete symbol of home.

3 COMPARISON

Sid, like Harris, is good-looking and well groomed.

GUIDED READING

LITERAL QUESTION

1a. Before Powell can answer Harris's question as to whether he is thirsty, what does Harris say? ("We'll stop by the house and get a drink.")

INFERENTIAL QUESTION

1b. What does this quick response imply? (Harris is anxious to stop at the house.)

AT A GLANCE

- Powell says that he is researching the old fort nearby.
- Sid brings them cold water to drink.

1 **POINT OF VIEW**

The first-person narrator draws us into the story through a personal confidence.

"He's gone to Denver to an auction. He and Zene Mulkey flew."

"It's a little lonesome out here by yourself, isn't it?" I asked.

"She doesn't mind," Harris said to me, then to her, "Dr. Powell's from California. He's come out to see the fort."

"Are you a history teacher?" she asked.

"Sometimes," I said. "Right now I'm writing a book on some of the old outposts in this part of the country. Doing research."

"Oh," she said, and gave a little shrug. "I'll fix some cold water."

We went into a big room that opened off the kitchen. There was a well at one end of the room and the wall of the kitchen was rock.

"This used to be the sleeping porch a long time ago. Before air conditioning," the boy said. "Mr. Cabe says the well was enclosed because of the Indians."

1 I doubted this but didn't say anything. You learn not to disturb family legends when you're a historian. It looked to me as if the well had been dug close to the house for convenience and whoever added the porch room enclosed it for the same reason.

The girl brought out a big enamel pitcher of ice water with some glasses. Suddenly I felt as if I could drink it all.

"I've lost my hump," I said, over my third glass.

"Your hump?" the girl looked toward me.

"That's what we used to say when I was a kid. Your hump was what kept you from getting thirsty. We thought a camel's hump was full of water."

GUIDED READING

LITERAL QUESTION

1a. When Powell asks Sid whether she is lonesome, what answer does he get? (Harris says, "She doesn't mind.")

INFERENTIAL QUESTION

1b. What does this answer reveal about the young couple? (Harris is presumptuous in speaking for Sid, but she does not contradict him. He seems to know her well.)

"Did you live out here?"

1 "I was born in Taylor County."

"You don't live there now though, do you?"

"No. I left to go to college and never moved back."

"Mr. Cabe says the stone for this house came from the old fort," the boy interjected.

"I was wondering if it didn't," I said.

"There's some frosted glass around the front door that's supposed to be from the fort, too," the girl said.

"How far is the fort from here?" I asked.

"Not far. Just across the river over there," the girl said, pointing out the direction of the back door.

"Can we drive it?" I asked.

The boy answered. "No, you've got to wade the river. Road's been washed out for years."

2 The girl turned to him coldly. "You can drive there, too. You can go through the Lambert and drive there. You just came the wrong way to get there in an automobile."

The boy grinned. "We're not in an 'automobile.' We're in a pickup."

"All right, or in a pickup either." She reached out a bare, red-toed foot and kicked at a magazine. She must have been reading it when we drove up.

"It's pretty over there," she said, not looking at either of us but concentrating on the movement of the magazine with her toe. "I go there all
3 the time. Ride over. Especially the graveyard. Down where Spring Creek runs into the Clear Fork. Daddy says it's dangerous because of the copperheads but I go there anyway."

"It's too hot," the boy said. "Too hot and muggy." He looked toward me. "The fort's on a flat that backs up against the hill. It's a lot lower than it is here. It doesn't get any breeze."

"Yes," I smiled in historical superiority, "General Pomeroy used to complain in his letters to his wife about how hot it got. 'Sweaty as a well,' he wrote to her."

The girl looked up. "Was General Pomeroy really at this fort . . . the famous one?"

"He was commander here just before the Civil War. Spent nearly two years."

"Well, good," she smiled. "I've lived here all my life and I never have known for sure. I thought it was just a kind of legend."

"I knew it," the boy said, without looking at her.

"General Pomeroy might have spent a lot of his time right where we're sitting," I said. "He wrote his wife that when the nights were too hot, he'd take his gear to what he called 'the Red Bluff beyond the River' and sleep."

"I know where that is," the girl said. "It's the place around behind the cowsheds. It's real high above the river."

"That may be the spot," I told her. "Of course, in a hundred and some-odd years things can change a lot. The river may have cut the bluff down years ago."

"It doesn't change that much around here," she said. "Nothing does."

"I don't think that's the bluff," the boy said.

"Why?" she turned toward him fiercely. "You don't know anything about it. Dr. Powell said it was. He knows a lot more about it than you do. You're just an . . . an ignorant cowboy," she bit her lower lip, "that's all you are. You don't want to be anything else."

"I still don't think that's the bluff," the boy said, not looking at her. "General Pomeroy would have had to come plumb around to the shallows to get across. He wouldn't have walked that far just for a cool place to sleep."

4 "He had a horse," she said tautly.

"He wouldn't have saddled up a horse just for that."

"Things were different then. He had aides and servants to saddle his horse. You heard what Dr. Powell said. The river might have been different."

She looked at me as if she were demanding I support her statement.

I ducked out. "All he wrote his wife was that he oftentimes took his bedroll and spent the night on the red bluff beyond the river. I just assumed it might be here, if the fort lies below this land."

The girl looked at the boy sullenly. When she turned back to me I could see tears gathering on

AT A GLANCE

- Powell tells Sid that he left to go to college and never returned.
- Harris tells Powell that they cannot drive to the fort because the road has been washed out, but Sid tells them there is another way to drive there.
- Sid and Harris argue over which bluff General Pomeroy used to sleep on before the Civil War.

1 DIALOGUE

Harris quickly changes the subject when Powell talks about how he left home to go to college and never returned. This dialogue implies that Sid might be having similar thoughts.

2 PLOT: RISING ACTION

Harris knows the land better than almost anyone else. He has come the wrong way on purpose.

3 CHARACTERIZATION

Sid's willingness to risk encountering copperheads is an indication of her lack of fear and of her feeling at home with the land.

4 CONFLICT

The argument that springs up over General Pomeroy suggests the tension between Harris and Sid. They seem willing to argue over nearly anything.

GUIDED READING

LITERAL QUESTIONS

1a. Why can Powell and Harris not get to the fort? (The road has been washed out for years.)

2a. What does Sid call Harris? ("an ignorant cowboy")

INFERENTIAL QUESTIONS

1b. What does this information suggest about the reason for the trip to the ranch? (Harris probably has come to see Sid.)

2b. Why does she say this? (She is probably angry and frustrated that Harris is not what she wants him to be.)

AT A GLANCE

- When Sid states her desire to leave, Powell tells how Pomeroy's son brought his bride there.
- The bride went back to Virginia to have a baby; Sid says she would have got a divorce.
- Sid and Harris argue over whether or not she really wants to go.
- She tells Powell that she would marry Harris if he were different.

1 CONTRAST

Harris sees Sid as being strong and loyal, unlike the weak woman who went back to Virginia to have her baby.

2 CHARACTERIZATION

Harris is confident and believes he knows Sid well. When she states that she will go away and get married, he just grins.

3 CONFLICT

Sid reveals her internal conflict. She wants more out of life and scorns Harris's desire to stay on the land, but she also loves him.

the bottom rims of her deep blue eyes.

"Do you write for the movies or TV, Dr. Powell?" she asked.

"No, just history books. I don't even write historical novels."

"And you've come all the way out here just to write a history book?"

"Partly. It's sort of a homecoming for me, coming from near here. I've got to go other places, too."

"If I left here I'd never come back," she said. "I wouldn't come back to write a book or do anything else. I'd go away and I'd stay wherever it was I went."

"Why, this is wonderful country, Miss Cabe," I said. "The old fort over there, just across the river . . . it has a lot of romance connected to it. General Pomeroy's son Catlett brought his beautiful young bride here on their honeymoon. She was daughter of the governor of Virginia."

"He brought her here to live?" the girl asked.

"Yes, and she was just about your age. Cat Pomeroy was a soldier, too. A lieutenant under his father."

"I'd die before I'd let a man bring me to a place like this," she said.

"Well, I'll admit, she didn't stay long. She went back to Virginia."

"Did she divorce him?"

"Oh, no. She just went back there to have a baby and live while her husband was on frontier duty."

"I'd have divorced him," the girl said firmly.

1 "You wouldn't have done any such thing," the boy said suddenly. "You'd have come out here and lived at that fort with him and liked it, heat and all. And you wouldn't have run back to Virginia just to have a baby, neither."

She shook her head violently. "I would have, and someday when I leave I'll show you. I'll never set foot here again."

The boy watched her. "You couldn't do that. You can't even spend a weekend in Dallas without wanting to come back. Your daddy told me so. He said, 'I can't get a room on the west side of the hotel or old Sid'll spend all her time gazing out the window tryin' to see home."

She was crying. "That's a lie you made up. Every word of it. It's Daddy wants to come back early. Not me."

"And you wait," the boy continued, "when you go off to that girls' college this fall, you'll be home Christmas and you'll say, 'Oh, Harris, I don't want to go back.' You'll flat hate it, being gone from here."

2 "I won't!" she was crying hard. "I'll go away and get married to somebody in another place. Anywhere but here."

The boy watched her. They acted as if they were going to do something more, but finally the boy stood up and grinned.

"Well, I guess we better get going."

"I suppose we'd better," I said, standing also. I felt to blame for the little domestic quarrel, as it were. "Thanks again for the water, Miss Cabe," I said. "You saved our lives."

Harris stood there running his tongue over his lips. "All right," he said, then turned to me and motioned, "come on," and walked out the door.

"I'm sorry, Sid," I said. "I didn't mean to start a fuss between you and Harris."

She shook her head, and her hair fell golden around her face. She wiped her tears away with her bare hand, pushing her hair back at the same time.

"You didn't start anything, Dr. Powell. You just got in on something. You better go on before he runs off and leaves you." She tossed her head

3 and looked at me. "He's just a cowboy. All he thinks about is land and cattle. That's all he wants out of life. Just like my daddy. He won't even get any more education. Thinks he knows everything he needs to know." She looked at me sadly. "I'd marry him if he was different."

I took her hand, "Goodbye, Sid."

"Come back again sometime," she said, sniffing.

The boy was seated in the pickup when I walked out. His rodeo hat was pushed down on his forehead.

"Why don't we wade across from here?" I asked.

"Naw. Get in. We'll drive."

GUIDED READING

LITERAL QUESTIONS

1a. What does Harris say that Sid cannot do? (spend a whole weekend in Dallas without wanting to come home)

2a. How does Sid answer Harris's assertion? ("That's a lie you made up.")

INFERENTIAL QUESTIONS

1b. What is he suggesting? (Sid loves the land as much as he does and can never leave it.)

2b. Why does she react so strongly? (She seems to realize that Harris is right, although she does not want him to be.)

"I thought you couldn't get there driving?"

"You can if you go through the Lambert."

"Have we got time?"

"It's not far. It's no further than through the Cabe if you start for there in the first place."

I smiled. "There must not be any cute girls at the Lambert ranch."

My humor failed again. "There isn't anything at the Lambert but cattle and cowmen," he said. "It's a big spread. A genuine ranch, not anything TV dreamed up. I'll guarantee you, I'd like to think I'd ever run something just half as big as the Lambert."

I decided I'd better make my amends to the boy, too.

"Harris," I said, "I apologize for what happened. I didn't realize I would bring up a sore subject, telling about the old fort."

"You didn't. We go through it all the time. In fact, you might have done her some good. That
1 story about the general's son bringing his bride out here . . . she'll go to thinking about it and next time I see her, she'll be telling me how much tougher she is than some Virginia aristocrat." He nodded his head in a strong affirmative. "And, by God, she is."

He wheeled the pickup around and we bounced down another gravelly hill to take up the pursuit of a pair of faint creases in the dry grass. It didn't look like a road to me. But the boy knew where he was going. I leaned back and let him drive.

STUDY QUESTIONS

Recalling

1. What brings Dr. Powell to the area of Cabe Ranch? How long has he been away?
2. How does Dr. Powell feel as he and Harris drive to the Cabe Ranch?
3. What surprises Dr. Powell about the Cabes' ranch house?
4. What does Dr. Powell tell Sid and Harris about General Pomeroy? What does he tell them about Pomeroy's son, Cat?
5. What happened to Cat Pomeroy's wife?
6. Where is Sid going in the fall? Does she plan to return?
7. What does Sid say to Dr. Powell about Harris?
8. How does Harris think the story of Cat Pomeroy's wife will affect Sid?

Interpreting

9. Why did Dr. Powell leave Taylor County?
10. What is the relationship between Sid and Harris?
11. What evidence does Harris provide to demonstrate that Sid loves her home?
12. Harris says that Sid is stronger than any Virginia aristocrat. Why does she need strength?

Extending

13. At the end of the story, Dr. Powell says that Harris knows where he is going. What does Harris want from life? What characteristics will help him reach his goals?

AT A GLANCE

- When Powell apologizes to Harris, he replies that the conflict is nothing new and that Powell's story may actually have done some good.
- They drive on toward the fort.

1 CHARACTERIZATION

Harris's concluding words show his understanding of the girl as well as his admiration for her.

REFLECTING ON THE STORY

What does the narrator mean when he says that the boy "knew where he was going"? Explain your answer. (Students may suggest that the narrator means that the boy knows the roads but also knows exactly what he wants out of life and how to get it.)

STUDY QUESTIONS

1. research at an old fort; at least twenty-five years
2. excitedly content
3. its beauty
4. He slept on a bluff above the river; he brought his beautiful young wife to the fort.
5. She returned to Virginia.
6. college; no
7. He's just a cowboy who only thinks of land and cattle; just like her father; won't get any more education. She'd marry him if he were different.
8. She will decide that she's stronger than any Virginia aristocrat.
9. He didn't fit in; loved history and books instead of horses; didn't try to understand other boys.
10. They are in love, but Sid does not want to marry a cowboy like Harris.
11. can't spend a weekend in Dallas without wanting to come back
12. lonely, harsh life if she marries him
13. to run a big ranch, to marry Sid; pride, toughness, single-mindedness

AT A GLANCE

- Bet wakes her nine-year-old son Arnold, dresses him, and unsuccessfully tries to feed him breakfast.
- He becomes alarmed when she tells him they are going out.

LITERARY OPTIONS

- characterization
- stream of consciousness

THEMATIC OPTIONS

- endurance
- active participation vs. passive acceptance

1 CHARACTERIZATION

Arnold's too-clean clothes and lack of age-appropriate skills indicate that he is severely retarded.

2 SETTING

The brief description of their surroundings suggests that mother and son exist on the edge of poverty.

Anne Tyler *born 1941*

Anne Tyler's prose is as precise and orderly as her life. Tyler says that she writes every weekday from Monday to Thursday. On Friday she shops and does errands. Her precision allows her to pack her writing with a wealth of detail without losing the clear sense of the narrative. Tyler says that writing allows her to meet her readers on "neutral ground," to share a life that belongs to neither the writer nor the reader.

Tyler was born in Minnesota, grew up in North Carolina, and is considered a southern writer. Critics frequently compare her work with that of Eudora Welty and Carson McCullers. Her novels include *Searching for Caleb* (1975), *Dinner at the Homesick Restaurant* (1982), and *The Accidental Tourist* (1985). In her short stories Tyler often describes one day that in effect defines a character's entire life.

■ What do you know about the rest of Bet's life at the end of "Average Waves in Unprotected Waters"?

Anne Tyler

Average Waves in Unprotected Waters

As soon as it got light, Bet woke him and dressed him, and then she walked him over to the table and tried to make him eat a little cereal. He wouldn't, though. He could tell something was up. She pressed the edge of the spoon against his lips till she heard it click on his teeth, but he just looked off at a corner of the ceiling—a knobby child with great glassy eyes and her
1 own fair hair. Like any other nine-year-old, he wore a striped shirt and jeans, but the shirt was too neat and the jeans too blue, unpatched and unfaded, and would stay that way till he outgrew them. And his face was elderly—pinched, strained, tired—though it should have looked as unused as his jeans. He hardly ever changed his expression.

She left him in his chair and went to make the beds. Then she raised the yellowed shade, rinsed a few spoons in the bathroom sink, picked up some bits of magazines he'd torn the night before. This was a rented room in an ancient, crum-
2 bling house, and nothing you could do to it would lighten its cluttered look. There was always that feeling of too many lives layered over other lives, like the layers of brownish wallpaper her child had peeled away in the corner by his bed.

She slipped her feet into flat-heeled loafers and absently patted the front of her dress, a worn beige knit she usually saved for Sundays. Maybe she should take it in a little; it hung from her shoulders like a sack. She felt too slight and frail, too wispy for all she had to do today. But she reached for her coat anyhow, and put it on and tied a blue kerchief under her chin. Then she went over to the table and slowly spun, modeling the coat. "See, Arnold?" she said. "We're going out."

Arnold went on looking at the ceiling, but his gaze turned wild and she knew he'd heard.

She fetched his jacket from the closet—brown corduroy, with a hood. It had set her back

GUIDED READING

LITERAL QUESTION

1a. How does Bet feel as she pats the front of her dress? ("too slight and frail" for all she has to do)

INFERENTIAL QUESTION

1b. What does this comment suggest about the events to come? (They will require all her strength; they will be very difficult for her.)

1 half a week's salary. But Arnold didn't like it; he always wanted his old one, a little red duffel coat he'd long ago outgrown. When she came toward him, he started moaning and rocking and shaking his head. She had to struggle to stuff his arms in the sleeves. Small though he was, he was strong, wiry; he was getting to be too much for her. He shook free of her hands and ran over to his bed. The jacket was on, though. It wasn't buttoned,
2 the collar was askew, but never mind; that just made him look more real. She always felt bad at how he stood inside his clothes, separate from them, passive, unaware of all the buttons and snaps she'd fastened as carefully as she would a doll's.

She gave a last look around the room, checked to make sure the hot plate was off, and then picked up her purse and Arnold's suitcase. "Come along, Arnold," she said.

He came, dragging out every step. He looked at the suitcase suspiciously, but only because it was new. It didn't have any meaning for him. "See?" she said. "It's yours. It's Arnold's. It's going on the train with us."

But her voice was all wrong. He would pick it up, for sure. She paused in the middle of locking the door and glanced over at him fearfully. Anything could set him off nowadays. He hadn't noticed, though. He was too busy staring around the hallway, goggling at a freckled, walnut-framed mirror as if he'd never seen it before. She touched his shoulder. "Come, Arnold," she said.

They went down the stairs slowly, both of them clinging to the sticky mahogany railing. The suitcase banged against her shins. In the entrance hall, old Mrs. Puckett stood waiting outside her door—a huge, soft lady in a black crepe dress and orthopedic shoes. She was holding a plastic bag of peanut butter cookies, Arnold's fa-
3 vorites. There were tears in her eyes. "Here, Arnold," she said, quavering. Maybe she felt to blame that he was going. But she'd done the best she could: baby-sat him all these years and only given up when he'd grown too strong and wild to manage. Bet wished Arnold would give the old lady some sign—hug her, make his little crowing noise, just take the cookies, even. But he was too excited. He raced on out the front door, and it
4 was Bet who had to take them. "Well, thank you, Mrs. Puckett," she said. "I know he'll enjoy them later."

"Oh, no . . ." said Mrs. Puckett, and she flapped her large hands and gave up, sobbing.

They were lucky and caught a bus first thing. Arnold sat by the window. He must have thought he was going to work with her; when they passed the red-and-gold Kresge's sign, he jabbered and tried to stand up. "No, honey," she said, and took hold of his arm. He settled down then and let his hand stay curled in hers awhile. He had very small, cool fingers, and nails as smooth as thumbtack heads.

At the train station, she bought the tickets and then a pack of Wrigley's spearmint gum. Arnold stood gaping at the vaulted ceiling, with his head flopped back and his arms hanging limp at his sides. People stared at him. She would have liked to push their faces in. "Over here, honey," she said, and she nudged him toward the gate, straightening his collar as they walked.

He hadn't been on a train before and acted a little nervous, bouncing up and down in his seat and flipping the lid of his ashtray and craning forward to see the man ahead of them. When the train started moving, he crowed and pulled at her sleeve. "That's right, Arnold. Train. We're taking a trip," Bet said. She unwrapped a stick of chewing gum and gave it to him. He loved gum. If she didn't watch him closely, he sometimes swallowed it—which worried her a little because she'd heard it clogged your kidneys; but at least it would keep him busy. She looked down at the top of his head. Through the blond prickles of his hair, cut short for practical reasons, she could see his skull bones moving as he chewed. He was so thin-skinned, almost transparent; sometimes she imagined she could see the blood traveling in his veins.

When the train reached a steady speed, he grew calmer, and after a while he nodded over against her and let his hands sag on his knees. She watched his eyelashes slowly drooping—two colorless, fringed crescents, heavier and heavier, every now and then flying up as he tried to fight off sleep. He had never slept well, not ever, not

AT A GLANCE

- Bet struggles to get Arnold into his coat, and they set out.
- Mrs. Puckett tries to give Arnold cookies, but he ignores her.
- Bet and Arnold board the train, and the trip begins.

1 POINT OF VIEW

The third-person narration is limited to Bet and her thoughts, which center almost exclusively on Arnold—what he likes, what he wants, and how to manage him.

2 THEME

That Arnold stands "separate" from his clothes is a reflection both of his disability and of the strain that his condition puts upon the mother-child relationship.

3 CONFLICT

The encounter with Mrs. Puckett reveals the central problem of the plot: Arnold is being institutionalized because he is now too big and strong for Bet to manage at home.

4 CHARACTERIZATION

Bet's words to Mrs. Puckett show her awareness of others' feelings and her innate graciousness.

GUIDED READING

LITERAL QUESTIONS

1a. What does Bet wish Arnold would give Mrs. Puckett? (some sign such as a hug, his crowing noise, or taking the cookies)

2a. What does Bet want to do to the people who stare at Arnold? (push their faces in)

INFERENTIAL QUESTIONS

1b. Why might she feel that way? (She wants to make the old woman feel better.)

2b. What does this comment suggest about her? (She is maternal and fiercely protective of her son.)

AT A GLANCE

- Arnold sleeps, and Bet recalls how her husband left them.
- She thinks of her former life with her parents, now dead.
- When Arnold wakes, Bet wonders how to amuse him.
- The conductor confronts a woman who has no ticket.

1 PLOT: FLASHBACK

The sleeping Arnold triggers memories of an earlier time, before his disability was known. The flashback explains why Bet has been living alone with Arnold. Her husband, unable to accept the handicapped child, has left them.

2 STREAM OF CONSCIOUSNESS

Bet's wandering thoughts show how distraught she is. Her father's life was ruled by the sea. Her life is ruled by her son.

3 CHARACTERIZATION

Bet has been essentially passive, unable to take hold of life, which, like the sea, seems to slam into her. Her staunchness is apparent in her life to date with Arnold.

4 THEME

As the flashback concludes, Bet realizes that all her life she has simply endured for the sake of enduring.

even as a baby. Even before they'd noticed anything wrong, they'd wondered at his jittery, jerky catnaps, his tiny hands clutching tight and
1 springing open, his strange single wail sailing out while he went right on sleeping. Avery said it gave him the chills. And after the doctor talked to them Avery wouldn't have anything to do with Arnold anymore—just walked in wide circles around the crib, looking stunned and sick. A few weeks later, he left. She wasn't surprised. She even knew how he felt, more or less. Halfway, he blamed her; halfway, he blamed himself. You can't believe a thing like this will just fall on you out of nowhere.

She'd had moments herself of picturing some kind of evil gene in her husband's ordinary, stocky body—a dark little egg like a black jelly bean, she imagined it. All his fault. But other times she was sure the gene was hers. It seemed so natural; she never could do anything as well as most people. And then other times she blamed their marriage. They'd married too young, against her parents' wishes. All she'd wanted was to get away from home. Now she couldn't remember why. What was wrong with home? She thought of her parents' humped green trailer, perched on cinder blocks near a forest of masts in Salt Spray, Maryland. At this distance (parents dead, trailer rusted to bits, even Salt Spray changed past recognition), it seemed to her that her old life had been beautifully free and spacious. She closed her eyes and saw wide gray
2 skies. Everything had been ruled by the sea. Her father (who'd run a fishing boat for tourists) couldn't arrange his day till he'd heard the marine forecast—the wind, the tides, the small-craft warnings, the height of average waves in unprotected waters. He loved to fish, offshore and on, and he swam every chance he could get. He'd tried to teach her to body surf, but it hadn't worked out. There was something about the breakers: She just gritted her teeth and stood staunch and let them slam into her. As if standing
3 staunch were a virtue, really. She couldn't explain it. Her father thought she was scared, but it wasn't that at all.

She'd married Avery against their wishes and been sorry ever since—sorry to move so far from home, sorrier when her parents died within a year of each other, sorriest of all when the marriage turned grim and cranky. But she never would have thought of leaving him. It was Avery who left; she would have stayed forever. In fact,
4 she did stay on in their apartment for months after he'd gone, though the rent was far too high. It wasn't that she expected him back. She just took some comfort from enduring.

Arnold's head snapped up. He looked around him and made a gurgling sound. His chewing gum fell onto the front of his jacket. "Here, honey," she told him. She put the gum in her ashtray. "Look out the window. See the cows?"

He wouldn't look. He began bouncing in his seat, rubbing his hands together rapidly.

"Arnold? Want a cookie?"

If only she'd brought a picture book. She'd meant to and then forgot. She wondered if the train people sold magazines. If she let him get too bored, he'd go into one of his tantrums, and then she wouldn't be able to handle him. The doctor had given her pills just in case, but she was always afraid that while he was screaming he would choke on them. She looked around the car. "Arnold," she said, "see the . . . see the hat with feathers on? Isn't it pretty? See the red suitcase? See the, um . . ."

The car door opened with a rush of clattering wheels and the conductor burst in, singing "Girl of my dreams, I love you." He lurched down the aisle, plucking pink tickets from the back of each seat. Just across from Bet and Arnold, he stopped. He was looking down at a tiny black lady in a purple coat, with a fox fur piece biting its own tail around her neck. "You!" he said.

The lady stared straight ahead.

"You, I saw you. You're the one in the washroom."

A little muscle twitched in her cheek.

"You got on this train in Beulah, didn't you. Snuck in the washroom. Darted back like you thought you could put something over on me. I saw that bit of purple! Where's your ticket gone to?"

She started fumbling in a blue cloth purse. The fumbling went on and on. The conductor shifted his weight.

GUIDED READING

LITERAL QUESTIONS

1a. How does Bet's old life seem to her? (beautifully free and spacious)

2a. What would Bet never have considered in her marriage to Avery? (leaving him)

INFERENTIAL QUESTIONS

1b. Why is this description ironic? (Her old life was drab—a trailer on cinder blocks. Still, it was better than what she had after she left home.)

2b. With what qualities of her personality is this consistent? (She takes whatever comes, grits her teeth, and endures.)

"Why!" she said finally. "I must've left it back in my other seat."

"What other seat?"

"Oh, the one back . . ." She waved a spidery hand.

The conductor sighed. "Lady," he said, "you owe me money."

"I do no such thing!" she said. "Viper! Monger! Hitler!" Her voice screeched up all at once;
1 she sounded like a parrot. Bet winced and felt herself flushing, as if *she* were the one. But then at her shoulder she heard a sudden, rusty clang, and she turned and saw that Arnold was laughing. He had his mouth wide open and his tongue curled, the way he did when he watched "Sesame Street." Even after the scene had worn itself out, and the lady had paid and the conductor had moved on, Arnold went on chortling and la-la-ing, and Bet looked gratefully at the little black lady, who was settling her fur piece fussily and muttering under her breath.

From the Parkinsville Railroad Station, which they seemed to be tearing down or else remodeling—she couldn't tell which—they took a taxicab to Parkins State Hospital. "Oh, I been out there many and many a time," said the driver. "Went out there just the other———"

But she couldn't stop herself; she had to tell him before she forgot. "Listen," she said, "I want you to wait for me right in the driveway. I don't want you to go on away."

"Well, fine," he said.

"Can you do that? I want you to be sitting right by the porch or the steps or whatever, right where I come out of, ready to take me back to the station. Don't just go off and———"

"I *got* you, I got you," he said.

She sank back. She hoped he understood.

Arnold wanted a peanut butter cookie. He was reaching and whimpering. She didn't know what to do. She wanted to give him anything he asked for, anything; but he'd get it all over his
2 face and arrive not looking his best. She couldn't stand it if they thought he was just ordinary and unattractive. She wanted them to see how small and neat he was, how somebody cherished him.

But it would be awful if he went into one of his rages. She broke off a little piece of cookie from the bag. "Here," she told him. "Don't mess, now."

He flung himself back in the corner and ate it, keeping one hand flattened across his mouth while he chewed.

The hospital looked like someone's great, pillared mansion, with square brick buildings all around it. "Here we are," the driver said.

"Thank you," she said. "Now you wait here, please. Just wait till I get———"

"*Lady,*" he said. "I'll wait."

She opened the door and nudged Arnold out ahead of her. Lugging the suitcase, she started toward the steps. "Come on, Arnold," she said.

He hung back.

3 "Arnold?"

Maybe he wouldn't allow it, and they would go on home and never think of this again.

But he came, finally, climbing the steps in his little hobbled way. His face was clean, but there were a few cookie crumbs on his jacket. She set down the suitcase to brush them off. Then she buttoned all his buttons and smoothed his shirt collar over his jacket collar before she pushed open the door.

In the admitting office, a lady behind a wooden counter showed her what papers to sign. Secretaries were clacketing typewriters all around. Bet thought Arnold might like that, but

AT A GLANCE

- Arnold is distracted by the woman, and Bet is grateful.
- They take a taxi to a state hospital; she makes the driver agree to wait for her.
- She urges Arnold up the steps.

1 CHARACTERIZATION

Bet's discomfort at a discussion in which she has no part further evidences her insecurity. She seems accustomed to taking blame, even for problems not of her own making.

2 CONFLICT

Bet feels torn between two negative alternatives: having Arnold arrive looking uncared-for or having him arrive in a rage. Her thoughts demonstrate the continual battle her life with Arnold has been.

3 CHARACTERIZATION

Bet is terribly guilty about what she is doing; making any decision is difficult for her, and this one is especially so. For a woman who finds strength in endurance, the inability to endure her own son is devastating. She hopes Arnold will refuse to go and thus take the decision out of her hands.

GUIDED READING

LITERAL QUESTIONS

1a. How did Bet look at the tiny black lady? (gratefully)

2a. What does Bet ask the taxi driver to do? (wait)

INFERENTIAL QUESTIONS

1b. Why does she feel this way? (The scene the woman caused distracted Arnold and kept him from causing a scene of his own.)

2b. What does her request suggest about her emotions? (She is anxious and desperately afraid of being stranded outside the hospital. She may fear that she will change her mind.)

AT A GLANCE

- She takes Arnold inside and signs commitment papers.
- A nurse takes them to a children's ward, and Bet says good-bye to Arnold.
- At the station she panics when she finds that the train will be twenty minutes late.

1 SETTING

The details of the hallway show the hard impersonality and institutional coldness of the hospital.

2 CONTRAST

Bet's attitude of warmth and caring for her son contrasts with that of the nurse, whose abstracted remarks suggest that she will humor Bet and then do what is expedient.

3 CHARACTERIZATION

Bet's overreaction reflects her ragged emotional state. She is afraid to have twenty minutes alone. She wants to get away as soon as possible so that she will not have time to think about what she has done.

instead he got lost in the lights—chilly, hanging ice-cube-tray lights with a little flicker to them. He gazed upward, looking astonished. Finally a flat-fronted nurse came in and touched his elbow. "Come along, Arnold. Come, Mommy. We'll show you where Arnold is staying," she said.

They walked back across the entrance hall, then up wide marble steps with hollows worn in them. Arnold clung to the bannister. There was a smell Bet hated, pine-oil disinfectant, but Arnold didn't seem to notice. You never knew; sometimes smells could just put him in a state.

The nurse unlocked a double door that had chicken-wired windows. They walked through a corridor, passing several fat, ugly women in shapeless gray dresses and ankle socks. "Ha!" one of the women said, and fell giggling into the arms of a friend. The nurse said, "*Here* we are." She led
1 them into an enormous hallway lined with little white cots. Nobody else was in it; there wasn't a sign that children lived here except for a tiny cardboard clown picture hanging on one vacant wall. "This one is your bed, Arnold," said the nurse. Bet laid the suitcase on it. It was made up so neatly, the sheets might have been painted on. A steely-gray blanket was folded across the foot. She looked over at Arnold, but he was pivoting back and forth to hear how his new sneakers squeaked on the linoleum.

"Usually," said the nurse, "we like to give new residents six months before the family visits. That way they settle in quicker, don't you see." She turned away and adjusted the clown picture, though as far as Bet could tell it was fine the way it was. Over her shoulder, the nurse said, "You can tell him goodbye now, if you like."

"Oh," Bet said. "All right." She set her hands on Arnold's shoulders. Then she laid her face against his hair, which felt warm and fuzzy. "Honey," she said. But he went on pivoting. She straightened and told the nurse, "I brought his special blanket."

"Oh, fine," said the nurse, turning toward her again. "We'll see that he gets it."

"He always likes to sleep with it; he has ever since he was little."

2 "All right."

"Don't wash it. He hates if you wash it."

"Yes. Say goodbye to Mommy now, Arnold."

"A lot of times he'll surprise you. I mean there's a whole lot to him. He's not just———"

"We'll take very good care of him, Mrs. Blevins, don't worry."

"Well," she said. "'Bye, Arnold."

She left the ward with the nurse and went down the corridor. As the nurse was unlocking the doors for her, she heard a single, terrible scream, but the nurse only patted her shoulder and pushed her gently on through.

In the taxi, Bet said, "Now, I've just got fifteen minutes to get to the station. I wonder if you could hurry?"

"Sure thing," the driver said.

She folded her hands and looked straight ahead. Tears seemed to be coming down her face in sheets.

Once she'd reached the station, she went to the ticket window. "Am I in time for the twelve-thirty-two?" she asked.

"Easily," said the man. "It's twenty minutes late."

"What?"

"Got held up in Norton somehow."

3 "But you can't!" she said. The man looked startled. She must be a sight, all swollen-eyed and wet-cheeked. "Look," she said, in a lower voice. "I figured this on purpose. I chose the one train from Beulah that would let me catch another one back without waiting. I do not want to sit and wait in this station."

"Twenty *minutes*, lady. That's all it is."

"What am I going to do?" she asked him.

He turned back to his ledgers.

She went over to a bench and sat down. Ladders and scaffolding towered above her, and only ten or twelve passengers were dotted through the rest of the station. The place looked bombed out—nothing but a shell. "Twenty minutes!" she said aloud. "What am I going to do?"

Through the double glass doors at the far end of the station, a procession of gray-suited men arrived with briefcases. More men came behind them, dressed in work clothes, carrying folding

GUIDED READING

LITERAL QUESTIONS

1a. What does Bet do in the cab? (She stares straight ahead, hands folded, and weeps.)

2a. What does she learn at the station? (The train will be twenty minutes late.)

INFERENTIAL QUESTIONS

1b. What do her actions suggest? (She is still enduring, but this time she endures the pain of leaving her child.)

2b. Why does this information present a problem? (She has planned the trip so that she will not have to wait there; she wants to get away, perhaps so that she will not be tempted to change her mind.)

chairs, black trunklike boxes with silver hinges, microphones, a wooden lectern, and an armload of bunting. They set the lectern down in the center of the floor, not six feet from Bet. They draped the bunting across it—an arc of red, white, and blue. Wires were connected, floodlights were lit. A microphone screeched. One of the workmen said, "Try her, Mayor." He held the microphone out to a fat man in a suit, who cleared his throat and said, "Ladies and gentlemen, on the occasion of the expansion of this fine old railway station———"

"Sure do get an echo here," the workman said. "Keep on going."

The mayor cleared his throat again. "If I may," he said, "I'd like to take about twenty minutes of your time, friends."

He straightened his tie. Bet blew her nose,
1 and then she wiped her eyes and smiled. They had come just for her sake, you might think. They were putting on a sort of private play. From now on, all the world was going to be like that—just something on a stage, for her to sit back and watch.

STUDY QUESTIONS

Recalling

1. Where is Bet taking Arnold as the story opens? What details tell the reader that Arnold is not a normal child? What is Bet afraid of in her relations with Arnold?
2. Where is Arnold's father? What caused Arnold's condition? How does Bet feel about the cause?
3. What amuses Arnold on the train? How does Bet want Arnold to look at the hospital?
4. What sorrows has Bet experienced in her life? Why did she marry?
5. What instructions does Bet give the cab driver?
6. Describe the hospital and the nurse Bet meets. How does the nurse respond to Bet's attempts to tell her about Arnold?
7. What occurs during the twenty minutes Bet has to wait at the train station? What is her response to the start of the speech?

Interpreting

8. How does the reader know that Bet loves Arnold? Why does Bet have to give him up? Why is Mrs. Puckett upset that Arnold is leaving?
9. Why was Bet unable to learn to body surf? Why did she stay in an expensive apartment after Avery left? In what other ways has Bet "stood staunch" in her life?

Extending

10. The hospital will not allow Bet to visit Arnold for six months. What do you think Arnold will be like in six months? What will Bet be like?

COMPOSITION

Writing About a Title

■ The title of a story often aids the reader in interpreting the events, understanding the characters, and grasping the story's theme. Write a brief composition explaining the possible meanings of the title "Average Waves in Unprotected Waters." Begin by finding the words of the title in the story. How does Bet respond to waves? What might waves represent? What would "unprotected waters" then symbolize?

Imagining a Character's Thoughts

■ In the story "Average Waves in Unprotected Waters" we see how carefully Bet has prepared and planned for Arnold's trip to the hospital. She has even made arrangements so that she will have no wait at the train station. How did Bet make the decision to commit Arnold to the hospital? In some ways this is the only decision she has made alone in her life. Write several paragraphs presenting Bet's thoughts as she comes to realize that she can no longer care for Arnold. What emotions does she experience? What doubts and changes of mind?

AT A GLANCE

- The mayor and his aides arrive at the station and set up microphones for a speech.
- Gratefully, Bet turns her attention to them.

1 CHARACTERIZATION

Bet is still taking a passive role in life. Instead of starting to participate, she intends to be a spectator.

REFLECTING ON THE STORY

What is the significance of the title? (Students may suggest that the unprotected waters represent life. The waves are the hardships of life.)

STUDY QUESTIONS

1. to a hospital to live; his glassy eyes, unchanging expression, wild gaze, moaning and rocking; a tantrum she will not be able to control
2. He left the family; it was inherited; blames herself, her husband, and the marriage
3. an altercation between a woman and the conductor; as if someone cherished him
4.
   - marriage was not successful; her parents both died soon after; Arnold was born retarded
   - She married to get away from her parents but can no longer remember why.
5. to wait
6. The hospital is cold and sterile; the nurse, brusque. The nurse is not really interested in hearing about Arnold.
7. The mayor is making a speech; she smiles because the speech is something she can watch passively.
8.
   - her care, attempts to please him, grief
   - She can no longer control him and has no babysitter.
   - She used to babysit but he became too wild.
9. let waves slam into her; took comfort from enduring; kept Arnold long as possible
10. Arnold—much more withdrawn, probably drugged, may not remember Bet; Bet—loving and hurt, may feel guilt

COMPOSITION: GUIDELINES FOR EVALUATION

WRITING ABOUT A TITLE

Objective

To discuss the meaning of a story's title

Guidelines for Evaluation

- suggested length: two to three paragraphs
- should cite reference to the title in story
- should note that Bet let the waves slam into her
- should suggest reasonable meanings for the title's symbols

IMAGINING A CHARACTER'S THOUGHTS

Objective

To write an essay describing a character's thoughts

Guidelines for Evaluation

- suggested length: two to three paragraphs
- should reflect understanding of Bet
- should illustrate the difficulty of Bet's decision

Photograph © 1982 by Jill Krementz

John Updike *born 1932*

"We must write where we stand," John Updike once said. "Wherever we do stand, there is life: And an imitation of the life we know, however narrow, is our only ground." In his writing Updike gives us "the life we know," revealing the universal through the fine details of the everyday.

John Updike was born in the small town of Shillington, Pennsylvania. When he was thirteen, his family moved to a farm. Both locations, lightly disguised, provide the setting for much of his early fiction. Updike graduated from Harvard and attended the Ruskin School of Drawing and Fine Art in England. He worked first as a cartoonist, then as a staff writer, for the *New Yorker,* the magazine in which many of his stories first appeared.

Updike is a prolific and popular writer, and his published works include novels, collections of stories, poems, essays, and reviews. His novels, however, have won him the greatest acclaim. They include *The Centaur* (1963), *Couples* (1968), *The Coup* (1978), and the trilogy *Rabbit, Run* (1960), *Rabbit Redux* (1971), and *Rabbit Is Rich* (1981).

Several character types appear repeatedly in Updike's fiction. One is the sensitive, sometimes egotistical adolescent groping with uncertainty. Another is the former high school athlete, once a star, who now seems a misfit in the workaday adult world. A third type is the middle-class man or woman who has "missed the moment," lost the opportunity for a great achievement, and who now feels trapped and frustrated. Updike's stories place people like these in ordinary situations that occur in ordinary places such as the high school classroom, the local supermarket, the family car, the small apartment. His characters often seem to be not quite happy, not quite secure, not quite satisfied with their lives.

John Updike's technical skill is sometimes overlooked because he deals with such everyday subjects, but he has a keen eye for the revealing detail and a sharp ear for colloquial dialogue. His language is alive with original metaphors and phrasing, always witty, sometimes melancholy. He is expert at stream of consciousness, ironic twists, and comic situations. In "The Slump" Updike uses one of his favorite images—the world of sports as a metaphor for life, the athlete as a metaphor for the achiever in all of us.

■ Authors often use metaphors to make their point. Is this story really about baseball—or something much more important? What?

The Slump

1 They say reflexes, the coach says reflexes,
even the papers now are saying reflexes, but I
don't think it's the reflexes so much—last
night, as a gag to cheer me up, the wife walks
into the bedroom wearing one of the kids' rubber gorilla masks and I was under the bed in
six-tenths of a second, she had the stopwatch
on me. It's that I can't see the ball the way I
used to. It used to come floating up with all
2 seven continents showing, and the pitcher's
thumbprint, and a grass smooch or two, and
the Spalding guarantee in ten-point sans-serif,[1]
and *whop!* I could feel the sweet wood with
the bat still cocked. Now, I don't know, there's
3 like a cloud around it, a sort of spiral vagueness, maybe the Van Allen belt,[2] or maybe I lift
my eye in the last second, planning how I'll
round second base, or worrying which I do first, tip my cap or slap the third-base coach's hand. You can't see a blind spot, Kierkegaard[3] says, but in there now, between when the ball leaves the bleacher background and I can hear it plop all fat and satisfied in the catcher's mitt, there's somehow just nothing, where there used to be a lot, everything in fact, because they're not keeping me around for my fielding, and already I see the afternoon tabloid has me down as trade bait.

The flutters don't come when they used to. It used to be, I'd back the convertible out of the garage and watch the electric eye put the door down again and drive in to the stadium, and at about the bridge turnoff I'd ease off grooving with the radio rock, and then on the lot there'd be the kids waiting to get a look and that would start the big butterflies, and when the attendant would take my car I'd want

1. **ten-point sans-serif** [san ser′if]: referring to the size and style of the lettering.
2. **Van Allen belt:** belt of radiation around the earth.
3. **Kierkegaard** [kēr′kə gärd′]: Søren [sœ′rən] Kierkegaard (1813–1855), Danish philosopher.

AT A GLANCE

- A baseball player knows that the coaches and press think that his reflexes are now slow.
- The player thinks the problem is that he cannot see the ball the way he used to.
- He hears that he is trade bait and remarks that the "flutters" come at a different time now.

LITERARY OPTIONS

- symbol
- style: figurative language

THEMATIC OPTIONS

- fame vs. personal satisfaction
- pressure and performance

1 POINT OF VIEW

The story is written in the first person and sounds as though the narrator is speaking to someone. Perhaps he is speaking to himself, engaging in a soul-searching exercise.

2 SYMBOL

Emphasis on the seven continents being imprinted on the baseball implies that baseball has been the narrator's "world." It also suggests that the story is about life in general and not simply baseball.

3 CONTRAST

Updike dramatizes the change in the narrator by contrasting how the ball is seen as it comes in at ninety miles per hour when the player is in a slump *(cloud, spiral vagueness, Van Allen belt)* with the way it appears when he is hitting well *(thumbprint, grass smooch).*

GUIDED READING

LITERAL QUESTION

1a. These days, what does the narrator see around the ball? (a cloud, a sort of spiral vagueness, or a belt, like the Van Allen belt)

INFERENTIAL QUESTION

1b. How does the appearance of the ball relate to the way that the narrator feels? (It seems to symbolize fear that he is no longer a hitter, a role that has given him fame and an identity.)

AT A GLANCE

- Now he is relaxed until it is time to play; then the fear comes.
- He wonders if getting hit by a pitched ball could help to break his slump, but pitchers throw the ball straight over the plate because they know he is not hitting.
- What it is, he says, is not caring enough, knowing that the only real thing is the self, and that is not enough.

1 STYLE: FIGURATIVE LANGUAGE

The reference to emeralds suggests that baseball once was miraculous to the narrator, virtually overwhelming him.

2 THEME

Perhaps the core of the narrator's present fear is that he has become painfully aware of the human condition.

3 BACKGROUND

Baseball has traditionally boasted of superstitious practices that supposedly have improved a player's performance.

REFLECTING ON THE STORY

What is the real setting of this story? (Students may say that, on one level, the setting is the stadium, but they may realize the setting is really the player's mind—his attitudes, beliefs and feelings.)

to shout *Stop, thief,* and walking down that long cement corridor I'd fantasize like I was going to the electric chair and the locker room was some dream after death, and I'd wonder why the suit fit, and how these really immortal guys, that I recognized from the bubble-gum cards I used to collect, knew my name. *They* knew *me.* And I'd go out and the stadium
1 mumble would scoop at me and the grass seemed too precious to walk on, like emeralds, and by the time I got into the cage I couldn't remember if I batted left or right.

Now, hell, I move over the bridge singing along with the radio, and brush through the kids at just the right speed, not so fast I knock any of them down, and the attendant knows his Labor Day tip is coming, and we wink, and in the batting cage I own the place, and take my cuts, pop five or six into the bullpen as easy as dropping dimes down a sewer. But when the scoreboard lights up, and I take those two steps up from the dugout, the biggest two steps in a ballplayer's life, and kneel in the circle, giving the crowd the old hawk profile, where once the flutters would ease off, now they dig down and begin.

They say I'm not hungry, but I still feel hungry, only now it's a kind of panic hungry, and that's not the right kind. Ever watch one of your little kids try to catch a ball? He gets so excited with the idea he's going to catch it he shuts his eyes. That's me now. I walk up to the plate, having come all this way—a lot of hotels, a lot of shagging—and my eyes feel shut. And I stand up there trying to push my eyeballs through my eyelids, and my retinas register maybe a little green, and the black patch of some nuns in far left field. That's panic hungry.

Kierkegaard called it dread.[4] It queers the works. My wife comes at me without the gorilla mask and when in the old days, *whop!,* now she slides by with a hurt expression and a flicker of gray above her temple. I go out and ride the power mower and I've already done it so often the lawn is brown. The kids get me out of bed for a little fungo and it scares me to see them trying, busting their lungs, all that shagging ahead of them. In Florida—we used to love it in Florida, the smell of citrus and marlin, the flat pink sections where the old people drift around smiling with transistor plugs in their ears—we lie on the beach after a work-
2 out and the sun seems a high fly I'm going to lose and the waves keep coming like they've been doing for a billion years, up to the plate, up to the plate. Kierkegaard probably has the clue, somewhere in there, but I picked up *Concluding Unscientific Postscript*[5] the other day and I couldn't see the print, that is, I could see the lines, but there wasn't anything on them, like the rows of deep seats in the shade of the second deck on a Thursday afternoon, just a single ice-cream vendor sitting there, nobody around to sell to, a speck of white in all that shade, old Søren Sock himself, keeping his goods cool.

3 I think maybe if I got beaned. That's probably what the wife is hinting at with the gorilla mask. A change of pace, like the time DiMaggio[6] broke his slump by Topping's[7] telling him to go to a night club and get plastered. I've stopped ducking, but the trouble is, if you're not hitting, they don't brush you back. On me, they've stopped trying for even the corners; they put it right down the pike. I can see it in his evil eye as he takes the sign and rears back, I can hear the catcher snicker, and for a second of reflex there I can see it like it used to be, continents and cities and every green tree distinct as a stitch, and the hickory sweetens in my hands, and I feel the good old sure hunger. Then something happens. It blurs, skips, fades, I don't know. It's not caring enough, is what it probably is, it's knowing that none of it—the stadium, the averages—is really there, just *you* are there, and it's not enough.

---

4. **dread:** In *The Concept of Dread* Kierkegaard stated that profound fear is natural to the human condition.

5. ***Concluding Unscientific Postscript:*** one of Kierkegaard's major works.

6. **DiMaggio:** Joe DiMaggio (born 1914), New York Yankee baseball player (1936–1951).

7. **Topping's:** Dan Topping, one of a group that owned the Yankees between 1945 and 1964.

GUIDED READING

LITERAL QUESTION

1a. When do the narrator's "flutters" begin now? (They begin right before he bats.)

INFERENTIAL QUESTION

1b. What does the change in the time of the "flutters" suggest? (The flutters used to come from the awe that the player felt for the game and its heroes; now they reflect his fear that he is not up to the challenge.)

STUDY QUESTIONS

Recalling

1. According to the first paragraph, what do the coach and papers say has caused the narrator's slump? What does the narrator say has caused it?
2. How did the baseball appear when the narrator used to see it clearly (paragraph 1)? How does it appear now?
3. How did the narrator once feel when he gave his car to the stadium attendant? How does the narrator now greet the stadium attendant? When do the flutters begin now?
4. How do "they" explain the cause of the slump in paragraph 4? How does the narrator describe his present kind of hunger? What does he say Kierkegaard calls it?
5. What is the narrator's explanation of his slump in the final sentence?

Interpreting

6. What do the contrasts in paragraph 3 and 4 suggest about the changes that have occurred in the narrator's attitude toward playing baseball? What was his old "hunger" a hunger for?
7. With what is the baseball coming at the narrator compared twice in the story? What does this comparison suggest that the baseball represents? What does the narrator's "blind spot" suggest about his current attitude toward life?
8. Explain the philosophical implications of the final sentence with regard to the narrator's present condition—his "slump"—and its causes.

Extending

9. What does this story suggest to you about fame? About aging? About modern life in general? Do you agree with these suggestions? Why or why not?

VIEWPOINT

In assessing Updike's fiction Robert Detweiler has written:

> Updike's accomplishment is in dramatizing the eternal human problems in terms of arresting contemporary techniques. (He may often be writing about the same failings that bothered the Victorians, but he handles them in a modern manner.)
>
> *—John Updike*

■ What are the "eternal human problems" that are dramatized in "The Slump"? What is particularly "contemporary" in Updike's literary techniques?

COMPOSITION

Writing About Diction and Sentence Structure

■ Write a brief composition about the appropriateness of the language and sentence structure in "The Slump." Begin with a general statement about the character of the narrator and the subject of the story. Then show with examples how the language is natural for the narrator and appropriate for his subject. Continue by discussing how the sentence structure suits the temperament of the narrator at this point in his life. Conclude by relating the narrator's language and sentence structure to the total effect the story has on you.

Writing a Monologue

■ Invent a character who doubts his or her ability in an occupation, a sport, a school subject, or a social grace. Write a first-person monologue expressing that character's doubts, fears, and struggle to succeed. Keep the language consistent with the subject, the character's background, and the character's state of mind.

STUDY QUESTIONS

1. problem with reflexes; cannot see the ball the way he used to
2. "floating . . . all seven continents showing . . . pitcher's thumbprint . . . grass smooch . . . Spaulding guarantee"; vague
3. like he wanted to shout "Stop, thief"; with a wink; when he kneels in the batter's circle
4. he is "not hungry"; panic hunger; dread
5. not caring enough, knowing none of it is really there but you
6.
   - *before:* nervous, excited, eager; *now:* excitement gone, takes fame for granted, cannot rely on his own ability
   - success
7. the world; life; uncertain of life's meaning, his own purpose
8. experiencing the terror of the human condition, of knowing we live solitary lives that end in death
9. temporary, does not offer fulfillment; makes people more introspective about meaning of life; complex, remorseless; students may agree

VIEWPOINT

not understanding the meaning of life, not knowing one's place or purpose; metaphor of baseball, mix of elegant figurative constructions and informal speech

COMPOSITION: GUIDELINES FOR EVALUATION

WRITING ABOUT DICTION AND SENTENCE STRUCTURE

Objective

To evaluate diction/sentence structure in story

Guidelines for Evaluation

- suggested length: five to seven paragraphs
- should describe narrator, subject of story
- should relate language to narrator's character
- should relate language to subject of story
- should relate language to story's total effect

WRITING A MONOLOGUE

Objective

To write a monologue

Guidelines for Evaluation

- suggested length: five to eight paragraphs
- should reveal the character's problem and personality through his or her own words
- should use language that is appropriate to the character and the subject

AT A GLANCE

- A man goes by a florist in New York City and sees a moss rose, which the florist calls "portulaca."
- The man recalls his childhood, and thinks about the El that no longer runs on Third Avenue.

LITERARY OPTIONS

- epiphany
- symbol
- flashback

THEMATIC OPTIONS

- past and present
- urban living
- remembrance of things past

1 SPEAKER

The speaker is not from New York City but from somewhere in the country. The point of view is third-person, but the narrator gives the reader access to the main character's smallest thoughts.

2 SYMBOL

The elevated railroad tracks are still part of the life of the people who live on Third Avenue. In this story the defunct El is a symbol of impermanence.

William Goyen 1915–1983

Lyric and realistic, delicate and harsh, William Goyen's stories leave unforgettable impressions. His characters are revealed with a moving combination of precision and compassion.

Goyen was born in Trinity, Texas, and graduated from Rice University. He has taught at the New School for Social Research and at Columbia University in New York City. His works of fiction include *The House of Breath* (1950), *In a Farther Country* (1955), *The Faces of Blood Kindred* (1960), and *The Fair Sister* (1963).

The characters in Goyen's fiction have often lost their purposes in life, their ideals, or their capacity to communicate with one another. They search for some way of bridging the chasm between the past and present. Their stories are carefully told, the product of close observation and hard-earned craft. While many of Goyen's stories possess a gothic quality, "The Moss Rose" is quite realistic.

- Can you think of instances when someone has revealed more than he or she realized through seemingly unimportant observations?

William Goyen

The Moss Rose

"Portulaca," the Third Avenue man said to him at the door of his shop when he asked the name of what he thought was a box of moss-rose plants for sale on the sidewalk.

"Aren't they moss roses?" he asked.

"Portulaca," the man said.

"Do they have orange and yellow and crimson blossoms?"

"That's right," the man said.

"And they aren't moss roses?"

"Portulaca," he said again.

He went on up Third Avenue saying the word to himself as he walked, so as not to for-
1 get it. *Portulaca.* "I guess that's what they call them up here," he said to himself.

He had grown up with them—*moss roses*—always in some flower bed, by a grave, by a pump where the ground was moist, in a hanging kettle on a porch. They were a part of another landscape, a flower illustration of many remembered scenes in another country. Here they were, on Third Avenue in New York City. Or were they the same—could they be? Oh, he thought, I guess people up here know and have this common little flower—why shouldn't they? But such a name as they've given it! *Portulaca.*

2 The El[1] was quiet, the train was gone. Though the complicated and permanent-looking structure was there, soon it would be torn down. Third Avenue was quieter. People who had lived for years with the noise of the El interrupting their sleep and conversation and

1. **The El:** elevated railroad.

GUIDED READING

LITERAL QUESTION

1a. What is the other name for moss roses? (Portulaca)

INFERENTIAL QUESTION

1b. What do the names reveal about the setting of the story? (The New York name, *portulaca,* is more formal. The city's formality contrasts with the informality and perhaps greater warmth of the speaker's place of origin.)

who had learned naturally to scream above it, still spoke in Third Avenue voices; but the train, the reason, was gone.

The children yelled in resounding voices on the sidewalks, though the noise over which they yelled had vanished; and he wondered if ever their voices would soften or modulate. No, they would go on through life yelling with powerful voices developed against the monster
1 whose tracks they had been bred alongside. It would be the El going on through them; it was not really destroyed. They seemed the children of the El, and the tracks and platform had bred children who looked a little like them, curiously, as their parents did, so that their faces, bearing, physiognomy reflected the resisted
2 force—as people who live in constant wind or on stony landscapes reflect the natural phenomenon which opposes them in daily life.

These Third Avenue people had the same vagabond, noisy air and quality that the ramshackle train and platform symbolized. The El had created a genus of humanity, almost as the plow had shaped his own; they looked as if they had performed some laborious job with the El, as an instrument of their daily bread, although it did not feed them or reward them with anything but noise and dirt. Still it shaped a style of life for them. Over the years a race had adapted itself to an inhuman presence and had learned, almost as if by imitating or mimicking it, a mode of life that enabled them to absorb it into their daily life, and to endure. They were a kind of grimly happy, sailorlike, reckless people, carefree, poor, tough and loud-mouthed, big-throated and hoarse-voiced. The old, who had lived so long with it, seemed very tired by it. They sat in their straight chairs on the sidewalks or on the steps of their buildings and conversed in loud voices—a gypsy breed with their Third Avenue dog, again his own special breed: a serene, somewhat sad, seasoned hound, resigned, fearless and friendly.

Portulaca, he said, walking along. Little moss rose. Well, he was homesick. But wasn't everyone? he consoled himself. By a certain time something, some structure, in every life is gone, and becomes a memory. But it has caused something: a change, an attitude, an aspect. It is the effect of what was, he thought, going on, that is the long-lastingness in us.

Thinking this, he looked up at the sides of the buildings and saw that the "Portulaca" grew here and there on the Third Avenue people's fire escapes. It was a rather common summer flower on Third Avenue! Well, the moss rose belongs to them, too, as it did to the old guard back home, he thought. Somehow the lit-
3 tle moss rose was a part of any old order, any old, passing bunch, and it clung to those who represented the loss of old fixtures of everyday life, it was that faithful a friend. Now it seemed right that it grow along Third Avenue in boxes and pots on rusty and cluttered and bedraggled fire escapes, as it had in a house he knew once that was inhabited by a flock of raggle-taggle kinfolks, full of joy and knowing trouble and taggling and scrabbling along, a day at a time, toward a better day, surely, they avowed. So, in that old home far away, the moss rose used to look out on a train track, though the scarce train was an event when it chose to pass that way, as if it might be some curious animal out of the woods that had taken a daring path by the house. Still, something of the same configuration was here.

Portulaca! Little moss rose! he thought. The same patterns do exist all over the world, in cities and towns, wherever people live and arrange life around themselves, a bridge over a creek or a tunnel under a river, there is a way to manage. And a sudden sight of this human pattern in one place restores a lost recognition of it in another, far away, through an eternal image of a simple flower, in the hands and care
4 of both; and in a moment's illumination there was in him the certain knowledge of unity forever working to stitch and tie, like a quilt, the human world into a simple shape of repetition and variation of what seems a meaningless and haphazard design whose whole was hostile to its parts and seemed set on disordering them.

He went back to the shop and told the man

AT A GLANCE

- The man thinks about the way the El has shaped the lives of people.
- He thinks the moss rose does that, too, and he sees many of these plants on fire escapes and in windows.
- Then he remembers his own childhood.

1 THEME

The city molds people, and even after their lives change, it continues to live in them, like the El.

2 SIMILE

The effects of wind or sun in faces are easy to see; the effects of the El require greater observation and understanding to appreciate.

3 SYMBOL

The man thinks the moss rose represents old order—things that reflect the past and resist loss. This symbol engenders hope in the main character that nothing is ever really lost.

4 SYMBOL

Now the flower takes on its greater significance as a symbol of the striving and hope that drive the human spirit everywhere and in all circumstances.

GUIDED READING

LITERAL QUESTION

1a. What does the man see when he feels homesick? (He sees the pots of moss roses on fire escapes and in window boxes along Third Avenue.)

INFERENTIAL QUESTION

1b. In what way is everyone homesick? (We all change and lose parts of our lives; we are homesick for the past.)

AT A GLANCE

- The man buys a moss rose for his fire escape and plants it in a "discarded roasting pan."
- The plant reminds him of something.
- He remembers his dead sister, who gave him a moss rose years ago.

1 STREAM OF CONSCIOUSNESS

The man's thoughts move from the flower to the idea of change, and he sees that he must accept change as part of life.

2 EPIPHANY

The man also sees that some parts of the past can be tended and preserved. He will preserve the past by tending the flower.

3 FLASHBACK

His memory comes to him in a rush. He sees all the key details, and for a moment he is actually reliving the past.

4 THEME

After the splendor of the flashback, the reality of the present is contrasted with the beauty of the past. The memory of the moment remains, but everything else is changed.

he would like to try a Portulaca plant. On his fire escape, just off Third Avenue, it would grow and bloom the fragile starlike blossoms of the moss rose he had loved so deeply in another place and would love here as well, though it might be a little different from the old one—something in the leaf, slight but dif-
1 ferent. Yet, everything changes, he thought, slowly it all changes. Do we resign ourselves to that? Is youth passing when we see this—the fierce battle of youth that would not accept change and loss? But there is always the relationship of sameness, too, in all things, which identifies the old ancestor: the *relatedness;* we'll cling to that, to that continuous stem around which only the adornments change, he thought. What if the leaf is a little different? The family is the same . . . the bloom is akin—Portulaca or moss rose. Though the El
2 was gone and the house of kinfolk vanished, two beings as different as man and woman, he would water and tend and foster the old moss-rose family that was still going on.

Sitting on his fire escape, after planting the moss rose in a discarded roasting pan, he looked out through the grillwork of the fire escape and saw the gaunt white-headed man who resembled so much his grandfather in his small room across the courtyard through the Trees of Heaven,[2] where he sat night and day, serene and waiting. Where was his home? Did he know a land where the moss rose bloomed? In his waiting, in his drab, monotonous loneliness, there was a memory living, surely. Who knew, one day it might freshen in him at the sight of something that lingered in the world out of his past, right in the neighborhood, just out of his window, and gladden him for an hour.

Squatting on the fire escape, he thought of his own dreams and hopes. As he sat with the little plant, gazing at it for a long time, a memory rose from it like a vapor, eluded him, and sank back into it. He sat patiently, to catch the memory that glimmered over the petals. What hummingbird remembrance, elusive and darting from his mind, still took its flavor, its bit of sweetness, from the moss rose? And then it came up clear and simple to him, the memory in the moss rose.

It was in the back yard of The Place, as it was called by all who lived there, long ago, under a cool shade tree in Texas. A clump of moss roses grew, without anybody asking it to, in the moist ground around the pump like ringlets of hair wreathed with red and orange and yellow blossoms. He had hung the bucket by its handle over the neck of the pump, and Jessy his small sister held one of his hands while he jacked the pump with the other. The chinaberry trees were still fresh before the sun would make them limp, the chickens were pert, the dew was still on everything, even the woodpile, and the sand in the road still cool. Their old Cherokee rose, that his grandmother had planted when she was a young woman in this house, was gay and blooming at every leaf and thorn, and frolicking all over the fence, down and up and around, locking itself and freeing itself—it would quieten down in the hot afternoon.

Over the squeaking of the pump, he heard
3 a voice and a word . . . "star . . . star." He turned to Jessy and saw that she had picked one of the moss roses and offered it to him, a tiny red star, on the palm of her hand. The bloom was so wonderous and the gift so sudden that he had thought, at that moment, that all life might be something like this twinkling offering. When they went in, the bucket filled, and their mother asked what they had been doing, Jessy had answered, "Picking stars . . ."
4 Now the place was gone, the water dried up, no doubt, the moss rose finished. Jessy was dead these many years; moss roses grew around her small grave—unless they had been overcome by weeds; he had not gone back to that graveyard for a long time. Here on his fire escape (the landlady had once advertised it as a "renovated terrace") was a fragile remnant of that vanished world; he would tend it; it would no doubt bloom, in time. To find that simple joy again, what could he do to recapture it, to recapture what had been, long ago in the moss

2. **Trees of Heaven:** hardy shade trees, cultivated especially in cities because they resist pollution.

GUIDED READING

LITERAL QUESTION

1a. What does his sister give him in the memory? (She gives him a moss rose, which she calls a "star.")

INFERENTIAL QUESTION

1b. Why do you think this memory is important? (Answers will vary. The sister is dead; only her memory is left. He had believed in the wonder of life when they were both young. Her calling the moss rose a "star" was also a beautiful surprise.)

rose and in himself—that ready acceptance, that instantaneous belief, in that pure joy of morning, in one sweet summer, long ago at the water pump, holding his sister's tiny hand? All
1 that had followed, as he had grown, dimmed and tarnished that small blinking star: error and disenchantment and loss.

I used to dream of a little fresh sunrise town like that one where we stood once, at the water pump, he said to himself, where I would be, as fixed upon the ground as the moss rose round the pump, rising in the early morning in vigor to my work and moving and living round it, drawing more and more life to it, through me. Instead, work and life seem to have withdrawn from me more and more, to
2 have pushed life back from where it began, into cities and stone buildings, onto pavements, to have impoverished me even of memories that would save me despair, in a huge grassless city where no flowers bloom on the ground.

3 When the moss rose bloomed again for him, this time on a fire escape in a great city where he sat with gray streaks in his hair, he would be grateful for that. There might even grow another star to pick. So he would watch, day by day, for the flowers to appear, speaking patiently to himself, and again for the hundredth time, that some change was imperative round which to rebuild, out of which to call back the fullness of forgotten signs of love and visions of hope. Believe that it is right ahead, he said to himself, sitting with the plant on the fire escape. Start with one little plain, going-on thing to live around and to take up an old beginning from. Until slowly, slowly, hope and new life will grow and leaf out from it to many places and to many old forgotten promises.

AT A GLANCE

- The man looks at his life and sees it has worsened.
- He looks at the plant and sees it as a new beginning.
- The plant will be the first shoot from which new hopes will flower.

1 PLOT: CLIMAX

In the light of the memory of his sister's gift, he sees the rest of his life as a sort of failure.

2 THEME

He has moved away from flowers to concrete and stone. The life of the city has changed him, just as the El changed the Third Avenue people; it has taken something away from him, and he wants it back.

3 SYMBOL

The flower is a symbol for his hope, and he sees that it has the power to make him grateful again. Maybe it will even "grow another star to pick." The best of the past has returned to him.

REFLECTING ON THE STORY

The last paragraph is a key to the whole story. What do you think the author is trying to say in it? (He is probably trying to say it is never too late for hope, and that life goes on one day at a time. The plant is a small thing, but it prevails, and we can as well, if we remember and go on.)

GUIDED READING

LITERAL QUESTIONS

1a. Who is the speaker in the next-to-the-last paragraph? (It is the same man who has been in the story all along.)

2a. How does the man say he has been impoverished? (He says that he has lost the memories that would save him from despair.)

INFERENTIAL QUESTIONS

1b. Why do you think the story shifts to the first person? (The man is thinking, and he is revealing his deepest thoughts. The author may be suggesting that the man is fully in touch with his inner self.)

2b. What will he do about it? (He will tend the flower, and he will try to focus on small things, like the flower, and find his faith in them.)

STUDY QUESTIONS

1. moss rose; another landscape; Third Avenue in New York City
2. homesick; "certain knowledge of unity forever working to stitch and tie . . . the human world into a simple shape of repetition and variation"
3. stars; put in brother's hand; died many years ago
4. lives alone in city; once lived with family in country and dreamed of future in similar setting
5. moss rose to bloom; change around which to rebuild; "fullness of forgotten signs of love and visions of hope"; "it is right ahead"
6. ▪ noisy, unpleasant
   ▪ urban dwellers who must make themselves heard over noise of the city
   ▪ *rose:* fertile earth, beauty, nature; *el:* city (manmade, sterile, harsh); roses on fire escapes are bridge between worlds
7. unhappy, lonely, alienated; estranged from his roots
8. ▪ life a continuum with similar recurring patterns; past part of present
   ▪ will wait for moss rose to flower, will welcome changed circumstances as new foundation to build on
   ▪ link between past, present and future; life, hope, and purpose
9. Answers will vary. Students might mention learning from past mistakes.

VOCABULARY

1. (b) loud
2. (c) adjust
3. (a) features
4. (d) unkempt
5. (c) declared

STUDY QUESTIONS

Recalling

1. What does the main character call Portulaca? Of what are these plants a part, according to the ninth paragraph? Where is the man when he sees the plants in this story?
2. What does the main character decide he is as he muses over the word *Portulaca* (paragraph 13)? What "certain knowledge" does he get in "a moment's illumination"?
3. What did the main character's sister Jessy once call moss roses? What did she do with the moss rose she picked? What has happened to Jessy?
4. According to the final paragraphs, how has the character's life differed from what it once was and what he once dreamed it would be?
5. What will the man watch for, according to the last paragraph? What does he decide is "imperative"? What will it "call back"? What does he tell himself to believe?

Interpreting

6. Basically, what does the man think the residents of Third Avenue are like at the beginning of the story? What people or life style do the residents of Third Avenue represent? What is the relationship between the moss rose and the El?
7. What is the man himself like before he has his "moment's illumination"? What is significant about his not having visited his sister's grave for a long time?
8. Explain in your own words the knowledge the man receives in his "moment's illumination." What is his new attitude at the end of the story? What does the moss rose represent for him?

Extending

9. How do you think the past can be important in helping us live in the present? Do you agree that "the same patterns . . . exist all over the world, in cities and towns"? Why or why not?

VOCABULARY

Synonyms

A **synonym** is a word that has the same or nearly the same meaning as another word. *Comfort* and *solace* are synonyms. The words in capital letters are from "The Moss Rose." Choose the word that is nearest the meaning of each word in capitals, *as it is used in the selection.*

1. RESOUNDING: (a) twice (b) loud (c) vanishing (d) quickening
2. MODULATE: (a) model (b) harden (c) adjust (d) extinguish
3. PHYSIOGNOMY: (a) features (b) back (c) skeleton (d) torso
4. RAMSHACKLE: (a) stylish (b) old (c) fixed (d) unkempt
5. AVOWED: (a) moved (b) changed (c) declared (d) retired

COMPOSITION

Writing About a Symbol

▪ "The Moss Rose" is a tightly constructed story that centers on the symbol of the moss rose. It does, however, also use the elevated train as a symbol. Write a brief composition about the Third Avenue El in this story. First tell how it is brought into the story, and what function it serves. Then discuss what it contributes to the theme and the effect on the theme if the El were not included. *For help with this assignment, refer to Lesson 5 in the Writing About Literature Handbook at the back of this book.*

Writing About Memory

▪ Write a short composition, or a poem if you wish, about how the memory of something past can influence the behavior of a person in the present. For example, the memory of a triumphant moment can spur someone to try again a difficult task. Following Goyen's example in "The Moss Rose," create a specific situation that dramatizes the effect of a memory.

COMPOSITION: GUIDELINES FOR EVALUATION

WRITING ABOUT A SYMBOL

Objective

To analyze a symbol

Guidelines for Evaluation

- suggested length: four to six paragraphs
- should explain how the El functions on both the literal and figurative levels in the story
- should show how the El relates to theme of story
- should discuss how the theme would change if the El were not mentioned in the story

WRITING ABOUT MEMORY

Objective

To write about the influence of the past

Guidelines for Evaluation

- suggested length: four to six paragraphs
- should create a specific situation that dramatizes the effect of a memory
- should show memory affects present behavior
- should give the reader a sense of what the memory means to the writer

Raymond Carver *1938–1988*

Poet and short story writer Raymond Carver was born in 1938 in Clatskanie, Oregon, and the Pacific Northwest is reflected in much of his writing. He published three collections of poetry: *Near Klamath* (1968), *Winter Insomnia* (1970), and *At Night the Salmon Move* (1976).

After working as an editor for three years, Carver began lecturing on creative writing at the University of California at Santa Cruz. He later taught at the University of California at Berkeley. Carver won numerous awards for his writing, including a National Book Award nomination for fiction in 1977. His short stories appear in the collections: *Will You Be Quiet, Please?* (1976), *Furious Seasons* (1977) and *Where I'm Calling From* (1988). A collection of his poems, *A New Path to the Waterfall*, was also published in 1989.

■ Carver's style resembles that of Ernest Hemingway in its terse, masculine language. How does the voice of the speaker help you to form an image of him?

Raymond Carver

Everything Stuck to Him

1 She's in Milan for Christmas and wants to know what it was like when she was a kid.

Tell me, she says. Tell me what it was like when I was a kid. She sips Strega, waits, eyes him closely.

She is a cool, slim, attractive girl, a survivor from top to bottom.

That was a long time ago. That was twenty years ago, he says.

You can remember, she says. Go on.

What do you want to hear? he says. What else can I tell you? I could tell you about something that happened when you were a baby. It involves you, he says. But only in a minor way.

Tell me, she says. But first fix us another so you won't have to stop in the middle.

He comes back from the kitchen with drinks, settles into his chair, begins.

They were kids themselves, but they were crazy in love, this eighteen-year-old boy and this seventeen-year-old girl when they married. Not all that long afterward they had a daughter.

The baby came along in late November during a cold spell that just happened to coincide with the peak of the waterfowl season. The boy loved to hunt, you see. That's part of it.

2 The boy and girl, husband and wife, father and mother, they lived in a little apartment under a dentist's office. Each night they cleaned the dentist's place upstairs in exchange for rent and utilities. In summer they were expected to maintain the lawn and the flowers. In winter the boy shoveled snow and spread rock salt on the walks. Are you still with me? Are you getting the picture?

I am, she says.

That's good, he says. So one day the dentist finds out they were using his letterhead for their personal correspondence. But that's another story.

AT A GLANCE

- A young woman is visiting her divorced father.
- She asks him to tell her about her childhood.
- He tells her of a girl and a boy who are young, married, and in love.
- They have a new baby.

LITERARY OPTIONS

- point of view
- characterization
- plot

THEMATIC OPTIONS

- inevitability of change
- friendship and love
- family

1 POINT OF VIEW

The frame allows the father to look back on his younger self and share a moment with the daughter whom he does not really know.

2 THEME

The identification of the couple by the roles they play suggests the complexity of human relationships, particularly those within a family.

GUIDED READING

LITERAL QUESTION

1a. What does the young woman want to know? (what it was like when she was a child)

INFERENTIAL QUESTION

1b. What does this request suggest about her relationship with her father? (She does not know him very well; he has been out of her life for a long time.)

AT A GLANCE

- When Carl, an old friend, invites the boy to go hunting, the girl says that she will be fine with the baby.
- They put the baby to bed and fall asleep.
- The baby's cries awaken them.

1 PLOT: RISING ACTION

The conversation with Carl introduces a new, outside element into the cozy, idyllic life of the young couple.

2 CHARACTERIZATION

The boy's interest in Sally and Betsy reveals that although he is an adult biologically, he still needs to mature emotionally.

3 SYMBOL

The boy's vision of himself hunting geese provides a strong sensory image that suggests a momentary yearning for freedom from responsibility.

4 PLOT: CONFLICT

The baby's fitful crying disrupts the night and initiates the crisis.

He gets up from his chair and looks out the window. He sees the tile rooftops and the snow that is falling steadily on them.

Tell the story, she says.

The two kids were very much in love. On top of this they had great ambitions. They were always talking about the things they were going to do and the places they were going to go.

Now the boy and girl slept in the bedroom, and the baby slept in the living room. Let's say the baby was about three months old and had only just begun to sleep through the night.

On this one Saturday night after finishing his work upstairs, the boy stayed in the dentist's office and called an old hunting friend of his father's.

Carl, he said when the man picked up the receiver, believe it or not, I'm a father.

Congratulations, Carl said. How is the wife?

She's fine, Carl. Everybody's fine.

1 That's good, Carl said, I'm glad to hear it. But if you called about going hunting, I'll tell you something. The geese are flying to beat the band. I don't think I've ever seen so many. Got five today. Going back in the morning, so come along if you want to.

I want to, the boy said.

The boy hung up the telephone and went downstairs to tell the girl. She watched while he laid out his things. Hunting coat, shell bag, boots, socks, hunting cap, long underwear, pump gun.

What time will you be back? the girl said.

Probably around noon, the boy said. But maybe as late as six o'clock. Would that be too late?

It's fine, she said. The baby and I will get along fine. You go and have some fun. When you get back, we'll dress the baby up and go visit Sally.

The boy said, Sounds like a good idea.

2 Sally was the girl's sister. She was striking. I don't know if you've seen pictures of her. The boy was a little in love with Sally, just as he was a little in love with Betsy, who was another sister the girl had. The boy used to say to the girl, If we weren't married, I could go for Sally.

What about Betsy? the girl used to say. I hate to admit it, but I truly feel she's better looking than Sally and me. What about Betsy?

Betsy too, the boy used to say.

After dinner he turned up the furnace and helped her bathe the baby. He marveled again at the infant who had half his features and half the girl's. He powdered the tiny body. He powdered between fingers and toes.

He emptied the bath into the sink and went upstairs to check the air. It was overcast and cold. The grass, what there was of it, looked like canvas, stiff and gray under the street light.

3 Snow lay in piles beside the walk. A car went by. He heard sand under the tires. He let himself imagine what it might be like tomorrow, geese beating the air over his head, shotgun plunging against his shoulder.

Then he locked the door and went downstairs.

In bed they tried to read. But both of them fell asleep, she first, letting the magazine sink to the quilt.

4 It was the baby's cries that woke him up.

The light was on out there, and the girl was standing next to the crib rocking the baby in her arms. She put the baby down, turned out the light, and came back to the bed.

He heard the baby cry. This time the girl stayed where she was. The baby cried fitfully and stopped. The boy listened, then dozed. But the baby's cries woke him again. The living room light was burning. He sat up and turned on the lamp.

I don't know what's wrong, the girl said, walking back and forth with the baby. I've changed her and fed her, but she keeps on crying. I'm so tired I'm afraid I might drop her.

You come back to bed, the boy said. I'll hold her for a while.

He got up and took the baby, and the girl went to lie down again.

Just rock her for a few minutes, the girl said from the bedroom. Maybe she'll go back to sleep.

The boy sat on the sofa and held the baby. He jiggled it in his lap until he got its eyes to close, his own eyes closing right along. He rose care-

GUIDED READING

LITERAL QUESTIONS

1a. Whom does the boy telephone? (Carl, an old hunting friend of his father's)

2a. How does the boy feel when he watches the baby being bathed? (He marvels.)

INFERENTIAL QUESTIONS

1b. What is his reason for calling? (He tells the news of his new baby, but perhaps he also wants an invitation to go hunting.)

2b. What does this comment suggest about the boy's relationship with his family? (He loves them and is very involved with them.)

fully and put the baby back in the crib.

It was a quarter to four, which gave him forty-five minutes. He crawled into bed and dropped off. But a few minutes later the baby was crying again, and this time they both got up.

The boy did a terrible thing. He swore.

For God's sake, what's the matter with you? the girl said to the boy. Maybe she's sick or something. Maybe we shouldn't have given her the bath.

The boy picked up the baby. The baby kicked its feet and smiled.

1 Look, the boy said, I really don't think there's anything wrong with her.

How do you know that? the girl said. Here, let me have her. I know I ought to give her something, but I don't know what it's supposed to be.

The girl put the baby down again. The boy and the girl looked at the baby, and the baby began to cry.

2 The girl took the baby. Baby, baby, the girl said with tears in her eyes.

Probably it's something on her stomach, the boy said.

The girl didn't answer. She went on rocking the baby, paying no attention to the boy.

The boy waited. He went to the kitchen and put on water for coffee. He drew his woolen underwear on over his shorts and T-shirt, buttoned up, then got into his clothes.

What are you doing? the girl said.

Going hunting, the boy said.

I don't think you should, she said. I don't want to be left alone with her like this.

Carl's planning on me going, the boy said. We've planned it.

I don't care about what you and Carl planned, she said. And I don't care about Carl, either. I don't even know Carl.

You've met Carl before. You know him, the boy said. What do you mean you don't know him?

That's not the point and you know it, the girl said.

What is the point? the boy said. The point is we planned it.

The girl said, I'm your wife. This is your baby. She's sick or something. Look at her. Why else is she crying?

I know you're my wife, the boy said.

The girl began to cry. She put the baby back in the crib. But the baby started up again. The girl dried her eyes on the sleeve of her nightgown and picked the baby up.

The boy laced up his boots. He put on his shirt, his sweater, his coat. The kettle whistled on the stove in the kitchen.

3 You're going to have to choose, the girl said. Carl or us. I mean it.

What do you mean? the boy said.

You heard what I said, the girl said. If you want a family, you're going to have to choose.

They stared at each other. Then the boy took up his hunting gear and went outside. He started

4 the car. He went around to the car windows and, making a job of it, scraped away the ice.

He turned off the motor and sat awhile. And then he got out and went back inside.

The living room light was on. The girl was asleep on the bed. The baby was asleep beside her.

The boy took off his boots. Then he took off everything else. In his socks and his long underwear, he sat on the sofa and read the Sunday paper.

The girl and the baby slept on. After a while, the boy went to the kitchen and started frying bacon.

The girl came out in her robe and put her arms around the boy.

Hey, the boy said.

I'm sorry, the girl said.

It's all right, the boy said.

I didn't mean to snap like that.

It was my fault, he said.

You sit down, the girl said. How does a waffle sound with bacon?

Sounds great, the boy said.

She took the bacon out of the pan and made waffle batter. He sat at the table and watched her move around the kitchen.

AT A GLANCE

- They give up trying to sleep; the boy dresses to go hunting.
- The girl tells the boy to choose: his family or Carl.
- The boy goes out and starts the car; then he goes back inside and finds the girl and the baby asleep.
- The girl wakes; they make up.

1 PLOT: CONFLICT

The boy and the girl disagree about the baby's state, creating discord.

2 CHARACTERIZATION

The girl's maternal feelings cause her to identify with and focus on the baby, to the exclusion of the boy.

3 PLOT: CLIMAX

The girl's ultimatum pushes the situation as far as it can go. What began as an innocent outing has become an either/or situation involving their future.

4 PLOT: FALLING ACTION

By choosing to stay with the girl, the boy has clarified his priorities; but he also has given something up.

GUIDED READING

LITERAL QUESTIONS

1a. What does the girl say that the boy will have to do? (choose between them and Carl)

2a. After sitting awhile in the car, where does the boy finally go? (back inside)

INFERENTIAL QUESTIONS

1b. What more important choice is she asking him to make? (She is asking him to choose between his own pleasures and his responsibility to his family.)

2b. What does this action show about him? (He has chosen his family over his desire to do what he wants.)

AT A GLANCE

- The girl gives the boy a waffle.
- The boy turns his syrupy plate over on himself.
- They laugh and agree not to fight again.
- The man tells his adult daughter that things change.

REFLECTING ON THE STORY

What does the author achieve by identifying the characters in the man's story merely as "the boy" and "the girl"? (Students may note that it stresses how young they were and how different from the man who tells the story; it also suggests that they could have been anyone.)

STUDY QUESTIONS

1. a father and his daughter; she asks to hear about her childhood; story involves her, the man, and the daughter's mother
2. young, in love, ambitious, poor; hunt; above a dentist's office
3. a hunting friend; to go hunting
4. She is pleased for him; the baby cries all night.
5. with great concern; does not think anything is wrong, helps a little; must choose between his hunting trip or his family
6. Eager to please, she makes him a waffle; his plate spills, and the food sticks to his long underwear.
7. not with the man; living in Milan, seems prosperous
8. Her parents were so young; later they parted.
9. He is not with the girl's mother any more.
10. She does not want her father to see her emotion; perhaps she is aware that nothing can change now between her parents.
11. the world; the world away from the girl and her mother
12. Possible answer: "Why didn't you try harder?"

She put a plate in front of him with bacon, a waffle. He spread butter and poured syrup. But when he started to cut, he turned the plate into his lap.

I don't believe it, he said, jumping up from the table.

If you could see yourself, the girl said.

The boy looked down at himself, at everything stuck to his underwear.

I was starved, he said, shaking his head.

You were starved, she said, laughing.

He peeled off the woolen underwear and threw it at the bathroom door. Then he opened his arms and the girl moved into them.

We won't fight anymore, she said.

The boy said, We won't.

He gets up from his chair and refills their glasses.

That's it, he says. End of story. I admit it's not much of a story.

I was interested, she says.

He shrugs and carries his drink over to the window. It's dark now but still snowing.

Things change, he says. I don't know how they do. But they do without your realizing it or wanting them to.

Yes, that's true, only— But she does not finish what she started.

She drops the subject. In the window's reflection he sees her study her nails. Then she raises her head. Speaking brightly, she asks if he is going to show her the city, after all.

He says, Put your boots on and let's go.

But he stays by the window, remembering. They had laughed. They had leaned on each other and laughed until the tears had come, while everything else—the cold, and where he'd go in it—was outside, for a while anyway.

STUDY QUESTIONS

Recalling

1. Who are the two people talking at the beginning of the story? How do you know their relationship? Who are the people in the story the man tells?
2. Describe the couple in the story. What did the boy love to do? Where did the couple live?
3. Who is Carl? What is his invitation?
4. What is the girl's response to the boy's plans? What makes her change her mind?
5. How does the girl treat her baby? How does the boy respond to the girl's distress? What choice does she give him?
6. How does the girl act when the boy returns? What makes them laugh?

Interpreting

7. Where is the mother now? What clues are there that the boy has realized at least some of his ambitions?
8. Why did the daughter need to be a survivor?
9. What does the father mean when at the end of the story he says "Things change"?
10. Why does the daughter change the subject at the end?
11. What does the cold represent in the story?

Extending

12. What might the daughter have started to say at the end of the story? How do you think she feels about her father?

Photograph © 1982 by Jill Krementz

Mark Helprin *born 1947*

Mark Helprin's novel, *Refiner's Fire,* and his collections of short stories—*A Dove of the East* and *Ellis Island*—have won him widespread praise. A graduate of Harvard and a student of Middle Eastern culture, Helprin has published most of his stories in magazines, particularly the *New Yorker.*

The settings for Helprin's stories range from New York and Massachusetts to Europe, North Africa, and the Middle East. His characters vary just as much. His first collection included stories about a young musician in Paris, a cattle rancher in Jamaica, a young girl working in a typewriter-ribbon factory, a priest who goes to Rome to die, and a soldier about to take part in a Civil War battle. His stories have been described as creating "strange, magical worlds." They often seem to float somewhere between reality and the country of the imagination. Indeed, Helprin has been praised for his "celebration of the transforming power of imagination."

Permeating Helprin's best stories is the quality of love—love of men and women, of landscapes, of beauty, of courage. "White Gardens" is such a story. It portrays one of those moments "when that which is truly important arises," and we realize the power of the love of life itself.

Model for Active Reading

In this selection, and in one selection in each unit, you will find notes in the right-hand margin that highlight parts of the selection. These notes point out important ideas of the period—in this case, contemporary ideas—and draw your attention to literary elements and techniques covered in the Literary Focuses. Page numbers in the notes will refer you to more extensive discussions of these important ideas and elements.

■ Another author said, "It takes life to love life." Does love of life give life in this story?

AT A GLANCE

- In a hot church a young priest is giving a eulogy for six firefighters who died in the line of duty. He stumbles because he is so moved by the situation.
- Ironically the event occurs in a season that "makes one feel improperly immortal."

LITERARY OPTIONS

- symbolism
- setting and mood
- cause and effect

THEMATIC OPTIONS

- beauty of life
- inevitability of death
- difficulty of communication

Mark Helprin

White Gardens

It was August. In the middle of his eulogy the priest said, "Now they must leave us, to repose in white gardens," and then halted in confusion, for he had certainly meant green gardens. But he was not sure. No one in the overcrowded church knew what he meant by white gardens instead of green, but they felt that the mistake was in some way appropriate, and most of them would remember for the rest of their lives the moment afterward, when he had glanced at them in alarm and puzzlement.

Contemporary idea: Literature dramatizes the difficulty of expression and communication among people (page 758).

The stone church in Brooklyn,[1] on one of the long avenues stretching to the sea, was full of firefighters, the press, uncharacteristically quiet city politicians in tropical suits, and the wives and eighteen children of the six men who, in the blink of an eye, had dropped together through the collapsing roof of a burning building, deep into an all-consuming firestorm.

Everyone noticed that the wives of the firemen who had died looked exceptionally beautiful. The young women—with the golden hair of summer, in dark print dresses—several of whom carried flowers, and the older, more matronly women who were less restrained because they understood better what was to become of them, all had a frightening, elevated quality which seemed to rule the parishioners and silence the politicians.

The priest was tumbling over his own words, perhaps because he was young and too moved to be eloquent according to convention. He looked up after a long silence and said, simply, "repose of rivers . . ." They strained to understand, but couldn't, and forgave him immediately. His voice was breaking—not because so many were in the church, for in the raw shadow of the event itself, their numbers were unimpressive. It wasn't that the Mayor was in the crowd: the Mayor had become just a man, and no one felt the power of his office. It may have been the heat. The city had been under siege for a week. Key West[2] humidity and rains had swept across Brooklyn, never-ending, trying to cover it with the sea. The sun was shining now, through a powerful white haze, and the heat inside the church was phenomenal and frightening, ninety-five degrees—like a boiler room. All the seasons have their mystery, and perhaps the mystery of summer is that it overwhelms with easy life, and makes one feel improperly immortal.

Setting (page 148): The time and place of the story suggest and support the theme.

One of the wives glanced out a high window and saw white smoke billowing from a chimney. Even in this kind of weather, she

1. **Brooklyn:** one of the five boroughs of New York City.
2. **Key West:** westernmost island of the Florida Keys.

GUIDED READING

LITERAL QUESTION

1a. How does the congregation respond to "repose of rivers"? (They cannot understand him but forgive him.)

INFERENTIAL QUESTION

1b. Why do they forgive him? (The priest speaks from the heart.)

thought, they have to turn on the furnaces to make hot water. The smoke rushed past the masonry as if the chimney were the stack of a ship. She had been to a fireman's funeral before, and she knew what it was going to be like when the flag-draped coffin was borne from the church and placed on the bed of a shiny new engine. Hundreds of uniformed men would snap to attention, their blue hats aligning suddenly. Then the procession would flow away like a blue river, and she, the widow (for she was now the widow), would stagger into a waiting black car to follow after it.

She was one of the younger wives, one of those who were filled with restrained motion, one of the ones in a dark print dress with flowers. She was looking to the priest for direction, but he was coming apart, and as he did she could not keep out of her mind the million things she was thinking, the things which came to her for no reason, just the way the priest had said "white gardens," and "repose of rivers." She thought of the barges moving slowly up the Hudson in a tunnel of silver and white haze, and of the wind-polished bridges standing in the summer sun. She thought of the men in the church. She knew them. They were firefighters; they were rough, and they carried with them in the church more ambition, sadness, power, courage, greed, and anger than she cared to think about on this day. But despite their battalion's worth of liveliness and strength, they were drawn to the frail priest whose voice broke every now and then in the presence of the wives and the children and the six coffins.

She thought of Brooklyn, of its vastness, and of the things that were happening in Brooklyn, right then. Even as the men were buried, traffic on the streets and parkways would be thick as blood; a hundred million emotions would pass from soul to soul, into the air, into walls in dark hot rooms, into thin groves of trees in the parks. Even as the men were buried in an emerald field dazzling with row upon row of bone-white gravestones, there would be something of resurrection and life all over Brooklyn. But now it was still, and the priest was lost in a moment during which everyone was brought together, and the suited children and lovely wives learned that there are quiet times when the world is touched, and when that which is truly important arises to claim all allegiances.

"It is bitter," said the priest, finally in control of himself, "bitter that only through windows like these do we see clearly into past and future, that in such scenes we burn through our temporal[3]

Contemporary idea: A finely crafted modern style does not necessarily avoid emotional involvement (page 759).

Contemporary idea: Out of life's common events, not romanticized, come profound meanings (page 759).

3. **temporal:** worldly; not spiritual.

AT A GLANCE

- One of the widows, who has been to other funerals for firefighters, realizes she is no longer a spectator.
- She looks to the priest for direction, but he is coming apart.
- There is a moment of stillness in which everyone is brought together.

GUIDED READING

LITERAL QUESTIONS

1a. What words of the priest does the young widow think of? ("repose of rivers" and "white gardens")

2a. What happens in the moment the priest is lost? (Everyone is brought together.)

INFERENTIAL QUESTIONS

1b. Why are these images significant? (They remind her of the flow of life and of white gravestones—of life and eternity.)

2b. What do the wives and children learn? (how a tragedy unites people)

AT A GLANCE

- The priest concludes by saying there will always be both white and green gardens.
- The mourners receive this meaning as a revelation.

REFLECTING ON THE STORY

What does the priest's moment of confusion add to the story? (It makes his final eloquence all the more powerful because it shows that his revelation comes only after painful searching.)

STUDY QUESTIONS

1. church in Brooklyn; funeral of six firefighters
2. says *white,* not *green;* priest
3. "emerald field"; thick traffic, hundred-million emotions passed, resurrection and life
4. ▪ "We shall always have green gardens, and . . . white gardens, too."
▪ electrified
5. a "blue river"
6. firefighters who died in line of duty, always faced with question of mortality; save lives
7. deaths not in vain—part of life that continues in Brooklyn; part of something eternal
8. ▪ no
▪ yes
▪ death or afterlife
▪ Death and life both always with us.
9. ▪ bravery, self-sacrifice
▪ anonymity
▪ Answers will vary.

COMPARING WRITERS

Malamud uses life of shoemaker, assistant, daughter as means of showing importance of love and self-sacrifice. *Saroyan* uses humorous childhood memory of limerick contest to point out importance of flexibility, openness. *Updike* shows basic human predicament of modern life—inability to find meaning, fulfillment—through a baseball player's slump. *Goyen* uses small moment in man's life to talk about continuity and change. *Helprin* uses funeral, priest's slip of tongue to talk about immortality.

concerns to see that everything that was, is; and that everything that is, will always be." She looked at him, bending her head slightly and pursing her lips in an expression of love and sadness, and he continued. "For we shall always have green gardens, and we shall always have white gardens, too."

Now they knew what he meant, and it shot like electricity through the six wives, the eighteen children, and the blue river of men.

Symbol (page 190): The gardens, standing for two aspects of life, carry the theme of the story.

Revelation and epiphany (page 794): A flash of insight is the climax of the story.

STUDY QUESTIONS

Recalling

1. Where is the story set? For what reason are the people gathered there?
2. What apparent error does the priest make in the opening paragraph? To what are the firefighters drawn "despite their battalion's worth of liveliness and strength" (paragraph 6)?
3. According to the seventh paragraph, where will the men be buried? What three things does the young wife realize will happen in Brooklyn "even as the men are buried"?
4. What does the priest say when he is "finally in control of himself"? How do the congregation react to his final speech, according to the last paragraph?
5. What image is used twice in the story to describe the procession of firemen?

Interpreting

6. What is the significance of the profession of the men who have died and the way they died? Why are they important to the people?
7. What does the "resurrection and life all over Brooklyn" suggest about the death of the six firemen? How is the image of the "blue stream" related to this suggestion?
8. When the priest first uses "white gardens," are his words intentional? When he uses the term a second time, are his words intentional? What might he mean by "white gardens"? Why must those mourning the dead firemen think of "white gardens" as well as "green gardens"?

Extending

9. In what sense are these six firemen traditional heroes? In what sense are they modern heroes? Who, in your opinion, are some of the other heroes of the modern world, and why?

COMPOSITION

Writing About Color Symbols

■ Helprin uses colors in a poetic and symbolic way in "White Gardens." Write a brief composition on the use of colors in this story. First identify the story's uses of *white;* tell what you think it stands for and how it conveys the theme of the story. Then identify other colors used in the story. Tell what they symbolize and how they compare or contrast to the uses of white. *For help with this assignment, refer to Lesson 5 in the Writing About Literature Handbook at the back of this book.*

Writing a Description

■ Write a brief prose description, or a poem if you wish, using colors to create a vivid scene for your reader. Imagine the scene as if you were a painter choosing colors from your palette. Do not hesitate to name unusual colors or describe conventional colors in new ways. If you attach symbolic meanings to the colors, be sure your reader sees your reasons for doing so.

COMPARING WRITERS

■ The great modern philosopher George Santayana said, "The local is the only universal." Writers have always known that the great issues of life must be presented in concrete, immediate terms, but many modern writers seem to confine themselves deliberately to the domestic, the everyday, the very ordinary. Discuss how the short story writers on pages 786–837 use the ordinary to express the extraordinary. Describe the scenes and events in the stories. Then tell what insight or universal meaning the writer draws from each.

COMPOSITION: GUIDELINES FOR EVALUATION

WRITING ABOUT COLOR SYMBOLS

Objective

To write about color symbols

Guidelines for Evaluation

- suggested length: four to six paragraphs
- should identify the symbolic meanings of the colors in the story and show how they help convey the theme

WRITING A DESCRIPTION

Objective

To write a description using colors

Guidelines for Evaluation

- suggested length: two to four paragraphs or eight to twelve lines
- should describe colors in unusual ways
- should ascribe appropriate symbolic meanings to colors

Barry Lopez *born 1945*

Writer and photographer Barry Holstun Lopez finds most of his subjects in nature and the environment. He has written about the desert in *Desert Notes: Reflections in the Eye of a Raven* (1976) and the Arctic vastness in *Arctic Dreams* (1986). In 1978 he published a work of nonfiction called *Of Wolves and Men* that became a best seller. Two works of fiction, *River Notes: The Dance of Herons* (1979) and *Winter Count* (1981), have also been well received. In addition to his writings about nature, Lopez has published a collection of Native American tales.

■ In what situations could you picture yourself working so closely with a group of people that you could sense what to do next without talking about it?

Barry Lopez

from Arctic Dreams

1 We left our camp on Pingok Island one morning knowing a storm was moving in from the southwest, but we were not worried. We were planning to work in open water between the beach and the edge of the pack ice, only a few miles out, making bottom trawls from an open 20-foot boat. The four of us were dressed, as usual, in heavy clothes and foul-weather gear.

2 You accept the possibility of death in such situations, prepare for it, and then forget about it. We carried emergency and survival equipment in addition to all our scientific gear—signal flares, survival suits, a tent, and each of us had a pack with extra clothing, a sleeping bag, and a week's worth of food. Each morning we completed a checklist of the boat and radioed a distant base camp with our day plan. When we departed, we left a handwritten note on the table in our cabin, saying what time we left, the compass bearing we were taking, and when we expected to return.

My companions, all scientists, were serious about this, but not solemn or tedious. They forestalled trouble by preparing for it, and were guided, not deterred, by the danger inherent in
3 their work. It is a pleasure to travel with such people. As in other walks of life, the person who feels compelled to dramatize the risks or is either smugly complacent or eager to demonstrate his survival skills is someone you hope not to meet.

Our camaraderie came from our enthusiasm for the work and from exhilaration with the landscape, the daily contact with sea birds, seals, and

AT A GLANCE

- Four scientists set out from their Arctic island camp.
- They accept the dangers of their work and take precautions.
- They leave behind them information on their destination.

LITERARY OPTIONS

- suspense
- main idea
- purpose

THEMATIC OPTIONS

- the importance of comradeship
- human beings against nature

1 PURPOSE

The author's purpose is to share an exciting, suspenseful adventure and to tell about the conditions that accompany scientific expeditions in the Arctic.

2 PLOT: FORESHADOWING

The author's mention of the possibility of death foreshadows the team's experience.

3 AUDIENCE

The author relates his experience to other walks of life, thus bringing the audience closer to the narrative.

GUIDED READING

LITERAL QUESTION

1a. What do the men leave behind in their cabin when they leave? (a handwritten note)

INFERENTIAL QUESTION

1b. Why do they leave it there? (In case they do not return, someone will know where to start searching.)

AT A GLANCE

- They decide to work on despite high waves and the falling temperature.
- Their boat is trapped by ice.
- They pull the boat over an ice floe into open water, but this water is also closing up.
- They find a channel and chop their way through it.

1 MAIN IDEA

The mutual regard of the scientists and their ability to work together in a crisis are essential to their success.

2 SUSPENSE

Stating the possible dangers helps to set the stage for what may happen to the team and helps to build anticipation.

3 SUSPENSE

The narrative moves from problem to solution, with each solution leading to a new and perhaps graver problem.

4 MAIN IDEA

The group's silent teamwork demonstrates their closeness and spirit of comradeship.

fish. We rarely voiced these things to each other; they surfaced in a word of encouragement or understanding around rough work done in un-
1 ending dampness or cold. Our mutual regard was founded in the accomplishment of our tasks and was as important to our survival as the emergency gear stowed in a blue box forward of the steering console.

We worked through the morning, sorting the contents of bottom trawls and vertical plankton tows. Around noon we shut the engines off and drifted under overcast skies, eating our lunch. The seas were beginning to slap at the hull, but we had another couple of hours before they built up to three or four feet—our match, comfortably. We decided, then, to search for seals in the ice front before heading in. An hour later, by a movement of the ice so imperceptible it was finished before we realized it, we were cut off from the sea. The wind, compacting the ice, was closing off the channels of calm water where we had been cruising. We were suddenly 200 yards from open water, and a large floe, turning off the wind and folding in from the west, threatened to close us off even deeper in the pack. Already we had lost steerageway—the boat was pinned at that moment on all four sides.

In those first hours we worked wordlessly
2 and diligently. We all knew what we faced. Even if someone heard our distress call over the radio, we could not tell him precisely where we were, and we were in pack ice moving east. A three-day storm was coming on. The floes might crush the boat and drive it under, or they could force it out of the water where we would have it for shelter.

We took advantage of any momentary opening in the ice to move toward open water, widening the channels with ice chisels, pushing with the twin 90-horsepower engines, the four of us heaving at the stern and gunwales. We were angling for a small patch of water within the pack. From there, it seemed, after a quick reconnoiter ahead on foot, we might be able to get out to the open sea. Thirty feet shy of our patch of water, we doubted the wisdom of taking ice chisels to one particular chunk of weathered pressure ice that blocked our path. Fractured the wrong way, its center of gravity would shift and the roll could take the boat under. The only way around it was to pull the boat, which weighed 3000 pounds, completely out of the water. With an improvised system of ice anchors, lines, and block and tackle, and out of the terrific desire to get free, we set to. We got the boat up on the floe, across it, and back into the water.

Had that been open water, we would have cheered. As it was, we exchanged quick glances
3 of justifiable but not foolish hope. While we had been winching the boat over the ice toward it, this patch of water had been closing up. And another large floe still separated us from the ocean. Where the surf broke against it, it fell a sheer four feet to the sea. Even if we got the boat over that ice, we could never launch it from such a precipice.

Two stayed in the boat. I and one other went in opposite directions along the floe. Several hundred yards to the east I found a channel. I looked it over quickly and then signaled with the upraised shaft of my ice chisel for the others. It was barely negotiable to begin with, and in the few minutes it took to get the boat there, the channel closed. We put the prow of the boat against the seaward floe and brought both engines up to full power, trying to hold it against the wind. The ice beside it continued to move
4 east. The channel started to open. With the engines roaring, the gap opened to six feet. With a silent, implicit understanding each of us acted decisively. The man at the helm reversed the engines, heeled the boat around, and burst up the channel. We made 20 quick feet, careened the boat over on its port gunwale, and pivoted through a 120° turn. One ran ahead, chopping swift and hard at the closing ice with a chisel. Two of us heaved, jumping in and out of the boat, stabbing at chunks of ice closing on the props. One man remained at the throttles. Suddenly he lunged away, yanking the starboard engine clear of fouling ice. The man ahead threw his ice chisel into the boat and jumped across to help lift at the port gunwale. We could *feel* how close. The starboard side of the boat slid off the ice, into the water. The bow lifted on the open sea. There was

GUIDED READING

LITERAL QUESTIONS

1a. According to the narrator, what is as important to the team as their emergency gear? (mutual regard)

2a. What does the narrator find when he walks east along the ice? (a channel)

INFERENTIAL QUESTIONS

1b. Why is respect for one another so vital? (Their concern for one another helps them to act together in an emergency.)

2b. Why is his discovery important? (The channel represents a potential avenue out of the ice to the open sea.)

nothing more for our legs to strain against. We pulled ourselves over the gunwale and fell into the boat, limp as feed sacks. Exhausted. We were out.

1 We were out, and the seas were running six feet. And we were miles now from a shore that we could not see. In the hours we had been in the ice, the storm had built considerably, and we had been carried we did not know how far east. The seas were as much as the boat could handle, and too big to quarter—we had to take them nearly bow-on. The brief views from wave crests showed us nothing. We could not see far enough through the driving sleet and spray, and the arctic coast here lies too low, anyway. We could only hope we were east of Pingok, the westernmost of the barrier islands, and not to the west, headed down into Harrison Bay, where the wind has a greater fetch and the shore is much farther on.

We took water over the bow and shouted strategy to each other over the wind and the sound of engines screaming as the props came out of the water. We erected a canvas shelter forward to break the force of the sea and shed water. We got all the weight we could out of the bow. A resolute steadiness came over us. We were making headway. We were secure. If we did not broach and if we were far enough to the east, we would be able to run up on a leeward shore somewhere and wait out the storm.

We plowed ahead. Three of us stood hunched backward to the weather.

I began to recognize in the enduring steadiness another kind of calmness, or relief. The distance between my body and my thoughts slowly became elongated, and muffled like a dark, carpeted corridor. I realized I was cold, that I was shivering. I sensed the dry pits of warmth under my clothes and, against this, an opening and closing over my chest, like cold breath. I realized with dreamlike stillness that the whole upper
2 right side of my body was soaked. The shoulder seams of my foul-weather gear were torn open.

I knew I had to get to dry clothes, to get them on. But desire could not move my legs or arms. They were too far away. I was staring at someone, then moving; the soaked clothes were coming off. I could not make a word in my mouth. I felt suspended in a shaft in the earth, and then

AT A GLANCE

- Finally they reach the open sea.
- The waves are running six feet high.
- They plow ahead, hoping to reach land.
- The narrator realizes that he is soaked and freezing.

1 SUSPENSE

Ironically, the act that saved them from the ice has only brought them into a greater peril.

2 PURPOSE

The author's experience graphically illustrates the unexpected dangers of working in an Arctic environment: A ripped jacket can be fatal.

GUIDED READING

LITERAL QUESTION

1a. What does the author realize that he must do? (get into dry clothes)

INFERENTIAL QUESTION

1b. Why is this action so important? (In those temperatures he could freeze to death if he remains wet.)

imagined I was sitting on a bare earthen floor somewhere within myself. The knowledge that I was being slammed around like a wooden box in the bottom of the boat was like something I had walked away from.

In dry wool and protected by a tarp from the seas, I understood that I was safe; but I could not understand the duration of time. I could not locate any visual image outside myself. I concentrated on trying to gain a sense of the boat; and then on a rhythmic tensing and loosening of my muscles. I kept at it and at it, then I knew time was passing. There was a flow of time again. I heard a shout. I tried to shout myself, and when I heard an answer I knew that I was at the edge of time again, and could just step into it. I realized I was sitting up, that I was bracing myself against heavy seas.

The shouts were for the coast. We had found Pingok.

We anchored the boat under the lee shore and went into the cabin and changed clothes and fixed dinner. Our sense of relief came out in a patter of jokes at each other's expense. We ate quietly and went to bed and slept like bears in winter.

STUDY QUESTIONS

Recalling

1. What possibility do Lopez and the scientists face daily? What precautions do they take every day? How do they feel about the chance of dying?
2. How does the group get caught in the ice? How do they reach the sea? What problem do they face there?
3. How does Lopez experience the cold when he becomes wet?
4. How does Lopez know that he has returned to normal?

Interpreting

5. How does Lopez feel about the scientists? Why is their mutual regard important?
6. How does Lopez get into dry clothes?
7. Why do the members of the group tease one another while making dinner? Why does Lopez not give the names of any of his companions?

Extending

8. If you had to interview candidates for an Arctic project, what sorts of questions would you ask to see whether an applicant would be an asset to the group? Write three such questions.

LITERARY FOCUS

Narration

Narration is writing that tells a story, moving from event to event, usually in chronological order. Sometimes, however, an author may choose to start with the middle or end of the story and then work in the missing parts through flashbacks or other devices. A narration may be factual, or it may be a work of fiction. Some poetry is narrative because it tells a story. Narratives may be book-length, or they may be only a few paragraphs long.

Thinking About Narration

1. What length of time does Lopez describe? When does the selection begin? When does it end?
2. Look through the selections in this book, and find an example of a narrative poem. Then find a story that starts with the end of a series of events.

COMPOSITION

Writing About Nonfiction

■ One critic has commented that "a poet slips quietly out of Mr. Lopez's matter-of-fact prose." Write a brief composition beginning with these words: "Barry Lopez uses poetic language and descriptions in *Arctic Dreams* in order to . . ." Give examples of the kind of poetic language you find, and explain what each example achieves. *For help with this assignment, refer to Lesson 4 in the Writing About Literature Handbook at the back of this book.*

Writing a Narrative Essay

■ Write an essay of at least three paragraphs about a goal that you have reached. Describe the goal in the first paragraph, and explain what it meant to you. In the middle paragraphs describe how you achieved the goal. In the last paragraph explain how you felt when you attained the goal.

AT A GLANCE

- In dry clothes he concentrates on sensations within his body.
- The team finally finds Pingok Island and safety.

REFLECTING ON THE SELECTION

What might have happened to the team if mutual respect and comradeship had been lacking? (The crew might have not worked with split-second coordination and so would have perished.)

STUDY QUESTIONS

1. ■ death
   ■ carry emergency and survival equipment, complete a checklist of the boat, radio a base camp, leave notes
   ■ accept the possibility, prepare for it, and then forget it
2. They do not notice the movement of the ice; they move toward open water through any momentary opening; they are in heavy seas, and they do not know where they are.
3. calm and dreamy, cannot talk or move legs or arms, loses sense of time
4. He hears an answer when he tries to shout.
5. He respects them and enjoys working with them; all depend on each other.
6. One of the group helps him.
7. to communicate their relief and thanks to one another; individuals less important than the group
8. Sample questions: What was the most dangerous experience you have ever had? What do you think is your strongest point? Where do your weaknesses lie?

LITERARY FOCUS

1. one day; in the morning; that night
2. ■ *Narrative poems:* "The Raven," "Snow-Bound" "Janet Waking"
   ■ *Stories:* "To Build a Fire," "The Jilting of Granny Weatherall"

COMPOSITION: GUIDELINES FOR EVALUATION

WRITING ABOUT NONFICTION

Objective

To analyze a nonfiction work

Guidelines for Evaluation

- suggested length: three to five paragraphs
- should include examples of precise description and poetic language
- should explain what these add to the work

WRITING A NARRATIVE ESSAY

Objective

To write a narrative essay

Guidelines for Evaluation

- suggested length: three to five paragraphs
- should describe a goal of the writer
- should explain how the writer achieved the goal
- should describe the writer's feelings

Américo Paredes *born 1915*

Américo Paredes has the rare distinction of being professor of two different subjects at the University of Texas at Austin. He teaches both English and anthropology, two subjects that merge in his specialty: folklore. Folklore is the traditional beliefs, practices, legends, and tales that are usually passed orally from one generation to the next. Paredes, who is especially interested in the folklore of Mexican Americans, has written several books on the subject. He has also served as editor of the *Journal of American Folklore.*

■ Proverbs, or *dichos,* are one form of folklore. Can you think of any proverbs that you have heard? Where did you first hear them?

Américo Paredes

Dichos

Proverbs have been called "the wisdom of many and the wit of one." They are "the wit of one" because it was some one person, at some particular time and place, who put the thought of each proverb into just the right words. To put something into "just the right words" is to create poetry, and the unknown persons who created proverbs were poets in their own right. Proverbs are "the wisdom of many" because they express the feelings and attitudes of whole groups of people rather than just the feelings of an individual.
1 They are part of the literature of distinctive groups of people that we refer to as "folk." That is, proverbs are one of the basic forms of folk poetry, and a very ancient kind. Proverbs are found in the Old Testament, for example.

The formal word for "proverb" in Spanish is *refrán,* but most Mexicans and Mexican-Americans call them *dichos,* "sayings." They are a spe-
2 cial way of saying things, of making a point, and they are used in ordinary conversation everywhere that Mexican-Americans speak to each other in Spanish, whether on a farm in South Texas or at a steel mill in Gary, Indiana. To those unfamiliar with the culture, the effect of *dichos* is to make the language "colorful." To the sayer of *dichos,* they are a time-honored way of expressing himself, of putting over a point in just the right way.

Dichos do not contain absolute truths; that is, they are not a set of rules telling one exactly how to behave at all times. They are a storehouse of

AT A GLANCE

- Proverbs are one of the basic forms of folk poetry.
- Mexican-Americans call them *dichos,* sayings used in ordinary conversation that put over a point in just the right way.

LITERARY OPTIONS

- balance
- rhyme
- purpose

THEMATIC OPTIONS

- wisdom in proverbs
- cultural identity
- art and imagination

1 THEME

The author invokes the venerable tradition of proverbs to show that they are an important form of folk utterance.

2 AUDIENCE

Because the author presumes that many in his audience will be unfamiliar with Mexican-American culture, his explanation provides background.

GUIDED READING

LITERAL QUESTION

1a. What is the formal word for "proverb" in Spanish? (*refrán*)

INFERENTIAL QUESTION

1b. Why do you think Mexican-Americans prefer the word *dichos,* meaning "sayings"? (The informal word suits the way the proverbs are used in ordinary conversation.)

AT A GLANCE

- *Dichos* are a storehouse of good advice to be used according to specific situations.
- One kind of *dicho* is the "true proverb," a complete little poem that uses the same kinds of effects found in other poetry.
- The other kind of *dicho* is a "comparison," a phrase beginning with *como* (like) usually based on popular stories.
- Subjects of true proverbs include perseverence, poverty, and minding one's own business.

1 PURPOSE

The factual analysis of *dichos* conforms to the author's purpose: to present and explain this form of folk literature.

2 BALANCE

The two parts of the proverb illustrate balance. The repeated *a* sounds provide an assonance that unifies the point of this *dicho*.

3 RHYME

The balanced, contrasting halves of this *dicho* are rhymed. The rhyming of folk sayings, or repeating vowel sounds, helps to make them memorable—an advantage both in transmitting the culture and in making a point.

good advice to be used according to specific situations. That is why two *dichos* may give opposite advice. This is also true of proverbs in English; for example, "Look before you leap" and "He who hesitates is lost."

1 There are two kinds of *dichos* most commonly used. One is called by folklorists the "true proverb." It is always a complete statement, a sentence. It is also a complete little poem, using the same kinds of effects that are found in other poetry. One of the simplest poetic effects, and perhaps the oldest, is balanced structure—the balancing of the two parts of the *dicho* on either side of a center, like two weights on an old-fashioned type of scales. For example: *Arrieros somos / y en el camino andamos.*[1] This is the same type of structure used in the Old Testament, in the Psalms: "The Lord is my shepherd; / I shall not want."

Contrast may be added to balanced structure, and the effect is even more pleasing. In the following *dichos* the two underlined words are contrasted with each other: *Mucho ruido / y pocas nueces; A buena hambre / no hay mal pan.* Another effect is made by adding rhyme, as in much poetry we are familiar with: *Cada oveja / con su pareja; A Dios rogando / y con el mazo dando.* Other *dichos* may use alliteration, the repetition of the first sounds of words, rather than the final sounds as in rhyme—"rough and ready." Alliteration is not common in Spanish poetry, but assonance is used very frequently. In assonance, only the vowel sounds are matched (*olas* and *hoja,* for example), instead of vowel and consonant sounds, as we do to make rhymes (*olas* and *solas*). The following *dicho* uses both assonance and alliteration: *Quien da pan a perro ajeno / pierde el pan y pierde el perro.*

The other kind of *dicho* is known as a "comparison." It is not a complete sentence, but a phrase beginning with the word *como,* "like." Most *dichos* of this kind have stories behind them, stories that everybody knows, so that when somebody says, "I was left there like the man who whistled on the hill," everybody knows just how the speaker was left—holding the bag.

(These dichos *were collected and translated by Américo Paredes.)*

True Proverbs

A buena hambre no hay mal pan.
No food is bad when you're good and hungry.

A Dios rogando y con el mazo dando.
Pray to God, but keep hammering away (at your problem).

¿A dónde ha de ir el buey, que no ha de seguir arando?
Where can the ox go that he will not have to plow? (Where can a poor man go, that he will not be given the hardest kind of job for the lowest pay?)

2 *Ahora es cuando, yerbabuena, le has de dar sabor al caldo.*
Now is the time, peppermint, when you must flavor the soup. (Now is the time to do or die; now or never; put up or shut up.)

Al pan, pan y al vino, vino.
Let us call bread, bread and wine, wine. (Be realistic.)

Arrieros somos y en el camino andamos.
We are all drovers,[2] traveling down the same road. (We are all the same, living in the same hard world; we are all in it together; the world is not so wide that we will not meet again.)

Cada oveja con su pareja.
Each ewe to its ram. (To each his own.)

Cada quien en su casa, y Dios en la de todos.
Each man in his house, and God in all houses. (Let each man mind his own business, and God will smile on all of us.)

3 *Caras vemos, corazones no sabemos.*
We see their faces, but we do not know their hearts.

1. **Arrieros . . . andamos:** translations of proverbs appear below.

2. **drovers:** persons who drive livestock to market.

GUIDED READING

LITERAL QUESTION

1a. Of the two kinds of *dichos*, what is a complete statement called? (true proverb)

INFERENTIAL QUESTION

1b. Why is it called this? (The form is the same as the very ancient proverbs found in the Old Testament; it is the form we most readily recognize as being a proverb.)

Abuelitos Piscando Nopalitos (Grandparents Picking Cactus), Carmen Lomas Garza, 1979–1980.

Como quiera nace el maíz, estando la tierra en punto.
Nothing will keep the corn from growing, as long as the land is ready. (Nothing will stop us, if we have planned well.)

Cuando se pelean las comadres, salen las verdades.
When gossips fight, then truths will out.

1 *Da y ten, y harás bien.*
Give (some of your goods) and keep (a part), and you will do well.

2 *El flojo y el mezquino andan dos veces el camino.*
The sluggard and the miser travel the same road twice. (Lazy and stingy people do not give their all to what they do, so they often have to do it again.)

El pan ajeno hace al hijo bueno.
Another man's food will make your son good. (Going out into the world and earning his own keep makes a son more considerate of his parents.)

El que carga su costal sabe lo que lleva dentro.
He who shoulders the bag knows what he carries in it. (No one really knows your troubles except yourself.)

3 *El que con lobos anda, a aullar se enseña.*
He who runs with wolves will learn to howl. (If you run around with unsavory characters, you will pick up their ways.)

El que nace pa' tamal, del cielo le caen las hojas.
If you're born to be a *tamal,* heaven will send you the cornshucks. (Tamales are made wrapped in cornshucks, so they go together like hamburgers and buns. You will be what you're going to be, and circumstances will conspire to keep you from being anything else.)

El que no habla, Dios no lo oye.
If you don't speak up, God will not hear you. (You have to speak up for your rights, or you won't get them.)

Entre menos burros, más olotes.
The fewer donkeys, the more corncobs. (The fewer to share, the more to go around.)

Es poco el amor, ¡y gastándolo en celos!
So little love—why waste it in jealous quarrels? (Let us not waste the little we have.)

Haz bien, y no mires a quién.
Do good, without caring to whom.

Las cuentas claras y el chocolate espeso.
I like my accounts clear and my chocolate thick.

Lo pescaron en las tunas, con las manos coloradas.
They caught him in the prickly-pear patch, with his hands all red.

Los golpes hacen al buen vaquero.
Hard knocks make a good horseman.

Manso como un cordero, mientras hago lo que quiero.
I'm as gentle as a lamb, as long as I'm doing what I want to do.

Más vale pobre que solo.
It's better to be poor than to live alone.

AT A GLANCE

The true proverbs include such subjects as preparedness, gossip, sharing, good works, laziness, child-rearing, fate, assertiveness, quarreling, and hard times.

1 CONTRAST

The contrast of *da* (give) and *ten* (keep) adds a note of paradox. To succeed, one must do both, but in a balanced way. The two parts of this *dicho* also rhyme.

2 ASSONANCE

The long *o* sounds in *flojo, mezquino, dos,* and *camino* tend to slow down the pace of this *dicho* and underscore the theme of laziness.

3 ONOMATOPOEIA

The results of "running with wolves" are dramatized through the use of the verb *aullar,* which imitates a howling wolf.

GUIDED READING

LITERAL QUESTIONS

1a. What does one *dicho* say will happen if you are born to be a *tamal?* (Heaven will send you the cornshucks.)

2a. What is the meaning of *Haz bien, y no mires a quién? (Do good, without caring to whom.)*

INFERENTIAL QUESTIONS

1b. What attitude toward life is shared by this *dicho* and *¿A dónde ha de ir el buey, que no ha de seguir arando?* (Both show fatalism and acceptance of one's station in life.)

2b. What cultural value is demonstrated by this *dicho* and *Da y ten, y harás bien?* (Both *dichos* call for generosity toward others.)

AT A GLANCE

- The true proverbs comment on overreacting and drawing sound conclusions.
- Proverbs of comparison deal with anger, boredom, deprivation, and foolishness.

1 STYLE: CONTRAST

The antonyms *mucho* (much) and *pocas* (few) heighten the contrast between sound and result.

2 RESPONSE JOURNAL

The image of the merchant's burden reflects a particular culture. Ask students to make up a proverb that expresses the same insight in terms of their own culture.

REFLECTING ON THE SELECTION

What attitudes do the *dichos* suggest exist in the culture from which they come? (Students may find in the *dichos* a positive, commonsense approach that displays closeness to the land and faith in God.)

STUDY QUESTIONS

1. sayings; Mexican Americans and Mexicans; they add color and tradition to language
2. the true proverb—a complete statement— and the comparison—not a complete sentence but a phrase beginning with the word *como* ("like")
3. balanced structure, contrast, rhyme, assonance
4. Although they express the thoughts and feelings of whole groups of people, one person put those thoughts and feelings into words.
5. The advice may change depending on the circumstances.
6. *Dichos* and other types of folklore teach a great deal about the people who thought of them.
7. If students have trouble completing the assignment, suggest that they consult proverb books such as *Poor Richard's Almanack*.

1 *Mucho ruido y pocas nueces.*
Much noise and few nuts (harvested or shelled). (Much ado about nothing.)

No creas que la luna es queso, nomás porque la ves redonda.
Don't think the moon is made of cheese, just because you see it's round.

Comparisons

Como agua pa' chocolate.
Like water for making chocolate. (Very hot, that is. When someone is very angry, he is "like water for making chocolate.")

Como atole de enfermo.
Like a sick man's gruel. (This is all a sick man is fed, so it stands for something that is very boring, that you just can't stand any more.)

2 *Como el burro del aguador* (or *del zacatero*).
Like the water seller's (or the hay seller's) burro. (The poor burro carries water or hay on his back all day, for sale, but he never gets any of it. When you are close to something you want very much but cannot have it, you say you are like the water seller's burro.)

Como el que chifló en la loma.
Like the man who whistled on the hill. (There is a story about several thieves or smugglers who posted one man on a hill as a lookout. The lookout was supposed to whistle, to warn them if police were coming. But the others saw the police officers before the lookout did, and they ran away. When the lookout saw the officers, he began to whistle as loudly as he could; but nobody answered him. So he kept whistling and whistling until he was caught.)

STUDY QUESTIONS

Recalling

1. What does *dichos* mean? Who uses *dichos* in their speech? What effect do *dichos* have on the language?
2. What are the two most common forms of *dichos*? Give examples of each type.
3. What are some of the poetic effects that make *dichos* pleasing?

Interpreting

4. Why are *dichos* called "the wisdom of many and the wit of one"?
5. How is it possible that two *dichos* can give opposite advice?
6. What is the value of collecting and studying folklore such as *dichos?*

Extending

7. Make a collection of proverbs used by your family, neighbors, teachers, and other people you know. Present them to the class as a booklet, an audio or video tape, a skit, or in some other form.

LITERARY FOCUS

Exposition

Exposition is one of the four main types of prose writing. The others are description (see page 92), narration (see page 113), and persuasion (see page 22).

Most essays use exposition to give information or to explain the nature of a particular subject. If you were to write an essay describing some important aspects of modern dance technique or how to hit a backhand shot in tennis or make a pizza, your essay would be expository.

In "Dichos" Américo Paredes discusses a special form of Mexican-American folklore. To do so, he uses some important forms of exposition. He *defines dichos* and *illustrates* his definition with examples. He *analyzes* the poetic qualities of *dichos,* and he *classifies* a number of *dichos* according to type.

Thinking About Exposition

■ Identify sentences in "Dichos" that use the following methods of exposition: definition, illustration, and classification. Look for examples of exposition in other reading material.

LITERARY FOCUS

Examples:

- definition—"Proverbs are one of the basic forms of folk poetry. . . ."
- illustration—"This is also true of proverbs in English; for example. . . ."
- classification—The concluding part of the essay contains *dichos* classified by type.

Ralph Ellison *born 1914*

Ralph Ellison's central theme is freedom, not only social and political freedom but the inner freedom of the individual spirit. This is the freedom Ellison himself achieved when he decided, as he said, "to run the risk of his own humanity."

Ralph Ellison grew up in Oklahoma City, Oklahoma. He loved music from an early age, played the trumpet in high school, and was especially inspired by jazz. From 1933 to 1936 he studied music and composition at Tuskegee Institute in Alabama. A new interest in sculpture drew him to New York City, where he also performed as a jazz musician.

In New York Ellison met the writers Langston Hughes and Richard Wright, who inspired and encouraged him to write. Ellison had read widely in American literature and had been particularly influenced by T. S. Eliot's poem *The Waste Land.* Now Hughes and Wright pointed him toward other great writers—Dostoevsky, Conrad, Joyce, Faulkner, and Hemingway among them. As he studied their works, Ellison learned the lessons of modernism and began to write seriously himself.

Ellison's first novel, *Invisible Man,* appeared in 1952. For its intense, deeply affecting, sometimes harrowing portrayal of a young black man growing up in the South and in Harlem, it won the National Book Award and immediate recognition as a classic of modern literature. In a poll of two hundred writers and critics, *Invisible Man* was named the most distinguished novel published in America between 1945 and 1965.

Ellison has lectured widely on black culture and folklore and has taught literature and creative writing at numerous colleges and universities. His second book, *Shadow and Act* (1964), is a collection of interviews and essays, including "Hidden Name and Complex Fate"—in which the author ponders the significance of the name his father gave him.

■ How do you feel about your name? Does it suit you? If you could choose another, what would it be?

AT A GLANCE

- The author says we must learn to establish a unity between our names and ourselves.
- For blacks, European names represent a triumph of the spirit and selecting names with special associations is important.

LITERARY OPTIONS

- purpose
- illustration

THEMATIC OPTIONS

- the importance of names
- establishing a personal identity

1 ESSAY

In this, as in many essays, the main point is directly stated in the first paragraph or sentence.

2 ILLUSTRATION

The author begins with an example to illustrate his point. The little girl is making her name her own. Her game fulfills a basic need.

3 STYLE: FIGURES OF SPEECH

Our names can be masks to hide behind, shields to protect us from the outside world, and vessels to hold our family past. These metaphors imply that our names are separate from us and that our goal should be to integrate our names with our selves.

4 ILLUSTRATION

The example of Franklin D. Roosevelt Jones illustrates the suggestive power of names.

Ralph Ellison

from Hidden Name and Complex Fate

1 Our names, being the gift of others, must be made our own.

Once while listening to the play of a two-year-old girl who did not know she was under observation, I heard her saying over and over again, at first with questioning and then with
2 sounds of growing satisfaction, "I am Mimi Livisay? . . . *I* am Mimi Livisay. I *am* Mimi Livisay . . . I am *Mimi* Li-visay! I am Mimi . . ."

And in deed and in fact she was—or became so soon thereafter, by working playfully to establish the unity between herself and her name.

For many of us this is far from easy. We must learn to wear our names within all the noise and confusion of the environment in which we find ourselves; make them the center of all of our associations with the world, with man and with nature. We must charge them with all our emotions, our hopes, hates, loves,
3 aspirations. They must become our masks and our shields and the containers of all those values and traditions which we learn and/or imagine as being the meaning of our familial past. . . .

Perhaps, taken in aggregate, these European names which (sometimes with irony, sometimes with pride, but always with personal investment) represent a certain triumph of the spirit, speaking to us of those who rallied, reassembled and transformed themselves and who under dismembering pressures refused to die. "Brothers and sisters," I once heard a Negro preacher exhort, "let us make up our faces before the world, and our names shall sound throughout the land with honor! For we ourselves are our *true* names, not their epithets! So let us, I say, Make Up Our Faces and Our Minds!"

Perhaps my preacher had read T. S. Eliot, although I doubt it. And in actuality, it was unnecessary that he do so, for a concern with names and naming was very much a part of that special area of American culture from which I come, and it is precisely for this reason that this example should come to mind in a discussion of my own experience as a writer.

Undoubtedly, writers begin their *conditioning* as manipulators of words long before they become aware of literature—certain Freudians[1] would say at the breast.[2] Perhaps. But if so, that is far too early to be of use at this moment. Of this, though, I am certain: that despite the misconceptions of those educators who trace the reading difficulties experienced by large numbers of Negro children in Northern schools to their Southern background, these children are, in *their* familiar South, facile manipulators of words. I know, too, that the Negro community is deadly in its ability to create nicknames and to spot all that is ludicrous in an unlikely name or that which is incongruous in conduct. Names are not qualities; nor are words, in this particular sense, actions. To assume that they are could cost one his life many times a day. Language skills depend to a large extent upon a knowledge of the details, the manners, the objects, the folkways, the psychological patterns, of a given environment. Humor and wit depend upon much the same awareness, and so does the suggestive power of names.

4 "A small brown bowlegged Negro with the name 'Franklin D. Roosevelt Jones' might sound like a clown to someone who looks at him from the outside," said my friend Albert Murray, "but on the other hand he just might turn out to be a fireside operator. He might just lie back in all of that comic juxtaposition of

1. **Freudians** [froi′dē ənz]: adherents of the psychoanalytical theories and methods of Sigmund Freud (1856–1939).
2. **at the breast:** in earliest infancy.

GUIDED READING

LITERAL QUESTIONS

1a. What does the preacher say about names? ("let us make up our faces before the world, and our names shall sound throughout the land with honor")

2a. What might the small man with the name Franklin D. Roosevelt Jones sound like? (a clown)

INFERENTIAL QUESTIONS

1b. What does this statement imply about names? (Names are the representation of heroic deeds and actions.)

2b. Why is this so? (People might focus on the fact that the name of a great man was given to a person of little stature.)

names and manipulate you deaf, dumb and blind—and you not even suspecting it, because you're thrown out of stance by his name! There you are, so dazzled by the F. D. R. image—which you *know* you can't see—and so delighted with your own superior position that you don't realize that it's *Jones* who must be confronted."

1 Well, as you must suspect, all of this speculation on the matter of names has a purpose, and now, because it is tied up so ironically with my own experience as a writer, I must turn to my own name.

For in the dim beginnings, before I ever thought consciously of writing, there was my own name, and there was, doubtless, a certain
2 magic in it. From the start I was uncomfortable with it, and in my earliest years it caused me much puzzlement. Neither could I understand what a poet was, nor why, exactly, my father had chosen to name me after one. Perhaps I could have understood it perfectly well had he named me after his own father, but that name had been given to an older brother who died and thus was out of the question. But why hadn't he named me after a hero, such as Jack Johnson,[3] or a soldier like Colonel Charles Young, or a great seaman like Admiral Dewey, or an educator like Booker T. Washington, or a great orator and abolitionist like Frederick Douglass? Or again, why hadn't he named me (as so many Negro parents had done) after President Teddy Roosevelt?

Instead, he named me after someone called Ralph Waldo Emerson, and then, when I was three, he died. It was too early for me to have understood his choice, although I'm sure he must have explained it many times, and it was also too soon for me to have made the connection between my name and my father's love
3 for reading. Much later, after I began to write and work with words, I came to suspect that he was aware of the suggestive powers of names and of the magic involved in naming.

I recall an odd conversation with my mother during my early teens in which she mentioned their interest in, of all things, prenatal culture! But for a long time I actually knew only that my father read a lot, and that he admired this remote Mr. Emerson, who was something called a "poet and philosopher"—so much so that he named his second son after him.

I knew, also, that whatever his motives, the combination of names he'd given me caused me no end of trouble from the moment when I could talk well enough to respond to the ritualized question which grownups put to very young children. Emerson's name was quite familiar to Negroes in Oklahoma during those days when World War I was brewing, and adults, eager to show off their knowledge of literary figures, and obviously amused by the

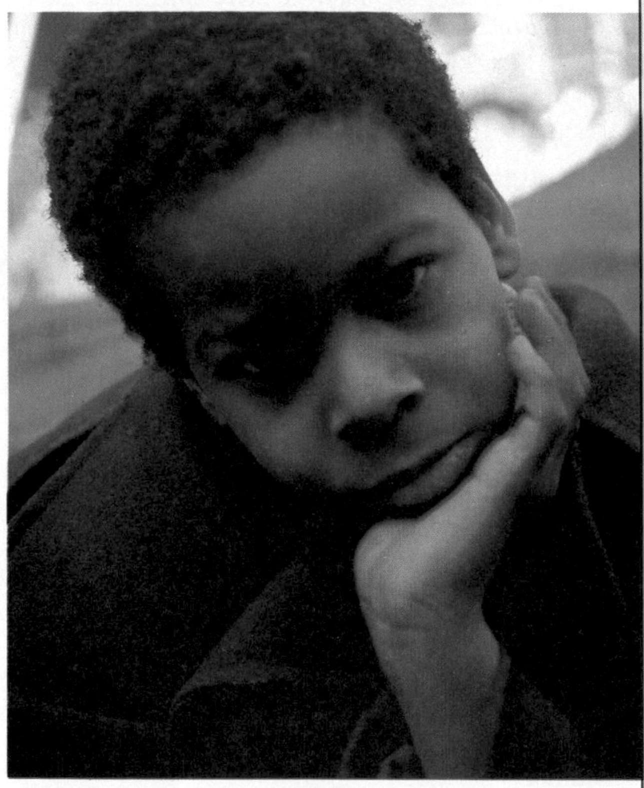

3. **Jack Johnson:** American boxing champion (1908–1915).

AT A GLANCE

- The author's father named him after Ralph Waldo Emerson, which puzzled the author.
- Since his father died when he was three, the author was unable to question him about the choice.
- The author knew only that his father read a lot and admired Emerson.

1 PURPOSE

Ellison's purpose is the personal one of considering whom he is and how his name has contributed to his identity.

2 THEME

Coming to grips with one's name and individual identity is not an easy task. The author relates that he was "uncomfortable" with his name, and it caused him much "puzzlement."

3 THEME

It is as a grown-up that the author became aware of his father's knowledge of the suggestive power of names.

RESPONSE JOURNAL

Have the students write a brief essay on their own names. Where do they come from? What expectations are contained in their names? Who chose them? Why?

GUIDED READING

LITERAL QUESTION

1a. What did the author come to suspect that his father was aware of? (the suggestive powers of names and the magic involved in naming)

INFERENTIAL QUESTION

1b. Why does he suspect this? (because he became a writer and lived up to his father's expectations)

AT A GLANCE

- When the author was a child, people used to laugh at his name.
- As a boy the author found a camera lens that he treasured even though he could never use it for its intended purpose; he had the same trouble dealing with his name.
- He cannot escape the obligation of trying to achieve some of the things Emerson asked of the American writer.

1 THEME

Establishing a personal identity is not an easy task.

2 COMPARISON

The lens was like the name—something mysterious and beautiful, but something the author really did not understand.

3 COMPARISON

The lens was something to be treasured, but something that could never be used as originally intended. The author's name is also something to be treasured, but something the author feels he can never live up to as his father intended.

REFLECTING ON THE SELECTION

How is this essay constructed to focus on the main point? (It begins with the main idea in the first sentence, and all the examples in the story stress or reinforce this idea.)

joke implicit in such a small brown nubbin[4] of a boy carrying around such a heavy moniker,[5] would invariably repeat my first two names and then to my great annoyance, they'd add "Emerson."

And I, in my confusion, would reply, "No, *no, I'm* not Emerson; he's the little boy who lives next door." Which only made them laugh all the louder. "Oh no," they'd say, *"you're* Ralph Waldo Emerson," while I had fantasies of blue murder.

For a while the presence next door of my little friend, Emerson, made it unnecessary for me to puzzle too often over this peculiar adult confusion. And since there were other Negro boys named Ralph in the city, I came to suspect that there was something about the combination of names which produced their laughter. Even today I know of only one other Ralph who had as much comedy made out of his name, a campus politician and deep-voiced orator whom I knew at Tuskegee, who was called in friendly ribbing, *Ralph Waldo Emerson Edgar Allan Poe,* spelled Powe. This must have been quite a trial for him, but I had been initiated much earlier.

During my early school years the name continued to puzzle me, for it constantly
1 evoked in the faces of others some secret. It was as though I possessed some treasure or some defect, which was invisible to my own eyes and ears; something which I had but did not *possess,* like a piece of property in South Carolina, which was mine but which I could not have until some future time. I recall finding, about this time, while seeking adventure in back alleys—which possess for boys a superiority over playgrounds like that which kitchen utensils possess over toys designed for in-
2 fants—a large photographic lens. I remember nothing of its optical qualities, of its speed or color correction, but it gleamed with crystal mystery and it was beautiful.

Mounted handsomely in a tube of shiny brass, it spoke to me of distant worlds of possibility. I played with it, looking through it with squinted eyes, holding it in shafts of sunlight, and tried to use it for a magic lantern. But most of this was as unrewarding as my attempts to make the music come from a phonograph record by holding the needle in my fingers.

I could burn holes through newspapers with it, or I could pretend that it was a telescope, the barrel of a cannon, or the third eye of a monster—*I* being the monster—but I could do nothing at all about its proper function of making images; nothing to make it yield its secret. But I could not discard it.

Older boys sought to get it away from me by offering knives or tops, agate marbles or whole zoos of grass snakes and horned toads in trade, but I held on to it. No one, not even the white boys I knew, had such a lens, and it was my own good luck to have found it. Thus I would hold on to it until such time as I could acquire the parts needed to make it function. Finally I put it aside and it remained buried in my box of treasures, dusty and dull, to be lost and forgotten as I grew older and became interested in music.

I had reached by now the grades where it was necessary to learn something about Mr. Emerson and what he had written, such as the "Concord Hymn" and the essay "Self-Reliance," and in following his advice, I reduced the "Waldo" to a simple and, I hoped, mysterious "W," and in my own reading I avoided his
3 works like the plague. I could no more deal with my name—I shall never really master it—than I could find a creative use for my lens. . . .

I could suppress the name of my namesake out of respect for the achievements of its original bearer but I cannot escape the obligation of attempting to achieve some of the things which he asked of the American writer. As Henry James suggested, being an American is an arduous task, and for most of us, I suspect, the difficulty begins with the name.

4. **nubbin:** something small or undeveloped.
5. **moniker:** slang for "name" or "nickname."

GUIDED READING

LITERAL QUESTIONS

1a. What toy does the author remember from his early days? (a large photographic lens)

2a. What did the author avoid "like the plague"? (He avoided the works of his namesake, Ralph Waldo Emerson.)

INFERENTIAL QUESTIONS

1b. How was this toy like his name? (They were both mysterious and special. They were both something no one else had. The author possessed both, but he could master neither.)

2b. Why do you think he did this? (He was afraid that he could not live up to his name.)

STUDY QUESTIONS

Recalling

1. What idea about names does Ellison introduce in his first sentence? In paragraph 4, what does he say we must learn?
2. What does Ellison say his name "constantly evoked" during his early school years (page 852)? What does he say possessing such a name was like?
3. What "mysterious object" did Ellison, as a boy, find in a "back alley"? Of what did it "speak to him"? What does he say he could *not* do with it? How did he react when other boys wanted him to trade it away?
4. What influenced Ellison to reduce "Waldo" to "W," according to page 852? To what does he compare his boyhood failure to "master" his name? What can he now not "escape," according to his final paragraph?

Interpreting

5. Identify three people or groups to which this essay pays tribute. What effects does Ellison suggest these people or groups had on forming his identity and career?
6. Consider the first five paragraphs of the essay. What modern need or dilemma does Ellison suggest is tied to the interest in one's name?
7. Why is Ellison's comparison between his name and his lens especially appropriate?
8. To what idea of Transcendentalism (page 154) is Ellison referring when he explains why he shortens his middle name to "W"? To what theme or concern of Emerson's does he refer in his last paragraph?
9. Basically, why does Ellison still feel he has been unable to "possess" his name?

Extending

10. People sometimes change their names from the names they are given at birth. Why do you think they do this, and how do such changes relate to the ideas expressed in this essay?

COMPOSITION

Writing About Nonfiction

■ Ellison covers many different topics in "Hidden Name and Complex Fate." He incorporates details, anecdotes, and opinions, all of which point toward the main topic—his name. Write a composition analyzing Ellison's purpose in this essay. How does he use his examples and opinions to help achieve his purpose? *For help with this assignment, refer to Lesson 4 in the Writing About Literature Handbook at the back of this book.*

Writing About Names

■ Choose a name that is interesting to you—the name of a person, a place, a group, or an organization. Write a composition about the meaning you find in it. Discuss its origin, its associations, and any hidden meaning it seems to have. Include in your composition your own observations about how our names affect our everyday experiences.

STUDY QUESTIONS

1. come from others, must be made our own; to wear names within noise of world, make them center of associations with world, man, nature
2. secret in others' faces; possessing some treasure or defect invisible to his own eyes and ears
3. photographic lens; "distant worlds of possibility"; make images; held on to it
4. "Self-Reliance"; failure to use lens to make images; the obligation of trying to achieve some things Emerson asked of the American writer
5. black community, author's father, Emerson; *community:* concern for names and naming; *father:* name, love of reading; *Emerson:* advice making it possible to chart own course and become an American writer.
6. to establish one's own identity
7. both treasured, neither used or appreciated to full potential
8. individualism
9. Full name brings with it a set of expectations from namesake, family, and society.
10. Answers will vary, but students should recognize that changing one's name is a way of expressing identity.

COMPOSITION: GUIDELINES FOR EVALUATION

WRITING ABOUT NONFICTION

Objective

To analyze a work of nonfiction

Guidelines for Evaluation

- suggested length: four to six paragraphs
- should identify Ellison's purpose
- should tell how Ellison achieves his purpose
- should cite specific examples and opinions from the essay

WRITING ABOUT NAMES

Objective

To write about a name

Guidelines for Evaluation

- suggested length: three to five paragraphs
- should tell why writer is interested in name
- should give background information about the name's history, meanings, and associations
- should tell how names affect our experiences

AT A GLANCE

- The author is a Kiowa Indian whose people live near a hill in Oklahoma named Rainy Mountain.
- He has gone back to visit his grandmother's grave.

LITERARY OPTIONS

- purpose
- style: figures of speech

THEMATIC OPTIONS

- mourning loss
- the power of culture and tradition

1 **SETTING**

A sense of place pervades this entire essay. The author acknowledges the importance of Rainy Mountain by describing it at the outset.

2 **STYLE: FIGURES OF SPEECH**

The first paragraph contains many vivid figures of speech. Here the simile compares the jumping of the grasshoppers to the popping of corn.

3 **PURPOSE**

One purpose of the essay is a personal one; to mourn the loss of the author's grandmother.

N. Scott Momaday *born 1934*

The novelist and poet N. Scott Momaday, a Kiowa Indian, acknowledges his vital interest in all aspects of American Indian history, culture, and art. Since 1963, along with writing, he has taught American Indian literature, folklore, and mythology.

Momaday was born in Lawton, Oklahoma. In addition to teaching, his father was a distinguished artist and his mother was a respected author. Momaday attended schools on Apache, Navaho, and Pueblo reservations in the Southwest before entering the University of New Mexico in 1952. He has written several highly acclaimed books, including *House Made of Dawn,* awarded the Pulitzer Prize for fiction in 1969, *Angle of Geese and Other Poems* (1974), *The Gourd Dancer* (1976), and *The Names* (1976).

Momaday is best known for *The Way to Rainy Mountain* (1969). This delicate and yet vibrant collection of imaginatively interwoven stories and legends of the Kiowa presents a picture of their history, mythology, and world view.

■ We all have our own "pasts," but, in addition, do we have a kind of "past" connected to the family and culture into which we are born?

N. Scott Momaday

from The Way to Rainy Mountain

1 A single knoll rises out of the plain in Oklahoma, north and west of the Wichita Range. For my people, the Kiowas,[1] it is an old landmark, and they gave it the name Rainy Mountain. The hardest weather in the world is there. Winter brings blizzards, hot tornadic winds arise in the spring, and in summer the prairie is an anvil's edge. The grass turns brittle and brown, and it cracks beneath your feet. There are green belts along the rivers and creeks, linear groves of hickory and pecan, willow and witch hazel. At a distance in July or August the steaming foliage seems almost to writhe in fire.
2 Great green and yellow grasshoppers are everywhere in the tall grass, popping up like corn to sting the flesh, and tortoises crawl about on the red earth, going nowhere in the plenty of time. Loneliness is an aspect of the land. All things in the plain are isolate; there is no confusion of objects in the eye, but *one* hill or *one* tree or *one* man. To look upon that landscape in the early morning, with the sun at your back, is to lose the sense of proportion. Your imagination comes to life, and this, you think, is where Creation was begun.

3 I returned to Rainy Mountain in July. My grandmother had died in the spring, and I wanted to be at her grave. She had lived to be very old and at last infirm. Her only living

1. **Kiowas** [kī′ō wäz]: Plains Indians who migrated from Montana and other western states to Oklahoma.

GUIDED READING

LITERAL QUESTION

1a. According to the author, what do you think when you look at the landscape early in the morning? (that this is where creation was begun)

INFERENTIAL QUESTION

1b. What does this tell you about the way Momaday feels about his homeland? (He reveres it.)

daughter was with her when she died, and I was told that in death her face was that of a child.

1 I like to think of her as a child. When she was born, the Kiowas were living the last great moment of their history. For more than a hundred years they had controlled the open range from the Smoky Hill River to the Red, from the headwaters of the Canadian to the fork of the Arkansas and Cimarron. In alliance with the Comanches, they had ruled the whole of the southern Plains. War was their sacred business, and they were among the finest horsemen the world had ever known. But warfare for the Kiowas was preeminently a matter of disposition rather than of survival, and they never understood the grim, unrelenting advance of the U.S. Cavalry. When at last, divided and ill-provisioned, they were driven onto the Staked Plains in the cold rains of autumn, they fell into panic. In Palo Duro Canyon they abandoned their crucial stores to pillage and had nothing then but their lives. In order to save themselves, they surrendered to the soldiers at Fort Sill and were imprisoned in the old stone corral that now stands as a military museum. My grandmother was spared the humiliation of those high gray walls by eight or ten years, but she must have known from birth the affliction of defeat, the dark brooding of old warriors.

Her name was Aho, and she belonged to the last culture to evolve in North America. Her forebears came down from the high country in western Montana nearly three centuries ago. They were a mountain people, a mysterious tribe of hunters whose language has never been positively classified in any major group. In the late seventeenth century they began a
2 long migration to the south and east. It was a journey toward the dawn, and it led to a golden age. Along the way the Kiowas were befriended by the Crows, who gave them the culture and religion of the Plains. They acquired horses, and their ancient nomadic spirit was suddenly free of the ground. They acquired Tai-me, the sacred Sun Dance doll, from that moment the object and symbol of their worship, and so shared in the divinity of the sun. Not least, they acquired the sense of destiny, therefore courage and pride. When they entered upon the southern Plains they had been transformed. No longer were they slaves to the simple necessity of survival; they were a lordly and dangerous society of fighters and thieves, hunters and priests of the sun. According to their origin myth, they entered the world through a hollow log. From one point of view, their migration was the fruit of an old prophecy, for indeed they emerged from a sunless world.

3 Although my grandmother lived out her long life in the shadow of Rainy Mountain, the immense landscape of the continental interior lay like memory in her blood. She could tell of the Crows, whom she had never seen, and of the Black Hills, where she had never been. I wanted to see in reality what she had seen more perfectly in the mind's eye, and traveled fifteen hundred miles to begin my pilgrimage.

Yellowstone, it seemed to me, was the top of the world, a region of deep lakes and dark timber, canyons and waterfalls. But, beautiful as it is, one might have the sense of confinement there. The skyline in all directions is close at hand, the high wall of the woods and deep cleavages of shade. There is a perfect freedom in the mountains, but it belongs to the eagle and the elk, the badger and the bear. The Kiowas reckoned their stature by the distance they could see, and they were bent and blind in the wilderness.

Descending eastward, the highland meadows are a stairway to the plain. In July the inland slope of the Rockies is luxuriant with flax and buckwheat, stonecrop[2] and larkspur. The earth unfolds and the limit of the land recedes. Clusters of trees, and animals grazing far in the distance, cause the vision to reach away and wonder to build upon the mind. The sun follows a longer course in the day, and the sky is immense beyond all comparison. The great billowing clouds that sail upon it are shadows

2. **stonecrop:** a flowering plant found on rocks and walls.

AT A GLANCE

- The author's grandmother was born a few years after the Kiowas were defeated.
- He likes to think of her as a child when the Kiowa were a proud, free people who had come from the high country of western Montana three centuries ago.
- The author traveled through the areas that his forebears had traversed on their journey.

1 FOCUS

The author moves back and forth from his grandmother to the Kiowa people. His grandmother is the concrete, or the particular, focus, and the Kiowa nation is the universal, or general, focus.

2 SYMBOL

All of the imagery is symbolic here. The dawn represents the direction east, as well as the dawn of culture. The gold is the color of the sunrise as well as the glory of the culture.

3 THEME

The traditions of the Kiowas are rooted in the lands they came from. Although his grandmother never saw the mountains, the story of the mountains has been handed down to her, and she sees them perfectly in her mind.

GUIDED READING

LITERAL QUESTIONS

1a. How does the myth say that the Kiowas came into the world? (They entered through a hollow log.)

2a. What did the author travel fifteen hundred miles to begin? (a pilgrimage)

INFERENTIAL QUESTIONS

1b. How is the myth a true observation? (The Kiowas came from the dark, cold world of the mountains to the sunny plains. They came out of ignorance, a kind of darkness, into the light.)

2b. Why might it have been important for him to do this? (He wanted to feel closer to his grandmother and his people.)

AT A GLANCE

- The author describes the landmarks he saw on his trip as he follows the path his people took.
- He tells a legend about Devil's Tower.
- His grandmother had been present at the last Sun Dance in 1890, when there were no more buffalo for the ceremony and the soldiers came to forbid the dance.

1 STYLE: FIGURES OF SPEECH

The simile underscores the majesty and power of the image of Devil's Tower.

2 SYMBOL

For the author the legend of Devil's Tower symbolizes the Kiowas' emergence as an enlightened, powerful people.

3 PURPOSE

The second purpose in the essay is to make the reading audience aware of the tragic loss of his people's way of life.

that move upon the grain like water, dividing light. Farther down, in the land of the Crows and Blackfeet, the plain is yellow. Sweet clover takes hold of the hills and bends upon itself to cover and seal the soil. There the Kiowas paused on their way; they had come to the place where they must change their lives. The sun is at home on the plains. Precisely there does it have the certain character of a god. When the Kiowas came to the land of the Crows, they could see the dark lees[3] of the hills at dawn across the Bighorn River, the profusion of light on the grain shelves, the oldest deity ranging after the solstices. Not yet would they veer southward to the caldron of the land that lay below; they must wean their blood[4] from the northern winter and hold the mountains a while longer in view. They bore Tai-me in procession to the east.

A dark mist lay over the Black Hills, and the
1 land was like iron. At the top of a ridge I caught sight of Devil's Tower upthrust against the gray sky as if in the birth of time the core of the earth had broken through its crust and the motion of the world was begun. There are things in nature that engender an awful quiet in the heart of man; Devil's Tower is one of them. Two centuries ago, because they could not do otherwise, the Kiowas made a legend at the base of the rock. My grandmother said:

Eight children were there at play, seven sisters and their brother. Suddenly the boy was struck dumb; he trembled and began to run upon his hands and feet. His fingers became claws, and his body was covered with fur. Directly there was a bear where the boy had been. The sisters were terrified; they ran, and the bear after them. They came to the stump of a great tree, and the tree spoke to them. It bade them climb upon it, and as they did so it began to rise into the air. The bear came to kill them, but they were just beyond its reach. It reared against the tree and scored the bark all around with its claws. The seven sisters were borne into the sky, and they became the stars of the Big Dipper.

2 From that moment, and so long as the legend lives, the Kiowas have kinsmen in the night sky. Whatever they were in the mountains, they could be no more. However tenuous their well-being, however much they had suffered and would suffer again, they had found a way out of the wilderness.

My grandmother had a reverence for the sun, a holy regard that now is all but gone out of mankind. There was a wariness in her, and an ancient awe. She was a Christian in her later years, but she had come a long way about, and she never forgot her birthright. As a child she had been to the Sun Dances; she had taken part in those annual rites, and by them she had learned the restoration of her people in the presence of Tai-me. She was about seven when the last Kiowa Sun Dance was held in 1887 on the Washita River above Rainy Mountain Creek. The buffalo were gone. In order to consummate the ancient sacrifice—to impale the head of a buffalo bull upon the medicine tree—a delegation of old men journeyed into Texas, there to beg and barter for an animal from the Goodnight herd. She was ten when the Kiowas came together for the last time as a living Sun Dance culture. They could find no buffalo; they had to hang an old hide from the sacred tree. Before the dance could begin, a company of soldiers rode out from Fort Sill under orders to
3 disperse the tribe. Forbidden without cause the essential act of their faith, having seen the wild herds slaughtered and left to rot upon the ground, the Kiowas backed away forever from the medicine tree. That was July 20, 1890, at the great bend of the Washita. My grandmother was there. Without bitterness, and for as long as she lived, she bore a vision of deicide.[5]

Now that I can have her only in memory, I see my grandmother in the several postures that were peculiar to her: standing at the wood stove on a winter morning and turning meat in

3. **lees:** sheltered sides, away from the wind.
4. **wean their blood:** become acclimated by removing themselves gradually.
5. **deicide** [dē′ə sīd]: killing of a god.

GUIDED READING

LITERAL QUESTIONS

1a. Why does the author say the Kiowas made a legend about the Devil's Tower? (because they could not do otherwise)

2a. Why does the author say the Sun Dances ended? (The soldiers prevented them.)

INFERENTIAL QUESTIONS

1b. What do you think he means by this? (The sight was overwhelming and inexplicable. They could neither ignore it nor understand it, so they made a story about it.)

2b. Why was this probably done? (By ending the dances, the army was destroying the cultural unity of the Kiowas and establishing dominance over them.)

a great iron skillet; sitting at the south window, bent above her beadwork, and afterwards, when her vision failed, looking down for a long time into the fold of her hands; going out upon a cane, very slowly as she did when the weight of age came upon her; praying. I remember her most often at prayer. She made long, rambling prayers out of suffering and hope, having seen many things. I was never sure that I had the right to hear, so exclusive were they of all mere custom and company. The last time I saw her she prayed standing by the side of her bed at night, naked to the waist, the light of a kerosene lamp moving upon her dark skin. Her long, black hair, always drawn and braided in the day, lay upon her shoulders and against her
1 breasts like a shawl. I do not speak Kiowa, and I never understood her prayers, but there was something inherently sad in the sound, some merest hesitation upon the syllables of sorrow. She began in a high and descending pitch, exhausting her breath to silence; then again and again—and always the same intensity of effort, of something that is, and is not, like urgency in the human voice. Transported so in the dancing light among the shadows of her room, she seemed beyond the reach of time. But that was illusion; I think I knew then that I should not see her again.

Houses are like sentinels in the plain, old keepers of the weather watch. There, in a very little while, wood takes on the appearance of great age. All colors wear soon away in the wind and rain, and then the wood is burned gray and the grain appears and the nails turn red with rust. The windowpanes are black and opaque; you imagine there is nothing within,
2 and indeed there are many ghosts, bones given up to the land. They stand here and there against the sky, and you approach them for a longer time than you expect. They belong in the distance; it is their domain.

Once there was a lot of sound in my grandmother's house, a lot of coming and going, feasting and talk. The summers there were full of excitement and reunion. The Kiowas are a summer people; they abide the cold and keep to themselves, but when the season turns and the land becomes warm and vital they cannot hold still; an old love of going returns upon them. The aged visitors who came to my grandmother's house when I was a child were made of lean and leather, and they bore themselves upright. They wore great black hats and bright ample shirts that shook in the wind. They rubbed fat upon their hair and wound their braids with strips of colored cloth. Some of them painted their faces and carried the scars of old and cherished enmities. They were an old council of warlords, come to remind and be reminded of who they were. Their wives and daughters served them well. The women might indulge themselves; gossip was at once the mark and compensation of their servitude. They made loud and elaborate talk among themselves, full of jest and gesture, fright and false alarm. They went abroad in fringed and flowered shawls, bright beadwork and German silver.[6] They were at home in the kitchen, and they prepared meals that were banquets.

There were frequent prayer meetings, and great nocturnal feasts. When I was a child I played with my cousins outside, where the lamplight fell upon the ground and the singing of the old people rose up around us and carried away into the darkness. There were a lot of good things to eat, a lot of laughter and surprise. And afterwards, when the quiet returned, I lay down with my grandmother and could hear the frogs away by the river and feel the motion of the air.

3 Now there is a funeral silence in the rooms, the endless wake of some final word. The walls have closed in upon my grandmother's house. When I returned to it in mourning, I saw for the first time in my life how small it was. It was late at night, and there was a white moon, nearly full. I sat for a long time on the stone steps by the kitchen door. From there I could see out across the land; I could see the long row of trees by the creek, the low light upon the rolling plains, and the stars of the Big Dipper. Once I looked at the moon and caught

6. **German silver:** alloy resembling real silver.

AT A GLANCE

- The author remembers his grandmother most often at prayer; the last time he saw her alive she was praying.
- He remembers the feasts in her house when he was a child.
- Now that she is dead, the house seems very small.

1 THEME

The author does not understand the language of his own people, but he senses the sadness in their prayers. He is an example of what has been lost to the culture of the Kiowas.

2 SYMBOL

The ghosts of his lost culture and the bones of his grandmother remain in his memory, just as the rotting houses symbolically stand in the distance, gone but not forgotten.

3 THEME

Now that his grandmother is dead, he sees how little there is of her home without her. It was her spirit, the spirit of the old ways, that made it seem large.

GUIDED READING

LITERAL QUESTIONS

1a. What are like sentinels of the plain? (the houses)

2a. What stars did the author see when he returned to his grandmother's house? (the stars of the Big Dipper)

INFERENTIAL QUESTIONS

1b. What do you think the author is trying to say with this observation? (He probably means that the houses are few and far between, lonely reminders of a dead culture.)

2b. Do you think that this matters to him? (Probably it does. The legend was about the Big Dipper, and the stars are his kinsmen. It makes him feel close to his grandmother and all Kiowas.)

AT A GLANCE

- The author sees a cricket, like a silhouette against the moon.
- At dawn he goes to his grandmother's grave.

1 THEME

The cricket is like the Kiowas. Their culture may be lost, but if they preserve some part of their tradition, they too will be made whole and eternal.

REFLECTING ON THE SELECTION

What do you think that the author has gained from writing this essay? (a feeling of greater closeness to his grandmother and his people and a sense of identity)

STUDY QUESTIONS

1. visit grandmother's grave
2. the last great moment of their history; affliction of defeat
3. seven sisters who became Big Dipper; kinsmen in the night sky
4. tribe dispersed by soldiers
5. long, rambling, exclusive of custom and company, sad-sounding; the reach of time; illusion
6. visits by War Lords, prayer meetings; seems small; Big Dipper; that the cricket has gone to moon to live and die, so its small definition is made whole and eternal
7. grandmother, the Kiowa; grandmother was living embodiment of Kiowa heritage
8. right to practice their religion; faith, traditions
9. Kiowa still have kinsmen in the night sky, people will continue in face of change; that they will struggle to maintain heritage, endure because human spirit is eternal
10. Answers will vary. Students should say it can describe traditions, customs, and events of a people.

sight of a strange thing. A cricket had perched upon the handrail, only a few inches away from me. My line of vision was such that the crea-
1 ture filled the moon like a fossil. It had gone there, I thought, to live and die, for there, of all places, was its small definition made whole and eternal. A warm wind rose up and purled[7] like the longing within me.

The next morning I awoke at dawn and went out on the dirt road to Rainy Mountain. It was already hot, and the grasshoppers began to fill the air. Still, it was early in the morning, and the birds sang out of the shadows. The long yellow grass on the mountain shone in the bright light, and a scissortail[8] hied above the land. There, where it ought to be, at the end of a long and legendary way, was my grandmother's grave. Here and there on the dark stones were ancestral names. Looking back once, I saw the mountain and came away.

7. **purled:** rippled.

8. **scissortail:** small gray and pink bird with a forked tail.

STUDY QUESTIONS

Recalling

1. Why did Momaday go to Rainy Mountain in July?
2. What does Momaday say the Kiowas were living when his grandmother was born (paragraph 3)? What does he say she must have known from birth?
3. What legend was inspired by Devil's Tower? What does Momaday say the Kiowas have as long as the legend lives?
4. What happened the last time the Kiowa came together as a living Sun Dance culture?
5. How does Momaday describe his grandmother's prayers on page 857? From what did she seem beyond reach the last time he saw her praying? What word does he use to contradict this perception?
6. Identify at least two events that once took place in Momaday's grandmother's house. What does Momaday notice about the house for the first time when he returns to it in mourning? What stars does he see above the plain that night? What thought does he have about the cricket he sees against the moon?

Interpreting

7. To what two things or people does Momaday pay respect in visiting Rainy Mountain? How are the two associated in his mind?
8. What did the Kiowa lose in 1890? What do the lifelong practices of Momaday's grandmother and her neighbors suggest the Kiowa did not lose?
9. What does the appearance of the Big Dipper in the next-to-last paragraph suggest? What does the image of the cricket suggest about Momaday's grandmother and her people?

Extending

10. How can literature help preserve the past?

COMPOSITION

Applying a Statement About Literature

■ It has been said that the subject of Momaday's writing is "a time that is gone forever, a landscape that is incomparable, and a human spirit which endures." Write a brief composition applying this statement to the selection from *The Way to Rainy Mountain.* First explain the comment in your own words. Then apply each part of the statement to specific examples from the selection. Conclude with your own observations about how the statement can apply to other works of literature as well. *For help with this assignment, refer to Lesson 9 in the Writing About Literature Handbook at the back of this book.*

Writing About Traditions

■ One of Momaday's greatest concerns is the survival of traditions. Write an informal essay about the survival of a tradition in your own time. You may want to write about a tradition you see fading away and that you would like to restore. Consider also writing about a tradition you would like to begin. Include your opinions on the meaning and value of the tradition.

COMPOSITION: GUIDELINES FOR EVALUATION

APPLYING A STATEMENT ABOUT LITERATURE

Objective

To apply general statement to particular work

Guidelines for Evaluation

- suggested length: five to eight paragraphs
- should paraphrase the statement
- should tell how essay discusses vanished time, incomparable landscape, enduring spirit
- should use examples for parts of statement

WRITING ABOUT TRADITIONS

Objective

To write about tradition

Guidelines for Evaluation

- suggested length: four to seven paragraphs
- should describe a tradition
- should consider the meaning of the tradition
- should tell why it should continue

Annie Dillard *born 1945*

In *An American Childhood,* published in 1987, Annie Dillard describes growing up in Pittsburgh, Pennsylvania. Dillard's given name was Meta Ann Doak, and her family was fairly well-to-do. She attended Hollins College in Virginia and earned a master's degree in English. In 1971 a camping trip inspired her first book, *Pilgrim at Tinker Creek,* which explores the natural life of a small valley in Virginia. It won the Pulitzer Prize in 1975. Her next book, *Holy the Firm* (1982), describes three days on an island and Dillard's thoughts about nature, life, and God. Dillard currently teaches writing at Wesleyan College in Middletown, Connecticut.

■ Annie Dillard tries to convince her students to "give their lives to something larger than themselves." She believes "you must give with your whole heart." How does the following extract from *An American Childhood* support that advice?

Annie Dillard

from An American Childhood

1 Some boys taught me to play football. This was fine sport. You thought up a new strategy for every play and whispered it to the others. You went out for a pass, fooling everyone. Best, you got to throw yourself mightily at someone's running legs. Either you brought him down or you hit the ground flat out on your chin, with your arms empty before you. It was all or nothing. If you hesitated in fear, you would miss and get hurt: You would take a hard fall while the kid got away, or you would get kicked in the face while the kid got away. But if you flung yourself wholeheartedly at the back of his knees—if you gathered and joined body and soul and pointed them diving fearlessly—then you likely wouldn't get hurt, and you'd stop the ball. Your fate, and your team's score, depended on your concentration and courage. Nothing girls did could compare with it.

Boys welcomed me at baseball, too, for I had, through enthusiastic practice, what was weirdly
2 known as a boy's arm. In winter, in the snow, there was neither baseball nor football, so the boys and I threw snowballs at passing cars. I got in trouble throwing snowballs, and have seldom been happier since.

On one weekday morning after Christmas, six inches of new snow had just fallen. We were standing up to our boot tops in snow on a front yard on trafficked Reynolds Street, waiting for
3 cars. The cars traveled Reynolds Street slowly and evenly; they were targets all but wrapped in red ribbons, cream puffs. We couldn't miss.

I was seven; the boys were eight, nine, and ten. The oldest two Fahey boys were there—Mikey and Peter—polite blond boys who lived near me on Lloyd Street, and who already had four brothers and sisters. My parents approved Mikey and Peter Fahey. Chickie McBride was there, a tough kid, and Billy Paul and Mackie Kean too, from across Reynolds, where the boys

AT A GLANCE

- As a child the author plays football with neighborhood boys.
- She loves flinging herself at her opponents.
- In winter they throw snowballs at cars.

LITERARY OPTIONS

- autobiography
- style

THEMATIC OPTIONS

- the joy of wholehearted action
- memory and time

1 AUDIENCE

The second-person pronoun, although used in its impersonal sense, involves the reader in the narrative.

2 PURPOSE

The transitional sentence, which pivots on the idea of "throwing," relates to the author's purpose of telling a humorous story that illustrates a point.

3 STYLE: METAPHOR

The comparison of cars to cream puffs and beribboned packages suggests the predatory glee with which the children viewed their targets.

GUIDED READING

LITERAL QUESTION

1a. What does the narrator call a "fine sport"? (football)

INFERENTIAL QUESTION

1b. Why does she have this opinion? (Everything in football depends on courage and determination; it is an activity into which she literally can throw herself.)

AT A GLANCE

- One day the children hit a passing car with a snowball.
- The driver gets out and starts chasing them.
- They scatter; he follows the author and Mikey Fahey.
- He pursues them through snowy backyards and finally catches them.

1 AUTOBIOGRAPHY

The interior thoughts and feelings of the author characterize the autobiography.

2 PURPOSE

The exaggeration ("the only time in all of life") captures the child's wonder at this unusual occurrence and creates humor, consonant with the purpose of entertainment.

3 AUTOBIOGRAPHY

The metamorphosis from a simple chase to "running for our lives" illustrates the author's vivid memory of a child's way of thinking and recalls the theme of wholehearted action.

4 STYLE: SENTENCE STRUCTURE

Long compound sentences joined with semicolons help to re-create the relentlessness of the chase.

5 THEME

At the height of the chase, the child discovers that the principle of flinging oneself wholeheartedly into life extends to those outside her immediate circle.

grew up dark and furious, grew up skinny, knowing, and skilled. We had all drifted from our houses that morning looking for action, and had found it here on Reynolds Street.

It was cloudy but cold. The cars' tires laid behind them on the snowy street a complex trail of beige chunks like crenellated[1] castle walls. I had stepped on some earlier; they squeaked. We could have wished for more traffic. When a car came, we all popped it one. In the intervals between cars we reverted to the natural solitude of children.

1 I started making an iceball—a perfect iceball, from perfectly white snow, perfectly spherical, and squeezed perfectly translucent so no snow remained all the way through. (The Fahey boys and I considered it unfair actually to throw an iceball at somebody, but it had been known to happen.)

I had just embarked on the iceball project when we heard tire chains come clanking from afar. A black Buick was moving toward us down the street. We all spread out, banged together some regular snowballs, took aim, and, when the Buick drew nigh, fired.

A soft snowball hit the driver's windshield right before the driver's face. It made a smashed star with a hump in the middle.

2 Often, of course, we hit our target, but this time, the only time in all of life, the car pulled over and stopped. Its wide black door opened; a man got out of it, running. He didn't even close the car door.

He ran after us, and we ran away from him, up the snowy Reynolds sidewalk. At the corner, I looked back; incredibly, he was still after us. He was in city clothes: a suit and tie, street shoes. Any normal adult would have quit, having sprung
3 us into flight and made his point. This man was gaining on us. He was a thin man, all action. All of a sudden, we were running for our lives.

Wordless, we split up. We were on our turf; we could lose ourselves in the neighborhood backyards, everyone for himself. I paused and considered. Everyone had vanished except Mikey Fahey, who was just rounding the corner of a yellow brick house. Poor Mikey, I trailed him. The driver of the Buick sensibly picked the two of us to follow. The man apparently had all day.

He chased Mikey and me around the yellow house and up a backyard path we knew by heart: under a low tree, up a bank, through a hedge, down some snowy steps, and across the grocery
4 store's delivery driveway. We smashed through a gap in another hedge, entered a scruffy backyard and ran around its back porch and tight between houses to Edgerton Avenue; we ran across Edgerton to an alley and up our own sliding woodpile to the Halls' front yard; he kept coming. We ran up Lloyd Street and wound through mazy backyards toward the steep hilltop at Willard and Lang.

He chased us silently, block after block. He chased us silently over picket fences, through thorny hedges, between houses, around garbage cans, and across streets. Every time I glanced back, choking for breath, I expected he would have quit. He must have been as breathless as we were. His jacket strained over his body. It was an immense discovery, pounding into my hot head
5 with every sliding, joyous step, that this ordinary adult evidently knew what I thought only children who trained at football knew: that you have to fling yourself at what you're doing, you have to point yourself, forget yourself, aim, dive.

Mikey and I had nowhere to go, in our own neighborhood or out of it, but away from this man who was chasing us. He impelled us forward; we compelled him to follow our route. The air was cold; every breath tore my throat. We kept running, block after block; we kept improvising, backyard after backyard, running a frantic course and choosing it simultaneously, failing always to find small places or hard places to slow him down, and discovering always, exhilarated, dismayed, that only bare speed could save us—for he would never give up, this man—and we were losing speed.

He chased us through the backyard labyrinths of ten blocks before he caught us by our jackets. He caught us and we all stopped.

1. **crenellated:** having squared-off notches at the top.

GUIDED READING

LITERAL QUESTION

1a. What does the narrator expect to see when she looks back? (that the man has quit chasing them)

INFERENTIAL QUESTION

1b. Why is the man's still being there important to her? (She discovers that an ordinary adult can throw himself wholeheartedly into life, a capacity she had believed belonged only to children.)

We three stood staggering, half-blinded, coughing, in an obscure hilltop backyard: a man in his twenties, a boy, a girl. He had released our jackets, our pursuer, our captor, our hero: He knew we weren't going anywhere. We all played by the rules. Mikey and I unzipped our jackets. I pulled off my sopping mittens. Our tracks multiplied in the backyard's new snow. We had been breaking new snow all morning. We didn't look at each other. I was cherishing my excitement. The man's lower pants legs were wet; his cuffs were full of snow, and there was a prow of snow beneath them on his shoes and socks. Some trees bordered the little flat backyard, some messy winter trees. There was no one around: a clearing in a grove, and we the only players.

It was a long time before he could speak. I had some difficulty at first recalling why we were there. My lips felt swollen; I couldn't see out of the sides of my eyes; I kept coughing.

"You stupid kids," he began perfunctorily.

We listened perfunctorily indeed, if we listened at all, for the chewing out was redundant, a mere formality, and beside the point. The point was that he had chased us passionately without giving up, and so he had caught us. Now he came down to earth. I wanted the glory to last forever.

But how could the glory have lasted forever? We could have run through every backyard in North America until we got to Panama. But when he trapped us at the lip of the Panama Canal, what precisely could he have done to prolong the drama of the chase and cap its glory? I brooded about this for the next few years. He could only have fried Mikey Fahey and me in boiling oil, say, or dismembered us piecemeal, or staked us to anthills. None of which I really wanted, and none of which any adult was likely to do, even in the spirit of fun. He could only chew us out there in the Panamanian jungle, after months or years of exalting pursuit. He could only begin, "You stupid kids," and continue in his ordinary Pittsburgh accent with his normal righteous anger and the usual common sense.

If in that snowy backyard the driver of the black Buick had cut off our heads, Mikey's and mine, I would have died happy, for nothing has required so much of me since as being chased all over Pittsburgh in the middle of winter—running terrified, exhausted—by this sainted, skinny, furious red-headed man who wished to have a word with us. I don't know how he found his way back to his car.

STUDY QUESTIONS

Recalling

1. What does Dillard enjoy about football? How does she say a person can make a tackle and not get hurt?
2. What activity do Annie and her friends take up during the snowy season? How old is Annie at the time of the chase through the snow? How does she describe the two boys from "across Reynolds Street"?
3. What are the children looking for on Reynolds Street? What surprises them when their snowballs hit a black Buick? How does the driver emerge from the car?
4. How is the driver dressed? How does young Annie think any normal adult would behave? How does the driver behave?
5. Which child does Annie follow? Describe the chase.
6. What is Annie's discovery during the chase? What emotions does she experience as she runs?
7. What happens when the driver catches the children? What does the word *perfunctorily* mean? What are the ways in which Annie thinks the glory of the chase could have lasted?

Interpreting

8. What does Annie's choice of companions tell you about her?
9. What does Dillard mean by "the natural solitude of children"?
10. Why do the children throw snowballs at cars?
11. Why does Dillard provide such a precise description of the chase?
12. Why does Dillard call the driver "sainted"?

AT A GLANCE

- The adult lectures the children perfunctorily; they listen the same way.
- The author feels that nothing in life has required as much of her since.

REFLECTING ON THE SELECTION

What idea about life does Annie Dillard illustrate with this story? (Dillard suggests that doing things passionately and fully is the most rewarding way to live.)

STUDY QUESTIONS

1. the tackling; by doing it wholeheartedly

2. throwing snowballs; seven; "dark and furious . . . skinny, knowing, and skilled"

3.
- action
- The car pulls over and stops.
- running

4. suit; would have made the children run and then quit; runs for blocks, catches them

5. Mikey Fahey; through backyards, up a woodpile, toward a steep hill

6. that the driver knows what Annie has learned from football; exhilaration, dismay

7. lectures them; done routinely; could have tortured them

8. did not always obey parents

9. Children can be together in a group, but each child is doing something different.

10. They are bored; it is a challenge.

11. The details make it seem real.

12. because of the joy he gave

AT A GLANCE

- The artist must help people to understand themselves.
- To achieve this goal, however, the artist must be alone.
- All societies do battle with their artists, for people would rather not face the knowledge that an artist reveals.

LITERARY OPTIONS

- point of view
- style

THEMATIC OPTIONS

- the goal of art
- the nature of society
- visions and ideals

1 PURPOSE

Baldwin's purpose is to explain and defend the role of the artist in America as necessary for a healthy society.

2 THEME

The role of the artist and the root of his antagonistic relationship to society is that of truth-teller—never a welcome role.

James Baldwin *1924–1987*

Recognized as one of the finest American writers, James Baldwin was also recognized for his work in the civil rights movement. Baldwin grew up in Harlem as one of nine children. In 1948, after graduating from high school and working at a series of jobs, he left the United States. He lived for ten years in Europe, during which time he published his first three books: two novels, *Go Tell It on the Mountain* (1953) and *Giovanni's Room* (1953), and a collection of essays, *Notes of a Native Son*. Baldwin returned to the United States in order to assume a more active role in the struggle for racial equality. Other collections of his essays are *Nobody Knows My Name* (1961) and *The Fire Next Time* (1963).

■ Why might an American writer's vision be different from the vision of a writer from another country?

James Baldwin

from Creative America

Perhaps the primary distinction of the artist is that he must actively cultivate that state which most men, necessarily, must avoid: the state of being alone. That all men *are*, when the chips are down, alone, is a banality—a banality because it is very frequently stated, but very rarely, on the evidence, believed. Most of us are not compelled to linger with the knowledge of our aloneness, for it is a knowledge that can paralyze all action in this world. There are, forever, swamps to be drained, cities to be created, mines to be exploited, children to be fed. None of these things can be done alone. But the conquest of the physical world is not man's only duty. He is also enjoined to conquer the great wilderness of him-
1 self. The precise role of the artist, then, is to illuminate that darkness, blaze roads through that vast forest, so that we will not, in all our doing, lose sight of its purpose, which is, after all, to make the world a more human dwelling place.

The state of being alone is not meant to bring to mind merely a rustic musing beside some silver lake. The aloneness of which I speak is much more like the aloneness of birth or death. It is like the fearful aloneness that one sees in the eyes of someone who is suffering, whom we cannot help. Or it is like the aloneness of love, the force and mystery that so many have extolled and so many have cursed, but which no one has ever understood or ever really been able to control. I put the matter this way, not out of any desire to create pity for the artist—God forbid!—but to suggest how nearly, after all, is his state the state of everyone, and in an attempt to make vivid his endeavor. The states of birth, suffering, love, and death are extreme states—extreme, universal, and inescapable. We all know this, but
2 we would rather not know it. The artist is present to correct the delusions to which we fall prey in our attempts to avoid this knowiedge.

It is for this reason that all societies have battled with that incorrigible disturber of the peace—the artist. I doubt that future societies will get on with him any better. The entire pur-

GUIDED READING

LITERAL QUESTION

1a. According to Baldwin, what state must the artist cultivate? (being alone)

INFERENTIAL QUESTION

1b. Why is solitude necessary for the artist? (Searching the inner recesses of self is of necessity a solitary job.)

pose of society is to create a bulwark against the inner and the outer chaos, in order to make life bearable and to keep the human race alive. And it is absolutely inevitable that when a tradition has been evolved, whatever the tradition is, the people, in general, will suppose it to have existed from before the beginning of time and will be most unwilling and indeed unable to conceive of any changes in it. They do not know how they will live without those traditions that have given them their identity. Their reaction, when it is suggested that they can or that they must, is panic. And we see this panic, I think, everywhere in the world today, from the streets of New Orleans to the grisly battleground of Algeria.[1] And a higher level of consciousness among the people is the only hope we have, now or in the future, of minimizing human damage.

1 The artist is distinguished from all other responsible actors in society—the politicians, legislators, educators, and scientists—by the fact that he is his own test tube, his own laboratory, working according to very rigorous rules, however unstated these may be, and cannot allow any consideration to supersede his responsibility to reveal all that he can possibly discover concerning the mystery of the human being. Society must accept some things as real; but he must always know that visible reality hides a deeper one, and that all our action and achievement rest on things unseen. A society must assume that it is stable, but the artist must know, and he must let us know, that there is nothing stable under heaven. One cannot possibly build a school, teach a child, or drive a car without taking some things for granted. The artist cannot and must not take anything for granted, but must drive to the heart of every answer and expose the question the answer hides.

I seem to be making extremely grandiloquent claims for a breed of men and women historically despised while living and acclaimed when safely dead. But, in a way, the belated honor that all societies tender their artists proves the reality
2 of the point I am trying to make. I am really trying to make clear the nature of the artist's responsibility to his society. The peculiar nature of this responsibility is that he must never cease warring with it, for its sake and for his own. For the truth, in spite of appearances and all our hopes, is that everything is always changing, and the measure of our maturity as nations and as men is how well prepared we are to meet these changes and, further, to use them for our health.

3 Now, anyone who has ever been compelled to think about it—anyone, for example, who has ever been in love—knows that the one face that one can never see is one's own face. One's lover—or one's brother, or one's enemy—sees the face you wear, and this face can elicit the most extraordinary reactions. We do the things we do and feel what we feel essentially because we must—we are responsible for our actions, but we rarely understand them. It goes without saying, I believe, that if we understood ourselves better, we would damage ourselves less. But the barrier between oneself and one's knowledge of oneself is high indeed. There are so many things one would rather not know! We become social creatures because we cannot live any other way. But in order to become social, there are a great many other things that we must not become, and we are frightened, all of us, of these forces within us that perpetually menace our precarious secu-
4 rity. Yet the forces are there: We cannot will them away. All we can do is learn to live with them. And we cannot learn this unless we are willing to tell the truth about ourselves, and the truth about us is always at variance with what we wish to be. The human effort is to bring these two realities into a relationship resembling reconciliation. The human beings whom we respect the most, after all—and sometimes fear the most—are those who are most deeply involved in this delicate and strenuous effort, for they have the unshakable authority that comes only from having looked on and endured and survived
5 the worst. That nation is healthiest which has the least necessity to distrust or ostracize or victimize these people—whom, as I say, we honor,

1. **Algeria:** North African country that won independence from France after an extremely violent revolution, 1954–1962.

AT A GLANCE

- The artist continually wars with society.
- The artist must make people see truths about themselves.

1 POINT OF VIEW

Baldwin's viewpoint is personal. He speaks for the artist in general, but his opinions are forged from his own experiences.

2 THEME

Baldwin views the artist as a gadfly, holding up unpopular truths to an unwilling society. Thus, the relationship is necessarily an uncomfortable one.

3 STYLE: ANALOGY

Baldwin introduces the concept of the artist as lover, the one who can clearly see the face of the beloved.

4 THEME

The necessity for truth, and concomitant unwillingness to face it, is the central problem with which the artist must grapple.

5 RESPONSE JOURNAL

Ask students to comment upon Baldwin's guideline for determining the "health" of a nation.

GUIDED READING

LITERAL QUESTION

1a. What does Baldwin say "goes without saying"? (If we understood ourselves better, we would damage ourselves less.)

INFERENTIAL QUESTION

1b. Why would this statement be true? (People often act without examining the premises that underlie their actions and thus make mistakes in judgment.)

AT A GLANCE

- The problems of being an American artist are particular, for America has repressed certain grim aspects of its past.
- An artist can reveal a society to itself and can make freedom real.

REFLECTING ON THE SELECTION

Does Baldwin view the position of the artist in American society as basically positive or negative? (Students may suggest that Baldwin finds it uncomfortable to be an artist but feels that the artist must pay this price to perform a necessary and rewarding role.)

STUDY QUESTIONS

1. being alone; like that of birth or death, or suffering, or love
2. to create order, make life bearable, keep the human race alive
3. Society must accept certain things as real and stable; the artist takes nothing for granted—visible reality hides a deeper one.
4. Artists are ostracized during life and honored after death.
5. moving beyond Old World concepts of race and class and caste; to make unflinching assessment of its past
6. To build, to make progress to pass on its traditions, society must accept that what we experience in the world is real.
7. Possible answers: greed, hatred, anger, lust
8. Emerging nations must unite and create traditions; do not want to see the darker side of their history.
9. Writers who would support Baldwin's ideas include Poe and Melville; writers who refute the ideas include Irving and Bellow.

VIEWPOINT

Baldwin would be pleased because it says that he is a successful artist by his own definition—one who fulfills his responsibility to society.

once they are gone, because somewhere in our hearts we know that we cannot live without them.

The dangers of being an American artist are not greater than those of being an artist anywhere else in the world, but they are very particular. These dangers are produced by our history. They rest on the fact that in order to conquer this continent, the particular aloneness of which I speak—the aloneness in which one discovers that life is tragic, and therefore unutterably beautiful—could not be permitted. And that this prohibition is typical of all emergent nations will be proved, I have no doubt, in many ways during the next fifty years. This continent now is conquered, but our habits and our fears remain. And, in the same way that to become a social human being one modifies and suppresses and, ultimately, without great courage, lies to oneself about all one's interior, uncharted chaos, so have we, as a nation, modified and suppressed and lied about all the darker forces in our history. We know, in the case of the person, that whoever cannot tell himself the truth about his past is trapped in it, is immobilized in the prison of his undiscovered self. This is also true of nations. We know how a person, in such a paralysis, is unable to assess either his weaknesses or his strengths, and how frequently indeed he mistakes the one for the other. And this, I think, we do. We are the strongest nation in the Western world, but this is not for the reasons that we think. It is because we have an opportunity that no other nation has of moving beyond the Old World concepts of race and class and caste, to create, finally, what we must have had in mind when we first began speaking of the New World. But the price of this is a long look backward whence we came and an unflinching assessment of the record. For an artist, the record of that journey is most clearly revealed in the personalities of the people the journey produced. Societies never know it, but the war of an artist with his society is a lover's war, and he does, at his best, what lovers do, which is to reveal the beloved to himself and, with that revelation, to make freedom real.

STUDY QUESTIONS

Recalling

1. What state does Baldwin say the artist must cultivate? What kind of aloneness does he describe?
2. What is the purpose of societies, according to Baldwin?
3. How does Baldwin say societies view reality? How does the artist view reality?
4. How do societies treat their artists, according to Baldwin?
5. What great opportunity does Baldwin say the United States has? What does it require?

Interpreting

6. Why must societies assume that some things are real?
7. Baldwin says that we fear certain forces within ourselves. What are some of these forces?
8. Why do emerging nations especially fear the artist?

Extending

9. Look through the biographies of the writers in this book, and select one author. Do more research on his or her life. Look for evidence to support Baldwin's theory that artists are victimized and ostracized. Write a short essay either presenting evidence that supports Baldwin or showing that his theory is not always correct.

VIEWPOINT

The writer Kay Boyle has said of Baldwin that he

> has told us things about ourselves with such clarity that we had to raise our hands to shield our eyes from the light.

- Why would Baldwin be pleased by this statement? How does it relate to his definition of an artist?

Saul Bellow *born 1915*

When leading authors and critics were asked to name the twenty best books written since World War II, four of Saul Bellow's novels—*Herzog* (1964), *Henderson the Rain King* (1959), *Seize the Day* (1956), and *The Adventures of Augie March* (1953)—made the list. Bellow is often referred to as the most important American writer of his generation. He is, as the critic Leslie Fiedler said, "of all our novelists the one we need most to understand."

Saul Bellow was born in Lachine, Quebec, Canada. Both his parents had emigrated there from Russia, where his father had been an importer of Egyptian onions. Growing up, Bellow learned four languages—English, Hebrew, Yiddish, and French. When he was nine, his family moved to Chicago, where, Bellow recalls, he spent most of his time in libraries. He attended the University of Chicago and then Northwestern University, from which he graduated in 1937 with honors in sociology and anthropology.

With a scholarship to the University of Wisconsin, Bellow was on his way toward an academic career in anthropology when he discovered a more urgent calling—literature. "Every time I worked on my thesis, it turned out to be a story," he told one interviewer. "I disappeared for the Christmas holidays and I never came back."

Bellow's first two novels, *Dangling Man* (1944) and *The Victim* (1947), won him a small following. *The Adventures of Augie March* won not only greater attention but the National Book Award as well, as did *Herzog* and *Mr. Sammler's Planet* (1970). His two most recent novels are *Humboldt's Gift* (1975), which was awarded the Pulitzer Prize, and *The Dean's December* (1982). In 1976 Bellow was awarded the Nobel Prize for Literature.

Saul Bellow's novels generally concern people alienated by their urban environments but not defeated by them. In novels filled with exuberance, comic invention, and intellectual brilliance, Bellow dramatizes the lives of characters who seem misplaced, disoriented, trapped. Yet these characters come face to face with others who are tough, energetic, and street-wise. As one writer put it, Bellow's achievement lies in his "combination of cultural sophistication and the wisdom of the streets."

In his Nobel Prize Acceptance Speech, Bellow explores the power and value of literature in our time. In stirring language he calls on writers—and on readers—to return to "the center," to the human concerns that are "simple and true."

■ Bellow uses the words "true impressions" to convey what literature must offer the reader. What does he mean by the term?

AT A GLANCE

The author says that although many books are written about the crises in modern society, the solutions put forth are not satisfactory.

LITERARY OPTIONS

- rhetorical technique
- style: repetition/parallelism
- persuasion

THEMATIC OPTIONS

- the writer's responsibility
- spiritual identity
- arts vs. science

1 STYLE: REPETITION/ PARALLELISM

The repetition of the word "their" and the parallel structure emphasize the list Bellow puts forth.

2 RHETORICAL TECHNIQUE

Posing a question and then answering it immediately is a rhetorical technique often used. It is an excellent way of engaging the listener's attention.

Saul Bellow receiving Nobel Prize for Literature from Sweden's King Karl Gustaf, December 1976.

Saul Bellow

from Nobel Prize Acceptance Speech

Every year we see scores of books and articles by writers who tell Americans what a state they are in. All reflect the current crises; all tell us what we must do about them—these analysts are produced by the very disorder and confusion they prescribe for. It is as a novelist that I am considering the extreme moral sen-
1 sitivity of our contemporaries, their desire for perfection, their intolerance of the defects of society, the touching, the comical boundlessness of their demands, their anxiety, their irritability, their sensitivity, their tender-mindedness, their goodness, their convulsiveness, the recklessness with which they experiment with drugs and touch-therapies[1] and bombs. . . .

2 And art and literature—what of them? Well, there is a violent uproar but we are not absolutely dominated by it. We are still able to think, to discriminate, and to feel. The purer, subtler, higher activities have not succumbed to fury or to nonsense. Not yet. Books continue to be written and read. It may be more difficult to cut through the whirling mind of a modern reader but it is still possible to reach

1. **touch-therapies:** any of various group psychotherapies in which patients touch one another as part of the treatment.

GUIDED READING

LITERAL QUESTION

1a. What are the writers of literature still able to do? (to think, to discriminate, and to feel)

INFERENTIAL QUESTION

1b. What will these writers be able to do that the others cannot? (come up with real solutions to the problems of the human condition)

the quiet zone. In the quiet zone we novelists may find that he is devoutly waiting for us. When complications increase, the desire for essentials increases too. The unending cycle of crises that began with the First World War has formed a kind of person, one who has lived through strange and terrible things, and in whom there is an observable shrinkage of prejudices, a casting off of disappointing ideologies, an ability to live with many kinds of madness, and an immense desire for certain durable human goods—truth, for instance; freedom; wisdom. I don't think I am exaggerating; there is plenty of evidence for this. Disintegration? Well, yes. Much is disintegrating but we are experiencing also an odd kind of refining process. . . .

1 Hegel[2] long ago observed that art no longer engaged the central energies of man. These energies were now engaged by science—a "relentless spirit of rational inquiry." Art had moved to the margins. There it formed "a wide and splendidly varied horizon." . . .

There were European writers in the Nineteenth Century who would not give up the connection of literature with the main human enterprise. The very suggestion would have
2 shocked Tolstoi and Dostoevski.[3] But in the West a separation between great artists and the general public took place. Artists developed a marked contempt for the average reader and the bourgeois[4] mass. The best of them saw clearly enough what sort of civilization Europe had produced, brilliant but unstable, vulnerable, fated to be overtaken by catastrophe.

Despite a show of radicalism and innovation our contemporaries are really very conservative. They follow their Nineteenth Century leaders and hold to the old standards, interpreting history and society much as they were interpreted in the last century. What would
3 writers do today if it occurred to them that literature might once again engage those "central energies," if they were to recognize that an immense desire had arisen for a return from the periphery, for what is simple and true?

Of course we can't come back to the center simply because we wish to, though the realization that we are wanted might electrify us. The force of the crisis is so great that it might summon us back. But prescriptions are futile. One can't tell writers what to do. The imagination
4 must find its own path. But one can fervently wish that they—that we—would come back from the periphery. We writers do not represent mankind adequately. What account do Americans give of themselves, what accounts of them are given by psychologists, sociologists, historians, journalists, and writers? In a kind of contractual daylight they see themselves in the ways with which we are desperately familiar. These images of contractual daylight, so boring to Robbe-Grillet[5] and to me, originate in the contemporary world view: We put into our books the consumer, civil servant, football fan, lover, television viewer. And in the contractual daylight version their life is a kind of death. There is another life coming from an insistent sense of what we are which denies these daylight formulations and the false life—the death-in-life—they make for us. For it is false, and we know it, and our secret and incoherent resistance to it cannot stop—that resistance arises from persistent intuitions. Perhaps humankind cannot bear too much reality, but neither can it bear too much unreality, too much abuse of the truth. . . .

What is at the center now? At the moment, neither art nor science but mankind determining, in confusion and obscurity, whether it will endure or go under. The whole species—everybody—has gotten into the act. At such a time it is essential to lighten ourselves, to dump encumbrances, including the encumbrances of education and all organized plati-

---

2. **Hegel** [hā'gəl]: Georg Wilhelm Friedrich [gā'ôrk vil'helm frē'drikH] Hegel (1770–1831), German philosopher.
3. **Tolstoi** [tōl'stoi] . . . **Dostoevski** [dos'tə yef'skē]: Leo Tolstoi (1828–1910) and Feodor [fyô'dôr] Dostoevski (1821–1881), Russian novelists.
4. **bourgeois** [bo͞or zhwä']: materialistic, conventional, middle-class.
5. **Robbe-Grillet** [rōb'grē yā']: Alain Robbe-Grillet (born 1922), French novelist.

AT A GLANCE

- Readers want to return to "durable human goods."
- Hegel observed that science has replaced art at the center of human interest.
- The author says we cannot return to the center just because we want to, but the force of the crisis may summon us back.
- The question of humanity's survival is at the center now.

1 STYLE: REPETITION

The repetition of "engaged" and "energies" in consecutive sentences makes for forceful rhetoric.

2 PERSUASION

To suggest that such literary giants as Tolstoi and Dostoevski are on his side provides strong support for Bellow's point. To put oneself in the company of genius is highly persuasive rhetoric.

3 RHETORICAL TECHNIQUE

Bellow believes that there is a yearning for spiritualism and that it is the writer's responsibility to address this issue. He states and restates this theme, a building block approach that is highly persuasive.

4 RHETORICAL TECHNIQUE

By identifying himself as part of the problem, Bellows comes across as modest, honest, and responsible. He may be all these things, but a sympathetic presentation of self is also a significant rhetorical device.

GUIDED READING

LITERAL QUESTIONS

1a. According to Hegel, what replaced art in engaging the central energies of man? (science)

2a. What idea would have shocked Tolstoi and Dostoevski? (the idea that literature was not connected with the main human enterprise)

INFERENTIAL QUESTIONS

1b. Why did this not work? (Science does not deal with "durable human goods" so it cannot come up with satisfactory solutions to the problems of the human condition.)

2b. Why do you think Bellow mentions these two writers? (They are both nineteenth-century writers, yet they wrote great books on the big themes, and neither was especially concerned with scientific truth.)

AT A GLANCE

- We have an immense longing for a real account of what human beings are and what life is for.
- Literature can show us "true impressions" of the human condition with all its complexity, pain, and confusion.
- Art, like Conrad said, can help us find what is essential and enduring.

1 PERSUASION

Bellow's admission that even he has had to revise his opinions creates an intimacy with the listener, this making that listener more receptive to his opinions.

2 STYLE: REPETITION

The repeated use of "disappointment" and the sequential use of "waiting to hear," "does not hear," and "cannot hear" emphatically set the stage for the significant statement which follows.

3 THEME

Bellow offers his definition of spirituality; he sees it as the promise of meaning, harmony, and justice.

REFLECTING ON THE SELECTION

What was Bellow's purpose in making this speech? (He wanted to use the opportunity to capture the attention of the world in order to convey a concept of importance to him; namely that writers must once again engage the "central energies" of their readers by addressing the human essentials.)

tudes, to make judgments of our own, to perform acts of our own. Conrad[6] was right to appeal to that part of our being which is a gift. We must look for that gift under the wreckage of many systems. The collapse of those systems may bring a blessed and necessary release from formulations, from misleading conceptions of
1 being and consciousness. With increasing frequency I dismiss as "merely respectable" opinions I have long held—or thought I held—and try to discern what I have really lived by, and what others really live by. As for Hegel's art freed from "seriousness" and glowing on the margins, raising the soul above painful involvement in the limitations of reality through the serenity of form, that can exist nowhere now, during this struggle for survival. However, it is not as though the people who engaged in this struggle had only a rudimentary humanity, without culture, and knew nothing of art. Our very vices, our mutilations, show how rich we are in thought and culture. How much we know. How much we can feel. The struggles that convulse us make us want to simplify, to reconsider, to eliminate the tragic weakness which prevented writers—and readers—from being at once simple and true.

Writers are greatly respected. The intelligent public is wonderfully patient with them,
2 continues to read them and endures disappointment after disappointment, waiting to hear from art what it does not hear from theology, philosophy, social theory, and what it cannot hear from pure science. Out of the struggle at the center has come an immense, painful longing for a broader, more flexible, fuller, more coherent, more comprehensive account of what we human beings are, who we are, and what this life is for. At the center humankind struggles with collective powers for its freedom, the individual struggles with dehumanization for the possession of his soul. If writers do not come again into the center it will not be because the center is pre-empted. It is not. They are free to enter. If they so wish.

The essence of our real condition, the complexity, the confusion, the pain of it is shown to us in glimpses, in what Proust[7] and Tolstoi thought of as "true impressions." This essence reveals, and then conceals itself. When it goes away it leaves us again in doubt. But our connection remains with the depths from which these glimpses come. The sense of our real powers, powers we seem to derive from the universe itself, also comes and goes. We are reluctant to talk about this because there is nothing we can prove, because our language is inadequate, and because few people are willing to risk the embarrassment. They would have to say, "There is a spirit" and that is taboo. So almost everyone keeps quiet about it, although almost everyone is aware of it.

The value of literature lies in these intermittent "true impressions." A novel moves back and forth between the world of objects, of actions, of appearances, and that other world from which these "true impressions" come and which moves us to believe that the good we hang onto so tenaciously—in the face of evil, so obstinately—is no illusion.

No one who has spent years in the writing of novels can be unaware of this. The novel can't be compared to the epic, or to the monuments of poetic drama. But it is the best we can do just now. It is a sort of latter-day lean-to, a hovel in which the spirit takes shelter. A novel is balanced between a few true impressions and the multitude of false ones that make up most of what we call life. It tells us that for every human being there is a diversity of existences, that the single existence is itself an illusion in part, that these many existences sig-
3 nify something, tend to something, fulfill something; it promises us meaning, harmony and even justice. What Conrad said was true, art attempts to find in the universe, in matter as well as in the facts of life, what is fundamental, enduring, essential.

6. **Conrad:** Joseph Conrad (1857–1924), English novelist of Polish birth, whose books often deal with honor, morality, alienation, and guilt.

7. **Proust** [proost]: Marcel Proust (1871–1922), French novelist.

GUIDED READING

LITERAL QUESTION

1a. What reason can writers not give for not coming again into the center? (that the center is pre-empted)

INFERENTIAL QUESTION

1b. Why is this reason not valid? (At first science was at the center, but it did not provide us with real solutions to the problems of the human condition. Now the question of humanity's survival is at the center. People would welcome a return to "durable human goods" to help them deal with their situation. Thus art can enter the center if it so desires.)

STUDY QUESTIONS

Recalling

1. What does Bellow say he is considering as a novelist (paragraph 1)? What does he say happens "when complications increase" (paragraph 2)? What sort of person does he say has been produced by the cycle of crises that began with World War I?
2. What did Hegel observe about art? What was Hegel's opinion about art "on the margin"?
3. According to page 867, what is at the center now, and what sort of people are involved in it? With what and for what does Bellow say humankind struggles "at the center"? With what and for what does he say the individual struggles?
4. What does Bellow say is shown to us "in glimpses"? What does he say literature can do in this regard? With which of Conrad's ideas about art does Bellow agree in his final sentence?

Interpreting

5. What kind of literature is Hegel's literature "on the periphery"? To what sort of audience does it appeal? Does Bellow approve of such literature?
6. Summarize Bellow's opinion of modern human beings. What does he believe that all of us understand, at least "in glimpses"?
7. For what kind of literature does Bellow argue?

Extending

8. Which twentieth-century American writers that you have read do you think are "on the periphery"? Which do you think address "the center"? Support your answers.

VIEWPOINT

Howard Harper, Jr., sees a pattern in the lives of the characters in Bellow's fiction:

> . . . the protagonist undergoes an internal crisis precipitated by external events; as he searches for a way out his existence becomes increasingly subjective and restricted; at last he recognizes and accepts the common humanity which his situation reveals to him, and in his subsequent commitment to the fullness of life he becomes free and fully human.
>
> —*Contemporary Literature*

■ Compare Harper's description of what happens to Bellow's characters with the struggles of modern people whom Bellow describes in his Nobel address. What is the "internal crisis" the modern world faces? In the speech what does Bellow say we need to "recognize and accept"? What "commitment" must we make to become "fully human"?

COMPOSITION

Writing About Literature and Its Period

■ Write a brief composition demonstrating how Bellow's Nobel address is deeply rooted in the contemporary experience. First identify the problems Bellow describes, and tell how they are like other statements of modern problems made in this unit. Then tell what solutions and sources of strength Bellow recommends and why they are particularly contemporary. Conclude with your own opinion of Bellow's assessment of the literature of our time. *For help with this assignment, refer to Lesson 10 in the Writing About Literature Handbook at the back of this book.*

Writing an Essay of Opinion

■ Throughout history writers have tried to describe the value of literature. Saul Bellow believes that the value of literature in our time lies in its ability to uncover a realm of "true impressions" that "moves us to believe that the good we hang onto . . . is no illusion." Write an essay telling what, in your opinion, is the value of literature. Make your essay formal or informal as you wish. Be sure, however, to give clear statements of your opinions and to back them up with examples whenever possible.

COMPARING WRITERS

■ Many of the nonfiction selections on pages 841–868 by Barry Lopez, Américo Paredes, Ralph Ellison, N. Scott Momaday, Annie Dillard, and Saul Bellow concern a figurative return to "the center," a search for or movement toward the essence or true identity of something important. Compare three authors in this section. What does each one seek? What is the essence or center that each values? What "road" does each take to reach his or her goal? How do their methods and approaches differ?

STUDY QUESTIONS

1. extreme moral sensitivity of contemporaries, desire for perfection; desire for essentials increases; less prejudiced, abandoned disappointing ideologies, able to live with madness, desires human values
2. no longer engaged in central energies of man; forms wide, splendidly varied horizon
3. question of humanity's survival involving the whole species; with collective powers for freedom; dehumanization for possession of soul
4. essence of real condition; move between world of objects, actions, appearances and world from which true impressions come; art attempts to find what is fundamental, enduring
5. doesn't deal with essentials of spirit; elite, intellectual; no
6. confused, in crisis, possess unknown strengths, desire essentials; true reality of life, human condition.
7. engaged, committed, at the center, addressed to essentials
8. Answer will vary according to student's experiences.

VIEWPOINT

spiritual disintegration, lack of contact with essentials; complexity, confusion, pain of our real condition; to continue seeking spiritual truth

COMPARING WRITERS

Ellison: personal identity through gaining understanding of his own name; *Momaday:* ethnic identity through understanding the lives of his ancestors; *Bellow:* spiritual understanding through literature

COMPOSITION: GUIDELINES FOR EVALUATION

WRITING ABOUT LITERATURE AND ITS PERIOD

Objective

To write about literature and its period

Guidelines for Evaluation

- suggested length: six to nine paragraphs
- should restate the problems Bellow identifies
- should tell how problems are representative
- should restate Bellow's recommended solutions and relate them to modern thinking in general
- should give personal evaluation of Bellow

WRITING AN ESSAY OF OPINION

Objective

To write an essay about the value of literature

Guidelines for Evaluation

- suggested length: four to six paragraphs
- should state an opinion about the value of literature
- should support the opinions with examples and reasons

ACTIVE READING

The Aural Imagination

After students have read this page, demonstrate the importance of the aural imagination in reading. Have volunteers choose passages from the selections for oral reading. A pair of students could rehearse the dialogue between Mrs. Miller and Miriam in Capote's "Miriam"; other students could prepare parts of the Lopez and Bellow selections; others could prepare narrative sections from the Goyen, Updike, or Saroyan selections. For a "before and after" comparison you might have one student read a passage first in a flat monotone and then expressively. To complete the lesson, remind the students that the aural imagination allows us to hear in our mind nuances and variations in tone even though we are reading silently.

ACTIVE READING

The Aural Imagination

Literature begins with a human voice speaking. Earlier in this book we talked about the sound of prose and the sound of poetry, to remind ourselves of the importance—and the pleasure—of *hearing* literature. The selections in this unit remind us once again how essential it is to hear not only the speakers of nonfiction and the songs of poets but also the variety of characters in fiction.

Just as we heard the emotion in Patrick Henry's speech, so we can hear the thoughtful eloquence in Saul Bellow's "Nobel Prize Acceptance Speech." Can we hear the speech *exactly* as he delivered it? No, not without listening to a tape recording which would allow us to hear his pauses and emphases. Still, we can hear in our mind's ear a plausible version of the sound and sense of that speech. We can hear the intense yet serene exhortation to modern writers and modern readers to seek the truth at the quiet center of our tumultuous contemporary world.

"Out of the struggle at the center has come an immense, painful longing for a broader, more flexible, fuller, more coherent, more comprehensive account of what we human beings are, and what this life is for."

In poetry too, of course, we listen for the music of the poem or the special tone of the poet. In Robert Hayden's "Those Winter Sundays" we give sound to the poet's plaintive question:

What did I know, what did I know
of love's austere and lonely offices?

The poem recreates the Sundays of the speaker's childhood not in a tone of fond reminiscence but rather in one of sadness and regret—regret for lost time and lost chances to express his love for his father.

Fiction writing makes a different kind of demand on our aural imagination. In fiction we want to hear the voice of imaginary characters, sometimes a great number of them, talking at once, having conversations, responding to each other. In A. C. Greene's "The Girl at Cabe Ranch," for example, the dialogue of the characters reveals an underlying emotional conflict between the ranch girl and the local boy, and the narrator gets caught in the crossfire.

"It doesn't change that much around here," she said. "Nothing does."

"I don't think that's the bluff," the boy said.

"Why?" she turned toward him fiercely. "You don't know anything about it. Dr. Powell said it was. He knows a lot more about it than you do. You're just an ignorant cowboy," she bit her lower lip, "that's all you are. You don't want to be anything else."

The emotion in the girl's voice far exceeds the ostensible subject of disagreement—the whereabouts of the bluff. Her tone as well as her words should alert us to the real source of tension between the boy and the girl.

How would you sound the final word in Truman Capote's "Miriam"? Miriam's "Hello" is not simple. The sound, the tone, must convey many implications. It is cheerful, youthful, and sinister—all at once.

Each of these works of fiction—in fact, any story or novel you will ever read—calls your aural imagination into action. It is through this use of your imagination that *you*—along with the writers you read—create the characters of fiction.

THE AMERICAN VOICE

Questions

The writers of our time are questioners. In our poetry, fiction, and nonfiction they ask who we are and who we are becoming. They ask what we should be doing and why we should do it. They wonder how we can become the heroes of our own lives.

Our writers ask questions about our identity, about our relationships with one another and with the natural world, about how we are trying to express ourselves. They know that only by asking questions can we begin to answer them.

Hayden
What did I know, what did I know
Of love's austere and lonely offices?

Ashbery
What's a plain level? It is that and other things,
Bringing a system of them into play. Play?

Carver
Tell me, she says. Tell me what it was like when I was a kid.

Dillard
But how could the glory have lasted forever?

Goyen
Yet, everything changes, he thought, slowly it all changes. Do we resign ourselves to that? Is youth passing when we see this—the fierce battle of youth that would not accept change and loss? . . .

Bellow
What is at the center now?

Throughout American literature the great artists have asked the most serious questions, and the greatest have achieved some answers. For the Puritans, the answer lay in a profound religious vision. For Emerson, the answer was a transcendental oneness with the universe. For Whitman, only a constant celebration of life was an adequate response. For Dickinson, intense personal commitment tempered with a cool sense of irony provided the greatest satisfaction. For Faulkner, a mythological world threw a light on reality. For Stevens, the power of the human imagination held the key.

There is no doubt that our writers will continue to ask questions and continue to offer answers about living. It is for this reason that we will continue to read them, need them, love them.

Key to Illustrations on Pages 756–757.

1		2		7
3	4	5		8
6				9

1. Computer map, photograph by Tom Tracy.
2. John Updike, photograph by Jill Krementz.
3. Liftoff of Apollo II, NASA photograph.
4. Children using computers, photograph by Mark Perlstein.
5. The St. Louis Arch, photograph by N. E. Warren.
6. William Saroyan, photograph by Jill Krementz.
7. Robert Penn Warren, photograph by Jill Krementz.
8. Dr. Sally Ride, first American woman in space, in the astronaut training module. Photograph by Katz.
9. Dr. Martin Luther King, Jr., photograph by Flip Schulke.

THE AMERICAN VOICE

Questions

Questions beget other questions as well as answers. Ask students what questions are on their minds. What do they think about? To what do they aspire? How does the process of asking questions lead to finding answers?

STUDENT'S RESOURCES: LESSONS IN ACTIVE LEARNING

A major goal of this literature series is to help students become active, independent learners. Resources on the following pages are designed to help students develop and refine the skills that mature learners use constantly as they interact with literature. Such learners know how to *manage* their assignments by applying these skills:

- speaking and listening skills
- thinking skills
- writing skills
- research skills

Students will be able to refer to these pages throughout the term—not just in connection with a single literary selection. In other words, students can use this *easy-to-find reference-and-practice guide* continually, as they experience all the literature they read. With outstanding literature, on the one hand, and a comprehensive resource guide, on the other, this literature series provides the means for you and your students to deal with both *ideas* and *skills*.

In addition, these pages also include the following elements, designed for successful teaching and learning:

- Literary Terms Handbook
- Glossary
- Vocabulary Review
- Index of Titles by Theme
- Index of Titles by Genre
- Index of Skills
- Index of Authors and Titles

STUDENT'S RESOURCES

LESSONS IN ACTIVE LEARNING

SPEAKING AND LISTENING HANDBOOK

THINKING SKILLS HANDBOOK

WRITING ABOUT LITERATURE HANDBOOK

SPEAKING AND LISTENING HANDBOOK

This handbook enables students to practice and improve their speaking and listening skills while studying literature. The four lessons in the handbook cover a wide range of interrelated speaking and listening skills:

- public speaking
- listening/discussion
- oral interpretation of literature
- collaborative learning

Each literature-based lesson is set up in a step-by-step format so that students can easily work on the skill on their own. The final step in each lesson is a transfer activity in which the student is directed to apply the skill to a variety of selections in the anthology. In other words, the lessons are designed to be used or referred to many times—as often as you wish your students to work with a particular speaking or listening skill.

In addition to this handbook, speaking and listening skills are practiced in the Additional Projects listed in the unit booklets in *Teacher's Classroom Resources*. The blackline masters Outline for Organizing a Speech About Literature and Questions for Preparing an Oral Interpretation of Drama (TCR 7, pages 40–41) and Overhead Transparency 30 will prove helpful as your students work with the lessons in this handbook.

LESSON 1

The first lesson gives students an opportunity to work with public speaking—perhaps the activity they most often associate with speaking and listening. Here students practice techniques of preparing and delivering a speech and, at the same time, examine literature from new perspectives.

SPEAKING AND LISTENING HANDBOOK

LESSON 1: *A Persuasive Speech About Literature*

OVERVIEW

You will present a speech in which you will persuade your audience to accept your view of what happens to a character in a story, play, or poem *after the work ends*. To support the epilogue you envision, you will, of course, draw evidence from the story, play, or poem itself. (An **epilogue** is a short section that follows the formal ending of a literary work and tells what happens to the characters thereafter.) The purpose of this assignment is to prove that you can pay close enough attention to details so that you really get to know the character.

PREPARING THE SPEECH

1. **Ask probing questions.**
   The following questions may help you as you try to project what happens to a character after the last page of the selection:

   a. If the author were to have continued the story line, what would have happened next?
   b. What do I imagine the character doing one hour, one day, one month, one year, or one decade from the point at which the story line ends?

2. **Check your hypothesis against the evidence in the selection—and common sense.**
   The most important point to keep in mind is that the developments you project for the character must be "in character." You should not propose an epilogue in which a character does something totally out of line with how he or she performs in the author's work. You may draw on real-life experiences to defend your epilogue, citing examples of how people you know act.

3. **Decide upon an effective opening and an effective closing.**
   A sensible way to begin this speech is to ask your audience a direct question. For example, if you choose to speak about Truman Capote's story "Miriam," you might come right out and ask, "Does Miriam stay or not?" Such a question should make your audience curious; they will pay attention to your opinion and reasons.

   The conclusion of your speech must increase your persuasive impact. It is particularly important in this kind of speech that you do not simply fade away at the end. You must leave your audience believing in your view.

A SAMPLE SPEECH

Suppose you were to think about Sinclair Lewis' story "The Hack Driver." This story lends itself to thinking about an epilogue because it stops so abruptly and yet contains many hints within it as to what might happen next.

As you consider the general questions suggested under "Preparing the Speech," you may actually find yourself asking such specific questions as the following:

- Does the narrator remain a lawyer?
- Does he learn not to be so naive, remain in the city, and advance to a higher position in his law firm?
- Does he conclude, as a result of his experiences in the story, that he must learn rural ways and decide to move to a small town to practice law?

Testing all possibilities against the story itself, you may conclude that the narrator remains a lawyer and continues to reside in a large city. The evidence in support of that epilogue includes the opening paragraph: Based on that paragraph, you may argue, the narrator must have remained a lawyer in a big city because only by so doing would he have learned what he claims to have learned about dining in large, posh homes. Other parts of the story also support the position that the narrator remains a big-city lawyer.

You may also cite an example or two from real life to support your version of the narrator's future. Perhaps you know a lawyer who, though a country romantic in some ways, has spent his career in a competitive city law practice.

As you think about various openings and conclusions, you may create the following outline:

I. Opening: Ask a question to involve audience. For "The Hack Driver": If you'd been made fun of on the job, would you recommit yourself to doing a good job, or would you give up your dream altogether?

II. Body

A. Summary of story as author wrote it

B. Statement of issue: What does the character do immediately or over the course of the next few months or years?

C. Justification of proposed epilogue

1. Evidence from story

2. Evidence from real life

III. Closing

Statement of appreciation of original story and solicitation of support for proposed epilogue

DELIVERING THE SPEECH

In actually giving your speech, you can follow several pointers to increase your persuasiveness.

1. Present your proposed epilogue clearly. You will want to use vivid description—as vivid as the author's descriptions in the original work. Your audience cannot be expected to accept an epilogue that they do not fully understand.
2. Be very familiar with the selection and with your own ideas. You must show the audience that you command great knowledge of the work. You may look at notes, and you may read an excerpt from the work, but make sure your speech is extemporaneous—prepared but spontaneous.
3. Demonstrate personal conviction by believing in your proposed epilogue. Only if you are committed will your audience believe you. Show your enthusiasm by speaking briskly, letting your pitch relay your excitement, standing with confidence, and making plenty of eye contact.

ASSIGNMENT

You may choose to present a persuasive speech about what happens to the narrator of "The Hack Driver." Here are other ideas for a persuasive speech about an epilogue, and you will be able to come up with many ideas of your own based on the literature in this book.

- For the story "Miriam": Will Miriam remain in Mrs. Miller's life?
- For "Driving to Town Late to Mail a Letter": What does the speaker do after he mails the letter?
- For "A Pair of Silk Stockings": What does Mrs. Sommers do when the cable car gets to her stop?

LESSON 2

Listening and discussion skills form the second strand of the handbook. Listening is critical to clear communication; after all, listening is the first step in responding. Discussion is equally essential to the study of literature. Without developed discussion skills students' insights into and responses to literature can never be shared.

LESSON 2: *A Panel Discussion About Literature*

OVERVIEW

A group of five or six students will conduct a panel discussion concerning one of the authors in this book. The students will, in effect, have become experts on the author. They may have become experts in different aspects of the author's life and works, but they will share a great deal of general knowledge about the author. The panel discussion will consist primarily of spontaneous remarks by the panel members in response to questions posed by a moderator and by the panel members themselves.

PLANNING A PANEL DISCUSSION

The group must meet together before the panel discussion itself is held.

1. **Select an author to discuss, and formulate a discussion question.**

   The group may select an author to discuss based on enjoyment of a work by the author, an interesting statement about the author, a biographical note, or a reference book.

   In deciding what to discuss about this author, the group should look for a question that is significant. Only if a question meets this criterion is it really worth pursuing because only then will the individual members of the panel find enough to talk about and to form different opinions about.

   The question can deal with a matter of fact or a matter of value. The first seeks to find out why something is so; the second seeks to discover whether or why something is good or bad.

   Examples of Questions of Fact
   - Why was Melville's novel *Moby-Dick,* now considered one of the greatest American novels, not recognized as great for almost a century? [This question grows out of the biographical headnote on page 203.]
   - What role did the black experience and life in the Harlem section of New York City play in shaping Langston Hughes's writing?

   Examples of Questions of Value
   - What is Mark Twain's place in American literature?
   - Does E. E. Cummings' unusual syntax and spacing of words and letters contribute to a deeper poetic experience?

2. **Research the question.**

   Each member of the panel, including the moderator, must do his or her own research on the author and must read some more of the author's work. You can begin with reference works such as an encyclopedia, the *Dictionary of American Biography*, and *Webster's Biographical Dictionary*, but you will have to go much further and check books such as the *Oxford Companion to American Literature*, biographies, and books of criticism.

   Each member will probably learn many of the same facts and interpretations as the others, but each member will probably also come across some data that the others do not. As a result, each person will have something unique to add to the panel discussion.

3. **Set an agenda.**

   After the individuals do their research, the group will have to meet again. This time they will brainstorm in order to come up with an agenda. An agenda is the list of subordinate questions they want to discuss in order to deal with the overall discussion question (see number 1, above). The moderator, or discussion leader, will be the one primarily responsible for making sure the group follows the agenda, but the entire group can help to determine the agenda.

   Example: Assume your overall discussion question is "How could Emily Dickinson, a poet who lived such an isolated life, reveal so much life experience in her poems?" The following subordinate questions would help focus the panel discussion:

   - Did Dickinson in fact live an isolated life?
   - Was Dickinson a recluse?

- What kinds of experiences *does* Dickinson reveal in her poems, and are the experiences unlikely to have been known to her?

GUIDELINES FOR THE MODERATOR

1. Set up the room to establish a good climate for discussion. Arrange chairs and tables so that the panel members are facing the audience and can be seen and heard well.
2. Present the discussion question clearly. Explain why it is important.
3. Briefly introduce each panel member.
4. Follow the agenda in asking questions. You can direct a question to a particular member of the panel. Then see if anyone else on the panel has something to add to that particular question or to a related question.
5. Allow panelists to ask one another related questions, but always try to keep the discussion on track.
6. Summarize the answers to questions frequently, pointing out where there is agreement among the panelists and where there is disagreement.
7. At the appropriate time open the discussion to the audience. Let them ask questions.
8. At the end of the discussion, state what has been accomplished and thank everyone for participating, including the audience.

GUIDELINES FOR THE PANELISTS

1. Be prepared. You must be familiar with the basic facts of the author's life and his or her writing. Remember, though, that you should not simply repeat what someone else has already said. Try to contribute new information or insights. To do so, you will, of course, have had to do a great deal of research before the panel discussion.
2. Present your ideas and opinions clearly.
3. Take responsibility for contributing to the discussion. Do not withdraw from the discussion.
4. Do not monopolize the conversation or force your views on the rest of the group.
5. Listen carefully to the other panel members. Remember that they may have read some sources that you have not. They may have thought of something that you have not. Listening carefully to them will stimulate your own thinking.

GUIDELINES FOR THE AUDIENCE

After a twenty-minute panel discussion, about seven or eight minutes should be set aside for audience questions and responses from the panelists. The moderator will open the discussion to the audience and recognize members of the audience.

1. Ask a question rather than make a long statement.
2. You may direct your question to an individual panel member or to the panel as a whole, in which case the moderator can ask which panelist wants to respond.
3. You may ask a follow-up question or allow another member of the audience to ask a question.

ASSIGNMENTS

1. You may want to participate in a panel discussion of one of the questions listed under *Examples* earlier in this lesson.
2. You may want to participate in a panel discussion that explores the connection between one of the writers in this book and the state you live in—whether the author was born there or wrote there. For example, to what extent is Carl Sandburg an Illinois poet?
3. You may want to participate in a panel that considers similarities between an author in this book and a contemporary writer not included in this anthology. Are there similarities, for example, between the writing of Edgar Allan Poe and your favorite contemporary science-fiction writer?

LESSON 3

Oral interpretation—the performance of literature—is gaining increased attention as another avenue to the understanding and appreciation of literature. As students work on their oral presentations of poems, short stories, etc., they find themselves reading more closely and thinking about literature more critically than ever before.

LESSON 3: *Oral Interpretation of Drama*

OVERVIEW

You will choose a scene from one of the two plays in this book, *Our Town* by Thornton Wilder and *The Glass Menagerie* by Tennessee Williams, and read it aloud to the class. The scene you select must have two characters in it. You will *not* present a full-blown production with acting and staging; you will present just a reading—but one that will give your audience insight into the play. Your scene should run about five minutes.

Giving an oral reading of a play emphasizes its language and helps bring the play to life. A single reader performing a scene between two characters gives us a sense of the whole, an idea of the shape of the scene, and an appreciation of the writer's style.

PREPARING AN ORAL INTERPRETATION OF A SCENE

1. **Cutting and adapting a scene**

First you will have to choose a scene from the play. These two plays have many scenes between two people.

Examples

- George and Emily discussing their future life together in the drugstore while having a soda (Act 2 of *Our Town*)
- Amanda coming home to confront her daughter Laura, who has not been going to the typing school as she was supposed to (Scene 2 of *The Glass Menagerie*)

You may have time to present only a portion of a scene, not the entire scene. You will want to find a good beginning and a good ending place so that your excerpted scene will have a feeling of completion. You may also cut out a section of the scene to make it fit within the time limit, as long as the scene still makes sense with the lines cut. Sometimes you can use a transitional sentence to tie together parts of the scene. You can say, for example, "We pick up the scene later as. . . ."

Consider also which stage directions to retain and which to cut. If the stage direction is merely a note on how to say the line, then simply apply it to your reading of the line. On the other hand, some stage directions cannot be made clear just by your reading of the dialogue. In these cases you will want to read the stage directions as part of the scene.

Finally, type your script, double-spaced, or print it neatly so that you can read it easily. On your typed or printed script mark important reading cues about voice and gestures.

2. **Characterization**

The most important task of the oral interpreter is to make the characters clear to the audience. You want to read the lines of dialogue as if they were being spoken by the character.

First, consider the character's sex, age, and personality. Then consider more specifically the character's particular state of mind and intention within the scene you are reading.

Example: Tom is quite different in Scene 3 of *The Glass Menagerie*, when he is upset with his mother, from the way he is in Scene 5, when he tries to make up with her. He is basically the same person and character in both scenes, but his mood and intentions are different.

Consider also how the character moves, stands, and gestures. What kind of an expression does the character's face show? Does the character gesture a lot or very little? What are two or three typical gestures that he or she might use? What person in real life does the character remind you of? Use some of that real person's gestures, facial expressions, and ways of talking to flesh out the character in your reading. Sometimes just the beginning of a gesture is enough to suggest the complete gesture to the audience, who will complete the gesture in their own imagination as you read the scene to them.

Example: The script indicates that in the last scene of *Our Town* Emily cries. The interpreter may read the stage direction stating that Emily cries and then give only a hint of beginning to cry—or *wanting* to cry—in her voice and eyes while reading the lines.

3. **Character differentiation**
When you are reading a scene with more than one character speaking, you must maintain a distinction between the characters so that the audience can tell them apart and know which one is speaking at any given moment. There are two ways to distinguish characters.

   a. Strongly create the characterizations: Be very definite as to each character's traits and way of speaking and gesturing.
   b. Place each character in a different space. When you read character A—Amanda, for instance—look up from your script slightly to your right; when you read character B—Tom—look up from the script slightly to your left. The audience will then get used to this convention and will know as you begin to speak, or even before you speak, which character you are reading by the direction you are looking in.

4. **Character interaction**
   a. *Use focus.* Focus refers to establishing an image of the other character—the one being spoken to—in the space before you as you read the line of dialogue. As you read the line, you actually pretend that you are talking to someone and that you can actually see that person in front of you. With focus you can indicate whether that person is sitting down or standing up, whether the person is shorter or taller than the character you are reading, whether the person is near or far away.
   b. *Use effective cue pick-up.* The last thing the previous character says is the cue for the next character to speak. There should usually not be a pause between the characters' lines. The next character should begin speaking immediately. Otherwise you will set up a deadly, unnatural rhythm and destroy the illusion that the characters are talking to each other.

5. **Realizing the structure of the scene**
Every scene has a way of beginning, of warming up, of reaching small climaxes, and then of reaching a major climax—or emotional high point. Sometimes a scene ends on this emotional high note, as in Scene 3 of *The Glass Menagerie*, when Tom runs out of the apartment. Often there is a period of falling action, to bring the scene back to a resting point, to give a feeling of completion. You want to realize these highs and lows as you read the scene. Do not start out at a high point, but gradually build up to it. Your voice may grow louder and faster and become more intense. If you start out too fast, high, and intense, you will have nowhere to build to—nothing left for the climax.

6. **Preparing an introduction to your reading**
Set the scene for the audience. Tell them which characters are in your scene. Your audience may have already read the scene, or they may not have. You do not want to explain the scene; you will do that in your reading. But you want to set the tone, tell them what they need to know to understand what is happening, and get them interested.

ACTIVITIES

Here are suggested two-character scenes for you to read to the class.

Our Town

- Mrs. Webb and Emily, Act 1, pages 680–681
- George and Emily in the drugstore, Act 2, pages 692–695

The Glass Menagerie

- Amanda and Laura, Scene 2 (typing school)
- Tom and Amanda, beginning Scene 6 (Tom lets Amanda know that he's invited someone home to meet Laura.)
- Jim and Laura, Scene 7 (Jim gets Laura to dance and breaks the horn off her unicorn.)

LESSON 4

Only by working together can students gain new and varied perspectives. Collaborative learning by its very nature is usually an oral language activity. Here students see how to work efficiently, imaginatively, and productively in small groups to explore literature in innovative ways.

LESSON 4: *Group Oral Interpretation (Poetry)*

OVERVIEW

Working in a group of five to eight students, you will select a poem from this anthology and read it aloud to the class. As a group you will divide the sentences, lines, and words of the poem and assign them to different readers. As you transform the poem into a performance, you may even add sounds and movements that will extend the poem's visual and auditory images. Your audience should be able to understand and appreciate the poem—maybe even see it in a new way—as a result of your performance.

PREPARING AN ORAL PRESENTATION

1. **Analyze the poem.**
   You must understand the poem because your understanding will become the basis for your performance. As a group study the poem—its images, organization, word choice, sound and rhythm, speaker, title—and arrive at an interpretation of the poem.

2. **Develop a performance concept.**
   At this point you have to start thinking about how many individual voices will read the poem and whether there will be any unison reading. You will have to work through the poem word by word and line by line to decide which voice should say what.

   Then you will consider staging the poem. What kinds of movement and sound effects should accompany particular parts of the poem?

3. **Rehearse the poem.**
   Sound: You want to blend individual voices so that your performance is smooth. Yet you also want to feature contrasts among voices. While you want each person and each word to be heard, you may also want to allow voices to overlap at times and to blend words with other sounds.

   Movement: Choreograph the movements so that they are smooth and precise. Timing is very important. Make sure your movements are in the rhythm of the poem and that they support the words of the poem. Make sure your movements have variety.

   Pacing: As stated before, you must work to achieve smoothness and variety at one and the same time. Remember that pauses can achieve suspense and suggest emphasis—pauses of sound, pauses of movement.

   Dress: At times clothing can lend a certain feel to a performance. You may want to consider the colors of what your group wears as it performs.

   Memorization: Since smoothness is so important to a performance of poetry, you should either memorize your lines during the rehearsal or write them out neatly on small cue cards to read from during the performance.

ASSIGNMENTS

1. Perform "The Death of the Ball Turret Gunner," as is scripted in this lesson.
2. Working in a group, prepare an alternative scripting of "The Death of the Ball Turret Gunner," and perform that version.
3. Select one of the following poems from this book—or any other poem from this book—to perform with a group:
   - Carl Sandburg's "Jazz Fantasia"
   - Langston Hughes's "Dream Variations"
   - Walt Whitman's "I Hear America Singing"
   - Emily Dickinson's "I felt a Funeral, in my Brain"
   - William Carlos Williams' "The Artist"
   - Margaret Walker's "Lineage"
   - Gwendolyn Brooks's "Strong Men, Riding Horses"

MODEL SCRIPTING

For the poem "The Death of the Ball Turret Gunner" by Randall Jarrell (page 561), one performance concept features three voices and a chorus. One voice is the ball turret gunner himself, and the other two voices echo his experience. The chorus is made up of three people (CHORUS 1, CHORUS 2, and CHORUS 3), who create the sounds of fighter planes and machine-gun fire—sounds that in this performance actually cause the ball turret gunner to wake up (line 3 of Jarrell's poem). According to this performance concept, the image of the gunner waking up to the machine-gun fire is emphasized; in fact, the performance begins with that image and then moves back to line 1. Eventually, the performance arrives at line 5, spoken in a detached manner—as if a comment on the first four lines of the poem.

CHORUS (sounds of World War II fighter planes)
CHORUS 1: YYYYeeeEEEOOOOwwwwwww
Yyyyngngngeeuuuu
CHORUS 2: Yyyyngngngeeeuuuuuuwwwww
CHORUS 3: NGNGNGNGeeeOOOOOOwwww

*

CHORUS 1: d-d-d-d-d-d-d-d d-d-d-d-d
CHORUS 2: g-g-g-g-g-g-g-g-
CHORUS 3: b-b-b-b-b-b-b-b-b-b
VOICE 1 *(has been hunched in fetal position; startled; sits up suddenly):* I woke!
VOICE 2: to black flak
VOICE 3: and the nightmare fighters.

Repeat from *

CHORUS 1: d-d-d-d-d-d-d-d d-d-d-d-d
CHORUS 2: g-g-g-g-g-g-g-g-
CHORUS 3: b-b-b-b-b-b-b-b-b-b

Again VOICE 1, *having assumed fetal position; sits up startled, suddenly.*
VOICE 1: I woke!
VOICE 2: I woke!
VOICE 3: I woke!
VOICE 1: I woke!

Pause.

CHORUS *sounds softer*

VOICES 2 *and* 3 *cradle* VOICE 1 *in fetal position.*
VOICE 1: From my mother's sleep
VOICE 2: mother's sleep
VOICE 1: I fell into the State
VOICE 2 *and* VOICE 3 *(stand, salute):* State!
VOICE 1: And I hunched in its belly
VOICE 2: hunched in its belly
VOICE 1: till my wet fur froze.
VOICE 3: froze.

All three voices look down as if from great heights.

VOICE 1: Six miles from earth
VOICE 2: Six miles
VOICE 3: Six miles
VOICE 1: loosed from its dream of life *(Voice 1 rolls one way, then the other.)*
VOICE 2: loosed from its dream of life
VOICE 3: loosed from its dream of life
CHORUS: d-d-d-d-d-d-/g-g-g-g-g-g-/b-b-b-b-b- *(strong)*
VOICE 1 (sits up suddenly): I woke!
VOICE 2: I woke!
VOICE 3: I woke!
VOICE 1: I woke!
VOICE 2: to black flak
VOICE 3: and the nightmare fighters.
VOICE 1: I woke to black flak and the nightmare fighters.

Sudden pause./Silence.

VOICE 1 *(no emotion; sitting up; to audience):* When I died they washed me out of the turret with a hose.

VOICE 2 *and* VOICE 3 *look at each other; shrug.*
VOICE 2: Washed me out of the turret.
VOICE 3: With a hose.

Pause.

Each of the six lessons in this handbook serves to integrate a particular thinking skill with the experience of literature. Each lesson is literature-based and demonstrates to the student that the active reader is a thinking reader, that the *results* of thinking are both understanding and enjoyment. The step-by-step format of each lesson allows for either teacher involvement or student independence. Gradually, as students continue to use the procedures shown in the lessons, they can grow more and more independent as thinkers about literature and as confident, thinking young adults.

Each lesson is structured in the following way:

- DEFINITION—A clear, jargon-free definition that expresses the thinking skills in students' own terms.
- EXAMPLE—A model of the thinking skill being applied in a literature-based situation. Each example emphasizes the students' own experience in using the skill.
- EXPLANATION—A detailed "walk-through" of the example, demonstrating and discussing each individual step in the application of the thinking skill.
- PROCEDURES—A list and summary of the individual steps used in the example and the explanation. Identifying procedures is an essential step in thinking about thinking and vital to the students' developing independence.
- ACTIVITIES—All activities are literature-based. Those activities keyed to specific literary selections give the student an opportunity to follow the correct procedures in thinking about some aspect of the selection. Those activities not keyed to specific literary selections provide the opportunity to transfer the thinking skill to a new literary situation.

THINKING SKILLS HANDBOOK

LESSON 1: *Logical Reasoning*

DEFINITION

Logical reasoning is a way to explain exactly why you believe that something is true. When you reason logically, you state the necessary conditions for the explanation to be true. Then you show that these necessary conditions do exist. When you reason logically, however, you must be sure that both you and your audience agree on the same set of assumptions. This means that you agree about what is important in the particular situation you are considering.

EXAMPLE

The importance of a person in the history of a nation can be shown in many ways. National holidays may commemorate a birthday; a portrait may appear on a coin or stamp; places may bear the name; songs, poetry, or other literary works may be written to show appreciation or respect. The assumption is that holidays, coins, stamps, and place names are rare and important to the nation.

EXPLANATION

According to the conditions necessary for importance, George Washington is important in American history. There are sufficient examples to support this belief. His portrait appears on money and stamps; cities and a state are named after him; novels, songs, and poetry have been written about him.

PROCEDURES

When you intend to use logical reasoning to convince an audience that something is true or important, you will find the following steps helpful:

1. **State what you believe** to be true.
2. **Identify all of the conditions that are necessary** for the situation to be true.
3. Show how the necessary conditions have been met. **Give specific examples that are sufficient evidence** to support your position.
4. **Identify the important assumptions** your audience must share in order for your position to be convincing.

ACTIVITY I. REASONING LOGICALLY ABOUT CULTURAL CHANGE

There are many examples of cultural change in the literature in the first two units of this book—"Early America" (pages 1–47) and "Reason and Revolution" (pages 48–97). Select two examples that illustrate an important change in American literature or culture.

1. For each example, **state what you believe** to be the situation prior to the change. Describe the situation after the change took place.
2. **List the conditions that would be necessary** if a particular change is to be considered important. **Identify the assumptions** you are making about importance.
3. **Show that the two examples meet the necessary conditions** for importance.
4. **Write a brief statement** supporting your contention that these two changes were important to American literature or culture.

ACTIVITY II. REASONING LOGICALLY ABOUT NATURE IN LITERATURE

Several of the articles in these units refer to the natural world of plants and animals. The purpose of this activity is to identify a literary position regarding nature. How do these writers feel about nature? Is it something to be exploited? Is it revered? What other opinions are expressed or implied?

The detailed lessons in this handbook are not the only application of thinking skills in the literature series. Throughout each book students also practice and reinforce thinking skills through the following features:

- Purpose-setting questions
- Study Questions divided into Recalling, Interpreting, and Extending categories
- Thinking About . . . questions within Literary Focuses
- Models for Active Reading
- Thinking Skills blackline masters, TCR 7, pages 42–44
- Thinking Skills Overhead Transparency 31

1. **Find two selections** in which the writers refer to the natural world. Do they appear to express the same attitude? Or do they see things differently? **State your belief** about their positions regarding relationships between people and nature.

2. **List the conditions** that are necessary for you to reason logically that an author holds a particular position about people and nature. Prepare a chart that displays these conditions.

3. **Show how each selection is appropriate** to illustrate that author's position.

4. **Write a brief statement** in which you make a reasoned argument that these writers viewed nature in a specific way.

ACTIVITY III. REASONING LOGICALLY ABOUT THE IDEA OF OPPORTUNITY

Many people came to America because they believed that there were greater opportunities for them.

1. **Find an example** of a writer who considered the wider range of opportunities an attraction.

2. **Identify the conditions** that help you recognize the author's attraction to opportunities of America.

3. **Demonstrate that the writer met the necessary conditions** of being attracted by the opportunities. Remember, the ideas may be implied or stated.

4. **Write a brief statement** in which you support your position that the writer was attracted to America by the opportunities the country offered.

LESSON 2: *Inductive Inquiry*

DEFINITION

Inductive inquiry is a way to *discover* meaning by observation. As you examine several examples of an idea, you discover the characteristics which the examples share—that is, what they have in common. Once you have discovered what is special, or characteristic, about the idea you are examining, you can also tell how that idea differs from similar ideas.

EXAMPLE

The units in this book called "New England Renaissance" and "Conflict and Celebration" contain many literary selections that describe conflicts. In other words, the literary selections provide information which helps you to develop an idea of what conflict means and how it is represented in literature. Your experience of literature—combined with your knowledge of conflicts that occur in the real world and all your personal experience of conflicts—can help you to *discover* that conflicts in literature have certain characteristics in common. To identify those characteristics, you need to **inquire** systematically into the idea of conflict in literature.

EXPLANATION

In order to **inquire** deliberately into the idea of conflict in literature, you first need to **identify some examples** of conflict. Using literary selections you have read, you might list three examples of conflict—say, Ahab against Moby Dick in Melville's *Moby-Dick*, the Union against the Confederacy in Lincoln's Gettysburg Address, and the Soul against Society in Emily Dickinson's poetry. Your next step is to **identify the general characteristics** of each example. Then, after you have identified those characteristics, you **identify which characteristics are common** to all of the examples.

A chart will **display** all of the characteristics in a practical and efficient way to reveal the pattern you are looking for. A chart that displays the general characteristics of conflicts in literature might look like this one:

Characteristics	Conflict 1	Conflict 2	Conflict 3
Two or more people	–	+	+
Significant issue	+	+	+
Physical setting	+	+	–
Verbal argument	–	+	–
Physical violence	+	+	–
Different values	+	+	+
Different goals	+	+	+

The plus and minus signs indicate whether or not a conflict has (+) or does not have (–) that characteristic. Observing the chart, you see that three characteristics—different values, different goals, and perception of the issue as significant—are common to all the examples you examined. Therefore, it is likely that a conflict represented in literature would have those characteristics.

It is also useful to **test your findings** against examples that are not likely to share the characteristics. In this case, you might test your findings about conflict against an example of cooperation. Add one more column to your chart for a non-example (for instance, Whittier's *Snow-Bound*).

Characteristics	Conflict 1	Conflict 2	Conflict 3	Non-example
Two or more people	–	+	+	+
Significant issue	+	+	+	+
Physical setting	+	+	–	+
Verbal argument	–	+	–	–
Physical violence	+	+	–	–
Different values	+	+	+	–
Different goals	+	+	+	–

Observing this chart, you see that even though the non-example does share some characteristics of conflicts, it does not fit the **pattern** of differing values and goals. You will want to expand your list of characteristics and add more examples and non-examples to make the basis of your inquiry stronger.

PROCEDURES

1. In order to inquire into a particular idea, first **examine several familiar examples** of the idea.
2. **List all the general characteristics** you can think of that are true of each of the examples.
3. **Display the list** in a way that helps you see the pattern of common characteristics.
4. **Identify the pattern** of common characteristics.
5. **Test your findings** by comparing what you found to be true of the idea with the characteristics of a closely related non-example. When you do this, you will find some combination of characteristics which is special to your idea and which does not occur in the non-example.

ACTIVITY I. INQUIRING INTO THE IDEA OF COURAGE IN LITERATURE

The purpose of this activity is to apply the steps of inductive inquiry to discover the characteristics of courage in American literature from 1840 to 1880.

1. **Identify five examples** of courage as expressed in literature from the units "New England Renaissance" (page 153) and "Conflict and Celebration" (page 231).
2. Look at each example separately and **list all the general characteristics** of each example. You may want to include such characteristics as a significant goal, major obstacle, life-and-death situation, fear, acting alone, and acting with others.
3. **Display the list** in a way that helps you see the pattern of common characteristics. Use a chart or invent another kind of display.
4. **Identify the pattern** of common characteristics.
5. **Test your findings** by comparing what you found to be true of the examples with the characteristics of a closely related non-example. (Consider initiative or responsibility.)
6. **Write a brief summary** of the characteristics of courage as you find it in the literature of this period. Support your findings with the specific examples you used as the basis for your inquiry.

ACTIVITY II. INQUIRING INTO THE APPEAL OF A CHARACTER

The purpose of this activity is to apply the steps of inductive inquiry to discover why one literary character is more appealing to you than other literary characters.

1. **Identify at least five examples** of literary characters who appeal to you in some way.
2. **List all the general characteristics** of each character. You may want to consider age, nationality, intelligence, strength, beauty, occupation, sense of adventure, and wisdom.
3. **Display the list** in a way that helps you see the pattern of common characteristics.
4. **Identify the pattern** of most commonly occurring characteristics.
5. **Test your findings** by comparing what you find to be true of the examples with the characteristics of a closely related non-example. (Consider a character who appeals to you in only a limited way.)
6. **Write a brief summary** of the characteristics that most appeal to you. Support your findings with the examples you used as the basis for your inquiry.

LESSON 3: *Problem Solving*

DEFINITION

Problem solving is a way of thinking that involves a group of skills. Regardless of the type of problem, good problem solvers attack problems systematically rather than in a haphazard fashion. These are the basic steps in problem solving:

Stating the goal

Identifying the givens, the things that cannot be changed

Identifying the obstacles

Developing the plan, including consideration of all the options

Carrying out the plan

Checking the results

The good problem solver knows both the *specifics* of the problem and the *procedures* of the problem solving. Problems are solved in specific contexts and they are solved by orderly thinking.

EXAMPLE

The man in Jack London's story "To Build a Fire" (page 355) must survive in a frozen wilderness long enough to reach the nearest camp. The problem he must solve is a matter of life or death.

EXPLANATION

The man knows that he must reach the camp or he will die. Reaching the camp is the **goal.** He considers the **givens** of his situation: He is alone; he thinks it is fifty degrees below zero (it is actually seventy-five degrees below zero); with no mishaps he should arrive at the camp by 6 p.m. He considers the **obstacles**: He must avoid the traps of snow and thin ice.

The man has a **plan,** a series of steps to overcome each of the obstacles. He stays alert and observant; he steps gingerly and tests his footing; he compels his dog to go in front; he plans to follow the time-tested procedures for survival in the frozen wilderness.

However, the man is not able to **carry out the plan.** He has not considered the extent of the seriousness of his situation; he fails to follow all the correct procedures. By the time he is aware of the failure of his plan, he knows that, as a **result,** his problem is not solved and it is too late to attempt any other solution.

PROCEDURES

1. **State a goal.**
   Identify what you want to do or to achieve.
2. **List the givens.**
   What information is available to you as you start to think about reaching the goal? Are you looking at the problem in its full context, considering the situation completely?
3. **List the obstacles.**
   What will prevent you from reaching the goal? Obstacles may be easy to see and clearly stated. They may also be unstated or hidden. You may have to think very carefully to identify them.
4. **Identify the methods.**
   What will you do to reach a solution? What is your plan of attack? What specific steps will you follow to eliminate each obstacle? What if new obstacles appear? Can you realistically confront several obstacles simultaneously?
5. **Carry out the plan.**
6. **Check the results.**
   Have you solved the problem? How will you be sure? Did you follow the best plan? Was there a better way to solve the problem?

ACTIVITY I. IDENTIFYING PROBLEM SOLVING IN A WORK OF REALIST LITERATURE

The purpose of this activity is to identify and describe the way a problem is faced in a particular work of Realist literature.

Choose one of the short stories or poems you have read in the unit called "Regionalism and Realism." Identify each step of the problem-solving process as it is presented in the selection.

1. What is the **goal**?
2. What are the **givens** of the situation, the conditions that cannot be changed? What is the context, the particular situation in which the problem exists?
3. What are the **obstacles**? Are all the obstacles obvious? Are some hidden?
4. What is the **plan** used to reach the goal? In the plan, what steps are to be followed and in what order?
5. Is the **plan carried out**?
6. **Check the results.** Is the problem solved? If not, why not? Were the givens or the obstacles wrongly identified? Were the methods incorrectly chosen? Was the plan not carried out properly? Could the plan ever have been successful?

ACTIVITY II. DESCRIBING PROBLEM SOLVING IN ANY WORK OF LITERATURE

The purpose of this activity is to identify and describe the steps of the problem-solving process in any work of literature in this book or any work of literature you have read.

1. Select a work of literature and identify the **goal,** the problem to be solved in the main action of the plot.
2. State the **givens** in the situation.
3. State the **obstacles** to solving the problem.
4. Identify the **methods,** or the **plan,** used to solve the problem.
5. Tell whether the **plan is carried out.**
6. Check the **results** by telling whether or not the problem is solved. If the problem is not solved, tell what change in the methods or plan you would make in order to solve it.

LESSON 4: *Representation*

DEFINITION

Representation involves changing the way that you perceive or understand information. A representation can be *internal*—a network of ideas or series of images. Or a representation can be *external*—a drawing, picture, or graphic organizer. Both internal and external representations are developed by asking yourself what are the important elements and how are they related.

Graphic representations make it easier to *select* what is important, *integrate* and *organize* the different parts, and *summarize.*

EXAMPLE

Toni noticed that many of the poems in this book can be compared and contrasted. She knew that the hard part in comparing and contrasting anything is figuring out the points of comparison. However, she had developed a strategy that worked fairly well. She noticed that there are a limited number of important elements or characteristics for a given genre such as poetry, fiction, and nonfiction. Important elements of poetry, for example, included the selection of the speaker, sound devices, imagery, figurative language, and theme. Toni's strategy was to set up a compare-and-contrast chart, comparing the poems on each of these characteristics.

	Poem 1	Poem 2
Speaker		
Sound devices		
Imagery		
Figurative language		
Theme		

EXPLANATION

In this example Toni used a chart or graphic representation to organize her thinking and her composition. She used this graphic to guide the selection of notes, to summarize what was important, and to sequence the organization of her essay.

Another graphic representation is the "spider map." Spider maps such as the one below are helpful to pull together what you know about a given concept. The concept word goes in the middle and information about the concept is placed on lines around the box, resembling a spider with many legs. Spider maps are also useful for representing or mapping a theme, a description of something, or a problem.

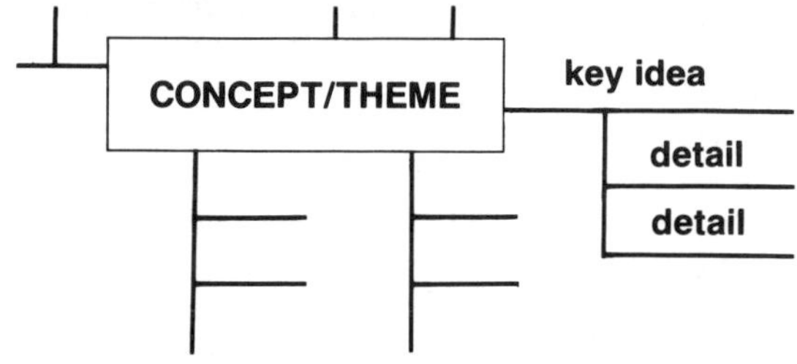

PROCEDURES

1. Decide whether the task you have to do involves a single concept, problem, theme, or description. If so, state it in the box.

2. Brainstorm on your own, with a group of students, or with your teacher to identify categories of information that go on the lines attached to the box. Start with what you already know about it. Then decide what questions you would like to know about it. Try to distinguish key ideas from details. Select the most important ideas and place them on the "legs" of the spider map—one category per line. In this brainstorming stage, consider all categories, but realize that not all of them will turn out to be useful.

3. Keep these categories of information in mind as you review your textbook and any notes or activities. Take notes on the spider map. Add any new categories as you continue your review.

4. When you have finished taking notes, ask yourself which categories are most important. Eliminate unimportant categories. Ask yourself how the remaining categories are related.

5. You may want to re-draw the map, placing related items near each other, and then think about the overall order of the lines.

ACTIVITY I. REPRESENTING THE CONCEPT OF IMAGISM

Construct a spider map for the concept of *imagism.* For the brainstorming phase, read or reread the definition of imagism, imagist selections, your notes from class discussions, and any other sources suggested by your teacher. Additionally, use the categories in the example above to ask yourself questions.

1. How do imagist poets select the speaker and what impact does that have on the poem?
2. How do imagist poets use sound devices? How does this differ from other types of poetry?
3. How do imagist poets use figurative language?
4. What kinds of themes do imagist poets use?

Add the information from these questions to your spider map.

ACTIVITY II. REPRESENTING THE CONCEPT OF MODERNISM

Construct a spider map for the general concept of modernism, using the general procedures above. For the brainstorming phase, read or reread the definition of modernism, modernist selections, your notes from class discussions, and any other sources suggested by your teacher.

ACTIVITY III. REPRESENTING MODERNIST POETRY

Construct a chart showing how the concept of modernism is revealed in poetry. To do this, answer each of the following questions.

1. How do modernist authors select the speaker?
2. How do modernist authors use sound devices? How does this differ from other types of poetry?
3. How do modernist authors use figurative language?
4. What kinds of themes do modernist poems use?

Your chart should have three columns: column A (selection of the speaker, sound devices, figurative language, and themes); column B (the information for each category); column C (examples in each category)

Write a brief summary of your chart giving examples from the selections you have read.

ACTIVITY IV. REPRESENTING MODERNIST FICTION

Construct a chart showing how the concept of modernism relates specifically to fiction. To do this answer the following questions.

1. What kind of character traits do modernist authors emphasize?
2. What techniques of characterization do modernists use?
3. Do modernists use specific types of settings? Explain.
4. What kind of events and plots do modernists emphasize?
5. What themes do modernist authors emphasize in fiction?
6. Discuss the tone in modernist works of fiction.

Construct a chart with three columns to summarize and represent answers to your questions: column A (character traits, techniques of characterization, settings, events and plots, themes, tone, and point of view); column B (answers to those questions); column C (examples).

Write a summary of your chart illustrating each characteristic with examples of fiction.

LESSON 5: *Evaluation*

DEFINITION

Evaluations are decisions about the value, excellence, beauty, effectiveness, truthfulness, or reliability of something or someone. The ability to make proper evaluations is a form of good thinking.

Proper evaluations rest on the thoughtful application of appropriate **criteria**—rules, tests, or standards for making judgments. Such judgments are calm and deliberate, not emotional and impulsive. When you were a child, others evaluated for you. As you mature, you assume more and more of the responsibility for performing your own evaluations.

EXAMPLE

Tad has saved his money to buy a car. He sees a car he wants to buy on a used car lot. The price is quite attractive because it is lower than Tad expected.

EXPLANATION

Tad's impulse is to buy the car immediately because it looks great and is just what he wants. But Tad asks his older sister whether he should buy the car. His sister tells Tad that before he buys the car he should check the car's electrical system, exhaust system, transmission, brakes, front-end alignment, and tires. These items constitute the proper criteria for evaluating an automobile. Tad decides to ask the dealer to have the car inspected at Tad's expense to see whether it will pass state standards for license. The dealer will not agree to have the state inspection done. Thus Tad decides not to buy the car. The reason Tad does not buy the car is that he is not able to apply appropriate criteria for judging the car's value by himself. He suspects that the car will not pass state inspection; that is probably why the dealer refused his request. It would suggest there are some serious problems with the car. Good evaluation—good thinking—saved Tad from making a potentially expensive error.

PROCEDURES

1. **Determine the reason or purpose** for evaluation.
2. **Identify the criteria**—the rules, tests, or standards to be applied in judging.
3. **Apply the criteria,** or find a way to have the criteria applied.
4. **Draw a conclusion.** The evaluation is the outcome based on the application of criteria.

ACTIVITY I. EVALUATING LITERATURE FOR USE ON TELEVISION

The purpose of this activity is to evaluate the qualities of the literary selections in the unit on "Midcentury Voices" (pages 538–755) for adaptation to a television-show format. Work in groups.

1. The television production studio has scheduled one forty-five-minute time slot for a production of a literary selection from "Midcentury Voices: 1930–1960." Which selection should be televised?
2. **Develop a set of criteria** for making a television production from a literary work. Consider such possible criteria as length, accessibility to a popular audience, theme, genre, and interest level. What other criteria are important to you? Criteria should enable the group to eliminate many of the literary pieces in this unit and should focus the group's attention on the best possibilities for this production.
3. **Apply the criteria** for selection to the most likely literary works in the unit. Each group may **select only one literary work.**
4. After the selection is made, group members should prepare to **defend the criteria** used to make the selection in each case.

ACTIVITY II. COMPARING AND COMBINING CRITERIA

1. **List the literary work** chosen by each group in Activity I.
2. When the literary work each group selected is displayed on the chalkboard, **a member from each group reads the criteria** the group used.
3. The class should **note similarities and differences** among sets of criteria used by each group.
4. The whole class should now **make one set of criteria** from among all criteria of all groups. The class can now apply one set of criteria to each group's selections.
5. After a common set of criteria has been determined, **apply the criteria** to each literary work listed in Step 1.
6. **Write the final selection of the literary work and the criteria** used on the chalkboard.

LESSON 6: Synthesis

DEFINITION

Synthesis involves the creation of something new, a pattern or perspective that was not present until you created it. Synthesis requires a complex combination of skills to organize ideas from different sources. This new pattern may be stated in various forms: an essay, a definition, a point of view, a play or poem, a work of art.

Note: An essay on one perspective is not a synthesis because it represents only one point of view. A synthesis must contain elements from more than one source or point of view.

EXAMPLE

Several of the selections in the unit called "In Our Time" focus on personal identity. Carl's group was asked to write an essay on the different meanings of the word *identity.* This is an example of synthesis because the group would need to define identity as it is used in each selection. Then, they would need to compare and contrast the various definitions to create a summary of the different meanings. What is new is the unified statement of different meanings that emerged from the analysis.

EXPLANATION

The task is to combine information from several different sources and organize it into a new statement. In other words, it is a task of synthesis. The *purpose* is clear—to examine a topic or a situation and clarify it for an audience by presenting a conclusion. The thinker must *identify the elements* that contribute to the situation. The thinker must *state a relationship* between the elements—tell how they are related or opposed or associated in some way. The thinker must *construct an original product*—a conclusion which expresses the relationship. The conclusion is a synthesis, a combining of information into something new that did not exist before. The most helpful synthesis will act as a jumping-off point for further thought.

PROCEDURES

1. Establish a purpose for the product. This step is given in the activities below.
2. Identify the elements to be combined.
3. State a relationship among the elements and represent the statement in a graphic if possible.
4. Construct an original product that expresses the relationship.

ACTIVITY I. DEVELOPING A STATEMENT OF THE WRITING PROCESS

The purpose of this activity is to increase awareness of the skills, strategies, and concepts involved in the writing process.

Note: This activity involves inviting model writers to visit the class.

1. **Brainstorm to identify categories** of model writers who may be invited to visit the class (e.g., journalists, local writers, English teachers, college professors, etc.).
2. **Identify individuals** within each category who could visit. **Select a panel** of three writers to visit.
3. Before they arrive, **brainstorm to identify questions** to ask them about the process of writing. Some sample questions are
   a. Who is your audience? What do you need to know about your audience as you plan and write a given work?
   b. What do you do to prepare for writing on a given topic? How long might these preparations take?
   c. Where and when do you do the thinking for your writing?
   d. How do you decide on organizational patterns and develop them on a given subject?
4. **Prioritize and organize your questions.**

5. **Develop a plan** for the interview.
   a. Who will ask the questions?
   b. How long will each speaker have?
   c. How will the interview be summarized and reported?
6. **Conduct the interview**, taking notes on the speakers' comments.
7. **Develop a group report** of the interview.
8. **Write a brief individual statement** about what you learned and/or how you might try specific strategies or concepts.

ACTIVITY II. ANALYZING THEMES IN A UNIT

The purpose of this analysis is to decide which themes are most important in the literature you have studied in the unit "In Our Time."

1. **Review each of the selections** you have read in "In Our Time."
2. **Brainstorm to identify the most common and/or most important themes** (Procedure 2).
3. **List the theme(s)** and/or key concepts.
4. **Ask yourself** whether the concepts/themes fall into any categories or patterns. For example, a number of the themes deal with the heritage of different cultures (e.g., "The First Seven Years" and *The Way to Rainy Mountain*).
5. As a group, **construct a chart** listing the most common themes in each genre.
6. As a group, **select the four of these themes** that you think are most important to society. Support your selections with reasons.
7. As individual students, **select one theme**, and **write a statement** explaining in your own words why this theme is important to society.
8. **Share your statement** with other students.

WRITING ABOUT LITERATURE HANDBOOK

The Writing About Literature Handbook guides students through the types of writing assignments that they are most likely to encounter in literature classes. Ten lessons show students how to write analyses of literary works, each lesson focusing on a different aspect of literary criticism. The handbook follows a writing-process approach to the various assignments, beginning with prewriting and continuing through writing and revising. Clearly sequenced instructions with specific examples reinforce students' familiarity with the writing process. Each lesson is cross-referenced to appropriate assignments throughout this book. In addition, to help students complete their assignments, your teacher's resource materials contain Writing About Literature blackline masters corresponding to each lesson in this handbook.

DEVELOPING A THESIS STATEMENT

Focusing on the task of formulating and supporting a thesis statement in a literary essay, this first lesson introduces students to a writing-process approach to writing about literature. Under "Assignments" on the following page, you will find cross-references to appropriate Composition assignments throughout this textbook. In addition, in your *Teacher's Classroom Resources* you will find the Checklist for Developing a Thesis Statement (TCR 7, page 45), Checklist to Explore a Literary Work (TCR 7, page 55) and Checklist for Revising a Paper About a Literary Work (TCR 7, page 56).

WRITING ABOUT LITERATURE HANDBOOK

LESSON 1: *Developing a Thesis Statement*

The **thesis statement** of a composition, which usually occurs in the introductory paragraph, announces the topic of the composition and your reason for writing about it. It sets forth the thesis, or proposition, that you will defend. For example, after reading an excerpt from Mark Twain's *Life on the Mississippi* (page 289 in this book), you may decide to write a composition about symbolism in the work. Symbolism, then, is the *topic.* What you will say about the topic is the *thesis,* and you will state the thesis in a *thesis statement.* Note that a thesis statement may contain more than one main clause and may even, at times, be two sentences long.

> *Example:* The Mississippi River possesses rich symbolic significance in Mark Twain's *Life on the Mississippi;* the author uses the river to reflect on his emergence into adulthood and on the passing of boyhood dreams.

A thesis statement is *not* merely a fact; it is a position, or interpretation, based on the facts of the literary selection. In other words, you would not have much of a thesis statement if you were to write, "The Mississippi River is prominent in Mark Twain's *Life on the Mississippi.*" That statement is merely a fact, not a position, or interpretation, based on the facts of the work.

The purpose of the thesis statement is to alert your audience to what they will read and the nature of what to expect in the following paragraphs. Each of those paragraphs will have its own topic sentence and will provide support for the opening thesis statement.

CONCEPTS TO REMEMBER

A thesis statement is far more detailed and specific than a general topic.

Byrd's *Progress to the Mines*

a. *General Topic:* Everyday life in the southern colonies

b. *Thesis Statement:* Byrd's *Progress to the Mines* shows that landowners in the southern colonies enjoyed a fairly high standard of living, enabling them to achieve a degree of everyday elegance and civility beyond the reach of the Puritan farmers in the north.

TYPICAL ESSAY QUESTION

The most challenging essay question may be the kind that asks you to create a thesis statement and to go on to support the thesis statement. Such an assignment may be worded as follows:

> Develop a thesis statement about a piece of literature, and in a brief essay defend your thesis with examples from the work.

PREWRITING

Assuming you have read a work carefully, ask yourself some or all of the following questions or other, similar questions.

1. What is the most intriguing literary element or aspect of the work?
2. Why is this element or aspect of the work interesting?
3. Can you support your idea about the element you have selected? What support can you find in the text itself? If it is part of the assignment, what evidence can you find in secondary sources, such as the author's biography or critics' writings?
4. What are some of the arguments against your thesis statement? How would you go about responding to these arguments?

The following example shows a thesis statement generated for the excerpt from the *Walum Olum,* which appears on page 8 of this book.

Example: In the *Walum Olum* the Delaware Indians demonstrate that they have a highly sophisticated, complex world view by presenting the great manito as a living paradox—a single force that contains all opposites.

WRITING AN ESSAY PARAGRAPH BY PARAGRAPH

1. Begin the introductory paragraph with the thesis statement. Fill out the introductory paragraph with definitions of terms or with clarification of your thesis statement.
2. In the following paragraphs give at least two specific examples from the *Walum Olum* to support your thesis statement.
3. In your concluding paragraph repeat your thesis statement in different words, and indicate that the preceding paragraphs have shown that the thesis statement is defensible.

WRITING A ONE-PARAGRAPH ANSWER

All the preceding advice on structure applies as well to written responses that are only one paragraph long. If you are limited to one paragraph, begin with a strong topic sentence. Each of your following sentences should develop one aspect of the topic sentence. You can conclude this one-paragraph response with a **clincher** sentence, which sums up the evidence you have presented.

REVISING AND EDITING

Use the following checklist to revise your writing. If you answer "yes" to each question on the list, you will submit an essay that your audience will find interesting and logical.

I. Organization
   a. Does your thesis statement in the introductory paragraph relate directly to the assignment?
   b. Are the ideas mentioned in the thesis statement then taken up in the following paragraphs with a topic sentence for each paragraph?
   c. Is there clear movement from paragraph to paragraph by means of transitions?
   d. Does the final paragraph offer a restatement of the thesis statement along with additional insights?

II. Content
   a. Does the essay as a whole adequately answer the question posed in the assignment?
   b. Is each idea adequately developed with supporting details from the literature rather than simply stated and restated in different ways without evidence?

III. Grammar, Usage, Mechanics
   a. Is each sentence complete (no fragments, no run-ons)?
   b. Have you avoided errors in the use of verbs (especially subject-verb agreement), pronouns, and modifiers?
   c. Have you correctly capitalized and punctuated all sentences?
   d. Are all words spelled correctly?

IV. Word Choice, Style
   a. Have you used words that are appropriate for your audience and your purpose?
   b. Have you avoided slang and clichés unless (and this should be rare) you are using them for a very special purpose or effect?
   c. Have you eliminated wordiness and vagueness?
   d. Have you varied sentence length and structure while checking for parallelism?

ASSIGNMENTS

1. Write a composition supporting the thesis statement given here for the *Walum Olum.*
2. Do one of the assignments called "Developing a Thesis Statement" that appear after the selections by John Smith (page 22), Nathaniel Hawthorne (page 191), John Ashbery (page 773), and Bernard Malamud (page 794).

WRITING A COMPARISON/ CONTRAST

This lesson guides students through the process of comparing and contrasting two literary works. The lesson reinforces the textbook's teaching about the basic elements of fiction and, especially, poetry. Since the lesson uses examples from "Listen! Rain Approaches" and "Calling One's Own," you may want to assign those works before you teach this lesson. Under "Assignments" on the following page, you will find cross-references to Composition assignments in this textbook that focus on comparing and contrasting. In addition, in your *Teacher's Classroom Resources* you will find the Chart for Writing a Comparison/Contrast (TCR 7, page 46; Overhead Transparency 32), Checklist to Explore a Literary Work (TCR 7, page 55) and Checklist for Revising a Paper About a Literary Work (TCR 7, page 56).

Lesson 2: *Writing a Comparison/Contrast*

When you are studying two literary works, a very effective way to clarify your understanding of each is to compare and contrast their similarities and differences. Whether the works are stories, novels, or poems, you can examine their content and techniques to see how they are alike and how they differ in relation to each other.

CONCEPTS TO REMEMBER

1. *To compare* in this lesson means "to examine two or more literary works for the purpose of noting similarities." *To contrast* means "to examine two or more literary works for the purpose of noting differences."
2. In stories and novels you can compare and contrast these elements: plot, characters, settings, points of view, tones, themes, symbols, and irony.
3. In poetry you can compare and contrast these elements: speakers, sound devices, rhythm, rhyme, imagery, and figurative speech.

TYPICAL ESSAY QUESTION

When you are asked to compare and contrast two literary works, you will often have to answer an essay assignment like this one:

> Select two pieces of literature that you have read. Compare and contrast the two pieces by pointing out the similarities and differences in content and literary techniques.

PREWRITING

1. Use the following questions and others like them to compare and contrast two works.
   a. What plot elements in each are similar?
   b. How are the characters similar or different? Do the characters change, or do they remain the same throughout the story?
   c. From what point of view is each story told?
   d. What is the setting of each piece? In what year does it take place?
   e. The tone of each piece may be serious, comic, straightforward, ironic, angry, etc. Are the tones of the two pieces alike or different?
   f. What theme is each author expressing?
   g. What symbols are used? How?
   h. How is irony used in each piece?
   i. What is the total impact of each piece?
2. Use the following questions and others like them to compare and contrast two poems.
   a. Does each poem focus on the actions of a character? On a place? On a thing? On an event?
   b. Does each poem focus on an idea? A feeling?
   c. What is your emotional response to each?
   d. On what does each poem cause you to reflect?
   e. Who is the speaker in each poem?
   f. What sound devices are used in each?
   g. What kind of rhyme and rhythm is used?
   h. How does each poem use imagery?
   i. What figures of speech are used in each?
3. Prepare a chart (see the opposite page) on which to record your answers to the questions in Prewriting Step 1 or Step 2 and to any other questions that you have devised.

WRITING PARAGRAPH BY PARAGRAPH

1. Begin your introductory paragraph with a thesis statement that restates the main points of the assignment. State the major similarities and differences in meaning and technique.

   Example: Although the two American Indian poems "Listen! Rain Approaches!" and "Calling One's Own" have different subjects and themes, different lengths, and different voices, they are similar in their attention to nature, their dependence upon imagery, and the repetition of lines or words.

2. Use one of the following options for organizing the body of the essay:

   Option A

   Introductory paragraph
   Next paragraph: Tell about one selection.
   Next paragraph: Tell about the second selection.
   Next paragraph: Discuss similarities and differences based on two preceding paragraphs.
   Concluding paragraph

SIMILARITIES AND DIFFERENCES IN POEMS

SELECTIONS: (1) "Listen! Rain Approaches!" and (2) "Calling One's Own"

	SPEAKER	SOUND	IMAGERY / FIGURATIVE LANGUAGE	THEME OR MEANING
SELECTION 1	Speaker calls to reader/listener directly.	*Irregular rhythm:* gives impression of gusts of wind *Parallel construction* in the two stanzas: gives feeling of cycle *Assonance:* East, bean	*Visual image:* fields of green crops literally tied with lightning and then with rainbow *Sound image:* bluebird as herald, announcing beginning and end of storm with equal joy	Poem describes an event; we reflect on nature's cycle. Rain is a life force that connects and is necessary to all living things. The storm is a process that we all must endure, and it has beauty from beginning to end.
SELECTION 2	Speaker addresses the beloved, not the reader, directly.	*Rhythm:* relatively even, with variations *Alliteration:* "*B*ehold me! *b*lood of my *b*eating heart!" "A *sh*ining river the *sh*adows of clouds darken." *Repetition of words:* "Awake" at beginning and end	*Visual image:* "A shining river the shadows of clouds darken"; "A forest streams to the sun in the moon of bright nights." *Smell image:* "fragrance of flowers in the morning" *Touch image:* "Furrows the cold wind drew" *Metaphors:* beloved called "flower of the forest"; "sky treading bird of the prairie"; "The breath of your mouth is the fragrance of flowers. . . ." *Personification:* "my heart sings"; "the water's face"; "Earth smiles"; "waters smile"	Poem describes effect of love in terms of nature: Nearness of loved one makes the world beautiful; anger of loved one is like storm darkening the world.

Option B

Introductory paragraph
Next paragraph: Discuss the similarities in meaning and elements in each selection.
Next paragraph: Discuss the differences in meaning and elements in each selection.
Concluding paragraph

3. In the concluding paragraph use different words to remind readers of your thesis. Focus on whether the two selections are more alike or more different.

REVISING AND EDITING

See page 895 for detailed reminders about improving your writing.

ASSIGNMENTS

1. Use the preceding chart to write a comparison/contrast for the two poems.
2. Do one of the "Writing a Comparison/Contrast" assignments that follow the selections by Bradford (page 29), Byrd (page 39), Robinson (page 391), Hemingway (page 496), Weidman (page 588), Welty (page 621), and Agee (page 632).

CITING EVIDENCE

This lesson guides students through the process of selecting specific evidence from a literary work in support of a generalization. The lesson teaches students the difference between a paraphrase and a direct quotation, along with the use of footnotes and bibliographies. Since the lesson uses examples from "Speech in the Virginia Convention," you may want to assign that work before you teach this lesson. Under "Assignments" on the following page, you will find cross-references to Composition assignments in this textbook that focus on citing evidence. In addition, in your *Teacher's Classroom Resources* you will find the Chart for Citing Evidence (TCR 7, page 47; Overhead Transparency 33) and the Checklist for Revising a Paper About a Literary Work (TCR 7, page 56).

LESSON 3: *Citing Evidence*

When you write a paragraph or an essay of literary analysis, you must provide details—evidence—in support of the generalization you have made in your topic sentence or thesis statement. Compare the following two paragraphs. Sample A consists only of general statements which just repeat the idea of the topic sentence but do not bolster or advance the idea. Sample B is stronger and more substantial.

Sample A

In his "Speech at the Virginia Convention" Patrick Henry offers several arguments for his position in favor of fighting the British. He wants his listeners to agree with his position. He feels it is necessary to take up arms against the British, and he cites arguments to persuade his listeners to agree with him.

Sample B

In his "Speech at the Virginia Convention" Patrick Henry offers several arguments for his position in favor of fighting the British. First of all, he explains that although it is natural to have hope, the colonists must face facts and admit that the British ministry has been planning the use of force by making "warlike preparations which cover our waters and darken our land." Second, he points out that the colonists have already tried and exhausted the approach of talking with the British. He says, ". . . we have been trying that for the last ten years." Third, Henry reminds his listeners of the importance of maintaining freedom. Fourth, Henry aruges that they are "armed in the holy cause of liberty" and that "God . . . will raise up friends to fight our battles for us."

CONCEPTS TO REMEMBER

Evidence may be in the form of a paraphrase or in the form of a direct quotation.

1. A **paraphrase** is a restatement in your own words of the sense of a piece of writing. When you paraphrase, you should indicate the source either within the context of your paraphrase (Paraphrase A) or in a footnote or endnote that you refer your reader to by placing a raised numeral at the end of your paraphrase (Paraphrase B).

Paraphrase A

In his speech before the delegates of the 1775 Virginia Convention, Patrick Henry states unequivocally that the matter they are deciding is nothing less than whether the colonists can consider themselves free people or slaves.

Paraphrase B

Some patriots such as Patrick Henry believed that they had to decide how to view themselves—as free people or as slaves.[1]

2. When you use a **direct quotation,** you use precisely the same words and the same word order as your source. Remember to use quotation marks or set off longer quotations, quote the author exactly, and indicate any omission by the use of ellipses and any addition by the use of brackets.

Direct Quotation A

In "The Devil and Tom Walker" Washington Irving describes Tom Walker's wife and the relationship between the husband and wife by writing that she was ". . . a termagant, fierce of temper, loud of tongue, and strong of arm. . . . and his [Tom's] face sometimes showed signs that their conflicts were not confined to words."

Direct Quotation B

In an effort to convince his listeners that all efforts have been exhausted in dealing with the king of England, Patrick Henry reminds them:

> We have petitioned; we have remonstrated; we have supplicated; we have prostrated ourselves before the throne. . . . Our petitions have been slighted . . . our supplications have been disregarded; and we have been spurned with contempt from the foot of the throne![1]

TYPICAL ESSAY QUESTION

You should always cite evidence in support of your thesis statement. Some essay questions make a particular point of reminding you to do so. The following essay assignment is an example.

CITING EVIDENCE **SELECTION:** "Speech in the Virginia Convention" **THESIS:** Patrick Henry offers several arguments for his position in favor of fighting the British.		
ARGUMENT	**SUPPORTING QUOTATION**	**SUPPORTING PARAPHRASE**
The British preparations	p. 67: "those warlike preparations which cover our waters and darken our land. . ."	The British are gathering the navy and the army.
Uselessness of talking	p. 67: "And what have we to oppose them? Shall we try argument? Sir, we have been trying that for the last ten years. Have we anything new to offer upon the subject? Nothing."	We have already tried to reason with the British but to no avail. There is nothing left to discuss.
The goal of the colonists	p. 67: "If we wish to be free, if we mean to preserve inviolate those inestimable privileges for which we have been so long contending, if we mean not basely to abandon the noble struggle in which we have been so long engaged, and which we have pledged ourselves never to abandon until the glorious object of our contest shall be obtained—we must fight!"	Freedom is precious and has long been our goal; we must not give up.
The strength of the colonists	p. 68: "Sir, we are not weak, if we make a proper use of those means which the God of nature hath placed in our power. Three millions of people, armed in the holy cause of liberty, and in such a country as that which we possess, are invincible by any force which our enemy can send against us. Besides, sir, we shall not fight our battles alone."	The colonists have God on their side in this battle.

Write a brief essay in which you give your opinion or make a generalization about a particular piece of literature. First clearly state your opinion. Then cite specific examples to support it.

PREWRITING

1. Gather material in support of your thesis by reading and rereading the piece of literature.
2. Prepare a chart on which you can list (on the left) the arguments you will present in support of your thesis. In the middle column add exact quotations that defend each argument you list. In the right-hand column, offer a paraphrase of each quotation. Then when you write your first draft, you will have options to pick from as you cite evidence. The chart at the top of this page was prepared during prewriting by the person who later produced Sample B, which appears near the beginning of this lesson.

USING FOOTNOTES OR ENDNOTES AND BIBLIOGRAPHY ENTRIES

A **footnote** or **endnote** gives source information for a statement in your composition. It tells who wrote the source, the title of the source, where it was published, by whom, and when. Footnotes appear at the bottom of the page that contains the idea or quotation taken from a source. Endnotes appear on a page at the end of your composition.

A **bibliography** is an alphabetical arrangement by last name of author of all the sources used in writing a composition. The bibliography appears at the end of the composition.

ASSIGNMENT

Do one of the assignments called "Citing Evidence" that appear after the selections by Jonathan Edwards (page 45), Thomas Jefferson (page 80), and Robert Penn Warren (page 765).

WRITING ABOUT NONFICTION

This lesson guides students through the process of writing about a nonfiction work. The lesson reinforces the textbook's teaching about the author's purpose and the use of supporting information such as facts, statistics, and details to accomplish this purpose. Since the lesson uses examples from *The Journal* of Christopher Columbus, you may want to assign that work before you teach this lesson. Under "Assignments" on the following page, you will find cross-references to Composition assignments in this textbook that focus on writing about nonfiction. In addition, in your *Teacher's Classroom Resources* you will find the Chart for Writing About Nonfiction (TCR 7, page 48; Overhead Transparency 34) and Checklist for Revising a Paper About a Literary Work (TCR 7, page 56).

LESSON 4: *Writing About Nonfiction*

Nonfiction comes in several different forms—for example, the biography, the autobiography, the essay, the diary, the journal. Nonfiction works may be only a few paragraphs long, or they may be book length. When you write about any kind of nonfiction, however, you can use the same kind of analysis. You can discuss the author's purpose in writing the piece and show how the author achieves that purpose.

CONCEPTS TO REMEMBER

1. The **purpose** of a piece of nonfiction is the central idea, or general statement about life, that the author wishes to make.
2. To communicate the purpose, the author uses various techniques such as sensory details, facts, statistics, examples, and opinions.

TYPICAL ESSAY QUESTION

When you are asked to write about a piece of nonfiction, you are often answering an assignment such as the following:

> Select a piece of nonfiction that you have read. An author always has a purpose in writing nonfiction. To accomplish this purpose, the author may use various techniques such as sensory details, facts, statistics, examples, and opinions.
>
> What is the purpose of the piece of nonfiction you have read? Cite with examples the particular techniques that the author uses to accomplish the purpose of the piece.

PREWRITING

1. To determine the author's purpose in writing a work of nonfiction, ask yourself the following questions:
   a. What, if anything, does the title suggest about the author's opinion of the subject of the essay, diary, or journal or about the person in the biography or autobiography?
   b. What opinion about life in general is suggested by the experiences that the author relates?
   c. What opinion about the subject or about people in general is suggested by details (including sensory details, facts, statistics, examples, and opinions)?
   d. What ideas about the world in general are suggested by details of setting?
   e. What tone, or attitude, toward the subject is revealed by the author's style?
2. Based on your answers to the preceding questions, prepare a statement of the author's purpose, and, on a chart like the one on the following page, record the techniques that the author uses to achieve that purpose. The filled-in chart represents an analysis of a section of *The Journal* of Christopher Columbus, adapted into a modern version by William Carlos Williams (page 15).

WRITING PARAGRAPH BY PARAGRAPH

1. Begin the introductory paragraph with a thesis statement. It should specify the author's purpose and state which techniques are used to accomplish this purpose.

   Example: In *The Journal* Christopher Columbus sets out to record the crew's despair, his desperate attempts to keep up the morale of his crew, and the joy of the discovery of land at last. The author uses sensory details, facts, statistics, examples, and opinions that help make the piece not just a dry captain's log but a story of suspense and drama.
2. In each of the body paragraphs, show how the author uses one technique to make the purpose clear.
3. In the concluding paragraph restate in other words the thesis statement from the introductory paragraph. Here you might include your own reaction to the author's efforts—a summary of your own opinion of the work.

REVISING AND EDITING

See page 895 for detailed reminders about improving your writing.

PURPOSE AND TECHNIQUES

SELECTION: from *The Journal*

PURPOSE: To record the facts and events of Columbus' voyage as well as Columbus' and the crew's feelings as they encountered difficulties, disappointments, and the discovery of a strange new land and people.

SENSORY DETAILS	FACTS	STATISTICS
"The sea water was found to be less salt. . . . This I caused the men to taste." "The breezes were always soft." "Bright green trees, the whole land so green . . ."	*He documents clues in the search for land:* "We observed much more weed appearing . . . a live crab." "On that morning appeared a white bird . . . not in the habit of sleeping on the sea." *Discoveries:* "their legs are straight, all in one line and no belly. They came to the ship in canoes, made out of the trunk of a tree, all in one piece. . . ." "There are also whales. I saw no beasts on land save parrots and lizards."	Keeps log including dates, course, number of leagues traveled Reduces number of leagues to lessen the distance so as not to upset the men at thought of how far from Spain they really are

EXAMPLES	OPINIONS
Of joy: "Martin Alonzo . . . with joy called out that he had sighted land. . . ." *Of despair:* ". . . what had been said to be land was only clouds . . . despair of the crew redoubled at this disappointment." *Of his attempts to keep up morale:* "I comforted them as best I could, begging them to endure a while longer for all that would be theirs in the end." *Of delightful new discoveries:* "The fish so unlike ours that it is wonderful. Some are the shape of dories and of the finest colors, so bright that there is not a man who would not be astounded."	*Feelings of despair and determination at "endless" journey:* "I fell on my knees and gave thanks to the Lord, so heavy had been my burdens these latter days at the despair among the men and the murmurs among them that I should have to turn back. . . . The crew here became even louder in their complaints but I gave as little heed as I was able though many were now openly mutinous and would have done me harm if they dared." *Of the new land:* "Gardens of the most beautiful trees I ever saw. I saw many trees very unlike those of our country. Branches growing in different ways and all from one trunk; one twig is one form and another is a different shape and so unlike that it is the greatest wonder in the world to see the diversity. . . ." ". . . I walked among the trees which was the most beautiful thing which I had ever seen."

ASSIGNMENTS

1. Use the above chart for *The Journal* to write an essay in which you discuss the author's purpose and the techniques he used to achieve that purpose.
2. Do the first Composition assignment for the selection by Patrick Henry (page 69), Thomas Paine (page 84), Henry David Thoreau (page 180), Frederick Douglass (page 244), William Faulkner (page 653), Jack Kerouac (page 660), Barry Lopez (page 844), or Ralph Ellison (page 853), or select another nonfiction work from this book and write an essay in which you discuss the author's purpose and the techniques used to achieve that purpose.

WRITING ABOUT A QUOTATION OR A SYMBOL

This lesson guides students through the process of writing about a symbol or a quotation in a literary work. The lesson reinforces the textbook's teaching about symbolism and about figurative and vivid language. Under "Assignments" on the following page, you will find cross-references to Composition assignments in this textbook that focus on symbols or quotations. In addition, in your *Teacher's Classroom Resources* you will find the Checklist for Writing About a Quotation or a Symbol (TCR 7, page 49) and Checklist for Revising a Paper About a Literary Work (TCR 7, page 56).

LESSON 5: *Writing About a Quotation or a Symbol*

Often a quotation from a piece of literature stands out. Whether the work is fiction, poetry, or nonfiction, sometimes just one line sums up its whole meaning so vividly that the line itself comes to represent the entire work. In the same way, a writer may use a symbol to create a vivid impression in a reader's mind. Just as a quotation can summarize an idea or opinion in a dramatic way, so a symbol can come to represent the message that the writer wishes to communicate. Because quotations and symbols express the writer's meaning so clearly and concisely, you should learn how to analyze them and relate them to a work as a whole.

CONCEPTS TO REMEMBER

1. A powerful quotation may have vivid adjectives and strong action verbs. It may use strong parallel structure that gives dramatic rhythm to a sentence. It may use metaphorical language. It may appeal strongly to the reader's emotions or senses. It may have a universal meaning.
2. A **symbol** is something that stands for itself but also for something larger than itself. It may be a person, an animal, an inanimate object, or an action. A writer often uses a concrete object to express an abstract idea, a quality, or a belief. A symbol may also appeal to a reader's emotions and can provide a dramatic way to express an idea, communicate a message, or clarify meaning.

TYPICAL ESSAY QUESTION

When you are asked to write about a quotation or a symbol, you may find an essay question such as this:

> Identify a quotation [or symbol] from a piece of literature. Explain the specific meaning of the quotation [or symbol] in the piece of literature. Then discuss the significance of the quotation [or symbol] in the work as a whole, explaining how it relates to a theme or main idea of the work.

PREWRITING

For a quotation

1. Identify a quotation from a given work of literature. Ask yourself the following questions if you need help in selecting a quotation that would be a good subject for an essay:
   a. Is there a sentence that has gained fame?
   b. Is there a sentence with strong parallel structure, emotional appeal, or notable simplicity?
   c. Does the work begin or end with a particularly impressive statement?

   For example, in considering Patrick Henry's speech at the Virginia Convention (page 66), you can select "give me liberty or give me death!" It is already famous, but even if it were not famous it would be a good quotation to discuss because of its strong parallelism, simplicity, and placement at the end of the speech.
2. Explain in your own words the meaning of the quotation. That is, restate any figurative language, and fill in any information your reader may need in order to understand the quotation. Make sure you explain when, where, and why the statement was made. For example, if you were working with the quotation "give me liberty or give me death!" you could explain that Henry, speaking in 1775, means he would rather die than live in America under the oppression of England.

For a symbol

1. Identify a symbol from a piece of literature. Look for a concrete object that seems to stand for something abstract above and beyond its concrete meaning. Ask yourself the following questions for help in selecting a symbol:
   a. Does the title of the selection alert you to symbolism? For example, the title of Hawthorne's story "The Minister's Black Veil" (page 182) might alert you to an object with a symbolic meaning in the story.
   b. Has the author given particular emphasis to one object or other detail and thereby perhaps raised it to the level of a symbol? For example, in Benjamin Franklin's *Autobiography* (page 58) the writer develops in great detail the incident of the puffy rolls.
   c. Does the object seem to be representative of something *of another kind*? Remember

that you would not say a robin is symbolic of all birds; a robin is merely representative of all birds. You would, however, say that a robin is symbolic of spring; a robin is an animal, whereas spring is an aspect of time, something *of different kind.*

2. Explain the meaning of the symbol. That is, tell what abstract idea, quality, or belief is called to mind by the given person, animal, object, or action. For example, the puffy rolls and Franklin's actions with them seem to symbolize the young man's generosity.

For both a quotation and a symbol

3. Identify a main idea or theme of the piece of literature by asking yourself questions such as the following. Remember that a main idea or theme should be stated in a complete sentence as a *general* truth.
   a. What ideas about life does the selection's title suggest?
   b. What do the particular *events* and *conflicts* reveal about life in general?
   c. What might these particular *people* or *characters* with these personality traits tell us about life in general?
   d. What view of the world do the *setting* and its details offer us?

   For example, answers to these questions should help you see the following main ideas:

   Revolution may be the only resort people have if they want to obtain freedom from oppression.—Henry

   Young men can be both absurd and sincere.—Franklin

4. Once you have identified the main idea or theme of the work, make notes on how the quotation or symbol relates to the work as a whole. Ask the following questions:
   a. Does the quotation or symbol *summarize* the theme or main idea?
   b. Does the quotation or symbol *illustrate* the theme or main idea?

WRITING PARAGRAPH BY PARAGRAPH

1. Begin your introductory paragraph with a thesis statement that tells what quotation or symbol you are going to write about and that identifies a theme or main idea of the literary work.

   Examples

   For a quotation: Patrick Henry's famous quotation "give me liberty or give me death!" is the dramatic statement with which he ends his impassioned speech to the Virginia Convention. The speech as a whole argues that at times people must pick up arms if they are to have the freedom they crave.

   For a symbol: In his *Autobiography* Benjamin Franklin gives prominence to the story of the puffy rolls, which serve as a symbol of young Franklin's actions. The writer sees himself and young men in general as capable of acting both absurdly and sincerely.

2. In the next paragraph tell the specific meaning of the quotation or symbol. Explain, if necessary, how you arrived at your understanding of the quotation or symbol.
3. In the next paragraph explain in what way the quotation or symbol fits into the literary work as a whole.
4. In your concluding paragraph you might tell how the analysis of the quotation or symbol has helped you understand better the nature of the piece as a whole. Decide whether the quotation or symbol added anything to the piece.

REVISING AND EDITING

See page 895 for detailed reminders about improving your writing.

ASSIGNMENTS

1. Using the information in this lesson, write an essay explaining the significance of the Henry quotation or the Franklin symbol.

2. Do one of the assignments called "Writing About a Quotation" or "Writing About a Symbol" that appear after the selections by James Fenimore Cooper (page 118), Sarah Orne Jewett (page 333), Jack London (page 366), Theodore Roethke (page 552), Walter Van Tilburg Clark (page 627), William Goyen (page 832), and Mark Helprin (page 840), or select another piece of literature from this book, and write about a symbol or a quotation within the work.

WRITING ABOUT THEME

This lesson guides students through the process of writing about the theme of a literary work. The lesson reinforces the textbook's teaching about stated and implied theme, about single and multiple themes, and about the relationship between theme and the other elements of a literary work. Since the lesson uses examples from "The Devil and Tom Walker," you may want to assign that story before you teach this lesson. Under "Assignments" on the following page, you will find cross-references to Composition assignments in this textbook that focus on theme. In addition, in your *Teacher's Classroom Resources* you will find the Chart for Writing About Theme (TCR 7, page 50; Overhead Transparency 35) and the Checklist for Revising a Paper About a Literary Work (TCR 7, pages 55–56).

LESSON 6: *Writing About Theme*

The **theme** of a literary work is its underlying central idea or generalization about life. A theme, therefore, is more than just the specific topic or subject of a story. Whether the work is a novel, short story, or play, its theme expresses an opinion or raises a question about human nature or the meaning of human experience. For example, the subject of a short story called "Through the Tunnel" is "a young boy's trials and success at swimming through an underwater passage." The theme might be stated this way: "A young person must take risks and develop courage in order to achieve independence and adulthood." You may or may not agree with the theme, but if the selection is well written, you will gain a fresh and moving insight into the human condition, and you will be able to write about that.

CONCEPTS TO REMEMBER

1. Most pieces of literature have only one theme, although the theme can be worded in several ways. Some works, however, may contain several themes; such is the case with a long, complex novel.
2. Sometimes the theme may be clearly stated. Usually, however, the theme is implied or suggested through other elements. The author uses characterization, setting, events, point of view, and tone to develop the theme.

TYPICAL ESSAY QUESTION

When you are asked to write about the theme of a selection, you are often answering an essay assignment such as the following:

> Identify the theme of a work of literature. Show how the author illuminates this theme through characterization, setting, events, point of view, and tone.

PREWRITING

1. Identify the subject of a selection that you have read. The selection may have more than one subject, but select only one. For example, the subject of "The Devil and Tom Walker" (page 105) is "Tom's bargain with the Devil."
2. Keeping the subject in mind, ask yourself the following questions so that you can move beyond the subject of the selection to its theme.
   a. What do various characters (or the main character) think, say, and do about the subject?
   b. What are character's key traits? Does the character change at all?
   c. How do the time, place, clothing, and other details of setting serve as a suitable background for the work's subject?
   d. What do the events and conflicts have to do with the subject matter?
   e. What do the selection's climax and resolution have to do with the selection's subject matter?
   f. From whose point of view is the story told, and how does this point of view affect you?
   g. What tone does the writer use, and how does that tone affect your reaction to the subject matter?
3. Prepare a chart to record your answers to the questions in Prewriting Step 2. The chart on the opposite page is a sample prepared for "The Devil and Tom Walker."
4. Examine the completed chart, and try to develop a statement of the theme of the selection. For example, for "The Devil and Tom Walker" you might state the theme as follows: "Those who are consumed by greed are doomed to suffer the consequences of their greed—the corruption of all that is good in human nature and the inevitable destruction of the soul."

WRITING PARAGRAPH BY PARAGRAPH

1. Begin your introductory paragraph with a thesis statement that restates the main ideas of the assignment. Indicate what the theme of the selection is, being certain to state the theme in terms of a generalization about human nature or experience. Then show how the theme is illuminated through the other elements of the selection.

   Example: The theme of "The Devil and Tom Walker" is that those who are consumed by greed are doomed to suffer the consequences of their greed, including the corruption of all that is good in human nature and the inevitable destruction of the

EVENTS ILLUMINATING THEME
SELECTION: "The Devil and Tom Walker"
SUBJECT OF STORY: Tom Walker's bargain with the Devil

CHARACTERIZATION	SETTING	EVENTS
Tom Walker's traits: Extremely miserly and greedy—so miserly he starves his horses and lives in what looks like bleak poverty. Although he has a moral streak (would not become a slave trader), he is pitiless toward those who owe him money. *Tom's wife's traits:* Even greedier than he; obstinate, shrewish; quite willing to sell her soul to the Devil to gain riches.	*House:* First setting evokes feeling of gloom. Tom's "forlorn-looking" house with "air of starvation" is symbol of Tom's miserly, bleak existence. *Scene of meetings with the Devil:* Swamp and dark woods ominous and foreboding, gloomy, full of quagmires, pits; quagmires are symbols of irrevocable doom.	*Conflicts:* Refuses to sell his soul—to spite his wife, who is anxious for him to do it. Then Tom's greed and pleasure at the Devil's having taken his wife overcome his reluctance. *Climax:* He becomes rich, but as he gets old, becomes afraid. Becomes fanatically religious in attempt to cheat the Devil. His own greed tricks him into calling forth the Devil. *Resolution:* The Devil appears and carries him off forever.
POINT OF VIEW	**TONE**	
Omniscient point of view: Narrator tells about all events and what the characters think and feel. Describes characters in detail so that we have very clear pictures of Tom, his wife, and the Devil.	Tone is simple, direct, with a slight touch of ironic humor, especially in description of characters. Tone conveys sense of inevitability: Tom cannot change the consequences of what he has done.	

soul. All the elements in the story—characterization, setting, events, point of view, and tone—contribute to the sense of doom and ultimate retribution as the Devil comes to claim Tom's soul.

2. In the next paragraph focus on how the characters, setting, and events reveal and bring to life the generalization which you feel the selection makes.
3. In the next paragraph focus on how the point of view illustrates the theme.
4. In the next paragraph focus on how the tone clarifies the theme.
5. In the concluding paragraph restate your thesis statement. Explain whether the elements of the selection led you to understand a theme new to you or whether they helped renew an awareness that you had.

REVISING AND EDITING

See page 895 for detailed reminders about improving your writing.

ASSIGNMENTS

1. Use the chart for "The Devil and Tom Walker" to write about theme. How do characterization, setting, events, point of view, and tone illustrate the theme that greedy people cannot escape the consequences of their greed?

2. Choose the first Composition assignment for the selection by William Cullen Bryant (page 124), Willa Cather (page 535), John Steinbeck (page 601), or Truman Capote (page 810), or select another piece of literature from this book, and show how all the other elements illuminate its theme.

WRITING ABOUT POETRY

This lesson guides students through the process of writing about a poem. The lesson reinforces the textbook's teaching about speaker, sound devices, imagery, and figurative language. Since the lesson uses examples from the poem "Thanatopsis," you may want to assign that poem before you teach this lesson. Under "Assignments" on the following page, you will find cross-references to Composition assignments in this textbook that focus on writing about poetry. In addition, in your *Teacher's Classroom Resources* you will find the Chart for Writing About Poetry (TCR 7, page 51; Overhead Transparency 36), Checklist to Explore a Literary Work (TCR 7, page 55) and Checklist for Revising a Paper About a Literary Work (TCR 7, page 56).

LESSON 7: Writing About Poetry

Poetry is very much like music in the way it uses rhythm and sound to capture a mood, convey feelings, and communicate a message. Composers use various musical techniques to create a song; poets use various literary techniques to convey the sense, or meaning, of a poem. These techniques include choice of the speaker, sound, imagery, and figurative language. Poets emphasize different techniques in different poems depending on which they feel work best to express the meaning of the poem. You should learn to think about all these techniques so that when you write an essay about a poem, you will be able to show the connection between the techniques of the poem and its meaning.

CONCEPTS TO REMEMBER

1. The **speaker** of the poem is the voice of the poem. Sometimes the speaker is the poet himself or herself; sometimes the speaker is a character or thing created by the poet.
2. Among the sound devices that a poet may use are **onomatopoeia** (a word or phrase that actually imitates or suggests the sound of what it describes); **alliteration** (the repetition of initial consonant sounds); **consonance** (the repetition of similar consonant sounds preceded by different accented vowels); **assonance** (the repetition of vowel sounds).
3. Other aspects of sound in poetry are **rhyme** (the repetition at regular intervals of similar or identical sounds) and **rhythm** (the pattern created by arranging stressed and unstressed syllables).
4. A poem's images may appeal to one or more senses.
5. The most common kinds of figurative language available to a poet are metaphor, simile, and personification. (**Metaphor** is a figure of speech in which two unlike things are compared without the use of *like* or *as;* **simile** is a comparison using *like* or *as;* **personification** is a figure of speech in which an animal, object, or idea is described as having human form or characteristics.)

TYPICAL ESSAY QUESTION

When you are asked to write about poetry, you are often answering an assignment such as the following one:

> Select a poem that you have read. What is the meaning of the poem? What techniques does the poet use to reveal this meaning? Techniques include the selection of the speaker, sound devices, imagery, and the use of figurative language.

PREWRITING

1. Use the following questions to help you determine the meaning of the poem:
   a. Does the poem focus on the actions of a character?
   b. Does the poem describe a person, place, or thing?
   c. Does the poem focus on an idea? Does it focus on a feeling?
   d. What emotional response does the poem seem to call up in you?
   e. After your immediate emotional response to the poem, on what does the poem cause you to reflect?
2. Prepare a chart on which to record your statement of the meaning of the poem and your observations about the techniques of the poem. The following chart represents an analysis of "Thanatopsis" by William Cullen Bryant (page 120). Each column deals with one of the poetic techniques.

THE MEANING AND TECHNIQUES OF A POEM SELECTION: "Thanatopsis" MEANING: Do not fear death, for it is a part of life and a part of nature's endless cycle of life and death.			
SELECTION OF SPEAKER	**SOUND**	**IMAGERY**	**FIGURATIVE LANGUAGE**
Narrator addresses reader/listener with a soothing, teacherlike tone.	*Rhythm:* varies; generally iambic pentameter, but the stress pattern varies, particularly at the end of a line. *Alliteration:* "move in majesty"; "Old Ocean's"; "favorite phantom"; sound contributes to a peaceful mood.	Images paint a picture of eternal nature—timeless, majestic, all life united in earth: "Old Ocean's gray and melancholy waste"; "vales stretching in pensive quietness"; "hills rock-ribbed and ancient."	*Metaphors:* "the narrow house" (coffin); "the great tomb of man" (earth); earth as "couch," or bed; "silent halls of death" *Main metaphor:* earth as tomb for all *Personification:* "She [Nature] has a voice of gladness and a smile."

WRITING PARAGRAPH BY PARAGRAPH

1. Begin your introductory paragraph with a thesis statement, which should restate the main points of the assignment. Indicate that the various techniques used by the poet all serve to enhance and present effectively the underlying meaning of the poem.

   Example: In "Thanatopsis" by William Cullen Bryant, the speaker tells us that we should not fear death but accept it peacefully as part of nature's eternal cycle of life and death. All the poetic techniques illustrate the timeless glory of nature, the oneness of all living things with nature, and the eternal cycle of life and death.

2. In each of the following paragraphs, discuss one or two of the techniques that the poet uses to underscore the poem's meaning—choice of speaker, sound devices, imagery, and figurative language. Show how each technique enhances the meaning, which you have discussed in your introductory paragraph.
3. In the next paragraph discuss further the meaning of the poem.
4. In the concluding paragraph restate your thesis statement. You might here go into greater detail on the emotional impact of the poem—now that you have analyzed the elements used to create emotion in the poem.

ASSIGNMENTS

1. Use the chart for "Thanatopsis" to write an essay about poetry. What is the meaning of the poem? What techniques does the poet use to reveal this meaning?
2. Do the assignment called "Writing About Poetry" that appears after the selections by Edgar Allan Poe (page 134), Walt Whitman (page 273), Ezra Pound (page 413), and T. S. Eliot (page 420), or write about another poem in this book.

WRITING ABOUT THE TOTAL EFFECT

This lesson guides students through the process of writing about the total effect of a literary work. The lesson reinforces the textbook's teaching about how various literary elements interact in producing a particular impact on the reader. Since the lesson uses examples from *The Deerslayer,* you may want to assign that work before you teach this lesson. Under "Assignments" on this page, you will find cross-references to Composition assignments in this textbook that focus on the total effect. In addition, in your *Teacher's Classroom Resources* you will find the Chart for Writing About the Total Effect (TCR 7, page 52; Overhead Transparency 37), Checklist to Explore a Literary Work (TCR 7, page 55) and Checklist for Revising a Paper About a Literary Work (TCR 7, page 56).

LESSON 8: *Writing About the Total Effect*

Color, light, texture and line—painters use these visual elements and others to create visions of their world. Like painters, writers have a palette. Their literary palette includes plot, characters, setting, point of view, tone, theme, symbol, and irony. A skillful writer combines these elements to create a total effect or impact on the reader. To see just how the writer achieves this impact, you can study the work and analyze each element's contribution to the whole. Often you will find that, as in a painting, one element dominates. However, all the elements are deftly woven together to support that key element. In this way the author—or painter—creates a unified effect.

CONCEPTS TO REMEMBER

Review the lessons dealing with writing about the various literary elements individually. Review the definitions and important concepts in each lesson.

TYPICAL ESSAY QUESTION

When you are asked to write about the total effect of a selection, you are often answering an essay question such as the following:

> Select a piece of literature that you have read. What is the total effect of the piece—that is, what is its impact on the reader? How does the author use the following literary elements to achieve this effect: plot, character, setting, point of view, tone, theme, symbol, and irony?

PREWRITING

1. Ask yourself the following questions as you reflect on the piece of literature:
   a. What is the impact of the work? Specifically, does the work irritate you, delight you, sadden you? Does it surprise you, or does it support an opinion or impression you already had? Does the work remind you of something else or contrast greatly with something else?
   b. Which literary element dominates?
   c. How do the other literary elements support or relate to the dominant element?
2. Prepare a chart on which to record your answers to the questions in Step 1. The chart should have columns for the question, the answer, and the details that support your answer. Remember that more than one answer may be possible; however, any answer should be supported with details. For the excerpt from *The Deerslayer* on page 115, a chart might look like the one on the following page.

WRITING PARAGRAPH BY PARAGRAPH

1. Begin the introductory paragraph with a thesis statement. The thesis statement should express the total effect of the work on the reader and note that all the key literary elements work together to create this impact.

   Example: The dominant literary element of *The Deerslayer* is character, but all the elements work together to create the total effect of the piece, which causes the reader to ponder the rules for survival in the wilderness and the definition of a "man."

2. In the next paragraph focus on the dominant literary element, and show by the inclusion of details how it contributes to the total effect.
3. In the following paragraphs discuss additional literary elements, and show by the inclusion of details how each element supports or relates to the dominant element.
4. In the concluding paragraph remind your audience that all the elements work together to produce the total impact.

REVISING AND EDITING

See page 895 for detailed reminders about improving your writing.

ASSIGNMENTS

1. Use the chart for *The Deerslayer* to write about the total effect of the work. How does the author use the key elements to achieve this effect?
2. Do the assignment called "Writing About the Total Effect" that appears after the selections by Edgar Allan Poe (page 149), Elizabeth Enright (page 637), and William Faulkner (page 651), or select another piece of literature from this book, and show how all the elements combine to achieve the total effect.

ANALYSIS OF THE TOTAL EFFECT SELECTION: from *The Deerslayer*		
QUESTIONS	**ANSWER**	**DETAILS**
A. WHAT IS THE IMPACT OF THE WORK?	Reader is struck by the difference in the two frontiersmen's attitudes toward killing and what makes a "man."	*Deerslayer:* "I hold it unlawful to take the life of man, except in open and generous warfare." *Harry:* "I shall not frequent your society long, friend, unless you look higher than four-footed beasts to practice your rifle on."
B. WHAT IS THE DOMINANT LITERARY ELEMENT?	*Character:* The author describes in great detail the differences in appearance, manner, and attitudes between Deerslayer and Harry. The basic conflict between these two is introduced by these descriptions.	*Deerslayer:* slight frame, "unusual agility"; expression of "guileless truth . . . earnestness of purpose . . . sincerity of feeling"; smart, neat *Harry:* "a dashing, reckless, offhand manner . . . gigantic frame . . . good-humored and handsome"; rough but not vulgar, thanks to "so noble a physique"; carelessly dressed
C. HOW DO THE OTHER ELEMENTS SUPPORT THE STORY?	*Plot:* The device of having the two men pause to eat in a clearing after having lost their way in the forest provides the opportunity to introduce two adversary characters.	"Both set themselves about making the preparations for their usual frugal but hearty meal. We will profit by this pause . . . to give the reader some idea of the appearance of the men."
	Setting: The lonely wilderness of the frontier is suitable backdrop for the conflict between Deerslayer and Harry.	"affording forest covers to the . . . native warrior as he trode the secret and bloody warpath"
	Point of view: Omniscient narrator underscores conflict by letting us into each character's mind.	*Deerslayer's mind:* "collision between mortification and correct feeling . . . , uprightness of heart soon getting the better of false pride and frontier boastfulness." *Harry's mind:* "as if he felt a noble scorn for the trifling accessories of dress and ornaments"
	Tone: serious, foreboding of conflict and tragedy to come	"He was as zealous a friend as his companion was dangerous as an enemy."
	Theme: conflict of opinion about how to survive in nature and about what makes a hero	Descriptions of dress, physical appearance, manners, and conversation all develop the conflicts between Deerslayer and Harry.
	Symbol: Deer—Deerslayer shot the deer that the two men eat. They disagree about whether shooting deer proves manhood.	*Harry:* "Fall to, and prove your manhood on this poor devil of a doe with your teeth, as you've already done with your rifle." *Deerslayer:* "Nay, nay, Harry, there's little manhood in killing a doe, and that too out of season. . . ."
	Irony: The peaceful setting contrasts with the conversation (situational irony).	"Centuries of summer suns"; "noble oaks and pines"; "brilliant light of a cloudless day in June"

APPLYING A STATEMENT ABOUT LITERATURE

This lesson focuses on the task of using a generalization about life or literature to illuminate a single literary work. Since the lesson uses examples from *Life on the Mississippi,* you may want to assign that work before you teach this lesson. Under "Assignments" on this page, you will find cross-references to Composition assignments in this textbook that focus on applying a statement to a literary work. In addition, in your *Teacher's Classroom Resources* you will find the Chart for Applying a Statement About Literature (TCR 7, page 53; Overhead Transparency 38) and Checklist for Revising a Paper About a Literary Work (TCR 7, page 56).

LESSON 9: *Applying a Statement About Literature*

Sometimes a statement about life or literature in general can illuminate a particular work of literature. The statement seems to penetrate to the heart of a situation or lay bare the essential meaning of a piece of literature. It is your job to explain precisely why the general statement fits the specific piece of literature so well.

TYPICAL ESSAY QUESTION

A common essay question involves giving you a statement, asking you to explain the meaning of the statement, and then requesting you to show how the statement relates to a work you select or to a work specified in the essay question.

Example: As people mature, they sometimes form bittersweet memories of the dreams and adventures of childhood. Using *Life on the Mississippi,* show how this statement applies to Mark Twain's life.

PREWRITING

1. To make sure you understand the general statement and can do the first part of the assignment, paraphrase the statement and define any key terms in the statement.

   Example: As people grow up, they can see the pain as well as the joy of certain childhood experiences, plans, and illusions. They can look back with both a realization of how naive they were and a fondness for the way they were.

2. Prepare a chart that helps you focus on the essay assignment and the piece of literature. The left column will contain questions to help you connect the essay assignment to specific literary elements in the work. In the middle column jot down quotations or other specifics from the work as answers to the questions on the left. Cite specifics from *throughout* the work; remember that giving only one specific is not sufficient evidence to prove a point. In the right column explain more fully the relationship of evidence from the middle column to the essay question and to the particular piece of literature. The chart on the following page was filled in after rereading Mark Twain's *Life on the Mississippi* (page 289).

WRITING PARAGRAPH BY PARAGRAPH

1. Begin the introductory paragraph with a thesis statement that ties the given statement to a specific work.

   Example: The events, characters, setting, and point of view in Mark Twain's *Life on the Mississippi* illustrate that as people mature, they sometimes form bittersweet memories of the dreams and adventures of childhood.

   The rest of this paragraph might offer a quick summary of the work or a generalization about its main idea or theme. In addition, you might paraphrase any part of the thesis statement to assure that your audience knows precisely what it is you are setting out to prove.

2. In each of the following paragraphs, discuss how the given statement about the work connects with a specific literary element in the work. Be sure to cite examples of each literary element.
3. In the concluding paragraph emphasize that the evidence presented from the work demonstrates the applicability of the statement to this particular piece of literature.

REVISING AND EDITING

See page 895 for detailed reminders about improving your writing.

ASSIGNMENTS

1. Use the chart on the following page to write a well-developed essay about the application of the following statement to Mark Twain's *Life on the Mississippi:* As people mature, they sometimes form bittersweet memories of the dreams and adventures of childhood.
2. Do the first Composition assignment for the selection by Bret Harte (page 324), Thornton Wilder (page 711), or N. Scott Momaday (page 858). Or select another piece of literature from this book, and find a statement that applies to it. Then explain what the statement means and how it relates to the piece.

APPLICATION OF GENERAL STATEMENT TO SPECIFIC WORK

SELECTION: from *Life on the Mississippi*

GENERAL STATEMENT: As people mature, they sometimes form bittersweet memories of the dreams and adventures of childhood.

LITERARY ASPECT	EVIDENCE FROM WORK	RELATIONSHIP OF EVIDENCE AND STATEMENT
WHAT *EVENTS* IN THE WORK DOES THE STATEMENT BRING TO MIND?	Twain's comrades' changing ambitions (clown, minstrel, pirate, steamboatman) Arrival of boat: "the people fasten their eyes upon the coming boat as upon a wonder they are seeing for the first time" Trying to learn the river: "I entered upon the small enterprise . . . with the easy confidence of my time of life." "It was pleasant enough information, but I could not see the bearing of it." "Here was something fresh—this thing of getting up in the middle of the night to go to work."	On the one hand, Twain sees how daily events seemed serious to young boys but implies that day-to-day life was really carefree. On the other hand, Twain implies that he did not take seriously enough certain important events.
WHAT DETAILS ABOUT *CHARACTERS* DOES THE STATEMENT BRING TO MIND?	". . . the captain stands by the big bell, calm, imposing, the envy of all." ". . . an envied deckhand stands picturesquely . . ." "I was stung, but I was obliged to admire [Mr. Bixby's] easy confidence."	Twain sees that as a boy he romanticized all the people he looked up to, painfully wishing he could be like them. He also realizes that he was generous and right in giving them credit for jobs well done.
WHAT DETAILS ABOUT *SETTING* DOES THE STATEMENT BRING TO MIND?	Major setting = river: "I could make neither head nor tail of it. . . . My heart broke again, for it was plain that I had to learn this troublesome river *both* ways." Secondary setting = boats: The young apprentice is enthralled by glamour of the big New Orleans boat ("here was a sumptuous glass temple") and degrades the *Paul Jones*.	Twain remembers how the river caused him grief but also how the whole experience elated him.
WHAT DOES THE *POINT OF VIEW* HAVE TO DO WITH THE STATEMENT?	"If I had really known what I was about to require of my faculties, I should not have had the courage to begin." "I was set aside in disgrace. . . ." "I used to have fine inspirations of prudence in those days."	First-person point of view is what makes this piece a candidate for consideration in light of the statement. It allows us to see the examples of "bittersweet memories" and of Twain's recognizing both his naiveté and his fondness for his younger self.

WRITING ABOUT LITERATURE AND ITS PERIOD

This lesson focuses on the task of writing about a literary work within its historical and cultural context. Since the lesson uses examples from *Walden,* you may want to assign that work before you teach this lesson. Under "Assignments" on the next page, you will find cross-references to Composition assignments in this textbook that focus on applying a statement to a literary work. In addition, in your *Teacher's Classroom Resources* you will find the Chart for Writing About Literature and its Period (TCR 7, page 54) and Checklist for Revising a Paper About a Literary Work (TCR 7, page 56).

LESSON 10: *Writing About Literature and Its Period*

Great writers, whether of fiction or nonfiction, can enter into a dialogue with their age. Their works reflect—indeed, sometimes create—the religious, economic, social, and political developments of a period.

CONCEPTS TO REMEMBER

1. You learn about a period through literature (a primary source) or through analyses of the period such as history textbooks (secondary sources). Make sure that you look carefully at a work of literature and not "read more into it" than is really there. Some works of literature are more characteristic of their periods than other works. On the other hand, some works of literature seem almost as though they could have been created during any period.
2. When thinking about literature and its period, you must remember to pay particular attention to the writer's tone, or attitude. In order to understand how the work relates to the period, you have to determine if the author is being satiric, supportive, optimistic, or pessimistic—to mention just a few possible tones.

TYPICAL ESSAY QUESTION

When you are asked to write about literature and its period, you are often answering an essay question like this one:

> Write an essay showing how an author exemplifies a given literary period. Identify the period. State each characteristic of the period, and for each give examples from the work under discussion.

PREWRITING

1. Identify the literary or historical period during which the piece of literature was created. List the major characteristics of the period.
2. Ask yourself the following questions or similar ones as you read or reread a piece of literature:

   a. *Social Customs* What manners and customs of the time does the work present? What seems to be the author's attitude toward them? What does the work say or imply about interpersonal relationships, roles, occupations, and social responsibilities?

   b. *Economy* What attitude does the author seem to have toward the economic conditions of the age (toward trade and working conditions, toward agrarian or industrial pressures)? What information about these conditions does the author supply?

   c. *Politics* What is the author's reaction to the political situation? Specifically, what does the author seem to think about the ruling powers? The laws? Other political systems?

   d. *Philosophy and Religion* Does the work present religious beliefs accepted during the period in question? Do scenes take place within traditional religious institutions? How are religious people characterized? What seems to be the author's attitude toward the human ability to do good or evil? What seems to be the author's attitude toward the interaction of human beings and the natural world?
3. Prepare a chart that will help you to focus on the most important parts of the essay question. At the top of the chart, identify and define the period. In the left column list ideas about the period that you have been able to determine based on either secondary sources or on answers to the questions in Prewriting Step 2. In the right column cite specifics, including direct quotations from the work, for each of the generalizations on the left. Such a chart for the excerpt from Thoreau's *Walden* (page 174) might look like the one on the following page.

WRITING PARAGRAPH BY PARAGRAPH

1. Begin the introductory paragraph with a thesis statement that identifies the period. In addition, the thesis statement should indicate that the work being analyzed exemplifies key characteristics of that period.

   Example: The American Transcendentalism movement of the mid-1880s has several characteristics that are notably present in Thoreau's *Walden,* particularly an emphasis on idealism, individualism, optimism, and the unity of God, nature, and humanity.

LITERATURE AND ITS PERIOD	
SELECTION: Excerpts from *Walden*	
PERIOD: The age of Transcendentalism—a period of Romantic optimism and extraordinary creativity in American culture (approximately 1840–1860), which laid particular emphasis on idealism, individualism, and the unity of God, nature, and humanity	
CHARACTERISTICS OF THE PERIOD	**EXAMPLES FROM THE WORK**
Romantic optimism belief in human perfectibility and in ability of mind and spirit to transcend matter	"But alert and healthy natures remember that the sun rose clear. It is never too late to give up our prejudices." "What old people say you cannot do, you try and find that you can. Old deeds for old people, and new deeds for new." ". . . if one advances confidently in the direction of his dreams, and endeavors to live the life which he has imagined, he will meet with a success unexpected in common hours."
Idealism natural world a reflection of universal truths possibility of reaching high spiritual goals	"I went to the woods because I wished to live deliberately, to front only the essential facts of life, and see if I could not learn what it had to teach." ". . . if it were sublime, to know it by experience . . ." "If you have built castles in the air, your work need not be lost. . . ."
Individualism self-reliance controlling one's own destiny energy and self-motivation	"I should not talk so much about myself if there were anybody else whom I knew as well." ". . . I desire that there may be as many different persons in the world as possible; but I would have each one be very careful to find out and pursue his own way. . . ." "If a man does not keep pace with his companions, perhaps it is because he hears a different drummer."
Unity of God, nature, and humanity inseparability of the divine and the human	"The winds which passed over my dwelling were such as sweep over the ridges of mountains, bearing the broken strains, or celestial parts only, of terrestrial music."

2. In each of the following paragraphs, discuss one or more of the major characteristics of the period, and cite examples from the work that illustrate that particular characteristic.
3. In the concluding paragraph reiterate that this author and the specific work being studied exemplify key characteristics of the period.

REVISING AND EDITING

See page 895 for detailed reminders about improving your work.

ASSIGNMENTS

1. Write a well-developed essay in which you identify characteristics of American Transcendentalism and show how Thoreau's *Walden* exemplifies key characteristics of that period.
2. Do one of the assignments called "Writing About Literature and Its Period" that follow the selections by Hamlin Garland (page 353) Adrienne Rich (page 779), and Saul Bellow (page 869), or show how another piece of literature from this book exemplifies its period.

RESEARCH PAPER CASEBOOK

The Research Paper Casebook guides students through the process of writing a research paper that focuses on a literary topic. Clearly sequenced instructions with specific examples reinforce students' familiarity with the process of formulating a research topic, gathering information on that topic, digesting that information, writing and revising a paper, and documenting outside sources.

In addition to offering instruction, this casebook actually guides students through the process of doing research and writing a paper on a *specific topic:* "Nature's Lessons in the Poetry of Robert Frost." In this casebook you will find several articles of literary criticism focusing on the role of nature in Frost's poetry. In addition, students are encouraged to go beyond the sources provided as they develop their ideas on the topic.

RESEARCH PAPER CASEBOOK

A literary research paper, like any other research paper, deals with a limited topic and draws upon information found in print and nonprint sources. But a literary research paper uses this information in a particular way. While an ordinary research paper—one on the U.S. Electoral College, for instance—will be based upon the information the researcher discovers in books, periodicals, and interviews with experts, a literary research paper—on Ernest Hemingway's short stories, for example—will be based on the researcher's own analysis of the stories. The information the researcher finds in critical books and articles or in film adaptations of Hemingway's fiction will support and, at times, extend the literary analysis, but it will not form the basis of the paper.

To write a literary research paper, you will follow a writing process. The details of this process may vary among researchers; and if your teacher wants you to employ a special method, follow his or her directions.

The casebook is divided in two parts: The first part describes a writing process for literary research papers, using the Robert Frost poems collected in this textbook as its subject; the second part presents a series of critical articles on Frost's poetry. Thus, the casebook gives you everything you need to write a 1500-word research paper on Frost's poetry. If you wish to write about other literature or use other critical articles, however, you may follow the general guidance here and locate your own critical articles.

THE TOOLS OF LITERARY RESEARCH

In a literary research paper you will draw upon two types of information: the textual details you discover in your primary source(s) and the critical arguments you encounter in your secondary sources. The **primary source** is the work of literature you are discussing. For example, if you are writing a research paper about Robert Frost's poetry, your primary source will consist of the collection of poems you analyze. In addition, you may want to consider a recording of Robert Frost reading from his poetry or letters that Frost wrote to friends as supplemental primary sources. **Secondary sources** are books, articles, or reviews written about your primary source(s). A secondary source may be a biography of the author, an encyclopedia article, an essay of literary criticism, or a review of a stage or film production of your literary text(s). Consult your library's catalog listing and periodical indexes.

Catalog listing

Whether your library has a card catalog or a computerized system, the catalog listing will tell you which books on your topic are available in your library. The following types of books will be useful for a literary research paper.

- Encyclopedias: A general work, such as *Collier's Encyclopedia,* or a literary one, such as *Benet's Readers' Encyclopedia,* will provide useful introductory information.
- Various editions of the text(s) you are researching: Review their critical introductions or check for bibliographies and critical articles in the appendices.
- Critical books on the author, literary text(s), or topic: For example, Richard Poirier's book, *Robert Frost: The Work of Knowing,* may be useful for a paper on Frost's poetry.
- Casebooks and anthologies of criticism on the author, text(s), or topic: For instance, *Robert Frost: A Collection of Critical Essays,* edited by James M. Cox, provides a good overview of criticism on Frost's poetry.
- Bibliographies on the author or text(s) you are researching: Annotated bibliographies are most helpful because they describe the arguments of the secondary sources they list.

Periodical indexes

You will find these indexes in either the periodical or the reference section of your library. The indexes will help you locate articles written about your author, text(s), or topic. Articles are important sources of recent information, and they are often more closely related to your topic than are book-length studies.

- *Humanities Index:* This index lists articles written on literary topics. Find the entry for your author(s); then check the title of your text(s) or the topic.
- *The Readers' Guide to Periodical Literature* or *The New York Times Index:* These indexes will help you locate special sources (reviews of Frost's books, for example).

PREWRITING: SELECTING AND LIMITING A TOPIC

Choose the work(s).

You may write about poetry, drama, or prose fiction. You may analyze one author or compare two authors.

Choose an area of investigation.

After choosing the work(s), consider which aspect of this literature most interests you. If you have decided to write a paper on Robert Frost's poetry, for example, ask yourself whether you are most interested in the speakers, themes, or poetic techniques in the poetry.

Focus on a topic

After you have chosen an area, do some broad reading to get a sense of what others have said on the subject. If you are writing about Frost's poetry, you may skim the sources in the casebook provided in this book. Otherwise, use the catalog listing in your library to locate information in encyclopedias, other casebooks and collections of essays, and various editions of your author's works.

After reading several sources you should be ready to narrow your topic. For example, if you began your broad reading with an interest in Robert Frost's poetic themes, the following passage from the *Collier's Encyclopedia* entry for the poet may have interested you:

> Frost's poetry offered little assurance that this was the most comforting and serene of all possible worlds. In contrast to the Georgian poets, he offered a world of trying situations, of temptations, of oppositions of the will, of little peace and few reconciliations, a world of which nature—New England nature—was the constant sign, symbol, and metaphor.

If you then looked at discussions of Frost's use of nature, you may have noticed that critics often evaluate the interaction of a poem's speaker and nature. At this point, you may decide to focus on one aspect of this interaction. For example, you may look at the speaker's alienation from nature or analyze nature as a teacher in Robert Frost's poetry. In either case, you have focused on a limited topic:

GENERAL: Poetic Themes in Frost's Poetry
LESS GENERAL: Nature in Frost's Poetry
LIMITED: Nature as Teacher in Frost's Poetry

To make sure that enough material is available on your limited topic, visit your library. A research paper of fifteen hundred words should draw on at least four sources of information (in addition to the literature being analyzed); the longer your paper, the more sources you will find helpful. If you choose to write about nature in Frost's poetry, you may use the casebook provided as your library. In it you will find adequate information on your topic. Of course, you may supplement these articles with additional sources from your library.

PREWRITING: CONTROLLING IDEA

Your controlling idea is the central thought you want to develop in your paper. An effective controlling idea will (1) state the main point of your paper, (2) suggest your opinion or attitude about the topic, and (3) indicate the path your research will follow. Research on the topic of "Nature as Teacher in Robert Frost's Poetry" may begin with this controlling idea: "Through the use of nature as theme and symbol, Robert Frost questions the extent to which we can learn lessons from our environment."

PREWRITING: RESEARCHING YOUR TOPIC

During this stage of the process, you will determine the subtopics for your research, create a working bibliography of sources, and take notes from your secondary and primary sources. You will be gathering and organizing a large amount of information during this stage of prewriting. For efficiency, use note cards—you will need 3″ x 5″ and 4″ x 6″ cards—to record the information.

Determine your subtopics.

Decide what questions you will need to answer in order to develop your controlling idea. For example, look at the sample controlling idea for a research paper on Frost's poetry. In order to develop this idea effectively, you will need to gather notes that can help you to answer questions such as the following:

- Where and how is nature used as a theme in Frost's poetry?
- Where and how is nature used as symbol in Frost's poetry?
- Where is nature the speaker's teacher?
- What are the specific lessons nature teaches the speaker?
- Where is nature unable to teach the speaker?
- What are the specific lessons nature cannot teach?

When you are satisfied with your research questions, write each of them on its own note card (4″ x 6″ size). Refer to these cards as you continue your research.

Create a working bibliography.

After you have determined your subtopics, gather the primary and secondary sources you will consult in your research. Write the bibliographic information for each possible source on its own index card (3″ x 5″ size). In that way, you will be able to sort and alphabetize the cards as necessary. Use the following samples as your guide:

Bibliography Card: A Book-Length Study

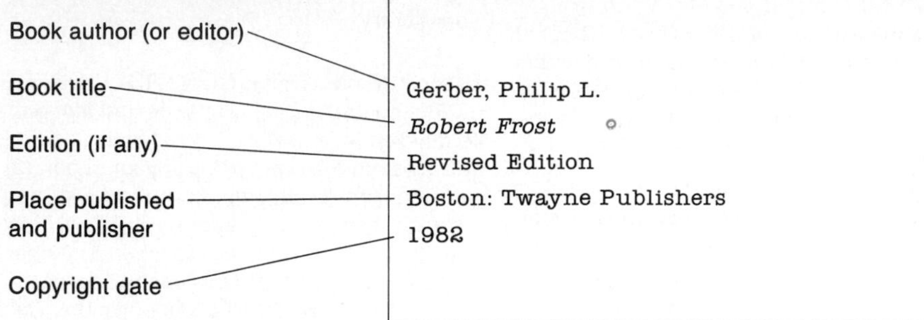

Bibliography Card: A Section of a Book

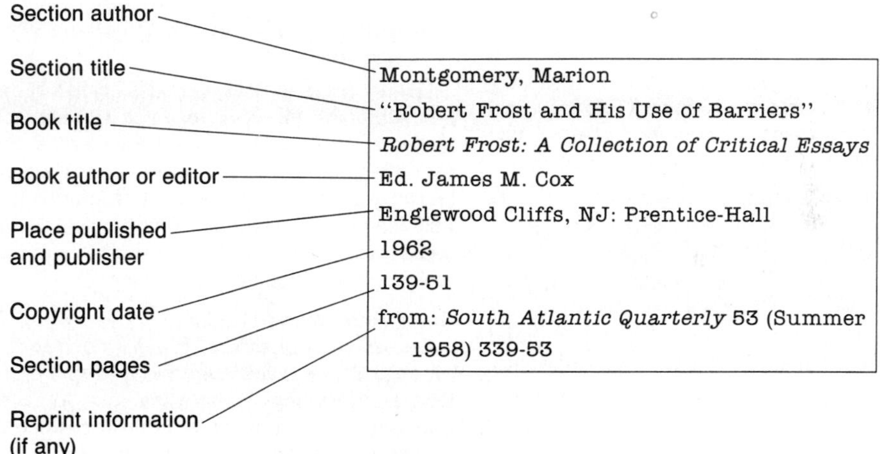

Bibliography Card: An Article in a Magazine or Journal

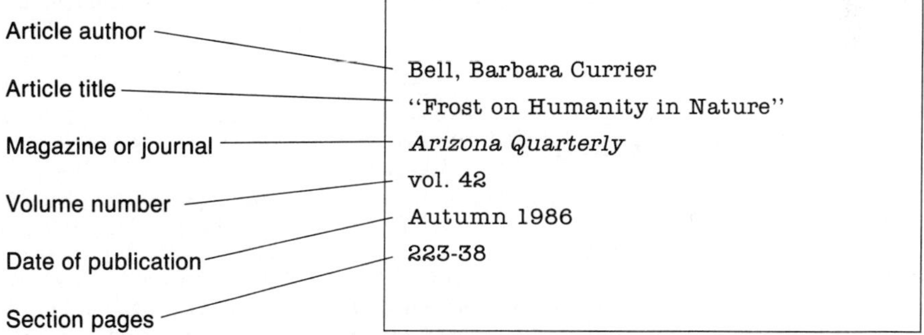

Remember, in a 1500-word research paper, you will refer to at least one primary source and four secondary sources. Gather more than four secondary sources at this stage, however. When you read these sources, you will probably find that one or more of them is not actually relevant to your topic.

Take notes from your secondary sources.

Summarize by restating only the main points and important details. For example, here is a passage from Philip Gerber's *Robert Frost:*

> Nature does not exist to work continual miracles of revelation. Nor will it impart transcendental truths to any poor, bare, forked creature who straggles near a brook or tuft of flowers. For nature is hard as she is soft. She can destroy and thwart, disappoint, frustrate, and batter. She may prove as flinty as the rocky soil of New England, and as difficult to till profitably. On the other hand, the poet is unwilling to declare outright that man is marooned on a desert isle called "earth." His experience with the world would not permit him to go that far—not as far, for instance, as Robinson Jeffers.
>
> Others might cry that man perches on a cinder drifting in the void, dying even as it cools—but not Robert Frost. Others might see nature possessed of unmitigable violence matched only by the brutality of society, but Frost is far too much like Emerson to drift in that direction. Again, neither a radical nor a conservative, he steers a middle path. Nature is at once harsh and mild. Man's relation to nature, as to his fellows, is both together and apart.

One way to summarize the Gerber passage follows:

> Robert Frost thinks nature exists neither to soothe nor to brutalize humans. He finds that nature can be harsh or mild and that humans live in nature but are not completely united with it.

The summary includes the main points and the most important details from Gerber's passage. Most of the notes you take from secondary sources will be summaries.

Paraphrase by restating an author's ideas in your own words. Here is a sample paraphrase of the Gerber passage you read above:

> In Frost's poems nature does not exist for the sole purpose of teaching humans transcendental truths. Nature can buffet humans about and frustrate their attempts to live in harmony with her. Still, Frost does not go so far as to say that humans are completely divorced from nature. Unlike others, Frost does not dwell on nature's potential for violence. Instead, he sees both sides of nature, the harsh and the mild; and sees humans at once in nature and still separate from it.

Here many more of Gerber's thoughts are retained but translated into the researcher's own words.

Directly quote a source by presenting the writer's exact words. As you examine your secondary sources, you may come across an especially relevant or powerful phrase, sentence, or passage that you may want to include exactly in your paper. Copy the quotation carefully, and enclose it within quotation marks. Here is an example of a note that directly quotes the Gerber passage:

> In Robert Frost's poetry nature can frustrate humans as easily as it can reveal truths to them. Yet Frost does not feel that humans are "marooned on a desert isle called 'earth.' " Instead he sees nature as both harsh and mild; and he sees humans at once in nature and separate from it.

As you can see, the researcher quoted one striking phrase and summarized the remainder of Gerber's passage. The strategy is a good one because an effective literary research paper should highlight its writer's argument and the words of the literary text(s) being discussed. Direct quotation of secondary sources should be used sparingly.

Use a note card (4″ x 6″) like the one on page 918 to record your summaries, paraphrases, or direct quotations. At the top write the subtopic that the note addresses, and number each card (s1, s2, s3, and so on) for easy reference. (The *s* stands for secondary.) Under the note write the name of the author and source page number. If you are using more than one work by an author, include a brief title reference with the author's last name (Gerber, *Robert Frost* 132). At the bottom of the card, write any ideas that come to mind about how you may use the information.

Remember, whether you summarize, paraphrase, or directly quote your source, you will have to credit the author's ideas in your paper. If you do not properly credit your sources, you are **plagiarizing,** or stealing, the thoughts or words you use.

When you have finished taking notes from your secondary sources, review your note cards, grouping them with the research question each of the notes answers and putting aside any notes that do not address one of your questions. Review each question

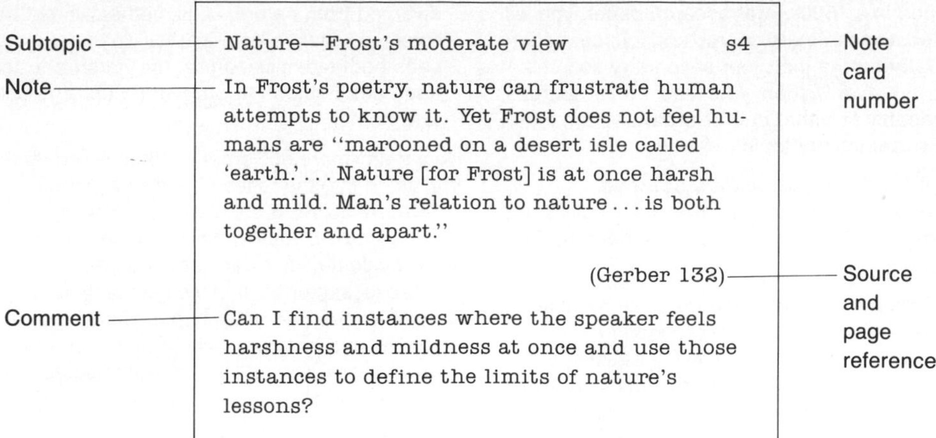

and the notes that address it. If you do not have notes for one or more of your research questions, you may (1) consult other secondary sources for information, (2) wait to search in your primary source(s) for textual details that address the question, or (3) discard the question because it is no longer relevant to your research paper. Next, turn to the group of cards that address issues not covered by your questions. Decide whether you should revise your questions to include the notes in this group or whether you should add one or more research questions to the list you generated earlier.

Subtopic
Nature—Frost's moderate view
s4
Note card number
Note
In Frost's poetry, nature can frustrate human attempts to know it. Yet Frost does not feel humans are "marooned on a desert isle called 'earth.' . . . Nature [for Frost] is at once harsh and mild. Man's relation to nature . . . is both together and apart."
(Gerber 132)
Source and page reference
Comment
Can I find instances where the speaker feels harshness and mildness at once and use those instances to define the limits of nature's lessons?

Take notes from your primary source(s)

During this stage of the process, you will be employing the skills you practiced in "Lesson 3: Citing Evidence" of the "Writing About Literature Handbook." Before you begin to take notes, consider what you want to find in your primary source(s). Review your research questions and secondary-source note cards, paying particular attention to any comments you noted. For example, in the sample secondary-source note card above, the comment asks if instances of nature as harsh and mild can be located and whether those instances will help to define the limits of nature's lessons. If you are researching the extent to which nature is a teacher in Frost's poetry, you may want to begin by searching for examples of nature's harshness and mildness.

Follow a procedure like the one you used for secondary sources. Decide whether summary, paraphrase, or direct quotation will make the most effective note. If you want to take down a direct quotation, copy the passage exactly, making only the most necessary changes by inserting information in brackets or by omitting part of the passage and marking the deletion with ellipses. Use note cards (4″ x 6″) to record your notes. Number each card (p1, p2, p3, and so on) for easy reference (the *p* stands for *primary*); record precisely where you find the note (title and line numbers for a poem; title and page numbers for a short story; act, scene, and line numbers for a play; page and chapter number for a novel).

After arranging your primary-source notes effectively, review your controlling idea, research questions, and secondary-source notes to begin to understand how you can combine all of your research. Consider, for example, whether your primary-source notes are related to or different from the arguments put forward by other critics. As you compare and contrast your analysis with that offered in your secondary sources, you should begin to see your paper taking shape.

PREWRITING: ORGANIZING YOUR RESEARCH

A useful way to organize all of your notes is to make an outline. An effective outline, one that blends your analysis of primary source(s) with the arguments offered in secondary sources, will guide you as you write the first draft of your research paper. Let your purpose, audience and controlling idea, as well as your notes, guide you.

If you are writing a research paper on the extent to which nature is a teacher in Robert Frost's poetry, you may consult your secondary source notes to see what critics have said about the unsuccessful search for absolute meanings by the speakers in Frost's poetry. As you review your notes, you may decide that the first major point of your outline will be as follows:

I. The search for meaning in the woods
   A. Frost's speakers often stand at edge peering into the woods.
      1. Lovely "dark and deep" nature is tempting.
      2. Speaker often unable to take full advantage of scene.
         a. Promises to keep
         b. Cannot walk two paths and one traveler be
   B. Speaker longs for woods to speak to him.
      1. To tell him which path to take
      2. To tell him they are bent because boys swing on birches
   C. Poems resolve in emphasis not on nature but on "I."

The second major point of this outline would most likely address other searches for meaning in the snow or in the waters that are prevalent in Frost's poems.

When you have drafted a complete outline, review your purpose, audience, controlling idea, and research questions to make sure that you have developed your thoughts fully. Make any necessary revisions, and then turn to your primary- and secondary-source notes. Group the note cards with the sections of the outline to which they pertain, and check to make sure that you have enough information to develop the points of your outline. Return to your primary and secondary sources for additional information if you find that some points need to be supported with more evidence. When you are satisfied with your outline, you may begin to write your first draft.

WRITING: DRAFTING YOUR RESEARCH PAPER

Introduction

Begin by considering how you are going to reword your controlling idea in order to make it an effective thesis statement. (You may want to review "Lesson 1: Developing a Thesis Statement" in the "Writing About Literature Handbook.") Then decide how you can best lead up to that statement with information that sets a context.

Body

The body is the major portion of your research paper. Follow the guidance of your outline as you discuss significant points and provide supporting evidence to develop your thesis statement effectively. As you write, keep your purpose squarely in mind, for it is in the body of your paper that you must provide the information that will help you achieve your goals.

When you use evidence from a primary or secondary source, follow the summary, paraphrase, or direct quotation with parentheses in which you write the number of the note card from which you took the reference (p1, s3, and so on). You will credit your sources fully as you revise.

Conclusion

Like the introduction, the conclusion to a 1500-word research paper will probably be one paragraph in length. In it you should restate your thesis in a way that will impress readers with the force of your argument. Do not simply repeat your thesis and major points. Instead, summarize your argument and emphasize it in a fresh way. Remember, this is the last paragraph your audience will read. Make it clear and convincing.

REVISING: CONTENT, STYLE, AND MECHANICS

The following revising questions will help you:

1. How effective is my introduction? Where have I clearly stated my thesis? Where have I set the context for my argument?
2. Did I omit any of the points or details of my outline?
3. What details and examples have I included to support general statements? Should I add details and examples from the note cards I did not use in my first draft?
4. Are my ideas clearly and logically presented? Do I need better transitions between sections of my paper?
5. How can I make my conclusion more effective? Does it sum up my main points? Does it reinforce my purpose?
6. Which sentences can I make clearer and easier to understand?
7. Where can I improve my word usage or vary my sentence structure to make the paper more interesting to read?
8. Is my paper free from errors in spelling, punctuation, capitalization, grammar, and usage?

When you are satisfied with your style and have corrected all mechanical problems in your draft, make a final pass through your paper, checking the accuracy of your citations against your note cards and inserting parenthetical documentation in place of the note-card numbers you used in writing the draft.

DOCUMENTATION

Parenthetical documentation provides brief source information in parentheses within the body of a research paper. For more complete source information, readers consult the alphabetized bibliography (often titled "Works Cited") at the end of the paper.

Most parenthetical documentation will consist of the last name of the author(s) and a page number (Gerber xxx). There are several exceptions, however:

- If a book has no author, use the editor's name.
- If a book has no author or editor, use its title in abbreviated form, if possible (*Collier's* 428).

Robert W. French argues that Frost cannot be thought of as a poet who celebrates nature because Frost's poems often look at the dark or complex aspects of nature (155).

Frost never simply celebrates nature in his poetry (French 155), as one can see in the following lines from "Stopping by Woods on a Snowy Evening."

Place parentheses before the punctuation mark that concludes the sentence, clause, or phrase containing the source you are crediting.

Despite the fear expressed in a poem like "Desert Places," Philip Gerber argues that Frost does not think humans are "marooned on a desert isle called 'earth' " (132).

Close quotation marks of a direct quotation before the parentheses; put concluding punctuation after the parentheses.

Frost's speakers often feel that an absence of meaning is suggested by the combination of snow and night:

> And lonely as it is, that loneliness
> Will be more ere it will be less—
> A blanker whiteness of benighted snow
> With no expression, nothing to express.
> ("Desert Places" 9–12)

Put the parentheses after the closing punctuation of set-off passages. Note title and line numbers of poems.

Lily Bart, the heroine of Edith Wharton's novel *The House of Mirth,* is presented with a vision of the continuity of life in the figures of Nettie Struther and her newborn daughter (337; pt. II, ch. 13).

In a novel, note page and chapter number, separated by a semicolon. Where necessary, include any part number with chapter number.

As Brutus says, "'tis a common proof / that lowliness is young ambition's ladder / Whereto the climber upward turns his face" (*Julius Caesar* 2.1.21–23).

Note act, scene, and line numbers in drama.

- If you have two authors with the same last name, use each author's complete name (Barbara Currier Bell 223).
- If you are using more than one work by an author, include an abbreviated title in the parentheses (Gerber, *Robert Frost* 132).
- If the sentence in your draft names the author (and, where appropriate, the title) of the source, you may omit the name (or title) from the parenthetical documentation.

As you insert parenthetical references, check the accuracy of your information and the form of each of your direct quotations.

Direct Quotations

Unless you wish to give them special emphasis, direct quotations of four or fewer lines of prose (approximately fifty words) and three or fewer lines of poetry or drama are included in the body of the paper; longer quotations are indented ten spaces from the left margin and set off from the body. All quotations included in the body of the paper are marked with quotation marks; do not use quotation marks when you set off passages. When lines of poetry and drama are included in the body of the paper, a slash (/) indicates line breaks.

List of works cited

Finally, create your list of works cited, or list of texts to which your parenthetical documentation refers. Gather together the bibliography cards for the sources you have used in your paper, double-checking your final draft to make certain that you have not overlooked any sources. Arrange the cards in alphabetical order according to the last name of the author, and create your list from the cards.

Proofread the "Works Cited" section carefully, place it at the end of your paper (making a photocopy of the entire paper, if you wish, for your files), and fasten the draft together. You may now publish your research paper, or submit it to your teacher.

SAMPLE BIBLIOGRAPHY

Works Cited

Bell, Barbara Currier. "Frost on Humanity in Nature." Arizona Quarterly. 42 (Autumn 1966): 223–238.

French, Roberts W. "Robert Frost and the Darkness of Nature." The English Record. Winter 1978. Reprinted in Critical Essays on Robert Frost. Ed. Philip Gerber. Boston: G. K. Hall, 1982. 155–162.

Frost, Robert. Poems from The Poetry of Robert Frost. Ed. Edward Connery Lathem. New York: Holt, Rinehart and Winston, 1967. Reprinted in American Literature. New York: Scribner Laidlaw, 1989. 465–473.

Gerber, Philip L. Robert Frost. rev. ed. Boston: Twayne, 1982.

Montgomery, Marion. "Robert Frost and His Use of Barriers: Man vs. Nature Toward God." South Atlantic Quarterly. 53 (Summer 1958): 339–353. Reprinted in Robert Frost: A Collection of Critical Essays. Ed. James M. Cox. Englewood Cliffs, NJ: Prentice-Hall, 1962. 138–150.

Ulanov, Barry. "Robert Frost." Collier's Encyclopedia. New York: Macmillan Ed. Co., 1983 ed. Vol. 10: 428–430.

SECONDARY SOURCES

The following five articles about Robert Frost along with the poems on pages 465–473 form a resource bank for a research paper. Throughout the reprinted articles you will find italicized page numbers. Each number indicates that the text following it appears on that page in the book or journal from which the article is reprinted. You will need this page information when you cite a secondary source.

SOURCE: Ulanov, Barry. "Robert Frost." *Collier's Encyclopedia.* New York: Macmillan Ed. Co., 1983 ed. Vol 10: 428–430.

page 428

FROST, ROBERT (1874–1963), American poet, whose works won four Pulitzer Prizes (1924, 1931, 1937, and 1943). Frost drew his inspiration and symbols from the New England countryside and his diction and rhythms from colloquial New England speech. Although he used simple words and basic ideas, his poems are eloquent and at times profound.

Robert Lee Frost was born in San Francisco on Mar. 26, 1874. He was named after Robert E. Lee, the commander of the Confederate armies. When Frost was 11, his father died of tuberculosis. Young Frost and his mother traveled to Massachusetts, where his father had wanted to be buried. There they remained, and Frost attended school in Lawrence.

For Frost, New England was a world of farms, factories, mills, country newspapers, small private schools, and great universities. All of these he sampled before giving himself entirely to poetry. He made brief attempts at obtaining college degrees, first at Dartmouth in 1892 and then at Harvard from 1897 to 1899. He worked in a Massachusetts mill as a bobbin boy and helped his mother run a small private school in Lawrence. He edited a country newspaper and tried to make a career as a poultry farmer. In 1895 he married, eventually having four children. Dispirited by his failure to find his true vocation, he took his family to England in 1912 and settled in Beaconsfield for a three-year stay. In England Frost achieved his earliest success. His first book of poems, *A Boy's Will* (1913), was printed by the first English publisher to whom he submitted it. Another collection, *North of Boston,* won conspicuous success the following year. His work was associated with that of the Georgian poets, soft-voiced celebrants of the English countryside whose poems appeared in Edward Marsh's five anthologies of *Georgian Poetry* (1912 to 1922). The poets included Robert Graves, Rupert Brooke, Wilfred Owen, Edmund Blunden and Edward Thomas. Thomas (1878–1917) was a particularly close friend and a significant influence in Frost's development as a poet. They brought to each other different kinds of country to muse upon, from which to draw various textures of irony, comfort, loneliness, and compassion. Thomas' death in the war deprived Frost of one of the

page 429

major figures of his middle age. He would not again see Thomas (as he wrote in his tribute "To E.T.") "pleased once more with words of mine."

In 1915 Frost returned to the United States. He bought a farm in New Hampshire, but neither its yield nor that of his poetry was enough to support his family. For additional income he lectured and gave readings of his poetry at universities. Eventually, he associated himself with a number of institutions, becoming one of the first campus "poets-in-residence" in the United States.

Frost's poetry offered little assurance that this was the most comforting and serene of all possible worlds. In contrast to the Georgian poets, he offered a world of trying situations, of temptations, of oppositions of the will, of little peace and few reconciliations, a world of which nature—New England nature—was the constant sign, symbol, and metaphor. "Every poem," he summed up in 1946, late in his career, "is an epitome of the greatest predicament; a figure of the will braving alien entanglements." His viewpoint was expressed with special clarity in such poems as "Mowing," "Revelation," and "Reluctance" in *A Boy's Will* and such dramatic monologues and dialogues as "Mending Wall," "The Death of the Hired Man," "Home Burial," and "The Wood-Pile" in *North of Boston.*

Frost had an unerring ear for the colloquial. He heard what people said to each other in his country world north of Boston, and he recorded it. He had, to the point of genius, what he called "The ruling passion in man...a gregarious instinct to keep together by minding each other's business." The recordings, the selections, the minding of other people's business continued in *Mountain Interval* (1916) with "The Road Not Taken," "An Old Man's Winter Night," "Birches," "Putting in the Seed," "Snow," and "A Time to Talk." In "A Time to Talk," which exemplifies Frost's economy of statement, he explains:

When a friend calls to me from the road
And slows his horse to a meaning walk,
I don't stand still and look around
On all the hills I haven't hoed.
And shout from where I am, 'What is it?'

No, Frost says succinctly in the remaining half of the poem; he digs his hoe in the ground, moves to the stone wall characteristic of New Hampshire and Vermont farms, and prepares "for a friendly visit."

The volume that followed, *New Hampshire* (1923), won for Frost in 1924 the first of his four Pulitzer Prizes. It contained engrossing narratives, such as "Paul's Wife" and "The Witch of Coös," as well as tidy, compact meditations. These poems, variously philosophical and psychological, include, "Fragmentary Blue," "Fire and Ice," "Nothing Gold Can Stay," and "Stopping by Woods on a Snowy Evening," perhaps the best known and most often anthologized of Frost's short poems. Its ending says much about Frost's approach to his patch of New England, to his craft, and to his solitude. As a play on one rhyme, without ever falling into doggerel, it is also a remarkably skilled performance:

The woods are lovely, dark and deep.
But I have promises to keep,
And miles to go before I sleep,
And miles to go before I sleep.

The title poem in *New Hampshire* is one of Frost's most explicit statements of creed. He elects New Hampshire and Vermont as "the two best states in the Union," rejects radical cures for human ills, declares how much he would "hate to be a runaway from nature," and rests finally upon a kind of stoicism. He accepts pain or pleasure with indifference but expects more of the former than of the latter:

I make a virtue of my suffering
From nearly everything that goes on round me.
In other words, I know wherever I am,
Being the creature of literature I am.
I shall not lack for pain to keep me awake.

Frost's ability to adapt traditional blank-verse measures to the cadences of New England speech is demonstrated with virtuoso frills in the title poem of *West-Running Brook* (1928). He was equally adept in the use of rhymes executed with a terseness that reflected his taciturn personal manner, his stoical reluctance to cry out against the pains of life. His Spartan use of rhyme can best be seen in the gem of the *West-Running Brook* collection, the celebrated "Acquainted with the Night."

The full range of Frost's work appeared in the first edition of his *Collected Poems* (1930), and for this volume, he won, in 1931, his second Pulitzer Prize. In honor of his next collections, *A Further Range* (1936) and *A Witness Tree* (1942), he was awarded two more Pulitzer Prizes. There

page 430

followed two plays in blank verse. The first, *A Masque of Reason* (1945), seemed to many critics to make less of the character and concerns of Job than might have been expected of Frost. The second and more successful play was *A Masque of Mercy* (1947), in which a modern treatment of Scriptural figures deepens and extends Frost's stoicism into a philosophy of maturity and stature.

Frost's final volumes of poetry, *Steeple Bush* (1947) and *In the Clearing* (1962), contain poems equal to his best known earlier works. The masterpiece of the first collection is "Directive." In this complex poem, dramatic monologues, sly wit, and philosophical rejections are mixed in words and images so rich in possible meanings and countermeanings that no summary of content, or even of technique, seems possible; every quotation suffers out of context. Perhaps the last two lines can be set off by themselves, however. Frost says of the fluid of a "broken drinking goblet like the Grail": "Here are your waters and your watering place." And then he advises: "Drink and be whole again beyond confusion."

Frost's refusal to be overcome by pain and suffering, the insistence on a constant resource against "alien entanglements," and a precise use of native speech and rhythm equal to the expression of refusal and resource were among the things that made him the logical choice of President John F. Kennedy to compose a poem for his inauguration in 1961. Frost died in Boston, Mass., on Jan. 29, 1963.

SOURCE: Montgomery, Marion. "Robert Frost and His Use of Barriers: Man vs. Nature Toward God." *South Atlantic Quarterly.* 53 (Summer 1958): 339–353. Reprinted in *Robert Frost: A Collection of Critical Essays.* Ed. James M. Cox. Englewood Cliffs, NJ: Prentice-Hall, 1962. 138–150.

page 145

[A] concern with barriers is the predominant theme in Frost's poetry. The barriers fall into several categories. First of all there is the great natural barrier, the void between man and the stars, a barrier which man continually, and sometimes foolishly, tries to bridge in his attempt to escape his limited haunt. The very stars, because of their remoteness, reduce man if he confuses distance and size with his own nature. . . .

But the remoteness of the stars is also something which man may lean his mind on and be stayed. What is more disturbing to man than the barrier of space is the barrier between man and the immediate

page 146

natural world, for it is in this realm of desert places that most of man's "gardening" takes place. This is where the "breathless swing between subject matter and form" becomes most apparent. And it is the struggle in this sphere which reveals what men are. In "Brown's Descent," the old farmer maintains his fight against the physical world, grimly and determinedly. Though he slides all the way down the mountain on the icy snow, he never gives up his struggle against gravity; and he wins, too. For finally, bowing to natural laws, he goes around the mountain and re-establishes himself on top. Nature's laws are inexorable, but man is armed against them: he can make allowances. These are those souls, of course, who are content to have a barrier stand as a continual challenge which they never quite accept; such is the old teamster of "The Mountain" who lives and works in the shade of the mountain he always intends to climb but never does. And there are those who accept the challenge and go down in defeat; the deserted village of the "Census-Taker" with its gaunt and empty buildings is evidence of such failure. The woman in "A Servant to Servants" has lost out to the wilderness by losing her sanity. Her days are spent alone, caring for the house while the men are away, and the emptiness of the world has overcome her. There are others on the border-line of tragic failure. The "Hill Wife," though not out of her mind, still has a fear of her house once she has left it deserted and has to return to it. When she comes back she has to reconquer it:

> They learned to rattle the lock and key
> To give whatever might chance to be
> Warning and time to be off in flight.

Courage is needed to reclaim the house. The preacher in the long poem "Snow" insists on going into the heart of the blizzard when he could remain overnight with his neighbors with no inconvenience to them or himself. But he must go and conquer the blizzard. Wherever there is failure, wherever the natural world has won out, there are always the young who follow to restore where their fathers failed. In "Generations of Men" the boy and girl meet for the first time at the ruins of an old homeplace, sit on the edge of the cellar, and talk about families and the decayed place. In the end they are in love, or about to fall in love, and have made a pact to return and rebuild the old homeplace . . .

SOURCE: Gerber, Philip L. *Robert Frost,* rev. ed. Boston: Twayne, 1982.

page 132

Nature, for Frost, is scarcely what it was for Bryant and other worshippers of the woods of the nineteenth century. The landscape is no panacea to soothe the ills and cares of society; the natural features do not invariably solace with warm companionship or bring a flush of hope to the pallored cheeks of despair. Nature does not exist to work continual miracles of revelation. Nor will it impart transcendental truths to any poor, bare, forked creature who straggles near a brook or tuft of flowers. For nature is hard as she is soft. She can destroy and thwart, disappoint, frustrate, and batter. She may prove as flinty as the rocky soil of New England, and as difficult to till profitably. On the other hand, the poet is unwilling to declare outright that man is marooned on a desert isle called "earth." His experience with the world would not permit him to go that far—not as far, for instance, as Robinson Jeffers.

Others might cry that man perches on a cinder drifting in the void, dying even as it cools—but not Robert Frost. Others might see nature possessed of unmitigable violence matched only by the brutality of society, but Frost is far too much like Emerson to drift in that direction. Again, neither a radical nor a conservative, he steers a middle path. Nature is at once harsh and mild. Man's relation to nature, as to his fellows, is both together and apart.

In keeping with his legacy from Emerson, Frost visualizes man always cradled within nature, totally immersed in environment. Nature is first of all the open book with lessons on every page awaiting the sensible reader. The need for self-reliance and individualism becomes apparent even to the least perceptive. The lesson of mutability is taught by repetition of days, seasons, years.

Beyond this, man learns his limitations, another lesson for survival. What man can do and cannot do; where he is allowed to stray and where he is prohibited; the length, breadth, height, and depth of his domain:

page 133

these recognitions must be absorbed. At war against nature's posted territories is man's unquenchable desire to reach beyond his grasp. He longs to break through the barriers set against him. If a thing is impossible, then this is what he lusts after. If a further step is mined with danger, then it is the one he must take. With the example of a peach tree carried perhaps too far north to survive the intense cold of winter, Frost illustrates man's refusal to accept decreed limits. The tree may live, but most probably will freeze, and all to satisfy the farmer's passion:

> Why is his nature forever so hard to teach
> That though there is no fixed line between wrong
> and right,
> There are roughly zones whose laws must be
> obeyed.

Limits imposed by nature are variously obeyed. "The Mountain" describes a hill-country township so dominated by the "black body" of the mountain Hor emanating from its center that:

> "Hor is the township, and the township's Hor—
> *And* a few houses sprinkled round the foot,
> Like boulders broken off the upper cliff"

An elderly citizen recognizes the limits which Hor places upon expansion by pointing out that sixty voters cast ballots in the last election, and "We can't in nature grow to many more" because "that thing takes all the room!" The land is vertical and stony; the few hill intervals are already under cultivation. There simply is no room for expanding the agriculture needed to sustain the population. Like it or not, man must accept. His alternative is to defeat himself in the attempt to do otherwise.

Man learns also, and quickly enough, that he cannot range beyond what his own physical nature permits. The woods tramper in "The Road Not Taken," coming upon a fork in the path, recognizes to his sorrow that he cannot travel both roads "and be one traveler." Not often is it given to man to have things all his own way. He learns not only that choices must be made but that his decisions prove irrevocable. Neither can he expect to pluck all the treasure from a lode. Time, space, and capability see to that; they set the zones within which nature allows

page 134

man to harvest. The eye is doomed always to encompass more than the arms can glean.

"After Apple-Picking" doubtless contains the best presentation of this theme. The harvester, long before his plan is carried out, finds himself blocked from success by winter's approach and physical weariness. "I am overtired/Of the great harvest I myself desired." The same limitless ambition that impels one man to plant his peach tree too far north causes another to formulate a plan of superhuman capacity. Here, too, nature imposes her zones by dragging across man's path roadblocks labeled *halt.* Why should it be cause for cynicism that his "missiles always make too short an arc"? Out of this failure, man learns his human limits, painful lessons sometimes, like a child's finger burnt on the stove. But he learns. If he accepts and profits, then he has good reason for rejoicing:

May something go always unharvested!
May much stay out of our stated plan,
Apples or something forgotten and left,
So smelling their sweetness would be not theft.[1]

page 135

[N]ature is not to be worshipped as a benevolent deity. But neither is nature to be tarred as a black-browned adversary, hands loaded with thunderbolts to hurl toward man's obliteration. Rather, both elements are present. Nature becomes friend and foe together:

page 136

There is much in nature against us. But we
  forget:
Take nature altogether since time began,
Including human nature, in peace and war,
And it must be a little more in favor of man.

In tune with this evaluation, cited from the poem "Our Hold on the Planet," Frost displays nature as being predominantly man's benefactor. Nature provides, in Emerson's terms, "all sorts of things and weather" to fashion the year and sphere amenable to man's pursuits.

This same world that spills the cornucopia stands alert to remind one of "the line where man leaves off and nature starts" by nipping apples at the stem before there are hours enough left to harvest them. When man asks for rain, the world answers with a vengeance, sending "a flood and bid us be damned and drown." This is the nature of "Snow," raising its voice to a thin pitch, asserting its heavy power, bombarding man with plummeting thermometers and towering drifts:

"This house is frozen brittle, all except
This room you sit in. If you think the wind
Sounds further off, it's not because it's dying;
You're further under in the snow—that's all—
And feel it less. Hear the soft bombs of dust
It burst against us at the chimney mouth,
And at the eaves."

page 137

If nature showers gifts and also confounds those gifts, so are the actions of man toward nature double-edged. On the one hand, man assumes the stewardship of his environment. On the other, he pillages the natural scene....

The men who keep vigil over the world include the...orchard owner who, leaving his trees to the winter, knows he will be haunted by the danger of their being prematurely warmed by a February sun masquerading as April. If the trees are induced to bud out of season they place themselves in jeopardy of freezing in the first subzero gale. "Good-by and keep cold" is this man's parting word as he commits his trees to the snow and to providence.

This theme becomes most emphatic in verses devoted to preservation of clear running water, emblematic of the life-gift of the natural world. In these poems Frost's reverence for nature most closely approximates the religious. A double motif of winter and spring dominates, with scene after scene of death closing in upon the year and of snow piling over trees, road, hill, and roof. Ultimately springtime thaws release a "wet stampede" which resurrects grass and flowers, causes birds to "redouble song and twitter," and most significantly gives fresh tune and speed to the racing brooks....

page 139

Of more than passing significance is his choice of epigraph for *A Boy's Will.* "The Pasture" encompasses not only his passion for tending the fount of life but also includes his invitation to the reader to participate:

I'm going to clean the pasture spring;
I'll only stop to rake the leaves away
(And wait to watch the water clear, I may):
I sha'n't be gone long.—You come too.

That quatrain might serve as motto for the entire Frost canon. His retention of its leading position in *Collected Poems* and in *Complete Poems* could affirm its import. Dependence upon running water is reasserted in "Going for Water." When the local well is dry, inhabitants seek their sustenance from the woods-hidden brook with tinkling fall and "drops that floated on the pool like pearls." At all costs, these brooks must be

page 140

kept clear and flowing. So much depends upon them,

and not only for material subsistence: "It is from this in nature we are from."

For the most part, man as "tenant farmer" of his environment performs his function with love and ability. But there are occasions when his depredations come close to wiping out every brave deed. He is capable of callously disposing of a brook's "immortal force" by running roughshod over it with his houses, curbs, and streets, throwing the brook

> Deep in a sewer dungeon under stone
> In fetid darkness still to live and run—
> And all for nothing it had ever done
> Except forget to go in fear perhaps.[2]

Man's sins against water fade to child's play beside his brooding urge to play with fire. Sometimes on a local scale, for his amusement, or even more to scare away his desert places and create a lighted clearing in the dark, a man builds a bonfire on the hills. Then "something or someone" blows a gust that spreads the torch well beyond the natural hearth he thought would contain it:

> The place it reached to blackened instantly.
> The black was almost all there was by daylight,
> That and the merest curl of cigarette smoke—
> And a flame slender as the hepaticas,
> Blood-root, and violets so soon to be now.
> But the black spread like black death on the
> ground,
> And I think the sky darkened with a cloud
> Like winter and evening coming on together.[3]

. . . . .

page 142

Among the traditional symbols employed by Frost to depict his thoughts on the eternal, his reliance upon stars stands out. Stars figure prominently in his poetry, either as centers of interest or as background. *The Poetry* is quite literally a star-ridden book. These are the lights that brighten the black desert spaces of the sky like street lamps, the stars whose unchanging courses impress the sense of never-ending serenity upon a man who looks up by chance at the constellations. They are "old skymarks in the blue" whose friendly constancy can be relied upon as a palliative against the "shocks and changes" of earth.

page 143

In choosing something like a star to place their faith in, mortals gain an antidote for earth's excesses. Some go mad for stars. Not content to view them with the naked eye, they must approach a more perfect vision:

> I knew a man who failing as a farmer
> Burned down his farmhouse for the fire
> insurance,
> And spent the proceeds on a telescope
> To satisfy a life-long curiosity
> About our place among the infinities.[4]

And when the arsonist has collected his six hundred dollars insurance money and squandered it on a star-splitting telescope, he spends his evenings searching up its brass barrel at the sky. What more does he discover?

> We've looked and looked, but after all where are
> we?
> Do we know any better where we are
> And how it stands between the night tonight
> And a man with a smoky lantern chimney?
> How different from the way it ever stood?[5]

Frost's reply is, of course, that man doesn't know any better where he is. He can't. Bound by the globe, with his feet planted in soil, he cannot approach the stars closely enough . . . .

page 145

In star, snow, and water man locates scraps of heaven's light. He clings tenaciously to them, as reluctant to let them pass as the old woman in "The Night Light" resists extinguishing her lamp—and for the same reason:

> She always had to burn a light
> Beside her attic bed at night.
> It gave bad dreams and broken sleep,
> But helped the Lord her soul to keep.

page 146

> Good gloom on her was thrown away.
> It is on me by night or day,
> Who have, as I suppose, ahead
> The darkest of it still to dread.

Enveloped in darkness which threatens to close in tightly, engulfing him, man must have some candle, however small and meager, to burn against the black. Lights provide security to push back the terror. They furnish knowledge to dissipate fear—to give the faint hope of eternity which subdues apprehension.

That an "enormous Outer Black" exists to make light essential is evident throughout the range of his poetry. At many times and in many places he has observed the night make threatening gestures. He has watched dark waters of the sea batter the cliffs of man's continent "as if a night of dark intent was coming." He has seen a woman driven mad with fear by the night brushing tree-fingers across her windowpane. He has followed an apple-picker overcome by twilight and discerned an appalling "design of darkness" even in a pure white scene, where an albino spider, moth, and flower combine "like the ingredients of a witches' broth."

The predominant image of darkness recurs like a major theme against which all else is variation. Dark woods, mixing fear and desire, typify the great concern of man for knowledge of the unknown that awaits him. Dark woods, full of mystery and promise, draw man like a filing to the magnet. They do their best to suck him in. He can only plant his feet in resistance, wanting all the while to enter but in mortal terror of setting a single toe past the forest's rim.

For fifty years this pattern repeats itself in poems which at times are so similar that they read like variants. The very first verse of Frost's first book recounts this wish to enter the woods, "into my own":

One of my wishes is that those dark trees,
So old and firm they scarcely show the breeze,
Were not, as 'twere, the merest mask of gloom,
But stretched away unto the edge of doom.

I should not be withheld but that some day
Into their vastness I should steal away,
Fearless of ever finding open land,
Or highway where the slow wheel pours the sand.

page 147

"A Dream Pang," also in *A Boy's Will,* tells of the wanderer in a dream who came to the forest edge, looked and pondered, "but did not enter, though the wish was strong."

"Stopping by Woods on a Snowy Evening" in *New Hampshire,* the most expert of all versions of the enticements of the dark woods, again looks upon a traveler mesmerized by the black trees yet unwilling to enter. This time, with his "promises to keep," the traveler has a ready rationalization for withstanding the bait. In *A Further Range,* "Desert Places" reproduces a scene almost identical to "Stopping by Woods":

Snow falling and night falling fast, oh, fast
In a field I looked into going past,
And the ground almost covered in snow,
But a few weeds and stubble showing last.

The woods around it have it—it is theirs.
All animals are smothered in their lairs.
I am too absent-spirited to count;
The loneliness includes me unawares.

This time the traveler feels no need to enter the black woods. Accustomed to contemplation of the "empty spaces between stars," he has already passed far beyond the mere echo of outer blackness which the woods represent. He does not need them to scare him. "Come In" adds emphasis to the inviting quality of the forest's "pillared dark." Dusk has fallen. Thrush music beckons from the branches, even though it is too dark in the woods for birds:

Almost like a call to come in
To the dark and lament.

But no, I was out for stars:
I would not come in.

It happens too often for coincidence that Frost's forest images carry light as an antidote—the blue sky, snow, water, or the stars. And in his last treatment of this theme, in the title poem of his final volume, *In The Clearing,* the human beings living in the woods possess two means of protection against hazard: lamp and clearing. The lamp is lit against the dark, but it is the clearing that provides the greater security:

page 148

They've been here long enough
To push the woods back from around the house
And part them in the middle with a path. . . .
All they maintain the path for is the comfort
Of visiting with the equally bewildered.
Nearer in plight their neighbors are than
distance.

In his poems Frost never enters these dark woods, although his life was spent approaching them and peering in as far as human eyes can see. This is not far or deep enough to return with any secrets found.

1. Frost, *The Poetry. . . ,* p. 305. ("Unharvested" 11–14)
2. Ibid., p. 231. ("A Brook in the City" 16–19)
3. Ibid., p. 131. ("The Bonfire" 48–55)
4. Ibid., p. 168. ("New Hampshire" 301–305)
5. Ibid., p. 179. ("The Star Splitter" 95–99)

SOURCE: French, Roberts W. "Robert Frost and the Darkness of Nature." *The English Record.* Winter 1978. Reprinted in *Critical Essays on Robert Frost.* Ed. Philip Gerber. Boston: G. K. Hall, 1982. 155–162.

page 155

Rightly or wrongly, Robert Frost has achieved a reputation as a poet of nature; and it is true that one tends to think of him posed against the landscapes of rural New England. He may in his poems be looking at birches, or stopping by woods on a snowy evening, or picking apples, or listening to the thrush or the oven bird; wherever he is, he seems to be participating in the life of nature, deriving sustenance from it, and finding in it a deeply satisfying source of pleasure.

Certainly Frost's poetry is filled with the imagery of nature; but to think of him as a "nature poet," or as a celebrant of nature, is to distort his poetry by overlooking its darker complexities. While Frost has written poems that express a certain joy in nature—"Mowing," for example, or "Putting in the Seed," or "Two Look at Two"—he is far from being a lover of nature; reading through his works, one finds that a major tone involves feelings of profound uneasiness, even of fear, toward nature. Frost may present himself in a natural landscape, but he is far from comfortable there. . . .

page 156

"Birches," for example—one of his best-known and most misunderstood poems—is not a poem about birches, primarily, but about the desirability of escaping from this world, if only temporarily; "I'd like to get away from earth awhile," he writes, "And then come back to it and begin over." Birch trees provide the poet with a useful metaphor, since a properly chosen birch tree will lower a person back to earth if he climbs it high enough; but the poem shows no great feeling for such trees, or for any trees. The dominant mood, rather, is one of confused exhaustion; the poet is "weary of considerations," "And life is too much like a pathless wood. . . ."

Elsewhere Frost expresses a darker attitude toward nature; indeed, the word "dark" in its various forms occurs with remarkable frequency in Frost's nature poetry. "An Old Man's Winter Night," for example, begins with this line: "All out-of-doors looked darkly in at him. . . ." The line accurately summarizes the poem: Nature seems to be watching the old man, poised like an enemy, hostile, waiting for a sign of weakness. The old man is only human; he struggles as he can to keep going, but his powers are declining while those of nature remain constant. He is fighting a battle that he cannot win; and in him there is a representation of us all. We may erect our pitiful defenses—friends, a house, a fire—but in time they will all prove inadequate; for nature will insist on death, and nature will have its way.

In "An Old Man's Winter Night" nature is a malevolent voyeur; in "Storm Fear" nature is portrayed as an active, diabolical opponent:

> When the wind works against us in the dark,
> And pelts with snow
> The lower chamber window on the east,
> And whispers with a sort of stifled bark,
> The beast,
> 'Come out! Come out!'—
> It costs no inward struggle not to go,
> Ah, no!. . . .

Nature is bestial, savage, intent on luring man to his destruction; and even worse, nature is portrayed as scheming and deceptive, whispering its cruel invitations to disaster. Faced with such active malevolence, the poet feels a deep sense of human inadequacy. What chance is there against such an opponent? One can only try to survive from day to day, but the uncertainty of the struggle leaves the poet troubled: "And my heart

page 157

owns a doubt / Whether 'tis in us to arise with day / And save ourselves unaided." . . .

page 158

In Frost's poetry even such a natural process as the cycle of seasons seems bent on destruction. Conventional thought recognizes a pattern that moves from birth (spring) to maturity (summer) through aging (autumn) to death (winter); the pattern reaches its height with the maturity of summer, then declines into the death of winter. In Frost's poems, however, the downward movement begins almost immediately; it seems as if the earth is hostile to the delicacy and beauty that humans value, so soon do the destructive processes exert their powers. Frost's finely crafted little poem "Nothing Gold Can Stay" provides a clear statement of this theme:

Nature's first green is gold,
Her hardest hue to hold.
Her early leaf's a flower;
But only so an hour.
Then leaf subsides to leaf.
So Eden sank to grief,
So dawn goes down to day.
Nothing gold can stay.

page 161

Once in Frost's poetry there seems to be something of an invitation from nature; and that is in "Come In," when the poet, standing by the edge of the woods, hears the song of the thrush:

Far in the pillared dark
Thrush music went—
Almost like a call to come in
To the dark and lament

It is almost a call, however, not a call; and even if it were one, it would not be entirely attractive, for it would be a call to come into the *dark* (a word used twice in this stanza and four times in the twenty lines of the poem); furthermore, it would be a call to lament, not to rejoice. Understandably, nature's offerings have little appeal, and the poet chooses to go in another direction:

But no, I was out for stars:
I would not come in.
I meant not even if asked,
And I hadn't been.

The exclusion from nature is complete; the poet remains outside.

This poem may suggest another, the more famous "Stopping by Woods on a Snowy Evening," a work which summarizes neatly Frost's sense of distance from nature. Again the poet is standing outside the woods, looking in; and again it is dark— "the darkest evening of the year." He feels the attractions of the scene, for "The woods are lovely, dark and deep"; and the darkness appeals to him. He seems to be in a melancholy, pensive mood, one that finds congenial the sombre stillness of the woods; but he cannot stay. Turning away from nature, he chooses the world of humanity.

SOURCE: Bell, Barbara Currier. "Frost on Humanity in Nature." *Arizona Quarterly.* 42 (Autumn 1966): 223–238.

page 223

Robert Frost was one of America's greatest nature poets. Not only did he take most of the subjects for his poems from nature, but he chose the relationship between humanity and nature to be his ruling theme.[1] This is known by any experienced reader of Frost's poems. That Frost challenged comfortable clichés about humanity in nature is also known. Count the number of times Frost critics apply the adjective "dark." . . . I propose a way of looking at his skepticism in more detail. Or, to borrow the terms of a line from *Hamlet* that Frost admired,[2] I propose a way of looking in more detail at what Frost had "heard" about humanity in nature and how much he believed it.

Through history, human beings have imagined a limited number of basic relationships between themselves and the natural world. The variations on these relationships, or roles, are myriad; nonetheless, the number of bases from which the variations are formed is not large. The six referred

[1]The best single source for anyone beginning a study of criticism on Frost as nature poet is Donald J. Greiner, *Robert Frost: The Poet and His Critics* (Chicago: American Library Association, 1974), esp. Chapter 5, "Robert Frost as Nature Poet," pp. 207–48. I have relied throughout on Greiner's fine review. One effect of this essay should be to resolve some of the disagreements between critics that Greiner describes, by providing an expanded set of terms in which to cast their discussions. But to do the remapping case by case would be too lengthy here.

[2]Reginald L. Cook, *The Dimensions of Robert Frost* (New York: Holt, Rinehart and Winston, Inc., 1958), p. 177, says that this line, used as the epigraph to this paper, was one of Frost's favorite quotations ["So I have heard and do in part believe it" (*Hamlet* I. i. 165)].

page 224

to here as the ones Frost had "heard" may, for convenience, be labeled "Defender," "Master," "Seer," "Sharer," "Steward," and "Sufferer."[3]

Frost believed in none of these roles, as can most clearly be seen when they are differentiated. Take first his thoughts about the roles in which humanity and nature are at odds. Since the main line of Frost criticism argues, in its customary broad terms, that the poet saw a disjunction between humanity and nature ("alienation," "dissociation," and "otherness" being but a few of the related words used to express the notion), it may come as a surprise that Frost actually was as skeptical about roles in which humanity opposed nature as he was about roles in which the two were allied.

The Sufferer pits humanity against the wild. According to this role, human beings are impotent in the midst of an overpowering and uncaring nature. Their physical existence makes little difference and their moral existence even less. Nature, in other words, is not responsible for humanity; it follows its own inner course, one to which humans must submit simply as natural beings, on a par with animals or stones. . . . Frost's counter to this role can be illustrated by "On the Heart's Beginning to Cloud the Mind."[4] The poem shows a traveler musing about a small light that he sees flickering from a house across the dark Utah desert. In the first third or so of the poem he fancies a pitiful tale behind it. He imagines

[3]Many times critics tend to link these roles with certain periods or cultures. I will not do so. Although the roles *are* expressed differently depending on the period and the culture in which they appear, and although certain of the roles gain prominence at different times and places, they can be treated independently of those variables.

[4]*The Poetry of Robert Frost,* ed. Edward Connery Lathem (New York: Holt, Rinehart and Winston, 1969), p. 290. All references to Frost's poetry are to this edition and will be cited parenthetically in the text.

A note should be made about the selection of this and the other five poems to be discussed. First, "single-issue" poems have been chosen: those that critique just one role for humanity in nature. They are the exception rather than the rule, for Frost's better-known, "greater," poems play off a variety of roles for humanity in nature (e.g., "Directive"), or create other possibilities, such as the radical internalization of role(s) (e.g., "Desert Places"). Yet the only way of establishing a set of terms for understanding complexity in detail is to begin with simple referents. The second criterion used for selecting the poems was length. Short poems were favored over long ones, lest this essay turn into a book.

page 225

its flickering represents the inhabitants', or all humans', life of "brute despair," suffering at the hands of a dark, vast universe and as vulnerable as a candle flame, their fragile lives liable to be snuffed out any moment.

The line "But my heart was beginning to cloud my mind," stops this sentimental pity. The remaining two-thirds of the poem sketch "a tale of a better kind," as Frost imagines confident human beings out there. Their light flickers not from any weakness on their part but merely from the motion of trees across their windows. Their "life is not so sinister-grave"; they are not even particularly lonely. Above all, they have God-like control, as Frost indicates by reference again to the light. The lines "I pass, but scarcely pass no doubt,/ When one will say, 'Let us put it out' " echo the biblical reference to God's last judgment.

The structure of the poem reinforces this point. Its stress on the word "please," with its connotations of ease, pleasure, and free will,[5] could hardly be more opposed to the notion of suffering.

"On the Heart's Beginning to Cloud the Mind," which comes from a group of poems under the heading "Taken Doubly," presents an argument that initially can be explained as simple "pro" and "con." To paraphrase, Frost says, "Anyone who *thinks* about humanity in nature will stop wallowing around in despair and consider humanity's more aggressive and hopeful lot."

A second role in which humanity and nature are at odds, and about which Frost expresses disbelief, is the Defender. Here, nature is not indifferent or uncaring, but hostile. It is "out to get" human beings, and usually succeeds. Almost sure to be overwhelmed, humanity sometimes fights back in the spirit of crusade, but its more frequent feeling is terror.

The poem in which Frost addressed this role most imaginatively is "Design" (p. 302). It describes a death scene in nature—moth, spider, flower—in such a way that the

[5]"Please" is the only repeated rhyme out of twenty-two in the poem and coincides with the only near-repeated lines in the poem. "The people can burn it as long as they please" (1. 16); "They can keep it burning as long as they please" (1. 24); "They can put it out whenever they please" (1. 25). The "please" rhyme is also the only extra rhyme in the poem. That is, 1. 25 adds a third "eeze" to 11. 23 and 24, whereas all the other rhymes are couplets.

page 226

reader is led as far as the penultimate line to conclude death results from a "Design of darkness to appall." Frost poses the view that "darkness," either dark, evil nature itself, or a dark, evil force driving nature, threatens humanity. This clear statement of what is here termed the Defender, Frost undercuts in the last line, which is an implied question: "If design govern in a thing so small." A heavy burden of meaning accrues to this line, some of which will be discussed later; at least in its simplest effect it is a brilliant poetic monkey wrench. As Randall Jarrell writes, "[the poem's] whole appalling categorical machinery of reasoning-out, of conviction, of condemnation . . . is suddenly made merely hypothetical, a possible contradicted shadow, by one off-hand last-minute qualification: one that dismisses it. . . ."[6] So much for the Defender.

The third role pitting humanity vs. nature that Frost disbelieved is the Master. In this role, unlike the Sufferer and the Defender, separation from nature does not render humanity inferior. The Master's place is to dominate. Human beings act as if they were all-important and all-powerful, while nature is regarded as a huge but relatively undifferentiated body of energy and raw material "out there" for humanity to exploit at will. Although human beings playing the Master have a hard time making nature their servant, the trouble arises from a temporary ignorance of the size of the task and not from any serious opposition on nature's part or question about humanity's power. Given time, the Master will control the universe. A poem that illustrates Frost's treatment of this role is "Good-By and Keep Cold" (p.228).

[6]Randall Jarrell, *Poetry and the Age* (New York: Alfred A. Knopf, 1953), pp. 48–49. This point of Jarrell's, as well as the other interpretive points made about "Design" in this paragraph, have been kept summary because critical discussion of the poem elsewhere has been so extensive.

page 227

A farmer is addressing the problem of how his orchard will get through the winter. He starts out acting like a domineering parent, saying good-bye to his "young" orchard with his main thought the trouble it can get into once it is out of his sight: a repeated phrase and feeling of "I don't want" (things to go wrong) governs the first two-thirds of the poem. The farmer even imagines ordering around other "simpleminded" creatures: he would lecture grouse, rabbit, and deer against interference with his plan. He emphasizes how he's laid out the orchard so as to minimize problems, and he ends his commands in a reductive, threatening tone. Finally, when he describes the business that takes him away from the orchard, it turns out to be an activity widely associated with the Master role, namely cutting down trees.

Only in the poem's last five lines does this petty tyrant acknowledge any limitation in his mastery, concluding with the thought, "But something has to be left to God." This ending admits two interpretations, one "straight," and one ironic—no surprise in a work by Frost. The straight reading would have the farmer developing a critical sense of his own about the Master role. He voices a tentative awareness of nature's otherness or uncontrollability, and, with a combination of regret and relief, yield's humanity's mastery over nature to that of a higher power. The ironic reading of the ending, on the other hand, would have the farmer yielding only a bone. He briefly imagines the possibility of perfect mastery over nature through a fanciful thought-control, but discards the possibility as not worth the effort. "Leave the leftovers up to God."

No matter which interpretation of the ending the reader favors, straight or ironic, Frost's message is the same: humanity as Master is way too pretentious. Canute-like posturing is ridiculed here. The poem's modified anapestic tetrameter and simple succession of rhyming couplets, which create a singsong sound, help make the farmer seem quite as childish as he takes nature to be. Whatever the proper role may be for humanity in nature, in the first analysis, Frost says it cannot be this one.

page 228

Turn now to the roles in which humanity and nature are continuous, or allied. These customarily are bunched together as "Romanticism," and Frost's disbelief of Romanticism is familiar ground. We can distinguish between three different versions of human affinity with nature, however, and see how Frost expressed his uneasiness about each one.

Acting the role of Steward, human beings care for the natural world. They do so not because they are inherently more powerful, but because they follow a preordained plan, usually set by some transcendent power. For the Steward, nature is a complex but unified, or harmonized, whole that is highly ordered: specifically, a hierarchy. The Steward helps to carry out the set of rules laid down for each level of nature, including humanity's own. Strong correspondences obtain from level to level, so that a sense of stasis pervades this role and it encourages anthropomorphism.

"The Need of Being Versed in Country Things" (pp.241–42) takes the Steward ironically. The central image here is of a smoothly ordered and fruitful farm that has been destroyed. Before the fire that was the cause, human life (the house) and nature's, as tended by humanity (the barn), had been in symmetry. Now, instead of being comfortably paired with the house, the barn looks over at a chimney, the symbol of destruction, and has itself been deserted by humanity and nature alike. The image of the barn in its prime (stanza three) is utopian. We see a human structure opening wide to receive nature's harvest, yielded up jointly to human and natural labor. A team of horses pulling in a load of hay: hardly any symbol could be better for stewardship. It puts together the power of nature, whether in the growth of the seed or the muscles of the horses; the control of humanity; and the good purpose of the activity both humanity and nature share. The whole picture seems like a hymn to husbandry. Certainly it is a vision over whose disappearance human beings would weep, and, according to the presumptions of the Steward, nature would weep, too, since nature is literally undone without human care. Frost's choice of phoebes to represent nature in this

page 229

poem is important: they are among the most domestic of country birds.

The consolation in stanza five of nature's and humanity's creations alike providing shelter or vantage for the phoebes is still appropriate to the role of the Steward. The last stanza gives the ironic skew, however. Frost writes, "One had to be versed in country things/Not to believe the phoebes wept" (p.242). The inference is that a person knowledgeable about country things would not believe the phoebes wept, or, by extension, that those most often called upon to play the Steward role in everyday life are least likely to believe its claims. At the simplest level of argument here, Frost can be said to blow up the Steward "balloon" through most of the poem, then puncture it in the last two lines.

A role resembling the Steward that Frost also questions is the Sharer. In this role, humanity comes even closer to nature. All living and nonliving beings are seen to follow the *same* law, and nature itself holds sway, instead of some further power. Nature's order is not as determined, static, or hierarchical as in the Steward. Energy replaces harmony as the unifying principle. A sense of growth, development, or unfolding pervades this role; it, too, encourages anthropomorphism.

In "Maple" (pp.179–88), a woman by that name tries to find a meaning for her life in nature, since her mother had given her the tree's name at birth, but had died shortly after, before being able to tell anyone what she was trying to signify. Maple's name not only constitutes the whole of her relationship with her mother, but it also determines her relationship with her father, who withdraws from her intense questions. It even determines her relationship with strangers, their first reaction being to remark on her unusual name or to get it wrong. Finally, it determines her marriage, for she is attracted to the man who becomes her husband by his apparently chance comment that she reminds him of a maple. But Maple does not know what her name means. Her attempt to find out becomes itself her identity, and her difficulties are the main subject of Frost's poem: the mystery of meaning. First, Maple can find no obvious commonsense

page 230

interpretation of her name. Then, she gets the suggestion of a biblical interpretation, but its significance escapes her. When she turns to nature, she finds no "special tree" (p.183) that her mother may have named her for, and has other difficulties.... [T]oward the end, Frost shows her and her husband "hover[ing] for a moment near discovery/Figurative enough to see the symbol,/But lacking faith in anything to mean/The same at different times to different people" (p.184). So the poem, which is generally about the problem of meaning, is more specifically about the hazards of understanding symbols and even more particularly about the hazards of understanding symbols taken from nature, the most common kind. Since the reason for artists' tendency to draw symbols from nature is the view that human beings and the natural world share a common being, the view embodied in the Sharer role, "Maple" makes the Sharer seem a problem. The irony Frost notes at the end of the poem is that a meaningless name for a child actually leaves "more to nature and happy chance" (p.185) than a name filled with an uncertain meaning based on some mistaken notion that human beings can somehow be equated with natural ones. "Maple" can be interpreted, in the first instance, to criticize the Sharer role insofar as Frost implies, against the romantic notion of correspondence, that nature is much more than what it holds in common with humanity.

The last role for humanity in nature that Frost took issue with is the Seer. According to this role, nature remains much the same as for the Sharer, except that it is pictured more generally or abstractly. Its material features increasingly yield to symbolic ones, and particular dynamic features of growth yield to general ones of flux or cycle. As for humanity, it continues to be integrated with nature, but

page 231

differs from the Sharer by sitting silently at the center. Humanity's "seeing" in this role is not simple observation. It is a mystical seeing, where the eye represents the soul. Humanity literally *becomes* nature: not actively, by entering into the play of natural law, but passively, by meditatively turning its "close-up" into a full-field view. The oneness of humanity's vision matches the oneness of nature, so that the experience of seeing is both total and timeless.

A poem that counters this role is "The Mountain" (pp.40–44). Here, a traveler and a farmer discuss the local landmark that gives the poem its name. The traveler has been impressed by the way it dominates the area and wonders whether it can be climbed. The farmer tells him about certain features of the mountain worth seeing, but says he has never climbed it himself and is discouraging about the possibilities of getting up. After their talk, he leaves the somewhat puzzled traveler in the dust.

No place is more often symbolically linked with revelation about humanity in nature than the top of a mountain. From this vantage, a human being can lay claim to seeing nature whole, thereby arriving at the most comprehensive understanding about what the role of humanity in nature might be. Frost connoted insight of this kind through mountain imagery in many poems, and here the traveler's wish to climb the mountain for the view suggests his attempt at fulfiling the Seer role. Although what the farmer stresses as important to see, alternatively, is a brook, this curious water is not as symbolically different from the mountaintop as it first appears. Its source is linked to a fountain, the traditional source of sacred waters, and its seemingly magical properties also make it seem revelatory.[7]

Frost's critique of the Seer comes through the farmer. The structure of the poem, almost entirely dialogue, emphasizes exchange of views, an argument. The farmer is the opposite of the traveler in several ways, but most importantly in his attitude toward the mountain, which he regards not as a

[7]The brook has avatars in even more Frost poems than does the mountain. For a reading of "The Mountain" that provides more background detail, although it is not quite the same as my reading, see Darrell Abel, "'Unfriendly Nature' in the Poetry of Robert Frost," *Colby Library Quarterly,* 17 (1981), 204–10.

page 232

challenge, but as a put-down: "That thing takes all the room!" (p.41). Although he is curious about it, he has never climbed all the way up; it is emphasized, too, that his forays were for material, not spiritual, sustenance. He not only discourages the traveler from going up, but faintly ridicules his own thoughts of trying to do so: it would be unreal for one who has spent his life farming suddenly to take to the mountains. Next to the traveler, the farmer seems admirably practical and sage. "Don't run around with your head in the clouds, my boy" could be a paraphrase of his advice, at a first approximation. The implication is that the Seer role, with its dramatic "highs," is less workable a way for humanity to act towards nature than the farmer's way, which involves slow, small, and earthbound routines....

Not only does Frost disbelieve every role he has heard imagined for humanity in nature so far, he disbelieves the possibility of humanity's ever knowing its "true" place in nature at all. In one critic's paraphrase, "The only meaning one can find in nature is that imposed upon it by the human mind."[8] Or, in Frost's own words: "I think there's probably nothing 'up there' but a stockpile of nature observations that came from earth."[9] This radical skepticism has been articulated so clearly and frequently in its outline as to have become virtually synonymous with certain Frost poems (e.g., "All Revelation," "For Once, Then, Something," "A Cabin in the Clearing").

But Frost *did* in part, believe. His "yea-saying," indeed, is what sets him apart from the main philosophical tradition of

page 233

skepticism to which he otherwise belongs.... The way Frost defended himself against wholesale disbelief in nature's order, according to the conventional wisdom, was by exercising limited belief in the ordering power of the human mind, particularly as represented by art.

[8]John F. Lynen, *The Pastoral Art of Robert Frost,* Yale Studies in English, Vol. 147 (New Haven: Yale University Press, 1960), p. 145.

[9]Elizabeth Shepley Sergeant, *Robert Frost: The Trial by Existence* (New York: Holt, Rinehart and Winston, 1960), p. 309.

LITERARY TERMS HANDBOOK

In this handbook you will find all of the reading and literary terms taught in this book. Each entry defines a term and then briefly discusses it, elaborating with examples from the selections. Each entry ends with a cross-reference to the pages that teach the literary term and, in some cases, to related entries in this handbook.

READING AND LITERARY TERMS HANDBOOK

ALLEGORY *A story with a symbolic meaning used to teach a moral principle.* Many of Hawthorne's stories, such as "The Minister's Black Veil" (p. 182), are allegories dealing with pride, isolation, and love.

See page 181.

ALLITERATION *The repetition of sounds at the beginnings of words and of sounds within words.* Notice the repetition of the *s* sound in these lines from "Sucess is counted sweetest" (p. 281):

Success is counted *sweetest*
By those who ne'er *succeed*

See page 131.

ALLUSION *A short reference to a person, a place, an event, or another work of literature.* The reference, which the reader is expected to know, clarifies a point or expands its meaning. For example, in Masters' "Cassius Hueffer" (p. 439) the poet uses a famous line from Shakespeare's *Julius Caesar* to shed additional light on the complex personality of Cassius Hueffer:

"His life was gentle, and the elements so mixed in him
That nature might stand up and say to all the world,
This was a man."

See page 29.

ALMANAC *An annual collection of statistics, weather forecasts, current events, and other useful or entertaining information.* Franklin's *Poor Richard's Almanack* remains interesting reading today.

See page 57.

AMERICANISM *A word or phrase that has originated in America:* for example, *Sun Belt, slam-dunk, hot dog.*

See page 273.

ANALOGY *A comparison made between two things to show the similarities between them.* Analogies explain something unfamiliar by comparing it to something familiar. In *Of Plymouth Plantation* (p. 24), for example, Bradford draws an analogy between the Puritans' "wandering" and that of the Israelites in Egypt:

When they had wandered in the desert wilderness out of the way, and found no city to dwell in, both hungry and thirsty, their soul was overwhelmed in them.

See page 39.
See also SIMILE, METAPHOR.

ANAPEST *A poetic foot consisting of two unstressed syllables followed by a stressed syllable* (˘ ˘ ʹ).

See page 123.

ANECDOTE *A short account of an interesting event in someone's life.* Anecdotes are used to raise or illustrate a point, to explain an idea, or to describe personality. In "My Father Sits in the Dark" (p. 585) the author explains his father's habit with an anecdote that begins: "Once I left him there and went to bed. . . . I went to the kitchen. There he was. . . ."

See page 584.

ANTAGONIST *A person or force that opposes the protagonist in a story or drama.* The antagonist in "To Build a Fire" (p. 355), for example, is the bitter cold and snow of the Klondike against which the man (the protagonist) must struggle.

See page 665.
See also PLOT, CONFLICT.

APHORISM *A short, pointed statement expressing a wise or clever observation about life.* For example:

No gains without pains.

—Poor Richard's Almanack

APOSTROPHE *A figure of speech in which a writer directly addresses an inanimate object, idea, or absent person.* In "Oread" (p. 428), for example, the poet addresses the sea:

Whirl up, sea—
whirl your pointed pines

See page 220.

ASIDE *In drama a short speech spoken by a character in an undertone or directly to the audience so that other characters on stage do not hear it.*

ASSONANCE *The repetition of similar vowel sounds in a line of poetry.* For example:

And the Raven, never fl*itt*ing, st*ill* *is* s*itt*ing, st*ill* *is*
s*itt* *ing*

—"The Raven"

See page 131.
See also ALLITERATION, CONSONANCE, REPETITION.

AUTOBIOGRAPHY *The story of a person's life told by the person who lived it.* An autobiography, such as Ben Franklin's, contains objective facts as well as subjective feelings.

See page 58.
See also BIOGRAPHY.

BIOGRAPHY *A factual account of a person's life written by someone other than the subject.* A biography that comments on the subject's work as well as life is called a **critical biography.**

See page 244.
See also AUTOBIOGRAPHY.

BLANK VERSE *Unrhymed iambic pentameter.* Blank verse attempts to suggest spoken English; every line, therefore, need not be perfectly regular. Robert Frost's "Birches" (p. 472) is written in blank verse:

When I see birches bend to left and right
Across the lines of straighter darker trees

See page 123.
See also METER, FOOT, SCANSION.

CAESURA *The pause or break in a line of poetry, usually created by punctuation.* The caesura falls generally, but not necessarily, at the middle of a line. For example:

Once upon a midnight dreary, // while I pondered,
weak and weary

—"The Raven"

See page 215.
See also METER.

CHARACTER *A person in a literary work.* Some characters are **flat**—built around a single trait, quality, or idea. **Stereotypes**, or **stock characters**, such as the noble hero and fiendish villain are usually flat characters. Butler, the landowner in Hamlin Garland's "Under the Lion's Paw" (p. 341), is a flat character.

A **round character** possesses a variety of traits, often complex and contradictory, making the character more like a real human being. The boy in "The Bear" (p. 640), for example, is a round character who exhibits conflicting behavior and attitudes.

See page 323.
See also CHARACTERIZATION.

CHARACTERIZATION *The ways an author develops the personalities of characters.* In **direct characterization** the writer states a character's personality. For example, in "To Build a Fire" (p. 355):

The man was without imagination.

In **indirect characterization** the writer reveals personality through physical description, action, thoughts, speech, or perceptions of the character or of other characters. Most frequently the reader must infer the personality from these suggestions. For example, the sensitivity of the narrator in "My Father Sits in the Dark" (p. 585) is revealed through his thoughts about his father.

See page 323.
See also CHARACTER.

CHORUS *In drama one or more characters who comment on the action.* In classical Greek drama the chorus is made up of a number of people. In *Our Town* (p. 670) the Stage Manager functions as a chorus.

CLASSICISM *A form of art that stresses reason and order over emotion and personal concerns.* The literature and art of ancient Greece and Rome are considered classical. The movement of the eighteenth century to imitate the balanced, orderly rationality of the ancients was called **neoclassicism.** Romanticism was in part a reaction to the neoclassic movement.

See page 101.

CLIMAX *The point of highest dramatic tension or excitement in a literary work.* The climax of "To Build a Fire" (p. 355), for example, occurs when the man loses his last match while alone in the bitter cold. He and the reader realize this means he is doomed.

See page 323.
See also PLOT, CONFLICT.

COLLOQUIAL LANGUAGE *The everyday language we use in conversation.* Mark Twain mastered the art of rendering colloquial speech in print. For example:

" 'What might it be that you've got in the box?' And Smiley says, sorter indifferent-like, 'It might be a parrot, or it might be a canary, maybe, but it ain't—it's only just a frog.' "

—"The Celebrated Jumping Frog of Calaveras County"

See page 305.
See also REGIONALISMS, DIALECT.

CONCEIT *A lengthy, unusual comparison, often extended throughout an entire poem.* In "Huswifery" (p. 33), for example, the poet speaks of himself as an instrument in God's hands, the way a spinning wheel is an instrument in a housewife's hands. The comparison runs through the entire poem.

See page 34.
See also METAPHOR.

CONFESSIONAL POETRY *A type of modern poetry in which poets speak with openness and frankness about their own lives.* Robert Lowell, John Berryman, Sylvia Plath, and Anne Sexton are the most important American confessional poets.

See page 553.

CONFLICT *The struggle that the protagonist of a story or drama undergoes.* The conflict can be external or internal, taking place within the character's mind. Each event in a plot relates to the conflict. In "The Bear" (p. 640), for example, the boy struggles to hunt the bear and to understand what the bear means to him.

See page 323, 365.
See also ANTAGONIST.

CONNOTATION *The suggestions or associations carried with a word beyond its denotation, or literal meaning.* For example:

> The *summer* soldier and the *sunshine* patriot will, in this crisis, shrink from the service of their country. . . .
>
> —"The American Crisis"

The connotations of *summer* and *sunshine* suggest that the author is referring to people who are soldiers and patriots only during good times.

See page 211.

CONSONANCE *The repetition of consonant sounds in a line of poetry.* For example:

> *B*eat! *b*eat! drums!—*b*low! *b*ugles! *b*low!
>
> —"Beat! Beat! Drums!"

See page 131.
See also ASSONANCE, ALLITERATION.

COUPLET *Two consecutive lines of poetry that rhyme.* For example, these lines from "To My Dear and Loving Husband" (p. 31):

> If ever two were one, then surely we.
> If ever man were loved by wife, then thee.

See page 87.

DACTYL *A poetic foot consisting of one stressed syllable followed by two unstressed syllables.* (′ ˘ ˘).

See page 123.
See also FOOT.

DENOTATION *The literal meaning, or dictionary definition, of a word.*

See page 211.
See also LITERAL LANGUAGE, CONNOTATION.

DENOUEMENT *The resolution of a story, as the conflict is resolved and the knot of the plot is untied.* After the climax of "The Far and the Near" (p. 603), when the trainman discovers that his "dream family" is quite ordinary, he comes to some conclusions about himself and his future.

See page 323.
See also PLOT.

DESCRIPTION *Writing that creates a picture of a person, place, or thing.* The specific details of description enhance poems, stories, and nonfiction. Columbus, for example, uses vivid and concrete details as he describes in his *Journal* (p. 15) a type of tree he had never before seen:

> . . . thus one branch has leaves like those of a cane, and others like those of a mastic tree; and on a single tree there are five different kinds.

See page 92.
See also IMAGE, NARRATION, EXPOSITION, PERSUASION.

DIALECT *The way of speaking and writing that is particular to a specific region of the country.* Mark Twain was a successful writer of dialect, capturing subtle differences of pronunciation and vocabulary. For example:

> . . . he was the curiosest man about always betting on anything that turned up you ever see. . . .
>
> —"The Celebrated Jumping Frog of Calaveras County"

See page 118.

DIALOGUE *The conversation of characters in a drama, short story, novel, or dramatic poem.*

See page 665.

DICTION *The choice of words to fit the character, theme, setting, or subject in a poem, story, essay, or play.* Notice how Emily Dickinson chooses words that intensify the violence of the action in "Apparently with no surprise" (p. 278):

The Frost *beheads* it at its play—
In accidental *power*—
The blonde *Assassin* passes on—

See page 211.

DRAMA *A story acted out with spoken dialogue before an audience.* The dramatist, or playwright, usually provides dialogue and stage directions that give instructions about scenery, costumes, gestures, movements, and lighting.

See page 665.

DRAMATIC MONOLOGUE *A long speech by one character in a play or poem, usually revealing the character's thoughts.* "The Love Song of J. Alfred Prufrock" (p. 415), is a dramatic monologue in which the speaker reveals his fears and frustrations.

See page 419.

DRAMATIC POEM *A poem that reveals character through dialogue and monologue.* While there is some narrative in a dramatic poem, the focus is on character, not events. In "The Love Song of J. Alfred Prufrock" (p. 415), for example, Prufrock speaks to himself and to the reader; he also imagines conversations with other people.

See page 286.
See also NARRATIVE POEM, LYRIC POEM.

END-STOPPED LINE *A line of poetry that ends with a pause both in punctuation and in thought.* For example:

By the rude bridge that arched the flood,
Their flag to April's breeze unfurled

—"Concord Hymn"

See page 215.
See also RUN-ON LINE.

EPIC *A long narrative poem that traces the adventures of a hero.* Composed during ancient and medieval times, epics usually intertwine myth and history, reflecting the values of the societies in which they originate. In epics gods and goddesses often intervene in the affairs of humans, as they do in Homer's *Iliad* and *Odyssey.* Though usually referred to as a myth, the *Walum Olum* of the Delaware Indians may also be considered an epic. Other than some long works by American Indians, however, there are no genuine American literary epics, though Longfellow's *Song of Hiawatha* (1855) attempted to imitate epic form and style.

See also NARRATIVE POEM.

EPIPHANY *A term used by Irish writer James Joyce to describe the moment of revelation or recognition in which a character in a story perceives an essential truth.* In Saroyan's "There Was a Young Lady of Perth" (p. 796), for instance, during one brief moment the narrator realizes that he does not need a life of fame and fortune.

See page 794.

ESSAY *A moderately brief nonfiction work that deals with a particular topic.* Essays may be classified as formal or informal. A **formal essay** is a carefully structured attempt to instruct or persuade. It has a serious tone and presents its argument logically. Ralph Waldo Emerson's *Nature* (p. 161) is a formal essay on the subject of the relationship between the human world and the natural world.

An **informal essay** usually attempts to entertain the reader while exploring a given topic. Its tone is light, its structure somewhat sprawling. Because the informal essay often makes personal references, it is sometimes called the **personal essay.** "Hidden Name and Complex Fate" (p. 850) is an informal essay presenting the author's personal view on the subject of names.

See page 664.

EXPOSITION *Writing that aims to explain or inform; also, in a work of fiction the background information vital to the reader's understanding of the story.* The exposition generally comes at the beginning of a story, presenting the characters and situation. The opening paragraph of "A Worn Path" (p. 615), for example, introduces the reader to the time, place, and central character.

See pages 323, 848.
See also DESCRIPTION, NARRATION, PERSUASION, PLOT.

FABLE *A tale, usually ending with a moral, in which animals behave as if they were human beings.* Some of the most famous fables are those of the Greek writer Aesop and those of the French writer

LaFontaine. Mark Twain openly called his fable "A Fable."

See page 303.

FIGURATIVE LANGUAGE *Language that is not meant to be taken literally.* Often figurative language uses a concrete image to express an abstract idea: for example, "Love your Neighbor; yet don't pull down your Hedge." In this proverb from *Poor Richard's Almanack* (p. 57), "Hedge" is not meant literally. It is an image representing the idea of protection of privacy.

See also LITERAL LANGUAGE, SIMILE, METAPHOR.

FIGURE OF SPEECH *A word or expression that is not meant to be taken literally.* **Similes** and **metaphors** are figures of speech.

See page 164.
See also FIGURATIVE LANGUAGE.

FLASHBACK *An interruption in a narrative to show an event that happened earlier.* This technique is used in stream-of-consciousness writing, as well as in generally conventional narratives. For example, in "The Jilting of Granny Weatherall" (p. 576), Granny remembers scenes of her past life that make her final moments in the story more meaningful.

See page 583.

FOIL *A character who through contrast underscores the characteristics of another.* The dog in "To Build a Fire" (p. 355), for example, exhibits a caution and respect for the cold of the Klondike that the man obviously lacks.

See page 600.
See also CHARACTERIZATION.

FOOT *The basic unit of meter in a line of poetry.* Usually a foot consists of one stressed syllable and one or two unstressed syllables. Common feet in American poetry are:

The **iamb**, an unstressed syllable followed by a stressed syllable. For example:

> Ănd só / măy yóu / whŏév / ĕr dáres / dĭsgráce
>
> —"To His Excellency, General Washington"

The **trochee,** a stressed syllable followed by an unstressed syllable. For example:

> Ónce ŭp / ón ă / mídnĭght / dréarў / ás Ĭ
>
> —"The Raven"

The **anapest,** two unstressed syllables followed by a stressed syllable. For example:

> Whĕn thĕ heárt / ĭn hĭs breást / lĭke ă tríp / hămmĕr beáts
>
> —"A Fable for Critics"
> James Russell Lowell

The **dactyl,** a stressed syllable followed by two unstressed syllables. For example:

> Thís ĭs thĕ / fórĕst prĭm / évăl. Thĕ / múrmŭrĭng / pínes ănd thĕ / hémlŏcks
>
> —"Evangeline"
> Henry Wadsworth Longfellow

The **spondee,** two stressed syllables. For example:

> Ĭn áll / hĭs cóurse; / nŏr yét / ĭn thĕ / cóld gróund
>
> —"Thanatopsis"

See page 123.
See also METER.

FORESHADOWING *A method of increasing suspense by presenting events or characters in such a way as to hint at what is going to happen to them.* Foreshadowing often contains a large element of irony. For example, in Thomas Wolfe's "The Far and the Near" (page 603), the trainman's disappointment is foreshadowed when his vision of the little house is said to be fixed in his mind as "something beautiful and enduring, something beyond all change."

See page 810.

FRAME STORY *A story that serves as a framework within which another story is told.* "In Dreams Begin Responsibilities" (p. 606) uses a frame story.

See page 613.

FREE VERSE *Poetry that has an irregular rhythm and line length and that avoids a predetermined verse structure.* Free verse uses the cadences of natural speech and rarely rhymes. Walt Whitman's poetry, for example, is free verse:

> This is the city and I am one of the citizens,
> Whatever interests the rest interests me, politics,
> wars, markets, newspapers, schools—
>
> —"Song of Myself"

See page 265.
See also METER, RHYTHM.

HAIKU *A Japanese verse form consisting of three lines, usually describing an image of a subject in na-*

ture. The first line is limited to five syllables, the second line to seven syllables, and the third line to five syllables. Haiku influenced the Imagist poets.

See page 413.

HEROIC COUPLET *A pair of rhymed lines in iambic pentameter.* For example:

> I prize / thy love / more than / whole mines / of gold
> Or all / the ri / ches that / the East / doth hold.
> —"To My Dear and Loving Husband"

See page 87.
See also RHYTHM.

IAMB *A poetic foot consisting of an unstressed syllable followed by a stressed syllable (˘ ′).*

See also FOOT, IAMBIC PENTAMETER.

IAMBIC PENTAMETER *A line of poetry composed of five iambic feet.*

> Proceed / great chief / with vir / tue on / thy side
> —"To His Excellency, General Washington"

See page 394.
See also METER, BLANK VERSE, HEROIC COUPLET.

IMAGE *A "picture" in the reader's mind created by words.* Images can describe the sensory experiences of seeing, hearing, tasting, smelling, feeling. In Columbus' *Journal* (p. 15), for example, the image helps the reader "see" the canoes approaching:

> . . . made out of the trunk of a tree, all in one piece, and wonderfully worked, propelled with a paddle like a baker's shovel . . .

Ezra Pound said that an image "presents an intellectual and emotional complex in an instant of time."

See page 34.
See also IMAGERY.

IMAGERY *The collection of mental pictures, or images, in a literary work.* Visual imagery is most common, but a writer can also suggest images that appeal to the senses of sound, taste, smell, and touch. Consider this image of sight:

> The purple petals, fallen in the pool,
> Made the black water with their beauty gay.
> —"The Rhodora"

See page 227.
See also DESCRIPTION.

IMAGISM *An influential literary movement that took place in Europe and America from about 1910 to 1920.* The Imagist poet creates a single sharp image that evokes an emotional response in the reader. Invented by Ezra Pound and furthered by H. D., Imagism was in part a reaction to the "bad habits" of nineteenth-century poets who were too explicit in their commentary and too repetitious in their subjects, patterns, and meters. Pound's "In a Station of the Metro" (p. 410) is the most famous example of Imagism.

See page 413.

IRONY *The awareness—by author, character, or reader—of a contrast or a difference between the way things seem and the way they really are.*

Verbal irony occurs when words that appear to be saying one thing mean something quite different. In W. H. Auden's "Unknown Citizen" (p. 547), for example, the poet suggests that something very definitely is wrong, making the last lines ironic:

> Was he free? Was he happy? The question is
> absurd:
> Had anything been wrong, we should certainly have
> heard.

Situational irony occurs when what is expected to happen is not what actually comes to pass. In "The Far and the Near" (p. 603), for example, the trainman is sadly surprised to find the dull and ordinary where he expected the romantic and beautiful.

Dramatic irony occurs when events that mean one thing to the characters mean something quite different to the reader. *Our Town* (p. 670) is full of dramatic irony. The breakfast scenes, for example, seem ordinary to the characters, but the audience sees the universal elements and significance in the actions.

See page 391.

JOURNAL *A daily record of events kept by an individual who is a participant in or witness to these events.* Journals are often valuable historical documents. Mary Chesnut's *Journal* gives us a view of the Civil War by one who lived through it.

See page 252.

LIMERICK *A humorous five-line poem in which the first, second, and fifth lines rhyme and have the rhythm ˘ ′/ ˘ ˘ ′/ ˘ ˘ ′, and the third and fourth lines rhyme with each other and have the rhythm ˘ ˘ ′/ ˘ ˘ ′.* Saroyan uses the limerick in "There Was a Young Lady of Perth" (p. 796). A sample limerick:

> There was an old man of Peru
> Who dreamt he was eating his shoe.

He awoke in the night
In a terrible fright,
And found it was perfectly true!

See page 795.

LITERAL LANGUAGE *Language that means exactly what it says.*

See page 164.
See also FIGURATIVE LANGUAGE.

LYRIC POEM *A poem that expresses primarily the personal thoughts and feelings of the poet.* Lyric poems are short and attempt to achieve a single, unified effect. "Success is counted sweetest" (p. 281) is an example of a lyric poem.

See page 287.
See also NARRATIVE POEM, DRAMATIC POEM.

METAPHOR *A comparison that identifies one thing with another, seemingly very different thing.* For example, in *Of Plymouth Plantation* (p. 24), to emphasize how vast the Pilgrims' troubles were, Bradford speaks of "a sea of troubles."

See page 39.
See also SIMILE, ANALOGY, CONCEIT.

METER *A generally regular pattern of stressed and unstressed syllables in a line of poetry.* Meter is determined by the number and kind of feet in a line. For example, the meter of Longfellow's "Psalm of Life" (p. 213) is trochaic tetrameter: Each line has four (tetra) trochaic feet (one stressed syllable followed by one unstressed syllable).

See page 122.
See also SCANSION, FOOT, BLANK VERSE.

MODERNISM *A collective term for the radically new ideas, forms, styles, and attitudes that revolutionized all the arts during the first three decades of our century.* American writers, many of whom traveled frequently to Europe, experimented with new, more objective styles and freer-flowing forms in poetry, drama, and fiction. World War I triggered a shift in values, and writers of the period were quick to reflect the change. The complacency and optimism of previous generations were replaced by a more desperate attempt to make sense of the modern world.

See page 401.

MOTIVATION *The reason or group of reasons why a character in fiction acts in a certain way.* Motivation makes characters believable. Sometimes the author will state directly why a character behaves in a certain way. Jack London, for example, explains his character's risking his life in the cold in "To Build a Fire" (p. 355): "The trouble with him was that he was without imagination."

Many times the author implies the motivation, enabling readers to draw it out of their knowledge of the character. For example, in "The First Seven Years" (p. 787) readers infer why Sobel quit his job.

See page 339.
See also CHARACTER.

NARRATION *Writing that tells a story, moving from event to event, usually in chronological order.* A narrative may be factual, like "The Alligators of East Florida" (p. 89), or fictional, like "The Fall of the House of Usher" (p. 135).

See page 113.
See also DESCRIPTION, EXPOSITION, PERSUASION.

NARRATIVE POEM *A poem that tells a story.* The **epic** is a long poem of heroic adventure. The **ballad** is a shorter narrative poem, often set to music. "Janet Waking" (p. 449) is a narrative poem.

See page 286.
See also DRAMATIC POEM, LYRIC POEM.

NARRATOR *One who narrates, or tells, a story.* Ishmael, a character in *Moby-Dick*, is the narrator. A story may be narrated in the first person or the third person. The author may serve as narrator. Sometimes even a play may have a narrator, as in *Our Town* (p. 670).

See also POINT OF VIEW.

NATURALISM *A literary movement that portrays people caught within forces of nature or society that are beyond their understanding or control.* Naturalism was an outgrowth of Realism, responding to theories in science, psychology, human behavior, and social thought current in the late nineteenth century. The naturalist uses a quasi-scientific "facts-only" approach, heavy in detail. While the subject matter of naturalistic writing is often grim, the purpose generally is to highlight ills so that they can be corrected. Hamlin Garland's "Under the Lion's Paw" (p. 341), for example, dramatizes the plight of farmers.

See page 311.

NOVEL *A book-length prose fiction.* Types of novels include the **picaresque,** a loose series of episodes recounting the adventures of wanderers and lovable rogues; **sentimental,** a highly emotional tale of romance and tears; **gothic,** a tale of mystery and fear; **philosophical,** a story that raises profound questions about life and humankind; **psychological,** a narrative that probes the complexity of its characters' thinking, behavior, and motivation; **realistic,** a story that focuses objectively on ordinary life; **naturalistic,** a story of characters trapped by overwhelming forces of nature or society; **regional,** a tale in which the peculiarities of a particular setting play a major role; **satiric,** or novel of **social witticism,** a story whose purpose is to uncover evils in society for the purpose of correction; **stream-of-consciousness,** a narrative told through the free-flowing consciousness of the narrator.

See page 395.
See also REALISM, REGIONALISM, NATURALISM.

OCTAVE *An eight-line poem or stanza.*

See SONNET.

ONOMATOPOEIA *The use of words with sounds that suggest their meanings.* For example:

So strong you *thump* O terrible drums—

—"Beat! Beat! Drums!"

See page 131.

ORAL TRADITION *Stories, songs, tales, and myths of a people passed down by word of mouth from one generation to another.* Much American Indian literature was originally preserved in the oral tradition.

See page 14.

ORATORY *Formal public speaking, often characterized by a blend of argument and emotion.* Orators such as Patrick Henry (p. 65) greatly influenced the shaping of America in its early years.

See page 68.
See also PERSUASION.

PARALLELISM *The repetition of phrases or sentences so that the repeated parts are alike in structure or meaning.* Parallelism gives emphasis to thoughts especially in persuasive writing. For example:

To err is human, to repent divine; to persist,
devilish.

—*Poor Richard's Almanack*

See page 84.

PARODY *A humorous imitation.* A parody imitates another work's plot, characters, or style, usually through exaggeration. "The Fall of the House of Usher" by Reed Whittemore (p. 565) parodies the plot of Poe's story of the same title.

See page 566.

PERSONIFICATION *A figure of speech in which human qualities are given to objects, animals, and ideas.* For example:

Earth smiles—the waters smile—even the sky of clouds smiles—

—"Calling One's Own"

See page 220.
See also METAPHOR.

PERSUASION *Writing that attempts to sway the reader to think or act in a particular way.* In "The Beauty of the World" (p. 44), for example, Jonathan Edwards tries to convince people of the superiority of spiritual beauty, so they will strive to be holy and virtuous.

See page 22.

PLOT *In a short story, novel, or play the series of events that leads from beginning to end.* Each event is related to the **conflict,** the struggle that the main character undergoes. Usually a plot begins with **exposition,** the background of setting and situation. Some interesting element, the **narrative hook,** draws readers into the story. Events that contribute to the conflict are called the **rising action,** leading to the **climax,** or point of highest dramatic tension. The **falling action** presents the results of the climax, and the **resolution** gives the final outcome. The resolution is sometimes called **denouement,** meaning "untying," since the term refers to the untying of the "knot" of the plot.

See page 323.

POINT OF VIEW *The relationship of the storyteller, or narrator, to the story.* A story has a **first-person point of view** if one of the characters, referred to as "I," tells the story, as in "My Father Sits in the Dark" (p. 585).

A story has a **limited third-person point of view** if the narrator reveals the thoughts of only one character but refers to that character as "he" or "she." "The Celebrated Jumping Frog of Calaveras County" (p. 298), for example, is told from a limited third-person point of view.

A narrator who tells the thoughts of all the characters and who tells things that no one character could know uses the **omniscient** (all-knowing), or **third-person,**

can be read in one sitting. A short story generally contains the following major elements:

Plot—the series of events leading from beginning to end.
Characterization—the way an author develops the personalities of characters.
Setting—the time and place in which events occur.
Point of view—the perspective of the storyteller, or narrator.
Theme—the main idea of the story.
Style—the writer's way of writing, determined by the diction, structure, imagery, etc.

See page 323.
See also NOVEL.

SIMILE *A figure of speech that states a comparison by using* like *or* as *to indicate the comparison.* For example:

When you look upon me I am satisfied as
flowers that drink dew.

—"Calling One's Own"

See page 39.
See also METAPHOR, ANALOGY.

SOLILOQUY *A long speech spoken by a character who is alone on stage.* This speech usually reveals the private thoughts and emotions of the character.

See also DRAMATIC MONOLOGUE.

SONNET *A lyric poem of fourteen lines written in iambic pentameter.* **Shakespearean,** or **English, sonnets** have three quatrains (groups of four lines) followed by a rhymed couplet, with the rhyme scheme *abab cdcd efef gg.* The English sonnet presents its main thought in the three quatrains, with a conclusion presented in the couplet.

Petrarchan, or **Italian, sonnets** divide into a group of eight lines, or octave, followed by a group of six lines, or sestet. The rhyme scheme for the octave is *abba abba* and for the sestet *cdecde* or *cd cd ee.* In the Italian sonnet the octave presents a single thought, with the sestet expanding, contradicting, or developing it in some other way.

Jean Toomer's "November Cotton Flower" (p. 443) is a modified Shakespearean sonnet. Paul Laurence Dunbar's "Douglass" (p. 393) is a Petrarchan sonnet.

See page 394.

SPEAKER *The voice of a poem, sometimes that of the poet, sometimes that of a fictional person or even a thing.* The speaker's words communicate a particular tone, or attitude, toward the subject of the poem. For example, the speaker in Masters' "Lucinda Matlock" (p. 440) is a woman whose tone is vigorous and full of the love of life.

See also POINT OF VIEW.

SPIRITUAL *A folk song, generally dealing with earthly bondage or religious faith.* "Go Down, Moses" (p. 237) is a famous spiritual.

See page 236.

SPONDEE *A poetic foot consisting of two stressed syllables (' ').*

See page 123.

STAGE DIRECTIONS *Instructions written by the playwright about scenery, costumes, gestures, movements, and lighting for a play or drama.* In *Our Town* (p. 670), for example, the directions about the lack of scenery, the stage manager's hat and pipe, and the use of chairs are examples of stage directions.

STANZA *A group of lines forming a unit in a poem.* Stanzas usually contain from two to eight lines and often have a definite rhyme scheme. The stanzas in "The Raven" (p. 127) have six lines and a rhyme scheme of *abcbbb.*

Common stanzas are the **couplet,** two lines; the **tercet,** three lines; the **quatrain,** four lines; the **sestet,** six lines; the **octave,** eight lines.

See page 170.

STREAM OF CONSCIOUSNESS *A technique of writing that imitates the flow of thoughts, feelings, images, and memories through the mind of a character in a work of fiction.* The traditional chronological narrative is replaced by a seemingly jumbled collection of things running through the mind, forcing the reader to piece together the "plot" of an incident. "The Jilting of Granny Weatherall" (p. 576), for example, is the stream of Granny's thoughts.

See page 582.
See also FLASHBACK.

STYLE *A writer's characteristic way of writing determined by his diction, imagery, tone, and choice of literary devices.* Frost's style, for example, has a natural rhythm and conversational tone, with many images of nature. Wallace Stevens is more abstract in his imagery; his lines are tighter. Cummings' style is easily recognized for its lack of conventional form, punctuation, and capitalization.

See page 384.

SUSPENSE *That quality in a story that makes the reader uncertain or tense about the outcome of events.* In one type of suspense, readers do not know what will happen next, as in "The Portable Phonograph" (p. 623). In a second type of suspense, readers know the plot but wonder about *how* things will happen.

See page 787.
See also FORESHADOWING.

SYMBOL *A person, place, or thing that has meaning in itself and also stands for something other than itself.* Symbols often help convey meaning in stories and poems. For example, the flag in "Success is counted sweetest" (p. 281) is a physical object, but it symbolizes the conquest of one army over another:

Not one of all the purple Host
Who took the Flag today
Can tell the definition
So clear of Victory.

See page 190.

THEME *The main idea that the writer of a literary work communicates to the reader.* The theme is usually expressed as a statement about life. Some stories have a **stated theme,** announced explicitly, usually at the end of the story. Most stories have **implied themes** revealed indirectly through the unfolding of the events. The implied theme of Ernest Hemingway's "In Another Country" (p. 490), for example, is that pain and loss, especially during war, can numb the spirit.

See page 323.
See also PLOT.

TONE *The attitude the writer takes toward his or her subject, characters, and readers.* The Declaration of Independence, for example, has a formal tone:

> When in the course of human events it becomes necessary for one people to dissolve the political bands which have connected them to another . . .

Twain's autobiography reflects a personal, affectionate tone:

> The moment we were underway I began to prowl about the great steamer and fill myself with joy. She was as clean and as dainty as a drawing room. . . .
>
> —*Life on the Mississippi*

See page 474.

TRANSCENDENTALISM *An American philosophical and artistic attitude based on the belief that the most fundamental truths about life and death can be reached only by going beyond the world of the senses.* Knowledge of this kind comes not through the mind's logic but through a deep, free intuition that Transcendentalists recognized as the "highest power of the Soul." The essays of Emerson convey much of the Transcendentalist philosophy.

See page 154.

TROCHEE *A poetic foot consisting of a stressed syllable followed by an unstressed syllable (′ ˘).*

See page 123.
See also FOOT.

VILLANELLE *A poem of nineteen lines divided into five tercets (three-line stanzas) and a final quatrain, using the rhyme scheme* aba aba aba aba aba abaa. There are only two rhymes in a villanelle, and eight of the nineteen lines are repeated. Lines 6, 12, and 18 repeat line 1; lines 9, 15, and 18 repeat line 3. Auden's "If I Could Tell You" (p. 546) is an example of a modern villanelle.

GLOSSARY

In this Glossary you will find the more difficult words in the selections in this book, along with pronunciations and definitions of the words as they are used in the selections. In addition, you will find the Glossary words for each selection listed with the teacher's materials for that selection in your teacher's resource materials.

GLOSSARY

The following glossary lists words from the selections that may be unfamiliar to you. Although many of the words have several different meanings, they are defined only as they are used in the selections. Some words may be familiar to you in other contexts but may have unusual meanings in the text.

Each glossary entry contains a pronunciation, a part of speech, and a definition. Some words are used in more than one way in the textbook and therefore have more than one definition and occasionally more than one part of speech. Related words are often combined in one entry: The main form (for example, the adjective *callow*) is defined, and another form (for example, the noun *callowness*) is run on after the main definition. Adverbs ending in *-ly* are usually run on after the definition of the adjective form.

Some unusual words or meanings of words are labeled ARCHAIC (old-fashioned), OBSOLETE (no longer in use), RARE, or POETIC. Other special usage labels include COLLOQUIAL, SLANG, CHIEFLY BRITISH, MILITARY, and so on. Occasionally an unfamiliar idiomatic expression is used within a selection; in such cases the main word of the expression is listed, followed by a definition of the idiom.

The following abbreviations are used in this glossary:

n.	noun	*conj.*	conjunction
v.	verb	*prep.*	preposition
adj.	adjective	*interj.*	interjection
adv.	adverb	*pl.*	plural
pron.	pronoun	*n.pl.*	plural noun

A

abase [ə bās′] *v.* to humiliate; degrade.
abate [ə bāt′] *v.* to lessen; reduce.
abdicate [ab′də kāt′] *v.* to give up (a high office or throne).
abeyance [ə bā′əns] *n.* the state of being stopped temporarily.
abhorrence [ab hôr′əns, -hor′-] *n.* hatred or disgust.
abject [ab′jekt, ab jekt′] *adj.* having lost one's spirit and self-respect; wretched.
abominate [ə bom′ə nāt′] *v.* to hate.
absolve [ab zolv′, -solv′] *v.* to set free from responsibility or blame.
abut [ə but′] *v.* to be next to; border on.
accolade [ak′ə lād′, -läd′] *n.* a sign of respect or praise.
acquiesce [ak′wē es′] *v.* to agree or accept quietly.
acquire [ə kwīr′] *v.* to gain possessions. **—acquirer,** *n.*
acrid [ak′rid] *adj.* bitter; sharp.
admonish [ad mon′ish] *v.* **1.** to caution; warn. **2.** to scold mildly. **—admonition** [ad′mə nish′ən], *n.*
adversity [ad vur′sə tē] *n.* a state of misery or trouble.
affinity [ə fin′ə tē] *n.* connection; similarity.
affliction [ə flik′shən] *n.* something that causes pain, distress, or suffering.
affright [ə frīt′] *v.* ARCHAIC. to terrify. —*n.* ARCHAIC. great fear.
affront [ə frunt′] *v.* to insult. —*n.* an insult.
agate [ag′it] *n.* a hard stone with striped or patterned colors.
aggregate [ag′rə git, -gāt′] *n.* a group of things taken as a whole; total.
aghast [ə gast′] *adj.* horrified.
alacrity [ə lak′rə tē] *n.* readiness; promptness; eagerness.
albino [al bī′nō] *n.* a person lacking in normal coloring and therefore having whitish skin and hair and pink eyes.
align [ə līn′] *v.* to line up; straighten. **—alignment,** *n.*
allege [ə lej′] *v.* to declare or state positively but without proof.
alleviate [ə lē′vē āt′] *v.* to lesson; relieve. **—alleviation,** *n.*
allot [ə lot′] *v.* to assign.
allurement [ə loor′mənt] *n.* attraction; temptation.
allusion [ə lo͞o′zhən] *n.* a casual or indirect reference.
almshouse [ämz′hous′] *n.* ARCHAIC. a publicly supported home for the poor.
altercation [ôl′tər kā′shən, al′-] *n.* an angry, noisy argument.
altitude [al′tə to͞od′, tūd′] *n.* height.
anathema [ə nath′ə mə] *n.* a curse.
angling [ang′gling] *n.* fishing with a hook and line.
annex [ə neks′] *v.* to add on.
anon [ə non′] *adv.* at another time; soon.
ante [an′tē] *v.* to put up (money) for a bet.
anthropological [an′thrə pə loj′i kəl] *adj.* relating to the study of mankind.
antipathy [an tip′ə thē] *n.* a strong dislike.
apex [ā′peks] *n.* the highest point; climax.
apotheosis [ə poth′ē ō′sis, ap′ə thē′ə-] *n.* the perfect example or model.
appease [ə pēz′] *v.* **1.** to make calm or quiet. **2.** to gain favor by pleasing acts. **—appeasingly,** *adv.*
appellation [ap′ə lā′shən] *n.* a name.
apprehension [ap′ri hen′shən] *n.* fear of something that might happen. **—apprehensive,** *adj.*
arbitrary [är′bə trer′ē] *adj.* based on someone's choice or whim.
arduous [är′jo͞o əs] *adj.* difficult.
armistice [är′mi stis] *n.* a temporary stopping of fighting; truce.
armorial [är môr′ē əl] *adj.* relating to or bearing a coat of arms, a design representing a family.
aromatic [ar′ə mat′ik] *adj.* having a strong, pleasant smell.
array [ə rā′] *n.* fine clothing.
articulate [är tik′yə lit] *adj.* clearly separated.
artifice [är′tə fis] *n.* trickery.
askance [ə skans′] *adv.* with distrust or disapproval.
aspire [əs pīr′] *v.* to have an ambition to achieve something.
assail [ə sāl′] *v.* to attack with actions or words.
assent [ə sent′] *v.* to agree. —*n.* agreement; consent.
assiduous [ə sij′o͞o əs] *adj.* careful and persistent; hardworking.
asunder [ə sun′dər] *adv.* info pieces; apart.
atone [ə tōn′] *v.* to make up for; repay. **—atonement,** *n.*
audacious [ô dā′shəs] *adj.* bold; fearless; daring. **—audaciously,** *adv.*
auditor [ô′də tər] *n.* a listener.
auger [ô′gər] *n.* a tool for making holes; drill.
aught [ôt] *n.* anything.
austere [ôs tēr′] *adj.* strict; harsh; self-denying.
avail [ə vāl′] *v.* to be of use or help.
averse [ə vurs′] *adj.* not willing; opposed.
avow [ə vou′] *v.* to declare.

B

balk [bôk] *v.* to frustrate or block.
barbaric [bär bar′ik] *adj.* primitive; savage.
bark [bärk] *n.* a boat.
batter [bat′ər] *v.* to beat; pound.
bearing [bār′ing] *n.* connection to the subject; relevance.
bedraggled [bi drag′əld] *adj.* falling apart; broken down.
befall [bi fôl′] *v.* to happen.
beguile [bi gīl′] *v.* to pass (time) pleasantly.
belie [bi lī′] *v.* to disguise; give a false impression of.
belligerent [bə lij′ər ənt] *adj.* wanting to fight; hostile.
beneficence [bə nef′ə səns] *n.* kindness; generosity.
bereaved [bi rēvd′] *adj.* having suffered a loss, especially through death.
blanch [blanch] *v.* to turn white or pale.
blight [blīt] *adj.* something that damages or destroys.
blithe [blīth, blīth] *adj.* lighthearted; carefree.
boatswain [bō′sən, bōt′swān′] *n.* a ship's officer who is in charge of some equipment and directs the crew.
bracken [brak′ən] *n.* a growth of large, thick ferns.
brook [brook] *v.* to put up with; tolerate. **—brook no quarter** to tolerate no mercy or consideration.
bulwarks [bool′wərks] *n.pl.* the side of a ship above the deck.
burdock [bur′dok] *n.* a plant with clusters of purple flowers with prickles.

C

cadaverous [kə dav′ər əs] *adj.* like a corpse; pale. **—cadaverousness,** *n.*
calamity [kə lam′ə tē] *n.* disaster.
callus [kal′əs] *n.* a hard, thick patch of skin.
capitulate [kə pich′ə lāt′] *v.* to surrender.
caravel [kar′ə vel′] *n.* a small sailing ship, especially one of the 15th and 16th centuries.
career [kə rēr′] *v.* to rush at top speed.
carrion [kar′ē ən] *n.* the flesh of dead animals.
casing [kā′sing] *n.* a frame.
castanets [kas′tə nets′] *n.pl.* an instrument consisting of two small, rounded pieces of wood, bone, ivory, etc., that are tied to the thumb and clicked together with the hand.
causeway [kôz′wā′] *n.* a raised road, usually across water or swampland.
cavalcade [kav′əl kād′, kav′əl kād′] *n.* a group, as a procession, moving along in sequence.
cavity [kav′ə tē] *n.* a hole.
cavort [kə vôrt′] *v.* to leap; prance.
celestial [sə les′chəl] *adj.* relating to the sky or heaven.
celibacy [sel′ə bə sē] *n.* the state of being unmarried.
censer [sen′sər] *n.* a container for burning incense.
censure [sen′shər] *n.* an official statement of disapproval.
chase [chās] *n.* animals to be hunted.
chattel [chat′əl] *n.* a possession.
chink [chingk] *n.* a crack.
chronic [kron′ik] *adj.* constant; always present.
cipher [sī′fər] *v.* to do arithmetic; calculate; figure.
civility [si vil′ə tē] *n.* politeness.
clerical [kler′i kəl] *adj.* of a clergyman.
coalesce [kō′ə les′] *v.* to come together; blend into a whole.
collocation [kol′ə kā′shən] *n.* arrangement.
comely [kum′lē] *adj.* attractive; handsome or pretty.
commendable [kə men′də bəl] *adj.* worthy of praise.
commendation [kom′ən dā′shən] *n.* recommendation; praise.
commensurate [kə men′sər it, -shər-] *adj.* equal; corresponding in degree.
commiseration [kə miz′ə rā′shən] *n.* an expression of sorrow or compassion for someone; sympathy.
commodity [kə mod′ə tē] *n.* a useful item; product.
compact [kəm pakt′] *v.* to press firmly together; make solid. *—n.* an agreement, a contract.
complacent [kəm plā′sənt] *adj.* satisfied.
comport [kəm pôrt′] *v.* to agree; match.
comprised [kəm prīzd′] *adj.* included.
compulsion [kəm pul′shən] *n.* the act of forcing or being forced.
concentric [kən sen′trik] *adj.* having the same center.
conciliate [kən sil′ē āt′] *v.* to win the friendliness or calm the anger of.
concision [kən sizh′ən] *n.* the act of stating in few words; briefness.
condescension [kon′di sen′shən] *n.* the act of lowering oneself to do something.
conducive [kən doo͞′sive, -dū′-] *adj.* helping to bring about.
confirmed [kən furmd′] *adj.* firmly set; unchanging; habitual.
confound [kən found′, kon-] *v.* to mix up; confuse.
conjecture [kən jek′chər] *n.* the act of guessing possible reasons or conclusions.
connivance [kə nī′vəns] *n.* a secret plan; scheme.
consort [kən sôrt′] *v.* to spend time together; be a companion.
consternation [kon′stər nā′shən] *n.* shock or dismay that leads to confusion.
constituent [kən stich′oo͞ ənt] *n.* a person represented by another.
consummate [*v.*, kon′sə māt′; *adj.*, kən sum′it, kon′sə mit] *v.* to complete; accomplish. *—adj.* excellent; expert.
contempt [kən tempt′] *n.* scorn; disdain.
contend [kən tend′] *v.* to struggle; fight.
contractual [kən trak′choo͞ əl] *adj.* of or like a contract, or formal agreement.
contrivance [kən trī′vəns] *n.* a machine.
contrive [kən trīv′] *v.* to plan; scheme.
convulse [kən vuls′] *v.* to shake or disturb violently.
convulsive [kən vul′siv] *adj.* marked by violent action or emotion. **—convulsiveness,** *n.*
corollary [kôr′ə ler′ē, kor′-] *n.* something that results.
countenance [coun′tə nəns] *n.* a person's face.
course [kôrs] *v.* to move rapidly; race.
covert [kuv′ərt, kō′vərt] *adj.* secret; stealthy. **—covertly,** *adv.*
crackle [krak′əl] *v.* to make a series of slight, sharp sounds.
craze [krāz] *v.* to make tiny cracks in.
credulity [kri doo͞′li tē, -dū′-] *n.* willingness to believe too easily.
crescendo [kri shen′dō] *adj.* increasing in loudness.

> **at**; **ā**pe; c**ä**r; end; m**ē**; **i**t; **ī**ce; h**o**t; **ō**ld; f**ô**rk; w**oo**d; f**oo͞**l; **oi**l; **ou**t; **u**p; **ū**se; t**u**rn; **ə** in **a**go; tak**e**n, penc**i**l, lem**o**n, circ**u**s; **b**at; **ch**in; **d**ear; **f**ive; **g**ame; **h**it; **hw** in **wh**ite; **j**oke; **k**it; **l**id; **m**an; **n**ot; si**ng**er; **p**ail; **r**ide; **s**at; **sh**oe; **t**ag; **th**in; **th**is; **v**ery; **w**et; **y**es; **z**oo; **zh** in trea**s**ure; **KH** in lo**ch**, German a**ch**; **N** in French bo**n**; **œ** in French f**eu**, German sch**ö**n

crestfallen [krest′fô′lən] *adj.* discouraged; depressed.
crypt [kript] *n.* an underground room or enclosed space.
cyclonic [sī klon′ik] *adj.* like a cyclone.
cynicism [sin′ə siz′əm] *n.* doubt of the sincerity or truth of the motives or values of others.

D

dapple [dap′əl] *v.* to mark with spots.
daub [dôb] *v.* to paint roughly or messily.
decline [di klīn′] *v.* to slope down.
deem [dēm] *v.* to think; judge; consider.
deferential [def′ə ren′shəl] *adj.* respectful.
degenerate [di jen′ər it] *adj.* fallen to a lower condition.
dehumanization [dē hū′mə niz ā′shən, dē ū′-] *n.* the taking away of qualities that make one a human being or an individual.
delectable [di lek′tə bəl] *adj.* delightful; delicious.
demeanor [di mē′nər] *n.* behavior; manner.
denominate [di nom′ə nāt′] *v.* to call; name.
denunciation [di nun′sē ā′shən] *n.* an accusation; criticism.
depository [di poz′ə tôr′ē] *n.* a place for storing things safely.
depravity [di prav′ə tē] *n.* wickedness; immorality.
depreciate [di prē′shē āt′] *v.* to make seem of little value.
deputation [dep′yə tā′shən] *n.* a group of people given authority to represent others.
derision [di rizh′ən] *n.* the act of laughing at or making fun of.
designation [dez′ig nā′shən] *n.* a distinguishing name or title.
desolate [des′ə lit] *adj.* lonely; uninhabited. **—desolation** [des′ə lā′shən], *n.*
destine [des′tin] *v.* to fix beforehand; predetermine.
destitute [des′tə to͞ot′, -tūt′] *adj.* lacking.
devise [di vīz′] *v.* LAW. to leave to in a will.
diffident [dif′ə dənt] *adj.* lacking self-confidence; shy. **—diffidently,** *adv.*
diffusion [di fū′zhən] *n.* a spreading out.
digress [di gres′, dī-] *v.* to wander from the subject being discussed.
dilate [dī lāt′, di-] *v.* to enlarge or widen.
dilatory [dil′ə tôr′ē] *adj.* delaying; slow.
diligent [dil′ə jənt] *adj.* careful; persistent; hard-working.
dirge [durj] *n.* a slow, mournful piece of music.
disavow [dis′ə vou′] *v.* to deny responsibility for or connection with.
discern [di surn′, -zurn′] *v.* to perceive; detect; make out.
disconsolate [dis kon′sə lit] *adj.* unable to be comforted; hopelessly sad. **—disconsolately,** *adv.*
discourse [dis′kôrs′] *n.* **1.** conversation. **2.** a long talk or lecture. —*v.* to talk; converse.
discrete [dis krēt′] *adj.* separate.
discriminate [dis krim′ə nāt′] *v.* to show prejudice.
disintegrate [dis in′tə grāt′] *v.* to break up; come apart. **—disintegration,** *n.*
disjointed [dis join′tid] *adj.* not continuous or logical; disconnected. **—disjointedly,** *adv.*
dismast [dis mast′] *v.* to remove the mast of (a ship); take away or destroy the long pole supporting the sails.
disparage [dis par′ij] *v.* to speak of as having little value; belittle.
dispel [dis pel′] *v.* to break up and drive away; cause to disappear.
disposed [dis pōzd′] *adj.* willing; inclined.
disposition [dis′pə zish′ən] *n.* usual behavior or attitude; character.
dissolution [dis′ə lo͞o′shən] *n.* a breaking up; ending; dissolving.
dissonant [dis′ə nənt] *adj.* not in harmony. **—dissonance,** *n.*
dissuade [di swād′] *v.* to persuade not to do something.
distraught [dis trôt′] *adj.* very troubled or confused.
ditty [dit′ē] *n.* a little song.
diverge [di vurj′, dī-] *v.* to move in different directions.
divest [di vest′, dī-] *v.* to deprive.
divulge [di vulj′] *v.* to reveal; disclose.
dog days uncomfortably hot days of July and August.
doltish [dōl′tish] *adj.* stupid.
dominion [də min′yən] *n.* rule; power.
draggle [drag′əl] *v.* to make dirty by dragging on the ground.

E

ecclesiastical [i klē′zē as′ti kəl] *adj.* relating to the church.
eddy [ed′ē] *n.* a water or air current moving in a circular motion —*v.* to move in a circular motion.
educe [i do͞os′, i dūs′] *v.* to draw out; extract.
efface [i fās′] *v.* to wipe out; erase.
egotism [ē′gə tiz′əm, eg′ə-] *n.* conceitedness; self-centeredness.
élan [ā län′] *n.* spirit; energy; enthusiasm.
elevation [el′ə vā′shən] *n.* great joyfulness or liveliness.
elliptic [i lip′tik] *adj.* oval.
elongate [i lông′gāt] *v.* to lengthen.
elude [i lo͞od′] *v.* to avoid being seen or understood by. **—elusive** [i lo͞o′siv], *adj.*
emaciated [i mā′shē ā′tid] *adj.* extremely thin.
embassy [em′bə sē] *n.* a group of people representing others.
encumbrance [en kum′brəns] *n.* something that holds one back; a burden.
endow [en dou′] *v.* to provide.
engender [en jen′dər] *v.* to produce; cause.
enigmatic [en′ig mat′ik, ē′nig-] *adj.* mysterious; puzzling.
enmity [en′mə tē] *n.* hatred.
entreaty [en trē′tē] *n.* a humble request.
entrenchment [en trench′mənt] *n.* a trench or ditch used for protection.
enumeration [i no͞o′mə rā′shən, i nū′-] *n.* a list.
envoy [en′voi, än′-] *n.* a messenger.
ephemeral [i fem′ər əl] *adj.* lasting only a short time; fleeting.
epithet [ep′ə thet′] *n.* a descriptive word or phrase coming before or after or replacing a name.
equanimity [ēk′wə nim′ə tē, ek′-] *n.* calmness; self-control.
equity [ek′wə tē] *n.* fairness; justice.
equivocal [i kwiv′ə kəl] *adj.* having more than one meaning; ambiguous.
eradicate [i rad′ə kāt′] *v.* to pull out by the roots.
eruptive [i rup′tiv] *adj.* bursting out.
ethereal [i thēr′ē əl] *adj.* **1.** delicate; exquisite. **2.** relating to the upper regions of space; heavenly.
eulogy [u′lə jē] *n.* a statement praising someone who has died.
evanescent [ev′ə nes′ənt] *adj.* impermanent; fleeting. **—evanescently,** *adv.*
evangelist [i van′jə list] *n.* a preacher.
evince [i vins′] *v.* to give evidence of; indicate.

exhilaration [ig zil′ə rā′shən] *n.* a lively, excited feeling.
exhort [ig zôrt′] *v.* to attempt to persuade; urge strongly.
expatriate [eks pā′trē āt′] *v.* to force to leave one's country; exile.
expedient [iks pē′dē ənt] *adj.* useful for achieving a purpose; advantageous. —*n.* something useful for achieving a purpose. **—expediency,** *n.*
expeditionary [eks′pə dish′ə ner′ē] *adj.* relating to a journey.
expire [iks pīr′] *v.* to die.
expletive [eks′plə tiv] *n.* an exclamation or curse.
expostulation [iks pos′chə lā′shən] *n.* protest; objection.
extemporize [iks tem′pə rīz′] *v.* to make or do without preparation or to fill an immediate need; improvise.
extenuate [iks ten′ū āt′] *v.* to make seem less serious.
extort [iks tôrt′] *v.* to take by force or threats.
exude [ig zo͞od′, ik so͞od′] *v.* to drip or ooze out.
exult [ig zult′] *v.* to be joyful; rejoice. **—exultation** [eg′zul tā′shən, ek′sul-] *n.*

F

facilitate [fə sil′ə tāt′] *v.* to make easier.
facsimile [fak sim′ə lē] *n.* a copy.
faculty [fak′əl tē] *n.* a power of the mind.
fantasize [fan′tə sīz′] *v.* to imagine; daydream.
farce [färs] *n.* a ridiculous display; pretense.
fatuous [fach′o͞o əs] *adj.* foolish. **—fatuousness,** *n.*
feign [fān] *v.* ARCHAIC. to imagine.
felicitous [fi lis′ə təs] *adj.* **1.** suitable; appropriate. **2.** happy; fortunate.
felonious [fə lō′nē əs] *adj.* POETIC. wicked; villainous.
fervid [fur′vid] *adj.* showing great feeling or intensity.
figurative [fig′yər ə tiv] *adj.* not actual or literal; metaphoric. **—figuratively,** *adv.*
figure [fig′yər] *n.* a series of dance steps.
firmament [fur′mə mənt] *n.* the sky.
fissure [fish′ər] *n.* a deep crack.
fitful [fit′fəl] *adj.* stopping and starting; irregular.
flail [flāl] *n.* a tool made up of a freely swinging stick at the end of a long handle, used to separate grains from their husks.
flay [flā] *v.* **1.** to skin. **2.** to scold harshly.
flush [flush] *adv.* in line; level.
folio [fo′lē ō′] *n.* a book of the largest standard size.
forbear [fôr bār′] *v.* to keep from doing; resist.
formulate [fôr′myə lāt′] *v.* to reduce to a fixed phrase or rule.
forthwith [fôrth′with′, -with′] *adv.* immediately.
founder [foun′dər] *v.* to sink.
foundry [foun′drē] *n.* a place where metal is melted and formed into shapes.
fracas [frā′kəs] *n.* a loud disturbance.
freight [frāt] *v.* to load.
fritter [frit′ər] *v.* to waste little by little.
frugality [fro͞o gal′ə tē] *n.* thriftiness; unwastefulness.
fungo [fun′gō] *n.* a ball tossed up by a batter and hit for practice.

G

garrulous [gar′ə ləs, gar′yə-] *adj.* talkative.
gauge-cock [gāj′kok] a valve or faucet that is used to determine the amount of liquid in a container.
genealogist [jē′nē ol′ə jist, -al′-, jen′ē-] *n.* someone who traces the descent of a person or family from ancestors.
geological [jē′ə log′i kəl] *adj.* relating to the study of the structure and development of the earth's crust.
gill [gil] *n.* the organ for breathing in fish.
girt [gurt] *v.* to surround.
goad [gōd] *v.* to push; poke; urge.
gossamer [gos′ə mər] *adj.* delicate; filmy.
grapple [grap′əl] *v.* to struggle.
grog [grog] *n.* an alcoholic drink.
guileless [gīl′lis] *adj.* not sly or crafty; candid.

H

hack [hak] *n.* a carriage that can be rented.
handselled [han′səld] *adj.* related to beginnings; original.
haply [hap′lē] *adv.* ARCHAIC. by chance or luck.
hardihood [här′dē hood′] *n.* boldness; courage.
hazard [haz′ərd] *v.* to risk.
heather [heth′ər] *n.* an evergreen plant with stalks of small pinkish flowers, common in the British Isles.
heft [heft] *n.* weight; heaviness.
heliotrope [hē′lē ə trōp′, hēl′yə-] *n.* a plant with clusters of white or purplish flowers.
hie [hī] *v.* to move quickly; hurry.
hoary [hôr′ē] *adj.* **1.** white or gray with age. **2.** old; ancient.
hobgoblin [hob′gob′lin] *n.* a cause of concern or needless anxiety.
husband [huz′bənd] *v.* to handle economically.

I

ideology [ī′dē ol′ə jē, id′ē-] *n.* the ideas or theories that make up a political or social system.
illimitable [i lim′i tə bəl] *adj.* that cannot be limited or measured.
illiterate [i lit′ər it] *adj.* unable to read or write.
imbue [im bū′] *v.* to fill; spread through.
imminent [im′ə nənt] *adj.* about to happen; threatening.
immitigable [i mit′i gə bəl] *adj.* that cannot be made less severe or painful.
immune [i mūn′] *adj.* protected against or unaffected by something harmful.
impalpable [im pal′pə bəl] *adj.* that cannot be touched.
impassive [im pas′iv] *adj.* not showing any feelings. **—impassiveness,** *n.*
impenetrable [im pen′ə trə bəl] *adj.* that cannot be passed through.
imperceptible [im′pər sep′tə bəl] *adj.* extremely small or slow; not noticeable.
impersonate [im pur′sə nāt′] *v.* to act the part of; imitate.
impetuous [im pech′o͞o əs] *adj.* rushing forcefully; violent.
impetus [im′pə təs] *n.* a spurring to action; incentive.
impious [im′pē əs] *adj.* not showing respect for God.
implement [im′plə mənt] *n.* **1.** a tool. **2.** something used to achieve a purpose.
implication [im′plə kā′shən] *n.* something hinted or suggested.

at; āpe; cär; end; mē; it; īce; hot; ōld; fôrk; wood; fo͞ol; oil; out; up; ūse; turn; ə in ago; taken, pencil, lemon, circus; bat; chin; dear; five; game; hit; **hw** in **wh**ite; joke; kit; lid; man; not; singer; pail; ride; sat; shoe; tag; thin; this; very; wet; yes; zoo; **zh** in trea**s**ure; KH in lo**ch**, German a**ch**; N in French bo**n**; œ in French f**eu**, German sch**ö**n

importunate [im pôr′chə nit] *adj.* bothersomely urgent; demanding.
impotent [im′pət ənt] *adj.* weak; helpless.
imprecation [im′pri kā′shən] *n.* a curse.
impregnable [im preg′nə bəl] *adj.* that cannot be entered by force or captured; unconquerable.
impressible [im pres′ə bəl] *adj.* able to be marked by pressing or influenced.
impropriety [im′prə prī′ə tē] *n.* improper behavior.
inaccessible [in′ək ses′ə bəl] *adj.* unreachable.
inaccommodate [in′ə kom′ə dāt] *adj.* unsuitable; unfit.
inanimate [in an′ə mit] *adj.* not living.
incantation [in′kan tā′shən] *n.* the chanting of magical spells or charms.
incense [in sens′] *v.* to anger greatly.
incertitude [in sur′tə to͞od′, -tūd′] *n.* uncertainty; doubt.
incessant [in ses′ənt] *adj.* never stopping; constant. **—incessantly,** *adv.*
incongruous [in kong′gro͞o əs] *adj.* inconsistent; inappropriate.
incorrigible [in kôr′ə jə bəl, -kor′-] *adj.* not capable of being corrected or improved.
indecorous [in dek′ər əs, in′di kôr′əs] *adj.* not proper or well-mannered.
indolence [ind′əl əns] *n.* laziness.
indomitable [in dom′ə tə bəl] *adj.* that cannot be controlled or conquered.
ineffable [in ef′ə bəl] *adj.* that cannot be put into words; indescribable.
inexplicable [in′iks plik′ə bəl, in eks′pli kə-] *adj.* not explainable or understandable.
infelicitous [in′fə lis′ə təs] *adj.* not appropriate.
inferential [in′fə ren′shəl] *adj.* concluded or figured out from facts or assumptions. **—inferentially,** *adv.*
infest [in fest′] *v.* to spread over; overrun.
ingenuity [in′jə no͞o′ə tē, -nū′-] *n.* cleverness.
ingenuous [in jen′ū əs] *adj.* open; simple; naive.
iniquity [in ik′wə tē] *n.* wickedness.
inordinate [in ôr′də nit] *adj.* excessive.
inscrutable [in skro͞o′tə bəl] *adj.* difficult to understand; mysterious.
insensible [in sen′sə bəl] *adj.* **1.** not capable of feeling. **2.** not aware. **—insensibly,** *adv.*
insidious [in sid′ē əs] *adj.* sly; deceitful.
insipid [in sip′id] *adj.* bland; tasteless.
insistent [in sis′tənt] *adj.* standing firmly; persistent.
insolence [in′sə ləns] *n.* disrespectfulness; impertinence.
inspiration [in′spə rā′shən] *n.* a breathing in.
intercept [in′tər sept′] *v.* NOW RARE. to interfere with; hinder.
interment [in tur′mənt] *n.* burial.
intermittent [in′tər mit′ənt] *adj.* stopping at intervals; going on and off.
interpose [in′tər pōz′] *v.* to come between; interrupt.
intimate [in′tə māt′] *v.* to hint; suggest.
intractable [in trak′tə bəl] *adj.* difficult to handle or work with.
introspective [in trə spek′tiv] *adj.* looking inward; examining one's own thoughts and feelings.
invariable [in vār′ē ə bəl] *adj.* not changing; always the same. **—invariably,** *adv.*
inviolable [in vī′ə lə bəl] *adj.* that must not be disturbed or debased; sacred.
inviolate [in vī′ə lit, -lāt′] *adj.* whole; pure; sacred.
irreproachable [ir′i prō′chə bəl] *adj.* faultless.
irruption [i rup′shən] *n.* OBSOLETE. a violent outburst: variation of **eruption.**
isolate [ī′sə lāt, is′ə-] *adj.* separated from others.

J

jaded [jā′did] *adj.* worn out; exhausted.
jag [jag] *n.* a sharp point that juts out.
jeopardy [jep′ər dē] *n.* great danger.
jocular [jok′yə lər] *adj.* **1.** joking; merry. **2.** like a joke; funny.
juxtapose [juks′tə pōz′] *v.* to put next to one another.

K

kindred [kin′drid] *adj.* similar; related.

L

languid [lang′gwid] *adj.* lacking liveliness.
lapse [laps] *n.* the passing of time.
latter-day [lat′ər dā′] *adj.* modern.
lattice [lat′is] *n.* a structure made of crossed strips of wood or metal, used as a screen, shutter, etc.
laurel [lôr′əl, lor′-] *n.* **1.** an evergreen tree or bush with large leaves and yellowish flowers. **2.** a wreath or crown made of laurel leaves and worn as a symbol of honor.
lean-to [lēn′to͞o′] *n.* a small, rough building with a roof that slopes in one direction, the higher end leaning against a wall or other support.
levy [lev′ē] *v.* to conduct or wage (war).
libel [lī′bəl] *v.* to write or print damaging information about a person.
license [lī′səns] *n.* freedom.
lineage [lin′ē ij] *n.* family descent; ancestry.
literalist [lit′ər əl ist] *n.* a realist.
livid [liv′id] *adj.* grayish or whitish; pale. **—lividly,** *adv.*
loll [lol] *v.* to hang loosely; droop.
lowering [lo′ə ring] *adj.* dark; threatening.
lucid [lo͞o′sid] *adj.* **1.** clear; understandable. **2.** thinking clearly; rational. **—lucidity,** *n.*
ludicrous [lo͞o′də krəs] *adj.* ridiculous.
lugubrious [loo go͞o′brē əs, -gū′-] *adj.* exaggeratedly sad or mournful. **—lugubriousness,** *n.*
lurid [loor′id] *adj.* glowing through smoke or haze.
lusty [lus′tē] *adj.* strong; vigorous. **—lustily,** *adv.*

M

mace [mās] *n.* a heavy club.
magnanimity [mag′nə nim′ə tē] *n.* generosity and forgivingness; nobility.
malediction [mal′ə dik′shən] *n.* a curse.
malevolence [mə lev′ə ləns] *n.* ill will; spite.
mangy [mān′jē] *adj.* low; contemptible.
manifest [man′ə fest] *v.* to show; reveal.
mansion [man′shən] *n.* a dwelling, usually large and luxurious.
mantle [mant′əl] *n.* something that covers or envelops.
mar [mär] *v.* to damage; spoil.
martial [mär′shəl] *adj.* relating to war.
materialist [mə tēr′ē ə list] *n.* a person more interested in possessions and physical comfort than in ideas and beliefs.
maudlin [môd′lin] *adj.* foolishly sentimental.

maul [môl] *n.* a heavy hammer.
maxim [mak′sim] *n.* a short statement expressing a rule or principle; saying.
mayhem [mā′hem, mā′əm] *n.* LAW. the injuring or crippling of a person.
mean [mēn] *adj.* average.
means [mēnz] *n.pl.* **1.** something used to achieve a purpose. **2.** resources.
mediate [mē′dē āt′] *v.* to settle differences; bring opposing sides together. **—mediator,** *n.*
mentor [men′tər] *n.* an adviser or teacher.
mercenary [mur′sə ner′ē] *n.* a soldier paid to fight in the army of a foreign country.
meteorological [mē′tē ər ə loj′i kəl] *adj.* referring to weather.
meticulous [mi tik′yə ləs] *adj.* extremely concerned or careful about details.
miasma [mī az′mə, mē-] *n.* fumes coming from a swamp or from decaying matter, once thought to be poisonous.
mimic [mim′ik] *v.* to copy; imitate.
minister [min′is tər] *v.* to give; provide.
ministry [min′is trē] *n.* the members of a government administration.
misanthropic [mis′ən throp′ik, miz′-] *adj.* having hatred or contempt for people.
misgiving [mis giv′ing] *n.* a feeling of doubt or worry.
mitigate [mit′ə gāt′] *v.* to make less intense or painful.
mobile [mō′bəl, -bēl] *adj.* able to move or flow; changeable.
mode [mōd] *n.* a way of doing something; method.
moderate [mod′ər it] *adj.* mild. **—moderately,** *adv.*
modulate [moj′ə lāt′] *v.* to change in pitch or intensity.
molder [mōl′dər] *v.* to crumble; decay.
morass [mə ras′] *n.* an area of soft, wet ground; marsh.
mottled [mot′əld] *adj.* spotted or streaked with color.
mutation [mū tā′shən] *n.* a change.
myriad [mir′ē əd] *adj.* very many; countless.
mystic [mis′tik] *adj.* mysterious.
mystical [mis′ti kəl] *adj.* relating to experiences beyond human reasoning; spiritual; mysterious.

N

natty [nat′ē] *adj.* neat; trim.
nectar [nek′tər] *n.* a delicious drink.
nocturne [nok′turn′] *n.* a dreamy, romantic musical composition appropriate to the evening.

O

obdurate [ob′dər it, ob′dyər-] *adj.* stubborn; unbending; hardened.
obeisance [ō bā′səns, ō bē′-] *n.* a respectful movement or gesture; bow.
obliterate [ə blit′ə rāt′] *v.* to wipe out; erase.
obscurity [əb skyoor′ə tē] *n.* darkness; unclearness; cloudiness.
obtrude [əb trood′] *v.* to call attention to or force on others without being asked.
obtuse [əb toos′, -tūs′] *adj.* slow in understanding; insensitive.
occult [ə kult′, ok′ult] *adj.* relating to things beyond normal experience; secret; mysterious.
octavo [ok tā′vō, -tä′-] *n.* a book about six by nine inches in size.
omnipotent [om nip′ət ənt] *adj.* having unlimited power.
onset [ôn′set′, on′-] *n.* beginning.
oppress [ə pres′] *v.* **1.** to rule over or keep down unfairly or cruelly. **2.** to weigh down; depress. **—oppressive,** *adj.*
orifice [ôr′ə fis, or′-] n. a hole; opening.
ostentation [os′tən tā′shən] *n.* a showing off; pretentiousness. **—ostentatious,** *adj.*
oust [oust] *v.* to drive out.
overbearing [ō′vər bār′ing] *adj.* arrogant.

P

pall [pôl] *n.* a cloth used to cover a coffin.
pallid [pal′id] *adj.* pale; whitish.
palpable [pal′pə bəl] *adj.* understandable; obvious.
palsy [pôl′zē] *n.* a condition marked by a shaking or trembling of a part of the body.
parable [par′ə bəl] *n.* a short story that illustrates a basic truth or moral principle.
paradoxical [par′ə dok′sə kəl] *adj.* seemingly contradictory or nonsensical but probably true.
parley [pär′lē] *n.* a conference for settling a dispute.
parsimony [pär′sə mō′nē] *n.* thriftiness; stinginess; miserliness.
passivity [pa siv′ə tē] *n.* lack of resistance; tendency to give in; meekness.
pathos [pā′thos] *n.* a feeling of sympathy or compassion.
patriarch [pā′trē ärk′] *n.* a father, founder, or leader; respected old man.
peat [pēt] *n.* partially decayed plant matter that is dried and used as a fuel.
pedestrian [pə des′trē ən] *adj.* moving on foot; walking.
pension [pen′shən] *v.* to grant (someone who has retired) regular payments of money.
pensive [pen′siv] *adj.* dreamily or sadly thoughtful. **—pensively,** *adv.*
pent [pent] *adj.* kept in; shut up.
penumbra [pi num′brə] *n.* the partially shaded area surrounding an area of total eclipse or shadow.
perdition [pər dish′ən] *n.* hell.
peremptory [pə remp′tər ē] *adj.* not permitting argument or delay; commanding. **—peremptorily,** *adv.*
perennial [pə ren′ē əl] *adj.* present all year.
periphery [pə rif′ər ē] *n.* the edge; perimeter.
perpetual [pər pech′oo əl] *adj.* eternal.
pertinacity [purt′ən as′ə tē] *n.* firmness; stubbornness.
perturbation [pur′tər bā′shən] *n.* the state of being disturbed or upset.
perusal [pə roo′zəl] *n.* study; examination.
pervade [pər vād′] *v.* to spread throughout.
perversion [pər vur′zhən, -shən] *n.* distortion.
pestilent [pes′tə lənt] *adj.* deadly.
phenomenon [fə nom′ə non′, -nən] *n., pl.* **phenomena** a fact or event that can be observed.
phosphorescent [fos′fə res′ənt] *adj.* shining or glowing after exposure to light.

at; **ā**pe; c**ä**r; **e**nd; m**ē**; **i**t; **ī**ce; h**o**t; **ō**ld; f**ô**rk; w**oo**d; f**oo**l; **oi**l; **ou**t; **u**p; **ū**se; t**ur**n; **ə** in **a**go; tak**e**n, penc**i**l, lem**o**n, circ**u**s; **b**at; **ch**in; **d**ear; **f**ive; **g**ame; **h**it; **hw** in **wh**ite; **j**oke; **k**it; **l**id; **m**an; **n**ot; si**ng**er; **p**ail; **r**ide; **s**at; **sh**oe; **t**ag; **th**in; **th**is; **v**ery; **w**et; **y**es; **z**oo; **zh** in trea**s**ure; **KH** in lo**ch**, German a**ch**; **N** in French bo**n**; **œ** in French f**eu**, German sch**ö**n

phraseology [frā′zē ol′ə jē] *n.* wording.
physiognomy [fiz′ē og′nə mē, -on′ə mē] *n.* features; expression; appearance.
pilfer [pil′fər] *v.* to steal.
pinnacle [pin′ə kəl] *n.* a peak.
pittance [pit′əns] *n.* a small amount of money.
platitude [plat′ə to͞od′, -tūd′] *n.* a dull, commonplace remark or idea.
plunge [plunj] *v.* to throw oneself; rush.
politic [pol′ə tik] *adj.* carefully polite.
pomp [pomp] *n.* showiness; splendor.
poncho [pon′chō] *n.* a garment made of a piece of waterproof material with a hole for the head, worn as a raincoat.
ponderous [pon′dər əs] *adj.* heavy and clumsy.
poop [po͞op] *n.* a raised deck at the back of a ship.
portend [pôr tend′] *v.* to give a sign or warning of (a future happening).
portent [pôr′tent] *n.* a sign or warning of something that will happen; omen.
posterity [pos ter′ə tē] *n.* descendants.
precipitous [pri sip′ə təs] *adj.* extremely steep; almost straight up and down.
precocious [pri kō′shəs] *adj.* more mature than is usual for one's age.
predecessor [pred′ə ses′ər] *n.* one who came before.
predispose [prē′dis pōz′] *v.* to make inclined (to do something) ahead of time.
pre-empt [prē empt′] *v.* to take or claim before others can.
prerogative [pri rog′ə tiv] *n.* a special right or power.
presage [pres′ij, pri sāj′] *v.* to give a sign or warning of (a future happening).
prescience [prē′shē əns, presh′ē-] *n.* knowledge of events before they happen.
presume [pri zo͞om′] *v.* to do without permission; be overly bold; dare.
prevail [pri vāl′] *v.* to triumph.
prevalent [prev′ə lənt] *adj.* common.
pristine [pris′tēn] *adj.* pure; unspoiled.
procure [prə kyoor′] *v.* to get; obtain.
prodigy [prod′ə jē] *n.* RARE. an amazing occurrence.
profuse [prə fūs′] *adj.* abundant.
progenitor [prō jen′ə tər] *n.* source; forerunner; ancestor.
prolixity [prō lik′sə tē] *n.* wordiness.
propitious [prə pish′əs] *adj.* favorable; gracious.
prostrate [pros′trāt] *adj.* lying flat or with the face down. —*v.* to cause to lie flat or give in; make humble.
protract [prō trakt′] *v.* to draw out; lengthen.
proverbial [prə vur′bē əl] *adj.* of a proverb or saying.
prowess [prou′is] *n.* extraordinary ability or skill.
proximity [prok sim′ə tē] *n.* nearness.
prudence [pro͞od′əns] *n.* carefulness; caution.
psalm [säm, sälm] *n.* a religious song or poem.
psalmist [sä′mist, säl′mist] *n.* one who writes psalms.
pullet [pool′it] *n.* a young hen.
puny [pū′nē] *adj.* small; weak; unimportant. **—punily,** adv.

Q

quaff [kwäf, kwaf] *v.* to drink thirstily.
quagmire [kwag′mīr′, kwog′-] *n.* soft, wet ground that one's feet sink into.
quartermaster [kwôr′tər mas′tər] *n.* a person on a ship who takes care of navigation and signals.
quarto [kwôr′tō] *n.* a book about nine by twelve inches in size.
querulous [kwer′ə ləs, kwer′yə-] *adj.* complaining; irritable.

R

rally [ral′ē] *v.* to recover; revive.
ramshackle [ram′shak′əl] *adj.* appearing ready to fall apart; rickety.
rapt [rapt] *adj.* showing great joy or pleasure.
ravenous [rav′ə nəs] *adj.* extremely hungry. **—ravenously,** *adv.*
reaffirm [rē′ə furm′] *v.* to declare again to be true.
recluse [rek′lo͞os, ri klo͞os′] *n.* a person who lives shut off from the world.
recoil [ri koil′, rē′koil′] *n.* the distance that a gun jumps back when fired.
recompense [rek′əm pens′] *v.* to repay. —*n.* repayment.
reconnoiter [rē′kə noi′tər, rek′ə-] *v.* to explore an area for information about the enemy.
recreate [rek′rē āt′] *v.* to refresh by play or relaxation.
rectitude [rek′tə to͞od′, -tūd′] *n.* correctness.
recumbent [ri kum′bənt] *adj.* lying down; resting.
redolent [red′əl ənt] *adj.* filled with a certain quality; suggestive.
redoubtable [ri dou′tə bəl] *adj.* causing fear.
reft [reft] *adj.* robbed or deprived.
regalia [ri gā′lē ə, -gāl′yə] *n.pl.* badges, symbols, or clothing indicating a certain position.
regenerate [ri jen′ə rāt′] *v.* to renew; reform; improve.
reign [rān] *n.* the period of rule or dominance.
reiterate [rē it′ə rāt′] *v.* to repeat.
relent [ri lent′] *v.* to become less stern or stubborn; soften.
relief [ri lēf′] *n.* clearness of outline; contrast.
relinquish [ri ling′kwish] *v.* to give up; surrender. **—relinquishment,** *n.*
remonstrance [ri mon′strəns] *n.* protest.
remonstrate [ri mon′strāt] *v.* to protest.
render [ren′dər] *v.* to represent in a picture; portray.
renovate [ren′ə vāt′] *v.* to make like new.
repast [ri past′] *n.* a meal.
replenish [ri plen′ish] *v.* to fill or supply again, as with fuel.
replete [ri plēt′] *adj.* filled.
reprieve [ri prēv′] *n.* a postponement of punishment.
resignation [rez′ig nā′shən] *n.* unresisting or passive acceptance.
resolve [ri zolv′] *v.* to decide.
resounding [ri zoun′ding] *adj.* ringing; echoing.
respite [res′pit] *n.* a period of rest or relief.
reticent [ret′ə sənt] *adj.* reluctant to speak; reserved.
retina [ret′ən ə] *n.* the part of the eye that is sensitive to light and receives the image formed by the lens.
retract [ri trakt′] *v.* to take back.
retrospection [ret′rə spek′shən] *n.* the act of looking back on the past.
revel [rev′əl] *v.* to celebrate wildly and noisily. **—reveler,** *n.*
rhetoric [ret′ər ik] *n.* showy language.
ricochet [rik′ə shā′] *n.* a slanting rebound of an object off a surface.
rife [rīf] *adj.* abundant; filled (with).
rift [rift] *v.* to break open; split.
ritualize [rich′o͞o ə līz] *v.* to make into a formal ceremony or custom.

rote [rōt] *n.* a repetitive or routine procedure. **—by rote** by memory rather than with thought.
rout [rout] *n.* a fast, confused running away or retreat.
rude [rood] *adj.* roughly made or done.

S

sagacious [sə gā'shəs] *adj.* having sound judgment; wise. **—sagacity** [sə gas'ə tē], *n.*
sally [sal'ē] *v.* to go out; set out; leave.
sanctify [sangk'tə fī'] *v.* to make holy.
sanctity [sangk'tə tē] *n.* holiness.
savant [sa vänt', sə-, sav'ənt] *n.* a person with great learning or knowledge.
scant [skant] *v.* to give less than enough.
scoff [skof, skôf] *v.* to show contempt; jeer.
scruple [skroo'pəl] *v.* to hesitate to do something because it may be wrong.
scuttle [skut'əl] *v.* to move with short, rapid steps.
semblance [sem'bləns] *n.* appearance; likeness.
sententious [sen ten'shəs] *adj.* fond of using trite phrases or maxims. **—sententiously,** *adv.*
sepulcher [sep'əl kər] *n.* a grave or tomb.
sepulchral [si pul'krəl] *adj.* tomblike; gloomy.
servile [sur'vil, -vīl] *adj.* slavelike.
sexton [seks'tən] *n.* a church official who takes care of church property.
shag [shag] *v.* to run after balls during practice.
shoal [shōl] *adj.* shallow.
shroud [shroud] *n.* a cloth for wrapping a dead body for burial.
shy [shī] *v.* to jump back suddenly when frightened.
simper [sim'pər] *v.* to say with a silly smile.
sinew [sin'ū] *v.* to strengthen or support.
singular [sing'gyə lər] *adj.* strange; remarkable.
skein [skān] *n.* a coil of thread or yarn.
skim [skim] *v.* to glide.
skirt [skurt] *v.* to move along the edge; pass around.
skulk [skulk] *v.* to move or hide stealthily or fearfully.
slough[1] [sluf] *n.* a snake's outer skin.
slough[2] [slou] *n.* an area of deep mud.
smite [smīt] *v.* to strike hard.
solace [sol'is] *v.* to comfort; console. *—n.* comfort; relief.
solicitous [sə lis'ə təs] *adj.* full of concern or anxiety. **—solicitude,** *n.*
soliloquy [sə lil'ə kwē] *n.* the act of talking to oneself.
solstice [sol'stis] *n.* either of two times during the year (**summer solstice** and **winter solstice**) when the sun is farthest from the equator.
sooth [sooth] *n.* ARCHAIC. truth.
sophistication [sə fis'tə kā'shən] *n.* the state of being cultured and experienced.
sough [sou, suf] *v.* to make a sighing or rustling sound. **—soughingly,** *adv.*
souvenir [soo'və nēr', soo'və nēr'] *n.* something kept as a reminder of a person or event.
spasmodic [spaz mod'ik] *adj.* happening in short, violent bursts; stopping and starting.
specific [spi sif'ik] *n.* a remedy for a particular ailment.
specter [spek'tər] *n.* a ghost. **—spectral** [spek'trəl], *adj.*
speculative [spek'yə lā'tiv, -lə tiv] *adj.* relating to thinking about or considering something.
spoil [spoil] *n.* something looted or robbed.
spook [spook] *v.* COLLOQUIAL. to become frightened; jump suddenly because of fright.
squander [skwon'dər] *v.* to spend foolishly; waste.
stance [stans] *n.* the placement of the body or feet.
statistician [stat'is tish'ən] *n.* a person who collects and organizes numerical data about a subject.
staunch [stônch, stänch] *adj.* firm; loyal; determined. **—staunchness,** *n.*
stereotyped [ster'ē ə tīpt', stēr'-] *adj.* typical; not individual.
strand [strand] *n.* a string or thread.
stratum [strā'təm, strat'əm, strä'təm] *n., pl.* **strata** a layer.
stricken [strik'ən] *adj.* strongly affected or distressed by something unpleasant, painful, etc.
strife [strīf] *n.* struggle; conflict.
stringency [strin'jən sē] *n.* harshness; strictness.
stubble [stub'əl] *n.* the bottoms of stalks of grain left after harvesting.
subjugation [sub'jə gā'shən] *n.* the state of being ruled over or controlled.
sublime [səb līm'] *adj.* lofty; noble; glorious.
subsistence [səb sis'təns] *n.* means of living; livelihood.
subterranean [sub'tə rā'nē ən] *adj.* underground; hidden.
succor [suk'ər] *n.* help or relief.
suffer [suf'ər] *v.* to allow.
sufferance [suf'ər əns, suf'rəns] *n.* toleration.
suffice [sə fīs'] *v.* **1.** to be enough. **2.** to satisfy.
suit [soot] *v.* ARCHAIC. to agree; correspond.
sumptuous [sump'choo əs] *adj.* luxurious; splendid.
sundry [sun'drē] *n.* some number; various ones.
supine [soo pīn'] *adj.* not active; not resisting or caring; meek. **—supinely,** *adv.*
supple [sup'əl] *adj.* able to bend easily; limber; flexible.
supplication [sup'lə kā'shən] *n.* the act of asking humbly for something.
suppress [sə pres'] *v.* to hold back or keep in.
surcease [sur sēs'] *n.* an end; stopping.
surmise [sər mīz'] *v.* to guess; imagine.
sward [swôrd] *n.* grassy ground.
swathe [swoth, swôth] *v.* to wrap.
synchronize [sing'krə nīz'] *v.* to cause to happen together or at the same speed.
synopsize [si nop'sīz] *v.* to shorten; summarize.

T

tablet [tab'lit] *n.* a flat piece of wood, stone, etc.
tacit [tas'it] *adj.* not stated but suggested or understood.
taint [tānt] *n.* a hint of decay or contamination.
temerity [tə mer'ə tē] *n.* foolhardy boldness; recklessness.
temperance [tem'pər əns, tem'prəns] *n.* restraint; moderation.
tempered [tem'pərd] *adj.* having been brought to the correct texture or hardness.
tenacious [ti nā'shəs] *adj.* tending to hang on and not give up; stubborn. **—tenaciously,** *adv.*

at; **ā**pe; c**ä**r; **e**nd; m**ē**; **i**t; **ī**ce; h**o**t; **ō**ld; f**ô**rk; w**oo**d; f**oo**l; **oi**l; **ou**t; **u**p; **ū**se; t**u**rn; **ə** in **a**go; tak**e**n, penc**i**l, lem**o**n, circ**u**s; **b**at; **ch**in; **d**ear; **f**ive; **g**ame; **h**it; **hw** in **wh**ite; **j**oke; **k**it; **l**id; **m**an; **n**ot; si**ng**er; **p**ail; **r**ide; **s**at; **sh**oe; **t**ag; **th**in; **th**is; **v**ery; **w**et; **y**es; **z**oo; **zh** in trea**s**ure; **KH** in lo**ch**, German a**ch**; **N** in French bo**n**; **œ** in French f**eu**, German sch**ö**n

tensile [ten′sil, -sīl] *adj.* pulled tightly; taut.
tenuity [ti no͞o′ə tē, -nū′-, te-] *n.* thinness.
tenuous [ten′ū əs] *adj.* weak; flimsy.
tenure [ten′yər] *n.* the conditions under which or length of time for which an office or position is held.
terrestrial [tə res′trē əl] *adj.* earthly.
testimonial [tes′tə mō′nē əl] *n.* a showing of appreciation.
thanatopsis [than′ə top′sis] *n.* a view of death.
thither [thith′ər] *adv.* there.
thoroughfare [thur′ə fâr′] *n.* a main street.
thrall [thrôl] *adj.* ARCHAIC. enslaved.
throe [thrō] *n.* a sudden, sharp pain or muscular contraction.
timorous [tim′ər əs] *adj.* fearful; timid.
toilsome [toil′səm] *adj.* involving work; difficult.
torpidity [tôr pid′ə tē] *n.* lack of energy or interest; dullness.
torpor [tôr′pər] *n.* a state of inactivity, or sluggishness.
torrential [tô ren′chəl, tə-] *adj.* streaming violently or rapidly.
transcendent [tran sen′dənt] *adj.* beyond ordinary experience or physical existence.
transfigure [trans fig′yər] *v.* to change the appearance of.
transient [tran′shənt] *adj.* staying for a short time; temporary.
transition [tran zish′ən] *n.* a moving from one condition or stage to another.
transpire [tran spīr′] *v.* to happen.
transverse [trans vurs′, tranz-] *adj.* going across.
travail [trə vāl′, trav′āl] *n.* **1.** difficult work. **2.** great pain.
trellis [trel′is] *n.* a structure made of crossed strips of wood, on which vines grow.
tremor [trem′ər] *n.* a trembling or shaking.
tremulous [trem′yə ləs] *adj.* trembling; shaking.
trepidation [trep′ə dā′shən] *n.* fear; anxiety.
trestle [tres′əl] *n.* a framework for supporting something.
tribute [trib′ūt] *n.* something given or done as a sign of respect or gratitude.
triviality [triv′ē al′ə tē] *n.* the state of being ordinary or unimportant.
type [tīp] *n.* a thing or person that represents another.
typify [tip′ə fī′] *v.* to represent; symbolize.

U

unaccountable [un′ə koun′tə bəl] *adj.* unexplainable; mysterious.
unction [ungk′shən] *n.* strong feeling or intensity in one's speech or behavior.
undeviating [un dē′vē ā′ting] *adj.* not turning to the side or branching off.
undistracted [un′dis trak′tid] *adj.* not having one's attention drawn to something else.
undulation [un′jə lā′shən, -dyə-] *n.* a wavelike motion.
unfurl [un furl′] *v.* to open; unroll.
ungainly [un gān′lē] *adj.* awkward or unattractive.
unitary [ū′nə ter′ē] *adj.* being one; single.
unnerve [un nurv′] *v.* to frighten or upset.
unobtrusive [un′əb tro͞o′siv] *adj.* not calling attention to itself.
unperverted [un′pər vur′tid] *adj.* not turned from what is good or right.
unprecedented [un pres′ə den′tid] *adj.* not having happened before; without match; new.
unremitting [un′ri mit′ing] *adj.* not letting up; constant.
unseared [un sērd′] *adj.* not scorched or withered.
unseemly [un sēm′lē] *adj.* not proper.
unsubstantiality [un′səb stan′shē al′ə tē] *n.* unreality.
unwonted [un wôn′tid, -wōn′-] *adj.* not common or usual.
urn [urn] *n.* a pot for serving hot drinks.

V

vagabond [vag′ə bond′] *adj.* like a person who moves from place to place; wandering.
vagary [və gār′ē, vā′gər ē] *n.* a strange action or idea.
vainglory [vān′glôr′ē, vān glôr′ē] *n.* boastful conceit; vanity.
vale [vāl] *n.* CHIEFLY POETIC. a valley.
valid [val′id] *adj.* sound; convincing; correct.
vanquish [vang′kwish, van′-] *v.* to defeat; conquer.
vaulted [vôl′tid] *adj.* having an arched ceiling.
vehement [vē′ə mənt] *adj.* having great force or feeling. **—vehemently,** *adv.*
venerable [ven′ər ə bəl] *adj.* deserving respect because of age, character, or achievements.
vent [vent] *n.* a way for passage; outlet.
verisimilitude [ver′ə si mil′ə to͞od′, -tud′] *n.* the appearance of truth or reality.
verity [ver′ə tē] *n.* a belief or principle accepted as true.
vernacular [vər nak′yə lər] *adj.* the language commonly spoken by people in a particular place.
vest [vest] *v.* to give a person or group the right to or control of.
vibrancy [vi′brən sē] *n.* the quality of pulsating with life or energy.
vicarious [vī kār′ē əs, vi-] *adj.* acting in place of another. **—vicariously,** *adv.*
vindictive [vin dik′tiv] *adj.* wanting revenge; vengeful.
virtuosity [vur′cho͞o os′ə tē] *n.* great skill in music, art, etc.
visage [viz′ij] *n.* a person's face.
vituperative [vī to͞o′pə rā′tiv, -pər ə tiv, -tū′-, vi-] *adj.* harshly insulting or scolding.
vociferation [vō sif′ə rā′shən] *n.* a loud outcry.
volatility [vol′ə til′ə tē] *n.* the state of flying or moving around constantly; liveliness; explosiveness.
volley [vol′ē] *n.* a burst of bullets, words, etc., sent out at once.

W

waft [waft, wäft] *v.* to send or carry gently through or as if through air or water.
waggery [wag′ər ē] *n.* mischievous playfulness or joking.
wax [waks] *v.* to become; grow.
wean [wēn] *v.* to accustom (someone) gradually to stopping or losing something.
whetstone [hwet′stōn′, wet′-] *n.* a stone for sharpening blades.
whirr [hwur, wur] *v.* to move rapidly with a buzzing sound.
wily [wi′lē] *adj.* sly; crafty. **—wiliness,** *n.*
wistful [wist′fəl] *adj.* longing sadly; yearning. **—wistfully,** *adv.*
wont [wōnt, wônt, wunt] *adj.* accustomed; used.
wrangle [rang′gəl] *v.* to quarrel or argue noisily.
wreak [rēk] *v.* to let out or express fully; inflict.
wreathe [rēth] *v.* to twist or coil.
wrought [rôt] past tense and past participle of **work.**

Z

zenith [zē′nith] *n.* the point in the sky directly above the observer.

VOCABULARY REVIEW

In addition to the words listed in the Glossary and the words covered in the word study sections throughout this book, each of the following words is presented to help you prepare for standardized tests of verbal skills. The page numbers at the right tell where you can find these words treated in *American Literature.*

accolades	651
admonish	64
adversity	29
affronted	711
altitude	660
anachronism	651
angling	22
array	87
avowed	832
barbaric	211
barnacles	560
battered	560
beating	287
belied	601
billow	287
blight	124
bolt	535
calamities	29
censure	64
chaff	535
coalesced	651
conclusion	287
contempt	455
crackled	366
desolation	660
diligent	711
disconsolately	601
discourse	29
discriminate	455
freighted	366
geological	211
gills	560
hazard	22
hazard	29
heather	287
heft	287
hoary	124
hollow	211
immune	601
impenetrable	660
implements	535
incessantly	39
incorrigible	64
infested	560
ingenuity	64
insensible	124
insolence	455
jeopardy	39
juxtaposed	651
lugubriousness	711
magnanimity	22
martial	87
maul	535
modulate	832
Muse	87
onset	287
oust	39
overbearing	601
pall	124
pensive	87
phenomena	455
physiognomy	832
plunged	366
poncho	660
posterity	22
precipitous	660
propitious	87
ramshackle	832
recompense	22
rectitude	64
regalia	651
reprieve	39
resolved	39
resounding	832
retract	601
savant	711
sepulchral	211
skim	366
skirted	366
stricken	211
succor	29
treading	287
triviality	455
unobtrusively	711
vales	124
venerable	560

INDEX OF TITLES BY THEME

This index groups all of the selections in this book according to the themes that they portray. Every selection is listed at least once; many are listed more than once. You may want to use this Index to help students examine the presentation of a particular theme in different selections.

INDEX OF TITLES BY THEME

THE POWER OF NATURE

SELF-RELIANCE

FRIENDSHIP AND LOVE

FAMILY PORTRAITS

GROWTH AND CHANGE

MEMORY AND TIME

CONFLICT AND RESOLUTION

LOSS AND RECOVERY

ART AND IMAGINATION

VISIONS AND IDEALS

INDEX OF TITLES BY GENRE

INDEX OF TITLES BY GENRE

This index classifies all of the selections in this book according to genre. Every selection is listed once. You may want to use this Index to help students examine the differences between types of literature.

SHORT STORY

SONG

SPEECH

INDEX OF SKILLS

Page numbers in boldface italics indicate entries in the Writing About Literature Handbook.
Page numbers in italics indicate entries in the Literary Terms Handbook.

See the Table of Contents for list of complete *lessons* on Speaking and Listening Skills, Thinking Skills, Researching Skills, and Writing Skills.

LITERARY SKILLS

INDEX OF SKILLS

This index lists the Literary Skills, Composition Skills, and Vocabulary Skills taught in this book, along with the pages on which those skills are taught or reinforced. For example, every Composition assignment in this book is listed in the Composition Skills section of this index. Page numbers in boldface indicate entries in the Writing About Literature Handbook. Page numbers in italics indicate entries in the Reading and Literary Terms Handbook.

COMPOSITION SKILLS

Page numbers in bold face italics indicate entries in the Writing About Literature Handbook.

ANALYTICAL

CREATIVE

VOCABULARY SKILLS

TEST-TAKING SKILLS

WORD STUDY

INDEX OF AUTHORS AND TITLES

This index is an alphabetical listing of all the selections and authors included in this book. Page numbers in italics indicate biographical information.

INDEX OF AUTHORS AND TITLES

Page numbers in italics indicate biographical material.

TEACHER'S PERSONAL RECORD

Most Successful Assignments and Projects

Page Notes

TEACHER'S PERSONAL RECORD

Most Successful Assignments and Projects

Page Notes

TEACHER'S PERSONAL RECORD

Most Successful Pairings or Groupings of Selections

TEACHER'S PERSONAL RECORD

Most Successful Pairings or Groupings of Selections

TEACHER'S PERSONAL RECORD

Original Assignments and Projects

Literary work being taught	My original assignment or project

TEACHER'S PERSONAL RECORD

Original Assignments and Projects

Literary work being taught	My original assignment or project

TEACHER'S PERSONAL RECORD

Additional Resources

Literary work being taught	Title and location of article, illustration, recording, film, etc.

TEACHER'S PERSONAL RECORD

Additional Resources

Literary work being taught	Title and location of article, illustration, recording, film, etc.

E. Dickinson William Faulkner

Gerard M. Hopkins S.J. Mark Twain Rudyard Kipling

Gwendolyn Brooks Randall Jarrell Joseph Conrad.

Stephen Spender C Brontë Virginia Woolf

John Keats Arthur Conan Doyle Sidney Lanier

A Bradstreet

A Lincoln Henry W. Longfellow Marianne Moore

James Joyce Fredk Douglass W Blake J. Austen

Wallace Stevens Phillis Wheatley

C Brontë F Scott Fitzgerald